Strategic Logistics Management

THE MCGRAW-HILL/IRWIN SERIES IN MARKETING

FOURTH EDITION

Strategic Logistics Management

James R. Stock
Professor of Marketing and Logistics
Department of Marketing
College of Business Administration
University of South Florida

Douglas M. Lambert
Raymond E. Mason Professor of Transportation and Logistics,
and Director, The Global Supply Chain Forum,
Fisher College of Business
The Ohio State University
and
Prime F. Osborn III Eminent Scholar Chair in Transportation,
Professor of Marketing and Logistics, and
Director, The International Center for Competitive Excellence
University of North Florida

Boston Burr Ridge, IL Dubuque, IA Madison, WI New York
San Francisco St. Louis Bangkok Bogotá Caracas Kuala Lumpur
Lisbon London Madrid Mexico City Milan Montreal New Delhi
Santiago Seoul Singapore Sydney Taipei Toronto

McGraw-Hill Higher Education

*A Division of The **McGraw-Hill** Companies*

Photo Credits

Chapter Openers 1, 3, 4, 8, 15, 17: © Gail Mooney; 18: Corbis; 2: Ohio State University Photo Services; 5: © David Pollack/The Stock Market; 6: © Will & Deni McIntyre/Photo Researchers, Inc.; 7: Courtesy Harley-Davidson; 9: NASA; 10: © Mitch Kazar/Stone; 11: © Roger Tully/Stone; 12: Courtesy CSX; 13: © Peter J. Schulz/Courtesy O'Hare Airport, Dept. of Aviation; 14: © Michael Newman/PhotoEdit; 16: © Bruce Ayres/Stone

STRATEGIC LOGISTICS MANAGEMENT
Published by McGraw-Hill, an imprint of The McGraw-Hill Companies, Inc. 1221 Avenue of the Americas, New York, NY, 10020. Copyright © 2001, 1993, 1987, 1982, by The McGraw-Hill Companies, Inc. All rights reserved. No part of this publication may be reproduced or distributed in any form or by any means, or stored in a database or retrieval system, without the prior written consent of The McGraw-Hill Companies, Inc., including, but not limited to, in any network or other electronic storage or transmission, or broadcast for distance learning.
Some ancillaries, including electronic and print components, may not be available to customers outside the United States.

This book is printed on acid-free paper.

1 2 3 4 5 6 7 8 9 0 CCW/CCW 0 9 8 7 6 5 4 3 2 1 0

ISBN 0-25-613687-4

Vice president/Editor-in-chief: *Robin J. Zwettler*
Senior sponsoring editor: *Rick Adams*
Developmental editor: *Christine Parker*
Marketing manager: *Kim Kanakes*
Production manager: *Jim Labeots*
Production supervisor: *Michael McCormick*
Freelance design coordinator: *Artemio Ortiz*
Supplement coordinator: *Rose Range*
Media technology producer: *Burke Broholm*
Photo research coordinator: *Judy Kausal*
Cover image: *Copyright © 2000 PhotoDisc, Inc. All rights reserved.*
Compositor: *Shepherd Incorporated*
Typeface: *10/12 Times Roman*
Printer: *Courier, Westford*

Library of Congress Cataloging-in-Publication Data

Stock, James R.
   Strategic logistics management / James R. Stock, Douglas M. Lambert.--4th ed.
      p. cm.
   Includes index.
   ISBN 0-256-13687-4 (alk. paper)
   1. Business logistics. 2. Physical distribution of goods--Management. I. Lambert, Douglas M. II. Title.

HF5415.7 .S86 2001
658.5--dc21

00-046625

To Bernard J. La Londe

About the Authors

James R. Stock is Professor of Marketing and Logistics at the College of Business Administration, University of South Florida. Dr. Stock held previous faculty appointments at Michigan State University, University of Oklahoma, and the University of Notre Dame. From 1986 to 1988 he held the position of Distinguished Visiting Professor of Logistics Management, School of Systems and Logistics, at the Air Force Institute of Technology, Wright-Patterson Air Force Base. Dr. Stock is the author or co-author of over 90 publications including books, monographs, articles, and proceedings papers. He is author of *Development and Implementation of Reverse Logistics Programs* and *Reverse Logistics;* co-author of *Distribution Consultants: A Managerial Guide to Their Identification, Selection, and Use;* and co-author of *Fundamentals of Logistics Management.* He currently serves as editor of *The International Journal of Physical Distribution and Logistics Management.* He received the Armitage Medal (1988) from the SOLE—The International Society of Logistics in recognition of his scholarly contributions to the discipline. His areas of expertise include reverse logistics, supply chain management, and the marketing–logistics interface. He has lectured on various logistics topics throughout Europe and Africa. Dr. Stock holds BS and MBA degrees from the University of Miami (Florida) and the Ph.D. from The Ohio State University.

Douglas M. Lambert is the Raymond E. Mason Professor of Transportation and Logistics and Director of The Global Supply Chain Forum, Fisher College of Business, The Ohio State University. He is also the Prime F. Osborn III Eminent Scholar Chair in Transportation, Professor of Marketing and Logistics, and Director of The International Center for Competitive Excellence at the College of Business Administration, University of North Florida. From 1983 to 1985 he was PepsiCo Professor of Marketing at Michigan State University. Dr. Lambert has served as a faculty member for over 500 executive development programs in North America, South America, Europe, Asia, and Australasia and he has given more than 100 presentations to professional associations around the world. He is the author of *The Development of an Inventory Costing Methodology, The Distribution Channels Decision, and The Product Abandonment Decision* and co-author of *Management in Marketing Channels, Fundamentals of Logistics Management, Strategic Logistics Management,* and *Supply Chain Directions for a New North America.* He has authored or co-authored more than 150 publications. In 1986 Dr. Lambert received the Council of Logistics Management's Distinguished Service Award, "the highest honor that can be bestowed on an individual for achievement in the physical distribution/logistics industry," for his contributions to logistics management and has also received the CLM's Founders Award (1997) and Doctoral Research Grant (1975). He holds an honors BA and MBA from the University of Western Ontario and a Ph.D. from The Ohio State University. Dr. Lambert is co-editor of *The International Journal of Logistics Management.*

Brief Contents

Contents

3 Customer Service   95

Preface

Notable changes occurring in the global marketplace since the publication of the first three editions of this book (1982, 1987, and 1993) have included e-commerce and widespread use of the Internet, increased interest in supply chain management, a continued explosion of computer and information technology worldwide, development of 24-hour markets with many organizations operating worldwide, and a continued corporate emphasis on quality and customer satisfaction. Trade agreements such as North America Free Trade Agreement (NAFTA), European Union, ASEAN, and Mercosur have enabled corporations to implement regional, if not entirely global, logistics strategies.

The fourth edition of *Strategic Logistics Management* has been significantly expanded to reflect these and the many other changes that have occurred, as well as to include state-of-the-art logistics information and technology. The basic tenets of the previous editions have been retained, but new material has been added to make the book more managerial, integrative, and "cutting edge." *Strategic Logistics Management* is still the only text that takes a marketing orientation and views the subject from a customer satisfaction perspective. While emphasizing the marketing aspects of logistics, it integrates all of the functional areas of the business as well as incorporating logistics into supply chain management.

Logistics is big business. Its consumption of land, labor, capital, and information—coupled with its impact on the world's standard of living—has enormous implications. During the last quarter of the twentieth century, logistics increased in importance from a function that was perceived as barely necessary to: (1) an activity where significant cost savings could be generated; (2) an activity that had enormous potential to impact customer satisfaction and hence increase sales; and (3) a marketing weapon that could be effectively utilized to gain a sustainable competitive advantage.

Strategic Logistics Management approaches the topic from a managerial perspective. Each chapter introduces basic logistics concepts in a format that is useful for management decision making. Of course, the basics—terms, concepts, and principles—are covered, but they are examined in light of how they interrelate and interface with other functions of the firm. In each chapter we have included examples of corporate applications of these concepts to illustrate how logistics activities can be managed to properly implement the marketing concept. These examples are incorporated into the narrative and highlighted in several boxed exhibits within each chapter—*Global, Technology,* and *Creative Solutions.*

This book includes a good balance of theory and practical application. All the traditional logistics activities have been included. However, there are several important topics that are unique to this text or are approached in a different way. For example, the financial control of logistics is interwoven throughout all chapters, and specifically examined in a separate chapter, *Financial Control of Logistics Performance.* We have purposely taken this approach because of the impact of logistics on the firm's profitability. Because logistics ultimately affects marketing's ability to generate and satisfy demand—and thus create customer satisfaction—the customer service activity is emphasized early in the book. Customer service can be considered the output of the logistics function. For this reason, customer service provides a focal point for the entire book, and customer service implications are considered in each of the 18 chapters, including a separate chapter, *Customer Service.* Since it is unlikely that great customer service will receive its appropriate level of reward unless it is measured and sold both inside and outside of the firm, this edition also includes a chapter on *Measuring and Selling the Value of Logistics.*

A number of important topics not covered in many other logistics texts, or covered only superficially, are given significant treatment in this book, including: supply chain management; measuring and selling the value of logistics; order processing and management information systems; e-commerce and the Internet; reverse logistics and packaging; financial control of logistics performance; logistics organizations; and global logistics. Our goal in covering these topics, in addition to the traditional activities, is to provide readers with a grasp of the total picture of logistics within the context of supply chain management processes.

There are a number of worthwhile improvements in the fourth edition. We have included many more references and examples from general business and other literature because of the impact of logistics on a variety of business processes. This edition extensively covers the academic and trade literature in the area of logistics, and includes the most up-to-date information and examples. Readers will notice the significant number of citations from the year 2000. We have retained those elements that are "timeless" and those that made the previous editions successful.

There are several new and expanded features in this edition. We have added to and updated the Suggested Readings at the end of each chapter. Margin notes have been increased, and charts, figures, and graphs have been updated and revised where necessary. The use of several boxed exhibits in each chapter highlights key elements of logistics development. We believe that this edition is more readable for both the instructor and student. This edition includes 15 cases, three more than in the previous edition. Several of the cases are new to this edition, while others have been updated and/or modified. Our aim has been to present instructors and students with the best textbook on the market. We believe we have succeeded.

The pragmatic, applied nature of the book, its managerial orientation, and its how-to appendices make it a must-have reference book for present and future logistics professionals. The end-of-the-chapter questions, boxed exhibits, and the case material help readers apply the material presented in each chapter. The questions, problems, and cases are structured to challenge readers' managerial skills. They are integrative in nature and examine issues that are important to today's logistics executive.

The text is the primary element in a complete package of teaching and learning resources. The supporting items include:

- An Instructor's Manual that contains lecture material in the form of additional examples and vignettes, suggested answers to the end-of-chapter questions, and commentaries on the case material.

- A Test Bank of approximately 1,500 objective questions. The questions are coded to indicate the type (definition, concept, application) and text location.
- A PowerPoint presentation of over 270 slides with additional graphics and exhibits for each chapter.
- An Instructor's Resource CD-ROM containing the Instructor's Manual in electronic format, CompuTest (an electronic Test Bank), and the PowerPoint presentation.
- A video program to accompany the text.
- A website with downloadable supplement files, links to additional resources and readings, Internet exercises, You Make the Call, and other online features.

James R. Stock
Douglas M. Lambert

Acknowledgments

Any work of this magnitude is seldom the exclusive work of one or two individuals. Several individuals and corporations provided material such as cases and exhibits for this edition of the textbook including: William C. Copacino, Andersen Consulting; Robert V. Delaney, Cass Logistics, Inc.; George A. Gecowets, Council of Logistics Management; Harvard Business School Publishing; Gary Ridenhower, 3M; Rohm and Haas Company; Richard Ivey School of Business; Stanford University Graduate School of Business; Target Stores; and Elaine M. Winter, Council of Logistics Management.

A number of academic colleagues have provided invaluable input. We are grateful to the following persons for graciously providing us with comments, exhibits, case materials, and other assistance: M. Eric Johnson, The Tuck School at Dartmouth; Donald J. Bowersox, Michigan State University; Martin G. Christopher, Cranfield School of Management; Robert L. Cook, Central Michigan University; Martha C. Cooper, The Ohio State University; John T. Gardner, SUNY at Brockport; David A. Haas, Kutztown University; Steve Hagel, Auburn University at Montgomery; Jim Heatherington, Oklahoma City University; Terence F. Henderson, Swinburne University; Sid Huff, Richard Ivey School of Business; Fraser Johnson, Richard Ivey School of Business; J. E. Kangas, GMI Engineering Institute; Matt Monroe, Bloomfield College; Terrance L. Pohlen, University of North Florida; E. Powell Robinson Jr., Texas A&M University; Dale Rogers, University of Nevada; Anthony D. Ross, Texas A&M University; Philip B. Schary, Oregon State University; Doris Shaw, Kent State University; Jay U. Sterling, University of Alabama; James Underwood, University of Southwest Louisiana; and Douglas E. Zemke, Millikin University. Our students at the University of South Florida, The Ohio State University, and the University of North Florida, and former students at Michigan State University, Air Force Institute of Technology, and University of Oklahoma have had a strong influence on the content of this book.

We are thankful for the assistance of Rick Adams, Senior Sponsoring Editor, Christine Parker, Developmental Editor, Craig Leonard, Project Manager, Kathy Little, Indexer, all at McGraw-Hill Higher Education; Nina McGuffin, Consultant; and Professor Drew Stapleton, University of Wisconsin.

Jim Stock wishes to thank his parents, William and Frances Stock, who have been a constant source of inspiration and encouragement over the years. They instilled in him the notion that of the two ways to accomplish a task—the easy way and the right way—

it is always best to do it right the first time. Appreciation is also given to Herbert and Bettye Townsend, the parents of his wife, Katheryn, who during their lives provided testimonies of hard work and a concern for others. Their continual support will be sorely missed, but their daughter will carry on their proud tradition. Katheryn has been a constant companion, providing love and encouragement, as well as moral support and manuscript assistance. Special thanks go to his daughter, Elizabeth, and his son, Matthew, for giving up so many hours of time with their daddy so that he could write. He would also like to thank his colleagues at the University of South Florida, including Dean Robert L. Anderson of the College of Business Administration and William B. Locander, Chairman, Department of Marketing.

Doug Lambert wishes to thank his parents, John and Mary Lambert, who in life and in death were examples of dignity and grace. They have always been a source of love and encouragement. Their many positive influences have contributed significantly to whatever success he has enjoyed thus far in life. His wife, Lynne, was a steadfast source of love and friendship. She provided encouragement to get the job done and welcome diversions. He would also like to give recognition to a number of other special individuals in his life. General Raymond E. Mason and his wife Margaret are generous supporters of the OSU Logistics program and are great examples of how one should live life. Grace Osborn, who has become our "southern mamma," offers love, encouragement, and advice. She is truly amazing. At The Ohio State University, Dean Joseph A. Alutto deserves recognition for his support of the vision for the OSU Logistics program. Professor Robert Burnkrant, Chair of the Department of Marketing and Logistics, has provided continuous encouragement and support. It is also important to recognize the outstanding colleagues in the Department of Marketing and Logistics, particularly Martha Cooper, Walter Zinn, Keely Croxton, and Thomas Goldsby. In addition, the support of Carol Newcomb, Executive Director of Executive Education at the Fisher College of Business, is appreciated. All of this support has made the OSU Logistics program larger and stronger than ever. At the University of North Florida, Dean Earle C. Traynham and Professor Robert Pickhardt, Chairman, Department of Management, Marketing and Logistics, are appreciated for providing a most supportive and collegial environment that fosters faculty productivity. Recognition must be given to colleagues, especially Terrance L. Pohlen, C. Donald Wiggins, and Timothy E. Jares. His office managers at OSU and UNF, Karen Papritan and Marian Kuhn, somehow manage to keep him organized and moving forward. Holding two chairs and leading two programs is possible with their support. Marian carries the additional burden of serving as Operations Manager for *The International Journal of Logistics Management,* which he co-edits with Martin Christopher. Veronica Mai and Li Chen, formerly MBA students at the Fisher College of Business, provided assistance with research, typing, and proofing of chapters for the fourth edition and their help is greatly appreciated. The executives, more than 20,000, who have attended his seminars over the years have influenced his thinking about logistics. Finally, he would like to thank the members of The Global Supply Chain Forum: 3M; Cemex Mexico; Coca-Cola, USA; Colgate-Palmolive Company; CSX; Fletcher Challenge Building; Ford Motor Company; Goodyear Tire and Rubber Company; Hewlett-Packard; International Paper; Limited Distribution Services; Lucent Technologies; McDonald's; New Holland of Mexico; Taylor Made-adidas Golf Company; and Whirlpool. It is Forum research that provided the basis for Chapter 2, *Supply Chain Management,* the Partnership Model in Chapter 12, as well as Chapter 17. The friendship and guidance provided by the individuals who represent these organizations are a major part of his personal and professional life.

Finally, we wish to express our appreciation to Bernard J. La Londe, Emeritus Professor, Fisher College of Business, The Ohio State University. It was his love for the discipline of logistics and his leadership during and since our doctoral programs at The Ohio State University that have made this text a reality. For those who know "Bud," no explanation is necessary. For those who have missed the experience, no words can explain it.

To all those persons who provided assistance and to the publishers and authors who graciously granted permission to use their material, we are indeed grateful. Of course, responsibility for any errors or omissions rests with the authors.

J. R. S.
D. M. L.

Strategic Logistics Management

Logistics' Role in the Economy and the Organization

Chapter Outline

Chapter Objectives

- To identify how logistics affects the economy and the performance of organizations.
- To briefly explore how logistics has developed over time.
- To understand how logistics contributes to value creation (value-added).
- To understand the concept of the systems approach as it relates to logistics and marketing, the total cost concept, and profitability.
- To show how to implement the integrated logistics management concept using total cost analysis.
- To show how to recognize areas in which logistics performance can be improved.

Introduction

Logistics Has Many Implications for Consumers

The logistics process affects almost every sphere of human activity, directly or indirectly. Few areas of business have as significant an impact on a society's standard of living as logistics. As customers, we tend to notice logistics only when there is a problem:

- A consumer uses the Internet to purchase a birthday gift for a family member and the item arrives too late, even though timely delivery was promised.
- A product advertised in a weekend newspaper insert is not available when a customer attempts to purchase it at a local retail store.
- A shipment of medical supplies and food intended for distribution to victims of a natural disaster in a foreign country cannot be delivered to those in need because transport equipment and storage facilities are not available or are inadequate.
- An automobile plant is shut down when a trucker's strike halts shipment of the supplies of parts and equipment essential to operate a just-in-time manufacturing system.
- An order is delivered to the wrong customer, and it takes several days for the mistake to be corrected; in the meantime, a substitute shipment must be sent by air express, resulting in additional costs to the seller.

We often don't think of the role that logistics has in our lives until something goes wrong. Fortunately, such occurrences are the exception rather than the rule.

Because of the significant impact logistics has on society, industries, organizations, and individuals, we take a general approach in this initial chapter. Specifically, the chapter focuses on the following: presenting a basic explanation of the logistics process, explaining the systems approach as it applies to logistics, exploring the role of logistics in the economy and organizations, exploring how logistics has developed over time, summarizing the importance of integrated logistics management, examining how organizations use total cost analysis, exploring how organizations can measure logistics process outcomes, and examining the key trends and current issues affecting logistics.

Definition of Logistics Management

A first step in gaining an understanding of the logistics process is to have a clear understanding of what *logistics management* means. Logistics management has many names, including:

Business logistics	Logistics
Channel management	Materials management
Distribution	Physical distribution
Industrial logistics	Quick-response systems
Logistical management	Supply chain management

The most commonly accepted term among practicing logisticians is *logistics management*. The Council of Logistics Management (CLM), a leading organization for logistics professionals with a current membership of over 15,000, defines the term as follows:

**Logistics Management
Defined**

Logistics management is that part of the supply chain process that plans, implements, and controls the efficient, effective flow and storage of goods, services, and related information from the point-of-origin to the point-of-consumption in order to meet customers' requirements.[1]

**Logistics Is Relevant
to All Types
of Organizations**

This definition includes the flow of goods, services, and information in both the manufacturing and service sectors. Manufacturing entities include all types of companies, producing goods as divergent as automobiles, computers, cosmetics, artificial limbs, aircraft, and food items. The service sector includes entities such as government organizations, hospitals, banks, universities, retailers, and wholesalers.[2] Examples from these various manufacturing and service sectors will be used throughout the book to illustrate the relevance of logistics management to a variety of operations.

**Inputs into the Logistics
System**

Figure 1–1 illustrates some of the many activities included within logistics management. Inputs to the logistics process include natural, human, financial, and information resources. Logistics practitioners plan, implement, and control these inputs in various forms, including raw materials (e.g., subassemblies, parts, packing materials, basic commodities); in-process inventory (i.e., products partially completed and not yet ready for sale); and finished goods (i.e., completed products ready for sale to intermediate or final customers).

**Outputs of the Logistics
System**

The outputs of the logistics system include competitive advantage for the organization resulting from a marketing orientation and operational efficiencies and

FIGURE 1–1

*Components of logistics
management*

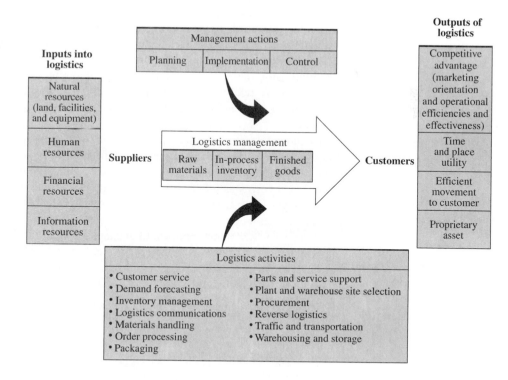

---

[1]Council of Logistics Management <http://www.clm1.org>.

[2]Peter A. Smith, Jack Barry, Joseph L. Cavinato, John J. Coyle, Steven J. Dunn, and William Grenoble, *Logistics in Service Industries* (Oak Brook, IL: Council of Logistics Management, 1991), p. xvii.

effectiveness, time and place utility, and efficient movement to the customer. Another output occurs when the logistics service mix is such that logistics becomes a proprietary asset of the organization. These outputs are made possible by the effective and efficient performance of the 13 logistics activities shown at the bottom of Figure 1–1. Each of these activities will be briefly explained later in this chapter and more thoroughly in other chapters of this textbook.

Systems Approach/Integration

The systems approach is a critical concept in logistics. Logistics is, in itself, a system; it is a network of related activities with the purpose of managing the orderly flow of material and personnel within the logistics channel.

The Systems Approach Defined

The systems approach is a simplistic yet powerful paradigm for understanding interrelationships. The *systems approach* simply states that all functions or activities need to be understood in terms of how they affect, and are affected by, other elements and activities with which they interact. The idea is that if one looks at actions in isolation, he or she will not understand the big picture or how such actions affect, or are affected by, other activities. In essence, the sum, or outcome of a series of activities, is greater than its individual parts.[3]

While it might be desirable to have high inventory levels in order to improve customer order fulfillment, high inventory levels increase storage costs as well as the risk of obsolescence. Those unfavorable factors must be "traded off" with the favorable aspects of a decision before arriving at a decision on inventory levels. Without considering the impact of decisions on the larger system, such as the firm or the distribution channel, suboptimization often occurs. That means while the individual activities in that system appear to be operating well, the net result on the total system is relatively poor performance. To understand the opportunities for improvement, and the implication of those opportunities, the system must be viewed as a whole.

Systems Must Be Viewed as a Whole

Without understanding the supply chain implications of logistics decisions to improve service levels, excess inventory will begin to build up at the links along the supply chain. This excess inventory will tend to increase costs throughout the supply chain, but it serves as a buffer to protect against the uncertainty of how other chain members will behave. Thus, the system as a whole is less efficient than it could otherwise be. To get around that issue, organizations like Hewlett-Packard's DeskJet Division have taken a systems approach to managing inventories in the supply chain.

The systems approach is at the core of the next several topics discussed. The systems approach is key to understanding the role of logistics in the economy, its role in the organization, including its interface with marketing, the total cost concept, and logistics strategy.

[3]For a more thorough discussion of the systems approach, see C. W. Churchman, *The Systems Approach and Its Enemies* (New York: Basic Books, 1979); R. L. Ackoff, "Science in the Systems Age: Beyond IE, OR and MS," *Operations Research* 21, no. 3 (1973), pp. 661–71; Heiner Müller Merback, "A System of Systems Approaches," *Interfaces* 24, no. 4 (July–August 1994), pp. 16–25; and Peter Senge, *The Fifth Discipline* (New York: Doubleday/Currency, 1990).

Logistics' Role in the Economy

The rising affluence of consumers has led to increasing national and international markets for goods and services. Thousands of new products and services have been introduced in the past decade and are currently sold and distributed to customers in every corner of the world. To meet the challenges of expanded markets and the proliferation of new products and services, business firms have increased in size and complexity. Multiple-plant operations have replaced single plants. The distribution of products from point-of-origin to point-of-consumption has become an enormously important component of the gross domestic product (GDP) of industrialized nations.

In the United States, for example, logistics now contributes approximately 9.9 percent of GDP. Table 1–1 shows that U.S. industries in 1999 spent an estimated $554 billion on freight transportation; more than $332 billion on warehousing, storage, and inventory carrying costs; and more than $40 billion to administer, communicate, and manage the logistics process—a total of $921 billion.[4] Investment in transportation and distribution facilities, not including public sources, is estimated to be in the hundreds of billions of dollars. Considering its consumption of land, labor, and capital, and its impact on the standard of living, logistics is clearly big business.

Logistics Is a Significant Component of GDP

As a significant component of GDP, logistics affects the rate of inflation, interest rates, productivity, energy costs and availability, and other aspects of the economy. One study reported that the average U.S. organization could improve its logistics productivity by 20 percent or more. Improvements in a nation's productivity have positive effects

TABLE 1–1   Components of 1999 Logistics Costs
$ Billions

Inventory carrying costs (All business inventory: $1.376 trillion)	
Interest	$ 70
Taxes, obsolescence, depreciation, insurance	187
Warehousing	75
Subtotal	$332
Transportation costs	
Motor carriers:	
Truck—intercity	$300
Truck—local	150
Subtotal	$450
Other carriers:	
Railroads	$ 35
Water (international 16; domestic 9)	22
Oil pipelines	9
Air (international 7; domestic 19)	26
Forwarders	6
Subtotal	$ 98
Shipper-related costs	$ 5
Logistics administration	$ 35
Total logistics cost	$920

Source: Robert V. Delaney and Rosalyn Wilson, *11th Annual "State of Logistics Report,"* Washington, D.C., National Press Club (June 5, 2000), Figure 10.

[4]Robert V. Delaney and Rosalyn Wilson, *11th Annual "State of Logistics Report,"* remarks to the National Press Club, Washington, DC (June 5, 2000), Figure 10.

on the prices paid for goods and services, the balance of national payments, currency valuation, the ability to compete effectively in global markets, industry profits (higher productivity implies lower costs of operation to produce and distribute an equivalent amount of product), the availability of investment capital, and economic growth—leading to a higher level of employment.

Perhaps the best way to illustrate the role of logistics in the U.S. economy is to compare logistical expenditures with other societal activities. The amount spent on business logistics is 10 times that spent on advertising, twice that spent on national defense, and equal to that spent on medical care.[5]

In 1981, logistics expenditures accounted for around 16.5 percent of GDP. If logistics expenditures were still that high (instead of the current figure of 9.9 percent of GDP), approximately $300 billion additionally would have been spent on logistics in the United States in 1999. This would translate into higher prices for consumers, lower profits for businesses, or both. The result would be a lower overall standard of living and/or a smaller tax base. Thus, improving the efficiency of logistics operations makes an important contribution to the economy as a whole.

Logistics also supports the movement and flow of many economic transactions; it is an important activity in facilitating the sale of virtually all goods and services. To understand this role from a systems perspective, consider that if goods do not arrive on time, customers cannot buy them. If goods do not arrive in the proper place, or in the proper condition, no sale can be made and thus all economic activity throughout the supply chain will suffer.

Logistics' Role in the Organization

In recent years, effective logistics management has been recognized as a key element in improving both the profitability and the competitive performance of firms. In the late 1980s and early 1990s, customer service took center stage in many organizations. Even organizations that had previously adhered to the "marketing concept" (defined below) were reexamining what it meant to be customer driven. The trend toward a strong customer focus continues today. Coupled with operational efficiencies and effectiveness, a marketing orientation provides organizations with opportunities to gain competitive advantage.

Logistics Leads to Competitive Advantage

The Marketing Concept   The *marketing concept* is a "marketing management philosophy that holds that achieving organizational goals depends on determining the needs and wants of target markets and delivering the desired satisfactions more effectively and efficiently than competitors."[6] In other words, the marketing concept holds that a business exists to meet customer needs. The three critical elements of the marketing concept (customer satisfaction, integrated effort, and company profit) are shown in Figure 1–2. Logistics plays a key role in each of these elements in several ways.

---

[5]Robert V. Delaney, "CLI's 'State of Logistics' Annual Report," press conference remarks to the National Press Club, Washington, DC (June 15, 1990), p. 4.

[6]Phillip Kotler and Gary Armstrong, *Principles of Marketing,* 5th ed. (Englewood Cliffs, NJ: Prentice Hall, 1999), p. 14.

Figure 1–2

*Marketing/logistics
management concept*

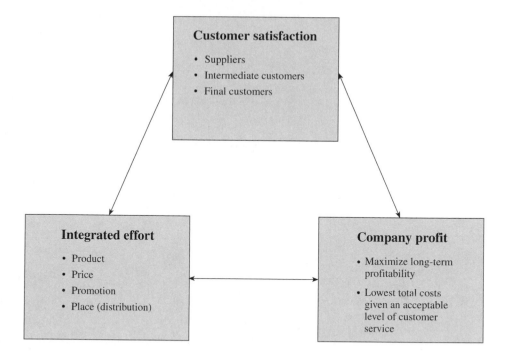

Figure 1–2

*Marketing/logistics
management concept*

**The Four Ps of the
Marketing Mix**

In order for a firm to be successful, any marketing effort must integrate the ideas of having the right *product,* at the right *price,* combined with the right *promotion,* and available in the right *place*—these are the four Ps of the marketing mix. Logistics plays a critical role, particularly in support of getting the product to the right place. As we will note later with regard to utility creation, a product or service provides customer satisfaction only if it is available to the customer when and where it is needed. Achieving customer satisfaction requires an integrated effort both internally and externally (with suppliers and ultimate customers).

**Making Trade-Offs in
Logistics Is Important**

Also, it is important to understand that a central goal of an organization is to maximize long-term profitability or, in the public or nonprofit sectors, effective budget allocation. One of the key ways to accomplish that, as shown in Figure 1–3 and presented a bit later, is through examining trade-offs among alternatives, thereby reducing the overall total cost of activities within a system.

To better explain Figure 1–3, the sections below explore the manner in which each of the major elements of the marketing mix interact with, and are affected by, logistics operations.

Product.   *Product* refers to the set of utilities or characteristics a customer receives as a result of a purchase. In an effort to lower price, management may decide to reduce product quality, eliminate product features, reduce the breadth of product offerings, reduce customer service or warranty support, or increase the time between model changes. However, any of these actions may reduce the attraction of the product for consumers, creating a loss of customers and thereby a reduction in long-term profits. To avoid making poor decisions, management needs to understand the trade-offs and interrelationships between logistics and other marketing activities.

Pricing Considerations

Price.   The amount of money a customer pays for a product or service is typically referred to as its *price.* Price factors include discounts for buying in quantities or for

FIGURE 1–3

*Cost trade-offs in
marketing and logistics*

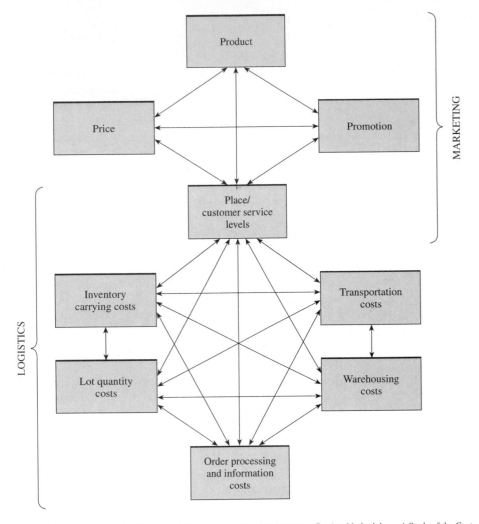

Source: Adapted from Douglas M. Lambert, *The Development of an Inventory Costing Methodology: A Study of the Costs
Associated with Holding Inventory* (Chicago: National Council of Physical Distribution Management, 1976), p. 7.

belonging to a certain class of customers, discounts for prompt payment, rebates, consignment arrangements, and delivery costs.

A supplier may attempt to increase sales by reducing the price of its product or by
changing the terms or service offering. Unless demand for the item in question is very
elastic (that is, sales change dramatically due to changes in price), such a strategy may
create higher unit sales but not necessarily higher profit—the sales may not increase
enough to offset the lower price. This is particularly true in mature industries, where
customer demand is relatively fixed and the competition may follow the price decrease.
In such cases the sales and the profitability of the entire industry may suffer.

Promotion.   *Promotion* of a product or service encompasses both personal selling and
advertising. Whereas increasing advertising expenditures or the size of the direct sales
force can have a positive impact on sales, there is a point of diminishing returns. At this
point, the extra money being spent does not yield high enough increases in sales and/or

profits to justify the added expense. It is important for organizations to understand when they reach this point so that they can avoid misallocating funds. A prudent idea may be to reallocate extra advertising funds to, perhaps, employee training. The sales force, for example, could be trained to provide more value-added services to the customer or to make the customer more aware of the value-added the firm currently provides through superior logistics.

Selling Value-Added to Customers

Place. Expenditures in the *place* component of the marketing mix support the levels of customer service provided by the organization. This includes on-time delivery, high order-fill rates, and consistent transit times. Customer service is an output of the logistics system and represents the firms expenditure for logistics. On the other hand, when the organization performs well on all the elements of the marketing mix, customer satisfaction occurs.

Customer Service Is an Output of the Logistics System

For many organizations, customer service may be a key to gaining competitive advantage.[7] By adjusting customer service levels to meet what the customer desires and is willing to pay for, the organization may simultaneously improve service levels and reduce costs. All of the logistics trade-offs illustrated in the bottom of Figure 1–3 must be considered in terms of their impact on customer service. In order to accomplish this analysis, the *total cost concept* (discussed later in this chapter) must be used.

Additionally, when combined with operational efficiencies and effectiveness from the adoption and implementation of technology and various management strategies such as supply chain management (SCM), total quality management (TQM), just-in-time (JIT), and quick response (QR), organizations can develop competitive advantage. Technology and management strategies will be discussed later in this chapter and throughout this text.

Logistics Adds Time and Place Utility

Manufactured products possess some value or utility because an assembled item is worth more than its unassembled components or raw materials. A completed automobile, for example, is much more valuable to a consumer than its unassembled parts would be. The value, or utility, of making materials available in a completed state is called *form utility.* To the customer, however, the product not only must have form utility but also must be in the right place, at the right time, and be available to purchase. The value added to products beyond that added by manufacturing (form utility) may be called *place, time,* or *possession utility.*[8] The logistics activity provides place and time utility, while other marketing activities provide possession utility.[9]

Management is quite concerned with the value added by logistics, because improvements in place and time utility are ultimately reflected in the firm's profits. Both cost savings in logistics and a stronger marketing position due to an improved logistics system can cause improved bottom-line performance. The more logistics contributes to the value of a product, the more important logistics management is.

---

[7]Joseph B. Fuller, James O'Conor, and Richard Rawlinson, "Tailored Logistics: The Next Advantage," *Harvard Business Review* 71, no. 3 (May–June 1993), pp. 87–98.

[8]See L. D. H. Weld, *The Marketing of Farm Products* (New York: Macmillan, 1916).

[9]The official definition of *marketing* by the American Marketing Association is "the process of planning and executing the conception, pricing, promotion, and distribution of ideas, goods, and services to create exchanges that satisfy individual and organizational objectives." See "AMA Board Approves New Marketing Definition," *Marketing News* 19, no. 5 (March 1, 1985), p. 1.

Place Utility   *Place utility* is the value created or added to a product by making it available for purchase or consumption in the right place. Logistics is directly responsible for adding place utility to products as it efficiently moves raw materials, in-process inventory, and

Time Utility   finished goods from point-of-origin to point-of-consumption. *Time utility* is the value created by making something available at the right time. Products are not as valuable to customers if they are not available precisely when they are needed. For example, a food-processing company must have raw materials (food items), packaging materials, and other items available before the production process begins—or, if already begun, before existing supplies run out. Failure to receive these items at the proper time can cause costly production shutdowns and place the firm at a competitive disadvantage. As the remaining chapters of this book will show, logistics activities combine to add place and time utility to products.

Possession Utility   *Possession utility* is the value added to a product by allowing the customer to take ownership of the item. Possession utility is a result not of logistics but of the offering of credit, quantity discounts, and delayed payments that enable the customer to assume possession of the product. The logistics and marketing processes culminate in possession utility.

Logistics Allows Efficient Movement to the Customer

E. Grosvenor Plowman said that the "five rights" of a logistics system are supplying the

**Five Rights
of a Logistics
System**   *right product* at the *right place* at the *right time* in the *right condition* for the *right cost* to those customers consuming the product.[10]

The term *right cost* deserves consideration. While Plowman's first four rights are analogous to the form, time, place, and possession utilities created by manufacturing and marketing, the addition of the cost component is immensely important to the logistics process. Donald Parker voiced the significance of the cost aspect almost four decades ago:

> Improvements in marketing efficiency and reductions in marketing costs still lie in the future, representing a major frontier for cost economies . . . There is room for substantial improvement, particularly in the performance of the physical distribution functions of marketing which constitute a major part of the total marketing costs.[11]

In a similar fashion, Peter Drucker stated:

> Almost 50 cents of each dollar the American spends for goods goes for activities that occur after the goods are made, that is, after they have come in finished form . . . Economically . . . distribution is the process in which physical properties of matter are converted into economic value; it brings the customer to the product.[12]

While some might disagree with Drucker's 50-cents estimate, the cost involved in adding time and place utility is substantial. Because the control of costs is one of top management's most significant concerns in the new millennium, efficient and effective control of the logistics function can have a substantial impact.

---

[10]George A. Gecowets, "Physical Distribution Management," *Defense Transportation Journal* 35, no. 4 (August 1979), p. 5.

[11]Donald D. Parker, "Improved Efficiency and Reduced Cost in Marketing," *Journal of Marketing* 26, no. 2 (April 1962), p. 16.

[12]Peter F. Drucker, "The Economy's Dark Continent," *Fortune* 65, no. 4 (April 1962), p. 103.

Logistics Is a Proprietary Asset

An efficient and economical logistics system is similar to a tangible asset on a corporation's books. Logistics competency cannot be readily duplicated by the firm's competitors. If a company can provide its customers with products quickly and at low cost, it can gain market share advantages over its competitors. It might be able either to sell its product at a lower cost as a result of logistics efficiencies or to provide a higher level of customer service, thereby creating goodwill. Although no organizations presently identify this "asset" on their balance sheets, it theoretically could be shown as an *intangible asset,* a category that includes such items as patents, copyrights, and trademarks.

Development of Logistics Management

Logistics activity is literally thousands of years old, dating back to the earliest forms of organized trade. Yet as an area of study, logistics first began to gain attention in the early 1900s in the distribution of farm products, as a way to support an organization's business strategy and provide time and place utility. To understand the important role of logistics management in today's business enterprise, it is worthwhile to examine its historical development.

Historical Development

In 1901, John F. Crowell discussed the costs and factors affecting the distribution of farm products in the U.S. government's *Report of the Industrial Commission on the Distribution of Farm Products.*[13] Later, in his *Approach to Business Problems* (1916), Arch W. Shaw discussed the strategic aspects of logistics.[14] During that same year, L. D. H. Weld introduced the concepts of marketing utilities (time, place, possession) and channels of distribution.[15] In 1922, Fred E. Clark identified the role of logistics in marketing.[16] And in 1927, the term *logistics* was defined in a way similar to its use today:

An Early Definition of Logistics

> There are two uses of the word distribution that must be clearly differentiated . . . first, the use of the word to describe physical distribution such as transportation and storage; second, the use of the word distribution to describe what is better termed marketing.[17]

With the onset of World War II, logistics was further developed and refined. Because logistics efforts clearly contributed to the Allied forces victory in World War II, logistics began to receive increased recognition and emphasis. Similarly, in the Persian Gulf War in 1990–91, the ability to efficiently and effectively distribute and store supplies and personnel was a key factor in the success of the U.S. Armed Forces.[18]

---

[13]John F. Crowell, *Report of the Industrial Commission on the Distribution of Farm Products,* vol. 6 (Washington, DC: U.S. Government Printing Office, (1901).

[14]Arch W. Shaw, *An Approach to Business Problems* (Cambridge, MA: Harvard University Press, 1916).

[15]L. D. H. Weld, *The Marketing of Farm Products* (New York: Macmillan, 1916).

[16]Fred E. Clark, *Principles of Marketing* (New York: Macmillan, 1922).

[17]Ralph Borsodi, *The Distribution Age* (New York: D. Appleton, 1927), p. 19.

[18]William G. Pagonis, *Moving Mountains: Lessons in Leadership and Logistics from the Gulf War* (Boston: Harvard Business School Press, 1992).

Used in conjunction with a new corporate philosophy that originated in the 1950s—the marketing concept—logistics came to be associated to an even greater degree with the customer service and cost components of a firm's marketing efforts.

A 1956 study of the economics of air freight added a new dimension to the field of logistics: the concept of *total cost analysis.*[19] Air freight is a high-cost form of transportation. However, air freight, when used instead of other modes of transportation, could result in lower inventory and warehousing costs because it allows a firm to distribute its product directly to its customers.

First Text on Logistics Management Is Published

The 1960s saw a number of developments in logistics. In 1961, Edward Smykay, Donald Bowersox, and Frank Mossman wrote one of the first texts on logistics management.[20] The book examined logistics from a systems or companywide perspective and discussed the total cost concept. That is also the time when Peter Drucker, a noted business expert, author, and consultant, stated that logistics was one of the last real frontiers of opportunity for organizations wishing to improve their corporate efficiency.[21] These factors combined to increase the interest in logistics.

The National Council of Physical Distribution Management (renamed the Council of Logistics Management in 1985) was formed in 1963 "to develop the theory and understanding of the [logistics] process, promote the art and science of managing [logistics] systems and to foster professional dialogue and development in the field operating exclusively without profit and in cooperation with other organizations and institutions."[22]

During the remainder of the 1960s and on into the 1980s, a multitude of textbooks, articles, monographs, journals, and conferences were devoted to the subject of logistics management. One of the earliest writings to examine the connection between accounting and logistics was Michael Schiff's *Accounting and Control in Physical Distribution Management,* published in 1972.[23] The study was instrumental in creating an awareness that accounting and financial information are vital to the logistics activity. In 1976, La Londe and Zinszer published their landmark study, *Customer Service: Meaning and Measurement,* the first detailed exploration of the topic of customer service.[24] As part of the marketing concept, customer satisfaction requires a complete understanding of customer service. These studies continue to influence the logistics profession.

Transportation Deregulation

Beginning in the late 1970s and continuing throughout the 1980s, logistics management in the United States was significantly affected by deregulation of the transportation industry. The Airline Deregulation Acts of 1977 and 1978, the Staggers Rail Act of 1980, the Motor Carrier Act of 1980, and the Shipping Act of 1984 removed or modified the existing economic sanctions on air, rail, motor, and ocean transport, respectively. The effects on carriers and shippers have been profound.

In the case of carriers, deregulation has resulted in increased inter- and intrafirm competition; greater pricing freedom (i.e., establishing and modifying rates); more

---

[19]Howard T. Lewis, James W. Culliton, and Jack D. Steele, *The Role of Air Freight in Physical Distribution* (Boston: Harvard Business School, 1956).

[20]Edward W. Smykay, Donald J. Bowersox, and Frank H. Mossman, *Physical Distribution Management* (New York: Macmillan, 1961).

[21]Drucker, "The Economy's Dark Continent," pp. 103, 265–70.

[22]Information supplied by the Council of Logistics Management indicates a 1999 membership of over 15,000 logistics practioners, consultants, and educators.

[23]Michael Schiff, *Accounting and Control in Physical Distribution Management* (Chicago: National Council of Physical Distribution Management, 1972).

[24]Bernard J. La Londe and Paul H. Zinszer, *Customer Service: Meaning and Measurement* (Chicago: National Council of Physical Distribution Management, 1976).

flexibility in routing and scheduling; an increased need to become marketing oriented; and a need to be creative in terms of marketing mix offerings. Shippers have more carriers from which to choose. New and varied types of services are now available. Most rates are now negotiated and involve long-term agreements or contracts. Service levels provided by carriers vary widely depending on the origin/destination combination.

Technology

Computer technology and distribution software are two other factors that have caused businesses to become more interested in logistics management. The development of computer technology, particularly the microcomputer, has allowed executives to implement logistics management much more effectively and efficiently than ever before. Firms can improve their cost efficiency because of the speed and accuracy of the computer; they can use sophisticated techniques to manage and control activities such as production scheduling, inventory control, and order processing. In fact, such advances, and the resulting impact on the firm's marketing, production, and financial activities, have been instrumental in creating top management awareness of logistics.

Global Competition

The development and expansion of global competition began in the 1970s and accelerated in the 1990s. Firms have increasingly become more international, as evidenced by the growth in foreign sourcing of raw materials, component parts, subassemblies, and labor.[25] Companies have penetrated new markets throughout the world.

For example, the United States became an attractive market for many Asian and European firms producing automobiles, electronics, and computers in the 1970s and 1980s. Similarly, markets in Western Europe (as a result of the formation of the European Union in 1992), China, the former Soviet Union, and Eastern Europe are increasingly becoming significant markets for companies producing a variety of goods and services. Enterprising firms throughout the world have recognized the need to become more globally oriented. In many instances, companies have discovered that their international markets exhibit higher growth rates and sales volumes than domestic markets.

During the 1990s, market changes accelerated, resulting in further recognition that logistics could help create sustainable competitive advantages for organizations. Developments in electronic commerce, reengineering, and supply chain management have revolutionized all facets of business, including logistics. During the first decade of the 2000s, the application and refinement of these technologies and approaches will provide significant potential benefits to organizations and their customers.

Table 1–2 identifies some of the most important events in the development of logistics management.[26]

Factors Underlying the Development of Interest in Logistics Management

A number of factors underlie the recognition of the importance of logistics management: advances in computer technology and quantitative techniques; development of the systems approach and total cost analysis concept; recognition of logistics' role in the firm's customer service program; erosion of many firms' profits because of their failure to examine functional areas where cost savings might be realized; profit leverage resulting from increased logistics efficiency; general economic conditions since the 1950s; and recognition that logistics can help create a competitive advantage in the marketplace.

---

[25]Graham Sharman, "The Rediscovery of Logistics," *Harvard Business Review* 62, no. 5 (September–October 1984), pp. 71–79.

[26]An interesting overview of the developments that have occurred in logistics since the early 1960s is provided in "The Times, They've Been A-Changin'," *Logistics Management* 36, no. 1 (January 1997), pp. 52–55.

TABLE 1–2   **Historical Development of Logistics Management**

Year(s)	Event	Significance
1901	John F. Crowell, *Report of the Industrial Commission on the Distribution of Farm Products,* vol. 6 (Washington, DC: Government Printing Office)	The first text to deal with the costs and factors affecting the distribution of farm products.
1916	Arch W. Shaw, *An Approach to Business Problems* (Cambridge, MA: Harvard University Press)	Text discussed the strategic aspects of logistics.
1916	L. D. H. Weld, *The Marketing of Farm Products* (New York: Macmillan)	Introduced the concepts of marketing utilities and channels of distribution.
1922	Fred E. Clark, *Principles of Marketing* (New York: Macmillan)	Text defined marketing as those efforts that affect transfers in the ownership of goods and care of their physical distribution.
1927	Ralph Borsodi, *The Distribution Age* (New York: D. Appleton)	One of the first books to define the term *logistics* similar to its present usage.
1941–45	World War II	Military logistics operations demonstrated how distribution activities could be integrated into a single system.
1950s	Development of the marketing concept	Corporations began to emphasize customer satisfaction at a profit. Customer service later became the cornerstone of logistics management.
1954	Paul D. Converse, "The Other Half of Marketing," *Twenty-Sixth Boston Conference on Distribution* (Boston: Harvard Business School)	A leading authority pointed out the need for academicians and practitioners to examine the physical distribution side of marketing.
1956	Howard T. Lewis, James W. Culliton, and Jack D. Steele, *The Role of Air Freight in Physical Distribution* (Boston: Harvard Business School)	Introduced the concept of total cost analysis to the area of logistics.
Early 1960s	Introduction of Raytheon Company's "unimarket" concept	Earliest reported company effort to adopt and implement logistics management concept. Raytheon utilized one distribution center for U.S. market in combination with an air freight transportation system.
Early 1960s	Michigan State University and Ohio State University institute undergraduate and graduate programs in logistics	First formal educational programs developed to train logistics practitioners and educators.
1961	Edward W. Smykay, Donald J. Bowersox, and Frank H. Mossman, *Physical Distribution Management* (New York: Macmillan)	One of the first texts on physical distribution. Discussed the systems approach and the total cost concept.
1962	Peter F. Drucker, "The Economy's Dark Continent," *Fortune* 65, no. 4 (April 1962)	A leading authority pointed out the importance of distribution in the United States. It is felt by many that this article had a significant impact on practitioners.
1963	National Council of Physical Distribution Management founded (became Council of Logistics Management in 1985)	The first organization to bring together professionals in all areas of logistics for the purpose of education and training.

(continued)

TABLE 1–2   (continued)

Year(s)	Event	Significance
1972	Michael Schiff, *Accounting and Control in Physical Distribution Management* (Chicago: National Council of Physical Distribution Management)	Created awareness of the importance of accounting and financial information for making optimal logistics decisions.
1976	Douglas M. Lambert, *The Development of an Inventory Costing Methodology: A Study of the Costs Associated with Holding Inventory* (Chicago: National Council of Physical Distribution Management)	Identified the cost components of one of the largest logistics expense items and developed a methodology whereby firms could calculate inventory carrying costs.
1976	Bernard J. La Londe and Paul H. Zinszer, *Customer Service: Meaning and Measurement* (Chicago: National Council of Physical Distribution Management)	First comprehensive state-of-the-art appraisal of the customer service activity in major corporations.
1970s–80s	Development and implementation of MRP, MRP II, DRP, DRP II, Kanban, and JIT	Widespread implementation of these techniques highlighted the need for Integrating logistics activities and maximizing their effectiveness. They also pointed out the relationships between logistics and other business functions such as marketing and manufacturing.
Late 1970s–early 1980s	Deregulation of U.S. transportation	Significantly reduced the economic regulation of the transportation sector. Increased competition and had substantial impact on prices and service levels of carriers. Made the transportation aspect of logistics significantly more important. Provided a model for other countries in their deregulation efforts.
1980s	Use of computers, especially PCs, increases dramatically	Technological advances, coupled with declining prices, allow organizations to utilize computers. Provided the capability to more effectively integrate logistics activities. Allowed cost trade off decisions to be made more quickly and optimally. Improved logistics efficiency and productivity.
1985	Michael E. Porter, *Competitive Advantage* (New York: The Free Press)	Introduced the "value chain" concept that provided a framework for organizations to develop competitive strategies. Significantly, it included inbound and outbound logistics as key components of marketing strategy. Created major awareness that logistics could help organizations create and maintain competitive advantage.
1987	Malcolm Baldrige National Quality Award established by U.S. Congress	Promoted quality awareness, recognized quality achievements of U.S. organizations and publicized successful

(continued)

TABLE 1–2   (concluded)

Year(s)	Event	Significance
		quality initiatives. A significant portion of the scoring system for the award was based on logistics outputs, including an organization's knowledge of its customers, overall customer service systems, and responsiveness and an ability to meet customer requirements and expectations.
1990s	Market restructuring occurs in global regions of Asia, Europe, and North America	Events such as NAFTA, Europe 1992, and the Asian financial crisis result in major changes in global markets and infrastructures.
1990s	Electronic commerce (e.g., Internet, EDI, e-mail) becomes globally accepted for communications	Instantaneous and low-cost communication systems allow organizations to develop and maintain contact. Such systems allow for the development of 24-hour, seven-day-a-week business hours.
1993	Michael Hammer and James Champy, *Reengineering the Corporation: A Manifesto Business Revolution* (New York: HarperCollins)	Many organizations evaluate their business processes to determine if there is a better way of performing them. Logistics is a major functional area where reengineering efforts result in significant improvements.
Mid-1990s	Supply chain management approach is recognized as an important concept. Its development and implementation are initiated in many industries.	The notion that multiple organizations and functional areas can integrate their efforts to optimize their individual and combined performances leads to the development of a systems approach throughout the entire channel of distribution.

Cost and Service Impacts.   Identifying the cost and service impacts of the logistics process was an important first step in achieving recognition for logistics. For example, logistics costs, as a percentage of product value, for a producer of industrial nondurable goods (raw materials and industrial products used in the manufacture of end products), can be much higher than logistics costs for a pharmaceutical company. Generally, the product value (measured in dollars per pound) is much higher for pharmaceuticals than for industrial nondurables such as chemicals or fuel. As a result, logistics costs will be a smaller percentage of a firm's sales dollar for the pharmaceutical company, but service considerations are becoming increasingly important.

Logistics Costs as a Percentage of Product Value

To illustrate, suppose a product shipment is valued at \$10,000 for the pharmaceutical company and another is valued at \$2,000 for the industrial nondurables company. Because of factors such as market conditions, level of competition, transportation modes, product perishability (i.e., damageability and shelf life), inventory carrying costs, and handling characteristics, the pharmaceutical company pays \$500 to distribute its product while the industrial nondurable goods firm pays \$250. In absolute terms, the pharmaceutical company pays more, but in relative terms it pays only 5 percent of the product value, whereas the industrial nondurable goods firm pays 12.5 percent of the product value.

Profit Squeeze.   In addition to the logistics expense of the firm, the profit squeeze and potential profit leverage that can result from increased efficiency in logistics have contributed significantly to the development of interest in logistics management. During the 1980s and 1990s many firms found it increasingly difficult to maintain traditional profit levels and growth rates because of increasing domestic and foreign competition, saturated markets, government regulation, and other factors.

Strategies for Increasing Profitability

An organization can pursue one or more of three basic strategies in a profit-squeeze situation. First, it can attempt to generate additional sales volume through increased marketing efforts. However, this may be very difficult and costly. Incremental sales increases in saturated or highly competitive markets are hard to achieve. In low-growth markets, the rate of growth may be less than the firm needs to generate additional sales. Even in high-growth market situations, a firm may be unable to achieve desired sales increases because of resource problems, competition, and other market conditions.

A second way to improve profitability may be to increase the price of the firm's product. Again, such increases may not be possible given market conditions. Depending on demand elasticity, price increases may not have the desired impact on sales. Typically firms hesitate to increase prices unless higher costs of materials, production, or labor make those increases unavoidable. Therefore, a third strategy—that of reducing the firm's costs of doing business—has been the one most companies have pursued.

As firms have looked inward, they have attempted to identify areas for cost savings and/or productivity increases. Many companies have found it difficult to reduce costs in manufacturing because they are already mechanized and highly efficient. They can increase productivity to reduce the cost of manufacturing, but the incremental costs of this approach can be quite high. There are some industries where significant production efficiencies are being achieved, but this is not the case in many others.

In the marketing area, many firms are unwilling to reduce marketing activities, especially advertising, because they fear an adverse reaction in the marketplace. Companies that market consumer goods in highly competitive industries (e.g., Procter & Gamble, Lever Brothers, General Motors, Ford Motor Company, McDonald's) typically hesitate to reduce marketing expenditures. In fact, they usually increase the size of their gross marketing budgets each year.

Profit Impact of Logistics Cost Savings

In many organizations, logistics is one of the most promising areas where significant cost savings can be achieved. And in some instances, such cost savings can have a far greater impact on the firm's profitability than increasing sales volume would have. A survey of chief executive officers of *Fortune* 500 manufacturing and service firms indicated that the CEOs believed that the most important way to improve company profitability was through cost cutting or cost control.[27] Thus, despite all the talk and emphasis on other issues, such as quality and customer service, which CEOs rated as second and third in importance, cost cutting was still seen as the most important factor.

There are many costs associated with a sale, such as the cost of goods sold and logistics-related costs. Thus, a $1.00 increase in sales does not result in a $1.00 increase in profit. In the case where an organization's before-tax profit margin (sales revenue less costs) is 2 percent, the firm receives a before-tax profit of only 2 cents from each

---

[27]"CEO's Still Don't Walk the Talk," *Fortune* (April 18, 1994), pp. 14–15.

sales dollar (see Table 1–3). Yet any dollar saved in logistics does not require sales increase or decreases in other costs to generate the savings. Therefore, a dollar saved in logistics costs is a dollar increase in profit! As a result, a reduction in logistics costs has much more leverage, dollar for dollar, than does an increase in sales. As the cost savings become larger, so does the commensurate sales increase.

For example, during the 1960s, a large appliance firm found that its logistics activities were not integrated under a single logistics executive, but were dispersed among many different functional areas throughout the organization. Some logistics elements fell under the jurisdiction of manufacturing, others under marketing, and others within finance. Top management discovered that the company was spending almost $20 million on logistics activities, yet no one was managing logistics as a major cost center. The firm created a senior-level logistics executive position and placed all logistics activities under that individual.

With management attention now specifically addressing logistics, the firm was able to eliminate duplicate activities, exercise better control over logistics activities, and reduce costs. During the first full year of implementation of the new logistics organizational structure, the firm realized cost savings of approximately $10 million. The savings had a sizable impact on profitability, one that the firm could not have achieved through an equivalent level of additional sales. Competition, slow market growth rates, and limited company resources would have precluded any significant sales increases.

Computer and Information Technology.   In the 1970s, information technology began to explode. This gave organizations the ability to better monitor transaction-intensive activities such as the ordering, movement, and storage of goods and materials. This information, combined with the availability of computerized quantitative models, increased the ability to manage flows and to optimize inventory levels and movements. Systems such as materials requirements planning (MRP, MRP II), distribution resource planning (DRP, DRP II), and just-in-time (JIT, JIT II) allow organizations to link many materials management activities, from order processing to inventory management, ordering from the supplier, forecasting, and production scheduling.

E-Commerce   Advances in electronic commerce (e.g., Internet, e-mail) have allowed organizations to better manage their activities and have been instrumental in allowing them to attain a national and/or global market presence. In combination with an increased emphasis on customer service, growing recognition of the systems approach and total

TABLE 1–3   **Profit Leverage Provided by Logistics Cost Reductions**

If Net Profit on the Sales Dollar Is 2.0 Percent, Then . . .	
A Saving of	*Is Equivalent to a Sales Increase of*
$ 0.02	$ 1.00
2.00	100.00
200.00	10,000.00
2,000.00	100,000.00
20,000.00	1,000,000.00
200,000.00	10,000,000.00
$2,000,000.00	$100,000,000.00

Source: Adapted from Bernard J. La Londe, John R. Grabner, and James F. Robeson, "Integrated Distribution Systems: A Management Perspective," *International Journal of Physical Distribution Management* 1, no. 1 (October 1970), p. 46.

cost concept, and the realization that logistics could be used as a strategic competitive weapon, these organizations were able to better develop fully integrated logistics systems.

World-Class Competitors

Competitive Pressures.   With rising interest rates and increasing energy costs during the 1970s, logistics received attention as a major cost driver. In addition, logistics costs became a more critical issue for many organizations due to the globalization of industry. This has affected logistics in two primary ways. First, the growth of world-class competitors from other nations has caused organizations to look for new ways to differentiate their organizations and product offerings. Logistics is a logical place to look, because domestic organizations should be able to provide more reliable, responsive service to nearby markets than overseas competitors can. Second, as organizations increasingly buy and sell offshore, the supply chain between the organization and those with whom it does business becomes longer, more costly, and more complex. Excellent logistics management is needed to fully leverage global opportunities.

More Complex Supply Chain

Shifting of Channel Power from Manufacturers to Retailers

Shifts in Channel Power.   Within the supply chain, the shifting of channel power from manufacturers to retailers, wholesalers, and distributors has also had a profound impact on logistics. When competition rises in major consumer goods industries, there is a shakeout of many suppliers and manufacturers, so that few leading competitors remain. Those remaining are intensely competitive and offer very high quality products. In many cases, the consumer sees the leading brands as substitutes for each other. A reduction in brand loyalty decreases manufacturers' power. This increases the retailer's power, because sales are determined by what is in stock rather than by what particular brands are offered.

In sum, along with the environment in which it is planned, implemented, and controlled, logistics is changing. Changes will continue to occur, probably at an increasing pace. The breadth and scope of these and other changes will place logistics at the forefront of organizational strategies and programs.

Key Logistics Activities

The following activities (as listed in Figure 1–1, p. 3) are involved in the flow of products from point-of-origin to point-of-consumption:

Major Logistics Activities

- Customer service
- Demand forecasting
- Inventory management
- Logistics communications
- Materials handling
- Order processing
- Packaging
- Parts and service support
- Plant and warehouse site selection
- Procurement
- Reverse logistics
- Traffic and transportation
- Warehousing and storage

While not all organizations may explicitly consider every one of these activities to be part of logistics, they all affect the logistics process. We will discuss each activity briefly below and in more detail in subsequent chapters.

Customer Service

Good Customer Service Supports Customer Satisfaction

Customer service has been defined as "a customer oriented philosophy that integrates and manages all elements of the customer interface within a predetermined optimum cost-service mix."[28] Customer service acts as the binding and unifying force for all of the logistics management activities (see Chapter 3).

Customer satisfaction, of which customer service is an integral part, occurs if the organization's overall marketing efforts are successful. Each component of the logistics system can affect whether a customer receives the right product, at the right place, in the right condition, for the right cost, at the right time. Thus, customer service involves successful implementation of the integrated logistics management concept in order to provide the necessary level of customer satisfaction at the lowest possible total cost.

Demand Forecasting

Demand forecasting involves determining the amount of product and accompanying service that customers will require at some point in the future. The need to know precisely how much product will be demanded is important to all facets of the firm's operations—marketing, manufacturing, and logistics. Forecasts of future demand determine promotional strategies, allocation of the sales force, pricing, and market research activities. Sales forecasts determine production schedules, purchasing and acquisition strategies, and in-plant inventory decisions.

Logistics management forecasts of demand determine how much of each item produced by the company must be transported to the various markets the firm serves. Also, logistics management must know where the demand will originate so that the proper amount of product can be placed or stored in each market area. Accurate estimates of future demand enable logistics managers to allocate resources (budgets) to activities that will service that demand. Decision making under uncertainty is less than optimal because it is extremely difficult to allocate resources among logistics activities without knowing what products and services will be needed. Therefore, it is imperative that organizations undertake some type of demand forecasting and communicate the results to the marketing, manufacturing, and logistics departments. Sophisticated computer models, trend analysis, sales force estimates, or other methods can help develop such forecasts.

Forecasting is a complex issue, with many interactions among functions and forecast variables. This topic will be explored in greater depth in Chapters 6 and 7.

Inventory Management

The inventory control activity is critical because of the financial necessity of maintaining a sufficient supply of product to meet both customers' needs and manufacturing requirements. Raw materials and parts, work-in-process, and finished goods inventories

---

[28]La Londe and Zinszer, *Customer Service: Meaning and Measurement,* p. iv.

all consume physical space, personnel time, and capital. Money tied up in inventory is not available for use elsewhere.

Financial Impacts of Inventories

Inventory management involves trading off the level of inventory held to achieve high customer service levels, with the cost of holding inventory, including capital tied up in inventory, warehousing costs, and obsolescence. In some cases, these costs can exceed 50 percent of the cash value of inventory on an annual basis![29] Successful inventory control involves determining the level of inventory necessary to achieve the desired level of customer service while considering the cost of performing other logistics activities.

Given the high cost of items such as high-tech merchandise, automobiles, and seasonal goods that rapidly become obsolete, organizations such as Hewlett-Packard, Xerox, and Sears have increased their attention to inventory management.[30] Inventory issues will be explored in Chapters 5 and 6.

Logistics Communications

Success in today's business environment requires the management of a complex communications system. Effective communication must take place among:

Effective Communication Is Necessary

1. The organization, its suppliers, and its customers.
2. The major functions within the organization, such as logistics, engineering, accounting, marketing, and production.
3. The 13 various logistics activities listed above.
4. The various aspects of each logistics activity, such as coordinating warehousing of material, work-in-process, and finished goods.
5. Various members of the supply chain, such as intermediaries and secondary customers or suppliers, who may not be directly linked to the firm.

Communication is the vital link between the entire logistics process and the firm's customers. Accurate and timely communication is the cornerstone of successful logistics management. The following example illustrates this point:

Communication at Sequent Computer Systems

Sequent Computer Systems is a provider of "data-center ready" open systems. The firm recognized its need to communicate order information quickly, clearly, and accurately. In combination with SonicAir, a third-party provider that delivers Sequent's spare and replacement parts to its customers, a real-time electronic data interchange (EDI) system was developed. "The communications system developed between the two companies is simple and straightforward. When a Sequent customer requires a part, an order is generated identifying the part number, quantity, and customer information. The order then is electronically transmitted to the SonicAir facility in Louisville, and a confirmation is posted acknowledging the transmission. A dispatcher receives the order within a few minutes and sends back an order acceptance. SonicAir then ships the order and sends confirmation of delivery to Sequent upon customer receipt." The results have been faster response time, more accurate orders, and tighter inventory control.[31]

---

[29]Douglas M. Lambert, *The Development of an Inventory Costing Methodology: A Study of the Costs Associated with Holding Inventory* (Chicago: National Council of Physical Distribution Management, 1976).

[30]Tom Davis, "Effective Supply Chain Management," *Sloan Management Review* 34, no. 4 (Summer 1993), pp. 35–46.

[31]Francis J. Quinn, "Communicating in Real Time," *Logistics Management and Distribution Report* 37, no. 1 (January 1998), p. 71.

A firm's communications system may be as sophisticated as a computerized management information system (MIS) or as simple as word-of-mouth communication between individuals. Whatever the system, vital information must be available and communicated to the appropriate individuals. Information systems will be discussed in Chapter 4.

Materials Handling

Materials handling is concerned with every aspect of the movement or flow of raw materials, in-process inventory, and finished goods within a plant or warehouse (see Chapter 11). The objectives of materials handling are to:

Objectives of Materials Handling

- Eliminate handling wherever possible.
- Minimize travel distance.
- Minimize work-in-process.
- Provide uniform flow free of bottlenecks.
- Minimize losses from waste, breakage, spoilage, and theft.

A firm incurs costs every time an item is handled. Since handling generally adds no value to a product, it should be kept to a minimum. For items with low unit value, the proportion of materials handling costs to total product cost can be significant. By carefully analyzing material flows, materials management can save the organization significant amounts of money.

Order Processing

Components of Order Processing

A customer's order triggers the logistics process and directs the actions to be taken in satisfying order demand. The components of order processing may be broken down into three groups: (1) *operational elements,* such as order entry/editing, scheduling, order-shipping set preparation, and invoicing; (2) *communication elements,* such as order modification, order status inquiries, tracing and expediting, error correction, and product information requests; and (3) *credit and collection elements,* including credit checking and accounts receivable processing/collecting.[32]

The speed and accuracy of a firm's order-processing activities have a great deal to do with the level of customer service the company provides. Because the order-processing cycle is a key area of customer interface with the organization, it can have a big impact on a customer's perception of service, and therefore satisfaction.[33]

Automation in Order Processing Is Widely Used

Computers and electronic commerce can help reduce the time between order placement and product shipment. In many cases, orders can be transmitted from a buyer's computer directly to a seller's computer; this is referred to as electronic data interchange (EDI). Orders can also be placed via other electronic means such as the Internet or facsimile (fax) machine. Computerized systems, although initially expensive to the company, can substantially improve both order-processing accuracy and response time. Frequently, savings in other logistics expenses (e.g., inventory, transportation,

[32]A. T. Kearney, Inc., *Measuring Productivity in Physical Distribution* (Chicago: National Council of Physical Distribution Management, 1978), p. 191.

[33]Benson P. Shapiro, V. K. Rangan, and J. J. Sviokla, "Staple Yourself to an Order," *Harvard Business Review* 70, no. 4 (July–August 1992), pp. 113–22.

warehousing) or increased sales from improved customer service will justify the cost of the computerized order-processing system (see Chapter 4).

Packaging

Functions of Packaging

Packaging performs two basic functions—marketing and logistics. In a marketing sense, the package acts as a form of promotion or advertising. Its size, weight, color, and printed information attract customers and convey information about the product. In logistics, packaging serves a dual role. First, the package protects the product from damage while it is being stored or transported. Second, proper packaging can make it easier to store and move products, thereby reducing materials handling costs. Chapter 11 will examine packaging issues.

When firms are involved in international marketing, packaging becomes even more important. Products marketed in foreign countries travel greater distances and undergo more physical handling than those marketed domestically. In many countries, management must deal with a lack of adequate materials handling equipment and must rely on inadequately trained personnel. In general, domestic packaging is not strong enough to withstand the rigors of international distribution.

Parts and Service Support

In addition to the movement of raw materials, in-process inventory, and finished goods, logistics must be concerned with the many activities involved in the repair and servicing of products. Logistics' responsibility does not end when the product is delivered to

Service after the Sale

the customer. Part of a firm's marketing activity is to provide customers with service after the sale. This can involve providing replacement parts when products break down or malfunction. Automobile dealerships, for example, must have efficient service departments that offer complete servicing and auto repair. Having adequate supplies of spare and replacement parts is vital to the service and repair activity, and logistics is responsible for making sure those parts are available when and where the customer needs them.

In the industrial marketplace, where the product may be a piece of manufacturing equipment, downtime can be extremely costly to the customer if product failure results in a production-line slowdown or shutdown. The firm supplying spare or replacement parts must be able to respond quickly and decisively. Adequate parts and service support are extremely important whenever postsale support is part of the firm's marketing effort.

Finally, if the firm is involved in any kind of product stewardship program, there is a responsibility to provide after-sales support of products, often for extended periods of time. This will require strategies and programs that are coordinated with other reverse logistics activities.

Plant and Warehouse Site Selection

Whether facilities are owned, leased, or rented, the location of plants and warehouses (storage facilities) is extremely important. The strategic placement of plants and warehouses can assist firms in improving customer service levels. Proper facility location can also allow lower volume-related transportation rates in moving product from plant to warehouse, plant to plant, or warehouse to customer (see Chapter 10).

**Considerations
in Site Selection**

The first consideration in selecting a site is the location of the firm's target markets. The needs of the customers and the location of raw materials, component parts, and subassemblies are also major considerations, for the company must be concerned with inbound movement and storage of materials in addition to outbound flows. Other important factors include labor rates; transportation services; city, county, and state taxes; security; legal concerns; local factors (e.g., attitude of the community toward new industry); land cost; and availability of utilities.

As an illustration of the importance of site selection, Intel Corporation had to determine a location for its new semiconductor manufacturing facility. The company received bids from a number of major cities, including Portland, Oregon; Austin, Texas; and Chandler, Arizona. Ultimately, Intel chose the Arizona location because it already had a facility nearby, the area was growing and had an attractive labor force, the town provided tax and other incentives, and Intel had a good relationship with local government.[34]

Procurement

Every company relies to some extent on materials and services supplied by other firms. In most industries, companies spend 40 to 60 percent of their revenues for materials and services from outside sources.[35] This process of acquiring materials and services to ensure the operating effectiveness of the firm's manufacturing and logistics processes is termed *procurement.* The procurement function includes the selection of supply source locations, determination of the form in which the material is to be acquired, timing of purchases, price determination, and quality control (see Chapter 12).

The changing economic environment of recent years, marked by wide variations in availability and cost of materials, has made procurement even more important in the logistics process. As organizations form long-term relationships with fewer key suppliers, procurement continues to grow in importance to the organization.

Reverse Logistics

The handling of return goods, as well as salvage and scrap disposal, is part of the larger process referred to as *reverse logistics,* which is an important component of logistics. Buyers may return items to the seller due to product defects, overages, shipping errors, trade-ins, or other reasons. Return goods handling has been likened to going the wrong way on a one-way street because the great majority of product shipments flow in one direction. Most logistics systems are ill equipped to handle product movement in a reverse channel.

Product Returns

In many industries in which customers return products for warranty repair, replacement, remanufacturing, or recycling, reverse logistics costs are high relative to forward logistics costs. Moving a product back through the system from the consumer to producer may cost as much as five to nine times more than moving the same product from producer to consumer. Often the returned goods cannot be transported, stored, or handled as easily as original goods, resulting in higher per-unit costs.

---

[34]"Intel Building $1.5 Billion Plant," *Rocky Mountain Construction* 74, no. 24 (December 20, 1993), p. 15; and William Carlisle, "States Are Closing Firms' 'Candy Store,'" *Arizona Republic* (July 24, 1994), pp. 1E–2E.

[35]Michiel Leenders and Harold E. Fearon, *Purchasing and Materials Management,* 10th ed. (Homewood, IL: Richard D. Irwin, 1993).

Reverse logistics also involves removal and disposal of waste materials from the production, distribution, or packaging processes. If waste materials cannot be used to produce other products, they must be disposed of in some manner. Whatever the by-product, the logistics process must effectively and efficiently handle, transport, and store it. If the by-products are reusable or recyclable, logistics manages their transportation to remanufacturing or reprocessing locations. Often, these activities are outsourced by the company to various third parties.[36]

Reverse logistics promises to become even more important as customers increase their demand for flexible and lenient return policies and as recycling and other environmental issues become more significant.

Traffic and Transportation

One major component of the logistics process is the movement or flow of goods from point-of-origin to point-of-consumption, and perhaps their return as well. The traffic and transportation activity involves managing the movement of products and includes selecting the method of shipment (air, rail, water, pipeline, truck, intermodal); choosing the specific path (routing); complying with various local, state, and federal transportation regulations; and being aware of both domestic and international shipping requirements.

Transportation is often the single largest cost in the logistics process. Therefore, it is an important component that must be managed effectively. Transportation issues are presented in Chapters 8 and 9.

Warehousing and Storage

Products must be stored at the plant or in the field for later sale and consumption unless customers need them the instant they are produced. Generally, the greater the time lag between production and consumption, the larger the level or amount of inventory required. Warehousing and storage activities involve the management of the space needed to hold or maintain inventories. Specific storage activities include decisions as to whether the storage facility should be owned, leased, or rented; layout and design of storage facilities; product mix considerations (e.g., what products should be stored?); safety and maintenance procedures; personnel training; and productivity measurement. These topics will be examined in Chapter 10.

Why Should Logistics Activities Be Integrated?

Logistics is a system or a process with many components or subprocesses. It is a network of related activities that have as a primary purpose to manage an orderly flow of materials and personnel within a firm, and the supply chain. This is illustrated in Figure 1–4, which shows a simplified example of the network of relationships that logistics has to manage in a portion of a supply chain.

Basically, the integrated logistics management concept refers to administering the various activities as an integrated system. In firms that have not adopted a systems

---

[36]James R. Stock, *Development and Implementation of Reverse Logistics Programs* (Oak Brook, IL: Council of Logistics Management, 1998), pp. 87–90.

FIGURE 1–4

*Logistics manages the flow
through the supply chain*

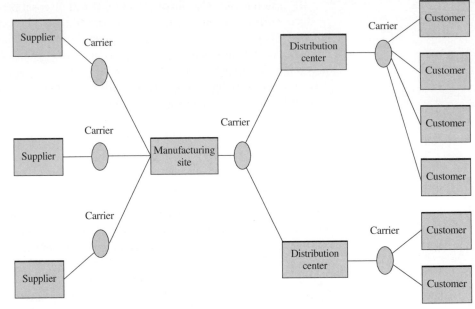

While the flow is primarily left to right, logistics is also responsible for returns, or movements from
right to left, hence the term *reverse logistics* has developed.

approach, logistics is often a fragmented and uncoordinated set of activities spread
throughout various organizational functions, with each individual function having its
own budget, set of priorities, and measurement systems. A number of firms, such as
Herman Miller, 3M, Quaker Oats, and Whirlpool Corporation, have found that total
logistics costs can be reduced by integrating such logistics-related activities as customer service, transportation, warehousing, inventory management, order processing
and information systems, and production planning and purchasing. Without this integrated approach, inefficiencies can result, such as inventory building up at the following critical business interfaces:

**Critical Business
Interfaces**

- Supplier–purchasing
- Purchasing–production
- Production–marketing
- Marketing–distribution
- Distribution–intermediary (wholesaler and/or retailer)
- Intermediary–customer

Excess inventories cost firms money (see Chapters 5 and 6). To illustrate, in a manufacturing environment, inventory buildups occur for one or more of the following reasons:

**Reasons for Inventory
Buildup**

1. Purchasing management is often rewarded for achieving low per-unit costs
   for raw materials and supplies.
2. Production management is usually compensated for achieving the lowest
   possible per-unit production costs.
3. Salespeople like to have market presence by positioning large inventories of
   product in the field, as close to the customer as possible. This allows

salespeople to offer the fastest possible order cycle time and to minimize the difficulties associated with forecasting customers' needs.

4. In some companies, transportation is the only logistics cost that is closely monitored. Transportation managers have more incentive to ship products by truckload or by railcar in order to obtain the lowest possible freight rates. Generally, these large shipments of products require increased inventories at both origin and destination points (e.g., manufacturer, wholesaler, retailer).

5. Both customers and intermediaries may attempt to reduce their inventories by purchasing more frequently, thereby forcing their inventories and their associated carrying costs back toward manufacturers. This is particularly true when intermediaries are concerned with cash flow.

Benefits of Integration   In addition to improving the flow of inventory, integration improves transport and warehouse asset utilization, and often eliminates the duplication of effort. For example, rather than having the purchasing department negotiate with inbound carriers and the logistics department negotiate with outbound carriers, one organization can negotiate for both inbound and outbound transportation. This typically results in lower overall freight rates because of the larger quantities involved. It also allows the firm and its carriers to more effectively and efficiently plan transportation. The central coordination of the various logistics activities forces cost trade-offs to be made between and among logistics activities such as customer service, transportation, warehousing, inventory management, order processing, production planning, and purchasing.

Global

Why Be Concerned with Reverse Logistics and Environmental Issues?

NKL, a vertically integrated Norwegian food cooperative, believes that reverse logistics and environmental programs can provide the company with competitive advantage. Specifically, NKL has identified four factors contributing to the creation of competitive advantage:

- The firm's retail shops can promote its environmental position.
- The company will attract customer groups who want to do "green" shopping.
- Being a "green" retail shop will result in cost reductions in a number of areas.
- "Green" shops will provide a positive profile in the community.

NKL experienced a 220 percent increase in the sales of environmental products during 1997, and has relied on 1.5 million reusable containers for fruits and vegetables (representing 14,000 tons or 70 percent of all Norwegian fruits and vegetables) to reduce costs and improve order cycle times. Additionally, NKL increased its use of rail transport from 50 to 60 percent (resulting in lower costs, less pollution, and better energy efficiency) and provided environmental training to more than 6,500 company employees.

Source: James R. Stock, *Development and Implementation of Reverse Logistics Programs* (Oak Brook, IL: Council of Logistics Management, 1998), p. 41.

The Total Cost Concept

Total cost analysis is the key to managing the logistics function. One of the major goals of the organization should be to reduce the total cost of logistics activities rather than focusing on each activity in isolation.[37] Attempts to reduce the cost of individual activities may lead to increased total costs.[38] For example, consolidating finished goods inventory in a small number of distribution centers will reduce inventory carrying costs and warehousing costs but may lead to a substantial increase in freight expense or a lower sales volume as a result of reduced levels of customer service. Similarly, savings associated with large-volume purchases may be less than the associated increase in inventory carrying costs.

Figure 1–5 identifies the six major cost categories of logistics. Management must consider the total of all the logistics costs described in the figure. Reductions in one cost invariably lead to increases in the costs of other components. Effective management and real cost savings can be accomplished only by viewing logistics as an integrated system and minimizing its total cost given the firm's customer service objectives.

The Relationship of Logistics Activities to Logistics Costs

Logistics costs are driven or created by the activities that support the logistics process. The major cost categories—customer service, transportation, warehousing, order processing and information, lot quantity, and inventory carrying (see again Figure 1–5)—are discussed in the following paragraphs.

Customer Service Levels.   The key cost trade-off associated with varying levels of customer service is the cost of lost sales. Customer service costs include order fulfillment costs, as well as costs for parts and service support. They also include costs associated with return goods handling, which has a major impact on a customer's perception of the organization's service, as well as the ultimate level of customer satisfaction.

Cost of Lost Sales

The cost of lost sales includes not only the lost contribution of the current sale but also potential future sales. Companies may lose future sales due to negative word-of-mouth publicity from former customers. One estimate indicated that every disgruntled customer tells an average of nine others about his or her dissatisfaction with the product or service.[39] It is no wonder that it is extremely difficult to measure the true cost of customer service!

The Objective Is to Minimize Total Costs Given the Customer Service Objectives

Thus, the best approach is to determine desired levels of customer service based on customer needs, and to consider how those needs will be affected by expenditures on other areas of the marketing mix. As we said earlier, the idea is to minimize the total cost, given the customer service objectives. Because each of the other five major

---

[37]This section draws heavily on Lambert, *The Development of an Inventory Costing Methodology*, pp. 5–15, 59–67.

[38]Joseph Cavinato, "A Total Cost/Value Model for Supply Chain Competitiveness," *Journal of Business Logistics* 13, no. 2 (1992), pp. 285–301.

[39]George R. Walter, *Upside-Down Marketing* (New York: McGraw-Hill, 1994), summarized by *Audio-Tech Books* 3, no. 2 (March 1994), p. 8.

FIGURE 1–5

How logistics activities drive total logistics costs

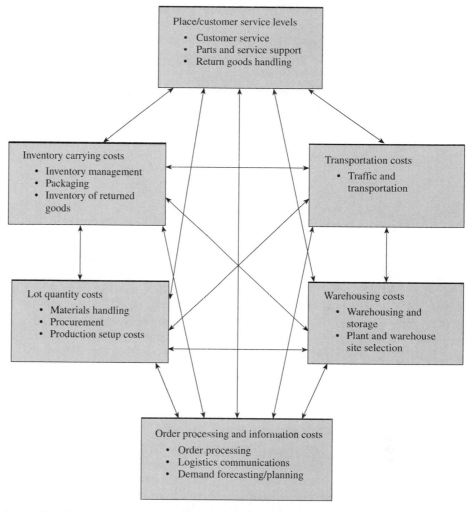

Source: Adapted from Douglas M. Lambert, *The Development of an Inventory Costing Methodology: A Study of the Costs Associated with Holding Inventory* (Chicago: National Council of Physical Distribution Management, 1976), p. 7.

logistics cost elements work together to support customer service, logistics managers need good data regarding expenditures in each category.

Transportation Costs.   Expenditures that support transportation can be viewed in many different ways, depending on the unit of analysis. Costs can be categorized by customer, by product line, by type of channel, by carrier, by direction (inbound versus outbound), and so on. Costs vary considerably with volume of shipment, weight of shipment, distance, and points of origin and destination. Costs and service also vary considerably with the mode of transportation chosen (see Chapters 8 and 9).

Warehousing Costs.   Warehousing costs are created by warehousing and storage activities, and by the plant and warehouse site selection process. Included are all of the costs that vary due to a change in the number or location of warehouses (see Chapter 10).

Order-Processing/Information Systems Costs.   Order-processing and information systems costs are related to activities such as processing customer orders, distribution communications, and demand forecasting. Investing in order processing and information systems is extremely important to support good customer service levels and control costs. Order-processing costs include order transmittal, order entry, order verification, order handling, and related internal and external costs such as notifying carriers and customers of shipping information and product availability. Shippers and carriers have invested a great deal in improving their information systems to include such technology as electronic data interchange (EDI), satellite data transmission, and bar coding and scanning for shipments and sales. There has also been a growth in sophisticated information technology such as decision support systems, artificial intelligence (AI), Internet access, and expert systems (see Chapter 4).

Examples of Order Processing Costs

Lot Quantity Costs.   The major logistics lot quantity costs are due to production and procurement activities. Lot quantity costs are production- or purchasing-related costs that vary with changes in production lot size or order size or frequency. They include:

Components of Lot Quantity Costs

1. Production setup costs.
    a. Time required setting up a line or locating a supplier and placing an order.
    b. Scrap due to setting up the production line.
    c. Operating inefficiency as the line begins to run, or as a new supplier is brought on board.
2. Capacity lost due to downtime during changeover of line or changeover to a new supplier.
3. Materials handling, scheduling, and expediting.
4. Price differentials due to buying in different quantities.

These costs must not be viewed in isolation, for they may also affect many other costs. For example, a consumer goods manufacturer that produces large production runs may get good prices from suppliers, and have long efficient production runs, but may also require more storage space to handle large runs. Customer service levels may suffer as order fulfillment declines, because goods are produced infrequently, in large batches, with inventory going to zero and creating stockout situations in between runs. This may increase information and order-processing costs, as customers frequently call to check on availability of back-ordered products, and cancel back orders.

Transportation costs may also rise as customers are sent partial or split shipments. Inventory carrying costs may rise as large quantities of inventory are held until depleted, due to large batch sizes. The impact of one cost on another must be explicitly considered.

Inventory Carrying Costs.   The logistics activities that may influence inventory carrying costs include inventory control, packaging, and salvage and scrap disposal. Inventory carrying costs are made up of many elements. Next to the cost of lost sales, inventory carrying costs are the most difficult to determine. For decision-making purposes, the only relevant inventory costs to consider are those that vary with the amount of inventory stored. These costs will be explored in detail in Chapter 5. The four major categories of inventory carrying costs are:

**Components
of Inventory
Carrying Costs**

1. *Capital cost,* or *opportunity cost,* which is the return that the company could make on the money that it has tied up in inventory.

2. *Inventory service cost,* which includes insurance and taxes on inventory.

3. *Storage space cost,* which includes those warehousing space-related costs that change with the level of inventory.

4. *Inventory risk cost,* including obsolescence, pilferage, movement within the inventory system, and damage. Proper packaging can reduce the cost of damage and pilferage, ease movement, and help prevent product obsolescence.

Logistics and Corporate Profit Performance—the Strategic Profit Model

**Strategies to Improve
Cash Flow and ROA**

In an uncertain economic environment, top management will be even more interested in properly managing assets and cash flow. The two most common strategies used to improve cash flow and return on assets (ROA) are (1) reducing accounts receivable and (2) reducing the investment in inventory. Table 1–4—which contains financial data for selected manufacturers, wholesalers, and retailers—provides insight into why this is so. It shows that accounts receivable ranged from 2.0 to 39.4 percent of total assets for manufacturers and from 0.0 to 60.7 percent of total assets for service firms. Inventories ranged from 1.5 to 26.2 percent of total assets for manufacturers and from 13.0 to 48.6 percent of total assets for service firms. Together, accounts receivable and inventories ranged, respectively, from 3.5 to 45.2 percent and from 33.9 to 80.5 percent of total assets.

When top management mandates a reduction in accounts receivable and/or inventories, its objectives are to improve cash flow and to reduce the company's investment in assets. Usually, management assumes that revenues and other costs will remain the same. But reduction in the terms of sale, or even enforcement of the stated terms of sale, in effect changes the price component of the firm's marketing mix. Additionally, simply reducing the level of inventory can increase the cost of logistics if current inventories have been set at a level that allows the firm to achieve least total cost logistics for a desired level of customer service.

The arbitrary reduction of accounts receivable and/or inventories in the absence of technological change or reengineering of the logistics process can have a devastating impact on corporate profit performance. For example, if a manufacturer changes its terms of sale, the effect on wholesalers and retailers will be twofold.

**Impacts of a Change
in Terms of Sale**

First, the change alters the manufacturer's price and therefore the competitive position of its products, which may lead to decreased sales. Second, it further complicates the cash flow problems of the manufacturer's customers. Forcing faster payment of invoices causes supply chain members to improve their cash flow by reducing their inventories of the manufacturer's products. They do so by placing smaller, more frequent orders, which may increase total logistics costs for both the manufacturer and its customers. This situation may also result in stockouts of the manufacturer's products at the wholesale or retail level of the channel, further reducing sales volume.

Similarly, a manufacturer's policy of arbitrarily reducing inventory levels to increase inventory turns, in the absence of a system change, may increase transportation costs and/or production setup costs as the logistics system scrambles to achieve the specified customer service levels with lower inventories (assuming the company was

TABLE 1–4   Selected Financial Data for Manufacturers, Wholesalers, and Retailers
$ Millions, 1998

	Sales	Net Profits	Net Profits as a Percentage of Sales	Total Assets	Accounts Receivable	Inventory Investment	Accounts Receivable as a Percentage of Assets	Inventories as a Percentage of Assets
Manufacturers								
Abbott Labs	$11,883.0	2,094.5	17.6%	12,061.1	1,782.3	1,280.0	14.8%	10.6%
Borden	3,481.6	278.2	8.0	3,049.7	n/a	n/a	n/a	n/a
Clorox	2,741.3	298.0	10.9	3,030.0	428.5	211.9	14.1	7.0
Ford Motor	122,937.0	6,920.0	5.6	85,079.0	3,513.0	5,468.0	4.1	6.4
General Electric	53,404.0	8,203.0	15.4	304,012.0	6,125.0	4,473.0	2.0	1.5
General Mills	6,033.0	421.8	7.0	3,861.4	394.1	389.7	10.2	10.1
Goodyear	13,155.1	558.7	4.2	9,917.4	1,733.6	1,835.2	17.5	18.5
Halliburton	8,818.6	454.4	5.2	5,603.0	2,205.0	326.9	39.4	5.8
Honeywell	8,027.5	471.0	5.9	6,411.4	1,837.8	1,028.0	28.7	16.0
NCR	6,589.0	7.0	0.1	5,293.0	1,471.0	489.0	27.8	9.2
Newell	3,234.3	290.4	9.0	3,943.8	524.6	625.2	13.3	15.9
Pfizer	12,504.0	2,213.0	17.7	15,336.0	2,527.0	1,773.0	16.5	11.6
Sara Lee	20,011.0	(523.0)	–2.6	10,989.0	1,800.0	2,882.0	16.4	26.2
Xerox	18,166.0	1,452.0	8.0	27,732.0	6,744.0	2,792.0	24.3	10.1
Service Firms								
Baxter	6,138.0	300.0	4.9	8,707.0	1,739.0	1,208.0	20.0	13.9
Bergen Brunswig	17,121.7	3.1	0.0	3,003.2	958.6	1,458.3	31.9	48.6
Target Stores	27,757.0	751.0	2.7	14,191.0	1,555.0	3,251.0	11.0	22.9
Fleming	15,372.7	25.4	0.2	3,924.0	334.3	1,018.7	8.5	26.0
Kmart	32,183.0	249.0	0.8	13,558.0	0.0	6,367.0	0.0	47.0
Nordstrom	4,851.6	186.2	3.8	2,865.2	664.4	826.0	23.2	28.8
Sears	41,296.0	1,188.0	2.9	38,700.0	23,494.0	5,044.0	60.7	13.0
Wal-Mart	117,958.0	3,526.0	3.0	45,384.0	976.0	16,497.0	2.2	36.3
Winn-Dixie	13,617.5	204.4	1.5	3,068.7	196.2	1,404.9	6.4	45.8

Sources: Various corporate annual reports, 10-K reports, websites, and other publications.

efficiently and effectively distributing its product prior to the policy change). Alternatively, pressure to reduce expenses may preclude the use of premium transportation or increased production setups to achieve the desired customer service levels.

One useful way to determine how a proposed systems change will influence profit performance and return on assets is by using the *strategic profit model* (see Figure 1–6). The strategic profit model demonstrates that return on net worth—that is, the return on shareholders' investment plus retained earnings—is a function of three factors management can control: net profit, asset turnover, and financial leverage.

Net Profit

Net profit as a percentage of sales is a measure of how efficiently and effectively products are manufactured and sold. However, net profit alone is not a satisfactory measure of performance. For example, would it be better to purchase stock in a company with a 2 percent net profit or one with a 10 percent net profit?

FIGURE 1–6

Strategic profit model

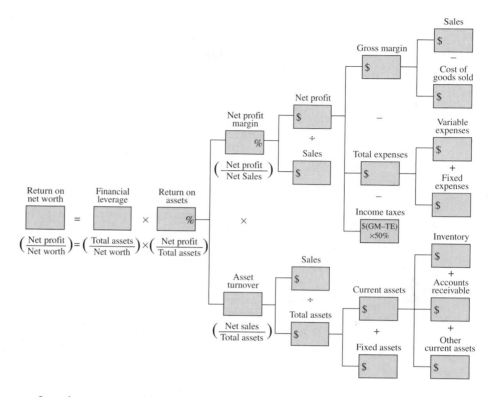

In order to answer this question, we would need to know the firms' sales volumes as well as the investment required to achieve that level of sales. We should also measure how efficiently management uses its assets.

Asset Turnover

Asset turnover, sales divided by total assets, shows how efficiently assets are employed in order to generate a level of sales.

Return on Assets

Return on assets (ROA), which is determined by multiplying the net profit margin by asset turnover, relates profitability to the value of the assets employed. For this reason, it is the best single measure of corporate performance. This yardstick allows the comparison of alternatives, whether they are similar or different projects or companies. However, as with any measure of performance, return on assets should not be used in isolation, since it may vary considerably as a result of industry conditions or the level of capital investment.

A firm can improve its return on assets by increasing net profit and/or reducing the assets it employs. In other words, increasing either net profit margins or asset turnover, keeping other things constant, will lead to higher return on assets.

Financial Leverage

Financial leverage is calculated by dividing total assets by the firm's net worth. It measures how management uses outside financing to increase the firm's return on net worth.

Net worth or shareholders' equity equals the shareholders' investment in capital stock plus retained earnings. Simply stated, if a company can borrow money at a cost of 10 percent before taxes and 5 percent after taxes, and can invest the funds in assets that provide a return of 15 percent after taxes, earnings per share will be larger if the firm finances its growth by borrowing money and using cash from operations, rather than by selling more shares. It should be noted, however, that it is possible for management to use too much financial leverage (i.e., borrow too much money) and create cash flow problems for the firm if sales decline.

Return on Net Worth

The important measure for shareholders is return on net worth (RONW), which equals net profit divided by shareholders' equity. It can be determined by multiplying the ROA by the financial leverage ratio.

TABLE 1–5   Income Statement and Balance Sheet of L and S Incorporated

L AND S INCORPORATED
INCOME STATEMENT
FOR THE YEAR ENDED DECEMBER 31, 2000
(000s)

Sales revenues		$100,000
Cost of goods sold		55,000
Gross margin on sales		45,000
Operating expenses:		
Variable expenses	$15,000	
Fixed expenses	20,000	35,000
Net profit before taxes		10,000
Income taxes		5,000
Net profit		$ 5,000

L AND S INCORPORATED
BALANCE SHEET
AS OF DECEMBER 31, 2000
(000s)

Assets			Liabilities and Stockholders' Equity		
Current assets:			Liabilities:		
Cash		$ 1,000	Accounts payable		$ 8,000
Accounts receivable		8,000	Notes payable, current		2,000
Inventories		15,000	Total current liabilities		$10,000
Other current assets		1,000	Long-term notes		15,000
Total current assets		$25,000	Total liabilities		$25,000
Fixed assets:					
Land		$ 4,000			
Plant and equipment		25,000			
Less:			Stockholders' Equity:		
Accumulated			Capital stock	$ 5,000	
depreciation	10,000	15,000	Retained earnings	20,000	25,000
Other fixed assets (net)		6,000	Total liabilities and		
Total assets		$50,000	stockholders' equity		$50,000

Using the Strategic Profit Model: An Example

The following example illustrates how the strategic profit model can be used. Table 1–5 contains a simplified income statement and balance sheet for L and S Incorporated. Figure 1–7 shows how the pertinent data from these financial statements can be transferred to the strategic profit model. The top portion of the model contains information from the income statement, and the bottom portion contains data from the asset side of the balance sheet.

Since financial leverage is a strategic decision made by top management, most operations managers must improve ROA to increase return on net worth. This can be accomplished by (1) increasing net profit margin or (2) increasing asset turnover. Net profit is a function of the sales volume achieved and expenses incurred to obtain that level of sales. Asset turnover is a function of sales volume and the level of assets employed. In other words, management can improve ROA by accomplishing one of the following objectives while holding the others constant: (1) increasing sales, (2) reducing expenses, or (3) reducing the level of assets employed.

Figure 1–7 shows that ROA for L and S Incorporated is 10 percent. If management wants to increase this figure to 12 percent, how can it do so? One method would be to increase sales by 7 percent, to $107 million. This would result in a corresponding 7 percent increase in cost of goods sold (COGS) and variable expenses, but net profit after taxes would increase to $6.05 million from $5.0 million (see Figure 1–8). The net profit margin would increase to 5.65 percent from 5.0 percent, and asset turnover would

FIGURE 1–7

Strategic profit model with financial data for L and S Incorporated ($ millions)

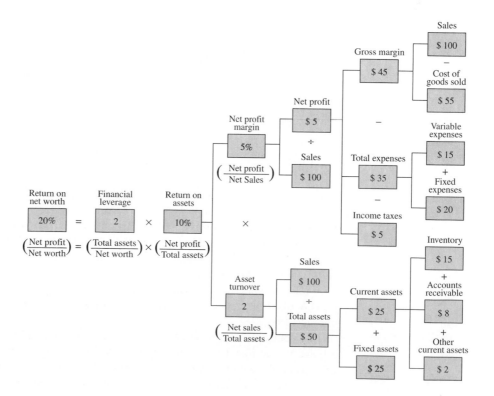

FIGURE **1–8**

*Strategic profit model
with financial data for
L and S Incorporated
after a sales increase
of 7 percent ($ millions)*

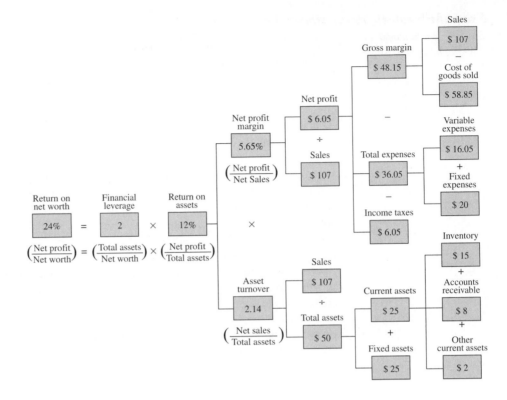

increase to 2.14 from 2.0. The result would be a 12 percent ROA. Since financial lever-age would remain the same, RONW would increase to 24 percent.

The second method of achieving the 24 percent return on net worth would be for management to reduce one or more of the following expenses by $2 million:

- Cost of goods sold (COGS)
- Variable expenses
- Fixed expenses

The $2 million reduction in expenses would increase net profit after taxes by $1 mil-lion, to $6 million. Since asset turnover would not change, ROA would be increased to 12 percent. Financial leverage would not change, and RONW would be 24 percent.

The third way to achieve the desired rate of ROA would be to reduce assets by $6 million. Assume that this could be accomplished by reducing inventories by $4 mil-lion and accounts receivable by $2 million. Also assume that the proceeds would be used to retire $6 million of debt bearing an interest rate of 12 percent. The result would be to increase ROA to 12.17 percent (see Figure 1–9). However, paying off loans of $6 million would reduce financial leverage to 1.76 (44 ÷ 25) and would result in a RONW of 21.4 percent. Typically, it is better to invest in more productive assets than to retire debt.

Of course, management could use any combination of the three methods above to achieve the desired 12 percent figure. Since logistics costs may represent as much as 25 percent of the cost of doing business and 30 percent of a manufacturer's assets, better management of the logistics function offers significant potential for improving RONW.

FIGURE 1–9

Strategic profit model with financial data for L and S Incorporated after reducing current assets by $6 million and paying off debt at 12 percent interest ($ millions)

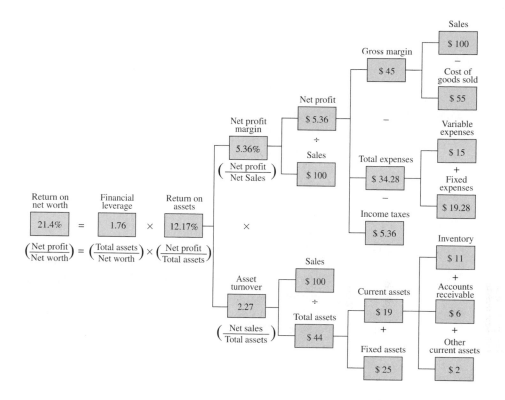

Future Challenges and Areas for Logistics Performance Improvement

Logistics professionals will face many complex challenges in this new millennium. Significant challenges will occur in the following areas: supply chain management (SCM), strategic planning, total quality management (TQM), just-in-time (JIT), quick response (QR), efficient consumer response (ECR), logistics as a competitive weapon, accounting for logistics costs, logistics as a boundary-spanning activity, global logistics, increasing skill requirements, logistics information systems, strategic alliances and partnerships, outsourcing, technology, e-commerce, and green marketing and reverse logistics.

These themes will be integrated throughout this text to provide continuity and an understanding of how some of these issues affect the performance and perceived importance of various logistics activities.

Supply Chain Management

Supply chain management (SCM) has been defined in several ways, including:

> The process for designing, developing, optimizing, and managing the internal and external components of the supply system, including material supply, transforming materials and distributing finished products or services to customers, that is consistent with overall objectives and strategies.[40]

---

[40]Robert E. Spekman, John W. Kamauff Jr., and Niklas Myhr, "An Empirical Investigation into Supply Chain Management," *International Journal of Physical Distribution and Logistics Management* 28, no. 8 (1998), p. 631.

Managing a set of three or more organizations directly linked by one or more of the upstream and downstream flows of products, services, finances, and information from a source to a customer.[41]

As we will discuss in Chapter 2, the optimal definition of SCM is different than both of these perspectives:

Definition of Supply Chain Management

The integration of key business processes from end user through original suppliers that provides products, services, and information that add value for customers and other stakeholders.[42]

An approach embraced by the business community in the 1990s, SCM focuses on the contributions of many firms and functions in providing customers with high-quality products and services. Although difficult to implement, SCM offers significant potential to customers and firms within the supply chain. The coordination of supply chain member organizations, coupled with shared real-time information, should result in both cost and service synergy.

SCM at Cisco Systems

For example, in 1996 Cisco Systems, a leading supplier of networking equipment and network management for the Internet, did not have online capability. "Today," according to a recent article, "it does billions of dollars a year in business—as much as 80 percent of that through the Web. In the process, the company has linked to suppliers and distributors, and developed other advanced supply chain practices that have reduced operating costs by an estimated $250 million a year."[43] It is because of the enormous potential to improve service and reduce costs that many organizations are examining the concept of SCM.[44]

Strategic Planning

Increasingly, logistics is participating in the formulation of competitive strategy (e.g., budgets, business plans).[45] Activities such as logistics budgeting and control, inventory planning and positioning, and customer service have become important parts of the organization's strategic planning process. Bergen Brunswig, a multibillion-dollar drug wholesaler, reported that logistics participation in strategic planning was so critical that the vice president of logistics attended corporate strategy meetings and served on a task force that thought strategically about the future.[46]

Strategic Planning at Bergen Brunswig

Total Quality Management

Total quality management (TQM) is a general business philosophy that can be applied to all facets of the enterprise, including manufacturing, marketing, and logistics. As a

---

[41]J. T. Mentzer, W. DeWitt, J. S. Keebler, S. Min, N. W. Nix, C. D. Smith, and Z. G. Zacharia, "A Unified Definition of Supply Chain Management," working paper, University of Tennessee, 1999.

[42]Douglas M. Lambert, Martha C. Cooper, and Janus D. Pagh, "Supply Chain Management: Implementation Issues and Research Opportunities," *International Journal of Logistics Management* 9, no. 2 (1998), p. 1.

[43]Robin Palmer, "The Five Stages of Supply Chain Management," *Supply Chain Technology News* 1, no. 2 (November/December 1999), p. 38.

[44]See Donald J. Bowersox, David J. Closs, and Theodore P. Stank, *21st Century Logistics: Making Supply Chain Integration a Reality* (Oak Brook, IL: Council of Logistics Management, 1999); and James S. Keebler, Karl B. Manrodt, David A. Durtsche, and D. Michael Ledyard, *Keeping Score: Measuring the Business Value of Logistics in the Supply Chain* (Oak Brook, IL: Council of Logistics Management, 1999).

[45]Martha C. Cooper, Daniel E. Innis, and Peter R. Dickson, *Strategic Planning for Logistics* (Oak Brook, IL: Council of Logistics Management, 1992), p. 10.

[46]Ibid., p. 105.

way of doing business, TQM should be embedded in all aspects of logistics operations. TQM requires that logistics management be proactive in performing the right activity, the right way, the first time, and in continuing to perform it to the required level.

Malcolm Baldrige National Quality Award

As an example, logistics has received increased corporate attention because of the emergence of various quality awards such as the Malcolm Baldrige National Quality Award (United States), the European Quality Award (Europe), and the Deming Award (global). The Baldrige Award, managed by the U.S. Department of Commerce, recognizes companies that have attained a high level of excellence and competitive advantage in domestic and world markets. Many organizations are using the award criteria to evaluate and improve their logistics processes and procedures, even if they do not intend to apply for the award.[47]

Logistics plays a pivotal role in a firm's winning the Baldrige Award. A significant portion of the score used in granting the award is based on customer satisfaction. Through creation of customer service, logistics contributes significantly to marketing's ability to satisfy customers. The "Customer and Market Focus" and "Customer Focused Results" categories of the award examine the company's knowledge of the customer, overall customer service systems, responsiveness, and ability to meet requirements and expectations.[48] Without a good logistics system, coupled with the inclusion of logistics in the strategic planning process, a firm cannot hope to score well in this important area.

ISO 9000 Programs

In addition to various quality awards, there are also a number of quality certification programs, the most recognized being the 9000 series of the International Organization for Standardization (ISO). The ISO 9000 series is an internationally recognized certification program whereby firms' quality processes are audited to verify whether they have effective, well-documented quality processes in place. It was born in Europe in an effort to support trade among European Economic Community members.[49] While not all firms attempt to obtain ISO certification, the standards have influenced how many companies approach quality issues, specifically within logistics (e.g., warehousing and transportation).[50]

Just-in-Time

Just-in-time (JIT) is an inventory management philosophy that attempts to minimize inventories through the elimination of safety stocks (i.e., extra product to cover unexpected variations in demand). Under a JIT approach, products, components, or other materials are delivered at the precise moment an organization needs them, or as close to that moment as possible.

---

[47]David Greisling, "Quality: How to Make It Pay," *Business Week* (August 8, 1994), pp. 54–59.

[48]*Malcolm Baldrige National Quality Award 2000 Criteria* (Milwaukee, WI: American Society for Quality, 1999).

[49]James R. Evans and William M. Lindsay, *The Management and Control of Quality,* 2nd ed. (St. Paul, MN: West Publishing, 1993), pp. 412–15.

[50]See Toby B. Gooley, "ISO 9000 Is Coming!" *Traffic Management* 34, no. 2 (October 1995), pp. 77–80; Samuel K. M. Ho, "Change for the Better via ISO 9000 and TQM," *Management Decision* 37, no. 4 (1999), pp. 381–85; and Lance L. Whitcre, *ISO 9000: Certifying Quality in Warehousing and Distribution* (Oak Brook, IL: Warehousing Education and Research Council, March 1994).

**Effects of JIT
on Logistics**

As we will discuss in Chapters 11 and 12, JIT has profound effects on logistics systems. JIT requires close coordination of demand needs among functional areas (e.g., logistics, manufacturing, marketing) and with other channel members (e.g., carriers, suppliers). JIT also represents a significant opportunity for logistics to contribute to the organization's success by reducing inventory and its associated costs, while maintaining or improving customer service levels.

Quick Response

Quick response (QR) is a retail sector strategy that combines a number of tactics to improve inventory management and efficiency while speeding inventory flows. Most QR is between manufacturer and retailer only. When fully implemented, QR applies JIT principles throughout the entire supply chain, from raw material suppliers through final customer.

The concept works by combining electronic data interchange (EDI) with barcoding technology. Sales are captured immediately. This information can be passed on to the manufacturer, who can then notify its raw material suppliers and schedule production and deliveries as required to meet replenishment needs. This allows inventory to be reduced while speeding response time, lowering the number of stockouts, reducing handling, and minimizing obsolescence. Although QR began in the textile/apparel industry, it is now being applied by many industries in the retail sector. The consumer packaged goods sector, especially the grocery industry, has implemented an adaptation of QR called efficient consumer response (ECR).

Cross-Docking

QR has had a major impact on logistics operations. Rather than "storing" products, distribution centers are now charged with "moving" products. This frequently entails cross-docking, a process that involves unloading inbound product, sorting products for individual stores, and reloading the shipments onto trucks destined for a particular store. No warehousing or storage of the product occurs, except for a few hours or, at most, a day.[51]

**Floor-Ready
Merchandise**

To further improve retail efficiency, some suppliers are shipping goods prehung and preticketed. Such goods, known as "floor-ready merchandise," are growing in popularity. As a result of QR, Mercantile Stores has reduced the number of distribution centers it owns from 12 to 8.[52] A retailing executive has commented that merchandise routinely spends an additional three days in the distribution center (DC) if it does not have retail price tickets and the proper hangers.[53] Thus, floor-ready merchandise leads to the further reduction in the number of DCs, since processing time is greatly reduced.

Efficient Consumer Response

The benefits of efficient consumer response (ECR) were first identified in a 1993 study. The study concluded that a savings of $30 billion was possible in the consumer

---

[51]For an overview of cross-docking, see Tom Andel, "Define Cross-Docking before You Do It," *Transportation and Distribution* 35, no. 11 (November 1994), pp. 93–98; and "Implementing a Cross-Docking Program," *Distribution Center Management* 30, no. 5 (May 1995), p. 3.

[52]Gary Robins, "Less Work, More Speed," *Stores* (March 1994), p. 24.

[53]Susan Reda, "Floor-Ready Merchandise," *Stores* (April 1994), p. 41.

Technology

Quick Response, Canadian Style

Executives at Toronto-based Hudson's Bay Co. left the pioneering spirit to US retailers when it came to developing Quick Response technology. They sat on the sidelines watching and learning from their US counterparts for years.

Then, in late 1991 the decision was made to implement QR technology and Hudson's Bay executives quickly made up for lost time. Everything from UPC codes to floor-ready processes was set up and put into effect in less than two years. Ironically, as US retailers and manufacturers hammer out guidelines for floor ready merchandise today, they're looking to their neighbors to the north for tips.

According to Peggy Macek, director of merchandise systems at Hudson's Bay Co., getting suppliers to comply with the various standards, including floor ready merchandise processing, involves a lot of partnering and understanding, and a bit of clout and coercion as well.

"We made it very clear to our suppliers what we expected of them, and gave them guidelines for making it happen. To our way of thinking there was no sense talking QR without having merchandise floor ready, and we did our best to help them see the benefits of coming on line," says Macek.

"There were suppliers who balked initially, but we're the largest retailer in Canada. They quickly came to the conclusion that you can't fight city hall."

No doubt, the fact that The Bay cut off one of its largest suppliers for one month for refusing to comply

with standards sent a clear message to Canadian manufacturers.

Currently, the retailer requires suppliers to price merchandise prior to shipping. Hangers have been standardized by merchandise type, and shipping cartons are moving through the DC without being opened.

While the Canadian retail scene is quite different from the US—fewer retailers and manufacturers are more spread out, for example—the benefits realized by The Bay are significant.

"We're saving millions of dollars in distribution functions," reports Macek. "We used to have five distribution centers. Now, because of the technology that's been implemented and the speed with which we can push goods through the pipeline, we were able to shut down three DC's."

In the past, it took as long as two to three weeks for product to get from the DC to the selling floor at The Bay. Today, product bound for stores in Toronto and Montreal is usually on the selling floor within a day or two of arriving at the DC. Stores located in more remote areas of the country can have product on the selling floor five to six days after arrival at the DC.

Hudson's Bay Co., the oldest retailer in North America, had total sales in excess of $5 billion in 1993. The retailer operates 102 full-line department stores called The Bay, and a discount store division known as Zellers.

Source: Stores (April 1994), p. 42.

packaged goods industry if the majority of the companies implemented ECR strategies.[54]

"ECR envisions a direct link among the consumer household, the retail store, the distributor and the supplier. ECR further envisions that connection to be a speedy, accurate, paperless flow of information driving the movement of product matched precisely to consumer [needs]. The vision requires a major shift in the way trading partners think."[55]

---

[54]Richard J. Sherman, "ECR Vision to Reality: Creating Innovative Strategies to Astonish Customers," *Annual Conference Proceedings of the Council of Logistics Management* (Cincinnati, OH, October 16–19, 1994), p. 142.

[55]Ibid., p. 143.

ECR includes the following strategies:[56]

Strategies of Efficient Consumer Response

1. Widespread implementation of electronic data interchange up and down the supply chain, between both suppliers and distributors, and distributors and customers.

2. Greater use of point-of-sale data obtained by greater and more accurate use of bar coding.

3. Cooperative relationships among distributors, suppliers, and customers.

4. Continuous replenishment of inventory and flow-through distribution.

5. Improved product management and promotions.

By applying the fourth point, continuous replenishment and flow-through distribution, inventory can be managed on a JIT basis, resulting in cost savings and service improvements.

Logistics as a Competitive Weapon

Just like a good product, promotion, and/or pricing strategy, logistics can be a source of competitive advantage for a firm. However, relative to other components of the marketing mix, logistics is the most difficult to duplicate. Competitors can develop competing products in a short time. Many brands are losing their advantages over non-branded items as more and more products become undifferentiated (i.e., generic). Promotional efforts can be matched by others who have the same access to advertising agencies, mass media, and other promotional activities. Because prices can be changed almost instantaneously, advantages arising from price reductions are very short-lived.

Logistics Competence Cannot Be Easily Duplicated

In contrast, logistics competence cannot be duplicated easily or inexpensively by competitors in the short term.

In an environment characterized by strong and sophisticated competitors, each trying to develop sustainable competitive advantage, many organizations have recognized that logistics competency holds the key to developing or maintaining continued business success. Improving customer service through logistics reengineering, employee training and empowerment, computerized information systems, and other efforts can provide an organization with competitive advantage.

The power of logistics in achieving an organization's customer service goals and supporting customer satisfaction has received an increased amount of attention in the press in the past few years.[57] Organizations that understand and use the potential of logistics as a competitive weapon include logistics as a key component of their marketing and overall business strategies.

Even though others might attempt to duplicate the efforts of the successful organization, those with the advantage will be engaged in programs of continuous improvement. While they may become smaller, differences among competitors will be maintained as long as the leading firm is pursuing continuous improvement. In an increasingly sophisticated marketplace, customers will be able to recognize smaller and smaller differences between competitors.

---

[56]Carol Casper, "ECR: Waiting to Move Center Stage?" *Industrial Distribution* (February 1994), pp. 83–85.

[57]See Ulf Casten Carlberg, "Information Systems Must Offer Customized Logistics and Increase Profitability," *Industrial Engineering* 26, no. 6 (June 1994), pp. 23–30; Daniel Innis and Bernard J. La Londe, "Customer Service: The Key to Customer Satisfaction, Customer Loyalty and Market Share," *Journal of Business Logistics* 15, no. 1 (1994), pp. 1–28; and "Logistics Mandate Is Customer Satisfaction," *Transportation and Distribution* 34, no. 12 (December 1993), pp. 28–30.

Organizations that view logistics as an offensive marketing weapon (i.e., as a strategy that can provide them with sustainable competitive advantage) are likely to make logistics an integral part of their organizational strategy.

Accounting for Logistics Costs

Integrated logistics management is based on total cost analysis, as described earlier in this chapter. Historically however, the necessary cost data have not been available, and the lack of data has prevented many firms from achieving least total cost logistics. The availability of logistics cost information should be a primary concern of management. Developing logistics cost information for decision making and control is one of the most critical tasks organizations face.

Activity-Based Costing

In general, accounting systems have not adapted enough to accurately account for the many trade-offs inherent in logistics activity and logistics decision making. Timely, accurate, meaningful logistics information is rarely available in practice. However, this is beginning to change as more organizations implement accounting systems that capture detailed information and use activity-based costing (ABC) systems to allocate costs to activities on an accurate and meaningful basis.[58] There is much work that remains to be done in this area. Some of the issues associated with the use of ABC in logistics are presented in Chapter 16.

The future potential of the integrated logistics management concept depends on the ability of organizations to obtain accurate real-time accounting information. Also, while many firms are using profitability (full cost) and contribution reports, the quality of those reports varies widely. It is not sufficient merely to have logistics accounting systems in place. Reports must be generated from such information and given to executives who have a need to know. Only then can optimal logistics cost trade-offs be made.

Logistics as a Boundary-Spanning Activity

Logistics Plays a Key Role throughout the Supply Chain

Logistics plays a key role throughout the supply chain, spanning boundaries within and between all members of it. Outside of the organization, logistics interfaces with customers, transportation carriers, warehousing firms, suppliers, vendors, and other third parties in the order-processing, order fulfillment, and product delivery cycles.

Inside the organization, logistics interfaces with all major functional areas. For example, it interfaces with finance in the planning process and in analysis of capital expenditures for logistics investments (e.g., buildings, equipment, and technology). Logistics interfaces with accounting in establishing logistics costs (e.g., transportation, distribution, storage) for various products, customers, and distribution channels, and it requires information from accounting regarding budgets and actual expenditures.

Logistics must work closely with production/operations because it receives order releases for materials from production and needs to make certain that the items required are ordered, transported, and received on time. Logistics often manages the flow of materials and/or work-in-process within the organization and must coordinate with production in terms of stocking and shipping finished products as they become available.

---

[58]Terrance Lynn Pohlen, *The Effect of Activity-Based Cost on Logistics Management,* an unpublished doctoral dissertation, Ohio State University, 1993; and Philip G. Deely, "Activity-Based Costing: What to Measure and How," *Annual Conference Proceedings of the Council of Logistics Management* (Cincinnati, OH, October 16–19, 1994), pp. 211–18.

**New-Product
Development**

Logistics should also be involved with all facets of new-product development such as product and packaging engineering. It is vital that logistics be represented in the new-product development process, because this will ensure that potential logistics problems will be eliminated or minimized.[59] Logistics input is critical with respect to the designing proper distribution channels, forecasting inventory requirements, insuring the availability of production materials, and configuring product packaging for maximum handling, transport, and storage within the distribution channel.

Global Logistics

As we noted briefly earlier in this chapter, an increasing number of organizations have become involved in some form of international marketing, manufacturing, and/or distribution. This trend should continue. With this expansion into global markets comes a need to develop worldwide logistics networks and information systems. The logistics executive will have to acquire additional skills and competencies in many areas (e.g., international finance, import and export documentation, political science, foreign business practices, and international customs and cultures). As organizations expand internationally, integrated logistics management and total cost trade-off analysis become even more complex and difficult to manage.

Future trends that will likely have an impact on organizations operating globally include the following:

Global Trends

1. An increasing number of logistics executives who have international responsibility and authority.
2. Increased standardization of international paperwork and documentation, especially the shipping bill of lading, coupled with reduced amounts of paper transactions.
3. An increasing number of smaller firms engaging in exporting with larger firms through licensing, joint ventures, or direct ownership.
4. A growing number of logistics service providers that are owned and operated on a global scale.
5. Increasing vertical integration of the channel of distribution, which will include channel members from many countries (especially in the acquisition of raw material supply sources).
6. Growth and development of global supply chains.

As organizations identify target markets in other parts of the world, they will have to establish logistics systems that meet the needs of a variety of customers. One of the most significant factors influencing expansion into international markets will be the increasing sophistication and expertise of logistics executives.

Increasing Skill Requirements

As rising costs threaten to increase the percentage of each sales dollar that firms spend for logistics activities, the logistics function will continue to gain visibility within the organization. Many logistics executives are positioned at senior levels (e.g., director, vice president) within their organizations.

---

[59]Phillip R. Witt, *Cost Competitive Products* (Reston, VA: Reston, 1986).

**Educational Needs
of Logistics Executives**

Studies have revealed broad ranges of responsibility. Vice presidents, directors, and managers spent a significant portion of their time outside traditional logistics activities, often involved in packaging, product planning, and sales forecasting. With this responsibility has come the need for academic training in information technology, global logistics, corporate finance, supply chain management, marketing management, and human resources.

Highlighting this continuing need of logistics executives to gain expertise in a larger number of areas was the response to a question on a recent survey relating to the factors that would affect the future growth and development of logistics. Among the factors mentioned by executives were information technology, supply chain management, cost/financial impacts, globalization, customer value, and e-business/commerce. Each of these factors will require executive expertise in a number of areas.[60]

With specific regard to supply chain management, logistics executives will require new skills in order to integrate supply chain thinking into strategic planning and operations. Five specific tasks will be important: (1) designing supply chains for strategic advantage, where innovation is vital to competitive advantage; (2) implementing collaborative relationships, which will replace command-and-control relationships; (3) forging partnerships; (4) managing information; and (5) measuring and managing prices and costs to make money.[61]

Logistics Information Systems

"Many logistics experts believe that the correct identification, integration, and implementation of information technology tools is the single most important issue facing logistics managers today and into the foreseeable future."[62]

Part of an organization's ability to use logistics as a competitive weapon is based on its ability to assess and adjust actual logistics performance in real time. This means the ability to monitor customer requirements, production demands, and inventory levels as they occur; to act in a timely manner to prevent product stockouts; and to maintain timely communication with customers. This requires integrated logistics information systems. Such systems not only must be integrated internally to take into account marketing and production activities but must also be integrated with others in the supply chain, to provide accurate information throughout the channel, from the earliest supplier through the ultimate customer.

**How Wal-Mart Uses
Electronic Information**

Information systems can link a variety of information technologies. Wal-Mart, for example, uses EDI to communicate with suppliers. It receives information from suppliers relating to shipment status, delivery schedules, quantities, and even billing/invoicing. Wal-Mart also uses bar-code readers in their retail store checkout lanes for capturing real-time sales information, which, in turn, is downloaded to suppliers. Suppliers

---

[60]Bernard J. La Londe and Terrance L. Pohlen "The 1999 Ohio State University Survey of Career Patterns in Logistics," *Annual Conference Proceedings of the Council of Logistics Management* (Toronto, Ontario, October 17–20, 1999), pp. 359–77.

[61]"Up Front: An Executive Summary of Industry News," *Logistics Management and Distribution Report* 37, no. 12 (December 1998), p. 5.

[62]Richard L. Dawe, Max Day, and Bill Goldsborough, "Using Information Technology to Improve Logistics Productivity," *Annual Conference Proceedings of the Council of Logistics Management* (Chicago, IL, October 5–8, 1995), p. 123.

use this information to determine which products to ship to Wal-Mart. Orders are created automatically. This system provides suppliers with rapid feedback on sales so that they can anticipate production requirements based on accurate, timely sales data. They also receive payments earlier, which helps their cash flow. Wal-Mart benefits in that it no longer has to place orders directly with many suppliers and can keep inventory levels to a minimum. Both strategies reduce Wal-Mart's costs and improve customer service levels.

Strategic Alliances, Partnerships, and Outsourcing

During the 1980s, many firms began to outsource various logistics activities to third parties and examine the viability of developing strategic alliances and partnerships with them. Stated simply, they were involved in a "make or buy" decision within logistics rather than manufacturing. As companies have been confronted with competitive pressures, shrinking budgets, downsizing, and a need to improve customer service levels, they have been outsourcing part or all of their logistics activities to third parties.

To illustrate, a firm may find it advantageous to contract with a specific transportation carrier to service a particular market segment, even though the company has a large private motor carrier fleet. Some customers may be located in remote areas where servicing them with the firm's private fleet may be too costly. In such a case, it would be more beneficial for the firm to have an outside transportation carrier make deliveries to those customers rather than trying to do it themselves.

Historically, traditional relationships between shippers and logistics service providers have been arm's-length transactions; that is, each entity has attempted to maximize its own interests with little regard for how the relationship might benefit or penalize the other party. In the last few decades, however, firms and logistics service providers have begun to recognize the benefits that can result from outsourcing and developing partnerships or alliances. In science, a relationship that benefits both parties is termed *symbiosis.*[63]

Relationship Marketing   A concept that goes beyond outsourcing is *relationship marketing,* a form of *partnering.* This concept of establishing close, long-term working relationships with suppliers of goods or services has been embraced by Bose Corporation in JIT II. A manufacturer of audio equipment, Bose uses the concept of an "in-plant," where key suppliers or service providers are actually on location at Bose's facility. Bose has such a relationship with Roadway Express, Inc. Bose has stated that the relationship has created efficiency between it and the carrier, resulting in improved communications, better service, and shared cost savings.[64]

The use of outsourcing and the number of alliances or partnerships is increasing each year, as more organizations recognize the symbiotic benefits that can arise from working in concert rather than independently. All indications point toward the continuation of this trend in the foreseeable future. For example, with the emergence of

Virtual Corporations   *virtual corporations* (i.e., entities that can respond quickly to emerging markets because

---

[63]For an excellent discussion of outsourcing issues, see Arnold B. Maltz, "Outsourcing the Warehousing Function: Economics and Strategic Considerations," *Logistics and Transportation Review* 30, no. 2 (1994), pp. 245–66.

[64]William J. Warren, "JIT II Puts Bose a Little Ahead of the Cutting Edge," *American Shipper* 33, no. 12 (December 1991), p. 47.

they concentrate on creative design and marketing, while contracting out other necessary business functions), more firms will rely on outsourcing logistics activities from third parties. Ensemble, a subsidiary of the greeting card company Hallmark, is responsible for new-product creation. It identifies market needs and develops products to fit those needs. All manufacturing and logistics activities are outsourced to third parties.[65]

Technology

Technology has had an impact on all facets of business, but in the logistics area the impact has truly been significant. The diffusion of technology is changing the way companies do business and the way firms relate to customers and suppliers.[66] Computers, the Internet, and information and communication systems are being increasingly used in every logistics activity, including transportation, warehousing, order processing, materials management, purchasing, and procurement.

Traditional methods of managing logistics activities are proving inadequate in today's fast-paced economy, and executives have been forced to innovate. If firms do not respond appropriately, they may face loss of market share, creating for themselves positions of competitive disadvantage. Fortunately, assistance is available due to recent innovations and developments in technology.

Technological Developments

The proliferation of technological developments in areas that support logistics include artificial intelligence (AI), electronic data interchange (EDI), bar-code scanning, local area networks (LANs), point-of-sale data gathering, radio frequency equipment, satellite data transmission, and warehouse management systems (WMS) software. Many manufacturing and merchandising firms have employed new technology to reap financial and customer service benefits.

Toys "R" Us Uses Technology in Its Distribution Centers

One such firm has been Toys "R" Us, one of the largest toy retailers in the world. In 1990, the firm decided to employ state-of-the-art technology in one of its distribution centers in California. At a cost of over $40 million, the 612,000-square-foot facility was equipped with over 80,000 pallets, or stage bins, by stacking them 50 feet high. The venture was very successful, as evidenced by comments of the Toys "R" Us president at the firm's annual stockholders' meeting:

> Operators get the goods with cherry picker-type trucks guided by wires in the floor and use laser scanners to identify the cartons. The [distribution] center holds 45% more merchandise than the company's existing warehouses and takes up two-thirds the space. It lets the company get toys out of the warehouse and onto store shelves faster, keeping handling costs low and enabling Toys "R" Us consistently to beat anyone else's prices.[67]

Information via Satellite at J. C. Penney

Similarly, J. C. Penney uses satellite transmissions to interface with its stores and its customers. Buyers place orders with company headquarters or directly with suppliers who are linked to Penney via an electronic ordering system. "These satellite feeds allow the retailer not only to cut travel time among buyers but also to react faster to changes in styles and give each store an individual look."[68]

---

[65]James Aaron Cooke, "Virtual Companies Need Real Logistics Support," *Logistics Management* 36, no. 11 (November 1997), pp. 47–49.

[66]For a brief discussion of some technological trends, see Peter Bradley, "We've Only Just Begun . . . ," *Logistics Management* 36, no. 1 (January 1997), pp. 63–64.

[67]Susan Caminiti, "The New Champs of Retailing," *Fortune* 122, no. 7 (September 24, 1990). p. 94.

[68]Ibid., pp. 94, 98.

E-Commerce

An increasing amount of products are being sold to consumers and businesses via the Internet, presently more than 2 billion orders per year.[69] The significant growth in what is referred to as e-commerce makes logistics efficiency and effectiveness paramount. Simply, organizations must develop optimal fulfillment infrastructures that maximize customer service and minimize costs. In such an environment, fast and accurate information systems are vital.

Information Requirements in an E-Commerce Supply Chain

In an e-commerce environment, the information requirements for an organization operating within a supply chain include:

- Ability to process a large number of stockkeeping units (SKUs).
- Ability to manage an accelerated replenishment cycle.
- High level of inventory accuracy.
- Ability to provide value-added customer services.
- Providing of real-time order and inventory data.[70]

Many organizations have begun to use e-commerce, some exclusively so. Amazon.com, the largest online seller of books and media, has annual revenues exceeding $1 billion. Dell Computer realizes more than $500 million from its Internet marketing efforts, and Gateway (computers) has revenues of more than $250 million.[71] Revenues for Internet-related businesses are expected to increase significantly during the next decade. In 1999, estimated Internet revenues were $500 billion.[72]

Green Marketing and Reverse Logistics

Green marketing, which deals with environment-related marketing issues, has been an area that has gained increased awareness, especially in Europe. Transportation and disposal of hazardous materials are frequently regulated and controlled. Organizations around the world are increasingly required to remove and dispose of packaging materials used in the manufacture, storage, or movement of their products. These issues, if not addressed correctly, complicate the tasks of logistics by potentially increasing costs and having negative customer service implications.

Environmental Issues Are Becoming More Important

Reverse Logistics Defined

The logistics activity corresponding to green marketing is referred to as *reverse logistics* (see Figure 1–10). Reverse logistics includes product returns, source reduction, recycling, materials substitution, reuse of materials, waste disposal, and refurbishing, repair, and remanufacturing. When viewed from a business logistics perspective, the relevant issues are those of cost, customer service, profitability, partnerships/alliances, and competitive advantage.

As an activity, program, or process, reverse logistics interfaces with every other functional area within the organization, such as accounting/finance, manufacturing, marketing, packaging engineering, and purchasing and procurement. Decisions made in logistics and the other functional areas affect the ability of the organization to conserve resources, generate additional revenues, and achieve green marketing goals and objectives.[73]

---

[69]Lisa H. Harrington, "Fast, First, Frightened," *Supply Chain Technology News* 2, no. 1 (January 2000), p. 39.

[70]Ibid., p. 40.

[71]Lisa H. Harrington, "Whatever the Customer Wants, the Customer Gets," *Supply Chain Technology News* 1, no. 2 (November/December 1999), p. 34.

[72]"Revenues for Internet-Related Businesses Will Rise by 68 Percent," *Competitive Edge* (Winter 1999), p. 20.

[73]Stock, *Development and Implementation of Reverse Logistics Programs,* p. 21.

FIGURE 1–10

Reverse logistics within one portion of a typical supply chain

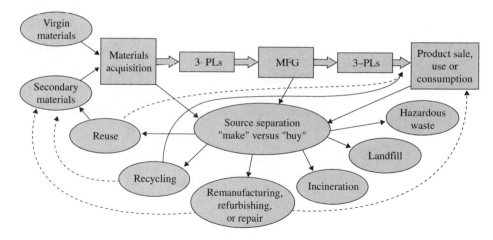

Source: James R. Stock, *Development and Implementation of Reverse Logistics Programs* (Oak Brook, IL: Council of Logistics Management, 1998), p. 22.

Creative Solutions

Creating Partnerships That Generate Solutions Within and Outside the Realm of Logistics

Traditionally, shippers look for a combination of the highest service levels and lowest costs in a logistics partnership. IBM, Xerox, and Airborne Express have taken that a step—or rather several steps—further. The companies have created a partnership that generates solutions both within and outside the realm of logistics.

For example, IBM has helped Airborne upgrade its information-management system. Airborne offered to fuel IBM and Xerox executive aircraft under its fuel contract. And through an agreement with Airborne, both Xerox and IBM may offer discounted express-air rates to their other business partners.

The partnership grew out of benchmarking meetings held jointly by Xerox and IBM in 1995. Both companies concluded that there might be synergies they could achieve with the air-express transportation used for parts distribution. [Many parts centers were in essentially identical locations.]

As the companies examined the overlapping distribution systems, several issues came to the surface

that offered potential cost and/or service improvements:

- Were there potential warehouse consolidation opportunities?

- When there were more than a single warehouse in an area, would it make sense to utilize the most sophisticated (e.g., state-of-the-art) facility?

- Couldn't a single air carrier gain advantages by servicing more single pickup and delivery points, rather than multiple locations?

Airborne Express became the air carrier of choice because they already had developed relationships with both Xerox and IBM. By reducing redundant operations and eliminating non–value-added distribution activities, the three partners together have saved $10 million. IBM and Xerox now co-locate inventory at parts centers in St. Louis, MO, and Seattle, WA.

Source: Jim Thomas, "Imagination Unlimited," *Logistics Management and Distribution Report* 37, no. 9 (September 1998), pp. 71–74.

Summary

In this chapter, we introduced the concept of logistics and described its development and relevance to the organization and economy as a whole. The concept of the systems approach was introduced, and related to logistics' interface with marketing and other functions. We emphasized the key role of logistics in customer service. The systems approach was also related to the total cost concept and the principle of trade-offs, as it relates to both the performance of logistics activity and the costs associated with such activity. The key logistics costs identified were inventory carrying costs, customer service, transportation, warehousing, order processing/information systems costs, and lot quantity costs.

In the chapter we described the importance of the integrated logistics management concept and the reasons for its growth. We saw how a firm could implement integrated logistics management using total cost analysis and how it can measure the impact of logistics decisions on corporate profit performance. Examples showed how firms have implemented logistics management. Finally, the chapter closed with a summary of future challenges for logistics professionals.

Clearly, there are many opportunities and challenges that face the logistics function in the future. We will begin to describe these in more depth in Chapter 2, which focuses on supply chain management.

Suggested Readings

Andersson, Jesper. "On Activity Based Costing in Supply Chains." In *Proceedings of the 11th Annual Conference for Nordic Researchers in Logistics,* ed. Everth Larsson and Ulf Paulsson. (Lund, Sweden: Lund University, 1999), pp. 141–56.

Andranski, Joseph C. "Foundations for Successful Continuous Replenishment Programs." *The International Journal of Logistics Management* 5, no. 1 (1994), pp. 1–8.

Blanchard, Dave. "Best Practices: Knowledge Management (From Data to Knowledge)." *Supply Chain Technology News* 2, no. 1 (January 2000), pp. 19–25.

Bowersox, Donald J.; David J. Closs; and Theodore P. Stank. *21st Century Logistics: Making Supply Chain Integration a Reality.* Oak Brook, IL: Council of Logistics Management, 1999.

Bowersox, Donald J.; Patricia J. Daugherty; Cornelia I. Dröge; Richard N. Germain; and Dale S. Rogers. *Logistical Excellence: It's Not Business as Usual.* Burlington, MA: Digital Press, 1992.

Clarke, Mike P. "Virtual Logistics: An Introduction and Overview of the Concepts." *The International Journal of Physical Distribution and Logistics Management* 28, no. 7 (1998), pp. 486–507.

Cooke, James Aaron. "To Outsource or Not to Outsource?" *Logistics Management & Distribution Report* 37, no. 10 (October 1998), pp. 57–59.

Emerson, Carol J., and Curtis M. Grimm. "The Relative Importance of Logistics and Marketing Customer Service: A Strategic Perspective." *Journal of Business Logistics* 19, no. 1 (1998), pp. 17–32.

Gentry, Connie. "The Dot.Com Dash," *Inbound Logistics* 20, no. 4 (April 2000), pp. 32–64.

Leenders, Michiel, and Harold E. Fearon. *Purchasing and Materials Management.* 11th ed. Burr Ridge, IL: Richard D. Irwin, 1997.

LeMay, Stephen A., and Jon C. Carr. *The Growth and Development of Logistics Personnel.* Oak Brook, IL: Council of Logistics Management, 1999.

The Logistics Forum Research Report. New York: Richmond Events, 1999.

Martin, James D. "CEOs and Logistics: Thinking Out of the Box." *Inbound Logistics* 17, no. 6 (June 1997), pp. 22–28.

Schwartz, Beth M. "From the End of the Supply Chain and Into the Abyss." *Supply Chain Technology News* 2, no. 5 (May 2000), pp. 27–29, 34–35.

Shapiro, Benson P.; V. K. Rangan; and J. J. Sviokla. "Staple Yourself to an Order." *Harvard Business Review* 70, no. 4 (July–August 1992), pp. 113–22.

Smith, Peter A.; Jack Barry; Joseph L. Cavinato; John J. Coyle; Steven J. Dunn; and William Grenoble. *Logistics in Service Industries.* Oak Brook, IL: Council of Logistics Management, 1991, p. xvii.

Stock, James R. "Logistics Thought and Practice: A Perspective." *International Journal of Physical Distribution and Logistics Management* 20, no. 1 (1990), pp. 3–6.

———. *Development and Implementation of Reverse Logistics Programs.* Oak Brook, IL: Council of Logistics Management, 1998.

Questions and Problems

1. How do improvements in logistics productivity affect the economy as a whole, as well as the position of individual consumers?

2. How is logistics related to the marketing effort? Be sure to discuss customer service, customer satisfaction, integration of efforts, and cost and performance outputs.

3. What are the different types of utility, and how does logistics directly or indirectly affect each one?

4. Why has logistics been receiving more attention as a strategic function of the organization?

5. What is the profit leverage effect of logistics, and what are the greatest cost savings opportunities for logistics?

6. Based on the example shown in Table 1–3 and described on pp. 17–18, what is the increase in sales necessary to have the same impact on before-tax profits as a savings in logistics of $350,000 if the net profit on sales is 7 percent?

7. Discuss the key challenges facing logistics today. Identify what you see as the greatest area of opportunity for logistics, and explain why you chose this area.

8. How have the role and performance of logistics been enhanced by the growth of technology, particularly information technology? What do you see as key trends in the future?

9. Of the 13 logistics activities listed in Figure 1–1 and described on pp. 19–25, which do you believe will experience the most change in the next five years or so? Why?

Supply Chain Management

Chapter Objectives

- To familiarize the reader with the concept of supply chain management (SCM).
- To show the role of logistics in supply chain management.
- To show how supply chain management can play a key role in achieving corporate success.
- To describe the factors that influence supply chain network structure, supply chain business processes, and supply chain management components.
- To present supply chain design considerations.
- To illustrate how to implement logistics cost trade-offs within a supply chain.

Introduction

In any society—industrialized or nonindustrialized—goods must be transported from the place they are produced to the place they are consumed. Except in very primitive cultures, where each family meets its own household needs, the exchange process is the cornerstone of economic activity. Exchange takes place when there is a discrepancy between the amount, type, and timing of goods available and the goods needed. If one or more individuals or organizations within the society have a surplus of goods that someone else needs, there is a basis for exchange. When many exchanges take place between producers and consumers, the alignment of firms that bring products or services to market has been called the *supply chain,* the *demand chain,* or the *value chain.* In this book we will use the term *supply chain* to represent this alignment of firms.

Supply chain management is a term that has grown significantly in use and popularity since the late 1980s, although considerable confusion exists about what it actually means. Many people are using the term as a substitute or synonym for *logistics.* However, the definition of supply chain management used in this book is much broader than that of logistics.

What Is Supply Chain Management?

Supply chain management is the integration of key business processes from end user through original suppliers that provides products, services, and information that add value for customers and other stakeholders.[1]

Supply Chain Management Processes

A number of important differences exist between the above definition of supply chain management and the Council of Logistics Management's definition of logistics. First and foremost, supply chain management is the management of eight key business processes:

1. Customer relationship management.
2. Customer service management.
3. Demand management.
4. Order fulfillment.
5. Manufacturing flow management.
6. Procurement.
7. Product development and commercialization.
8. Returns.

Key requirements for successful implementation of supply chain management are executive support, leadership, commitment to change, and empowerment. These requirements will be described along with the key processes later in this chapter.

Thus, supply chain management (SCM) is a highly interactive, complex systems approach and requires simultaneous consideration of many trade-offs. As shown in Figure 2–1, SCM spans organizational boundaries as it considers trade-offs both within

---

[1]Douglas M. Lambert, Martha C. Cooper, and Janus D. Pagh, "Supply Chain Management: Implementation Issues and Research Opportunities," *The International Journal of Logistics Management* 9, no. 2 (1998), p. 1. Website: <http://www.ijlm.org>.

FIGURE 2–1

Supply chain management: Integrating and managing business processes across the supply chain

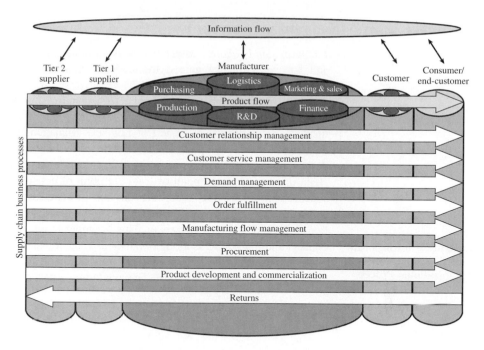

Source: Douglas M. Lambert, Martha C. Cooper, and Janus D. Pagh, "Supply Chain Management: Implementation Issues and Research Opportunities," *The International Journal of Logistics Management* 9, no. 2 (1998), p 2.

and among organizations regarding where inventory should be held and where activities should be performed.

Product Flows Follow Information Flows

In addition to the eight business processes, Figure 2–1 illustrates the product flows and information links that must take place in a supply chain. Information is not a process, but it is a key enabler of supply chain integration. Remember that product flows take place only after information flows are initiated.

Due to the dynamic nature of the business environment, management must regularly and frequently monitor and evaluate the performance of the supply chain. When performance goals are not met, management must evaluate possible supply chain alternatives and implement changes. SCM is particularly important in mature and declining markets and during periods of economic slowdown, when market growth cannot conceal inefficient practices. It is also critical in new-product and market development, when the organization is making decisions related to supply chain configuration.

This chapter begins with an explanation of the differences between SCM and logistics. Next, issues related to the structure of the supply chain are presented. Then the supply chain business processes, along with business process chains, are described. Sections on the management components of SCM and supply chain design follow. The chapter closes with sections on performance considerations in supply chain management, reengineering improvement into the supply chain, and implementing integrated supply chain management; these sections draw heavily on the experience of 3M.

Supply Chain Management versus Logistics[2]

The term s*upply chain management* was introduced by consultants in the early 1980s[3] and has subsequently gained tremendous attention.[4] Since 1989, academics have attempted to give structure to SCM.[5]

Until recently most practitioners,[6] consultants,[7] and academics[8] viewed SCM as not appreciably different from the contemporary understanding of logistics management, as defined by the Council of Logistics Management (CLM) in 1986.[9] That is, SCM was viewed as logistics outside the firm to include customers and suppliers. As defined by the Council of Logistics Management, *logistics* always represented a supply chain orientation, from point of origin to point of consumption. Then why the confusion? It is probably due to the fact that logistics is a functional silo within companies and is also a bigger concept that deals with the management of material and information flows across the supply chain. This is similar to the confusion over marketing as a concept and marketing as a functional area. Thus, the quote from the CEO, "Marketing is too important to be left to the marketing department." Everybody in the company should have a customer focus. The marketing concept does not apply just to the

Logistics Is a Corporate Function and an Interorganizational Process

---

[2]This section is taken from ibid., pp. 2–5.

[3]R. Keith Oliver and Michael D. Webber, "Supply Chain Management: Logistics Catches Up with Strategy," *Outlook* (1982), cited in Martin G. Christopher, *Logistics: The Strategic Issue* (London: Chapman and Hall, 1992).

[4]Bernard J. La Londe, "Supply Chain Evolution by the Numbers," *Supply Chain Management Review* 2, no. 1 (1998), pp. 7–8.

[5]For example, Graham C. Stevens, "Integration of the Supply Chain," *International Journal of Physical Distribution and Logistics Management* 19, no. 8 (1989), pp. 3–8; Denis R. Towill, Mohamed M. Naim, and J. Wikner, "Industrial Dynamics Simulation Models in the Design of Supply Chains," *International Journal of Physical Distribution and Logistics Management* 22, no. 5 (1992), pp. 3–13; Lisa M. Ellram and Martha C. Cooper, "The Relationship Between Supply Chain Management and Keiretsu," *The International Journal of Logistics Management* 4, no. 1 (1993), pp. 1–12; and Christian Bechtel and Jayanth Jayaram, "Supply Chain Management: A Strategic Perspective," *The International Journal of Logistics Management* 8, no. 1 (1997), pp. 15–34.

[6]Tom Davis, "Effective Supply Chain Management," *Sloan Management Review* 34, no. 4 (Summer 1993), pp. 35–46; Bruce C. Arntzen, Gerald G. Brown, Thomas P. Harrison, and Linda L. Trafton, "Global Supply Chain Management at Digital Equipment Corporation," *Interfaces* 25, no. 1 (1995), pp. 69–93; Hau L. Lee and Corey Billington, "The Evolution of Supply Chain Management Models and Practice at Hewlett-Packard," *Interfaces* 25, no. 5 (1995), pp. 42–63; and Robert C. Camp and Dan N. Colbert, "The Xerox Quest for Supply Chain Excellence," *Supply Chain Management Review,* Spring 1997, pp. 82–91.

[7]John W. Scharlacken, "The Seven Pillars of Global Supply Chain Planning," *Supply Chain Management Review* 2, no. 1 (1998), pp. 32–40; Gene Tyndall, Christopher Gopal, Wolfgang Partsch, and John Kamauff, *Supercharging Supply Chains* (New York: John Wiley & Sons, Inc., 1998); and William C. Copacino, *Supply Chain Management: The Basics and Beyond* (Boca Raton, FL: St. Lucie Press, 1997).

[8]Marshall L. Fisher, "What Is the Right Supply Chain for Your Product?" *Harvard Business Review* 75, no. 2 (March–April 1997), pp. 105–16; Hau L. Lee and Corey Billington, "Managing Supply Chain Inventory: Pitfalls and Opportunities," *Sloan Management Review* 33, no. 3 (Spring 1992), pp. 65–73; Robert B. Handfield and Ernest L. Nichols Jr., *Introduction to Supply Chain Management* (Upper Saddle River, NJ: Prentice Hall, 1999); and Donald J. Bowersox and David J. Closs, *Logistical Management—The Integrated Supply Chain Process* (New York: McGraw-Hill, 1996).

[9]That definition read as follows:

> The process of planning, implementing, and controlling the efficient, cost-effective flow and storage of raw materials, in-process inventory, finished goods, and related information flow from point-of-origin to point-of-consumption for the purpose of conforming to customer requirements.

What's It All About? (Oak Brook, IL: Council of Logistics Management, 1986).

marketing department. It is everybody's responsibility to focus on serving the customer's needs.

Executives in companies leading the drive to implement SCM visualize the necessity to integrate all key business operations across the supply chain.[10] This broader understanding of SCM is likewise the core message in the following statement by James E. Morehouse, vice president of A. T. Kearney, Inc.: "For companies to survive and prosper, they will need to operate their supply chains as extended enterprises with relationships which embrace business processes, from materials extraction to consumption."[11] Thus, SCM has been reconceptualized from integrating *logistics* across the supply chain to integrating and managing *key business processes* across the supply chain.[12] Based on this emerging distinction between SCM and logistics, CLM modified the definition of logistics in 1998. The modified definition (given in Chapter 1, and shown below) explicitly declares CLM's position that logistics management is only a part of SCM.

In 1998 CLM Revised the Definition of Logistics

Logistics is that part of the supply chain process that plans, implements, and controls the efficient, effective flow and storage of goods, services, and related information from the point-of-origin to the point-of-consumption in order to meet customers' requirements.[13]

Managing the supply chain is a very complicated task and even managing logistics from point-of-origin to point-of-consumption is a lot easier to write on a piece of paper than it is to actually do. Imagine the degree of complexity you will face if you are actually going to manage all suppliers back to the point-of-origin and all products and services out to the point-of-consumption. It is probably easier to understand why executives would want to manage their supply chains to the point-of-consumption because whoever has the relationship with the end user has the power in the supply chain. Intel has created a relationship with the end user by having computer manufacturers place a label stating "intel inside" on their computers. This affects the computer manufacturer's ability to switch chip suppliers. But managing all tier 1 suppliers' networks to the point-of-origin is an enormous undertaking. Managing the entire supply chain is a very difficult and challenging task, as illustrated in Figure 2–2.

The supply chain network structure will have a different look depending on who is the focal company, that is, the company whose management is mapping the supply chain. For example, if the focal company is a retailer such as Wal-Mart, the consumer "cloud" on the far right would be moved next to the black box in the center of the chart. If the focal company was a farmer, suppliers beyond tier 1 would not be included in the supply chain map. Tier 1 suppliers are those from whom the focal company purchases products and services. Tier 2 suppliers are the suppliers to tier 1 suppliers and so on.

---

[10]Lawrence C. Giunipero and Richard R. Brand, "Purchasing's Role in Supply Chain Management," *The International Journal of Logistics Management* 7, no. 1 (1996), pp. 29–37; and Donald J. Bowersox, "Lessons Learned from World Class Leaders," *Supply Chain Management Review* 1, no. 1 (1997), pp. 61–67.

[11]*Annual Conference Program* (Oak Brook, IL: Council of Logistics Management, 1998), p. 11.

[12]Martha C. Cooper, Douglas M. Lambert, and Janus D. Pagh, "Supply Chain Management: More Than a New Name for Logistics," *The International Journal of Logistics Management* 8, no. 1 (1997), pp. 1–13.

[13]The revised definition was presented at the annual business meeting of the Council of Logistics Management in Anaheim, California, October 1998. The definition is posted on the CLM's website: <http://www.clm1.org>.

FIGURE 2–2

Supply chain network structure

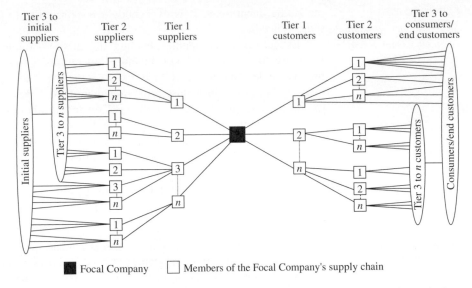

Focal Company   Members of the Focal Company's supply chain

Source: Douglas M. Lambert, Martha C. Cooper, and Janus D. Pagh, "Supply Chain Management: Implementation Issues and Research Opportunities," *The International Journal of Logistics Management* 9, no. 2 (1998), p. 3.

The early marketing channel researchers such as Wroe Alderson and Louis P. Bucklin conceptualized the key factors for why and how channels are created and structured.[14] From a supply chain standpoint these researchers were basically on the right track, particularly in the areas of (1) identifying who should be a member of the marketing channel, (2) describing the need for channel coordination, and (3) drawing actual marketing channels. However, for the last 30 years the channel researchers studied power and conflict, with questionable results, and ignored two critical issues. First, they did not build on the early contributions by including suppliers to the manufacturer, and thus neglected the importance of a total supply chain perspective. Second, they focused on marketing activities and flows across the channel, and overlooked the need to integrate and manage multiple key processes across companies.

Unlike the marketing channel literature, a major weakness of the SCM literature to date is that the authors appear to assume that everyone knows who the members of the supply chain are. There has been little effort to identify specific supply chain members, key processes that require integration, or what management must do to successfully manage the supply chain. The SCM framework presented here encompasses the combination of three closely interrelated elements: the structure of the supply chain, the supply chain business processes, and the supply chain management components (see Figure 2–3). We believe that the combination of these three elements captures the essence of SCM.

The supply chain structure is the network of members and the links between members of the supply chain. Business processes are the activities that produce a specific output of value to the customer. The management components are the managerial variables

A Supply Chain Management Framework

---

[14]Wroe Alderson, "Marketing Efficiency and the Principle of Postponement," *Cost and Profit Outlook* 3 (September 1950); Reavis Cox and Wroe Alderson, *Theory in Marketing* (Chicago: Richard D. Irwin, 1950); and Louis P. Bucklin, *A Theory of Distribution Channel Structure* (Berkley, CA: Institute of Business and Economic Research 1966).

FIGURE 2–3

Supply chain management framework: Elements and key decisions

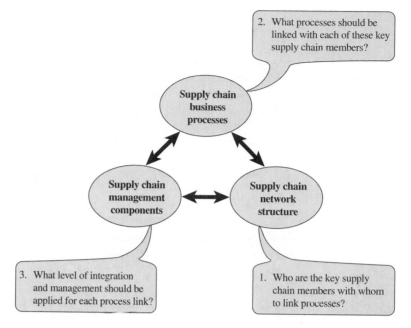

Source: Douglas M. Lambert, Martha C. Cooper, and Janus D. Pagh, "Supply Chain Management: Implementation Issues and Research Opportunities," *The International Journal of Logistics Management* 9, no. 2 (1998), p. 4.

by which the business processes are integrated and managed across the supply chain. In combination, the SCM definition and this new framework move the SCM philosophy to its next evolutionary stage.

Keys to the Implementation of SCM

The implementation of SCM involves identifying the supply chain members with whom it is critical to link, what processes need to be linked with each of these key members, and what type or level of integration applies to each process link. The objective of SCM is to maximize competitiveness and profitability for the company as well as the whole supply chain network, including the end customer. Consequently, supply chain process integration and reengineering initiatives should be aimed at boosting total process efficiency and effectiveness across members of the supply chain.

Channel Structure

The theory on channel structure described in the marketing literature provides a useful foundation for studying supply chain structure. According to this literature, channel structure may be viewed as a function of product life cycle, logistics systems, effective communication networks,[15] product characteristics,[16] and/or firm size.[17] However, the

---

[15]Ronald Michman, "Channel Development and Innovation," *Marquette Business Review,* Spring 1971, pp. 45–49; and Lisa M. Ellram and Martha C. Cooper, "Supply Chain Management, Partnerships and the Shipper–Third Party Relationship," *The International Journal of Logistics Management* 1, no. 2 (1990), p. 2.

[16]Leo Aspinwall, "The Characteristics of Goods and Parallel Systems Theories," in *Marketing Management,* ed. Eugene Kelley and William Lazer (Homewood, IL: Richard D. Irwin, 1958), pp. 434–50.

[17]Robert E. Weigand, "The Marketing Organization, Channels and Firm Size," *Journal of Business* 36 (April 1963), pp. 228–36.

most detailed theory of channel structure was developed by Bucklin.[18] He stated that the purpose of the channel is to provide consumers with the desired combination of its outputs (lot size, delivery time, and market decentralization) at minimal cost. Consumers determine channel structure by purchasing combinations of service outputs. The best channel has formed when no other group of institutions generates more profits or more consumer satisfaction per dollar of product cost. Bucklin concluded that functions will be shifted from one channel member to another in order to achieve the most efficient and effective channel structure.

Bucklin's Theory of Channel Structure

Given a desired level of output by the consumer and competitive conditions, channel institutions will arrange their functional tasks in such a way as to minimize total channel costs. This shifting of specific functions may lead to the addition or deletion of channel members.

In deciding when and where to use channel intermediaries, the firm is really considering the make-versus-buy, or "outsourcing," decision. Does the organization need to develop the required skills and capabilities internally, or can it be done faster and more efficiently by using a third party?

Outsourcing

Approximately $40 billion of logistics services in the United States are being outsourced.[19] And there are significant opportunities to outsource additional logistics services. Some examples of outsourcing are the following:

- A large pharmaceutical company outsources its worldwide distribution, providing on-site pharmacists at some centers to dispense high-value products.
- A third party handles the entire finished goods inventory for a large women's clothing company. When garments are purchased by a retailer, the distributor attaches the store's private label, refreshes the garment, packs it in the store's packaging, and ships to the retailer.
- A mail-order retailer is having FedEx handle not only its shipments but also storage and management of its inventory.
- In addition to handling store replenishment and delivery of product to consumers for a tool manufacturer, UPS now is going to handle the warehouse. If the retail store needs product, an order that reaches the distribution center by 9:00 P.M. will be at the store by the next morning.[20]

Outsourcing Should Be Evaluated in Supply Chain Design

As these examples show, outsourcing represents an opportunity that should be considered in both supply chain design and evaluation of existing supply chains. In addition, the role of the distributor is changing. In some cases, consolidation of suppliers and customers has reduced the value and functionality of distributors.

For example, Wal-Mart's large stores, which use direct distribution, replace small stores that may have used distributors. Similarly, advanced technology like electronic data interchange (EDI) trades information for inventory, reducing the need to hold inventory at distributors, as well as at retailers. Better information technology and

---

[18]Bucklin, *A Theory of Distribution Channel Structure.*

[19]*Third-Party Logistics* (Piper Jaffray Equity Research, January 1999), p. 18.

[20]Helen L. Richardson, "How Much Should You Outsource?" *Transportation and Distribution* 35, no. 9 (September 1994), p. 61.

increased service offerings by carriers (such as cross-docking) also reduce the need for distributor's services.[21]

Postponement and Speculation

Postponement

Bucklin's theory of channel structure is based on the concepts of postponement and speculation.[22] Costs can be reduced by (1) postponing changes in the form and identity of a product to the last possible point in the marketing process, and (2) postponing inventory location to the last possible point in time, since risk and uncertainty costs increase as the product becomes more differentiated. Postponement results in savings because it moves differentiation nearer to the time of purchase, when demand is more easily forecast. This reduces risk and uncertainty costs. Logistics costs are reduced by sorting products in large lots in relatively undifferentiated states. Third-party service providers can support postponement by mixing pallets for individual customers as orders are received, by repackaging product to fit specific customer or country requirements, and by performing final assembly or customization in the field.

Companies can use postponement to shift the risk of owning goods from one channel member to another. That is, a manufacturer may refuse to produce goods until it receives firm orders; an intermediary may postpone owning inventories by purchasing from sellers who offer faster delivery, by purchasing on consignment, or by purchasing only when a sale has been made; and consumers may postpone ownership by buying from retail outlets where the products are in stock.

An excellent example of postponement is the mixing of paint colors at the retail store. Rather than having to forecast the exact colors that consumers will want to buy, the retailer waits until the time of purchase to mix paint in the color a consumer wishes to acquire. Other examples include color panels in the front of built-in kitchen appliances that enable the same unit to be any one of a number of colors; the centralization of slow-selling products in one warehouse location; and the assembly of products only after orders have been received.

Speculation

Speculation is the opposite of postponement: that is, a channel institution assumes risk rather than shifting it. Speculation can reduce marketing costs through (1) the economies of large-scale production; (2) the placement of large orders, which reduces the costs of order processing and transportation; (3) the reduction of stockouts and their associated cost; and (4) the reduction of uncertainty. To reduce the need for speculative inventories, managers in many firms are exploring strategies of time-based competition.[23] By using time-based competition, management can significantly reduce the firm's time to manufacture products, while reducing inventory, improving inventory turns, reducing cost of ownership, and improving customer satisfaction.

---

[21]Copacino, *Supply Chain Management: The Basics and Beyond,* pp. 173–75.

[22]Louis P. Bucklin, "Postponement, Speculation and the Structure of Distribution Channels," *Journal of Marketing Research* 2, no. 1 (February 1965), pp. 26–31.

[23]See, for example, Robert Handfield, "The Role of Materials Management in Developing Time-Based Competition," *International Journal of Purchasing and Materials Management* 29, no. 4 (Winter 1991), pp. 2–10; Maynard Rafuse, "Reducing the Need to Forecast," *The International Journal of Logistics Management* 6, no. 2 (1995), pp. 103–8; and Martin Christopher and Helen Peck, "Managing Logistics in Fashion Markets," *The International Journal of Logistics Management* 8, no. 2 (1997), pp. 63–74.

Time-to-Market Pressures

Speed as a Competitive Advantage

Speed can be used as a source of competitive advantage. This is true in virtually all market sectors: services, manufacturing, and retailing. Retailers have been leaders in the area of time-based competition, relying heavily on advanced computer systems involving bar coding and EDI to support quick response. (This will be described further in Chapter 4.) The use of such systems is growing among carriers. But computer systems alone are not enough for companies facing time-to-market pressures; fundamental changes in operational relationships are required. These changes include information sharing among suppliers, manufacturers, and retailers; the information may concern lead times, forecasts of sales, production, purchase needs, shipping, new-product plans, and payment.

Some of the benefits of effective time-based management are:

- Enhanced customer value through better responsiveness.
- Reduced inventory requirements due to shorter lead times.
- Reduced "cost-added" or duplicate functions.
- Improved product freshness or quality through reduced handling and lower inventories.
- Improved competitive position.
- Increased responsiveness to changing market needs.
- Improved productivity.

Other Issues Affecting Channel Structure

Additional factors that can influence channel structure include the following:

- Technological, cultural, physical, social, and political factors.
- Physical factors such as geography, size of market, location of production centers, and concentration of population.
- Local, state, and federal laws.
- Social and behavioral variables.

For example, social, cultural, political, and economic variables may support channels that are not necessarily as efficient or effective as they should be.

Supply Chain Network Structure[24]

One key element of managing the supply chain is to have an explicit knowledge and understanding of how the supply chain network structure is configured. The three primary structural aspects of a company's network structure are (1) the members of the supply chain, (2) the structural dimensions of the network, and (3) the different types of process links across the supply chain. These three issues are all related to the first element: supply chain network structure, as was shown in Figure 2–3. Now, each issue will be addressed.

---

[24]This section is taken from Lambert, Cooper, and Pagh, "Supply Chain Management: Implementation Issues and Research Opportunities," pp. 5–9.

Identifying Supply Chain Members

**Who Is a Member
of the Supply Chain?**

When determining the network structure, it is necessary to identify who the members of the supply chain are. Including all types of members may cause the total network to become highly complex, since it may explode in the number of members added from tier to tier.[25] To integrate and manage all process links with all members across the supply chain would, in most cases, be counterproductive, if not impossible. The key is to sort out some basis for determining which members are critical to the success of the company and thus should be allocated managerial attention and resources.

Marketing channel researchers identify members of the channel based on who takes part in the various marketing flows, including product, title, payment, information, and promotion flows.[26] Each flow includes relevant members, such as banks for the payment flow and advertising agencies for the promotion flow. The channel researchers have sought to include all members taking part in the marketing flows, regardless of how much impact each member has on the value provided to the end customer or other stakeholders.

The members of a supply chain include all companies or organizations with whom the focal company interacts directly or indirectly through its suppliers or customers, from point-of-origin to point-of-consumption. However, to make a very complex network more manageable, it seems appropriate to distinguish between primary and supporting members.

Primary Members

Primary members of a supply chain are all those autonomous companies or strategic business units who actually perform operational and/or managerial activities in the business processes designed to produce a specific output for a particular customer or market. In contrast, the *supporting members* of a supply chain are companies that simply provide resources, knowledge, utilities, or assets for the primary members of the supply chain.

Supporting Members

For example, supporting companies include agents that lease trucks to the manufacturer; banks that lend money to a retailer; the building owners who provide warehouse space; and companies that supply production equipment, print marketing brochures, or provide temporary secretarial assistance. These supply chain members support the primary members now and in the future. Resource, knowledge, utility, or asset providers are important, if not vital, contributors to a company and the supply chain, but they do not directly participate in or perform activities in the value-adding processes of transforming inputs to outputs for the end customer.

**The Same Company
Can Perform Primary
and Supportive
Activities**

The same company can perform both primary and supporting activities. Likewise, the same company can perform primary activities related to one process and supporting activities related to another process. An example is an original equipment manufacturer (OEM) that buys some critical and complex production equipment from a supplier. As the OEM develops new products, it works very closely with the equipment supplier; thus, the supplier is a primary member of the OEM's product development process. However, when looking at the manufacturing flow management process, the supplier is a supporting member, not a primary member, since supplying the equipment does not in itself add value to the output of the processes, even though the equipment does add value.

---

[25]Martha C. Cooper, Lisa M. Ellram, John T. Gardner, and Albert M. Hanks, "Meshing Multiple Alliances," *Journal of Business Logistics* 18, no. 1 (1997), pp. 67–89.

[26]Louis W. Stern, Adel El-Ansary, and Anne Coughlan, *Marketing Channels,* 5th ed. (Englewood Cliffs, NJ: Prentice Hall, 1996) pp. 8–22.

It should be noted that the distinction between primary and supporting chain members is not obvious in all cases. Nevertheless, this distinction provides a reasonable managerial simplification and yet captures the essential aspects of who should be considered a key member of the supply chain. The approach for differentiating types of members is similar to Porter's method of distinguishing between value-adding and support activities in his "value chain" framework.[27]

The definitions of primary and supporting members make it possible to define the point-of-origin and the point-of-consumption of the supply chain. The point-of-origin of the supply chain occurs where no primary suppliers exist. All suppliers to the point-of-origin members are solely supporting members. The point-of-consumption is where no primary customers exist and the product or service is consumed.

The Structural Dimensions of the Network

Three structural dimensions of the network are essential when describing, analyzing, and managing the supply chain: the horizontal structure, the vertical structure, and the horizontal position of the focal company within the end points of the supply chain.

Three Structural Dimensions

The term *horizontal structure* refers to the number of tiers across the supply chain. The supply chain may be long, with numerous tiers, or short, with few tiers. The *vertical structure* refers to the number of suppliers/customers represented within each tier. A company can have a narrow vertical structure, with few companies at each tier level, or a wide vertical structure, with many suppliers or customers at each tier level. The third structural dimension is the company's *horizontal position* within the supply chain. A company can be positioned at or near the initial source of supply, at or near to the ultimate customer, or somewhere between these end points of the supply chain.

Different combinations of these structural variables are possible. For example, a long, narrow network structure on the supplier side can be combined with a short, wide structure on the customer side. Increasing or reducing the number of suppliers and/or customers will affect the structure of the supply chain. As companies move from having multiple to having single-source suppliers, the supply chain will become narrower. Outsourcing logistics, manufacturing, marketing, or product development activities is another example of decision making that likely will change the supply chain structure. It may increase the length and width of the supply chain, as well as influence the horizontal position of the focal company in the supply chain network.

Supply chains with too many tier 1 customers or suppliers will strain corporate resources and limit the number of process links the focal company can integrate and closely manage beyond tier 1. In general, managers in companies with wide vertical structures actively manage only a few tier 2 customers or suppliers. Some companies have transferred the servicing of small customers to distributors, thus moving the small customers further down the supply chain from the focal company. This principle, known as *functional spin-off,* is described in the channels literature,[28] and can be applied to the focal company's network of suppliers as well as to its customers.

Supply chains look different from each company's perspective, since management in each sees its firm as the focal company and therefore views membership and network structure differently. Thus, the perceived supply chain network structure is arbitrary.

---

[27]Michael E. Porter, *Competitive Advantage—Creating and Sustaining Superior Performance* (New York: The Free Press, 1984), p. 36.

[28]Stern, El-Ansary, and Coughlan, *Marketing Channels,* p. 20.

However, because each firm is a member of the other's supply chain, it is important all managers understand their interrelated roles and perspectives. The reason for this is that the integration and management of business processes across company boundaries will be successful only if it makes sense from each company's perspective.[29]

Types of Business Process Links

Four Types of Business Process Links

Integrating and managing all business process links throughout the entire supply chain is usually not appropriate. Since the drivers for integration are situational, and therefore different from process link to process link, the levels of integration also will vary from link to link, and over time. Thus, some links are more critical than others.[30] As a consequence, a crucial task is to allocate scarce resources among the different business process links across the supply chain. Four fundamentally different types of business process links can be identified between members of a supply chain.[31] These are managed business process links, monitored business process links, not-managed business process links, and nonmember business process links.

Managed Process Links.   *Managed process links* are links that the focal company finds important to integrate and manage. This might be in collaboration with other member companies of the supply chain. In the supply chain drawn in Figure 2–4, the managed process links are indicated by the thickest solid lines. The focal company will integrate and manage process links with tier 1 customers and suppliers. As indicated by the remaining thick solid lines in Figure 2–4, the focal company is actively involved in the management of a number of other process links beyond tier 1.

Monitored Process Links.   Compared to managed process links, *monitored process links* are not as critical to the focal company; however, it is important to the focal company that these process links be integrated and managed appropriately between the other member companies. Thus, the focal company, as frequently as necessary, simply monitors or audits how each process link is integrated and managed. The thick dashed lines in Figure 2–4 indicate the monitored process links.

Not-Managed Process Links.   *Not-managed process links* are links in which the focal company is not actively involved, nor are they critical enough to use resources for monitoring. In other words, the focal company either fully trusts the other members to manage the process links appropriately or, because of limited resources, leaves it up to them. The thin solid lines in Figure 2–4 indicate the not-managed process links. For example, a manufacturer has a number of suppliers for cardboard shipping cartons. Usually the manufacturer will not choose to integrate and manage the links beyond the cardboard supplier all the way back to the growing of the trees. The manufacturer wants certainty of supply but does not find it necessary to integrate and manage the links beyond the cardboard supplier.

---

[29]Cooper, Ellram, Gardner, and Hanks, "Meshing Multiple Alliances."

[30]Håkan Håkansson and Ivan Snehota, *Developing Relationships in Business Networks* (London: Routledge, 1995).

[31]Lambert, Cooper, and Pagh, "Supply Chain Management: Implementation Issues and Research Opportunities," pp. 7–9.

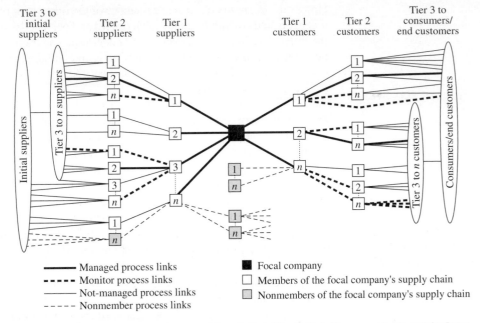

Source: Douglas M. Lambert, Martha C. Cooper, and Janus D. Pagh, "Supply Chain Management: Implementation Issues and Research Opportunities," *The International Journal of Logistics Management* 9, no. 2 (1998), p. 7.

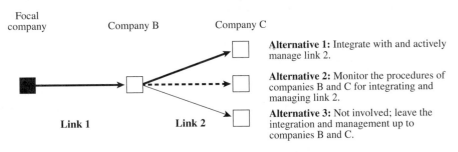

Source: Douglas M. Lambert, Martha C. Cooper, and Janus D. Pagh, "Supply Chain Management: Implementation Issues and Research Opportunities," *The International Journal of Logistics Management* 9, no. 2 (1998), p. 8.

The three alternatives for integrating and managing links are illustrated in Figure 2–5. Company A may chose to integrate with and actively manage link 2 (alternative 1). Or company A could chose not to integrate, but only to monitor the procedures of companies B and C for integrating and managing link 2 (alternative 2). Both alternatives 1 and 2 necessitate some level of resource allocation from company A. Finally, company A can chose not to be involved and leave the integration and management of link 2 up to companies B and C (alternative 3).

Nonmember Process Links.   Managers understand that their supply chains are influenced by decisions made in other, connected supply chains. For example, a supplier to the focal company is also a supplier to the chief competitor. Such a supply chain structure may have implications for the supplier's allocation of manpower to the focal company's product development process, or availability of products in times of shortage, and/or protection of confidentiality of information. This leads us to identify a fourth type of business link, *nonmember process links.* Nonmember process links are process links between members of the focal company's supply chain and nonmembers of the supply chain. Nonmember links are not considered as links of the focal company's supply chain structure, but they can and often will affect the performance of the focal company and its supply chain. The thin dashed lines in Figure 2–4 illustrate examples of nonmember process links.

Managing the Supply Chain Can Yield Significant Benefits

Based on the process links just described, there is variation in how closely companies integrate and manage links further away from the first tier. In some cases, companies work through or around other members or links in order to achieve specific supply chain objectives, such as product availability, improved quality, and reduced overall supply chain costs. For example, a tomato ketchup manufacturer in New Zealand conducts research on tomatoes in order to develop plants that provide larger tomatoes with fewer seeds. The manufacturer's contracted growers are provided with young plants in order to ensure the quality of the output. Since the growers tend to be small, the manufacturer negotiates contracts with suppliers of equipment, fertilizer, chemicals, and so on. The farmers are encouraged to purchase their raw materials and machinery using the contract rates. This results in higher quality raw materials and lower prices without sacrificing the margins and financial strength of the growers.

There are several examples of companies that discovered the importance of managing beyond tier 1 suppliers for critical times. One example involves a material used in the manufacture of semiconductors. The manufacturer had six tier 1 suppliers from which to purchase the material. However, when shortages occurred, it became apparent that all six of the tier 1 suppliers purchased from the same tier 2 supplier. It turned out that the most critical relationship was with the tier 2 supplier.

Supply Chain Business Processes[32]

Successful supply chain management requires a change from managing individual functions to integrating activities into key supply chain processes. Traditionally, both upstream and downstream portions of the supply chain have interacted as disconnected entities receiving sporadic flows of information over time.

The purchasing department placed orders as requirements became necessary, and marketing interfaced with various distributors and retailers in an attempt to satisfy customer demand. Orders were periodically given to suppliers who had no visibility of demand at the point of sale or use. Satisfying the customer often required expedited operations throughout the supply chain as member firms reacted to unexpected changes in demand.

The Customer Is the Primary Focus in Supply Chain Management

Operating an integrated supply chain requires continuous information flows, which in turn help create the best product flows. The customer remains the primary focus of the process. However, improved links with suppliers are necessary since controlling uncertainty in customer demand, manufacturing processes, and supplier performance is critical to effective supply chain management. Achieving a good cus-

---

[32]This material is adapted from Douglas M. Lambert, Larry C. Guinipero, and Gary J. Ridenhower, "Supply Chain Management: A Key to Achieving Business Excellence in the 21st Century," unpublished manuscript, 1998. All rights reserved.

tomer-focused system requires processing information both accurately and on time, for quick response systems require frequent changes in response to fluctuations in customer demand.

Key Supply Chain Processes Identified at 3M

In many major corporations, such as 3M, management has reached the conclusion that optimizing the product flows cannot be accomplished without implementing a process approach to the business. In 1995, supply chain excellence along with customer loyalty were identified as key for corporate success by 3M's chairman. The goal was "to be the most innovative enterprise in the world" and "the preferred supplier in the markets we serve." The supply chain excellence initiative challenged the 3M businesses to implement a process approach. The processes identified by the corporate supply chain group were similar to those recommended in this chapter. In fact Gary Ridenhower of 3M led this group and he has had a great impact on our thinking with regard to supply chain management. The results in the 3M businesses that have implemented supply chain management using the process approach have been dramatic in terms of cost reductions and service improvements.

While the specific processes identified by individual firms may vary somewhat from the eight that were listed in Figure 2–1 (p. 55) and are described in the sections below, we believe that these processes are applicable to any manufacturing firm and that using similar processes facilitates supply chain integration.

Of course, performance metrics that traditionally capture individual firm results must be changed to reflect process performance across the supply chain, and rewards and incentives must be aligned to these metrics in order to bring about change.

Customer Relationship Management

Partnering Programs with Key Customers

The first step toward integrated SCM is to identify key customers or customer groups that are critical to the organization's business mission. The corporate business plan is the starting point for this identification. Customer service teams develop and implement partnering programs with key customers. Product and service agreements specifying the levels of performance are established with these key customer groups. In many cases the agreements will be tailored to meet the needs of key individual customers.

New customer interfaces lead to improved communications and better predictions of customer demand, which in turn lead to improved service for customers. Customer service teams work with customers to further identify and eliminate sources of demand variability. Managers undertake performance evaluations to analyze the levels of service provided to customers as well as customer profitability.

Customer Service Management

A Single Source of Customer Information

Customer service management provides a single source of customer information. It becomes the key point of contact for administering the product and service agreement. Customer service provides the customer with real-time information on promised shipping dates and product availability through interface with the organization's production and distribution operations.

Managing customer service in an SCM environment requires an online, real-time system to provide product and pricing information to support customer inquiries and facilitate order placement. After-sales service is also a requirement. Finally, the technical customer service group must be able to efficiently assist the customer with product applications and recommendations.

Technology

The Value Chain Initiative

The goal in supply chain management is to link together the ultimate consumer, the supplier of original materials, and all trading partners in between with a seamless information flow. The charter of the Value Chain Initiative (VCI) is to migrate a high-level uninterrupted data stream from raw materials to the consumer's hands using the Internet, a communications medium that promises to revolutionize business/commerce protocols worldwide. The goal is to extend the powerful Microsoft Windows NT client/server technology to all facets of the supply chain and to make these data accessible, in real time!

Today's supply chain data stream is largely paper-based and event driven. Hence, it is essentially a static or "EDI-like" data stream. After an event has occurred, the opportunity to make or save money has elapsed with the event.

The goal of the VCI data stream is to give decision makers access to and control over data prior to an event,

so that the ability to dynamically model or reallocate these resources is continuously available. Most retailers/manufacturers know that by saving nickels and dimes at the lower reaches of the supply chain they can migrate these incremental savings all the way up to the highest levels, where they eventually will amount to millions in new or "rediscovered" savings and profits.

Why is this the "value chain"? Because providing the power to control these far-flung resources makes them assets rather than liabilities. Making this value available by leveraging existing internal IT investment is truly a sound business reason to embrace the VCI.

Source: From a presentation by Mark Waller, of Microsoft Corporation, at The Global Supply Chain Forum winter meeting. The Ohio State University, February 12, 1997.

Demand Management

The Demand Management Process Is Key for Success

Managers at Hewlett-Packard have determined that inventory is either essential or the result of variability in the system.[33] *Essential inventory* includes work-in-process in factories and products in the pipeline moving from location to location. Periodic review systems lead to certain amounts of incoming inventory stock. *Inventory due to variability* is present due to variances in process, supply, and demand. Customer demand, characterized by irregular order patterns, is by far the largest source of variability. Given this variability in customer ordering, demand management is a key to an effective SCM process.

The demand management process must balance the customer's requirements with the firm's supply capabilities. Part of managing demand involves attempting to determine what customers will purchase, and when. A good demand management system uses point-of-sale and "key" customer data to reduce uncertainty and provide efficient flows throughout the supply chain.

Marketing requirements and production plans should be coordinated throughout the enterprise. Thus, multiple sourcing and routing options are considered at the time of order receipt, which allows market requirements and production plans to be coordinated

---

[33]Davis, "Effective Supply Chain Management."

across the organization. In very advanced SCM systems, customer demand and production rates are synchronized to manage inventories globally.

Customer Order Fulfillment

The Objective Is to Provide a Seamless Process

Another key to effective SCM is meeting or exceeding "customer need dates." It is important to achieve high order fill rates on either a line-item or an order basis. Performing the order fulfillment process effectively requires integration of the firm's manufacturing, distribution, and transportation plans. As previously described, partnerships should be developed with key supply chain members and carriers to meet customer requirements and reduce total delivered cost to customer. The objective is to develop a seamless process from the supplier to the organization and then on to its various customer segments.

Manufacturing Flow Management

Matching Demand and Production Capability

The manufacturing process in make-to-stock firms traditionally produced goods and supplied them to the distribution channel based on historical forecasts. Products were pushed through the plant to meet a schedule. Often the wrong mix of products was produced, resulting in unneeded inventories, excessive inventory carrying costs, markdowns, and transshipments of product.

With SCM, product is pulled through the plant based on customer needs. Manufacturing processes must be flexible to respond to market changes. This requires the ability to perform rapid changeover to accommodate mass customization. Orders are processed on a just-in-time basis in minimum lot sizes. Production priorities are driven by required delivery dates. One of the keys to operating with mass customization and small lot sizes is that managers must concentrate on keeping setup/changeover costs very low. This may require the reengineering of processes, changes in product design, and attention to product sequencing. To ignore these measures is to elevate costs beyond a competitive position.

At 3M, manufacturing planners work with customer planners to develop strategies for each customer segment. Changes in the manufacturing flow process lead to shorter cycle times, meaning improved responsiveness to customers.

Procurement

Supplier Development

Strategic plans are developed with suppliers to support the manufacturing flow management process and the development of new products. Suppliers are strategically categorized according to their contribution and importance to the organization. In companies whose operations extend worldwide, sourcing should be managed from corporate headquarters on a global basis.

Long-term partnerships are developed with a small core group of suppliers. The desired outcome is a win–win relationship. This represents a change from the traditional bid-and-buy system. Involving a key supplier early in the design cycle can lead to dramatic reduction in product development cycle times. Having early supplier input reduces time by getting the required coordination between engineering, purchasing, and the supplier prior to design finalization.

The purchasing function develops rapid communication mechanisms such as EDI and Internet links to quickly transfer requirements. These rapid communication tools provide a means to reduce time and money spent on the transaction portion of the purchase. Purchasers can focus their efforts on managing suppliers as opposed to placing and expediting orders.

Product Development and Commercialization

Customers and Suppliers Must Be Integrated into the Product Development Process

If new products are the lifeblood of a corporation, then product development is the lifeblood of a company's new products. Customers and suppliers must be integrated into the product development process in order to reduce time to market. As product life cycles shorten, the right products must be developed and successfully launched in ever shorter time frames in order for the organization to remain competitive.

Managers of the product development and commercialization process must:

- Coordinate with customer relationship management to identify articulated and unarticulated customer needs.
- Select materials and suppliers in conjunction with procurement.
- Develop production technology in manufacturing flow to assess manufacturability and integration into the best supply chain flow for the product/market combination.

Returns

Managing the returns channel as a business process offers organizations the same opportunity to achieve a sustainable competitive advantage as managing the supply chain from an outbound perspective.[34] Effective process management of the returns channel enables identification of productivity improvement opportunities and breakthrough projects.

"Return to Available" Is a Critical Cycle Time Measurement

At Xerox, returns are managed in four categories: equipment, parts, supplies, and competitive trade-ins. "Return to available" is a measure of the cycle time required to return an asset to a useful status. This metric is particularly important for those products where customers are given an immediate replacement in the case of product failure. Also, equipment destined for scrap and waste from manufacturing plants is measured in terms of the time it takes for the organization to receive cash.

Summary of Supply Chain Business Processes

Focusing efforts on these key business processes, which extend from the end users to original suppliers, provides the foundation for a supply chain management philosophy. The goals or outcomes of these processes are to:

- Develop customer-focused teams that provide mutually beneficial product and service agreements to strategically significant customers.
- Provide a point of contact that efficiently handles inquiries from all customers.
- Continuously gather, compile, and update customer demand to match requirements with supply.
- Develop flexible manufacturing systems that respond quickly to changing market conditions.

---

[34]John A. Clendein, "Closing the Supply Chain Loop: Reengineering the Returns Channel Process," *The International Journal of Logistics Management* 8, no. 1 (1997), pp. 75–85.

Localizing Generic Products at Hewlett-Packard

In an industry characterized by punishingly short product life cycles and extreme unpredictability, getting the right products to the right market on time is an absolute imperative. For computer equipment manufacturer Hewlett-Packard the need to manufacture and deliver products quickly, reliably, and ever more cost effectively has led to the development of capabilities that put the company at the very forefront of global supply chain management.

Product complexity was a hidden enemy for Hewlett-Packard, for while the company served a global marketplace with seemingly global products, these products were almost always tailored to meet local specifications. They had to be delivered with power cords and transformers to meet the local voltage, and supplied with keyboards, manuals, and operating software in the appropriate local language. This meant that instead of dealing with a single product line, produced and distributed to meet an overall global forecast, Hewlett-Packard was producing differently configured machines to meet estimated demand in each of a number of relatively small markets. But the smaller the market, the more erratic the order patterns were likely to be, and the more difficult it was to predict demand accurately.

The uncertainty reverberated back through every stage of the supply chain, leading to exaggerated safety stocks, and increased risk of obsolete stock or of expensive reworking for internal and external suppliers alike. There were, for example, five physically separate Hewlett-Packard facilities contributing to the manufacture and distribution of its best-selling family of low-cost DeskJet printers, resulting in a pipeline that was nearly six months long.

Supplying the European market, with its tightly packed cluster of nations and linguistic differences, was particularly troublesome, with huge safety stocks needed to meet Hewlett-Packard's goal of 98 percent service levels. Product managers, while wishing to lessen their exposure to variability in the supply chain, were eager to reduce the amount of inventory in the system, freeing up cash for other uses. An investigation of how current service levels might be maintained at lower cost was commissioned.

Under the then-current system, the printers were "localized" at the central factory, leaving packaged for sale in the country of destination. Stockpiles of each of the different language variants were held at regional distribution centers, ready to meet sudden fluctuations in demand. A question that quickly arose concerned the value of switching production over to a single form of generic printer, with localization postponed until the distribution-center stage, thereby delaying the point of commitment until a firm order had been received.

Hewlett-Packard had been honing its inventory network modeling skills for some time, and was able to apply these skills to modeling the DeskJet supply chain. The results indicated that costs of safety stocks could be significantly reduced if a generic printer was introduced. First, safety stocks could be lowered from seven weeks of finished goods to around five weeks of the generic version, as fewer generic printers would be required to maintain service levels. Second, the cost of each unit stockpiled would be reduced because less value had been added by this point. Anticipated savings were in excess of $30 million per year, on current volumes. The costs associated with performing the localization process at the distribution centers were slightly higher than if performed by the factory, and higher overall inventories of localization materials would be required with the dispersal of this activity. But these costs were dwarfed by the overall savings on inventory of product. Also, savings amounting to several million dollars per annum were identified from reduced shipping costs. The generic printers could be packed more densely and transported more cheaply.

The logic of switching to a generic printer for the European market was unimpeachable. The U.S. market already had its own factory-produced version of the generic printer, so ostensibly there seemed to be no case for extending the practice to the European market. Surely there could be no benefit in postponing completion for such a large and homogeneous market? Not so. An extension of the DeskJet study evaluated a proposal to factory-produce two versions of the printer, an ultra-low-cost U.S. version and a generic one to serve the rest of the world. This proposal was rejected, however, because of the potential strategic time advantage offered by a singly generic printer strategy. The critical factor here was the increased unpredictability of even regional forecasts (for the Americas, Asia, and Europe) when set against a forecast for overall global demand. If, contrary to all earlier indications, demand for a new product failed to materialize in, say, the United States,

---

Localizing Generic Products at Hewlett-Packard *continued*

while in the rest of the world sales took off at an unprecedented rate, pipelines would already be filled to meet predicted demand. A generic printer strategy would allow the immediate diversion of stocks to wherever they were required, at minimal cost and with minimal delay and loss of service. Contrast this with the prospect of reworking unneeded stocks before redirection, or waiting until forecasted output could meet demand. In a market with nar-

rowing windows of opportunity, the risk of the latter was deemed to be too great. Hewlett-Packard introduced its global generic printer.

Source: Adapted from Martin Christopher, Marketing Logistics (Oxford, UK: Butterworth Heinemann, 1997), pp. 128–30. Based on material contained in Tom Davis, "Effective Supply Chain Management," Sloan Management Review 34, no. 4 (Summer 1993), pp. 35–46. Reprinted by permission of the publisher. Copyright 1993 by Sloan Management Review Association. All rights reserved.

- Manage supplier partnerships that allow for quick response and continuous improvement.
- Fill 100 percent of customer orders accurately and on time.
- Minimize the return-to-available cycle time.

A responsive, flexible, integrated supply chain can accomplish these objectives. Since, as previously mentioned, these processes cut across business functions, it is important to examine or reengineer each key process using a systematic approach.

Business Process Chains[35]

Every Company Is Involved in Supply Chain Relationships

Thousands of activities are performed and coordinated within a company, and every company is in some way involved in supply chain relationships with other companies.[36] When two companies build a relationship, certain of their internal activities will be linked and managed between the two companies.[37] Since both companies have linked some internal activities with other members of their supply chain, a link between two companies is thus a link in what might be conceived as a supply chain network. For example, the internal activities of a manufacturer are linked with and can affect the internal activities of a distributor, which in turn are linked with and can affect the internal activities of a retailer. Ultimately, the internal activities of the retailer are linked with and can affect the activities of the end customer.

Håkansson and Snehota stress that "the structure of activities within and between companies is a critical cornerstone of creating unique and superior supply chain performance."[38] Executives in leading companies believe that competitiveness and profitability can increase if internal key activities and business processes are linked and managed across multiple companies. Thus, "successful supply chain management

---

[35]This section is taken from Lambert, Cooper, and Pagh, "Supply Chain Management: Implementation Issues and Research Opportunities," pp. 9–11.

[36]Donald J. Bowersox, "Integrated Supply Chain Management; A Strategic Perspective," *Annual Conference Proceedings* (Chicago: Council of Logistics Management, 1997), pp. 181–89; George E. Stigler, "The Division of Labor Is Limited by the Extent of the Market," *Journal of Political Economy* 59, no. 3 (1951), pp. 185–93; and R. H. Coase, "The Nature of the Firm," *Economica* 4 (1937), pp. 386–405.

[37]Håkansson and Snehota, *Developing Relationships in Business Networks*.

[38]Ibid.

**There Is a Lack
of Consistency in How
Companies in a Supply
Chain Structure
Activities**

requires a change from managing individual functions to integrating activities into key supply chain business processes."[39]

Companies in the same supply chain may have different activity structures. Some companies emphasize a functional structure, some a process structure, and others a combined structure of processes and functions. Companies often have different numbers of processes consisting of different activities and links between activities. Further, different names are used for similar processes, and similar names for different processes. This lack of intercompany consistency is a cause of significant friction and inefficiencies in supply chains. At least with functional silos (corporate departments that are internally focused), there is generally an understanding of what functions like marketing, manufacturing, and accounting represent. If each firm identifies its own set of processes, how do we communicate and how do we link these processes across firms? A simplified illustration of such a disconnected supply chain is shown in Figure 2–6.

A process can be viewed as a structure of activities designed for action with a focus on end customers and on the dynamic management of flows involving products, information, cash, knowledge, and ideas.

In an exploratory study involving 30 successful supply chain redesign practitioners, Fred Hewitt found that companies identified between 9 and 24 internal business processes. The two most commonly identifiable processes were order fulfillment and product development.[40]

FIGURE 2–6

*Supply chain
management: The
disconnects*

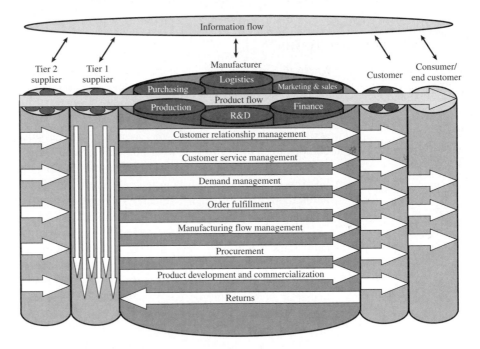

Source: Douglas M. Lambert, Martha C. Cooper, and Janus D. Pagh, "Supply Chain Management: Implementation Issues and Research Opportunities," *The International Journal of Logistics Management* 9, no. 2 (1998), p. 10.

---

[39]Lambert, Guinipero, and Ridenhower, "Supply Chain Management: A Key to Achieving Business Excellence in the 21st Century."

[40]Fred Hewitt, "Supply Chain Redesign," *The International Journal of Logistics Management* 5, no. 2 (1994), pp. 1–9.

Internal Coordination Is a Prerequisite for Successful Supply Chain Management

A prerequisite for successful SCM is to coordinate activities within the firm. One way to do this is to identify the key business processes and manage them using cross-functional teams. In some cases the internal business processes have been extended to suppliers and managed to some extent between the two firms involved. This may imply that when a firm takes a leadership role, its internal business processes can become the supply chain business processes. The obvious advantage of this is that each member of the band is playing the same tune.

The number of business processes that it is critical or beneficial to integrate and manage between companies will likely vary. In some cases it may be appropriate to link just one key process, and in other cases to link multiple or all key business processes. However, in each specific case, it is important that executives thoroughly analyze and discuss which key business processes to integrate and manage. The next section addresses the major components for integrating and managing a supply chain network.

The Management Components of Supply Chain Management

The management components of SCM are the third element of the SCM framework (see again Figure 2–3). An essential underlying premise of the SCM framework is that certain management components are common across all business processes and members of the supply chain.[41] We believe these common management components to be critical and fundamental for successful SCM, since they essentially represent and determine how each process link is integrated and managed. The level of integration and management of a business process link is a function of the number and level, ranging from low to high, of components added to the link.[42] Consequently, adding more management components or increasing the level of each component can increase the level of integration of the business process link.

The literature on SCM, business process reengineering, and buyer–supplier relationships suggests numerous possible components that must receive managerial attention when managing supply chain relationships.[43] Each component can have several subcomponents whose importance can vary depending on the process being managed. But the primary components are

- Planning and control methods.
- Work flow/activity structure.
- Organization structure.
- Communication and information flow facility structure.
- Product flow facility structure.

---

[41]Cooper, Lambert, and Pagh, "Supply Chain Management: More Than a New Name for Logistics."

[42]Douglas M. Lambert, Margaret A. Emmelhainz, and John T. Gardner, "So You Think You Want a Partner?" *Marketing Management* 5, no. 2 (Summer 1996), pp. 25–41; and Cooper, Ellram, Gardner, and Hanks, "Meshing Multiple Alliances."

[43]See literature review by Cooper, Lambert, and Pagh, "Supply Chain Management: More Than a New Name for Logistics"; Lambert, Emmelhainz, and Gardner, "So You Think You Want a Partner?"; Rasmus F. Olsen and Lisa M. Ellram, "A Portfolio Approach to Supplier Relationships," *Industrial Marketing Management* 26 (1997), pp. 101–13; and Peter W. Turnbull, "A Review of Portfolio Planning Models for Industrial Marketing and Purchasing Management," *European Journal of Marketing* 24, no. 3 (1990), pp. 7–22.

- Management methods.
- Power and leadership structure.
- Risk and reward structure.
- Culture and attitude.

Each component is briefly described next.

Planning and Control Methods

Planning and control of operations are keys to moving an organization or supply chain in a desired direction. The extent of joint planning will have a significant impact on the success of the supply chain. Different components may be emphasized at different times during the life of the supply chain, but planning transcends the phases.[44] The control aspects can be operationalized as the best performance metrics for measuring supply chain success.

Work Flow/Activity Structure

The work flow/activity structure indicates how the firm performs its tasks and activities. The level of integration of processes across the supply chain is a measure of organizational structure. All but one of the literature sources examined for this chapter cite work structure as an important component.

Organization Structure

Organizational structure can refer to the individual firm and the supply chain. The use of cross-functional teams suggests a process approach. When these teams cross organizational boundaries, such as in-plant supplier personnel, the supply chain should become more integrated.

Communication and Information Flow Facility Structure

The information flow facility structure is key. The kind of information passed among supply chain members and its timeliness have a strong influence on the efficiency of the supply chain. This may well be the first component integrated across part or all of the supply chain.

Product Flow Facility Structure

Product flow facility structure refers to the network structure for sourcing, manufacturing, and distribution across the supply chain. With reductions in inventory, fewer warehouses would be needed. Inventory is necessary in the system, but some supply chain members may keep a disproportionate amount of inventory. Since it is less expensive to have unfinished or semifinished goods in inventory than finished goods, upstream members may bear more of this burden. Rationalizing the supply chain network has implications for all members.

---

[44]Martha C. Cooper and Lisa M. Ellram, "Characteristics of Supply Chain Management and the Implications for Purchasing and Logistics Strategy," *The International Journal of Logistics Management* 4, no. 2 (1993), pp. 13–22.

Product structure issues include how coordinated new-product development is across the supply chain and the product portfolio. Lack of coordination in new-product development can lead to inefficiencies in production, but there is also the risk of giving away proprietary corporate information. The complexity of the product will likely affect the number of suppliers for the different components and the challenge of integrating the supply chain.

Management Methods

Management methods include the corporate philosophy and management techniques. It is very difficult to integrate a top-down organization structure with a bottom-up structure. The level of management involvement in day-to-day operations can differ across supply chain members.

Power and Leadership Structure

The power and leadership structure across the supply chain will affect its form. One strong leader will drive the direction of the supply chain. In most supply chains studied to date, there are one or two strong leaders among the firms. The exercise or the lack of power can affect the level of commitment of other supply chain members. Forced participation will encourage exit behavior, given the opportunity.[45]

Risk and Reward Sharing

The anticipation of sharing of risks and rewards across the supply chain affects the long-term commitment of its members. A fire at a Toyota supplier demonstrated Toyota's commitment to its suppliers and the assistance from other members of the chain.

Culture and Attitude

The importance of corporate culture and its compatibility across supply chain members cannot be overestimated. Meshing both cultures and individuals' attitudes is time-consuming but is necessary at some level for the supply chain to perform as a coordinated network. Aspects of culture include how employees are valued and incorporated into the management of the firm.

Two Categories of Management Components

Figure 2–7 illustrates how the management components can be divided into two groups, to point out some basic differences. The first group, the physical and technical group, includes the most visible, tangible, measurable, and easy-to-change components. Much of the literature on change management[46] shows that if this group of management

---

[45]Ian R. Macneil, *The New Social Contract: An Inquiry into Modern Contractual Relations* (New Haven, CT: Yale University Press, 1980); and Oliver E. Williamson, *Markets and Hierarchies: Analysis and Antitrust Implications* (New York: Free Press, 1975).

[46]Dennis T. Jaffe and Cynthia D. Scott, "Reengineering in Practice: Where Are the People? Where Is the Learning?" *Journal of Applied Behavioral Science* 34, no. 3 (1998), pp. 250–67; Dorine C. Andrews and Susan K. Stalick, *Business Reengineering: The Survival Guide* (Englewood Cliffs, NJ: Yourdon Press, 1994); Michael Hammer, "Reengineering Work: Don't Automate, Obliterate," *Harvard Business Review* 68, no. 4 (1990), pp. 104–12; Michael Hammer and James Champy, *Reengineering the Corporation: A Manifesto for Business Revolution* (New York: Harper Business, 1993); and Stephen Towers, *Business Process Re-engineering: A Practical Handbook for Executives* (Stanley Thorns, 1994).

FIGURE 2–7

Supply chain management:
Fundamental management
components

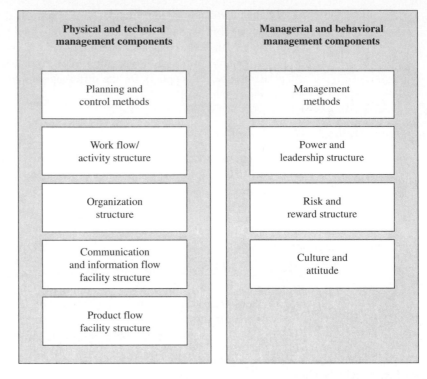

Source: Douglas M. Lambert, Martha C. Cooper, and Janus D. Pagh, "Supply Chain Management: Implementation Issues and Research Opportunities," *The International Journal of Logistics Management* 9, no. 2 (1998), p. 12.

components is the only focus of managerial attention, managing the supply chain will most likely be doomed to fail.

The second group is comprised of the managerial and behavioral components. These components are less tangible and visible and are often difficult to assess and alter. The managerial and behavioral components define the organizational behavior and influence how the physical and technical management components can be implemented. If the managerial and behavioral components are not aligned to drive and reinforce an organizational behavior supportive to the supply chain objectives and operations, the supply chain will likely be less competitive and profitable. If one or more components in the physical and technical group are changed, management components in the managerial and behavioral group likewise may have to be readjusted. Consequently, the groundwork for successful SCM is established by understanding each of these management components and their interdependence. Hewitt stated that true intra- and intercompany business process management, or redesign, is likely to be successful only if it is recognized as a multicomponent change process, simultaneously and explicitly addressing all SCM components.[47]

The physical and technical components are best understood, and applied or managed, at the farthest points up and down the supply chain. For example, one company integrated its demand management process across four links by applying the following components: planning and control methods, work flow/activity structure, communication and

[47]Hewitt, "Supply Chain Redesign."

information flow facility structure, and product flow facility structure. However, the managerial and behavioral components were not linked across these firms. In general, managers do not understand managerial and behavioral components, and encounter more difficulties in their implementation, compared to physical and technical components.

Supply Chain Design

The Majority of Supply Chains Were Not Designed

Even though leading-edge firms are doing more planning of their supply chains, evidence suggests that the majority of supply chains were not designed but rather developed over time. Although companies like Hewlett-Packard[48] and Digital Equipment Corporation[49] plan new channels/supply chains and use supply chain management strategies to modify existing networks, these examples appear to be the exception rather than the rule.

Current practice reveals a lack of planning by most firms. Better management of supply chains can create many benefits. For example, in many cases organizations do not know about all of the supply chain alternatives when they initially negotiate structural arrangements; thus the resulting decisions may later prove to be less than optimal. Identifying suboptimal supply chain arrangements and making structural changes will lead to increased profitability.

In addition, unanticipated changes in the environment may make it necessary to reconsider the supply chain and reevaluate partnership arrangements. Environmental factors include changes in end-consumer needs, markets, products and product lines, the competitive situation, the economy, and government regulation and incentives.

Supply chain strategy must be aligned with overall corporate strategy. Supply chain performance goals must be stated in operational terms, such as projected market coverage, sales and service support, sales volume, profitability, inventory turns, cash-to-cash cycle times, and return on investment. The supply chain strategy includes decisions regarding intensity of distribution, use of direct or indirect channels, the services of intermediaries in each geographic area, and implementation plans.

Management of a firm must become involved in the supply chain design process when it is considering new-product introductions or when existing supply chains are falling short of performance objectives. The supply chain design process consists of the following steps:[50]

Steps in the Supply Chain Design Process

1. Establish supply chain objectives.
2. Formulate a supply chain strategy.
3. Determine supply chain structure alternatives.
4. Evaluate supply chain structure alternatives.
5. Select supply chain structure.
6. Determine alternatives for individual supply chain members.
7. Evaluate and select individual supply chain members.

---

[48]Lee and Billington, "Managing Supply Chain Inventory: Pitfalls and Opportunities"; and Davis "Effective Supply Chain Management."

[49]Arntzen, Brown, Harrison, and Traffton, "Global Supply Chain Management at Digital Equipment Corporation."

[50]Adapted from Douglas M. Lambert, *The Distribution Channels Decision* (New York: National Association of Accountants; Hamilton, Ontario: Society of Management Accountants of Canada, 1978), pp. 44–45.

8. Measure and evaluate supply chain performance.
9. Evaluate supply chain alternatives when performance objectives are not met or when attractive new options become available.

The manufacturer, wholesaler, or retailer may lead the design process, depending on the relative market power, financial strength, and availability of desired supply chain members.

The Manufacturer's Perspective

A manufacturer has market power when customers demand its product. In this case, retailers and consequently wholesalers are anxious to market the manufacturer's existing and new products because such products will draw customers. Increasingly the consolidation of manufacturers, wholesalers, and retailers on both national and global bases has resulted in a power shift to retailers since they have access to larger numbers of consumers. The consolidation of manufacturers results in a reduced set of global suppliers that produce brands that consumers increasingly view as substitutes. The store brands of retailers such as Wal-Mart have become national and in some cases global brands themselves, which has further contributed to the weakening of traditionally strong manufacturer brands.

A small manufacturer of a little-known brand may find it difficult to attract supply chain members for its existing or new product offerings. Such a manufacturer lacks market power when entering supply chain negotiations. Also, since financial resources determine a manufacturer's ability to perform marketing functions internally, small manufacturers usually cannot afford to distribute directly to retailers or geographically dispersed industrial customers and must therefore rely on wholesalers. Furthermore, in some locations acceptable intermediaries may not be available in every line of trade. Firms in this situation include some manufacturers of electrical supplies and small hand tools.

Even the manufacturer of a full line of products who has geographically concentrated customers may find direct channels less profitable than indirect channels for some of the products and customers. For example, many pharmaceutical companies have increased their use of wholesalers, even in concentrated market areas, because of the high customer service levels required.

The Wholesaler's Perspective

Wholesalers make it possible to efficiently provide possession, time, and place utility. Wholesalers are economically justified because they improve distribution efficiency by "breaking bulk," building assortments of goods, and providing financing for retailers or industrial customers.

Wholesalers' market power is greatest when retailers order a small amount of each manufacturer's products, or when the manufacturers involved have limited financial resources. For some products, such as Whirlpool appliances and some lines of jewelry and fashion apparel, per-unit prices and margins may be large enough to enable the manufacturer to sell directly to retailers, even when the number of items sold to each retailer is small. But manufacturers of low-value or low-margin items such as cigarettes and some food items may find it profitable to sell only through wholesalers, even though each retailer may order in relatively large quantities.

Wholesalers' and distributors' financial strength determines the number of services they can perform. Each service represents a profit opportunity as well as an associated risk and cost. The presence or absence of other firms offering comparable services influences the market power of individual wholesalers. Traditionally wholesalers have been regional in scope. In some industries, such as pharmaceuticals, wholesaler mergers have occurred. Cardinal Health, McKesson, and Bergen Brunswig are large pharmaceutical wholesalers that have become national in scope. Together they control over one-half of the wholesale drug business in the United States.

The Retailer's Perspective

Retailers exist when they provide convenient product assortment, availability, price, and image within a given geographic market. The degree of customer preference (loyalty due to customer service and price/value performance) that a retailer enjoys in a specific area directly affects its ability to negotiate supply chain relationships. The retailer's financial capability and size also determine its degree of influence over other supply chain members.

Supply Chain Design Considerations

Among the factors management must consider when establishing a supply chain are market coverage objectives, product characteristics, customer service objectives, and profitability.[51]

Market Coverage Objectives

In order to establish market coverage objectives, management must consider customer buying behavior, type of distribution, supply chain structure, and the degree of control necessary for success.

Customer Buying Behavior.   The buying motives of potential customer segments must be determined in order to design a supply chain that can perform most efficiently and effectively. This analysis enables the designer to determine the retail segments most capable of reaching the target markets. Industrial marketers also must identify potential users and determine how these customers will make the purchase decision. The industrial purchaser's decision-making process depends on whether the firm is a user, an original equipment manufacturer, or a distributor.

Intensive Distribution

Type of Distribution.   There are basically three types of distribution that can be used to make products available to consumers:

1. Intensive distribution.
2. Selective distribution.
3. Exclusive distribution.

In *intensive distribution,* products are sold to as many appropriate retailers or wholesalers as possible. Intensive distribution is appropriate for products such as chewing gum,

---

[51]The material in this section is adapted from Donald J. Bowersox, M. Bixby Cooper, Douglas M. Lambert, and Donald A. Taylor, *Management in Marketing Channels* (New York: McGraw-Hill, 1980), Chapter 7, pp. 201–9.

candy bars, soft drinks, bread, film, and cigarettes where the primary factor influencing the purchase decision is convenience. Industrial products that may require intensive distribution include pencils, paper clips, transparent tape, file folders, typing paper, transparency masters, screws, and nails.

Selective Distribution

In *selective distribution,* the number of outlets that may carry a product is limited, but not to the extent of exclusive dealing. By carefully selecting wholesalers and retailers, the manufacturer can concentrate on potentially profitable accounts and develop solid working relationships to ensure that the product is properly merchandised. The producer may also restrict the number of retail outlets if the product requires specialized servicing or sales support. Selective distribution may be used for product categories such as clothing, appliances, televisions, stereo equipment, home furnishings, and sports equipment.

Exclusive Distribution

When a single outlet is given an exclusive franchise to sell the product in a geographic area, the arrangement is referred to as *exclusive distribution.* Products such as specialty automobiles, some major appliances, some brands of furniture, and certain lines of clothing that enjoy a high degree of brand loyalty are likely to be distributed on an exclusive basis. This is particularly true if the consumer is willing to overcome the inconvenience of traveling some distance to obtain the product. Usually, exclusive distribution is undertaken when the manufacturer desires more aggressive selling on the part of the wholesaler or retailer, or when channel control is important. Exclusive distribution may enhance the product's image and enable the firm to charge higher retail prices.

Sometimes manufacturers use multiple brands in order to offer exclusive distribution to more than one retailer or distributor. Exclusive distribution occurs more frequently at the wholesale level than at the retail level. Anheuser-Busch, for example, offers exclusive rights to distributors, who in turn use intensive distribution at the retail level (in states such as Florida where this is allowed). In general, exclusive distribution lends itself to direct channels (manufacturer to retailer). Intensive distribution is more likely to involve indirect channels with two or more intermediaries.

Supply Chain Structure.   With customer requirements and the type of distribution determined, management must select supply chain institutions for both inbound and outbound portions of the supply chain. Factors to consider when selecting supply chain members include (1) financial strength, (2) capabilities, (3) ability to link up processes, (4) ability to grow with the business, and (5) competing supply chains.

Control.   In many cases, a firm may have to exercise some control over other members of the supply chain to ensure product quality or postpurchase services. The need for control stems from management's desire to protect the firm's long-term profitability.

Product Characteristics

Product characteristics are a major consideration in supply chain design. Nine product characteristics should be analyzed by the designer: (1) the product's value, (2) the technicality of the product, (3) the degree of market acceptance, (4) the degree of substitutability, (5) the product's bulk, (6) the product's perishability, (7) the degree of market concentration, (8) seasonality, and (9) the width and depth of the product line.

Value.   Products with a high per-unit cost require a large inventory investment. Consequently, high-value products typically will require shorter supply chains (fewer members) in order to minimize total inventory investment. But supply chains tend to be longer when the unit value is low, unless sales volume is high. In general, intensive distribution is used for low-value products.

The product's value also influences its inventory carrying cost and the desirability of premium transportation. Low-value, low-margin grocery products may be shipped by rail car and stored in field warehouses. High-value component parts and products such as high-fashion merchandise may be shipped by air freight to minimize in-transit inventories and reduce inventory carrying costs and markdowns.

Technicality.   Highly technical products usually require demonstration by a salesperson as well as prepurchase and postpurchase service that often requires repair parts to be stocked. Technical products include such items as home computers, high-priced stereo components, expensive cameras and video equipment, imported sports cars, and a multitude of industrial products. Generally, direct channels and selective or exclusive distribution policies are used for these kinds of products.

Market Acceptance.   The degree of market acceptance determines the amount of selling effort required. If a leading manufacturer offers a new product and plans significant introductory advertising, customer acceptance will be high and intermediaries will want to carry the product. But new products with little market acceptance and low brand identification require aggressive selling.

Substitutability.   Product substitutability is closely related to brand loyalty. When brand loyalty is low, product substitution is likely and intensive distribution is required. Firms place a premium on point-of-purchase displays in high-traffic areas. To gain support from wholesalers or retailers, the producer may offer higher-than-normal margins. Selective or exclusive distribution makes product support easier.

Bulk.   Generally, low-value, high-weight products are restricted to markets close to the point of production. These products often require special materials-handling skills. With low weight and small cubes, more units can be shipped in a truck, rail car, or container, thereby reducing the per-unit cost of transportation. Tank-truck shipment of orange juice concentrate from Florida to northern markets for packaging is an example of moving a product closer to the point of consumption to overcome value and bulk restrictions.

Perishability.   Perishability refers to physical deterioration or to product obsolescence caused by changing customer buying patterns or technological change. Perishable products are usually sold on a direct basis in order to move product through the supply chain more quickly and reduce the potential for inventory loss.

Market Concentration.   When the market is concentrated in a geographic area, short supply chains may be the most effective and efficient method. When markets are widely dispersed, however, specialized intermediaries are necessary; they can capitalize on the efficiencies associated with moving larger quantities. Because of widely dispersed markets, many food-processing companies use brokers to market their products. This factor also explains the existence of pooling agencies, such as freight forwarders and local cartage firms, which aggregate small shipments into truckload or carload units for movement to distant points.

Seasonality.   Seasonality must be considered when applicable. For some products, sales volumes peak at certain times of the year (such as toy sales at Christmas); in other cases, raw materials, such as fresh fruits and vegetables, may only be available at specific times. Both cases require out-of-season storage. Manufacturers must invest in warehouses, use third parties, or provide incentives to intermediaries that perform the storage function. For example, manufacturers might offer a seasonal discount or consignment inventories to wholesalers or retailers who agree to take early delivery.

Width and Depth.   The width and depth of a supplier's product line influence supply chain design. A manufacturer of products with low per-unit values may use intensive distribution with direct sales if the product line is broad enough to result in a relatively large average sales volume. Grocery manufacturers such as Kellogg and General Foods are examples. Usually, a manufacturer of a limited line of products will use wholesalers to achieve adequate market coverage at a reasonable cost.

Customer Service Objectives

Customer service represents the place component of the marketing mix. Customer service can be used to differentiate the product or influence the market price—if customers are willing to pay more for better service. In addition, the supply chain structure will determine the costs of providing a specified level of customer service.

Customer Service Measures

Customer service is a complex subject, and will be covered in detail in Chapter 3. However, it is usually measured in terms of (1) the level of product availability, (2) the speed and consistency of the customer's order cycle, and (3) the communication that takes place between seller and customer. Management should establish customer service levels only after carefully studying customer needs.

Availability.   The most important measure of customer service is inventory availability within a specified order cycle time. A common measure of availability is the number of orders shipped complete within a specified time period as a percentage of total orders received. The measure(s) selected should reflect the customer's view of customer service. The best measure of customer service reflects the product's importance to the customer and the customer's importance to the company.

Order Cycle.   The order cycle is the time that elapses between the customer's order placement and the time the product is received. The ability to consistently achieve the targeted order cycle time influences the amount of inventory held throughout the supply chain. Consequently, the speed and consistency of the order cycle are prime factors in supply chain design. Most customers prefer consistent service to fast service, since the former allows them to plan inventory levels to a greater extent than is possible with a fast but highly variable order cycle.

Communication.   Communication refers to the firm's ability to supply timely information to the customer regarding such factors as order status, order tracking, back-order status, order confirmation, product substitution, product shortages, and product information requests. The use of automated information systems usually results in fewer errors in shipping, picking, packing, labeling, and documentation. The ability of supply chain members to provide good communications systems is a major factor in supply chain design.

Supply Chain Performance Measurement

The literature rarely focuses on measuring supply chain performance for a number of reasons:

1. Measuring supply chain performance is difficult.
2. Some aspects of supply chain performance are difficult to quantify, making it difficult to establish a common performance standard.
3. Differences in supply chains make it difficult to establish standards for comparison.

One measure of supply chain performance is the extent to which the company's target end-user markets are being satisfied, given the firm's goals and objectives. This would include measures of product availability, adequacy of customer service, and strength of brand image.

Measures of Supply Chain Structure Efficiency

Next, management must analyze supply chain structure to determine whether the corporate strategy has been successfully implemented. Measures of structure efficiency include member turnover, competitive strength, and related issues. When management evaluates supply chain structure, it must compare the firm's ability to perform the activities internally with another member's ability to perform these activities.

Some potential quantitative measures of supply chain performance include logistics cost per unit, cash-to-cash cycle, and total days of inventory in the supply chain. Qualitative measures that managers may use when reevaluating the supply chain and specific members include degree of coordination, degree of conflict, and availability of information as needed. Management should set objectives for the supply chain and individual members and measure actual performance against planned performance. Also, evaluation measures should be developed over time and be used to isolate potential problem areas. Perhaps the best measures of performance are the value created for customers and the profitability of the supply chain and its members.

Recall that in Chapter 1 we introduced the integrated logistics management concept and the cost trade-offs required in a logistics system (see Figure 2–8). Cost trade-off analysis can be performed either within a single firm or across firms in the supply chain. For the individual firm, the goal is to find the most efficient way to offer the desired level of customer service. For the supply chain, the goal is to improve overall efficiency by reallocating functions, and therefore costs, among its members. The level of customer service offered by the individual member firms will have a significant impact on other members and total supply chain performance.

For example, a manufacturer whose product availability is poor and order cycle times are inconsistent may force wholesalers to carry more inventory as safety stock in order to offer an acceptable level of service to the retailers. In this case, lower logistics costs for the manufacturer were achieved at the expense of other members of the supply chain, and the entire supply chain may be less efficient.

Information Technology Can Increase Supply Chain Efficiency and Effectiveness

However, if management concentrates on systems changes that improve logistics efficiency or effectiveness, it may be possible to satisfy all of the firm's objectives. For example, by linking members of the supply chain, using advanced information technology, and sharing key data, a firm may be able to achieve some or all of the following: (1) increased customer service levels, (2) lower inventories, (3) speedier collections, (4) decreased transportation costs, (5) lower warehousing costs, (6) improvement in cash flow, and (7) high return on assets. Thus, all supply chain decisions are best viewed from a systems perspective, as an integrated whole.

FIGURE 2–8

*Cost trade-offs required
in marketing and logistics*

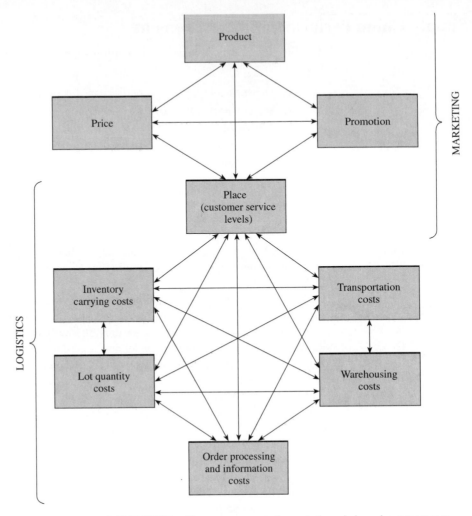

MARKETING OBJECTIVE: Allocate resources to the marketing mix in such a manner as to
                        maximize the long-term profitability of the firm.
LOGISTICS OBJECTIVE: Minimize Total Costs given the customer service objective where
                        Total costs = Transportation costs + Warehousing costs +
                        Order processing and information costs + Lot quantity costs +
                        Inventory carrying costs.

Source: Adapted from Douglas M. Lambert, *The Development of an Inventory Costing Methodology: A Study of the Cost
Associated with Holding Inventory* (Chicago: National Council of Physical Distribution Management, 1976), p. 7.

A manufacturer has minimal additional cash invested in inventory held by the customer rather than in the manufacturer's warehouse. Furthermore, the non–cost-of-
money components of inventory carrying cost are shifted to the next level of the supply chain. However, this may not be most efficient for the supply chain as a whole, as
the value of inventory increases as it gets closer to the consumer because of markups
by each subsequent member or value added at various stages in the supply chain. The
supply chain would be better off as a whole to have inventory held in the least valuable
forms. In addition, the less differentiated the inventory has become, the more likely, in

general, that it can be used in a different application. This was explained earlier in this chapter when we described postponement. The cost of carrying inventory at various locations within the supply chain will be described in detail in Chapter 5, which deals with the financial impact of inventory.

In addition to rethinking traditional strategies for improving supply chain cash flow and return on assets, supply chain leaders may wish to consider automating and integrating the information systems within the supply chain. This can reduce lead-time variability and create time for planning. If the organization improves communications flows throughout the supply chain, all members will be able to reduce inventories while improving customer service.

In addition, the extra planning time that results due to increased communication speed will allow freight consolidations, warehousing cost savings, and lower lot quantity costs. Customer service levels can be improved and total operating costs reduced— truly a unique opportunity.

In the last section of this chapter, we will describe how leading-edge firms are implementing an integrated approach to managing the supply chain.

Reengineering Improvement into the Supply Chain

A critical part of streamlining supply chains involves reengineering the key processes to meet customer needs. Reengineering is a process aimed at producing dramatic changes quickly. Michael Hammer and James Champy define it as the fundamental rethinking and radical redesign of business processes to achieve dramatic improvements in critical contemporary measures of performance such as cost, quality service, and speed.[52] Improvement through reengineering cannot be accomplished haphazardly. These changes must be supported at the top and driven through an overall management plan.

Three Stages in the Reengineering Process

A typical reengineering process proceeds through three stages:

(1) Fact finding.
(2) Identifying areas for improvement to business process redesign.
(3) Creative improvements.

The fact-finding stage is a very detailed examination of the current systems, procedures, and work flows. Key focus is placed on separating facts from opinions.

Armed with the facts collected in the first stage, the reengineering team identifies areas for improvement. The team analyzes where value was added for the final customer with particular emphasis on customer contact points and product information transfers that are currently ineffective or inefficient. After identifying improvement points, the reengineering team enters the creative phase of redesigning business process and information flow. The outcomes of the creative phase will fundamentally change both the nature of the work and how it is performed.

Figure 2–9 illustrates a general plan for undertaking the reengineering process. Organizational energy needs to focus on the firm's mission statement. The mission statement drives the business requirements in the organization. A complete assessment is made of the firm's culture, strategies, business practices, and processes.

---

[52]Hammer and Champy, *Reengineering the Corporation.*

FIGURE 2–9

*Reengineering SCM
process flow chart*

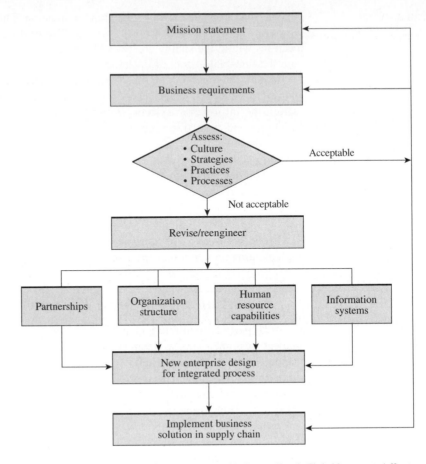

If this analysis proves acceptable, management implements its business solution across the supply chain. Typically, improvements are required in one of the areas to enhance supply chain performance. An example of this reengineering is the new Mercedes-Benz microcar, which is based on the principle of systems supply.[53] This reengineering of the process results in delegating more design activities to suppliers, reducing the amount of engineering and labor at the primary manufacturer. The result is passing the savings of these efficiencies along to the customer in the form of increased value.

Implementing Integrated Supply Chain Management

Implementing SCM requires changing the focus of an organization from function to process. Figure 2–10 illustrates how each of six typical functions in an organization maps with the seven key processes.

---

[53]J. L. Coleman, A. K. Bhattacharya, and G. Brace, "Supply Chain Reeingineering: A Supplier's Perspective," *The International Journal of Logistics Management,* 6, no. 1 (1995), pp. 85–92.

FIGURE 2–10

Implementation of supply chain management

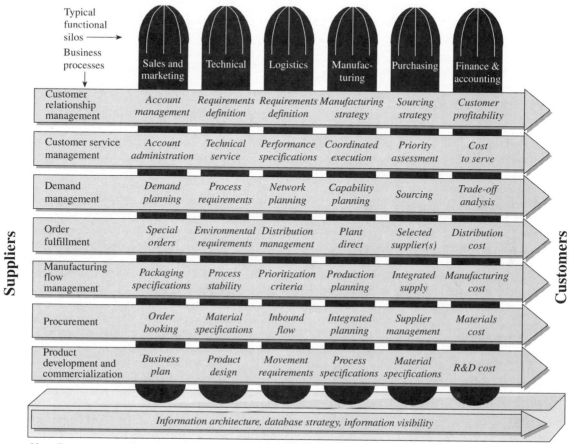

Note: Process sponsorship and ownership must be established to drive the attainment of the supply chain vision and eliminate the functional barriers that artificially separate the process flows.

For example, in the customer relationship management process, sales and marketing provides the account management expertise, engineering provides the specifications that define the requirements, logistics provides knowledge of customer service requirements, manufacturing provides the manufacturing strategy, purchasing provides the sourcing strategy, and finance and accounting provides customer profitability reports. The customer service requirements must be used as inputs to manufacturing, sourcing, and logistics strategies.

If the proper coordination mechanisms are not in place across the various functions, the process will be neither effective nor efficient. With a process focus, all functions that touch the product or provide information must work together. For example, sales/marketing data fed through a production schedule are used to assess specific order levels and timing of requirements. These orders drive production requirements, which in turn are transmitted upstream to suppliers.

Creative Solutions

How Milliken Drives Supply Chain Integration

In 1981 U.S. textile and apparel producers enjoyed an 80 percent share of their domestic market. Six years later, their share was 60 percent. Protectionist legislation slowed this decline, but profits went in to free fall, plunging from $1.9 billion in 1987 to $600 million in 1991.[1]

In 1986 the industry commissioned consultants Kurt Salmon Associates to study U.S. apparel industry supply chains. The results were alarming. The supply chains were too long and too badly coordinated to respond effectively to marketplace demands. Time to market averaged 1.25 years from textile loom to store rack. Industrywide, the cost of this inefficiency was estimated to be approximately $25 billion per year, around 20 percent of the industry's total turnover.[2] The supply chain could not absorb these costs, so they had been passed on to the customer—until imports became a threat.

The U.S. industry had to find new ways of working if it was going to survive. Several pilot studies were commissioned to determine if pipelines could be shortened by collaboration between retailers, apparel manufacturers, and textile producers. Among the first to participate in the pilot studies was Milliken & Co., the country's largest textile producer.

Milliken's performance before embarking on the experiment was as follows: Milliken received incoming orders—slowly—by mail. Weaving would normally be completed eight weeks after the yarn became available. Dyeing and finishing took a further four to five weeks. The stock would be forwarded to the central warehouse until required by the customer. Throughput times were around 18–20 weeks from receipt of order. Keeping the factory operating at maximum capacity was the overriding priority.

After Milliken, an apparel manufacturer could take around 18–20 weeks from receipt of cloth to get the clothing to a retailer.[3] The retailers, fearing stockouts, regularly overordered, increasing their carrying costs and resulting in markdowns of excess stock. If the retailer's inventories got too high the retailer would cut back on purchasing, leaving the manufacturers with excess stock. They in turn would cancel fabric orders, leaving Milliken holding unwanted inventory.

In the pilot study, Milliken partnered with apparel manufacturer Seminol and with Wal-Mart stores. Consultants monitored a single product line (basic slacks), measuring the sales and profit improvement delivered by the implementation of quick response. The results showed increased sales of 31 percent and a 30 percent improvement in inventory turns.[4]

This exercise taught Milliken to look beyond its immediate customer—the apparel producer who paid the fabric invoice—so as to be responsive to the end consumers' requirements. If point-of-sale information could be shared between the partners, long-range forecasting, overstocking, and order cancellations would no longer be necessary. Milliken began seeking out like-minded supply chain partners who were willing to set aside short-term self-interest to create integrated supply chains.

The lessons learned in the apparel industry were used to improve other areas of Milliken's textile business. For example, the company approached one of its customers, a retailer of oriental-style rugs, with an offer to manufacture the rugs to order by quick response, and ship them by UPS direct to the customer's home. The retailer would have to forward its customer orders to Milliken on a daily basis, and keep it fully informed of planned promotional activity. The retailer hesitated at first, but then agreed. The move allowed the retailer to eliminate its entire inventory of the product, keeping only display items, while cutting delivery times and costs since the rugs no longer passed through its distribution center.

---

[1]Walecia Konrad, "Why Leslie Wexner Shops Overseas," *Business Week* (February 1992), p. 33.
[2]George Stalk Jr. and Thomas M. Hout, *Competing against Time* (New York: Free Press, 1990), p. 249.
[3]"Time Based Competition" (video), Harvard Business School Management Programmes, 1993, Program 2.
[4]Stalk and Hout, *Competing against Time,* p. 252.

Source: Adapted from Martin Christopher, *Marketing Logistics* (Oxford, UK: Butterworth Heinemann, 1997), pp. 81–84.

The increasing use of outsourcing has accelerated the need to coordinate supply chain processes. As the organization becomes more dependent on outside suppliers, coordination mechanisms must be developed within the organization. Where to place these coordination mechanisms and which team and functions are responsible become critical decisions.

Any of several process redesign and reengineering techniques can be applied by management. Chrysler Corporation's development of the Neon was accomplished through the efforts of 150 internal employees. This core group leveraged their efforts to 600 engineers and 289 suppliers, as well as Chryler's line employees. Concurrent engineering techniques required the involvement of personnel from all key functional areas working with suppliers to develop the vehicle in 42 months. The use of concurrent engineering resulted in the avoidance of later disagreements, misunderstandings, and delays.

All firms within the supply chain will have their own functional silos that must be overcome and a process approach accepted in order to successfully implement SCM. The requirements for successful implementation of SCM include:

Requirements for Successful Supply Chain Management

- Executive support, leadership, and commitment to change.
- An understanding of the degree of change that is necessary.
- Agreement on the SCM vision and the key processes.
- Commitment of the resources and empowerment necessary to achieve the stated goals.

Summary

In this chapter we saw that:

1. Supply chain management is different from managing logistics in the supply chain.
2. Various supply chain structures are used.
3. Supply chain management is a process-oriented approach to manage relationships in the supply chain; leading-edge firms such as 3M are implementing SCM.
4. Communications can improve the efficiency and effectiveness of the supply chain.
5. A number of factors influence supply chain design, evolution, and performance.
6. The implementation of integrated supply chain management requires a process management team structure.

Now that we have established the necessary background in supply chain management and the role of logistics in the supply chain, we will describe the major logistics activities in depth, beginning in Chapter 3 with the subject of customer service.

Suggested Readings

Abrahamsson, Mats, and Staffan Brege. "Structural Changes in the Supply Chain." *The International Journal of Logistics Management* 8, no. 1 (1997), pp. 35–44.

Andraski, Joseph C. "Foundations for Successful Continuous Replenishment Programs." *The International Journal of Logistics Management* 5, no. 1 (1994), pp. 1–8.

Ballou, Ronald H., Stephen M. Gilbert, and Ashok Mukherjee. "New Managerial Challenges from Supply Chain Opportunities." *Industrial Marketing Management* 29, no. 1 (2000), pp. 17–18.

Bechtel, Christian, and Jayanth Jayaram. "Supply Chain Management: A Strategic Perspective." *The International Journal of Logistics Management* 8, no. 1 (1997), pp. 15–34.

Berry, Danny, and Denis R. Towill. "Material Flow in Electronic Product Based Supply Chains." *The International Journal of Logistics Management* 3, no. 2 (1992), pp. 77–94.

Bhattacharya, Arindam K., Julian L. Coleman, Gordon Brace, and Paul J. Kelly. "The Structure Conundrum in Supply Chain Management." *The International Journal of Logistics Management* 7, no. 1 (1996), pp. 39–48.

Bowersox, Donald J., M. Bixby Cooper, Douglas M. Lambert, and Donald A. Taylor. *Management in Marketing Channels.* New York: McGraw-Hill, 1980.

Bucklin, Louis P. *A Theory of Distribution Channel Structure.* Berkeley, CA: Institute of Business and Economic Research, University of California, 1966.

Burgess, Rachel. "Avoiding Supply Chain Management Failure: Lessons from Business Process Reengineering." *The International Journal of Logistics Management* 9, no. 1 (1998), pp. 15–23.

Cavinato, Joseph L. "Identifying Interfirm Total Cost Advantages for Supply Chain Competitiveness." *The International Journal of Purchasing and Materials Management* 27, no. 4 (Fall 1991), pp. 10–15.

Christopher, Martin. "The Agile Supply Chain: Competing in Volatile Markets." *Industrial Marketing Management* 29, no. 1 (2000), pp. 37–44.

Christopher, Martin, and Lynette Ryals. "Supply Chain Strategy: Its Impact on Shareholder Value." *The International Journal of Logistics Management* 10, no. 1 (1999), pp. 1–10.

Clendenin, John A. "Closing the Supply Chain Loop: Reengineering the Returns Channel Process." *The International Journal of Logistics Management* 8, no. 1 (1997), pp. 75–85.

Closs, David, Anthony S. Roath, Thomas J. Goldsby, James A. Eckert, and Stephen M. Swartz. "An Empirical Comparison of Anticipatory and Response-Based Supply Chain Strategies." *The International Journal of Logistics Management* 9, no. 2 (1998), pp. 21–34.

Coleman, Julian L., Arindam K. Bhattacharya, and Gordon Brace. "Supply Chain Reengineering: A Supplier's Perspective." *The International Journal of Logistics Management* 5, no. 2 (1994), pp. 1–10.

Cooper, Martha C., and Lisa M. Ellram. "Characteristics of Supply Chain Management and the Implications for Purchasing and Logistics Strategy." *The International Journal of Logistics Management* 4, no. 2 (1993), pp. 13–24.

Cooper, Martha C., Douglas M. Lambert, and Janus D. Pagh. "Supply Chain Management: More Than a New Name for Logistics." *The International Journal of Logistics Management* 8, no. 1 (1997), pp. 1–14.

Ellinger, Alexander E. "Improving Marketing/Logistics Cross-Functional Collaboration in the Supply Chain." *Industrial Marketing Management* 29, no. 1 (2000), pp. 85–96.

Ellram, Lisa M., and Martha C. Cooper. "Supply Chain Management, Partnerships and the Shipper-Third Party Relationship." *The International Journal of Logistics Management* 1, no. 2 (1990), pp. 1–10.

———. "The Relationship Between Supply Chain Management and Keiretsu." *The International Journal of Logistics Management* 4, no. 1 (1993), pp. 1–12.

Fernie, John, and Clive Rees. "Supply Chain Management in the National Health Service." *The International Journal of Logistics Management* 6, no. 2 (1995), pp. 83–92.

Gattorna, John. *Strategic Supply Chain Alignment: Best Practice in Supply Chain Management.* Hampshire, England: Gower Publishing Limited, 1998.

Guinipero, Larry C., and Richard R. Brand. "Purchasing's Role in Supply Chain Management." *The International Journal of Logistics Management* 7, no. 1 (1996), pp. 29–38.

Gunn, T. G. *In the Age of the Real-Time Enterprise.* Essex, VT: Omneo, 1994.

Hewitt, Fred. "Supply Chain Redesign." *The International Journal of Logistics Management* 5, no. 2 (1994), pp. 1–10.

Hines, Peter. "Integrated Materials Management: The Value Chain Redefined." *The International Journal of Logistics Management* 4, no. 1 (1993), pp. 13–22.

Hines, Peter, Nick Rich, John Bicheno, David Brunt, David Taylor, Chris Butterworth, and James Sullivan. "Value Stream Management." *The International Journal of Logistics Management* 9, no. 1 (1998), pp. 25–42.

Horscroft, Peter, and Alan Braithwaite. "Enhancing Supply Chain Efficiency: The Strategic Lead Time Approach." *The International Journal of Logistics Management* 1, no. 2 (1990), pp. 47–52.

Houlihan, John B. "International Supply Chains: A New Approach." *Management Decision* 26, no. 3 (1988), pp. 13–19.

Jenkins, Gareth P., and Derek S. Wright. "Managing Inflexible Supply Chains." *The International Journal of Logistics Management* 9, no. 2 (1998), pp. 81–88.

Johnson, D. T., and A. Simpson. "International Service Parts Management." *Annual Conference Proceedings of the Council of Logistics Management,* vol. 2 (Oak Brook, IL: Council of Logistics Management, 1993), pp. 331–46.

Johnston, Russell, and Paul R. Lawrence. "Beyond Vertical Integration: The Rise of the Value-Adding Partnership." *Harvard Business Review* 66, no. 4 (July–August 1988), pp. 94–101.

La Londe, Bernard J., and Terrance L. Pohlen. "Issues in Supply Chain Costing." *The International Journal of Logistics Management* 7 (1991), pp. 1–12.

Lambert, Douglas M., and Martha C. Cooper. "Issues in Supply Chain Management." *Industrial Marketing Management* 29, no. 1 (2000), pp. 65–83.

Lamming, Richard. *Beyond Partnerships.* Englewood Cliffs, NJ: Prentice Hall, 1993.

Lancioni, Richard A. "New Developments in Supply Chain Management for the Millennium." *Industrial Marketing Management* 29, no. 1 (2000), pp. 1–6.

Lancioni, Richard A., Michael F. Smith, and Terrence A. Oliva. "The Role of the Internet in Supply Chain Management." *Industrial Marketing Management* 29, no. 1 (2000), pp. 45–56.

Mallen, Bruce. *Principles of Marketing Channel Management.* Lexington, MA: Lexington Books, 1977.

Mason-Jones, Rachel, Mohammed M. Naim, and Denis R. Towill. "The Impact of Pipeline Control on Supply Chain Dynamics." *The International Journal of Logistics Management* 8, no. 2 (1997), pp. 47–62.

Moon, Mark A., John T. Mentzer, and Dwight E. Thomas Jr. "Customer Demand Planning at Lucent Technologies." *Industrial Marketing Management* 29, no. 1 (2000), pp. 19–26.

Pano, Robin. "Pull Out the Stops in Your Network." *Transportation and Distribution* 35, no. 8 (August 1994), pp. 38–40.

Stern, Louis W., Adel I. El-Ansary, and Anne Coughlan. *Marketing Channels,* 5th ed. Englewood Cliffs, NJ: Prentice Hall, 1996.

Trafton, L., and M. McElroy. "Logistics Network Design and Pipeline Optimization: The Optimizer." *Proceedings of the Annual Conference of the Council of Logistics Management,* vol. 2 (Oak Brook, IL: Council of Logistics Management, 1993), pp. 375–95.

Treacy, M., and F. Wiersma. "Customer Intimacy and Other Value Disciplines." *Harvard Business Review* 71, no. 1 (January–February 1993), pp. 84–93.

Webber, Mary Margaret. "Calculating the Cost of Variances in the Supply Chain." *Industrial Marketing Management* 29, no. 1 (2000), pp. 57–64.

Wilding, Richard D. "Chaos Theory: Implications for Supply Chain Management." *The International Journal of Logistics Management* 9, no. 1 (1998), pp. 43–56.

Van Hoek, Remko L. "Reconfiguring the Supply Chain to Implement Postponed Manufacturing." *The International Journal of Logistics Management* 9, no. 1 (1998), pp. 95–110.

Van Hoek, Remko L., and Harm A. M. Weken. "The Impact of Modular Production on the Dynamics of Supply Chains." *The International Journal of Logistics Management* 9, no. 1 (1998), pp. 95–110.

Questions and Problems

1. Define *supply chain management.* What are the differences/similarities between logistics and supply chain management?

2. What is the role of outsourcing in supply chain management?

3. Give an example of (*a*) a firm that uses postponement and (*b*) a firm that uses speculation in the supply chain.

4. Describe the four types of business process links and give an example of a situation when each would be appropriate.

5. Identify the eight supply chain processes and explain why they are cross-functional.

6. What difficulties might be expected when management attempts to implement a business process approach with members of the firm's supply chain?

7. Explain how product characteristics influence supply chain design.

8. How can communications technology be used to improve supply chain efficiency and effectiveness?

9. What are some of the difficulties you would expect to encounter in trying to measure supply chain performance?

10. What are the major obstacles to successfully implementing supply chain management?

CHAPTER 3

Customer Service

Chapter Outline

Chapter Objectives

- To define customer service.
- To show the importance of the customer service function to a firm's marketing and logistics efforts.
- To show how to calculate cost/revenue trade-offs.
- To show how to conduct a customer service audit.
- To identify opportunities for improving customer service performance.

Introduction

A world-class organization must provide high levels of logistics service to customers. Both knowing customer expectations and understanding the firm's performance (relative to that of competitors) on logistics service attributes are vital to achieving service excellence.[1] As domestic competition, international competition, and customer demands increase, management must use logistics as a weapon to create a sustainable competitive advantage in the marketplace.

As we noted in Chapter 1, customer service represents the output of the logistics system and the place component of the firm's marketing mix. It is a measure of the effectiveness of the logistics system in creating time and place utility for a product. The level of customer service determines not only whether existing customers will remain customers but also how many potential customers will become customers. Thus, customer service has a direct impact on a firm's market share,[2] its total logistics costs, and ultimately its profitability. For this reason, it is imperative that customer service be an integral part of the design and operation of any logistics system.

What Is Customer Service?

The importance of a marketing orientation for business success has been well documented.[3] How management allocates scarce resources to the components of the marketing mix—product, price, promotion, and place—will determine a company's market share and profitability. Figure 3–1 summarizes the cost trade-offs that management must make.

The place component represents the manufacturer's expenditure for customer service, which can be thought of as the output of the logistics system. Customer service is the interface of logistics with marketing. Although customer service is the output of the logistics system, customer satisfaction results when the company performs well on all components of the marketing mix. For many firms providing excellent customer service may be the best method of gaining a competitive advantage.[4] A firm may be able to improve its market share and profitability significantly by spending more than competitors on customer service and logistics. By systematically adjusting the customer service package, however, the firm may improve service and reduce the total costs of logistics. When evaluating alternative customer service strategies, management should try to maximize the firm's long-run profitability.

As we said in Chapter 1 when we introduced the total cost concept, management must consider the *total* of all the logistics costs described in Figure 3–1. Reductions in one cost invariably lead to increases of other costs. Effective management and real cost

---

[1]James R. Stock and Douglas M. Lambert, "Becoming a 'World Class' Company with Logistics Service Quality," *The International Journal of Logistics Management* 3, no. 1 (1992), p. 73.

[2]The relationship between customer service and market share has been documented in Jay U. Sterling, "Integrating Customer Service and Marketing Strategies in a Channel of Distribution: An Empirical Study," unpublished Ph.D. dissertation, Michigan State University, 1985.

[3]Thomas J. Peters and Robert H. Waterman Jr., *In Search of Excellence* (New York: Harper & Row, 1982).

[4]Jay U. Sterling and Douglas M. Lambert, "Establishing Customer Service Strategies Within the Marketing Mix," *Journal of Business Logistics* 8, no. 1 (1987), pp. 1–30.

FIGURE 3–1

*Cost trade-offs in
marketing and logistics*

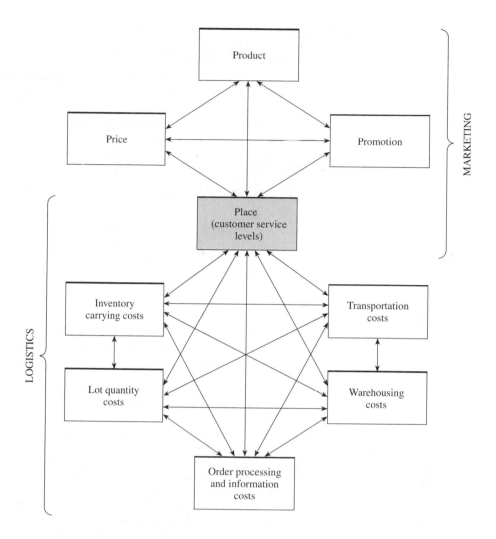

MARKETING OBJECTIVE: Allocate resources to the marketing mix in such a manner as to
                       maximize the long-term profitability of the firm.
LOGISTICS OBJECTIVE: Minimize Total Costs given the customer service objective where
                       Total costs = Transportation costs + Warehousing costs +
                       Order processing and information costs + Lot quantity costs +
                       Inventory carrying costs.

Source: Adapted from Douglas M. Lambert, *The Development of an Inventory Costing Methodology: A Study of the Cost
Associated with Holding Inventory* (Chicago: National Council of Physical Distribution Management, 1976), p. 7.

savings can be accomplished only by viewing logistics as an *integrated system* and
minimizing its total cost, given the firm's customer service objectives. It is impossible
to design an efficient and effective logistics system without first establishing the firm's
customer service objectives.

   Determining the customer service objectives is the first step in logistics system
design. Until we have taken this step, we cannot make decisions about transportation,
warehousing, inventory investment, ordering strategies, or production.

Definition of Customer Service

Customer service can be defined as

> a process which takes place between buyer, seller, and third party. The process results in a value added to the product or service exchanged. This value added in the exchange process might be short term as in a single transaction or longer term as in a contractual relationship. The value added is also shared, in that each of the parties to the transaction or contract is better off at the completion of the transaction than they were before the transaction took place. Thus, in a process view: Customer service is a process for providing significant value-added benefits to the supply chain in a cost effective way.[5]

Customer Service Can Impact Demand

Successful implementation of the marketing concept requires both obtaining customers and keeping them, while satisfying the firm's long-range profit and return on investment objectives. Creating demand—obtaining customers—is often thought of solely in terms of promotion (selling and advertising), product, and price, but customer service can have a significant impact on demand.[6] In addition, customer service determines whether customers will remain customers.

Elements of Customer Service

A number of elements are commonly associated with customer service, although the degree of importance attached to any of them varies from company to company depending on customer needs. Bernard J. La Londe and Paul Zinszer categorized the elements of customer service into three groups: pretransaction, transaction, and posttransaction (see Figure 3–2).[7]

Three Groups of Customer Service Elements

Pretransaction Elements.   The pretransaction elements of customer service tend to be nonroutine and policy related, and they require management input. These activities, although not specifically involved with logistics, have a significant impact on product sales. The specific elements of pretransaction customer service include the following:

1. *A written statement of customer service policy.* The customer service policy statement would (*a*) be based on customer needs, (*b*) define service standards, (*c*) determine who reports the performance measurements to whom and with what frequency, and (*d*) be operational or capable of being implemented.

2. *Customers receive service policy statement.* It makes little sense to provide a level of service designed to improve market penetration and then fail to inform the customer of what is being provided. Giving customers a written statement reduces the likelihood that they will have unrealistic expectations of performance. The statement must provide the customer with information on how to communicate with the firm if specified performance levels are not attained.

3. *Organization structure.* Although no one organization structure is best suited to successful implementation of all customer service policies, the structure

---

[5]Bernard J. La Londe, Martha C. Cooper, and Thomas G. Noordewier, *Customer Service: A Management Perspective* (Chicago: Council of Logistics Management, 1988), p. 5.

[6]Sterling and Lambert, "Establishing Customer Service Strategies Within the Marketing Mix."

[7]Bernard J. La Londe and Paul H. Zinszer, *Customer Service: Meaning and Measurement* (Chicago: National Council of Physical Distribution Management, 1976), pp. 272–82.

Figure 3–2

*Elements of customer
service*

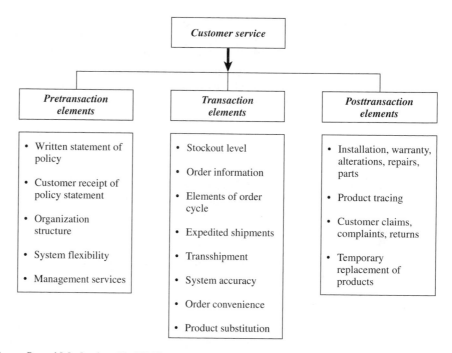

Source: Bernard J. La Londe and Paul H. Zinszer, *Customer Service: Meaning and Measurement* (Chicago: National
Council of Physical Distribution Management, 1976), p. 281.

selected should facilitate communication and cooperation among those
functions involved in implementing the customer service policy. In addition,
the firm should provide customers with the name and phone number of a
specific individual who can satisfy their need for information. The
individuals who manage the customer service components must have the
appropriate responsibility and authority, and must be rewarded in a manner
that encourages them to interface with other corporate functions.

**Achieving Customer
Service Objectives
Should Be a High-Level
Responsibility**

4. *System flexibility.* To effectively respond to unplanned events, such as
snowstorms, shortages of raw materials or energy, and strikes, the system
must be flexible.

5. *Management services.* Management services—such as training manuals and
seminars designed to help the customer improve inventory management,
ordering, or merchandising—are elements of customer service.

All of the above pretransaction elements of customer service are essential components of a successful marketing strategy.

Transaction Elements.   Transaction elements are the activities normally associated
with customer service. They include the following:

1. *Stockout level.* The stockout level is a measure of product availability. Stockouts
should be recorded by product and by customer in order to determine where problems
exist. When stockouts occur, the firm can maintain customer goodwill by arranging for
suitable product substitution or expediting the shipment when the product is received in
stock.

2. *Order information.* Order information is the ability to provide the customer with fast and accurate information about inventory status, order status, expected shipping and delivery dates, and back-order status. A back-order capability allows the firm to identify and expedite orders that require immediate attention. The firm can use the number of back orders and their associated order cycle times to measure system performance. The ability to back-order is important because the alternative may be to force a stockout. The firm should record the number of back orders by customer and by product categories to identify and correct poor system performance.

The Order Cycle Defined

3. *Elements of the order cycle.* The *order cycle* is the total time that elapses from customer initiation of the order until delivery to the customer. Individual components of the order cycle include order communication, order entry, order processing, order picking and packing, and delivery. Because customers are mainly concerned with total time, it is important to monitor and manage each of the components of the order cycle to determine the cause of any variations.

4. *Expedited shipments.* Expedited shipments are those that receive special handling in order to reduce the normal order cycle time. Although expediting costs considerably more than standard handling, it may cost less than losing a customer. It is important for management to determine which customers qualify for expedited shipments and which do not. Presumably, such a policy would be based on how much a given customer contributes to the manufacturer's profitability.

5. *Transshipment.* Transshipment is the transporting of product between field locations to avoid stockouts. Transshipments are often made in anticipation of customer demand.

6. *System accuracy.* System accuracy—the accuracy of quantities ordered, products ordered, and billing—is important to both the manufacturer and the customer. Errors should be recorded and reported as a percentage of the number of orders handled by the system.

7. *Order convenience.* Order convenience refers to the degree of difficulty that a customer experiences when placing an order. Problems that result from confusing order forms or nonstandard terminology can lead to poor customer relations. An appropriate performance measurement is the number of convenience-related problems as a percentage of the number of orders. These problems can be identified and reduced or eliminated by conducting field interviews with customers.

Product Substitution Can Improve Customer Service

8. *Product substitution.* Substitution occurs when the product a customer ordered is replaced by the same item in a different size or by another product that will perform as well or better. For example, a customer may order a case of Ivory shampoo for normal hair in 15-ounce bottles. If the customer is willing to accept 8-ounce or 20-ounce bottles during a stockout, the manufacturer can increase the customer service level as measured by product availability within some specified time period. Figure 3–3 shows an example in which two product substitutions allow the manufacturer to increase the customer service level from 70 percent to 97 percent with no change in inventory. If the firm attained a 97 percent customer service level without product substitution, two product substitutions would enable it to maintain the same service level with a 28 percent reduction in inventory.

In order to develop an appropriate product substitution policy, the manufacturer should work closely with customers to inform them or gain their consent. It should also keep product substitution records to monitor performance. A successful product substitution program requires good communication between the manufacturer and customers.

FIGURE 3–3

Impact of substitution on service level

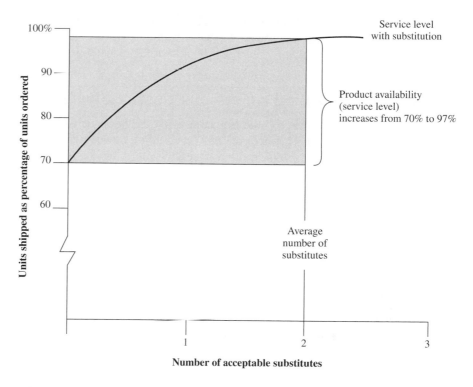

The transaction elements of customer service are the most visible because of the direct impact they have on sales.

Posttransaction Elements.   The posttransaction elements of customer service support the product after it has been sold. The specific posttransaction elements include:

1. *Installation, warranty, alterations, repairs, and parts.* These elements of customer service can be a significant factor in the decision to purchase; they should be evaluated similarly to the transaction elements. To perform these functions, the firm needs (*a*) assistance in seeing that the product is functioning as expected when the consumer begins using it; (*b*) availability of parts and repair personnel; (*c*) documentation support for the field force, as well as accessibility to a supply of parts; and (*d*) an administrative function that validates warranties.[8]

2. *Product tracing.* Product tracing is another necessary component of customer service. In order to avoid litigation, firms must be able to recall potentially dangerous products from the marketplace as soon as problems are identified.

3. *Customer claims, complaints, and returns.* Usually, logistics systems are designed to move products in one direction—toward the customer. Nevertheless, almost every manufacturer has some goods returned, and the nonroutine handling of these items is expensive. A corporate policy should specify how to handle claims, complaints, and returns. The company should maintain data on claims, complaints, and returns in order to provide valuable consumer information to product development, marketing, logistics, and other corporate functions.

---

[8]Ibid., p. 278.

4. *Temporary product replacement.* A final element of customer service is temporary placement of product with customers waiting for receipt of a purchased item or waiting for a previously purchased product to be repaired.

Methods of Establishing a Customer Service Strategy

A firm's entire marketing effort can be rendered ineffective by poorly conceived customer service policies. Yet customer service is often a forgotten component of the marketing mix, and the level of customer service is often based on industry norms, management judgment, or past practices—not on what the customer wants, or what would maximize corporate profitability.[9] What is the advantage of having a well-researched and needed product, priced to sell and promoted well, if customers cannot find it on the shelf at the retail level? However, placing too much emphasis on customer service will needlessly reduce corporate profits. It is essential that a firm adopt a customer service policy that is based on customer needs, is consistent with overall marketing strategy, and advances the corporation's long-range profit objectives.

Four Methods of Developing a Customer Service Strategy

A number of methods have been proposed to aid in establishing a profitable customer service strategy. But the following four methods have the most merit: (1) determining channel service levels based on knowledge of consumer reactions to stockouts; (2) analyzing cost/revenue trade-offs; (3) using ABC analysis of customer service; and (4) conducting a customer service audit.

Consumer Reactions to Stockouts

In consumer goods companies, customer service levels are measured between the manufacturer and its intermediaries. These measures exclude the consumer—the person who purchases the product at the retail level. However, a stockout at the manufacturer–wholesaler interface does not always result in the wholesaler's stocking out the retail accounts it services—depending on the amount of safety stock the wholesaler carries. The retailer's inventories also may prevent the consumer from facing a stockout at that level.

One way to establish the level of customer service that should be provided to wholesalers and retailers is to determine what the consumer is likely to do in the event of a stockout. Figure 3–4 illustrates consumers' possible reactions to a stockout at the retail level. For example, a consumer enters a retail store to purchase Ivory shampoo for normal hair in a 15-ounce bottle. If the item is unavailable, the customer can go to another store to purchase the product. It may not be worth making such a trip for a bottle of shampoo, but there are a number of products for which customers are willing to switch stores.[10]

For Some Products Consumers Are Willing to Switch Stores

Most manufacturers of infant formula, for example, do not advertise their products to consumers in national media. They spend the bulk of their promotion dollars in giving the product to hospitals and doctors who, in turn, give it to new mothers. Because of the high perceived risk associated with the purchase of a nutritional product for a

[9]Harvey M. Shycon and Christopher R. Sprague, "Put a Price Tag on Your Customer Service Levels," *Harvard Business Review* 53, no. 4 (July–August 1975), pp. 71–78.

[10]Consumers may be quite willing to switch stores for a shampoo with special properties, such as one that will solve a dandruff problem.

FIGURE 3–4

*Model of consumer
reaction to a repeated
stockout*

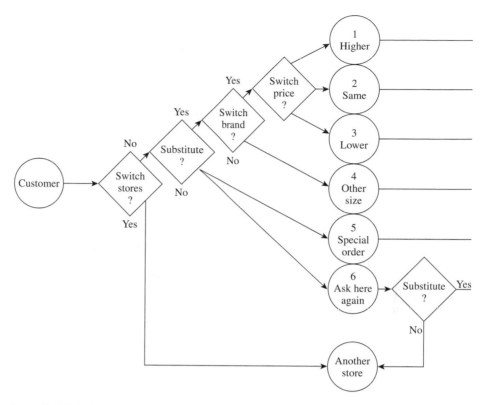

Source: Clyde K. Walter, "An Empirical Analysis of Two Stockout Models," unpublished Ph.D. dissertation, Ohio State University, 1971.

baby, the mother will request the brand given to her by the doctor or hospital.[11] Although the leading brands of products may have identical ingredients, the consumer would rather switch stores than switch brands.

Thus, information on consumer reactions to stockouts is critical to formula manufacturers in setting customer service strategy. While the penalty for stocking out the retailer may be very low, the manufacturer will incur a high cost if it stocks out a doctor or a hospital. If a service failure causes a doctor to switch from Ross Laboratories' product, Similac, to Mead Johnson's product, Enfamil, Ross Laboratories will lose the business of all mothers that doctor treats in the future. Similarly, if a hospital stops stocking a brand as a result of poor product availability or any other problem with customer service, the firm will lose future contributions to profit from mothers who give birth at that hospital and use an infant formula. While it may be difficult to determine the exact cost of losing the business of a doctor or hospital, the customer service implications are clear. Hospitals and doctors require a high level of customer service, which may include lead times of 48 hours and 99 percent in-stock availability.

Retailers, in contrast, will most likely lose the sale if they experience a stockout on Similac. Since retail management must be conscious of how its store is positioned

---

[11]In fact, many doctors further reduce the likelihood of brand switching by telling the mother not to switch the brand of formula.

compared to competitors, it must be concerned about the frequency of stockouts on items for which consumers are willing to switch stores. Frequent stockouts on such items could cause consumers to permanently switch their shopping loyalties to another store.[12] With this information, the manufacturer could set a longer order cycle for retailers, but use the additional time to reduce variability in lead times and provide high levels of in-stock availability. While the retailers would be required to adjust to longer lead times, the greater stability and high levels of in-stock availability would enable them to satisfy their customers without maintaining excessive inventories.

In Most Stockout Situations Consumers Will Not Switch Stores

In most stockout situations, however, consumers are not willing to accept the inconvenience of switching retail outlets. This brings us to the second decision point in Figure 3–4, substitution. At this point, the consumer must decide if substitution is acceptable. The consumer who wanted to purchase Ivory shampoo may be willing to postpone the purchase until the next shopping trip if he or she still has some shampoo left at home. If not, the consumer may substitute another brand. It is unlikely that consumers would place special orders for products like shampoo.

Whirlpool and Sears Study Consumer Needs

For some items, however, the majority of consumers are willing and may even expect to place a special order. In the early 1970s, Whirlpool and Sears, in a study of consumer purchase behavior, found that the majority of consumers did not expect to take delivery of major appliances the same day. In fact, most consumers were willing to wait from five to seven days for delivery. This study had significant implications for the companies' logistical systems. First, only floor models of appliances were necessary at the retail level. Second, retail distribution centers needed to carry only fast-moving standard items.

All other products were manufactured and/or shipped from the manufacturer's mixing warehouse only when the manufacturer received orders from retailers. Once manufactured, the product was shipped to the manufacturer's mixing warehouse, from there to a Sears distribution center, and from the distribution center to the consumer. All of this took place within the required five to seven days.

Implementation of this system substantially reduced systemwide inventories without sacrificing the necessary customer service. Sears no longer had to predict the color, size, and features desired by consumers at each retail outlet. By 1984 the system had undergone a number of refinements, and in major U.S. markets, Sears customers received 48- to 72-hour delivery on Kenmore appliances. In addition, Sears established similar programs with vendors of other products. While this type of system may not be possible for all consumer products, it illustrates how consumer research can be used to establish customer service strategy.

Usually, consumers will switch stores when they experience a stockout on an item with a high level of brand preference (such as infant formula). But for other products, consumers will substitute size or brand. Recall that Figure 3–3 showed how customer service levels could be increased from 70 percent to 97 percent with no corresponding increase in inventories if customers were willing to accept two product substitutions. When this is the case, customer service levels should be measured not according to each stock-keeping unit (such as the 15-ounce bottle of Ivory shampoo for normal hair), but according to all units of that product (all sizes of Ivory shampoo for normal hair).[13]

---

[12] A study of 7,189 shoppers found that those experiencing stockouts left the store with a lower image of the store and less satisfaction and purchase intentions. See Paul H. Zinszer and Jack A. Lesser, "An Empirical Evaluation of the Role of Stockout on Shopper Patronage Process," *1980 Educators' Conference Proceedings* (Chicago: American Marketing Association, 1980), pp. 221–24.

[13] Stock-keeping units (SKUs) are individual units of product that differ from others in shape, size, color, or some other characteristic.

The final option for consumers who face a retail stockout is to switch brands. They may switch to a same-price, higher-price, or lower-price brand. When substitution takes place, the retailer does not lose a sale. Depending on the substitution strategy the consumer employs, the seller may not experience any negative impact on either sales or profits; for instance, the consumer may substitute an item that sells for a higher price or may buy one national brand instead of another.

Consumers May Switch Brands When Faced with a Stockout

If the manufacturer knows that consumers are willing to substitute size, it should use this information to convince retailers and wholesalers that they too should accept these substitutes.[14] If brand switching takes place, however, the manufacturer definitely loses at least the contribution to profit from this one purchase. By stocking out and putting the consumer in the position of switching brands, the manufacturer is allowing the competitor to conduct product sampling and receive compensation for it. In addition, the substituted brand may become the consumer's first choice in the future. If this happens, the manufacturer loses the present value of all future contributions to profit that it would have realized had the consumer not changed his or her purchase behavior. These amounts are difficult, or impossible, to determine.[15]

Cost/Revenue Trade-Offs

The sum of the expenditures for such logistics activities as transportation, warehousing, order processing and information systems, production setups and purchasing, and inventory management can be viewed as the company's expenditure for customer service.

What Increase in Sales Volume Is Required to Break Even on the Customer Service Improvements?

In order to achieve least-cost logistics, management must minimize total logistics costs, given a specified level of customer service. Consequently, the costs associated with improving the level of service can be compared to the increase in sales required to recover the additional costs. For example, many times managers will try to improve customer service levels by increasing inventory investment. Figure 3–5 shows how inventories will increase at an increasing rate as customer service levels are increased. This curve can be calculated based on average demand, average lead time, and variability in demand and lead time. (We will show you how to develop this curve in Chapter 6.) However, because in many companies managers do not mathematically determine the relationship between customer service levels and inventory, the actual inventory investment will be greater than necessary. In Figure 3–5, if company A moved from its current position on the left of the curve to a place on the curve, it could reduce inventory, improve service, or combine an inventory reduction and a service improvement.

Consider a company that is currently offering a 95 percent customer service level—by its own measures—and doing so at least total cost. If sales management insists that service levels be increased to 98 percent to achieve the company's market-penetration objectives, the cost of the most efficient logistics method can be calculated for the new service objective and compared to the current cost.

---

[14]For a review of the literature on consumer response to stockouts as well as a proposed research methodology, see W. E. Miklas, "Measuring Customer Response to Stockouts," *International Journal of Physical Distribution and Materials Management* 9, no. 5 (1979), pp. 213–42.

[15]For an example of how 1,182 consumers responded when faced with stockouts of products they had intended to buy, see Larry W. Emmelhainz, James R. Stock, and Margaret A. Emmelhainz, "Retail Stockouts: Now What?" *Annual Conference Proceedings* (Oak Brook, IL: Council of Logistics Management, 1989), pp. 71–79.

FIGURE 3–5

*The relationship between
customer service and
inventory investment*

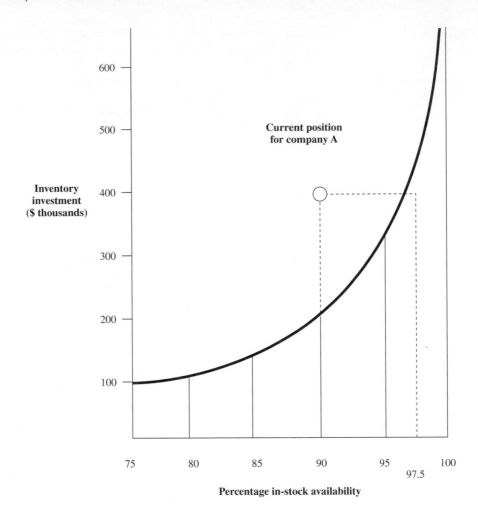

Assume that the cost of the most efficient logistics system for a 98 percent service goal is $2 million higher than the existing system's cost. If each dollar of additional sales yields a 25 percent contribution to fixed costs and profit—that is, for each $1 in revenue, the company incurs 75 cents in out-of-pocket manufacturing, marketing, and logistics costs—what additional sales volume will the company need to recover the increase in logistics costs? We can calculate the point at which the company breaks even on the service improvement by dividing the $2 million increase in costs by the 25 percent contribution margin. The company needs a sales increase of $8 million per year. We can estimate the likelihood that this will occur by determining what $8 million represents as a percentage increase in sales. A 2 percent increase in sales volume might be viewed as likely, whereas a 20 percent sales increase might be considered unlikely, given the competitive situation. Figure 3–6 shows the impact of customer service level on revenues, logistics costs, and profits. The goal is to implement a customer service strategy that will maximize profits. For any given level of customer service, the goal within logistics should be to minimize the total costs of providing that level of service. However, as service levels increase, the total of the associated logistics costs will increase at an increasing rate and diminishing returns will result in terms of the impact of service on revenues.

FIGURE 3–6

The impact of incremental customer service levels on revenues, logistics costs, and profits

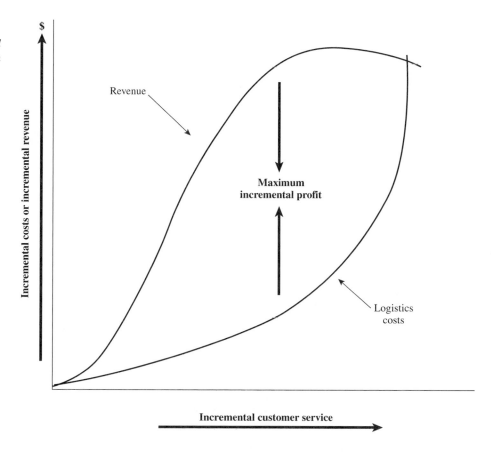

Another method of determining the cost/revenue trade-offs of alternative levels of customer service is to take advantage of unplanned decreases in service levels caused by such events as strikes, snowstorms, shortages, or quality inspection failures. "Before," "during," and "after" measures of retail sales associated with such an event can provide the manufacturer with valuable insights into the impact of various customer service levels on retail sales.

Although the manufacturer's ultimate goal should be to provide needed products to the ultimate consumer, manufacturers rarely engage in direct transactions with ultimate consumers. Usually manufacturers reach consumers through intermediaries such as wholesalers and retailers. For this reason, it is important to determine how retailers or wholesalers will react to service failures. In case studies of six wholesaling institutions, all with annual sales exceeding $500 million, Marcus Bennion found that a number of short-run and long-run reactions were possible when buyers encountered a stockout (see Figure 3–7).[16] For example, in response to a stockout, a short shipment, or an order cycle failure, in the short run a buyer could choose to back-order the desired products or substitute another product. The specific reaction will be influenced by the type of service failure and the time constraints of the buyer. The record of service performance of the supplier will influence the decision to seek a long-run solution. Long-run

It Is Also Important to Determine How Intermediaries React to Service Failures

[16]Marcus Lyndsay Bennion, "An Investigation of Wholesale Buyer Reaction to Manufacturer Customer Service Failures in the Grocery Channel," unpublished Ph.D. dissertation, Michigan State University, 1980.

FIGURE 3–7

Generalized model of reactions to customer service failures

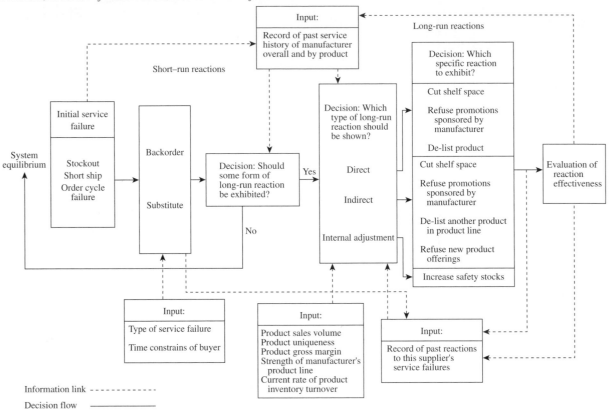

Source: Marcus Lyndsay Bennion, "An Investigation of Wholesale Buyer Reaction to Manufacturer Customer Service Failures in the Grocery Channel," unpublished Ph.D. dissertation, Michigan State University, 1980, p. 163.

reactions fall into three categories: direct, indirect, and internal adjustment. *Direct* reactions include cutting the shelf space devoted to the product, refusing to participate in the manufacturer's promotions, or de-listing the product. *Indirect* reactions include cutting shelf space, refusing to participate in promotions, de-listing another of the manufacturer's products, and refusing new product offerings. Typically, the *internal adjustment* would be to increase inventories that are known as safety stocks. In order to evaluate the costs and benefits of various service policies, the manufacturer must determine its customers' reactions.

ABC Analysis

In Chapter 1, we used the abbreviation ABC for activity-based costing. Here, ABC analysis is used to denote a tool for classifying items or activities according to their relative importance. (Category A items are more important than category B items, and so on.) The ABC analysis used to improve customer service efficiency is similar to the ABC analysis used for inventory planning, which we will describe in Chapter 6. The logic behind this approach is that some customers and products are more profitable than others. Thus, a company should maintain higher levels of customer service for the most

TABLE 3–1   A Customer–Product Contribution Matrix

Customer Category	Product Category			
	A	B	C	D
I	1	2	6	10
II	3	4	7	12
III	5	8	13	16
IV	9	14	15	19
V	11	17	18	20

Source: Bernard J. La Londe and Paul H. Zinszer, *Customer Service Meaning and Measurement* (Chicago: National Council of Physical Distribution Management, 1976), p. 181.

profitable customer–product combinations. Profitability should be measured on a contribution basis, excluding joint costs and fixed overhead allocations. (We will describe a method for obtaining profitability on a segmental basis in Chapter 16.) Trends in profitability also should be measured or estimated so that the firm can consider potential growth.

Customer–Product Contribution Matrix

Table 3–1 illustrates a customer–product contribution matrix that can be used to classify customers and products according to their impact on the manufacturer's profit performance. It is interpreted as follows:

1. Category A includes the firm's most profitable products, followed by categories B, C, and D. The products in category A represent a small percentage of the total product line.

2. Products in category D represent the firm's least profitable products. Typically, 80 percent of the product line falls into this category.

3. Customers in category I are the most profitable for the manufacturer; they may number no more than 5 or 10.

4. Customers in category V are the least profitable customers because they purchase in small quantities or generate small annual sales volume. The price and service concessions they receive could total hundreds or thousands of dollars. Category V usually contains the majority of customers.

5. The most profitable customer–product combination occurs when products in category A are sold to customers in category I (priority number 1). The next most profitable combination occurs when products in category B are sold to customers in category I. The next most profitable are products in category A sold to customers in category II, and so on until the least profitable customer–product relationship—when products in category D are sold to customers in category V (priority number 20).

The customer–product contribution matrix is put into operation in a manner similar to that shown in Table 3–2. Priority range 1–5 is assigned an in-stock standard of 100 percent and a delivery standard of 48 hours, and orders are shipped complete 99 percent of the time. The reason the order completeness standard is not 100 percent when the in-stock standard is 100 percent is that customers in category I also order products in priority range 6–10. The lowest priority range, 16–20, has an in-stock standard of 90 percent, a delivery standard of 120 hours, and an order completeness standard of 93 percent.

TABLE 3–2   Making the Customer–Product Contribution Matrix Operational

Priority Range	In-Stock Standard	Delivery Standard	Order Completeness Standard
1–5	100.0%	48 hours	99%
6–10	97.5	72 hours	97
11–15	95.0	96 hours	95
16–20	90.0	120 hours	93

Source: Bernard J. La Londe and Paul H. Zinszer, *Customer Service Meaning and Measurement* (Chicago: National Council of Physical Distribution Management, 1976), p. 182.

This method recognizes the need to provide the most profitable customers with service levels that encourage repeat business. A drawback to this method is that priority ranges do not order products; customers order products. Management does not want to stock out the firm's most profitable customers on its most profitable products or the less profitable products if these customers are measuring suppliers on orders shipped complete. Less profitable accounts can be made more valuable by reducing the costs of servicing them. For example, one method of making unprofitable accounts profitable is to limit the time when orders can be placed and then consolidate those orders for shipment to customers. By requiring that small customers in a specific geographic area place their orders biweekly on Mondays for delivery the following Friday, a firm can increase its profitability. Benefits to the customer include reduced order cycle variability; higher levels of in-stock availability; and, if the customer pays the freight, reduced transportation costs. Large, profitable customers can place their orders at any time and receive delivery within the agreed-on lead time.

The Customer Service Audit

The customer service audit is used to evaluate the level of service a company is providing and to serve as a benchmark for appraising the impact of changes in customer service policy. The audit is designed to identify the important elements of customer service, the manner in which performance is controlled, and the internal communication system. Audit procedures should comprise four distinct stages: an external customer service audit, an internal customer service audit, the identification of potential solutions, and the establishment of customer service levels.[17]

Four Stages of a Customer Service Audit

Objective of the External Customer Service Audit

The External Customer Service Audit.   The starting point in any thorough study of customer service is the external audit. The key objectives of an external audit are (1) to identify the elements of customer service that customers believe to be important when making the decision to buy and (2) to determine how customers perceive the service being offered by each of the major vendors in the market.

The first step of an external audit is the identification of the customer service variables that are most important to the firm's customers. For a consumer packaged-goods

[17]The following material is adapted from Douglas M. Lambert and Douglas E. Zemke, "The Customer Service Component of the Marketing Mix," *Proceedings of the Twentieth Annual Conference of the National Council of Physical Distribution Management,* 1982, pp. 1–24.

The Value of Customer Retention

Though the subject of customer service has received considerable attention during the past decade, customer loyalty is just beginning to emerge as a critical concern for a broad group of companies. As these companies begin to quantify the real value of customer retention (and the real cost of losing a customer), it becomes clear that an effective customer-retention strategy can significantly improve financial performance.

Recent research in the area of customer retention has confirmed the obvious: Companies that do a better job of keeping their customers generate better financial results than do companies with poor retention records. What is not obvious is the truly shocking magnitude of the impact that customer retention has on profits. Some analysts have estimated that a 5 percent reduction in the number of customers lost can increase profits by 50 percent—or more. Another important finding is that the profit generated by the average customer generally increases in each of the first four or five years of the vendor–customer relationship.

There are several reasons customer retention has such a powerful impact on financial performance. First, the cost of acquiring a new customer is significant in most industries. If you add up the various expenses associated with customer acquisition—such as the costs of advertising, promotion, closing, and setup for a new customer—you quickly gain an appreciation of the great impact customer acquisition can have. For example, I recently assessed the cost of customer acquisition in food retailing as being more than $300. As happens in many industries, this customer-acquisition cost may well equal a full year's net profit from that same customer.

In addition to the cost of acquisition, the value a satisfied customer generates for a company can include the margin on base purchases, the opportunity to generate

incremental sales, reduced operating costs, and referrals.

My colleague Scott Puopolo has developed an approach to assessing the lifetime value of a customer. This powerful analysis helps our clients understand and develop strategies for retaining the most-profitable customers, as well as develop strategies to increase the profitability of less-profitable customers. Furthermore, it promotes insight into the true cost of a lost customer.

Logistics managers can play a leading role in developing a customer-retention program because they are at the core of many elements of customer service. To be effective, such a program should:

- Quantify the value of different customer segments, with explicit consideration of the cost of customer acquisition and of a customer's lifetime value.

- Assess the reasons why customers have defected. This often includes debriefing lost customers to understand the source of their dissatisfaction.

- Analyze how customers are being served, what their needs are, what their concerns are, and their level of satisfaction with service performance. This can best be accomplished through ongoing customer focus groups, customer surveys, and transaction surveys.

Most companies lose from 10 to 20 percent or more of their customer base annually. If a company can cut this defection rate in half, it may double profits. Logistics programs can play a key role in contributing to profits by building customer loyalty, enhancing customer retention, and reducing customer defections.

Source: William C. Copaccino, "The Value of Customer Retention," *Logistics Management* 35, no. 5 (May 1997), p. 37.

firm, the relevant customer service variables might include the following: average order cycle time, order cycle variability, number of orders shipped complete, in-stock variability, accuracy in filling orders, order status information, action on complaints, returns policy, remote order transmission (computer-to-computer order entry), ability to expedite emergency orders, billing procedures, palletized and unitized loads for handling efficiency, speed and accuracy in billing, handling of claims, availability of inventory status, freight pickup allowances for distributors wishing to pick up freight at the manufacturers' warehouses, backhaul policy, and ability to select the carrier.

It is important to develop the list of variables based on interviews with the firm's customers. A list such as the one above, or one created by management, might serve as a useful starting point in discussions with customers. If marketing executives are involved, the list could be expanded to include other marketing mix components, such as product quality, price, terms of sale, quantity discount structure, number of sales calls, cooperative advertising, and national advertising support for the product.

Advantages of Including the Marketing Function

There are three advantages to including the marketing function. First, marketing involvement facilitates the implementation of trade-offs within the marketing mix. Second, marketing often has considerable expertise in questionnaire design, which is the next step in the process. Third, marketing's involvement adds credibility to the research findings, which increases acceptance and facilitates successful implementation.

Alternatives to using the corporate market research department include using an outside market research firm; a local university where the research might be conducted by an MBA class, a doctoral student, or a professor; or a consulting firm or vendor with specific expertise. The advantages of using one of these alternatives are that the company sponsoring the research does not have to be identified and that assistance is available for developing the questionnaires. Identifying the sponsoring firm may bias responses, and questionnaire length and clarity will influence the response rate.

Identifying the Research Sponsor May Bias Responses

It should be emphasized that the variables used in the external audit must be specifically tailored to the industry under study. Using variables from past research instruments, especially those designed for different industries with different supply chain structures, would lead to misinterpretation and nonresponse.[18] In addition, because the quantity and type of variables used to select and evaluate vendors are complex, simple replication of previous research endeavors is not possible.

For example, in a comprehensive study in the plastics industry, 110 variables were categorized by marketing mix components as follows: product (21), price (14), promotion (29), and customer service (46). Similar research in the office systems industry was conducted prior to the plastics industry research. However, in the plastics industry research, only 34 variables were the same as those used in the office systems research, 12 were revised from variables used in the office systems research, and 64 were specific to the plastics industry. While almost one-half of the price, promotion, and customer service variables were similar to those used in the office systems research, 17 of the 21 product variables were different.[19]

Variables Are Industry Specific

When the relevant customer service elements have been determined, the second step in the external audit procedure is to design a questionnaire to gain feedback from a statistically valid sample of customers. The appendix to this chapter contains an example of a questionnaire designed to determine the importance customers attach to marketing variables. Customers were asked to circle, on a scale of 1 to 7, the number that best expressed the importance they attached to each variable. The survey defined an important variable as possessing significant weight in the evaluation of suppliers, whereas an unimportant variable did not.[20]

---

[18]Sterling and Lambert, "Establishing Customer Service Strategies Within the Marketing Mix."

[19]Douglas M. Lambert and Thomas C. Harrington, "Establishing Customer Service Strategies Within the Marketing Mix: More Empirical Evidence," *Journal of Business Logistics* 10, no. 2 (1989).

[20]Although a considerable body of research in service quality in service industries uses expectations scales with *strongly agree* and *strongly disagree* as the anchor points, research has shown that results obtained are the same as those obtained using importance scales. See Douglas M. Lambert and M. Christine Lewis, "A Comparison of Attribute Importance and Expectation Scales for Measuring Service Quality," in *Enhancing Knowledge Development in Marketing,* ed. William Bearden et al. (Chicago, IL: American Marketing Association, 1990), p. 291.

An important consideration in the external audit is determining competitive performance ratings for major suppliers. This can be accomplished by asking respondents to evaluate major suppliers' performance on each of the variables (see Part A of the questionnaire in the appendix). Responses to these questions help the firm compare customers' perceptions of supplier performance. Obviously suppliers want to score high on variables that are highest in importance to customers.

Overall Satisfaction with Suppliers Should Be Determined

The questionnaire should include items that require respondents to rate their overall satisfaction with each supplier and indicate the percentage of business they allocate to each supplier (see Part B of the questionnaire). Also, the questionnaire should seek to obtain specific levels of expected performance for key variables, such as the number of sales calls (see Part C of the questionnaire).

Finally, the questionnaire should include demographic information that will enable the firm to determine whether there are significant differences in response by such variables as type of account (wholesaler, retailer, etc.); market served (national versus regional); specific geographic location; sales volume; sales growth; profit as a percentage of sales; and sales volume of each vendor's products (see Part D of the questionnaire in the appendix).

Pretesting Is a Must

Before mailing the questionnaire, the firm should pretest it with a small group of customers to ensure that the questions are understandable and that important variables have not been ignored. The mailing list can be developed from an accounts receivable list; a sales/marketing department list of prospects; or lists of contracts, projects, bids lost, or inactive accounts. The accounts receivable list enables stratification of the sample to achieve an adequate number of large, medium, and small customers. If management wants an analysis of inactive accounts, it can send color-coded questionnaires to identify these accounts.

External Audit Enables Management to Identify Problems and Opportunities

The results of the customer service survey used in the external audit enable management to identify problems and opportunities. Table 3–3 illustrates the type of information that can be provided. The survey from which this table was developed evaluated both customer service and other marketing mix variables. The two columns on the left side of Table 3–3 show that the ranking of the variables was not influenced by the order in which the questions appeared on the questionnaire.

In this example, 7 of the 12 variables with the highest mean customer importance scores were customer service variables. This result highlights the importance of customer service within the firm's marketing mix. A small standard deviation in customer importance ratings means that there was little variation in the respondents' individual evaluations of a variable's importance. For variables with a large standard deviation, however, it is important to use the demographic information to determine which customers want which services. The same argument holds for the last variable, "Store layout planning assistance from manufacturer." For example, do large-volume, high-growth customers rate this higher in importance than small customers do?

Logistics Dominates the List of Most Important Variables

The previously described study in the plastics industry revealed similar results regarding the importance of customer service. The 18 variables rated as most important by the respondents (those with a mean score of 6.0 or more on a scale of 1 to 7) consisted of 9 logistics/customer service variables (accuracy in filling orders, consistent lead times, ability to expedite emergency orders in a fast responsive manner, information provided when order is placed—projected shipping date, advance notice of shipping delays, information provided when order is placed—projected delivery date, action on complaints, length of promised lead times, and information provided when order is placed—inventory availability); 5 product quality variables (supplier's resins are of consistent quality, processability of the resin, supplier's resins are of consistent

TABLE 3-3 Overall Importance Compared to Selected Performance of Major Manufacturers as Evaluated by Dealers

Rank	Variable Number	Variable Description	Overall Importance—All Dealers Mean	SD	Mfr. 1 Mean	SD	Mfr. 2 Mean	SD	Mfr. 3 Mean	SD	Mfr. 4 Mean	SD	Mfr. 5 Mean	SD	Mfr. 6 Mean	SD
1	9	Ability of manufacturer to meet promised delivery date (on-time shipments)	6.4	0.8	5.9	1.0	4.1	1.6	4.7	1.6	6.6	0.6	3.7	1.8	3.3	1.6
2	39	Accuracy in filling orders (correct produce is shipped)	6.4	0.8	5.6	1.1	4.7	1.4	5.0	1.3	5.8	1.1	5.1	1.2	4.4	1.5
3	90	*Competitiveness* of price	6.3	1.0	5.1	1.2	4.9	1.4	4.5	1.5	5.4	1.3	4.4	1.5	3.6	1.8
4	40	Advance notice on shipping delays	6.1	0.9	4.6	1.9	3.0	1.6	3.7	1.7	5.1	1.7	3.0	1.7	3.1	1.7
5	94	Special pricing discounts available on contract/project quotes	6.1	1.1	5.4	1.3	4.0	1.7	4.1	1.6	6.0	1.2	4.7	1.5	4.5	1.8
6	3	Overall manufacturing and design *quality* of product relative to the price and range involved	6.0	0.9	6.0	1.0	5.3	1.3	5.1	1.2	6.5	0.8	5.2	1.3	4.8	1.5
7	16	Updated and current price data, specifications and promotion materials provided by manufacturer	6.0	0.9	5.7	1.3	4.1	1.5	4.8	1.4	6.3	0.9	4.9	1.7	4.3	1.9
8	47	*Timely* response to requests for assistance from manufacturer's sales representative	6.0	0.9	5.2	1.7	4.6	1.6	4.4	1.6	5.4	1.6	4.2	2.0	4.3	1.7
9	14	Order cycle consistency (small variability in promised versus actual delivery)	6.0	0.9	5.8	1.0	4.1	1.5	4.8	1.4	6.3	0.9	3.6	1.7	4.4	1.7
10	4b	Length of promised order cycle (lead) times (from order submission to delivery) for base line/in-stock ("quick ship") product	6.0	1.0	6.1	1.1	4.5	1.4	4.9	1.5	6.2	1.1	4.3	1.7	3.7	2.0
11	54	Accuracy of manufacturer in forecasting and committing to estimated shipping dates on contract/project orders	6.0	1.0	5.5	1.2	4.0	1.6	4.3	1.4	6.3	1.1	3.8	1.7	3.5	1.6
12	49a	Completeness of order (% of line items eventually shipped complete)—made to order product (contract orders)	6.0	1.0	5.5	1.2	4.3	1.2	4.7	1.3	6.0	1.1	4.4	1.4	4.0	1.6
50	33a	Price *range* of product line offering (e.g., low, medium, high price levels) for major vendor	5.0	1.3	4.4	1.5	4.6	1.6	5.1	1.5	5.2	1.4	4.3	1.6	3.9	1.6
101	77	Store layout planning assistance from manufacturer	2.9	1.6	4.2	1.7	3.0	1.5	3.4	1.6	4.7	1.6	3.0	1.4	3.4	1.2

Note: Mean (average score) based on a scale of 1 (not important) through 7 (very important).

Source: Douglas M. Lambert and Jay U. Sterling, "Developing Customer Service Strategy," unpublished manuscript, 1986. All rights reserved.

color, supplier's resins are of consistent melt flow, and overall quality of resin relative to price); 2 price variables (competitiveness of price and adequate advance notice of price changes); and 2 promotion variables (quality of the sales force—honesty, and quality of the sales force—prompt follow-up).[21]

It should be noted that the "honesty of the sales force" variable was to a large extent a logistics variable. The in-depth interviews revealed that the honesty variable was related to the degree of accurate information about product availability and delivery provided by the sales force. Because inventory records were not on-line and real-time, customers would be told that inventory was available when in fact it had been sold, and the batch process system had not updated the inventory levels. Customers did not realize that there was a problem until the product did not arrive.

Although the mix of most important attributes is somewhat different for the plastics and office systems industries, there was a good deal of similarity on those attributes that were the most important. To make the office systems numbers a little more comparable to the 18 attributes rated 6.0 or above in the plastics industry, the top 16 variables were selected. Of the 16 most important attributes in the office systems industry, 10 were logistics; and of the top 18 attributes in the plastics industry, 9 were logistics. Table 3–4 reveals that the following variables were the same: ability to meet promised delivery date, accuracy in filling orders, advance notice of shipping delays, action on customer service complaints, information on shipping date, length of promised lead times for in-stock products, overall quality relative to price, competitiveness of price, and prompt follow-up from the sales force. These variables have also been identified as the most important attributes in other industries.

TABLE 3–4   A Summary of the Most Important Variables Common to the Office Systems Industry and Plastics Industry

| | Number of Variables | | |
Marketing Mix Component	*Office Systems*	*Plastics*	*Common Variables*
Logistics/customer service	10	9	Ability to meet promised delivery date
			Accuracy in filling orders
			Advance notice of shipping delays
			Action on customer service complaints
			Information on shipping date
			Length of promised lead times for in-stock products
Product	3	5	Overall quality relative to price
Price	2	2	Competitiveness of price
Promotion	1	2	Prompt follow-up from sales force
Total	16	18	

[21]Lambert and Harrington, "Establishing Customer Service Strategies Within the Marketing Mix," p. 50.

Six logistics variables were the same in both industries. However, it would be a mistake to think that it is only necessary to consider variables that are similar across industries, because in the office systems industry there are four variables, as important as the six common variables, that would not be considered. In the plastics industry three variables would be ignored that are every bit as important as the six common variables. This is why a customer service study has to be industry specific.

In terms of product, there was one variable that was similar in both industries: overall quality relative to price. In terms of price, there was only one match: competitiveness of price. With regard to promotion, the variable that was common to both industries was prompt follow-up from the sales force. The other promotion variable was honesty of the sales force, and the office systems industry is the only industry of 15 studied where honesty of the sales force was not one of the most important decision criteria. In every other industry, sales force honesty was a key attribute, which implies that salespeople make promises that their companies cannot keep even on their best day. "You want the product on Friday, no problem," they would say, even when the company could not get the product there on Friday in the best of circumstances.

Importance Ratings Cannot Be Used Alone

Most customer service studies emphasize the importance ratings of the variables being researched, which assumes that the variables rated the highest in importance determine the share of business given to each vendor. But this may not be true, for one or more of the following reasons:

- All of an industry's major suppliers may be performing at "threshold" levels, or at approximately equal levels, which makes it difficult to distinguish among suppliers.
- Variables for which there are significant variances in supplier performance may be better predictors of market share than the variables described above.
- Customers may rate a variable as extremely important, but there may be few or no suppliers who are providing satisfactory levels of service for that variable. Such variables offer opportunities to provide differential service in the marketplace.
- A variable may be rated low in importance with a low variance in response. In addition, there may be no single supplier providing adequate service levels. Therefore, customers do not recognize the advantages of superior service for that variable. If one vendor improved performance, it could lead to gains in market share.[22]

Both Importance Measures and Performance Measures Are Required

In order to determine what variables represent the best opportunity for increasing market share and/or profitability, both importance and performance measures are necessary. For this reason, Table 3–3 contains customer (dealer) evaluations of perceived performance for the firm being researched and its five major competitors. This gives management some insight into the relative competitive position of each supplier, as viewed by the firm's customers. It is important that management determine what it is that the top-rated supplier is doing to create this perception. Management also must consider what actions it can take to improve customer perceptions of its service.

The company must compare customer perceptions of service to internal measures of performance. This may show that the customer is not aware of the service being provided or that management is measuring service performance incorrectly.

---

[22]Sterling and Lambert, "Establishing Customer Service Strategies Within the Marketing Mix."

The Internal Customer Service Audit.   The internal customer service audit requires a review of the firm's current practices. This will provide a benchmark for appraising the impact of changes in customer service strategy.[23] The internal customer service audit should provide answers to the following questions:

**Internal Audit
Questions**

- How is customer service currently measured within the firm?
- What are the units of measurement?
- What are the performance standards or objectives?
- What is the current level of attainment—results versus objectives?
- How are these measures derived from corporate information flows and the order processing system?
- What is the internal customer service reporting system?
- How do each of the functional areas of the business (e.g., logistics, marketing) perceive customer service?
- What is the relation between these functional areas in terms of communications and control?[24]

**Purpose of Internal
Audit**

The overall purpose of the internal audit is to identify inconsistencies between the firm's practices and its customers' expectations. It is also important to verify customer perceptions, since customers may perceive service performance to be worse than it really is. In such a situation, the firm should change customer perceptions rather than the level of service provided.

The communications system largely determines the sophistication and control of customer service within a company. As La Londe and Zinszer stated, "Without good control of information flow within the firm and between the firm and its customers, the customer service function is usually relegated to reporting performance level statistics and reacting to special problems."[25] That is why an internal audit must evaluate both the communications flow from customers to the company and the communications flow within the company, and must review the customer service measurement and reporting system. The internal audit should give top management a clear understanding of the firm's communications with customers.

Most communications between customer and firm can be grouped into the following eight categories relating to the ordering-shipping-billing cycle: order entry; post-order entry inquiries and changes; delivery; postdelivery reports of damages, shortages, or overages; billing; postbilling dispute; payment delay; and payment.[26] The extent to which these communications are organized and managed can significantly affect both market share and profitability. The audit will help assess the effectiveness and cost of these communications.

**Management Interviews
Are a Good Source
of Data**

Management interviews are another way to gather data. Interviews should be conducted with managers responsible for order processing, inventory management, warehousing, transportation, customer service, accounting/finance, production, materials

---

[23]This section is adapted from Douglas M. Lambert and M. Christine Lewis, "Managing Customer Service to Build Market Share and Increase Profit," *Business Quarterly* 48, no. 3 (Autumn 1983), pp. 50–57.

[24]Ibid., p. 52.

[25]La Londe and Zinszer, *Customer Service,* p. 168.

[26]Lambert and Lewis, "Managing Customer Service," p. 53.

management, and sales/marketing. Such interviews help determine how managers of each of these functions perceive customer service, communicate with customers, and interface with other functional areas. Specifically, the interviews address:

- Definition of responsibilities.
- Size and organizational structure.
- Decision-making authority and processes.
- Performance measurements and results.
- Definition of customer service.
- Management's perception of how customers define customer service.
- Plans to alter or improve customer service.
- Intrafunctional communications.
- Interfunctional communications.
- Communications with key contacts such as consumers, customers, common carriers, and suppliers.

Management must evaluate the customer service measurement and reporting system in order to determine how customer service is measured, the units of measurement, performance standards employed, current results, the corporate function controlling each activity, sources of data, reporting formats and compilation methods, reporting frequency, distribution of reports, and transmission methods. It is equally important to understand how customers obtain information from the company. Thus, the internal audit should determine the types of information available to customers, the person in the company who provides each type of information, the way in which customers reach these departments, the average time taken to respond to customer inquiries, and the accessibility of needed information to the person(s) responsible for answering the inquiry. Appendix A of Chapter 18 provides an example of the questions that can be asked during an internal customer service audit.

Identifying Potential Solutions.   The external audit enables management to identify problems with the firm's customer service and marketing strategies. Used in combination with the internal audit, it may help management adjust these strategies and vary them by segment in order to increase profitability. But if management wants to use such information to develop customer service and marketing strategies for optimal profitability, it must use these data to benchmark against its competitors.

The most meaningful competitive benchmarking occurs when customer evaluations of competitors' performance are compared to each other and to customers' evaluations of the importance of supplier attributes.[27] Once management has used this type of analysis to determine opportunities for gaining a competitive advantage, every effort should be made to identify best practices, that is, the most cost-effective uses of technology and systems, regardless of the industry in which they have been successfully implemented. Noncompetitors are much more likely to share their knowledge with each other, and it is possible to uncover opportunities for significant competitive advantage over industry rivals.

---

[27]The material in this section is adapted from Douglas M. Lambert and Arun Sharma, "A Customer-Based Competitive Analysis for Logistics Decisions," *International Journal of Physical Distribution and Logistics Management* 20, no. 1 (1990), pp. 17–24.

**A Method
for Competitive
Benchmarking**

A method for competitive benchmarking is presented with data collected from a segment of the chemical industry. The analysis involves a comparison of the performance of two major suppliers in the industry. The products marketed by these firms were considered to be commodities. In this example only two firms are analyzed, but the analysis can be expanded to more than one competitor or more than one segment.

The first step is to generate a table with importance evaluations for each of the variables as well as the performance evaluations of the firm and its major competitor, as in Table 3–5. To simplify the data for this example, only customer service attributes are considered and only 10 are included. Attributes were sorted by mean importance rating (to the customers) and a systematic random sample of 10 measures was selected. The selection ensured that the analysis and discussion were based on a set of attributes that were representative of the full range of importance to customers.

**The Competitive
Position Matrix**

The next step is to prepare a competitive position matrix that has two dimensions: importance and relative performance. The performance is determined by calculating the difference in the evaluation of the sponsor company less the evaluation of the major competitor. The nine cells in the matrix can be grouped into three broad categories:

1. Competitive advantage.
   a. Major strength (high importance, high relative performance).
   b. Minor strength (low importance, high relative performance).
2. Competitive parity.

TABLE 3–5   **Importance and Performance Evaluations for Selected Customer Service Attributes**

			Performance Evaluation		
No.	*Attribute*	*Importance*	*Company A*	*Company B*	*Relative Performance*
1	Accuracy in filling orders	6.42	5.54	5.65	−0.11
2	Ability to expedite emergency orders in a fast, responsive manner	6.25	4.98	5.23	−0.25
3	Action in complaints (e.g., order servicing, shipping, product)	6.07	4.82	5.18	−0.36*
4	Accuracy of supplier in forecasting and committing to shipping date for custom-made products	5.92	4.53	4.73	−0.20
5	Completeness rate (percentage of order eventually shipped)	5.69	5.29	5.27	+0.02
6	Rapid adjustment of billing and shipping errors	5.34	4.64	4.90	−0.24
7	Availability of blanket orders	4.55	5.03	4.15	+0.88†
8	Frequency of deliveries (supplier consolidates multiple/split shipments into one larger, less frequent shipment)	4.29	5.07	5.03	+0.04
9	Order processing personnel located in your market area	3.58	5.33	5.21	+0.12
10	Computer-to-computer order entry	2.30	4.07	3.53	+0.54†

*Performance evaluations of A and B are significantly different at $p \leq 0.05$.
†Performance evaluations of A and B significantly different at $p \leq 0.01$.

Source: Douglas M. Lambert and Arun Sharma, "A Customer-Based Competitive Analysis for Logistics Decisions," *International Journal of Physical Distribution and Logistics Management* 20, no.1 (1990), p. 18.

3. Competitive disadvantage.
    a. Major weakness (high importance, low relative performance).
    b. Minor weakness (low importance, low relative performance).

The first and most important cell represents the major strengths of the company. The attributes in this cell need to be emphasized in the communications with customers. The second most important cell represents the major weaknesses of the company. These need to be improved, or customers need to be convinced that these attributes are not important. The minor-strengths cell represents those things that the firm does well but that customers believe are not important. Customers need to be convinced that these attributes are important to them, or expenditures need to be reduced.

Options for Preparing a Competitive Position Matrix

The competitive position matrix can be created in a variety of ways, based on the objectives of the manager. For example, the company can be compared to the average of all competitors for the entire industry. This matrix provides a representation of the company's competitive position in the entire market. A second option is to compare the company to the average of all competitors for each segment. This matrix provides a representation of the company's competitive position in each segment and suggests segment-specific strategies. A third option is to compare the company to a specific competitor for a group of accounts. This matrix provides a representation of the company's competitive position relative to a specific competitor for a group of customers that purchase from both firms. This enables management to develop customer segment and competitor-specific strategies. Performing the analysis using specific competitors will allow management to target the primary customers of those competitors when the firm is the second or third source of supply. It also provides information that can be used to design strategies to protect the firm's primary customers from competitive threats.

Refer back to Table 3–5, which presents the relative performance of company A when compared to company B. As can be seen from the table, firms A and B are very similar in performance evaluations, the maximum and minimum differences being 0.88 and 0.02, respectively, on a seven-point scale. The evaluations are statistically different for three of the attributes. The competitive position matrix is presented in Figure 3–8, which shows that the performance of the major competitors was viewed as virtually identical by customers. In addition, no managerially useful differences in performance evaluations could be found based on geography, customer type, or sales volume.

The top cell in the competitive parity column suggests that performance improvements should be made on attributes 1, 2, 3, 4, 5, and 6 as long as the incremental costs associated with achieving these improvements are not greater than the incremental revenues earned by doing so. For example, implementation of a service quality program in the distribution center may result in a significant improvement in the accuracy in filling orders, and this achievement may be at a relatively low cost or no net cost to the firm. On the other hand, accuracy in forecasting and committing to shipping date for custom-made products may require a new forecasting package and/or production planning model. Also, improving the order completeness rate may require new computer systems or significant increases in inventory. In summary, there are two variables that can be manipulated. First, the preference can be improved by actually performing better or by changing the buyers' perceptions regarding the firm's performance, if their perceptions can be shown to be incorrect using the firm's internal performance data. Second, the importance of an attribute can be changed by proving to the customer why it should be more or less important than the customer perceives it to be.

As will be shown, there is a danger to using the competitive position matrix by itself to identify strategic opportunities for gaining a competitive advantage. It is nec-

FIGURE 3–8

Competitive position matrix

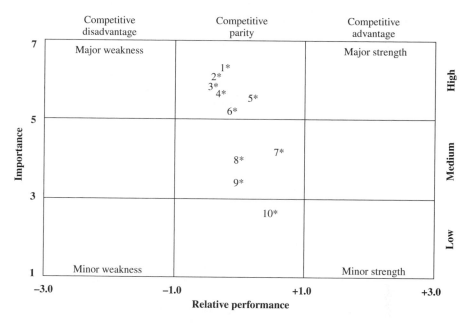

* Denotes attribute number

Source: Douglas M. Lambert and Arun Sharma, "A Customer-Based Competitive Analysis for Logistics Decisions," *International Journal of Physical Distribution and Logistics Management* 20, no. 1 (1990), p. 21.

essary to develop a performance evaluation matrix to be used in conjunction with the competitive position matrix. The performance evaluation matrix is obtained by creating a three-by-three matrix with the importance of each attribute and evaluation of the performance of the company as two dimensions. The matrix is divided into nine cells as follows:

- Maintain/improve service (high importance, high performance).
- Improve service (high importance, medium performance).
- Definitely improve service (high importance, low performance).
- Improve service (medium importance, low performance).
- Maintain service (medium importance, medium performance).
- Maintain service (low importance, low performance).
- Reduce/maintain service (medium importance, high performance).
- Reduce/maintain service (low importance, medium performance).
- Reduce/maintain service (low importance, high performance).

The performance evaluation matrix presented in Figure 3–9 shows that company A was not meeting customer expectations on four of the six variables rated highest in importance by customers and was exceeding expectations on the two least important variables (those evaluated as 2.30 and 3.58 in importance). Similar results were found for the other vendors evaluated by the respondents: No vendor was performing up to customer expectations on all of the variables rated high in importance by customers, and all were performing above expectations on the variables that were rated lowest in importance. A cautionary note is in order: High standard deviations in importance or

FIGURE 3–9

Performance evaluation matrix

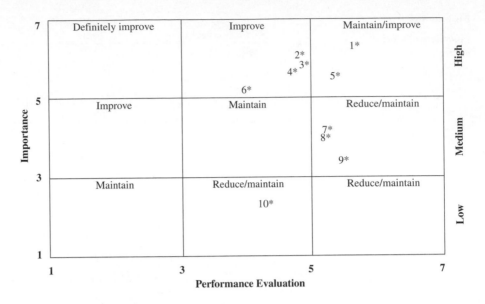

* Denotes attribute number

Source: Douglas M. Lambert and Arun Sharma, "A Customer-Based Competitive Analysis for Logistics Decisions," *International Journal of Physical Distribution and Logistics Management* 20, no. 1 (1990), p. 21.

performance evaluations make it necessary to determine if market segments exist. If segments do exist, this analysis must be performed by market segment.

Figure 3–9 implies that if marketing resources were being allocated in the most efficient and effective manner, all of the numbers should fall on the diagonal. That is, we would want to perform at a level of five or more on those variables that customers evaluated as high in importance, between three and five for those variables rated as medium in importance, and so on. However, as will be shown in step four, this may not be the ideal strategy when the information contained in Figure 3–8 is also considered.

The Two Matrices Must Be Used Together

The two matrices (Figures 3–8 and 3–9) must be used together because the competitive position matrix by itself also may result in incorrect conclusions about areas of improvement. For example, the competitive position matrix implies that management should increase expenditures on attributes 1, 2, 3, 4, 5, and 6 in an effort to make them major strengths. In fact, all six attributes appear to offer comparable opportunities. However, the performance evaluation matrix suggests that attributes 2, 3, 4, and 6 offer the greatest opportunities for building a competitive advantage.

The competitors were evaluated very similarly on all of the attributes. Consequently, the performance evaluation matrix needs to be studied to identify the areas that offer the greatest opportunity for improvement. In some cases the entire industry may be performing badly on an attribute, and improving the firm's performance may represent a substantial opportunity to gain a competitive advantage. As an example, customers felt that accuracy in filling orders (attribute 1) was one of the most important attributes of customer service (6.4 on a 7-point scale). However, the company and its major competitor were rated at virtually the same level of performance on this attribute (5.5 and 5.7, respectively), and there is a definite opportunity for improvement. When Figures 3–8 and 3–9 are considered simultaneously, it can be seen that attribute 5 does not represent the same potential for improvement as attributes 1, 2, 3, 4, and 6. This is

FIGURE 3–10

Strategic opportunities for a competitive advantage

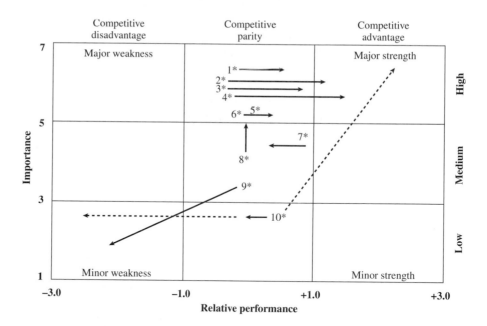

* Denotes attribute number

⟵ Indicates desired shift in relative performance

◀- - - - Indicates potential opportunities that may be revealed within specific customer segments

Source: Douglas M. Lambert and Arun Sharma, "A Customer-Based Competitive Analysis for Logistics Decisions," *International Journal of Physical Distribution and Logistics Management* 20, no. 1 (1990), p. 23.

because company A is performing close to customer expectations on attribute 5. While Figure 3–9 suggests that the firm can reduce its expenditures on attributes 7, 8, 9, and 10, Figure 3–8 suggests that caution be exercised with attributes 8, 9, and 10 since reductions in expenditures may result in relative competitive weaknesses. Clearly, care must be exercised in interpreting the data with respect to some attributes. For example, "computer-to-computer order entry" received a low overall importance score. However, this attribute may be of vital importance to a small number of large customers. Failure to implement computer-to-computer ordering systems might result in losing these customers. On the other hand, small molders and extruders might view this technology as "star wars." For most of these customers, simply having someone at the vendor location answer the telephone and input the order using a computer with online capability is all that is necessary. However, some may find it appealing to place their orders using the Internet. More in-depth study would be required to determine if expenditures can be reduced without significantly affecting the purchase decision.

Figure 3–10 provides the greatest insight into where expenditures can be changed to achieve a competitive advantage because it illustrates the strategic opportunities for gaining a competitive advantage based on the importance of the attributes to customers and the firm's performance relative to its major competitor. Figure 3–10 shows that attributes 1, 2, 3, 4, or 6 can become relative competitive strengths and that attributes 2 and 4 have the potential to become major strengths and a source of competitive advantage. In order to make attributes 1, 3, 5, and 6 into major strengths, customers would have to be convinced that these attributes are more important to them. Otherwise, a relative competitive performance of more than +1.0 would require that company A's performance exceed customer expectations. Emphasis on attribute 7 should be reduced for all customers unless there is a segment of profitable customers that views this attribute to be high in importance. If such a segment exists, attribute 7 should be stressed for this segment. Customers should be shown why frequency of deliveries (attribute 8) is more important to them than they currently believe it is. Typically, when multiple/split shipments are consolidated into a larger, less frequently scheduled delivery, customers prefer the service because of the consistency, which increases their ability to plan. Also, customers should be convinced that it is not necessary to have order processing personnel located in local markets (attribute 9), and expenditures for local order entry should be reduced. High levels of performance with centralized order processing personnel would change customer perceptions about the need for a local presence. Analysis of segments may reveal that attribute 10 should be moved to the major strength category for large profitable customers and that expenditures should be reduced for small molders and extruders who rate computer-to-computer capability as low in importance.

The performance evaluation matrix and the competitive position matrix can be used together to guide the development of logistics strategy for competitive advantage. It is important to emphasize that a company's logistics strategy needs to be designed giving full consideration to the basic strategy of the company and also the costs involved in a change in strategy. Within the customer service package, it may be possible to lengthen lead times for certain customers and use the additional planning time to provide these customers with higher levels of in-stock availability and more consistent delivery. This may improve service without increasing costs and may thereby improve profitability. If the improvement in service leads to increased sales, profits will increase further.

In situations in which customers would prefer lower levels of marketing services in exchange for higher levels of customer service, the firm's marketing mix should be adjusted. Of course, the power structure within the firm determines the extent to which this is possible.

Service Performance Standards and the Measurement of Performance

Establishing Customer Service Levels.   The final steps in the audit procedure are the actual establishment of service performance standards and the ongoing measurement of performance. Management must set target service levels for segments such as type of customer, geographic area, channel of distribution, and product line. It must inform all employees responsible for implementing the customer service levels and develop compensation schemes that encourage attainment of the customer service objectives. Formal reports that document performance are a necessity. Finally, management must repeat the entire procedure periodically to ensure that the customer service package reflects current customer needs. In fact, it is the collection of customer information over time that is most useful in guiding corporate strategy.

Implementation.   There are a number of keys to successful implementation of a customer service audit (see Table 3–6). To ensure successful implementation, it is important to have a broad team of people involved in the project. It is necessary to get input from top managers. Also, marketing and sales managers should be involved as well, but not salespeople. The worst thing that can happen is for a salesperson to call on a customer who shows him or her the survey form and says, "Look what I received! Do you know anything about it?" If the salesperson says, "Yes, it is my company that is send-

TABLE 3–6   Implementation: Keys to Success

- Broad-based team involvement supports buy-in and quality.
- Data collection requires considerable time and effort.
- Analysis covering the total marketing mix minimizes second-guessing.
- The focus should be on gaps that provide the greatest opportunities.
- Gaps may be caused by real or perceived causes—responses vary.
- Current customers provide easier opportunity for more business than new customers.
- Converting strategic implications to operational outcomes facilitates implementation.
- Change takes time.
- Commitment from the top is essential.
- The marketplace is dynamic and thus requires ongoing monitoring.

ing the survey," the whole idea of conducting an anonymous survey is lost. So, with the exception of salespeople, a broad base of support—including sales management, market research, and manufacturing—is necessary so that when it comes to time to implement the results, the support will be there.

Conducting a thorough customer service audit is going to take at least six months. So be patient; it is not something you can do well in two or three weeks. Analysis covering the total marketing mix minimizes second-guessing. It is typical to be able to answer many questions about the business after the research is completed if the survey is comprehensive, even though those questions were not asked at the beginning of the research. Consider all of the buying influences. Later, if additional questions are asked about how customers buy, it will be possible to answer them. A useful way to start is to ask managers to come up with a list of questions they would like to have answered about the business so that there are sections of the questionnaire that address those issues. If managers believe that major changes are going to take place in an industry, prepare a list of statements about the future and ask the respondents to agree or disagree with the statements. For example, "Every supplier in this industry will be using EDI within three years" (Agree/Disagree). If there are going to be some major changes that are not common practice now but might affect the future business, it is possible to have a separate section in the questionnaire to tap into those future issues. It is important not to implement a customer service strategy that would make the firm the leader now but that would become outdated a year or two years from now, because of some changes in the industry that were not anticipated.

The focus should be on gaps that provide the greatest opportunities, for either building the business or protecting existing business. Gaps may result from real or perceived causes, and responses would vary. If there is a large gap on an attribute and the firm's internal performance measure shows that it is performing better than customers think, you would want to change the customers' perceptions rather than change what the firm is doing.

Current customers provide an easier opportunity for more business than new customers. So a customer who is buying only 10 percent of the requirements from the firm should be encouraged through better customer service to buy 30 percent of its requirements from the firm; this is an easier method of increasing sales and profitability than trying to develop business with a new customer.

The strategy must be converted to operational details with which employees can identify. If the goal is to obtain better performance on an aspect of customer service, determine what has to improve to make that happen. It is at that level where performance must be measured. To keep from becoming discouraged, remember that change takes time and that you must stay the course.

Commitment from the top is essential. The customer service audit should not be considered a logistics study but rather a corporate study. This will facilitate implementation of the findings. Typically, there are a lot of implications for marketing and sometimes for manufacturing, so if top management is not committed to make the firm customer focused, then it may not be possible to implement programs based on the findings of the survey. There may be a number of things that logistics cannot accomplish on its own.

Customer service strategies must change as customers' expectations increase. Customer satisfaction is a moving target. For this reason it will be necessary to repeat the survey periodically. The marketplace changes, and competitors get better, so studying the customer base is an ongoing project. Following a major survey, you can conduct a quarterly survey in which you identify the firm and ask the customers to evaluate the firm's performance on the attributes that needed improvement. This way you can determine whether your strategy is working without having to wait three years to do another major benchmarking study.

Developing and Reporting Customer Service Standards

Once management has determined which elements of customer service are most important, it must develop standards of performance. Designated employees should regularly report results to the appropriate levels of management. Customer service performance can be measured and controlled by:

Measuring and Controlling Customer Service Performance

- Establishing quantitative standards of performance for each service element.
- Measuring actual performance for each service element.
- Analyzing variance between actual services provided and the standard.
- Taking corrective action as needed to bring actual performance into line.[28]

For the company to obtain information about speed, dependability, and condition of the delivered product, customer cooperation is essential. Customers must be convinced that the firm's service measurement and monitoring will help improve future service.

Figure 3–11 contains a number of possible measures of service performance. The manufacturer must place emphasis on individual elements according to what its customers believe to be important. Improving such service elements as inventory availability, delivery dates, order status, order tracing, and back-order status requires good communications between the manufacturer and its customers.

Automated Order Processing Improves Customer Service

Order processing offers significant potential for improving customer service because many companies have not kept pace with new technology. Consider the possibilities for improved communications if customers can either phone their orders to customer service representatives who have computer terminals or input orders on their own terminals. The representatives or the computer can provide immediate information on

[28]William H. Hutchinson Jr. and John E Stolle, "How to Manage Customer Service," *Harvard Business Review* 46, no. 6 (November–December 1968), pp. 85–96.

FIGURE 3–11

*Possible measures
of customer service
performance*

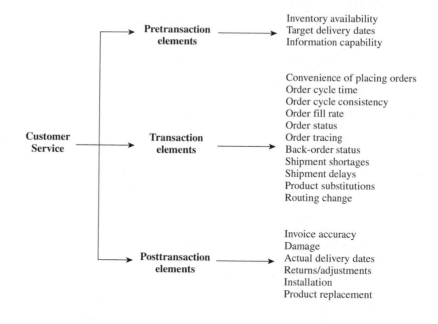

Customer
Service

Pretransaction
elements
- Inventory availability
- Target delivery dates
- Information capability

Transaction
elements
- Convenience of placing orders
- Order cycle time
- Order cycle consistency
- Order fill rate
- Order status
- Order tracing
- Back-order status
- Shipment shortages
- Shipment delays
- Product substitutions
- Routing change

Posttransaction
elements
- Invoice accuracy
- Damage
- Actual delivery dates
- Returns/adjustments
- Installation
- Product replacement

FIGURE 3–12

*Examples of customer
service standards*

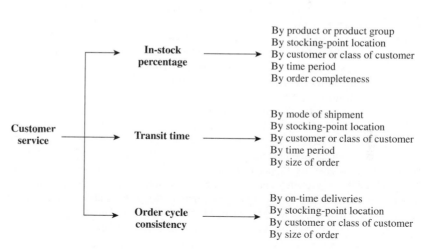

Customer
service

In-stock
percentage
- By product or product group
- By stocking-point location
- By customer or class of customer
- By time period
- By order completeness

Transit time
- By mode of shipment
- By stocking-point location
- By customer or class of customer
- By time period
- By size of order

Order cycle
consistency
- By on-time deliveries
- By stocking-point location
- By customer or class of customer
- By size of order

inventory availability and can arrange product substitution in a stockout. Customers also can be given target delivery dates.

Figure 3–12 gives examples of customer service standards. A firm's standards should reflect what customers need rather than what management thinks customers need. Designated employees should measure and compare performance to the standard, and report this information to the appropriate levels of management on a regular and timely basis.

The firm's order processing and accounting information systems can provide much of the information necessary for developing a customer–product contribution matrix and meaningful customer service management reports. We will describe these important interfaces in detail in Chapter 4 and Chapter 16.

Technology

"What Does No. 1 Do for an Encore?"

Dell is now the largest merchant on the Internet, selling $6 million worth of gear daily. And all of this after three previous years of similar pyrotechnics. That's why Dell ranks No. 1 on the *Business Week* Info Tech 100 list of top performers.

So what does the company do for an encore? Ask CEO Michael S. Dell, and he'll tell you with his typical straight face: more of the same. Well, sure, that's what you'd expect him to say. Except Dell—whose direct-manufacturing model shook up the industry by redefining customer service as the speedy delivery of custom-built PCs—now wants to get even more up close and personal with buyers. "Our industry has generally neglected the customer. I want to take the customer experience to a whole new level," Dell says.

That's not just marketing mumbo jumbo. For Dell, it's a new battle cry. The 33-year-old CEO sees customer service as the "next battleground for market share." And nowhere will that be more true, say analysts, than in the consumer and home-office PC markets, which Dell is just beginning to target. "The consumer and home-office markets are going to be where the growth is, and that's where I want us to go next to keeping growing," Dell declares.

The message isn't lost on the troops at Dell's suburban Austin, Tex., headquarters. Pinned to a wall amid a sea of cluttered cubicles is a photograph of Dell. Someone has drawn a hat on him, the kind worn by Uncle Sam. A slogan scrawled below reads: "Michael wants YOU to OWN your relationship with the customer." Just in case there's any doubt, Dell has tied bonuses and profit-sharing to service improvements of at least 15% this year. Success will be measured by shipping deadlines, fixing machines on the first try, and getting repair people to customers within 24 hours.

Dell's new customer-service plan: Use the Internet to automate and customize service, in much the same way that Dell streamlined and customized PC production. The do-it-the-customer's-way mantra has created for Dell the tightest—and most envied—relationship with buyers in the PC business. By using communications links over speedy private networks and the vast Internet, Dell plans not only to provide personalized Web pages for non-corporate customers but also to answer knotty service questions with the lightning speed that only the Net can deliver. "All our customers have individual files with us online," says Scott Eckert, director of Dell Online. "Why not expand those files for a new kind of direct-service model, one that will enable conversations with customers about service, industry trends, and new products—or even, say, weather and news someday?"

To Dell, the benefits of dispensing more service over the Net are twofold: "It can be a great relief valve for disgruntled customers," says Mehta—and a relief for shareholders, too. Doug Chandler, a customer-service analyst at International Data Corp., estimates that phone calls to give service and support can cost PC companies $25 apiece. Dell's online service operation, he says, saves a bundle—thousands of calls per week and potentially millions of dollars. If that's extended to include a greater percentage of Dell's customers, it could save millions more.

Source: Marcia Stepanek, "What Does No. 1 Do for an Encore?" *Business Week,* no. 3602 (1998), p. 112.

Impediments to an Effective Customer Service Strategy

Many companies lack an effective customer service strategy. Even the best-managed firms may have difficulty in avoiding the many impediments to successful implementation of the firm's customer service strategy.

Failing to segment markets in terms of the service offered may be a costly mistake. For example, larger more profitable customers may receive a lead time of three days when smaller customers may have a lead time of five days and only receive deliveries on a specific day each week. Management often hesitates to offer different levels of service for fear of violating the Robinson-Patman Act, which requires that firms cost-justify such policies. However, most firms do not have the necessary cost information to do so.[29] Nevertheless, management can segment markets based on customers' evaluations of the importance of marketing services, and can obtain the necessary financial data using sampling techniques.

Salespeople Often Create Unrealistic Expectations

Salespeople can misuse customer service by promising faster delivery to obtain an order. But most customers value reliability and consistency in filling orders more than speed of delivery. Consequently, ad hoc attempts to decrease the order cycle will increase transportation costs for the expedited shipments; order-assembly costs also rise because of the disruption of normal workflow. In addition, neither the customer nor the company has much to gain. When salespeople override customer service policies on shipping dates, lead times, shipping points, modes of transportation, and units of sale, they disrupt other customers' orders and cause an increase in logistics costs. In other situations, salespeople have been known not to "sell" the services being provided by the company.[30]

A firm's customer service standards and performance expectations are affected substantially by the competitive environment and what is perceived to be traditional industry practices. Consequently, it is imperative that management understand industry norms, expectations, and the costs of providing high levels of customer service. Evidence suggests that many firms do not measure the cost-effectiveness of service levels and lack an effective way of determining competitive service levels. In many cases, information provided by a sales organization often is concerned with raising service levels. Another source of information is industry anecdotes about outraged customers. The net result is that management may overreact to imprecise cues from the marketplace, or even from within their own organizations.[31]

Considering the vast sums of money firms spend on research and development and advertising, it makes little sense for a company to inadequately study the levels of customer service necessary for profitable long-range business development.

Finally, the economic environment since the late 1970s has caused top management to push for more inventory turns and lower accounts receivable. As we saw in Chapter 1, both of these reactions can lead to decreased levels of customer service and, eventually, lower corporate profitability.

Improving Customer Service Performance

An Effective Customer Service Strategy Requires a Thorough Understanding of Customers

An effective customer service strategy must be based on an understanding of how customers define *service.* The customer service audit and surveys of customers are imperative. Once management has determined the firm's customers' view of service, it must select a customer service strategy that advances the firm's objectives for long-range profit and return on investment. The optimum customer service level is not always the lowest cost level but rather the one that retains the "right" or "desired" customers.

---

[29]See Douglas M. Lambert, *The Distribution Channels Decision* (New York: National Association of Accountants, and Hamilton, Ontario: The Society of Management Accountants of Canada, 1978); Douglas M. Lambert and John T. Mentzer, "Is Integrated Physical Distribution Management a Reality?" *Journal of Business Logistics* 2, no. 1 (1980), pp. 18–27; and Douglas M. Lambert and Howard M. Armitage, "Distribution Costs: The Challenge," *Management Accounting,* May 1979, pp. 33–37, 45.

[30]Douglas M. Lambert, James R. Stock, and Jay U. Sterling, "A Gap Analysis of Buyer and Seller Perceptions of the Importance of Marketing Mix Attributes," in *Enhancing Knowledge Development in Marketing,* ed. William Bearden et al. (Chicago: American Marketing Association, 1990), p. 208.

[31]La Londe, Cooper, and Noordewier, *Customer Service: A Management Perspective,* p. 29.

The development of an effective customer service program also requires the establishment of customer service standards that do the following:

- Reflect the customer's point of view.
- Provide an operational and objective measure of service performance.
- Provide management with cues for corrective action.[32]

In addition, management should measure and evaluate the impact of individual logistics activities—such as transportation, warehousing, inventory management, production planning/purchasing, and order processing—on the level of customer service. Designated employees should report achievements regularly to the appropriate levels of management. Management should compare actual performance to standards and take corrective action when performance is inadequate. For management to be successful and efficient, a firm needs timely information. It also is necessary to hold individuals accountable for their performance, since information alone does not guarantee improved decision making.

The Perfect Order: Achievement of the Service Promise on Each and Every Occasion

Achievement of the service promise on each and every occasion has been termed "the perfect order."[33] Achieving the perfect order means that each element of the service package has been performed to customer specifications. One common definition of the perfect order is an order delivered on time, complete, and error free. On-time delivery is measured against the agreed-on lead time, completeness is measured by order fill, and *error free* includes the avoidance of error in invoices as well as other sources of quality failure in the order fulfillment process.

This is quite a challenging measure for even the best-run organizations. The overall level of service performance during a period is determined by the *combined* effect of each separate element of the perfect order. Hence performance levels on each element should be multiplied together to provide the real level of service achievement:

$$\text{Perfect order achievement} = \% \text{ on time} \times \% \text{ complete} \times \% \text{ error free}$$

Let's say that during the past 12 months the actual performance in meeting one customer's requirement was as follows:

90 percent on-time delivery.

80 percent complete.

70 percent error and damage free.

In this case the actual service performance in terms of perfect order achievement would be 90 percent $\times$ 80 percent $\times$ 70 percent, which is approximately 50 percent.

How can organizations get anywhere close to achieving the perfect order? The answer lies in some of the lessons to be learned from total quality management (TQM). For many years managers of production facilities have recognized that the only way that 100 percent quality output can be achieved from any process is through the continuous control of that process.

If the Process Is under Control, Then the Quality of the Output Can Be Guaranteed

In a production environment managers will seek to understand the critical elements of a process where, if a failure occurs, the quality of the output would be affected. Then, understanding these critical potential fail points, the priority is to monitor and control

---

[32]La Londe and Zinszer, *Customer Service,* p. 180.

[33]Adapted from Martin Christopher, *Marketing Logistics* (Oxford, England: Butterworth-Heinemann, 1997), pp. 40–43.

them constantly. Typically, statistical process control (SPC) methods are used. The techniques of process control also can be applied to the control of service processes.

First, the processes must be clearly understood and defined. This will involve the detailed mapping and flow-charting of each aspect of the service processes, for example, the order management process. Typically, once the results of these process mapping exercises are available, managers are surprised at the complexity of the processes. A benefit of performing this exercise can be that reengineering takes place to simplify and streamline the processes.

The identification of the critical fail points in a service process can be facilitated by the use of cause-and-effect analysis using a *fishbone diagram.* This simple device is based on the 80/20 concept, which suggests that 80 percent of the problems that arise in any process are the result of 20 percent of the causes.

If we take as an example an investigation into the failure to meet the customer's requested delivery date, we might find a number of frequently occurring causes, such as the product not being available, poor carrier performance, or lead times that are too short. Then, we investigate the reasons for these failures. By plotting the causes and effects in the form of a fishbone diagram we can begin to identify the key areas where management attention must be focused if failure is to be reduced or eliminated. Figure 3–13 gives an example of a simplified fishbone diagram.

By focusing on the critical areas, the firm will find ways to introduce fail-safe systems. In any case it is vital that these critical points be monitored continuously so that potential problems can quickly be identified. The methods of statistical process control can be used to establish control limits within which these activities must be performed. (SPC will be described in Chapter 16.) Managers who are serious about perfect order achievement will develop the appropriate measurements and will incorporate these into their portfolio of key performance indicators.

FIGURE 3–13

An example of cause-and-effect analysis using a fishbone diagram

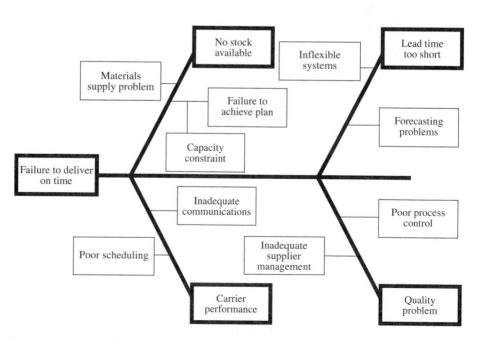

Source: Martin Christopher, *Marketing Logistics* (Oxford, England: Butterworth-Heinemann, 1997), p. 43.

How IBM Gets Closer to Its Worldwide Customers

Worldwide, IBM receives more than 50,000 customer complaints (excluding calls to the company's toll-free technical support system) each year. IBM customers receive surveys with 10 specific questions on product quality and customer satisfaction. Teams of IBM employees from different areas across the company read surveys from those customers with whom they have previously dealt. Each team is empowered to take immediate action, if necessary, to solve a customer's complaint.

Each year IBM conducts some 40,000 customer interviews in 71 countries and in 26 languages. A central database catalogs the data and makes it available to a team of managers who generate companywide initiatives. That database contains, according to Ned Lautenbach, IBM's senior vice president of sales and distribution, "every known problem that we've ever encountered, so we can go in, respond, and fix the customer's problems quickly. We set a goal in every country we do business in to be the best in our class in customer satisfaction. That's the case in more than half of the counties where we operate, twice as many as just three or four years ago."

As a major outgrowth of this new company attitude to customer service, IBM now allocates over 1,200 employees from IBM Research to work with specific customers, often at the customer's site, on providing solutions such as creating algorithms for scheduling and ordering tickets. In addition, IBM has developed new technology that enables financial service companies to offer their clients better investment strategies such as online trading and risk-management system. "IBM Research now devotes approximately 25 percent of its resources to funding this customer support," says Lautenbach. "It used to be zero percent or almost zero. So it's a dramatic change."

Another dramatic change is IBM's "Customer First" initiative. Begun in 1996, this program gives each frontline employee the authority without prior management approval to spend up to *$5,000 per incident* to solve problems for a customer on the spot.

More complex problems call for the frontline employee to elicit the help of an IBM executive. Managers from various regions in North America or from other countries constitute Customer Action Councils (CACs). Every council meets monthly to discuss with frontliners those issues that require extensive research, product development, or expenditures. As Jim Waugh, director of customer satisfaction for North America, describes them, the CACs offer senior management a way of saying to employees, "Bring us your problems, and we'll solve them together."

In addition, IBM's "Partnership Executive" program assigns 470 executives to more than 1,300 customer accounts, including many Fortune 500 companies and IBM's strategic business partners. These executives themselves function as "points of contact," much as their frontline counterparts. Each IBM executive in this program visits twice a year with client executives at each partner company to further strengthen customer relationships, which Lautenbach calls "the most valuable assets we have today at IBM."

As the central part of its restructure, providing excellence in customer service has enabled IBM to regain lost ground and reach new levels of success. The company has mastered this best practice by creating personalized, profitable relationships between employees and customers, and a strong sense of cooperation among its frontline and management staff, and establishing a training program that enables employees to better enhance the customer's experience with IBM products and services.

"Over the last four or five years," says Waugh, "what customers expect hasn't changed. They want an approachable company, knowledgable follow-up, and basically a perfect encounter every time. That's impossible, of course, but we at IBM are getting closer."

Source: Robert Hiebeler, Thomas B. Kelly, and Charles Ketteman, *Best Practices: Building Your Business with Customer-Focused Solutions* (New York: Simon & Schuster, 1998), pp. 168–70.

Global Customer Service Issues

Taking a global perspective requires searching for common market demands world-wide, rather than dividing world markets into separate entities with very different product needs.[34] On the other hand, different parts of the world have different service needs related to such concerns as information availability, order completeness, and expected lead times.[35] In addition, the local congestion, infrastructure, communications, and time differences may make it impossible to achieve the same levels of customer service globally. Service should match local customer needs and expectations to the greatest degree possible. So while a compelling argument can be made for the implementation of a centrally coordinated global logistics strategy, the one activity that should be conducted locally is establishing the customer service strategy.

Coca-Cola Services Japan and the United States Differently

For example, Coca-Cola provides very different types of service in Japan than in the United States. The drivers of Coca-Cola delivery trucks in Japan focus on providing merchandising in supermarkets, helping in processing bills in small mom-and-pop operations, and responding to signals from communication systems in vending machines so that time is not wasted delivering to full machines.[36] Tailoring the service to the country creates the most efficient and effective customer service policy, rather than simply implementing the same strategy worldwide.

Summary

This chapter opened with a description of how to define customer service. Although the importance of the individual elements of customer service varies from company to company, we described the common elements that are of concern to most companies. We also saw the necessity for a customer service strategy consistent with marketing and corporate strategies. The successful implementation of the integrated logistics management concept depends on management's knowledge of the costs associated with different system designs, and of the relationship between system design and customer service levels. We saw how management can obtain better knowledge of the costs and revenues associated with different levels of customer service, and how it can implement cost/service trade-offs.

The customer service audit is a method of determining the existing service levels, determining how performance is measured and reported, and appraising the impact of changes in customer service policy. Questionnaires are a means of finding out what management and customers view as important aspects of customer service.

---

[34]Martin Christopher, "Customer Service Strategies for International Markets," *Annual Proceedings of the Council of Logistics Management* (Oak Brook, IL: Council of Logistics Management, 1989), p. 327.

[35]For some global examples, see Mauro Caputo and Valeria Mininno, "Internal, Vertical and Horizontal Logistics Integration in Italian Grocery Distribution," *International Journal of Physical Distribution and Logistics Management* 26, no. 10 (1996), pp. 64–90; Jae-Il Kim, "Logistics in Korea: Current State and Future Directions," *International Journal of Physical Distribution and Logistics Management* 26, no. 10 (1996), pp. 6–21; and Andrei N. Rodnikow, "Logistics in Command and Mixed Economics: The Russian Experience," *International Journal of Physical Distribution and Logistics Management* 24, no. 2 (1994), pp. 4–14.

[36]Joseph B. Fuller, James O'Conor and Richard Rawlinson, "Tailored Logistics: The Next Advantage," *Harvard Business Review* 71, no. 3 (May–June 1993), p. 88.

Although customer service may represent the best opportunity for a firm to achieve a sustainable competitive advantage, many firms implement customer service strategies that are simply duplicates of those implemented by their major competitors. The audit framework represented in this chapter can be used by management to collect and analyze customer and competitive information.

We saw that there are some common roadblocks to an effective customer service strategy—as well as some ways to improve performance. In Chapter 4 we will show you how order processing and information systems influence the efficiency and effectiveness of the logistics function.

It is not enough to simply provide customers with superior customer service. It is necessary to identify the value provided to the customers and sell the value proposition that is being offered. This topic will be addressed in Chapter 17.

Suggested Readings

Daugherty, Patricia J.; Theodore P. Stank; and Alexander E. Ellinger. "Leveraging Logistics/Distribution Capabilities: The Effect of Logistics Service on Market Share." *Journal of Business Logistics* 19, no. 2 (1998), pp. 35–52.

Emerson, Carol J., and Curtis M. Grimm. "The Relative Importance of Logistics and Marketing Customer Service." *Journal of Business Logistics* 19, no. 1 (1998), pp. 17–32.

Gilmour, Peter. "Customer Service: Differentiating by Market Segment." *International Journal of Physical Distribution and Materials Management* 12, no. 3 (1982), pp. 37–44.

Harding, Forest E. "Logistics Service Provider Quality: Private Measurement, Evaluations and Improvement." *Journal of Business Logistics* 19, no. 1 (1998), pp. 103–20.

La Londe, Bernard J., and Martha C. Cooper. *Partnerships in Providing Customer Service: A Third-Party Perspective.* Chicago: Council of Logistics Management, 1989.

La Londe, Bernard J.; Martha C. Cooper; and Thomas G. Noordewier. *Customer Service: A Management Perspective.* Chicago: Council of Logistics Management, 1988.

Levy, Michael. "Toward an Optimal Customer Service Package." *Journal of Business Logistics* 2, no. 2 (1981), pp. 87–109.

Levy, Michael; John Webster; and Roger A. Kerin. "Formulating Push Marketing Strategies: A Method and Application." *Journal of Marketing* 47, no. 1 (Winter 1983), pp. 25–34.

Maltz, Arnold, and Elliot Maltz. "Customer Service in the Distributor Channel: Empirical Findings." *Journal of Business Logistics* 19, no. 2 (1998), pp. 103–32.

Mathe, Hervé, and Roy D. Shapiro. "Managing the Service Mix: After Sale Service for Competitive Advantage." *The International Journal of Logistics Management* 1, no. 1 (1990), pp. 44–50.

Ozment, John, and Douglas N. Chard. "Effects of Customer Service on Sales: An Analysis of Historical Data." *International Journal of Physical Distribution and Materials Management* 16, no. 3 (1986), pp. 14–28.

Perreault, William D., and Frederick A. Russ. "Improving Physical Distribution Service Decisions with Trade-Off Analysis." *International Journal of Physical Distribution and Materials Management* 7, no. 3 (1977), pp. 117–27.

Sterling, Jay U., and Douglas M. Lambert. "Customer Service Research: Past, Present and Future." *International Journal of Physical Distribution and Materials Management* 19, no. 2 (1989), pp. 3–23.

———. "Establishing Customer Service Strategies Within the Marketing Mix." *Journal of Business Logistics* 8, no. 1 (1987), pp. 1–30.

van der Veeken, Danielle J. M., and Werner G. M. M. Rutten. "Logistics Service Management: Opportunities for Differentiation." *The International Journal of Logistics Management* 9, no. 2 (1998), pp. 91–98.

Zemke, Ron, and John A. Woods. *Best Practices in Customer Service,* New York: HRD Press, 1998.

Questions and Problems

1. Explain why customer service should be integrated with other components of the marketing mix when management develops the firm's marketing strategy.

2. Explain the importance of the pretransaction, transaction, and posttransaction elements of customer service.

3. Customer service has been referred to as the output of the firm's logistics system. What exactly does this mean? What are the benefits that customers normally expect from this output? What techniques are available to the logistics executive to help in the construction of the most profitable package of customer service?

4. Explain how ABC analysis can be used to improve the efficiency of the customer service activity.

5. Why is the customer service audit important when establishing a corporation's customer service strategy?

6. How should management go about improving customer service performance?

7. It was suggested that customer service decisions should be left to managers at the individual country level rather than centralized as part of the implementation of a global logistics strategy? Why would this be the case?

8. Show how management can use cost/revenue trade-offs to determine whether customer service levels should be increased from 95 percent to 98 percent in-stock availability, given the following information:

    a. Transportation costs would increase by $135,000.

    b. Inventory levels would increase by $3 million.

    c. Warehousing costs would increase by $15,000.

    d. Inventory carrying cost as a percentage of inventory value is 35 percent.

    e. Annual sales are currently $50 million.

    f. The contribution margin on the company's products averages 30 percent of the selling price.

Survey of Marketing and Distribution Practices in the Blood Banking Reagent Industry

UNF
UNF
UNF
UNF
UNF
UNF
UNF
UNF
UNF
UNF
UNF
UNF
UNF
UNF
UNF

Department of Management, Marketing and Logistics
University of North Florida, Jacksonville, Florida

SURVEY OF MARKETING AND DISTRIBUTION PRACTICES IN THE BLOOD BANKING REAGENT INDUSTRY

PART A: IMPORTANCE OF FACTORS CONSIDERED WHEN SELECTING AND EVALUATING SUPPLIERS OF BLOOD BANKING REAGENTS

INSTRUCTIONS

Listed on the following pages are various factors often provided by **suppliers** of reagents to their customers. **This Section involves two tasks.** Each task will be explained separately.

The first task involves your evaluation of the various factors that you might consider when you select a new reagent supplier, or when you evaluate the performance of one of your current suppliers. Please circle on a scale of 1 to 7, the number which best expresses the *importance* of each of these factors. If a factor is not used or possesses very little weight in your evaluation of suppliers, please circle number 1 (not important). A rating of 7 (very important) should be reserved for those factors that would cause you to *reevaluate* the amount of business done with a supplier, or cause you to drop the supplier in the event of inadequate performance.

The second task is to *evaluate the current performance of three major suppliers.* Please list below in the spaces labeled "Supplier A", "Supplier B" and "Supplier C" three major suppliers of reagents. If you use fewer than three suppliers, please evaluate only those that you use. Next, using the scale labeled PERCEIVED PERFORMANCE, please insert the number between 1 and 7 which best expresses your perception of the supplier's current performance under the appropriate supplier heading. If you perceive that a supplier's performance is poor, insert a 1. Reserve a rating of 7 for excellent performance. If a service is not available from a supplier, please write NA, NOT AVAILABLE, in the appropriate space.

Please identify your major suppliers below:
SUPPLIER A (**the largest amount** of your reagent purchases are from this supplier): _____
SUPPLIER B (**second largest amount** of your reagent purchases are from this supplier): _____
SUPPLIER C (**third largest amount** of your reagent purchases are from this supplier): _____

EXAMPLE	Not Important		IMPORTANCE			Very Important		PERCEIVED PERFORMANCE SUPPLIERS (Scale of 1 to 7)		
FACTORS CONSIDERED	1	2	3	4	5	6	7	A	B	C
• Product Quality	1	2	3	4	5	6	⑦	7	6	6
• Average Lead Time	1	2	3	4	⑤	6	7	6	5	2

FACTORS CONSIDERED	Not Important		IMPORTANCE			Very Important		PERCEIVED PERFORMANCE SUPPLIERS (Scale of 1 to 7)		
	1	2	3	4	5	6	7	A	B	C
1. Accurate and timely billing (invoicing)	1	2	3	4	5	6	7	___	___	___
2. Lowest Price	1	2	3	4	5	6	7	___	___	___
3. Computer-to-computer order entry	1	2	3	4	5	6	7	___	___	___
4. Consistent lead times (supplier consistently meets promised delivery date)	1	2	3	4	5	6	7	___	___	___
5. Cash discounts for early payment or prepayment	1	2	3	4	5	6	7	___	___	___
6. Ability of supplier to meet specific service and delivery needs	1	2	3	4	5	6	7	___	___	___
7. Order processing personnel are located in:										
• your city	1	2	3	4	5	6	7	___	___	___
• your state	1	2	3	4	5	6	7	___	___	___
• one centralized U.S. location	1	2	3	4	5	6	7	___	___	___
8. Rapid adjustment of billing errors (due to pricing errors)	1	2	3	4	5	6	7	___	___	___
9. Supplier absorbs cost of expedited freight and handling when the supplier experiences a stockout	1	2	3	4	5	6	7	___	___	___

FACTORS CONSIDERED	Not Important 1	2	3	IMPORTANCE 4	5	6	Very Important 7	PERCEIVED PERFORMANCE SUPPLIERS (Scale of 1 to 7) A	B	C
10. Adequate identification/ labeling of shipping carton	1	2	3	4	5	6	7	___	___	___
11. Participation of vendor in conventions	1	2	3	4	5	6	7	___	___	___
12. Adequate advance notice of price changes provided	1	2	3	4	5	6	7	___	___	___
13. Supplier adequately tests new products before delivering to market	1	2	3	4	5	6	7	___	___	___
14. Availability of status information on orders	1	2	3	4	5	6	7	___	___	___
15. Number of tests per 10ml. bottle	1	2	3	4	5	6	7	___	___	___
16. Long term (longer than 1 year) contractual relationship available with supplier	1	2	3	4	5	6	7	___	___	___
17. Supplier holds dedicated inventory in return for a commitment to buy	1	2	3	4	5	6	7	___	___	___
18. Adequate availability (supplier's ability to deliver) of new products at time of introduction	1	2	3	4	5	6	7	___	___	___
19. Supplier's adherence to special shipping instructions	1	2	3	4	5	6	7	___	___	___
20. Availability of educational material from supplier	1	2	3	4	5	6	7	___	___	___
21. Bar code location: • outer carton	1	2	3	4	5	6	7	___	___	___
• on the product itself	1	2	3	4	5	6	7	___	___	___
22. Supplier offers monoclonal reagents	1	2	3	4	5	6	7	___	___	___
23. Supplier combines purchases of different products in order to compute volume discount	1	2	3	4	5	6	7	___	___	___
24. Product stability (shelf life) • Red cells	1	2	3	4	5	6	7	___	___	___
• Antiserum	1	2	3	4	5	6	7	___	___	___
25. Free WATS line (800 number) provided • for entering orders	1	2	3	4	5	6	7	___	___	___
• for technical or repair service	1	2	3	4	5	6	7	___	___	___
26. Quality/cleanliness of packaging materials	1	2	3	4	5	6	7	___	___	___
27. Supplier sponsored technical seminars: • at user's location	1	2	3	4	5	6	7	___	___	___
• at supplier's location	1	2	3	4	5	6	7	___	___	___
28. Supplier gives you an adequate period of price protection after a price increase is announced	1	2	3	4	5	6	7	___	___	___
29. Supplier's warehousing facility is located in your immediate area	1	2	3	4	5	6	7	___	___	___
30. Coded products (type of code used): • bar coding	1	2	3	4	5	6	7	___	___	___
• color coding	1	2	3	4	5	6	7	___	___	___
31. Availability of published price schedule	1	2	3	4	5	6	7	___	___	___
32. Sales rep has authority to negotiate special prices	1	2	3	4	5	6	7	___	___	___
33. Availability of blanket purchase orders	1	2	3	4	5	6	7	___	___	___
34. Damage-free shipments	1	2	3	4	5	6	7	___	___	___

FACTORS CONSIDERED	Not Important 1	IMPORTANCE 2	3	4	5	6	Very Important 7	PERCEIVED PERFORMANCE SUPPLIERS (Scale of 1 to 7) A	B	C
35. Supplier replaces entire allotment when there is evidence of defective product	1	2	3	4	5	6	7	___	___	___
36. National trade journal advertising by supplier	1	2	3	4	5	6	7	___	___	___
37. Sales representative characteristics:										
• accessibility	1	2	3	4	5	6	7	___	___	___
• honesty	1	2	3	4	5	6	7	___	___	___
• product knowledge	1	2	3	4	5	6	7	___	___	___
• industry knowledge	1	2	3	4	5	6	7	___	___	___
• technical knowledge	1	2	3	4	5	6	7	___	___	___
• concern/empathy	1	2	3	4	5	6	7	___	___	___
38. Development of new products by supplier	1	2	3	4	5	6	7	___	___	___
39. Prompt handling of claims due to overages, shortages or shipping errors	1	2	3	4	5	6	7	___	___	___
40. Extended dating programs (supplier allows more than 60 days for payment)	1	2	3	4	5	6	7	___	___	___
41. Order processing personnel can provide information on:										
• product characteristics	1	2	3	4	5	6	7	___	___	___
• technical questions	1	2	3	4	5	6	7	___	___	___
• inventory availability	1	2	3	4	5	6	7	___	___	___
• projected shipping date	1	2	3	4	5	6	7	___	___	___
• projected delivery date	1	2	3	4	5	6	7	___	___	___
• availability of substitute products	1	2	3	4	5	6	7	___	___	___
42. Availability of technical materials from supplier	1	2	3	4	5	6	7	___	___	___
43. Quantity discount structure based on total annual purchases	1	2	3	4	5	6	7	___	___	___
44. Length of promised lead times (from order submission to delivery):										
• Normal orders	1	2	3	4	5	6	7	___	___	___
• Emergency orders	1	2	3	4	5	6	7	___	___	___
45. Supplier absorbs cost of freight and handling on returns due to damage or product shipped in error	1	2	3	4	5	6	7	___	___	___
46. Action on complaints related to order servicing and shipping	1	2	3	4	5	6	7	___	___	___
47. Dealing directly with the supplier (vs. distributor)	1	2	3	4	5	6	7	___	___	___
48. Contact with supplier's top management	1	2	3	4	5	6	7	___	___	___
49. Assistance/counselling provided by supplier on:										
• credit	1	2	3	4	5	6	7	___	___	___
• inventory management	1	2	3	4	5	6	7	___	___	___
• technical assistance	1	2	3	4	5	6	7	___	___	___
• data management	1	2	3	4	5	6	7	___	___	___
• work flow improvement	1	2	3	4	5	6	7	___	___	___
50. Consistency of supplier's delivered product after initial evaluation of samples by my facility	1	2	3	4	5	6	7	___	___	___
51. Supplier reacts quickly to competitive price reductions	1	2	3	4	5	6	7	___	___	___
52. Advance information (literature, specs, prices, etc.) on new product introductions	1	2	3	4	5	6	7	___	___	___
53. Supplier sponsored entertainment	1	2	3	4	5	6	7	___	___	___
54. Product reliability (consistent performance from shipment to shipment)	1	2	3	4	5	6	7	___	___	___

FACTORS CONSIDERED	IMPORTANCE Not Important 1	2	3	4	5	Very Important 6	7	PERCEIVED PERFORMANCE SUPPLIERS (Scale of 1 to 7) A	B	C
55. Environmental considerations	1	2	3	4	5	6	7	___	___	___
56. Technical service personnel characteristics:										
• accessibility	1	2	3	4	5	6	7	___	___	___
• responsiveness	1	2	3	4	5	6	7	___	___	___
• problem-solving capability	1	2	3	4	5	6	7	___	___	___
• product knowledge	1	2	3	4	5	6	7	___	___	___
• follow up	1	2	3	4	5	6	7	___	___	___
• new techniques/ methods	1	2	3	4	5	6	7	___	___	___
57. Quality/durability of reagent packaging (protects integrity of reagent during shipping)	1	2	3	4	5	6	7	___	___	___
58. Accuracy in filling orders (correct reagent is shipped)	1	2	3	4	5	6	7	___	___	___
59. Frequency of deliveries (supplier consolidates multiple and/or split shipments into one larger, less frequent shipment)	1	2	3	4	5	6	7	___	___	___
60. Service support if salesperson is not available	1	2	3	4	5	6	7	___	___	___
61. Assistance from supplier in handling carrier loss and damage claims	1	2	3	4	5	6	7	___	___	___
62. Sensitivity (specifity) of reagent	1	2	3	4	5	6	7	___	___	___
63. Advance notice of shipping delays	1	2	3	4	5	6	7	___	___	___
64. Supplier provides promotional gifts (calendars, mugs, etc.)	1	2	3	4	5	6	7	___	___	___
65. Availability of quality control information from supplier	1	2	3	4	5	6	7	___	___	___
66. Supplier sponsored training	1	2	3	4	5	6	7	___	___	___
67. Supplier has complete assortment of reagents	1	2	3	4	5	6	7	___	___	___
68. Ability of supplier to respond to changes in requested delivery dates	1	2	3	4	5	6	7	___	___	___
69. Prompt and comprehensive response to competitive bid quotations	1	2	3	4	5	6	7	___	___	___
70. Competitiveness of price	1	2	3	4	5	6	7	___	___	___
71. Supplier expedites emergency orders in a fast, responsive manner	1	2	3	4	5	6	7	___	___	___
72. Timely response to requests for assistance from supplier's sales representative	1	2	3	4	5	6	7	___	___	___
73. Prompt notification of technical analysis results	1	2	3	4	5	6	7	___	___	___
74. Supplier's ability to work with you to improve your processes (work flow)	1	2	3	4	5	6	7	___	___	___
75. Supplier provides references for consultation service	1	2	3	4	5	6	7	___	___	___
76. Quantity discount structure based on size of individual order	1	2	3	4	5	6	7	___	___	___
77. Number of sales calls you personally receive per year from supplier's sales representatives	1	2	3	4	5	6	7	___	___	___
78. Supplier provides timely notification of product problems	1	2	3	4	5	6	7	___	___	___
79. Freight paid by supplier	1	2	3	4	5	6	7	___	___	___
80. Supplier does not raise prices more than once per year	1	2	3	4	5	6	7	___	___	___

PART B: MEASUREMENT OF OVERALL PERFORMANCE

---

1. Please indicate the percent that each supplier currently represents of your annual requirements, as well as the percent that you would *prefer* to give each supplier under ideal conditions in the future (Your totals should add to 100%).

	Current %	Ideal (Preferred) %
SUPPLIER A (the **largest amount** of your REAGENT purchases are from this supplier):	_____ %	_____ %
SUPPLIER B (**second largest amount** of your REAGENT purchases are from this supplier):	_____ %	_____ %
SUPPLIER C (**third largest amount** of your REAGENT purchases are from this supplier):	_____ %	_____ %
Other Suppliers	_____ %	_____ %
	100 %	100 %

2. Please mark a point anywhere on the lines below that best expresses your *level of satisfaction* with the above suppliers. If you are extremely dissatisfied with a supplier's performance, a mark should be placed very near the left end of the line (labeled Poor). If you are exceptionally pleased with the Supplier's performance, a mark should be placed very near the right end of the line (labeled Excellent). A midpoint has been placed on the line to correspond with a "Satisfactory" performance level.

OVERALL SUPPLIER PERFORMANCE

	Poor	Satisfactory	Excellent
SUPPLIER A	I_____-_____I		
SUPPLIER B	I_____-_____I		
SUPPLIER C	I_____-_____I		

	SUPPLIER A	SUPPLIER B	SUPPLIER C
3. Would you recommend this supplier to another laboratory?	___ Yes ___ No	___ Yes ___ No	___ Yes ___ No
4. Have you ever reported a problem to this supplier over the service you received?	___ Yes ___ No	___ Yes ___ No	___ Yes ___ No
5. Did this supplier respond adequately to the problem you reported?	___ Yes ___ No	___ Yes ___ No	___ Yes ___ No
6. What percentage of your shipments are received on-time from your major suppliers during a typical month?	_____ %	_____ %	_____ %

7. If your major supplier is a DISTRIBUTOR (rather than a manufacturer), what is the **primary** reason you buy from them? (Check *only one* item)

_____ faster delivery	_____ price	_____ only available source of preferred reagents
_____ small quantities	_____ local service	_____ other (Specify) _____

8. For the three suppliers that you have evaluated, please give the lowest price supplier a score of 0 %. For the others, indicate the percentage premium that you pay for their services. If two or more suppliers offer the same price, give them the same score. (EXAMPLE: If Supplier B was the lowest price supplier, they would be assigned a 0; if Supplier A's price was 2 % higher than Supplier B's, they would be assigned a 2 %; if Supplier C charged the same price as Supplier A they would also be assigned a 2 %; if Supplier C's price was 3% higher than Supplier B's, it would be assigned a 3%).

SUPPLIER A _____ %   SUPPLIER B _____ %   SUPPLIER C _____ %

PART C: EXPECTED PERFORMANCE LEVELS
Please provide the following information with respect to the levels of customer service that you need from your suppliers of blood banking reagents. **Supplier A** *is identified as the supplier from whom you make your largest amount of* **reagent** *purchases.*

---

1. How many sales contacts do you receive from **SUPPLIER A** during a typical year?
   a. face-to-face calls :   _____ per year   b. telephone calls :   _____ per year

2. How many sales contacts would you **prefer** to receive from **SUPPLIER A** during a typical year?
   a. face-to-face calls :   _____ per year   b. telephone calls :   _____ per year

3. What response time do you expect and currently receive from **SUPPLIER A** 's sales representative?

	Expect	Currently Receive
a. Response time in Emergency situations	_____ hours	_____ hours
b. Response time in Non - emergency situations	_____ hours	_____ hours

4. How much advance notice do you *need* from **SUPPLIER A** on price changes?
   _____ days   _____ weeks   _____ months

5. How much advance notice do you *currently receive* from **SUPPLIER A** on price changes?
    _____days   _____weeks   _____months

6. Under **normal conditions**, how frequently do you submit orders to **SUPPLIER A**? (Check one)
    a. Several times a day   _____   b. Once a day   _____   c. Several times a week   _____
    d. Once a week   e. Several times a month   _____   f. Once a month   _____
    g. Other (please specify)   _____

7. Under **normal conditions,** what is the total average lead time (from time order is placed to day received) in calendar days :
    a. that you *need* from **SUPPLIER A**?   _____ days
    b. that you *actually receive* from **SUPPLIER A**?   _____ days

8. How many orders do you place with **SUPPLIER A** in a typical month?   _____ orders.

9. What is the maximum number of days beyond the promised delivery date that you consider to be an acceptable delay?   _____ days

10. Once you have placed an order, how long does it take to receive notification from **SUPPLIER A** as to the expected (promised) delivery date? *(Please specify the number of minutes, hours or days. If none is provided, answer "N")*
    _____ minutes   _____hours   _____days

11. Please indicate the percentage of your reagent orders that are initially transmitted to **SUPPLIER A** by each of the following:
    a. U.S. Mail .... _____ %
    b. TWX, FAX machine and/or other communication terminal........... _____ %
    c. Toll-free telephone line   (paid by supplier)............................ _____ %
    d. Other telephone communication (paid by you)......................... _____ %
    e. Hand delivered to manufacturer's sales rep............................ _____ %
    f. Other (Specify) _____ _____ %
    TOTAL   **100   %**

12. What percentage of your orders are "emergency" orders that require expedited service?   _____ %

13. For products that are available from more than one supplier, identify the percentage of times that the following alternatives are used in the event that your order cannot be filled by the committed and/or requested delivery date?
    a. Backorder (hold until all product is available and ship complete) .. _____%
    b. Cancel unavailable items and ship balance by committed date..... _____%
    c. Split ship (ship quantities as they become available)................. _____%
    d. Cancel order and go to another supplier .... _____%
    e. Purchase unavailable items from another supplier..................... _____%
    f. Other (Specify)_____ _____%
    TOTAL   **100%**

14. What terms of payment (e.g. 2/10, net 30) are *offered* by your major suppliers for *early payment*?

		Discount %	Number of days	Net No. of days
a.	**SUPPLIER A**	_____%	_____	_____
b.	**SUPPLIER B**	_____%	_____	_____
c.	**SUPPLIER C**	_____%	_____	_____

15. What payment terms do you *actually receive* from **SUPPLIER A** :   number of days _____   % discount for early payment _____

16. What percentage premium for handling and freight **should** a supplier charge you for an emergency, expedited order?   _____ %

17. What is the typical **dollar value** of your average order of reagents from **SUPPLIER A**? $ _____.00

18. What is the **minimum dollar value** order **SUPPLIER A** will ship? $ _____.00

19. What percentage of the product is delivered by **SUPPLIER A**'s promised delivery date? _____ %

20. What percentage of **SUPPLIER A's** products arrive damage free? _____ %

21. Do you evaluate suppliers using: *(check one)*   a. Formal process/system _____   b. Informal process/system _____
                                                        c. No evaluation process/system _____   d. Don't know/uncertain_____

22. How frequently do you evaluate supplier performance: (check *one*)
    a. constantly ___   b. weekly ___   c. monthly ___   d. quarterly ___   e. annually ___   f. never ___

23. What proportion of your orders do you realistically need to have within: same day   _____ %
                                                                                       1 day   _____ %
                                                                                       3 days   _____ %
                                                                                       5 days   _____ %
                                                                                       7 days   _____ %
                                                                                       10 days or more _____ %
                                                                                       TOTAL   **100%**

24. In your evaluation of supplier performance, which of the following factors do you consider? (Please check all that apply)
    a. Fill rate on first shipment _____   b. Lead time _____   c. Lead time variability _____   d. Accuracy in invoicing _____
    e. Quality of products shipped _____   f. Damage _____   g. Others (Please List)_____

PART D: DEMOGRAPHIC DATA
This information is required in order to identify major market segments and to provide more meaningful analyses of the previous sections. Please use approximate figures in the event that exact data are not readily available.

---

1. What has been the average rate of growth in your purchases of reagents for the company over the last 5 years? *(indicate decline in purchases with a negative sign)* _____ %

2. What is your approximate annual budget for reagents ? $ _____ .00

3. How much reagent inventory (average number of days of supply of product) do you carry ? _____ days

4. How many supply sources of reagent products have you added and deleted during the last 12 months, 2 years and 5 years?

	Last 12 Months	Last 2 Years	Last 5 Years
Suppliers added	_____	_____	_____
Suppliers deleted (dropped)	_____	_____	_____

5. What percentage of your operating cost is represented by your purchases of reagents ? _____ %

6. Please indicate your overall evaluation of each of the following reagent suppliers.

SUPPLIER	Insufficient Information To Evaluate	Very Unfavorable						Very Favorable
Baxter Dade	_____	1	2	3	4	5	6	7
Gamma Diagnostics	_____	1	2	3	4	5	6	7
Immucor	_____	1	2	3	4	5	6	7
Organon Teknika (BCA)	_____	1	2	3	4	5	6	7
Ortho Diagnostic Systems	_____	1	2	3	4	5	6	7
Other _____	_____	1	2	3	4	5	6	7

7. Please indicate the major specialty(s) of your hospital (you may check more than one):
    ___ Trauma Center   ___ Cancer Research/ Treatment   ___ Open-Heart Surgery   ___ Neonatal Intensive Care
    ___ Burn Center   ___ Organ/ Tissue Transplants   ___ Obstetrics   ___ Medical Technical Facility/ Affiliation
    ___ Other _____   ___ Other _____

		Yes	No	Uncertain
8.	Do you have the authority to select (or specify) a specific (preferred) supplier of reagents?.......	_____	_____	_____
9.	Do you have the authority to **reject** a specific supplier of reagents?...................................	_____	_____	_____
10.	Does your institution belong to a **buying group** or **organization** which makes volume purchases from laboratory suppliers?..	_____	_____	_____

   If yes, to which buying group do you belong? _____

11. How do you order reagents from suppliers?   _____ personally order reagents directly from suppliers
                                                        _____ place orders through institution's purchasing department

12. What is your position or title? _____
    How long have you held this position? _____ years

13. What is your highest education level?   High School Diploma _____   Community College Degree _____
                                            Undergraduate (bachelors) degree _____   Graduate degree _____

14. Please indicate the percentage of your time devoted to: a. administrative duties   _____ %
                                                                b. laboratory (i.e. "bench") work   _____ %
                                                                                              100   %

15. What are the first three numbers of your zip code? _____

Thank you for you participation and cooperation in completing this survey. Your time and effort are sincerely appreciated.
Please return the questionnaire in the envelope provided or mail to:

DOUGLAS M. LAMBERT, Ph.D and RONALD ADAMS, Ph.D
Department of Management, Marketing and Logistics • College of Business Administration
University of North Florida • Jacksonville, Florida 32216 • Phone : (904) 620-2585

CHAPTER 4

Order Processing and Information Systems

Chapter Objectives

- To show how the order processing system can influence performance of the logistics function.
- To show how order processing systems can be used to improve customer communications and increase efficiency in many areas of logistics.
- To show how the order processing system can form the basis of a logistics information system at the strategic and tactical levels.
- To show how information technology supports time-based competition.
- To show how advanced information technologies support logistics and supply chain integration.

Introduction

The order processing system is the nerve center of the logistics system. A customer order serves as the communications message that sets the logistics process in motion. The speed and quality of the information flows have a direct impact on the cost and efficiency of the entire operation. Slow, erratic communications can lead to not only lost customers but also excessive transportation, inventory, and warehousing costs, as well as possible production inefficiencies caused by frequent line changes. The order processing and information system forms the foundation for the logistics and corporate management information systems. It is an area that offers considerable potential for improving logistics performance. In fact, research on world-class logistics practices cited logistics information systems as a key to competitiveness.[1]

Electronic Commerce

The term *electronic commerce (e-commerce)* encompasses a wide range of tools and techniques used to conduct business in a paperless environment. E-commerce is having a significant impact on how organizations conduct business. The Internet allows firms to transfer information inexpensively and effectively throughout the world, making e-commerce a key contributor to supply chain integration.

Going beyond transaction processing and tracking, computer-based decision support systems (DSSs) support the executive decision-making process. A DSS is an integrative system that provides information to decision makers; without a DSS, many choices would not be possible.

Faced with time-based competition, organizations are increasingly using information technologies as a source of competitive advantage. Systems such as quick response (QR), just-in-time (JIT), and efficient consumer response (ECR) are integrating a number of information-based technologies in an effort to reduce order cycle times, speed responsiveness, and lower supply chain inventory. In addition, more sophisticated applications of information technology such as decision support systems, artificial intelligence, and expert systems are being used directly to support decision making in logistics.

Order processing and information systems play a key role in achieving customer service goals at competitive cost. As Figure 4–1 shows, the costs of information exist in a trade-off environment with the costs of transportation, warehousing, inventory, and lot quantity considerations. In addition, the order processing and information systems have a direct impact on the customer service levels achieved by the firm and the total supply chain. Information system costs can be substituted for the much higher costs of transportation or inventory. In this chapter we will describe the critical role that information plays in integrating logistics within the firm and within the supply chain.

Customer Order Cycle

The *customer order cycle* starts with the placement of the order and ends when the product is received and placed into the customer's inventory. The typical order cycle consists of the following components: (1) order preparation and transmittal, (2) order receipt and order entry, (3) order processing, (4) warehouse picking and packing, (5) order transportation, and (6) customer delivery and unloading.

Six Components of the Order Cycle

---

[1]Global Logistics Research Team, Michigan State University, *World Class Logistics: The Challenge of Managing Continuous Change* (Oak Brook, IL: Council of Logistics Management, 1995), pp. 137–64.

FIGURE 4-1

Cost trade-offs in marketing and logistics

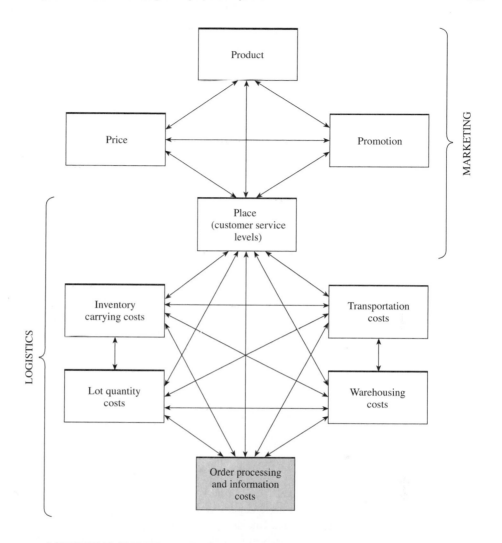

MARKETING OBJECTIVE: Allocate resources to the marketing mix in such a manner as to maximize the long-term profitability of the firm.

LOGISTICS OBJECTIVE: Minimize Total Costs given the customer service objective where Total costs = Transportation costs + Warehousing costs + Order processing and information costs + Lot quantity costs +

Source: Adapted from Douglas M. Lambert, *The Development of an Inventory Costing Methodology: A Study of the Cost Associated with Holding Inventory* (Chicago: National Council of Physical Distribution Management, 1976), p. 7.

Figure 4–2 illustrates the flow associated with the order cycle. In this example, the total order cycle is eight days, from the customer's point of view. However, many manufacturers make the mistake of measuring and controlling only the portion of the order cycle that is internal to their firm. That is, they monitor only the time that elapses between receipt of the customer order and shipment of the product. The example in Figure 4–2 shows shortcomings of this approach. The portion of the total order cycle that is internal to the manufacturer (steps 2, 3, and 4) amounts to only three of the eight days. This ratio is not unusual for companies that do not have an automated order entry and processing system. Improving the efficiency of the three-day portion of the order

Figure 4–2

Total order cycle: A customer's perspective

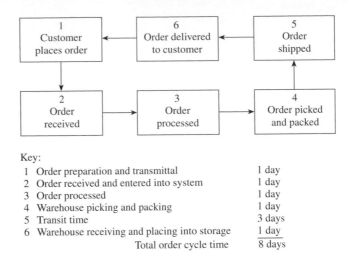

Key:

1	Order preparation and transmittal	1 day
2	Order received and entered into system	1 day
3	Order processed	1 day
4	Warehouse picking and packing	1 day
5	Transit time	3 days
6	Warehouse receiving and placing into storage	1 day
	Total order cycle time	8 days

cycle that is controlled by the manufacturer may be costly compared to eliminating a day from the five days not directly under the manufacturer's control. For example, it may be possible to reduce transit time by as much as one day by monitoring carrier performance and switching business to those carriers with the fastest and most consistent transit times.

However, a change in the method of order placement and order entry may have the potential for the most significant reduction in order cycle time. An advanced order processing system could reduce the total order cycle by as much as two days. In addition, the improved information flows could enable management to more efficiently execute the warehousing and transportation, reducing the order cycle by another one or two days.

Order Cycle Variability

Figure 4–2 treats the performance of order cycle components as though no variability occurred. Figure 4–3 illustrates that variability is likely to occur for each component of the order cycle and for the total. In our example, the actual order cycle could range from a low of 3.5 days to as many as 20 days, with the most likely length being 8 days. Variability in order cycle time is costly to the manufacturer's customer; the customer must either carry safety stock to cover for possible delays or lose sales as a result of stockouts.

In Figure 4–3, if the average order cycle time is 8 days but can be as long as 20 days, the customer must maintain additional inventory equivalent to 12 days' sales just to cover variability in lead time. If daily sales equal 20 units and the company's economic order quantity is 160 units—an 8-day supply—the average cycle stock is 80 units (one-half the order quantity). The additional inventory required to cover the order cycle variability of 12 days is 240 units. Excluding demand uncertainty, average inventory will increase from 80 units to 320 units due to the variability in the order cycle.

Which has the greatest impact on the customer's inventory—a three-day reduction in the order cycle, or a three-day reduction in order cycle variability? If the customer continued to order the economic order quantity of 160 units, a three-day reduction in the order cycle would result in little or no change in inventories. The customer would simply wait three days longer before placing an order. In contrast, if the customer ordered 100 units every five days instead of 160 units every eight days, the average cycle stock would be 50 units rather than 80 units, but safety stock of 240 units would

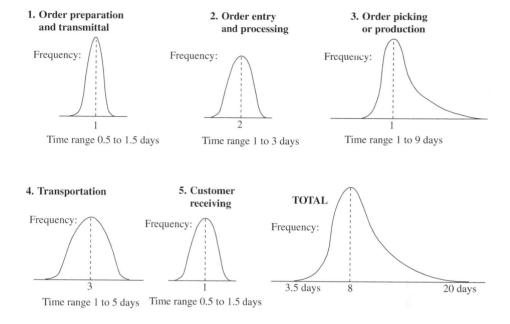

be required to cover the possibility of the order arriving 12 days late. The result would be a reduction in total average inventory of 30 units, from 320 to 290 units. However, a three-day reduction in order cycle variability would reduce safety stocks by 60 units and result in a total average inventory of 260 units (80 + 180). The reduction in safety stock has twice the impact of the reduction in cycle stock. This example should make clear why order cycle consistency is preferred to fast delivery.

In the next two sections we will look at how customer orders enter the order processing function and the typical path taken by a customer's order.

How Do Customer Orders Enter the Firm's Order Processing Function?

Methods of Order Entry

There are a number of ways in which a customer order can be placed, transmitted, and entered into a manufacturer's order processing function. Traditionally, customers wrote down orders and gave them to salespeople or mailed them to the supplier. The next level of sophistication was telephoning the order to the manufacturer's order clerk, who wrote it up. An advanced system might have customers telephoning orders to customer service representatives located at the manufacturer's headquarters and equipped with computer terminals. This type of system allows the customer service representative to determine whether the ordered products are available in inventory. The items are then deducted from inventory so that they are not promised to another customer. If there is a stockout on the item, the representative can arrange product substitution while the customer is still on the telephone, or can inform the customer when the product will be available. In effect, this type of system eliminates the first two days of the order cycle described in Figure 4–2.

Electronic Methods of Order Entry Are Becoming More Common

Electronic methods, such as an electronic terminal with information transmitted by telephone lines, and computer-to-computer hookups are becoming more widely used in order to gain the maximum speed and accuracy in order transmittal and order entry. Increasingly, companies are making it possible for customers to place their orders using the Internet. We will describe these types of systems in more detail later in this chapter.

There is a direct trade-off between inventory carrying costs and communications costs. However, the more sophisticated the communications system becomes, the more vulnerable the company becomes to any internal or external communications malfunction. This is due to the fact that, with advanced order processing systems and lower inventory levels, safety stocks are substantially reduced, leaving the customer with minimal protection against stockouts that result from any variability in the order cycle time. In many supply chains, significant potential exists for using advanced order processing to improve logistics performance.

The Path of a Customer's Order

When studying a firm's order processing system, it is important to understand the information flow that begins when a customer places an order. Figure 4–4 represents one interpretation of the path that a customer's order might take. In the first step, the customer recognizes the need for certain products and transmits an order to the supplying manufacturer. The various methods of order transmittal will be described in detail later in this chapter.

Once the manufacturer receives the order and enters it into the order processing system, it must make various checks to determine (1) whether the desired product is available in inventory in the quantities ordered, (2) whether the customer's credit is satisfactory to accept the order, and (3) whether the product is scheduled for production if not currently in inventory. The inventory file is then updated, product is back-ordered if necessary, and production is issued a report showing the inventory balance. Management can also use the information on daily sales as an input to its sales forecasting package. Order processing next provides information to accounting for invoicing, acknowledgment of the order to send to the customer, picking and packing instructions to enable

FIGURE 4–4

The path of a customer's order

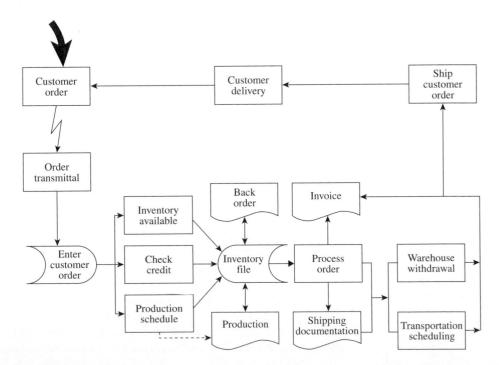

warehouse withdrawal of the product, and shipping documentation. When the product has been pulled from warehouse inventory and transportation has been scheduled, documentation is sent to accounting so that invoicing may proceed.

The Communications Function

Four Ways to Evaluate Alternative Methods of Order Transmittal

The primary function of the order processing system is to provide a communication network that links the customer and the supplier. Management should evaluate various methods of order transmittal for consistency of message delivery. Usually, greater inconsistency is associated with slower methods of order transmittal. Manual methods of order transmittal require more handling by individuals, and consequently there is greater chance of a communication error. Management can evaluate methods of order transmittal on the basis of speed, cost, consistency, and accuracy. Order transmittal should be as direct as possible; transmitting orders electronically rather than manually minimizes the risk of human error.

In addition, the order processing system can communicate useful sales information to marketing (for market analysis and forecasting), to finance (for cash-flow planning), and to logistics or production (for production planning and scheduling—see Table 4–1). Finally, the order processing system provides information to those employees who assign orders to warehouses, clear customer credit, update inventory files, prepare warehouse picking instructions, and prepare shipping instructions and the associated documentation. Communication is extremely important because it sets the logistics system in motion.

Advanced Order Processing Systems

Computers Have Improved Order Processing Systems

No component of the logistics function has benefited more from the application of electronic and computer technology than order entry and processing. Some advanced systems are so sophisticated that the only human effort required is to enter the order and monitor the results.

TABLE 4–1   **Management Information Provided by an Advanced Order Processing System**

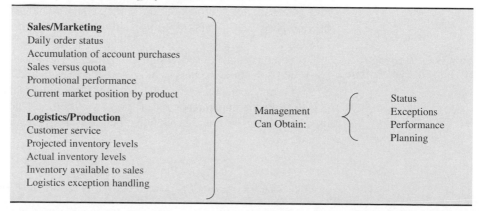

At one level of advanced order processing systems, customers and salespeople transmit orders to distribution centers or corporate headquarters via a toll-free number. The order clerk is equipped with a data terminal and can both enter and access information in real time. As soon as the order clerk enters the customer code, the order format, including the customer's name, billing address, credit code, and shipping address, is displayed on the screen. The clerk receives the rest of the order information verbally and enters it on the terminal; it is displayed along with the header information. Deviations from standard procedure, such as products on promotion, special pricing arrangements, and allocations, may be highlighted on the computer screen to ensure that the order clerk grants them special attention. The system can match order quantity against a list of minimum shipment quantities to ensure that the order meets the necessary specifications. The clerk may then read the order back to the customer. When the order meets all criteria for accuracy and completeness, it is released for processing.

A major chemical company replaced a manual system with a system using computer input similar to the one just described. Prior to the new order entry system, employees took orders over the phone and recorded them on a form by hand. The orders were then transferred to another form for keypunching, and finally were batch-processed into the system. The computer order entry system was cost-justified based on its savings over the manual system. As a result, sales increased by 23 percent with no increase in order processing costs. An additional benefit was that customer billing took place the day after the product was shipped, rather than five days later. This improved cash flow.

Figure 4–5 shows a typical supply chain for a retail product. Consumer demand flows from the retailer to the distributor to the manufacturer to the manufacturers' suppliers, and product flows in the reverse direction. However, Figure 4–6 more accurately depicts what takes place. Retailers place orders with distributors at periodic intervals in a manner that represents throwing orders over a wall. The distributor has no idea what the orders will look like until they arrive. There is no visibility in terms of the actual volume of sales at retail. In a similar fashion, distributors throw orders over a wall to the manufacturers, and the manufacturers repeat this practice with their suppliers. Each member of the supply chain forecasts using historical data assuming that future sales will be similar to past sales. Obviously, if there is any volatility in sales, this method spells disaster in terms of unnecessarily high inventory levels and markdowns to unload slow-moving or inactive stock.

Figure 4–7 illustrates what is possible. Each member of the supply chain receives timely information on what is actually selling at the retail level and adjusts its operations accordingly. Point-of-sale data are captured by retailers and are used to synchronize materials flows throughout the supply chain. Manufacturers plan short-term production according to what is being sold at retail rather than forecasts based on past sales.

An Advanced System at Manville Canada, Inc.

A company that has successfully implemented an advanced order transmittal, order entry, and order processing system is Manville Canada, Inc.[2] Manville Canada invested $750,000 in a computer system that paid for itself in less than two years.

Prior to the implementation of the new system, a customer would telephone an order for fiberglass home insulation—one of Manville Canada's products—to one of

---

[2]This example was furnished by Donald J. Allison, former vice president–corporate business logistics, Manville Canada, Inc.

FIGURE 4–5

Traditional supply chain flows

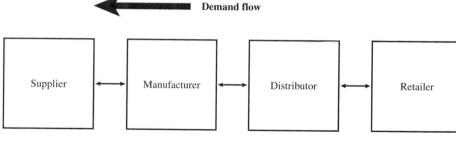

Demand flow

Supplier ⟷ Manufacturer ⟷ Distributor ⟷ Retailer

Product flow

FIGURE 4–6

Barriers to information flows in a traditional supply chain

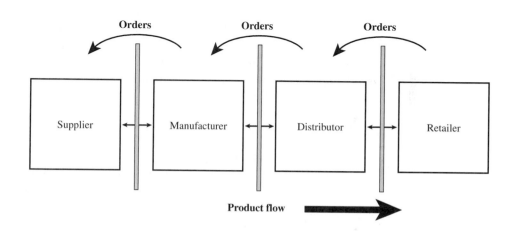

Orders   Orders   Orders

Supplier ⟷ Manufacturer ⟷ Distributor ⟷ Retailer

Product flow

FIGURE 4–7

Information-based supply chain flows

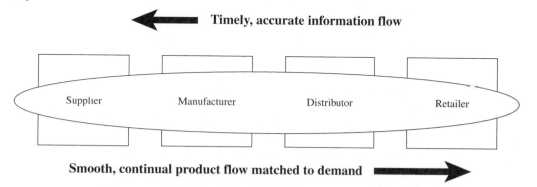

Timely, accurate information flow

Supplier   Manufacturer   Distributor   Retailer

Smooth, continual product flow matched to demand

three customer service clerks located in Toronto. One of these clerks was assigned to the telephone, while the other two were kept busy writing orders. The telephone clerk received the order and passed it on to one of the others for processing. Information required to complete the order was obtained from different files in many locations and manually filled in on each order set.

When this process was completed, the clerks sent the order to the order and billing department, where it was typed and sent to the shipping location. Once the order was shipped, shipping returned the order form and a shipping document to the customer service clerks, who verified and forwarded them to the billing department to be typed again.

The three customer service clerks could process an average of 12 orders per day, with overtime required during peak periods. This piecemeal method of handling customer orders created a considerable amount of pressure and resulted in a relatively high incidence of human error.

With the new system, customers telephone orders to customer service clerks, who enter the name of the customer on a video display screen. At this point, all pertinent customer information is displayed on the screen and applied to the order. When the product is entered, all inventory, price, and other related information about that item is displayed and applied to the order.

When all items have been added to the order, the total weights and percentages of a truckload shipment are calculated. If the order is for less than a truckload quantity, the customer is told the cost of increasing the order to truckload as well as the discount that would occur. In this way, customer service clerks provide an inside sales function. The computer also calculates the total value of the order and compares this to the credit limit that has been established for that customer. If the securement amount is greater than the credit limit, the order is placed on credit hold pending review by the credit manager. (The company refers to orders received as *securements*. As orders come in, they are accumulated, measured, and reported on securement reports. Once the customer is billed, the order is counted as a sale.)

Once the order is completed, the shipping documents, such as packing slips and bills of lading, are printed at the shipping locations. At each shipping location, the shipping date, along with such data as the quantity shipped, carrier, carrier number, and products substituted, is entered into a terminal. At this point inventory files are automatically updated.

The customer service clerk reviews and verifies all information on the order and releases the order for billing. The billing is then printed out automatically by the computer—in French and English—and mailed to the customer. The computer also generates accounts receivable and sales detail reports. If required, a back order is created.

Benefits associated with the new system are numerous. Edits built into the system reduced billing errors by as much as 85 percent. With a 5 percent reasonability factor built into the system, it is able to detect errors made by clerks as they are processing the order through its various stages. The system has also streamlined Manville Canada's organization by 19 people and has largely eliminated time- and space-consuming typing and filing. The level of customer service has been improved. In addition, the company's cash flow has been accelerated by several days because of the system's ability to generate customer billings the same day the shipment is made. The company has also integrated the system with its inventory management system.

As orders are placed and shipped, inventory backlogs are automatically updated. This feature provides accurate data for production scheduling and a great variety of other reports: marketing-securement and billing reports, exception reports showing beyond-normal transportation costs, and carrier revenue reports.

Interfaces are also possible between similar systems that have been set up in the Toronto-, Montreal-, and Edmonton-based operations. This allows orders to be placed from any one region to any other region in the Canadian operation. It also permits total control of the order by the customer service clerk who has responsibility for that customer regardless of where in Canada the order will be shipped. The flow of an order through the Manville Canada system is shown in Figure 4–8.

FIGURE 4–8

An advanced order processing system, implemented at Manville Canada, Inc.

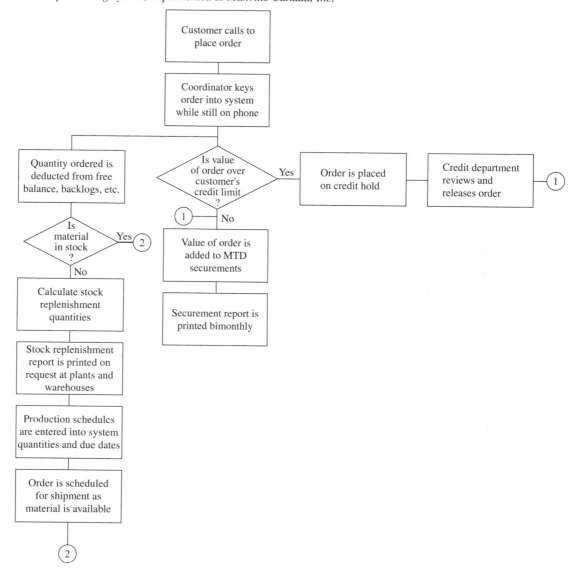

Source: Donald J. Allison, former vice president–corporate business logistics, Manville Canada, Inc.

(continued)

**The Order Sets
the Logistics System
in Motion**

Generally, the more rapid a form of order transmittal is, the more it costs. Likewise, electronic order entry may be more costly than simpler systems when viewed strictly on the basis of price. However, the logistics system cannot be set into motion until the order is entered at the processing point; an increase in order processing speed, accuracy, and consistency will make it possible to reduce inventories throughout the system while maintaining the desired customer service level. In addition, management can use the time saved in order transmittal and entry to realize transportation consolidation opportunities. As an alternative strategy, the firm could decrease the order cycle time offered to its customers, which would allow customers to hold less inventory. In addition, a reduction in the order cycle time would result in lower in-transit inventories

FIGURE 4–8

(continued)

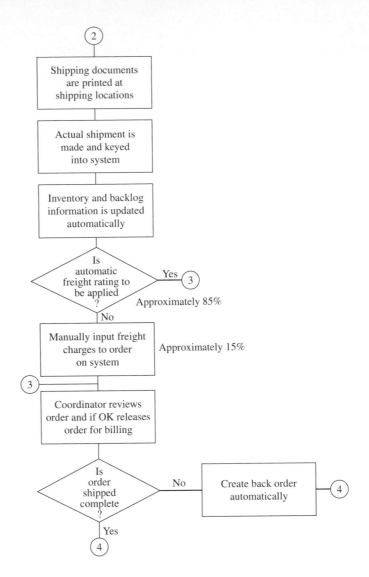

if customers reduced the quantities ordered. But we have seen that most customers prefer a consistent order cycle to a shorter one. Therefore, in the event of a decrease in lead time due to faster order transmittal and order entry, a firm's best strategy would be to keep the planning time made available and reduce costs by lowering inventory levels and reducing freight costs. The reduction in other logistics costs will more than offset the increased communications expenditures.

Inside Sales/Telemarketing

**Benefits
of Telemarketing**

Inside sales/telemarketing is an extension of the automated order processing systems we have discussed. It enables the firm to (1) maintain contact with existing customers who are not large enough to justify frequent sales visits; (2) increase contact with large, profitable customers; and (3) efficiently explore new market opportunities. Customer contacts

FIGURE 4–8

(concluded)

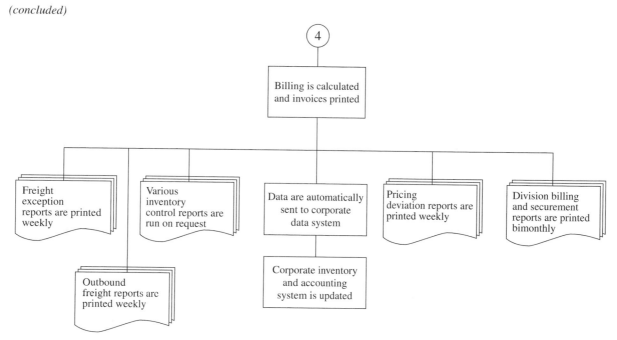

made by telephone from an inside sales group will achieve the desired market coverage in an economical, cost-effective manner. In addition, the use of data terminals for direct order input integrates inside sales with logistics operations. One of the major cost advantages of inside sales/telemarketing comes from the associated logistics efficiencies.

Inside sales/telemarketing can be cost-justified on the basis of increased sales, reduced expenses, or a combination of the two. If management desires to build sales volume, it may not reduce the selling expenses associated with the existing sales force. Inside sales may simply increase the firm's total selling expenses, and increased sales volume will be required to justify the additional expense. In most cases, however, expense reductions are possible if the program is implemented correctly. One method of improving efficiency is to place all small customers on scheduled deliveries in order to reduce transportation costs and other logistics costs. Justifying the expenditure for inside sales solely on projected sales increases is risky, to say the least. Many factors may prevent the company from achieving the desired sales increase, which may cause management to abandon the program in periods of financial difficulty. Programs that increase profitability by reducing costs will be retained, however.

An important step in cost justification is to conduct a pilot project. In this way, management can substantiate and project the program costs, as well as the cost savings from logistics and selling efficiencies, and the profit contribution from sales increases, for the national program. States or other market areas that are comparable in past sales history, market penetration, competition, and other important variables should be selected as control markets (old system) and test markets (proposed inside sales program). Control and test markets should also reflect the firm's total business so that it can make projections based on the pilot.

Electronic Data Interchange

Definition of EDI
Electronic data interchange (EDI) can be defined as "the interorganizational exchange of business documentation in structured, machine-processable form,"[3] or simply, one computer communicating directly with another computer. As illustrated in Figure 4–9, EDI replaces verbal and written communications with electronic ones. Since EDI transmissions are computer to computer, fax transmissions do not qualify. Also, the transmission is of standard business documents or forms. Thus, sending informal e-mail messages does not fit the definition of EDI.

EDI transmissions allow a document to be directly processed and acted on by the receiving organization. Depending on the sophistication of the system, there may be no human intervention at the receiving end. EDI specifically replaces more traditional transmission of documents, such as mail, telephone, and fax.

FIGURE 4–9

EDI versus traditional methods

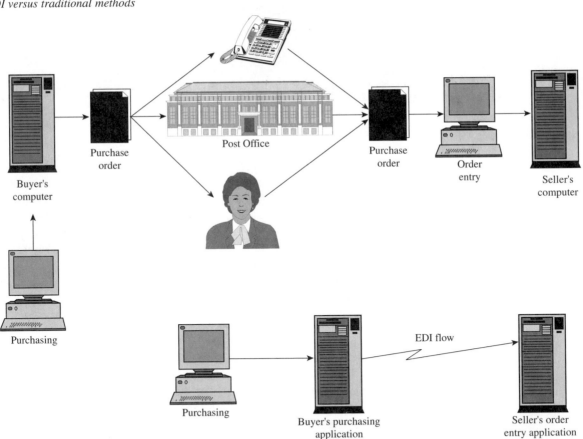

Source: Margaret A. Emmelhainz, *Electronic Data Interchange: A Total Management Guide* (New York: Van Nostrand Reinhold, 1990), p. 5.

---

[3]Margaret A. Emmelhainz, *Electronic Data Interchange: A Total Management Guide* (New York: Van Nostrand Reinhold, 1990), p. 4.

In the following pages, we will describe EDI standards, various types of EDI systems, the benefits of EDI implementation, electronic mail, and the Internet.[4]

EDI Standards.   For EDI to function properly, computer language compatibility is required. First, the users must have common communication standards. Documents are transmitted at a certain speed over particular equipment, and the receiver's equipment must be able to accept that speed. Also, the users must share a common language or message standard or have conversion capabilities. This means that EDI trading partners must have a common definition of words, codes, and symbols, as well as a common format and order of transmission.

EDI Protocols

There are a number of EDI protocols in use today. Some are unique systems created by and for a particular company. Some standards have been adopted by an industry. The American National Standards Institute (ANSI) has proposed the use of the ANSI X12 standard, which is a form of EDI that supports virtually all standard customer-order-associated documents. However, many industry associations have established their own standards for EDI, which are to be used by firms within their industry. Examples include the grocery, automotive, retail, warehousing, chemical, and wholesale drug industries.

Types of EDI Systems.   While several types and variations of EDI systems are in use, the main ones are proprietary systems, value-added networks (VANs), and industry associations. The difference between a proprietary system and a VAN is illustrated in Figure 4–10.

Value-Added Networks (VANs)

FIGURE 4–10

Typical EDI configurations

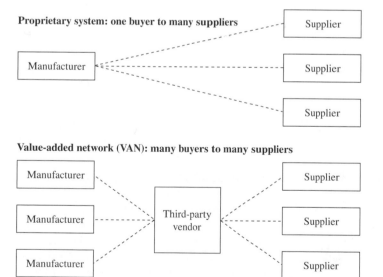

Source: GE Information Service, as reported in Lisa H. Harrington, "The ABC's of EDI," *Traffic Management* 29, no. 8 (August 1990), p. 51.

---

[4]This material is adapted from Lisa M. Ellram and Laura M. Birou, *Purchasing for Bottom-Line Impact* (Burr Ridge, IL: Irwin Business One, 1995).

Technology

One Industry's Approach to eProcurement

The Automotive Industry Action Group (AIAG), a trade association for all trading partners in the auto industry, has developed a common, standards-based network, the Automotive Network eXchange (ANX). ANX will provide automotive trading partners with a single, secure network for electronic commerce and data transfer for procurement, engineering, and other time-critical data. The AIAG has contracted with Bellcore, a leading provider of communications software and engineering, to oversee the ANX.

According to Brian Whittle, Bellcore's general manager for the project, the value proposition to the trading partners is the consolidation of multiple networks. "Auto suppliers and OEMs have had one-to-one applications for each type of data moving between trading partners," says Whittle. "The result is the complex, redundant, and costly system of multiple connections that currently exists throughout the automotive supply chain."

For example, Whittle says, a supplier has one system for moving CAD engineering specifications to one OEM and a different system for another OEM. For purchasing applications, suppliers have entirely different networks for each OEM with which they work.

"Sixty percent of the cost of networking in the auto industry is spent on supporting these redundant networks," says Whittle. "With ANX, there is a single connection that eliminates the need for a great deal of hardware, software, and networking."

The savings of creating uniform, or at least similar, data methods among trading partners is substantial, according to Whittle. He says that a recent study of how seats were supplied to the OEMs showed that if all OEMs and their suppliers handled communications for these components in the same way, the industry would save $1 billion, or $71 per vehicle. In addition, cycle time would be reduced by a factor of four.

ANX went live on November 1, 1998, after an extensive certification and testing phase. There currently are 22 trading partners on ANX, with 100 coming on at a rate of about one per day. An additional 3,500 other vendors have been sponsored, or invited by an OEM to join the system.

Source: Thomas A. Foster, "Global eProcurement Solutions," *Supply Chain Management Review Global Supplement* 3, no. 1 (1999), p. 21.

Proprietary Systems   *Proprietary systems* involve an EDI system that is owned, managed, and maintained by a single company that buys directly from a number of suppliers or receives orders directly from customers. Proprietary systems work best when the company that owns the system is large and powerful relative to suppliers and can encourage them to be part of the network.

The advantage to the owner of the system is control. The disadvantage is that the system may be expensive to establish and maintain internally, and suppliers may not want to be part of a unique system that requires a dedicated terminal.

Value-Added Networks   *Value-added networks (VANs),* also known as third-party networks or many-to-many systems, are the most widely used EDI systems. When a VAN is used, all of the EDI transmissions go through a third-party firm, which acts as a central clearinghouse.

For example, a buying firm sends a number of purchase orders (POs) to different suppliers through a VAN. The VAN sorts the POs by supplier and transmits them to the appropriate supplier. The value-added occurs when buyers and suppliers use incompatible communication or message standards. The VAN performs translation so that the user does not need to worry about system compatibility with its trading partners. This represents a big advantage over proprietary systems.

In addition, the users do not need to have expertise in EDI standards and issues since VANs provide turnkey, off-the-shelf systems, which lowers start-up costs and reduces start-up time.

A value-added network generally utilizes a mailbox feature. With the mailbox, the receiver picks up the documents whenever it chooses. This may be at a regular time several times a day, to allow those sending the documents to plan accordingly. This gives the receiving firm flexibility, particularly if orders are placed or released to be filled at certain times. The user's system does not need to be cluttered with information that will not be acted on immediately.

Another advantage of a VAN is that it can receive from and transmit to proprietary systems. This means that the supplier who has a customer or customers with proprietary systems does not need to have a dedicated terminal or direct link to each system. Many major corporations, such as General Motors and Coca-Cola, have chosen the VAN route for EDI.[5]

EDI and the Internet

Using EDI over the Internet is rapidly becoming a reality. After initial software purchase and systems setup, EDI over the Internet is virtually free, whereas VANs charge for services. An Internet Engineering Task Force—made of prominent companies such as Compaq, Hewlett-Packard, Digital Equipment Corporation, Microsoft, and Oracle—is working to ensure the capability of EDI products on the Internet.[6]

Major corporations such as NASA Goddard, AVEX Electronics, and UNISYS use the Internet for EDI, and it is likely just a matter of time before the Internet completely replaces VANs.[7]

Benefits of EDI Implementation.   Electronic data interchange is complex, but once in place it tends to be a very easy system with which to interface and communicate. The potential benefits of EDI are:

EDI Has Many Potential Benefits

- Reduced paperwork.
- Improved accuracy due to a reduction in manual processing.
- Increased speed of transmission of the order and other data.
- Reduced clerical/administrative effort in data entry, filing, mailing, and related tasks.
- Increased opportunity for proactive contribution by employees because less time is spent on clerical tasks.
- Reduced costs of order placement and related processing and handling.
- Improved information availability due to speed of acknowledgments and shipment advises.
- Reduced workload and improved accuracy of other departments through linking EDI with other systems, such as bar-coding inventory and electronic funds transfers (EFTs).
- Reduced inventory due to improved accuracy and reduced order cycle time.

---

[5]Mike Cassidy, "The Catalyst to Electronic Commerce," *EDI World,* April 1996, pp. 14–16.
[6]Rik Drummond, "EDI over the Internet Inter-operability," *EDI World,* April 1996, p. 8.
[7]Newton D. Swain, "Surfing for EDI information," *EDI World,* April 1996, p. 12; Howard Smith, "Caught in the Web," *EDI World,* July 1996, pp. 44–48.

One expert estimates that EDI can reduce the cost of processing a purchase order by 80 percent.[8] It is also possible to significantly reduce inventory as a result of improved inventory accuracy and reduced order cycle time. There are numerous examples of successful EDI implementation.

EDI at Oregon Steel Mills

Oregon Steel Mills, a small manufacturer of steel plate used in construction and military applications, implemented EDI in its traffic department. Using only personal computers, the firm transmitted bills of lading electronically to its major rail carrier. Errors were reduced, railcar tracing took minutes instead of hours, manpower requirements in the traffic department were reduced, and customer service levels were improved.[9]

Major retailers and manufacturers require that their suppliers provide specific barcode labeling and EDI advance shipment notices, which has had a great impact on warehouse operations and information systems.[10]

EDI at Baxter Healthcare

The labor-intensive nature of the transportation sector and its heavy paperwork made the transportation industry one of the first to turn to EDI. Baxter Healthcare uses EDI to communicate information on pickup and load status every 500 miles. All of the company's major carriers are set up on freight payment EDI and electronic funds transfer (EFT), and the company is moving toward self-invoicing, shipper-initiated billing.[11] Canadian National Railroad uses EDI to facilitate the movement of shipments between the United States and Canada.

EDI has become widely used within the supply chain for consumer and industrial goods. Firms such as Eastman Kodak, Xerox, American Express, Ford, and Honda of America use EDI for the majority of their products moving within their respective supply chains.[12]

Electronic Mail and the Internet.   A variation of EDI, *electronic mail,* involves electronic transmission of a variety of data and has become an important form of data transmission. The electronic mail market is a multibillion dollar business that has experienced tremendous growth. Electronic mail usually occurs over the Internet. Many individuals and organizations subscribe to online services such as America Online, Prodigy, and Gateway, which gives them access to many data sources and services (some for a fee) and allows them to send e-mail to Internet users at other organizations throughout the world.[13] Many companies, such as MCI, solicit bids and interact regularly with suppliers via e-mail.

Electronic Mail at United Van Lines

One of the major reasons for the growth in e-mail, in addition to the speed and accuracy of its data transmission, is cost savings. United Van Lines of St. Louis has been using e-mail for a number of years and has achieved significant cost savings as a result. Under its previous manual systems, United Van Lines spent several dollars to transmit a single communication. With electronic mail, the cost has been reduced to 30 cents a transmission.

---

[8]James Carbone, "Make Way for EDI," *Electronics Purchasing,* September 1992, pp. 20–24.

[9]"EDI Proves 'Godsend' to One-Man Department," *Traffic Management* 28, no. 8 (August 1989), pp. 56–67.

[10]Tim Stevens, "R_x for Logistics," *Industry Week,* September 18, 1995, p. 51.

[11]Ann Saccomano, "A Primer on Warehousing Information Technology," *Traffic World,* April 1996, pp. 24–26.

[12]Michael Hammer and James Champy, *Reengineering the Corporations* (New York: HarperCollins, 1993), pp. 90–91.

[13]For an extensive listing of data sources see Harley Hahn and Rick Stout, *The Internet Yellow Pages* (Berkeley, CA: Osborne McGraw-Hill, 1994).

Internet and E-Commerce

The auto industry has been slow to implement advanced communications systems, but that is changing. Ford Motor Company has announced that it plans to use the Internet to streamline suppliers and distribution of automobiles. Customers will be able to configure automobiles online and have them custom-made and delivered right to their doorstep in days (see Box 4–1 for more details). Ford is attempting to achieve a sustainable competitive advantage by transforming the entire supply chain for automobiles.

Box 4–1

At Ford, E-Commerce Is Job 1

The Rust Belt is approaching Net-speed. It was June 1999 when a Ford Motor Co. task force made a presentation to Chief Executive Jacques A. Nasser and his top managers. Originally assigned to study how the Internet could improve manufacturing, the team had gone all out, showing Nasser a computer simulation of the auto company of the future. The vision was breathtaking: factories that built cars to order, dealerships that reported problems instantly so that plants could make adjustments, and suppliers that controlled inventories at Ford factories—much the way retailer Wal-Mart Stores Inc. does when it gives vendors responsibility for stocking its store shelves. "We were mesmerized," says Alice Miles, a veteran Ford purchasing manager. Nasser gave it an instant thumbs-up. "This is nothing short of reinventing the auto industry," he says.

Since then, the old-line Ford has been latching on to the Net like some new dot-com. In January 2000 Ford showed off futuristic "24/7" concept vehicles packed with cyber-goodies such as Internet connections and e-mail. Miles now heads auto-xchange, a newly created online trading mart for Ford's 30,000 suppliers. And in an effort to wire up its far-flung workforce of 350,000 people, Ford announced on February 8, 2000, that it would offer each of them a home computer, a printer, and Internet access for $5 a month.

Some 90 years after Ford led the world into the era of mass manufacturing, the No. 2 auto maker wants to reprise its trailblazing role—and cash in the way it did decades ago. By using the Net to bust up bureaucracy and unleash radically new ways of planning, making, and selling cars, Ford could become a model of efficiency in the Internet Age. Streamlining suppliers and distribution using the Web could amount to savings equal to 25% of the retail price of a car, says analyst Jonathan Lawrence of Dain Rauscher. The auto-xchange mart could generate $3 billion in transaction fees within five years—of which Ford would get a hefty cut. And that doesn't take into account the monthly service fees of $20 to $25 that Ford could collect if drivers should want to hop on to the Net while roaring down the highway . . .

Nasser's vision is a sweeping one. He pictures the day when a buyer hits a button to order a custom-configured Ford Mustang online, transmitting a slew of information directly to the dealer who will deliver it, the finance and insurance units who will underwrite it, the factory that will build it, the suppliers that provide its components, and the Ford designers brainstorming future models. To buyers, it will mean getting just what they ordered delivered right to their doorstep in days.

Out in Front

Plenty of old-line manufacturers are moving into cyberspace, but none so boldly or so broadly as Ford. And, with the exception of archrival General Motors Corp., none on such a huge scale. In 1999, GM launched e-GM, an initiative to link its suppliers and dealers and to forge Net ties with consumers at their PCs and in their cars. GM, however, has not yet announced plans to wire up its entire workforce . . .

DaimlerChrysler and Toyota Motor Corp. are pursuing online ventures and experiments, but on a much smaller scale. Jurgen Hubbert, a member of DaimlerChrysler's management board, says he's not worried about rushing into grand Internet deals: "Why jump into this sort of business when nobody makes money?" he asks.

So far, Wall Street isn't impressed, either . . . Analysts wonder if Nasser has bitten off more than he can chew. While tantalized by the potential of e-business, they worry that all the cyberdazzle will distract Ford from its bread-and-butter task of designing and building cars and trucks.

Certainly, there are plenty of risks. Skeptics wonder if consumers really want vehicles loaded with costly gadgetry that may be prone to technical problems and obsolescence. "People want to bring their portable communications devices with them," says DaimlerChrysler Chairman Robert Eaton. "Are we going to embed all those devices in every car? No." And some suppliers fret that the big cost savings Ford says will result from its

continued

At Ford, E-Commerce Is Job 1 *continued*

online bazaar auto-xchange could instead squeeze vendors to the breaking point.

And for all its potential, e-commerce may find itself up against the biggest roadblock of all: a century-old industry with an infrastructure that impedes change. Slick new online ways to sell cars directly to buyers collide with an entrenched dealer base protected by tough state franchise laws. And systems that are capable of building custom cars actually clash with the economics of the high fixed costs that prod plant managers to run factories at full tilt.

It's not just ignorance that has made the Rust Belt slow to imitate such tech idols as Dell Computer Corp. Detroit is saddled with a much more complex manufacturing task than that faced by any computer outfit. Starting from scratch allowed Dell to create a state-of-the-art, direct-sales model. Over a 16-year period it has been able to tune its ordering and manufacturing processes—and update them for the Web. That's how it was able to custom assemble more than 25,000 different computer configurations for buyers last year. The company deals with hundreds of suppliers, but about 90% of its parts and components come from two dozen companies. And it works closely with them to make sure the parts are designed for snap-in assembly and for just-in-time delivery to its factories.

But even Dell's level of complexity is mere child's play compared with the challenges in the build-to-order auto business. Cars can contain 10,000 parts and, across Ford's entire line, some 1 million possible variations. Ford's F-150 full-size pickup truck, alone, is offered in well over 1,000 possible combinations of engine, transmission, body style, and color—without counting the truck's optional features.

To pull off the monumental task, Nasser has created a business group called ConsumerConnect that is driving the e-business efforts across company lines. He also went outside the company to find the team he wanted to lead it. Brian P. Kelley, 39, a former General Electric Co. appliance sales boss who was known there for championing customer communications and launching a GE Web site, was named to head ConsumerConnect last September. Since then, Kelley has recruited dozens of other Net whizzes from the likes of Whirlpool, Booz, Allen & Hamilton, and Procter & Gamble. Says Michelle Guswiler, director of corporate initiatives: "We see ourselves as a kind of Alpha squad, here to lead change and help make the cultural difference required to bring Ford into the 21st century."

One of ConsumerConnect's most promising efforts is auto-xchange, an online trading site where its 30,000 suppliers can be linked to Ford for quicker communication, better prices, and faster delivery. Analysts say auto-xchange could save Ford $8 billion in procurement prices, and nearly $1 billion more from reduced overhead, paperwork, and other transaction efficiencies each year. Ford owns a majority of auto-xchange, with Silicon Valley giants Oracle Corp. and Cisco Systems Inc. each having a stake.

The troika's plans for auto-xchange are much dreamier yet. They hope it will become so popular that everyone in the auto industry will use it to barter for parts and office supplies. Indeed, Wall Street is expecting that Ford will take auto-xchange public by 2001, when it would have estimated revenues of more than $500 million.

Bird's-Eye View

To make Ford's e-commerce ventures robust, there's a lot that must go on under the hood. Oracle is doing the heavy lifting on the software and databases needed to swap information and conduct transactions seamlessly. Cisco will provide much-needed networking expertise. And Microsoft Corp.'s CarPoint, an auto sales and information Web site, will help Ford develop a build-to-order service. Internet service provider UUNet, PC maker Hewlett-Packard, and middleman PeoplePC signed on to put Ford's sprawling workforce online . . .

Other tech partners are helping Ford get closer to its customers. Online Powerhouses Yahoo! and Priceline. com, along with Denver-based call-center wizard TeleTech, will design systems that deliver highly personalized warranty, loan, repair, and customized services based on more detailed knowledge of driver lifestyles and buying habits. "It could give us a bird's-eye view of what consumers want out of a car before we build it," says Ford design chief J Mays.

Meanwhile, ConsumerConnect and Ford's Visteon auto-parts unit are teaming up to wire future Fords for e-mail and news, voice-recognition systems, and satellite phone services that will, says Kelley, "turn the family car into a Web portal on four wheels." The payoff: a whole array of new services in a marketplace where basic car prices are declining. Better yet, Web services and phones can be sold on a subscription basis, generating monthly fees that keep cash flowing into Ford's coffers for the life of the car.

At Ford, E-Commerce Is Job 1 *concluded*

Given the risks, why does Nasser chance it—especially since Ford is already the most profitable player in the global auto industry? The Net offers a chance to reinvent manufacturing. Forget marginal efficiency improvements. At stake here is the holy grail of carbuilding: Changing from the century-old "push" model to a streamlined "pull" system would save auto makers billions of dollars. Traditionally, an auto plant cranks at full capacity—building a predetermined mix of cars—and ships them to dealers who then rely on strong-arm tactics or fat rebates to move the ones customers don't want.

Pinpoint Tailoring

In a pull model, customers decide what they want built. That could shorten the current 64-day average time from customer order to delivery, freeing a good chunk of the $60 billion now tied up in U.S. completed-vehicle inventories, say Ernst & Young auto consultant Lee A. Sage.

To do this, carmakers would need to deliver those cars swiftly. And they would need to tailor vehicles and pricing with pinpoint accuracy, or high-overhead factories would sit idle. Kelley says Ford hopes to deliver its first high-volume built-to-order vehicles within two years. The company would probably first offer certain popular combinations for quick delivery, taking more time for unusual configurations. Ford hopes to see the results in its bottom line within five years. By then, Kelley says, Ford's Net initiatives could save the company billions in waste.

Reinventing manufacturing while juggling high-tech alliances may be a Herculean task, but Nasser figures he has no choice. Still, Nasser is determined to forge ahead. "We're going to turn the old ways on their ears," he says. "It might not happen right away, but change is inevitable." Judging by Ford's progress since last June, Nasser intends to make sure the company wastes no time making it happen.

Source: Kathleen Kerwin, Marcia Stepanek, and David Welch, "At Ford, E-Commerce Is Job 1," *Business Week,* February 28, 2000, pp. 74–78.

Integrating Order Processing and the Company's Logistics Management Information System

The Order Processing System Initiates Many Activities

The order processing system initiates such logistics activities as:

- Determining the transportation mode, carrier, and loading sequence.
- Assigning inventory and preparing picking and packing lists.
- Carrying out warehouse picking and packing.
- Updating the inventory file, subtracting actual products picked.
- Automatically printing replenishment lists.
- Preparing shipping documents (a bill of lading if using a common carrier).
- Shipping the product to the customer.

Other computerized order processing applications include maintaining inventory levels and preparing productivity reports, financial reports, and special management reports.

Order Processing Provides Important Information to the MIS

Processing an order necessitates the flow of information from one department to another, as well as the referencing or accessing of several databases—such as customer credit status, inventory availability, and transportation schedules. The information system may be fully automated or manual; most are somewhere in between. Depending on the sophistication of the order processing system and the corporate management information system (MIS), the quality and speed of the information flow will vary, affecting the manufacturer's ability to achieve transportation consolidations and the lowest possible inventory levels. Generally, manual systems are very slow and error prone. The time required to complete various activities tends to be quite long and variable, and information delays occur frequently. Such a system seriously restricts a company's ability to implement integrated logistics management—specifically, to reduce total costs while maintaining or improving customer service. Some common problems include the inability to detect pricing errors, access timely credit information, or determine inventory availability. Negative results include invoice errors, payment delays, and inappropriate rejection of an order due to incorrect inventory information. Lost sales and higher costs combine to reduce the manufacturer's profitability.

Indeed, timely and accurate information has value. Information delays hamper the completion of all activities that follow them in the process. Automating and integrating the order process frees time and reduces the likelihood of information delays. Automation helps managers integrate the logistics system and allows them to reduce costs through reductions in inventory and freight rates. The communications network is clearly a key factor in achieving least total cost logistics.

Basic Need for Information

Benefits of a Logistics MIS

A logistics management information system is necessary in order to provide management with the knowledge to exploit new markets; to make changes in packaging design; to choose between common, contract, or private carriage; to increase or decrease inventories; to determine the profitability of customers; to establish profitable customer service levels; to choose between public and private warehousing; and to determine the number of field warehouses and the extent to which the order processing system should be automated. To make these strategic decisions, management must know how costs and revenue will change given the alternatives being considered.

Once management has made a decision, it must evaluate performance on a routine basis in order to determine (1) whether the system is operating in control and at a level consistent with original profit expectations, and (2) whether current operating costs justify an examination of alternative systems. This is referred to as *operational decision making*. The order processing system can be a primary source of information for both strategic and operational decision making.

An advanced order processing system is capable of providing a wealth of information to various departments within the organization. Terminals for data access can be made available to logistics management, production management, and sales/marketing management. The system can provide a wide variety of reports on a regularly scheduled basis, as well as status reports on request. It can also accommodate requests for all current reports, as well as a variety of data including customer order history, order status, and market and inventory position.

Designing the Information System

The design of a logistics management information system should begin with a survey of customer needs and a determination of standards of performance for meeting these needs. Next, customer needs must be matched with the current abilities of the firm, and current operations must be surveyed to identify areas that will require monitoring. It is important at this stage to interview various levels of management. In this way, the firm

Knowledge of Customer Needs Is the First Step in System Design

can determine what strategic and operational decisions are made, and what information is needed for decision making and in what form. Table 4–2 illustrates the various types of strategic and operational decisions that management must make within each of the functions of logistics.

TABLE 4–2   Typical Strategic and Operational Decisions by Logistics Function

Decision Type	Customer Service	Transportation	Warehousing	Order Processing	Inventory
Strategic	Setting customer service levels	Selecting transportation modes	Determination of number of warehouses and location	Extent of mechanization	Replenishment systems
		Freight consolidation programs	Extent of warehouse automation	Centralized or decentralized	Safety stock levels
		Common carriers versus private trucking	Public versus private warehousing		
Operational	Service level measurements	Rate freight bills	Picking	Order tracking	Forecasting
		Freight bill auditing	Packing	Order validation	Inventory tracking
		Claims administration	Stores measurement	Credit checking	Carrying-cost measurements
		Vehicle scheduling	Warehouse stock transfer	Invoice reconciliation	Inventory turns
		Rate negotiation	Staffing	Performance measurements	
		Shipment planning	Warehouse layout and design		
		Railcar management	Selection of materials-handling equipment		
		Shipment routing and scheduling			
		Carrier selection	Performance measurements		
		Performance measurements			

A Common Database Is Needed

The next stage is to survey current data processing capabilities to determine what changes must be made. Finally, a common database must be created and management reports designed, considering the costs and benefits of each. Figure 4–11 identifies the basic features of an integrated information system. A good system design must support the management uses previously described, and must have the capability of moving information from locations where it is collected to the appropriate levels of management. Telephones, teletypewriters, personal conversations, and computer-to-computer linkups are just a few of the means by which information can be transferred. In addition to information processing, the computerized information system must have a storage capability in order to hold information until it is required for decision making.

Sources of Data

Data for a logistics management information system can come from many sources. The most significant sources of data for the common database (see Figure 4–11) are (1) the order processing system, (2) company records, (3) industry data, and (4) management data.

The order processing system is capable of providing data such as customer locations, items demanded, revenue by customer and item, sales patterns (when items are ordered), order size, and salesperson. Company records can be used to provide manufacturing and logistics cost information, the cost of capital, company resources, and the amount spent on various items such as insurance, taxes, obsolescence, and damage.

FIGURE 4–11

The logistics information flow

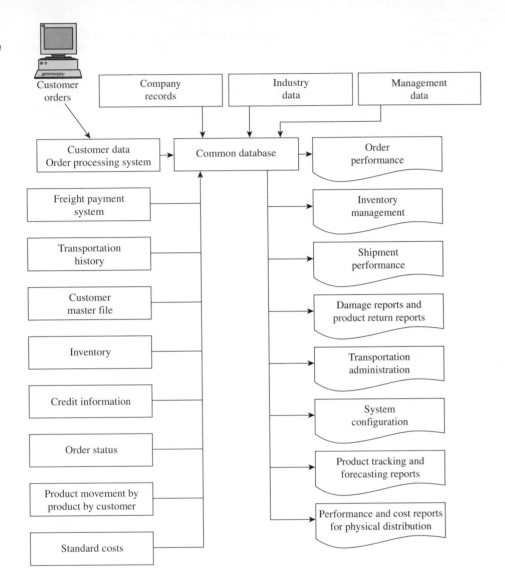

FIGURE 4–11

The logistics information flow

Industry data can be obtained from trade and professional organizations. Firms such as A. C. Nielsen Company sell statistics on competitors and their relative market shares. Professional journals and trade publications are a useful source of data; they may report on research projects and surveys of current practices. Statistics compiled by the federal government may also be of significant value, since they report such statistics as population shifts, inventory levels, housing starts, and consumer-credit expenditures.

Management can also provide the computerized database with useful input. This input may include likely reactions by competitors, future trends in sales, government policy, availability of supplies, and the probable success of alternative strategies.

Usually, the database contains computerized data such as the freight payment system, transportation history, inventory status, open orders, deleted orders, and standard costs for various logistics activities, as well as for marketing and manufacturing. The computerized information system must be capable of (1) data retrieval, (2) data processing, (3) data analysis, and (4) report generation.

Capabilities of a Computerized Information System

Using Information to Speed Execution

Most of the managerial challenges at Dell Computer have to do with what we call velocity-speeding the pace of every element of our business. Life cycles in our business are measured in months, not years, and if you don't move fast, you're out of the game. Managing velocity is about managing information—using a constant flow of information to drive operating practices, from the performance measures we track to how we work with our suppliers.

Performance Metrics

At Dell, we use the balance sheet and the fundamentals of the P&L on a monthly basis as tools to manage operations. From the balance sheet, we track three cash-flow measures very closely. We look at weekly updates of how many days of inventory we have, broken out by product component. We can then work closely with our suppliers so we end up with the right inventory. When it's not quite right, we can use our direct-sales model to steer customers toward comparable products that we do have. So we use inventory information to work both the front and back ends at the same time.

We also track and manage receivables and payables very tightly. This is basic blocking and tackling, but we give it a high priority. The payoff is that we have a negative cash-conversion cycle of five days—that is, we get paid before we have to pay our suppliers. Since our competitors usually have to support their resellers by offering them credit, the direct model gives us an inherent cost advantage. And the more we can shorten our cash-collection cycle, the greater our advantage.

The real-time performance measures in the P&L that we regard as the best indicators of the company's health are our margins, our average selling price, and the over-head associated with selling. We split the P&L into these core elements by customer segment, by product, and by country. These metrics can alert us instantly to problems, for example, with the mix of products being sold in any particular country.

Working with Suppliers

The greatest challenge in working with suppliers is getting them in sync with the fast pace we have to maintain. The key to making it work is information. The right information flows allow us to work with our partners in ways that enhance speed, either directly by improving logistics or indirectly by improving quality.

Take our service strategy, for example. Customers pay us for service and support, and we contract with third-party maintainers (TPMs) to make the service calls. Customers call us when they have problems, and that initial call will trigger two electronic dispatches—one to ship the needed parts directly from Dell to the customers' sites and one to dispatch the TPMs to the customers. Our role as information broker facilitates the TPMs' work by making sure the necessary parts will be on-site when they arrive.

But our role doesn't stop there. Because poor quality creates friction in the system, which slows us down, we want to capture information that can be used to fix problems so they won't happen again. So we take back the bad part to diagnose what went wrong, and we feed that information back to our suppliers so they can redesign the component. Clearly, we couldn't operate that way if we were dealing with hundreds of suppliers. So for us, working with a handful of partners is one of the keys to improving quality—and therefore speed—in our system.

Source: Kevin Rollins, *Harvard Business Review* 76, no. 2 (March–April 1998), p. 81.

Data retrieval is the capability of recalling data such as freight rates, standard warehousing costs, or the current status of a customer order. Basically, the data are still in their raw form; the computerized records allow fast and convenient access to the information.

Data processing is the capability to transform the data to a more useful form by relatively simple and straightforward conversion. Examples of data processing capability include preparation of warehousing picking instructions, preparation of bills of lading, and printing purchase orders.

Data analysis refers to taking the data from orders and providing management with information for strategic and operational decision making. A number of mathematical and statistical models are available to aid the firm's management, including linear programming and simulation models. Linear programming is probably the most widely used strategic and operational planning tool in logistics management. It is an optimization technique that subjects various possible solutions to constraints that are identified by management. Simulation is a technique used to model a situation so that management can determine how the system's performance is likely to change if various alternative strategies are chosen. The model is tested using known facts. Although simulation does not provide an optimal solution, the technique allows management to determine satisfactory solutions from a range of alternatives. A number of simulation models are available for purchase if the firm does not have the resources to develop its own.[14]

The last feature of an information system is *report generation.* Typical reports that can be generated from a logistics management information system include order performance reports; inventory management reports; shipment performance reports; damage reports; transportation administration reports; system configuration reports, which may contain the results of data analysis from mathematical and statistical models; and cost reports for logistics.

Using Logistics Information Systems to Support Time-Based Competition

Customers are becoming increasingly demanding. They want consistent delivery times; consistent order cycles; and excellent communications regarding in-stock availability and expected shipment arrival. In order to meet these demands, it is necessary to implement integrated logistics systems supported by integrated logistics information systems. These applications are aided by a number of technologies, such as bar coding, EDI, point-of-sale (POS) data gathering and transmission, and electronic funds transfer (EFT). Bar coding and POS technology can be linked to support quick response or efficient consumer response (ECR), considerably reducing the total order cycle time.

Bar Coding.   Bar codes can be seen on virtually all types of consumer packaged goods. A bar code is a sequence of parallel bars of various widths, with varying amounts of space between the bars. The pattern and spacing of the bars convey information such as letters, numbers, and special characters. These bars are optically read by scanning them with a beam of light. The information contained in the bars is either read directly into a computer or stored and downloaded into the computer system at a later time.

Texas Instruments Has Linked EDI and Bar Coding

Texas Instruments has linked EDI and bar coding in the order placement and management of office supplies, with positive results. The firm reduced cash tied up in inventory by $2 million, freed up 40,000 square feet of warehouse space, reassigned 11 employees away from office supply control, and reduced cycle time by more than one-third. Further, bar coding inbound shipments enabled the entire materials function to get more accurate accounts of actual receipts. The bar-code error rate has been estimated at from 1 in 10,000 to 1 in 1 million, compared with 1 in 25 or 30 for manually keyed data.[15]

---

[14]See *Logistics Software* (Oak Brook, IL: Council of Logistics Management, 1998).

[15]Ed Hatchett, "Combining EDI with Bar-Coding to Automate Procurement," *1992 National Association of Purchasing Management Conference Proceedings* (Tempe, AZ: National Association of Purchasing Management, 1992), pp. 45–50.

Emery Worldwide is spending $70 million to upgrade the information systems associated with its bar code–based package tracking system. The bar-code tracking system upgrade is a two-pronged program. Within Emery's Dayton, Ohio, hub, 120 holographic bar-code scanners are being installed to speed data capture for the 5.2 million pounds of packages that pass through daily. And throughout the country, 3,000 pen-based, portable wide area network terminals are being given to drivers for real-time exchange of package and routing data. There are benefits for Emery and customer alike.

Emory Worldwide Uses Scanners to Improve Labor Productivity and Routing

At the Dayton hub, "the new scanners will improve labor efficiencies and result in higher throughput with greater accuracy and reduced costs," says Tim Wendling, vice president of hub operations. "[On the road,] the system will allow us to shift from territory based driver routes to dynamic routing, resulting in greater driver productivity and significant increases in aircraft usage efficiencies." Wendling also expects to see an improvement "in customer service levels by substantially improving Emery's understanding of routing volumes early in the day." The rollout of the holographic scanners and portable terminals was expected in late 1999.

Information Provides Real-Time Update on Location of Package

Installation of the fixed-position scanners in the hub started in 1998. During the day, about 25,000 packages weighing a total of 1.5 million pounds pass through the center. The night is much busier. More than 50,000 packages weighing 3.7 million pounds arrive and leave. Emery specializes in heavy packages (those that weigh more than 5 pounds).

The information is used to update customers on the progress of their packages through Emery's delivery system. By knowing as early as possible what packages are due for delivery at each location daily, the company can assign routes to drivers based on volume rather than a geographic area. In addition to capturing data from each package on delivery, the terminals' 2.4 GHz radios exchange data with the service center over a wide area network. As a result, a driver can receive updated pickup and delivery schedules throughout the day. Availability of those data means that customers can get a real-time update on the location of a specific package. In addition, Emery knows sooner and more completely what has been picked up that day and will need to be shipped that night.[16]

Receiving also can be automated, which further contributes to cycle time reduction and data accuracy. Bar-code data can be used by the accounts payable department for generating checks and reconciling invoices with purchase orders and receiving. Bar coding represents a logical extension of the organization's information systems and a link with EDI.

Bar-code technology is advancing rapidly. Two-dimensional bar codes are gaining acceptance; these codes are capable of handling 100 times more data in the same space than ordinary bar codes.[17]

Point-of-Sale Data.   Point-of-Sale (POS) data gathering is simply the scanning of bar codes of items sold, generally at the retail level. The data may be transmitted to the relevant supplier, who can replenish the inventory based on sales. This type of system is used by Wal-Mart. In other cases, the retailer may prefer to intervene and use POS data to place the order itself.

POS Data Gathering at Wal-Mart

---

[16]Gary Forger, "How Emery Knows Where Your Package Is Every Step of the Way," *Modern Materials Handling* 54, no. 2 (1999), pp. A10–A11.

[17]Saccomano, "A Primer on Warehousing Information Technology," pp. 24–26; and Ginger Koloszyc, "New 2D Bar-code Standard Seen Benefiting Retail," *Stores* 80, no. 12 (1998), pp. 28–30.

Quick response (QR) and efficient consumer response (ECR) integrate the above technologies in an effort to speed time to market. Thus, they support time-based competition while reducing inventories and improving or maintaining customer service. For example, Levi Strauss & Company has integrated its customer order processing systems using a QR system called LeviLink. Retailers can order directly using EDI or allow Levi Strauss to place the orders for them. Invoices are transmitted by means of EDI, and customers can pay using electronic funds transfer.

The company has experienced increased sales with lower inventory levels, improving profits by 35 percent. Retailers benefit because LeviLink creates an electronic packing slip that can be verified by scanning bar-coded carton labels. This saves time in counting and matching paperwork such as the packing slip, invoice, and receiving document. Bar coding speeds stocking of products to shelves, freeing the retail employees to spend more time on the floor helping customers.[18]

Integrated information systems directly support an organization's total quality management (TQM) efforts by providing more accurate order fill. This occurs because the more automated the system, the less chance there is for human error. Such systems improve the quality of customer service by reducing order cycle time and improving order cycle consistency. In addition, they create the ability to provide the customer with real-time information regarding inventory availability, order status, and shipment status.

While the types of systems described focus on day-to-day operations, logistics information systems can be used to support strategic decision making. Other systems, such as decision support systems (DSSs) and artificial intelligence (AI) provide a great deal of flexibility and support for logistics decisions based on logistics information. DSSs and AI are presented briefly in the next sections.

Decision Support Systems

Decision support systems (DSSs) encompass a wide variety of models, simulations, and applications that are designed to ease and improve decision making. These systems incorporate information from the organization's database into an analytical framework that represents relationships among data and simulates different operating environments such as vehicle routing and scheduling. They may also incorporate uncertainty and what-if analyses, and use algorithms or heuristics. DSSs actually present an analysis and, based on the analysis, recommend a decision.

Artificial intelligence tools can be incorporated into DSS, which may contain decision analysis frameworks, forecasting models, simulation models, and linear programming models. They can be used to assist in a wide variety of logistics decisions, such as evaluating alternative transportation options, determining warehouse location, and setting levels of inventory.

While the use of DSSs is not currently widespread, it appears to be growing as the potential contribution becomes more understood, and computing costs continue to decline. Figure 4–12 shows the components of a DSS.

A DSS is applications oriented. More specifically, a DSS has the following objectives:

- To assist logistics executives in their decision processes.
- To support, but not replace, managerial judgment.
- To improve the effectiveness of logistics decisions.[19]

---

[18]Don Tapscott and Art Caston, *Paradigm Shift: The Promise of New Information Technology* (New York: McGraw-Hill, 1993), pp. 116–17.

[19]Eframin Truban, *Decision Support and Expert Systems* (New York: Macmillan, 1988), p. 8.

Decision support system

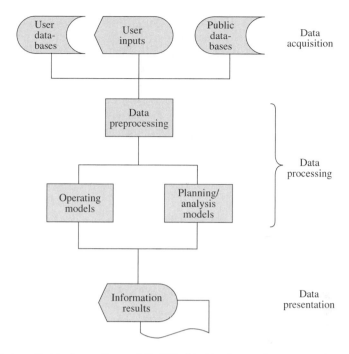

Source: Allan F. Ayers, *Decision Support Systems: A Useful Tool for Manufacturing Management* (King of Prussia, PA: K. W. Tunnell Company, 1985), p. 2.

Perhaps the most critical element of a DSS is the quality of the data used as input into the system. ADSS requires information about the environment that is both internal and external to the organization. Thus, an important first step in DSS planning, implementation, and control is to have good external information. This is described in Chapter 18 in conjunction with strategic planning. Models are also needed to provide data analysis.

Modeling can be defined as the process of developing a symbolic representation of a total system. A model must accurately represent the "real world" and be managerially useful. The purpose of models has been described as

The Purpose of Models

essentially . . . to replicate reality and assess the behavior of that reality if changes are introduced. A model supports, rather than replaces, the managerial decision-making process. By using a model, we are able to establish a current situation and then play "what-if" games. This "what-if" ability is significant. It allows us to quickly consider many different alternatives and test the outcome.[20]

Modeling at Pet Inc.

An interesting example of the use of logistics modeling in a corporate acquisition occurred in 1989 when Pet Inc., a manufacturer of specialty foods, acquired Van de Kamp's Frozen Seafood. Before the acquisition was completed, Pet used its in-house logistics model to evaluate the cost and service implications. Within three days after the acquisition, all of Van de Kamp's orders were being processed on Pet systems and all products were being distributed through Pet's logistics system.

---

[20]John H. Campbell, "The Manager's Guide to Computer Modeling," *Business* 32, no. 4 (October–December 1982), p. 11.

What's the payoff from this successful integration of systems and operations? From a quantitative standpoint, monthly inventories in 1989 dropped an average of nearly $1.5 million compared to the previous year. This was achieved despite a 10 percent increase in the number of cases sold.

Pet realized the highest inventory turnover rate in the company's history at 5.34. And the case-fill ratio has consistently hit the target of 98 percent. Notably, the distribution department accomplished this with no increase in manpower.[21] The company anticipated expanding its use of computer models to aid its marketing and logistics processes.

Artificial Intelligence and Expert Systems

Developed in the field of computer science, artificial intelligence (AI) is

Artificial Intelligence (AI) Defined

concerned with the concepts and methods of inference by a computer and the symbolic representation of the knowledge used in making inferences. The term *intelligence* covers many cognitive skills, including the ability to solve problems, to learn, to understand language, and in general, to behave in a way that would be considered intelligent if observed in a human.[22]

AI is a comprehensive term encompassing a number of areas, including computer-aided instruction, voice synthesis and recognition, game-playing systems, natural language translators, robotics, and expert systems (ES).[23] While the number of AI applications is limited, the potential in logistics is staggering. AI has been used to model response-time requirements for customer delivery; model transportation costs and times for various transportation models, locations, and routing; determine which warehouses should serve which plants, with which products, and what inventory levels; model customer service response with various levels of reliability; and perform sensitivity analysis to determine how much inputs can vary without affecting the structure of the optimal solution.[24]

Of specific interest to logistics executives are the subareas of AI known as *expert systems (ES),* natural language recognition, and neural networks. An ES is defined as

Expert Systems (ES) Defined

a computer program that uses knowledge and reasoning techniques to solve problems normally requiring the abilities of human experts. An expert system is an artificial intelligence (AI) program that achieves competence in performing a specialized task by reasoning with a body of knowledge about the task and the task domain.[25]

Expert systems are capable of being applied to a variety of problems in marketing and logistics, including interpretation, monitoring, debugging, repair, instruction, and control.[26]

Expert Systems at Xerox Corporation, Digital Equipment Corporation, and Eastman Kodak Company

Xerox Corporation, the multibillion-dollar office products equipment manufacturer and winner of the Malcolm Baldrige National Quality Award, has used expert systems to manage its vehicle routing and scheduling. Digital Equipment Corporation, the computer manufacturer, has used an ES to reduce work-in-process cycle times from

---

[21]Francis J. Quinn, "A Model Distribution System," *Traffic Management* 29, no. 6 (June 1990), p. 34.

[22]Mary Kay Allen and Omar Keith Helferich, *Putting Expert Systems to Work in Logistics* (Oak Brook, IL: Council of Logistics Management, 1990), p. A6.

[23]Omar K. Helferich, Stephen J. Schon, Mary Kay Allen, Raymond L. Rowland, and Robert L. Cook, "Applications of Artificial Intelligence—Expert System to Logistics," *Proceedings of the Annual Conference of the Council of Logistics Management,* vol. 1 (Oak Brook, IL: Council of Logistics Management, 1990), pp. 45–86.

[24]Paul S. Bender, "Using Expert Systems and Optimization Techniques to Design Logistics Strategies," *Proceedings of the Annual Conference of the Council of Logistics Management* (Oak Brook, IL: Council of Logistics Management, 1994), pp. 231–39.

[25]Allen and Helferich, *Putting Expert Systems to Work in Logistics,* p. A10.

[26]See Paul Harmon and David King, *Expert Systems* (New York: John Wiley, 1985), p. 94.

35 to 5 days by better managing work-in-process inventory and flows between operations. Eastman Kodak Company, the multinational firm that produces film and cameras, uses expert systems in its distribution centers to improve worker productivity in picking and palletizing products for shipment. For example, the training period for new employees was reduced from 6–12 weeks to 1–2 days.[27]

Five criteria aid decision makers in determining whether expert systems should be used to solve a particular logistics problem. If any of the criteria are met, an ES may be appropriate:

When Should an Expert System Be Used?

1. The task or problem solution requires the use of human knowledge, judgment, and experience.
2. The task requires the use of heuristics (i.e., rules of thumb) or decisions based on incomplete or uncertain information.
3. The task primarily requires symbolic reasoning instead of numerical computation.
4. The task is neither too easy (taking a human expert less than a few minutes) nor too difficult (requiring more than a few hours for an expert to perform).
5. Substantial variability exists in people's ability to perform the task. Novices gain competence with experience; experts are better than novices at performing the task.[28]

Artificial Intelligence and EDI Work Together at Benetton

If an ES is appropriate, the next decisions facing the logistics executive are whether the system can be economically justified and whether EDI can be combined with other systems such as artificial intelligence. At Benetton, the Italian clothing manufacturer, computers not only determine what will be included in upcoming production runs but also designate optimum routing for all finished goods.

At each Benetton store, the point-of-sale cash registers maintain a running inventory of item sales, which they transmit by way of EDI to computers in branch offices. The branch offices, in turn, transmit the data to the central office computer, which uses AI and a modeling program to make decisions on production runs. If red sweaters are selling fast, the computer tells the manufacturing system to design and produce more red sweaters. The system then determines how the shipments will be routed to the store, freeing the traffic department—which consists of only six people—to spend its time researching new routing and handling problems.[29]

Mead Corporation Uses Natural Language Processing

Natural Language Recognition.   Mead Corporation, a paper producer, has used the natural language capabilities of AI to make data stored within its computer system much more accessible to employees. It used to be that a simple request, like "Find the past use of a commodity," could take an hour, as workers sorted through pages and pages of reports. Mead's Decision Support Department suggested that the firm create an online database that would be voice accessible, using natural language processing. Since the advent of this system, workers can access the data in three minutes rather than in an hour, simply by verbally asking the system a question. This has contributed tremendously to the productivity of the purchasing function as well as other areas within the firm.[30]

---

[27]Allen and Helferich, *Putting Expert Systems to Work in Logistics,* pp. 14, 44–45.

[28]Ibid., p. 115.

[29]Marsha Johnston, "Electronic Commerce Speeds Benetton Business Dealings," *Software Magazine,* January 1994, pp. 93–95.

[30]Gary M. Bramble, Bette Clark, and Robert Florimo, "Artificial Intelligence in Purchasing," *1990 National Association of Purchasing Management Conference Proceedings* (Tempe, AZ: MAPM, 1990), pp. 186–90.

Neural Networks.   Neural networks are still in the development stages. They can be considered an offshoot of expert systems because they aid in decision making through the use of logic and rules. A key difference is that neural networks actually create their own rules based on past decisions and outcomes, rather than relying on an "expert." Once developed, these systems will be excellent for any repetitive activity that requires analysis of large amounts of data, more than a human could process effectively. As such, neural networks could be used to alert management to potential problems in supplier performance patterns, quality, delivery, invoicing, and similar issues. Airlines are "training" neural networks to forecast passenger traffic.[31]

Database Management

As previously mentioned, computers are excellent at managing data. A database management system allows application programs to retrieve required data stored in the computer system. The types of data stored were shown in Figure 4–12. A database management system must store data in some logical way, showing how different pieces of data are related, in order for retrieval to be efficient. This is a critical issue in logistics because of the large volume of data generated that may require analysis at a later date. For example, a buyer may want to see a history of order cycle times and fill rates of suppliers with whom orders for a particular item have been placed in the past six months.

Database Management Systems Must Perform Many Tasks

The database management system must be able to use the item number to reference the orders and "pull up" the pertinent data. If the buyer sees that two suppliers have been used, the buyer will want the system to provide a transaction history for those suppliers over a given time period. The database management system must have the flexibility to sort data in a variety of ways that are meaningful to the user.

Relational database structures are popular today because they allow access to and sorting of data by relating the data to other data. Increasingly, companies are using what is known as a local area network (LAN). This consists of a minicomputer linked to a number of microcomputers or terminals that allow access to a common database, software, and other systems features.[32] LANs give microcomputers the power of mainframe systems.

Regardless of the sophistication of the software and hardware, a system cannot provide good results if the data in the system are not accurate and timely. Thus, systems integrity is vital. If people do not use the system consistently (e.g., do not scan each bar-coded item individually), the system will quickly become inaccurate. Data accuracy problems are very difficult, costly, and time-consuming to correct.

Enterprise Resource Planning

Enterprise resource planning (ERP) products are

> enterprise-wide transactional tools which capture data and reduce the manual activities and tasks associated with processing financial, inventory and customer-order information.
>
> One of the fundamental keys to improving core business processes for most organizations is fast and accurate integration, capture and retrieval of information. ERP systems achieve a high level of integration by utilizing a single data model, developing a common understanding of what the shared data represent and establishing a set of rules for accessing data. ERP systems within a single company utilize a common database as the basis for com-

---

[31]Kyundo Nam and Thomas Schaefer, "Forecasting International Airline Passenger Traffic Using Neural Networks," *Logistics and Transportation Review* 31, no. 3 (1995), pp. 239–51.

[32]Ellram and Birou, *Purchasing for Bottom-Line Impact,* p. 149.

munication within the organization, with individual information systems accessing data via any number of standard networking protocols.

Although the concept of a single data model across a supply chain is an elegant solution to the problem of sharing data, it has proved difficult to implement, even inside large enterprises. Unlike today's ERP systems, supply chain solutions must be able to cope with the complexity of integrating information across any number of disparate information systems spanning the entire length of the supply chain. This issue has been partially addressed—previously by EDI and, more recently, by universal acceptance of the Internet and associated protocols as a standard communications mechanism between businesses. However, communications have been limited to standard transactional information, not proactive decision-support data.

While integration of key business transactions across the supply chain is crucial to success, it is only part of the equation when the desired outcome is a fully integrated supply chain management solution.[33]

SAP AG, a German firm, is the world leader in providing ERP software.[34] Its flagship product is known as R/3. Many of the world's largest companies use the software, including, in the United States, Baxter Healthcare, Exxon, and even the software giant Microsoft. The software consists of four major modules: Financial Accounting, Human Resources, Manufacturing and Logistics, and Sales and Distribution.

The software is designed to operate in a three-tier client/server configuration. As shown in Figure 4–13, the core of the system is a high-speed network of database servers. These database servers are special computers designed to efficiently handle a large database of information. The applications, which consist of the modules listed above, can be run on separate computers. The applications are networked around the database cluster

FIGURE 4–13

SAP triple client/server configuration

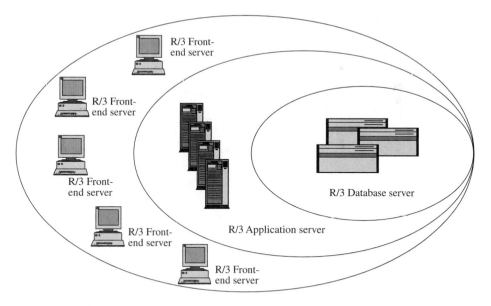

Source: Jonathan Blain, *Using SAP R/3* (Indianapolis, IN: Que, 1996), p. 42; and Nancy H. Bancroft, *Implementing SAP R/3: How to Introduce a Large System into a Large Organization* (Greenwich, CT: Manning Publications, 1996), as reported in Richard B. Chase, Nicholas J. Aquilano, and F. Robert Jacobs, *Production and Operations Management,* 8th ed. (Burr Ridge, IL: Richard D. Irwin, 1998), p. 655.

---

[33]Bruce Richmond, Ann Burns, Jay Mabe, Linda Nuthall, and Rick Toole, "Supply Chain Management Tools," in *Strategic Supply Chain Alignment,* ed. John L. Gattorna (Hampshire, England: Gower, 1998), pp. 512–13.

[34]The rest of the section is adapted from Richard B. Chase, Nicholas J. Aquilano, and F. Robert Jacobs, *Production and Operations Management,* 8th ed. (Burr Ridge, IL: Richard D. Irwin, 1998), pp. 654–56.

TABLE 4–3   SAP R/3 Application Modules

SAP Application	Program
Cross application (CA)	Business Process Technology (CA-BPT)
	CAD Integration (CA-CAD)
Project system (PS)	Project Planning (PS-PLN)
	Project Execution/Integration (PS-EXE)
Logistics general (LO)	Logistics Information System (LO-LIS)
	Master Data (LO-MD)
Human resources (HR)	Workforce Planning (PD-WFP)
Personnel administration (HR-PA)	Time Management (PA-TIM)
	Incentive Wages (PA-INW)
Production planning (PP)	Sales and Operations Planning (PP-SOP)
	Master Planning (PP-MP)
	Capacity Requirements Planning (PP-CRP)
	Material Requirements Planning (PP-MRP)
	Kanban/Just-in-Time Production (PP-KAB)
	Repetitive Manufacturing (PP-REM)
	Assembly Orders (PP-ATO)
	Production Planning for Process Industries (PP-PI)
	Plant Data Collection (PP-PDC)
Materials management (MM)	Material Requirements Planning (MM-MRP)
	Purchasing (MM-PUR)
	Inventory Management (MM-IM)
	Warehouse Management (MM-WM)
	Electronic Data Interchange (MM-EDI)
Quality management (QM)	Planning Tools (QM-PT)
	Inspection Processing (QM-IM)
	Quality Control (QM-QC)
	Quality Certificates (QM-CA)

Source: Adapted from Richard B. Chase, Nicholas J. Aquilano, and F. Robert Jacobs, *Production and Operations Management,* 8th ed. (Burr Ridge, IL: Richard D. Irwin, 1998), p. 655.

and have independent access to it. Users communicate with the applications through the front-end servers, which typically are PCs running Microsoft Windows NT.

The R/3 applications are fully integrated so that data are shared among all applications. If, for example, an employee posts a shipping transaction in the Sales and Distribution module, the transaction is immediately seen by Accounts Payable in the Financial Accounting module, and by Inventory Management in the Materials Management module. The Manufacturing and Logistics module has applications that support many of the topics described in this book. Table 4–3 shows the impressive list of features that are packaged with the software. Similar lists could be developed for the Accounting, Finance, and Marketing functional areas. However, many users of SAP also use "bolt-on" software provided by i^2 Technologies or Manugistics, which support more supply chain–specific applications.

In a sense, SAP has changed the face of information technology. We now have an enterprisewide integrated system, and management can now consider the automation of the firm's basic business processes. However, it is not really this simple. The problem is that many of the applications do not line up with the way companies operate. The SAP consultants argue that the modules are designed around industry "best practices." But this, in many cases, means that a firm wishing to use SAP needs to change its

FIGURE 4–14

Typical view of enterprise applications

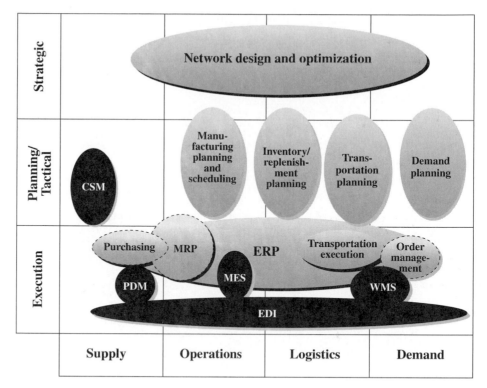

Key: CSM = Component Source Management
      MES = Manufacturing Execution System
      PDM = Product Data Management
      WMS = Warehouse Management System

Source: Mary Lou Fox, Senior Vice President of Product and Industry Marketing, Manugistics, Inc., 1999.

practices to those implemented by the SAP programmers. This can be a painful and time-consuming process.

Figure 4–14 is a representation of how ERP systems and EDI are positioned relative to other logistics management and supply chain management tools that will be described in later chapters of this text. The figure shows the applications within the firm that must be integrated prior to implementation across the supply chain.

Financial Considerations

Cost Justification for an Advanced Order Processing System

Of course, it will be necessary to justify an advanced order processing system or any other investment in information systems through a cost/benefit analysis. The costs of developing the system, start-up costs, can be justified by discounting the improvement in cash flows associated with the new system and comparing them to the initial investment. In most cases, cash flow will improve by changing to an advanced order processing system if the volume of orders processed is large. In smaller operations, this may not be true if the proposed system is more than the company needs.

In any case, the difference in cash flow that results from implementing the proposed system can be calculated using the framework shown in Figure 4–1 (p. 147). It is important, when the cash flow is calculated, to include in the analysis only those costs

FIGURE 4–15

Total order cycle with variability both before and after implementing an advanced order processing system

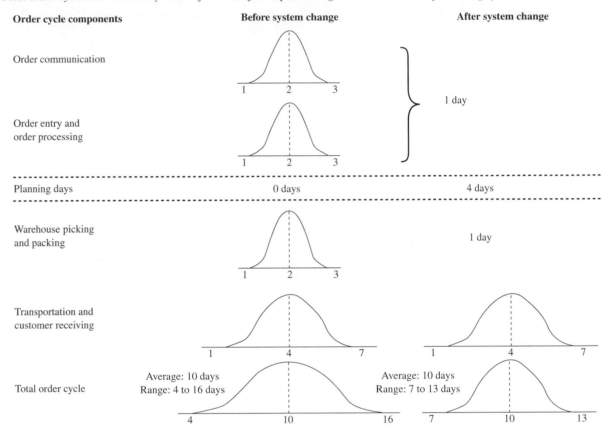

that will change with the system change. Usually, the most significant cost differences will occur in the order processing, inventory, transportation, and warehousing cost components. More information on measuring and selling the value of logistics will be provided in Chapter 17.

Figure 4–15 illustrates how an advanced order processing system can free time for planning. By reducing order communication, order entry, and order processing time from an average of four days to one day, on the average three days are made available for planning. This planning time means that sales forecasting and production scheduling receive sales information three days sooner, as do the managers of logistics activities such as warehousing, transportation, and inventory management. The advance notice at field warehouses allows the more productive allocation of orders to level volume. In any case, it is possible to plan so that all orders are shipped from warehouse locations after the sixth day. In essence, then, four days are available for planning warehouse picking and packing, consolidating transportation, and reducing levels of safety stock. This assumes, of course, that the manufacturer's customers find a 10-day order cycle acceptable, and a reduction in order cycle is not given to them. If transportation and customer receiving are the only variabilities remaining in the order cycle, variability in the total order cycle can be reduced from 6 days (when the order cycle ranged from 4 to 16 days) to 3 days (with the order cycle ranging from 7 to 13 days). This improvement in order cycle consistency allows the manufacturer's customers to cut their safety stocks by half. In fact, the increased planning time often results in a reduction in transit time and transit time variability. In this example, the results might be an additional day of planning time, and a customer order cycle ranging from 9 to 11 days. In any case, the entire channel of distribution becomes more efficient and realizes cost savings as a result of the advanced order processing application. In addition, the improved customer service may create increased sales and market share for the manufacturer.

Generally, the fixed costs associated with an advanced order processing system are higher than those incurred by a manual system. However, the variable costs per order are significantly less with the advanced system. We will expand this type of cost analysis in Chapter 16, which deals specifically with the calculation of logistics cost savings.

Summary

In this chapter we saw how the order processing system can directly influence the performance of the logistics function. We also examined how order processing systems can be used to improve customer communications and total order cycle time, and/or lead to substantial inventory reductions and transportation efficiencies. Information is vital for the planning and control of logistics systems, and we saw how the order processing system can form the basis of a logistics information system.

Modern computer technology and communication systems make it possible for management to have the information required for strategic and operational planning of the logistics function. The latest technology in information systems can significantly improve the quality of decision making. We also described decision support systems and other information-related tools for logistics management. In Chapter 5 we will look at the financial impact of holding inventory and show you how to calculate inventory carrying costs.

Suggested Readings

Bookbinder, James H., and David M. Dilts. "Logistics Information Systems in a Just-in-Time Environment." *Journal of Business Logistics* 10, no. 1 (1989), pp. 50–67.

Bundy, William. "Leveraging Technology for Speed and Reliability." *Supply Chain Management Review* 3, no. 1 (1999), pp. 62–69.

Emmelhainz, Margaret A. "Strategic Issues of EDI Implementation." *Journal of Business Logistics* 9, no. 2 (1988), pp. 55–70.

Fontanella, John. "The Web-Based Supply Chain." *Supply Chain Management Review* 3, no. 4 (2000), pp. 17–20.

Henriott, Lisa L. "Transforming Supply Chain into e-Chains." *Supply Chain Management Review Global Supplement* 3, no. 1 (1999), pp. 15–18.

Lewis, Ira, and Alexander Talalayevsky. "Logistics and Information Technology: A Coordination Perspective." *Journal of Business Logistics* 18, no. 1 (1997), pp. 141–57.

Mulligan, Robert M. "EDI in Foreign Trade: Case Studies in Utilization." *The International Journal of Physical Distribution and Logistics Management* 28, no. 9/10 (1998), pp. 794–804.

Murphy, Paul R., James M. Daley, and Patricia K. Hall. "EDI Issues in Logistics." *Journal of Business Logistics* 19, no. 2 (1998), pp. 89–102.

Salcedo, Simon, and Ann Grackin. "The e-Value Chain." *Supply Chain Management Review* 3, no. 4 (2000), pp. 63–70.

Schary, Philip B., and James Coakley. "Logistics Organization and the Information System." *The International Journal of Logistics Management* 2, no. 2 (1991), pp. 22–29.

Sheffi, Yosef. "The Shipment Information Center." *The International Journal of Logistics Management* 2, no. 2 (1991), pp. 1–12.

Weiss, Martin A. "Implications of Electronic Order Exchange Systems for Logistics Planning and Strategy." *Journal of Business Logistics* 5, no. 1 (1984), pp. 16–39.

Williams, Lisa R., George D. Magee, and Yoshinori Suzuki. "A Multidimensional View of EDI: Testing the Value of EDI Participation to Firms." *Journal of Business Logistics* 19, no. 2 (1998), pp. 73–87.

Williams, Lisa R., and Kant Rao. "Information Technology Adoption: Using Classical Adoption Models to Predict AEI Software Implementation." *Journal of Business Logistics* 19, no. 1 (1998), pp. 5–16.

Questions and Problems

1. What do wholesalers and retailers perceive to be the order cycle provided to them by a manufacturer?

2. Explain the impact of order cycle variability on the inventory levels of wholesalers and retailers.

3. How is logistics performance affected by the order processing system used?

4. What are the primary advantages associated with the implementation of an integrated and automated order processing system?

5. Electronic data interchange applications have experienced significant growth in recent years. Why do you believe this growth in EDI has occurred? What are the primary benefits of EDI? Do you think that the growth rate in EDI applications will be sustained? Why or why not?

6. In this chapter, we described how Ford Motor Company was planning to use e-commerce to link with customers and suppliers. One of management's goals was to use the Internet to enable Ford to build cars to individual customer orders. What are the logistics implications of this strategy for Ford, its customers and suppliers, and the efficiency of the entire supply chain?

7. How does the order processing system form the foundation of the logistics management information system?

8. How is the logistics management information system used to support planning of logistics operations?

9. Explain how point-of-sale data and bar coding contribute to supply chain integration.

10. Company X operates an order processing department whose costs consist of monthly lease charges, indirect labor (customer service reps and data entry clerks), supervisory salaries, and a charge for general corporate burden. The division is treated as a cost center whose expenses are first accumulated and then allocated back to other cost and profit centers on the basis of their ability to bear such charges.

    The company is currently investigating ways in which a more equitable order processing charge can be assessed to its user divisions. As a first step, you have been asked to investigate the behavior of costs in the department to determine if there is a significant relationship between volume (as measured by orders processed) and total departmental cost. You have secured the following data (which have been adjusted for inflation):

Quarter	Number of Orders Processed	Departmental Cost
1	40,000	44,000
2	64,000	52,000
3	52,000	40,000
4	90,000	68,000
5	50,000	48,000
6	58,000	48,000
7	76,000	61,000
8	88,000	64,000
9	62,000	54,000
10	85,000	60,000
11	72,000	54,000
12	80,000	68,000

    Determine the breakdown of fixed and variable expenses by:

    a. Analyzing the change in costs with respect to volume changes in each year.

    b. Drawing a scatter diagram on the accompanying graph and making reasonable inferences regarding cost behavior.

    Note: If you need to refresh your memory about regression analysis and scatter diagrams (graphing the data), see Chapter 5.

11. Show the impact that implementation of an automated order processing system would have on a manufacturer's return on investment, given the following information:

The analysis of costs in an order processing departmnet—scatter diagram approach

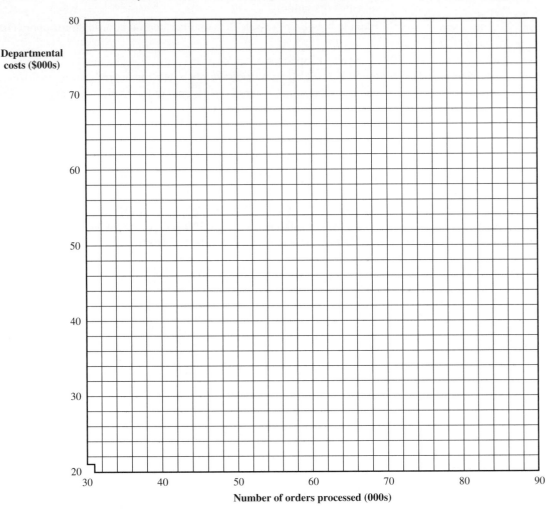

a. Net profit after taxes is $2 million.

b. Return on assets is currently 10 percent.

c. With the current system, customer orders are mailed; salespeople collect them and either hand-carry them to sales offices (where they are telephoned or mailed to headquarters) or telephone or mail orders directly to headquarters.

d. With the proposed order processing system, customers will telephone orders to inside salespeople (customer service representatives) equipped with computer terminals, who immediately input the order.

e. The proposed order processing system will provide management with four additional planning days and eliminate two days of variability in the order cycle.

f. The planning time made available by the proposed order processing system will enable management to reduce inventories by $2 million; achieve $450,000 in transportation savings as a result of consolidations; and reduce handling charges in public warehouses by $75,000 as a result of direct plant-to-customer shipments.

g. The proposed system will increase order processing costs by $225,000 per year.

h. The non–cost-of-money components of inventory carrying costs are 5 percent of the inventory value.

i. The company is experiencing capital rationing and could achieve a 20 percent after-tax rate of return on additional capital if it were available.

12. Explain how the proposed order processing system described in question 11 would affect the customer service levels provided by the manufacturer.

Chapter Outline

Chapter Objectives

- To show how inventory investment influences corporate profit performance.
- To show how inventory management contributes to least total cost logistics.
- To show how to calculate inventory carrying costs.
- To show the impact of inventory turns on inventory carrying costs in total and per unit.
- To show how inventory carrying costs will differ according to a firm's position in the supply chain.

Introduction

Inventory represents the largest single investment in assets for most manufacturers, wholesalers, and retailers. Highly competitive markets have led to a proliferation of products, as companies attempt to satisfy the needs of diverse market segments. In addition, in most industries, customers have become accustomed to high levels of product availability. For many firms, the result has been higher inventory levels. In manufacturing companies, inventory investment is typically 10 percent or more of total assets and in some cases can exceed 20 percent of total assets. For wholesalers and retailers, inventory investment as a percentage of total assets is usually more than 20 percent and may approach 50 percent (see Table 5–1).

Inventory Must Compete with Other Investments

Inventory management therefore is an important activity. The capital invested in inventories must compete with other investment opportunities available to the firm, and the out-of-pocket costs associated with holding inventory can represent a significant cost of doing business. Management must know inventory carrying costs to make informed decisions about logistics system design, customer service levels, the number and location of distribution centers, inventory levels, inventory storage, transportation modes, production schedules, and minimum production runs. For example, ordering in smaller quantities on a more frequent basis will reduce inventory investment but will typically result in higher ordering costs and increased transportation costs. It is necessary to compare the savings in inventory carrying costs to the increased costs of ordering and transportation to determine how the decision to order in smaller quantities will affect profitability. A determination of inventory carrying costs is also necessary for new-product evaluation, the evaluation of price deals and discounts, make-versus-buy decisions, and profitability reports. From a total supply chain standpoint, the inventory carrying costs at different tiers will have a significant impact on where inventories should be positioned within the supply chain. It is thus imperative to take a detailed look at inventory carrying costs.

Financial Aspects of Inventory Strategy

The quality of inventory management and the inventory policies a firm sets can have a significant impact on corporate profitability and management's ability to implement least total cost logistics.

Inventory and Corporate Profitability

Excessive Inventories Can Lower Profitability

Inventory represents a significant portion of a firm's assets. Consequently, excessive inventory levels can lower corporate profitability in two ways: (1) net profit is reduced by out-of-pocket costs associated with holding inventory, such as insurance, taxes, storage, obsolescence, damage, and interest expense, if the firm borrows money specifically to finance inventories; and (2) total assets are increased by the amount of the inventory investment, which decreases asset turnover. The result is a reduction in return on assets and return on net worth.

For example, ABC Company's financial data are summarized in Figure 5–1. As a result of poor forecasting, lack of attention to inventory management, and the absence of an integrated systems approach to the management of logistics, the company's inventory is $6 million too large. What would be the impact on profitability and return on net worth of a change in management practice if (1) the cash made available from

TABLE 5–1 Selected Financial Data for Manufacturers, Wholesalers, and Retailers for 1998
($ Millions)

Companies	Sales	Cost of Goods Sold	Net Profits	Net Profits as a Percentage of Sales	Total Assets	Inventory Investment	Inventories as a Percentage of Assets	Number of Inventory Turns
Manufacturers								
Abbott Laboratories	$ 12,478	$ 5,394	$ 2,333	18.7%	$ 13,216	$ 1,411	11%	3.8
Clorox	2,741	1,193	298	10.9	3,030	212	7	5.6
Colgate Palmolive	8,972	4,290	849	9.5	7,685	746	10	5.8
Ford Motor	144,416	104,782	22,071	15.3	237,545	5,656	2	18.5
General Electric	100,469	31,772	9,296	9.3	355,935	6,049	2	5.3
General Mills	6,246	2,594	535	8.6	4,140	427	10	6.1
Goodyear Tire & Rubber	12,626	9,673	682	5.4	10,589	2,165	20	4.5
Harris Corp.	3,939	2,165	133	3.4	3,784	604	16	3.6
Lucent	30,147	16,156	970	3.2	26,720	3,081	12	5.2
3M	15,021	8,744	1,175	7.8	14,153	2,219	16	3.9
Procter & Gamble	37,154	21,064	3,780	10.2	30,966	3,284	11	6.4
Pfizer	13,544	2,094	3,351	24.7	18,302	1,828	10	1.2
Sara Lee	20,012	12,208	1,191	6.0	10,580	2,624	25	4.7
Whirlpool	10,323	7,805	325	3.2	7,935	1,100	14	7.1
Xerox	19,449	5,724	395	2.0	30,024	3,269	11	1.8
Wholesalers and Retailers								
Baxter International	$ 6,599	$ 3,623	$ 315	4.8%	$ 10,085	$ 1,324	13%	2.7
Bergen Brunswig	17,122	16,371	3	0.02	3,003	1,458	49	11.2
CVS	15,274	11,144	383	2.5	6,736	3,190	47	3.5
Dayton Hudson	30,951	22,634	935	3.0	15,666	3,475	22	6.5
Fleming Companies	15,069	13,594	511	3.4	3,491	984	28	13.8
Kmart	33,674	26,319	518	1.5	14,166	6,536	46	4.0
Nordstrom	4,852	3,296	186	3.8	2,865	826	29	4.0
Sears, Roebuck	41,322	27,257	1,048	2.5	37,675	4,816	13	5.7
Wal-Mart Stores	117,958	93,438	3,526	3.0	45,384	16,497	36	5.7
Winn-Dixie	13,617	9,994	199	1.5	3,069	1,405	46	7.1

Note: Ending inventory figures are used for inventory investment. All figures are for 1998.

the $6 million reduction in inventory were used to repay a bank loan at 10 percent interest; and (2) the total of the other out-of-pocket costs saved by the reduction in inventory equaled 5 percent of the inventory value? Figure 5–2 gives the answers:

- Current assets and total assets are reduced by $6 million.
- Asset turnover increases from 1.67 times to 1.85 times.
- Total expenses are reduced by $900,000 ($600,000 in fixed interest expense plus $300,000 in other fixed expenses).
- Net profit before taxes increases by $900,000, but income taxes increase by $450,000, resulting in an increase in after-tax net profit of $450,000.
- Net profit margin increases from 5 percent to 5.45 percent.
- Return on assets increases from 8.35 percent to 10.08 percent.

FIGURE 5–1

*The strategic profit model
with financial data
for ABC Company
($ millions)*

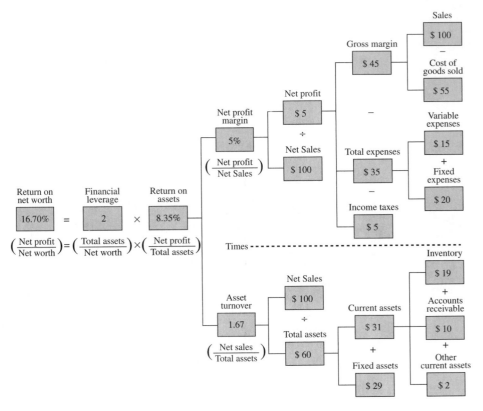

Note: Income taxes are assumed to equal 50 percent of net profit before taxes.

- Financial leverage declines from 2 to 1.8.
- Return on net worth increases from 16.70 percent to 18.15 percent.

Capital Rationing Raises the Cost of Carrying Inventory

If the company is experiencing capital rationing, however—that is, if there is not enough money to invest in all of the new projects available—then management has to decide where to invest the money from the inventory reduction and at what rate of return. For example, if ABC were to invest the money in plant modernization that would reduce manufacturing costs and yield a 20 percent after-tax return (which equals 40 percent before tax), this opportunity cost should be reflected in the analysis. Excluding the cost of capital, the out-of-pocket costs associated with the inventory investment equal 5 percent of the inventory value. How will a $6 million reduction in inventory affect the company's return on net worth? Figure 5–3 shows that

- Current assets are reduced by the $6 million inventory reduction, and fixed assets are increased by $6 million, the cost of the plant modernization.
- Total assets and asset turnover remain the same.
- As a result of improved production efficiency, the cost of goods sold is reduced by $2.4 million ($6 million × 40 percent) and gross margin increases from $45 million to $47.4 million.

FIGURE 5–2

*Impact of inventory
reduction on ABC
Company's net worth
when bank loan is repaid
($ millions)*

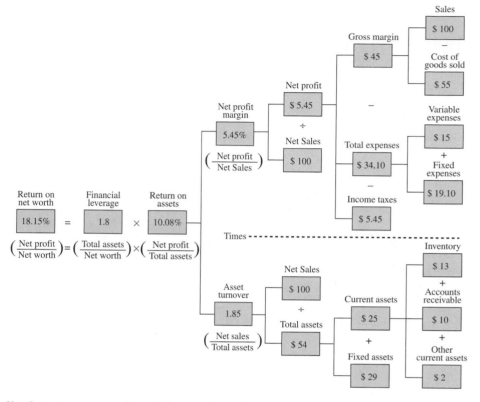

Note: Income taxes are assumed to equal 50 percent of net profit before taxes.

- Fixed expenses and total expenses are reduced by $300,000 in inventory-
  related expenses ($6 million × 5 percent).
- Net profit before taxes increases by $2.7 million but income taxes increase by
  $1.35 million, resulting in an increase in after-tax net profit of $1.35 million.
- Net profit margin increases from 5 percent to 6.35 percent.
- Return on assets increases from 8.35 percent to 10.60 percent.
- Financial leverage remains at 2.
- Return on net worth increases from 16.70 percent to 21.20 percent.

Both examples show that holding too much inventory can erode net profits and
return on net worth. However, as can be seen from Figures 5–2 and 5–3, companies
experiencing capital rationing will benefit the most from inventory reductions. In order
to establish the optimal inventory stocking strategy, management has to think in terms
of the cost trade-offs required in a logistics system.

Inventory and Least Total Cost Logistics

**Inventory Carrying
Costs Impact
Logistics Policies**

Least total cost logistics is achieved by minimizing the total of the costs illustrated in Figure 5–4 for a specified level of customer service. However, successful implementation of

FIGURE 5–3

*Impact of inventory
reduction on ABC
Company's net worth
when capital rationing
exists ($ millions)*

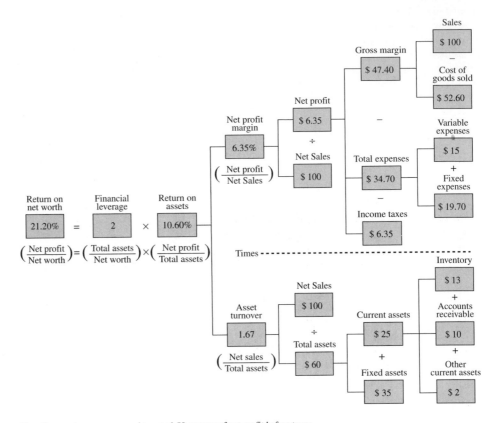

Note: Income taxes are assumed to equal 50 percent of net profit before taxes.

cost trade-off analysis requires that adequate cost data be available to management. Management should not set inventory levels and inventory turnover policies arbitrarily, but instead with full knowledge of inventory carrying costs and total logistics system costs.

The cost of carrying inventory has a direct impact not only on the number of warehouses that a company maintains but also on all of the firm's logistics policies. Given the same customer service level, low inventory carrying costs lead to multiple warehouses and a slower mode of transportation, such as railroads. High inventory carrying costs, on the other hand, result in a limited number of stock locations and require a faster means of transportation, such as motor or air carriers, in order to minimize total costs. Without an accurate assessment of the costs of carrying inventory, it is unlikely that a company would choose the logistics policies that would minimize costs.

In addition, knowledge of the cost of carrying inventory is required to accurately determine economic manufacturing quantities, economic order quantities, and sales discounts, all of which are usually calculated on the basis of estimated costs in the majority of companies that use these formulas. (We will discuss these formulas in Chapter 6.)

FIGURE 5–4

Cost trade-offs required in marketing and logistics

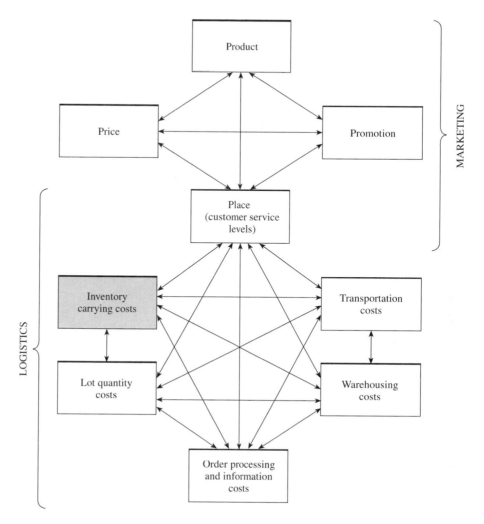

MARKETING OBJECTIVE: Allocate resources to the marketing mix in such a manner as to maximize the long-term profitability of the firm.

LOGISTICS OBJECTIVE: Minimize Total Costs given the customer service objective where Total costs = Transportation costs + Warehousing costs + Order processing and information costs + Lot quantity costs + Inventory carrying costs.

Source: Adapted from Douglas M. Lambert, *The Development of an Inventory Costing Methodology: A Study of the Cost Associated with Holding Inventory* (Chicago: National Council of Physical Distribution Management, 1976), p. 7.

Inventory Carrying Costs

Inventory carrying costs, the costs associated with the quantity of inventory stored, include a number of different cost components and generally represent one of the highest costs of logistics.[1] The magnitude of these costs and the fact that inventory levels

---

[1]This section draws heavily from Douglas M. Lambert, *The Development of an Inventory Costing Methodology: A Study of the Costs Associated with Holding Inventory* (Chicago: National Council of Physical Distribution Management, 1976).

are influenced by the configuration of the logistics system demonstrate the need for an accurate assessment of inventory carrying costs, if the appropriate trade-offs are to be made within the firm and within the supply chain. Nevertheless, most managers who consider the cost of holding inventory use estimates or traditional industry benchmarks.

What Is the Cost of Carrying Inventory?

We have seen how inventory levels can affect corporate profit performance, and have described the need for assessment of inventory carrying costs in logistics system design. The next question might be: What inventory carrying cost percentages are managers currently using for logistics system design decisions (cost trade-off analysis) and such things as determining economic order quantities and sales discounts?

Unfortunately, in many companies inventory carrying costs have never been calculated, even though these costs are both real and substantial. When inventory carrying costs are calculated, they often include only the current interest rate plus such expenditures as insurance and taxes. Also, many managers use traditional textbook percentages or industry averages. All of these approaches have problems.

Textbook Carrying Costs Are Suspect

First, there are only a few special circumstances in which the current interest rate is the relevant cost of money (we will explore these shortly). Traditional textbook percentages also have serious drawbacks. Table 5–2 contains a number of estimates of inventory carrying costs that are widely referenced in logistics and inventory management literature.

The 12 to 34 percent range presented by George Aljian's *Purchasing Handbook* covers a range so large that picking a number within the range would allow a manager to cost-justify almost any inventory policy.[2] The 1960 *Harvard Business Review* article by John Magee has the same shortcoming as the Aljian publication, but Magee recognized that the cost of money should be applied only to the out-of-pocket investment in inventory.[3] In the 1974 *Management Accounting* article by Thomas Hall, carrying cost was calculated to be 20.4 percent, but Hall added an after-tax cost of capital to the other components, which were pretax numbers.[4] In addition, he included in the calculations storage costs that were not variable with the quantity of inventory held.

The publications listed in Table 5–2 cover the years 1951 to 1999. However, most of the carrying costs percentages used during that period were about 25 percent. If 25 percent was an accurate number in 1951, how could it be accurate in 1990, when during that period the prime interest rate fluctuated between 3 percent and 20 percent?

Inventory Carrying Costs Should Not Be Based on Industry Averages

Finally, there is the method of using inventory carrying costs that are based on industry averages. Businesspeople, for the most part, seem to find comfort in such numbers, but many problems are inherent with this practice. For example, would the logistics executive of a cosmetics manufacturer want to compare his or her firm to Avon, a company that sells its products door to door, or Revlon, a company that sells its products through major department stores? Or—even worse—would the executive use an average of the two companies? This latter approach, of course, would compare the executive's firm to a nonentity—no company at all.

Even if two companies are very similar in terms of the manufacture and distribution of their products, the availability of capital may lead to two very different inventory strategies. That is, one firm may experience shortages of capital—capital rationing—and

[2]George W. Aljian, *Purchasing Handbook* (New York: McGraw-Hill, 1958), pp. 9–29.

[3]John F. Magee, "The Logistics of Distribution," *Harvard Business Review* 38, no. 4 (July–August 1960), p. 99.

[4]Thomas W. Hall, "Inventory Carrying Costs: A Case Study," *Management Accounting* 55, no. 7 (January 1974), pp. 37–39.

TABLE 5–2   **Estimates of Inventory Carrying Cost**

Author	Publication	Estimate of Carrying Costs as a Percentage of Inventory Value
L. P. Alford and John R. Bangs (eds.)	*Production Handbook* (New York: Ronald Press, 1955), p. 397	25%
George W. Aljian	*Purchasing Handbook* (New York: McGraw-Hill, 1958), pp. 9–29.	12–34
Dean S. Ammer	*Materials Management* (Homewood, IL: Richard D. Irwin, 1962), p. 137.	20–25
Donald J. Bowersox and David J. Closs	*Logistical Management* (New York: McGraw-Hill, 1996), pp. 254–58.	19.25*
Joseph L. Cavinato	*Purchasing and Materials Management* (St. Paul, MN: West Publishing, 1984), p. 284.	25
John J. Coyle, Edward J. Bardi, and C. John Langley Jr.	*The Management of Business Logistics,* 6th ed. (St. Paul, MN: West Publishing, 1996), pp. 200–7.	25
Gordon T. Crook	"Inventory Management Takes Teamwork," *Purchasing,* March 26, 1962, p. 70.	25
Thomas W. Hall	"Inventory Carrying Costs: A Case Study," *Purchasing,* March 25, 1962, p. 70.	20.4
J. L. Heskett, N. A. Glaskowsky Jr., and R. M. Ivie	*Business Logistics,* 2nd ed. (New York: Ronald Press, 1973), p. 20.	28.7
James C. Johnson, Donald F. Wood, Daniel L. Wardlow, and Paul R. Murphy Jr.	*Contemporary Logistics,* 7th ed. (Upper Saddle River, NJ: Prentice Hall, 1999), pp. 302–4.	25
John F. Magee	"The Logistics of Distribution," *Harvard Business Review,* July–August 1960, p. 99.	20–35
Benjamin Melnitsky	*Management of Industrial Inventory* (Conover-Mast Publication, 1951), p. 11.	25
Thomson M. Whitlin	*The Theory of Inventory Management* (Princeton, NJ: Princeton University Press, 1957), p. 20.	25

*19.25% is given as an average, with a range of 9% to 50%.

the other may have an abundance of cash. The former has a cost of money for inventory decisions of 40 percent pretax, which is the rate of return the company is earning on new investments. The latter has a cost of money of 5 percent pretax, which is the interest rate the company is earning on its cash. If both of these companies are well managed, which one is likely to have the most inventory? The company with the 5 percent cost of money will. Because of the lower cost of money, this company will increase inventory levels, move toward transporting carload and/or truckload quantities of its products, and have longer production runs. The company with the 40 percent cost of money will have lower inventories but will accomplish it by incurring higher production setup costs, higher transportation costs, and/or more stockouts. Each company may have what represents least total cost logistics, and yet one may turn its inventories 12 times per year and the other 6 times. Transportation costs as a percent of sales may be significantly higher for the company with the 40 percent cost of money. However, if either company were to change any component of its logistics system in order to match the other's performance, total costs could increase and return on net worth could decrease.

Calculating Inventory Carrying Costs

**Four Components
of Inventory
Carrying Costs**

Each company should determine its own logistics costs and strive to minimize the total of these costs, given its customer service objectives. Inventory carrying costs should include only those costs that vary with the quantity of inventory and that can be categorized into the following groups: (1) capital costs, (2) inventory service costs, (3) storage space costs, and (4) inventory risk costs.

Capital Costs on Inventory Investment.   Holding inventory ties up money that could be used for other types of investments. This reasoning holds for internally generated funds as well as capital obtained from sources external to the firm, such as debt from banks and insurance companies or from the sale of common stock. Consequently, the company's opportunity cost of capital—the rate of return that could be realized from some other use of the money—should be used to accurately reflect the true cost involved. In companies experiencing capital rationing—that is, in most companies—the *hurdle rate* (which is the minimum rate of return on new investments) should be used as the cost of capital. When capital rationing is not in effect, it is necessary to determine where the cash from a reduction in inventory would be invested. If the money would be invested in marketable securities, then that is the rate of return for inventory carrying cost purposes. If the money would be placed in a bank account or used to reduce some form of debt, then the appropriate interest rate applies. The same logic applies for increases in inventories. What rate of return will be forgone on the cash invested in inventory?

Some companies differentiate among projects by categorizing them according to risk and looking for rates of return that reflect the perceived level of risk. For example, management could group projects into high, medium, and low categories of risk. High-risk projects might include investments in new products, since market acceptance is difficult to predict, or new equipment for the plant, if technology is changing so rapidly that the equipment could be obsolete soon. The desired rate of return on high-risk projects might be 25 percent after tax. Medium-risk projects, on the other hand, may be required to obtain an 18 percent after-tax return. Low-risk projects, which may include such investments as warehouses, private trucking, and inventory, might be expected to achieve an after-tax return of 10 percent. In such a company, corporate aversion to risk may require that cash made available by a reduction in inventory be used for another low-risk category investment. Consequently, the cost of money for inventory carrying costs would be 10 percent after taxes, which equals 20 percent before taxes (assuming a 50 percent tax rate).[5] All inventory carrying cost components must be stated in before-tax numbers, because all of the other costs in the trade-off analysis, such as transportation and warehousing, are reported in before-tax dollars.

In some very special circumstances, such as the fruit-canning industry, short-term financing may be used to finance the seasonal buildup of inventories. The seasonal building of inventory stands in contrast to the inventories determined by the strategic deployment of product to achieve least total cost logistics. In the latter case, any change in inventory will affect the quantity of inventory carried throughout the year and usually will compete with other long-term investments for funding. In the former situation, the inventory buildup is short-term and the actual cost of borrowing is the acceptable cost of money.

---

[5]If the marginal tax rate is not 50 percent, simply divide the after-tax rate of return by 1 minus the marginal tax rate.

Once management has established the cost of money, it must determine the out-of-pocket (cash) value of the inventory for which the inventory carrying cost is being calculated. For wholesalers or retailers, the out-of-pocket value of the inventory is the current replacement cost of the inventory, including any freight costs paid, or the current market price if the product is being phased out. In the case of manufacturers, it is necessary to know which costing alternative is being used. For example, is the company using direct costs to determine the inventory value, or is it using some form of absorption costing?

Direct versus Absorption Costing

Direct costing is a method of cost accounting based on segregating costs into fixed and variable components. For management planning and control purposes, the fixed–variable cost breakdown yields more information than that obtained from current financial statements designed for external reporting. Under direct costing, the fixed costs of production are excluded from inventory values, and therefore inventory values more closely reflect the out-of-pocket cost of their replacement. With *absorption costing* (otherwise known as full costing or full absorption costing), which is the traditional approach used by most manufacturers, fixed manufacturing overhead is included in the inventory value.

In addition to the distinction between direct costing and absorption costing, companies may value inventories based on actual costs or standard costs. There are four distinct costing alternatives:

1. *Actual absorption costing* includes actual costs for direct material and direct labor, plus predetermined variable and fixed manufacturing overhead.
2. *Standard absorption costing* includes predetermined direct material and direct labor costs, plus predetermined variable and fixed overhead.
3. *Actual direct costing* includes actual costs for direct material and direct labor, plus predetermined variable manufacturing overhead; it excludes fixed manufacturing overhead.
4. *Standard direct costing* includes predetermined costs for direct material and direct labor, plus predetermined variable manufacturing overhead; it excludes fixed manufacturing overhead.

The preceding material on methods of inventory valuation supports the conclusion that using industry averages for inventory carrying costs is not a good policy. This is because the various component percentages may not be calculated using comparable inventory valuation systems.

The situation is complicated even further if one considers the various methods of accounting for inventory. Most manufacturing companies use one of the following three methods of accounting for inventory:

Three Methods of Accounting for Inventory

1. *First-in, first-out (FIFO):* Stock acquired earliest is assumed to be sold first, leaving stock acquired more recently in inventory. Under FIFO, inventory is valued near the current replacement cost.
2. *Last-in, first-out (LIFO):* Sales are made from the most recently acquired stock, leaving items acquired in the earliest time period in inventory. This method attempts to match the most recent costs of acquiring inventory with sales. In periods of rising prices, LIFO will result in lower inventory valuation, higher cost of goods sold, and lower profits than the FIFO method. The converse is true when prices are declining.
3. *Average cost:* This method could be a moving average, in which each new purchase is averaged with the remaining inventory to obtain a new average price, or a weighted average, in which the total cost of the opening inventory plus all purchases is divided by the total number of units.

Neither FIFO nor LIFO isolates and measures the effects of cost fluctuations. However, when standard costing is used, the currently attainable standards, when compared to actual costs, provide a measure of cost variance—gains or losses—that can be reported separately.[6]

Determining the Cash Value of Inventory

For the purposes of calculating inventory carrying costs, it is immaterial whether the company uses LIFO, FIFO, or average cost for inventory valuation. The value of the inventory for calculating carrying costs is determined by multiplying the number of units of each product in inventory by the standard or actual direct (variable) costs associated with manufacturing the product and moving it to the storage location. The way a manufacturer decreases its inventory investment is to sell a unit from inventory and not produce a replacement. Hence, the cash made available is equal to the cash saved by not replacing the unit. Similarly, inventories are increased by manufacturing more product than is currently demanded. Consequently, in either case, it is the current manufacturing costs that are relevant for decision making, since these are the costs that will be incurred if inventories are increased or not incurred if inventory is decreased. Likewise, if products are held in field locations, the transportation cost incurred to move them there plus the variable costs associated with moving them into storage are costs that are inventoried, just as are direct labor costs, direct material costs, and the variable manufacturing overhead. For example, the out-of-pocket value of a unit of product stored in a public warehouse is equal to the variable manufacturing costs, plus the transportation from the plant to the warehouse and the handling charge paid to the public warehouse.

The implicit assumption is that a reduction in finished goods inventory will lead to a corresponding reduction in inventory throughout the manufacturer's internal logistics system (see Figure 5–5). That is, a one-time reduction in finished goods inventory results in a one-time reduction in raw materials purchases, as inventory is pushed back through the system. Similarly, a planned increase in finished goods inventory results in a one-time increase in the quantity of raw materials purchased and subsequently pushed through the system. If we multiply the one-time change in inventory value, a balance sheet account, by the opportunity cost of money, the resulting figure reflects the annual cost of having the money invested in inventory; this cost is a profit and loss statement account. All other components of the inventory carrying cost are annual costs that affect the profit and loss statement, as do the other logistics cost categories such as transportation, warehousing, lot quantity, and order processing.

In summary, many businesspeople think that inventory is a relatively liquid and riskless investment. For this reason, they feel that they can justify a somewhat lower return on inventory investments. However, inventory requires capital that could be used for other corporate investments, and by having funds invested in inventory a company forgoes the rate of return that it could obtain with such investments. Therefore, the company's opportunity cost of capital should be applied to the investment in inventory. The cost of capital should be applied to the out-of-pocket investment in inventory. Although most manufacturers use some form of absorption costing for inventory, only variable (direct) manufacturing costs are relevant. That is, the company's minimum acceptable rate of return, or the appropriate opportunity cost of money, should be applied only to the variable costs directly associated with the inventory. In the case of wholesalers and retailers, or the purchased materials of manufacturers, the out-of-pocket investment in

Capital Costs Equal the Opportunity Cost of Money, Times the Out-of-Pocket Investment in Inventory

---

[6]Students who want to read more about direct and absorption costing and the methods of accounting for inventory should refer to Charles T. Horngren, George Foster, and Srikant Datar, *Cost Accounting: A Managerial Emphasis,* 9th ed. (Englewood Cliffs, NJ: Prentice Hall, 1996).

FIGURE 5–5

Inventory positions in the manufacturer's logistics system

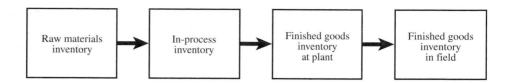

Assumptions: A one-time increase (decrease) in finished goods inventory results in a one-time increase (decrease) in raw materials purchased.

inventory is simply the current replacement cost plus transportation costs if they are not included in the purchase price of the products.

Inventory Service Costs.   Inventory service costs are comprised of ad valorem (personal property) taxes and fire and theft insurance paid as a result of holding the inventory. Taxes vary depending on the state in which inventories are held. Tax rates can range from zero in states where inventories are exempt to as much as 20 percent of the assessed value. In general, taxes vary directly with inventory levels. Many states exempt inventories from taxation if they are placed into storage for subsequent shipment to customers in another state. Thus, with proper planning a company can minimize this component when establishing a warehousing network.

Taxes

Insurance

Insurance rates are not strictly proportional to inventory levels, since insurance is usually purchased to cover a certain value of product for a specified time period. Nevertheless, an insurance policy will be revised periodically based on expected inventory level changes. In some instances, an insurance company will issue policies in which premiums are based on the monthly amounts insured. Insurance rates depend on the materials used in the construction of the storage building, its age, and considerations such as the type of fire prevention equipment installed.

The actual dollars spent on both insurance and taxes during the past year can be calculated as a percentage of that year's inventory value and added to the cost of money component of the carrying cost. If budgeted figures are available for the coming year, they can be used as a percentage of the inventory value based on the inventory plan—the forecasted inventory level—in order to provide a future-oriented carrying cost. In most cases, there will be few if any significant changes from year to year in the tax and insurance components of the inventory carrying cost.

Storage Space Costs.   We will consider four general types of facilities: (1) plant warehouses, (2) public warehouses, (3) rented or leased (contract) warehouses, and (4) company-owned (private) warehouses.

Plant Warehouses

The costs associated with plant warehouses are primarily fixed. If any costs are variable, they are usually variable with the amount of product that moves through the facility (throughput) and not with the quantity of inventory stored. If there are some variable costs such as the cost of taking inventory or any other expenses that would change with the level of inventory, management should include them in inventory carrying costs. Fixed charges and allocated costs are not relevant for inventory policy decisions. If the firm can rent out the warehouse space or use it for some other productive purpose instead of using it for storing inventory, and if the associated opportunity costs are not readily available to the manager, then it may make sense to use the allocated costs as surrogate measures. However, the best approach would be to estimate the appropriate opportunity costs.

Public Warehouses

Public warehouse charges are usually based on the amount of product moved into and out of the warehouse (handling charges) and the amount of inventory held in storage (storage charges). In most cases, handling charges are assessed when the products are moved into the warehouse and storage charges are assessed on a periodic basis, such as monthly. Sometimes, the first month's storage also must be paid when the products are moved into the facility. In effect, this makes the first month's storage a handling charge since it must be paid on every case of product regardless of how long it is held in the warehouse.

The use of public warehouses is a policy decision management makes because it is the most economical way to provide the desired level of customer service without incurring excessive transportation costs. For this reason, handling charges, which represent the majority of costs related to the use of public warehouses, should be considered as throughput costs; that is, they should be thought of as part of the warehousing cost category of the cost trade-off analysis, and not part of inventory carrying costs. Only charges for warehouse storage should be included in inventory carrying costs, since these are the public warehouse charges that will vary with the level of inventory.

In situations where a throughput rate (handling charge) is given based on the number of inventory turns, it is necessary to estimate the storage cost component by considering how the throughput costs per case will change if the number of inventory turns changes. Of course, the public warehouse fees that a company pays when its inventory is placed into field storage should be included in the value of its inventory investment.

Rented or Leased Warehouses

Rented or leased warehouse space is normally contracted for, and the contract is in force for a specified period of time. The amount of space rented is based on the maximum storage requirements during the period covered by the contract. Thus, warehouse rental charges do not fluctuate from day to day with changes in the inventory level, although rental rates can vary from month to month or year to year when a new contract is negotiated. Most costs, such as rent payment, the manager's salary, security costs, and maintenance expenses, are fixed in the short run. But some expenses, such as warehouse labor and equipment operating costs, vary with throughput. During the term of the contract, few if any costs vary with the amount of inventory stored.

All of the costs of leased warehouses could be eliminated by not renewing the contract and are therefore a relevant input for logistics decision making. However, operating costs that are not variable with the quantity of inventory stored, such as those outlined in the preceding paragraph, should not be included in the carrying costs. Rather, these costs belong in the warehousing cost category of the cost trade-off analysis. The inclusion of fixed costs, and those that are variable with throughput in inventory carrying costs, has no conceptual basis. Such a practice is simply incorrect and will result in erroneous decisions.

Company-Owned Warehouses

The costs associated with company-owned warehouses are primarily fixed, although some may be variable with throughput. All operating costs that can be eliminated by closing a company-owned warehouse or the net savings resulting from a change to public warehouses should be included in warehousing costs and not in inventory carrying costs. Only those costs that vary with the quantity of inventory belong in inventory carrying costs. Typically, in company-owned warehouses, these costs will be negligible.

Inventory risk costs vary from company to company, but typically include charges for (1) obsolescence, (2) damage, (3) shrinkage, and (4) relocation of inventory.

Obsolescence

The cost of *obsolescence* is the cost of each unit that must be disposed of at a loss because it can no longer be sold at regular price. Obsolescence cost is the difference between the original cost of the unit and its salvage value, or the original selling price and the reduced selling price if the price is lowered (marked down) to move the product. This figure may or may not show up on the profit and loss statement as a separate item. Usually, obsolescence costs are buried in the cost of goods manufactured account or the cost of goods sold account. Consequently, managers may have some difficulty arriving at this figure.

Damage

The cost of *damage* should be included only for the portion of damage that is variable with the amount of inventory held. Damage incurred during shipping should be considered a throughput cost, since it will continue regardless of inventory levels. Damage attributed to a public warehouse operation is usually charged to the warehouse operator if it is above some specified maximum amount. Often damage is identified as the net amount after claims.

Shrinkage

Shrinkage has become an increasingly important problem for American businesses. Many authorities think inventory theft is a more serious problem than cash embezzlement. Theft is far more common and involves far more employees, and it is hard to control. However, shrinkage costs may be more closely related to company security measures than inventory levels, even though they will definitely vary with the number of warehouse locations. It varies by industry, but security is a major issue in both materials management and transportation. In some companies, security costs related to inventories are a significant expense that varies with the amount of inventories. Shrinkage can also result from poor record keeping, or shipping wrong products or quantities to customers. In many companies, shrinkage costs are more likely to vary with the number of warehouse locations than the amount of inventory, and management finds it more appropriate to assign some or all of these costs to the warehousing cost category.

Relocation Costs

Relocation costs are incurred when inventory is transshipped from one warehouse location to another to avoid obsolescence. For example, products that are selling well in the Midwest may not be selling on the West Coast. By shipping the products to the location where they will sell, the company avoids the obsolescence cost but incurs additional transportation costs. Transshipments to avoid obsolescence or markdowns are the result of having too much inventory, and the cost should be included in inventory carrying costs. Often, transshipment costs are not reported separately, but are simply included in transportation costs. In such cases, a managerial estimate or a statistical audit of freight bills can isolate the transshipment costs. The frequency of these types of shipments will determine which approach is most practical in any given situation. That is, if such shipments are rare, the percentage component of the carrying cost will be very small and a managerial estimate should suffice.

In some cases, firms may incur transshipment costs as a result of inventory stocking policies. For example, if inventories are set too low in field locations, stockouts may occur and may be rectified by shipping product from the nearest warehouse location that has the item(s) in stock. The transportation costs associated with transshipments to avoid stockouts are a result of decisions that involve trade-offs between transportation costs, warehousing costs, inventory carrying costs, and/or stockout costs. They are transportation costs and should not be classified as inventory carrying costs.

Since managers do not always know just how much of damage, shrinkage, and relocation costs are related to the amount of inventory held, they may have to determine mathematically whether a relationship exists. For example, a cost for damage may be available, but the amount of this cost due to the volume of inventory may not be known. Damage can be a function of such factors as throughput, general housekeeping, the quality and training of management and labor, the type of product, the protective packaging used, the material handling system, the number of times that the product is

TABLE 5–3   **Damage and Corresponding Inventory Levels at Various Points in Time**

	Time Periods						
	1	*2*	*3*	*4*	*5*	*6*	*7*
Y, damage ($ 000)	80	100	70	60	50	70	100
X, inventory ($ millions)	11	15	13	10	7	9	13

handled, how it is handled, and the amount of inventory (which may lead to damage as a result of overcrowding in the warehouse). To say which of these factors is most important and how much damage each one accounts for is extremely difficult. Even an elaborate reporting system may not yield the desired results, as employees may try to shift the blame for the damaged product. The quality of damage screening during the receiving function, and the fact that higher inventories may hide damaged product until inventories are reduced, may contribute to the level of damage reported, regardless of the cause.

Using Regression Analysis to Determine Inventory-Related Costs

To determine the portion of a cost that is variable with inventory, an analyst can use regression analysis or plot the data graphically.[7] Consider the damage rates and inventory levels shown in Table 5–3. Simple linear regression can be used as a tool for segregating the portion of a cost component that is related to the level of inventory held. The principal objective in simple linear regression analysis is to establish a quantitative relationship between two related variables. In order to establish the relationship between two variables, X and Y, a number of paired observations similar to those in Table 5–3 must be obtained.

For example, we are able to obtain the total damage figure in dollars for a number of time periods, but we do not know how much of this damage is directly related to the level of inventory. The first pair of observations ($Y = 80$, $X = 11$) indicates that $80,000 worth of damage occurred in the period when inventory was $11 million.

Now the data can be plotted on graph paper, with each pair of observations represented by a point on the chart (see Figure 5–6). A point is obtained by plotting the independent variable, X, along the horizontal axis and the dependent variable, Y, along the vertical axis. When all the pairs of observations have been plotted, a straight line is drawn that attempts to minimize the distance of all the points from the line. (The statistical technique referred to as least-squares regression minimizes the sum of the squared distances of all of the points from the line.)

Once this has been done, any two points, A and B, should be selected on the estimated regression line. The increment in the damage from A to B and the change in the inventory from A to B should be expressed as a percentage:

$$(\Delta D / \Delta I) \times 100\% = \frac{\$10,000 \times 100\%}{\$2,000,000} = 0.5\%$$

[7]For more information on regression analysis, refer to any basic statistics book. For example, see Terry Sincich, *A Course in Modern Business Statistics*, 2nd ed. (San Francisco: Delien Publishing Company, 1994).

FIGURE 5–6

Graphing the relationship between damage and inventory levels

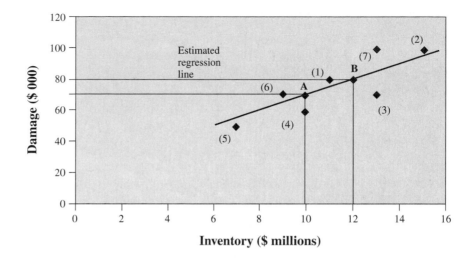

The 0.5 percent can be interpreted as the percentage of the inventory investment that is damaged because product is being held in inventory. This percentage can be added to the other cost components to determine the total carrying cost percentage. Note that if damage does in fact increase with increased levels of inventory, then the estimated regression line must move upward to the right. A line that is vertical, horizontal, or sloping downward from the left indicates that such a relationship does not exist. The ability to successfully fit a line through the plotted points will depend on the degree of correlation, that is, the strength of the relationship present. If the points are scattered all over, this indicates that no relationship exists. A moderate correlation exists when the points are all situated relatively close to the estimated regression line. A perfect correlation exists when all of the points fall on the line. This is a correlation of 1.0. The closer the correlation is to 1.0, the stronger the relationship.

Figure 5–7 summarizes the method that should be used to calculate inventory carrying costs. The model is normative, because using it will lead to a carrying cost that accurately reflects a firm's costs.

Industry Examples

Now let's examine an actual application of the method of calculating inventory carrying costs for a manufacturer of packaged goods, followed by an example from the bulk chemicals industry.

A Consumer Packaged Goods Industry Example

Using the method summarized in Figure 5–7, the consumer packaged goods manufacturer found it necessary to calculate costs for the following four basic categories: (1) capital costs, (2) inventory service costs, (3) storage space costs, and (4) inventory risk costs.

Capital Costs.   In order to establish the opportunity cost of capital—the minimum acceptable rate of return on new investments—an interview was conducted with the company's comptroller. Due to capital rationing, the current hurdle rate on new investments

FIGURE 5–7

*Normative model
of inventory carrying
cost method*

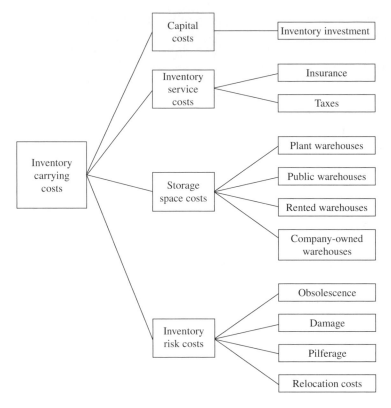

Source: Douglas M. Lambert, *The Development of an Inventory Costing Methodology: A Study of the Costs Associated with Holding Inventory* (Chicago: National Council of Physical Distribution Management, 1976), p. 68.

was 15 percent after taxes (30 percent before taxes). The company conducted a post-audit of most projects in order to substantiate the rate of return. This was required by corporate policy, and in the majority of cases the desired rate of return was achieved, although there was considerable variability on individual marketing projects. The difficulty in estimating the rate of return on marketing projects was caused by the inability to forecast the market's acceptance of new products. Consequently, the cost of money used for inventory carrying costs was set at 30 percent before taxes. A before-tax cost of money is required, since all of the other components of inventory carrying cost and the other cost categories in logistics cost trade-off analysis, such as transportation and warehousing, are before-tax numbers.

**A Before-Tax Cost
of Money is Required**

The opportunity cost of capital should be applied only to the out-of-pocket investment in inventory. This is the direct variable expense incurred up to the point at which the inventory is held in storage. In other words, it was necessary to obtain the average variable cost of products delivered to the warehouse location. Since the company used standard fully allocated manufacturing cost for valuing inventory, it was necessary to investigate the standard cost for each product in order to determine the variable manufactured cost per unit. Using the company's inventory plan for the coming year, it was possible to calculate the average inventory for each product. This can be determined for each storage location and for the total system.

Next, the average transportation cost per case of product was added to the variable manufactured cost. This was necessary because the transportation cost must be paid just

TABLE 5–4   **Adjusting the Cost of Money to Fit the Method**
             of Inventory Valuation

One Method	
Inventory at full cost	$10,000,000
Variable cost is 80% of full cost	× 80%
Inventory at variable cost	$ 8,000,000
Cost of money before tax is 30%	× 30%
Cost of money associated with the inventory investment	$ 2,400,000
Another Method	
Cost of money before tax	30%
Variable cost is 80% of full cost	80%
Inventory at full cost	$10,000,000
Adjusted cost of money	× 24%
Cost of money associated with the inventory investment	$2,400,000

like the manufacturing labor and raw material costs. Finally, if any warehousing costs are incurred moving product into storage in field locations, these costs should be added on a per-case basis to the standard variable manufactured cost. When public warehousing is used, any charges paid at the time products are moved into the facility should be added on a per-case basis to all products held in inventory. In the case of corporate facilities, only variable out-of-pocket costs associated with moving the products into storage should be included.

The company had $10 million in average system finished goods inventory valued at full manufactured cost. Annual sales were $175 million, or approximately $125 million at manufactured cost. The inventory value based on variable manufacturing costs and the forecasted product mix was $7 million. The $7 million was the average annual inventory held at plants and field locations in order to achieve least cost logistics. The variable costs associated with transporting the strategically deployed field inventory and moving it into public warehouses totaled $800,000. Therefore, the average system inventory was $7.8 million when valued at variable cost delivered to the storage location.

Calculating the Non–Cost-of-Money Components

All of the remaining inventory carrying cost components should be calculated as a percentage of the variable delivered cost ($7.8 million), and added to the capital cost percentage. In some companies, however, inventory reports may value products only at full standard manufactured cost, and the cost or time involved in changing reporting practices may seem high relative to the benefits to be gained. If a firm faces this type of situation, the cost of money can be adjusted when the carrying cost is developed in order to reflect that it is being applied to a value larger than the cash generated by a reduction in inventory. Table 5–4 shows methods of adjusting the carrying cost calculation to represent only variable costs.

The assumptions are that variable costs are 80 percent of full cost and that the cost of money is 30 percent before taxes or 15 percent after taxes. If the inventory shown on management reports is valued at $10 million at full cost, a manager could take 80 percent of this amount and then apply the 30 percent cost of money. This would yield a capital cost of $2.4 million. Another alternative is to adjust the cost of money at the time the inventory carrying cost is developed. By taking 80 percent of the 30 percent cost of money, the adjusted cost of money, 24 percent, can be applied to the inventory value shown on the management reports. This method also yields a capital cost of $2.4 million. If full cost is used and the cost of money is appropriately adjusted, all remaining cost components should be calculated as a percentage of the full cost inventory value.

Inventory Service Costs.   Return to the example of the manufacturer of packaged goods, with system inventories of $7.8 million valued at variable cost delivered to the storage location. Taxes for the year were $90,948, which is 1.17 percent of the $7.8 million inventory value; this figure was added to the 30 percent capital cost (see Table 5–5). Insurance costs covering inventory for the year were $4,524, which is 0.06 percent of the inventory value.

Storage Space Costs.   The storage component of the public warehouse in cost was $225,654 for the year, which equals 2.89 percent of the inventory value. Variable storage costs in plant warehouses should include only those costs that are variable with the amount of inventory stored. The vast majority of plant warehousing expenses were fixed in nature. Those costs that were variable fluctuated with the amount of product moved into and out of the facility (throughput) and were not variable with inventory levels. Consequently, variable storage costs were negligible in plant warehouses.

Inventory Risk Costs.   Obsolescence cost, which is the cost of holding products in inventory beyond their useful life, was being tracked in this company and represented 0.80 percent of inventory for the past 12 months.

Shrinkage and Damage Costs.   Shrinkage and damage costs were not recorded separately. Regression analysis would have been a possible means of isolating the portion of these costs that were variable with inventories. However, management was confident that no more than 10 percent of the total shrinkage and damage, $100,308, was related to inventory levels. Therefore, a managerial estimate of 10 percent was used. This was equal to 1.29 percent of the inventory value of $7.8 million.

Relocation Costs.   Those costs incurred transporting products from one location to another to avoid obsolescence were not available. Management said that such costs were incurred so infrequently that they were not recorded separately from ordinary transportation costs.

Inventory Carrying Cost Was Calculated to Be 36 Percent

Total Inventory Carrying Costs.   When totaled, the individual percentages gave an inventory carrying cost of 36.21 percent. Thus, management would use a 36 percent inventory carrying cost when calculating cost trade-offs in the logistics system. Inventory carrying cost calculations for six additional packaged goods companies are included in the appendix to this chapter.

Table 5–5 summarizes the data collection procedure that the consumer packaged goods company used. Notice the distinction between the cost of money component of inventory carrying costs and all of the other component costs. All of the non–cost-of-money components (steps 3 through 10 of Table 5–5) are annual expenses. Consequently, they appear on the profit and loss statement and affect the firm's net profit. Inventory, however, is a balance sheet account. Inventory becomes an expense only when it is sold and the cost of the inventory is matched with the revenue generated by its sale. Usually, the inventory is replaced when it is sold and the inventory account on

TABLE 5–5   Summary of Data Collection Procedure

Step No. Cost Category	Source	Explanation	Amount (Current Study)
1. Cost of money	Comptroller	This represents the cost of having money invested in inventory and the return should be comparable to other investment opportunities.	30% pretax
2. Average monthly inventory valued at variable costs delivered to the distribution center	1. Standard cost data—comptroller's department 2. Freight rates and product specs are from distribution reports 3. Average monthly inventory in cases from printout received from sales forecasting	Only want variable costs since fixed costs go on regardless of the amount of product manufactured and stored—follow steps outlined in body of report.	$7,800,000 valued at variable cost delivered to the DC. (Variable manufactured cost equaled 70% of full manufactured cost. Variable cost FOB the DC averaged 78% of full manufactured cost.)
3. Taxes	The comptroller's department	Personal property taxes paid on inventory	$90,948, which equals 1.17%
4. Insurance	The comptroller's department	Insurance rate/$100 of inventory (at variable costs)	$4,524, which equals 0.06%
5. Recurring storage (public warehouse)	Distribution operations	This represents the portion of warehousing costs that is related to the volume of inventory stored.	$226,654 annually, which equals 2.89%
6. Variable storage (plant warehouses)	Transportation services	Only those costs that are variable with the amount of inventory stored should be included.	Nil
7. Obsolescence	Distribution department reports	Cost of holding product inventory beyond its useful life.	0.80% of inventory
8. Shrinkage	Distribution department reports	Requires managerial judgment to determine the portion attributable to inventory storage.	$100,308, which equals 1.29%
9. Damage	Distribution department reports	Requires managerial judgment to determine the portion attributable to inventory storage.	
10. Relocation costs	Not available	Only relocation costs incurred to avoid obsolescence should be included.	Not available
11. Total carrying costs	Calculate the numbers generated in steps 3, 4, 5, 6, 8, 9, and 10 as a percentage of average inventory valued at variable cost delivered to the distribution center and add them to the cost of money (step 1).		36.21%

the balance sheet remains the same. If the inventory is not replaced, the cash account increases by the amount not spent on the inventory.

While cash, like inventory, is a balance sheet account, the rate of return earned on the cash does affect the profit and loss statement. Multiplying the cash value of a decrease or an increase in inventory by the opportunity cost of money presents the change in inventory as a profit and loss statement "expense"; this can be added to the other expenses, such as insurance and taxes. The out-of-pocket expenses (non–cost-of-money components) associated with inventory must simply be calculated as a percentage of inventory investment (cash value) and added to the cost of money to determine the total inventory carrying cost percentage.

Up to this point, we have assumed that the company has a relatively homogeneous product line, that is, that products are manufactured at each plant location, shipped in mixed quantities, and stored in the same facilities. Consequently, if the company has a 12-month inventory plan, and standard costs are available, a weighted-average inventory carrying cost can be used for all products and locations. This figure would require updating on an annual basis when the new inventory plan, updated standard costs, and the previous year's expenditures for insurance, taxes, storage, and inventory risk costs become available.

Inventory Carrying Costs May Vary by Storage Location

Management at General Mills, Inc., calculated an inventory carrying cost for each location where products were stored, and found considerable variations.[8] Since the costs have to be collected by storage location, minimal additional effort is required to fine-tune the numbers for decisions regarding a specific location or type of inventory. If the differences are minimal, the weighted-average inventory carrying cost will be sufficient.

In companies with heterogeneous product lines, however, inventory carrying costs should be calculated for each individual product. For example, bulk chemical products cannot be shipped in mixed quantities or stored in the same tanks. For this reason, transportation and storage costs should be included on a specific product/location basis, rather than using an average transportation and storage cost as one would for homogeneous products. The next section contains an industry example from the bulk chemicals industry, which will clarify the distinction between homogeneous and heterogeneous products.

A Bulk Chemicals Industry Example

Due to the vastly different nature of bulk chemical products—in terms of storage requirements, shrinkage, and terminal locations—and because of the absence of an inventory forecast, it was necessary to determine an inventory carrying cost figure for each major product or class of products. There was an additional problem caused by the fact that the selling price per ton, the full manufactured cost, and variable costs per ton varied by plant and also varied within a plant throughout the year.

This example will focus on two products manufactured by the industrial chemicals division. One product was selected because it had a relatively low variable cost of production and the other was chosen because its variable cost of production represented a substantially higher percentage of the full manufactured cost. The two products were representative of the range of products manufactured by the company in terms of cost and shipping and storage requirements. Since the variable costs of transportation were different for each stocking point and represented a significant component of the inventory value at field terminals, inventory carrying costs were calculated for each storage location. In this example inventory carrying costs are presented for the manufacturing location and are calculated as a percentage of the variable manufactured costs.

---

[8]William R. Steele, "Inventory Carrying Cost Identification and Accounting," *Proceedings of the Sixteenth Annual Conference of the National Council of Physical Distribution Management* (Chicago: National Council of Physical Distribution Management, 1979), pp. 75–86.

Capital Costs. An interview with the comptroller revealed that a 20 percent return after taxes was required on new investments of more than $500,000. As a result of this meeting, it was established that the opportunity cost of capital would be 20 percent after taxes or 40 percent before taxes. The opportunity cost of capital should be applied only to the out-of-pocket investment in inventory. The first step was to determine the standard variable costs of each product and to express these costs as a percentage of full manufactured costs and average net back per ton, which is the average selling price less the selling expenses per ton.[9] Since monthly reports valued inventory at average net back, all components of inventory carrying costs were expressed as a percentage of average net back per ton as well as variable costs and full manufactured costs (see Tables 5–6 and 5–7). Depending on where inventory is held, however, the variable costs as a percentage of average net back per ton may change. This is because transportation costs should be added to field inventory.

TABLE 5–6   Inventory Carrying Costs for Product LMN

	Percentage based on average net back per ton ($393)	Percentage based on budgeted full manufacturing cost per ton ($138.51)	Percentage based on variable costs per ton ($80.43)
I. Capital costs			
Capital cost (minimum acceptable rate of return = 20% after taxes, 40% before taxes)	8.188%[a]	23.227%[b]	40.000%
II. Inventory service costs			
Insurance	0.265	0.752	1.295
Taxes (vary with location— average)	0.274	0.777	1.338
III. Storage space costs[c]	—	—	—
IV. Inventory risk costs			
Obsolescence	—	—	—
Pilferage (shrinkage)	3.220	9.137[d]	15.735
Damage	—	—	—
Relocation costs	—	—	—
Total (before taxes)	11.947%	33.893%	58.368%
Inventory carrying costs (per ton)	$46.95	$46.95	$46.95

[a]Based on variable costs of $80.43 per ton and average net back per ton of $393. Variable costs = 20.47% of average per ton net back. Therefore, capital costs = 0.2047 × 40% = 8.188% of average net back per ton.

[b]Budgeted full manufacturing costs were $138.51. Variable costs as a percentage of full manufacturing costs = 58.068%. Therefore capital costs = 0.58068 × 40% = 23.227%.

[c]Fixed over the relevant range of inventory levels.

[d]Calculated on the basis of tons of shrinkage as a percent of average inventory in tons. Applied to full manufacturing costs as a surrogate for variable manufacturing costs plus transportation, and adjusted to corresponding percentage based on net back and variable costs per ton.

Source: Douglas M. Lambert, *The Development of an Inventory Costing Methodology: A Study of the Costs Associated with Holding Inventory* (Chicago: National Council of Physical Distribution Management, 1976), pp. 167–68.

---

[9]During a period of shortages in the chemical industry, the firm began to value inventory investment on management reports at average net back per ton. Since the firm was able to sell the product held in inventory, holding inventory in anticipation of future orders from existing customers prevented immediate sales to new customers. Thus average net back per ton, the selling price less the out-of-pocket costs associated with making the sale (such as sales commissions and freight) was used to represent the cash value of the inventory.

TABLE 5–7   **Inventory Carrying Costs for Product XYZ**

	Percentage based on average net back per ton ($50.84)	Percentage based on budgeted full manufacturing cost per ton ($28.89)	Percentage based on variable costs per ton ($2.34)
I. Capital costs			
Capital cost (minimum acceptable rate of return = 20% after taxes, 40% before taxes)	1.841%[a]	3.240%	40.000%
II. Inventory service costs			
Insurance	0.265	0.466	5.757[b]
Taxes (vary with location—average)	0.270	0.482	5.865
III. Storage space costs[c]	—	—	—
IV. Inventory risk costs			
Obsolescence	—	—	—
Pilferage (shrinkage)	0.730	1.284[d]	15.852
Damage	—	—	—
Relocation costs	—	—	—
Total (before taxes)	3.106%	5.472%	67.474%
Inventory carrying costs (per ton)	$1.58	$1.58	$1.58

[a]This depends on the percentage of average net back per ton that variable manufacturing costs plus variable transportation costs represent. For product held at the plant and based on $2.34 per ton variable cost and $50.84 average net back per ton, variable costs = 0.04602 × = 40% = 1.841%. For field inventory, transportation costs would be added before calculating the variable cost percentage.

[b]Based on variable costs of $2.34 per ton and average net back of $50.84. Variable manufacturing costs = 4.602% of average per ton net back. Consequently, 0.265% of $50.84 = 5.757% of $2.34 and 0.270% of $50.84 = 5.865% of $2.34. Full manufacturing costs were $28.89 per ton, and percentages based on this figure were calculated in a manner similar to the percentages based on average net back per ton.

[c]Fixed over the relevant range of inventory levels.

[d]Calculated on the basis of tons of shrinkage as a percent of average inventory in tons. Applied to full manufacturing costs as a surrogate for variable manufacturing costs plus transportation, and adjusted to corresponding percentage based on net back and variable costs per ton.

Source: Douglas M. Lambert, *The Development of an Inventory Costing Methodology: A Study of the Costs Associated with Holding Inventory* (Chicago: National Council of Physical Distribution Management, 1976), pp. 165–66.

Inventory Service Costs.   The company was self-insured for $250,000 of finished-product inventory at each warehouse location, but for inventory over $250,000 at any specific location the insurance rate was $0.265 per $100 of average inventory. Since the cost of the insurance on the first $250,000 of inventory was not readily available, the $0.265 per $100 figure was used in the calculation of inventory carrying costs with the realization that it may be fractionally below or above the actual figure.

Taxes paid on inventory vary depending on the state and city in which the terminal is located. The actual tax rate payable for each location should be used when determining specific sites for the terminals. In this case, management believed that tax rates would not change for the coming year, so the average tax figure for the preceding year was used. Based on average monthly inventory figures and taxes for the preceding year, this represented 0.274 percent of inventory valued at average net back. Since taxes represented such a small portion of the total carrying cost, it was unlikely that using the actual taxes for each location would significantly alter the carrying cost percentage.

Storage Space Costs.   The costs associated with plant storage tanks were fixed, and therefore not relevant for decisions related to increasing the level of inventory in any particular storage tank. If an increase in inventory required additional plant storage and the installation of new tanks, a capital budgeting decision would be required. Once an additional storage tank was built, changes in the level of product held in the tank would not affect the storage costs.

A similar argument held for rented terminal space, since the cost of such space was fixed on an annual basis. The cost per gallon might decrease as larger quantities of storage space were contracted, but usually the total annual cost was insensitive to the quantity of product held within a given tank. Handling costs were related to sales (throughput), and not to the quantity of product held in storage. The manager of warehouse and terminal operations said that in some instances it was necessary to guarantee four turns of inventory per year. A logistics analyst confirmed that, although terminal lease costs were required when making a decision to locate a terminal, once the terminal was on-stream its costs were considered fixed when deciding if other customers should be routed through the terminal.

Inventory Risk Costs.   Obsolescence was not a factor, since the company was experiencing a "seller's market" for its products due to product shortages in the chemical industry. In a "buyer's market," however, the obsolescence costs should be measured.

Damage that resulted while the product was in the custody of a carrier was claimed, and was therefore not a significant cost. Managing the claims function has costs attached to it, of course. But the variable cost of making these claims against carriers should not be included in inventory carrying costs, since the majority of these claims are related to throughput and not the amount of inventory held.

All other shrinkage costs amounted to 1.51 percent of the average inventory for all products; however, they varied substantially by product. The wide fluctuation in the price of each product, caused by such factors as the plant in which it was produced and the supply–demand relationship, made the dollar shrinkage figure as determined by management extremely tenuous. For this reason a weighted-average cost per ton was calculated for the two products being studied (see Table 5–8). However, this problem could be avoided by just considering the shrinkage in tons as a percentage of average annual inventory in tons. This yields a percentage figure that is independent of dollars.

Relocation Costs.   Those costs incurred transporting products from one storage location to another to avoid obsolescence were believed to be negligible and were not included.

Inventory Carrying Costs May Differ by Product

Total Inventory Carrying Costs.   The total inventory carrying cost figure to be used for decision making was 58.37 percent of variable costs before taxes for product LMN, and 67.47 percent of variable costs before taxes for product XYZ. These percentages may seem high, but they apply only to the variable costs associated with the inventory, and not to full manufactured costs. For example, if these figures were calculated as percentages of the full manufactured costs, they would be 33.89 percent and 5.47 percent, respectively. As percentages of the average net back per ton, they would be 11.95 percent for product LMN and 3.11 percent for product XYZ, even though the inventory carrying costs, expressed in dollars, were $46.95 per ton for product LMN and $1.58 per ton for product XYZ (see again Tables 5–6 and 5–7, respectively).

All of the percentages were calculated under the assumption that the inventory would be stored at the plant. However, if the inventory was located in field warehouses, the variable costs would include transportation costs plus any charges associated with moving the product into storage, and would represent a higher percentage of

TABLE 5–8   **Terminal Inventory and Shrinkage for the Year**

	Product XYZ			Product LMN			
	Dollars	*Tons*	*Dollars per Ton*	*Dollars*	*Tons*	*Dollars per Ton*	*Total*
January							
February							
March							
April							
May							
June							
July							
August							
September							
October							
November							
December							
Monthly average							
Annual average							
Percent shrinkage	*			*			

*Best number to use since it is independent of the price per ton (since percentage can be applied to any value of inventory). However, this percentage should only be applied to out-of-pocket costs. Since variable manufacturing costs do not include transportation costs, it is recommended that this shrinkage percentage be applied to full manufacturing costs (surrogate measure for variable manufacturing cost plus transportation). From *Summary of Warehouse Valuation,* report from Distribution Accounting.

Source: Douglas M. Lambert, *The Development of an Inventory Costing Methodology: A Study of the Costs Associated with Holding Inventory* (Chicago: National Council of Physical Distribution Management, 1976), p. 164.

full manufactured cost and average net back per ton. It was recommended that the percentage based on variable costs be used when calculating inventory carrying costs.

This chemical industry example clearly illustrates why it is a mistake to use an inventory carrying cost percentage that is an industry average or textbook percentage. Not only were the inventory carrying costs significantly different for each of the products considered, but the carrying costs varied widely for each product depending on the method of inventory valuation used.

These two examples should have clarified the method and how it can be applied. At this point, readers should be able to calculate an inventory carrying cost percentage for a company.

The Impact of Inventory Turnover on Inventory Carrying Costs

Increasing Inventory Turns May Reduce Profits

In Chapter 1 we saw that, in many firms, management attempts to improve profitability by emphasizing the need to improve inventory turnover. But pushing for increased inventory turnover without considering the impact on total logistics system costs may actually lead to decreased profitability.

For example, Table 5–9 illustrates the impact that increased inventory turnover has on total carrying costs.[10] For a product, product category, division, or company with

---

[10]This example is adapted from Douglas M. Lambert and Robert H. Quinn, "Profit Oriented Inventory Policies Require a Documented Inventory Carrying Cost," *Business Quarterly* 46, no. 3 (Autumn 1981), pp. 64–65.

TABLE 5–9   The Impact of Inventory Turns on Inventory Carrying Costs

Inventory Turns	Average Inventory	Carrying Cost at 40 Percent	Carrying Cost Savings
1	$750,000	$300,000	—
2	375,000	150,000	$150,000
3	250,000	100,000	50,000
4	187,500	75,000	25,000
5	150,000	60,000	15,000
6	125,000	50,000	10,000
7	107,143	42,857	7,143
8	93,750	37,500	5,357
9	83,333	33,333	4,167
10	75,000	30,000	3,333
11	68,182	27,273	2,727
12	62,500	25,000	2,273
13	57,692	23,077	1,923
14	53,571	21,428	1,649
15	50,000	20,000	1,428

Source: Douglas M. Lambert and Robert H. Quinn, "Profit Oriented Inventory Policies Require a Documented Inventory Carrying Cost," *Business Quarterly* 46, no. 3 (Autumn 1981), p. 65.

sales of $750,000 at cost, inventory turn would equal 1 if the average inventory were $750,000. If the inventory carrying costs were 40 percent, they would represent $300,000 annually. Increasing inventory turns from 1 to 2 would lead to a $150,000 decrease in inventory carrying costs; this would represent a 50 percent savings. Improving turns from 6 to 12 also would result in a 50 percent reduction in inventory carrying costs, but it would represent a much smaller savings of $25,000. Many times management finds itself in a position where inventory turns are expected to increase each year. If the company is inefficient and has too much inventory, increasing inventory turns will lead to increased profitability. However, continued improvements in inventory turns, in the absence of process change, will eventually result in the firm cutting inventories below the optimal level. If a logistics system is currently efficient and the goal is to increase turns from 11 to 12, the annual savings in carrying costs would be $2,273. Care must be taken that transportation costs, lot quantity costs, warehouse picking costs, and order processing and information costs do not increase by more than this amount; that lower customer service levels do not result in lost profit contribution in excess of the carrying cost savings; or that some combination of the above does not occur.

Figure 5–8 illustrates the relationship between inventory carrying costs and the number of inventory turnovers, using the data that were presented in Table 5–9. The example shows that improvements in the number of inventory turns has the greatest impact if inventory is turned less than 8 times per year. In fact, beyond eight turns the curve becomes relatively flat. Increasing inventory turns from 5 to 6 times generates the same savings in inventory carrying costs as does improving them from 10 to 15 times. An increase in inventory turns from 1 to 2 will cut inventory carrying costs by one-half. In order to save the other half, all of the remaining inventory must be eliminated. Every time inventory turns are doubled, one-half as much money is saved as with the previous doubling of turns. Beyond 8 turns the curve begins to flatten out. This is not an argument for being satisfied with 8 turns, but rather if the firm is achieving 8 turns, the

FIGURE 5–8

Relationships between inventory turns and inventory carrying costs

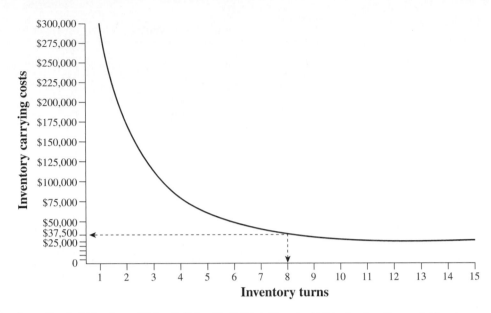

Source: Douglas M. Lambert and Robert H. Quinn, "Profit Oriented Inventory Policies Require a Documented Inventory Carrying Cost," *Business Quarterly* 46, no. 3 (Autumn 1981), p. 65.

goal should be to achieve 16 or 24 turns, not 9. Improving turns to 16 or 24 cannot be achieved by incremental improvements but requires breakthrough thinking such as information sharing in the supply chain. When establishing inventory turnover objectives, it is necessary to fully document how each alternative strategy will increase the other logistics costs and compare this to the savings in inventory carrying costs.

Inventory Carrying Cost per Unit

For a number of management decisions it may be useful to calculate inventory carrying costs on a per-unit basis. The inventory carrying costs associated with each item sold can vary dramatically for high-turnover items versus low-volume, low-turn items. The previous analysis of inventory carrying costs and inventory turns is repeated using a carrying cost per unit example in order to illustrate this point. For example, if the variable manufacturing cost of an item is $100 and the annual inventory carrying cost is 30 percent, the monthly cost to carry the item in inventory is $2.50 ($30 ÷ 12). Annual turns of 1 (12 months in inventory) would consume $30 in carrying costs, whereas 2 turns per year would cost $15; 4 turns, $7.50; and 8 turns, $3.75 (see Figure 5–9). It is not uncommon for some items in a product line to turn less than once a year. When inventory carrying costs are included in product profitability reports, low inventory turns can place a product in a loss position. One inventory turn per year would result in a charge of $30 in inventory carrying costs for every unit sold. In contrast, 15 turns per year would result in a charge of only $2 per unit. This example should make it clear how inventory turns affect the profitability of each item sold. In Chapter 6 we will review methods for improving the profitability of products by better managing inventories.

Inventory Carrying Costs within the Supply Chain

Supply Chain Goal: Improve Overall Efficiency

The cost trade-offs required in a logistics system (see again Figure 5–4) can be performed either within a single firm, between different levels of the supply chain, or for

FIGURE 5–9

Annual inventory carrying costs compared to inventory turns

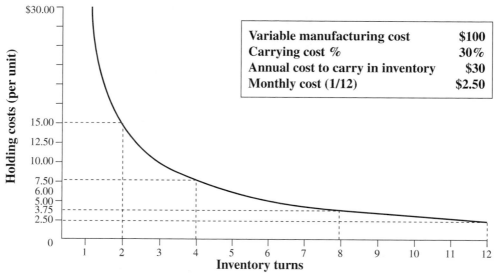

Variable manufacturing cost	$100
Carrying cost %	30%
Annual cost to carry in inventory	$30
Monthly cost (1/12)	$2.50

Source: Jay U. Sterling and Douglas M. Lambert "Segment Profitability Reports: You Can't Manage Your Business Without Them," unpublished manuscript, 1992.

the entire supply chain. For the individual firm, the goal is to find the most efficient way to offer the desired level of service. For the supply chain, the goal is to improve overall efficiency by reallocating functions, and therefore costs, among its members. The level of customer service offered by the manufacturer, for example, will have a significant impact on other members of the supply chain.

A manufacturer whose product availability is poor and whose order cycle time is inconsistent may force wholesalers to carry more inventory as safety stock in order to offer an acceptable level of service to the retail level of the channel. In this case, lower logistics costs for the manufacturer were achieved at the expense of the other members of the supply chain and the entire supply chain may be less efficient.

However, if management concentrates on systems changes that improve logistics efficiency or effectiveness, it may be possible to satisfy all of the firm's objectives. For example, many companies have not kept pace with technology in the area of order processing. As we described in Chapter 4, by replacing an outdated order processing and information system with advanced technology, a firm may be able to achieve some or all of the following: (1) increased customer service levels, (2) lower inventories, (3) speedier collections, (4) decreased transportation costs, (5) lower warehousing cost, and (6) improvements in cash flow and return on assets.

Information Technology Can Increase Supply Chain Efficiency and Effectiveness

The manufacturer has minimal additional cash invested in inventory held by the customer rather than in the manufacturer's warehouse. Furthermore, the non–cost-of-money components of inventory carrying cost are shifted to the next level of the supply chain. For this reason, supply chain efficiency may be increased if the manufacturer owns the customer's inventory until it is consumed. Figure 5–10 illustrates how inventory increases in value as it moves closer to the final consumer. The supplier's variable product costs are $5, but the manufacturer's are $11. The manufacturer's variable manufactured costs—that is, out-of-pocket cash invested in inventory—is $25, but the

Why More Inventory Ownership Is Being Shifted to Suppliers

Is shifting inventory ownership/responsibility to the supplier a legitimate inventory reduction practice?

According to practitioners, it's definitely a means to reduce inventory levels and investment and increase inventory velocity and turns. Even if the supplier or distributor attaches a fee for this "service," it is still less than the 25% to 40% inventory carrying cost that holding the inventory would cost. In some cases, shifting inventory is a reaction to the many suppliers who express reluctance to engage a vendor management inventory (VMI) initiative.

By shifting inventory ownership/responsibility back to the supplier, the inventory managers may be signaling more forceful VMI and supply chain initiatives for the future. A number of practitioners also are insisting on some "value-added" activities. For example, these are inventory managers' views on the subject:

Leveraging the Volume of MRO Buys

"We've shifted inventory ownership and management responsibility to several of our key suppliers," describes a purchasing manager at a large packaging manufacturer. "We have leveraged our volume of inventories of MRO items by utilizing fewer sources and requiring them to provide higher levels of value-added services for this increased volume." While time savings have not been calculated, he notes costs savings average 10% to 20%.

Supply Chain Review Initiates a Change in Policy

"We shifted inventory usage/ownership to subcontractors that previously were supplied inventory consigned by us," according to a manager of international sub-contracts at a midsize maker of portable power devices. "A review of our supply chain revealed a significant amount of inventory was purchased and then consigned to subcontractors who didn't have the partnerships and alliances with our suppliers. The change in practice has lowered our inventory investment more than 25%."

Consigned Inventory a Partial Answer

"We have moved to a consignment inventory arrangement in which the material is located in our facility, but the ownership rests with our supplier," explains a materials manager at a small manufacturer of lighting systems. "The arrangement provides us with benefits such as increased inventory turns, and we don't have to include it as 'our' inventory until we use it, and the supplier replaces only what we use." However, "It still consumes floor space in our facility."

Third Party Provider Comments on "Shifting" Trend

"For the organizations we serve, most of them are shifting the inventory responsibility to us," according to the vice president, supply chain solutions. "The gain for us is . . . the visibility of the inventory and all its uses without suffering the waves of inventory based on forecasts, orders that haven't arrived, and so forth."

Reduced Space Available Forces Move to Supplier Partnership

"We began to shift more of our inventory to a third-party logistics/warehouse provider while also insisting that the supplier maintain ownership of the inventory," describes a manager of material distribution at a utility company. "We entered into a partnership arrangement with that supplier."

Shift Ownership, but Share Schedules

"When we began to shift inventory ownership to our suppliers, we also introduced them to our production plans and schedules through EDI and autofaxing," says a planning facilitator at a mid-sized producer of fluid control devices. "This effort was the beginning of a trading partner relationship. Part of the arrangement called for a quarterly discussion of service, delivery, and other appropriate items."

Source: Adapted from the *Inventory Reduction Report,* Issue 99-2, February 1999, pp. 1 and 7. Reprinted by permission. © Joe Mazel, IOMA's Inventory Reduction Report. (212) 244-0360. http://www.ioma.com/.

FIGURE 5–10

*Inventory positions
and major flows
in a supply chain*

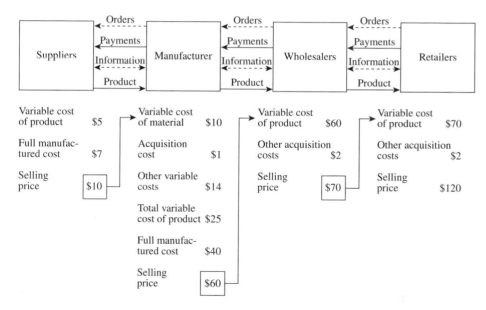

Source: Adapted from Douglas M. Lambert and Mark L. Bennion, "New Channel Strategies for the 1980s," in *Marketing Channels: Domestic and International Perspectives,* ed. Michael G. Harvey and Robert F. Lusch (Norman: Center for Economic and Management Research, School of Business Administration, University of Oklahoma, 1982), p. 127.

wholesaler's investment is $62. Similarly, the retailer's cost is $82. When a manufacturer holds the customer's inventory, minimal additional out-of-pocket costs are incurred, and the non–cost-of-money components of inventory carrying costs are shifted.

**Inventory Location
Affects Total Supply
Chain Costs**

The location of inventory within the supply chain affects total supply chain costs and the level of customer service provided to end consumers. Generally, the closer to the consumer the product is held, the higher the inventory carrying cost. If extending the terms of sale encourages other channel members to purchase larger quantities or accept a longer order cycle, or if increased sales result from the higher service levels, the entire supply chain may be more profitable. Firms that respond to a market's challenges with innovative new strategies reap the rewards.

In addition to rethinking traditional strategies for improving cash flow and return on assets, supply chain leaders may wish to consider automating and integrating the information systems within the supply chain. This can reduce lead time, as well as lead time variability, and create time for planning. The latest communications technology offers a unique opportunity for improving the efficiency and effectiveness of the supply chain. If communications flows throughout the supply chain are improved, all members will be able to reduce inventories while improving customer service. In addition, the planning time that results will allow freight consolidations, warehousing costs savings, and lower lot quantity costs.[11] The benefits of integrated information systems were described in detail in Chapter 4.

Usually, increased customer service levels create increased expenses, and sales must increase just to break even on the service improvement. However, by improving communications, a firm can improve customer service levels and reduce total operating costs—truly a unique opportunity.

---

[11]For an example of how consumer products companies are responding to this need for improved information flows in the supply chain, see <www.transora.com>.

Technology

Shell Improves Value through "Supplier Managed Inventory"

With the development of new software programs, more and more suppliers are offering programs that virtually eliminate the purchase order, redundant paper processing, and the need for huge amounts of "safety inventory."

One major practitioner of managed customer inventory is the Shell Chemical Co. It now has a number of vendor managed inventory programs in operation for customers in the pharmaceuticals, automotive, consumer goods, chemicals, and industrial goods industries. Under a new automated replenishment system called Supplier Managed Inventory (SMI)—many customers supplied by Shell Chemical no longer place orders for whole lines of products offered by Shell. Instead, Shell anticipates demand and proactively replaces inventory based on information supplied by the customer.

SMI was the product of a series of reengineering efforts aimed at reducing costs in Shell's production planning and operations processes. After much study, Shell concluded that if it had a better understanding of its customers' usage patterns, it could forecast its own production more accurately and thus rationalize the inventory it carried in its plants.

As Ken Valentine, a marketing director, reasoned, the best way to understand customer use would be to actually take on the job of supply management for customers—at once providing a new value-added service and gaining key insights into customer demand. "What's more," he reasoned, "by managing inventory for its customers, Shell would be rewarded with more business. . . . in what's largely a commodity business."

Shell then marshaled its resources in an effort to develop an infrastructure needed to provide such a value-added service. The result: A "Lotus Notes"–based on-line tool-dubbed "SIMON"—for Shell Inventory Managed Order Network—that allows customers and Shell to share information. Each night, SIMON, a Notes client at the customer site, reads four pieces of information from the customer company's information system: day's consumption, current inventory levels, status on new product that arrived and was unloaded that day, and the customer's forecast.

Through a process called "replication," all of the updated data is selectively copied each night from the customer's plant to Shell's Lotus Notes servers in Houston. An automatic upload of data from all of the SMI customers occurs as a batch job into Shell's SAP system. SAP's MRP then calculates a new re-supply plan that is available to the account services representative each morning.

At the end of each month, SIMON calculates consumption based on the figures the customer has supplied. The customer then electronically pays Shell based on that calculation. No invoice is needed because both Shell and the SMI customer are reviewing the same data in SIMON.

In return for this service, the customer agrees to use Shell as the sole supplier for the products managed through SMI. This is necessary because the customer pays based on consumption, not according to how much product is shipped to the plant. If products from multiple suppliers were mingled in the tank, there would be no way to differentiate consumption of Shell's product.

Major benefits listed by Shell include a major reduction in the total amount of inventory carried by customers, reduced supplier inventory (because of more accurate forecast and consumption information), and a dramatic reduction in transaction processing.

Source: "Shell Improves Value through "Supplier Managed Inventory," *Purchasing* 128, no. 8 (November 27, 1997), p. 79.

Summary

In this chapter we saw how to determine the impact of inventory investment on a firm's corporate profit performance. We also examined the way in which inventory policy affects least total cost logistics, and described a methodology that can be used to calculate inventory carrying costs. Finally, we looked at the relationship between inventory turnover and inventory carrying costs.

By now it should be apparent that inventory is a costly investment. With an awareness of this fact, and a knowledge of the procedures used to determine inventory carrying costs, we are ready to take a detailed look at inventory management. That is the subject of Chapter 6.

Suggested Readings

Edelman, Martin P. "Use of the Inventory Turnover Measurement." *Hospital Material Management Quarterly* 12, no. 1 (1990), pp. 50–56.

Huq, Faizul, and William E. Pinney. "Impact of Short-Term Variations in Demand on Opportunity Costs in a Just-in-Time Kanban System." *Production and Inventory Management Journal* 37, no. 4 (1996), pp. 8–13.

Lambert, Douglas M. *The Development of an Inventory Costing Methodology: A Study of the Costs Associated with Holding Inventory.* Chicago: National Council of Physical Distribution Management, 1976.

Lambert, Douglas M., and John T. Mentzer. "Inventory Carrying Costs: Current Availability and Uses." *International Journal of Physical Distribution and Materials Management* 9, no. 6 (1979), pp. 256–71. Reprinted in Martin Christopher, ed. "New Horizons in Distribution and Materials Management." *International Journal of Physical Distribution and Materials Management* 12, no. 3 (1982), pp. 56–71.

Ptak, Carol A. "A Comparison of Inventory Models and Carrying Costs." *Production and Inventory Management Journal* 29, no. 4 (1988), pp. 1–3.

Sheffi, Yosef, Babak Eskandari, and Haris N. Koutsopoulos. "Transportation Model Choice Based on Total Logistics Costs." *Journal of Business Logistics* 9, no. 2 (1988), pp. 137–54.

Steele, William R. "Inventory Carrying Cost Identification and Accounting." *Proceedings of the Sixteenth Annual Conference of the National Council of Physical Distribution.* Chicago: National Council of Physical Distribution Management, 1979, pp. 75–86.

Questions and Problems

1. Explain how excessive inventories can erode corporate profitability.

2. Many businesspeople rely on industry averages or textbook percentages for the inventory carrying cost that they use when setting inventory levels. Why is this approach wrong?

3. Explain how you would determine the cost of capital that should be used in inventory decisions.

4. How would you determine the cash value of a manufacturer's finished goods inventory investment? How would this differ in the case of a wholesaler or retailer?

5. What is the difference between the transportation cost component of logistics cost trade-off analysis and the transportation cost included in the inventory valuation (cash value)?

6. What problems do you foresee in gathering the cost information required to calculate inventory carrying costs for a company?

7. Describe the circumstances under which inventory carrying costs can vary within a given manufacturing company. Explain why total inventory carrying costs decrease, but at an ever-slower rate, as inventory turnovers increase. Consider raw materials, goods in process, and finished goods inventories in your answer.

8. Using the following data, determine the fixed and variable warehousing costs for this plant warehouse:

Month	Number of Loads Shipped	Total Plant Warehousing Cost
January	$ 750	$ 9,200
February	1,080	10,800
March	1,010	11,400
April	840	9,900
May	860	10,900
June	830	10,800
July	970	11,200
August	920	10,000
September	1,160	11,000
October	1,200	12,300
November	1,100	11,600
December	510	9,300

9. *a.* Calculate the inventory carrying cost percentage for the ABC Company given the following information:

   - Finished goods inventory is $28 million valued at full manufactured cost.
   - Based on the inventory plan, the weighted-average variable manufactured cost per case is 65 percent of the full manufactured cost.
   - The variable transportation cost incurred to move the inventory from plants to warehouse locations close to customers was $1.5 million.
   - The variable cost of moving the inventory into these warehouse locations was calculated to be $300,000.
   - The company was currently experiencing capital rationing and new investments were required to earn 15 percent after taxes.
   - Personal property taxes paid on inventory were approximately $200,000.
   - Insurance coverage to protect against loss of inventory was $100,000.
   - Storage charges at public warehouses totaled $500,000.
   - Variable storage in plant warehouses was considered to be negligible.
   - Obsolescence was $100,000.
   - Shrinkage was $100,000.
   - Damage related to inventory storage was $50,000.
   - Transportation costs associated with the relocation of field inventory to avoid obsolescence was $50,000.
   - The marginal tax rate is 40 percent.

   b. Would it be a good decision to spend $720,000 per year in increased production setup costs and premium transportation costs in order to achieve an inventory reduction of 10 percent?

10. Calculate the impact on return on net worth of a new information system, given the following information about the Jacksonville Manufacturing Company:

    - Sales are $100 million.
    - Net profit is $2 million after taxes.

- Asset turnover is 2.5 times.
- Financial leverage is 2.
- Taxes are 50 percent of net income.
- The new system will provide management with the additional days for planning logistics operations.
- Inventories will be reduced by $2 million, valued at variable costs delivered to the storage location.
- The company's inventory carrying cost is 36 percent, which is comprised of a pretax cost of money of 30 percent and non–cost-of-money components of 6 percent of the inventory value.
- Transportation consolidations made possible by the additional planning time will reduce transportation costs by $430,000 per year.
- Warehousing costs of $150,000 will be eliminated.
- The new order processing system will cost $300,000 per year more than the existing system.

11. Using your answer from question 10, what percentage increase in sales would be necessary in order to realize the same increase in return on net worth?

12. Why is it that managers want to push inventory back on suppliers? Is this good or bad? Evaluate General Motors' strategy of pushing inventories of parts and components back to suppliers and finished automobiles out to the dealer network. Typically dealers hold 60 to 120 days' supply of vehicles.

APPENDIX

INVENTORY CARRYING COSTS—SIX CASE STUDIES

In order to provide further knowledge on how to calculate inventory carrying costs, this appendix presents data from six case studies of manufacturers of packaged goods. Although some of the companies had substantial institutional sales, most of their sales were in the household consumer market. All of the companies had sales of over $1 billion annually.

Three of the firms used public warehouses to satisfy 100 percent of their field warehousing requirements. One company used leased facilities exclusively and another used public warehouses and corporate-managed facilities on a 50-50 basis. The sixth company used private, leased, and public warehouses on a 10 percent, 40 percent, and 50 percent basis, respectively. In addition to plant warehouses, the number of field warehouses used by the respondents ranged from 5 to over 20, with two companies falling into the last category.

The data collected from the six companies are shown in Table 5A–1. The results support the contention that each company should calculate its own figure, since individual carrying cost

TABLE 5A–1   Summary of Inventory Carrying Cost Data from Six Packaged Goods Companies

Inventory Carrying Cost Components	Company A	Company B	Company C	Company D	Company E	Company F
I. Capital costs	40.00%	29.00%	25.50%	8.00%	30.00%	26.00%
II. Inventory service costs						
Insurance	0.09	0.21	1.69	0.13	0.02	4.55
Taxes	1.90	0.46	0.09	1.22	0.03	0.33
III. Storage space costs						
Recurring storage	0.74	—	0.57	2.68	0.46	2.93
IV. Inventory risk costs						
Obsolescence	—	—	—	0.79	1.70	n.a.
Damage	0.23	0.40	0.50	1.39	0.12	—
Shrinkage	—	—	—	—	0.33	—
Transhipment costs	—	—	—	n.a.	0.30	—
Total inventory carrying costs (before taxes)[a]	42.96%[b]	30.07%	28.35%	14.21%[c]	32.96%	33.81%[d]
Inventory carrying cost previously used	9.5%	15%	20%	8%	25%	15%
Method of inventory valuation	Full manufactured cost	Variable cost delivered to the customer	Actual variable costs of production	Full manufactured cost	Variable cost delivered to distribution center	Full manufactured cost
Time required for data collection	16 hours	70 hours[e]	40 hours	30 hours	20 hours	20 hours
Average inventory of division or product studied	$10,000,000	$25,000,000	$8,000,000	$500,000	$45,000,000	$2,000,000

[a]As a percentage of the variable costs delivered to the distribution center. (This allows comparison to be made across all companies.)

[b]Inventory carrying costs were 35.44% of the full manufactured cost.

[c]Inventory carrying costs were 14.10% of the full manufactured cost.

[d]Inventory carrying costs were 27.32% of the full manufactured cost.

[e]But only 20 hours per year required for update.

percentages ranged from a low of 14 percent to a high of 43 percent before taxes. Unusual cost-of-money numbers such as those for companies B, C, and F (29.11 percent, 25.50 percent, and 26.00 percent, respectively) occur when the marginal tax rate is not 50 percent. This is a result of the fact that the after-tax cost of money must be divided by one minus the marginal tax rate in order to obtain the before-tax cost of money. All other costs are already before taxes.

With few exceptions, the data were readily available in each of the companies; however, a number of minor data-collection problems were experienced:

1. One company did not have a specific hurdle rate for new investments. Another company used a hurdle rate of 20 percent but was required to pay its corporate head office only 8 percent for money that was invested in inventories or accounts receivable. Consequently, the 8 percent figure was used since it reflected the division's true cost.

2. The inventory investment data and the insurance and taxes on the inventory investment were readily available in most cases. But in one company three days' work was required to determine accurately a tax calculation of 0.46 percent of the inventory value. Since a small percentage error would have little impact on a carrying cost of 30 percent, it was recommended that, in the future, the percentage of total inventory represented by each product group be applied to the total tax figure. This procedure would require approximately 15 minutes.

3. The variable costs associated with the amount of inventory held were available in every company; however, the costs of damage and shrinkage, and to some extent the cost of obsolescence, required managerial estimates. In only one company were these costs not recorded.

4. Relocation costs, which are the costs associated with the transshipment of inventory from one stocking location to another to avoid obsolescence, were believed to be negligible.

For all six companies, the time required to calculate the carrying cost figures was minimal. However, some caution should be exercised in viewing the time required for data collection as the absolute maximum. This is because the times reported assume a certain level of sophistication in terms of the corporate accounting system. In a less sophisticated company it is conceivable that substantial additional effort may be required in order to accurately trace some of the cost components. For example, in situations in which inventory risk costs represent a substantial proportion of the total inventory carrying costs, a managerial estimate of the proportion of these costs related to the level of inventory held would not suffice. Consequently, it would be necessary to implement a reporting system that would accurately reflect these costs, or to use regression analysis to determine the portion of these costs that were variable with the quantity of inventory.

Table 5A–2 contains a summary of where in each of the six organizations the individual carrying cost components were obtained. This table should be of considerable use as an indicator of where in a company one might look for specific inventory carrying cost components.

Finally, there was one minor problem in terms of using the inventory carrying cost percentage in economic order quantity (EOQ) analysis. If the quantity generated from this formula required that additional fixed storage space be added, then the EOQ should be recalculated, including an estimated annual cost for the additional facilities. Should the EOQ change appreciably, a number of additional recalculations would be necessary in order to find the best trade-off between order quantity and the additional capital costs.

TABLE 5A–2 Summary of Data Collection Procedures Showing Source of Data

Step No.	Cost Category	Explanation	Company A	Company B	Company C	Company D	Company E	Company F
1.	Cost of money	This represents the cost of having money invested in inventory and the return should be comparable to investment opportunities	Corporate controller	Divisional vice president and general manager	Vice president and controller	Vice president, controller and treasurer	Manager, financial analysis	Vice president and controller
2.	Average monthly inventory valued at variable costs delivered to the distribution center	Only want variable costs since fixed costs remain the same regardless of inventory levels	Standard costs from accounting Inventory plan from logistics Location of inventory and freight rates from logistics	Monthly computer printout	Director of logistics planning from monthly inventory printout	Standard cost data from controller's dept. Freight rates and product specs from logistics reports Average monthly inventory in cases from sales forecasting	Inventory planning manager	From budget report
3.	Taxes	Personal property taxes paid on finished goods inventory	Manager, corporate taxes	Property tax representative	Director, corporate insurance	Controller's department	Manager, ad valorem taxes	From budget
4.	Insurance	Insurance paid on inventory investment	Budgeted figures from logistics	Manager, corporate insurance	Director, corporate insurance	Controller's department	Assisant treasurer	From budget
5.	Variable storage	Only include those costs that are variable with the amount of inventory stored	Manager, materials management	Warehouse managers	Director, distribution center operations	Logistics	Year-end summary of monthly report	Logistics report

224

#	Item					
6.	Obsolescence	Obsolescence due to holding inventory	Manager, materials management planning and analysis			Reclamation expense report
7.	Shrinkage	Shrinkage related to volume of inventory	Manager, claims shrinkage and damage	Actual numbers not available, estimates used, from manager of logistics planning	From logistics department reports	Reclamation expense report
8.	Damage	Damage that is attributable to the level of inventory held				Manager, materials handling systems
9.	Relocation costs	Only relocation costs that result to avoid obsolescence	Manager, logistics research	Not available	Not available	Inventory planning manager
10.	Total carrying cost percentage	Calculate the numbers generated in steps 3 to 9 as a percentage of average inventory, and add to cost of money (step 1)				

Logistics reports or knowledge of managers

Chapter Outline

Chapter Objectives

- To show how the basic concepts of inventory management are applied.
- To show how to calculate safety stocks.
- To show how production policies influence inventory levels.
- To show how inventories and customer service levels are interrelated.
- To show how to recognize poor inventory management.
- To show how to improve inventory management.
- To show how profit performance can be improved by systems that reduce inventories.

Introduction

In Chapter 5 we saw that inventory is a large and costly investment. Better management of corporate inventories can improve cash flow and return on investment. Nevertheless, most companies (retailers, wholesalers, and manufacturers) suffer through periodic inventory rituals; that is, they institute crash inventory reduction programs every few years: "[The reduction programs] usually last two or three months and are characterized by top management edicts, middle management lip service—and insufficient knowledge of how to control inventory investment at all levels."[1]

Obviously, a more coherent program of inventory management is necessary. This chapter will provide the reader with the knowledge required to improve the practice of inventory management.

Basic Inventory Concepts

In this section, we will consider basic inventory concepts such as the reasons for holding inventory and the various types of inventory.

Why Hold Inventory?

Five Reasons for Holding Inventory

Formulation of an inventory policy requires an understanding of the role of inventory in manufacturing and marketing. Inventory serves five purposes within the firm:

1. It enables the firm to achieve economics of scale.
2. It balances supply and demand.
3. It enables specialization in manufacturing.
4. It provides protection from uncertainties in demand and order cycle.
5. It acts as a buffer between critical interfaces within the supply chain.

Economies of Scale.   Inventory is required if a firm is to realize economies of scale in purchasing, transportation, and manufacturing. For example, raw materials inventory is necessary if the manufacturer is to take advantage of the per-unit price reductions associated with volume purchases. However, increasingly when purchased volumes are sufficiently large, purchase contracts are being negotiated based on annual volumes, not the amount purchased on an individual order. Nevertheless, purchased materials have a lower transportation cost per unit if ordered in larger volumes. The reason for this lower per-unit cost is that full truckload and railcar shipments receive lower transportation rates than smaller shipments of less than truckload (LTL) or less than carload (LCL) quantities. When suppliers are located in the same geographic area, it may be possible to consolidate small volumes into one large shipment. This will be described in detail in Chapter 8.

The reasons for holding finished goods inventory are similar to reasons for holding raw materials inventory. Transportation economies are possible with large-volume shipments, but in order for a firm to take advantage of these economical rates, larger quantities of finished goods inventory are required at manufacturing locations and field warehouse locations, or at customers' locations. An alternative to shipping large cus-

---

[1]Professor Jay U. Sterling, University of Alabama.

tomer orders only is to consolidate a number of customer orders into one shipment for the long-distance shipment and pay for local delivery in the local market.

Finished goods inventory also makes it possible to realize manufacturing economies. Plant capacity is greater and per-unit manufacturing costs are lower if a firm schedules long production runs with few line changes. Manufacturing in small quantities leads to short production runs and high changeover costs. However, the production of large quantities may require that some of the items be carried in inventory for a significant period of time before they can be sold. The production of large quantities may also prevent timely and responsive recovery on items that experience a stockout, since large production runs mean that items will be produced less frequently. The cost of maintaining this inventory must be compared to the production savings realized. Although frequent production changeovers reduce the quantity of inventory that must be carried, and shorten the lead time that is required in the event of a stockout, they require time that could be used for manufacturing a product. When a plant is operating at or near capacity, frequent line changes may mean that contribution to profit is lost because there is not enough product to meet demand. In such situations, the cost of lost sales plus the changeover costs must be compared to the increase in inventory carrying costs that would result from longer production runs. While these trade-offs exist in the short term, in the long term management should invest in manufacturing technology that enables quick changeover and the efficient production of small quantities.

Balancing Supply and Demand.   Seasonal supply and/or demand may make it necessary for a firm to hold inventory. For example, a producer of a premium line of boxed chocolates experiences significant sales volume increases at Christmas, Valentine's Day, Easter, and Mother's Day. The cost of establishing production capacity to handle the volume at these peak periods would be substantial. In addition, substantial idle capacity and wide fluctuations in the labor force would result if the company were to produce to demand. The decision to maintain a relatively stable workforce and produce at a somewhat constant level throughout the year creates significant inventory buildup at various times during the year, but at a lower total cost to the firm. The seasonal inventories are stored in a freezer warehouse built adjacent to the plant.

In contrast, demand for a product may be relatively stable throughout the year, but raw materials may be available only at certain times during the year. Such is the case for producers of canned fruits and vegetables. This makes it necessary to manufacture finished products in excess of current demand and hold them in inventory, unless the raw materials can be purchased from parts of the world with different growing seasons. In this case, increased acquisition costs must be compared to the inventory carrying costs associated with local supply.

Specialization.   Inventory makes it possible for each of a firm's plants to specialize in the products that it manufactures. The finished products can be shipped to large mixing warehouses, from which customer orders and products for field warehouses can be shipped. The economics that result from the longer production runs, as well as savings in transportation costs, more than offset the costs of additional handling. Companies such as Whirlpool Corporation have found significant cost savings in the operation of consolidation warehouses that allow the firm to specialize manufacturing by plant location. The specialized facilities are known as *focused factories.*[2]

Focused Factories

_____

[2]See Wickham Skinner, "The Focused Factory," *Harvard Business Review* 52, no. 3 (May–June 1974), pp. 113–21.

**Raw Materials
Inventory**

Protection from Uncertainties.   Inventory is also held as protection from uncertainties. *Raw materials inventories* in excess of those required to support production can result from speculative purchases made because management expects either a future price increase or a strike, for example. Other reasons include seasonal availability of supply, such as in the case of fruits or vegetables for canning, or a desire to maintain a source of supply. Regardless of the reason for maintaining a raw materials inventory, the costs of holding the inventory should be compared to the savings realized or costs avoided by holding it.

**Work-in-Process
Inventory**

Work-in-process inventory is often maintained between manufacturing operations within a plant to avoid a shutdown if a critical piece of equipment were to break down, and to equalize flow, since not all manufacturing operations produce at the same rate. The stockpiling of work-in-process within the manufacturing complex permits maximum economies of production without work stoppage. Increasingly, management is working to eliminate the manufacturing bottlenecks that lead to work-in-process inventories. This will be dealt with further in Chapter 7.

Inventory planning is critical to successful manufacturing operations since a shortage of raw materials can shut down the production line or lead to a modification of the production schedule; these events may increase expenses or result in a shortage of finished product. While shortages of raw materials can disrupt normal manufacturing operations, excessive inventories can increase costs and reduce profitability by increasing inventory carrying costs.

**Finished Goods
Inventory**

Finally, *finished goods inventory* can be used as a means of improving customer service levels by reducing the likelihood of a stockout due to unanticipated demand or variability in lead time. If the inventory is balanced, increased inventory investment will enable the manufacturer to offer higher levels of product availability and less chance of a stockout. A balanced inventory is one that contains items in proportion to expected demand.

A Buffer throughout the Supply Chain.   Inventory is held throughout the supply chain to act as a buffer for the following critical interfaces:

- Supplier–procurement (purchasing).
- Procurement–production.
- Production–marketing.
- Marketing–distribution.
- Distribution–intermediary.
- Intermediary–consumer/user.

Because members of the supply chain are separated geographically, it is necessary for inventory to be held throughout the supply chain in order to successfully achieve time and place utility (see Chapter 1).

Figure 6–1 shows the typical inventory positions in a supplier-manufacturer-retailer-consumer supply chain. Raw materials must be moved from a source of supply to the manufacturing location, where they will be input into the manufacturing process. In many cases this will require holding work-in-process inventory.

Once the manufacturing process has been completed, product must be moved into finished goods inventory at plant locations. The next step is the strategic deployment of finished goods inventory to field locations, which may include corporate-owned or leased distribution centers, public warehouses, wholesalers' warehouses, and/or retail chain distribution centers. Inventory is then positioned to enable customer purchase.

FIGURE 6–1

The logistics flow

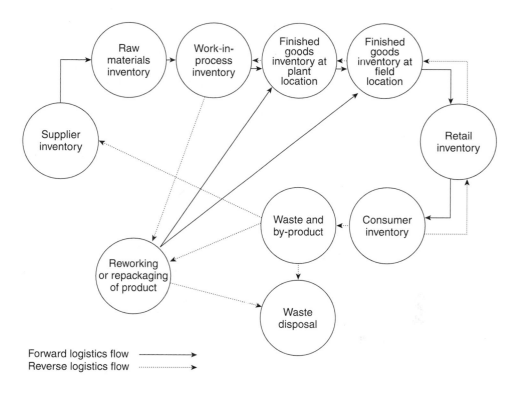

Forward logistics flow ⟶
Reverse logistics flow ·····⟶

**No Product Moves
until Information Moves**

Similarly, the customer maintains an inventory to support individual or institutional consumption.

All of these product flows are the result of a transaction between the manufacturer and the customer, or a decision by the ultimate consumer or user to purchase the product. The entire process depends on a communications network that moves information from the customer to the firm, through the firm back to the customer, and to the firm's suppliers. Clearly, communications is an integral part of managing logistics in the supply chain.

Often it is necessary to move a product backward through the supply chain for a variety of reasons. For example, a customer may return a product because it is damaged, or a manufacturer may need to recall a product because of defects. This, as we explained in Chapter 1, is referred to as *reverse logistics.*[3]

Finally, another aspect that promises to become a bigger factor in the future is waste disposal. One specific example involves "bottle laws," such as those enacted in Michigan, Vermont, Oregon, and Iowa. As sensitivity to litter from packaging and concern over resource use increase, environmentalists and concerned citizens in other states—if not nationally—are likely to push for such laws. To date, these laws have applied only to beer and soft-drink containers, but other packaging materials may become future targets.

---

[3]James R. Stock, *Development and Implementation of Reverse Logistics Programs* (Oak Brook, IL: Council of Logistics Management, 1998).

Types of Inventory

Six Types of Inventory

Inventories can be categorized into the following types, signifying the reasons for which they are accumulated: cycle stock, in-transit inventories, safety or buffer stock, speculative stock, seasonal stock, and dead stock.

If Demand and Lead Time Are Constant, Only Cycle Stock Is Necessary

Cycle Stock.   Cycle stock is inventory that results from the replenishment process and is required in order to meet demand under conditions of certainty—that is, when the firm can predict demand and replenishment times (lead times) perfectly. For example, if the rate of sales for a product is a constant 20 units per day and the lead time is always 10 days, no inventory beyond the cycle stock would be required. While assumptions of constant demand and lead time remove the complexities involved in inventory management, let's look at such an example to clarify the basic inventory principles. Figure 6–2 shows three alternative reorder strategies. Since demand and lead time are constant and known, orders are scheduled to arrive just as the last unit is sold. Thus, no inventory beyond the cycle stock is required. The average cycle stock in all three examples is equal to half of the order quantity. However, the average cycle stock will be 200, 100, or 300 units depending on whether management orders in quantities of 400 (Part A), 200 (Part B), or 600 (Part C), respectively.

In-Transit Inventories.   In-transit inventories are items that are en route from one location to another. They may be considered part of cycle stock even though they are not available for sale and/or shipment until after they arrive at the destination. For the calculation of inventory carrying costs, in-transit inventories should be considered as inventory at the place of shipment origin since the items are not available for use, sale, or subsequent reshipment.

Variability in Demand Increases Safety Stock

Safety or Buffer Stock.   Safety or buffer stock is held in excess of cycle stock because of uncertainty in demand or lead time. The notion is that a portion of average inventory should be devoted to cover short-range variations in demand and lead time. Average inventory at a stock-keeping location that experiences demand or lead-time variability is equal to half the order quantity plus the safety stock. For example, in Figure 6–3, the average inventory would be 100 units if demand and lead time were constant. But if demand was actually 25 units per day instead of the predicted 20 units per day with a 10-day lead time, inventory would be depleted by the 8th day (200/25). Since the next order would not arrive until the 10th day (order was placed on day zero), the company would experience stockouts for two days. At 25 units of demand per day, this would be a stockout of 50 units in total. If management believed that the maximum variation in demand would be plus or minus 5 units, a safety stock of 50 units would prevent a stockout due to variation in demand. This would require holding an average inventory of 150 units.

Variability in Lead Time Increases Safety Stock

Now consider the case in which demand is constant but lead time can vary by plus or minus 2 days (Part B of Figure 6–3). If the order arrives 2 days early, the inventory on hand would be equal to a 12-day supply, or 240 units, since sales are at a rate of 20 units per day and 40 units would remain in inventory when the new order arrived. However, if the order arrived 2 days late, on day 12—which is a more likely occurrence—the firm would experience stockouts for 2 days (40 units). If management believed that shipments would never arrive more than 2 days late, a safety stock of 40 units would ensure that a stockout due to variation in lead time would not occur if demand remained constant.

Figure 6–2

The effect of reorder quantity on average inventory investment with constant demand and lead time

A. Order quantity of 400 units

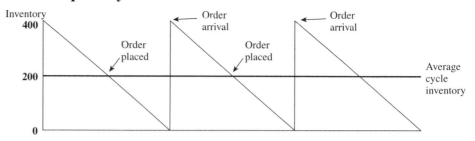

B. Order quantity of 200 units

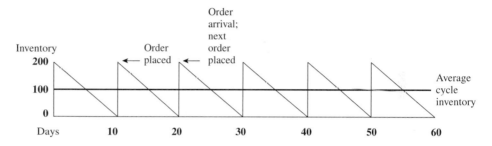

C. Order quantity of 600 units

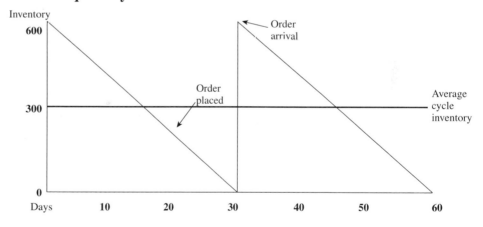

Demand and Lead-Time Variability Are Facts of Life

In most business situations management must be able to deal with variability in demand and lead time. Forecasting is rarely accurate enough to predict demand, and demand is seldom, if ever, constant. In addition, transportation delays along with supplier and production problems make lead-time variability a fact of life. Consider Part C of Figure 6–3, in which demand uncertainty (Part A) and lead-time uncertainty (Part B) are combined.

Combined uncertainty is the worst of all possible worlds. In this case demand is above the forecast by the maximum, 25 units instead of 20 units per day, and the incoming order arrives two days late. The result is a stockout period of four days at 25 units

FIGURE 6–3

Average inventory investment under conditions of uncertainty

A. With variable demand

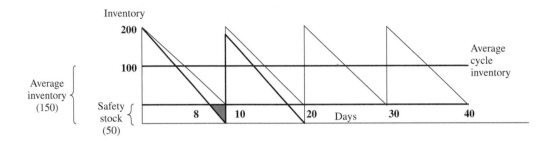

B. With variable lead time

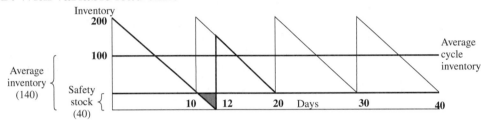

C. With variable demand and lead time

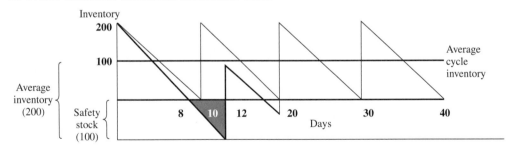

per day. If management wanted to protect against the maximum variability in both demand and lead time, the firm would need a safety stock of 100 units. This policy (no stockouts) would result in an average inventory of 200 units.

In summary, variability in demand and lead time results in either safety stocks or stockouts. Although it may not be possible to eliminate variability in demand, forecasting can be used to better predict demand, resulting in less safety stock. However, by using the services of transportation companies that deliver consistently on time and by selecting suppliers that have consistent, reliable lead times, it is possible to eliminate the safety stocks associated with lead-time variability. Referring back to Part C of Figure 6–3, the elimination of lead-time variability would reduce safety stocks from

100 units to 50 units (see Part A of Figure 6–3) and overall inventories from 200 units to 150 units—or 25 percent reduction in total inventory.

Speculative Stock.   Speculative stock is inventory held for reasons other than satisfying current demand. For example, materials may be purchased in volumes larger than necessary in order to receive quantity discounts, because of a forecasted price increase or materials shortage, or to protect against the possibility of a strike. Production economics may also lead to the manufacture of products at times other than when they are demanded. Finally, goods may be produced seasonally for consumption throughout the year, or at a constant level in anticipation of seasonal demand in order to maintain a stable workload and labor force.

Seasonal Stock.   Seasonal stock is a form of speculative stock that involves the accumulation of inventory before a season begins in order to maintain a stable labor force and stable production runs or, in the case of agricultural products, inventory accumulated as the result of a growing season that limits availability throughout the year.

Dead Stock.   Dead stock is the set of items for which no demand has been registered for some specified period of time. Such stock might be obsolete on a total company basis or at just one stock-keeping location. If it is the latter, the items may be either transshipped to another location to avoid the obsolescence penalty or marked down and sold at the current location.

Basic Inventory Management

The Objectives of Inventory Management

Inventory is a major use of capital and, for this reason, the objectives of inventory management are to increase corporate profitability, to predict the impact of corporate policies on inventory levels, and to minimize the total cost of logistics activities.

Corporate profitability can be improved by increasing sales volume or cutting inventory costs. Increased sales are often possible if high levels of inventory lead to better in-stock availability and more consistent service levels. Low inventory levels can reduce fill rates on customer orders and result in lost sales. However, the costs associated with high levels of inventory usually exceed the benefits derived. Methods of decreasing inventory-related costs include such measures as reducing the number of back orders or expedited shipments, purging obsolete or dead stock from the system, or improving the accuracy of forecasts. Transshipment of inventory between field warehouses and small-lot transfers can also be reduced or eliminated by better inventory planning. Better inventory management can increase the ability to control and predict the reaction of inventory investment to changes in management policy. For example, how will a change in the corporate hurdle rate influence the quantity of inventory held?

Finally, total cost integration should be the goal of inventory planning. That is, management must determine the inventory level required to achieve least total cost logistics, given the required customer service objectives.

Inventory managers must determine how much inventory to order and when to place the order. As a means of illustrating the basic principles of reorder policy, let's consider inventory management under conditions of certainty and uncertainty. This latter case is the rule rather than the exception.

Inventory Management under Conditions of Certainty

Ordering Costs

Replenishment policy under conditions of certainty requires the balancing of ordering costs against inventory carrying costs.[4] For example, a policy of ordering large quantities infrequently may result in inventory carrying costs in excess of the savings in ordering costs. Ordering costs for products purchased from an outside supplier typically include (1) the cost of transmitting the order, (2) the cost of receiving the product, (3) the cost of placing it in storage, and (4) the cost associated with processing the invoice for payment.

In the case of restocking its own field warehouses, a company's ordering costs typically include (1) the cost of transmitting and processing the inventory transfer; (2) the cost of handling the product if it is in stock, or the cost of setting up production to produce it, and the handling cost if the product is not in stock; (3) the cost of receiving at the field location; and (4) the cost of associated documentation. Remember that only direct out-of-pocket expenses should be included. These costs were explained in detail in Chapter 4.

Economic Order Quantity.   The best ordering policy can be determined by minimizing the total of inventory carrying costs and ordering costs using the economic order quantity (EOQ) model.

The EOQ Model

Referring to the example given in Figure 6–2, two questions seem appropriate:

1. Should we place orders for 200, 400, or 600 units, or some other quantity?
2. What is the impact on inventory if orders are placed at 10-, 20-, or 30-day intervals, or some other time period? Assuming constant demand and lead time, sales of 20 units per day and 240 working days per year, annual sales will be 4,800 units.[5] If orders are placed every 10 days, 24 orders of 200 units will be placed. With a 20-day order interval, 12 orders of 400 units are required. If the 30-day order interval is selected, 8 orders of 600 units are necessary. The average inventory is 100, 200, and 300 units, respectively. Which of these policies would be best?

The cost trade-offs required to determine the most economical order quantity are shown graphically in Figure 6–4. By determining the EOQ and dividing the annual demand by it, we can identify the frequency and size of the order that will minimize the two costs.

The EOQ in units can be calculated using the following formula:

$$\text{EOQ} = \sqrt{\frac{2PD}{CV}}$$

where

P = The ordering cost (dollars per order)
D = Annual demand or usage of the product (number of units)
C = Annual inventory carrying cost (as a percentage of product cost or value)
V = Average cost or value of one unit of inventory

---

[4]When the supplier pays the freight cost.
[5]For this example, it was assumed that the plant was closed for four weeks during each year. In an industrial application we would use the actual number of working days for the firm in question.

Figure 6–4

*Cost trade-offs
to determine the most
economical order quantity*

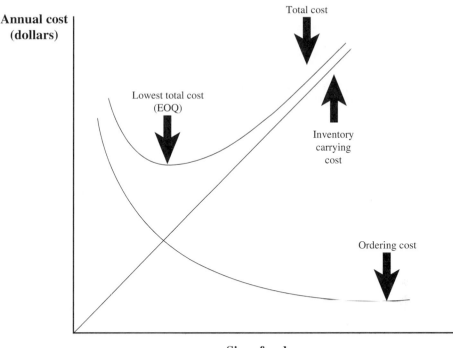

Figure 6–5 contains the mathematical derivation of the EOQ model, which was one of the first operations research applications.

Now, using the EOQ formula, we will determine the best ordering policy for the situation described in Figure 6–2:

V = $100 per unit
C = 25 percent
P = $40
D = 4,800 units

$$EOQ = \sqrt{\frac{2(\$40)(4,800)}{(25\%)(100)}}$$

$$= \sqrt{\frac{384,000}{25}}$$

$$= 124 \text{ units}$$

If 20 units fit on a pallet, then the reorder quantity of 120 units (due to rounding) would be established. This analysis is shown in tabular form in Table 6–1.

The EOQ model has received significant attention and use in industry; however, it is not without its limitations. The simple EOQ model is based on the following assumptions:

1. A continuous, constant, and known rate of demand.

2. A constant and known replenishment or lead time.

3. A constant purchase price that is independent of the order quantity or time.

FIGURE 6–5

Mathematical derivation of the economic order quantity model

Total annual cost (TAC) $= \left[\dfrac{Q \times V \times C}{2}\right] + \left[\dfrac{P \times D}{Q}\right]$

Where: Q **= The average number of units in the economic order quantity during the order cycle**

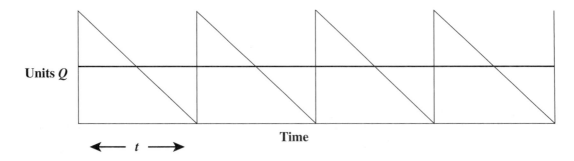

Units Q

$\longleftarrow\ t\ \longrightarrow$ **Time**

Mathematical solution:

$$\frac{dTAC}{dQ} \ = \ \frac{VC}{2} \ - \ \frac{PD}{Q^2}$$

Set = Zero: $\dfrac{VC}{2} \ - \ \dfrac{PD}{Q^2} \ = \ 0$

$$\frac{VC}{2} \ = \ \frac{PD}{Q^2}$$

$$Q^2 \ = \ \frac{2PD}{CV}$$

$$Q \ = \ \sqrt{\frac{2PD}{CV}}$$

4. A constant transportation cost that is independent of the order quantity or time.
5. The satisfaction of all demand (no stockouts are permitted).
6. No inventory in transit.
7. Only one item in inventory, or at least no interaction.
8. An infinite planning horizon.
9. No limit on capital availability.

It would be extremely rare to find a situation where demand is constant, lead time is constant, both are known with certainty, and costs are known precisely. However, the simplifying assumptions are of great concern only if policy decisions will change as a

TABLE 6–1   Cost Trade-Offs Required to Determine the Most Economic Order Quantity

Order Quantity	Number of Orders (D/Q)	Ordering Cost [P ×(D/Q)]	Inventory Carrying Cost ($\frac{1}{2}Q \times C \times V$)	Total Cost
40	120	$4,800	$ 500	$5,300
60	80	3,200	750	3,950
80	60	2,400	1,000	3,400
100	48	1,920	1,250	3,170
120	40	1,600	1,500	3,100
140	35	1,400	1,750	3,150
160	30	1,200	2,000	3,200
200	24	960	2,500	3,460
300	16	640	3,750	4,390
400	12	480	5,000	5,480

result of the assumptions made. The EOQ solution is relatively insensitive to small changes in the input data. Referring back to Figure 6–4, we can see that the EOQ curve is relatively flat around the solution point. This is borne out in Table 6–1. Although the calculated EOQ was 124 units (rounded to 120), an EOQ variation of 20 units or even 40 units does not significantly change the total cost.

Adjusting EOQ for Volume Discounts

Adjustments to the EOQ.   Typical refinements that must be made to the EOQ model include adjustments for volume transportation rates and for quantity discounts. The simple EOQ model did not consider the impact of these two factors. The following adjustment can be made to the EOQ formula so that it will consider the impact of quantity discounts and/or freight breaks:[6]

$$Q_1 = 2\frac{rD}{C} + (1-r)Q_0$$

where

Q_1 = The maximum quantity that can be economically ordered to qualify for a discount on unit cost
r = The percentage of price reduction if a larger quantity is ordered
D = The annual demand in units
C = The inventory carrying cost percentage
Q_0 = The EOQ based on current price

Calculating the EOQ

Using the modified EOQ formula, we will determine the best ordering policy for the Johnson Manufacturing Company. Johnson Manufacturing produced and sold a complete line of industrial air-conditioning units that were marketed nationally through independent distributors. The company purchased a line of relays for use in its air conditioners from a manufacturer in the Midwest. It ordered approximately 300 cases of

---

[6]See Robert G. Brown, *Decision Rules for Inventory Management* (New York: Holt, Rinehart & Winston, 1967), pp. 205–6.

24 units each, 54 times per year; the annual volume was about 16,000 cases. The purchase price was $8.00 per case, the ordering costs were $10.00 per order, and the inventory carrying cost was 25 percent. The relays weighed 25 pounds per case; Johnson Manufacturing paid the shipping costs. The freight rate was $4.00 per hundredweight (cwt) on shipments of less than 15,000 pounds, $3.90 per cwt on shipments of 15,000 to 39,000 pounds, and $3.64 per cwt on orders of more than 39,000 pounds. The relays were shipped on pallets of 20 cases.

First, it is necessary to calculate the transportation cost for a case of product without discounts for volume shipments. Shipments of less than 15,000 pounds—600 cases—cost $4.00 per cwt, or $1.00 ($4.00/100 lbs. × 25 lbs.) per case.

Therefore, without transportation discounts for shipping in quantities above 15,000 pounds, the delivered cost of a case of product would be $9.00 ($8.00 plus $1.00 transportation), and the EOQ would be:

$$EOQ = \sqrt{\frac{2PD}{CV}}$$

$$= \sqrt{\frac{2(\$10)(16,000)}{(25\%)(\$9.00)}}$$

$$= \sqrt{\frac{320,000}{2.25}}$$

$$= 377, \text{ or } 380 \text{ rounded to the nearest full pallet}$$

If the company shipped in quantities of 40,000 pounds or more, the cost per case would be $0.91 ($3.64/100 lbs. × 25 lbs.). The percentage price reduction, *r,* made possible by shipping at the lowest freight cost is:

$$\frac{\$9.00 - \$8.91}{\$9.00 \times 100} = 1.0\% \text{ reduction in delivered cost}$$

The adjusted EOQ is calculated as follows:

$$Q_1 = 2\frac{(0.01)(16,000)}{0.25} + (1 - 0.01)(380)$$

$$= 1,280 + 376$$

$$= 1,656, \text{ or } 1,660 \text{ rounded to the nearest full pallet}$$

While the largest freight break results in only a 1 percent reduction in the delivered cost of a case of the product, the volume of annual purchases is large enough that the EOQ changes significantly, from 380 cases to 1,660 cases.

An alternative to using the above formula would be to perform an analysis similar to the one shown in Table 6–1 and add a column that includes the annual transportation cost associated with each of the order quantities. The total annual costs would include the transportation costs associated with different order quantities. The Johnson Manufacturing example is shown in tabular form in Table 6–2, which illustrates that transportation costs have a significant impact on the purchase decision. The purchase of the EOQ of 380 cases per order would require 43 orders per year, or the purchase of 16,340 cases in the first year. Therefore, this option is not as attractive as the 400-case order quantity, which would require 40 orders to purchase the necessary 16,000 cases

TABLE 6–2   Cost Trade-Offs Required to Determine the Most Economic Order Quantity with Transportation Costs Included

A	B	C (A × $8)	D (B × C)	E	F	G	H	I
Possible Order Quantity	Number of Orders per Year	Purchase Price per Order	Value of Orders Year One	Transportation Cost per Order	Annual Ordering Cost	Annual Transportation Cost	Inventory Carrying Cost[d]	Total Annual Costs[e]
300	54	$ 2,400	$129,600	$ 300[a]	$540	$16,200	$ 338	$17,078
380	43	3,040	130,720	380[a]	430	16,340	428	17,198
400	40	3,200	128,000	400[a]	400	16,000	450	16,850
800	20	6,400	128,000	780[b]	200	15,600	898	16,698
1,200	14	9,600	134,400	1,170[b]	140	16,380	1,346	17,866
1,600	10	12,800	128,000	1,458[c]	100	14,580	1,782	16,462[f]
2,000	8	16,000	128,000	1,820[c]	80	14,560	2,228	16,868

[a]Orders for less than 15,000 lbs. (600 cases) have a rate of $4.00/cwt, which equals $1.00/case.
[b]Orders weighing between 15,000 lbs. and 39,000 lbs. (600 cases and 1,560 cases) have a rate of $3.90/cwt, which equals $0.975/case.
[c]Orders weighing 40,000 lbs. or more (1,600 cases) have a rate of $3.64/cwt, which equals $0.91/case.
[d]Inventory carrying cost = 1/2 (C + E) (25%).
[e]I = F + G + H.
[f]Lowest total cost.

and is $348 less expensive. However, with the transportation costs included, 10 orders of 1,600 cases yields the lowest total cost.

It is also possible to include purchase discounts by adding a column, "Annual Product Cost," and appropriately adjusting the inventory carrying cost and total annual costs columns. Once again, the desired EOQ would be the order quantity that resulted in the lowest total cost.[7]

EOQ with Incremental Replenishment.[8]   The basic EOQ model assumes that each order is delivered at a single point in time (instantaneous replenishment). However, when a firm is both a producer and user, or when deliveries are spread over time, inventories are replenished over time instead of instantaneously.

If usage and production (or delivery) rates are equal, there will be no inventory buildup, because all output will be used immediately and the issue of lot size does not come up. Usually, the production or delivery rate exceeds the usage rate, creating the situation depicted in Figure 6–6. In the typical production case, production occurs over only a portion of each cycle because the production rate is greater than the usage rate, and usage occurs over the entire cycle. During the production phase of the cycle, inventory builds up at a rate equal to the difference between production and usage rates. For example, if the daily production rate is 20 units and the daily usage rate is 5 units,

[7]For additional examples of special purpose EOQ models, refer to Richard B. Chase, Nicholas J. Aquilano and F. Robert Jacobs, *Production and Operations Management,* 8th ed. (Burr Ridge, IL: McGraw-Hill/Irwin, 1998), pp. 586–98.

[8]This section is adapted from: William J. Stephenson, *Production/Operations Management,* 6th ed. (Burr Ridge, IL: McGraw-Hill/Irwin, 1999), pp. 572–73.

FIGURE 6–6

EOQ with incremental replenishment

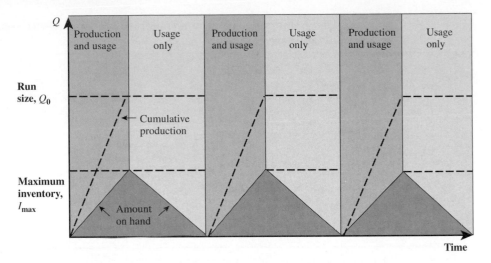

Source: William J. Stephenson, *Production/Operations Management,* 6th ed. (Burr Ridge, IL: Irwin/McGraw-Hill, 1999), p. 573.

inventory will build up at the rate of 20 − 5 = 15 units per day. As long as production occurs, the inventory level will continue to build; when production ceases, the inventory level will begin to decrease. Hence, the inventory level will be maximum at the point where production stops. When the amount of inventory on hand is exhausted, production is resumed, and the cycle repeats itself.

If a company makes the product, there are no ordering costs, but with every run there are setup costs—the costs required to prepare the equipment for the job, such as cleaning, adjusting, and changing tools and fixtures. Setup costs are similar to ordering costs because they are independent of the lot (run) size. They are treated in the formula in exactly the same way. The larger the run size, the fewer the number of runs needed and the lower the annual setup cost. The number of runs is demand divided by the EOQ (D/Q), and the annual setup cost is equal to the number of runs per year times the setup cost per run: $(D/Q)S$.

Total cost (TC) is:

$$TC_{min} = \text{Carrying cost } + \text{ Setup cost}$$

$$= \left(\frac{I_{max}}{2}\right)CV + \left(\frac{D}{Q_0}\right)S$$

where

I_{max} = Maximum inventory

The economic run quantity is:

$$Q_0 = \sqrt{\frac{2PD}{CV}} \sqrt{\frac{p}{p-u}}$$

where

p = Production or delivery rate
u = Usage rate

The cycle time (the time between orders or between the beginnings of runs) for the economic run size model is a function of the run size and usage (demand) rate:

$$\text{Cycle time} = \frac{Q_0}{u}$$

Similarly, the run time (the production phase of the cycle) is a function of the run size and the production rate:

$$\text{Run time} = \frac{Q_0}{p}$$

The maximum and average inventory levels are:

$$I_{max}\ \frac{Q_0}{p}(p - u)\ \text{and}\ I_{average} = \frac{I_{max}}{2}$$

Inventory Management under Uncertainty

As we have noted, managers rarely, if ever, know for sure what demand to expect for the firm's products. Many factors including economic conditions, competitive actions, changes in government regulations, market shifts, and changes in consumer buying patterns may influence forecast accuracy. Order cycle times are also not constant. Transit times vary, it may take more time to assemble an order or wait for scheduled production on one occasion than another, supplier lead times for components and raw materials may not be consistent, and suppliers may not have the capability of responding to changes in demand.

Consequently, management has the option of either maintaining additional inventory in the form of safety stocks (as was shown in Figure 6–3) or risking a potential loss of sales revenue due to stockouts at a distribution center. We must thus consider an additional cost trade-off: inventory carrying costs versus stockout costs.

The uncertainties associated with demand and lead time cause most managers to concentrate on when to order rather than on the order quantity. The order quantity is important to the extent that it influences the number of orders, and consequently the number of times that the company is exposed to a potential stockout at the end of each order cycle. The point at which the order is placed is the primary determinant of the future ability to fill demand while waiting for replenishment stock.

Fixed Order Point, Fixed Order Quantity Model

One method used for inventory control under conditions of uncertainty is the *fixed order point, fixed order quantity model.* With this method, an order is placed when the inventory on hand and on order reaches a predetermined minimum level required to satisfy demand during the order cycle. The economic order quantity will be ordered whenever demand drops the inventory level to the reorder point.

Fixed Order Interval Model

In contrast, a *fixed order interval model* compares current inventory with forecast demand, and places an order for the necessary quantity at a regular, specified time. In other words, the interval between orders is fixed. This method facilitates combining orders for various items in a vendor's line, thereby qualifying for volume purchase discounts and freight consolidation savings. Figure 6–7 illustrates the two methods.

Part A of Figure 6–7 shows that replenishment orders are placed on days 15, 27, and 52, respectively, under the fixed order point, fixed order quantity model. In contrast, when the fixed order interval model is used (Part B), orders are placed at 20-day intervals on days 15, 35, and 55. With the fixed order interval model it is necessary to forecast demand for days 20 through 40 on day 15, for days 40 through 60 on day 35, and

FIGURE 6–7

*Inventory management
under uncertainty*

A. Fixed order point, fixed order quantity model

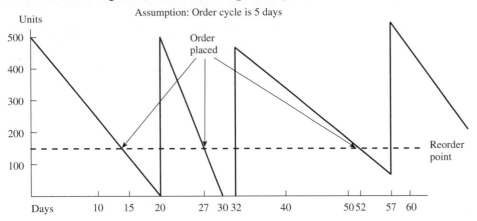

B. Fixed order interval model

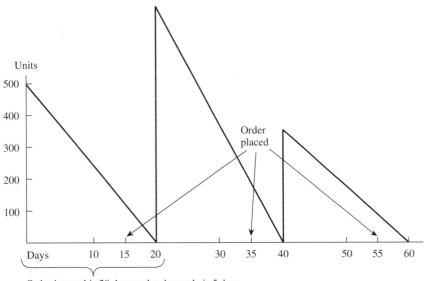

so on. The fixed order interval system is more adaptive, in that management is forced to consider changes in sales activity and make a forecast for every order interval.

Calculating Safety Stock Requirements

**How to Determine
the Amount
of Safety Stock**

The amount of safety stock necessary to satisfy a given level of demand can be determined by computer simulation or statistical techniques. In this illustration we will address the use of statistical techniques. In calculating safety stock levels it is necessary to consider the joint impact of demand and replenishment cycle variability. This can be accomplished by gathering statistically valid samples of data on recent sales volumes and replenishment cycles. Once the data are gathered it is possible to determine safety stock requirements by using the following formula:[9]

$$\sigma_c = \sqrt{\overline{R}(\sigma_S^{\,2}) + \overline{S}^{\,2}(\sigma_R^{\,2})}$$

where

> σ_c = Units of safety stock needed to satisfy 68 percent of all probabilities (one standard deviation)
> $\overline{R}$ = Average replenishment cycle
> σ_S = Standard deviation of daily sales
> $\overline{S}$ = Average daily sales
> σ_R = Standard deviation of the replenishment cycle

Assume that the sales history contained in Table 6–3 has been developed for market area 1. The next step is to calculate the standard deviation of daily sales as shown in Table 6–4. From this sample we can calculate the standard deviation of sales. The formula is:

$$\sigma_S = \sqrt{\frac{\Sigma fd^2}{n-1}}$$

where

> σ_s = Standard deviation of daily sales
> f = Frequency of event
> d = Deviation of event from mean
> n = Total observations

TABLE 6–3   Sales History for Market Area 1

Day	Sales in Cases	Day	Sales in Cases
1	100	14	80
2	80	15	90
3	70	16	90
4	60	17	100
5	80	18	140
6	90	19	110
7	120	20	120
8	110	21	70
9	100	22	100
10	110	23	130
11	130	24	110
12	120	25	90
13	100		

---

[9]Robert Hammond of McKinsey and Company, Inc., as reported in Robert Fetter and Winston C. Dalleck, *Decision Models for Inventory Management* (Homewood, IL: Richard D. Irwin, 1961), pp. 105–8. For an application of the formula in a simulation model, see Walter Zinn, Howard Marmorstein, and John Charnes, "The Effect of Autocorrelated Demand on Customer Service," *Journal of Business Logistics* 13, no. 1 (1992), pp. 173–92.

TABLE 6–4   Calculation of Standard Deviation of Sales

Daily Sales in Cases	Frequency (f)	Deviation from Mean (d)	Deviation Squared (d^2)	fd^2
60	1	−40	1,600	1,600
70	2	−30	900	1,800
80	3	−20	400	1,200
90	4	−10	100	400
100	5	0	0	0
110	4	+10	100	400
120	3	+20	400	1,200
130	2	+30	900	1,800
140	1	+40	1,600	1,600
$\bar{S} = 100$	$n = 25$			$\Sigma fd^2 = 10,000$

Applying this formula to the data yields a standard deviation of sales approximately equal to 20 units:

$$\sigma_S = \sqrt{\frac{10,000}{25-1}}$$

$$= 20$$

This means that 68 percent of the time, daily sales fall between 80 and 120 units (100 units ± 20 units). Two standard deviations' protection, or 40 units, would protect against 95 percent of all events. In setting safety stock levels, however, it is important to consider only events that exceed the mean sales volume. Thus, a safety stock level of 40 units actually affords protection against almost 98 percent of all possible events (see Figure 6–8). Given a distribution of measurements that is approximately bell-shaped, the mean, plus or minus one standard deviation, will contain approximately 68 percent of the measurements. This leaves 16 percent in each of the tails, which means that inventory sufficient to cover sales of one standard deviation in excess of mean daily sales will actually provide an 84 percent customer service level. (If the sample does not represent a normal distribution, refer to a basic statistics book for an alternative treatment.)

The same procedure can be used to arrive at the mean and standard deviation of the replenishment cycle. Once this is accomplished, the formula shown previously can be used to determine safety stock requirements at a certain level of demand. For example, analysis of replenishment cycles might yield the results shown in Table 6–5. The standard deviation of the replenishment cycle is:

$$\sigma_R = \sqrt{\frac{\Sigma fd^2}{n-1}}$$

$$\sigma_R = \sqrt{2.67}$$

$$= 1.634$$

The average replenishment cycle is:

$$(\bar{R}) = 10$$

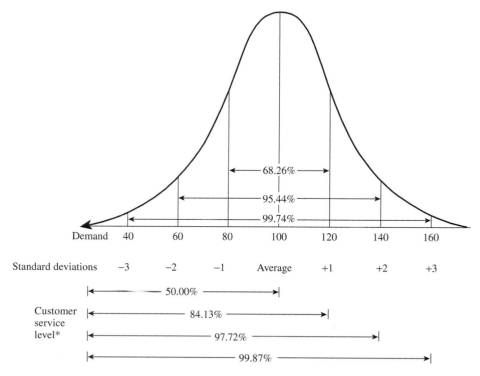

FIGURE 6–8

*Area relationships
for the normal
distribution*

*As measured by the percentage of order cycles that will not suffer from stockouts. It is the probability that no stockout will occur during a replenishment cycle.

TABLE 6–5   Calculation of Standard Deviation of Replenishment Cycle

Lead Time in Days	Frequency (f)	Deviation from Mean (d)	Deviation Squared (d²)	fd²
7	1	−3	9	9
8	2	−2	4	8
9	3	−1	1	3
10	4	0	0	0
11	3	+1	1	3
12	2	+2	4	8
13	1	+3	9	9
$\bar{R} = 10$	$n = 16$			$\Sigma fd^2 = 40$

The combined safety stock required to cover variability in both demand and lead time can be found using the formula:

$$\sigma_c = \sqrt{\bar{R}(\sigma_S)^2 + \bar{S}^2(\sigma_R)^2}$$

$$= \sqrt{10(20)^2 + 100^2(1.634)^2}$$

$$= \sqrt{30{,}700}$$

$$= 175 \text{ cases}$$

Thus, in a situation in which daily sales vary from 60 to 140 cases and the inventory replenishment cycle varies from 7 to 13 days, a safety stock of 175 cases will allow the manufacturer to satisfy 84 percent of all possible occurrences. To protect against 98 percent of all possibilities, 350 cases of safety stock are required. Table 6–6 shows alternative customer service levels and safety stock requirements.

In order to establish the average inventory for various levels of customer service, we must first determine the EOQ. The projected yearly demand is found by multiplying the average daily demand by 250 working days,[10] which equals 25,000 cases (250×100). The inventory carrying cost was calculated to be 32 percent, the average value of a case of product was $4.37, and the ordering cost was $28. The average inventory required to satisfy each service level is shown in Table 6–7.

Note that the establishment of a safety stock commitment is really a policy of customer service and inventory availability. Although we have demonstrated a quantitative method of calculating safety stock requirements to protect the firm against stockouts at various levels of probability, additional calculations are necessary in order to determine the specific fill rate when stockouts occur. Fill rate represents the percentage of units demanded that are on hand to fill customer orders.

TABLE 6–6   Summary of Alternative Service Levels and Safety Stock Requirements

Service Level	Number of Standard Deviations (σ_c) Needed	Safety Stock Requirements (cases)
84.1%	1.0	175
90.3	1.3	228
94.5	1.6	280
97.7	2.0	350
98.9	2.3	403
99.5	2.6	455
99.9	3.0	525

TABLE 6–7   Summary of Average Inventory Levels Given Different Service Levels

Service Level	Average Cycle Stock ($\frac{1}{2} \times EOQ$)	Safety Stock (units)	Total Average Inventory (units)
84.1%	500	175	675
90.3	500	228	728
94.5	500	280	780
97.7	500	350	850
98.9	500	403	903
99.5	500	455	955
99.9	500	525	1,025

[10]For this example the average number of working days was assumed to be 250.

Calculating Fill Rate

Fill rate represents the magnitude of the stockout. If a manager wants to hold 280 units as safety stock, what will the fill rate be?[11] The fill rate can be calculated using the following formula:

$$FR = 1 - \frac{\sigma_c}{EOQ}[I(K)]$$

where

> FR = Fill rate
>
> σ_c = Combined safety stock required to consider both variability in lead time and demand (one standard deviation)
>
> EOQ = Order quantity = 1,000 (in this example)
>
> $I(K)$ = Service function magnitude factor (provided by Table 6–8), based on desired number of standard deviations.

K (the safety factor) is the safety stock the manager decides to hold divided by σ_c. Returning to the question presented above, the manager's economic order quantity (EOQ) is 1,000. The safety stock determined by the manager is 280 units. Therefore, K is equal to 280 divided by 175, or 1.60. If $K = 1.60$, Table 6–8 can be used to identify $I(K) = 0.0236$ (see last column of Table 6–8).

Now the fill rate can be calculated using the formula:

$$FR = 1 - \frac{\sigma_c}{EOQ}[I(K)]$$

$$= 1 - \frac{175}{1000}(0.0236)$$

$$= 1 - 0.0041$$

$$= 0.9959$$

Thus, the average fill rate is 99.59 percent. That is, of every 100 units of product A demanded, 99.59 will be on hand to be sold if the manager uses 280 units of safety stock and orders 1,000 units each time.[12]

If the manager wants to know how much safety stock of product A to hold to attain a 95 percent fill rate, the same formula can be used:

$$FR = 1 - \frac{\sigma_c}{EOQ}[I(K)]$$

$$I(K) = (1 - FR)\left(\frac{EOQ}{\sigma_c}\right)$$

$$I(K) = (1 - 0.95)\left(\frac{1,000}{175}\right)$$

$$= (0.05)(5.714)$$

$$= 0.2857$$

---

[11]This example was provided by Professor Robert L. Cook, Central Michigan University, Mount Pleasant, Michigan.

[12]If demands, lead times, order quantities, or safety stocks significantly change, the fill rate percentage will also change.

TABLE 6–8   Inventory Safety Stock Factors

$\sigma \begin{cases} \textit{Safety} \\ \textit{Factor} \\ K \end{cases}$	*Stock Protection (Single Tail σ)*	*Stockout Probability F(K)*	*Service Function (Magnitude Factor) Partial Expectation I(K)*
0.00	0.5000	0.5000	0.3989
0.10	0.5394	0.4606	0.3509
0.20	0.5785	0.4215	0.3067
0.30	0.6168	0.3832	0.2664
0.40	0.6542	0.3458	0.2299
0.50	0.6901	0.3099	0.1971
0.60	0.7244	0.2756	0.1679
0.70	0.7569	0.2431	0.1421
0.80	0.7872	0.2128	0.1194
0.90	0.8152	0.1848	0.0998
1.00	0.8409	0.1591	0.0829
1.10	0.8641	0.1359	0.0684
1.20	0.8849	0.1151	0.0561
1.30	0.9033	0.0967	0.0457
1.40	0.9194	0.0806	0.0369
1.50	0.9334	0.0666	0.0297
1.60	0.9454	0.0546	0.0236
1.70	0.9556	0.0444	0.0186
1.80	0.9642	0.0358	0.0145
1.90	0.9714	0.0286	0.0113
2.00	0.9773	0.0227	0.0086
2.10	0.9822	0.0178	0.0065
2.20	0.9861	0.0139	0.0049
2.30	0.9893	0.0107	0.0036
2.40	0.9918	0.0082	0.0027
2.50	0.9938	0.0062	0.0019
2.60	0.9953	0.0047	0.0014
2.70	0.9965	0.0035	0.0010
2.80	0.9974	0.0026	0.0007
2.90	0.9981	0.0019	0.0005
3.00	0.9984	0.0014	0.0004
3.10	0.9990	0.0010	0.0003
3.20	0.9993	0.0007	0.0002
3.30	0.9995	0.0005	0.0001
3.40	0.9997	0.0003	0.0001
3.50	0.9998	0.0002	0.0001
3.60	0.9998	0.0002	
3.70	0.9999	0.0001	
3.80	0.9999	0.0001	
3.90	0.9999	0.0001	
4.00	0.9999	0.0001	

Source: Professor Jay U. Sterling, University of Alabama; adapted from Robert G. Brown, *Materials Management Systems* (New York: John Wiley & Sons, 1977), p. 429.

The corresponding *K* value from Table 6–8 is approximately 0.25. Since *K* is equal to the safety stock the manager decides to hold divided by σ_c, the safety stock required to provide a 95 percent fill rate is 44 units (175×0.25).

How Much to Order: Fixed Order Interval Model[13]

Orders Are Placed at Fixed Time Intervals

The fixed order interval model is used when orders must be placed at fixed time intervals such as weekly or twice a month. The question to be answered at each other point is: How much should be ordered for the next (fixed) interval? If demand is variable, the order size will tend to vary from cycle to cycle. This is quite different from an EOQ/ROP (reorder point) approach in which the order size generally remains fixed from cycle to cycle, while the length of the cycle varies (shorter if demand is higher than average, and longer if demand is less than average).

Reasons to Use the Fixed Order Interval Model

In some cases, a supplier's policy might encourage orders at fixed intervals. Even when that is not the case, grouping orders for items from the same supplier can produce savings in shipping costs. Furthermore, some situations do not readily lend themselves to continuous monitoring of inventory levels. Many retail operations including drugstores and small grocery stores fall into this category. The alternative for them is to use fixed-interval ordering, which requires only periodic checks of inventory levels.

Determining the Amount to Order

If both the demand rate and lead time are constant, the fixed-interval model and the fixed-quantity model function identically. The differences in the two models become apparent only when examined under conditions of variability. Like the ROP model, the fixed-interval model can have variations in demand only, in lead time only, or in both demand and lead time. However, for simplicity we will focus only on *variable demand and constant lead time.*

In the fixed-quantity arrangement, orders are triggered by a *quantity* (ROP), while in the fixed-interval arrangement orders are triggered by a *time* (see again Figure 6–7). Therefore, the fixed-interval system must have stockout protection for lead time plus the next order cycle, but the fixed-quantity system needs protection only during lead time because additional orders can be placed at any time and will be received shortly (lead time) thereafter. Consequently, there is a greater need for safety stock in the fixed-interval model than in the fixed-quantity model.

Both models are sensitive to demand experience just prior to reordering, but in somewhat different ways. In the fixed-quantity model, a higher-than-normal demand causes a *shorter time* between orders, whereas in the fixed-interval model, the result is a *larger order size.* Another difference is that the fixed-quantity model requires close monitoring of inventory levels in order to know *when* the amount on hand has reached the reorder point. The fixed-interval model requires only a periodic review (i.e., physical inspection) of inventory levels just prior to placing an order to determine how much is needed.

Order size in the fixed-interval model is determined by the following computation:

$$\begin{matrix} \text{Amount} \\ \text{to order} \end{matrix} = \begin{matrix} \text{Expected demand} \\ \text{during protection} \\ \text{interval} \end{matrix} + \begin{matrix} \text{Safety} \\ \text{stock} \end{matrix} - \begin{matrix} \text{Amount on hand} \\ \text{at reorder time} \end{matrix}$$

$$= \overline{S}(\text{OI} + \overline{R}) + z\sigma_S \sqrt{\text{OI} + \overline{R}} - A$$

[13]This section is adapted from Stephenson, *Production/Operations Management,* 6th ed., pp. 586–89.

where

$\overline{S}$ = Average daily sales

$\overline{R}$ = Average replenishment cycle

z = Number of standard deviations

OI = Order interval (length of time between orders)

A = Amount on hand at reorder time

As in previous models, we assume that demand during the protection interval is normally distributed.

Given the following information, determine the amount to order:

$\overline{S}$ = 30 units per day

σ_s = 3 units per day

$\overline{R}$ = 2 days

Desired service level = 99 percent

Amount on hand at reorder time = 71 units

OI = 7 days

z = 2.33 for 99 percent service level

$$\begin{array}{c}\text{Amount}\\\text{to order}\end{array} = \overline{S}(OI + \overline{R}) + z\sigma_s \sqrt{OI + \overline{R}} - A$$

$$= 30(7 + 2) + 2.33(3)\sqrt{7 + 2} - 71$$

$$= 220 \text{ units}$$

Benefits and Disadvantages

The fixed-interval system provides the tight control needed for A items in an ABC classification due to the periodic reviews it requires. In addition, when two or more items come from the same supplier, grouping orders can yield savings in ordering, packing, and shipping costs. Moreover, it may be the only practical approach if inventory withdrawals cannot be closely monitored.

However, the fixed-interval system necessitates a larger amount of safety stock for a given risk of stockout because of the need to protect against shortages during an entire order interval plus lead time (instead of lead time only), and this increases the inventory carrying cost. Also, there are the costs associated with the periodic reviews.

Inventories and Customer Service

The establishment of a service level, and thus a safety stock policy, is really a matter of managerial judgment. Factors management should consider include customer relations and the ability of the firm to support continuous production.

In many companies, management improves customer service levels by simply adding safety stock. This is because the cost of carrying inventory has often not been calculated for the firm or has been set arbitrarily at an artificially low level. Figure 6–9 graphically illustrates the relationship between customer service levels and inventory investment shown in Table 6–7. (Ignore the dotted line and arrows in Figure 6–9 at this time.)

Although inventory investment figures will vary from situation to situation, relationships similar to those in the example will hold. As customer service levels move toward 100 percent, inventory levels increase disproportionately. It becomes obvious

FIGURE 6–9

Relationship between inventory investment and customer service levels

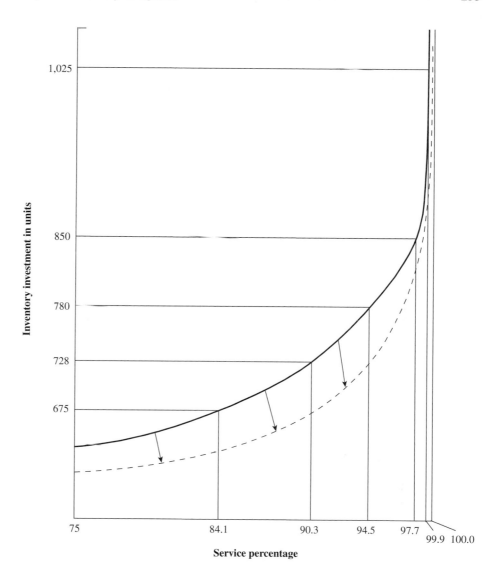

that customer service levels should not be improved solely by the addition of inventory. The need to develop an accurate inventory carrying cost for the purpose of planning should be clear.

One way of resolving this problem is to substitute transportation costs for inventory carrying costs by using premium transportation to improve customer service. Another possibility is to recognize the wide differences in demand levels and demand variation associated with each product and set inventory levels accordingly. Managers often make the mistake of treating all products the same. Generally, a more economical policy is to stock the highest volume items at retail locations, high- and moderate-volume items at field warehouse locations, and slow-moving items at centralized locations. The centralized location may be a distribution center or a plant warehouse. This type of multi-echelon stocking procedure is referred to as ABC analysis; we will discuss it later in this chapter. The dotted line in Figure 6–9 shows how the relationship between inventory investment and customer service levels can be shifted using some of these strategies.

Production Scheduling

Logistics Policy Changes Can Increase Production Costs

Earlier in this chapter, we described how inventory levels can be influenced by production policies. The reverse is also true. In many cases changes in logistics policy—especially those that decrease inventory levels—can create significant increases in total production costs that are beyond the control of manufacturing management. For example, General Mills, Inc., had a production operations division that manufactured and distributed products for the various marketing divisions of the firm. Consequently, the logistics function received a sales forecast from marketing, and, given the divisions' inventory deployment policies and the objective to minimize total logistics costs, manufacturing was told how many units of each item to produce. Manufacturing then established a production schedule.

The system was not without its problems, however. Manufacturing performance was judged by comparing actual production costs to the cost arrived at by multiplying the various units produced by the standard manufacturing cost for each product. The standard cost was a full cost standard comprised of (1) direct materials, (2) direct labor, (3) variable overhead, and (4) fixed overhead. The overhead costs included production setup costs that were based on a projected number of setups for each product for the year, divided by the estimated number of units produced during the year.

Logistics Decisions Can Influence Manufacturing Costs

Logistics influenced the number of setups actually incurred by manufacturing, but the standard cost was not changed during the year to reflect this. Since the number of setups incurred would influence manufacturing performance, plant management resisted policies that would change the projected number of setups. The solution was to maintain two separate standard costs for each product. One was a variable cost per unit excluding a setup component, and the other was a standard setup cost for each product. Manufacturing performance was judged on the ability to manufacture a specified quantity efficiently. Logistics was charged with the responsibility of considering setup costs in the analysis when inventory policies were determined.

An inventory policy decision that reduces logistics costs by less than the increase in production setup cost results in lower overall profit performance for the company. For this reason, logistics managers must be aware of the impact of their decisions on the efficiency of manufacturing operations and consider associated changes in manufacturing costs when establishing logistics policies.

Symptoms of Poor Inventory Management

How to Recognize Poor Inventory Management

This section deals with how to recognize situations where inventories are not being managed properly. Recognition of problem areas is the first step in determining where opportunities exist for improving logistics performance.

The following symptoms may be associated with poor inventory management:

1. Increasing numbers of back orders.
2. Increasing dollar investment in inventory with back orders remaining constant.
3. High customer turnover rate.
4. Increasing number of orders being canceled.
5. Periodic lack of sufficient storage space.
6. Wide variance in inventory turnover among distribution centers and among major inventory items.

7. Deteriorating relationships with intermediaries, as typified by dealer cancellations and declining orders.

8. Large quantities of obsolete items.

In many instances inventory levels can be reduced by one or more of the following steps:

**Ways to Reduce
Inventory Levels**

1. Multi-echelon inventory planning. ABC analysis is an example of such planning.

2. Lead-time analysis.

3. Delivery-time analysis. This may lead to a change in carriers or negotiation with existing carriers.

4. Elimination of low turnover and/or obsolete items.

5. Analysis of pack size and discount structure.

6. Examination of returned goods procedures.

7. Encouragement/automation of product substitution.

8. Installation of formal reorder review systems.

9. Measurement of fill rates by stock-keeping unit (SKU).

10. Analysis of customer demand characteristics.

11. Development of a formal sales plan and source demand by a predetermined logic.

Global

DHL Helps Fujitsu Enhance Global Service

Fujitsu Personal Systems (FPS) is a wholly owned subsidiary of Fujitsu with headquarters in California, USA. This division of Fujitsu produces hand-held computers, of the type used by sales people or service engineers. Manufacturing takes place in Japan, but markets are worldwide.

In order to service their European customers better, Fujitsu established a partnership with DHL. Products flow through the DHL Express Logistics Center (ELC) in Brussels, Belgium, for overnight delivery to FPS's European customers. The ELC carries out incoming quality and functional inspection, kitting and configuration and repair. The ELC has a 400 square meter technical support facility with a full "clean room" environment. Fully qualified technicians are employed by DHL having been trained by Fujitsu engineers and the facility is an approved Fujitsu repair center. All work carried out in the center carries the full Fujitsu warranty.

Kitting and configuration of products in the ELC enables Fujitsu to hold lower inventories for a given service level, as the ELC is able to customize the basic mod-els and ship the same day. DHL now undertakes all order processing and inventory management on behalf of FPS in Europe.

Spare computers are kept in the ELC as partly configured inventory. When a salesperson's machine breaks down in the field, the ELC is notified. A spare machine is plugged into the customer's global telecommunications network and receives a download of the appropriate database for that salesperson from the customer's mainframe computer in the USA. The ELC technician verifies that the machine functions correctly before it is packed and shipped for next day delivery to the salesperson.

Recently, DHL joined FPS in a joint sales presentation to a potential FPS customer. The customer was seeking a supplier of hand-held computers for its European sales force and gave the order to Fujitsu on the basis of its after-sales service capability (provided by DHL).

Source: Martin Christopher, *Marketing Logistics* (Oxford, England: Butterworth-Heinemann, 1997), pp. 131–32.

In many companies the best method of reducing inventory investment is to reduce order cycle time by using advanced order processing systems. If the order cycle currently offered to customers is satisfactory, the time saved in order transmittal, order entry, and order processing can be used for inventory planning. The result will be a significant reduction in inventory.

Improving Inventory Management

Inventory management can be improved by using one or more of the following techniques: ABC analysis (similar to the ABC analysis for customer service described in Chapter 3), forecasting, enterprise resource planning (ERP) systems (first described in Chapter 4), and advanced order processing systems.

ABC Analysis

**Pareto Principle—
The 80/20 Rule**

In the 18th century, Villefredo Pareto, in a study of the distribution of wealth in Milan, found that 20 percent of the people controlled 80 percent of the wealth. This logic of the few having the greatest importance and the many having little importance has been broadened to include many situations and is termed the Pareto Principle. This is true in our everyday lives (such as, most of the decisions we make are relatively unimportant but a few shape our future), and is certainly true in inventory systems.[14]

The logic behind ABC analysis is that 20 percent of the firm's customers or products account for 80 percent of the sales and perhaps an even larger percentage of profits. The first step in ABC analysis for inventory planning is to rank products by sales, or preferably by contribution to corporate profitability if such data are available. The next step is to check for differences between high-volume and low-volume items that may suggest how certain items should be managed.

Inventory levels increase with the number of stock-keeping locations.[15] By stocking low-volume items at a number of logistics centers, the national demand for these products is divided by the number of locations. Each of these locations must maintain safety stock. If one centralized location had been used for these items, the total safety stock would be much lower. For example, if only one centralized warehouse is used and sales are forecast on a national basis, a sales increase in Los Angeles may offset a sales decrease in New York. However, safety stock is required to protect against variability in demand, and there is greater variability in demand when national demand is subdivided into regions. The total system inventory will increase with the number of field warehouse locations, because the variability in demand must be covered at each location; that is, a sales increase in one market area will not be offset by a sales decrease in another market.

When a firm consolidates slow-moving items at a centralized location, transportation costs often increase. However, these costs can be offset by lower inventory carrying costs and fewer stockout penalties. Customer service can be improved through consolidation of low-volume items, thus decreasing the probability of experiencing a stockout. ABC analysis is a method for deciding which items should be considered for centralized warehousing.

---

[14]Chase, Aquilano, and Jacobs, *Production and Operations Management,* p. 606.

[15]While average inventory at each facility decreases as the number of warehouse locations increases, total system inventory (all facilities) increases.

**An Example
of ABC Analysis**

At this point let's consider an example of ABC analysis.[16] An analysis of sales volume by product revealed that A items accounted for 5 percent of items and contributed 70 percent of sales, B items accounted for 10 percent of items and added an additional 20 percent of sales, while C items accounted for the 65 percent of the items remaining and contributed only 10 percent of sales. The last 20 percent of the items had no sales whatsoever during the past year (see Figure 6–10)! This statistical distribution is almost always found in companies' inventories.[17] The "degree of concentration of sales among items will vary by firm, but the shape of the curve will be similar."[18]

For A items, a daily or continuous review of inventory status might be appropriate. B items might be reviewed weekly, while the C items should receive the least attention. Different customer service levels could be established for each category of inventory. An order fill rate of 98 percent might be set for A items, 90 percent for B items, and 85 percent for C items. This policy would result in an overall customer service level of 95 percent, as shown in Table 6–9. By focusing attention on the A items, management places greater emphasis on the products that contribute the most to sales and profitability.

Similarly, the amount of safety stock is less when lower volume items are stocked in fewer locations. If the firm made use of 20 distribution centers, A items might be stocked in all 20 warehouses, B items in 5 regional warehouses, and C items stocked only at the factory. Although transportation costs for B and C items are greater, the

FIGURE 6–10

ABC parts classification

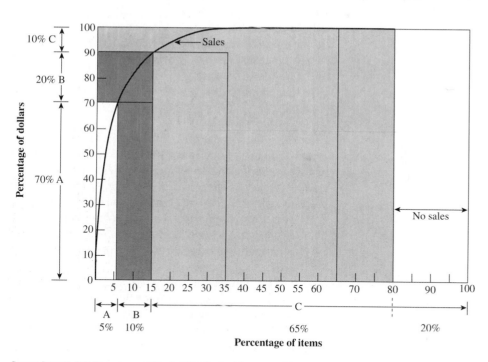

Source: Lynn E. Gill, "Inventory and Physical Distribution Management," in *The Distribution Handbook,* ed. James F. Robeson and Robert G. House (New York: The Free Press, 1985), p. 664. Copyright © 1985 by The Free Press, a Division of Macmillan, Inc. Reprinted by permission of the publisher.

---

[16]This example is adapted from Lynn E. Gill, "Inventory and Physical Distribution Management," in *The Distribution Handbook,* ed. James F. Robeson and Robert G. House (New York: The Free Press, 1985), pp. 664–67.

[17]It is referred to as lognormal distribution.

[18]Gill, "Inventory and Physical Distribution Management," p. 664.

TABLE 6–9   **Customer Service Level Using ABC Analysis**

Category	Percentage of Sales	Customer Service Level	Weighted Customer Service Level
A	70%	98%	68.6%
B	20	90	18.0
C	10	85	8.5
	100% Overall service level: 95.1%		

Source: Lynn E. Gill, "Inventory and Physical Distribution Management," in *The Distribution Handbook,* ed. James F. Robeson and Robert G. House (New York: The Free Press, 1985), p. 664. Copyright © 1985 by The Free Press, a Division of Macmillan, Inc. Reprinted by permission of the publisher.

inventory reductions are usually more than enough to make a selective stocking policy worthwhile. Management can test alternative inventory policies for their impact on customer service and profitability. For example, how would the deletion of slow-moving items affect inventory? What impact would a 25 percent increase in sales have on inventory?

A Distribution-by-Value Report Forms the Basis of an ABC Analysis

A distribution-by-value report forms the basis of an ABC analysis (see Table 6–10). The report is prepared by listing annual sales for each item in descending sequence. In order to simplify this example, some items were omitted from the sequence. Distribution-by-value reports are easy to prepare on computerized inventory systems. Each of the cumulative totals is also shown as a percentage of total items and as a percentage of total sales.

Forecasting

Forecasting the amount of each product that is likely to be purchased is an important aspect of inventory management. One forecasting method is to survey buyer intentions by mail questionnaires, telephone interviews, or personal interviews. These data can be used to develop a sales forecast. This approach is not without problems, however. It can be costly, and the accuracy of the information may be questionable.

Another approach is to solicit the opinions of salespeople or known experts in the field. This method, termed *judgment sampling,* is relatively fast and inexpensive. However, the data are subject to the personal biases of the individual salespeople or experts.

Forecasting for Groupings of SKUs Increases Forecast Accuracy

Most companies simply project future sales based on past sales data. Because most inventory systems require only a one- or two-month forecast, short-term forecasting is therefore acceptable. A number of techniques are available to aid the manager in developing a short-term sales forecast.[19] A method for developing the forecast is shown in Figure 6–11. Rather than trying to forecast at the stock-keeping unit (SKU) level, which would result in large forecast errors, management can improve forecast accuracy significantly by forecasting at a much higher level of aggregation. For example, in Figure 6–11 the forecast is developed at the total company or product line level using a forecasting model. The next step is to break that forecast down by product class and SKU, based on sales history. The inventory is then pushed out from the central distribution center to branch/regional distribution centers using one of the following methods:

---

[19]For excellent in-depth coverage of various forecasting methods, see Steven C. Wheelwright and Spyros Makridakis, *Forecasting Methods for Management,* 5th ed. (New York: John Wiley & Sons, 1989).

TABLE 6–10   Distribution-by-Value Report

Rank of Items	Part Number	Annual Dollar Sales	Cumulative Dollar Sales	Cumulative Percent Items	Cumulative Percent Sales	Classification
1	K410	$126,773	$ 126,773	0.01	1.74	A
3	9999	74,130	285,602	0.02	3.92	A
5	410	44,800	397,075	0.03	5.45	A
8	2300	32,666	510,732	0.05	7.01	A
16	K820	22,838	730,034	0.10	10.02	A
35	2601	16,899	1,158,439	0.22	15.90	A
60	K53	13,009	1,467,356	0.39	20.14	A
90	5401	10,988	1,889,201	0.58	25.93	A
126	1101	9,388	2,191,561	0.82	30.08	A
168	K860	7,879	2,610,494	1.09	35.83	A
219	1302	6,538	2,936,895	1.42	40.31	A
279	3600	5,639	3,307,741	1.81	45.40	A
321	5601	5,017	3,567,115	2.08	48.96	A
351	K350	4,619	3,642,887	2.28	50.00	A
438	1603	3,823	4,047,249	2.84	55.55	A
543	540P	3,118	4,438,494	3.52	60.92	A
674	2305	2,496	4,837,759	4.37	65.91	A
839	920L	2,000	5,231,186	5.44	70.01	A
1000	K82T	1,635	5,508,045	6.48	75.60	B
1261	1304	1,186	5,784,905	8.18	79.40	B
1394	1806	1,017	5,908,764	9.04	81.10	B
1632	5304	831	6,127,337	10.58	84.10	B
1823	2600	693	6,312,395	11.82	86.64	B
2452	3501	463	6,570,312	15.90	90.18	B
2698	4200	357	6,775,043	17.49	92.99	C
2920	460P	300	6,787,428	18.93	93.16	C
3186	131M	250	6,906,187	20.66	94.79	C
3506	4304	207	6,953,544	22.73	95.44	C
4442	410G	116	7,130,588	28.80	97.87	C
5202	3500	78	7,150,989	33.73	98.15	C
5414	K542	71	7,176,762	35.11	98.50	C
5688	3402	60	7,193,246	36.88	98.73	C
6048	110G	50	7,198,345	39.22	98.80	C
6256	1308	45	7,208,546	40.56	98.94	C
6386	110P	42	7,210,732	41.41	98.97	C
6437	2306	41	7,212,917	41.74	99.00	C
6493	920K	40	7,249,346	42.10	99.50	C
7711	83J4	8	7,261,732	50.00	99.67	C
9253	172R	6	7,266,103	60.00	99.73	C
12318	4404	1	7,285,775	79.87	100.00	C
12970	X438	0	7,285,775	84.10	100.00	C
15422	999J	0	7,285,775	100.00	100.00	C

Source: Adapted from Lynn E. Gill, "Inventory and Physical Distribution Management," in *The Distribution Handbook,* ed. James F. Robeson and Robert G. House (New York: The Free Press, 1985), p. 666. Copyright © 1985 by The Free Press, a Division of Macmillan, Inc. Reprinted by permission of the publisher.

- *Going rate*—the rate of sales that the SKU is experiencing at each location.
- *Weeks/months of supply*—the number of weeks/months of sales based on expected future sales that management wishes to hold at each location.
- *Available inventory*—currently available inventory less back orders.

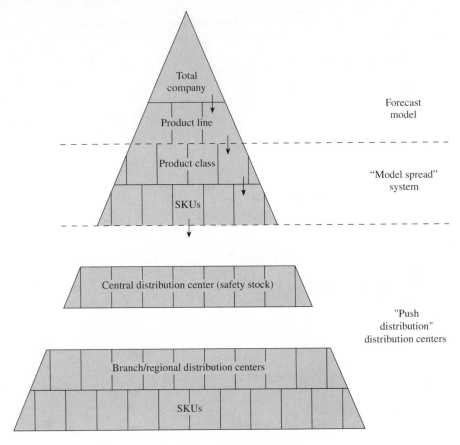

Source: Professor Jay U. Sterling, University of Alabama. Used with permission.

The only certainty when developing a forecast is that the forecast will not be 100 percent accurate. For this reason, many firms are developing strategies that focus on reducing the total time from sourcing of materials to delivery of the final product. The shorter this time period can be made, the less critical forecasting becomes, because the firm can respond more quickly to changes in demand. Time-based competitive strategies will be discussed in detail in Chapter 18.

How ERP Systems Contribute to Improved Inventory Management[20]

As we noted in Chapter 4, the German firm SAP AG is the world leader in enterprise resource planning (ERP) software. Although there are many other firms that also provide ERP systems, there is widespread agreement that SAP AG has set new standards in the information technology market with R/3, its client/server application software system. Over 100,000 companies are using R/3 applications worldwide. Leading companies in industries such as high technology, consumer goods, and chemicals, as well as numerous small and medium-sized firms, have adopted this software. Of the four

---

[20]This is adapted from Chase, Aquilano, and Jacobs, *Production and Operations Management*, pp. 669–75. For a detailed summary of available inventory software see Andersen Consulting, *Logistics Software* (Oak Brook, IL: Council of Logistics Management, 1998).

Collaborative Forecasting and Replenishment Internet Protocol

Retailers and manufacturers compensate for poor forecasting by overstocking merchandise. This is called the safety stock or buffered inventory—fancy words for waste and inefficiency. In 1996 about $700 billion of the $2.3 trillion retail supply chain inventory was in safety stock. That is, almost 30% was tied up due to waste and inefficiency.

The CFAR (Collaborative Forecasting and Replenishment) Internet protocol was codeveloped by Benchmark Partners and software vendor SAP AG in 1996 to eliminate the waste and inefficiency of safety stock. Wal-Mart and Warner-Lambert use the CFAR protocol to download

their forecasting models (spreadsheets) directly to suppliers bypassing the truckers and warehouses thus cutting costs.

Warner-Lambert loads forecast data it receives from Wal-Mart into its demand planning software. The planning software automates—and eliminates—the process of estimating the size of an order. In addition, it takes advantage of volume discounts, delivery schedules, and it negotiates the lowest price.

Source: T. G. Lewis, *The Friction Free Economy: Marketing Strategies for a Wired World* (Harper Business, 1997).

Manufacturing and Logistics

major modules in R/3 (see p. 177), the Manufacturing and Logistics and the Sales and Distribution modules offer significant opportunities to better manage corporate inventories.

The *Manufacturing and Logistics* segment is the largest and most complex of the four modules. It is comprised of five major components: materials management (MM), plant maintenance (PM), quality management (QM), production planning and control (PP), and a project management system (PS). Each component is divided into subcomponents. Materials management includes consumption-based planning, purchasing, vendor evaluation, and invoice verification. It also includes inventory and warehouse management to manage stock until usage dictates the cycle should begin again. Electronic Kanban/just-in-time delivery is supported by the module.

Production planning and control supports both discrete and process manufacturing processes. Repetitive and configure-to-order approaches are provided. These modules support all phases of manufacturing, providing capacity leveling and requirements planning, material requirements planning, product costing, bills of material explosion and implosion, computer-aided design (CAD) dialog interface, and engineering change management. The system allows users to link rework orders to production schedules. Orders can be generated from internal sales orders or from links to a website.

Sales and Distribution

The *Sales and Distribution* module provides prospective customers and customer management, sales order management, configuration management, distribution, export controls, shipping, and transportation management, as well as billing, invoicing, and rebate processing. As with all SAP modules, these can be implemented globally. For example, an order may be received in Hong Kong. If the products are not available locally, they may be internally procured from warehouses in other parts of the world and shipped to arrive together at the Hong Kong customer's site. When implementing the Sales and Distribution module, the company structure must be represented in the system so that, for example, R/3 knows where and when to recognize revenue. It is possible to represent the structure of the firm from the point of view of accounting, materials management, or sales and distribution. Also, these structures can be combined.

Creative Solutions

Saturn's Happy Dealers

General Motors' wholly owned subsidiary Saturn designs, manufactures and markets automobiles in the U.S. market through independently owned dealers. When GM created Saturn, one of its primary business objectives was to provide a high, luxury-car level of after-sale customer support, even though the Saturn product line is priced in the $13,000 to $20,000 range. Traditionally, manufacturers utilizing the dealer channel model took responsibility for managing their own parts inventories and relied on their dealers to manage parts inventories owned and held by the dealers.

Saturn took a different approach. The company and its dealers are linked by a sophisticated information system that enables Saturn to "see" the part inventory availability and sales data of each of its dealers. It uses this information to create replenishment orders to restock dealer inventories of service parts. This new approach ensures that all service parts supply chain planning decisions are driven by customer demand, thereby reducing inventory through-out the supply chain and improving parts availability to customers. Saturn dealers parts availability, as experienced by customers, is consistently in the 90 to 95 percent range versus typical inventory availability levels of 70 to 80 percent. This exceptionally high level of parts availability is not achieved by maintaining excessive inventories. Typically Saturn dealer parts inventory "turnover" (i.e., parts sales divided by inventory) is six to seven turns per year, compared to an industry norm of two to four turns per year.

This innovative supply chain relationship redefined the channel dealer model and has prompted both Saturn's competitors and other firms outside the automotive industry who utilize the dealer channel model to pursue similar operating strategies.

Source: Robert Evans and Doug Castek, "Customer Support Logistics: The Key to Customer Satisfaction," in *Strategic Supply Chain Alignment: Best Practice in Supply Chain Management,* ed. John Gattorna (Hampshire, England: Gower, 1998), pp. 65–66.

When a sales order is entered, it automatically includes the correct information on pricing, promotions, availability, and shipping options. Batch order processing is available for specialized industries such as food, pharmaceutical, or chemical. Users have the ability to reserve inventory for specific customers, request production of subassemblies, or enter orders that are assemble-to-order, build-to-order, or engineer-to-order as well as special customized orders.

As we noted in Chapter 4, the modules are built on what SAP considers industry best practices. The SAP research and development group continually looks for better ways to carry out a particular process or subprocess. System upgrades are designed to reflect the newest best practices.

Order Processing Systems

Many companies have not undertaken comprehensive and ongoing analysis and planning of inventory policy because of a lack of time and lack of information.[21] Many times a poor communications system is a contributing factor. A primary goal of inventory management is to achieve an optimum balance between inventory carrying costs

---

[21] Adapted from materials provided by Douglas E. Zemke, Dean, Tabor School of Business, Milliken University.

and customer service. The essential task of determining the proper balance requires continuous and comprehensive planning. It hinges on the availability of information. Communications make information available. Linking members of the supply chain with timely and accurate product usage information can reduce the time needed to perform certain elements of the order cycle, including order entry, order processing, and inventory replenishment. Further, variability in the replenishment cycle can be reduced. In this way, the firm can gain substantial cost savings by reducing its levels of safety stock as well as the inventories of its customers and suppliers.

Improved Information System Can Reduce Inventory Requirements

In addition, better information systems can reduce message errors and unexpected time delays. This facilitates better decision making and improves internal coordination in the firm. The result is reduced inventories and faster invoicing, which improves cash flow.

With full, up-to-the-second information on orders, raw materials inventory and production scheduling can be better managed. The distribution center can meet customer commitments without increasing inventories. More accurate invoices can be prepared, customers can be invoiced sooner, and payments can be received more quickly with fewer reconciliations. When reconciliations are necessary, they can be resolved much more quickly. Reduced inventories and faster invoicing improve cash flow. Inventory management is improved by placing vital information into the hands of the decision makers and by providing them with the necessary time to use this information in planning inventory strategies.

Impact of an Inventory Reduction on Corporate Profit Performance

In order to illustrate the impact of an inventory reduction on corporate profit performance, consider the case of XYZ Company, whose financial data are presented in summary in Figure 6–12. The company has sales of $100 million, less $60 million cost of goods sold, yielding a gross margin of $40 million. When variable expenses of $18 million, fixed expenses of $18 million, and income taxes of $2 million are deducted, the net profit is $2 million, which gives a net profit margin of 2 percent of sales.

On the balance sheet portion of the model, current assets of $22 million are comprised of inventory of $14 million, accounts receivable of $6 million, and other current assets of $2 million. The current assets plus $18 million of fixed assets result in total assets of $40 million and asset turnover of 2.5 times. The net profit of 2 percent multiplied by the asset turnover of 2.5 times equals a return on assets of 5 percent. The financial leverage of 2 to 1 boosts the return on net worth to 10 percent.

How Would a Logistics System Change Affect Corporate Return on Net Worth?

The question for consideration is: How would a change in the order processing system affect the performance of the logistics function and affect corporate return on net worth? In order to answer this question, the following information about the company is required:

1. Customers place orders once per week, though sometimes less frequently particularly right after the end of a quarter. Approximately 36 percent of the company's sales take place in 20 days per year. There is no visibility of customer product usage on a daily or even weekly basis. It is assumed that customer sales equal the ordered quantities.

2. The company does not calculate inventory carrying costs. If it did so, the non–cost-of-money components of inventory carrying costs, such as insurance, taxes, variable storage costs, obsolescence, shrinkage, and damage, would be 5 percent of the average inventory value. The fact that the

FIGURE 6–12

The strategic profit model with financial data for XYZ Company—before system change (financial data in $ millions)

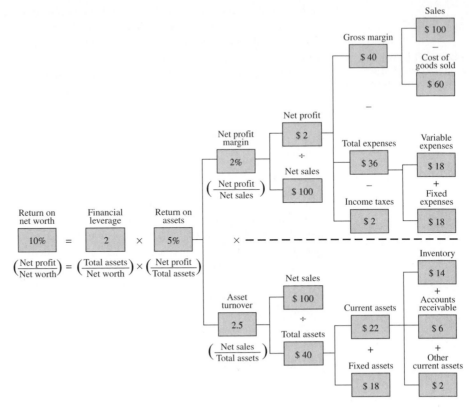

Note: Income taxes are assumed to equal 50 percent of net profit before taxes.

company does not specifically identify inventory carrying costs does not make these costs any less real. They are still incurred.

3. The company is experiencing capital rationing. That is, there is a shortage of capital for investment in new projects, and investments promising a return of 20 percent after taxes or 40 percent before taxes cannot be undertaken. If the capital were available, management could invest up to $5 million in plant modernization, which would generate a return of 40 percent before taxes. If such an investment were made, it would be depreciated on a straight-line basis over a 10-year period ($500,000 per year if the investment were $5 million).

If the company's information system is improved to be able to accept point-of-sale data from large retailers and materials requirements from key original equipment manufacturers, management can use the information to plan production and restock field inventories, resulting in a $5 million reduction in inventories on a companywide basis. The $5 million obtained from the inventory reduction would be available for investment in the new plant equipment that was previously rejected due to the shortage of capital.

Finally, it is estimated that the annual cost of the proposed system change will be $750,000. What is the financial impact of the proposed system on after-tax return on net worth? Figure 6–13 provides the answer.

Figure 6–13

The strategic profit model with financial data for XYZ Company—after system change (financial data in $ millions)

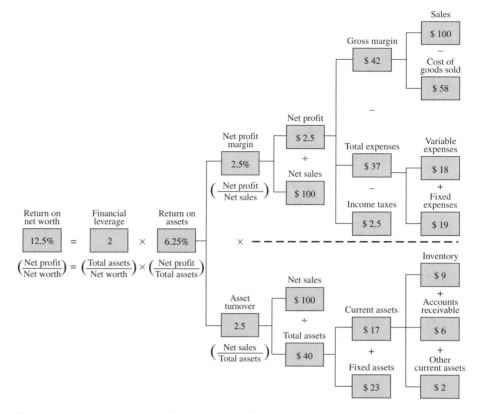

Note: Income taxes are assumed to equal 50 percent of net profit before taxes.

First, consider the impact on asset turnover. Inventory is reduced by $5 million—from $14 million to $9 million—thereby reducing current assets to $17 million. However, total assets remain unchanged at $40 million because the capital from the inventory reduction is used to buy $5 million of plant equipment; this purchase increases fixed assets by $5 million. So the asset is merely switched from a current asset to a fixed asset. Because sales and total assets are unchanged, asset turnover remains at 2.5 times.

The proposed system will affect a number of profit and loss statement accounts. The new plant equipment will reduce production costs and generate a 20 percent return after taxes, which is 40 percent before taxes, or $2 million. As a result, the cost of goods sold is reduced to $58 million from $60 million, increasing the gross margin to $42 million. Expenses that are variable with sales remain the same. But those that are variable with inventory, or with the non–cost-of-money, out-of-pocket costs associated with the $5 million inventory reduction, reduce fixed expenses by $250,000. However, the increased information system expenditure of $750,000 per year, plus depreciation on the new plant equipment of $500,000 per year, raises the fixed expenses by $1.25 million, so that the fixed expenses increase to $19 million and total expenses to $37 million. Net profit before taxes is increased from $4 million to $5 million, resulting in income taxes of $2.5 million. Net profit after taxes is $2.5 million, and the net profit margin is 2.5 percent. Consequently, return on assets is increased from 5 percent to 6.25 percent. Since corporate financing is not affected, financial leverage stays at 2 to 1, and return on net worth increases from 10 percent to 12.5 percent.

FIGURE 6–14

The strategic profit model with financial data for XYZ Company—after system change, assuming repayment of bank loan (financial data in $ millions)

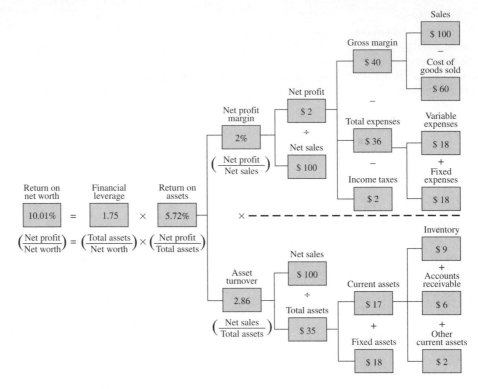

Note: Income taxes are assumed to equal 50 percent of the net profit before taxes.

The purpose of this exercise was twofold. First, it illustrated how the strategic profit model can be used to identify the impact of a change in logistics operations on return on assets and return on net worth. The example also showed that even though a firm may not calculate inventory carrying costs, the costs are indeed real. The cost of money for inventory carrying cost purposes should always reflect how the money would be used if it were not invested in inventory.

In the example, it was assumed that the money could be reinvested in a project that would yield 20 percent after taxes. Figure 6–14 shows what the return on net worth would be if the money were used to reduce bank loans by $5 million. It is assumed that the interest rate on the loan was at 10 percent. Of course, this is a pretax expense.

Since the money is being used to reduce debt, total assets decrease by $5 million, to $35 million, and asset turnover increases from 2.5 times to 2.86 times. In this example gross margin is unchanged. Fixed expenses are decreased by $750,000—a $250,000 reduction in non–cost-of-money, inventory-related expenses, plus a $500,000 decrease in interest expense. However, the increase in information system and communication costs of $750,000 negates the decrease in expenses and results in no change in the total. Net profit margin remains at 2.0 percent, and return on assets becomes 5.72 percent. The reduction in debt lowers financial leverage from 2 to 1 ($40 million to $20 million) to 1.75 to 1 ($35 million to $20 million). The impact on return on net worth is a marginal increase from 10 percent to 10.01 percent.

Notice once again how changes in inventory levels, resulting from revisions in the logistics system, can influence corporate return on net worth.

Summary

In this chapter we examined the basic concepts of inventory management. The EOQ model was introduced, along with methods for adjusting it. In addition, we described demand and order cycle uncertainty and examined a method for considering both types of uncertainty when calculating safety stock requirements. We also saw that the traditional approach to improving customer service, increasing inventory investment, is costly and inefficient. We described the impact of inventory investment on production scheduling and looked at some symptoms of poor inventory management.

The chapter concluded with an explanation of techniques that can be used to improve inventory management, and a method for determining the impact of an inventory reduction on corporate profit performance. In Chapter 7, we will see how a knowledge of materials management can improve logistics performance.

Suggested Readings

Chase, Richard B., Nicholas J. Aquilano, and F. Robert Jacobs. *Production and Operations Management,* 8th ed. Burr Ridge, IL: Richard D. Irwin, 1998.

Evers, Philip T., and Frederick J. Bier. "Operational Aspects of Inventory Consolidation Decision Making." *Journal of Business Logistics* 19, no. 1 (1998), pp. 173–89.

Flores, Benito E., and D. Clay Whybark. "Forecasting 'Laws' for Management." *Business Horizons* 28, no. 4 (July–August 1985), pp. 48–53.

Georgoff, David M., and Robert G. Murdick. "Managers' Guide to Forecasting." *Harvard Business Review* 64, no. 1 (January–February 1986), pp. 110–20.

Jain, C. L. "Myths and Realities of Forecasting." *Journal of Business Forecasting* (Fall 1990), pp. 18–29.

Langley, C. John, Jr. "The Inclusion of Transportation Costs in Inventory Models: Some Considerations." *Journal of Business Logistics* 2, no. 1 (1980), pp. 106–25.

Lee, Hau. "Postponement for Mass Customization." In *Strategic Supply Chain Alignment,* ed. John Gattorna. Hampshire, England: Gower Publishing, 1998, pp. 77–91.

Mentzer, John T., and R. Krishnan. "The Effect of the Assumption of Normality on Inventory Control/Customer Service." *Journal of Business Logistics* 6, no. 1 (1985), pp. 101–20.

Merrills, Roy. "How Northern Telecom Competes on Time." *Harvard Business Review* 89, no. 4 (July–August 1989), pp. 108–14.

O'Neil, Brian F., and Gerald O. Fahling. "A Liquidation Model for Excess Inventories." *Journal of Business Logistics* 3, no. 2 (1982), pp. 85–103.

Pagh, Janus D., and Martha C. Cooper. "Supply Chain Postponement and Speculation Strategies: How to Choose the Right Strategy." *Journal of Business Logistics* 19, no. 2 (1998), pp. 13–33.

Rafuse, Maynard. "Reducing the Need to Forecast." *The International Journal of Logistics Management* 6, no. 2 (1995), pp. 103–8.

Tersine, Richard J., and Michele G. Tersine. "Inventory Reduction: Preventive and Corrective Strategies." *The International Journal of Logistics Management* 1, no. 2 (1990), pp. 17–24.

Tyagi, Rajesh, and Chandrasekhar Das. "Extension of the Square-Root Law for Safety Stock to Demands with Unequal Variance." *Journal of Business Logistics* 19, no. 2 (1998), pp. 197–203.

Van Hoek, Remko I., Harry R. Cammandeur, and Bart Vos. "Reconfiguring Logistics Systems Through Postponement Strategies." *Journal of Business Logistics* 19, no. 1 (1998), pp. 33–54.

Wilkinson, Gary F. "Why Did You Use That Forecasting Technique?" *Journal of Business Forecasting* (Fall 1988), pp. 2–4.

Zinn, Walter. "Developing Heuristics to Estimate the Impact of Postponement on Safety Stock." *The International Journal of Logistics Management* 1, no. 2 (1990), pp. 11–16.

Questions and Problems

1. Why is inventory so important to the efficient and effective management of a firm?

2. How does uncertainty in demand and lead time affect inventory levels?

3. How does the economic order quantity (EOQ) model mathematically select the most economical order quantity?

4. One of the product lines carried by Farha Wholesale Foods was a line of canned fruit manufactured by California Canners, Inc. Mr. Jones, the canned goods buyer, knew that the company did not reorder from its suppliers in a systematic manner and wondered if the EOQ model might be appropriate. For example, the company ordered 250 cases of fruit cocktail each week, and the annual volume was about 13,000 cases. The purchase price was $10 per case, the ordering cost was $15 per order, and the inventory carrying cost was 45 percent. California Canners, Inc., paid the transportation charges, and there were no price breaks for ordering quantities in excess of 250 cases. Does the economic order quantity model apply in this situation? If so, calculate the economic order quantity.

5. Explain the basic differences between a fixed order point, fixed order quantity model, and a fixed order interval inventory model. Which is likely to lead to the largest inventory levels?

6. Calculate the economic order quantity, the safety stock, and the average inventory necessary to achieve a 98 percent customer service level, given the following information:

   a. The average daily demand for a 25-day period was found to be:

Day	Units Demanded	Day	Units Demanded	Day	Units Demanded
1	8	11	7	21	7
2	5	12	8	22	8
3	4	13	12	23	8
4	6	14	9	24	10
5	9	15	10	25	11
6	8	16	5		
7	9	17	8		
8	10	18	11		
9	7	19	9		
10	6	20	7		

   b. There is no variability in order cycle.

   c. The ordering cost is $20 per order.

   d. The annual demand is 2,000 units.

   e. The cost is $100 per unit.

    f. The inventory carrying cost is 35 percent.

    g. The products are purchased FOB destination.

7. Recalculate your answer to question 6, *a–g,* given the following sample of replenishment cycles:

Replenishment Cycle	Lead Time in Days	Replenishment Cycle	Lead Time in Days
1	10	10	9
2	12	11	8
3	11	12	10
4	10	13	11
5	10	14	9
6	9	15	9
7	8	16	10
8	12	17	11
9	11	18	10

8. Given your calculations in questions 6 and 7, what will the actual fill rate be if management is willing to hold inventory equal to one week's sales as safety stock?

9. What is the cost saving to the customer resulting from a manufacturer's ability to reduce variability by two days, given the following information:

    a. Average sales of 40 cases per day.

    b. Purchase price per case is $45.

    c. Transportation cost per case is $5.

    d. The order cycle is 10 days.

    e. Inventory carrying cost is 40 percent.

    How does this compare with the cost saving associated with a two-day reduction in the order cycle with no change in order cycle variability?

10. Using the financial data in Figure 6–11, show the impact of a $4 million reduction in inventory, given that:

    a. Inventory carrying costs are 45 percent, which includes 5 percent for non–cost-of-money components.

    b. The average variable cost of the inventory delivered to the storage location is 70 percent of full manufactured cost.

    c. The inventory reduction is accomplished by eliminating rail shipments, which represent 30 percent of all shipments, and shipping all products by truck. As a result, transportation costs increase by $350,000.

11. As the inventory planning team for Cook Department Stores, one of your primary responsibilities is to aid department managers with inventory decisions. The electronics department manager has come to your group with a desire to improve department inventory planning and profitability. The department stocks a VCR brand named Super View.

    a. Super View financial data:

Selling price/unit	$555.00
Cost of goods sold including delivery costs at current level of operations and under current inventory policies	$495.00

b. Super View sales data (representative 10-day sales—assume Cook Department Store is open 360 days/year):

Sales/Day	Number of Days (f)
1	2
2	2
6	2
10	2
16	2

c. Super View lead-time data (Super View is supplied directly from Tokyo, Japan, by Syonara Manufacturing):

Delivery pattern:	Sample of 10 order cycles in days
Super View:	9, 9, 42, 13, 22, 33, 11, 18, 36, 27

d. Current Super View service and inventory policies:

Order policy:	EOQ: Orders are equal to the average demand during average lead time
Fill rate:	99 percent

e. The following inventory carrying-cost figures were collected (corporate opportunity cost of capital was 37%, pretax):

Inventory taxes	1.6%
Insurance	0.4
Recurring storage	3.3
Obsolescence	0.7
Damage	2.0

f. The manager has several questions regarding inventory policy:

(1) Which one of the following Super View fill rates (99 percent, 95 percent, 91 percent, or 87 percent will result in the highest annual profit?

(2) Syonara Manufacturing stated that for an additional increase in price of 1.5 percent, they can hire more dependable international carriers and cut the lead-time standard deviation in half. Should the electronics department manager accept or reject the offer? (Assume their current 99 percent fill rate and ordering policies.)

(3) There are five Cook Department Store branches in the Detroit area (see Table 1). Corporate management wants to compare the annual profitability of two strategies:

• Provide a 99 percent fill rate for Super View by stocking the appropriate number of units of safety stock at each branch store; or

• Provide a 99 percent fill rate for Super View at the local area distribution center, which serves all 5 branches, and expedite safety stock when needed to each individual branch at a total expediting cost of $150.00 per week.

Which strategy will be most profitable, assuming that there will be no lost sales if the second strategy is employed?

TABLE 1   **Super Value Sales**
(per day, each branch store)

	Store				
Day	*1*	*2*	*3*	*4*	*5*
1	1	1	1	16	16
2	2	2	2	10	10
3	6	6	6	6	6
4	10	10	10	2	2
5	16	16	16	1	1
6	1	1	1	16	16
7	2	2	2	10	10
8	6	6	6	6	6
9	10	10	10	2	2
10	16	16	16	1	1
Average sales/Store	7	7	7	7	7
σ_s/Store	5.81	5.81	5.81	5.81	5.81

CHAPTER

7

Managing Materials Flow

Chapter Outline

Chapter Objectives

- To identify the activities of materials management.
- To examine the concept of total quality management (TQM).
- To identify and describe a variety of materials management techniques, including kanban/just-in-time systems, MRP, ERP, and DRP.

Introduction

Materials Management Defined

As defined in this book, logistics management is that part of the supply chain process that plans, implements, and controls the efficient flow and storage of goods, services, and related information from point-of-origin to point-of-consumption in order to meet customers' requirements.[1] An integral part of that flow, referred to as *materials management,* encompasses the administration of raw materials, subassemblies, manufactured parts, packing material, and in-process inventory.[2] Simply, materials management is concerned with those activities related to the physical supply of materials in an organization.

The importance of materials management to the total logistics process cannot be overstated. Although materials management does not *directly* interface with the final customer, the degree to which raw materials, component parts, and subassemblies are made available to the production process ultimately determines the availability of products to the customer. In essence, the internal customer is just as important as the final customer.

Importance of Materials Management

The decisions, good or bad, made in the materials management portion of the logistics process will have a direct effect on the level of customer service offered, the ability of the firm to compete with other companies, and the level of sales and profits achieved in the marketplace. Without efficient and effective management of inbound materials flow, the manufacturing process cannot produce products at the desired price and at the time they are required for distribution to the firm's customers. It is essential that the logistics executive understand the role of materials management and its impact on the organization's cost/service mix.

TABLE 7–1   Materials Management—Past, Present, and Future

	Past	*Present and Future*
Market	Seller's market	Buyer's market
	Low competition	Keen competition
	Restricted export	Global orientation
Products	Small assortment	Wide assortments
	Long life cycle	Short life cycle
	Low technology	High technology
Production	Full capacity load	Full capacity load
	Low flexibility	High flexibility
	Large lot sizes	Low lot sizes
	Long lead times	Short lead times
	Low costs	Low costs
	Make instead of buy	Buy instead of make
Service level	High service level	High service level
	High inventories	Low inventories
	Slow logistics process	Quick logistics process
	Slow transport time	Quick transport time
Information technology	Manual data processing	Electronic data processing
	Paper administration	Paperless factory
Enterprise strategy	Production-oriented	Market-oriented

Source: Hans F. Busch, "Integrated Materials Management," *International Journal of Physical Distribution and Materials Management* 18, no. 7 (1988), p. 28.

---

[1]Definition provided at Council of Logistics Management website <http://www.clm1.org>.

[2]Some organizations use the term *materials management* to refer to logistics. However, in the majority of companies, *logistics* is the broader term, with materials management being a subset of logistics.

Beginning in the 1980s, more and more firms recognized the importance of materials management. As business enterprises developed and matured, the role of materials management has expanded to meet the challenges of market-driven, rather than production-driven, economies. Table 7–1 identifies some of the differences between the historical role played by materials management within firms and the present and future environments in which materials will be brought into firms' production processes.

While many things such as the need to reduce costs and provide high levels of customer service will continue to remain important, future environments will be characterized by a changing set of priorities and issues. Some of these issues include global orientation, shorter product life cycles, lower levels of inventories, electronic commerce, and a market-oriented focus. We discussed these and other factors in Chapter 1 and will continue to mention them throughout the book.

This chapter identifies the various components of materials management and discusses how to effectively manage materials flow within a manufacturing environment. We will examine specific management strategies and techniques used in the planning, implementation, and control of materials flow within organizations.

Scope of Materials Management Activities

Materials management is typically comprised of four basic activities:

1. Anticipating materials requirements.
2. Sourcing and obtaining materials.
3. Introducing materials into the organization.
4. Monitoring the status of materials as a current asset.

The definition of materials management used in this chapter describes the activity as an organizational system with the various functions as subsystems. The objective of materials management is to

Objectives of Materials Management

solve materials problems from a total company viewpoint by coordinating performance of the various materials functions, providing a communications network, and controlling materials flow.[3]

The specific objectives of materials management will tie in very closely to the firm's main objectives of achieving an acceptable level of profitability and/or return on investment, and to remain competitive in a marketplace characterized by increasing competition.

Figure 7–1 highlights the major objectives of materials management: low costs, high levels of service, quality assurance, low level of tied-up capital, and support of other functions. Each objective is clearly linked to the overall corporate goals and objectives.

The main objective—to make a substantial contribution to profit—is reached by optimizing the procurement, management and allocation of material as a productive resource. Hence it is the aim of integrated materials management to achieve optimum supply by reconciling the conflicting goals of low materials costs and overhead, and to achieve a high level of

[3]Michael Leenders and Harold E. Fearon, *Purchasing and Materials Management,* 10th ed. (Burr Ridge, IL: Richard D. Irwin, 1993), p. 5.

FIGURE 7–1

*The objectives of
integrated materials
management*

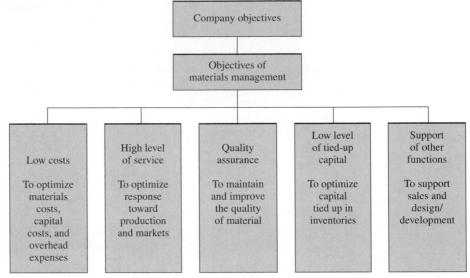

Source: MCB University Press Limited, Yunus Kathawala, and Heino H. Nauo, "Integrated Materials Management: A Conceptual Approach," *International Journal of Physical Distribution and Materials Management* 19, no. 8 (1989), p. 10.

customer service and a very low level of capital tied up in inventories. The optimization of the supply function and, thus, the addition of intangible value are achieved by totally controlling the flow of materials and information from the supply market through the company and finally to the point of sale.[4]

Materials management encompasses a variety of logistics activities. In a manner similar to the administration of finished goods distribution, the materials manager must be concerned with purchasing and procurement, inventory control, warehousing and storage, order processing, transportation, and almost every other logistics activity. The **Differences between Materials Management and Finished Goods Distribution** primary differences between the materials management process and the process that distributes finished goods are that the items being handled in materials management are raw materials, component parts, and subassemblies, and the recipient of the distribution effort is the production or manufacturing group rather than the final customer.

Integral aspects of materials management include purchasing and procurement, production control, inbound traffic and transportation, warehousing and storage, MIS control, inventory planning and control, and salvage and scrap disposal.

Purchasing and Procurement

The acquisition of materials has long been an important aspect of materials management and will continue to be in the future. Rapidly changing supply environments, periods of abundance and shortages, price fluctuations, and lead-time variability all provide ongoing challenges to organizations wishing to optimize materials management efforts.

Purchasing and Procurement Are Not the Same The terms *purchasing* and *procurement* arc often used interchangeably, although the activities do differ in scope. Purchasing generally refers to the actual buying of

---

[4]MCB University Press Limited, Yunus Kathawala, and Heino H. Nauo, "Integrated Materials Management: A Conceptual Approach," *International Journal of Physical Distribution and Materials Management* 19, no. 8 (1989), p. 10.

Technology

Internet 101—Enabling the Supply Chain

What is technology? To be clear, technology is nothing more than an enabler. If you have solid business and supply chain practices in place, the Internet can help you achieve successful results faster. If you have poor practices in place, the Internet can help you do poor things exponentially faster!

With regard to [the Internet and] procurement we see two major areas of growth, qualification and enablement. With regard to qualification, we are seeing companies now able to solicit to a much larger audience than during pre-Internet times. The Internet serves as a global recruiting field where manufacturers now have access to a much larger group of potential suppliers. This initial selection process allows the manufacturer to screen its potential suppliers to specific qualifica-

tion criteria. The benefit to the manufacturer is more potential suppliers and a more competitive environment to do business. The result of improved qualification is a general improvement in the quality of service delivered as we now see more requirements placed upon the supplier if they want to compete for the business. Likewise the benefit to the supplier is they have access to manufacturers previously unknown or unattainable.

Once qualified, the supplier has the opportunity to do business with the manufacturer.

Source: Kevin Q. Sullivan, "Internet 101—Enabling the Supply Chain," *Annual Conference Proceedings of the Council of Logistics Management* (Oak Brook, IL: Council of Logistics Management, 1998), pp. 331–32.

materials and those activities associated with the buying process. Procurement is broader in scope and includes purchasing, traffic, warehousing, and receiving inbound materials.

> Materials, product design and engineering, manufacturing, distribution and transportation, sales and marketing, data processing, financial and administrative functions—all are regularly purchased from external suppliers. The spread of outsourcing has given a new strategic importance to the purchasing function. In many cases, the purchase of goods and services from outside suppliers has become the dominant factor in a company's cost structure, representing up to 70 or 80 percent of overall expenditures. Two-thirds of the cost of new Boeing airplanes and three-fourths of the cost of one leading computer maker's PCs is spent on supplier-provided parts and subassemblies.[5]

Purchasing and procurement will likely increase in importance in the future (see Chapter 12). Many factors will influence this trend, including:

Reasons for the Rising Importance of Purchasing and Procurement

- Shorter product life cycles, rapid technological change, and more sophisticated customers have made flexibility and agility increasingly important in the purchasing process.
- Emergence of a global economy has forced companies to broaden their sourcing horizons and to locate potential suppliers around the world that can provide low-cost, high-quality goods and services.

---

[5]Scott A. Elliff and Robert Sabath, "Beyond Purchasing: Managing Procurement for Advantage," *Mercer Management Journal,* no. 4 (1995), p. 67.

TABLE 7–2   Purchasing versus Procurement

	Traditional Purchasing Function	Innovative Procurement Function
Organizational positioning	Back-office function	Strategic function
Role	Narrow	Broad
Visibility to top management	Low	High
Staff profile	Clerical	Professional
Culture	Reactive	Proactive
Buying process	Bureaucratic	Streamlined
Supplier relationships	Adversarial, inflexible	Cooperative, flexible
Performance criterion	Unit price	Overall cost and quality

Source: Scott A. Elliff and Robert Sabath, "Beyond Purchasing: Managing Procurement for Advantage," *Mercer Management Journal*, no. 4 (1995), p. 70.

- Revolution in information technology and telecommunications has provided low-cost, high-speed, automated alternatives to the manual activities that characterize the traditional purchasing department.[6]

Table 7–2 compares the traditional and limited role of purchasing with the innovative and expanded role of procurement. Procurement offers significant potential to organizations in their pursuit of supply chain excellence and optimal levels of customer service.[7]

Production Control

Production control is an activity traditionally positioned under manufacturing, although a few firms place it under logistics. Its position in the firm's organizational chart is probably not crucial, so long as both manufacturing and logistics have inputs into the production control activity.

Relationships between Logistics and Manufacturing

The role of production or manufacturing in the logistics process is twofold. First, the production activity determines how much and what kinds of finished products are produced. This, in turn, influences when and how the products are distributed to the firm's customers. Second, production directly determines the company's need for raw materials, subassemblies, and component parts that are used in the manufacturing process. Therefore, it is axiomatic that manufacturing and logistics jointly share production control decisions.

Inbound Logistics

Materials management is concerned with product flows into the firm. The materials manager's customer is the manufacturing or production department rather than the intermediate or final customer in the marketplace. Much like the firm's target markets, manufacturing requires certain levels of customer service. Manufacturing depends on

---

[6]Ibid., pp. 68–70.

[7]See Lisa H. Harrington, "Buying Better," *Industry Week* 246, no. 14 (July 21, 1997); and Shawn Tully, "Purchasing's New Muscle," *Fortune* 131, no. 3 (February 20, 1995), pp. 75–83.

the ability of materials management to adequately administer a variety of functions, including traffic and transportation, warehousing and storage, and MIS control.

Inbound Transportation
One of the most important activities administered by materials management is the inbound traffic and transportation function. Like their counterparts who are responsible for finished goods movement, materials managers must be aware of the various transport modes and modal combinations available to their companies, any regulations that might affect the transportation carriers their firm uses, the decision of private versus for-hire, leasing, evaluating mode and carrier performance, and the cost/service trade-offs involved in the inbound movement of product.

Differences between Inbound and Outbound Transportation
There are basically three major differences between the administration of inbound transportation and outbound transportation. First, the market demand that generates the need for outbound movement is generally considered to be uncertain and fluctuating. The demand with which the materials manager is concerned originates with the production activity and is much more predictable and stable than market demand. Therefore, transportation decisions made by the materials manager are not subject to the same types of problems his or her counterpart in the outbound traffic area will encounter.

Second, the materials manager is more likely to be concerned with bulk movements of raw materials or large shipments of parts and subassemblies. In addition, raw materials and parts have different handling and loss and/or damage characteristics, which will affect the entire mode/carrier selection and evaluation process. Third, firms generally exercise less control over their inbound transportation because purchasing procedures tend to look at "total delivered cost." A separate analysis of inbound costs is not performed as often or in as much depth. Thus, significant cost savings are possible.

Warehousing and Storage

Firms must place raw materials, component parts, and subassemblies in storage until they need those items in the manufacturing process. Unlike the warehousing of finished goods, which often occurs in the field, items awaiting use in the production process are usually either stored on-site, that is, at the point of manufacture, or delivered as needed by a just-in-time (JIT) supplier.

Warehousing in a JIT Environment
In firms using a JIT delivery system, the need for inbound warehousing is greatly minimized or eliminated altogether. In other firms, warehouses may be used extensively for the storage of inbound materials and thus the materials manager is usually much more concerned with warehousing and inventory costs because they account for a larger percentage of product value. Generally, finished goods are valued significantly higher than goods-in-process, raw materials, parts, or subassemblies. As a result, warehousing and storage costs are not as important, on a comparative basis, as they would be to the materials manager.

In addition, the warehousing requirements for raw materials and other items are usually quite different. For example, open or outside storage is possible with many raw materials, such as iron ore, sand and gravel, coal, and other unprocessed materials. Also, damage or loss due to weather, spoilage, or theft is minimal with raw materials because of their low value per pound.

Data and Information Systems

Information Needed by Materials Managers
The materials manager needs direct access to the firm's information system in order to properly administer materials flow into and within the organization. The types of information often needed by the materials manager include demand forecasts for production,

names of suppliers and supplier characteristics, pricing data, inventory levels, production schedules, transportation routing and scheduling data, and various other financial and marketing facts. Additionally, materials management supplies input into the firm's management information system. Data on inventory levels for materials, delivery schedules, pricing, forward buys, and supplier information are examples of some of the inputs provided by materials management.

> Integrated materials management constantly has a multitude of data to process, a task that would not be possible without EDP-supported program systems. Numerous software packages for individual functional elements of integrated materials management have been developed during the last few years, packages that have been tailored for particular branches of industry and particular company sizes. Thus, modern information technology will offer opportunities for the fast and safe transmission and processing of extensive amounts of data, both internally for users within the company and externally for suppliers and customers. Paperless communication is coming to the forefront whereby routine tasks in order processing and scheduling will be decisively facilitated. As a result, new information technology offers great opportunities for linking the planning, control and processing functions of materials management that were hitherto performed independently, thereby creating the foundation for the establishment of integrated materials management.[8]

With the proliferation of computerized information systems, including electronic databases, this facet of materials management will become more significant in the future.

Inventory Planning and Control

Inventory planning and control of raw materials, component parts, subassemblies, and goods-in-process are just as important as the management of finished goods inventory. Many of the concepts discussed in Chapters 5 and 6, such as ABC analysis, inventory carrying costs, and economic order quantity (EOQ), are directly applicable to materials management.

Just-in-time (JIT) systems, material requirements planning (MRP I), manufacturing resource planning (MRP II), enterprise resource planning (ERP), distribution requirements planning (DRP I), distribution resource planning (DRP II), and other systems or approaches can also improve the efficiency of inventory planning and control. We will briefly discuss these systems later in this chapter.

Reverse Logistics

One of the most important areas of materials management that a firm often overlooks or considers minor is that of reverse logistics. The disposal or recycling of scrap, surplus, or obsolete materials; the purchasing of remanufactured or refurbished goods; and the handling of product returns and defects are each aspects of a total reverse logistics program.[9] Such tasks were once considered incidental to other materials management activities, but have become more important because of environmental factors and

---

[8]MCB University Press Limited, Kathawala, and Nauo, "Integrated Materials Management: A Conceptual Approach," p. 15.

[9]A thorough overview of the logistics issues involved in product returns can be found in Dale S. Rogers and Ronald S. Tibben-Lembke, *Going Backwards: Reverse Logistics Trends and Practices* (Reno, NV: Reverse logistics Executive Council, 1999).

recognition of the revenue aspects of reverse logistics. Many customers now require suppliers to handle these tasks.

Many materials can be recycled or reused, resulting in added revenues and profits. For example, a film-processing firm had been selling the residual chemicals and materials that were by-products of its operations for relatively low prices. The firm invested in a machine that could separate the waste materials into its components. While the company was still able to sell some of the components to the same salvage firm that had previously been performing the separation process, one of the residues produced was silver, which the company subsequently sold to a precious metals dealer for a handsome profit. The separator machine paid for itself in less than two years.

Almost all firms generate surplus items, product returns, or waste materials as a by-product of their operations, whether they are manufacturers, retailers, or service organizations. The existence of such items can result from overoptimistic sales forecasts, changes in product specifications, errors in estimating materials usage, losses in processing, warranties, customer returns, overbuying due to forward buys, or quantity discounts on large purchases.[10]

The reverse logistics aspects of materials management will likely become much more important in the future. Reverse logistics will continue to be examined throughout this book.

Forecasting

One aspect of materials management that requires further emphasis is forecasting. Forecasting attempts to predict the future using either quantitative or qualitative methods, or some combination of both. The essence of forecasting is to aid in logistics decision making.[11]

Why Forecast?

The rationale for forecasting is twofold. First, proper control of materials management requires forward planning. Forward planning, in turn, requires good forecasts. The need for forward planning is great if the materials manager wishes to keep operations running smoothly, to adequately prepare for and meet future market conditions, and to minimize potential problems that can occur in materials acquisition.

Second, forecasting is needed if management is to be able to approximate the future with some degree of accuracy. Forecasting can provide an accurate picture of the future and, as such, provides the driving force for all forward-planning activities. In a study of the forecasting practices of a large number of companies, the most widely cited reasons for engaging in forecasting included:

1. Increasing customer satisfaction.
2. Reducing stockouts.
3. Scheduling production more efficiently.
4. Lowering safety stock requirements.
5. Reducing product obsolescence costs.
6. Managing shipping better.

---

[10]For a discussion of many issues relating to reverse logistics, see James R. Stock, *Development and Implementation of Reverse Logistics Programs* (Oak Brook, IL: Council of Logistics Management, 1998).

[11]A historical overview of forecasting and numerous examples are provided in Leslie Bernard Trustrum, F. Robert Blore, and William James Paskins, "Using Demand Forecasting Models," *Marketing Intelligence and Planning* 5, no. 3 (1987), pp. 5–15.

7. Improving pricing and promotion management.

8. Negotiating superior terms with suppliers.

9. Making more informed pricing decisions.[12]

Effective and efficient materials management requires many types of forecasts, including:

Types of Forecasts

- *Demand forecast.* Investigation of the firm's demand for the item, to include current and projected demand, inventory status, and lead times. Also considered are competing demands, current and projected, by industry and end product use.
- *Supply forecast.* Collection of data about current producers and suppliers, the aggregate current projected supply situation, and technological and political trends that might affect supply.
- *Price forecast.* Based on information gathered and analyzed about demand and supply. . . Provides a prediction of short- and long-term prices and the underlying reasons for those trends.[13]

Additionally, forecasts can be short term, midrange, or long term. The particular time frame most relevant to the firm will be selected:

Forecasting Time Frames

- *Long-term forecasts* usually cover more than three years and are used for long-range planning and strategic issues. These will naturally be done in broad terms—sales by product line or division, throughput capacity by ton per period or dollars per period, and so on.
- *Midrange forecasts*—in the one- to three-year range—address budgeting issues and sales plans. Again, these might predict more than demand.
- *Short-term forecasts* are most important for the operational logistics planning process. They project demands into the next several months and, in some cases, more than a year out. These are needed in units, by actual items to be shipped, and for finite periods of time—monthly or perhaps weekly.[14]

Organizations often use a variety of forecasting techniques, ranging from those based on general market information (from suppliers, sales force, customers, and others) to highly sophisticated computer algorithms. The specific technique or approach a firm selects should be appropriate for the unique characteristics of the company and its markets.

Total Quality Management (TQM)

Total quality management (TQM) has been defined as follows:

TQM Defined

TQM is both a philosophy and a set of guiding principles that represent the foundation of a continuously improving organization. TQM is the application of quantitative and human resources to improve the material services supplied to an organization, all the processes within the organization, and the degree to which the needs of the customer are met—now

---

[12]Glen Galfond, Kelly Ronayne, and Christian Winkler, "State-of-the-Art Supply Chain Forecasting," *PW Review* (November 1996), p. 3.

[13]Leenders and Fearon, *Purchasing and Materials Management,* p. 457.

[14]Allan F. Ayers, "Forecasting: Art or Reality?" *Transportation and Distribution* 35, no. 6 (June 1994), pp. 29–30.

Global

Certifying Quality with ISO 9000

ISO 9000? Total Quality Management? Quality Assurance? Quality System? Quality Policy? Depending upon the individuals you ask, these terms can conjure up many different, and sometimes conflicting, definitions.

Since 1987 one set of standards, the ISO 9000 series, has attempted to define a single definition for "quality" and a "quality system." The ISO 9000 series is a set of five international standards that establish the minimum requirements for an organization's quality system.

The five standards were authored by the International Organization for Standardization, headquartered in Geneva, Switzerland. Contrary to popular belief, ISO is not an acronym for the International Organization for Standardization. ISO is the official nickname, derived from *isos,* a Greek word meaning equal.

The standards themselves are numbered ISO 9000, 9001, 9002, 9003, and 9004. The ISO 9000 series was adopted by the United States as the ANSI/ASQC Q90 series of standards (ANSI is the American National Standards Institute, while ASQC is the American Society for Quality Control).

Each of the five standards has a particular application, explained as follows:

- ISO 9000/Q90 specifies the guidelines for selection and use of the other series standards.
- ISO 9001/Q91 specifies a quality system model for use by organizations that design/develop, produce, install, and service a product.
- ISO 9002/Q92 specifies a quality system model for use by organizations that produce and install a product or service.
- ISO 9003/Q93 specifies a quality system model for use by organizations that include final inspection and testing.
- ISO 9004/Q94 provides a set of guidelines for an organization to develop and implement a quality system, and interpret the other series standards.

When a firm becomes ISO 9000 certified they prove to an independent assessor that they meet all the requirements of either ISO 9001/Q91, ISO 9002/Q92, or ISO 9003/Q93. Generally, ISO 9000 certification is good for a period of three years.

Source: Lance L. Whitacre, *ISO 9000: Certifying Quality in Warehousing and Distribution* (Oak Brook, IL: Warehousing Education and Research Council, March 1994), pp. 5–6.

---

and in the future. TQM integrates fundamental management techniques, existing improvement efforts, and technical tools under a disciplined approach focused on continuous improvement.[15]

Another, more managerial definition, offered in the Procter & Gamble–sponsored *Report of the Total Quality Leadership and Steering Committee,* stated:

Total quality (TQ) is a people-focused management system that aims at continual increase of customer satisfaction at continually lower real cost. TQ is a total system approach (not a separate area or program), and an integral part of high-level strategy; it works horizontally across functions and departments, involves all employees, top to bottom, and extends backwards and forwards to include the supply chain and the customer chain. TQ stresses learning and adaptation to continual change as keys to organizational success.[16]

---

[15]Office of the Deputy Assistant Secretary of Defense for TQM, *Total Quality Management: A Guide for Implementation,* DOD 5000.51-G, final draft (Washington, DC: August 23, 1989).

[16]S. W. Becker, "TQM Does Work: Ten Reasons Why Misguided Attempts Fail," *Management Review* 82, no. 5 (May 1993), p. 30.

TABLE 7–3   Traditional Management and TQM Comparison

Traditional Management	*Total Quality Management*
Looks for "quick fix"	Adopts a new management philosophy
Fire-fights	Uses structured, disciplined operating methods
Operates the same old way	Advocates "breakthrough" thinking using small innovations
Randomly adopts improvement efforts	Sets the example through management action
Focuses on short-term gains	Stresses long-term, continuous improvement
Inspects for errors	Prevents errors
Throws resources at a task	Uses people to add value
Is motivated by profit	Focuses on the customer
Relies on programs	Is a new way of life

Source: James H. Saylor, "What Total Quality Management Means to the Logistician," *Logistics Spectrum* 24, no. 4 (Winter 1990), p. 20.

TQM has particular relevance and importance to materials flow within logistics. Many leading authorities have championed the importance of quality in business, including W. Edwards Deming and Philip B. Crosby.[17] Additionally, the Malcolm Baldrige National Quality Award program of the U.S. Department of Commerce has helped shape corporate thinking on quality issues. Traditional concepts about quality have been modified and enhanced to form the TQM approach outlined in Table 7–3.

The TQM approach stresses long-term benefits resulting from continuous improvements to systems, programs, products, and people. Improvements most often result from a combination of small innovations. A structured, disciplined operating method is used to maximize customer service levels.

Difficulties in TQM Implementation

While TQM has a number of obvious advantages to both organizations and customers, not all firms are successful in implementing it. Many reasons exist for the difficulty or lack of successful implementation, including too much training required, too little focus on human issues, underestimating the time and effort necessary, losing sight of the customer, trying to encompass too many elements, and lack of integration into the firm's core values and competencies.[18]

Table 7–4 identifies the relationships between TQM and logistics. Underlying the specific items listed in the table is the notion that quality is a philosophy of doing business. It is like the marketing concept, cost trade-off analysis, and the systems approach. Each is an orientation or approach to conducting business that influences how individuals, departments, and organizations plan, implement, and control marketing and logistics activities. Therefore, every person involved in logistics must understand his or her role in delivering a level of quality to suppliers, vendors, and final customers.

Keys to TQM Success

Central to TQM success is focus on continuous improvement that leads to higher quality and better customer support whether internal or external to the organization. It normally requires a cultural change, because most organizations today focus on activities rather than process improvement.

---

[17]See Howard S. Gitlow and Shelby J. Gitlow, *The Deming Guide to Quality and Competitive Position* (Englewood Cliffs, NJ: Prentice Hall, 1987); and Philip B. Crosby, *Quality Is Free* (New York: McGraw-Hill, 1979).

[18]Paul D. Larson and Ashish Sinha, "The TQM Impact: A Study of Quality Managers' Perceptions," *Quality Management Journal* 2, no. 3 (Spring 1995), p. 53.

TABLE 7–4   Direct Relationship between TQM and Logistics

TQM	*Logistics*
Provides a TQM management environment	Uses systematic, integrated, consistent, organization-wide perspective for satisfying the customer
Reduces chronic waste	Emphasizes "doing it right the first time"
Involves everyone and everything	Involves almost every process
Nurtures supplier partnerships and customer relationships	Knows the importance of supply and partnerships
	Key to customer relations. Customer relations are directly dependent on training, documentation, maintenance, supply support, support equipment, transportation, manpower, computer resources, and facilities
Creates a continuous improvement system	Uses logistics support analysis to continuously improve the system
Includes quality as an element of design	Influences design by emphasizing reliability, maintainability, supportability using the optimum mix of manpower and technology
Provides training constantly	Provides constant technical training for everyone
Leads long-term continuous improvement efforts geared toward prevention	Focuses on reducing life cycle costs by quality improvements geared to prevention
Encourages teamwork	Stresses the integrated efforts of everyone
Satisfies the customer (internal and external)	Places the customer first

Source: James H. Saylor, "What Total Quality Management Means to the Logistician," *Logistics Spectrum* 24, no. 4 (Winter 1990), p. 22.

> More importantly, TQM requires employee involvement to be successful. Without employee involvement, focus cannot be achieved . . . Senior management commitment and leadership is imperative to ensure follow-through of employee recommendations. Commitment at all levels is the "oil" that enables the organizational "engine" to work.[19]

As indicated earlier, TQM is a process. It involves almost every logistics activity and takes a systematic, integrated, consistent, organizationwide perspective for satisfying the customer. And TQM emphasizes continuous improvements. As shown in Figure 7–2, the process begins with a determination of logistics requirements (e.g., customer service levels, inventory levels, transportation strategies). Those requirements are specified as a result of a logistics audit that has examined the materials management and physical distribution aspects of the total logistics system.

After requirements are determined, the processes are continuously reviewed to develop ways to improve. For example, based on historical information, supplier evaluation criteria may be revised, inbound logistics strategies may be modified, or perhaps JIT relationships may be established with selected vendors or suppliers.

---

[19]Scott A. Wagoner, "Logistics and Quality Management: Leadership and the Process Improvement Link," *Logistics Spectrum* 23, no. 4 (Winter 1989), p. 13; also see Johann L. Von Flue, "Quality Management," *Logistics Spectrum* 24, no. 4 (Winter 1990), pp. 13–17.

FIGURE 7–2

TQM/logistics process

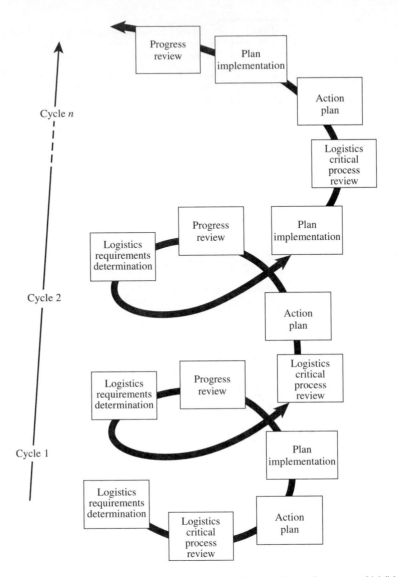

Source: Scott A. Wagoner, "Logistics and Quality Management: Leadership and the Process Improvement Link," *Logistics Spectrum* 23, no. 4 (Winter 1990), p. 15.

"An action plan . . . as well as process improvement recommendations [are] prepared. The action plan should be specified with step by step goals, completion dates, responsible personnel, and resource requirements. The logistics team then acts upon the plan with progress being reviewed regularly.[20] In essence, the process resembles the spiral shown in Figure 7–2.

Implementation of TQM within the materials management environment has resulted in significant benefits and improvements for many companies. McDonnell Douglas Corporation employed TQM concepts and reduced scrap by 58 percent. Boeing

---

[20]Wagoner, "Logistics and Quality Management," p. 15.

Ballistic Systems Division reduced parts and materials lead times by 30 percent and reduced material shortages from 12 percent to zero. AT&T reduced product defect rates and total process time by 30 percent and 46 percent, respectively. Hewlett-Packard reduced scrap by 75 percent and put 60 percent of its product failure rate through TQM improvements.[21]

In summary, TQM and logistics are interrelated. It is vital that managers administer and control materials flow using the concepts of TQM.

Administration and Control of Materials Flow

Measuring Performance of Materials Management

Like all of the functions of logistics, materials management activities must be properly administered and controlled. Proper administration and control require some methods to identify the firm's level of performance. Specifically, the firm must be able to *measure, report,* and *improve* performance.

In measuring the performance of materials management, the firm should examine a number of elements, including supplier service levels, inventory, prices paid for materials, quality levels, and operating costs.

Service levels can be measured using several methods, including:

- Order cycle time for each supplier.
- Variability in order cycle time for each supplier.
- Order fill rate for each supplier.
- Percentage of orders from each supplier that are overdue.
- Percentage of production orders not filled on time.
- Number of stockouts resulting from late deliveries from suppliers.
- Number of production delays caused by materials being out of stock.

Inventory is an important aspect of materials management and can be controlled using the following measures:

- Amount of dead stock.
- Comparison of actual inventory levels with targeted levels.
- Comparison of inventory turnover rates with data from previous time periods.
- Percentage of stockouts caused by improper purchasing decisions.
- Number of production delays caused by improper purchasing decisions.

Materials *price level* measures include gains and losses resulting from forward buying, a comparison of prices paid for major items over several time periods, and a comparison of actual prices paid for materials with targeted prices.

In the area of *quality control,* measures that can be used are the number of product failures caused by materials defects, and the percentage of materials rejected from each shipment from each supplier.

As an overall measure of performance, management can *compare the actual budget* consumed by materials management *to the targeted budget* allocated at the beginning of the operating period.

---

[21]See Joe W. Meredith and Benjamin S. Blanchard, "Concurrent Engineering: Total Quality Management in Design," *Logistics Spectrum* 24, no. 4 (Winter 1990), pp. 31–40; and R. I. Winner, J. P. Pennell, H. E. Bertrand, and M. G. Slusarczuk, *The Role of Concurrent Engineering in Weapons System Acquisition,* IDA Report R-338 (Alexandria, VA: Institute for Defense Analysis, December 1988).

**Materials Management
Operating Reports**

Once the company has established performance measures for each component of the materials management process, data must be collected and results reported to those executives in decision-making positions. The major operating reports that should be developed by materials management include (1) market and economic conditions and price performance, (2) inventory investment changes, (3) purchasing operations and effectiveness, and (4) operations affecting administration and financial activities. Table 7–5 presents a summary of the reports needed.

Finally, after performance has been measured and reported, the firm must improve it whenever possible. In order to initiate improvements, the materials manager must address certain key questions. These relate to how the product is produced and how inventories are controlled. Some of the questions to be examined are the following:

1. How much product is to be manufactured? What is forecasted demand? What is available capacity?

2. When are manufacturing plants to produce to meet demand? In what amount? At which facility?

TABLE 7–5   Operating Reports That Should Be Developed by Purchasing and Materials Management Functions

Market and Economic Conditions and Price Performance
- Price trends and changes for the major materials and commodities purchased. Comparisons with:
  1. Standard costs where such accounting methods are used.
  2. Quoted market prices.
  3. Target costs, as determined by cost analysis.
- Changes in demand–supply conditions for the major items purchased. Effects of labor strikes or threatened strikes.
- Lead-time expectations for major items.

Inventory Investment Changes
- Dollar investment in inventories, classified by major commodity and materials groups.
- Days' or months' supply, and on order, for major commodity and materials groups.
- Ratio of inventory dollar investment to sales dollar volume.
- Rates of inventory turnover for major items.

Purchasing Operations and Effectiveness
- Cost reductions resulting from purchase research and value analysis studies.
- Quality rejection rates for major items.
- Percentage of on-time deliveries.
- Number of out-of-stock situations that caused interruption of scheduled production.
- Number of change orders issued, classified by cause.
- Number of requisitions received and processed.
- Number of purchase orders issued.
- Employee work load and productivity.
- Transportation costs.

Operations Affecting Administration and Financial Activities
- Comparison of actual departmental operating costs to budget.
- Case discounts earned and cash discounts lost.
- Commitments to purchase, classified by types of formal contracts and by purchase orders, aged by expected delivery dates.
- Changes in cash discounts allowed by suppliers.

Source: Michael R. Leenders and Harold E. Fearon, *Purchasing and Materials Management,* 10th ed. (Burr Ridge, IL: McGraw-Hill/Irwin, 1993), p. 467.

3. When are raw materials to be ordered? In what quantities? From which source? With what provisions to remove shortages?

4. How large is preseason inventory buildup?

5. What are target inventory levels? Where should inventory be positioned? When should inventory be relocated?

6. How are customers allocated in periods of short supply?

7. How are backlogs managed?

8. What are information requirements? What record keeping and status reporting are needed? What cost data must be gathered?

9. When do plans and schedules get revised? What information is used? How far ahead are plans and schedules made?

10. Who sets management policy for product planning?

11. Who is responsible for planning—logistics, sales, production control?

12. Who is responsible for scheduling?[22]

Computers are also used to improve materials management performance. Systems that have gained acceptance in many firms are Kanban/just-in-time (JIT), MRP, ERP, and DRP.

Kanban/Just-in-Time Systems

Kanban at Toyota

Kanban.   Kanban and just-in-time (JIT) systems have become much more important in manufacturing and logistics operations in recent years. Kanban, also known as the Toyota Production System (TPS), was developed by Toyota Motor Company during the 1950s and 1960s. Figure 7–3 provides an overview of the original Kanban procedure. One writer described it as follows: "Kanban is basically the system of supplying parts and materials just at the very moment they are needed in the factory production process so those parts and materials are instantly put to use."[23] Through reduction of inventories, Toyota identified problems in supply and product quality, because problems were forced into the open. Safety stocks were no longer available to overcome supplier delays and faulty components, thus forcing Toyota to eliminate "hidden" production and supply problems.

Recently, Toyota has computerized its Kanban system and provides it online to suppliers.

> The data recording technology enables the system to incorporate about 100 times more data than Kanban cards. In addition to increasing the amount of information available to suppliers, the new system will slash lead times. With the Kanban card process, it's reported that it takes seven to eight hours for the card to reach the production point. Under the new system . . . parts suppliers receive ordering instructions online, print them out, and attach them to the ordered parts, which are then delivered to Toyota. According to one estimate, if Toyota sent all its transactions with a specific supplier electronically, that supplier would save 2,000 to 3,000 hours per month.[24]

---

[22]Provided by Professor Jay Sterling, University of Alabama.

[23]Bruce D. Henderson, "The Logic of Kanban," *The Journal of Business Strategy* 6, no. 3 (Winter 1986), p. 6.

[24]"Why Kanbans Are Now Catching the Attention of Inventory Managers," *Inventory Reduction Report,* Issue 99-2 (February 1999), p. 4.

FIGURE 7–3

Kanban card procedure

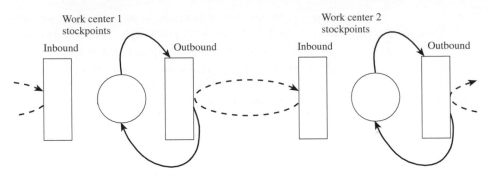

– – –   Move card path. When a container of parts is selected for use from an inbound stockpoint, the move card is removed from the container and taken to the outbound stockpoint of the preceding work center as authorization to pick another container of parts.

———   Production card path. When a container of parts is picked from an outbound stockpoint, the production card is removed and left behind as authorization to make a standard container of parts to replace the one taken.

The Kanban Card System

"Kanban" literally means "signboard" in Japanese. The system involves the use of cards (called "kanbans") that are attached to containers which hold a standard quantity of a single part number. There are two types of kanban cards: "move" cards and "production" cards.

When a worker starts to use a container of parts the move card, which is attached to it, is removed and is either sent to or picked up by the preceding, or feeding work center (in many cases this is the supplier). This is the signal—or "sign"—for that work center to send another container of parts to replace the one now being used. This replacement container has a production card attached to it which is replaced by the "move" card before it is sent. The production card then authorizes the producing work center to make another container full of parts. These cards circulate respectively within or between work centers or between the supplier and the assembly plant.

In order for Kanban to work effectively, these rules must be observed:

1. There can only be one card attached to a container at any one time.

2. The using (or following) work center must initiate the movement of parts from the feeding (or preceding) work center.
3. No fabrication of parts is allowed without a kanban production card.
4. Never move or produce other than the amount indicated by the kanban card.
5. Kanban cards must be handled on a first-in, first-out (FIFO) basis.
6. Finished parts must be placed at the location point indicated on the kanban card.

Because each kanban card represents a standard number of parts being made or used within the production process, the amount of work-in-process inventory can easily be controlled by controlling the number of cards on the plant floor. Japanese managers, by simply removing a card or two, can test or strain the system and reveal bottlenecks. Then they have a problem they can address themselves to—an opportunity to improve productivity, the prime goal of Kanban.

Source: "Why Everybody Is Talking About 'Just-in-Time,'" *Warehousing Review* 1, no. 1 (October 1984), p. 27. Reprinted by permission of the International Warehouse Logistics Association.

While the use of Kanban systems is most often associated with the automobile industry, it can apply to any manufacturing process involving repetitive operations. One company that has reaped the benefits of a Kanban system is OPW Fueling Components in Cincinnati, Ohio. The firm has realized a 10 percent reduction in inventory, increased its inventory turnover rates from an average of six to eight, and improved its on-time delivery to 95 percent.[25]

———

[25]Ibid., p. 3.

JIT.   Closely related to Kanban is just-in-time (JIT). Introduced in the 1970s, the concept or philosophy of JIT is not new. Many terms are used interchangeably for JIT, although they are not identical. In the food industry, efficient consumer response (ECR) is the preferred term, while in the retail sector, quick response (QR) is commonly used.[26]

JIT links purchasing and procurement, manufacturing, and logistics. Its primary goals are to minimize inventories, improve product quality, maximize production efficiency, and provide optimal customer service levels. It is basically a philosophy of doing business.

JIT Defined   JIT has been defined in several ways, including the following:

A method of inventory control with a focus on waste elimination.[27]

A program which seeks to eliminate non-value-added activities from any operation with the objectives of producing high-quality products (i.e., "zero defects"), high productivity levels, lower levels of inventory, and developing long-term relationships with channel members.[28]

At the heart of the JIT system is the notion that anything over the minimum amount necessary for a task is considered wasteful. This is in direct contrast to the traditional philosophy of "just-in-case" in which large inventories or safety stocks are held just in case they are needed. In JIT, the ideal lot size or EOQ is one unit, safety stock is considered unnecessary, and inventory should be eliminated.

Many companies in the United States have applied JIT procedures in recent years. Not every component can be handled by the various JIT approaches, but for items that are used repetitively and are not bulky or irregular in shape, the systems work extremely well.

Benefits of JIT   There are many benefits of JIT programs, including the following:

- Improved inventory turns.
- Improved customer service.
- Decreased warehouse space.
- Improved response time.
- Reduced logistics costs.
- Reduced transportation costs.
- Improved quality of vendor products.
- Reduced number of vendors.
- Reduced number of transportation carriers.[29]

JIT at Xerox Europe   An example of a firm that has achieved success through JIT is Xerox Europe (formerly Rank Xerox). As the largest Xerox company outside the United States, Xerox Europe (a joint venture between Xerox Corporation and Britain's Rank Corporation) produces and refurbishes midvolume copier equipment for distribution throughout the world.

In the 1980s, Xerox Europe implemented a JIT program. As part of the program, the firm also installed an automated materials handling system and information

---

[26]See Mike Jenkins, "The New Game and the New Players," *Logistics Today* (Summer 1998), pp. 1–2.

[27]Richard Germain, Cornelia Dröge, and Nancy Spears, "The Implications of Just-in-Time for Logistics Organization Management and Performance," *Journal of Business Logistics* 17, no. 2 (1996), p. 19.

[28]Larry C. Giunipero and Wai K. Law, "Organizational Support for Just-in-Time Implementation," *The International Journal of Logistics Management* 1, no. 2 (1990), pp. 35–36.

[29]Francis J. Quinn, Robert C. Lieb, and Robert A. Millen, "Why U.S. Companies Are Embracing JIT," *Traffic Management,* 29, no. 11 (November 1990), p. 34.

processing system. Production procedures were modified at the same time. As a result of the JIT program and other system changes, Xerox Europe realized the following benefits:

1. Its supplier base was reduced from 3,000 to 300.
2. Ninety-eight percent on-time inbound delivery was achieved, with 70 percent of materials arriving within an hour of the time they were needed.
3. Warehouse stock was reduced from a three-month to a half-month supply.
4. Overall material costs were reduced by more than 40 percent.
5. Most inbound product inspection stations were eliminated because of higher quality materials from suppliers.
6. Reject levels for defective or inferior materials fell from 17 percent to 0.8 percent.
7. Positions for 40 repack people were eliminated because of standardized shipment-packaging criteria.
8. Inbound transportation costs were reduced by 40 percent.
9. On-time inbound delivery performance was improved by 28 percent.[30]

Other companies that have successfully introduced JIT into their operations include Cummins Engine, Ford, General Motors, 3M, Textron, and Whirlpool. In sum, organizations that implement JIT will likely have one or more of the following characteristics:

1. Formalization of performance measurements.
2. Greater reliance on logistics personnel with specialized skills.
3. Delegation of decisions concerning strategic logistics issues down the organizational chart.
4. Greater involvement by senior executives from different functions in the creation of logistics strategy.
5. An increased span of control of senior logistics executives as size of the firm increases.
6. Improved perceptions of the organization's performance relative to the rest of the industry.[31]

Problems Associated with JIT

While the benefits arising from JIT are many, the approach may not be right for all firms, and the system has some inherent problems. These problems fall into three categories: production scheduling (plant), supplier production schedules, and supplier locations.

When leveling of the production schedule is necessary due to uneven demand, firms will require higher levels of inventory. Items can be produced during slack periods even though they may not be demanded until later, which results in larger inventories of end product. Also, finished goods inventory has a higher value because of its form utility, and thus there is a greater financial risk resulting from product obsolescence, damage, and loss. However, higher levels of inventory, coupled with a uniform production schedule, can be more advantageous than a fluctuating schedule with less

---

[30]Lisa H. Harrington, "Why Rank Xerox Turned to Just-in-Time," *Traffic Management* 27, no. 10 (October 1988), pp. 82–87.
[31]Germain et al., "Implications of Just-in-Time for Logistics," pp. 30–32.

inventory. In addition, when stockout costs are great because of production slowdowns or shutdowns, JIT may not be the optimal system. JIT reduces inventory levels to the point where there is little, if any, safety stock, and parts shortages can adversely affect production operations.

A second problem with JIT relates to supplier production schedules. Success of a JIT system depends on suppliers' ability to provide parts in accordance with the firm's production schedule. Smaller, more frequent orders can result in higher ordering costs, which must be taken into account when calculating any cost savings due to reduced inventory levels. Suppliers incur higher production and setup costs due to the large number of small lot quantities produced. Generally, the result can be an increase in the cost of procuring items from suppliers, unless suppliers are able to perceive the benefits they can receive from being part of a JIT system.

Supplier locations can be a third problem area. As distances between the firm and its suppliers increase, delivery times may become more erratic and less predictable. Transportation costs also increase as small shipments are made. Transit time variability can cause inventory stockouts that disrupt production scheduling. When this factor is combined with higher delivery costs per unit, total costs may be greater than savings in inventory carrying costs. Table 7–6 summarizes the areas of difficulty when attempting to implement JIT in a global arena.

Other problem areas that can become obstacles to JIT include organizational resistance, lack of systems support, misdefinition of service levels, lack of planning, and inventory being shifted to suppliers. Overcoming these and the previously discussed problems or obstacles requires cooperation and integration within and between organizations.

Logistics Implications of JIT

JIT has numerous implications for logistics executives. First, proper implementation of JIT requires that the firm fully integrate all logistics activities. Many trade-offs

---

TABLE 7–6   JIT and Logistics in Global Sourcing

Required Elements	*JIT*	*Global Purchasing*
Frequent deliveries	Essential	Difficult
Small lots	Essential	Difficult
Supplier location	Close	Far
Single sourcing	Common	High risk
Long-term relationship	Essential	Difficult
Early supplier involvement (ESI) in design, manufacturing, etc.	Possible and probable	Unlikely
Coordination and monitoring of schedules and markets	High	Difficult
Price	Less important	Central consideration
Transit loss/damage	Low	High
Information sharing	High	Low
Potential pipeline instability	Low	High
Quality	High	Variable
Supplier flexibility and reaction time	High	Low

Source: Ajay Das and Robert B. Handfield, "Just-in-Time and Logistics in Global Sourcing: An Empirical Study," *International Journal of Physical Distribution and Logistics Management* 27, nos. 3–4 (1997), p. 247.

are required, but without the coordination that integrated logistics management provides, JIT systems cannot be fully implemented.

Second, transportation becomes an even more vital component of logistics under a JIT system. In such an environment, the demands placed on the firm's transportation network are significant and include a need for shorter, more consistent transit times, more sophisticated communications, use of fewer carriers with long-term relationships, a need for efficiently designed transportation and materials handling equipment, and better transportation decision-making strategies.

Third, warehousing assumes an expanded role in a JIT system. A warehouse becomes a consolidation facility rather than a storage facility. Since many products come into the manufacturing operation at shorter intervals, less space is required for storage, but there must be an increased capability for handling and consolidating items. Different forms of materials handling equipment may be needed to facilitate the movement of many products in smaller quantities. The location decision for warehouses serving inbound material needs may also change because suppliers are often located closer to the manufacturing facility in a JIT system.

JIT II at Bose Corporation

JIT systems can also be combined with systems that plan and control material flows into, within, and out of manufacturing. These systems include JIT II, MRP, and DRP systems. JIT II applies JIT concepts to the purchasing function by having a representative of the supplier locate at the buying organization's facility. Developed by Bose Corporation, a global audio equipment manufacturer, this approach improves mutual understanding between the buyer and supplier, reduces waste and redundancy of efforts, improves supplier responsiveness, and creates a positive working environment.[32] MRP and DRP will be discussed in the following sections. Simply, DRP manages finished product inventory in distribution, while MRP manages material and in-process inventory for production.

MRP Systems

The abbreviation *MRP* has been used to signify systems called *material requirements planning (MRP I)* and *manufacturing resource planning (MRP II)*. MRP I developed into MRP II with the addition of financial, marketing, and purchasing components.

Basic Logic of MRP

MRP—An Example.[33]   The basic logic of MRP is a simple process that begins with customers and how well the organization can supply their demands. As an illustration, suppose a hypothetical company, Fine Line Industries, manufactures writing implements. Assume that you are the materials manager for Fine Line. The sales manager enters your office and announces that some pens have been sold. What information do you need? How many pens she's sold, to begin with, and when the customer wants them. Then you're going to want some specifics: Which pens are we talking about? How are they to be packaged? And, in practical terms, so we can start thinking about the proper priority to give the order, who is the customer?

For our purposes, in the basic logic of MRP, we need to know how many pens—let's use 20 for our example—and when the customer wants them—let's say next Friday. Of

---

[32]See Lance Dixon and Anne Millen Porter, *JIT II: Evolution in Buying and Selling* (Newton, MA: Cahners, 1994).

[33]The material in this section has been closely adapted from material included in Terry Lunn, with Susan A. Neff, "Basic Logic of MRP," Chapter 3 of *MRP: Integrating Material Requirements Planning and Modern Business* (New York: McGraw-Hill/Irwin, 1992), pp. 33–47.

course, the main question you have as materials manager is whether or not the company can fulfill the customer's requirements. The first thing that needs to be done would be to check inventory to see if there are finished pens in stock that are ready to ship. If so, then we would merely enter a shipping order and not have to get into our manufacturing planning logic.

However, let's say that no, we don't have any stock on hand. Where do we go from here? First, we have to ask whether we have the components we need to make the pens. Basically, there are three pen parts—the upper barrel, the ink cartridge, and the lower barrel. We need 20 pens next Friday for this customer, so how many upper barrels do we need? The answer, naturally, is 20, because we need one upper barrel per pen. Likewise, for the other components, we will need 20 ink cartridges and 20 lower barrels in order to satisfy the customer requirement.

Master Schedule

The example that has just been presented is the central logic of an MRP system. We have just encountered the three main *inputs* to that MRP system: What do we need in order to fill the customer demands? In our case, 20 pens next Friday. This is called the *master schedule.* Next, we check our inventory balances, and if we don't have the parts, we consult the bill of material and determine the quantity of each component required. The sum of the needs for each particular component is called the *gross requirement.* Throughout this first example, we are going to be looking at the requirement for upper barrels, and we know that we need 20 of them by next Friday.

Once this requirement is established, we subtract our inventory from it. We check the stockroom to see how many upper barrels are on the shelf. The stockroom tells us that we have 25 upper barrels on the shelf. Are we capable of delivering the pens by next Friday? Well, it depends on the available stock for the other two components, but we do have enough upper barrels to do the job. If we have 25 on hand, and we need to use 20 to fill the customer order, how many will we have left on the shelf next Friday? The answer, of course, is five.

Scheduled Receipt

What we have just done is commonly referred to as computing the *projected balance on hand.* Our current balance on hand is 25 and we can project the balance on hand next Friday to be 5. There is another element of our inventory information, however, that must be taken into account: Do we have any scheduled receipts for these upper barrels? A *scheduled receipt* is an order for material to replenish our stock. For example, if we purchase the upper barrel from a vendor, we might have an open purchase order with that vendor for a quantity to be delivered on a specific date; many companies call this a scheduled receipt. The term does have a broader implication, for if the part were manufactured in our own plant, we would call it an *open order.*

Open Order

Gross requirements reduce our projected balance on hand, whereas scheduled receipts increase the expected balance on hand. We should not limit our view to the period between now and next Friday; we should consider conditions that will occur further into the future. Therefore, we will look at our requirements, scheduled receipts, and the projected balance on hand over time. This can be called a *time-phased format.* In our example, each of these periods, or time buckets, represents one week. This is not a necessary condition; not only can the period be something other than a week, the period length can vary.

Time-Phased Format

We have checked our inventory records, and we have a scheduled receipt for 25 upper barrels coming in on week 2. We also want to look at our gross requirements over time. We already know about our requirement for 20 pens in week 1; other master schedule information tells us that there are 20 more needed in week 4. Of course, like many other companies, we do make things other than this one pen. We also make mechanical pencils. While the pencil has a number of components, right now we are going to focus on the upper barrel. If we were to take an upper barrel for the pencil, do you suppose it would fit on the top of a pen?

Our engineering department has designed these so that the upper barrels are interchangeable. Consequently, the requirements for upper barrels must include not only the requirements for our pens, but also for our pencils. We know about two pending orders for pencils: 20 pencils for week 3 and 5 pencils in week 6. Gross requirements means, simply, that we add together all of the requirements for upper barrels for pens and pencils, plus any other demands. All these requirements are then inserted into our time-phased format under the appropriate dates.

With these data, we can easily compute the projected balance on hand for each week across our time-phased format. The scheduled receipt in week 2 will raise our balance on hand from 5 to 30, and the gross requirement in week 3 will reduce the projected balance on hand from 30 to 10. We can anticipate what's going to happen in week. If we don't do something by then, our projected balance on hand will go into a negative condition. This means a shortage, and we will be unable to fulfill the requirement for the upper barrel because we will be 10 pieces short. This shortage is defined as a *net requirement* of 10.

Net Requirement

Net requirements refer to the quantity that we need in order to fulfill demands. We would show the net requirement for the part each week: In our example, there is a net requirement for 10 pieces in week 4 and five pieces in week 6. Net requirements mean that we must ensure that more upper barrels arrive into our stockroom so that we can satisfy our gross requirements. How do we do this? We order more upper barrels. This is often called replenishing stock, or a *replenishment stock order*.

Replenishment Stock Order

Lot Sizing

How many should we order at a time? The determination of this order quantity is known as *lot sizing*. For purposes of our example, we will set the lot size at 25. This can be determined by the length of the setup time in our shop, or perhaps by the packaging limitations of our vendor.

Planned Order Receipt

Logically, we are saying at this point that we are planning to have a receipt of 25 upper barrels come into the stockroom in week 4. This is called a *planned order receipt*. This represents the quantity anticipated for a specific need date.

You should keep in mind that the difference between a planned order receipt and a scheduled receipt is that the scheduled receipt represents an open order, while the planned order receipt has not yet been released to the shop floor or to the supplier.

Projected Available

Assuming that this planned order receipt will arrive in stock as planned, we can compute an amount called the *projected available*. The projected available takes the balance on hand plus any scheduled receipts minus the gross requirements plus any planned order receipts and records the resulting quantity for each week.

In order to have this planned order receipt come about, it is necessary to enter an order to replenish our stock. Our planned order receipt, using the lot size, tells us that the order should be 25 pieces, and that it is needed in week 4. Our next question, then, is, when shall we start this order so that it arrives in the stockroom in week 4?

Lead-Time Offset

The length of time from the start of the order to our finish date is called the *lead-time offset*. In most plants, this is the time between the date when the order is released and the receipt of the goods in the stockroom. If we make the part, it is called *manufacturing lead time,* and if we get the part from a vendor, it is known as *purchasing lead time.* In our example, we define our lead time as three weeks. Therefore, we compute that we should release the order in week 1 in order for it to arrive into the stockroom by week 4.

This is one of the key elements in the logic of an MRP system: The planned order receipt must be timed to meet the net requirement. We must release this order with a due date that matches the requirement need date. We use the time-phased format to enable us to look far enough into the future to create planned order releases that will get parts on their way into our stockroom soon enough to avert shortages. Also, we should look at any items whose due dates do not match the need date. MRP logic will suggest that we reschedule. In our example, we showed a scheduled receipt in week 2, but the part is not actually needed until week 3. MRP would suggest a reschedule notice to move that receipt out to week 3.

MRP Worksheet

What we really need to do is condense this information into a format that brings out the key items and shows us what actions we need to take. We don't need to see all of the detailed computations our computer is going to make as it produces its suggestions; we do need to see the results. There are four specific things we need to see: gross requirement, scheduled receipts, projected balance on hand, and planned order releases (see Figure 7–4).

In Figure 7–4, you will notice that the projected balance on hand number assumes that the planned order releases will arrive as anticipated in weeks 4 and 8. Hence, the balance on hand is shown to be increased by planned order receipts.

If the upper barrel were a purchased part, the MRP worksheet in Figure 7–4 would show us the action necessary to fulfill all our requirements. Looking at the planned order release in week 1 tells us we should now release a purchase order to our vendor to have the 25 upper barrels come into our stockroom in week 4. We should also consider delaying our existing scheduled receipt of 25 pieces, due in week 2, for one week, into week 3. Also, looking ahead, we will plan another order release for week 5 with delivery scheduled for week 8. We might consider a world-class strategy, where we would advise our vendor now of this future projected need.

On the other hand, if we manufacture upper barrels in our own plant, we need to proceed with this planning into the level of the components necessary to build the upper barrel. Our upper barrel is comprised of two components: the clip and the sleeve. MRP logic tells us that the planned order releases at one level create the gross requirement at

FIGURE 7–4

MRP worksheet (upper barrel)

						Period				
	Now	1	2	3	4	5	6	7	8	9
Requirement		20		20	20		5		20	
Scheduled Receipts			25							
On hand	25	5	30	10	15	15	10	10	15	15
Planned order releases		25				25				

Source: Terry Lunn, with Susan A. Neff, *MRP: Integrating Material Requirements Planning and Modern Business* (New York: McGraw-Hill/Irwin, 1992), p. 43.

FIGURE 7–5

Explosion

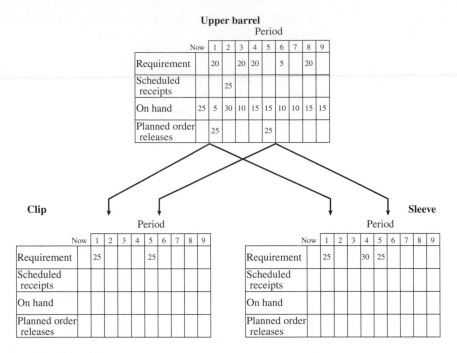

Upper barrel

Period	Now	1	2	3	4	5	6	7	8	9
Requirement		20		20	20		5		20	
Scheduled receipts			25							
On hand	25	5	30	10	15	15	10	10	15	15
Planned order releases		25				25				

Clip

Period	Now	1	2	3	4	5	6	7	8	9
Requirement		25				25				
Scheduled receipts										
On hand										
Planned order releases										

Sleeve

Period	Now	1	2	3	4	5	6	7	8	9
Requirement		25			30	25				
Scheduled receipts										
On hand										
Planned order releases										

Source: Terry Lunn, with Susan A. Neff, *MRP: Integrating Material Requirements Planning and Modern Business* (New York: McGraw-Hill/Irwin, 1992), p. 45.

the next level. Therefore, our planned order release for 25 upper barrels starting in week 1 gives us a requirement for 25 clips that have to be in our stockroom in week 1. There will be a second requirement for clips in week 5. There is a corresponding set of requirements for the sleeves, as shown in Figure 7–5.

We must emphasize that the gross requirements reflect the sum of all the needs for the particular part. In Figure 7–5, you see the requirement for 30 more sleeves in week 4 that must come from the planned order release for some other kind of upper barrel assembly than the one we have been discussing. It is important that we consider all the requirements for a part before computing the net requirements and making the planned order release. Some of these requirements may be independent demand seen as spare parts, which must be added to the dependent requirements.

The same logic continues for the clips, considering the gross requirements, balance on hand, and scheduled receipts to create planned order releases for the clips. The lot size for the clips may create a planned order release indicating the gross requirement for steel coil. The purpose of this is to ensure that we have sufficient raw materials on hand to manufacture enough clips.

This process of using planned order releases to calculate gross requirements may continue on down through the bill of material for many levels, until we arrive at the purchase level for every part needed in the manufacture of our product. This process is

Explosion   known as an *explosion.*

You may have noticed that the scheduled receipt for the upper barrels in week 2 does not show a requirement for the components. This is due to the assumption in the MRP logic that the components have already been issued from the stockroom to an existing shop order. The balance on hand for that component was already reduced when the parts were physically moved from the stockroom to the shop floor.

We can distill all of the elements of the MRP logic into an easily understood format. Starting with gross requirements, we subtract inventory, yielding net requirements. To the net requirements, we apply lot size and lead-time offset to arrive at planned order releases. Planned order releases at one level create gross requirements at the next level.

Outputs of MRP Systems

Using MRP logic, we can see the three main outputs are, first, planned order releases, used to release new orders either to our vendor or to our own shop. A second output, the reschedule notice, is used to suggest adjustments to scheduled receipts, matching the due date to the need date. Our third output is the data we will use to determine the amount of capacity required to implement our production schedules.

Still following this MRP logic, we can see that the gross requirements are derived initially from the master production schedule, which is one of the three main inputs into the MRP system. The second input is the inventory status, which we used to determine our balance on hand and our record of scheduled receipts. The third input, the bill of material, is used to convert planned order releases for assemblies into gross requirements for components.

MRP I.   Material requirements planning (MRP I) became a popular concept in the 1960s and 1970s. It consists of a (1) computer system, (2) manufacturing information system, and (3) concept and philosophy of management. MRP I uses an array of computer hardware and software. As an information system it focuses on inventory, production scheduling, and the administration of all manufacturing resources—people, dollars, equipment, and materials. As a management philosophy it is viewed as a means to an end.

Like other approaches, methods, and business philosophies, MRP I attempts to minimize inventories yet maintain adequate materials for the production process. Within an MRP I system, the master production schedule (as updated each week) directly initiates subsequent activities of the purchasing and manufacturing functions. An MRP I system is employed when (1) usage or demand of materials is discontinuous or highly unstable; (2) demand for materials depends on the production of other specific inventory items or finished products; and (3) purchasing/procurement, suppliers, and manufacturing possess the flexibility to handle order placements or delivery releases on a weekly basis.

MRP I systems offer many advantages over traditional systems, including:

- Improved business results (e.g., return on investment, profits).
- Improved manufacturing performance.
- Better manufacturing control.
- More accurate and timely information.
- Inventory reductions.
- Time-phased ordering of materials.
- Reductions in material obsolescence.
- Increased reliability.
- More responsiveness to market demand, and reduced production costs.

Disadvantages of MRP I

MRP I does have a number of drawbacks, and a firm considering adopting such a system should examine them. First, MRP I may not optimize materials acquisition costs. Because inventory levels are kept to a minimum, materials must be purchased more frequently and in smaller quantities. This results in increased ordering costs, unless these conditions are negotiated in contracts with suppliers. Higher transportation bills and higher unit costs may also be incurred because the firm is less likely to qualify for large volume discounts, unless suppliers offer cumulative quantity discounts. The company must weigh the anticipated savings from reduced inventory costs against the potentially greater acquisition costs resulting from smaller and more frequent orders.

Another possible disadvantage is the potential hazard of production slowdowns or shutdowns that may arise because of unforeseen delivery problems and supplier materials shortages. The availability of safety stocks gives production some protection against stockouts of essential material. As safety stocks are reduced, this level of protection is lost.

A final disadvantage of MRP I arises from the use of computer software packages. Organizations must determine whether standardized or custom-developed software will be used. Standardized programs are less expensive, but will likely not meet the specific requirements of user firms. Custom software is more expensive and takes longer to develop.

Figure 7–6 portrays the MRP I system and its outputs. The master production schedule serves as the major input into the MRP I system. Other inputs include the bill of materials file and the inventory records file. The bill of materials file contains the

FIGURE 7–6

Elements of an MRP I system

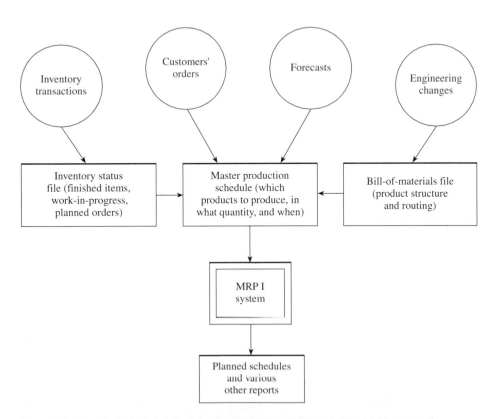

Source: MCB University Press Limited, Amrik Sohal, and Keith Howard, "Trends in Materials Management," *International Journal of Physical Distribution and Materials Management* 17, no. 5 (1987), p. 11.

component parts of the finished product, identified by part number. The inventory records file maintains a record of all inventories on hand and on order. It also keeps track of due dates for all component parts as well as finished goods.

Reports generated from MRP I systems include planning reports that can be used to forecast inventory and specify future requirements; performance reports for determining whether actual and programmed item lead times and actual and programmed quantity usages and costs agree; and exception reports, which point out discrepancies, such as errors, late or overdue orders, excessive scrap, or nonexistent parts.[34]

While MRP I is still being used by many firms, it has been updated and expanded to include financial, marketing, and logistics elements. This newer version is called manufacturing resource planning, or MRP II.

MRP II.   MRP II affects many functional areas of an organization, including engineering, finance, logistics, manufacturing, purchasing, and marketing.[35] It is a computer software package that includes the entire set of activities involved in the planning and control of production operations: production planning, resource requirements planning, master production scheduling, material requirements planning (MRP I), shop floor control, and purchasing (see Figure 7–7).

Benefits of MRP II

Organizations have reported a number of benefits associated with the implementation of MRP II systems, including:

- Inventory reductions of one-fourth to one-third.
- Higher inventory turnover ratio.
- Improved consistency in on-time customer delivery.
- Reduction in purchasing costs due to less expedited shipments.
- Minimization of workforce overtime.[36]

These benefits typically result in savings to a firm beyond the initial costs of implementing MRP II. Costs can easily exceed $750,000 during the first year of setup, although smaller companies may spend as little as $250,000. Therefore, the benefits must be tangible and sizable.

ERP Systems

Enterprise resource planning (ERP) is a system that includes the core accounting functions of accounts payable, accounts receivable, and general ledger, coupled with logistics functions, to manage the distribution and manufacturing components of the organization. According to one writer, "Integrated inventory handles finished goods, raw materials and sourced stock, all supported through a requisition system that can be driven from material requirements planning (MRP I) and sales forecasting . . . ERP becomes the facilitator of the organization, moving data from one function to another

---

[34]Leenders and Fearon, *Purchasing and Materials Management,* p. 211.

[35]See Paul A. Hoy, "The Changing Role of MRP II," *APICS Online Edition* 6, no. 6 (June 1996) <http://207.87.14.34/jun96/mrp.htm>.

[36]See Peter Duchessi and Charles M. Schaniger, "MRP II: A Prospectus for Renaissance," *Operations Research* 34, no. 3 (1994), pp. 325–51; and "Benefits Multiply with MRP II," *Modern Materials Handling* 48, no. 7 (July 1993), pp. 60–65.

FIGURE 7–7

Elements of an MRP II system

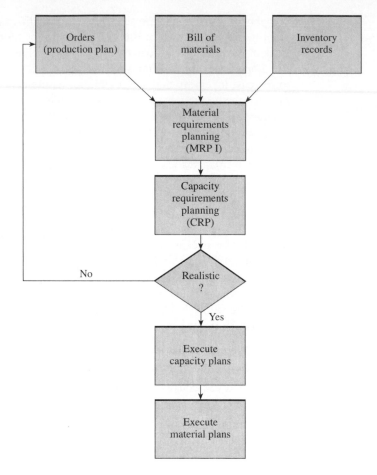

Source: Karl A. Hatt, "What's the Big Deal about MRP II?" *Winning Manufacturing* 5, no. 2 (1994), p. 2.

and managing the data centrally."[37] In essence, ERP is the newest generation of MRP systems. Other functions that might be supported in ERP can range from fixed assets to a warehouse management system (see Chapter 11).

ERP systems can interface with supply chain management (SCM) business solutions. For example, Coca-Cola Bottling Co. Consolidated, a North Carolina bottler of soft drinks, combined its ERP system with SCM software to centralize and streamline its planning activities for all of its branches. The combined systems "provide pre-configured business process integration intelligence that is customizable through a point-and-click interface to drive information and decisions through the supply chain."[38]

In Chapter 4 and again in Chapter 6, we described one particular application of ERP that has become widely used in many companies (e.g., Baxter, Exxon, Kodak, Microsoft) around the world: the suite of software developed by the German firm SAP

ERP Systems at Coca-Cola

SAP R/3— an Application of ERP

[37]Robert L. Olsen, *The Elements of Software Selection,* unnumbered and undated.
[38]"Coke Chooses Manugistics," *Supply Chain Technology News* 1, no. 2 (November–December 1999), p. 40.

AG. The SAP R/3 software is server-based, often used on personal computers running Microsoft Windows. The strength of the software is its ability to handle very large databases within four major modules: Financial Accounting, Human Resources, Manufacturing and Logistics, and Sales and Distribution.[39]

DRP Systems

DRP I Defined

DRP systems (DRP I and DRP II) are time-phased models that include demand forecasts, purchase orders, and customer orders for a facility. Distribution requirements planning (DRP I) has been defined as "a system of determining demands for inventory at distribution centers, consolidating the demand information backwards, and acting as input to the production and materials system."[40] The differences between DRP I and DRP II are as follows:

> Distribution resource planning (DRP II) is an extension of distribution requirements planning (DRP I). Distribution requirements planning applies the time-phased DRP I logic to replenish inventories in multi-echelon warehousing systems. Distribution resource planning extends DRP I to include the planning of key resources in a distribution system-warehouse space, manpower levels, transport capacity (trucks, railcars, etc.), and financial flows.[41]

In DRP II, logistics requirements drive the master schedule, which in turn drives the bill of materials, which controls material requirements planning. In essence, DRP I and DRP II are outgrowths of MRP I and MRP II, applied to the logistics activities of a firm. Figure 7–8 depicts the DRP II system schematically.

Although not shown in the figure, accurate forecasts are essential ingredients to successful DRP II systems: "A DRP [II] system translates the forecast of demand for each SKU [stock-keeping unit] at each warehouse and distribution center into a time-phased replenishment plan. If the SKU forecasts are not accurate, then the plan will not be accurate."[42]

An example of how DRP II works in a hypothetical company is shown in Box 7–1. The logic of Box 7–1 is evident in the real-world example of ICI Autocolour, a leading supplier of paints to the automotive trade in the United Kingdom and Europe. The company combined good forecasting tools, supply chain management principles, and DRP to control its many warehouses located throughout its market territories and to reduce overall inventory levels. These systems, techniques, and approaches allowed the firm to maintain inventory at the correct levels to allow for fluctuations in demand, improve inventory turnover rates, and at the same time provide adequate levels of service to its more than 200,000 customers worldwide.[43]

---

[39]Information on SAP AG and its software products can be found on its website <http://www.sap.com>.

[40]Joseph L. Cavinato, *Transportation-Logistics Dictionary,* 3rd ed. (Washington, DC: International Thomson Transport Press, 1989), p. 72; see also R. Neil Southern, *Transportation and Logistics Basics* (Memphis, TN: Continental Traffic Publishing, 1997), p. 28.

[41]John F. Magee, William C. Copacino, and Donald B. Rosenfield, *Modern Logistics Management: Integrating Marketing, Manufacturing, and Physical Distribution* (New York: John Wiley & Sons, 1985), p. 150.

[42]Mary Lou Fox, "Closing the Loop with DRP II," *Production and Inventory Management Review* 7, no. 5 (May 1987), pp. 39–41.

[43]"Global View," *Logistics Europe* 3, no. 3 (June 1995), pp. 46–48.

FIGURE 7–8

*Elements of a DRP II
system*

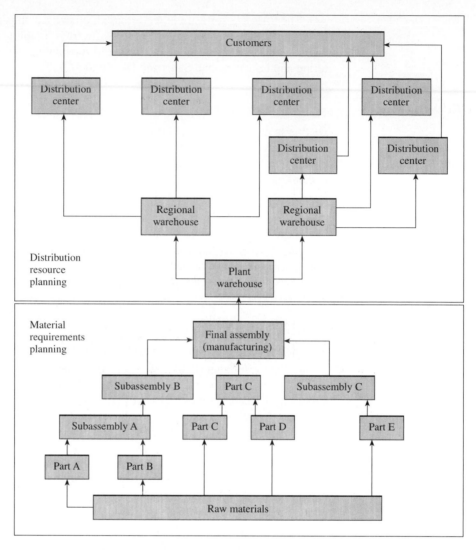

Source: "How DRP Helps Warehouses Smooth Distribution," *Modern Materials Handling* 39, no. 6 (April 9, 1984), p. 53.
Modern Materials Handling, copyright 1984 by Cahners Publishing Company, Division of Reed Holdings.

There are many potential benefits associated with the use of a DRP II system, especially in the marketing and logistics areas.

Marketing benefits include:

1. Improved service levels, resulting in on-time customer deliveries and fewer customer complaints. This is because managers can plan what is needed and then execute the plan. The firm's promises to customers are met, not missed.

2. The ability to plan promotions and new introductions effectively. This includes tying advertising into the planning process.

3. The ability to see in advance when a product will not be available, so that it is not being marketed aggressively when the supply is short. In most cases, using DRP means that companies can get the products they need. But even when this is not possible, at least marketing people are aware of the situation in advance and can take some other action.

Box 7–1

How DRP II Forecasts Demand—a Case History

BOSTON DISTRIBUTION CENTER
On hand balance: 352   Lead time: 2 weeks
Safety stock: 55   Order quantity: 500

	Past due	Week							
		1	2	3	4	5	6	7	8
Gross requirements		50	50	60	70	80	70	60	50
Scheduled receipts						500			
Projected on hand	352	302	252	192	122	542	472	412	362
Planned orders				500					

CHICAGO DISTRIBUTION CENTER
On hand balance: 220   Lead time: 2 weeks
Safety stock: 115   Order quantity: 800

	Past due	Week							
		1	2	3	4	5	6	7	8
Gross requirements		115	115	120	120	125	125	125	120
Scheduled receipts		800							
Projected on hand	220	905	790	670	550	425	300	175	855
Planned orders							800		

SAN DIEGO DISTRIBUTION CENTER
On hand balance: 140   Lead time: 2 weeks
Safety time: 2 weeks   Order quantity: 150

	Past due	Week							
		1	2	3	4	5	6	7	8
Gross requirements		20	25	15	20	30	25	15	30
Scheduled receipts						150			
Projected on hand	140	120	95	80	60	180	155	145	110
Planned orders				150					

CENTRAL SUPPLY FACILITY
On hand balance: 1250
Safety stock: 287
Lead time: 3 weeks
Order quantity: 2200

	Past due	Week							
		1	2	3	4	5	6	7	8
Gross requirements	0	0	0	650	0	0	800	0	0
Scheduled receipts									
Projected on hand	1250	1250	1250	600	600	600	2000	2000	2000
Master sched-rcpt							2200		
Master sched-start				2200					

→ To material requirements planning schedule ⟶

MMH, Inc., has three distribution centers (DCs) located across the Unites States, and a central supply facility at its manufacturing plant in Quebec, Canada. Here's how their distribution resource planning (DRP[II]) system works over an eight-week period:

The Boston DC has a safety stock level set at 55 units of widgets. When stock goes below that level, the DC sends out an order for 500 more widgets. The lead time for shipment from the central facility to the Boston DC is two weeks.

The DRP display for the Boston DC shows the demand forecast, called *gross requirements,* for eight weeks. Starting with an on-hand balance of 352 widgets, the DC forecasts that it will have only 42 widgets during week five (the 122 widgets on hand minus the 80 in gross requirements).

This is below the safety stock level, so DRP initiates a planned order of 500 widgets during week three (week five minus the lead time). Stock comes, as forecasted, and the DC is back to safe operating levels.

Widgets are a high-volume seller in Chicago, so the Chicago DC has a higher gross requirement than the Boston DC. It also orders more widgets at a time.

The DRP display for the Chicago DC shows that 800 widgets are already in transit (scheduled receipts) and due to arrive in week one. They do, and the next order, for 800 widgets, is placed in week six to satisfy the upcoming below-safety stock condition in week eight.

Through experience, the San Diego DC expresses their safety stock as safety time (two weeks).

Examining the DRP display, the DC realizes that without replenishment, 30 widgets (60 minus 30) would be remaining in week five, five widgets (30 minus 25) in week six, and a negative on-hand balance of ten (5 minus 15) in week seven. So, the DC initiates a planned order for 150 widgets in week three—week seven minus the safety time minus the lead time (four weeks total).

The DRP display for the central supply facility is similar to that for the DCs; however, it displays recommendations for the master schedule in terms of the start and receipt of manufacturing orders.

The gross requirements in the facility are caused by the DCs; the Boston and San Diego DCs produced demands for a total of 650 widgets in week three, while Chicago DC produced demands for 800 widgets in week six. The facility finds it will be a negative on-hand balance in week six. Therefore it initiates a master schedule order in week three of 2,200 widgets to cover the shortage.

Source: "How DRP Helps Warehouses Smooth Distribution," *Modern Materials Handling* 39, no. 6 (April 9, 1984), p. 57. *Modern Materials Handling,* copyright 1984 by Cahners Publishing Company, Division of Reed Holdings, Inc.

4. Better working relationships with the other functions of the company. This is because everyone is working with the same set of numbers, and because the causes of problems are more visible than before. With DRP, people can see why something went wrong, and they can do something about correcting it. Without such a tool, the situation is often so confused that it is never really obvious what went wrong and why.

5. The ability to offer customers not only a product but also a service in helping them manage their own inventory. A firm can do this by extending its DRP system into the customers' inventories.

Logistics benefits include:

1. Reduced freight costs to the distribution centers, due to fewer rush or premium freight shipments and better planning for loading trucks and rail cars.

2. Lower inventories. DRP can accurately tell *what* is needed and when, and keep this information up-to-date as changes occur.

3. Reduced warehouse space due to lower inventories, as mentioned above.

4. Better obsolescence control. DRP can monitor when the stock for each item in each distribution center will run out, and warn the planner of any obsolescence problems while there is still time to do something about it.

5. Reduced distribution cost from the DCs to the customers due to fewer back orders. DRP can have the right products in stock when they are needed, so they can all be shipped at the same time.

6. Better coordination and a more beneficial working relationship between distribution and manufacturing. With DRP, the people in manufacturing can truly see the needs of the distribution network, and they are kept up-to-date as things change. This nearly provides total communication of the distribution needs to manufacturing. In addition, the same system is used for both manufacturing and distribution. People understand one another and can work together better because they use the same system.

7. Better tools for budgeting. DRP is a very accurate simulation of distribution operation and, as such, it can be used to develop budgets.[44]

A DRP model can improve the performance of an organization. "Training and implementation can run from two to six months. The overall investment is a fraction of the enterprise solution while the benefits are substantial. This offers a significant opportunity for investment return in most organizations."[45] In many organizations, the DRP model becomes the stepping stone for adoption and implementation of supply chain management (SCM) models (see Chapter 2).

The Logistics–Manufacturing Interface

Systems such as Kanban, JIT, MRP, ERP, and DRP require that the logistics and manufacturing activities of a firm work together closely. Without such cooperative effort,

[44]Andre J. Martin and Darryl V. Landvater, *Distribution Resource Planning—Distribution Management's Most Powerful Tool* (Essex Junction, VT: Oliver Wight Limited Publications, Inc., 1983), pp. 4–6.

[45]Olsen, *The Elements of Software Selection.*

Joint Planning and Decision Making Are Necessary

the full advantages of such systems can never be realized. Conflicts, both real and perceived, must be minimized. This requires joint planning and decision making. There are a number of areas in which cooperation is necessary and great improvements can be made. The following actions can be of significant benefit:

- Logistics must support manufacturing's efforts to increase investment in equipment and computer hardware/software that will increase manufacturing flexibility and reduce replenishment lead times.

- Manufacturing and logistics must work together in the production scheduling area to reduce production planning cycle time. Logistics can provide input into production scheduling and system requirements.

- Strictly manufacturing or production orientations must be eliminated. Shortening lead times, setup times, and production run sizes will minimize average inventory levels and stockouts.

- Logistics must develop strategies to reduce vendor or supplier lead times for parts and supplies.

- Logistics must adopt the philosophy that slow movers (i.e., products with low inventory turnover ratios) should be produced only after orders are received. Inventories of those items should not be kept.

Technology

Seven Benefits of Information Technology

Here's at least seven ways that information technology can make you a more effective logistics manager.

1. **Greater accuracy.** Through elimination of manual data entry, information technology minimizes errors and gives you more accurate information. And this, in turn, translates to better management decisions.

2. **More economy.** By streamlining and automating data entry and exchange, technology delivers that accurate information at a far lower cost than manual approaches.

3. **Faster.** Bar-code scanners, EDI systems, satellite-tracking programs and the like transmit information instantaneously—far faster than a letter, fax, or even a phone call.

4. **Higher visibility.** Today's logistics technology gives you a systemwide view of your operations. Powerful software programs, for example, can afford an instant overview of the

inventory picture across warehouses, retail units, or sales territories.

5. **Immediate availability.** Technology gives logistics professionals instant access to information they need to manage their distribution centers, track their shipments, run their fleet, and audit freight bills.

6. **Tighter customer focus.** Fast communication of accurate, timely information is a key to customer satisfaction. Information technology is the enabler of this critical activity.

7. **Higher productivity.** By taking the manual, repetitive tasks out of the work equation, information technology frees up people to be a lot more innovative, customer-oriented, and productive.

Source: "Logistics Technology Takes Off!" *Traffic Management* 34, no. 10 (October 1995), p. S-4.

Creative Solutions

Excellence in Logistics Strategies

Sequent Computer Systems has a Preferred Logistics Supplier Program that concentrates business with a small number of high-performing suppliers. A commodity team manages the program.

"We have a formal program for order fulfillment reduction," says Sequent's Martha McMahon, Worldwide Logistics manager. "It's really a team effort within the organization and focuses on three main areas." Those areas include supply of materials and materials management.

Another area of focus is on linking with customers in the field. Sequent's "prelim" order program allows the company to see what potential orders are coming in and anticipate those material needs.

The third area involves the education of staff. "It's important for everyone to understand what the goals are,

why the goals have been set up, and also to monitor the progress on achieving those goals to keep everyone informed."

Sequent has achieved a significant reduction of order to shipment time from 35 days down to 7.5 days, which exceeds industry best in class by 10 days. Spare parts can be made available to customers within two to four hours if their computer goes down. Significant cost savings have resulted from the program, over $350,000 for the year and an inventory reduction of $3 million. On-time delivery is averaging 98 percent with preferred suppliers.

Source: Sarah A. Bergin, "Recognizing Excellence in Logistics Strategies," *Transportation and Distribution* 37, no. 10 (October 1996), p. 50. Reprinted from various editions of *Transportation & Distribution* and *Industry Week.* Copyright 1995 permission granted by Penton, Cleveland, Ohio.

Many other areas of logistics–manufacturing interface exist. It is important that each functional area of the firm examine its role in the JIT, MRP, ERP, or DRP system and identify how it can work individually and jointly to optimize the organization's strategic position.

Summary

This chapter examined the broad area of materials flow. We discussed the functions of purchasing and procurement, production control, inbound logistics, warehousing and storage, data and information systems, inventory planning and control, and materials disposal. The relationships between materials management and total quality management (TQM) were identified. The TQM process was discussed and some examples of its implementation were presented.

The administration and control of materials flow requires that the firm measure, report, and improve performance. Concepts and approaches being used or developed include Kanban/just-in-time, MRP, ERP, and DRP systems. Each system has been implemented by a variety of firms, with significant results. Advantages in computer technology have enabled many of the systems to be implemented successfully in manufacturing, retailing, and service firms. The impact on logistics has been substantial.

In Chapter 8 we will examine one of the most significant areas within organizations and one that directly interfaces with materials flow activities—transportation.

Suggested Readings

Chase, Richard B.; Nicholas J. Aquilano; and F. Robert Jacobs. *Production and Operations Management: Manufacturing and Services,* 8th ed., especially Chapter 16, "Inventory Systems for Dependent Demand MRP-Type Systems," pp. 624–67. New York: McGraw-Hill/Irwin, 1998.

Das, Ajay, and Robert B. Handfield. "Just-in-Time and Logistics in Global Sourcing: An Empirical Study." *International Journal of Physical Distribution and Logistics Management* 27, nos. 3–4 (1997), pp. 244–59.

Daugherty, Patricia J.; Dale S. Rogers; and Michael S. Spencer. "Just-in-Time Functional Model: Empirical Test and Validation." *International Journal of Physical Distribution and Logistics Management* 24, no. 6 (1994), pp. 20–26.

Demmy, W. Steven, and Arthur B. Petrini. "MRP II + JIT + TQM + TOC: The Path to World Class Management." *Logistics Spectrum* 26, no. 3 (Fall 1992), pp. 8–13.

Dixon, Lance, and Anne Millen Porter. *JIT II: Revolution in Buying and Selling.* Newton, MA: Cahners, 1994.

"Evolution Continues in MRP II Type Systems: New Functionality for Flexible Enterprise Management." *Manufacturing Systems* 12, no. 7 (July 1994), pp. 32–35.

Galfond, Glenn; Kelly Ronayne; and Christian Winkler. "State-of-the-Art Supply Chain Forecasting." *PW Review* (November 1996), pp. 1–12.

Germain, Richard; Cornelia Dröge; and Nancy Spears. "The Implications of Just-in-Time for Logistics Organization Management and Performance." *Journal of Business Logistics* 17, no. 2 (1996), pp. 19–34.

Ho, Samuel K. M. "Is the ISO 9000 Series for Total Quality Management?" *International Journal of Quality and Reliability Management* 11, no. 9 (1994), pp. 74–89.

Laskey, Fredcrick J. "Innovations in Business Process and Technology: Interdependent Forces Drive Change." In *Annual Conference Proceedings of the Council of Logistics Management* (Oak Brook, IL: Council of Logistics Management, 1999), pp. 99–108.

Masters, James M.; Greg M. Allenby; and Bernard J. La Londe. "On the Adoption of DRP." *Journal of Business Logistics* 13, no. 1 (1992), pp. 47–67.

Purchasing Magazine Just-in-Time USA. Newton, MA: Cahners, no date.

Sillince, J. A. A., and G. M. H. Sykes. "Integrating MRP II and JIT: A Management Rather Than a Technical Challenge." *International Journal of Operations and Production Management* 13, no. 4 (1993), pp. 18–31.

Simpson, Mike; Geoff Sykes; and Adini Abdullah. "Case Study: Transitory JIT at Proton Cars, Malaysia." *International Journal of Physical Distribution and Logistics Management* 28, no. 2 (1998), pp. 121–42.

Snehemay, Banejee, and Damodar Y. Golhar. "EDI Implementation: A Comparative Study of JIT and Non-JIT Manufacturing Firms." *International Journal of Physical Distribution and Logistics Management* 23, no. 7 (1993), pp. 22–31.

Sohal, Amrik S.; Liz Ramsay; and Danny Samson. "JIT Manufacturing: Industry Analysis and a Methodology for Implementation." *International Journal of Physical Distribution and Logistics Management* 23, no. 7 (1993), pp. 4–21.

Stevenson, William J. *Production/Operations Management,* 6th ed., especially Chapter 14, "Material Requirements Planning," pp. 617–55. New York: McGraw-Hill/Irwin, 1999.

Waters-Fuller, Niall. "The Benefits and Costs of JIT Sourcing: A Study of Scottish Suppliers." *International Journal of Physical Distribution and Logistics Management* 26, no. 4 (1996), pp. 35–50.

Questions and Problems

1. Discuss how forecasting has an important role in managing materials flow for a manufacturer. Briefly identify the various types of forecasts that can be used. Consider the relative time horizons of each type of forecast.

2. Identify how total quality management (TQM) differs from traditional management within a manufacturing or retailing firm, and indicate how TQM can be applied to logistics activities and processes.

3. The vice presidents of logistics and manufacturing of the XYZ Corp. have been approached by the chief operating officer (COO) with a question about whether the firm should adopt just-in-time (JIT) material supply techniques. What conditions in the firm's operations should the two vice presidents assess in formulating their response to the COO?

4. Discuss the role of vendors and suppliers in a JIT system within a supply chain. Identify areas where potential conflicts may occur.

5. MRP, DRP, and ERP are relatively recent systems innovations in materials management and manufacturing. Describe the types of situations where MRP, DRP, and ERP could be used in an organization.

CHAPTER 8 Transportation

Chapter Objectives

- To examine transportation's role in logistics and its relationship to the marketing activities of an organization.
- To identify various transport modes, intermodal combinations, and other transportation entities available for distributing products to customers.
- To summarize transportation regulation and deregulation, and their effects on shippers and carriers.
- To examine global aspects of transportation.

Introduction

**Transportation Costs
the United States
$529 Billion**

An industrialized society cannot exist without an efficient transportation system. We often assume that products will move from where they are produced to where they are consumed with a minimum of difficulty, in terms of both time and cost. In most industrialized economies transportation is so pervasive that we often fail to comprehend the magnitude of its impact on society. In the United States, transportation expenditures constitute approximately 6.0 percent of gross domestic product (GDP). In 1999, transportation costs amounted to $554 billion.[1]

Since 1970 the transportation sector has grown considerably. Figure 8–1 shows how freight transportation has grown over the years relative to U.S. gross domestic product. The rate of growth in the amount spent on freight transportation has been slower since 1980–81 due to economic deregulation of transportation, introduction of new technologies, and implementation of many leading-edge practices and management philosophies.

FIGURE 8–1

Freight transportation outlays versus GDP

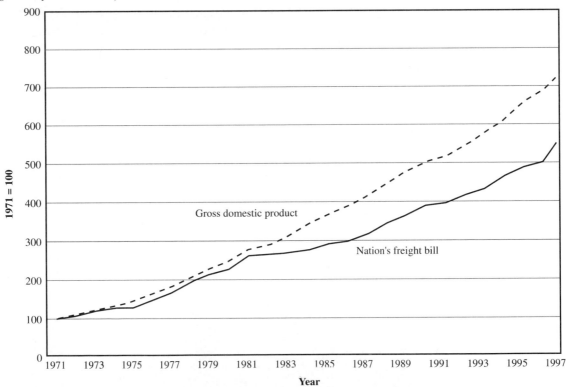

Source: Robert V. Delaney, "10th Annual State of Logistics Report," Press conference remarks to the National Press Club, Washington, DC (June 7, 1999), Figure 34.

---

[1]Robert V. Delaney, "11th Annual State of Logistics Report," Press conference remarks to the National Press Club, Washington, DC (June 5, 2000), Figure 12.

This chapter provides an overview of the transportation activity and its importance to logistics. The characteristics of the major transportation modes and intermodal combinations will be presented. We will also look at how transportation regulation and deregulation have developed historically and identify how the present regulatory environment affects shippers and carriers.

Time and Place Utility

Transportation Creates Value or Place Utility

Logistics involves the movement of products (raw materials, parts, supplies, and finished goods) from point-of-origin to point-of-consumption. A product produced at one point has very little value to the prospective customer unless it is moved to the point where it will be consumed. Transportation achieves this movement.

Transportation creates value or place utility. Time utility is primarily added by the warehousing and storage of products until they are needed by customers. Transportation is also a factor in the creation of time utility because it determines how fast and how consistently products move from one point to another. These factors are referred to as *time-in-transit* and *consistency of service.* If products are not available at the precise time they are needed, there may be expensive repercussions, such as lost sales, customer dissatisfaction, and production downtime.

Most logistics executives are familiar with the problems created by late arrival of needed items. United Parcel Service (UPS), Federal Express (FedEx), DHL, Roadway Package Express (RPS), and other overnight carriers have been successful because they can increase the time and place utilities of their customers' products through fast and consistent product delivery.

Transportation–Logistics–Marketing Interfaces

Customer Satisfaction Is a Component of the Marketing Concept

Transportation moves products to markets that are often far apart from each other. By doing so fast and efficiently, transportation increases customer satisfaction, an important component of the marketing concept.

Because transportation creates place utility and contributes to time utility—both of which are necessary for successful marketing—its availability, adequacy, and cost affect business decisions seemingly unrelated to managing the transportation function itself. Some of these decisions are described in the following paragraphs.

Product. What products should an organization produce? The ease or difficulty of transporting a product (e.g., due to physical characteristics), costs of transportation, transport equipment availability, and capacity of that equipment to move the product, will affect many components of product decision making.

Transportation Inefficiencies Increase Costs

Pricing. Since transportation is a variable expense of business, it has an obvious impact on the prices that an organization must charge for its goods and services in order to recoup its expenses and make a profit. Inefficiencies and excess costs incurred in transportation will cause upward pressure on prices.

Target Markets. Where should products be marketed or sold? The ability to service various markets depends on many factors, including the availability of adequate transportation, costs of transport, and ability of transportation options to provide timely delivery of products.

Purchasing/Procurement.   What to purchase can be greatly determined by transportation. Whether the products are parts, raw materials, supplies, components, or finished goods, the availability, adequacy, and cost of transportation influence the *what, when,* and *where* of purchasing and procurement.

Facility Location.   Transportation is one of many factors to be considered when making facility location decisions. Transportation availability, adequacy, and cost will affect the proximity of plants, warehouses, and retail locations to final customers.

Transportation Is More Important When Product Value Is Low

Transportation can account for 50 percent or more of the value of basic raw materials such as sand and coal. For such items as computers, business machines, and electronic components, transportation costs as a percentage of product value may be less than 1 percent. Generally, the effective and efficient management of transportation becomes more important to a firm as transportation's share of product value increases. While the absolute monetary cost of transportation will likely be larger for more expensive products, the percentage may be smaller. Conversely, for products of low value, transportation costs are usually a greater percentage of product value.

Successful management of all aspects of transportation is essential, including inbound costs for acquisition of raw materials, parts, and supplies, and outbound costs of shipping finished goods to customers. Thus, logistics executives must be aware of those factors that influence transportation costs.

Transportation Costs, Pricing, and Related Issues

Factors influencing transportation costs and pricing can be grouped into two major categories: product-related factors and market-related factors. These factors determine the choice between two basic pricing strategies of carriers: cost-of-service pricing and value-of-service pricing. A related issue is setting the terms of sale.

Many Factors Impact Transport Costs

Product-Related Factors.   Many factors related to a product's characteristics influence the cost and pricing of transportation. A company can use these factors to determine product classifications for rate-making purposes. They can be grouped according to (1) density, (2) stowability, (3) ease or difficulty in handling, and (4) liability.

Density

Density refers to a product's weight-to-volume ratio. Items such as steel, canned foods, building products, and paper goods have high weight-to-volume ratios; that is, they are relatively heavy given their size and thus have higher densities. In contrast, electronic products, clothing, luggage, and toys have low weight-to-volume ratios (they are relatively lightweight given their size). Generally, low-density products—those with low weight-to-volume ratios—tend to cost more to transport per pound (or kilo) than high-density products.

Stowability

Stowability, or cube utilization, is the degree to which a product can fill the available space in a transport vehicle. For example, grain, ore, and bulk petroleum have excellent stowability because they can completely fill the container (e.g., railcar, tank truck, pipeline) in which they are transported. Other items, such as automobiles, machinery, livestock, and people, do not have good stowability. A product's stowability depends on physical characteristics such as size, shape, and fragility.

Ease or Difficulty in Handling

Related to stowability is the *ease or difficulty in handling* the product. Items that are not easily handled are usually more costly to transport. Products that are uniform in size or shape (e.g., raw materials and items in cartons, cans, or drums), or products that can be manipulated with materials-handling equipment, require less handling expense and are therefore less costly to transport.

Technology

Routing Software Streamlines Service

After years of managing its service fleet manually, Whirlpool Corp. took a big step toward the future recently by installing a computerized routing, scheduling, and dispatch system . . . The system—called RIMMS (Resource in Motion Management System)—helps Whirlpool manage its entire service staff of 440 technicians around the United States.

Before installing RIMMS, local dispatchers in multiple locations across the country managed the coordination of the service fleet through a laborious "pins and map" method. Using RIMMS, however, the dispatchers can put their regional market knowledge to work more efficiently by applying the software's navigable map database.

Whirlpool decided to install RIMMS after successful testing in the Houston/Dallas/San Antonio market. . . . In that pilot program, Whirlpool reduced mileage for deliveries by an average of 10%, with mileage reductions ranging from 6% to 30% on individual delivery schedules/routes.

Whirlpool has already improved its responsiveness to customers with RIMMS. The software allows for real-time updates, enabling Whirlpool to make last-minute changes to routes and schedules, thereby better accommodating customer needs.

Source: "Routing Software Streamlines Service," *Transportation and Distribution* 38, no. 8 (August 1997), p. 41. Reprinted from various editions of *Transportation & Distribution* and *Industry Week.* Copyright 1995 permission granted by Penton, Cleveland, Ohio.

Liability

Liability is an important concern for many products such as those that have high value-to-weight ratios, are easily damaged, or are subject to high rates of theft or pilferage. In cases where the transportation carrier assumes greater liability (e.g., with computer, jewelry, and home entertainment products), a higher price will be charged to transport the product.

Other factors, which vary in importance depending on the product category, are whether the product is hazardous or needs strong and rigid protective packaging. Such factors are particularly important in the chemical and plastics industries.

Market-Related Factors. In addition to product characteristics, important market-related factors also affect transportation costs and pricing. The most significant are

Examples of Market-Related Factors

(1) the degree of intramode and intermode competition; (2) the location of markets (i.e., the distance goods must be transported); (3) the nature and extent of government regulation; (4) the balance or imbalance of freight traffic in a market; (5) the seasonality of product movements; and (6) whether the product is being transported domestically or internationally. These factors, in combination, affect the costs and pricing of transportation, and determine whether a transportation carrier will use a cost-of-service, value-of-service, or other type of pricing strategy.

Cost-of-Service Pricing

Cost-of-Service versus Value-of-Service Pricing. *Cost-of-service pricing* establishes transportation rates at levels that cover a carrier's fixed and variable costs, plus some profit margin. Naturally, this approach is appealing, because it establishes rate limits. It has some inherent difficulties, however.

First, a carrier must be able to identify its fixed and variable costs. This involves both a recognition of the relevant cost components and an ability to measure those costs reasonably accurately. Many transportation carriers cannot measure those costs precisely, at least in terms of cause and effect. Second, this approach requires that fixed costs be allocated to each freight movement (shipment). As the number of shipments increases, however, the allocation of fixed costs gets spread over a larger number of movements, and thus the fixed cost-per-unit ratio becomes smaller. As the number of shipments decreases, the ratio becomes larger. In the end, the allocation process becomes somewhat arbitrary unless exact shipment volume is known or can be accurately forecast.

Transportation costs can vary within the cost-of-service pricing approach because of two major factors: distance and volume. As distance increases, rates generally increase, although not as quickly. In their simplest form, distance rates are the same for all origin-destination pairs. An example of such a uniform rate is the postal rate charged for a one-ounce, first-class letter. Another distance measure is built on the tapering principle. Rates increase with distance, but not proportionally, because terminal costs and other fixed costs remain the same regardless of distance. Due to the higher fixed costs of rail relative to motor transportation, railroad rates experience a greater tapering with distance.

The second factor concerns the volume of the shipment. Economies of scale are present with large-volume shipments. The rate structure can reflect the volume in a number of ways. Rates may be based on the quantity of product shipped. Shipments above a specified volume receive truckload (TL) or carload (CL) rates,[2] and those between these extremes receive less-than-full-vehicle-load rates. High volumes can also be used as justification for quoting a shipper special rates on particular commodities.

Value-of-Service Pricing

A second method of transportation pricing is *value-of-service pricing*. This approach essentially charges what the market will bear, and is based on market demand for transportation service and the competitive situation. In effect, this approach establishes the upper limit on rates. Rates are set that will maximize the difference between revenues received and the variable cost incurred for transporting a shipment.

Example of Value-of-Service Pricing

For example, assume that two manufacturers compete for business in the same target market area. Manufacturer A, which is located in the target market area, sells its product for $2.50 a unit and earns a contribution of 50 cents per unit. If manufacturer B incurs the same costs as manufacturer A, exclusive of transportation costs, but is located 500 miles from the market, 50 cents per unit represents the maximum that manufacturer B can afford to pay for transportation to the target market. Also, if two forms of transportation available to manufacturer B are equal in terms of performance characteristics, the higher-priced service would have to meet the lower rate to be competitive. In most instances, competition will determine the price level when it lies between the lower and upper limits.

FOB Pricing.   The free on board (FOB) pricing terms offered by sellers to buyers have significant impacts on logistics generally, and transportation specifically. For example, a seller may quote a delivered price to the buyer's retail store location that includes not only the cost of the product but also the cost of moving the product to the retail store. This rather simple illustration highlights a number of important con-

---

[2]Smaller shipments transported by motor carriers are referred to as less-than-truckload (LTL). LTL can be defined as any quantity of freight weighing less than the amount required for the application of a truckload (TL) rate. Similarly, less-than-carload (LCL) rates would generally apply to rail shipments of less than one full rail car.

siderations for the buyer or consignee (i.e., the recipient of the product being distributed).

Why Terms of Sale Are Important

First, the buyer knows the final delivered price prior to the purchase. Second, the buyer does not have to manage the transportation activity involved in getting the product from the seller's location to the buyer's location. Third, and closely related to the second consideration, the buyer typically will not control the transportation decision.

While it is easier from a management perspective to purchase products FOB destination, the buyer's lack of control over the transportation function can potentially cause problems. The carrier selected by the shipper, for example, may provide poor service in the buyer's area, or may make deliveries at times that do not correspond to when the buyer would like to receive shipments. Buyers should always know the specifics regarding all shipments that include delivery to ensure that optimal decisions are being made on their behalf.

Figure 8–2 provides a simple overview of the major terms of sale for FOB shipping and their implications for buyers and sellers.

Delivered Pricing. In a delivered pricing system, buyers are given a price that includes delivery of the product. As mentioned in the discussion of FOB pricing, this form of pricing is, in essence, FOB destination. The seller secures the transportation

FIGURE 8–2

Examples of terms of sale and corresponding buyer and seller responsibilities

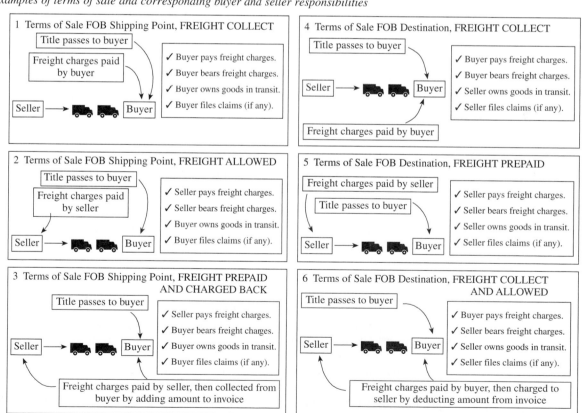

Source: Harold Fearon, Donald Dobler, and Ken Killen, *The Purchasing Handbook,* National Association of Purchasing Management, 1993, McGraw-Hill.

mode or carrier and delivers the product to the buyer. This option can be advantageous to one or both parties of the transaction, depending on which variation of delivered pricing is used by the seller.

Zone Pricing

Variations include zone pricing and basing-point pricing. *Zone pricing* is a method that categorizes geographic areas into zones. Each zone will have a particular delivery cost associated with it. The closer the zone to the seller, the lower the delivery cost; the farther away, the higher the delivery charge. Depending on the buyer's location in a particular zone, some buyers will be paying more per mile for delivery than others will.

Basing-Point Pricing

In a *basing-point pricing* system, the seller selects one or more locations that serve as points-of-origin. Depending on which origin is selected by the seller, the buyer will pay delivery costs from that point to its location. The seller will often use a manufacturing plant, distribution center, port, or free trade zone as a basing point. This method can be good or bad for the buyer depending on which basing point is selected. For example, a manufacturer may have a distribution center located in the same state as the buyer but may use the location of the corporate office located in another state as the basing point. The product may or may not actually originate at the basing point location.

Quantity Discounts.   Quantity discounts can be cumulative or noncumulative. *Cumulative quantity discounts* provide price reductions to the buyer based on the amount of purchases over some prescribed period of time. *Noncumulative quantity discounts* are applied to each order and do not accumulate over a time period.

Cumulative versus Noncumulative Quantity Discounts

From a transportation perspective, buyers purchasing products under a cumulative quantity discount system can order smaller quantities, paying the higher transportation costs for smaller shipments, and still gain a cost advantage. That is, the additional cost of transportation is less than the cost savings resulting from the quantity discount.

In contrast, if a noncumulative quantity discount is applied, the buyer must purchase sufficient quantities in order to obtain TL or CL rates for larger shipments. While transportation costs per item or per pound will be less for larger shipments, there will be additional costs incurred by the buyer (e.g., warehousing costs, inventory carrying costs). We will address these issues in later chapters, but note here that these costs have to be considered when buyers are placing larger, but fewer, orders with sellers.

In today's business environment, companies must be very responsive to customer demand in the marketplace. The trend is for companies to purchase smaller quantities, more often, and as quickly as possible, so it is more advantageous for the buyer to have a cumulative quantity discount applied.

Allowances.   Sometimes sellers will provide price reductions to buyers that perform some of the delivery function themselves. For example, when using a delivered pricing system, the seller assumes all costs of delivery and adds those costs to the price of the product. If the buyer is willing to assume some of the delivery functions, the seller will often provide some allowances, or price reductions, to the buyer.

Example of an Allowance

The most common allowances are provided for customer pickup of the product or unloading the carrier vehicle upon delivery at the customer's location. Pickup and unloading are services that cost money; buyers willing to perform these functions can earn price concessions from sellers.

The important element in deciding whether or not to take advantage of allowances is to know the costs associated with each delivery function. The allowance should be equal to, or greater than, the costs to the buyer for assuming these responsibilities.

Pricing and Negotiation.   During the past decade, shippers have tended to use fewer carriers[3] and to place greater emphasis on negotiated pricing.[4] The goal of the negotiation process is to develop an agreement that is mutually beneficial, recognizes the needs of the parties involved, and motivates them to perform. Because most negotiation is based on cost-of-service pricing, carriers must have fairly precise measures of their costs. Only then can carriers and shippers work together in an effort to reduce the carrier's cost base.

US West and CF MotorFreight Form an Alliance

US West has been very aggressive in developing an alliance with CF MotorFreight, its national LTL carrier. The company began by looking at its total cost of doing business with carriers, going beyond simply transportation price. The goal of the relationship is to reduce its total cost of doing business. US West and CF MotorFreight work together to take costs out of the supply chain. During the first two years of the relationship, US West's base transportation rate declined by 15 percent.[5]

Line-Haul Rates

Categories of Rates.   There are two types of charges assessed by carriers: *line-haul rates,* which are charged for the movement of goods between two points that are not in the same local pickup and delivery area, and *accessorial charges,* which cover all other payments made to carriers for transporting, handling, or servicing a shipment. Line-haul rates can be grouped into four types: (1) class rates, (2) exception rates, (3) commodity rates, and (4) miscellaneous rates. Note, however, that since the economic deregulation of most transportation in the United States, carriers have been discounting rates. In effect, the distinctions between the various types of rates have blurred as carriers actively market their services to shippers. Negotiated rates, permitted under deregulation, have become much more important than before.

Class Rates

Class rates reduce the number of transportation rates required by grouping products into classes for pricing purposes. A product's specific classification is referred to as its class rating. A basic rate would be Class 100, with higher numbers representing more expensive rates and lower numbers less expensive rates. The class rating of a product determines the rate per hundredweight (100 pounds) for moving it between any two points.

Exception Rates

Exception rates, or exceptions to the classification, provide the shipper with rates lower than the published class rates. Exception rates were introduced in order to provide a special rate for a specific area, origin-destination, or commodity when competition or volume justified the lower rate. When an exception rate is published, the classification that normally applies is changed. When an exception rate is used, usually all services associated with the shipment are the same as with the class rate.

---

[3]For a discussion of this trend and other issues relating transportation to customer service, see Bernard J. La Londe, Martha C. Cooper, and Thomas G. Noordewier, *Customer Service: A Management Perspective* (Oak Brook, IL: Council of Logistics Management, 1988).

[4]For a managerial discussion of carrier–shipper negotiation issues, see Joseph V. Barks, "Who's Getting a Bad Deal?" *Distribution* 93, no. 3 (March 1994), pp. 34–38; Jack Barry, "Advanced Negotiating: Preparation Is the Key," *Distribution* 87, no. 6 (June 1988), pp. 54–56; Robert J. Bowman, "Risk and Reward: How Shippers Are Negotiating the Best Possible Transportation Deals in a Time of Radical Change," *Distribution* 95, no. 4 (April 1996), pp. 42–49; and Joseph Cavinato, "Tips for Negotiating Rates," *Distribution* 90, no. 2 (February 1991), pp. 66–68.

[5]Peter A. Buxbaum, "Winning Together," *Transportation and Distribution* 36, no. 4 (April 1995), pp. 47–50.

Commodity Rates   *Commodity rates* apply when a large quantity of a product is shipped between two locations on a regular basis. These rates are published on a point-to-point basis.

Miscellaneous Rates   *Miscellaneous rates* include other rates that apply in special circumstances. For example, contract rates are those negotiated between a shipper and carrier and then formalized through a written contractual agreement between the two parties. Carriers are using these types of rates more often because of the growth of contract carriage. Freight-all-kinds (FAK) rates have developed in recent years and apply to shipments rather than products. They tend to be based on the costs of providing the transportation service; the products being shipped can be of any type. The carrier provides the shipper with a rate per shipment based on the weight of the products being shipped. The FAK rates have become very popular with wholesalers and manufacturers that ship a variety of products to retail customers on a regular basis.

Rate Bureaus.   Rate bureaus are organizations of common carriers within a single mode that establish and publish rates. Prior to 1980, rate bureaus in the United States established the overwhelming number of common carrier rates for motor, rail, and domestic water carriers. Since deregulation of the major transport modes, however, the majority of rates are being established or changed by individual carriers and shippers in consort, rather than by rate bureaus. Today, rate bureaus publish information on "official" rates (which are rarely the actual rates being charged). But they no longer exercise much control over the actual setting of rates.

Transportation Service Characteristics

As we have emphasized throughout this book, customer service is a vital component of logistics management. While each activity of logistics management contributes to the level of service a company provides to its customers, transportation's impact on customer service is one of the most significant.

The Most Important Service Characteristics   The most important transportation service characteristics affecting customer service levels are dependability (consistency of service); time-in-transit; market coverage (the ability to provide door-to-door service); flexibility (with respect to the variety of products that can be handled and meeting the special needs of shippers); loss and damage performance; and the ability of the carrier to provide more than just basic transportation service (i.e., to become part of a shipper's overall marketing program).

Each mode of transport has varying service capabilities. In the next section, we will examine the characteristics of many transportation options.

Transportation Carrier Characteristics

Many options are available for transporting products from one point to another. A firm may select any one or more of five basic transportation modes—motor, rail, air, water, or pipeline. Table 8–1 identifies the usage patterns of various transportation options throughout the world. Significant variations can and do exist.

In addition, certain modal combinations are available, including rail-motor, motor-water, motor-air, and rail-water. Such intermodal combinations offer specialized services (and sometimes lower costs) not generally available from a single transport mode. Finally, other transportation options exist, including indirect, special carriers, or non-operating third parties, which offer a variety of services to shippers. These transporters include freight forwarders, shipper cooperatives, parcel post, United Parcel Service (UPS), FedEx, and other specialty carriers.

TABLE 8–1   Freight Movements in 1989 (in Billion Ton-Kilometers)

	Road[a]	Rail[b]	Inland Waterway[b]	Seagoing	Inland Pipeline
European Community					
Belgium	31.0[c]	8.0[c]	5.3	—	1.0
Denmark	9.2[c]	1.7	0	2.0[c]	1.6[c]
FR of Germany	124.2	60.0[c]	54.0	0.6[c]	8.8[c]
France	116.7	52.3[c]	7.0[c]	—	31.0[c]
Greece	12.5[c]	0.6[c]	0	—	—
Irish Republic	4.0[c]	0.6[c]	—	—	—
Italy	165.0[c]	20.0[c]	0.1	36.0[c]	9.0[c]
Luxembourg	0.2[c]	0.7	0.4	0	—
Netherlands	22.1[c]	3.1	36.0	—	4.6
Portugal	12.05[c]	1.7	—	—	—
Spain	143	11.9	—	28.0[c]	4.8[c]
United Kingdom	134.3	17.0	0.3	56.2	9.1
Other Europe					
Austria	8.0[c]	11.2[c]	1.8[c,d]	0	5.3
Czechoslovakia	23.8	72.0	4.8[d]	0	9.0[c]
German DR[f]	16.9	59.0	2.3	—	4.3
Hungary	13.4	19.8	2.1[d]	0	3.4
Sweden	22.6[c]	19.2	0	8.0[c]	—
Switzerland	7.5[c]	8.2	0.1	0	1.1
Yugoslavia	25.0[c,e]	25.9	8.8	—	3.4
Rest of the World					
Japan	260.0[c]	23.0[c]	0	2405	—
United States	1,200.0[c]	1,500.0[c]	550.0[c]	900.0[c]	9205
Soviet Republics	510.0[c]	4,000.0[c]	239.6	—	1,422

[a]In vehicles above a size threshold that (for EC countries) may not exceed 3.5 tons net or 6 tons gross vehicle weight.
[b]Carried by national and foreign vehicles.
[c]Estimated from previous years.
[d]Transport by national shipping undertaken at home and abroad.
[e]For hire and reward only.
[f]Now unified with the Federal Republic of Germany.
Source: Kevin A. O'Laughlin, James Cooper, and Eric Cabocel, *Reconfiguring European Logistics Systems* (Oak Brook, IL: Council of Logistics Management, 1993), p. 72.

Legally Defined Forms of Transportation

Transportation carriers can be classified on the basis of their legally defined form or type: common, contract, exempt, or private. The first three forms are for-hire carriers; the last is shipper owned. For-hire carriers transport freight belonging to others and are subject to various federal, state, and local statutes and regulations. For the most part, private carriers transport their own goods and supplies in their own equipment and are exempt from most regulations, with the exception of those dealing with safety and taxation.

Deregulation has reshaped how logistics executives view the transport modes, particularly the legal forms of transportation. In principle, these legal designations no longer exist because of deregulation. For example, the distinction between common and contract motor carriers was eliminated by the Trucking Industry Regulatory Reform Act of 1994 (TIRRA). However, the terms are still used within the industry and do provide some guidance with respect to transportation type.

Common Carriers

Common carriers offer their services to any shipper to transport products, at published rates, between designated points. In order to legally operate, they must be granted authority from the appropriate federal regulatory agency. With deregulation, common carriers have significant flexibility with respect to market entry, routing, and pricing. Common carriers must offer their services to the general public on a nondiscriminatory basis—that is, they must serve all shippers of the commodities that their equipment can feasibly carry. A significant problem common carriers face is that they cannot predict the number of customers with certainty in advance, and thus future demand is uncertain. The result has been that many common carriers have entered into contract carriage.

Contract Carriers

A *contract carrier* is a for-hire carrier that does not hold itself out to serve the general public; rather it serves a limited number of shippers under specific contractual arrangements. The contract between the shipper and the carrier requires that the carrier provide a specified transportation service at a specified cost. In most instances, contract rates are lower than common carrier rates because the carrier is transporting commodities it prefers to carry for cost and efficiency reasons. An advantage is that the carrier knows the transport demand in advance.

Exempt Carriers

An *exempt carrier* is a for-hire carrier that transports certain products such as unprocessed agricultural products and related goods such as farm supplies, livestock, fish, poultry, and seeds. Carriers of newspapers are also given exempt status. The exempt status was originally established to allow farmers to transport their products using public roads; however, it has been extended to a wider range of products being transported by a variety of modes. In addition, local cartage firms operating in a municipality or a commercial zone surrounding a municipality are exempt.

Generally, exempt carrier rates are lower than common or contract carriage rates. However, because very few commodities are given exempt status, the exempt carrier is not a viable form of transport for most companies. In reality, however, because transportation deregulation has eliminated pricing regulations, almost all carriers can be considered exempt from pricing restrictions.

Private Carriers

A *private carrier* is generally not for hire and is not subject to federal economic regulation. With private carriage, the firm is primarily providing transportation for its own products. As a result, the company must own or lease the transport equipment and operate its own facilities. From a legal standpoint, the most important factor distinguishing private carriage from for-hire carriers is the restriction that the transportation activity must be incidental to the primary business of the firm.

Private carriage traditionally had advantages over other carriers because of the flexibility and economy it offered. However, with deregulation, common and contract carriage can often provide excellent service levels at reasonable costs. In Chapter 9, private versus for-hire transportation will be examined in depth.

Basic Transportation Modes

Five Basic Transportation Modes

There are five basic transportation modes: motor, rail, air, water, and pipeline.

Motor.   During the late 1960s, motor carriage replaced rail carriage as the dominant form of freight transport in the United States. Motor carriers transport over 75 percent of the nation's tonnage of agricultural products, such as fresh and frozen meats, dairy products, bakery products, confections, beverages, and cigars. Manufactured products transported by motor carriers include sporting and athletic goods, toys, watches, clocks, farm machinery, radios, televisions, CD players, personal computers, carpets and rugs, clothing, drugs, and office and accounting machines. In fact, the majority of consumer goods are transported by motor carriers.

Motor Carriers Compete with Air

Motor carriers often compete with air carriers for small shipments and rail carriers for large shipments. An efficient motor carrier can often compete with an air carrier on point-to-point service for any size shipment if the distances are less than 1,000 miles. This is because motor carriers can realize greater efficiencies in terminal, pickup, and delivery operations.

For example, Chattanooga Tent Company had to deliver a 60- by 150-foot tent to a religious organization that was holding a revival in New York City. "On the first night of the revival, an organ caught fire and destroyed a 30- by 60-foot section of the tent. With 1,500 people attending and rain threatening, the damaged section needed to be replaced immediately . . . Roberts Express delivered the replacement section overnight after driving 837 miles from Chattanooga to the Bronx. The new section of the tent was raised in time for the celebration to continue without interruption."[6]

Motor Carriers Compete with Rail

Motor carriers compete directly with railroads for shipments of truckload (TL) size that are transported longer distances, usually over 500 miles. However, rail is the dominant transportation mode when shipment sizes exceed 100,000 pounds. Motor carriers dominate in the movement of less-than-truckload (LTL) shipments.

The average length of haul for motor carriers is slightly more than 400 miles.[7] Some national carriers have average hauls several times as long, while some intracity carriers may average five miles or less. LTL shipments are generally of shorter haul than TL shipments, but significant variability exists. A little over 10 percent of the for-hire motor carriers in the United States are in the LTL business, but they account for more than a quarter of the revenues.[8]

Service Characteristics of Motor Carriers

Motor is more flexible and versatile than other transportation modes. The flexibility of motor carriers in the United States is made possible by a network of over 4 million miles of roads,[9] which enables them to offer point-to-point service between almost any origin-destination combination. Motor carriers are versatile in that they can transport products of varying sizes and weights over any distance. Virtually any product, including some for which equipment modifications are necessary, can be transported by motor carriage. The combination of flexibility and versatility of motor carriage has enabled it to become the dominant form of transport in the United States as well as in many other parts of the world.

Motor carriers offer customers fast, reliable service, with low levels of damage or loss. They generally give much faster service than railroads and compare favorably with air carriers on short hauls. Many motor carriers, particularly those involved in just-in-time programs, operate on a scheduled timetable. This results in very short and reliable

---

[6]Karen Thuermer, "Truckers Move Fast to Capture Lucrative Business," *Logistics Management and Distribution Report* 38, no. 2 (February 1999), p. 73.

[7]"News Capsule: In for the Long Haul," *Logistics Management and Distribution Report* 37, no. 4 (April 1998), p. 20.

[8]"News Capsule: Less Is More," *Logistics Management and Distribution Report* 37, no. 2 (February 1998), p. 18.

[9]Bureau of Transportation Statistics, *Pocket Guide to Transportation* (Washington, DC: U.S. Department of Transportation, December 1998), p. 3.

transit times. Loss and damage rates of motor carriers are substantially lower than for most rail shipments and are slightly higher than for air freight. No other transport mode can provide the market coverage offered by motor carriers.

The industry can be classified into two general categories of carriers: general freight carriers and specialized carriers. *General freight carriers* account for the majority of all truck revenues and include intercity common carriers and other general carriers. *Specialized carriers* generate the remaining revenues. These include carriers of heavy machinery, liquid petroleum, refrigerated products, agricultural commodities, motor vehicles, building materials, household goods, and other specialized items.

The amount of freight transported by motor carriers has steadily increased over the years. Motor carriage is a vital part of most firms' logistics networks, because the characteristics of the motor carrier industry are more compatible with the service requirements of customers than are other transportation modes. As long as it is able to provide fast, efficient service, at rates between those offered by rail and air, the motor carrier industry will continue to prosper.

Rail.   In many regions of the world, such as Europe and China, rail is the dominant transportation mode. In the United States, railroads carried over 1 trillion ton-miles of freight over a track network totaling approximately 175,000 miles in 1996.[10] Railroads accounted for slightly over one-third of the intercity freight traffic in ton-miles. Between World War II and the mid-1980s, railroad's share of the U.S. market declined significantly. Traffic dropped from two-thirds to less than one-quarter of the ton-mile traffic, until the downward trend was reversed. By 1996, railroads transported about 26 percent of intercity ton-miles, although this represented only 4 percent of the dollar value of all shipments.[11]

Most of the freight once shipped by rail has been shifted to motor carriers. Some traffic also has been lost to water and pipeline carriers, which generally compete with railroads for bulk commodities. The average length of haul for rail carriers is approximately 850 miles.[12]

Rail service is available in almost every major metropolitan center in the world, and in many smaller communities as well. However, the rail network is not nearly as extensive as the highway network in most countries. Therefore, rail transport lacks the versatility and flexibility of motor carriers because it is limited to fixed track facilities. As a result, rail transport, like air, water, and pipeline transport, provides terminal-to-terminal service rather than point-to-point service for most shippers (unless they have a rail siding at their facility).

Rail transport generally costs less (on a weight basis) than air and motor carriage.[13] For many shipments, rail does not compare favorably with other modes on loss and damage ratios. It has disadvantages compared to motor carriers in terms of transit time and frequency of service, although, since deregulation of the rail industry in 1980, railroads have improved significantly in these service areas. Trains travel on timetable

General Freight Carriers

Specialized Carriers

Service Characteristics of Rail

---

[10]Ibid.

[11]Ibid., p. 16.

[12]"News Capsule: In for the Long Haul," p. 20.

[13]In some transportation lanes (i.e., routes) and markets, motor carriers have been very price competitive with rail. In a few instances, motor carriers have been able to match or even undercut the rates charged by railroads.

schedules, but departures are less frequent than those of motor carriers. If a shipper has strict arrival and departure requirements, railroads are usually at a competitive disadvantage compared to motor carriers.

TOFC and COFC

Some of this disadvantage may be overcome through the use of trailer-on-flatcar (TOFC) or container-on-flatcar (COFC) services, which offer the economy of rail or water movements combined with the flexibility of trucking. Truck trailers or containers are delivered to the rail terminals, where they are loaded on flatbed railcars. At the destination terminal they are off-loaded and delivered to the consignee (i.e., the customer who receives the shipment). We will examine these services in further detail later in this chapter.

An additional area in which railroads suffer in comparison to motor carriers is equipment availability. Railroads use each other's railcars, and at times this equipment may not be located where it is most needed. Railcars may be unavailable because they are being loaded, unloaded, moved within railroad sorting yards, or undergoing repair. Other cars may be standing idle or lost within the vast rail network.

Recent Developments in the Rail Industry

A number of developments have helped the rail industry overcome some of these utilization problems. Advances have included computer routing and scheduling; upgrading of equipment, roadbeds, and terminals; improvements in railcar identification systems; the addition of cars owned or leased by the shipper; and the use of unit trains or dedicated through-train service between major metropolitan areas (nonstop shipments of one or a few shippers' products). Railroads own most of their car fleet, with the remainder either leased or owned by shippers. Shippers that own or lease cars are typically heavy users of rail and are especially sensitive to railcar shortages because of unique market or competitive conditions.

During the late 1980s, railroads recaptured some of the traffic lost to trucks, pipelines, and water carriers. The improvements listed above, along with better monitoring and control of rail fleets, were contributing factors to that success. Additionally, railroads placed more emphasis on customer service issues.

The president and CEO of the largest railroad in Canada, Canadian National, stated that the product being sold by rail was service, and that customers had "a right to expect customer focus, quality of service, performance standards, consistent delivery, accountability, transparency, competitive pricing, quality equipment, resourcefulness, [and] partnership."[14]

Finally, the relative energy-efficiency advantage railroads have over motor carriers and the continuing trend toward consolidation through mergers and acquisitions, coupled with deregulation of the rail industry, hold promise for a brighter future for this transportation mode.

Air. Domestically, air carriers transport less than 1 percent of ton-mile traffic, although that traffic represents more than 2 percent of the dollar value of all shipments. Firms spent $16 billion on freight shipments via air carriers in the first half of 1999.[15] Although increasing numbers of shippers are using air freight for regular service, most view air transport as a premium emergency service because of its higher cost. When products must be delivered to a distant location quickly, air freight offers the shortest time-in-transit of any transportation mode. For most shippers, however, these time-sensitive shipments are relatively few in number or frequency.

Air Is Best for Time-Sensitive Shipments

[14]"Railroad/Shipper Meeting Gets Mixed Reviews," *Railway Age* (October 1998), p. 20.
[15]"Heavy-Airfreight Market Lost Altitude Last Year," *Logistics Management & Distribution Report* 39, no. 5 (May 2000), p. 28.

Modern aircraft have cruising speeds of 500 to 600 miles per hour and are able to travel long distances both domestically and internationally. Domestic air freight directly competes with motor carriers. International freight movements are typically made via air or water. For most commercial airlines, the transportation of freight is incidental to passenger traffic. However, many companies transport nothing but cargo. The all-cargo carriers transport approximately 50 percent of all domestic air freight. This percentage represents a sizable increase over 1968, when only a small percentage of air freight was handled by the all-cargo carriers.

Product Characteristics Determine Use of Air

Air carriers generally transport high-value products. Air freight usually cannot be cost-justified for low-value items, because the greater cost of air freight would represent too high a percentage of product cost. For example, consider an electronics component and a textbook that weigh the same but differ significantly in selling price. If it costs the same to ship both of them from point A to point B by air freight, transportation charges will consume a greater portion of the textbook's total cost and a smaller portion of the electronic component's cost. Customer service considerations may influence the choice of transport mode in this situation, but only if service issues are more important than cost.

Air transport provides rapid time-in-transit, but terminal and delivery delays and congestion may appreciably reduce some of this advantage. On a point-to-point basis, motor transport can often match or outperform the total transit time of air freight.

Comparing Air and Motor Transport

Surface transportation via dedicated, well-managed carriers, such as contract or private carriage, can also compete favorably with air freight on short- to medium-length shipments, when total transit time (from pickup at vendor to delivery to customer) is considered. For example, a national retailer of women's fashion apparel regularly uses its contract carrier to deliver emergency shipments to West Coast stores from its national distribution center located in the Midwest. The company found that the time air shipments spent on the ground (e.g., pickup, delivery, waiting for scheduled aircraft departures), plus transit time, exceeded the total transit time provided by motor carriage.[16]

It is the total transit time that is important to the shipper rather than the transit time from terminal to terminal. Generally, the frequency and reliability of air freight service is very good. Service coverage is usually limited to movements between major points, although there is limited service to smaller cities.

The volume of air freight has grown over the years and shows continuing growth even in the face of costs higher than other transportation modes. Undoubtedly, as customers demand higher levels of service in the future, and the number of international shipments increases, air freight will continue to have a strategic role in the distribution plans of many organizations.

For example, in 1999, the Southern California Logistics Airport (SCLA) and SwissGlobalCargo/Panalpina (an integrated forwarder and leading air cargo service provider) inaugurated a dedicated air service that circles the globe every week on a scheduled route. Additionally, at the SCLA, a bonded warehouse, a U.S. customs clearance facility, and a foreign trade zone were opened.[17]

---

[16]Example provided by Professor Jay U. Sterling, University of Alabama.

[17]Press release of the Southern California Logistics Airport, "Southern California Logistics Airport and SwissGlobalCargo/Panalpina Establish Vital Transpacific Supply Chain Link Connecting Asia, Europe and South America" (October 20, 1999).

Water.   Water transportation can be broken down into several categories: (1) inland waterway, such as rivers and canals, (2) lakes, (3) coastal and intercoastal ocean, and (4) international deep sea. The first three categories of water carriage compete primarily with rail and pipeline, since the majority of commodities carried by water are semi-processed or raw materials transported in bulk.

Domestic water carriage by nature is suited for moving heavy, bulky, low-value-per-unit commodities that can be loaded and unloaded efficiently, usually by mechanical means in situations where speed is not of primary importance. Water transportation is also used where the commodities shipped are not particularly susceptible to shipping damage or theft, and where accompanying land movements are unnecessary. In the United States, organizations primarily use water transportation for inbound shipments. Often, water carriers transport bulk materials such as iron ore, grains, pulpwood products, coal, limestone, and petroleum internationally or domestically to points where they can be used as inputs into manufacturing processes. Internationally, water carriage is used for both inbound and outbound product shipments, and the range of products transported is much broader.

Other than deep-sea transport, water carriers are limited in their movement by the availability of lakes, rivers, canals, or intercoastal waterways. Reliance on water carriage to a greater or lesser degree depends on the geography of the particular location. In the United States, for example, approximately 508 billion ton-miles, or 15 percent of total intercity freight, is moved by water.[18]

Water Transport Is More Important in Western Europe

In Western Europe, water transport is much more important because of the vast system of navigable waterways and the accessibility to major population centers provided by water routes. In Germany, waterways account for about 20 percent of all freight transported, and in Norway and the Netherlands, the percentage is substantially higher.[19] The average length of haul varies tremendously depending on the type of water transport. For international ocean movements, the length of haul can be many thousands of miles.

VLCCs

Water carriage is perhaps the most inexpensive method of shipping high-bulk, low-value commodities. But because of the inherent limitations of water carriers, it is unlikely that water transport will gain a larger role in domestic commerce, although international developments have made marine shipping increasingly important. The development of very large crude carriers (VLCCs), or supertankers, has enabled marine shipping to assume a vital role in the transport of petroleum between oil-producing and oil-consuming countries. Because of the importance of energy resources to industrialized nations, water carriage will continue to play a significant role in the transportation of energy resources. In addition, container ships have greatly expanded the use of water transport for many products.

Containers in International Shipping

Many domestic and most international shipments involve the use of containers. The shipper in one country places cargo into an owned or leased container at its facility or at point-of-origin. Then the container is transported via rail or motor carriage to a water port for loading onto a container ship. After arrival at the destination port, it is unloaded and tendered to a rail or motor carrier in that country and subsequently delivered to the customer or consignee. The shipment leaves the shipper and arrives at the customer's location with minimal handling of the items within the container. The use of containers in intermodal logistics reduces staffing needs, minimizes in-transit damage and

---

[18]U.S. Bureau of the Census, *Statistical Abstract of the United States: 1999,* 119th ed. (Washington, DC: U.S. Government Printing Office, October 1999), p. 631.

[19]Alan C. McKinnon, *Physical Distribution Systems* (London: Routledge, 1989), p. 153.

pilferage, shortens time-in-transit because of reduced port turnaround time, and allows the shipper to take advantage of volume shipping rates.

Pipeline.   Pipelines transport approximately 19 percent of all domestic intercity freight traffic measured in ton-miles.[20] Pipelines are able to transport only a limited number of products, including natural gas, crude oil, petroleum products, water, chemicals, and slurry products. Natural gas and crude oil account for the majority of pipeline traffic.

Slurry products, usually coal slurry, account for only a small percentage of pipeline shipments. The coal is ground into a powder, suspended in water, transported through a pipeline, and at destination is removed from the water and readied for use. Considering the world's dependence on energy products, pipelines will continue to be an important transportation mode for a select group of products. This will be especially true for coal slurry, as some countries attempt to shift away from natural gas or petroleum-based energy systems toward coal-based systems.

Pipelines Provide High Service Levels

There are more than 114,000 miles of oil pipe and 260,000 miles of gas transmission pipe in the United States.[21] Pipelines offer shippers an extremely high level of service dependability at a relatively low cost. Pipelines are able to deliver their product on time because of the following factors:

- The flows of products within the pipeline are monitored and controlled by computer.
- Losses and damages due to pipeline leaks or breaks are extremely rare.
- Climatic conditions have minimal effects on products moving in pipelines.
- Pipelines are not labor-intensive and strikes or employee absences have little effect on them.

The cost and dependability advantages pipelines have over other transport modes has stimulated shipper interest in moving other products by pipeline. Certainly, if a product is, or can be, in liquid, gas, or slurry form, it can be transported by pipeline. As the costs of other modes increase, shippers may give additional consideration to pipelines as a mode of transport for nontraditional products.

Mode Selection.   All transport modes are viable shipping options for someone. Each mode transports a large amount of freight (see Table 8–2). The particular mode(s) a shipper selects depends on the characteristics of the mode(s) and the needs of the company and its customers. Table 8–3 summarizes the economic and service characteristics of the five basic modes of transportation. Sometimes, a transportation mode may be used in concert or jointly with others. We will discuss these *intermodal combinations* in the next section.

Intermodal Combinations

In addition to the five basic modes of transport, a number of intermodal combinations are available to shippers. The most common examples are trailer-on-flatcar (TOFC), or piggyback; container-on-flatcar (COFC); and roadrailers. Theoretically, intermodal

[20]U.S. Bureau of the Census, *Statistical Abstract of the United States: 1999,* p. 631.
[21]Ibid., p. 2.

TABLE 8–2   Estimated Distribution of Intercity Freight Ton-Miles

		Percentage of Total				
Mode	*1997 (billions of ton-miles)*	*1997*	*1990*	*1980*	*1960*	*1940*
Rail	1,421	38%	36%	38%	44%	61%
Motor carrier	1,051	28	25	22	22	10
Air	14	*	*	*	*	*
Water	508	15	16	16	17	19
Pipeline	628	19	23	24	17	10
Total	3,622	100	100	100	100	100

*Amount is less than 1.

Source: U.S. Bureau of the Census, *Statistical Abstract of the United States: 1999,* 119th ed. (Washington, DC: U.S. Government Printing Office, October 1999), p. 631; and "Railroads Gain Traffic Share but Lose Dollar Market Share," *On Track* 5, no. 16 (August 21, 1991), p. 1.

TABLE 8–3   Comparison of U.S. Domestic Transportation Modes

	Motor	*Rail*	*Air*	*Water*	*Pipeline*
Economic Characteristics					
Cost	Moderate	Low	High	Low	Low
Market coverage	Point-to-point	Terminal-to-terminal	Terminal-to-terminal	Terminal-to-terminal	Terminal-to-terminal
Degree of competition (number of competitors)	Many	Moderate	Moderate	Few	Few
Predominant traffic	All types	Low–moderate value, moderate–high density	High value, low–moderate density	Low value, high density	Low value, high density
Average length of haul	Short to long	Medium to long	Medium to long	Medium to long	Medium to long
Equipment capacity (tons)	10–25	50–12,000	5–125	1,000–60,000	30,000–2,500,000
Service Characteristics					
Speed (time-in-transit)	Moderate	Slow	Fast	Slow	Slow
Availability	High	Moderate	Moderate	Low	Low
Consistency (delivery time variability)	High consistency	Moderate consistency	High consistency	Low–moderate consistency	High consistency
Loss and damage	Low	Moderate–high	Low	Low–moderate	Low
Flexibility (adjustment to shipper's needs)	High	Moderate	Low–moderate	Low	Low

movements combine the cost and service advantages of two or more modes in a single product movement.

Piggyback (TOFC/COFC).   Although technically there are differences, most logistics executives refer to TOFC and COFC as piggyback service. This form of transportation involves the use of a motor carrier trailer or a container that is placed on a rail flatcar and transported between two or more terminals. Temporary axles can be placed under the containers so that they can be delivered by a truck or tractor. At the terminal facilities, a motor carrier performs the pickup and delivery functions. Piggyback service thus combines the low cost of long-haul rail movement with the flexibility and convenience of short-haul truck transportation.

Piggyback Usage Has Increased

In recent years shippers have increased their usage of piggyback service. Since the mid-1970s, there has been a significant increase in the use of piggyback. In 1999, 1,404.6 billion ton-miles of freight were transported by various intermodal combinations.[22] Figure 8–3 shows the upward trend in intermodalism since 1955. Intermodal business is the second largest source of revenue for U.S. railroads.[23] The future bodes well for the use of TOFC/COFC.

An Example of Intermodalism

An interesting example of intermodalism is the partnership that began in late 1989 between the Burlington Northern Santa Fe (BNSF) Railroad and J. B. Hunt Transportation Services. This combination of a large railroad company with a national truckload (TL) motor carrier has provided shippers with door-to-door intermodal services between California and the Midwest. The joint service provides unified communication and

FIGURE 8–3

Growth of intermodal transportation

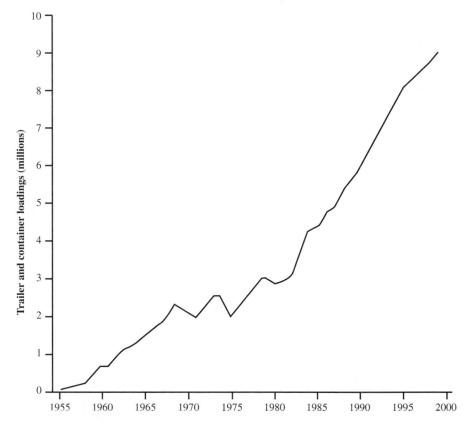

Source: Peter Bradley, "Railroads: The Big Get Bigger," *Logistics Management and Distribution Report* 37, no. 7 (July 1998), p. 39; "TM News Capsule," *Traffic Management* 29, no. 7 (July 1990), p. 19; and "US Intermodal Volume Sets Record," *American Shipper* 42, no. 2 (February 2000), p. 74.

---

[22]"US Intermodal Volume Sets Record," *American Shipper* 42, no. 2 (February 2000), p. 74.

[23]"Up Front," *Logistics Management and Distribution Report* 38, no. 5 (May 1999), p. 3.

billing systems, and expedited terminal procedures. BNSF transports freight on the long haul, while J. B. Hunt picks up and delivers between the customer and the railhead.[24]

Roadrailers Combine Motor and Rail

Roadrailers.   An innovative intermodal concept was introduced in the late 1970s. Roadrailers, or trailertrains as they are sometimes called, combine motor and rail transport in a single piece of equipment. As shown in Figure 8–4, the roadrailer resembles a conventional motor carrier (truck) trailer. However, the trailer has both rubber truck tires and steel rail wheels. Over highways, tractor power units transport the trailers in the normal way. But instead of placing the trailer on a flatcar for rail movement, the wheels of the trailer are retracted and the trailer rides directly on the rail tracks.

The advantages of this intermodal form of transport are that rail flatcars are not required and that it takes less time to change wheels on the trailer than to load and unload the trailer from the flatcar. The major disadvantage of roadrailers has been the added weight of the rail wheels, which has reduced fuel efficiency and resulted in higher costs for the highway portion of the movement.

FIGURE 8–4

Selected forms of intermodal transportation

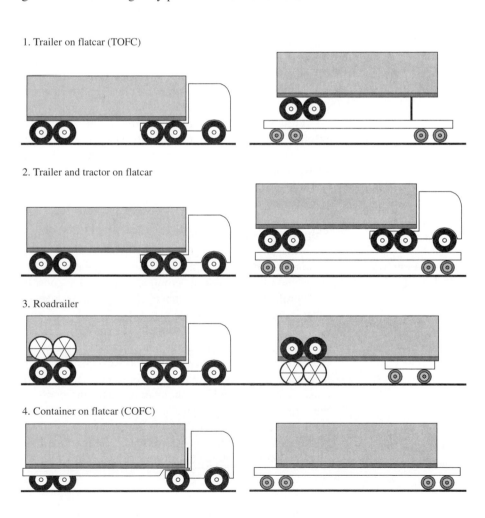

1. Trailer on flatcar (TOFC)

2. Trailer and tractor on flatcar

3. Roadrailer

4. Container on flatcar (COFC)

---

[24]Mitchell E. MacDonald, "Intermodal Battles a Perception Problem," *Traffic Management* 29, no. 5 (May 1990), p. 32.

Other variations of the roadrailer use trailers equipped only with collapsible highway wheels. When moving by rail, the trailers sit atop removable rail wheels. To date, the use of roadrailers has been very limited because of the costs of operation and equipment.

Other Transport Options

In addition to the intermodal combinations of piggyback and roadrailers, other important elements of the transportation system include the nonoperating third parties that may be unimodal or multimodal. The major options include freight forwarders (domestic and international), shippers' associations or cooperatives, transportation brokers, intermodal marketing companies (or shippers' agents), and third-party logistics service providers.[25]

Forwarders Provide Many Services

Freight Forwarders.   Although freight forwarders are not one of the five basic modes of transport, they are a viable shipping alternative for many companies. Forwarders act in much the same capacity as wholesalers in the marketing channel. They purchase transport services from any one or more of the five modes. They then consolidate small shipments from a number of shippers into large shipments that move at a lower rate. These companies offer shippers lower rates than the shippers could obtain directly from the carrier, because small shipments generally cost more per pound to transport than large shipments. In some instances, the freight forwarder can provide faster and more complete service than a carrier.

Freight forwarders can be domestic or international (foreign) depending on whether they specialize in shipments within a country or externally to other countries. Forwarders can also be surface and/or air freight forwarders depending on the specific transportation mode(s) they use. If they are involved in international shipments, forwarders will also provide documentation services, especially vital for firms with limited international marketing experience.

Shippers' Association Defined

Shippers' Associations or Cooperatives.   Another form of transportation intermediary is the shippers' association or cooperative. In its operations, it is much like a freight forwarder, but it differs in terms of how regulatory authorities perceive it. A shippers' association is defined as a "group of shippers that consolidates or distributes freight on a nonprofit basis for the members of the group in order to secure carload, truckload, or other volume rates or service contracts."[26]

Shippers' associations primarily use motor and rail carriers for transport. They are especially important to firms that ship small quantities of product to customers. Because small shipments are much more expensive to ship on a per-unit basis than large shipments, many companies band together to lower their transportation costs through consolidation (i.e., taking a number of small shipments and combining them into a single larger shipment). Typically, members of the shippers' association realize service level improvements in addition to lower rates.

Shippers' associations can also handle truckload shipments by purchasing large blocks of flatbed railcars at discount rates. They then fill the available cars with the

---

[25]For an overview of many of these transport options, see PricewaterhouseCoopers LLP, *The Emergence of Third-Party Logistics,* white paper (1999).

[26]"Associations Must Follow Rules: Justice Department Scrutinizes Operation of Shippers' Associations," *American Shipper* 41, no. 4 (April 1999), p. 71.

truck trailers (TOFC) of member companies. Both parties benefit as a result. Shippers are charged lower rates than they could get by themselves, while the railroads realize better equipment utilization and the economics of large, direct-route piggyback trains.

Transportation Brokers.   A transportation broker is someone who arranges for the transportation of products and charges a fee to do so. They are legal transportation entities, but are not carriers. One of the largest companies offering such services is C. H. Robinson Worldwide, Inc., with more than 17,000 contacts with motor carriers in North America and 119 offices worldwide.[27] Transportation brokerage works as follows: "The broker makes shipment arrangements and participates in the rate negotiation. A broker's agreement is typically established between the carrier and the broker, naming the broker as an agent of the carrier. This means that the broker is authorized to bill and receive payments on the carrier's behalf."[28]

Services Provided by a Broker

Shippers and carriers choose to use brokers for many reasons. Perhaps the most important has been the myriad of carrier options resulting from deregulation of the transportation sector. Brokers help carriers obtain return loads, or back hauls. This helps make carriers more efficient because their equipment is moving "full" rather than "empty."

In instances where shippers lack the necessary expertise, time, or personnel, brokers can be very useful. Shippers with minimal traffic support, or no traffic department at all, can use brokers to negotiate rates, oversee shipments, and do many of the things the shipper may not be able to do because of resource constraints. In these instances the broker replaces, partially or completely, the firm's own traffic department. Typically, this occurs only with small- and medium-sized shippers.

Intermodal Marketing, Companies or Shippers' Agents.   Intermodal marketing companies (IMCs), or shippers' agents, act much like shippers' associations or cooperatives. However, they specialize in providing piggyback services to shippers and thus are important intermodal links between shippers and carriers. IMCs purchase large quantities of TOFC/COFC services at discount and resell them in smaller quantities. As the use of intermodal transportation increases in the future, IMCs will become more important.

Third-Party Logistics Service Providers.   The use of third-party logistics service providers is growing very rapidly. Carrier-based examples of third parties include Ryder Logistics, ROLS (Caliber), Schneider Logistics, Customized Transportation, and Menlo Logistics.[29] For example, Sears (a mass merchandise retailer) and Menlo Logistics (a third-party logistics service provider) have established a mutually beneficial relationship in which Menlo provides significant transportation support for Sears, to the tune of 1.2 billion pounds of freight annually.[30]

---

[27]See the company's website <www.chrobinson.com>.

[28]Mike Prince, "Tools for More Effective Transportation Management," *Competitive Edge* (Winter 1998), p. 13.

[29]PricewaterhouseCoopers, *The Emergence of Third-Party Logistics,* p. 3.

[30]Thomas A. Foster, "How Sears Leverages Its LTL," *Distribution* 91, no. 9 (September 1992), pp. 46, 49–50. For additional examples of the use of third parties, see James Aaron Cooke, "Third Time's a Charm!" *Logistics Management* 35, no. 3 (March 1996), pp. 85–87; James Aaron Cooke, "Three 'Takes' on Third Party," *Logistics Management* 35, no. 5 (May 1996), pp. 53–55; and Toby B. Gooley, "Why GM Pushed Inbound Shipments Back Out the Door," *Traffic Management* 34, no. 6 (June 1995), pp. 49–52.

The Use of Third Parties Is Increasing

With the increasing emphasis on supply chain management, more companies are exploring the third-party option. For some firms, dealing with one third-party firm that will handle all of most of their freight offers a number of advantages, including the management of information by the third party, freeing the company from day-to-day interactions with carriers, and having the third party oversee hundreds or even thousands of shipments. Activities such as freight payment and dedicated contract carriage have been administered by third parties for many years. However, additional transportation and logistics activities are being outsourced. In some instances, entire logistics operations are being outsourced to third parties.

All of the transportation entities described in this section can be viable shipping options for a firm in the same way as the five basic transportation modes or intermodal combinations. The logistics executive must determine the optimal combination of transport alternatives that is right for his or her company.

Small Package Carriers.   For many shippers, such as electronics firms, catalog merchandisers, cosmetic companies, and textbook distributors, small package carriers such as parcel post and air express companies can be very important transportation options.

U.S. Postal Service

The U.S. Postal Service provides both surface and air parcel post services to companies shipping small packages. The advantages of parcel post are its low cost and wide geographical coverage, both domestically and internationally. Disadvantages include specific size and weight limitations, variability in transit time (especially internationally), higher loss and damage rates than many other forms of shipment, and inconvenience, since packages must be prepaid and deposited at a postal facility. Mail-order houses are probably the most extensive users of parcel post.

UPS

United Parcel Service (UPS) is a private business that, like parcel post, transports small packages using both air and ground transportation. It competes directly with parcel post and transports a majority of the small parcels shipped in the United States. The advantages of UPS include its low cost, wide geographic coverage internationally, and minimum variability in transit time. Its disadvantages include size and weight limitations (which are more restrictive than parcel post) and inconvenience (UPS will provide pickup for larger shippers, but smaller shippers must often deposit parcels at a UPS facility).

FedEx

Characterized by high levels of customer service, the air express industry has significantly expanded since its inception in 1973. The Federal Express Corporation (FedEx), one of the most well-known examples of an air express company, illustrates how the concept of supplying rapid transit with very high consistency has paid off. In 1999, FedEx had worldwide revenues of $18 billion, representing service to 210 countries. This represented more than 5 million daily express packages, transported by over 500 aircraft, and supported by thousands of vehicles.[31]

Many E-Commerce Companies Use Air Express

Because some firms need to transport products quickly, the air express industry is able to offer overnight or second-day delivery of small parcels to many locations throughout the world. Many of the e-commerce companies that sell books over the Internet—such as Amazon.Com, Borders Books, and Barnes & Noble—use air express for shipping their products to customers.[32]

---

[31]FedEx, annual reports, 1995 and 1999 <www.fdxcorp.com>.
[32]Marcia Jedd, "Internet Logistics: Booking Success," *Inbound Logistics* 19, no. 1 (January 1999), pp. 140–48.

Competition is fierce among the "giants" of the industry, including Airborne Express, DHL Airways, Emery Worldwide, FedEx, and UPS. In many instances, these companies also provide motor carrier transport by operating their own trucks, or having subsidiaries that provide rapid trucking service (e.g., RPS, operated by FedEx).

So long as there is a need to transport products quickly and with very high levels of service consistency, the air express companies will continue to provide a valuable service to many shippers.[33]

Transportation Regulation and Deregulation

There are two major areas of transportation regulation: economic and safety/environmental. All U.S. freight movements are subject to numerous safety and environmental regulations, but to relatively few economic regulations. Economic regulation has affected many logistics decisions in areas such as mode/carrier selection, carrier rates and services, routing and scheduling, and carrier service levels. Safety and environmental issues, such as labor standards, working conditions for transportation employees, hazardous materials shipments, vehicle maintenance, insurance, pollution, and other elements relating to public health and safety, have been the targets of a number of U.S. laws and regulations.

Regulatory History

Historically, the regulation, and subsequent deregulation, of the transportation sector has had an enormous impact on the activities of shippers and carriers. Table 8–4 presents a summary of the major economic and safety/environmental legislation in the United States.

Economic Deregulation

In general, economic regulation has exhibited periodic swings from regulation to deregulation and back again. The late 1970s to the 1990s was a period of economic deregulation in the United States, Canada, and elsewhere throughout the world. In contrast, safety and environmental regulations have been increasing in terms of their scope and breadth.

Government authorities have always viewed the transportation sector as an area that has to be maintained, protected, and promoted; hence, it has been viewed as a public utility. To achieve those objectives the government has sought to control the number of competitors, rates, and services offered.

Origins of U.S. Transportation Regulation

U.S. transportation regulation has developed primarily over the last 100 years: "It was first imposed by congressional action on railroads in 1887, on motor carriers in 1935, on U.S. flag carriers in 1936, on air carriers in 1938, on domestic water carriers in 1940, and on freight forwarders in 1942. As newer modes of transport developed, much the same type of regulation was applied to the newcomers despite quite variant economic characteristics of the modes and carriers."[34]

Major U.S. Regulatory Agencies

As Table 8–4 shows, a variety of legislation has been enacted during the past 100 years, with more likely during the new millennium. The major federal agencies that regulate transportation include the Surface Transportation Board (STB), Department

---

[33]For examples of how express carriers serve international customers in an e-commerce environment, see Gordon Forsyth, "Uncovering Cost," *American Shipper* 42, no. 2 (February 2000), pp. 24–28.

[34]Charles A. Taff, *Management of Physical Distribution and Transportation,* 7th ed. (Homewood, IL: Richard D. Irwin, 1984), p. 513.

TABLE 8–4   Historical Development of U.S. Transportion Regulation

Date(s)	Event	Significance
1887	Act to Regulate Commerce (Interstate Commerce Act)	The first legislation to regulate transportation. Created the Interstate Commerce Commission (ICC)—initially to administer the railroads, and later almost all forms of transportation.
1903	Elkins Act	Known as the "antirebate" act. Made both the carrier and the shipper equally guilty for violations of the Act to Regulate Commerce.
1906	Hepburn Act	Allowed ICC to prescribe the maximum rates carriers could charge. Also declared oil pipelines common carriers and thus subject to regulation by the ICC.
1910	Mann-Elkins Act	Gave the ICC power to suspend proposed carrier rate changes for a limited period if it felt the rate was unreasonable.
1916	Shipping Act	Established the U.S. Shipping Board (predecessor of the Federal Maritime Commission) to regulate the ocean transportation industry.
1920	Transportation Act	Attempted to restructure the railroad industry through consolidation. Also allowed railroad pooling arrangements in certain instances. "Rule of Rate-Making" provision of Interstate Commerce Act was changed to allow railroads to earn a fair return on their investment, to give the ICC authority to establish minimum rates, and to allow the ICC to prescribe the actual rates railroads could charge if existing rates were deemed unreasonable.
1935	Motor Carrier Act	Placed motor carriers under the jurisdiction of the ICC. Established four categories of motor carriers: Common, contract, private, and exempt. Carriers were required to have certificates of authority issued by the ICC in order to operate.
1938	Civil Aeronautics Act	Created the Civil Aeronautics Board (CAB) to regulate commercial aviation in the areas of rates, routes, and market entry.
1940	Transportation Act	Placed domestic water carriers, except those with exempt status, under ICC jurisdiction. Included a statement of the National Transportation Policy.
1942	Freight Forwarders Act	Included freight forwarders in the Interstate Commerce Act and thus made them subject to ICC regulation.
1948	Reed-Bulwinkle Act	Amended Interstate Commerce Act so as to allow the establishment of rate bureaus.
1958	Transportation Act	Modified the 1940 statement of the National Transportation Policy to include the issue of "umbrella" rate making. Also eased restrictions on abandonment of rail passenger service.
1966	Department of Transportation Act	Established the Department of Transportation (DOT).
1970	Rail Passenger Service Act	Created Amtrak for intercity passenger transport. Railroads were able to turn over their passenger service to Amtrak for a fee.
1973	Northeast Regional Rail Reorganization Act	Created the United States Railway Association (USRA) and the Consolidated Rail Corporation (Conrail) from the bankrupt Penn Central Railroad.
1974	Hazardous Materials Transportation Uniform Safety Act	A part of the Transportation Safety Act of 1974. Consolidated the regulation of hazardous materials under the Materials Transportation Bureau of DOT, established training requirements for firms, allowed DOT to regulate routing and loading/unloading of hazardous materials, and increased penalties for violation of the Act.

TABLE 8–4   (concluded)

Date(s)	Event	Significance
1976	Rail Revitalization and Regulatory Reform Act	Known as the "4-R Act." Provided government financial assistance to Conrail, Amtrak, and other railroads. Provided guidelines to the ICC on "just and reasonable" rates and defined "market dominance."
1977	Department of Energy Act	Created the Federal Energy Regulatory Commission (FERC) to regulate oil and natural gas pipelines.
1977, 1978	Airline Deregulation Acts	Freed all-cargo aircraft operations from CAB regulations. Allowed air carriers significantly greater pricing flexibility, market entry/exit, and routing. CAB restrictions were to be gradually removed and the CAB was abolished on January 1, 1985.
1978	The *Toto* Supreme Court Decision [Toto Purchasing and Supply, Common Carrier Application 128 MCC 873 (1978); Ex Parte Number MC-1 1 8]	Removed backhaul restrictions from private carriers.
1980	Motor Carrier Act	Comprehensive legislation deregulating the motor carrier industry. Major provisions allowed carriers to adjust their rates within a "zone of reasonableness" without ICC approval, reduced the authority of rate bureaus, provided greater flexibility in contract carriage, opened markets to greater competition through relaxed entry restrictions, and allowed intercorporate hauling by private carriers.
1980	Staggers Rail Act	Removed much of the ICCs authority over rail rates. Established a zone of rate flexibility. Reduced the importance of rate bureaus and authorized railroad contracts with shippers.
1980	Household Goods Transportation Act	Reduced government regulation of household movers in the areas of pricing, reporting requirements, liability (e.g., insurance), and customer payment.
1984	Shipping Act	Partially deregulated the ocean transport industry. Allowed carriers to pool or apportion traffic, allot ports and regulate sailings, publish port-to-port or point-to-point tariffs, and enter into confidential service contracts with shippers. Allowed shippers to form nonprofit groups to obtain volume rates.
1993	Negotiated Rates Act	The law provided mechanisms for the resolution of claims relating to negotiated rates of bankrupt motor carriers.
1994	Trucking Industry Regulatory Reform Act	Carriers no longer had to file their rates with the ICC or its replacement, the Surface Transportation Board.
1994	Federal Aviation Administration Authorization Act	Section 601 preempts state laws and regulations relating to prices, routes, and services of motor carriers. Also exempts air intermodal carriers from economic regulation by the individual states.
1995	ICC Termination Act	Eliminated the Interstate Commerce Commission and placed transportation regulation under the Surface Transportation Board of the Department of Transportation.
1998	Ocean Shipping Reform Act	Deregulated ocean liner shipping in the U.S. trades. Shippers can negotiate confidential contracts with Ocean carriers and tariff filing at the Federal Maritime Commission was ended.

of Transportation (DOT), Federal Maritime Commission (FMC), and Federal Energy Regulatory Commission (FERC).

The DOT regulates the safety aspects of transport modes and the economic aspects of air carriers. The STB, FMC, and FERC regulate economic aspects of the other modes. Environmentally, federal regulation of transportation is accomplished through laws such as the Occupational Safety and Health Act (OSHA), the Hazardous Materials Transportation Uniform Safety Act, and the National Environmental Policy Act.

Transportation is also regulated at the state level. It is beyond the scope of this book to examine the myriad of state regulations that exist, but carriers and shippers must be familiar with all regulations in states where they operate.

An important part of a logistics executive's responsibility is to keep abreast of regulatory changes because of their potential impact on the firm's logistics operations. An assessment of present and future changes is often enhanced by an awareness of past regulatory activity.

Impacts of Deregulation

Economic Deregulation Has Been the Trend

The degree to which the transportation sector has been regulated has varied over the years. Since 1977, the trend in the United States has been toward less economic regulation. Airlines were the first transport mode to be extensively deregulated, with the Federal Aviation Act being amended in 1977, followed by the passage of the Airline Deregulation Act of 1978. Railroads and motor carriers were next, with the passage of the Staggers Rail Act (1980) and the Motor Carrier Act of 1980. In 1984, the Shipping Act partially deregulated ocean cargo carriers. In the 1990s, further deregulation occurred through the Negotiated Rates Act of 1993, the Trucking Industry Regulatory Reform Act of 1994 (TIRRA), the Federal Aviation Administration Authorization Act of 1994 (including Section 601, which affected motor carriers), the ICC Termination Act of 1995, and the Ocean Shipping Reform Act of 1998.

Deregulation of the major transportation modes has had significant impact on motor, rail, air, and water carriers, and the shippers who use their services. Freight transportation has moved into a new age. The next decade promises to be an exciting time for carriers and shippers. We will begin by examining the motor carrier industry.

Motor Carrier Act of 1980

Motor.   The Motor Carrier Act of 1980 substantially reduced the amount of economic regulation of interstate trucking. The act specifically addressed restrictions on market entry, routing, intercorporate hauling, contract carriage, rates, and transportation brokers.

As a result of this legislation motor carriers have had to be cost-efficient in order to survive. For example, in the less-than-truckload (LTL) market between 1980 and 1989, approximately one-half of the largest motor carriers declared bankruptcy. The shakeout of unprofitable and inefficient motor carriers that characterized the first 10 years after deregulation (1980–89) has passed, and since 1990 the motor carrier industry has exhibited much more stability.

As a by-product of a more competitive environment, there have been significant developments in the areas of rates and service offerings. Rates for truckload (TL) and LTL have declined since 1984. Energy costs and other factors may cause these rates to increase, but the trend will likely continue downward (or perhaps stabilize) over the long term. Deregulation removed constraints on motor carriers' product, service, and price offerings, and new price/service trade-offs emerged.

During the 1990s, significant additional deregulation occurred, primarily through the Negotiated Rates Act of 1993, the Trucking Industry Regulatory Reform Act of 1994 (TIRRA), the amending of the Federal Aviation Administration Authorization Act of 1994, and the ICC Termination Act of 1995.

Economic Deregulation in the 1990s

- *Negotiated Rates Act of 1993:* It is common practice for carriers and shippers to negotiate rates for transportation services.

Difficulties arise, however, when motor carriers fail to properly file the negotiated rate with the ICC [now replaced by the STB] or when certain conditions trigger tariff provisions canceling tariff discounts. If a motor carrier ceases operation and files for bankruptcy, the receiver or trustee frequently retains an auditor to search the records of the carrier for instances in which the rates billed and collected were lower than the applicable rates on file . . . When these discrepancies are discovered, the receiver or trustee then files a collection action to recover the difference from the shipper. The shipper most often refuses to pay the claim, on the grounds that the shipper and the carrier had a valid agreement by which they both agreed to the lower rate . . . Rising numbers of motor carrier bankruptcies in recent years led to a large number of negotiated rates collection actions.[35]

The law provided mechanisms for the resolution of claims relating to negotiated rates.[36]

- *Trucking Industry Regulatory Reform Act of 1994 (TIRRA):* Carriers no longer must file their rates with the Interstate Commerce Commission (ICC). Only household goods movers must file with the ICC.

- *Federal Aviation Administration Authorization Act of 1994 (Section 601):* The law preempts state laws and regulations relating to prices, routes, and services of motor carriers. In essence, intrastate regulations of transportation were eliminated.[37]

The ICC Is Eliminated

- *ICC Termination Act of 1995:* Eliminated the Interstate Commerce Commission and placed transportation regulation under the Surface Transportation Board (STB) of the Department of Transportation (DOT).

The Results of Motor Carrier Deregulation

As a result of TIRRA and the ICC Termination Act, the following notable changes in trucking regulation occurred:

1. The distinction between common and contract carriers was eliminated. All motor carriers now are allowed to enter into contracts or to provide transportation that is not covered by contracts. The common carrier obligation to provide service on reasonable request remains.

2. All remaining motor carrier tariff-filing and rate regulations are repealed, except for those affecting non-contiguous domestic trade and individual household-goods movements.

3. The STB has broad exemption authority except with regard to cargo loss and damage, insurance, safety fitness, and antitrust immunity.

4. Responsibility for motor carrier registration is transferred to the DOT. New carriers no longer must seek a certificate of operating authority. Safety fitness and financial responsibility are the only requirements for registering.[38]

As a result of the most recent deregulation of motor carriers, the industry has seen the expansion of intrastate service by LTL carriers; introduction of a variety of new

---

[35]Small Business Legislative Council, *The Business Guide to the Negotiated Rates Act of 1993* (Park Ridge, IL: American Warehouse Association, 1993), p. 2.

[36]For a discussion of this act in some detail, see William J. Augello, *Doing Business Under the New Transportation Law: The Negotiated Rates Act of 1993* (Huntington, NY: Transportation Claims and Prevention Council, January 1994).

[37]Ray Bohman, "The Brave New World of Tariff-Free Pricing," *Traffic Management* 34, no. 6 (June 1995), pp. 41–45.

[38]Peter Bradley, "The ICC Fades Away, But Regulation Never Dies," *Traffic Management* 35, no. 2 (February 1996), p. 14.

intrastate pricing options; simplification of carrier service offer sheets and related charges; a switch from tariffs to pricing agreements with individual shippers; increased usage of "spot pricing," where pricing concessions are given to shippers in special circumstances; more innovative carrier pricing approaches; and increased offerings of new carrier services.

Rail.   Deregulation has had a significant impact on the railroads. Between 1975 and 1987, the number of railroad companies with operating revenues over $50 million (called Class I railroads) increased the amount of freight they transported in ton-miles by one-third. During the same period, track miles declined by 30 percent, there were 25 percent fewer freight cars and 29 percent fewer locomotives, and the number of railroad employees declined by 49 percent.[39]

Because of their increased rate flexibility and ability to enter into long-term contracts with shippers, railroads have offered a variety of cost-service packages, greatly increasing their customer focus.[40] Today, most rail rates are negotiated, and the number of rail-shipper contracts is increasing, so that contract carriage is the dominant method of shipping products by rail.

The Trend toward Megacarriers

Since 1980, there has been a trend toward large regional railroads, or megacarriers. The largest U.S. railroads (Burlington Northern/Santa Fe Railway Co., CSX Transportation, Norfolk Southern, and Union Pacific/Southern Pacific) transport the bulk of all rail shipments.[41] Mergers have allowed significant economies of scale, as well as the ability to provide single-line rates between many origin-destination pairs.

Specific deregulation of the rail industry includes the Staggers Rail Act and the ICC Termination Act.

Staggers Act Was First Major Attempt to Deregulate the Rail Industry

- *Staggers Rail Act of 1980:* Removed much of the federal regulatory agency control over rail rates. Established a zone of rate flexibility for carriers and reduced the importance of rate bureaus. Authorized long-term railroad contracts between shippers and carriers.
- *ICC Termination Act of 1995:* Eliminated the Interstate Commerce Commission and placed transportation regulation under the Surface Transportation Board (STB) of the Department of Transportation (DOT). Notable elements of the law included:

  1. Rail mergers will be reviewed by the STB. A 15-month time limit was established for reviewing rail mergers.
  2. "Tariff filing and most contract filing for railroads was eliminated, except where agricultural products are concerned. Carriers, however, must provide 20 days' advance notice of any rate increases or changes in service terms."[42]

Captive Shippers

One result of U.S. deregulation, stemming from several rail mergers and acquisitions, has been an increase in the number of *captive shippers.* These are companies in

---

[39]"The Staggers Rail Act: Why It Was Passed . . . What It Has Accomplished," Association of American Railroads Publication No. AAR6-040389 (1989), p. 8.

[40]Lewis M. Schneider, "New Era in Transportation Strategy," *Harvard Business Review* 63, no. 2 (March–April 1985), p. 122.

[41]Peter Bradley, "Railroads: The Big Get Bigger," *Logistics Management and Distribution Report* 37, no. 7 (July 1998), p. 37.

[42]Bradley, "The ICC Fades Away," p. 14.

a market being served by only one rail carrier; hence, no competitive choices are available to these firms. While it is uncertain whether these shippers are paying higher rates and/or receiving less service than shippers located in markets with multiple rail options, there is some pressure on the U.S. government to increase competition through some form of legislative relief (i.e., re-regulation). These issues might impact logistics executives in the future and will have to be monitored by those involved in the transportation mode selection process. (See Chapter 9 for a discussion of mode and carrier selection).

Air.   With the amending of the Federal Aviation Act in 1977, followed by the passage of the Airline Deregulation Act of 1978, the airline industry became the first transport mode to be substantially deregulated in the United States. For the most part, the impacts of deregulation on air carriers (including passengers and freight) have been mixed. Operating profits of the airline industry have been erratic.[43] The airline industry's unstable financial performance has been partly due to competitive pressures, general economic conditions, industry pricing practices, fluctuations in the cost of jet fuel, and equipment updating. However, deregulation itself has had a significant effect on the airline industry.

The major airline deregulation can be summarized as follows:

- *Amendment of the Federal Aviation Act in 1977:* Removed federal rate and operating authority regulations from all-cargo aircraft operations, including all-cargo airlines, FedEx, and any all-cargo operation of regularly scheduled airlines. Size restrictions on all-cargo aircraft were eliminated.
- *Airline Deregulation Act of 1978:* Deregulated the airline passenger industry, which, in turn, affected the freight transportation operations of scheduled airlines. Primary impacts were on passenger traffic with secondary impacts on freight traffic. All market entry and rate controls were eliminated.
- *Federal Aviation Administration Authorization Act of 1994:* Exempted air intermodal carriers from economic regulation by the individual states.

Water.   The final mode of transportation to be deregulated was the maritime shipping industry. The Shipping Act of 1984 was the principal vehicle for changing the regulatory environment in which ocean carriers operated. Ocean common carriers, or liners, are regulated by the Federal Maritime Commission (FMC).

- *Shipping Act of 1984:* Partially deregulated the ocean transport industry. Allowed carriers to pool or apportion traffic, allot ports and regulated sailings, publish port-to-port or point-to-point rates, and enter into confidential service contracts with shippers. Allowed shippers to form nonprofit groups to obtain volume rates.
- *Ocean Shipping Reform Act of 1998:* Shippers were allowed "to negotiate confidential contracts with ocean carriers and tariff filing at the Federal Maritime Commission (FMC) [was] ended."[44]

Shipping Conferences   Ocean carriers have traditionally formed groups called *conferences* for the purpose of establishing rates, deciding which ports to serve, pooling or consolidating cargo, and allocating revenues among participating carriers. Conferences were originally given

---

[43]"Uncertain Weather Patterns Ahead," *Distribution* 93, no. 6 (July 1994), pp. 49–54.
[44]*The National Industrial Transportation League annual report* (November 1998), p. 4.

limited antitrust immunity under the Shipping Act of 1916, and greater immunity under the Shipping Act of 1984.

Point-to-Point Rates   Liner rates can be adjusted up or down to meet shipper needs and market conditions without undue difficulty. The ability to publish *point-to-point rates* has facilitated intermodal movements, such as landbridge (ocean-land-ocean movement), microbridge (inland location-seaport-ocean movement), and minilandbridge (ocean via ship, land via rail movement), which are discussed below. As in the rail and trucking industries, contract carriage in the ocean transport sector will continue to increase in the future.[45]

In many instances, shippers have benefited from the economic deregulation of motor, rail, air, and ocean cargo carriers. Thus, the trend for the foreseeable future is likely to be further deregulation of the transportation sector. While any projections of future deregulation will be imprecise, it is certain that shippers and carriers will work together more closely than ever before.

Global Aspects of Transportation

Transportation managers of firms involved in international markets must be aware of the services, costs, and availability of transport modes within and between the countries where their products are distributed. As an example, air and water transportation are the major options available for the majority of international shipments, unless the countries happen to be contiguous. Within most countries, motor and rail shipments dominate. Management must consider many factors when it compares the various options. Many of these issues will be examined in Chapter 14.

Air and Water Transport Are Primary International Shipping Options

Differences that exist between transportation modes can be due to taxes, subsidies, regulations, government ownership of carriers, geography, and other factors that vary by country or geographic region. For example, because of government ownership or subsidies of railroads in Europe, rail service benefits from newer or better maintained equipment, track, and facilities that accompany the large budgets of governments. As we noted earlier, Japan and Europe use water carriage to a much larger degree than the United States or Canada due to the length and favorable characteristics of coastlines and inland waterways.

International Transportation Is More Expensive Than Domestic Transportation

Typically, international transportation costs represent a much higher percentage of merchandise value than is the case in domestic transportation. This is due to the longer distances involved, administrative requirements, and related paperwork that must accompany international shipments.[46]

Intermodal transportation is much more common in international movements, and even though rehandling costs are higher than for single mode movements, cost savings and service improvements often result. For example, there are three basic forms of international intermodal distribution (see Figure 8–5).

Landbridge   *Landbridge* is a service in which foreign cargo crosses a country en route to another country. For example, European cargo en route to Japan may be shipped by ocean to the U.S. East Coast, then moved by rail to the U.S. West Coast, and from there shipped by ocean to Japan.

---

[45]For some early indications of the impact of ocean transport deregulation, see Philip Damas, "Fewer Carriers, Higher Rates," *American Shipper* 42, no. 1 (January 2000), pp. 30–31.

[46]See Paul S. Bender, "International Logistics," in *The Distribution Management Handbook,* ed. James A. Tompkins and Dale Harmelink (New York: McGraw-Hill, 1994), pp. 8.5–8.6.

FIGURE 8–5

International distribution shipping options

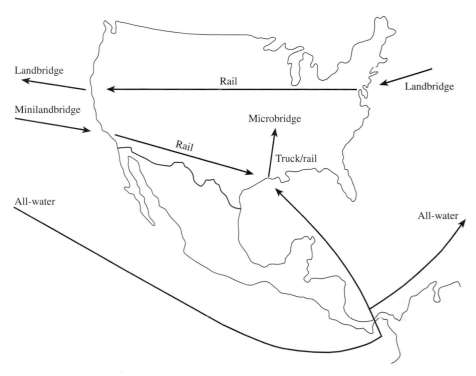

Source: David L. Anderson, "International Logistics Strategies for the Eighties," *Proceedings of the Twenty-Second Annual Conference of the National Council of Physical Distribution Management* (1984), p. 363. Used by permission of the Council of Logistics Management.

Minilandbridge

  Minilandbridge (also called *minibridge*) is a special case of landbridge, where foreign cargo originates or terminates at a point within the United States.

Microbridge

  Microbridge is a relatively new service being provided by ports on the U.S. West Coast. In contrast with minibridge, this service provides door-to-door rather than port-to-port transportation. The big advantage of microbridge is that it provides a combined rate including rail and ocean transportation in a single tariff that is lower than the sum of the separate rates.[47]

  A comparison of single-mode and intermodal movements between the Far East and the U.S. East Coast demonstrates the advantages of the latter. If we compare an all-water versus minilandbridge (MLB) movement for comparable shipments, the costs are approximately the same. But MLB is significantly faster, thus offering the opportunity to reduce order cycle times and improve customer service levels.

NAFTA

  Although the North American Free Trade Agreement (NAFTA) will be discussed in Chapter 14, it is of value to briefly identify some of its transportation implications here. Trade between the United States and Canada, and between Mexico and the United States, has grown significantly during the previous decade. More than 70 percent of the goods moving between the United States and Canada go by truck. Infrastructure

---

[47]Paul S. Bender, "The International Dimension of Physical Distribution Management," in *The Distribution Handbook,* ed. James A. Robeson and Robert G. House (New York: Free Press, 1985), pp. 791–92.

Global

Trading with Mexico

AES, a joint program of the U.S. Customs Service, Bureau of the Census, and other federal agencies, allows paperless export documentation. The program is designed to automate the submission and processing of Shippers Export Declaration (SED) forms. It has been estimated that 50 percent of the 500,000 SEDs processed by hand are incomplete or incorrect.

Roadway, a national trucking company, in combination with U.S. Customs and the Bureau of the Census launched the AES program, which worked as follows:

Step 1: Roadway delivers a shipment and the accompanying documents from its Laredo (Texas) terminal to the U.S. forwarding agent's warehouse in Laredo.

Step 2: The forwarding agent inspects the goods for compliance with Mexican laws and prepares additional documentation. Meanwhile, the Mexican customs broker pays duties and taxes, then releases the *pedimento* (import declaration) and other documents to the forwarding agent.

Step 3: When the shipment is ready to cross the border, the forwarding agent transmits AES export data and Mexican import data to the forwarders association's service center in Laredo. The center manages electronic transmission of shipment information for the group's members.

Step 4: The forwarders association transmits validated data to the AES Service Center in Washington, D.C. It also transmits Mexican import data to its sister organization in Mexico, the Nuevo Laredo Customs Brokers Association. The brokers transmit that information to the customs broker and to customs officials in Mexico.

Step 5: AES OKs the electronic SED and transmits a unique AES export authorization number to the forwarders association, which passes it on to Roadway and the forwarding agent.

Step 6: A local drayage driver picks up the freight and documents, which include the AES authorization number and a statement that the SED has been filed electronically.

Step 7: A U.S. customs agent at the border accepts the documents, then sends the driver on to Mexican customs. The agent enters the AES number in a computer, alerting the AES center in Washington that the shipment has left U.S. territory.

Step 8: The driver clears Mexican customs and delivers the trailer to Roadway's Nuevo Laredo terminal. Arrival confirmation is posted on Roadway's tracking system.

All parties are able to track merchandise every step of the way.

Source: "AES Pilot Program Fills Border Information Gap," *Logistics Management and Distribution Report* 38, no. 2 (February 1999), p. 91.

improvements at Montreal's airports now provide faster and more consistent access to one-third of the entire population of Canada and the United States. Additionally, a modern port at Vancouver, combined with low intermodal shipping rates on the Canadian Pacific and Canadian National railroads, allows for substantial movements of products from Asia into North America.[48]

In making traffic and transportation decisions, the logistics manager must know and understand the differences between the domestic and international marketplace. Modal availability, rates, regulatory restrictions, service levels, and other aspects of the transportation mix may vary significantly from one market to another.

---

[48]Anne Fitzgibbon, "Two-Way Transportation: US & Canada," *World Trade* 13, no. 2 (February 2000), pp. 50, 52.

Creative Solutions

Goodyear Tire & Rubber Company Takes a New Approach to Carrier Productivity

Before 1992, Goodyear took a very hard-line approach to negotiating with transportation providers, focusing only on rates. The negotiation process was really an "annual rate battle" that consumed a great deal of time in terms of preparation as well as the actual negotiation process itself. Then Rich Adante, vice president of materials management for Goodyear, realized how unproductive this approach really was. "We realized there could be strength in sharing information," he says, "and developing a relationship where each party knew more about the other's operation . . . we realized that how we worked impacted their business and cost structure."

Goodyear thus developed the following negotiating strategy:

1. Establish three-year, firm price LTL contracts.
2. Consolidate domestic LTL carriers, giving preferred carriers greater volume.
3. Pursue open-book negotiations with each party studying the others' processes for ways to reduce total system costs.

While this innovative approach was not well received by carriers initially, Yellow Freight System responded. They established a joint steering committee to reduce costs, with the agreement that it would be dissolved after one year if either side was dissatisfied. They worked together to establish key indicators of the success of the relationship. The chosen indicators included:

- Yellow's operating ratio.
- Percent on-time delivery versus Yellow's average.
- Average days in transit.
- Transfer data: cost per bill, per cwt.
- Pickup and delivery cost data: per bill, per cwt.

The relationship has progressed very positively. The two-way information sharing and joint management of continuous improvement efforts have created a commitment to the project and the relationship.

Source: Adapted from E. J. Muller, "A New Paradigm for Partnerships," *Distribution* 93, no. 1 (January 1994), pp. 45–48. Reprinted by permission of *Logistics Management & Distribution Report.*

Summary

In this chapter we examined the role of transportation in logistics. Transportation, together with warehousing, adds time and place utility to products. It also affects many decision-making areas of marketing and logistics, including new-product development, target market areas served, purchasing/procurement, facility location, and pricing.

We described the legal forms of transport (common, contract, exempt, and private) and discussed transportation pricing (cost-of-service versus value-of-service, and class, exception, and commodity rates).

The five basic modes of transportation—motor, rail, air, water, and pipeline—provide movement of products between where they are produced and where they are consumed. Each mode varies in its economic and service characteristics and has a different cost structure based on product- and market-related factors. Logistics executives must be aware of the characteristics of each mode as well as various intermodal combinations, nonoperating third parties, and other options (e.g., piggyback, containers, freight forwarders, IMCs, shippers' associations, brokers, UPS, parcel post).

Transportation regulation and deregulation were examined from a historical perspective. The two major types of regulations were discussed (economic and safety/environmental).

Deregulation of the major modes of transportation has had significant impact on motor, rail, air, and water carriers. Several of the most important transportation laws were briefly discussed. Some of the areas most affected by deregulation were rates, market entry, the use of contracts, routing and scheduling, mergers, service levels, and the use of brokers.

The material in this chapter will form the basis for our examination in Chapter 9 of the traffic management function from shipper and carrier perspectives. In addition, we will discuss other decision strategies in the transportation area.

Suggested Readings

Bigness, Jon. "In Today's Economy, There Is Big Money to Be Made in Logistics." *The Wall Street Journal,* September 6, 1995, pp. A1 and A11.

Cavinato, Joseph L. *Transportation-Logistics Dictionary,* 3rd ed. Washington, DC: International Thomson Transport Press, 1989.

Cooke, James Aaron. "Trucking into the 21st Century." *Logistics Management* 36, no. 11 (November 1997), pp. 50–53.

Coyle, John J.; Edward J. Bardi; and Robert A. Novack. *Transportation,* 5th ed. Cincinnati, OH: South-Western, 1999.

Cunningham, Francesca. "The Missing Links." *Logistics Europe* 4, no. 6 (December 1996), pp. 10–15.

Gillis, Chris, and Philip Damas. "Maersk Sealand: After the Deal." *American Shipper* 42, no. 2 (February 2000), pp. 52–58.

Hanna, Joe B.; Robert A. Kunkel; and Gregory A. Kuhlemeyer. "A Financial Analysis of the Interstate Commerce Commission (ICC) Termination Act of 1995 on the Motor Carrier Industry." *Journal of Transportation Management* 11, no. 1 (Spring 1999), pp. 23–36.

Harding, Forrest E. "Characteristics of the Market for International Airfreight in Intermodal Logistics." *Journal of Transportation Management* 9, no. 1 (Spring 1997), pp. 28–37.

Hoffman, Kurt C. "Land-Air Freight Partnerships Expand Carriers' Services." *Global Sites and Logistics* 3, no. 2 (March 1999), pp. 60–70.

Lieb, Robert C., and Luigi A. Peluso. "1999 CEO Perspectives on the Current Status and Future Prospects of the Third-Party Logistics Industry in the United States." *Proceedings of the Annual Conference of the Council of Logistics Management.* Oak Brook, IL: Council of Logistics Management, 1999, pp. 379–97.

———. "The Use of Third-Party Logistics Services by Large American Manufacturers: The 1999 Survey." *Proceedings of the Annual Conference of the Council of Logistics Management.* Oak Brook, IL: Council of Logistics Management, 1999, pp. 159–71.

Muller, Gerhardt. *Intermodal Freight Transportation,* 4th ed. Washington, DC: Eno Foundation, 1999.

Murphy, Paul R., and James M. Daley. "Examining International Freight Forwarder Services: The Perspectives of Current Providers and Users." *Journal of Transportation Management* 9, no. 1 (Spring 1997), pp. 19–27.

———. "Investigating Selection Criteria for International Freight Forwarders." *Transportation Journal* 37, no. 1 (Fall 1997), pp. 29–36.

NITL Ocean Shipping Reform Act (OSRA) Reference Book. Arlington, VA: National Industrial Transportation League, 1999.

Taylor, Stephen. "Shipping Forecast." *Logistics Europe* 5, no. 2 (April 1997), pp. 18–23.

Weart, Walter. "Intermodal: What Now?" *Inbound Logistics* 20, no. 3 (March 2000), pp. 24–35.

Wisner, Joel D., and Michael C. Majza. "Quality Assessment and Improvement Practices in the U.S. Railroad Industry." *Journal of Transportation Management* 11, no. 1 (Spring 1999), pp. 37–49.

Questions and Problems

1. Explain what is meant by *time utility* and *place utility,* and identify how the transportation function adds utility to products.

2. Basic transportation modes can be defined and compared based on their characteristics. Briefly discuss the economic and service characteristics of the five modes of transportation.

3. Although third parties are not one of the basic modes of transportation, they are a viable shipping option for many companies. Discuss the role and functions of third-parties in the transportation system.

4. In addition to the five basic transportation modes, there are a number of intermodal combinations. Among the most widely used are trailer-on-flatcar (TOFC) and container-on-flatcar (COFC). These combinations are referred to as *piggyback.* Describe piggyback movements from the perspectives of cost, service, and availability, and identify their major strengths and weaknesses.

5. There are three types of for-hire transportation carriers. Briefly identify and describe the characteristics of each. Identify the impacts, if any, that deregulation has had on each of them.

6. What is the difference between cost-of-service and value-of-service pricing? How does each one affect the rates charged by carriers?

Decision Strategies in Transportation

Chapter Objectives

- To provide a brief overview of the basics of traffic management.
- To identify the major transportation management activities of shippers and carriers.
- To identify areas of transportation affected by technology.
- To briefly overview how transportation productivity can be measured.
- To describe the transportation audit process.

Introduction

As an essential part of the logistics process and supply chain management, transportation must be effectively managed if organizations are to satisfy their customers and achieve acceptable rates of return on their investments.

Effective and efficient strategies are of paramount importance to both shippers and transportation carriers. Shippers must be aware of the opportunities and pitfalls of inbound and outbound transportation, mode/carrier selection, contracts, transportation brokers, private carriage options, carrier performance evaluation, and so on. Carriers must be experts in many areas, including marketing, pricing, negotiating, routing and scheduling, understanding customer needs, and managing human resources.

In this chapter we will describe the basics of traffic management, as well as some of the more important decision strategies facing shippers and carriers. We will examine the issues of transportation productivity, computer technology, and strategic planning, with a view toward evaluating transportation's role in logistics, marketing, and corporate strategies.

Traffic and Transportation Management

The strategies of carriers and shippers are very much interrelated. The competitive environment requires that transportation be an integral part of logistics strategy. Carriers must understand the role that transportation has in their customers' logistics systems. Logistics executives in shipper firms must be aware of how carriers assist in helping them to satisfy their customers' needs at a profit.

In many organizations, the traditional role of the traffic executive has been expanded considerably, with greater emphasis being placed on how transportation decisions affect the firm's marketing mix and aid in the creation of sustainable competitive advantage.

Transportation Must Interface with Many Functions

The transportation function must interface with other departments within and outside logistics, such as accounting (freight bills); engineering (packaging, transportation equipment); inventory management (raw materials, parts, components, finished goods); legal (warehouse and carrier contracts); manufacturing (just-in-time deliveries); purchasing (expediting, supplier selection); marketing/sales (customer service standards); receiving (claims, documentation); and warehousing (equipment supply, scheduling). Table 9–1 lists some of the areas within the supply chain affected by transportation.

Carrier–Shipper Relationships

The carrier–shipper relationship is an important one; it directly affects the transportation executive's ability to manage successfully. In the following sections, we will look at shippers' and carriers' perspectives of transportation management. Shipper issues to be addressed include inbound and outbound transportation, mode/carrier selection, contracts, outsourcing transportation, private carriage/leasing, and strategic partnerships and alliances. On the carrier side, the issues we will examine include pricing/negotiation, routing and scheduling, service offerings, competition, and marketing activities.

Prior to those discussions, we will present a brief overview of the most important transport documents and traffic management activities.

Basics of Traffic Management

It is beyond the scope of this text to examine the entire traffic management function or all of the transportation-related documents used in managing transportation. However,

TABLE 9–1   Areas in the Supply Chain Affected by Transportation

Planning	*Procurement*	*Manufacturing*	*Distribution*
Network and asset rationalization Lead times Vendor sourcing Economic order quantity	Landed costs Inbound in-transit inventory management Reduced raw material and work-in-process inventories	Interplant movements JIT and other specialized services	Load plans Pick lists Shipping documentation preparation Dock scheduling Outbound shipment management Mode/carrier selection

Source: Adapted from *The Emergence of Third-Party Logistics,* White Paper no. 4 (Atlanta, GA: PricewaterhouseCoopers, 1998), p. 5.

we can present an overview of the major elements of traffic management. This will highlight the myriad of tasks that comprise this important area of transportation management.

Documentation.   Traffic managers use several kinds of documents when shipping products to customers: bills of lading, freight bills, freight claims, and shipping manifests.

Bill of Lading

A *bill of lading* is the most basic transportation document. Simply, it is the contract between a carrier and shipper for transportation services. Typically, the bill of lading contains information about the origin of the shipment (e.g., the shipper's name and location), a description of the products being transported, the weight and quantity of products moved, contract terms, and the destination for the shipment. In essence, the bill of lading provides all information needed by the carrier to transport the shipment from origin to destination.

Also, the bill of lading is a receipt for the items being transported, and thus is very important in the claims process should products be damaged or lost in shipment. Figure 9–1 is an illustration of a typical bill of lading. While there will be some variation in the form and structure of bills of lading used by shippers and carriers, all will contain the same basic information. Many bills of lading are generated electronically and transmitted using EDI or the Internet.

Freight Bill

The *freight bill* is the carrier's invoice. Freight bills can be prepaid (i.e., shipper pays freight charges prior to shipment) or collect (i.e., consignee pays freight charges after arrival of the shipment). Most freight bills are generated electronically, which reduces preparation costs and clerical errors, and speeds up paperwork processing. The freight bill is a multipart document; besides invoicing, its purposes include arrival notification and delivery receipt.[1]

Shipping Manifest

When multiple shipments or stops occur on a single vehicle for transport, a *shipping manifest* is used. This document, used in combination with the bill of lading, lists transit stops, consignees, and product characteristics. In essence, the shipping manifest summarizes the multiple shipments that are being transported in a single move.

---

[1]Joseph L. Cavinato, *Transportation Logistics Dictionary,* 3rd ed. (Washington, DC: International Thomson Transport Press, 1989), p. 96.

FIGURE 9–1

Bill of lading

ABF Freight System, Inc.

Shipper Provided Bill of Lading
Not Negotiable — Original

ABF Freight System, Inc.
3801 Old Greenwood Road
Post Office Box 10048
Fort Smith, Arkansas 72903

Pro #:
B/L #:
SCAC: **ABFS**

PO Number:
Reference Numbers:

RECEIVED, subject to individually determined rates or contracts that have been agreed upon in writing between the carrier and shipper, if applicable, otherwise to the rates, classifications and rules that have been established by the carrier and are available to the shipper, on request; the property described below, in apparent good order, except as noted (contents and condition of contents of packages unknown) marked, consigned, and destined as shown below, which said carrier agrees to carry to destination, if on its route, or otherwise to deliver to another carrier on the route destination. Every service to be performed hereunder shall be subject to all the conditions not prohibited by law, whether printed or written, herein contained, including the back hereof, which are hereby agreed to by the shipper and accepted for himself and his assigns.

From: **Date:**
Street: **City:**   **State:**   **Zip:**

Consigned To:
                                    On Collect on Delivery Shipments, the letters "COD" must appear before the consignee's name

Destination Street:
City: **State:**   **Zip:**
Delivering Carrier:
Additional Shipment Information:

Collect on Delivery:	and remit to:		C.O.D. Charge	Shipper
Street:	City:	State:	to be paid by	Consignee

Hdlg. Units No. Type	Packages No. Type	HM (*)	Kind of Package, Description of Articles, Special Marks and Exceptions (Subject to Correction)	Weight (in lbs) *Subj. to Correction*	Class or Rate Ref. *For Info. Only*	Cube (in lbs) *Optional*

Total Handling Pieces: **Pieces:**   **Weight:**

(*) Mark X to designate Hazardous Materials as defined in DOT Regulations.

Note(1) Where the rate is dependent on value, shippers are required to state specifically in writing the agreed or declared value of the property as follows:

The agreed or declared value of the property is specifically stated by the shipper to be not exceeding _____ per _____."

NOTE (2) Liability Limitation for loss or damage on this shipment may be applicable. See 49 U.S.C. §14706(c)(1)(A) and (B)

NOTE (3) Commodities requiring special or additional care or attention in handling or stowing must be so marked and packaged as to ensure safe transportation with ordinary cara. See Sec. 2(e) of NMFC Item 360.

Freight Charges are PREPAID
unless marked collect
CHECK HERE IF COLLECT >>

FOR FREIGHT COLLECT SHIPMENTS:
If this shipment is to be delivered to the consignee, without recourse on the consignor, the consignor shall sign the following statement:

The carrier may decline to make delivery of this shipment without payment of freight and all other lawful charges.

(Signature of Consignor)

Notify if problem enroute or at delivery (for informational purposes only):
Send freight bill to:

Shipper: **Carrier: ABF Freight System, Inc.**
Per: **Per:**

Shipper Certification	Carrier Certification
This is to certify that the above named materials are properly classified, packaged, marked and labeled, and are in proper condition for transportation according to the applicable regulations and DOT.	Carrier acknowledges receipt of packages and required placards. Carrier certifies emergency response information was made available and/or carrier has the DOT emergency response guidebook or equivalent document in the vehicle.
Per: Date:	Per: Package Nos.:

Source: ABF Freight System, Inc. <http://www.abfs.com/forms/abfbol.jpg>.

Freight Claim

Although not used as frequently as the previous documents, the *freight claim* form is extremely important when loss or damage occurs in a transport move. Figure 9–2 shows a typical form used in the trucking industry, although such forms are uniform across all of the modes of transportation. Much of the identification information from the bill of lading is included on the freight claim form. Shippers must provide a detailed description of the loss or damage that occurred, as well as other accompanying materials to support the claim. Often, such forms are faxed or transmitted electronically to the carrier.

FIGURE 9–2

Claim form

STANDARD FORM FOR PRESENTATION OF LOSS AND DAMAGE CLAIM

To: ABF Freight System, Inc.
        Customer Service Department
        Post Office Box 10048
        Fort Smith, AR 72917-0048

_____
(Date)

_____
(Your File Reference)

_____
(Carrier's Freight Bill Number)

This claim is for: ☐ Damage   ☐ Loss

_____
(Shipper's Name)

_____
(Consignee's Name)

_____
(Point Shipped From)

_____
(Final Destination)

_____
(Date of Bill of Lading)

DETAILED STATEMENT SHOWING HOW AMOUNT CLAIMED IS DETERMINED
(Number and description of articles, nature and extent of loss or damage, invoice price of articles, amount of claim, etc.)
(ALL DISCOUNTS AND ALLOWANCES MUST BE SHOWN)

TOTAL AMOUNT CLAIMED	

The following documents are submitted in support of this claim:

☐ Original Bill of Lading
☐ Document bearing notation of loss or damage
☐ Carrier's Inspection Report Form

☐ Complete invoice or copy showing cost of goods
☐ Other:

Please add any comments in the space below:

_____
_____
_____
_____
_____
_____

ABF's goal is to conclude all claims within 30 days of receipt at its corporate offices in Fort Smith, Arkansas. Should you want to fax your claim, our number is 501-785-8800. DO NOT mail originals if you fax claim. Our telephone number is 501-785-8741.

_____
Your Company Name

_____
Street Address or Post Office Box

_____
City, State, Zip

_____
Your Name

_____   _____
Your Phone   Your Fax

PLEASE PRINT OR TYPE

CS-1   AB 101901

Source: ABF Freight System, Inc. <http://www.abfs.com/forms/LossDamageClaimForm.jpg>.

Traffic Management Activities.   In addition to the ones discussed in the next section of this chapter, basic traffic management activities include claims handling, freight bill auditing, carrier rate negotiation, and shipment tracing and expediting.

Claims Handling   *Claims handling* involves the actual recording, handling, and monitoring of product claims arising from carrier-responsible loss or damage. Accurate, real-time data collection and claims filing are key elements of the process. Additionally, firms must keep historical records of claims in order to identify trends in carrier loss or damage, and response times for claims payments.

Freight Bill Auditing

Freight bill auditing is a process carried out by shippers that ensures that the proper rates have been charged for each shipment. Because clerical errors and product rating misclassifications can occur, shippers must check for these potential problems. Organizations use manual or computerized audit approaches. There are also numerous third parties that provide freight bill auditing services.

Carrier Rate Negotiation

Because most shipments are moved under contract, *carrier rate negotiation* is an important traffic management activity. With transportation rates that can vary according to such factors as the specific carrier, geographic region, time of the year, level of inter- and intramode competition, and product characteristics, the best rate often is given to the best negotiator. Within an environment of supply chain management, partnerships, and strategic alliances, the optimal negotiation process should result in a win–win situation for all parties (e.g., shippers and carriers).

Shipment Tracing and Expediting

Shipment tracing and expediting have become much more significant than ever before because of the need for shippers and carriers to provide real-time information about orders and product shipments. Due to factors such as time compression of the order cycle, changing customer needs, quick response system requirements, and e-commerce, accurate and timely information is essential for effective and efficient traffic management. At times, it is imperative that the location of product in transit be known immediately. This capability is referred to as shipment tracing.

Additionally, when customers require more rapid transit times or a shortened order cycle, shipments must be moved more quickly through the supply chain. This facilitation of more rapid movement of products is referred to as shipment expediting.

Shipment tracing and expediting require monitoring and administration by dedicated personnel and equipment (e.g., computers and information systems). In addition, to be able to perform such activities successfully, both the shipper and carrier must act in partnership.

Shipper Perspectives

The development of an overall logistics strategy requires an understanding of the important issues of transportation. While there are many items that affect the transportation component of logistics, we will examine only selected ones here. They were chosen because they affect a large number of shippers and usually have a significant impact on customer service.

Transportation Impacts Cost and Service

Inbound and Outbound Transportation.   Transportation is one of the most significant areas of logistics management because of its impact on customer service levels and the firm's cost structure. Inbound and outbound transportation costs can account for as much as 10 to 20 percent of product prices, and sometimes even more. Effective management of transportation can result in significant improvements in profitability.[2]

CYDSA Increases Profits with Transportation Efficiencies

CYDSA, one of Mexico's largest private industrial conglomerates, specializing in chemicals, packaging materials, and textile products, conducted a thorough audit of its transportation activities as part of a larger logistics audit. As a result of discovering and taking advantage of a number of opportunities for reducing costs and improving service levels, CYDSA was able to reduce transportation charges within its textile sector by

---

[2]James Aaron Cooke, "Should You Control Your Inbound?" *Traffic Management* 32, no. 2 (February 1993), pp. 30–33.

more than 6 percent, or approximately $4 million. To achieve such savings, the firm implemented the following actions:

- It reduced the carrier supply base by 30 percent, from 171 suppliers to 120.
- It renegotiated rates, placing more volume with fewer carriers.
- It obtained commitments from carriers to improve service levels.
- It improved efficiency of LTL shipments.
- It developed synergies between company divisions on certain routes, resulting in the better use of carriers.[3]

Shippers can improve their transportation systems in many ways. Areas in which cost and service improvements can take place include routing and scheduling of vehicles, private fleet management, shipment consolidation, contract carriage, and rate negotiations.

Mode/Carrier Selection.   Economic and resource constraints mandate that organizations make the most efficient and productive mode and carrier choice decisions possible. Because of transportation's impact on customer service, time-in-transit, consistency of service, inventories, packaging, warehousing, and the environment, transportation decision makers must attempt to optimize the outcomes of the selection process. Quantitative and qualitative factors must be developed and evaluated. Sometime during the selection process, the factors identified in Table 9–2 will be considered.

TABLE 9–2   Cost and Service Factors Often Considered in Mode/Carrier Selection

Cost-Related Factors
Freight costs
Inventory carrying costs of inventory in the pipeline
Inventory carrying costs of cycle stock at the receiving location
Inventory carrying costs of the required safety stock at the receiving location
Investment cost required to produce the inventory to fill the pipeline

Service-Related Factors
Perceived quality of customer services (e.g., consistency of service, on-time pickups and deliveries, transit times, claims handling, shipment tracking and tracing)
Shipment tracking and tracing capabilities
Billing/invoicing accuracy
Electronic data interchange (EDI) capabilities
Potential to develop mutually beneficial long-term partnership
Cargo capacity limitations
Ability to provide service that does not damage goods while in transit
Customs clearance capabilities for international shipments
Impact on the shipper's negotiating position/leverage on other shipping activities

Source: Adapted from Matthew J. Liberatore and Tan Miller, "A Decision Support Approach for Transport Carrier and Mode Selection," *Journal of Business Logistics* 16, no. 2 (1995), p. 88.

[3]Eduardo Martinez, Adan D. Rodriguez, and James K. Wilson, "Quantifying Logistics and Its Effect on the Bottom Line: A Case Study," *Proceedings of the Annual Conference of the Council of Logistics Management,* (Oak Brook, IL: Council of Logistics Management, 1998), pp. 525–44.

Mode/Carrier Selection Process

Four distinct decision stages occur in the mode/carrier selection decision: (1) problem recognition, (2) search, (3) choice, and (4) postchoice evaluation.

Problem Recognition

Problem Recognition.   The problem recognition stage of the mode/carrier choice process is triggered by a variety of factors, such as customer orders, dissatisfaction with an existing mode, and changes in the distribution patterns of the firm. Typically, the most important factors are service related. In those instances where customers do not specify the mode and/or carrier, a search is undertaken for a feasible transportation alternative.

Search Process

Search Process.   The transportation executive scans a variety of information sources as inputs into the mode/carrier choice process. Possible sources include past experience, carrier sales calls, existing company shipping records, printed materials such as advertising brochures, and customers. The extent of the search process may be minimal if the decision maker uses only past experience as an information source. Examining sources can take a considerable amount of time.

Choice Process

Choice Process.   The task facing the transportation executive at this stage is to choose a feasible alternative from among the several modes and carriers that are likely to be viable options. Using the information previously gathered, the executive determines which options can meet the organization's requirements. Generally, if a mode or carrier is within an acceptable price range, service-related factors are the major determinants in mode/carrier choice. Tables 9–3 and 9–4 identify a number of selection criteria used in the evaluation of motor carriers and ocean container shipping, respectively.

Obtaining relevant information to select and evaluate carriers is critical. The appendix to this chapter presents one possible method for gathering such data.

There are similarities across modes in terms of the most important attributes used to select and evaluate carriers. Attributes such as on-time pickup and delivery, prompt response to customer inquiries, consistent transit times, and competitive rates are important irrespective of the mode or carrier being considered.[4]

The transportation executive then selects the mode or carrier that best satisfies the decision criteria, and the shipment is routed via that option. In cases in which a similar decision may occur in the future, such as with a repeat order from a customer, management may establish an order routine so that the same choice process will not have to be repeated. Order routines eliminate inefficiencies associated with making the same decision repeatedly.

Postchoice Evaluation

Postchoice Evaluation.   Once management has made its choice of mode and carrier, some evaluation procedure must be instituted to determine their performance. Depending on the individual firm, the postchoice evaluation process can range from being extremely detailed to being nonexistent. For most organizations, the degree of evalua-

---

[4]For a discussion of factors used in selecting other transportation modes and related transportation services, see Edward A. Morash and Roger J. Calantone, "Rail Selection, Service Quality, and Innovation," *Journal of the Transportation Research Forum* 32, no. 1 (1991), pp. 205–15; Paul R. Murphy and James M. Daley, "A Comparative Analysis of Port Selection Factors," *Transportation Journal* 34, no. 1 (Fall 1994), pp. 15–21; Paul R. Murphy and Patricia K. Hall, "The Relative Importance of Cost and Service in Freight Transportation Choice Before and After Deregulation: An Update," *Transportation Journal* 35, no. 1 (Fall 1995), pp. 30–38; and "What Do Air Shippers Want?" *Traffic Management* 31, no. 7 (July 1992), pp. 65–67.

TABLE 9–3   The Most Important Attributes Considered When Selecting and Evaluating LTL Motor Carriers

Attribute Description	Importance Mean*
Quality of dispatch personnel (honesty)	6.5
On-time pickups	6.5
On-time deliveries	6.5
Competitive rates	6.5
Accurate billing	6.4
Assistance from carrier in handling loss and damage claims	6.4
Prompt action on complaints related to carrier's service	6.4
Quality of drivers (honesty)	6.4
Prompt response to claims	6.4
Carrier's general attitude toward problems/complaints	6.3
Prompt availability of status information on delivery	6.3
Consistent (reliable) transit times	6.3

*Respondents were asked to indicate on a seven-point scale how important the attribute was in selecting a LTL motor carrier, from 1 (not important) to 7 (very important).

Source: Adapted from Douglas M. Lambert, M. Christine Lewis, and James R. Stock, "How Shippers Select and Evaluate General Commodities LTL Motor Carriers," *Journal of Business Logistics* 14, no. 1 (1993), p. 135.

TABLE 9–4   Containership Carrier Selection Criteria

Attribute Description	Importance Mean*
Transit time reliability/consistency	1.31
Equipment availability	1.41
Frequency of service	1.48
Willingness of carrier to negotiate rate changes	1.69
Quality of operating personnel	1.84
Total door-to-door transit time	1.97
Financial stability of carrier	1.97
Freight loss and damage	2.02
Shipment expediting	2.10
Shipment tracing	2.19
Willingness of carrier to negotiate service changes	2.22
Door-to-door transportation rates	2.24
Scheduling flexibility	2.24
Quality of carrier salesmanship	2.48

*Respondents were asked to indicate on a five-point scale how important the attribute was in selecting a carrier, from 1 (highest importance) to 5 (lowest importance).

Source: Adapted from John L. Kent and R. Stephen Parker, "International Containership Carrier Selection Criteria: Shippers/Carriers Differences," *International Journal of Physical Distribution and Logistics Management* 29, no. 6 (1999), p. 403.

tion lies somewhere between the two extremes. It is rare that an organization does not at least respond to customer complaints about its mode or carriers; this is one form of postchoice evaluation. Many firms use other techniques, such as cost studies, audits, on-time pickup and delivery performance, and damage/claims reviews. Some will statistically analyze the quality of a host of carrier service attributes in an application of *statistical process control* (which we will discuss in Chapter 16).

Statistical Process Control

In some cases, these evaluative procedures may lead to the problem recognition stage if the mode or carrier is performing unsatisfactorily. Firms that primarily use private carriage also employ many of these procedures as part of their self-evaluation.

Obtaining Feedback

An integral part of the mode/carrier choice is obtaining feedback. Information feedback can come from sources other than performance measures. The decision environment external to the selection decision also provides input into the process, such as sales personnel feedback and interdepartmental communications.

The feedback can be used as input at any point in the process. Feedback is invaluable because it occurs concurrently and independently of other performance measures. Choosing a mode or carrier is a universal process, in that while the factors entering into the process may vary by geographic location or industry, the basic structure of the decision remains consistent.

Mode and carrier selection is becoming much more important as shippers move toward the core carrier concept and reduce the number of carriers with whom they do business. By leveraging freight volumes to get bigger discounts and higher levels of service, shippers are able to reduce their transportation costs. At the same time, carriers benefit by having to deal with fewer shippers, each shipping larger volumes of product consistently, over longer periods of time.

Square D Reduces Its Number of Carriers

Square D [an electrical equipment manufacturer] reports that [it] has successfully reduced the number of carriers it uses. Five years ago as many as 1,500 carriers were involved in moving company goods. Today, 55 handle 98 percent of the freight. The savings also have been substantial . . . The program saved $3.5 million in transportation costs when first implemented three years ago. Today, the company's annual transportation costs have stabilized at a three-year-old level, while the volume of freight moved steadily increases.[5]

Contracts.   The use of contracts between shippers and carriers has become widespread in the United States since transportation deregulation began to occur in the late 1970s. Since 1980, when the Staggers Rail Act took effect, tens of thousands of rail contracts have been filed. Similar increases in the use of shipper-carrier contracts have occurred in the ocean and motor transportation sectors.

Advantages of Shipper/Carrier Contracts

The advantages of contracting are numerous. A good contract is the foundation of a successful strategic partnership or alliance between a shipper and a carrier.[6] Contracts permit shippers to exercise greater control over their transportation. They help assure predictability and guard against fluctuation in rates. In addition, contracting provides the shipper with service level guarantees and allows the shipper to use transportation to gain competitive advantage.

PMI Food Equipment Benefits from the Use of Contracts

Since 1981, Ohio-based PMI Food Equipment has used contractual agreements with its LTL carriers to transport its products to more than 400 distributors throughout the United States.[7] The firm provides commercial dishwashing, cooking, and refrigeration products to the food service market. With a core carrier base of four companies, PMI spends approximately $21 million annually on transportation, of which $12 million is LTL freight. Carriers are guaranteed a specified level of revenue in exchange for meeting the firm's service requirements.

---

[5]Mitchell E. MacDonald, "Why Shippers Are Cutting Carriers," *Traffic Management* 29, no. 4 (April 1990), p. 49.

[6]Douglas K. Cooper, "Contracts: Cementing a Dedicated Relationship," *Private Carrier* 32, no. 9 (September 1995), pp. 16–20, 38.

[7]Deborah Catalano Ruriani, "Nothing Beats a Good Solid Contract," *Inbound Logistics* 16, no. 9 (September 1996), p. 28.

Carrier–shipper contracts can prove valuable to both parties, but it is important that the contract include all of the relevant elements that apply to the shipping agreement. In soliciting carriers for possible contracting, a standard bid package or request for proposal (RFP) should be developed that includes the following components:

Standard Bid Package for Soliciting Carriers

- *Commitment clause.* The shipper commits to a certain volume of freight, and the carrier commits to providing the equipment necessary to move that volume.
- *Metrics clause.* The parties should establish how performance will be measured.
- *Pricing.* How much will the logistics service provider charge? Will charges be per shipment, or will a flat fee be charged for the contract's duration?
- *Controlling law.* Which state's law will govern the contract if there is a dispute?
- *Description of services.* What services are to be performed by the various parties to the contract?
- *Tender of goods.* What constitutes delivery? What happens if the party receiving the goods refuses to accept the shipment?
- *Liability.* Who is responsible if goods are damaged during shipment?
- *Confidentiality.* A clause is needed to ensure that any information designated as confidential stays that way and is not shared with other shippers or providers.
- *Length.* How long will the relationship exist? What are the ramifications if one party wants to terminate the contract before it expires?[8]

The same components in the RFP should also form the basis of the contract that is ultimately negotiated between the shipper and carrier. Contracts are legal documents and therefore binding.

The exact format for each carrier–shipper contract will vary, depending on the mode and carrier involved, characteristics of the shipping firm, products to be transported, level of competition, and other factors.

Outsourcing Transportation.[9]   The outsourcing of various logistics services, including transportation, has been a common practice for many years, although the practice is occurring more widely today. It has been estimated that the total third-party market opportunity is approximately $450 billion, of which only $18–$20 billion has been tapped.[10] Of the total market, transportation outsourcing comprises approximately 80 percent.

Size of Third-Party Market Is Significant

Among the many reasons why shippers would outsource transportation are cost savings, revenue-enhancing potential, transportation not being a core competency, internal problems associated with administering the transportation function, and logistics reengineering or redesign.[11]

Why Shippers Outsource Transportation

---

[8]Steven E. Salkin, "Breaking Up Is Hard to Do," *Logistics Management and Distribution Report* 38, no. 4 (April 1999), p. 76.

[9]For a comprehensive overview of the outsourcing literature, see Mohammed Abdur Pedersen and Richard Gray, "Outsourcing of Logistics Functions: A Literature Survey," *International Journal of Physical Distribution and Logistics Management* 28, no. 2 (1998), pp. 89–107.

[10]*The Emergence of Third-Party Logistics,* White Paper no.4 (Atlanta, GA: PricewaterhouseCoopers, 1998), p. 3.

[11]Sandor Boyson, Thomas Corsi, Martin Dresner, and Elliot Rabinovich, "Managing Effective Third Party Logistics Relationships: What Does It Take?" *Journal of Business Logistics* 20, no. 1 (1999), p. 81.

In simple terms, the transportation outsourcing decision is a "make-or-buy" decision. Can a third party do the same job for less and provide the same, or perhaps better, customer service? With outsourcing expected to grow at 15–20 percent annually within the United States, many organizations have determined that third parties are viable transportation options. Box 9–1 describes Xerox Corporation's decision to outsource transportation to Ryder.

Private Carriage/Leasing.   A private carrier can be any transportation entity that moves products for a manufacturing or merchandising organization that owns it, although the vast majority of private carriage is truck transport. While the equipment may transport nonowned goods in some cases, private carriers have traditionally been established to haul the products of their own enterprises. In fact, prior to deregulation of the transportation industry during the 1980s, it was extremely difficult for private carriers to haul any products that were not owned by the organization.

Private carriage should be viewed not strictly as a transportation decision but also as a financial decision. There are two steps in evaluating the cost of private carriage. The first is to conduct a feasibility study comparing current cost and service data of the organization's for-hire carriers with that of a private operation, and the second is to devise a plan of implementation and a procedure for system control.

The feasibility study should begin with an evaluation of the current transportation situation, along with corporate objectives regarding potential market expansion. Objectives should include a statement outlining past, current, and desired service levels, as well as a consideration of the business environment, such as legal restrictions and the general economic trends. There are 10 steps that an organization should follow to fully evaluate the private carriage option. These steps are discussed below.[12]

1. *Define the problem.* Difficulties can originate from one or more members of the transportation system—customer, carrier, or shipper. Does the customer receive adequate service and undamaged goods on time and at a reasonable cost? Does the carrier have the required route flexibility and operational capability to deliver the product economically? Does volume prevent delivery of the desired service level at a competitive price? Do the carrier's equipment and facilities meet the requirements of the channel members? The problem may also originate in the seller's operation; facility and dock equipment may be overburdened or underutilized, the organization may be responsible for management and scheduling problems, or it may simply have a poor logistics system.

2. *Develop transport objectives.* These objectives should center on two measures. The first is the customer service level—consistent and fast delivery, as well as additional services that may be required. The second should focus on the organization's cost objectives for the total logistics process—order processing, communications, warehousing, inventory, transportation, and the return of damaged goods. The enterprise should establish goals for each of these functions in terms of both effectiveness and efficiency.

3. *Collect pertinent information.* This requires the gathering of data relevant to the parties involved: inventory data, shipping procedures, product characteristics, origin and destination, volume and weight, and cost associated with the shipment of the products.

Most Private Carriage Is Via Truck

Private Carriage Is a Financial Decision

Cost and Service Objectives

---

[12]Private carriage has been a transportation option for many years, both before and after deregulation. An early published source document that outlines the steps in evaluating the private carriage option, which is still valid today, is Barrie Vreeland, *Private Carriage from A to Z* (New York: Commerce and Industry Association Institute, 1968), p. 6.

Box 9–1

A Case Study in Outsourcing: Ryder/Xerox

The Ryder/Xerox relationship began about 20 years ago when Ryder began to handle the delivery of Xerox products to customers. Under this original arrangement, Ryder managed 10 of Xerox's distribution centers, prepped the machines for the customer, delivered the machines to the customer, and removed old machines. This original business arrangement with Xerox generated about $12 million to $15 million in annual revenue for Ryder.

Ryder's relationship with Xerox began to significantly expand in the 1990s coincident with the trend of corporations implementing more sophisticated supply chain management strategies. In 1993, Xerox's Webster, New York, manufacturing facility had an inbound logistics system that was complex and inefficient. Webster was using in excess of 40 common less-than-truckload (LTL) and truckload carriers. Costs were high and customer requirements were not being met. Often, long queues of trucks would be idling on the Webster complex, waiting to be unloaded.

Following an internal assessment, Xerox decided supply chain logistics was not a core competency and decided to outsource Webster's inbound logistics. Xerox sent out requests for quotes (RFQs) to a number of 3PLs, including Ryder, to manage Webster's inbound logistics needs. Ryder was awarded the contract following a competitive bid process and subsequently designed a logistics system to support just-in-time inbound material management for the Webster facility. Ryder began operating this network in 1994 with guarantees to Xerox regarding time, cost, and continual improvements. Cost savings beyond a certain level are shared between Ryder and Xerox.

Clusters of Xerox suppliers are serviced by strategically located driver and equipment domiciles that operate closed loop routes to pick up components from these suppliers. Trailers are then hauled by Ryder tractors to the Ryder Logistics Center in Webster—a "relay" that is both fast and efficient. Components from remote suppliers arrive on LTL common carriers managed by Ryder. Similarly, Ryder schedules full-truckload common carrier shipments, just in time, directly to the appropriate receiving door within the Xerox complex.

Components from Pacific Rim countries arrive via sea container at the Port of Vancouver, then travel by rail across Canada. Xerox relies on Fritz Companies, Inc., to handle the coordination of the import/export process. At a railhead in Toronto, the containers are transferred to Ryder trucks for their trip through customs to the Logistics Center. Xerox manufacturing facilities in Canada also ship components to

the Center on Ryder-managed trucks. Likewise, sea container freight from Europe arrives at the Port of New York/New Jersey and is transported by Ryder trucks or Ryder-managed common carriers to the Logistics Center.

The "heart" of the inbound logistics system is the Logistics Center, located just one mile from the Webster complex. Here, Ryder professionals manage the system, monitor system performance and make adjustments and improvements. The Center also serves as a "cross dock" and reconfigures inbound loads into outbound shipments that go to the right receiving docks in the vast Xerox manufacturing complex, just in time.

Following the implementation of Ryder's logistics operation, Xerox has experienced a variety of improvements. Webster now receives fewer deliveries, eliminating tractor gridlock on the Webster campus while enabling Xerox to balance the workload of its receiving department. Delivery predictability has increased substantially, reducing internal fluctuations and improving on-time customer deliveries. Overall, Ryder's system has reduced inventory levels, reduced order cycle times, improved quality, and better synchronized supply chain flow between inbound freight and the manufacturing process, all resulting in lower costs and better service to Xerox. Following the initial realization of efficiency enhancements, Ryder has successfully demonstrated continuous year-over-year productivity improvement for Xerox through continuous system re-engineering.

Ryder's relationship with Xerox has continued to expand. In 1996, Ryder received another piece of business from Xerox, managing finished product, spare parts, and consumable distribution to serve customer delivery centers. In the summer of 1998, Ryder began to operate 20 high-velocity Xerox parts centers throughout the United States. Ryder now operates 38 different projects with Xerox that collectively generate about $60 million of business for Ryder. Ryder is also involved in Xerox's product development process to help it determine total landed cost of a potential product, including logistics costs. Ryder and Xerox continue to work together to determine new opportunities for supply chain improvement and Ryder expects to continue to gain share of Xerox's estimated $1 billion annual logistics budget.

Source: Gregory P. Konezny and Martin J. Beskow, *Third-Party Logistics: Improving Global Supply Chain Performance* (Minneapolis, MN: Piper Jaffray, Inc., January 1999), pp. 24–25. Reprinted by permission of U.S. Bancorp Piper Jaffray, Inc.

Management should take the customer's viewpoint when evaluating customer complaints, quantifiable service level data, and competitors' actions.

4. *Determine present cost.* It is necessary to use a total cost approach that not only determines the cost of transportation but also encompasses the total logistics network. The determination of operating costs should include the cost of order processing, packaging, shipping, transportation, and damaged goods and returns. In addition, the current cost of inventory investment, insurance, taxes, inventory risk, and building cost directly associated with the inventory function should be included. The determination of these current costs will serve as the point of comparison with the private carriage option and other possible alternatives.

Review Quantitative and Qualitative Data

5. *Analyze present operations.* The analysis of present operations includes the review of both the qualitative and quantitative data the organization has gathered in the attempt to uncover poor cost/service relationships. This step includes analysis of customer order patterns, transportation patterns, cyclical or seasonal variations, and potential for backhauls. Also included are evaluation of ton-mile cost and review of specific transportation costs that exceed standard.

6. *Develop alternatives.* This step begins with a review of cost service levels of functions in which problems have been identified; management then makes suggestions

Three Basic Alternatives

of alternative courses of action to solve those problems. Three basic alternatives are almost always available in this process: (1) do nothing, (2) invest the available capital in other areas of the organization that may yield an even higher return, or (3) use funds to improve the current system.

The improvement of distribution operations need not include implementation of a private carriage operation. Instead, the organization may make adjustments, such as improving order processing, negotiating new carrier rates, or improving packaging—all of which may yield the same benefits as private trucking or leasing, but at a much lower cost.

7. *Determine private fleet cost.* The organization should account for all costs associated with private carriage, as well as the effects these costs will have on the firm's total costs.[13] Any added savings or costs generated in inventory, personnel, or production because of the use of private carriage should be added to or deducted from the cost of this alternative. Costs for the private carriage function include equipment, labor, and other expenses such as maintenance, insurance, and vehicle taxes.

8. *Consider indirect factors.* Many nonmonetary factors may influence the decision to switch to a private carriage operation, including company image; competition; the advertising value of the vehicles; effects on employees and unions; management skills required to develop and control the system; carriers' willingness to accept remaining freight; potential for rate renegotiations; and corporate policies regarding equipment selection, maintenance, and replacement. A wide range of factors not under the firm's control, such as the legal, economic, and technical environments, must also be considered.

9. *Summarize alternatives.* The summary should outline the cost, capital requirements, and indirect factors (advantages and disadvantages) for (1) the present method, (2) an alternative method that would not be a major change from the existing operation but would be an improvement, and (3) a private carriage operation.

---

[13]For an interesting discussion on how Playtex Family Products Co. examined the costs of its private carriage operation, see Lisa H. Harrington, "How to Get the Most from Your Private Fleet Dollar," *Traffic Management* 30, no. 1 (January 1991), pp. 39–43.

10. *Make the decision.* The final step is to make a decision based on the summary as well as on other inputs from sources such as internal management, outside experts, and the experience of other firms that have had private carriage operations. Despite the quantitative information available, no decision can be cut and dried. A large number of factors depend on the decision maker's willingness to assume some level of risk.

In our discussion of the transportation selection decision, we saw that an organization must perform a cost/benefit analysis to determine whether it should use private carriage. Any financial analysis should consider the time value of money. Table 9–5 illustrates the analysis of cash flows that must be performed.

Cash Flow Considerations

The organization must calculate the net cash inflows (cash inflows minus cash outflows) for the life of the investment decision and discount them using the enterprise's minimum acceptable rate of return on new investment. The sum of these discounted cash flows must be compared to the initial capital requirement to determine whether the investment is financially sound.

Implementation and Control

If the organization makes the decision to engage in private carriage, its next step is to devise a plan of implementation and a procedure for system control. Implementation begins with a review of the structure of the organization or group responsible for operating the private fleet. Management assigns the activities to be performed to groups or

TABLE 9–5   Financial Considerations in the Decision to Switch to Private Carriage

	Amount
Capital Requirements	
Cost of buying or leasing fleet	_____
Cost of maintenance facilities	_____
Cost of terminal facilities	_____
Annual Cash Inflows	
Savings over using public carriers	_____
Reduction in lost sales	_____
Reduction in inventory carrying costs due to more efficient routing	_____
Total	_____
Annual Cash Outflows	
Fuel	_____
Labor—drivers	_____
Labor—maintenance and terminal	_____
Insurance—trucks	_____
—drivers	_____
—maintenance and terminal facilities	_____
License fees	_____
Parts supply	_____
Utilities	_____
Supervision	_____
Administrative—billing, telephone, accounting	_____
Total	_____
Annual cash inflows – Annual cash outflows	_____

individuals, and formulates a timetable for phasing in the project. Because of the risk involved, most organizations begin with a low level of activity, followed by intermediate reviews of results and subsequent modification of the plan. The process is repeated until full implementation is achieved.

Measuring Performance against Standards

Control of private carriage should center on measuring performance against standards, with the ability to identify specific problem areas. If management desires to use a total cost approach in order to charge cost against the product and customer, it can calculate a cost per mile, identifying the fixed cost associated with distribution of the product, and then adding the variable cost per mile. This information may also be useful to compare budgeted to actual expenditures, or to compare the private carriage operation to common carrier statistics and industry averages. The information generated is limited, however, due to the wide variations of cost and service requirements across industries and organizations.

Leasing

The leasing of equipment and/or personnel (e.g., drivers) is an important consideration in private carriage. Leasing provides ease of entry and predictable cost and service levels. In contracting for the use of a full-service fleet, even inexperienced managers can know the exact cost for transportation services, and can budget accordingly.

Other advantages of leasing include the ability to adjust vehicle resources for business cycles and seasonality through special lease agreements. Also, if the fleet is to be small, the organization will avoid investing in maintenance equipment and facilities. Another consideration is transportation obsolescence. New technology may render older vehicles obsolete, or the organization may outgrow its distribution and transportation system. Many companies are available that provide leased equipment, including Ryder, Penske Truck Leasing, and Rollins Leasing.

Whirlpool's Quality Express Program

As an example, Penske, a truck leasing company that operates over 115,000 trucks serving approximately 4,000 locations in the United States, provides vehicles to Whirlpool Corporation as part of the "Quality Express" program used by Whirlpool to distribute its products throughout the United States. The program includes eight regional distribution centers, 54 local distribution centers, a private fleet of 450 truck tractors and 1,200 trailers, and approximately 1,500 employees.[14]

Private fleet ownership may be preferable if capital is available and if it can be shown that vehicle investment will yield a favorable return. Other advantages might include the ability to buy needed equipment at a discount cost through reciprocity, the use of currently owned maintenance equipment and facilities, increased flexibility and freedom of use, and a potential to provide special customer services that a lessor would not allow.

Leasing Options

Another form of leasing occurs when the shipper either acquires both drivers and equipment from others or leases its drivers and equipment to a for-hire carrier. Organizations can "single-source lease" and "trip lease." These options promise to expand the flexibility of shippers with private fleets and to provide additional opportunities to reduce operating costs. The two leasing options can be defined as follows:

Single-source leasing: An arrangement under which a private carrier acquires both drivers and equipment from a single source for at least 30 days.

Trip leasing: An arrangement under which a private carrier leases its drivers and equipment to a for-hire carrier for a period of fewer than 30 days.

---

[14]News release from Penske Truck Leasing, December 21, 1998.

Third-Party Equity Loans

A third alternative form of equipment acquisition, and one that is particularly appealing from a cash flow viewpoint, involves *third-party equity loans* from a financial institution that include a "guaranteed buy-back" from the dealer at the termination of the useful life of the equipment. This type of lease is fairly common in the acquisition of computer equipment. Under this approach, monthly payments cover interest on the entire purchase price but only an amount of principal equal to the difference between the purchase price and the guaranteed buy-back. This significantly reduces an organization's cash flow outlays and results in lower interest rates if the enterprise has established a high credit rating with its financial institutions. By using this technique, a national clothing retailer was able to save over $250,000 in interest charges on a three-year equity loan for 22 truck tractors. In addition, the company minimized its risk by obtaining buy-back guarantees from the selected dealer equal to 58 percent of the purchase price of each tractor.[15]

Private carriage can hold tremendous promise for those shippers able to take advantage of its benefits. For others, for-hire carriers (common and contract) offer the most opportunities.

Partnerships/Alliances.   An effective logistics network requires a cooperative relationship between shippers and carriers. True strategic relationships between shippers and carriers are extremely rare. When such cooperation takes place, the shipper and carrier become part of a partnership or alliance. Companies that have implemented the concept include Black & Decker, GTE, IBM, Procter & Gamble, McKesson, Saturn, Xerox, and 3M.

Saturn and Ryder Form a Partnership

Saturn Corporation has a "world-class" production operation that is supported by truck distribution from Ryder Dedicated Logistics. "Under a fixed price contract, Ryder leverages its route-planning and vehicle-tracking skills to meet 15-minute delivery windows at Saturn's just-in-time (JIT) manufacturing facility."[16] Partly as a result of that partnership, Saturn has achieved 300 inventory turns annually.

Shipper–Carrier Partnerships at 3M

One company that has been long recognized for developing high-quality relationships with transportation carriers has been 3M Corporation. Continuing a shipper–carrier partnership program that began in the early 1980s, 3M has been able to realize significant benefits, including:

- Use of fewer carriers/suppliers—a reduction in the number of carriers used from more than 1,200 to fewer than 30.
- Reduction of transportation costs by almost 10 percent.
- Improvement in on-time delivery performance to approximately 98 percent.
- Reduction in freight claim amounts by 20 percent.
- Increase in productivity of 50 percent.

Steps in Establishing a Business Alliance

Establishing a business alliance is a process. As a general guideline, the process has three phases, consisting of eight steps or stages.[17] Figure 9–3 shows the phases and steps in logistics alliance formation.

---

[15]Material on third-party equity loans was obtained from Professor Jay U. Sterling, University of Alabama, and former director of distribution for The Limited Stores, Inc.

[16]A. T. Kearney, Inc., *Converging Technologies and Value Creation,* Position Paper No. 97-3 (1997), p. 4.

[17]Prabir K. Bagchi and Helge Virum, "Logistical Alliances: Trends and Prospects in Integrated Europe," *Journal of Business Logistics* 19, no. 1 (1998), pp. 205–8.

Figure 9–3

Steps in logistics alliance formation

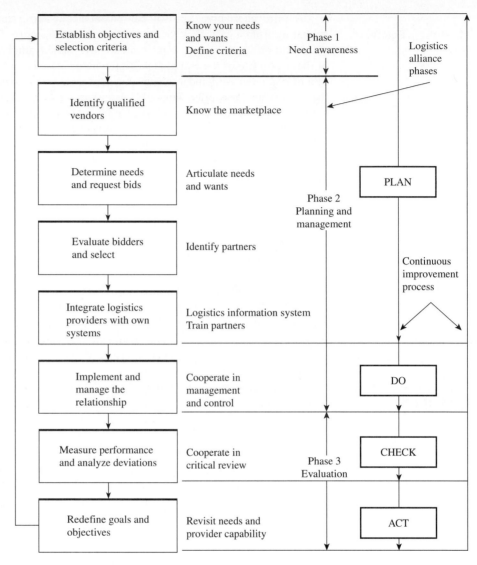

Source: Prabir K. Bagchi and Helge Virum, "Logistical Alliances: Trends and Prospects in Integrated Europe," *Journal of Business Logistics* 19, no. 1 (1998), p. 209.

In too many instances, shippers and carriers do not act in concert because of differences in perceptions, practice, or philosophy. Sometimes the notion "We never did it that way before" impedes cooperation and synergy. Such differences result in inefficiencies in the transportation system and conflicts between shippers and carriers.

"Partnershipping" Is a Philosophy

In essence, a successful partnership or alliance is more than just a set of plans, programs, and methods. Like the marketing concept, "partnershipping" is a philosophy that permeates an entire organization. It is a way of life that becomes part of the way a firm conducts its business. A model that can be used by management to determine when a partnership is appropriate and, if so, how it should be structured, is presented in Chapter 12 (pp. 508-512).

Carrier Perspectives

Core Carrier Concept

Pricing/Negotiation Issues.   Over the past two decades, shippers have tended to use fewer carriers, moving toward what has been termed the *core carrier concept.* As shippers have reduced the number of carriers they use, they have placed greater emphasis on negotiated pricing. Prior to deregulation of transportation in the United States, rate negotiations typically occurred only when contract carriage was being used. Today, most rates are the result of direct negotiation between carriers and shippers.[18]

Many contracts are developed as a result of a bidding process, which is a "structured method of negotiating the service–price agreement between shipper and carrier. A successful bid can form the basis for establishing a long-term working relationship."[19]

The issues identified in the previous discussion of contracts from the shipper's perspective would be included in the bid and negotiation processes. The negotiation process is a symbiotic one between carrier and shipper, and requires that carriers have fairly precise measures of their costs.

Cost Issues

There are three general types of costs that need to be considered:

1. *Fully allocated costs,* which include all costs involved in the movement or transport of a shipment.
2. *Semivariable costs,* which include all costs involved in the movement or transport of a shipment, except overhead-related expenses.
3. *Out-of-pocket costs,* which include only those costs requiring an actual expenditure of money to perform the movement or transport of a shipment.

Before negotiations begin, carriers need to establish their costs for providing specific types and levels of services. Since many negotiations are based on a "cost-plus" approach, knowing the cost base is imperative. It also allows carriers and shippers to work together in an effort to reduce that carrier's cost base. Many carriers are introducing or considering some very innovative pricing programs. For example, CSX Intermodal (CSXI) introduced a pricing program for new customers. First-time intermodal shippers were given a 10 percent savings over comparable motor carrier rates. Begun in the early 1990s, the CSXI program exceeded company expectations in terms of market response.[20]

Pricing at CSX Intermodal

Every pricing approach must be developed based on a thorough knowledge of the carrier's costs and the shipper's needs. Pricing today must be creative; that is, traditional approaches may not be appropriate. Pricing also will require cooperation between carriers and shippers.

Routing and Scheduling.   Considering the significant capital investments in equipment and facilities, along with operating expenses, carriers have long recognized the importance of good routing and scheduling in achieving acceptable levels of company profit and customer service. Because of the complexity of the routing and scheduling process when many transportation vehicles, customers, and routing combinations exist, computer models are often used to determine optimal routes and schedules.[21]

---

[18]For a managerial discussion of shipper–carrier negotiation issues, see Joseph V. Barks, "Who's Getting a Bad Deal?" *Distribution* 93, no. 3 (March 1994), pp. 34–38; and Roger J. Bowman, "Risk and Reward: How Shippers Are Negotiating the Best Possible Transportation Deals in a Time of Radical Change," *Distribution* 95, no. 4 (April 1996), pp. 42–49.

[19]Presentation by Jim Bowers, Pricing Systems & Publications Manager, Watkins Motor Lines, Inc., to the Central Florida Roundtable of the Council of Logistics Management, 1999.

[20]"CSXI Offering 10% Rate Reductions for New Customers," *On Track* 5, no. 5 (March 20, 1991), p. 4.

[21]For an example of a computerized routing and scheduling solution, see Tzong-Ru Lee and Ji-Hwa Ueng, "A Study of Vehicle Routing Problems with Load-Balancing," *International Journal of Physical Distribution and Logistics Management* 29, no. 10 (1999), pp. 646–58.

Benefits of Good
Routing and Scheduling

What can happen in a firm when good routing and scheduling decisions are made? Carriers, as well as companies operating private truck fleets, can achieve sizable benefits. For example, by prescheduling shipments into specific market areas, while simultaneously reducing the frequency of delivery, a vehicle's load factor[22] can be increased. The result is a cost saving to the carrier. A reduction in the frequency of pickups and deliveries can result in a reduction in the amount of transportation required to deliver the same amount of goods. Thus, the cost of transportation is reduced and productivity is increased.[23]

Other examples include the use of fixed routes instead of variable routes for some shipments, and changing customer delivery hours. If customers can accept shipments at off-peak hours, the carrier will have a larger delivery-time window, and thus can improve vehicle use and reduce equipment costs per delivery.[24]

In general, the benefits to a carrier of improved routing and scheduling include greater vehicle use, improved customer service, lower transportation expenses, reduced capital investment in equipment, and better decision-making capability. As an example, Baskin-Robbins, an ice-cream manufacturer with 2,500 stores in the United States, computerized its fleet routing and scheduling. The result was a 10 percent reduction in truck fleet miles, equaling an annual cost saving of $180,000.[25]

Baskin-Robbins
Computerizes
Its Routing
and Scheduling

Service Offerings.   One of the fundamental changes that have occurred in transportation has been the collaboration between carriers and shippers in developing a broad array of services tailored to the specific needs of shippers.

In the traditional areas of pickup and delivery, claims, equipment availability, time-in-transit, and consistency of service, competitive market pressures have necessitated improved service levels and consistency. Carriers have had to develop customer service packages that meet the needs of increasingly demanding customers. Such improvements have benefited shippers and have made it even more necessary for carriers to maximize efficiency and productivity levels in order to remain competitive and profitable.

Examples of carriers providing higher levels of traditional transportation services can be found in all modes. A. P. Moller-Maersk Line and Sea-Land Service Inc. (two international ocean marine transporters) began a vessel-sharing plan for the purpose of improving service levels. Some 50 vessels were being shared in the Pacific and Intra-Asia shipping trade lanes. The plan reduced the number of ships deployed and increased the number of transpacific sailings to five per week. At the same time, Maersk and Sea-Land continued to compete against each other.[26]

Formation of Maersk
Sealand

The relationship developed into an operating alliance in 1995. In late 1999, Maersk acquired the international business of Sea-Land and formed a new company, Maersk Sealand. Overnight, this new company became the largest U.S.-flag vessel operator,

---

[22]*Load factor* is defined as the amount (as a percentage) of the utilized space in a transport vehicle in relation to the total amount of available space. In general, a high load factor indicates that the transport vehicle is being used efficiently and effectively.

[23]A. T. Kearney, Inc., *Measuring and Improving Productivity in Physical Distribution Management* (Chicago: National Council of Physical Distribution Management, 1984), pp. 176, 178.

[24]Ibid., p. 182.

[25]"Routing Software Prevents Scheduling Meltdown," *Logistics Management* 35, no. 6 (June 1996), p. 85-S.

[26]Elizabeth Canna, "The Maersk/Sea-Land Deal," *American Shipper* 33, no. 5 (May 1991), p. 43.

controlling an estimated 12 percent of the world market, with more than 250 vessels and 500,000 containers.[27]

Nontraditional Services

Carriers have begun expanding into nontraditional areas such as warehousing, logistics consulting, import/export operations, and facility location analysis. In effect, the transportation carrier becomes a logistics service provider. For example, CSX Corporation, with over $10 billion in annual revenues, offers one-stop shipping that includes trains, trucks, barges, ocean containers, intermodal services, and distribution warehouses. Some of the operating companies of CSX include CSX Transportation (rail), CSX Intermodal (rail/truck), Customized Transportation (contract logistics), and American Commercial Lines (barge) in which the company owns a minority share. During 1999, the company expanded its operations significantly with the acquisition of a portion of another larger railroad, Conrail.[28]

Carriers Are Expanding Service Offerings

The trend is likely to continue, with carriers expanding their traditional and nontraditional service offerings to become, in effect, logistics service providers. In addition, competitive pressures will force overall carrier service levels to improve.

Competition.   Since economic deregulation of the U.S. transportation industry began in the late 1970s, carrier management has faced an environment characterized by increasing levels of competition. Greater freedom of entry into the marketplace has been one of the most significant results of deregulation legislation, bringing with it sizable increases in the number of competitors in most transport modes.

Competition Has Increased

Competition has also increased between transport modes. The ability of carriers from the various modes to price their services more flexibly, and to offer a greater number and variety of services, has created a much more competitive environment. Intermodal competition, especially between air-motor and motor-rail, has increased and is likely to become more intense.

Competitors are also much stronger than in the past. As a result of intramode mergers (e.g., the CSX–Conrail merger) and good marketing practices, many large regional and national carriers have emerged, primarily in the rail, motor, and airline industries, and have become market leaders in their respective target markets.

Air Carriers and E-Commerce

Additionally, the increases in Internet shopping and e-commerce have expanded global shipping opportunities for air carriers, which will likely result in a competitive advantage for air over ocean carriers. It has been estimated that one-third of the potential global e-commerce market is outside of North America, translating into a market of over $100 billion. During the year 2000, DHL Worldwide Express, FedEx, and UPS introduced technology targeted at serving the delivery needs of international e-commerce shippers.[29]

Carriers Discover Marketing

Marketing Activities.   Carriers have recognized the need to place greater emphasis on marketing, rather than purely selling, activities. Many factors have contributed to that realization, including economic deregulation, technology improvements, carrier mergers and acquisitions, increasing use of outsourcing, and higher levels of competition.

Transportation carriers in all modes have developed marketing goals, objectives, strategies, and tactics. The more successful carriers are those that have refocused

---

[27]Chris Gillis and Philip Damas, "Maersk Sealand: After the Deal," *American Shipper* 42, no. 2 (February 2000), pp. 52–58.

[28]CSX Corporation, 1999 annual report <http://www.csx.com>.

[29]Gordon Forsyth, "Uncovering Cost," *American Shipper* 42, no. 2 (February 2000), p. 24.

themselves from sales-oriented to marketing-oriented organizations. The former react to customer requests, while the latter anticipate customer needs. Sales-oriented carriers focus primarily on the transportation services they perform, with little attempt to integrate their activities with their customers' total distribution operations. Marketing-oriented carriers view themselves as partners in their customers' total logistics activities.

Market Segmentation   Many of the marketing-oriented carrier firms have developed market segmentation strategies that have permitted them to grow in size and profitability in the face of increased competition. A typical approach has been to segment markets by geographic location. Other approaches have included segmenting markets based on the level of service desired by customers. Much like price elasticity of demand, where the quantity demanded varies by price,[30] there is also service elasticity. The demand from carrier services has been shown to vary according to the level and scope of transportation services provided.

Carrier marketing activities will continue to gain importance, due in part to the structural changes that have taken place in the marketplace. Opportunities for higher carrier profits and market shares exist, but only for those firms that develop customer-focused programs. At the same time, carriers have to train their salespeople to sell "value-added" services, an approach to selling that differs from traditional carrier sales strategies.

Transportation Productivity

Both shippers and carriers are concerned with reducing costs and improving transportation productivity. Cost improvements can arise from a number of tactical or strategic improvements, including the following:

Cost Improvement Opportunities

Tactical Opportunities

- Understand current rates and leverage lower cost carriers that provide a consistent level of service.
- Ensure that your rates are under contract and that they are competitively priced.
- Ensure that you have a core carrier program.
- Control your inbound freight.
- Monitor carrier performance.
- Eliminate your freight bill audit function.

Strategic Opportunities

- Investigate the use of automated load planning tools.
- Integrate freight rates and transit times with order entry.
- Provide a transportation resource to the procurement function.
- Review the business case of maintaining your private fleet.
- Identify opportunities where you can work with your carriers to reduce their cost to serve you.[31]

---

[30]*Price elasticity of demand* is defined as the ratio of the relative change in quantity to the relative change in price. A price elasticity of greater than 1 means that sales increase (decrease) by more than price decreases (increases) in percentage terms. Elasticity of less than 1 means that sales increase (decrease) by less than the price decreases (increases) in percentage terms.

[31]*Transportation Management,* document published by PricewaterhouseCoopers LLP (1999), unnumbered.

Productivity improvements are absolutely vital to the success of any logistics system and can come from doing things right (i.e., efficiency) and doing the right things (i.e., effectiveness). It is primarily through improved effectiveness that shippers and carriers can achieve significant productivity gains.

**Productivity
Improvement
Opportunities**

Productivity improvements can be categorized into three groups:

1. Improvements in the transportation system's *design* and its methods, equipment, and procedures (e.g., inbound consolidation, company-operated over-the-road trucking, local pickup and delivery operations, and purchased for-hire transportation).

2. Improvements in the *use* of labor and equipment (e.g., breakbulk operations, backhaul use of fleet, routing and scheduling systems, tracing and monitoring systems, customer delivery hours, shipment consolidation/pooling, and driver use).

3. Improvements in the *performance* of labor and equipment (e.g., standards for driver activity, first-line management improvements, establishment of a transportation database, incentive compensation to encourage higher productivity and safety, and programs to increase fuel efficiency).[32]

**Measuring Carrier
Effectiveness**

From a shipper's perspective, data that measure carrier effectiveness and efficiency include claims and/or damage ratios, transit time variability, on-time pickup and delivery percentages, cost per ton-mile, billing accuracy, and customer complaint frequency. In many organizations, the data do not appear on a formal report, and therefore carrier performance is examined informally.

Carriers employ similar measures, although they view them from the perspective of a provider rather than a receiver of services. Additionally, some carriers measure monetary contributions by traffic lane, shipper, salesperson, or terminal. Those measures are used primarily for internal performance evaluations but may be provided to customers in special situations, such as in rate negotiations or partnership arrangements. The exact format for data collection is not as important as the need to have the information available in some form. According to A. T. Kearney, Inc.:

> Transportation measurement has evolved almost on a company-by-company basis . . . [Figure 9–4] displays a schematic representation of the evolution of effectiveness measurement. This evolutionary process may be viewed as occurring in four separate stages.

**Stages in Productivity
Measurement**

> Stage I is the development and use of raw data in terms of dollars. Characteristic of these data is that they are usually provided by some other functional area (e.g., sales or finance); [they are] usually financial in nature; and the time increment measured is relatively long (e.g., monthly or quarterly). At this stage, these cost data are often compared to some type of macro output such as dollar sales. Thus, a common Stage I measure might be total transportation costs as a percent of sales. Typically, outbound transportation is measured first. Only more sophisticated companies were found to be effectively capturing information about inbound freight costs and flows.
>
> In Stage II, physical measures and activity budgets are introduced for transportation activities. Units such as weight, stops, orders, miles, etc., are tracked within the transportation activities over shorter time intervals, such as days or weeks. At this point, these physical units can be measured against transportation labor and non-labor costs to track cost per pound, per mile, per stop, or per ton-mile. The introduction of time-phased activity budgets is now possible with this information.

---

[32]A. T. Kearney, Inc., *Measuring and Improving Productivity,* pp. 174–85.

FIGURE 9–4

Evolution of transportation productivity measurement

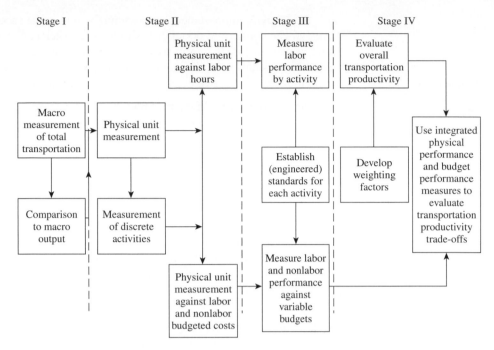

Source: A. T. Kearney, Inc., *Measuring and Improving Productivity in Physical Distribution* (Oak Brook, IL: National Council of Physical Distribution Management, 1984), p. 173.

Stage III begins with the establishment of empirical or historical "goals" for the overall transportation operation. These goals could be in the form of physical units or period operational cost, but in either case can now lead to the measurement of performance (actual versus standard) . . . The development of industrial engineered standards for labor and nonlabor inputs by activity is usually the next step in further sophistication. Transportation requirements can then be converted to standard hours of work, vehicle loads, or dollars of cost, for instance. This development leads to performance measurement of labor, and nonlabor inputs by activity against variable (i.e., volume-related) budgets. Included here would be actual versus budgeted cost analyses as well as variance analyses highlighting the reasons for budgetary variance (e.g., standard versus actual unit cost, standard versus actual output).

Stage IV is the last step in the development of a productivity measurement system. In Stage IV, physical performance data are merged with financial data to provide management with an overall view of the transportation operation. Armed with this type of measurement system, management is in a position to control ongoing operations as well as to test alternatives and seek trade-offs to present operations.[33]

Productivity measurement allows decision makers to plan, implement, and control components of their transportation networks better. Many of the significant results have been the direct result of computer technology.

---

[33]Ibid. pp. 171–72, 174.

Technology Issues

Electronic commerce (e-commerce) and computer usage have become widespread in logistics, especially in the area of traffic management. For example, companies use the Internet for communicating by e-mail, tracking and tracing shipments, obtaining industry and carrier news and information, and conducting database searches.[34] It has been estimated that up to 50 percent of all transactions between carriers and their customers are handled over the Internet.[35] Some specific uses of electronic technology include the following:

Uses of Electronic Technology in Transportation

- The National Transportation Exchange (NTE) has a website that identifies and sells unused trucking volume to its subscribers. Carrier members include contract carriers, dedicated carriers, and private fleet operators. Shippers include all manufacturing categories.[36]

- An Internet shipping database (www.compairdata.com) allows companies to compare global shipping services to and from selected ports. Targets of the Web-based subscription service include exporters, importers, forwarders, non-vessel-operating common carriers, ports, and shipping lines that require comparative, detailed information on international ocean liner services.[37]

- Emery Worldwide, an international air cargo carrier, established a service with SkyTel Communications that allowed shipment tracking using SkyTel's SkyWriter messaging service. Up to 30 shipments can be tracked using the shipment number, shipper reference number, or consignee reference number.[38]

- Schneider Logistics installed its SUMIT (Schneider's Utility for Managing Integrated Transportation) system at various General Motors Service Parts Organization locations to track parts throughout the supply chain. In combination with a parts delivery program that made daily deliveries to each location, the program decreased freight expenses by 25 percent, cut order cycle times in half, and reduced inventory levels.[39]

- RPS Inc., a subsidiary of FDX Corp., has a software package called Custom-CLEAR, which enables exporters to store international shipping data electronically and generate corresponding documents.[40]

- The U.S. Department of Transportation has an Internet library site (http://ntl.bts.gov/tris) that contains the world's largest bibliographic database on transportation.[41]

---

[34]Steve Salkin, "Back to Basics," *Logistics Management and Distribution Report* 38, no. 4 (April 1999), p. 99.

[35]Scott Moscrip, "What's It to Me? Internet Expertise Boosts Fleet Efficiency—And Job Security," *Business Trucking* 37, no. 10 (October 1999), p. 35.

[36]"Up Front," *Logistics Management and Distribution Report* 38, no. 3 (March 1999), p. 3.

[37]"Compare Global Shipping Services on the Internet," *American Shipper* 41, no. 4 (April 1999), p. 4.

[38]Peter Bradley, "Carriers Serve Up New Menu Choices," *Logistics Management and Distribution Report* 37, no. 11 (November 1998), p. 78.

[39]A. T. Kearney, Inc., *Converging Technologies and Value Creation,* p. 2.

[40]"RPS Introduces International Shipping Software," *Logistics Management and Distribution Report* 38, no. 4 (April 1999), p. 97.

[41]"DOT Announces New Internet Library Site," *National Industrial Transportation League Notice* 64 (January 14, 2000), p. 2.

- During the 1990s, UPS invested more than $1 billion per year in technology that would allow the company to better connect electronically with customers.[42]

Four Types of Transportation Software

Generally, computerized transportation activities can be categorized into four groups: transportation analysis, traffic routing and scheduling, freight rate maintenance and auditing, and vehicle maintenance. Andersen Consulting has conducted an annual survey of computer software for logistics for two decades and has described the four general groups as follows:

1. *Transportation analysis.* This software allows management to monitor costs and service by providing historical reporting of key performance indicators such as carrier performance, shipping modes, traffic lane use, premium freight usage, and backhauls.

2. *Traffic routing and scheduling.* Software in this area provides features such as the sequence and timing of vehicle stops, route determinations, shipping paperwork preparation, and vehicle availability.

3. *Freight rate maintenance and auditing.* These software systems maintain a database of freight rates used to rate shipments or to perform freight bill auditing. They compare actual freight bills with charges computed from the lowest applicable rates in the database. The systems can then pay, authorize payment, or report on exceptions.

4. *Vehicle maintenance.* Features commonly provided by these packages include vehicle maintenance scheduling and reporting.[43]

On some occasions, organizations will use transportation management systems (TMSs). These software systems, which determine the optimal methods to move products to final customers, work as follows: "The TMS receives orders from an order management system (OMS), then confirms shipping dates required to meet delivery promises, checks rates, assigns carriers and establishes pick-up and delivery schedules before releasing orders to the warehouse management system (WMS) for processing. Once orders have been processed and are ready to be shipped, the TMS manages the delivery and freight payment process."[44]

Pamida Holdings Uses Computerized Systems

Pamida Holdings, a general merchandise retailer with stores in 15 states, implemented a computerized transportation management system for its inbound and outbound routing and scheduling. The six-figure expenditure was recouped within the first 90 days following implementation.[45]

Supply Chain Management Software

In a study of chief information officers and chief financial officers of some of the nation's largest transportation and logistics service providers, KPMG, an international accounting, tax, and consulting firm, found that more than half of all firms planned to invest in supply chain management (SCM) software. Specifically within transportation, the areas where future software investment were likely to occur included air (cargo tracking, crew scheduling, supply chain planning, flight scheduling); marine (vessel

---

[42]Troy J. Strader, "Electronic Commerce in the Transportation Industry," *Transportation Trends* 1, no. 3 (September 1999), p. 7.

[43] Richard C. Haverly and James F. Whelan, *Logistics Software* (New York: Andersen Consulting, 1996), p. 9.

[44]"Glossary of Supply Chain Terms," *Supply Chain Yearbook 2000* (Winter 2000), p. 76.

[45]Deborah Catalano Ruriani, "Pamida's Big Payoff," *Inbound Logistics* 16, no. 8 (August 1996), pp. 32–35.

and land transport scheduling, shipment tracing/scanning); rail (car and locomotive fleet management); and motor (order entry and management).[46]

The level of computer technology use will vary between and within organizations. Despite such variations, it is clear that the use of technology is expanding at a rapid pace, especially in the area of transportation. This trend is likely to continue.[47]

International Transportation

Infrastructure Varies Globally

International transportation of goods can involve any of the five basic modes of transportation, although air and water carriage are perhaps the most important. Within countries, motor, rail, and water carriage are the most important freight transporters.

There can be significant differences between the transportation infrastructure found in countries throughout the world. Figure 9–5 shows a comparison of railway infrastructure between various countries. Variations in each of the transport modes will exist throughout the world and must be examined by logistics executives distributing products in those areas. Differences in taxes, transport subsidies, regulations, government ownership of carriers, geography, and other factors can significantly influence the modes and carriers selected for inbound and outbound freight movements.

As noted in Chapter 8, Rail service in the European Union (EU) is usually much better than in the United States because equipment, track, and facilities are in better condition as a result of government ownership or subsidies of the rail system. Japan and Europe use water carriage to a much larger degree than the United States or Canada due to the length and favorable characteristics of coastlines and inland waterways. Organizations shipping products between or within the borders of foreign countries need to thoroughly evaluate transport alternatives, costs, and services, because they are likely to differ.

Figure 9–5

Railway and road infrastructures throughout the world (km per million people)

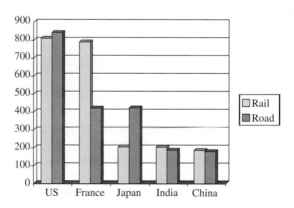

Source: Exel Logistics data as reported in Beth M. Schwartz, "Asia's Bumpy Road to Recovery," *Transportation & Distribution* 40, no. 10 (October 1999), p. 48. Reprinted from various editions of *Transportation & Distribution* and *Industry Week.* Copyright 1995 permission granted by Penton, Cleveland, Ohio.

---

[46]*Strategic Technology: A Survey of Top Transportation and Logistics Service Providers,* report published by KPMG LLP (1999), p. 12.

[47]For a discussion of the use of technology and the Internet in trucking, see Leslie Hansen Harps, "I-Trucking: Web Powers U.S. Truckers," *Inbound Logistics* 19, no. 9 (September 1999), pp. 30–42.

Technology

Help for the Cyber Shipper

Less-than-truckload (LTL) shippers are utilizing a variety of Internet services of carriers in their day-to-day management of traffic and transportation. The majority of carriers have websites that contain information helpful to transportation executives. Some of the Internet services provided by carriers include the following:

- Receive generic or customer-specific rate quotes and rate shipments.
- Request shipment pickup; send origin, destination, and other shipment information or schedule a pickup time.
- Fill out and transmit bills of lading.
- Trace and track shipments.
- Receive automatic e-mail notices of critical events, including delivery confirmation or notification of possible delays.

- Communicate electronically with all parties connected to a shipment, from sales through to accounts receivable.
- Retrieve information on the status of loss-and-damage claims.
- Make electronic freight payments.
- Retrieve documents.
- Produce carrier report cards. Shippers also can download and manipulate

batches of shipment information based on price, on-time percentage, claims, or other measurements used to track carrier performance.

Source: Jim Thomas, "Cyber Carriers," *Logistics Management and Distribution Report* 38, no. 4 (April 1999), p. 53.

In general, international transportation costs represent a much higher fraction of merchandise value than domestic transportation costs. This is primarily due to the longer distances involved, administrative requirements, and related paperwork that must accompany international shipments.[48]

In making traffic and transportation decisions, the logistics manager must consider the differences between the domestic and international markets. Mode availability, rates, regulatory restrictions, service levels, and other aspects of the transportation mix may vary significantly from one market to another. It is vital that the differences be known and understood so that an optimal transportation network can be established for each international market.

Evaluating International Transportation Options

When logistics executives evaluate international transportation options, their decisions are usually based on the following: cutting transportation/distribution costs, freeing up or reducing staff, focusing on core business, acquiring outside expertise, improving customer service and satisfaction, avoiding capital expenditures, and using providers' logistics information systems.[49] An expanded discussion of various global transportation issues can be found in Chapters 13 and 14.

---

[48]Paul S. Bender, "International Logistics," in *The Distribution Management Handbook,* ed. James A. Tompkins and Dale Harmelink (New York: McGraw-Hill, 1994), pp. 8.5–8.6.

[49]Gregory E. Burns, "Freight Forwarding/Logistics: Toward a New Era in Transportation," excerpt from industry report by Gerard Klauer Mattison & Co. (June 1997), Exhibit 24.

Global

Anyone Can Sell on the Web, But Can You Deliver Worldwide?

E-commerce retailers such as etoys.com and toysrus.com ship their products almost exclusively within North America, with some products being distributed to the UK. The major reasons for the lack of globalization are the costs associated with international distribution, difficulties in obtaining reasonable transport prices and high service levels, and problems associated with obtaining payments from customers located throughout the globe.

A New York–based company, Syntra Technologies, developed a Web-based system called Global Logistics System (GLS) that automates order fulfillment with suppliers and customers worldwide. Motorola, one user of GLS software, reduced its global shipping costs, lowered inventory levels from 45 days to 5 days, and cut supply chain order cycle time by one-half. According to a recent article:

Origin and destination, as well as intermediary countries crossed in-transit, have to be considered prior to fulfilling international orders. GLS addresses issues not only concerning what you are shipping, but also the country or person to whom you are shipping, and the transportation path the order must follow.

Unlike domestic shipments, international deliveries can transfer through multiple modes. Companies entering global markets need to be able to review various combinations of modes to decide the most efficient transportation options. By sending coordinated messages, GLS can reserve space on multiple modes to choreograph the ideal flow of products. Advanced shipping notices update carriers throughout the supply chain as the order progresses, facilitating proactive responses to any problems or delays that might arise.

Source: Connie Gentry, "Anyone Can Sell on the Web, But Can You Deliver Worldwide?" Inbound Logistics 19, no. 12 (December 1999), pp. 44–45. Reprinted with permission from *Inbound Logistics Magazine*—www.inboundlogistics.com.

The Transportation Audit

No single transportation system is best for all organizations, because each has its own unique set of products, markets, customers, and facilities. The individual company must develop a system that is optimal in terms of both cost and service. Each component of the logistics system is capable of being audited. The company should perform such an audit periodically. A transportation system audit provides the firm with an overview of the various transportation components of their logistics network and serves to identify and pinpoint the important areas of transportation decision making.

Components of the Transportation Audit

In conducting the audit, the firm needs to examine the cost and service aspects of the transportation system. Theoretically, the transportation decision is fairly simple: How should products be moved from suppliers to the firm and from the firm to customers? Unfortunately, reality is more complex than theory; customers order in different quantities and at varying times, they order different products, and they are geographically dispersed. Other complicating factors include multiple stocking points, varying inventory levels, and different mode/carrier options and characteristics.

A firm must consider many factors as it plans, implements, and controls its transportation system. Product considerations affect the selection of a particular mode or carrier. Some products, because of factors such as size, weight, durability, and value, are not compatible with certain transportation options. It is vital that the organization identify the product–mode interfaces that exist in order to select the modes and carriers offering the best cost and service packages.

Similarly, it is important to identify the characteristics of all potential modes or carriers. Usually there are a number of transportation options available, and it is essential that the organization explore each option sufficiently so that it can make optimal choices.

Even after a specific network is established, the system must be constantly monitored and evaluated. A thorough transportation system audit includes identification of performance standards; measurement of cost and service components; and procedures for planning, implementation, and control of the entire transportation network. Such an evaluation must take place within the context of the firm's overall logistics system. An audit provides numerous opportunities to improve both the efficiency and effectiveness of the transportation operating system.

Benefits of a Transportation Audit

Additionally, conducting a transportation audit will aid an organization in developing a transportation business plan. Such a plan outlines an approach for conducting transportation activities with vendors, suppliers, and customers. The steps or components of a successful business plan often include the following:

- Obtain input from internal and external customers about their service expectations and cost requirements.
- Compare the customers' service and cost requirements with the carrier marketplace.
- Set goals for timely completion of the business plan process assuring conformance to cultural, environmental, and ethical observances.
- Evaluate individual carrier short-term capabilities.
- Evaluate individual carrier long-term capabilities as an investment.
- Choose carrier candidates who objectively represent the best prospects for business and who are genuinely interested in [the firm's] business.
- Make agreements with carriers needed to achieve cost and service goals.[50]

An important part of a transportation audit is the measurement of customer perceptions of carriers and the services they provide. In the appendix to this chapter, a sample transportation customer service questionnaire is presented to illustrate the kinds of information necessary to effectively select and evaluate an LTL motor carrier. It should be noted that the transportation component cannot be examined in isolation. There are many questions included in the survey that relate to other logistics components, as well as various marketing issues (e.g., product, price, and promotion). The main reason for their inclusion is that any transportation decision made using the results of the survey will undoubtedly affect other areas of logistics.

Auditing More than Transportation

Similarly, other areas such as marketing will also be affected. Because organizations do not have unlimited resources, trade-offs will be required. Additional funds spent in one area may mean that expenditures in other areas must be reduced. In order to make the correct transportation decisions in light of the organization's other activities, the transportation manager must obtain information on a variety of factors.

Certainly, variations on this survey are possible for other types of transportation modes, carriers, and situations. Whatever format is used, however, it is important to collect information at regular intervals on service attribute importance and mode/carrier performance that will meet the specific needs of the firm and its customers.

---

[50]As stated in *Transportation Business Planning,* a publication of 3M, St. Paul, Minnesota (undated pamphlet).

Creative Solutions

How Rohm & Haas Used Technology and Reengineering to Save $100 Million

Rohm & Haas, a North American–based chemical manufacturer with sales of $4 billion worldwide, uses every mode of transportation in the distribution of its products. Its product lines include specialty chemicals used in acrylic paint, caulk, floor polish, lubricants, water softeners and purifiers, vinyl siding, vinyl blister packs, printed wiring boards, and semiconductors.

To obtain cost reductions and improve control of their global logistics network, Rohm & Haas employed a third-party provider of reengineering services to develop supply chain solutions for the company. Traditionally, Rohm & Haas developed computer software in-house, with modifications being made at its many locations to fit local conditions. This resulted in a lack of standardized data and difficulty in making comparisons of operations by location, product line, and so on.

After several years of effort, Rohm & Haas developed and implemented a global computer system network and for the first time was able to collect standard data from every location. As a result, several corporate activities were centralized. Accounts payable and other financial functions were consolidated into two regional centers—Europe and North America. However, some problems remained, even after the implementation of their global logistics network.

As stated by the corporate director of logistics and supply chain process for Rohm & Haas: "We learned, from 1991–94, that when you invest in extensive computer systems, you don't get compatible business processes along with them . . . If you haven't trained people in the business process that the system enables you to use—you'll have a system in place, but then everyone has to do extra work to satisfy it."

Using activity-based costing, Rohm & Haas discovered that they were spending $800 million on their supply chains. Some solutions that were developed from their partnership with the third-party provider included:

1. Improved transportation load factors for raw materials and supplies.
2. Leveraged volumes of freight and purchased transportation from fewer carriers.
3. Created employee awareness of the importance of "paying attention to the numbers" by a disciplined reshaping of major business practices.

As a result of all of the changes implemented by Rohm & Haas with its computer systems and process reengineering, $100 million of the $800 million was saved.

Source: Adapted from Robert Mottley, "How Rohm & Haas Saved $100 Million," *American Shipper* 41, no. 4 (April 1999), pp. 27–30. Reprinted by permission of *American Shipper.*

Summary

In this chapter we examined some basic traffic management documents and activities, including the major transportation management strategies of shippers and carriers. From a shipper perspective, the most important considerations are inbound and outbound transportation, mode/carrier selection, contracts, outsourcing, private carriage/leasing, and strategic partnerships/alliances. Important carrier perspectives include pricing/negotiation issues, routing and scheduling, service offerings, competition, and marketing activities.

We examined issues relating to productivity in transportation and looked at some examples of the benefits that technology has brought to the area, with a view toward computer technology's future role in traffic and transportation management. In reviewing a firm's transportation process, we presented the transportation audit as a useful tool.

Suggested Readings

Bowman, Robert J. "Small-Shipment Carriers Pick up the Pace—and Diversify Offerings." *Global Logistics & Supply Chain Strategies* 4, no. 4 (May 2000), pp. 60–68.

Boyson, Sandor; Thomas Corsi; Martin Dresner; and Elliot Rabinovich. "Managing Effective Third Party Logistics Relationships: What Does It Take?" *Journal of Business Logistics* 20, no. 1 (1999), pp. 73–100.

Crowley, James A. "Virtual Logistics: Transport in the Marketspace." *International Journal of Physical Distribution and Logistics Management* 28, no. 7 (1998), pp. 547–74.

D'Este, Glen. "An Event-Based Approach to Modelling Intermodal Freight Systems." *International Journal of Physical Distribution and Logistics Management* 26, no. 6 (1996), pp. 5–16.

Ernst & Whinney. *Transportation Accounting and Control: Guidelines for Distribution and Financial Management* (Oak Brook, IL: National Council of Physical Distribution Management, 1983).

Forsyth, Gordon. "Meet the Digital 3PL." *American Shipper* 42, no. 4 (April 2000), pp. 18–26.

Hanna, Joe B., and David J. Bloomberg. "An Examination of Risk and Resource Sharing Behavior Between LTL Trucking Companies and Warehouse Providers." *Journal of Transportation Management* 9, no. 2 (Fall 1997), pp. 16–24.

Kasarda, John D. "Transportation Infrastructure for Competitive Success." *Transportation Quarterly* 50, no. 1 (Winter 1996), pp. 35–50.

McConville, Daniel J. "Private Fleet Leasing: Two Sides to Teamwork." *Distribution* 96, no. 3 (March 1997), pp. 40–46.

Morash, Edward A., and Steven R. Clinton. "The Role of Transportation Capabilities in International Supply Chain Management." *Transportation Journal* 36, no. 3 (Spring 1997), pp. 5–17.

Nielsen, Lise Drewes. "Flexibility and Innovation in the Supply Chain—A Case Study of Transport Activities." In *Proceedings of the 11th Annual Conference for Nordic Researchers in Logistics,* ed. Everth Larsson and Ulf Paulsson (Lund, Sweden: Lund Institute of Technology, 1999), pp. 61–76.

Richardson, Barbara C. "Transportation Ethics." *Transportation Quarterly* 49, no. 2 (Spring 1995), pp. 117–26.

Rinehart, Lloyd M., and David J. Closs. "Implications of Organizational Relationships, Negotiator Personalities, and Contract Issues on Outcomes in Logistics Negotiations." *Journal of Business Logistics* 12, no. 1 (1991), pp. 123–44.

Swartz, George J., Jr., and William E. Miller. "The Three Dimensions of Third-Party Selection and Implementation." *Proceedings of the Annual Conference of the Council of Logistics Management* (Oak Brook, IL: Council of Logistics Management, 1997), pp. 461–74.

van Donselaar, Karel; Kees Kokke; and Martijn Allessie. "Performance Measurement in the Transportation and Distribution Sector." *International Journal of Physical Distribution and Logistics Management* 28, no. 6 (1998), pp. 434–50.

van Hoek, Remko I. "The Role of Transportation in Customized Supply Chains." *Journal of Transportation Management* 11, no. 1 (Spring 1999), pp. 50–64.

Weart, Walter. "Intermodal: What Now?" *Inbound Logistics* 20, no. 3 (March 2000), pp. 24–35.

Wicker, Gary. "How to Become a Carrier-Preferred Shipper." *Proceedings of the Annual Conference of the Council of Logistics Management* (Oak Brook, IL: Council of Logistics Management, 1998), pp. 565–71.

Wisner, Joel D., and Ira A. Lewis. "A Study of Quality Improvement Practices in the Transportation Industry." *Journal of Business Logistics* 18, no. 1 (1997), pp. 179–97.

Questions and Problems

1. Transportation carriers have become much more marketing-oriented. Briefly identify the major factors that caused this orientation, and describe the forms of marketing activity that have developed in the transportation industry. What would be the role of a carrier's sales force in this new marketing environment?

2. Most transportation executives believe that service factors are generally more important than cost factors in causing firms to switch from one transport mode to another. Identify how service factors would be more important than cost factors to a firm operating in a JIT environment.

3. In the evaluation of transportation modes, *consistency of service* is significantly more important to shippers than *time-in-transit*. Differentiate between the two terms, and identify some possible reasons why consistency of service is considered more important.

4. Private carriage should not be viewed only as a transportation decision; it is also a financial decision. If a firm was trying to determine whether to invest in a private fleet versus developing a partnership/strategic alliance with a carrier, what factors should be considered in making the decision?

5. Strategic partnerships and alliances are becoming more important as shippers and carriers increase their levels of cooperation. Briefly indicate some of the benefits that result for shippers and carriers entering into such arrangements.

6. What is the role of a transportation audit in a shipper firm? How does the transportation audit relate to logistics and other functional areas of the organization? What should be the major components of the transportation audit?

APPENDIX

SAMPLE TRANSPORTATION SERVICE QUALITY QUESTIONNAIRE

SURVEY OF HOW SHIPPERS SELECT AND EVALUATE GENERAL COMMODITIES LTL MOTOR CARRIERS

DEPARTMENT OF MANAGEMENT, MARKETING AND LOGISTICS, UNIVERSITY OF NORTH FLORIDA, JACKSONVILLE

PART A: FACTORS CONSIDERED WHEN SELECTING AND EVALUATING LTL MOTOR CARRIERS

INSTRUCTIONS: Listed on the following pages are various factors often provided by LTL motor carriers to their customers. **This section involves two tasks.** Each task will be explained separately. Do not evaluate small package services such as UPS or RPS.

The **first task** involves your evaluation of the various factors that your firm might consider when selecting a new LTL motor carrier, or when you evaluate the performance of one of your current carriers. Please **circle**, on a scale of 1 to 7, the number which best expresses the importance to your firm of each of these factors. If a factor is not used by your firm or has no importance in your evaluation of carriers, please circle number 1 (Not Important). If a factor is not currently provided by any of your carriers, please evaluate its importance to you if it was available. A rating of 7 (Very Important) should be reserved for those factors that would cause you to reevaluate the amount of business done with a carrier or cause you to drop a carrier in the event of inadequate performance.

The **second task** is to evaluate the current performance of three LTL motor carriers that you use. Please list below in the spaces labeled "Carrier A", "Carrier B" and "Carrier C" three *LTL motor carriers* used most frequently by your firm (if you use fewer than three LTL carriers, please evaluate those that you use). Next, using the scale labeled PERCEIVED PERFORMANCE, please **insert** the number between 1 and 7 which best expresses your perception of a carrier's current performance. If you perceive that a carrier's performance is poor, insert a 1. Reserve a rating of 7 for excellent performance. If a service is not available from a carrier, please write NA, "NOT AVAILABLE," in the appropriate space.

YOUR LTL CARRIERS:

CARRIER A (**the largest amount** of your freight is handled by this carrier)   = _____

CARRIER B (**the second largest amount** of your freight is handled by this carrier) = _____

CARRIER C (**the third largest amount** of your freight is handled by this carrier) = _____

Example:			IMPORTANCE					PERCEIVED PERFORMANCE OF CARRIERS (Scale of 1 to 7)		
	Not Important					Very Important				
FACTORS CONSIDERED	1	2	3	4	5	6	7	A	B	C
• Bar coding of shipments	1	2	③	4	5	6	7	*NA*	*2*	*NA*
• Reliability of transit times	1	2	3	4	5	⑥	7	*5*	*7*	*6*

	IMPORTANCE							PERCEIVED PERFORMANCE OF CARRIERS (Scale of 1 to 7)		
	Not Important					Very Important				
FACTORS CONSIDERED	1	2	3	4	5	6	7	A	B	C
1. Carrier's loss/damage history	1	2	3	4	5	6	7	__	__	__
2. Adequate advance notice of rate changes	1	2	3	4	5	6	7	__	__	__
3. Provides same day delivery	1	2	3	4	5	6	7	__	__	__
4. On-time deliveries	1	2	3	4	5	6	7	__	__	__
5. Prompt action on complaints related to carrier's service	1	2	3	4	5	6	7	__	__	__
6. Quality of dispatch personnel										
- knowledge of carrier's capabilities	1	2	3	4	5	6	7	__	__	__
- prompt notification of scheduling changes	1	2	3	4	5	6	7	__	__	__
- honesty	1	2	3	4	5	6	7	__	__	__
- knowledge of my business	1	2	3	4	5	6	7	__	__	__
- concern/empathy	1	2	3	4	5	6	7	__	__	__
- friendliness	1	2	3	4	5	6	7	__	__	__
7. Carrier sales rep provides assistance/counseling on:										
- transportation solutions	1	2	3	4	5	6	7	__	__	__
- inventory management	1	2	3	4	5	6	7	__	__	__
- customer reports (i.e. transit time analysis)	1	2	3	4	5	6	7	__	__	__
- inbound just-in-time systems	1	2	3	4	5	6	7	__	__	__
- rates and tariffs	1	2	3	4	5	6	7	__	__	__
- logistics training programs	1	2	3	4	5	6	7	__	__	__
- customer service problems	1	2	3	4	5	6	7	__	__	__
- EDI information systems and usage	1	2	3	4	5	6	7	__	__	__
- packaging to reduce damage	1	2	3	4	5	6	7	__	__	__
8. Competitive rates	1	2	3	4	5	6	7	__	__	__
9. Availability of rates on a diskette	1	2	3	4	5	6	7	__	__	__

FACTORS CONSIDERED	Not Important 1	2	3	4	5	6	Very Important 7	PERCEIVED PERFORMANCE OF CARRIERS (Scale of 1 to 7) A B C
10. Single point of contact with carrier to resolve operations problems	1	2	3	4	5	6	7	___ ___ ___
11. Rate structure simple and easy to understand	1	2	3	4	5	6	7	___ ___ ___
12. Electronic (on-line terminal) interface for:								
- pickup	1	2	3	4	5	6	7	___ ___ ___
- billing	1	2	3	4	5	6	7	___ ___ ___
- tracing	1	2	3	4	5	6	7	___ ___ ___
13. Frequency of sales calls you personally receive from carrier's sales representative	1	2	3	4	5	6	7	___ ___ ___
14. Lowest rates	1	2	3	4	5	6	7	___ ___ ___
15. Cash discounts for early payment or prepayment	1	2	3	4	5	6	7	___ ___ ___
16. Carrier has adequate interline arrangements	1	2	3	4	5	6	7	___ ___ ___
17. Literature/information available from carrier:								
- routing guide	1	2	3	4	5	6	7	___ ___ ___
- pricing	1	2	3	4	5	6	7	___ ___ ___
18. Availability of "released value" rates	1	2	3	4	5	6	7	___ ___ ___
19. Assistance from carrier in handling loss and damage claims	1	2	3	4	5	6	7	___ ___ ___
20. Pro number given at time of pickup	1	2	3	4	5	6	7	___ ___ ___
21. Quality of billing staff:								
- knowledge of carrier's billing procedures	1	2	3	4	5	6	7	___ ___ ___
- prompt follow-up	1	2	3	4	5	6	7	___ ___ ___
- honesty	1	2	3	4	5	6	7	___ ___ ___
- knowledge of my business	1	2	3	4	5	6	7	___ ___ ___
- concern/empathy	1	2	3	4	5	6	7	___ ___ ___
22. Ability to provide direct delivery without interlining	1	2	3	4	5	6	7	___ ___ ___
23. Information provided when pickup call placed:								
- projected pickup time	1	2	3	4	5	6	7	___ ___ ___
- projected delivery time	1	2	3	4	5	6	7	___ ___ ___
- rate information	1	2	3	4	5	6	7	___ ___ ___
24. On-time pickups	1	2	3	4	5	6	7	___ ___ ___
25. Bar coding to facilitate tracing	1	2	3	4	5	6	7	___ ___ ___
26. Carrier sponsored entertainment	1	2	3	4	5	6	7	___ ___ ___
27. Carrier's general attitude toward problems/complaints	1	2	3	4	5	6	7	___ ___ ___
28. Carrier's programs for claim prevention (i.e. truck alarms, surveillance equipment, statistical process control (SPC))	1	2	3	4	5	6	7	___ ___ ___
29. Prompt response to claims	1	2	3	4	5	6	7	___ ___ ___
30. Prompt and accurate response to billing inquiries	1	2	3	4	5	6	7	___ ___ ___
31. Promotional gifts (coffee mugs, golf balls, calendars, etc)	1	2	3	4	5	6	7	___ ___ ___
32. Sales rep available if customer service response is inadequate	1	2	3	4	5	6	7	___ ___ ___
33. Willingness to renegotiate rates	1	2	3	4	5	6	7	___ ___ ___
34. Length of promised transit times (from pickup to delivery)	1	2	3	4	5	6	7	___ ___ ___
35. If possible, advance notice of transit delays (e.g. weather, equipment breakdown, etc.)	1	2	3	4	5	6	7	___ ___ ___
36. Freight bill references your bill-of-lading or control number	1	2	3	4	5	6	7	___ ___ ___
37. Regular/scheduled check-in by driver for pickup	1	2	3	4	5	6	7	___ ___ ___
38. Single point of contact with carrier to resolve billing problems	1	2	3	4	5	6	7	___ ___ ___

FACTORS CONSIDERED	IMPORTANCE							PERCEIVED PERFORMANCE OF CARRIERS (Scale of 1 to 7)		
	Not Important 1	2	3	4	5	6	Very Important 7	A	B	C
39. Shipment security	1	2	3	4	5	6	7	—	—	—
40. Frequency of service to key points	1	2	3	4	5	6	7	—	—	—
41. Complete/understandable/legible freight bill	1	2	3	4	5	6	7	—	—	—
42. Quality of drivers:										
- knowledge of carrier's capabilities	1	2	3	4	5	6	7	—	—	—
- ability to handle problems	1	2	3	4	5	6	7	—	—	—
- honesty	1	2	3	4	5	6	7	—	—	—
- responsiveness to inquiries	1	2	3	4	5	6	7	—	—	—
- helpfulness	1	2	3	4	5	6	7	—	—	—
- friendliness/courtesy	1	2	3	4	5	6	7	—	—	—
- willingness to make inside deliveries	1	2	3	4	5	6	7	—	—	—
- appearance	1	2	3	4	5	6	7	—	—	—
- uniforms	1	2	3	4	5	6	7	—	—	—
43. Prompt availability of status information on:										
- shipment tracing	1	2	3	4	5	6	7	—	—	—
- delivery	1	2	3	4	5	6	7	—	—	—
- COD shipments	1	2	3	4	5	6	7	—	—	—
44. Liftgate availability for you and your customer	1	2	3	4	5	6	7	—	—	—
45. Provides new rate and discount sheets in a timely fashion	1	2	3	4	5	6	7	—	—	—
46. Carrier's ability to make pickups: before noon	1	2	3	4	5	6	7	—	—	—
: after 5:00 p.m.	1	2	3	4	5	6	7	—	—	—
47. Quantity discount structure based on:										
- size of shipment	1	2	3	4	5	6	7	—	—	—
- annual volume of shipments	1	2	3	4	5	6	7	—	—	—
48. Quality of sales force:										
- knowledge of carrier's capabilities	1	2	3	4	5	6	7	—	—	—
- prompt follow-up	1	2	3	4	5	6	7	—	—	—
- honesty	1	2	3	4	5	6	7	—	—	—
- concern/empathy	1	2	3	4	5	6	7	—	—	—
- friendliness	1	2	3	4	5	6	7	—	—	—
- knowledge of my business	1	2	3	4	5	6	7	—	—	—
- understanding of my customer's business	1	2	3	4	5	6	7	—	—	—
49. Timely response to requests for assistance from carrier's sales representative	1	2	3	4	5	6	7	—	—	—
50. Adequate geographical coverage:										
- major origins/destinations of your traffic	1	2	3	4	5	6	7	—	—	—
- remote regions	1	2	3	4	5	6	7	—	—	—
51. Prompt and comprehensive response to competitive bid quotations (i.e., contract discounts)	1	2	3	4	5	6	7	—	—	—
52. Accuracy of response to tracing inquiry (ETA)	1	2	3	4	5	6	7	—	—	—
53. Cleanliness of carrier's equipment	1	2	3	4	5	6	7	—	—	—
54. Carrier's reputation	1	2	3	4	5	6	7	—	—	—
55. Carrier's financial condition	1	2	3	4	5	6	7	—	—	—
56. Carriers ability to make deliveries: before noon	1	2	3	4	5	6	7	—	—	—
: after 5:00 pm	1	2	3	4	5	6	7	—	—	—
57. Ability of carrier to customize its services to meet specific and/or unique needs										
- handle emergency shipments	1	2	3	4	5	6	7	—	—	—
- handle hazardous materials	1	2	3	4	5	6	7	—	—	—
- adhere to special shipping instructions	1	2	3	4	5	6	7	—	—	—
- handle COD shipments	1	2	3	4	5	6	7	—	—	—
- rerouting/rescheduling	1	2	3	4	5	6	7	—	—	—
- inside deliveries	1	2	3	4	5	6	7	—	—	—
58. Carrier has satisfactory insurance coverage	1	2	3	4	5	6	7	—	—	—
59. Friendships with carrier personnel	1	2	3	4	5	6	7	—	—	—

			IMPORTANCE					PERCEIVED PERFORMANCE OF CARRIERS (Scale of 1 to 7)		
FACTORS CONSIDERED	Not Important 1	2	3	4	5	6	Very Important 7	A	B	C
60. Ability of carrier to deliver damage-free goods	1	2	3	4	5	6	7	___	___	___
61. Accurate billing	1	2	3	4	5	6	7	___	___	___
62. Low frequency of split shipments	1	2	3	4	5	6	7	___	___	___
63. Proof-of-delivery available with freight bill	1	2	3	4	5	6	7	___	___	___
64. Prompt advance notice of pickup delays	1	2	3	4	5	6	7	___	___	___
65. Carrier's policy on COD/refused/returned/unclaimed freight	1	2	3	4	5	6	7	___	___	___
66. Consistent (reliable) transit times	1	2	3	4	5	6	7	___	___	___
67. Ability of carrier to respond to all customer inquiries with:										
- a single point of contact	1	2	3	4	5	6	7	___	___	___
- immediate response	1	2	3	4	5	6	7	___	___	___
68. Ability to make and meet appointments for delivery	1	2	3	4	5	6	7	___	___	___
69. Accurate rating	1	2	3	4	5	6	7	___	___	___
70. Ability to handle call before deliveries	1	2	3	4	5	6	7	___	___	___
71. Safety rating	1	2	3	4	5	6	7	___	___	___
72. Sales rep has authority to negotiate rates	1	2	3	4	5	6	7	___	___	___
73. Carrier's ability to provide formal reports on:										
- billing accuracy	1	2	3	4	5	6	7	___	___	___
- claims experience	1	2	3	4	5	6	7	___	___	___
- on-time deliveries	1	2	3	4	5	6	7	___	___	___
- on-time pickups	1	2	3	4	5	6	7	___	___	___
- transit times	1	2	3	4	5	6	7	___	___	___

PART B: MEASUREMENT OF OVERALL PERFORMANCE

1. Please indicate the percent that each carrier currently represents of your annual requirements as well as the percent that you would prefer to give each carrier under ideal conditions in the future. (Your totals should add to 100%)

	Current %	Ideal (preferred) %
CARRIER A (the largest amount of your freight is handled by this carrier)	_____ %	_____ %
CARRIER B (the second largest amount of your freight is handled by this carrier)	_____ %	_____ %
CARRIER C (the third largest amount of your freight is handled by this carrier)	_____ %	_____ %
Other Carriers	_____ %	_____ %
	100 %	100 %

2. Please mark a point anywhere on the lines below that best expresses your level of satisfaction with the above carriers. If you are extremely dissatisfied with a carrier's performance, a mark should be placed very near the left end of the line (labeled Poor). If you are exceptionally pleased with the carrier's performance, a mark should be placed very near the right end of the line (labeled Excellent). A midpoint has been placed on the line to correspond with a ''Satisfactory'' performance level.

OVERALL CARRIER PERFORMANCE

	Poor	Satisfactory	Excellent
CARRIER A		———————————	———————————	
CARRIER B		———————————	———————————	
CARRIER C		———————————	———————————	

3. Would you recommend these carriers to another shipper?

CARRIER A	CARRIER B	CARRIER C
_____ Yes	_____ Yes	_____ Yes
_____ No	_____ No	_____ No

4. Have you ever reported to these carriers a problem with the service you received?

CARRIER A	CARRIER B	CARRIER C
_____ Yes	_____ Yes	_____ Yes
_____ No	_____ No	_____ No

5. What percentage of on-time performance do you currently receive from your major LTL carriers during a typical month?

CARRIER A: pickups _____% deliveries _____%
CARRIER B: pickups _____% deliveries _____%
CARRIER C: pickups _____% deliveries _____%

6. For the three carriers that you have evaluated, please give the lowest price carrier a score of 0%. For the others, indicate the percentage premium that you pay for their service. If two or more carriers have the same rates, please give them the same score.

CARRIER A: _____%
CARRIER B: _____%
CARRIER C: _____%

PART C: EXPECTED PERFORMANCE LEVELS OF LTL MOTOR CARRIERS

Please provide the following information with respect to the levels of customer service that you need from your LTL carriers.

1. How many contacts does your department receive from your major LTL carrier's sales rep during a typical month?
_____ face to face calls per month   _____ telephone calls per month

2. How many contacts would your department prefer to receive from your major LTL carrier's sales rep during a typical month?
_____ face to face calls per month   _____ telephone calls per month

3. What is the minimum number of contacts that your department would accept from your major LTL carrier's sales rep during a typical month?
_____ face to face calls per month   _____ telephone calls per month

4. What response time do you rexpect from a carrier's sales representative in:
a. Emergency situations _____ minutes   b. Non-emergency situations _____ hours

5. How much advance notice do you need from your carriers on price changes? _____ days

6. On the average, how soon do you expect a carrier to pick up your shipment after they have been notified?   _____ hours

7. What is the maximum number of hours beyond the promised delivery date that you consider to be an acceptable delay?   _____ hours

8. What terms of payment are offered by your major LTL carriers?
_____ % cash discount for early payment
_____ % discount

9. What percentage of shipments is delivered by the carrier's promised delivery date? _____%

10. What percentage of your products arrive damage free? _____%

11. What percentage of damage free service can be reasonably expected? _____%

12. Do you evaluate carriers using a: (Please check one)
a. Formal process/system _____   b. Informal process/system _____

13. How frequently do you evaluate carrier performance (please check one):
constantly _____   weekly _____   monthly _____   quarterly _____   annually _____   never _____

14. On-time delivery to your firm means plus-or-minus (please indicate the specific number of minutes, hours or days):
_____ minutes   _____ hours   _____ days

15. What is the percentage of on-time performance that you want from your major LTL carrier during a typical month?
pickups _____%   deliveries _____%

16. What is the minimum percentage of on-time performance that you would accept from your major LTL carrier during a typical month?
pickups _____%   deliveries _____%

17. What percentage increase in rates would you be willing to pay if a carrier was able to meet your service expectations? _____%

	Strongly Disagree						Strongly Agree
	1	2	3	4	5	6	7
18. In the next five years, bar coding is going to become much more important in my selection of a LTL carrier	1	2	3	4	5	6	7
19. I require written service standards from my carrier(s)	1	2	3	4	5	6	7
20. Within the next 3 years I will not give business to a carrier that does not use Statistical Process Control (SPC) and provide me with performance reports	1	2	3	4	5	6	7

PART D: DEMOGRAPHIC DATA

This information is required in order to identify major market segments and to provide more meaningful analyses of the previous sections. Please use approximate figures in the event that exact data are not readily available.

1. What is your firm's approximate annual gross sales volume? $_____

2. How long has your firm (division) been in business? (If your answer is 4 years or less, please omit answering question 3).   _____ years

3. What was the average rate of growth in gross sales for the company over the last five years?   _____%

4. What are your approximate annual freight bills: Corporate? $_____   At this location? $_____

5. How many manufacturing locations does your firm operate?   _____

6. For what percentage of inbound shipments is the carrier specified by suppliers?   _____%

7. For what percentage of outbound shipments is the carrier specified by customers?   _____%

8. Please indicate the percentage of your organization's product or raw material moved via:

	Inbound % of Tonnage		Outbound %of Tonnage	
	Today	1995	Today	1995
LTL Motor Carrier	_____	_____	_____	_____

9. How many total LTL shipments do you have in a typical month?
   _____ inbound shipments   _____ outbound shipments

10. What percentage of your LTL shipments are "emergency" orders that require expedited service?
    inbound _____% outbound _____%

11. What is the weight of your typical LTL shipment? _____ lbs.

12. What is the average value of your typical LTL shipment? $_____

13. Please indicate your overall evaluation of each of the following carriers.

CARRIERS:	Insufficient Information To Evaluate	Very Unfavorable 1	2	3	4	5	6	Very Favorable 7
AAA Cooper..	_____	1	2	3	4	5	6	7
Alterman	_____	1	2	3	4	5	6	7
Benton Bros..	_____	1	2	3	4	5	6	7
Carolina...	_____	1	2	3	4	5	6	7
Consolidated	_____	1	2	3	4	5	6	7
Estes	_____	1	2	3	4	5	6	7
Gator	_____	1	2	3	4	5	6	7
Old Dominion	_____	1	2	3	4	5	6	7
Overnite...	_____	1	2	3	4	5	6	7
Roadway	_____	1	2	3	4	5	6	7
Smalley	_____	1	2	3	4	5	6	7
Southeastern	_____	1	2	3	4	5	6	7
Southern Freight	_____	1	2	3	4	5	6	7
Super Transport	_____	1	2	3	4	5	6	7
Transus	_____	1	2	3	4	5	6	7
Watkins	_____	1	2	3	4	5	6	7
Yellow	_____	1	2	3	4	5	6	7
Other (please specify) _____ ..	_____	1	2	3	4	5	6	7

14. What industries do you serve? (Please indicate the percentage of your business represented by each of the following)

Automotive	_____%	Medical equipment	_____%
Chemicals/Plastics	_____%	Military	_____%
Computer	_____%	Paper Products	_____%
Construction	_____%	Petroleum	_____%
Consumer products	_____%	Pharmaceutical	_____%
Educational/Universities	_____%	Retail	_____%
Food products	_____%	Telecommunications	_____%
Industrial equipment	_____%	_____	_____%
Instrumentation	_____%		100 %

15. What is your position or title? _____

16. Please indicate your responsiblities (check all those that apply).
    _____ Accounts receivable   _____ International traffic   _____ Purchasing
    _____ Customer service   _____ Inventory control   _____ Shipping—Receiving
    _____ Distribution   _____ Materials management   _____ Traffic
    _____ Inbound carrier selection _____ Outbound carrier selection _____ Warehousing

17. What are the first three numbers of your zip code? _____

Thank you for your participation and cooperation in completing this survey. Your time and effort are sincerely appreciated. Please return the questionnaire in the envelope provided or mail to:

DOUGLAS M. LAMBERT, Ph.D. and JAMES R. STOCK, Ph.D.
Department of Management, Marketing and Logistics • College of Business Administration,
University of North Florida • 4567 St. Johns Bluff Road, South, Jacksonville, Florida 32216-6699

Chapter Outline

Chapter Objectives

- To show why warehousing is important in the logistics system.
- To identify the types of warehousing facilities that exist.
- To examine the primary functions of warehousing.
- To compare and contrast public versus private warehousing.
- To examine issues relating to warehouse facility development.
- To describe international warehousing issues.
- To provide an overview of the importance of productivity and accounting/control issues in warehouse management.

Introduction

**Warehousing
Is a Primary Link
between Producers
and Customers**

Warehousing is an integral part of every logistics system. It plays a vital role in providing a desired level of customer service at the lowest possible total cost (see Figure 10–1). Warehousing is a primary link between producers and customers. Over the years, warehousing has developed from a relatively minor facet of a firm's logistics system to one of its most important functions. We can define warehousing as that part of a firm's logistics system that stores products (raw materials, parts, goods-in-process, finished goods) at and between point-of-origin and point-of-consumption, and provides information to management on the status, condition, and disposition of items being

FIGURE 10–1

*Cost trade-offs required
in a logistics system*

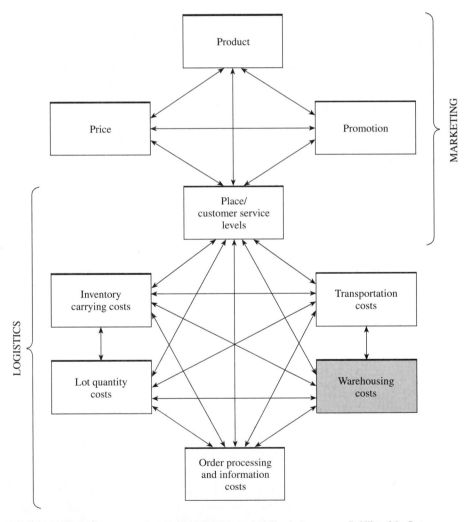

Marketing objective: Allocate resources to the marketing mix to maximize the long-run profitability of the firm.
Logistics objective: Minimize total costs given the customer service objective where: Total costs = Transportation costs + Warehousing costs + Order processing and information costs + Lot quantity costs + Inventory carrying costs.

Source: Adapted from Douglas M. Lambert, *The Development of an Inventory Costing Methodology: A Study of the Costs Associated with Holding Inventory* (Chicago: National Council of Physical Distribution Management, 1976), p. 7.

stored. The term *distribution center (DC)* is also used, but the terms are not identical; *warehouse* is the more generic term:

> Warehouses store all products, DCs hold minimum inventories and predominantly high-demand items. Warehouses handle most products in four cycles [receive, store, ship, and pick], DCs handle most products in two: receive and ship. Warehouses perform a minimum of value-added activity, DCs perform a high percentage of value adding, including possible final assembly. Warehouses collect data in batches, DCs collect data in real-time. Warehouses focus on minimizing the operating cost to meet shipping requirements, DCs focus on maximizing the profit impact of meeting customer delivery requirements.[1]

Nature and Importance of Warehousing

Warehousing is used for the storage of inventories during all phases of the logistics process. In simple terms, two basic types of inventory exist: (1) raw materials, components, and parts (physical supply); and (2) finished goods (physical distribution). There also may be goods-in-process inventory, although in many firms, goods-in-process constitute only a small portion of a company's total investment in inventories.

Why Hold Inventories?

Why is it necessary to hold inventories in storage? In general, the warehousing of inventories is necessary for the following reasons:

1. To achieve transportation economies.
2. To achieve production economies.
3. To take advantage of quantity purchase discounts and forward buys.
4. To maintain a source of supply.
5. To support the firm's customer service policies.
6. To meet changing market conditions (e.g., seasonality, demand fluctuations, competition).
7. To overcome the time and space differentials that exist between producers and consumers.
8. To accomplish least total cost logistics commensurate with a desired level of customer service.
9. To support the just-in-time programs of suppliers and customers.

How Are Warehouses Used?

Figure 10–2 identifies some of the uses of warehousing in a typical logistics system. Warehouses can be used to support manufacturing; to mix products from multiple production facilities for shipment to a single customer; to break bulk, or subdivide a large shipment of product into many smaller shipments to satisfy the needs of many customers; and to combine or consolidate smaller shipments of products into a higher-volume shipment.

In supporting manufacturing operations, warehouses often function as inbound consolidation points for the receipt of materials shipments from suppliers. As shown in Figure 10–2A, firms order raw materials, parts, components, or supplies from various suppliers, who ship truckload (TL) or carload (CL) quantities to a warehouse located in close proximity to the plant. Items are then transferred from the warehouse to the manufacturing plant(s).

---

[1]Richard L. Dawe, "Reengineer Warehousing," *Transportation and Distribution* 39, no. 1 (January 1995), p. 102.

FIGURE 10–2

Uses of warehousing in physical supply and physical distribution

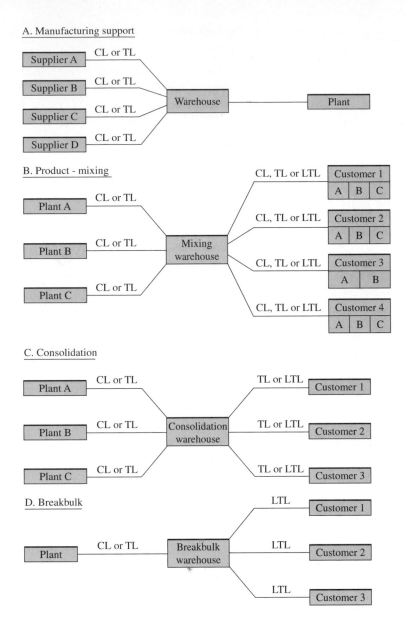

Mixing Warehouse

From an outbound perspective, warehouses can be used for product mixing, outbound consolidation, and/or breakbulk. Product mixing (Figure 10–2B) often involves multiple plant locations (e.g., plant A, plant B, and plant C) that ship products (e.g., product A, product B, and product C) to a central warehouse. Each plant manufactures only a portion of the total product offering of the firm. Shipments are usually made in large quantities (TL or CL) to the central warehouse, where customer orders for multiple products are combined or mixed for shipment.

When a warehouse is used for outbound consolidation (Figure 10–2C), TL or CL shipments are made to a central facility from a number of manufacturing locations. The warehouse then consolidates or combines products from the various plants into a single shipment to the customer.

Breakbulk Warehouse

Breakbulk warehouses (Figure 10–2D) are facilities that receive large shipments of product from a manufacturing plant. Several customer orders are combined into a single shipment from the plant to the breakbulk warehouse. When the warehouse receives the shipment, it is subdivided or broken down into smaller LTL shipments, which are sent to customers in the geographical area served by the warehouse.

Consolidation Warehouse

Transportation economies are possible for both the physical supply system and the physical distribution system. In the case of physical supply, small orders from a number of suppliers may be shipped to a consolidation warehouse near the source of supply; in this way the producer can achieve a truckload or carload shipment to the plant, which is normally a considerably greater distance from the warehouse. The warehouse is located near the sources of supply so that the less-than-truckload (LTL) rates apply only to a short haul, and the volume rate is used for the long haul from the warehouse to the plant.

Warehouses are used to achieve similar transportation savings in the physical distribution system. In the packaged goods industry, manufacturers often have multiple plant locations, with each plant manufacturing only a portion of the company's product line.[2] Usually, these companies also maintain a number of field warehouse locations from which mixed shipments of the entire product line can be made to customers. Shipments from plants to field warehouses are frequently made by rail in full carload quantities of the products manufactured at each plant. Orders from customers, comprised of various items in the product line, are shipped by truck at TL or LTL rates. The use of field warehouses results in lower transportation costs than direct shipments to customers. Savings are often significantly larger than the increased costs resulting from warehousing and the associated increase in inventory carrying costs.

Short production runs minimize the amount of inventory held throughout the logistics system by producing quantities near to current demand. But there are increased costs of setups and line changes associated with short production runs. Also, if a plant is operating near or at capacity, frequent line changes may leave the manufacturer unable to meet product demand. If so, the cost of lost sales—the lost contribution to profit on sales that cannot be made—could be substantial.

In contrast, the production of large quantities of product for each line change results in a lower per-unit cost on a full-cost basis, as well as more units for a given plant capacity. However, long production runs lead to larger inventories and increased warehouse requirements. Consequently, production cost savings must be balanced with increased logistics costs in order to achieve least total cost.

Warehousing is also necessary if a company is to take advantage of quantity purchase discounts on raw materials, component parts, or finished products. Not only is the per-unit price lower as a result of the discount, but if the company pays the freight, transportation costs will be less on a volume purchase because of transportation economies. Similar discounts and savings can accrue to manufacturers, retailers, or wholesalers. Once again, however, those savings must be weighed against the added costs that will be incurred as a result of larger inventories.

Holding inventories in warehouses may be necessary in order to maintain a source of supply. For example, the timing and quantity of purchases are important in retaining suppliers, especially during periods of shortages. It also may be necessary to hold an inventory of items that may be in short supply as the result of damage in transit, vendor stockouts, or a strike against one of the company's suppliers.

---

[2]Such plants are often referred to as "focused factories." For a description of focused factories, see W. Skinner, "The Focused Factory," *Harvard Business Review* 52, no. 3 (May–June 1974), pp. 113–21.

Customer service policies, such as a 24-hour delivery standard, may require a number of field warehouses in order to minimize total costs while achieving the standard. Changing market conditions may also make it necessary to warehouse products in the field, primarily because companies are unable to accurately predict consumer demand and the timing of retailer and wholesaler orders. By keeping some excess inventory in field warehouse locations, companies can respond quickly to meet unexpected demand. In addition, excess inventory allows manufacturers to fill customer orders when shipments to restock the field warehouses arrive late.

The majority of firms use warehousing in order to accomplish least total cost logistics at some prescribed level of customer service. The use of warehousing enables management to select the transport modes and inventory levels that, when combined with communication and order processing systems and production alternatives, minimize total costs while providing a desired level of customer service.

Factors that influence a firm's warehousing policies include the industry; the firm's philosophy; capital availability; product characteristics such as size, perishability, product lines, substitutability, and obsolescence rate; economic conditions; competition; seasonality of demand; use of just-in-time programs; technology; use of e-commerce;[3] and the production process being used.

Factors Influencing Warehousing

Four major factors have been identified that influence the nature and importance of warehousing, including:

- *Time* is one of the most important ingredients in effective warehousing. Therefore, the best warehouse operations are those designed to reduce every aspect of order cycle time.

- *Quality* is just as important as punctuality, and users of warehouse services now expect performance that approaches perfection.

- The emphasis in using warehouses is to improve *asset productivity*. Three critical functions are to reduce total cost, reuse, and recycle.

- To enter the 21st century, warehouse managers must develop a *new kind of workforce*, and requirements for both management and labor will change significantly.[4]

Additional factors that will influence warehousing in the 21st century include the following: focusing more on customer's needs through communication and value-added services; compression of operations and time (e.g., more frequent shipments, faster inventory turnover rates, smaller order sizes); continuous flow of information and products through the logistics system; cross-docking; electronic tracking and control of products; customized warehousing services (e.g., on-demand packaging, labeling, palletization); increasing use of automation; and greater importance of human capital and management leadership.[5]

---

[3]See "E-commerce and Warehousing," *Warehousing Forum* 14, no. 11 (October 1999), pp. 1–3.

[4]From an article by Bernard J. La Londe in *Warehousing Forum* 7, no. 9 (1992) and included in Kenneth B. Ackerman, *Warehousing Profitably: A Manager's Guide* (Columbus, OH: Ackerman Publications, 1994), p. 11.

[5]Brian Hudock, "10 Trends Warehouses Must Follow for 21st Century Success," publication of Tompkins Associates (1999). Also see "21st Century Corporate Strategy in the Warehouse," *Warehousing Forum* 15, no. 7 (June 2000), pp. 1–2.

Types of Warehousing

Direct Store Delivery

In general, firms have several warehousing alternatives. Some companies may market products directly to customers (a process called *direct store delivery*) and thereby eliminate warehousing in the field. Mail-order catalog companies are one example of an industry that uses warehousing only at a point-of-origin, such as sales headquarters or a plant. Most firms, however, warehouse products at some intermediate point between plant(s) and customers.

When a firm decides to store product in the field, it typically must choose whether to rent space, called *public warehousing,* or to own or lease space, called *private warehousing.*

Firms must examine important customer service and financial considerations to choose between public and private warehousing. These options will be described in detail later in this chapter. For now it is sufficient to identify the types of public warehouses that exist. Later in this chapter we will examine the specific aspects relating to the selection of one warehousing type versus another.

Types of Public Warehouses

There are six types of public warehouses: (1) general merchandise warehouses for manufactured goods, (2) refrigerated or cold storage warehouses, (3) bonded warehouses, (4) household goods and furniture warehouses, (5) special commodity warehouses, and (6) bulk storage warehouses. Each type provides users with a broad range of specialized services.

The *general merchandise warehouse* is probably the most common form. It is designed to be used by manufacturers, distributors, and customers for storing practically any kind of product.

Refrigerated or cold storage warehouses provide a temperature-controlled storage environment. Usually, they are used for preserving perishable items such as fruits and vegetables. However, a number of other items—such as frozen food products, some pharmaceuticals, photographic paper and film, and furs—require this type of facility.

Some general merchandise or special commodity warehouses are known as *bonded warehouses.* These warehouses undertake surety bonds from the U.S. Treasury and place their premises under the custody of an agent of the Treasury. Goods such as imported tobacco and alcoholic beverages are stored in this type of warehouse, although the government retains control of the goods until they are distributed to the marketplace. At that time, the importer must pay customs duties to the Internal Revenue Service. The advantage of the bonded warehouse is that import duties and excise taxes need not be paid until the merchandise is sold.

Household goods warehouses are used for storage of personal property rather than merchandise. The property is typically stored for an extended period of time as a temporary layover option. Within this category of warehouses, there are several types of storage alternatives. One is the open storage concept. The goods are stored on a cubic-foot or cubic-meter basis per month on the open floor of the warehouse. Household goods are typically confined to this type of storage. A second kind of storage is private room or vault storage, where users are provided with a private room or vault to lock in and secure goods. A third kind, container storage, provides users with a container into which they can pack goods. Container storage affords better protection of the product than does open storage.

Special commodity warehouses are used for particular agricultural products, such as grains, wool, and cotton. Ordinarily each of these warehouses handles one kind of product and offers special services particular to that product.

Bulk storage warehouses provide tank storage of liquids and open or sheltered storage of dry products such as coal, sand, and chemicals. The services provided by such warehouses may include filling drums from bulk or mixing various types of chemicals with others to produce new compounds or mixtures.

Cross-docking   Other options also exist, including *cross-docking* and *contract warehousing,* a variation of public warehousing. Cross-docking attempts to reduce the amount of time products are held in storage. In essence, the warehouse becomes a distribution mixing center. Products arrive in bulk and are immediately broken down and mixed in the proper range and quantity for customer shipment. Technically, the product never enters the warehouse.

Cross-docking has become an important option for many retailers. For example, Laney & Duke, a third-party warehousing company in Jacksonville, Florida, that handles Hanes brand products, tickets merchandise, places it on hangers, and boxes it up for individual Wal-Mart stores to replace items sold. The trailer leaves Jacksonville for the Wal-Mart distribution center where product is cross-docked to trucks for delivery to individual stores. At store locations, the boxes are opened and garments are ready to hang on display racks.

Contract Warehousing   Contract warehousing is a partnership arrangement between the user and provider of the warehousing service. It has been defined as a

> long-term mutually beneficial arrangement, which provides unique and specially tailored warehousing and logistics services exclusively to one client, where vendor and client share the risks, associated with the operation. [There is a] focus on productivity, service and efficiency, not the fee and rate structure itself.[6]

The growth of contract warehousing has exceeded that of public warehousing in general, and will likely continue to be the dominant form of nonowned warehousing in the foreseeable future.

Warehousing Operations

Warehousing serves an important role in a firm's logistics system. In combination with other activities, it provides the firm's customers with acceptable service levels.

Warehousing Tasks

Warehousing performs a wide variety of tasks, including:

- Receiving, put-away.
- Storage, inventory tracking.
- Order entry.
- Picking, staging, loading.
- Cross-docking.
- Return processing/recoupment.
- Packaging.
- Light assembly, blending, filling, kitting.

---

[6]Kenneth B. Ackerman, "Contract Warehousing—Better Mousetrap, or Smoke and Mirrors?" *Warehousing Forum* 8, no. 9 (August 1993), p. 1; also see Thomas W. Speh et al., *Contract Warehousing: How It Works and How to Make It Work Effectively* (Oak Brook, IL: Warehousing Education and Research Council, 1993).

- Labeling, shrink wrapping.
- Display building/promotions.
- Breakbulk and consolidation.
- Transportation (own fleet or outside carrier).
- Import/export services.
- Proof of delivery.
- Tracing/customer service/billing.
- Service reporting/carrier monitoring.
- Site location.
- Real estate management.
- Network analysis.
- Systems development.[7]

All of these services primarily emphasize product flow rather than storage. Fast and efficient movement of large quantities of raw materials, component parts, and finished goods through the warehouse, coupled with timely and accurate information about the products being stored, is the goal of every warehouse management effort.

Warehousing Functions

Three Functions of Warehousing

Warehousing has three basic functions: movement, storage, and information transfer. The movement function has been receiving the most attention in recent times, as organizations focus on improving inventory turns and speeding orders from manufacturing to final delivery. (See Figure 10–3 for an overview of warehousing functions and flows.)

FIGURE 10–3

Typical warehouse functions and flows

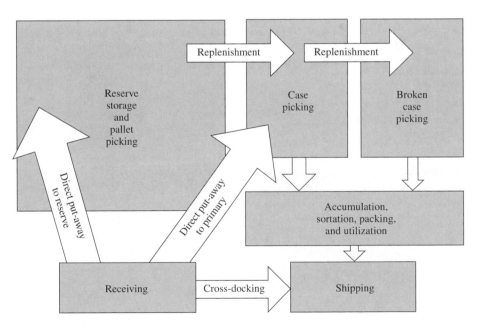

Source: James A. Tompkins, John A. White, Yavuz A. Bozer, Edward H. Frazelle, J. M. A. Tanchoco, and Jaime Trevino, *Facilities Planning,* 2nd ed. (New York: John Wiley & Sons, 1996), p. 392.

[7]Arnold Maltz, *The Changing Role of Warehousing* (Oak Brook, IL: Warehousing Education and Research Council, 1998), p. 35.

Movement.   The *movement* function can be further divided into several activities, including:

- Receiving.
- Transfer or put-away.
- Customer order picking/selection.
- Cross-docking.
- Shipping.[8]

The *receiving* activity includes the actual unloading of products from the transportation carrier. It also includes the updating of warehouse inventory records, inspection for damage, and verification of the merchandise count against orders and shipping records.

Transfer or *put-away* involves the physical movement of the product into the warehouse for storage, movement to areas for specialized services such as consolidation, and movement to outbound shipment. *Customer order picking* or *order selection* is the major movement activity and involves regrouping products into the assortments customers desire. Packing slips are also generated at this point.

Approaches to Order Picking

The task of order picking can be grouped into four categories: discreet picking, batch picking, zone picking, and wave picking.

- *Discreet picking* is [one] means of selecting an order. One order picker takes a single order and fills it from start to finish.
- With *batch picking* the order picker takes a group of orders, perhaps a dozen. A batch list is prepared that contains the total quantity of each SKU found in the whole group. The order picker then collects the batch and takes it to a staging area, where it is separated into single orders.
- *Zone picking* assigns each order selector to a given zone of the warehouse. Under a zone picking plan, one order picker selects all parts of the order that are found in a given aisle and then passes the order to another picker, who selects all of the items in another aisle, and so on. Under this system, the order is almost always handled by more than one individual.
- *Wave picking* groups shipments by a given characteristic, such as common carrier. For example, all of the orders for UPS might be picked in a single wave. A second wave would pull all of the orders destined for parcel post, and still other waves would select shipments routed by other carriers.[9]

Cross-docking

Cross-docking bypasses the storage activity by transferring items directly from the inbound receiving dock to the outbound or shipping dock (see Figure 10–4). A pure cross-docking operation would avoid put-away, storage, and order picking. Information transfer would become paramount due to the close coordination of shipments required.

This activity has become very commonplace in warehousing because of its impact on costs and customer service. For example, approximately 75 percent of food distribution warehouses are cross-docking products from supplier to retail food stores.[10]

---

[8]See James A. Tompkins et al., *Facilities Planning,* 2nd ed. (New York: John Wiley & Sons, 1996), pp. 389–450.

[9]Ackerman, *Warehousing Profitably,* p. 232.

[10]"Grocery Warehouses Turn to Cross-Docking," *Traffic Management* 34, no. 2 (February 1995), p. 77-S.

FIGURE 10–4

How cross-docking works

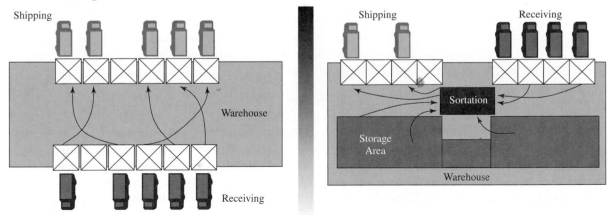

Under a cross-docking system, palletloads can be moved directly across the warehouse floor from receiving to shipping (left). Boxes, however, first must pass through a sortation system (right).

Source: James Aaron Cooke, "Cross-Docking Rediscovered," *Traffic Management* 33, no. 11 (November 1994), p. 51.

Eliminating the transfer or put-away of products reduces costs and the time goods remain at the warehouse, thus improving customer service levels.[11]

Cross-docking should be considered as an option by firms meeting two or more of the following criteria:

When Should Cross-Docking Be Considered?

- The destination of the inventory is known when it is received.
- Your customer is ready to receive the inventory immediately.
- You ship to fewer than 200 locations daily.
- Daily throughput exceeds 2,000 cartons.
- More than 70% of the inventory is conveyable.[12]
- You receive large quantities of individual items.
- The inventory arrives at your docks pre-labeled.
- Some inventory is time sensitive.
- Your distribution center is already near capacity.
- At least some of the inventory is pre-priced.[13]

---

[11]A large literature exists that overviews cross-docking. The interested reader is directed to the following sources: Tom Andel, "Define Cross-Docking Before You Do It," *Transportation and Distribution* 35, no. 11 (November 1994), pp. 93–98; *Crossdocking in the '90s,* Monograph Series No. M0020 (Raleigh, NC: Tompkins Associates, undated); Lisa Harrington, "Cross Docking Takes Costs Out of the Pipeline," *Distribution* 92, no. 9 (September 1993), pp. 64–66; "Implementing a Cross-Docking Program," *Distribution Center Management* 30, no. 5 (May 1995), p. 3; and James T. Westburgh, "Cross Docking in the Warehouse—An Operator's View," *Warehousing Forum* 10, no. 9 (August 1995), pp. 1–3.

[12]In theory, all products are capable of being moved within a warehouse via conveyors. However, some products can more easily be moved in this way. For example, items in cartons or totes are easily moved on conveyors; that is, they are "conveyable." Items that are heavy or irregularly shaped are more difficult to move in this fashion.

[13]"Receiving Is Where Efficiency Starts," *Modern Materials Handling* 50, no. 5 (Mid-April 1995), p. 9.

The last movement activity, *shipping,* consists of staging the product and physically moving the assembled orders onto carrier equipment, adjusting inventory records, and checking on orders to be shipped. It can also consist of sorting and packaging items for specific customers. Products are placed in boxes, cartons, or other containers; placed on pallets; stretch-wrapped (i.e., wrapped in a plastic film); and marked with information necessary for shipment, such as origin, destination, shipper, consignee (i.e., customer), and package contents.

Temporary Storage

Storage.   The second function of warehousing—storage—can be performed on a temporary or a semipermanent basis. *Temporary storage* emphasizes the movement function of the warehouse and includes only the storage of product necessary for basic inventory replenishment. The extent of temporary inventory storage depends on the design of the logistics system and the variability experienced in lead time and demand. A goal of cross-docking is to use only the temporary storage function of the warehouse.

Semipermanent Storage

Semipermanent storage is the storage of inventory in excess of that required for normal replenishment. It can also be referred to as buffer or safety stock. The most common conditions leading to semipermanent storage are (1) seasonal demand; (2) erratic demand; (3) conditioning of products such as fruits and meats; (4) speculation or forward buying; and (5) special deals, such as quantity discounts.

Information Transfer.   *Information transfer,* the third major function of warehousing, occurs simultaneously with the movement and storage functions. Managers always need timely and accurate information as they attempt to administer the warehousing activity. Information on inventory levels, throughput levels (i.e., amount of product moving through the warehouse), stockkeeping locations, inbound and outbound shipments, customer data, facility space utilization, and personnel is vital to the successful operation of a warehouse. Organizations are relying increasingly on computerized information transfer using electronic data interchange (EDI), the Internet, and bar coding to improve both the speed and accuracy of information transfer.

In spite of numerous attempts by firms to reduce the paperwork flow, the amount of paperwork is still significant. For this reason, and many others, firms have attempted to automate the clerical function whenever possible. The developments in electronic communications (e.g., e-mail) have been instrumental in reducing the clerical activities in all aspects of warehousing.

Successful completion of all of the warehousing activities already mentioned eliminates the need for *checking.* However, errors and mistakes do occur within any warehouse operation, and it is usually necessary to periodically conduct a check of previous activities. In some instances, this activity can be minimized in operations where employees are empowered to perform quality control at their respective levels within the warehouse. Teams, rather than individuals, may also perform this activity.

Examples of Warehousing Inefficiencies

Within the warehouse it is important to eliminate any inefficiencies in movement, storage, and information transfer. These can occur in a variety of forms, such as:

- Redundant or excessive handling.
- Poor utilization of space and cube.
- Excessive maintenance costs and downtime due to obsolete equipment.
- Dated receiving- and shipping-dock conditions.
- Obsolete computerized information handling of routine transactions.

Today's competitive marketplace demands more precise and accurate handling, storage, and retrieval systems, as well as improved packaging and shipping systems. It is therefore vital for a warehouse operation to have the optimal mix of manual (nonautomated) and automated handling systems. These issues are presented in more depth in Chapter 11. The next section compares and contrasts private versus public warehousing.

Public versus Private Warehousing

One of the most important warehousing decisions is whether public or private facilities should be used. In order to make the proper decision from both cost and service perspectives, the logistics executive must understand the advantages and disadvantages, as well as the financial implications, of each alternative.[14] Appendix A to this chapter illustrates the type of financial analysis that must be performed.

Many companies typically find it advantageous to use some combination of public and private warehousing. Private warehouses can be used to handle basic inventory levels required for least-cost logistics in markets where the volume justifies ownership. Public warehouses, a form of outsourcing, can be used in those areas where volume is not sufficient to justify ownership and/or to store peak requirements. Public warehouses typically charge on the basis of case or hundredweight stored or handled. Consequently, when the volume of activity is sufficiently large, public warehousing charges exceed the cost of a private facility, making ownership more attractive.

Advantages and Disadvantages of Public Warehousing

Advantages.   The benefits that may be realized if a firm uses public warehousing rather than private warehousing include (1) conservation of capital, (2) the ability to increase warehouse space to cover peak requirements, (3) reduced risk, (4) economies of scale, (5) flexibility, (6) tax advantages, and (7) specific knowledge of costs.

Conservation of Capital   One of the major advantages of public warehouses is that they require *no capital investment* on the part of the user. The user avoids the investment in buildings, land, and materials handling equipment, as well as the costs associated with starting up the operation and hiring and training personnel.

Meet Peak Requirements   If an organization's operations are subject to seasonality, the public warehouse option allows the user to contract for as much storage space as needed to *meet peak requirements.* A private warehouse, in contrast, has a constraint on the maximum amount of product that can be stored and is likely to be underutilized during a portion of each year. Since many organizations experience variations in inventory levels due to business cycles or seasonality in demand or production, sales promotions, or other factors, public warehousing offers the advantage of allowing storage costs to vary directly with volume.

Companies normally plan for a distribution facility to have a life span of 20 to 40 years. Consequently, by investing in a private warehouse, management assumes the risk that the facility will become obsolete due to changes in technology or changes in the volume of business. With public warehousing, the user can switch to another facility in a short period of time, usually within 30 days.

Economies of Scale   Public warehouses are able to achieve *economies of scale* that may not be possible for a small firm. Public warehouses handle the storage requirements of a number of

---

[14]See James Aaron Cooke, "Getting the Right Fit," *Traffic Management* 34, no. 2 (February 1995), Warehousing and Distribution Supplement, pp. 78–80.

firms at the same time and that volume allows the employment of a full-time warehousing staff. In addition, building costs are nonlinear, and a firm pays a premium to build a small facility. Additional economies of scale can be provided by using more expensive, but more efficient, materials handling equipment, and by providing administrative and other expertise.

Public warehouses are often able to offer a number of specialized services more economically than a private warehouse. These specialized services include the following:

- Broken-case handling, which is breaking down manufacturers' case quantities to enable orders for less-than-full case quantities to be filled.
- Packaging of manufacturers' products for shipping. Exel Logistics, a public warehousing and logistics services firm, has performed a variation of this service for the California Growers Association. Product was shipped to the Atlanta distribution center in "brights"—cans without labels—and the labels were put on the product at the warehouse as orders were received from customers.
- Consolidation of damaged product and product being recalled by the manufacturer for shipment to the manufacturer in carload or truckload quantities. In addition to the documentation and prepacking that may be necessary, the public warehouse frequently performs the rework of damaged product.
- Equipment maintenance and service.
- Stock spotting of product for manufacturers with limited or highly seasonal product lines. Stock spotting involves shipping a consolidated carload of inventory to a public warehouse just prior to a period of maximum seasonal sales.
- A breakbulk service whereby the manufacturer combines the orders of different customers located in a market and ships them at the carload or truckload rate to the public warehouse where the individual orders are separated and local delivery is provided.

A public warehouse can be very flexible and adaptable. For example, PRISM Team Services, a California-based food warehouse company, emphasizes value-added services such as just-in-time (JIT) delivery, plant production support, and export shipping.[15]

Economies of scale result from the consolidation of small shipments with other, noncompeting companies using the same public warehouse. The public warehouse consolidates orders of specific customers from the products of a number of different manufacturers on a single shipment. This results in lower shipping costs, as well as reduced congestion at the customer's receiving dock. Also, customers who pick up their orders at the public warehouse are able to obtain the products of several manufacturers with one stop, if the manufacturers all use the same facility.

Flexibility   Another major advantage offered by public warehouses is *flexibility.* Owning or holding a long-term lease on a warehouse can become a burden if business conditions necessitate changes in locations. Public warehouses require only a short-term contract, and thus short-term commitments. Short-term contracts available from public warehouses make it easy for firms to change field warehouse locations due to changes in the

---

[15]Ann Saccamano, "California Warehouse Operator Emphasizes Tailored Services, sans Bells and Whistles," *Traffic World* (May 8, 1995), pp. 66–67.

marketplace (e.g., population shifts), the relative cost of various transport modes, volume of a product sold, or the company's financial position.

In addition, a firm that uses public warehouses does not have to hire or lay off employees as the business volume changes. Because a public warehouse provides the personnel for extra services when they are necessary, the company does not have to hire extra full-time workers.

Public warehousing makes it possible for the manufacturer to experiment with a warehouse location to determine its contribution to the firm's logistics system, and to discontinue the operation with relative ease if cost savings or performance objectives are not realized.

Taxes

In most states a firm is at a definite advantage if it does not own property in the state, because such ownership means that the firm is doing business in the state and is thus subject to various state *taxes*. These taxes can be substantial. Consequently, if the company does not currently own property in a state, it may be advantageous to use a public warehouse. In addition, certain states do not charge property taxes on inventories in public warehouses; this tax shelter applies to both regular warehouse inventories and storage-in-transit inventories. A free-port provision enacted in some states allows inventory to be held tax free for up to one year. Finally, the manufacturer pays no real estate tax. Of course, the public warehouse pays real estate tax and includes this cost in its warehouse rates, but the cost is smaller on a per-unit throughput basis because of the significantly larger volume of business possible.

Storage and Handling Costs

When a manufacturer uses a public warehouse, *it knows its exact storage and handling costs* because it receives a bill each month. The manufacturer can also forecast costs for different levels of activity because the costs are known in advance. Firms that operate their own facilities often find it very difficult to determine the fixed and variable costs based on variability in volumes.

Communication Problems

Disadvantages. *Effective communication* may be a problem with public warehouses, because not all computer terminals and systems are compatible. A warehouse operator may hesitate to add another terminal for just one customer. In addition, the lack of standardization in contractual agreements makes communication regarding contractual obligations difficult. However, many of these problems have been overcome with the advent of e-mail, electronic data interchange (EDI), the Internet, and intranets.[16]

Availability of Specialized Services

Specialized services may not always be available in a specific location. Many public warehouse facilities only provide local service and are of limited use to a firm that distributes regionally or nationally. Consequently, a manufacturer that wants to use public warehouses for national distribution may find it necessary to deal with several different operators and monitor several contractual agreements. Also, some public warehouses may not offer certain services unless a sufficient number of their clients require it. Sometimes, a public warehouse and a client will cooperate to develop and financially support a new service.

---

[16]For discussions of the role of the Internet and e-commerce on warehousing, see George Anders, "Virtual Reality: Web Firms Go on Warehouse Building Boom," *The Wall Street Journal* (September 8, 1999), pp. B1 and B8; Rebecca Quick, "Behind Doors of a Warehouse: Heavy Lifting of E-Commerce," *The Wall Street Journal* (September 3, 1999), pp. B1 and B3; "Webhousing," *WERCSheet* 23, no. 4 (April 2000), pp. 1–5; and Doris E. Kilbane, "Terms of Endearment," *Operations & Fulfillment* 8, no. 3 (May/June 2000), pp. 110–20.

Space Availability

Finally, *public warehousing space* may not be available when and where a firm wants it. Shortages of space do occur periodically in selected markets, and this can adversely affect the logistics and marketing strategies of a firm. Unless an organization has developed a good relationship with a public warehouse in an area where a shortage exists, either space may not be available or the price of that space may be very high.

Advantages and Disadvantages of Private Warehousing

Degree of Control

Advantages.   In private warehousing, the company that owns the goods exercises a greater *degree of control* over their storage, handling, and management. The firm has direct control of, and responsibility for, the product until the customer takes possession or takes over delivery. This greater degree of control allows the firm to integrate the warehousing function more easily into the company's total logistics system.

Flexibility

With this warehouse control comes *flexibility*—not flexibility to reduce or increase storage space quickly, but flexibility to design and operate the warehouse to fit the specific needs of customers and the characteristics of the product. Organizations with highly specialized products requiring special handling or storage may not find public warehousing feasible because of facility or materials handling limitations. In such instances the firm must use private warehousing or ship direct to customers. The warehouse can also be modified through expansion or renovation to facilitate product changes, or it can be converted into a manufacturing plant or a branch office.

Cost

Another prominent advantage of private warehousing is that it can be *less costly* over the long term than public warehousing. Operating costs can be 15 to 25 percent lower if the company achieves sufficient throughput or utilization (i.e., high inventory turnover). The generally accepted industry norm for the utilization rate of a private warehouse is 75 to 80 percent. If an organization cannot achieve at least 75 percent utilization, it would generally be more appropriate to use public warehousing.

Human Resources

By employing private warehousing, an organization can make greater use of its present *human resources*. It can use the expertise of its technical specialists. In addition, the individuals working in the warehouse are company employees. Generally, there is greater care in handling and storage when the firm's own workforce operates the warehouse. On the other hand, some public warehouses allow a firm to use its own employees in the handling and storage of its products.[17]

Tax Benefits

An organization can also realize *tax benefits* when it owns its warehouses. Depreciation allowances on buildings and equipment can substantially reduce the cost of a structure or apparatus over its life.

Finally, there may be certain *intangible benefits* associated with warehouse ownership. When a firm distributes its products through a private warehouse, it can give the customer a sense of permanence and continuity of business operations. The customer sees the company as a stable, dependable, and lasting supplier of products. This can provide an organization with potential marketing advantages.

Flexibility

Disadvantages.   The major drawback of private warehousing is the same as one of its main advantages—*flexibility*. A private warehouse may be too costly because of its fixed size and costs. Irrespective of the level of demand the firm experiences, the size of the private warehouse is restricted in the short term. A private facility cannot expand

---

[17]For a discussion of human resource issues in warehousing, see "Alternatives to Traditional Labor," *WERCSheet* 20, no. 6 (June 1997), pp. 1–4.

and contract to meet increases or decreases in demand that might occur. When demand is low, the firm must still assume the fixed costs, as well as the lower productivity associated with unused warehouse space. This disadvantage can be minimized, however, if the firm is able to rent out part of its space, in essence acting like a public warehouse.

If a firm uses only private warehouses, it also loses flexibility in its strategic location options. Changes in market size, location, and preferences can be rapid and unpredictable. If an organization cannot adapt to these changes in its warehouse structure, it may lose a valuable business opportunity. Customer service and sales could also fall if a private warehouse cannot adapt to changes in the firm's product mix.

Investment   Because of the costs involved, many organizations are simply unable to generate enough capital to build or buy their own warehouse and make the investments needed in plant and equipment or new products. A private warehouse is a long-term, often risky *investment* that may be difficult to sell because of its customized design. Start-up is often a costly and time-consuming process due to the hiring and training of employees, as well as the purchase of materials handling equipment. And, depending on the nature of the organization, return on investment may be greater if funds are channeled into other profit-generating opportunities.[18]

Facility Development

One of the more important decisions facing logistics executives is how to determine the size and number of the organization's warehouses. In addition, where should those facilities be located? Finally, each warehouse must be laid out and designed properly in order to maximize efficiency and productivity. Examples of how to address some of these issues are presented in Appendix B at the end of this chapter.

Size and Number of Warehouses

Determining the size and number of warehouse facilities are interrelated decisions in that they typically have an inverse relationship; that is, *as the number of warehouses increases, the average size of each warehouse decreases.* The general trend is to have fewer, but larger, warehouses in an organization's distribution system.[19]

Factors Affecting   Many factors influence how large a warehouse should be, although it is first nec-
Warehouse Size   essary to define how size is measured. Size is often defined in terms of square footage of floor space, and sometimes in cubic space of the entire facility. Public warehouses often use square footage dimensions in their advertising and promotional efforts. Unfortunately, square footage measures ignore the capability of modern warehouses to store merchandise vertically. Hence, the cubic space measure was developed. Cubic space refers to the amount of volume available within a facility. It is a much more realistic size estimate because it considers more of the available usable space in a warehouse than square footage does.

---

[18]For a discussion of the public versus private warehousing decision, see Cooke, "Getting the Right Fit"; James Aaron Cooke, "How to Pick a Public Warehouse," *Traffic Management* 33, no. 1 (January 1994), Warehousing and Distribution Supplement, pp. 14–16; C. Alan McCarrell, "Monitoring Public Warehouses," *Warehousing Forum* 8, no. 4 (March 1993), pp. 1–4; Hugh L. Randall, "Contract Logistics: Is Outsourcing Right for You?" in *The Logistics Handbook,* ed. James F. Robeson and William C. Copacino (New York: Free Press, 1994), pp. 508–16; and William G. Sheehan, "Criteria for Judging a Public Warehouse," *Warehousing Forum* 11, no. 5 (April 1996), p. 3.

[19]"Facility Trends 1997–1999," *WERCwatch Report* (March 1999), p. 1.

Some of the most important factors affecting the size of a warehouse are:

1. Customer service levels.
2. Size of market(s) served.
3. Number of products marketed.
4. Size of the product(s).
5. Materials handling system used.
6. Throughput rate (i.e., inventory turnover).
7. Production lead time.
8. Economies of scale.
9. Stock layout.
10. Aisle requirements.
11. Office area in warehouse.
12. Types of racks and shelves used.
13. Level and pattern of demand.

Typically, as a company's service levels increase, it requires more warehousing space to provide storage for higher levels of inventory. As a warehouse serves more markets, additional storage space is normally required, unless cross-docking is used and/or throughput rates are increased. When an organization has multiple products or product groupings, especially if they are diverse, larger warehouses will be required in order to maintain minimum inventory levels of each product. Generally, greater space requirements are necessary when products are large; low throughput rates exist; production lead times are long; manual materials handling systems are used; the warehouse contains office, sales, or computer activities; or demand is erratic and unpredictable.

Warehouse Size and Materials Handling Equipment

To illustrate, consider the relation of warehouse size to the type of materials handling equipment used. As Figure 10–5 shows, the type of forklift truck a warehouse employs can significantly affect the amount of storage area necessary. Because of different capabilities of lift trucks, a firm can justify the acquisition of more expensive units when they are able to bring about more effective utilization of space. The four examples in Figure 10–5 illustrate the fact that warehouse layout and warehouse handling systems are integrally intertwined. The simplest type of forklift truck, the counterbalanced truck, requires 10,000 square feet of area and aisles that are 144 inches wide. At $30,000 or so, it is the least expensive forklift. The turret truck requires only 3,070 square feet to handle the same amount of product but costs $95,000 or more.[20] The warehouse decision maker must examine the cost trade-offs involved for each of the variety of available systems and determine which alternative is most advantageous from a cost/service perspective.

Demand also has an impact on warehouse size. Whenever demand fluctuates significantly or is unpredictable, inventory levels are higher because of safety stock requirements. The only exceptions to this are when the organization can manufacture or replenish products very quickly and meet stated customer service requirements. This results in a need for more space and thus a larger warehouse.

Demand and Warehouse Size

The space does not have to be private warehousing. However, many organizations use a combination of private and public warehousing. Figure 10–6 shows the relationship between demand and warehouse size. The hypothetical firm depicted in the figure uses

---

[20]See Thompkins et al., *Facilities Planning*, p. 237.

FIGURE 10–5

Narrow-aisle forklift trucks can reduce warehouse floor space

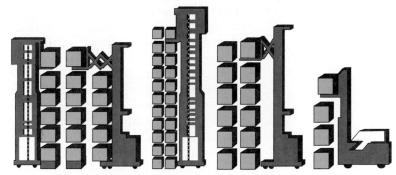

Type of truck	Deep reach	Turret	Reach-fork	Counter-balanced
Area required	5,550 sq. ft.	3,070 sq. ft.	6,470 sq. ft.	10,000 sq. ft.
Aisle width	102 inches	66 inches	96 inches	144 inches
Floor space saved	45%	70%	33%	———

Source: James Aaron Cooke, "When to Choose a Narrow-Aisle Lift Truck," *Traffic Management* 28, no. 12 (December 1989), p. 55.

FIGURE 10–6

The relationship of demand to warehouse size

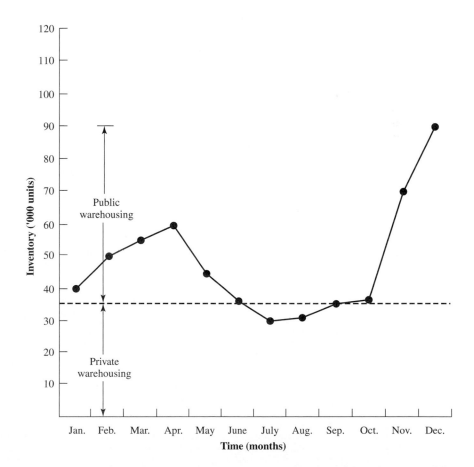

private warehousing to store 36,000 units of inventory. This results in full utilization of its facilities all year, with the exception of July and August. For months where inventory requirements exceed private warehousing space, short-term storage is rented from one or more public warehouses. In essence, the firm develops private facilities to accommodate a maximum level of inventory of 36,000 units.

Inventory velocity (as measured by turnover) and the maximization of "direct deliveries" to customers (bypassing a regional or wholesaler's warehouse) can also have great impact on the size of a warehouse. Whirlpool Corporation developed a computer program to simulate these two characteristics, as well as the warehousing space requirements (cube) of its total channel network (including wholesale distributors). The company calculated the square footage required for each of its factory-controlled and/or wholesale warehouses. It added space to the base requirements of each of its major product categories in order to provide for aisles and docks, as well as unused (empty) vertical and horizontal storage bays. By manipulating planned sales volumes, inventory turns, and bypassed orders shipped directly to dealers, it was able to accurately project future warehousing needs.[21]

Some factors that affect storage space requirements are listed in Table 10–1. Additionally, suggestions are shown that can result in less space being required for the storage of products. Although the items in Table 10–1 are specific to the United States, they would generally apply to warehouses located almost anywhere in the world.

Factors Influencing the Number of Warehouses

In deciding on the number of warehousing facilities, four factors are significant: cost of lost sales, inventory costs, warehousing costs, and transportation costs. Figure 10–7 depicts these cost areas, with the exception of cost of lost sales. Although lost sales are extremely important to a firm, they are the most difficult to calculate and predict, and they vary by company and industry. If the *cost of lost sales* appeared in Figure 10–7, it would generally slope down and to the right. The degree of slope, however, would vary.

TABLE 10–1   Determinants of Storage Space Requirements

These Situations Increase the Need for Storage Space	*These Situations Decrease the Need for Storage Space*
Market or company expansion	Decrease in production or sales
Shorter product life cycle	Decrease in number of SKUs
Increase in number of SKUs	Less volatile demand (including longer product life cycles)
Direct store delivery on a quick response basis	Customer handles store delivery
Elimination of distributors	Smaller manufacturing lot sizes
Expansion into specialized products	Smaller purchase amounts
Import/export items	Higher inventory turns
Lengthened production process	Better information
Increase in minimum manufacturing lot size	Quicker transportation
Requirement for faster response time	Cross-docking
Inflation/forward buying	Carrier performing consolidation

Source: Adapted from Arnold Maltz, *The Changing Role of Warehousing* (Oak Brook, IL: Warehousing Education and Research Council, 1998), p. 9.

---

[21]Illustration provided by Professor Jay U. Sterling, University of Alabama, and former director of logistics planning for Whirlpool Corporation.

The remaining components of the figure are more consistent across firms and industries. *Inventory costs* increase with the number of facilities, due to the fact that organizations usually stock a minimum amount (safety stock) of all products at every location (although some companies have specific warehouses dedicated to a particular product or product grouping). This means that both slow and fast turnover items are stocked, and thus more total space is required. *Warehousing costs* also increase, because more warehouses mean more space to be owned, leased, or rented. The costs tend to increase at a decreasing rate after a number of warehouses are brought online, particularly if the firm leases or rents space. Public and contract warehouses often offer quantity discounts when firms acquire space in multiple locations.

Transportation costs initially decline as the number of warehouses increase. But they eventually curve upward if too many facilities are employed due to the combination of inbound and outbound transportation costs. A firm must be concerned with the total delivered cost of its products and not just the cost of moving products to warehouse locations. In general, the use of fewer facilities means bulk shipments from the manufacturer or supplier. The shipments typically are rated on a truckload (TL) or carload (CL) basis, either of which provides a lower cost per hundredweight. When customer orders arrive, products are then shipped out of the warehouse on a less-than-truckload (LTL) basis, but are rated higher. After the numbers of warehouses increase to a certain point, the firm may not be able to ship its products in such large quantities and may have to pay a higher rate to the transportation carrier. Local transportation costs for delivery of products from warehouses to customers may also increase because of minimum charges that apply to local cartage.

FIGURE 10–7

Relationship between total logistics cost and the number of warehouses

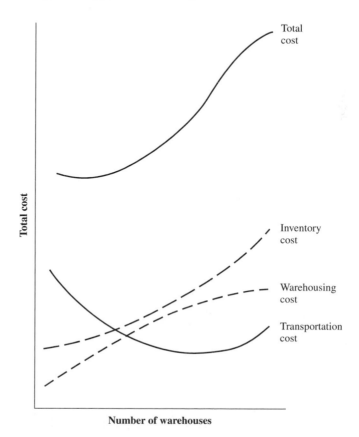

If the cost of lost sales is not included, the costs shown in Figure 10–7 indicate that having fewer warehouses is better than having many warehouses. However, customer service is perhaps the most important component of a firm's marketing and logistics systems. If the cost of lost sales is very high, a firm may wish to expand the number of warehouses. There are always cost/service trade-offs. Management must determine what level of customer service it desires and only then determine the optimal number of warehouses to service those customers.

Other factors affecting the number of warehouses are the purchasing patterns of customers, the competitive environment, and the use of computers and other information technology. If customers order small quantities frequently, an organization will sometimes need more warehouses located closer to the marketplace. An organization will usually have more warehouses if the level of competition is high. When competitors offer rapid delivery to customers, a firm may be forced to match the service level unless it possesses some other differential advantage. If transportation and order communication are slow, inefficient, or uncertain, then the only alternative might be additional warehouses.

Computers and information technology can help minimize the firm's number of warehouses by improving warehouse layout and design, inventory control, shipping and receiving, and the dissemination of information. The substitution of information for inventories, coupled with more efficient warehouses, tends to reduce the number of warehouses needed to service the firm's customers.

Location Analysis

Where Is the Best Place to Locate a Warehouse?

Where would be the best places to build warehouses that would service the greatest number of U.S. consumers? If a firm wished to locate facilities closest to its potential customers, using one or more warehouses in its logistics network, a number of sites would be possible. Table 10–2 identifies the best locations given various warehouse configurations. Bloomington, Indiana, is closer, on average, to the majority of the U.S. population than any other location.[22]

Nike Europe

With the creation of the European Union (EU), Nike Europe embarked on a strategy that would eliminate more than 20 warehouses scattered across the continent and consolidate operations into a single facility. The new facility was designed to handle all Nike apparel and the majority of the company's footwear. At the end of 1994, the new facility opened in Meerhout, Belgium. In total, the facility covered more than 70,000 square meters. According to an article describing the facility:

> At the heart of the warehouse is a 30 meter high bay storage cell (14,000 square meters in all, including footwear) with 10 storage and retrieval machines or stacker cranes available for handling apparel. Within the total product range of more than 20,000 lines (SKU's), the faster-moving products will be stored on pallets and the slow-moving lines held as individual cartons. Some 7 million items of apparel can be stocked.[23]

The Nike Europe warehouse is situated in a prime location. It is close to a major highway, an inland waterway (canal), and a rail terminal, and within an hour of the international port at Antwerp.

---

[22]"The 10 Best Warehouse Networks for 2000," Chicago Consulting <http://www.chicago-consulting.com/10best.htm>.

[23]"Nike's Dream," *Logistics Europe* 3, no. 1 (February 1995), p. 32.

TABLE 10–2   Best Warehouse Locations in the United States (2000)

Number of Warehouses in the Network	Shortest Average Distance to U.S. Population (Miles)	Best Warehouse Locations
1	797	Bloomington, IN
2	486	Chillicothe, OH
		Mojave, CA
3	376	Allentown, PA
		Mojave, CA
		McKenzie, TN
4	315	Hilltown, PA
		Mojave, CA
		Chicago, IL
		Meridian, MS
5	265	Madison, NJ
		Mojave, CA
		Chicago, IL
		Dallas, TX
		Macon, GA
6	237	Madison, NJ
		Pasadena, CA
		Chicago, IL
		Dallas, TX
		Macon, GA
		Tacoma, WA
7	218	Madison, NJ
		Pasadena, CA
		Chicago, IL
		Dallas, TX
		Gainesville, GA
		Tacoma, WA
		Lakeland, FL
8	203	Madison, NJ
		Pasadena, CA
		Chicago, IL
		Palestine, TX
		Gainesville, GA
		Tacoma, WA
		Lakeland, FL
		Denver, CO
9	188	Newark, NJ
		Pasadena, CA
		Rockford, IL
		Palestine, TX
		Gainesville, GA
		Tacoma, WA
		Lakeland, FL
		Denver, CO
		Mansfield, OH
10	174	Newark, NJ
		Alhambra, CA
		Rockford, IL
		Palestine, TX
		Gainesville, GA
		Tacoma, WA
		Lakeland, FL
		Denver, CO
		Mansfield, OH
		Oakland, CA

Source: "The 10 Best Warehouse Networks for 2000," Chicago Consulting <http//www.chicago-consulting.com/10best.htm>. Reprinted by permission of Chicago Consulting, Chicago, IL.

The site selection decision can be approached from both macro and micro perspectives. The *macro perspective* examines the issue of where to locate warehouses geographically (in a general area) to improve the sourcing of materials and the firm's market offering (improve service and/or reduce cost). The *micro perspective* examines factors that pinpoint specific locations within the larger geographic areas.

In his macro approach, Edgar Hoover identified three types of location strategies: (1) market positioned, (2) production positioned, and (3) intermediately positioned.[24]

Market Positioned Warehouses

The *market positioned* strategy locates warehouses nearest to the final customer. This maximizes customer service levels and enables the firm to use transportation economies—TL and CL shipments—from plants or sources to each warehouse location. The factors that influence the placement of warehouses near the market areas served include transportation costs, order cycle time, order size, local transportation availability, and customer service levels.

Production Positioned Warehouses

Production positioned warehouses are located close to sources of supply or production facilities. These warehouses generally cannot provide the same level of customer service as that offered by market positioned warehouses; instead, they serve as collection points or mixing facilities for products manufactured at a number of different plants. For multiproduct companies, transportation economies result from consolidation of shipments into TL or CL quantities. The factors that influence the placement of warehouses close to the point of production include perishability of raw materials, number of products in the product mix, assortment of products ordered by customers, and transportation consolidation rates.

Intermediately Positioned Warehouses

The final location strategy places warehouses at a midpoint between the final customer and the producer. Customer service levels for the *intermediately positioned* warehouses are typically higher than for the production positioned facilities and lower than for market positioned facilities. A firm often follows this strategy if it must offer high customer service levels and if it has a varied product offering being produced at several plant locations.

Another macro approach is to locate facilities using one of the following three strategies:[25]

1. Product warehouse strategy.
2. Market area warehouse strategy.
3. General purpose warehouse strategy.

Product Warehouse Strategy

Under the *product warehouse strategy,* the firm places only one product or product grouping in a warehouse. Each warehouse will therefore have a lot of one type of product but little or no inventory of other products. This can be a useful strategy when a firm has only a few products or product groupings that are high-turnover items. If the company has important customers that demand a specific product in the market area being served by the warehouse, or if it manufactures products that have distinctly different transportation freight classifications and size/weight/loadability characteristics, it may also consider the product warehouse strategy. This strategy has also been used for new-product introductions. Industries that employ this strategy include the farm equipment, appliance, electronics, apparel, and textile industries.

---

[24]Edgar M. Hoover, *The Location of Economic Activity* (New York: McGraw-Hill, 1948), p. 11.

[25]This discussion is based on a manufacturing plant location strategy proposed in Roger W. Schmenner, *Making Business Location Decisions* (Englewood Cliffs, NJ: Prentice Hall, 1982), pp. 11–15.

**Market Area
Warehouse Strategy**

A *market area warehouse strategy* positions full-line warehouses in specific market territories. Each facility stocks all the firm's products so that customers can receive complete orders from a single warehouse. Industries using this strategy include the beverage, food, paper products, glass, chemical, and furniture industries.

**General Purpose
Warehouse Strategy**

The *general purpose warehouse strategy* is similar to the previous approach in that facilities carry a full line of products. It differs, however, in that each warehouse serves all markets within a geographical market. Manufacturers of consumer packaged goods often employ this strategy.

A final macro approach includes the combined theories of a number of economic geographers. Many of these theories are based on distance and cost considerations.

Von Thunen's Model

Von Thunen called for a strategy of facility location based on cost minimization.[26] Specifically, he argued, when locating points of agricultural production, transportation costs should be minimized to result in maximum profits for farmers. His model assumed that market price and production costs would be identical (or nearly so) for any point of production. Since farmer profits equal market price minus production costs and transportation costs, the optimal location would have to be the one that minimized transportation expenditures.

Weber's Model

Weber also developed a model of facility location based on cost minimization.[27] According to Weber, the optimal site was the location that minimized "total transportation costs—the costs of transferring raw materials to the plant and finished goods to the market."[28] Weber classified raw materials into two categories according to how they affected transportation costs: location and processing characteristics. Location referred to the geographical availability of the raw materials. For items with very wide availability, few constraints on facility locations would exist. Processing characteristics were concerned with whether the raw material increased, remained the same, or decreased in weight as it was processed. If it decreased, facilities would best be located near the raw material source because transportation costs of finished goods would be less with lower weights. Conversely, if processing resulted in heavier finished goods, facilities would be best located near final customers. If processing resulted in no change in weight, locating at raw material sources or markets for finished goods would be equivalent.

Hoover's Model

Other geographers included the factors of demand and profitability in the location decision. Hoover examined both cost and demand elements of location analysis. Once again, his approach stressed cost minimization in determining an optimal location. Additionally, Hoover identified that transportation rates and distance were not linearly related; that is, rates increased with distance but at a decreasing rate. The tapering of rates over greater distances supported the placement of warehouses at the end points of the channel of distribution rather that at some intermediate location. In that regard, Hoover did not fully agree with Weber's location choices.

Greenhut's Model

Greenhut expanded the work of his predecessors by including factors specific to the company (e.g., environment, security) and profitability elements in the location choice. According to Greenhut, the optimal facility location was the one that maximized profits.[29]

---

[26]See *Von Thunen's Isolated State,* trans. C. M. Warnenburg and ed. Peter Hall (Oxford, England: Pergamon Press, 1966).

[27]See *Alfred Weber's Theory of the Location of Industries,* trans. Carl J. Friedrich (Chicago: University of Chicago Press, 1929).

[28]John J. Coyle, Edward J. Bardi, and C. John Langley, Jr., *The Management of Business Logistics,* 6th ed. (St. Paul, MN: West, 1996), p. 474.

[29]See Melvin L. Greenhut, *Plant Location in Theory and in Practice* (Chapel Hill: University of North Carolina Press, 1956).

**Center-of-Gravity
Approach**

Another approach, simplistic in scope, locates facilities based on transportation costs. Termed the *center-of-gravity approach,* it locates a warehouse or distribution center at a point that minimizes transportation costs for products moving between a manufacturing plant and the market. This approach can be viewed rather simply. Envision two pieces of rope being tied together with a knot and stretched across a circular piece of board, with unequal weights attached to each end of the rope. Initially, the knot would be located in the center of the circle. Upon the release of weights, the rope would shift to the point where the weights would be in balance. Adding ropes with varying weights would result in the same shifting of the knot (assuming the knots were all in the same place). If the weights represented transportation costs, then the position where the knot would come to rest after releasing the weights would represent the center of gravity, or the position where transportation costs would be minimized.[30]

The approach provides general answers to the warehouse location problem, but it must be modified to take into account such factors as geography, time, and customer service levels.

**Micro View
of Location Analysis**

From a micro perspective, more specific factors must be examined.[31] If a firm wants to use private warehousing, it must consider:

- Quality and variety of transportation carriers serving the site.
- Quality and quantity of available labor.
- Labor rates.
- Cost and quality of industrial land.
- Potential for expansion.
- Tax structure.
- Building codes.
- Nature of the community environment.
- Costs of construction.
- Cost and availability of utilities.
- Cost of money locally.
- Local government tax allowances.

If the firm wants to use public warehousing, it will be necessary to consider:

- Facility characteristics.
- Warehouse services provided.
- Availability and proximity to motor carrier terminals.
- Availability of local cartage.
- Other companies using the facility.
- Availability of computer services and communications.
- Type and frequency of inventory reports.

---

[30]For a similar discussion of the center-of-gravity approach, see Philip B. Schary, *Logistics Decisions* (Chicago: Dryden Press, 1984), p. 423.

[31]For a comprehensive discussion of the warehouse location decision, see "A Guide to Site Selection in the '90s," *Traffic Management* 34, no. 9 (September 1993) Warehousing and Distribution Supplement, pp. 20–23; Thomas L. Freese, "Site Selection," in *The Logistics Handbook,* ed. James F. Robeson and William C. Copacino (New York: Free Press, 1994), pp. 604–31; Steve Harris, "Site Unseen," *Operations & Fulfillment* 8, no. 1 (January/February 2000), pp. 54–57; Tan Miller, "Learning about Facility Location Models," *Distribution* 92, no. 5 (May 1993), pp. 47–50; and Robert Pano, "Pull Out the Stops in Your Network," *Transportation and Distribution* 35, no. 8 (August 1994), pp. 38–39.

Schmenner proposed an eight-step approach to a business location search that we can apply to the warehouse site selection decision (see Figure 10–8).[32] It has been used to select a site or location for a facility. The process includes the following steps:

Schmenner's Eight-Step Approach to Site Selection

1. After the firm has made the initial decision to establish a facility at a new location (not yet determined), it solicits input from those persons in the company affected by the decision.

FIGURE 10–8

Approach to site selection

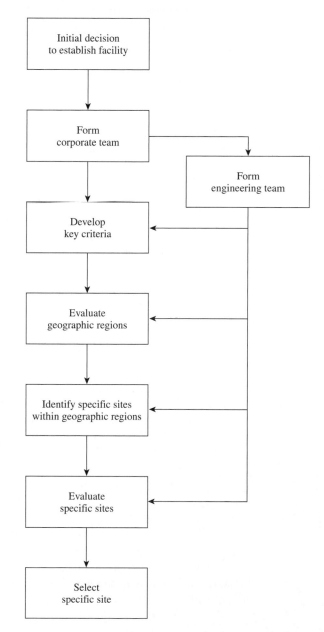

Source: Based on the site selection approach suggested by Roger W. Schmenner, *Making Business Location Decisions* (Englewood Cliffs, NJ: Prentice Hall, 1982), pp. 11–15.

---

[32]Adapted from Schmenner, *Making Business Location Decisions,* pp. 16–21.

2. Management designates a corporate team to examine potential sites and to collect information on selected attributes, such as land availability, labor requirements, transportation options, utilities, environmental factors, and products to be stored.

3. The firm establishes a separate engineering team to examine potential sites in terms of topography, geology, and facility design.

4. The corporate team develops a list of key criteria for the new location. Such criteria take into account the needs of all functional areas of the business.

5. The team evaluates geographic regions in view of the key criteria established; it identifies potential regional sites.

6. The team identifies specific sites within acceptable regional areas. Typically, it selects 10 or fewer sites for in-depth investigation.

7. The corporate team examines each prospective site, using the set of factors deemed to be important. The team makes frequent site visits and creates a ranking of potential locations.

8. The team selects a specific site from the recommended locations. This decision is often made by the person most directly affected, normally the senior logistics executive.

Each step in the process is interactive, progressing from the general to the specific. It may be a highly formal or informal process. The process can also be centralized at the corporate level, decentralized at the divisional or functional level, or some combination of each. What is important, however, is that even with the differences that exist among companies, most firms follow some type of logical process when making a location decision.

In some cases, firms use computer modeling approaches. Computerized location models can be classified into four categories: planar models, warehousing models, network models, and discrete or mixed-integer programming models.

Planar Models

Planar models are the simplest. They are optimization models in that they attempt to identify the best locations for the facilities:

> Typically a planar location problem involves the location of one or more new facilities in the plane, with costs incurred which depend upon an appropriately chosen "planar" distance (e.g., Euclidean distance) between the new facilities and existing facilities which have known planar locations. The new facilities are to be located so as to minimize an appropriately chosen total cost expression.[33]

Planar models can be very useful in identifying general locations for facilities and are widely used for this purpose. Identification of more specific locations usually involves more sophisticated modeling procedures.

Warehousing Models

Warehousing models are classified into two types: external location and internal location. External location models examine the issue of where to actually locate warehouses. Internal location models address the location of items inside the warehouse, that is, layout and design considerations (to be discussed in the next section of this chapter). The external models are often discrete or mixed-integer models, although they are often discussed separately.

---

[33]Richard L. Francis, Leon F. McGinnis, and John A. White, "Location Analysis," *European Journal of Operational Research* 12, no. 3 (March 1983), p. 222.

Network Models   Network models are similar to planar models, with one important exception; possible locations are constrained in that they must be on or near a transport network. While planar models identify optimal facility locations anywhere in the plane, network models only locate facilities on various transport networks such as roads, shipping lanes, rail lines, and air corridors. Therefore, the number of potential sites is more limited, although the sites determined by the model are much more realistic.

Discrete Models   Discrete models are the most realistic, but also the most complex, location models. They incorporate fixed and variable costs:

> To set up and operate a warehouse usually involves significant fixed costs that are not directly proportional to the level of activity. In many cases, the potential warehouse locations are limited to a few specific sites due to availability, capability, etc., and these sites each may have differing costs for acquiring the warehouse, differing costs for operating the warehouse, differing shipping costs, and differing capabilities . . . With discrete location problems, we are not so much moving specified facilities about to find their best locations . . . as we are selecting a few facilities from a finite set of candidate facilities.[34]

The combination of technology developments and lower prices for computers and related equipment has made it easier and less costly to use computer simulations to locate facilities. Because of these factors, combining customer service attributes with cost data on a multitude of location factors will be feasible using simulation.

Related to the location of facilities is the decision to design an optimal structure that maximizes efficiency and effectiveness. This is the warehouse layout and design decision.

Warehouse Layout and Design

Where should things be located in the organization's logistics system? More specifically, where should products be located within a warehouse? With an average warehouse containing approximately 22,000 SKUs, this is an important decision because it has a critical effect on system efficiency and productivity.[35] A good warehouse layout can (1) increase output, (2) improve product flow, (3) reduce costs, (4) improve service to customers, and (5) provide better employee working conditions.[36]

The optimal warehouse layout and design for an organization will vary by the type of products being stored, availability of financial resources, level and type of competition, and customer needs. Additionally, there are various cost trade-offs between labor, equipment, space, and information.[37] For example, as previously shown in Figure 10–5, the purchase of more expensive, yet more efficient, materials handling equipment can affect the optimal size of a warehouse facility. Installation of an automated conveyor system to reduce labor costs and raise productivity can affect the configuration of a warehouse.

Within a warehouse, randomized and dedicated storage are two examples of how products can be located and arranged.

---

[34]Ibid., p. 240.

[35]Philippe R. Hebert, "Manage Inventory? Better Find It First!" *Transportation and Distribution,* Buyer's Guide Issue (July 1995), p. 8. Also see James M. Apple, Jr., "Thoughts on Warehouse Layout," *Warehousing Forum* 15, no. 1 (December 1999), pp. 1–4.

[36]Greg Owens and Robert Mann, "Materials Handling System Design," in *The Distribution Handbook,* ed. James F. Robeson and William C. Copacino (New York: Free Press, 1994), pp. 519–45.

[37]See "Storage/Staging: Planning Pays Off," *Modern Materials Handling* 50, no. 5 (Mid-April 1995), pp. 12–15.

Randomized Storage   **Randomized Storage.**   Randomized, or floating slot, storage places items in the closest available slot, bin, or rack. Products are then retrieved on a first-in, first-out (FIFO) basis. This approach maximizes space utilization, although it requires longer travel times between order-picking locations. Randomized systems often employ a computerized automatic storage and retrieval system (AS/RS), which minimizes labor and handling costs.

Dedicated Storage   **Dedicated Storage.**   In dedicated, or fixed-slot, storage, products are stored in permanent locations within a warehouse. Three methods can be used to implement the dedicated storage approach, including storing items by (1) part number sequence, (2) usage rates, or (3) activity levels (e.g., grouping products into classes or families based on their level of activity or throughput rates).[38]

Compatibility   In terms of overall warehouse layout, products may be grouped according to their compatibility, complementarity, or popularity. *Compatibility* refers to how well products may be stored together. For example, pharmaceuticals cannot be stored with bagged agricultural chemicals in the United States because of federal regulations. And many years ago, before the development of newer paints, it was discovered that automobile tires and consumer appliances could not be stored together. Chemical vapors given off by the tires reacted with the pigments in the appliance paint, resulting in slight color changes. Appliances then had to be repainted or sold at a discount.

Complementarity   *Complementarity* refers to how often products are ordered together and therefore stored together. Computer disk drives, CD-ROMs, and monitors; pens and pencils; and desks and chairs are examples of complementary products that are usually stored close to each other.

Popularity   *Popularity* relates to the fact that products have different inventory turnover rates or demand rates. Another term used for this turnover rate is *velocity.* Items that are in greatest demand should be stored closest to shipping/receiving docks. Slow-moving items should be stored elsewhere, at more remote locations within warehouses.

Using the computer, it is possible to group products within a warehouse so that the following objectives are met:[39]

- Fast movers are placed nearest the outbound truck docks. This minimizes the distances traveled daily by materials handling equipment.
- Slow movers are located at points farthest from outbound shipping docks. This ensures that lengthy horizontal moves by materials handling equipment are minimized.
- The middle area of the warehouse is reserved for products received in periodic batches, products requiring rework before shipping, items compatible with fast-moving products, and backup overflow from fast-moving areas.
- Aisles are redesigned to facilitate the most efficient flow of product to and from dock areas.
- Storage areas are configured to match the velocity and dimensions of each major product, rather than designing all storage bins, racks, and floor storage

[38]For a brief discussion of random and dedicated storage, see Hebert, "Manage Inventory? Better Find It First!" pp. 7–9.

[39]For a discussion of how computers can be used to group products in a warehouse, see Richard A. Parrott, "Automated Space Planning for Warehousing," *Transportation and Distribution* 33, no. 7 (July 1992), pp. 54, 56; and Tompkins et al., *Facilities Planning,* pp. 418–34.

areas in the same dimensions. This facilitates the maximum use of available cubic space, because products are matched not only to the width of each slot but also to the depth and height of each storage slot.

An Example of Warehouse Redesign

Figure 10–9 depicts a 40′ × 40′ storage area before and after redesign.

In order to complete this warehouse interior redesign, all individual stockkeeping units (SKUs) were analyzed for a 12-month period. The following data were collected: total number of receipts and shipments; average size and frequency of receipts and shipments per day, week, and month; number of line items received and picked daily, weekly, and monthly; dimensions of the product; and materials handling capacity.

FIGURE 10–9

Two warehouse configurations

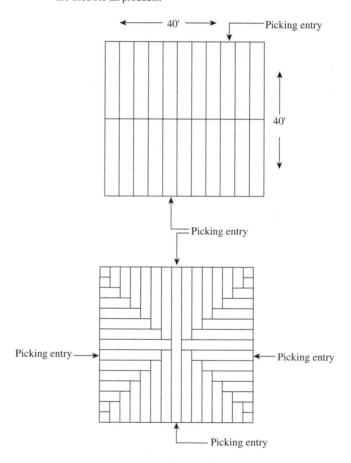

Before: Standard openings and depths are used for all products.

After: Both store widths and depths vary according to the volume (size) of receipts, velocity (frequency and size) of order pickups, and dimensions (widths) of the product.

Source: Professor Jay U. Sterling, University of Alabama, and former director of logistics planning for Whirlpool Corporation

Using this technique, a major manufacturer of consumer durable goods was able to increase the effective capacity of its major distribution center by 20 percent, and thereby forestall a planned expansion for several years. The firm also saved $200,000 per year in reduced labor and outside overflow warehousing.[40]

In addition to internal space layout, it is also important to analyze a warehouse's external configuration. Four aspects of external layout are critical: truck docks, rail requirements, external security measures, and physical features such as roof and windows. As an illustration, Table 10–3 presents an analysis of how an organization would

---

TABLE 10–3   An Example of External Warehouse Layout Analysis

Let's take a look at a hypothetical warehouse which handles 6,000,000 cases per year. This warehouse operates two shifts a day, five days a week. Seventy percent of inbound shipments are via truck; 90 percent of outbound shipments are via truck.

Trucks are unloaded at a rate of 200 cases per worker-hour for inbound shipments, and loaded at a rate of 175 cases per worker-hour for outbound shipments. Both inbound and outbound trucks are loaded with 500 cases. A 25 percent safety factor is desired due to the fact that the flow of trucks throughout the month is apt not to be uniform.

The determine the number of truck doors, you can work through the following calculations:

Step I: Determine Inbound Requirements
a. Percent inbound via truck × total inbound
     70 percent × 6,000,000 = 4,200,000 cases
b. Inbound cases/cases per truck
     4,200,000/500 = 8,400 inbound trucks
c. Hours per truck
     Cases per truck/inbound productivity
          500/200 = 2.5 hours per inbound truck
d. Total inbound truck hours (b × c)
     8,400 × 2.5 = 21,000 hours/year

Step II: Determine Outbound Requirements
a. Percent outbound via truck × total outbound
     90 percent × 6,000,000 = 5,400,000
b. Outbound cases/cases per truck
     5,400,000/500 = 10,800 trucks
c. Hours per truck
     Cases per truck/outbound productivity
          500/175 = 2.85 hours per outbound truck
d. Total outbound truck hours (b × c)
     10,800 × 2.85 = 30,780 hours/year

Step III: Total Hours Required

Inbound hours	21,000 hours
Outbound hours	30,780 hours
Subtotal	51,780 hours
Safefy factor for peaking (25 percent)	21,945 hours
Total hours	64,725 hours

Step IV: Hours Available per Year
     52 Weeks × hours per day × days per week
     52 × 16 (2 shifts) × 5 = 4,160
Step V: Doors Required
     Truck hours required/annual hours available
     64,725 hours/4,160 hours = 15.5 or 16 doors

Source: Howard P. Weisz, "Analyzing Your Warehouse's External Layout," *WERC Memo,* no. 4 (March 1985), pp. 1–2. Used with permission of Warehousing Education and Research Council, Inc.

[40]Illustration provided by Professor Jay U. Sterling, University of Alabama, and former director of logistics planning for Whirlpool Corporation.

determine the number of truck doors needed in a typical warehouse. Similar analyses could be performed for all facets of warehouse layout and design.

The entire area of facilities development—size and number of warehouses, location analysis, warehouse layout and design—is an important yet complex part of warehouse management.

In recent years, global issues have begun to play a much more significant role in warehouse decision making as organizations attempt to optimize their logistics networks.

International Dimensions of Warehousing

Usually, products will be stored at some point prior to their final consumption. Depending on the particular conditions in effect within each market area, products may be stored at different points within the channel of distribution.

For organizations located in Asia, warehouse sites may be selected in Bombay, Hong Kong, Kuala Lumpur, Manila, Melbourne, Shanghai, Singapore, and/or Tokyo. In South America, Buenos Aires, Bogotá, Caracas, and/or Rio de Janeiro may be the locations of choice. Africa offers warehouse choices in Cairo, Cape Town, Kinshasa, Lagos, and/or Nairobi. In Western Europe, organizations such as Philips (electronics), Nestlé (food), and Perstorp (chemicals) must store a variety of products at factories and warehouses throughout Western Europe in order to provide market coverage to the EU.

Many organizations with customers located in foreign markets, such as Hoffman-LaRoche (pharmaceuticals)[41] and Life Fitness (exercise bikes), have to determine the number of warehouse locations to use in various global regions because customers could just as easily purchase similar products from local competitors. The nuances of each world region must be considered when making optimal warehouse location decisions. Here are some examples:[42]

Examples of Warehousing throughout the World

- Hoffman-LaRoche consolidated inventories from several warehouses into only two: one for northern Europe, and one for southern Europe and the rest of the world. This was possible because of the unification of Europe in early 1993.

- Life Fitness has concentrated its European warehouse, office, and showroom in Rotterdam. This centralized inventory of generic products sold throughout Europe allows the firm to provide higher customer service levels while simultaneously reducing costs.

Warehousing Requirements Vary Globally

Due to differences in culture, technology, accepted practice, competition, and so on, warehousing requirements will likely vary across geographic regions of the world. For example, in Japan, Europe, and elsewhere, the retail network is composed of a great number of small shops, each having little capacity for inventory storage. As a result, such shops order frequently from distributors, manufacturers, or other channel intermediaries. The burden of storage is carried by the manufacturer or other channel members rather than the retailer. In the United States, because there are fewer, but larger, retail stores, the storage function is more easily shifted away from the channel intermediaries directly to the retailer.

The type of transportation equipment available in an area can affect warehouse decisions: "The wide variety of delivery vehicles used in some countries makes it difficult to standardize on warehouse designs and makes efficient loading and unloading

[41]See "Logistics Package," *Logistics Europe* 3, no. 4 (August 1995), pp. 30–32.

[42]Tom Andel, "Make the World Your Warehouse," *Transportation and Distribution* 38, no. 8 (August 1997), pp. 88–92.

Global

BBN Communications Serves Customers Worldwide

BBN Communications (Cambridge, Massachusetts) manufactures high-value telecommunications and networking equipment, "including components that allow a firm's satellite offices to combine all computer traffic on a local area network and communicate with the home office to share information." The firm was searching for ways to improve service levels to customers located in North America and Europe.

"BBN Communications' remote warehousing solution relies on same-day shipping and delivery of . . . components. BBN has established sites in London and Stuttgart for warehousing its high-value materials. Not only do these sites build a comfort level for the parts managers, but they also make life

easier on the BBN sales staff . . . There are hidden dollar savings to using a location within the EEC for warehousing parts. One never knows to which country a part might be sent and it is impractical to establish warehouses in every country. By establishing parts centers within the EEC, BBN pays duties only once on materials shipped into [another country] and stored at a parts bank.

So successful has the European parts bank been [the company] is considering establishment of a similar depot in Asia . . . either Singapore or Hong Kong—to take advantage of the duty free ports there, again bringing cost savings into the warehousing and distribution network."

Source: Renee Sall, "Case Study: BBN Communications," *Export Today* 9, no. 6 (July/August 1993), p. 45.

---

a challenge. Warehouses in many countries load straight from the ground, and some don't even use pallets."[43]

When an international firm needs warehousing facilities in a foreign market, it may find an abundance of sophisticated, modern warehouses in some industrial nations. In Japan and Western Europe, organizations use high-cube automated warehousing. This is due primarily to high land and labor costs, which require firms to build higher warehouses and use automation to minimize labor.

Quality and Availability of Warehousing Vary Widely

On the other hand, in less developed countries, storage facilities may be nonexistent or limited in availability or sophistication. In the latter instance, the product package or shipping container may have to serve the warehousing purpose. Packaging issues will be addressed in Chapter 11.

In the United States, many public warehouses provide services such as consolidation and breakbulk, customer billing, traffic management, packaging, import/export assistance, and product labeling. Public warehouses in many foreign markets may also provide services in addition to storage.[44]

Like all logistics activities, the warehousing and storage activity must be administered differently in each market. It is the responsibility of the logistics executive to recognize how the storage activity differs and to adjust the organization's strategy accordingly.

---

[43]Ibid., p. 92.

[44]For an example from Mexico, see Russ Dixon, "Logistics in Mexico: The Warehouse Solution," *Export Today* 9, no. 6 (July/August 1993), pp. 38–39.

Warehouse Productivity

To obtain maximum logistics efficiency, each component of the logistics system must operate at the highest levels. This means that high levels of productivity must be achieved, especially in the warehousing area. Productivity gains in warehousing are important to organizations (in terms of reduced costs) and to customers (in terms of improved customer service levels).

Productivity has been defined in many ways, but most definitions include the elements of real outputs and real inputs, utilization, and warehouse performance:

Productivity

Productivity is the ratio of real output to real input. Examples are cases handled per labor-hour and lines selected per equipment-hour.

Utilization

Utilization is the ratio of capacity used to available capacity. Examples are percentage of pallet spaces filled in a warehouse and employee-hours worked versus employee-hours available.

Performance

Performance is the ratio of actual output to standard output (or standard hours earned to actual hours). Examples are cases picked per hour versus standard rate planned per hour, and actual return on assets employed versus budgeted return on assets employed.[45]

Any working definition of productivity probably includes all three components because all are interrelated.[46] The expression "You can't manage what you don't measure" is just as true in warehousing as it is elsewhere. Most organizations use a variety of measures to examine warehouse productivity, and these measures tend to evolve over time in terms of their sophistication.[47]

Additionally, performance data must be available and used as the basis for corrective action. It is not sufficient merely to identify problem areas. It is also vital that organizations take appropriate actions to improve poor performance whenever possible. Therefore, decision strategies should be developed that will handle most problem areas before they develop. This is the essence of contingency planning and proactive management.

There is no single best approach that a firm can pursue in warehouse productivity measurement. Management action is determined by a variety of factors, such as customer service levels (e.g., shipping performance, error rates, order cycle time); inventory accuracy (e.g., correct quantities of each SKU at all warehouse locations); space utilization (e.g., the right inventory, square foot or cube utilization of facilities), and labor productivity (e.g., throughput rates).[48] It is universally accepted, however, that problems should be pinpointed based on cause and effect. Once they are pinpointed, the organization can institute various controls or corrective actions to improve warehouse productivity.

---

[45]A. T. Kearney, Inc., *Measuring and Improving Productivity in Physical Distribution* (Oak brook, IL: National Council of Physical Distribution Management, 1984), p. 188.

[46]For a discussion of various productivity measures, see Kenneth B. Ackerman, "Meeting the 'Process Needs' of Warehousing." *Warehousing Forum* 9, no. 5 (April 1994), pp. 1–3.

[47]A number of examples of productivity measurement approaches and systems are presented in "Benchmarking Warehouse Operations," *WERCwatch* (November 1999), pp. 1–11; "Establishing Metrics to Improve Performance," *WERCSheet* 22, no. 2 (February 1999), pp. 8–11; and "A Measure of Excellence," *WERCSheet* 21, no. 8 (September 1998), pp. 8–10.

[48]*The Journey to Warehousing Excellence,* Monograph Series No. M0003 (Raleigh, NC: Tompkins Associates, undated), p. 22; see also Kenneth B. Ackerman, "Benchmarking the Holy Grail," *Warehousing Forum* 11, no. 2 (Janaury 1996), pp. 1–2; and "How to Benchmark Warehouse Operations," *Distribution* 91, no. 9 (September 1992), pp. 60–64; and Catherine Cooper and Steve Mulaik, "Warehouse Management: Killer Clues," *Operations & Fulfillment* 8, no. 1 (January/February 2000), pp. 12–22.

Because warehousing is such a significant component of the logistics process in terms of its impact on cost and service, executives are acutely aware of the need to improve warehouse productivity.[49] There are many ways in which productivity can be improved, including methods-related, equipment-related, systems-related, and training/ motivation-related programs.[50]

Methods-Related Programs

Methods-related programs include those involving warehouse cube utilization, warehouse layout and design, methods and procedures analysis, batch picking of small orders, combined put-away/picking, wrap packaging,[51] unitization, inventory cycle counting, product line obsolescence, standardized packaging, and warehouse consolidation. More specifically, these methods-related programs have been found to improve productivity:

1. Expand existing warehouse storage capacity through the installation of narrow aisle equipment and racking, in lieu of standard equipment and racks.

2. Store materials multi-deep in flow bins or racks using handling equipment that reduces the number of aisles required to service a given number of storage units.

3. Use variable-height storage racks to accommodate additional pallets for greater cube utilization.

4. Install mezzanines over small pick areas, which results in greater small pick capacity in the same square foot (meter) area.

5. Locate fast-moving (high-turnover) products nearest to the shipping and receiving docks to minimize travel time in the warehouse.

6. Locate products requiring similar handing in the same area so as to maximize the use of equipment and personnel.

7. Develop work simplification procedures that allow employee performance standards to be increased.

8. Use batch picking of infrequently picked, slow-moving items.

9. Use materials handling equipment for both put-away and picking on a single trip, thus increasing equipment utilization.

10. Use stretch- and shrink-wrap packaging to reduce product handling requirements and shipping damage.

11. Group individual items in a shipment into larger units. Unitization can reduce handling costs by up to 90 percent.

12. Use inventory cycle counting, rather than curtailing operations for a yearly physical inventory, to improve labor costs and inventory availability.

13. Initiate programs that review product obsolescence and determine whether items can be eliminated from inventory.

14. Eliminate poorly located or uneconomic warehouses.

---

[49]For discussion of various methods for improving warehouse productivity, see Ackerman, *Warehousing Profitably,* pp. 11–16.

[50]This material was paraphrased from A. T. Kearney, Inc., *Measuring and Improving Productivity in Physical Distribution,* pp. 227–34. Used with permission of the Council of Logistics Management, formerly the National Council of Physical Distribution Management.

[51]Wrap packaging includes shrink and stretch film used to protect products from the elements and maintain product integrity during shipment and storage; it was designed to replace rigid, generally corrugated, packaging.

Equipment-Related Programs

Equipment-related programs include the use of optical scanners, automatic labeling devices, computer generated put-away and pick lists, automated materials handling equipment, communications devices, computers and AS/RS, carousels, and conveyors. Many of the specific types of equipment used in the warehouse will be explained in Chapter 11, but specific practices relating to equipment include the following:

1. Utilize electronic scanning devices for check-in and routing cartons in an automated warehouse.
2. Use automatic labelers for put-away lists to reduce location errors and improve labor productivity.
3. Generate on-line computer-sequenced put-away and pick lists that reduce search time for items.
4. Use automated rather than standard (nonautomated) materials handling equipment.
5. Install communication devices to allow constant contact between material handlers and other warehouse personnel.
6. Use computers in all phases of warehouse operations to increase speed and accuracy of information transfer.
7. Automate or semiautomate warehouse operations to reduce labor costs and improve efficiency.

Systems-Related Programs

Systems-related programs include the use of router/location systems, geographic or zone picking, and random location of products in the warehouse. Some of the specific order-picking approaches were presented earlier in this chapter, but others such as the following can be employed:

1. Use computer router/location systems to improve the levels of warehouse efficiency and effectiveness.
2. Monitor labor efficiency through the use of engineered labor standards.
3. Institute programs to provide a more constant order backlog from which to work. This order backlog can be provided by lengthening the time span during which the warehouse may hold an order, thus tending to level the load, or by encouraging customers to order less frequently and in larger quantities on specified days.
4. Pick items in specified areas of the warehouse and consolidate in a centralized location.
5. Use a computer to randomly assign items to any available space to increase warehouse cube utilization.

Training/Motivation-Related Programs

Training/motivation-related programs include employee training, management development programs, incentive systems, and awards recognition.[52] These programs can improve warehouse productivity:

1. Conduct formal training at periodic intervals on key warehouse tasks so as to improve employee productivity and safety.

---

[52]For a thorough discussion of training issues relating to warehousing, see Stephen A. LeMay and Jon C. Carr, *The Growth and Development of Logistics Personnel* (Oak Brook, IL: Council of Logistics Management, 1999), Chapter 5, "Warehousing," pp. 89–127.

Technology

Software with a Vroommmmmmmmmm—Porsche

In our automobile-dependent society, car owners hate being grounded while their vehicles languish in a repair shop, waiting for parts. For that reason, luxury-car maker Porsche decided to shift gears, so to speak, and find a way to speed up parts delivery to its North American dealers.

Porsche operates a parts facility in Reno, Nevada, for the North American market. That facility stores parts totaling $18 million in inventory value and representing approximately 35,000 SKUs, which are used to fill an average of 500 orders each day. In addition to standard maintenance items such as filters and gaskets, the warehouse stores components for engines, electrical systems, transmissions, drive lines, and clutches.

The majority of parts are shipped by sea directly from Germany to the West Coast and then moved by truck to the Nevada distribution center. As a rule, parts are individually packaged in Germany and consolidated into larger shipping containers for overseas transit.

Once Porsche's executives began looking for ways to improve parts service to dealers, they quickly concluded that warehouse-management systems (WMS) software would both give the distribution center more accurate information on stored parts and eliminate the need for paper documentation.

Along with the software, the company installed a radio-frequency data-collection (RFDC) system to handle up-to-the-minute inventory control. When a worker scans a bar-coded part in the receiving area, that information is relayed via radio waves to the computer that keeps tabs on parts in stock.

The WMS in conjunction with the RF system has expedited the process of receiving parts. In the past, it took Porsche as long as 10 days to log in a shipment. Now it's done in three days and there is almost simultaneous availability of parts to fill orders.

In addition to providing inventory visibility, the software has improved the automaker's accuracy in both its parts receiving and shipping operations. That means Porsche can provide its dealers with information on real-time availability of parts. As a result, it has reduced shipping errors and has lost fewer sales when items were placed on back order. Warehouse throughput has also improved by 17 percent.

Source: James Aaron Cooke, "Software with a Vroommmmmmmmmm," *Logistics Management* 37, no. 8 (August 1998), p. 103.

2. Conduct formal training of management personnel to improve leadership and communications skills.

3. Implement reward/incentive systems that provide bonuses or other compensation for performance above some specified standard.

4. Provide awards programs for recognizing specific individuals who perform well in their assigned tasks.

All of the preceding programs can be implemented individually by most organizations. However, most will employ several methods in combination to improve warehouse productivity.

Financial Dimensions of Warehousing

Financial control of warehousing is closely tied to logistics productivity and corporate profitability.[53] Before the various activities of warehousing can be properly integrated

---

[53]For a discussion of general financial issues associated with warehousing that are of interest to senior management, see James D. Krasner, "Satisfying the Chief Financial Officer," *Warehousing Forum* 10, no. 7 (June 1995), pp. 1–2.

into a single unified system, management must be aware of the cost of each activity. This is where financial accounting and control techniques become important.

One approach, which has proved very successful in the financial control of warehousing activities, is *activity-based costing (ABC).* Accurate and timely financial data allow warehouse executives to properly plan, administer, and control warehousing activities. Traditional costing systems, in place at many firms, often do not provide financial data in the proper form for use in making warehousing decisions. Frequently, it is difficult to identify how warehousing costs affect overall corporate profitability and how changes in costs in one area affect costs in another.

A large number of companies are implementing ABC in order to have better warehousing cost information. One writer describes ABC as follows:

Activity-Based Costing (ABC)

ABC is simply the tracing of overhead and direct costs to specific products, services or customers. The tracing of costs follows a two stage process. The first stage assigns resource costs based on the amount of each resource consumed in performing specific warehousing activities. The second stage assigns warehousing activity costs to the products, services or customers consuming the activities based on actual consumption.

ABC unbundles traditional cost accounts and re-orients costs to show how resources are actually consumed. [Figure 10–10] compares the two approaches.[54]

Four Levels of Sophistication in Warehouse Accounting and Control

Companies are often at various levels of sophistication in terms of warehouse accounting and control. Four levels of sophistication have been identified:

- *Level I:* Warehouse costs are allocated in total, using a single allocation base.
- *Level II:* Warehouse costs are aggregated by major warehouse function (e.g., handling, storage, and administration) and are allocated using a separate allocation base for each function.
- *Level III:* Warehouse costs are aggregated by major activity within each function (e.g., receiving, put-away, order pick) and are allocated using a separate allocation base for each activity.

Figure 10–10

A comparison of traditional costing versus activity-based costing

General ledger view of warehousing costs		Activity-based view of warehousing costs	
Storage and handling	$40.1	Dry storage	$25.0
General and administration	30.9	Refrigerated storage	8.1
		Receiving	20.0
Trucking and delivery	14.5	Shipping	18.8
		Billing	3.2
Freight consolidation	2.4	Delivery	6.0
		Packaging/stenciling	1.8
Value-added services	3.3	Freight consolidation	3.0
		Materials handling equipment	5.3
Total	**$91.2**	**Total**	**$91.2**

Source: Terrance L. Pohlen, "Activity Based Costing for Warehouse Managers," *Warehousing Forum* 9, no. 5 (May 1994), p. 1.

---

[54]Terrance L. Pohlen, "Activity Based Costing for Warehouse Managers," *Warehousing Forum* 9, no. 5 (May 1994), pp. 1–3; also see Lisa Ellram et al., "Understanding the Implications of Activity-Based Costing for Logistics Management," *Annual Conference Proceedings of the Council of Logistics Management* (Oak Brook, IL: Council of Logistics Management, 1994), pp. 11–25; and "Use ABC to Improve Supply Chain Management & Reduce Logistics Costs," *IOMA's Report on Managing Logistics,* Issue 99-07 (July 1999), pp. 2–3.

Creative Solutions

Less Warehousing, Better Distribution

Lincoln Electric is the world's leading manufacturer of welding equipment and supplies, as well as a major producer of electric motors. The company used to have 36 to 40 small area warehouses scattered around the country. Pricing policies were designed to encourage large orders that would simplify manufacturing and shipping to end users and stocking distributors.

Because the firm's local warehouses were not large enough to carry a complete stock to supply the growing needs of the distribution network, the company decided to consolidate its distribution in a much smaller number of larger, well-stocked regional distribution centers.

The first distribution center was set up in Cleveland, Ohio, toward the end of 1989. New centers were added to cover the rest of the country and corresponding local warehouses were closed when they became redundant. Not only did the consolidation reduce the degree to which inventory was dissipated in multiple locations, but it provided an opportunity to refocus the local facilities.

Currently there are six of the new regional distribution centers located across the United States and two in Canada. Others are planned for Philadelphia and Mexico, as well as parts of Europe and South America. The U.S. distribution centers range in size from 30,000 to 100,000 square feet and run with staffs that vary from three to about a dozen employees.

To get up and running faster, operations of some new distribution centers were contracted out, although each has at least one Lincoln Electric employee at the location.

By working more effectively with its distributors and helping them serve their end users better, Lincoln Electric is able to meet the broader needs of the entire arc welding market more effectively. The independent welding distributor can carry a lower level of inventory and rely on Lincoln Electric distribution centers to provide most items his or her customers need, usually in 24 to 72 hours.

Customers get more of the products they need to keep operating with minimal delay. Distributors can provide better customer service and turn inventories more often while maintaining smaller stocks and relying on the distribution centers for backup.

By improving the way it serves customers, Lincoln Electric receives greater efficiency, increased sales, and positive customer relations.

Source: John J. Hach, "Less Warehousing, Better Distribution," *Transportation and Distribution* 36, no. 3 (March 1995), pp. 108–15. Reprinted from various editions of *Transportation & Distribution* and *Industry Week*. Copyright 1995 permission granted by Penton, Cleveland, Ohio.

- *Level IV:* Costs are categorized in matrix form reflecting each major activity, natural expense, and cost behavior type. Separate allocations are developed for each cost category using allocation bases that reflect the key differences in warehousing characteristics among cost objectives.[55]

In a study of 140 companies in 19 types of industries, the accounting firm of Ernst and Whinney identified five key findings related to warehouse accounting and control:

1. The configuration of warehouse networks—numbers, sizes, and locations—[varies] widely between industries and often among firms in the same industry.
2. The way a company markets its products or merchandise is a major determinant of the overall warehouse network structure and function in successful companies.

---

[55]Ernst and Whinney, *Warehouse Accounting and Control: Guidelines for Distribution and Financial Managers* (Oak Brook, IL: National Council of Physical Distribution Management, 1985), p. 50. Used with permission of the Council of Logistics Management, formerly the National Council of Physical Distribution Management.

3. Specific warehouse networks and the positioning of warehouse management have generally evolved in response to external developments and pressures—not as a result of strategic distribution plans.

4. The functions of individual warehouses in the distribution network fall into major categories (e.g., stockpiling, consolidation, and distribution), each of which requires different types of information to manage effectively.

5. Warehouse operations encompass discrete activities that should be analyzed separately for both operational and financial management purposes.[56]

This is what accounting and control are all about. Simply stated, it is having the right kind of financial data available when and where they are needed, and in a form that is usable by as many functional areas of the organization as possible. Ultimately, such data are essential to making the necessary cost/service trade-offs within the warehousing activity and between other logistics functions. The accurate determination of logistics costs is the subject of Chapter 16.

Summary

In this chapter we described the importance of warehousing in the logistics system. Economies of scale, costs, and customer service are the most important considerations. The types of options available to a firm include public (rented) and private (owned or leased) warehousing. Logistics executives must understand the advantages and disadvantages of each option in order to make optimal warehouse management decisions.

The major functions of warehousing are movement, storage, and information transfer. Movement consists of receiving, transfer, order selection, and shipping. Storage can be temporary or semipermanent. Information transfer is the link between all of the activities that take place in the warehouse. Such activities can take place domestically or internationally.

Facility development is a large part of warehouse management. Decisions relating to the size and number of warehouses, location of facilities, and layout and design have significant impact on the organization's ability to satisfy its customers and make a profit. Various methods, techniques, and approaches relative to each decision area were described. Those topics led us to examine the issues of warehouse productivity, accounting, and control.

Within a warehouse, manual (nonautomated) or automated materials handling equipment can be employed. Standard equipment can be categorized by the function it performs: storage and order picking, transportation and sorting, or shipping. Automated equipment includes items such as automated storage and retrieval systems (AS/RS), carousels, conveyors, robots, and scanning systems. These items will be examined in Chapter 11.

Suggested Readings

Ackerman, Kenneth B. "The Deming Management Message: It Can Work in Your Warehouse!" *Warehousing Forum* 11, no. 4 (March 1996), pp. 1–2.

———."The Fundamentals of Warehousing." *Warehousing Forum* 14, no. 12 (November 1999), pp. 1–2.

---

[56]Ibid., p. 22.

————. "Leadership in the 21st Century Warehouse." *Warehousing Forum* 7, no. 6 (May 1992), pp. 1–3.

————. *Warehousing Profitably: A Manager's Guide [An Update].* Columbus, OH: Ackerman Publications, 2000.

Baker, C.M. "Case Study: Development of National Parts Distribution Center." *Proceedings of the Conference on the Total Logistics Concept.* Pretoria, Republic of South Africa, June 4–5, 1991.

Ballou, Ronald H., and James M. Masters. "Commercial Software for Locating Warehouses and Other Facilities." *Journal of Business Logistics* 14, no. 2 (1993), pp. 71–107.

Britt, Frank F. "A Profit Center Approach to Warehousing." *WERC Research Paper.* Oak Brook, IL: Warehousing Education and Research Council, 1990.

Cooke, James Aaron. "Re-inventing the Public Warehouse." *Logistics Management & Distribution Report* 39, no. 5 (May 2000), pp. 44–50.

Cooper, Catherine, and Steve Mulaik. "Warehouse Management: Killer Clues." *Operations & Fulfillment* 8, no. 1 (January/February 2000), pp. 12–22.

"Getting the Right Fit." *Traffic Management* 34, no. 2 (February 1995), Warehousing and Distribution Supplement, pp. 785–805.

Harmon, Roy L. *Reinventing the Warehouse: World Class Distribution Logistics.* New York: Free Press, 1993.

Ho, Peng-Kuan, and Jossef Perl. "Warehouse Location Under Service-Sensitive Demand." *Journal of Business Logistics* 16, no. 1 (1995), pp. 133–62.

Maltz, Arnold B. "The Relative Importance of Cost and Quality in the Outsourcing of Warehousing." *Journal of Business Logistics* 15, no. 2 (1994), pp. 45–62.

————. "Warehouse Systems and the Year 2000: What You Need to Do NOW!" *WERC Special Report,* January 1997.

"Mastering Technology." *WERCSheet* 22, no. 1 (January 1999), pp. 14–15.

"Mining for Gold," *WERCSheet* 23, no. 1 (January 2000), pp. 8–11.

Napolitano, Maida. *Using Modeling to Solve Warehousing Problems.* Oak Brook, IL: Warehousing Education and Research Council, 1998.

Newton, Chris. "Warehousing Isn't Just About Storage Anymore." *The Report on Supply Chain Management,* published by ARM Research, Inc. (October 1999), pp. 1–28.

van Oudheusden, Dirk L., and Peter Boey. "Design of an Automated Warehouse for Air Cargo: The Case of the Thai Air Cargo Terminal." *Journal of Business Logistics* 15, no. 1 (1994), pp. 261–85.

Pavis, Theta. "A New Era of Customer Service." *Warehousing Management* 7, no. 2 (March 2000), pp. 20–24.

Robeson, James F., and William C. Copacino, eds. *The Logistics Handbook.* New York: Free Press, 1994, especially Section VI, "Distribution Facilities Management," pp. 517–643.

Rogers, Dale S., and Patricia J. Daugherty. "Warehousing Firms: The Impact of Alliance Involvement." *Journal of Business Logistics* 16, no. 2 (1995), pp. 249–69.

Setting Continuous Improvement Priorities in Warehouse Operations, Monograph Series No. M0016. Raleigh, NC: Tompkins Associates Inc., undated.

Speh, Thomas W. *How to Determine Total Warehouse Costs.* Sarasota, FL: DCW-USA, Inc., 1990.

————. *Warehouse Inventory Turnover.* Oak Brook, IL: Warehousing Education and Research Council, 1999.

———— et al. *A Guide to Effective Motivation & Retention Programs in the Warehouse.* Oak Brook, IL: Warehousing Education and Research Council, 1999.

Tompkins, James A. "Enhancing the Warehouse's Role through Customization." *WERC Special Report,* February 1997.

Tompkins, James A., and Dale Harmelink, eds. *The Distribution Management Handbook.* New York: McGraw-Hill, 1994, especially Part 3, "Warehousing," pp. 16.1–22.36.

"Trends in Warehouse Management Systems." *Information Systems and Logistics: A Canadian Perspective.* White Paper published by Sistema Logistics, 1999, pp. 3–4.

"Warehouse Management Systems—The State of the Industry." *Parcel Shipping & Distribution* 6, no. 11 (October 1999), pp. 22–26.

"Warehousing After 2000." *Warehousing Forum* 14, no. 3 (February 1999), pp. 1–2.

"Warehousing's Evolution: Meeting Demands in the New Millennium." *WERCSheet* 23, no. 6 (June 2000), pp. 1–5, 7.

"What If? Today's Simulation Packages Can Give You the Answer to That and More." *WERCSheet* 22, no. 10 (November 1999), pp. 8–10.

"What's Your Pleasure? Today's Warehouses Deliver Service as Well as Product." *WERCSheet* 23, no. 1 (January 2000), pp. 1–4.

"WMS + TMS = Success." *WERCSheet* 23, no. 2 (February 2000), pp. 1–4.

Questions and Problems

1. Warehousing is used for the storage of inventories during all phases of the logistics process. Why is it necessary for a firm to store inventories of any kind, since inventory carrying costs can be very high?

2. Distinguish between private and public warehousing. What are the advantages and disadvantages of each type?

3. Discuss what is meant by cost trade-off analysis within the context of warehousing. Give at least two examples of the cost trade-offs involved in a firm's decision to use a combination of public and private warehousing, rather than public or private warehousing alone.

4. What are the three basic functions of warehousing? Briefly describe each function.

5. Identify and describe some of the more important factors that affect the size of an organization's warehouse or warehouses.

6. Explain the differences between the following types of facility location strategies: (*a*) market positioned; (*b*) production positioned; and (*c*) intermediately positioned.

7. How can warehouse layout and design affect productivity and efficiency?

8. Productivity has been defined as the ratio of real output to real input. In terms of the warehousing function, how could an organization measure the productivity level of its storage facilities?

APPENDIX A

CASE STUDY—PUBLIC VERSUS PRIVATE WAREHOUSING

This case highlights the comparison of leased, private warehousing to public warehousing. It also illustrates how the treatment of certain costs can influence the results of the analysis.

Synopsis

The company's warehouse facilities have reached capacity in the mid-Atlantic region. Currently, the firm owns and operates two facilities in the area and utilizes approximately 150,000 square feet of outside public warehouse space. The most pressing need is for overflow storage, which is currently being handled by the public warehouse. Overflow requirements are expected to grow substantially in the next several years.

A variety of options are considered initially by the task force charged with recommending a solution to the space requirements problem. It is estimated that approximately 210,000 square feet of space will be required in the mid-Atlantic region. The alternatives have been reduced to the following: (1) use public warehousing or (2) lease 210,000 square feet at $2.75/square foot on a five-year lease with a five year renewal option.

Financial Analysis

Alternative 1: Public Warehousing

A. Annual cost:

Handling charges, annual	=	$ 760,723
Storage charges, annual	=	413,231
Total	=	$1,173,954

B. The public warehousing costs are based on a careful review of public operators in the area. The costs shown in the analysis above are based on the rates for the lowest cost quotation received from the vendors in the feasible set.

Alternative 2: Lease a New Facility

A. Costs are estimated on the basis of past experience and forecasted levels of expense in this specific market.

Estimated yearly operating expenses—new facility:	=	$ 309,914

B. Investment in the new facility:
1. Capitalized lease

a. Annual lease payment	=	$ 577,500
b. Present value of 10 annual		
payments of $577,500	=	$3,547,600

2. The lease is capitalized, i.e., the leased asset (building) is treated as a fixed asset, and the present value of future lease payments is treated as a debt. Capitalization of the lease is required for auditing purposes by the Financial Accounting Standards Board and is used in this type of analysis because future lease payments are as binding as if money had been borrowed by the firm to purchase the building. The net effect is to treat the lease as an asset. In this situation, the company considers their investment in the asset to be the

Source: Reprinted with permission from *The Financial Evaluation of Warehousing Options: An Examination and Appraisal of Contemporary Practices,* Thomas Speh and James A. Blomquist, © 1988, Warehousing Education and Research Council, 1100 Jorie Blvd., Oak Brook, IL 60523-4413.

present value of the future lease payments (as will be discussed in the commentary, not all financial analysts would agree with treating the lease in this fashion). The discount rate used to determine the present value of the lease payments is typically the firm's after-tax cost of capital, adjusted according to the risk of the project.

3. Other fixed assets required for the new facility:

Handling equipment	$ 170,800
Computer systems	26,740
Rack	252,000
Total	$ 449,540

4. Start-up costs—new facility:

Product movement	$ 10,500

5. Initial cash outlay | $ 460,040 |

Yearly Savings, Lease versus Public

Annual public warehouse cost	=	$1,173,954
Annual private warehouse cost	=	309,914
Annual total savings	=	$ 864,040

Private cost appears understated, but the annual lease cost is not reflected in the annual operating cost because the lease is capitalized and treated as an investment.

TEN-YEAR CASH FLOWS (000s)

Year	Initial Outlay	Capitalized Lease	Savings: Lease versus Public	Pre-Tax Net Cash In/Out Flow	Tax Depreciation*	Savings Less Depreciation	Taxes 39%	Savings Less Depreciation and Taxes	Depreciation	After-Tax Net Cash In/Out Flow
0	$460	$3,548	$ 0	($4,008)	0					($4,008)
1	0	0	864	864	$136	$ 728	$ 284	$ 444	$136	580
2	0	0	864	864	109	755	294	461	109	570
3	0	0	864	864	71	793	309	484	71	555
4	0	0	864	864	50	814	317	497	50	547
5	0	0	864	864	45	819	319	500	45	545
6	0	0	864	864	25	839	327	512	25	537
7	0	0	864	864	22	842	328	514	22	536
8	0	0	864	864	3	861	336	525	3	528
9	0	0	864	864	0	864	337	527	0	527
10	0	0	864	864	0	864	337	527	0	527
Total	$460	$3,548	$8,640	$4,632	$461	$8,179	$3,190	$4,989	$461	$1,442

*Depreciation on rack, handling equipment, and computer hardware is factored in here to reflect the impact on cash flows as a result of the reduction of taxes.

For example:	Year 1
Savings	$ 864,040
Depreciation	– 135,839
Net Profit (before tax)	$ 728,201
Federal tax (39%)	– 283,998
Net Profit (after tax)	$ 444,203
Depreciation	+ 135,839
After tax cash flow	$ 580,042

Return on Investment

Internal Rate of Return (IRR)

A. Savings stream:

Year	Savings
0	($4,007,640)
1	580,042
2	569,222
3	554,768
4	546,741
5	544,587
6	536,774
7	535,654
8	528,146
9	527,065
10	527,065

B. IRR (after taxes) + 6.13%

Net Present Value

A. Discount rate: 11% after taxes

B. NPV of the 10-year savings stream (discounted at 11%)   =   ($692,941)

Decision

Use Public Warehousing. IRR and NPV for the private facility do not meet company standards.

Discussion

It is interesting to note that the leased facility generates significant yearly operating savings, yet the operating savings, as large as they are, do not generate a return on investment that exceeds the company's hurdle rate.

The cost elements included in the company's original analysis were all "hard dollars," and no incremental revenues were considered. The distribution function has its own capital "pool," but distribution projects must meet the hurdle rate that applies to all capital projects.

The lease capitalization in the case study provides an opportunity to review some fundamental financial concepts. As was described in the case, the lease is treated as an asset, and the present value of the future lease payments is shown as an asset on the balance sheet. The interesting point is that the company then treated the capitalized value of the lease as an *investment* in their cash flow analysis. That is, the capitalized lease is treated as a major cash outflow against which the cash savings will be compared to determine the rate of return.

Many managers would argue that the present value of the capitalized lease should not be treated as a lump sum cash outflow (i.e., as an investment). The present value of the annual lease payments is indeed a balance sheet item, but from a *cash flow perspective,* the annual lease payments should be treated as cash outflows in the years in which they are made. If the analysis of the leased space versus public warehousing alternative is recast to treat the lease payments as annual outflows, and the equipment outlay and start-up costs of $460,040 are treated as the initial investment, an entirely different decision would be reached. The data in the table below shows the revised analysis.

Ten-Year Cash Flow Analysis Using Annual Lease Payments ($000s)

Year	Public Warehouse Annual Cost	Annual Cost of Leasing (Lease cost + Operating costs)	Initial Investment	Pretax Savings: Lease versus Public	After-Tax Savings (Savings, less taxes, plus depreciation)
0			$460		
1	$1,174	$888		$286	$228
2	1,174	888		286	217
3	1,174	888		286	202
4	1,174	888		286	194
5	1,174	888		286	192
6	1,174	888		286	184
7	1,174	888		286	183
8	1,174	888		286	176
9	1,174	888		286	175
10	1,174	888		286	175
Net present value of the cash savings of lease vs. public over years 1–10 (hurdle rate of .11 after taxes)					$1,624 998
Internal rate of return (lease vs. public, after taxes)					29.99%

Note that the net present value of the savings between leasing and public warehousing is $1.6 million compared to the negative net present value in the original analysis. The revised IRR is almost 30 percent compared to the original IRR of 6.13 percent. Clearly, this analysis would support a decision to lease the space.

This case study illustrates how the treatment of different costs affects the outcome of the financial analysis. In this instance, the way in which the lease payments are treated dramatically affects the final decision. The results suggest that all personnel involved in the warehousing analysis process must constantly challenge and carefully evaluate the way in which various cost elements are conceptualized and brought into the analysis process.

APPENDIX B

CASE STUDY—WAREHOUSE CONSOLIDATION

This case focuses on the reconfiguration of the firm's warehouse network. The case illustrates the conservative approach that many firms take regarding the inclusion of service and revenue impacts in the quantitative financial analysis. Interestingly, third-party warehousing is not considered, even though the firm experiences widely varying sales volumes.

Synopsis

The company's distribution centers (DCs) are near their maximum storage capacity, and sales projections suggest that volume cannot be handled with existing facilities. A recent study of customer service, conducted by a well-known consulting firm, indicated that larger customers require much less stringent order cycle times than those currently being provided by the company. Consequently, the company has the opportunity to reduce the number of distribution centers and accept a longer cycle time in order to reduce costs.

Source: Reprinted with permission from *The Financial Evaluation of Warehousing Options: An Examination and Appraisal of Contemporary Practices,* Thomas Speh and James A. Blomquist, © 1988, Warehousing Education and Research Council, 1100 Jorie Blvd., Oak Brook, IL 60523-4413.

Currently, the southern region distribution center in Atlanta provides the lowest total delivered cost, and expanding the area served by the Atlanta DC would reduce total distribution costs. Savings from expanding the center's service area and the increased order cycle time could be applied to increasing the limited storage and throughput capacity at the Atlanta DC.

The Distribution Environment

The company manufactures and distributes a broad line of consumer products through grocery stores, retail drugstores, wholesalers, and mass merchandisers. Throughput is characterized by sharp peaks:

- The number of cases shipped varies from 80,000 to 740,000 per day.
- Sales peaks are reached toward the end of each quarter when volume per day increases by a factor of four.
- The number of pallets stored varies ± 15 percent from the average.
- For five or six months during peak storage times, the distribution centers are close to maximum capacity.

Annually, more than 1.2 million orders for 1,100 products are processed by the logistics function. Transportation is primarily by truck: over 8,000 trailers are moved per year. In total, over 300 million pounds of product are shipped to more than 40,000 domestic customers.

System Reconfiguration Analysis

The first phase of the analysis process utilized a network optimization model to evaluate two dozen network configuration alternatives. The optimal configuration had two fewer DCs than existed at the present time. The proposed alternative included:

- Closing a full-line DC in Harrisburg, PA.
- Closing an export DC in Baltimore, MD.
- Expanding the Atlanta DC by 150,000 sq. ft. (one-third), enabling the DC to service the northeast and export customers.

The facility in Baltimore is used to handle export distribution and help achieve consolidation economies. On an annual basis, the center makes slightly more than 1,800 shipments that contain 3,000 orders and weigh 4 million pounds. Almost two-thirds of the weight originates in other company facilities. This DC's operations will be merged into the Atlanta facility under the current proposal. Total costs will be reduced by integrating international distribution into the new Atlanta facility.

The major advantages of the proposal are centered on the following:

- Expanded storage capacity to accommodate long-term growth.
- Elimination of the need to use the Atlanta plant warehouse space.
- Reduced operating costs.
- Reduced safety stock.
- Expanded capacity to handle storage and throughput peaks.
- Enhanced service due to higher fill rates and improved picking accuracy.

The final aspect of the analysis was the capital expenditure and rate of return analysis.

Financial Analysis

Project to begin in April of 1988, with an estimated completion date of June 30, 1989. The project involves the construction of a 150,000 square foot expansion to the Atlanta DC.

Cash Flows Associated with This Alternative

A. Investment (in $000s):

Expand Atlanta DC building 150,000 square feet	$4,450
Roads and truck parking	400
Drainage system	120
Architect	249
Contingency	497
Conveyor system	2,100
Total investment capital	$7,816
($4,005,000 to be spent in 1988)	
($3,811,000 to be spent in 1989)	

B. One-time (start-up) expenses ($000s):

Severance	$ 670
Relocation	150
Vacancy	360
Miscellaneous	400
Total	$1,580

Severance expenses include the cost of settlement with employees not transferred from the old facilities to the expanded DC in Atlanta.

Relocation includes the costs of physically moving inventory from old locations to the new location.

Vacancy expenses are made up of the on-going costs of maintaining the Harrisburg facility until it is sold or subleased.

C. Annual net operating savings[1] (in $000s):

	Harrisburg	*Baltimore*	*Atlanta*	*Total*
Salaries/benefits	$463.00[2]	$ 38.60[3]	—	$ 501.60
Lease expense	490.00	124.00	—	614.00
Operating expenses	551.20	49.80	$60.40[4]	661.40
Transportation[5]	130.00	—	—	130.00
Net annual savings				$1,907.00

[1]These savings are "net," that is, operating costs at the new facility are subtracted from the savings at the other two facilities to arrive at a net savings figure.

[2]Includes the elimination of 23 hourly, 18 non-exempt, and 4 exempt personnel.

[3]Does not reflect a reduction in number of personnel, but includes savings due to lower pay scales in Atlanta.

[4]The plant warehouse in Atlanta would not be used for distribution.

[5]Transportation includes plant-to-DC and DC-to-customer. The $130,000 savings is a net figure reflecting the sizeable reduction in plant-to-DC transportation cost and a slight increase in DC-to-customer transportation cost associated with the new Atlanta facility.

D.   Asset liquidation ($000s):

Net book value of:	
Leasehold improvements	$129.00
Machinery and equipment	478.50
Furniture and fixtures	76.20
Total book value	$683.70
Less transfers to new facility:	
Computer system	($175.40)
Racks	(67.70)
Forklift and trucks	(26.70)
Conveyors	(66.70)
Label printer	(16.20)
Total transfer	($352.70)
Value of assets to be liquidated:	
($683.70 − $352.70)	$331.00
Less estimated sale proceeds:	−31.00
Net loss associated with asset liquidation	($300.00)

E.   Working capital:

Reduction in inventory (safety stock)	$2,075.00

F.   Annual out-of-pocket savings from inventory reduction:

Interest percentage = 13%	
Savings ($2,075 @ .13)	$ 270.00

The reduction of safety stock by consolidating into one DC has two effects:

    (1) It results in a one-time cash inflow when the inventory is reduced, and

    (2) It causes an annual cash inflow due to the reduction in annual interest expense.

G.   Annual depreciation ($000s):

Year 1	$100
Years 2–9	$269

Calculation of Net Cash Flows, 1988–1996

A.   Data ($000s):

	1988	1989	1990	1991	1992	1993	1994	1995	1996
Depreciation	$100	$269	$269	$269	$269	$269	$269	$269	$269
Tax rate*	46.6%	46.6%	48.5%	48.5%	48.5%	48.5%	48.5%	48.5%	48.5%
Deferred taxes[†]	($5)	$98	$207	$135	$85	$48	$48	$48	$3

*The analysis is based on pre-1987 tax rates.

[†]The deferred taxes shown in the third row above are a result of the tax impact from maintaining two sets of books. For internal reporting, assets are valued as close to their true value as possible. For external purposes (i.e., federal taxes), assets will be depreciated as quickly as is legally possible. If an asset is depreciated more quickly than the item actually depreciates in value, there will be a discrepancy between the two values. The deferred taxes reflect the cash flow impact of this difference.

B. Sample calculation of net cash flow:
1. Net cash flow would include:

Operating savings + Inventory savings (interest) = Total savings – Depreciation = Profit before tax – Federal tax	Calculate operating profit
= Profit after tax + Depreciation + Deferred tax = Net cash flow	Add back depreciation and deferred tax to obtain "cash flow"

2. Consider 1990 ($000s):

Operating savings	$1,907
+ Inventory savings (interest)	+ 270
= Total savings	$2,177
– Depreciation	– 269
= Profit before tax	$1,908
– Federal tax (48.5%)	– 925
= Profit after tax	$ 983
+ Depreciation	+269
+ Deferred tax	+207
= Net cash flow	$1,459

C. Total annual net cash flow ($000s), 1988–1996:

	1988	1989	1990	1991	1992	1993	1994	1995	1996
Operating savings	$ 0	$1,430	$1,907	$1,907	$1,907	$1,907	$1,907	$1,907	$1,907
Inventory savings (interest)	0	270	270	270	270	270	270	270	270
1-time expense	—	(1,580)	—	—	—	—	—	—	—
Asset loss	—	(300)	—	—	—	—	—	—	—
Depreciation	(100)	(269)	(269)	(269)	(269)	(269)	(269)	(269)	(269)
Profit before tax	(100)	(449)	1,908	1,908	1,908	1,908	1,908	1,908	1,908
Federal tax	(47)	(209)	(925)	(925)	(925)	(925)	(925)	(925)	(925)
Profit after tax	(53)	(240)	983	983	983	983	983	983	983
Depreciation	100	269	269	269	269	269	269	269	269
Deferred tax	(5)	98	207	135	85	48	48	48	3
Cash generated	42	127	1,459	1,387	1,337	1,300	1,300	1,300	1,255
Capital expense	(4,005)	(3,811)	—	—	—	—	—	—	—
Change in working capital	—	2,075	—	—	—	—	—	—	—
Net cash flow	($3,963)	($1,609)	$1,459	$1,387	$1,337	$1,300	$1,300	$1,300	$1,255

Return on Investment

Rate of Return Analysis

A. Net present value ($000s):
    1. Net cash flow

Year	Cash Flow
1988	(3,963)
1989	(1,609)
1990	1,459
1991	1,387
1992	1,337
1993	1,300
1994	1,300
1995	1,300
1996	1,255

    2. Hurdle rate = 14%
    3. Net present value @ 14%   = $1,449.80
B. Internal rate of return of the cash flow   =   20.3%
C. Payback period   =   5.7 years

Decision

Build the addition to the Atlanta DC as:

$$\text{IRR} > \text{Hurdle rate and NPV} > 0$$

Discussion

It is interesting to note that the current network would not accommodate the projected growth in the firm's sales volume. Yet there is no consideration given to including incremental revenue in the cash flow analysis. But it is possible to make a case for including incremental profits because sales presumably could not expand without an increase in the capacity of the warehousing network.

The approach shown here reflects the basic conservative stance that most firms take when analyzing warehousing capital projects. However, it could be argued that additional sales could be handled through temporary warehousing or increased productivity from the current system. The issue of incremental sales is difficult to resolve.

A significant advantage associated with the new facility is the enhancement of customer service. The new equipment to be installed in the Atlanta facility is expected to result in a higher percentage of completed orders and an increase in order-picking accuracy. Order fill and order accuracy are highly regarded by customers. However, the enhancements to service are not quantified or formally recognized in the financial analysis. Again, few managers are willing to take the risk of projecting the effect of service enhancements on revenue. As is obvious in the cash flow analysis, neither increased sales nor enhanced service were needed to produce a positive net present value. However, had this been a borderline project, cash flows associated with sales and service enhancements may have pushed the project into the favorable range.

The most intriguing aspect of this analysis is the fact that third-party warehousing was not considered in the feasible set of alternatives. The situation described in the case suggests that volume is extremely volatile, resulting in the need to build substantial excess warehouse capacity to handle peak periods. It could be argued that this situation is well-suited to third-party warehousing where peak requirements for one principal can be offset with opposite requirements of another principal. It would be interesting, in this situation, to calculate a rate of return on the private facility on the basis of the savings, vis-à-vis third-party warehousing. Here, the savings may not be significant due to the excess capacity required in the private warehousing scenario. Although corporate culture may argue for private warehousing, it would have been insightful to review the financial impacts of third-party warehousing.

Materials Handling, Computerization, and Packaging

Chapter Outline

Chapter Objectives

- To describe various types of nonautomated and automated materials handling systems.
- To examine the role of warehousing in a just-in-time (JIT) environment.
- To examine the role of packaging in warehousing and logistics.
- To overview the role of computer and information technology in warehouse management.

Introduction

The importance of warehousing in marketing and logistics strategies is increasing. Those who view warehousing as a means of achieving a competitive advantage expand the traditional perspective of warehousing (i.e., managing inventories) to include the management of information flows. In the modern warehouse, computerization and automation become essential ingredients of logistics success and, ultimately, competitive success.

This chapter integrates some of the key components that affect warehousing decisions. Some companies tend to view the warehousing decisions discussed in Chapter 10 (e.g., private versus public; facility location, size, and number) as separate from decisions about warehouse automation, materials handling systems, packaging, and warehouse computerization. Yet these decisions are very intertwined, as will be demonstrated in this chapter.

Materials Handling Equipment

The Materials Handling Institute, an industry trade association for manufacturers of materials handling equipment and systems, has estimated that "the hardware and software used to move, store, control, contain, and unitize materials in factories and warehouses exceeds $50 billion annually. Much of the growth in size and variety of the market is fueled by major changes in the requirements of warehouse and distribution operations (e.g., reduced order cycle times, reduced inventory levels, reduced order sizes, SKU proliferation)."[1]

Materials Handling Expenditures Exceed $50 Billion Annually

Materials handling equipment and systems often represent major capital outlays for an organization. Like the decisions related to the number, size, and location of warehouses, materials handling decisions can affect many aspects of logistics operations.

Manual or Nonautomated Systems

Manual or nonautomated materials handling equipment has been the mainstay of the traditional warehouse and will likely continue to be important even with the move toward automated warehouses. Generally speaking, manual systems do the best job when there is either very high or very low throughput of products in a warehouse. Manual systems provide a great deal of flexibility in order picking, since they use the very most flexible handling systems.

Equipment can be categorized according to the functions they perform: (1) storage and order picking, (2) transportation and sorting, and (3) shipping.

Storage and Order-Picking Equipment

Storage and order-picking equipment includes racks, shelving, drawers, and operator-controlled devices such as forklift trucks. Figure 11–1 identifies a number of forklift truck variations, including both powered and nonpowered units. These units are staples in a typical warehouse operation.

The *counterbalanced lift truck* is a common type of forklift truck. It can be powered by liquid propane, by gas or diesel engines, or by batteries. Units can have three or four wheels and pneumatic or cushion tires. *Tow tractors* are self-powered operator-driven

---

[1]Edward H. Frazelle and James M. Apple, Jr., "Materials Handling Technologies," in *The Logistics Handbook*, ed. James F. Robeson and William C. Copacino (New York: Free Press, 1994), p. 547.

FIGURE 11–1

Powered and nonpowered forklift trucks

Counterbalanced lift trucks

Sideloading lift trucks

Tow tractors

Electric-powered rider straddle trucks

Pallet trucks or "pallet jacks"

Orderpicker trucks

Reach trucks

Source: *Modern Materials Handling* <http://www.manufacturing.net/magazine/mmh/glossary/egtruck.htm>.

tractors used to tow wagons or carts. *Pallet trucks or jacks* are a basic type of unit load handler. They can handle loads of up to 10,000 pounds. For operating in narrow-aisle warehouses, *reach trucks* are useful for handling, storing, and retrieving pallets. *Sideloading lift trucks* are designed for operating in very narrow aisles at heights of 25 feet or higher. Rotating masts or forks allow the sideloading lift truck to stack pallets without turning. *Electric-powered rider straddle trucks* handle pallets in narrow-aisle storage-rack facilities. A load capacity of this equipment approximates two tons. The last forklift truck shown in Figure 11–1 is the *orderpicker truck.* These units put the forklift operator on an elevating platform along with the forks. When the forks are raised, so is the operator. The operator then picks the items from the storage racks or shelves and places them onto a pallet or into totes. There are many other examples of forklift trucks that are also used.[2]

Table 11–1 describes many different types of materials handling equipment. Storage racks normally store palletized or unitized loads. In most instances, some type of operator-controlled device places the load into the storage rack. Table 11–1 presents the type of materials stored, the benefits, and other information about each item. Figures 11–2 through 11–6 picture some of the more commonly used storage and order-picking equipment.

Storage Racks

The storage racks illustrated in Figure 11–2 are found in most warehouse facilities. They may be permanent or temporary and are placed within a warehouse for storage of products. They would be considered "standard" or "basic" components of a warehouse. All these storage racks are easily accessible by materials handling equipment such as forklift trucks.

Gravity flow storage racks, shown in Figure 11–3, are often used to store high-demand items. Products that are of uniform size and shape are well suited for this type of storage system. Items are loaded into the forward-sloping racks from the back and then flow to the front, where order-picking personnel can reach them.

Bin Shelving Systems

For small parts, bin shelving systems are useful. Figure 11–4 illustrates a typical bin configuration. Items are handpicked, so the height of the system must be within the physical reach of employees. Typically, the full cube of each bin cannot be used, so some wasted space exists. Bin shelving systems are relatively inexpensive compared to other storage systems, but they have limited usefulness beyond small parts storage.

Modular Storage

The modular storage drawers and cabinets shown in Figure 11–5 are used for small parts. They are similar in function to bin shelving systems, but they require less space and allow items to be concentrated into areas that are easily accessed by employees. The drawers are pulled out and items are then picked. By design, modular storage drawers must be low to the floor, often under five feet in height, so that employees can pick items from the drawers.

The previously described storage systems are classified as "fixed" systems because they are stationary. Others, classified as "movable," are not in fixed positions. The bin shelving systems shown in Figure 11–4 can be transformed from a fixed to a movable system, as illustrated in Figure 11–6. In the bin shelving mezzanine, wheels on the bottom of the bins follow tracks in the floors, allowing the bins to be moved and stacked together when not being accessed. This allows maximum utilization of space, because full-width aisles are not needed between each bin.

---

[2]See illustrations of various forklift trucks and related equipment at the following website: <http://www.manufacturing.net/magazine/mmh/glossary/egtruck.htm>. An overview of the costs of a variety of warehousing and distribution equipment can be found in *Rules of Thumb* (Woodbridge, NJ: Gross & Associates, 1999).

TABLE 11–1   Storage Guidelines for the Warehouse

Equipment	Type of Materials	Benefits	Other Considerations
Manual			
Racking: Conventional pallet rack	Pallet loads	Good storage density, good product security	Storage density can be increased further by storing loads two deep
Drive-in racks	Pallet loads	Fork trucks can access loads, good storage density	Fork truck access is from one direction only
Drive-through racks	Pallet loads	Same as above	Fork truck access is from two directions
High-rise racks	Pallet loads	Very high storage density	Often used in AS/R systems, may offer tax advantages when used in rack-supported building
Cantilever racks	Long loads or rolls	Designed to store difficult shapes	Each different SKU can be stored on a separate shelf
Pallet stacking frames	Odd-shaped or crushable parts	Allow otherwise unstackable loads to be stacked, saving floor space	Can be disassembled when not in use
Stacking racks	Odd-shaped or crushable parts	Same as above	Can be stacked flat when not in use
Gravity flow racks	Unit loads	High-density storage, gravity moves loads	FIFO or LIFO flow of loads
Shelving	Small, loose loads and cases	Inexpensive	Can be combined with drawers for flexibility
Drawers	Small parts and tools	All parts are easily accessed, good security	Can be compartmentalized for many SKUs
Mobile racking or shelving	Pallet loads, loose materials, and cases	Can reduce required floor space by half	Come equipped with safety devices
Automated			
Unit Load AS/RS	Pallet loads, and a wide variety of sizes and shapes	Very high storage density, computer controlled	May offer tax advantages when rack-supported
Car-in-lane	Pallet loads, other unit loads	High storage density	Best used where there are large quantities of only a few SKUs
Miniload AS/RS	Small parts	High storage density, computer controlled	For flexibility, can be installed in several different configurations
Horizontal carousels	Small parts	Easy access to parts, relatively inexpensive	Can be stacked on top of each other
Vertical carousels	Small parts and tools	High storage density	Can serve dual role as storage and delivery system in multifloor facilities
Man-ride machines	Small parts	Very flexible	Can be used with high-rise shelving or modular drawers

Note: This table is a general guide to the types of available storage equipment and where each is best used in the warehouse. Each individual storage application should be studied in detail with the equipment supplier before any equipment is specified.

Source: "Storage Equipment for the Warehouse," *Modern Materials Handling, 1988 Warehousing Guidebook* 40, no. 4 (Spring 1985), p. 53. *Modern Materials Handling,* Copyright 1985 by Cahners Publishing Company, Division of Reed Holding, Inc.

Products are picked from the various storage systems using some order-picking approach. In a manual system, the personnel doing the order picking go to stock: "They either walk and pick, or they use mechanized equipment to carry them to stock locations."[3] In many cases, the order picker retrieves items from a flow-through gravity storage rack (see Figure 11–3).

[3]"Orderpicking Systems to Boost Productivity," *Modern Materials Handling, 1985 Warehousing Guidebook* 40, no. 4 (Spring 1985), p. 56.

FIGURE 11–2

Nonautomated storage units—storage racks

Common rack designs

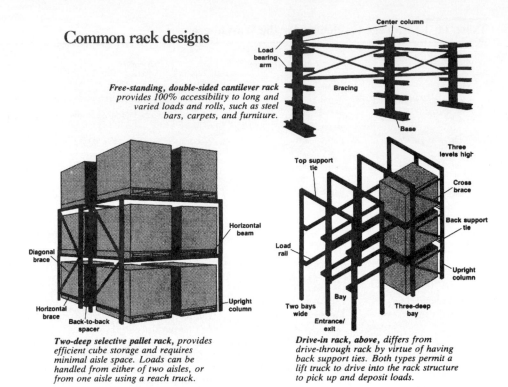

Free-standing, double-sided cantilever rack provides 100% accessibility to long and varied loads and rolls, such as steel bars, carpets, and furniture.

Two-deep selective pallet rack, provides efficient cube storage and requires minimal aisle space. Loads can be handled from either of two aisles, or from one aisle using a reach truck.

Drive-in rack, above, differs from drive-through rack by virtue of having back support ties. Both types permit a lift truck to drive into the rack structure to pick up and deposit loads.

Racks for flexibility

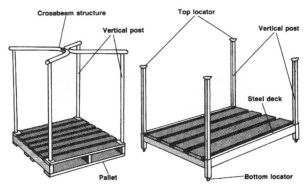

Pallet stacking frames attach directly to existing pallets, thus providing stack storage for otherwise unstackable loads.

Unitized portable racks enable heavy loads to be stacked, whether palletized or not. Racks can be nested if not disassembled.

Source: "The Trends Keep Coming in Industrial Storage Racks," *Modern Materials Handling* 40, no. 9 (August 1985), pp. 54–55. *Modern Materials Handling,* Copyright 1985 by Cahners Publishing Company, Division of Reed Holdings, Inc.

FIGURE 11–3

Gravity flow racks

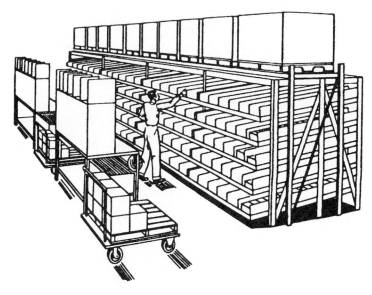

Source: Department of the Navy, Naval Supply Systems Command, Publication 529. From Edward H. Frazelle, *Small Parts Order Picking: Equipment and Strategy* (Oak Brook, IL: Warehousing Education and Research Council, 1988), p. 3. Reprinted with permission.

FIGURE 11–4

Bin shelving systems

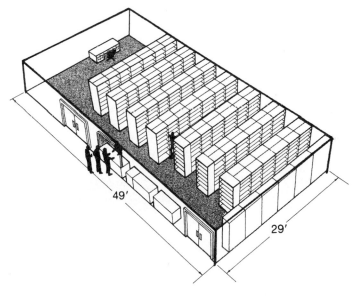

Source: Edward H. Frazelle, *Small Parts Order Picking: Equipment and Strategy* (Oak Brook, IL: Warehousing Education and Research Council, 1988), p. 1. Reprinted with permission.

Transportation and Storage Equipment

The order picker can use a large selection of powered and nonpowered equipment for *transporting and sorting* items located in the racks, shelves, and drawers. Examples of apparatus of this type include forklift trucks, platform trucks, hand trucks, cranes, and carts. This equipment performs multiple functions in addition to transportation and sorting, such as order picking.

Manual sorting of items is a very labor-intensive part of warehousing. It involves separating and regrouping picked items into customer orders. Personnel physically

FIGURE 11–5

Modular storage drawers and cabinets

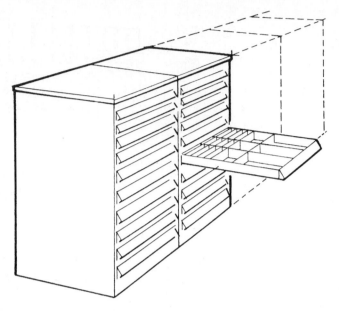

Source: Department of the Navy, Naval Supply Systems Command, Publication 529. From Edward H. Frazelle, *Small Parts Order Picking: Equipment and Strategy* (Oak Brook, IL: Warehousing Education and Research Council, 1988), p. 2. Reprinted with permission.

FIGURE 11–6

Bin shelving mezzanine

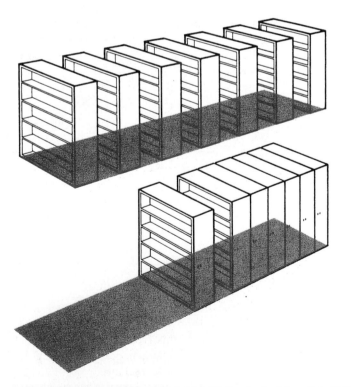

Source: Courtesy of White Storage & Retrieval Systems. From Edward H. Frazelle, *Small Parts Order Picking: Equipment and Strategy* (Oak Brook, IL: Warehousing Education and Research Council, 1988), p. 8. Reprinted with permission.

examine items and place them onto pallets or slip-sheets, or into containers for shipment to customers. This is a time-consuming process subject to human error. As a result, most firms attempt to minimize manual sorting whenever possible.

Shipping of products to customers involves preparing items for shipment and loading them onto transportation carriers. The powered and nonpowered equipment previously discussed are used. Additionally, equipment such as pallets, palletizers, strapping machines, and stretch wrappers are important. As we stated earlier, manual or nonautomated equipment is often used in combination with automated equipment.

Automated Systems

Automated storage and retrieval systems (AS/RS), carousels, case-picking and item-picking equipment, conveyors, robots, and scanning systems have become commonplace in warehousing. As a result, many organizations have been able to achieve improvements in efficiency and productivity.

For example, the Park Seed Company in South Carolina, the largest family-owned mail-order seed company in the world, must be able to fill customers' orders within 24 to 36 hours during the peak season of December to April. Because of increasing business, the firm replaced its 125-year-old wooden bin system with automated horizontal carousels. The result was five times the lines picked per hour per operator and a reduction in labor of one-third. Compared to the old system, picking speed increased from 180 to almost 1,000 lines picked per hour.[4]

Automated Storage and Order-Picking Equipment

Automated equipment can be grouped into the same categories used to discuss nonautomated equipment—storage and order picking, transportation and sorting, and shipping. Table 11–1 listed examples of automated storage and order-picking equipment. Bausch & Lomb, Chek Lap Kok Airport (Hong Kong), Compaq, General Electric, Nike, Packard Bell, Posten PaketFrakt (Sweden), Rothmans Tobacco (Netherlands), Toyota, and many other firms have employed automated systems with great success.

To illustrate, Packard Bell used automated materials handling equipment to facilitate the manufacture of computers in its Angers, France, facility. As one writer described it: "The system consists of five kitting (assembly) stations, 32 modular and interchangeable conveyor workstations where the computers are assembled and tested, and an in-line burn-in testing system."[5]

The Toyota Marketing Company's Parts Distribution Center in South Africa was partially automated at a cost of $5.6 million. Additional storage and handling facilities were added; new receiving, binning, and order processing systems were introduced; and a high-rise bulk warehouse was constructed. The benefits were significant and included the following:

1. Order processing productivity increased 300 percent.
2. Product damage rates declined by 50 percent.
3. Stock accuracy and service rates improved by 65 percent.
4. The work of three clerks was eliminated and an additional three clerks were reassigned to more essential tasks.[6]

---

[4]Ed Romaine, "How One Company Increased Its Pick Rate," *Parcel Shipping & Distribution* 2, no. 4 (July–August 1995), pp. 27–28.

[5]"Total Solutions: Problem Solving with Materials Handling Systems," *Modern Materials Handling* 50, no. 7 (June 1995), p. 22.

[6]C. M. Baker, "Case Study: Development of National Parts Distribution Center," *Proceedings of the Conference on the Total Logistics Concept* (Pretoria, South Africa, 1991).

Automation Helps Distribute Mazda Automobiles in Europe

Mazda Motors has a parts distribution center in Willebroek, Belgium, which is approximately halfway between Antwerp and Brussels. The facility occupies 230,000 square meters in total, with 40,000 square meters of warehousing space storing more than 115,000 different parts, servicing 32 distributors and a number of Mazda dealerships. Ninety-five percent of product shipments go by truck.

Within the warehouse,

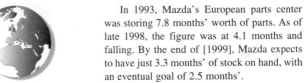

storage racks are carefully laid out according to the nature of each part. One section, a triple-decked mezzanine, is devoted exclusively to parts smaller than 60 centimeters. They are assigned slots by a computer program that takes into account order frequency, part size, and volume. Nearby, a series of high racks handles items of up to one meter, 80 centimeters in length.

Willebroek recently assumed even greater responsibility for serving Mazda's European customers. It has managed to convince distributors and dealers no longer to stock slow-moving items, which account for 75 percent of all aftermarket parts. That has freed up a substantial amount of space at dealerships, while giving Willebroek greater control over parts flow.

In 1993, Mazda's European parts center was storing 7.8 months' worth of parts. As of late 1998, the figure was at 4.1 months and falling. By the end of [1999], Mazda expects to have just 3.3 months' of stock on hand, with an eventual goal of 2.5 months'.

Willebroek employs bar-coding throughout its operation. Incoming orders are processed in batches at night, creating labels and detailed picking instructions for workers the next morning.

Each bar-coded label allows for manual backup in the event of a computer crash, which has already happened twice. In such cases, workers can simply peel off a section of the picking label and continue physical operations without interruption. They can even pack and ship without the need for invoices, which in any case aren't required for shipment within the European Union.

Mazda has seen a steady rise in productivity at Willebroek . . . In the last half of 1998, the Belgian facility chalked up a performance record of 84 line items per day per person. That compares with 53 line items in 1992. The current target is 90 line items."

Source: Adapted from Robert J. Bowman. "Lean on Automation, Mazda's Spare Parts Center Covers Europe," *Global Logistics and Supply Chain Strategies* 3, no. 2 (March 1999), pp. 18–26. Reprinted by permission of Global Logistics & Supply Chain Strategies, SupplyChain.com, and Supply Chain e-Business.

**Advantages
of Automated Systems**

**Disadvantages
of Automated Systems**

Automated systems can provide several benefits for warehouse operations, including operating cost savings, improved service levels, and increased control through more accurate and timely information. However, automated systems are not without disadvantages.

Typical problems faced by firms choosing to automate materials handling operations include the initial capital cost, downtime of equipment, maintenance interruptions, software-related problems (e.g., poor documentation, incompatibility, failure), capacity problems, lack of flexibility to respond to changing environment, maintenance cost, user interface/training, worker acceptance, and obsolescence (see Table 11–2).[7]

The initial capital cost outlay is the most significant obstacle. For example, a miniload AS/RS (see Figures 11–7 and 11–8), where a storage/retrieval (S/R) machine travels horizontally and vertically simultaneously in a storage aisle transporting containers to and from an order-picking station at one end of the system, generally costs between $150,000 and $300,000 per aisle.[8]

---

[7]Kofi Q. Dadzie and Wesley J. Johnston, "Innovative Automation Technology in Corporate Warehousing Logistics," *Journal of Business Logistics* 12, no. 1 (1991), p. 72.

[8]Edward H. Frazelle, *Small Parts Order Picking: Equipment and Strategy* (Oak Brook, IL: Warehousing Education and Research Council, 1988), p. 6.

TABLE 11–2   **Operational and Implementation Problems with Warehouse Automation Systems**

Problem Area	Percent Mentioning
1. Cost of equipment/financial justification	19.0%
2. Downtime or reliability of equipment/maintenance interruptions	10.0
3. Software-related problems, such as poor documentation, incompatibility, failure, or modification	8.0
4. Capacity problems, such as limited applications/integration of equipment into existing system	8.0
5. Lack of flexibility to respond to changing environment/not suitable for high degree of seasonality in business	6.0
6. Maintenance cost/maintenance parts	5.0
7. User interface/training to operate system/transition from manual to automated procedure	5.0
8. Worker acceptance of automation	4.0
9. No problems/we are adapting well	4.0
10. Lack of top management commitment	3.0
11. Obsolescence/need more up-to-date automation/need more automation	3.0

Source: Kofi Q. Dadzie and Wesley J. Johnston, "Innovative Automation Technology in Corporate Warehousing Logistics," *Journal of Business Logistics* 12, no. 1 (1991), p. 72.

FIGURE 11–7

Mini-load AS/RS

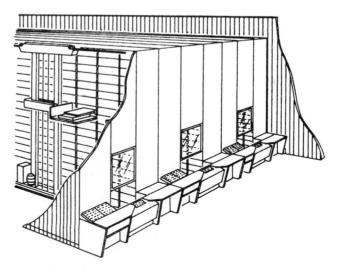

Source: Department of the Navy, Naval Supply Systems Command, Publication 529. From Edward H. Frazelle, *Small Parts Order Picking: Equipment and Strategy* (Oak Brook, IL: Warehousing Education and Research Council, 1988), p. 6. Reprinted with permission.

Such a system has been described as follows:

An Example of Unit Load AS/RSs

When the unit to pick is a full pallet or similar large load, the AS/RS offers complete automation from storage to retrieval, in minimal space. Unit load AS/RS's are installed to 100 feet high with aisles only inches wider than the load to be stored. The S/R machines operate at speeds much faster than industrial trucks and travel simultaneously in the horizontal and vertical directions. They are used when inventories, throughput, and space costs

FIGURE 11–8

Minimizing inventory at Apple Computer with a flexible miniload AS/RS

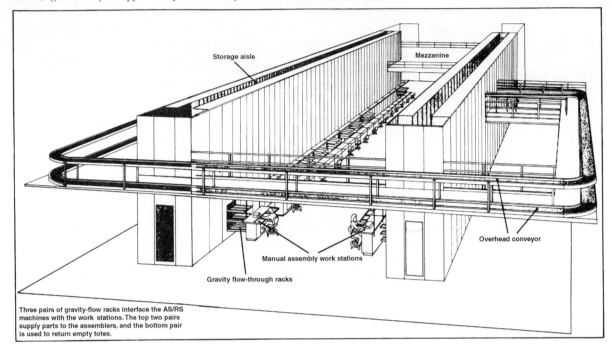

Three pairs of gravity-flow racks interface the AS/RS machines with the work stations. The top two pairs supply parts to the assemblers, and the bottom pair is used to return empty totes.

Source: "Mini-Load AS/RS Trims Inventory, Speeds Assembly," *Modern Materials Handling* 39, no. 13 (September 21, 1984), pp. 48–49. *Modern Materials Handling,* Copyright 1984 by Cahners Publishing Company, Division of Reed Holdings, Inc.

are high. In totally automated systems, AS/RS's are supplied by conveyors, automated guided vehicles, or electrified monorail systems.[9]

Carousels

Another form of AS/RS is the carousel.[10] Carousels are mechanical devices that house and rotate items for order picking. The most frequently used carousel configurations are the horizontal and vertical systems. Carousel systems have been successfully implemented in a variety of organizations, including Levi Strauss France and Raytheon.[11]

Horizontal Carousels

A *horizontal carousel* (see Figure 11–9) is a linked series of rotating bins of adjustable shelves driven on the top or bottom by a drive motor. Rotation takes place on an axis perpendicular to the floor at approximately 80 feet per minute. Costs for horizontal carousels begin at more than $7,000 per unit and can exceed $30,000. In some instances, used equipment can be purchased for much less.[12]

---

[9]*The Warehouse Manager's Guide to Effective Orderpicking,* Monograph Series no. M0008 (Raleigh, NC: Tompkins Associates, n.d.), p. 21. A review of several Internet sites of companies selling AS/RSs indicates that older systems can also be upgraded at costs ranging from $5,000 to $200,000, depending on the complexity of the system.

[10]See "Materials Issues: Carousels," *WERCSheet* 22, no. 10 (November 1999), pp. 13 and 16.

[11]For a brief discussion of the Levi Strauss France carousel system, see "Flexible Fashion," *Logistics Europe* 3, no. 3 (June 1995), p. 33.

[12]See Edward H. Frazelle and James M. Apple, Jr., "Materials Handling Technologies," in *The Logistics Handbook,* ed. James F. Robeson and William C. Copacino (New York: Free Press, 1994), p. 574; and SJF Material Handling Inc. <http://www.sjf.com>.

FIGURE 11–9

Horizontal carousels

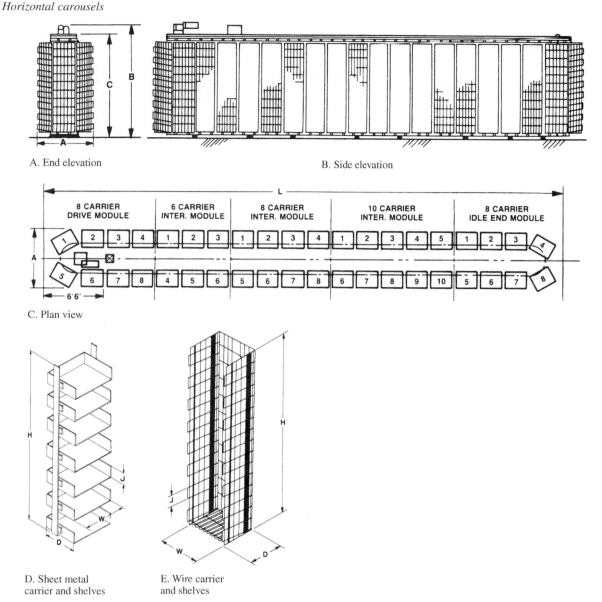

A. End elevation

B. Side elevation

C. Plan view

D. Sheet metal
carrier and shelves

E. Wire carrier
and shelves

Source: Courtesy of SPS Technologies, Inc. From Edward H. Frazelle, *Small Parts Order Picking: Equipment and Strategy* (Oak Brook, IL: Warehousing Education and Research Council, 1988), p. 4. Reprinted with permission.

Raytheon Company's Electromagnetic Systems Division (ESD) installed a horizontal carousel system with dramatic results. Productivity at the ESD facility increased 60 percent, and inventory accuracy rose from 85 percent to almost 98 percent.[13] Schematically, the ESD system is illustrated in Figure 11–10. A vertical carousel

[13]"Carousels Boost Productivity by 60%," *Modern Materials Handling* 42, no. 2 (February 1987), p. 59.

FIGURE 11–10

Raytheon's automated storeroom

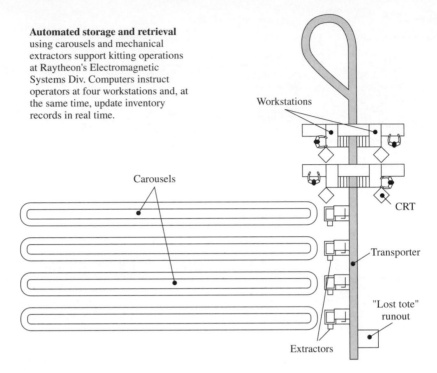

Automated storage and retrieval using carousels and mechanical extractors support kitting operations at Raytheon's Electromagnetic Systems Div. Computers instruct operators at four workstations and, at the same time, update inventory records in real time.

Workstations

Carousels

CRT

Transporter

"Lost tote" runout

Extractors

Source: "Carousels Boost Productivity by 60%," *Modern Materials Handling* 42, no. 2 (February 1987), p. 59. Reprinted with permission.

system was installed by Camco, Inc., Canada's largest producer of major appliances. An improvement of 200 percent was realized in the productivity of its small parts and order-picking operation.[14]

Tacony Corporation, a supplier of vacuum cleaner and sewing machine parts, fills and ships customer orders received by 1:00 P.M. the same day they are received. To provide such a high level of customer service from its five warehouses, Tacony installed horizontal carousel systems. Because 65 percent of the firm's items are small parts, a carousel system made sense. As a result of the installation, order pickers increased their pick rate from 350–400 items per day to 900–1000 items.[15]

Vertical Carousel

A *vertical carousel* (see Figure 11–11) is a horizontal carousel turned on its end and enclosed in sheet metal. As with horizontal carousels, an order picker operates one or multiple carousels. The order picker operating a keypad on the carousel's work surface indexes the carousels either automatically via computer control, or manually.[16] The cost of a vertical carousel begins at $10,000.[17]

The *transportation and sorting* activities are typically performed in combination with storage and order picking. The three most often used pieces of transportation equipment are conveyors, automatic guided vehicle systems (AGVSs), and operator-controlled

[14]"Appliance Maker Gets Higher Warehouse Productivity," *Material Handling Engineering* 42, no. 7 (July 1987), p. 50.

[15]"Ready for the Future," *WERCSheet* 22, no. 11 (December 1999), pp. 6–7.

[16]Frazelle, *Small Parts Order Picking*, pp. 4–5.

[17]Frazelle and Apple, "Materials Handling Technologies," p. 575.

FIGURE 11–11

Vertical carousel

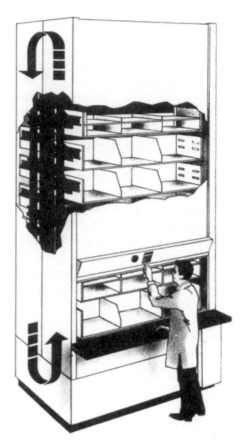

Source: Courtesy of Kardex Systems, Inc. From Edward H. Frazelle, *Small Parts Order Picking: Equipment and Strategy* (Oak Brook, IL: Warehousing Education and Research Council, 1988), p. 5. Reprinted with permission.

trucks or tractors. Sorting equipment can be specialized, such as a tilt-tray sorter with built-in diverting mechanisms, or it can be assembled from other components, such as conveyors and diverters.[18]

Pic 'N' Save Uses a Conveyor Sorting System to Handle 100 Cases per Minute

Pic 'N' Save Corporation, a division of Consolidated Stores, has developed a conveyor sorting system that handles over 100 cases per minute. The company has shipped up to 68,000 cases in one working day—a high level of productivity under normal conditions, but even more outstanding for Pic 'N' Save because the firm rarely has the same item in stock more than once. The company buys closeout goods (overruns, discontinued items, and style changes) from manufacturers and therefore has a wide variety of merchandise in inventory. Case goods are stored in a reserve storage area and are then moved to a picking area four levels high. After being picked, items move to a merge area, where they are sorted and shipped.[19]

---

[18]"Transportation and Sorting—Keys to Throughput," *Modern Materials Handling, 1985 Warehousing Guidebook* 40, no. 4 (Spring 1985), p. 75.

[19]"How We Sort Up to 135 Cases per Minute," *Modern Materials Handling* 40, no. 6 (May 1985), pp. 60–63.

Many other organizations use conveyors in their warehousing operations. The German building supplies company Moderne Bauelemente services more than 1,000 builder merchants with more than 1 million window frames, doors, and accessories. In the company's two distribution centers, conveyors are used to move pallets of products into automated high-bay storage areas that have 3,650 pallet locations, capable of storing one month's inventory.[20]

IKEA, the European furniture manufacturer, installed a conveyor system in its warehousing facility in Sweden. Bar-coded pallets enter the IKEA system and travel by conveyor to and from their storage locations. Computers control both the put-away and picking sequences. The firm has been able to achieve significant improvements in pick rate and reduce its production costs.[21]

Automatic Guided Vehicle System (AGVS)

Automatic guided vehicle systems (AGVSs) are "battery-powered driverless vehicles that are controlled by computers for task assignment, path selection, and positioning."[22] AGVSs are often used in automated warehouse operations involving AS/RSs. The benefits of AGVSs include "lower handling costs, reduced handling-related product damage, improved safety, the ability to interface with other automated systems, and reliability."[23] AGVSs cost about $30,000 for a single low-end model and around $70,000 for a more advanced model.[24]

Maybelline Uses an AS/RS and an AGVS to Pick 90,000 Items

Maybelline, a cosmetics manufacturer, uses a combination system that includes an AS/RS and an AGVS. The automated systems have increased the number of items picked per day by over 50 percent. On busy days, approximately 90,000 items are picked. Figure 11–12 shows the Maybelline operation and describes some of the specifics of the systems being used.[25]

Robots

The robot is another type of equipment used in many phases of materials handling. Robots have been used in the manufacturing process for some time. However, advances in robotics technology have enabled robots to be used in a larger number of applications.[26] Materials handling robots will continue to be used in many application areas (see Figure 11–13).

Shipping Automation

Automation in the *shipping* area has also occurred. The two aspects of the shipping activity that have been most affected by automation are packaging and optical scanning. We have previously discussed packaging by pass-through and rotary stretch-wrapping machines. We will further address the area of packaging later in this chapter.

Another aspect of shipping automation is documentation. As other components of the warehouse become automated, firms need to computerize their tracking and information systems. A. B. Oxford Cold Storage Company in Melbourne, Australia, uses radio frequency portable data terminals[27] and bar-code scanning to manage frozen and

[20]"Building Success." *Logistics Europe* 3, no. 5 (October 1995), pp. 29–32.
[21]Bill Redmond, "Under Pressure," *Logistics Europe* 5, no. 1 (March 1997), p. 35.
[22]David R. Olson, "Material Handling Equipment," in *The Distribution Management Handbook*, ed. James A. Tompkins and Dale Harmelink (New York: McGraw-Hill, 1994), p. 19.17.
[23]Less Gould, "Selecting an AGVS: New Trends, New Designs," *Modern Materials Handling* 50, no. 6 (May 1995), pp. 42–43.
[24]James Aaron Cooke, "Should You Automate Your Warehouse?" *Traffic Management* 34, no. 11 (November 1993), pp. 6-S–8-S.
[25]Gary Forger, "How Maybelline Ships Smaller, More Frequent Orders," *Modern Materials Handling* 50, no. 7 (June 1995), pp. 48–50.
[26]For a discussion of how robots can be used in a typical materials handling environment, see "Smooth WIP Flow with the Right Handling," *Modern Materials Handling* 50, no. 5 (April 1995), pp. 23–26.
[27]For a thorough discussion of radio frequency data communication in warehousing, see Bruce Richmond, *Radio Frequency Data Communication for Warehousing and Distribution* (Oak Brook, IL: Warehousing Education and Research Council, July 1993).

FIGURE 11–12

Using an AS/RS and an AGVS at Maybelline

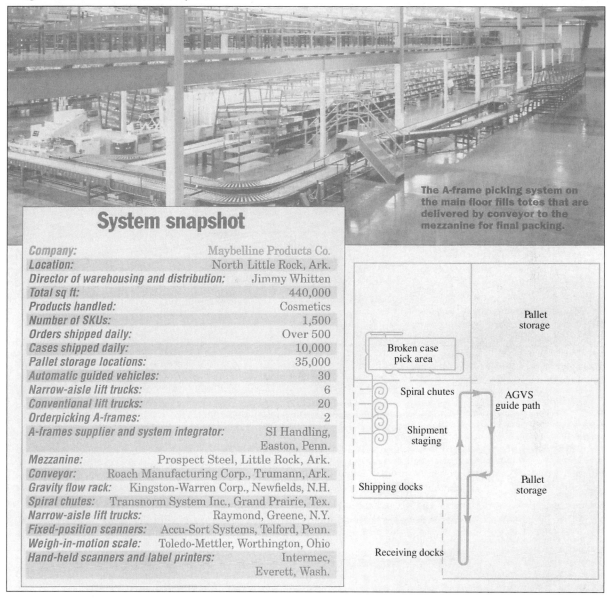

The A-frame picking system on the main floor fills totes that are delivered by conveyor to the mezzanine for final packing.

System snapshot

Company:	Maybelline Products Co.
Location:	North Little Rock, Ark.
Director of warehousing and distribution:	Jimmy Whitten
Total sq ft:	440,000
Products handled:	Cosmetics
Number of SKUs:	1,500
Orders shipped daily:	Over 500
Cases shipped daily:	10,000
Pallet storage locations:	35,000
Automatic guided vehicles:	30
Narrow-aisle lift trucks:	6
Conventional lift trucks:	20
Orderpicking A-frames:	2
A-frames supplier and system integrator:	SI Handling, Easton, Penn.
Mezzanine:	Prospect Steel, Little Rock, Ark.
Conveyor:	Roach Manufacturing Corp., Trumann, Ark.
Gravity flow rack:	Kingston-Warren Corp., Newfields, N.H.
Spiral chutes:	Transnorm System Inc., Grand Prairie, Tex.
Narrow-aisle lift trucks:	Raymond, Greene, N.Y.
Fixed-position scanners:	Accu-Sort Systems, Telford, Penn.
Weigh-in-motion scale:	Toledo-Mettler, Worthington, Ohio
Hand-held scanners and label printers:	Intermec, Everett, Wash.

Source: Gary Forger, "How Maybelline Ships Smaller, More Frequent Orders," *Modern Materials Handling* 50, no. 7 (June 1995), p. 49.

refrigerated food storage.[28] Items entering the warehouse are bar-code scanned and assigned storage locations by the computer. Additionally, the data collected become part of the warehouse information system that is used for a variety of purposes, including the preparation of many business-related documents.

---

[28]"RF Pacesetter Applies Hands-On Handling Experience," *Logistics and Materials Handling* 3, no. 7 (February 17, 1995), pp. 21–24.

FIGURE 11–13

Robots in the warehouse

Artist's conception of guided vehicles and robotics in the warehouse. An automatically guided and programmed lift truck is shown stacking a load into a pallet rack. The robot is shown on a floor-supported vehicle capable of raising and lowering; the robot is picking from gravity flow racks and building pallet loads.

Source: "Warehousing Flexibility Aided by Robots," *Material Handling Engineering* 40, no. 9 (September 1985), p. 103. Artwork by Steven Martin. Reproduced by permission of St. Onge Company, York, PA.

Computerized Documentation

Many companies are using various computerized documentation procedures. Whether such technology is being used by Avia Presto of Holland (air freight cargo handling),[29] the Royal Marines of Britain,[30] or the Barrow upon Soar site of British Gypsum Plaster production,[31] firms are recognizing the benefits associated with automating the materials handling process; these include increased productivity, reduced operating expenses, increased space utilization, increased customer service levels, and improved flow of materials.[32]

---

[29]Moyette Marrett-Gibbons, "Freight Flies Faster with Bar Code," *ID Systems* 4, no. 7 (September 1996), pp. 46–49.

[30]Paul Quinn, "Bar Code Moves Military Munitions," *ID Systems* 4, no. 7 (September 1996), pp. 42–44, 54.

[31]News release of British Gypsum, February 25, 1993, unnumbered.

[32]For examples, see Tom Andel, "Automatic Data Identification: For Your Own Good," *Transportation & Distribution* 34, no. 10 (October 1993), pp. 76–88; James Aaron Cooke, "Getting Your Money's Worth from Auto ID," *Traffic Management, Warehousing and Distribution Supplement* (March 1992), pp. 17–19; Gary Forger, "Our System Eliminates Errors and Cuts Our Customers' Costs," *Modern Materials Handling* 50, no. 6 (May 1995), pp. S-10–S-11; and "Wrap It All Up the Right Way in Shipping," *Modern Materials Handling* 50, no. 5 (April 1995), pp. 31–34.

The type and scope of benefits a company receives will vary depending on such factors as product characteristics, labor intensity, existing customer service levels, and present level of company expertise.

Warehousing in a Just-in-Time (JIT) Environment

As manufacturing and merchandising firms adopt and implement just-in-time (JIT) programs, logistics functions such as warehousing are directly affected. Because JIT stresses reduced inventory levels and more responsive logistics systems, greater demands are placed on warehousing to maximize both efficiency and effectiveness. Some examples of these demands include the following:[33]

JIT Places Added Demands on Warehousing and Materials Management

- *Total commitment to quality*—Warehouse employees must perform their tasks at levels specified by customers (inbound and outbound).
- *Reduced production lot sizes*—Items are packaged in smaller lots, and warehouse deliveries are smaller and in mixed pallet quantities.
- *Elimination of non-value-added activities*—Nonessential and inefficient physical movement and handling activities are identified and eliminated, resulting in improved facilities layout and warehouse operating efficiencies.

Zytec Corporation Uses JIT in Its Warehouse

Zytec Corporation, a manufacturer of power supplies for computers and medical equipment, successfully used its warehousing operations to support a JIT manufacturing system. Prior to implementing JIT, the firm's warehousing situation was described as follows:

> The raw materials and purchased parts warehouse at Zytec was out of control. Boxes of parts clogged every aisle and spilled into two additional buildings. The computer on-hand balances were seldom correct, destroying MRP credibility. Unable to trust the system, purchasing agents bought excess inventory to protect against stockouts. Lines were shut down due to parts "lost in the crib" and then worked overtime when hot parts were expedited. Three inventory analysts worked 13-hour days to correct on-hand balances verified by two full-time cycle counters, yet no improvements were visible.[34]

After identifying the problems and causes of the warehousing inefficiencies, process and procedure changes were implemented that resulted in a raw materials inventory reduction of $5 million (from $8.8 million to $3.8 million) and an increase in inventory accuracy from 98.5 to 99.6 percent. Only one facility was needed rather than the three that had previously been required.

Rio Bravo Electricos Uses JIT in Mexico

At Rio Bravo Electricos in Juarez, Mexico, the firm, which assembles electric wiring harnesses for General Motors vans, supplies its 36 subassembly and assembly lines with parts every two hours or so. A wiring harness can be assembled in one hour within the JIT environment.[35]

---

[33]See Robin G. Stenger and Robert E. Murray, "Using Warehousing Operations to Support a Just-in-Time Manufacturing Program," *WERC Technical Paper No. 20* (Oak Brook, IL: Warehousing Education and Research Council, 1987), pp. 1–2; and Louis Giust, "Just-in-Time Manufacturing and Material-Handling Trends," *International Journal of Physical Distribution and Logistics Management* 23, no. 7 (1993), pp. 32–38.

[34]Stenger and Murray, "Using Warehousing Operations," p. 2.

[35]Karen A. Auguston, "Feeding the JIT Pipeline from Across the Border," *Modern Materials Handling* 50, no. 6 (May 1995), pp. 34–35.

Delphi Packard Electric Systems and Its JIT Distribution Center

Similarly, Delphi Packard Electric Systems, also a manufacturer of wiring harnesses, uses JIT in its distribution center to move 99 percent of its product out of the facility within 24 hours. As described in an article about the company: "While the number of outbound shipments and stock keeping units have increased every year of the past decade at the company's El Paso, Texas distribution center, the amount of space devoted to storage has been steadily shrinking."[36] A brief overview of Delphi Packard's JIT distribution center is shown in Figure 11–14.

Packaging

Packaging is an important warehousing and materials management concern, one that is closely tied to warehouse efficiency and effectiveness. The best package optimizes service, cost, and convenience. Good packaging can have a positive impact on layout and design, as well as overall warehouse productivity.

Functions of Packaging

Packaging Serves Two Basic Functions: Marketing and Logistics

Packaging serves two basic functions: marketing and logistics. In its marketing function, the package provides customers with information about the product and promotes the product through the use of color, sizing, and so forth: "The [package] is the 'silent sales[person],' and it is the final interface between the company and its consumers . . . Consumers generally choose to buy from the image they perceive that a product has, and what they perceive is heavily influenced by the cues given on the product's packaging: brand name, color and display."[37]

From a logistics perspective, the functions of packaging are to organize, protect, and identify products and materials. In performing these functions, the package takes up space and adds weight. Industrial users of packaging strive to gain the advantages packaging offers while minimizing the disadvantages, such as added space and weight. We are getting closer to that ideal in several types of packaging, including corrugated containers, foam-in-place packaging, stretch wrapping, and strapping. Also, environmental aspects of packaging are important because of the issue of reverse logistics.[38]

Packaging Performs Six Logistics Functions

Within the general functions of packaging, six specific functions are performed:

- *Containment*—Products must be contained before they can be moved from one place to another. If the package breaks open, the item can be damaged or lost, or contribute to environmental pollution if it is a hazardous material.

- *Protection*—The contents of the package must be protected from damage or loss from outside environmental effects such as moisture, dust, insects, and contamination.

- *Apportionment*—The output must be reduced from industrial production to a manageable, desirable consumer size; that is, translating the large output of manufacturing into smaller quantities of greater use to customers.

---

[36]Karen A. Auguston, "A Focus on Throughput Scores a JIT Success," *Modern Materials Handling* 50, no. 6 (May 1995), pp. 36–38.

[37]Rod Sara, "Packaging as a Retail Marketing Tool," *International Journal of Physical Distribution and Logistics Management* 20, no. 8 (1990), p. 30.

[38]See Judith E. M. Klostermann and Arnold Tukker, eds., *Product Innovation and Eco-Efficiency* (Dordrecht, The Netherlands: Klower Academic Publishers, 1988); and James R. Stock, *Development and Implementation of Reverse Logistics Programs* (Oak Brook, IL: Council of Logistics Management, 1998).

FIGURE 11–14

A layout designed for quick handling, high throughput

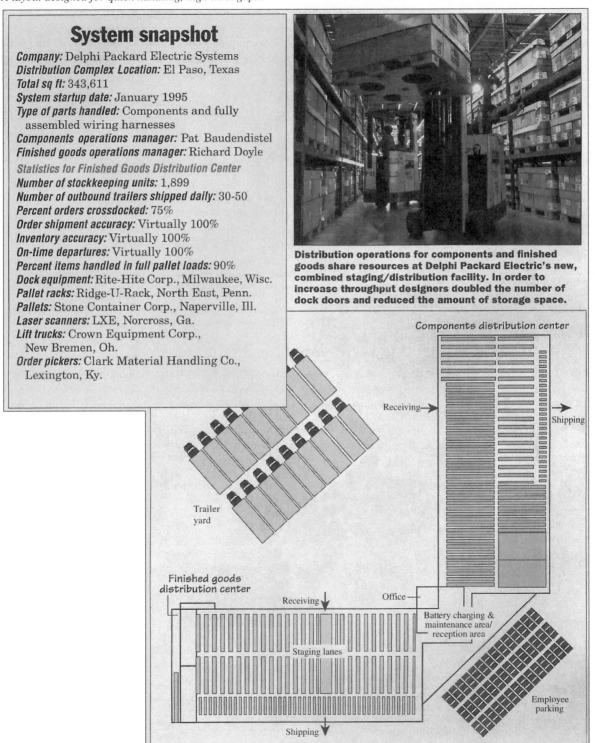

System snapshot

Company: Delphi Packard Electric Systems
Distribution Complex Location: El Paso, Texas
Total sq ft: 343,611
System startup date: January 1995
Type of parts handled: Components and fully assembled wiring harnesses
Components operations manager: Pat Baudendistel
Finished goods operations manager: Richard Doyle

Statistics for Finished Goods Distribution Center
Number of stockkeeping units: 1,899
Number of outbound trailers shipped daily: 30-50
Percent orders crossdocked: 75%
Order shipment accuracy: Virtually 100%
Inventory accuracy: Virtually 100%
On-time departures: Virtually 100%
Percent items handled in full pallet loads: 90%
Dock equipment: Rite-Hite Corp., Milwaukee, Wisc.
Pallet racks: Ridge-U-Rack, North East, Penn.
Pallets: Stone Container Corp., Naperville, Ill.
Laser scanners: LXE, Norcross, Ga.
Lift trucks: Crown Equipment Corp., New Bremen, Oh.
Order pickers: Clark Material Handling Co., Lexington, Ky.

Distribution operations for components and finished goods share resources at Delphi Packard Electric's new, combined staging/distribution facility. In order to increase throughput designers doubled the number of dock doors and reduced the amount of storage space.

Components distribution center

Receiving→   →Shipping

Trailer yard

Finished goods distribution center

Receiving↓   Office

Battery charging & maintenance area/ reception area

Staging lanes

Employee parking

Shipping↓

Source: Karen A. Auguston, "A Focus on Throughput Scores a JIT Success," *Modern Materials Handling* 50, no. 6 (May 1995), p. 37.

- *Unitization*—Primary packages can be unitized into secondary packages (e.g., placed inside a corrugated case), which can then be unitized into a stretch-wrapped pallet, and ultimately into a container loaded with several pallets. This reduces the number of times a product must be handled.
- *Convenience*—Packaging allows products to be used conveniently, that is, with little wasted effort by customers (e.g., blister packs, dispensers).
- *Communication*—Packaging allows the use of unambiguous, readily understood symbols such as a universal product code (UPC).[39]

The package should be designed to provide the most efficient storage. Good packaging interfaces well with the organization's materials handling equipment and allows efficient utilization of both storage space and transportation cube and weight constraints.

Trade-Offs in Packaging

An Example of Cost Savings through Packaging

Packaging trade-offs have frequently been ignored or downplayed in logistics decision making. However, like all logistics decisions, packaging affects both costs and customer service levels. From a cost perspective, suppose a company uses a carton that is $12'' \times 12'' \times 8''$ instead of a carton that measures $12'' \times 12'' \times 16''$. Assume the smaller carton costs 30 cents less. The smaller box also requires less loose fill, which can save a half cubic foot of dunnage costing 50 cents. In this hypothetical example, that represents a savings of 80 cents per carton. Multiplied by hundreds, thousands, or millions of packages distributed during a year and the savings add up pretty quickly.[40]

At the same time as costs are being reduced, service levels are being improved because customers are able to obtain more or the same amount of product in less space, enabling them to achieve cost savings through better space utilization of their facilities. The customer is also likely to realize fewer partial or split shipments from suppliers because more products can be placed on the transport vehicle that is making deliveries.

Packaging is becoming a more visible issue because of the current environmental concerns related to recycling and reuse of packaging.[41] Investing in efficient and effective packaging can save organizations money in several ways, including the following:

Benefits of Good Packaging

- Lighter packaging may save transportation costs.
- Careful planning of packaging size/cube may allow better warehousing and transportation space utilization.
- More protective packaging may reduce damage and requirements for special handling.
- Environmentally conscious packaging may save disposal costs and improve the company's image.
- Use of returnable containers provides cost savings as well as environmental benefits through the reduction of waste products.[42]

---

[39]Gordon L. Robertson, "Good and Bad Packaging: Who Decides?" *International Journal of Physical Distribution and Logistics Management* 20, no. 8 (1990), pp. 38–39.

[40]Toby B. Gooley, "Is There Hidden Treasure in Your Packaging?" *Logistics Management* 35, no. 12 (December 1996), p. 23.

[41]John H. Sheridan, "Pollution Prevention Picks Up Steam," *Industry Week* (February 17, 1992), p. 48; and Tom Andel, "Don't Recycle When You Can Recirculate," *Transportation and Distribution* 31, no. 9 (September 1991), pp. 68–72.

[42]For a discussion of returnable containers, see Tom Andel, "Conversion to Returnables Wins Believers," *Transportation & Distribution* 36, no. 9 (September 1995), pp. 94–100; and Leo Kroon and Gaby Vrijens, "Returnable Containers: An Example of Reverse Logistics," *International Journal of Physical Distribution and Logistics Management* 25, no. 2 (1995), pp. 56–68.

Some specific examples of cost savings and/or customer service improvements resulting from packaging modifications include the following:

- A frozen-foods supplier saved $3 million and a baked-goods company saved $1 million on annual freight costs by redesigning their packaging to better fit standard pallets. Both were able to put more product on a pallet and more pallets in each truck, thus greatly reducing the number of truckloads required.
- A pharmaceuticals company reduced freight costs on one product line by 25 percent by reducing the amount of packaging used—without compromising product protection.
- A manufacturer of electronic components changed its packaging for some products to reflect the average quantities ordered by customers. Customers liked the larger quantities, and the reduced number of packages per order improved inventory and order accuracy, and reduced packaging and transportation costs.[43]

Some examples of packaging and logistics cost trade-offs are shown in Table 11–3. As identified in the table, there are many important interfaces between packaging and areas such as transportation, inventory, warehousing, and information systems.[44]

Box 11–1 discusses some of the trade-offs between packaging materials and other logistics aspects as a result of the "green" movement.

TABLE 11–3 Packaging Cost Trade-Offs with Other Logistics Functions

Transportation	
Increased package information	Decreases shipment delays; decreases tracking of lost shipments
Increased package protection	Decreases damage and theft in transit but increases package weight and transport costs
Increased standardization	Decreases handling costs, vehicle waiting time for loading/unloading; increases modal choices for shipper and decreases need for specialized transport equipment.
Inventory	
Increased product protection	Decreases theft, damage, insurance; increases product availability (sales); increases product value and carrying costs
Warehousing	
Increased package information	Decreases order filling time, labor cost
Increased product protection	Increases (stacking), but decreases cube utilization by increasing the size of the product dimensions.
Increased standardization	Decreases materials handling equipment costs
Communications	
Increased package information	Decreases other communications about the product such as telephone calls to track down lost shipments

Logistics functions of packaging: informs; protects; standardizes package dimensions; enhances handling efficiency.

Source: Professor Robert L. Cook, Department of Marketing and Hospitality Services Administration, Central Michigan University, Mt. Pleasant, MI, 1991.

---

[43]Gooley, "Is There Hidden Treasure in Your Packaging?" p. 20.

[44]For specific company examples, see "Foam Protection Serves Electronic Parts Well," *Transportation & Distribution* 29, no. 3 (March 1989), pp. 57–58; Ronald Kopicki, Michael J. Berg, and Leslie Legg, *Reuse and Recycling—Reverse Logistics Opportunities* (Oak Brook, IL: Council of Logistics Management, 1993); Paul R. Murphy, Richard F. Poist, and Charles D. Braunschweig, "Role and Relevance of Logistics to Corporate Environmentalism: An Empirical Assessment," *International Journal of Physical Distribution and Logistics Management* 25, no. 2 (1995), pp. 5–19; and Helen L. Richardson, "Stop Damage at the Source," *Transportation & Distribution* 29, no. 3 (March 1989), pp. 30–32.

Box 11–1

Green Manufacturing Has Major Implications for Logistics

Design for disassembly is a hot new trend in manufacturing. The goal is to design, develop, and produce product with the goal of reducing the waste created when the product reaches the end of its useful life. That could involve recycling, refurbishing, or safely disposing of a product and its components. It also has major implications for how a company needs to design its logistics and purchasing systems.

Germany has been the leader in the green movement, requiring that manufacturers take back their product's packaging. To address this requirement, manufacturers banded together to form a private company that collects and recycles and disposes of packaging material. This has reduced the amount of waste due to packaging materials by 4 percent in the first two years of implementation.

It also has major implications for materials handling equipment and packaging design. For example, companies have been designing product to use less packaging. Colgate and several other manufacturers are now using a design for a toothpaste tube that stands on the cap. Thus, no box is needed.

Hewlett-Packard has designed work stations in a "green" way that has many implications for logistics. Instead of using metal internal "frames" to hold the parts in place, HP uses a polypropylene foam chassis with cutouts for each component and connection. This is so effectively protective that external packaging can be minimized—reduced by 30 percent. The product is lighter, which reduces transportation cost. Disassembly time has been reduced by 90 percent.

As components are reused, new ways of transporting, storing, and handling the unusable materials and inventory need to be found. Logistics will play a key role in this process.

Source: Gene Bylinsky, "Manufacturing for Reuse," *Fortune* (February 6, 1995), pp. 102–12. Copyright 1995 Time, Inc. Reprinted by permission.

Package Design

Factors Influencing Package Design

What is involved in designing the optimal package? In a very practical sense, the factors governing good package design include (1) standardization, (2) pricing, (3) product or package adaptability, (4) protective level, (5) handling ability, and (6) product packability. Today, reusability and recyclability are additional concerns. With the growth in automation and computerization of warehousing; ability to utilize high storage space and convey information are also key. The importance a firm places on each of the factors, as well as the cost/service trade-offs it makes, varies by company, by industry, and by geographic location. (See Box 11–2.)

Packaging and Logistics Cost Trade-Offs

For example, because of the difference in products (cost and physical characteristics), a food processing firm is more concerned than a computer manufacturer with having a package that minimizes shipping and storage costs. A computer manufacturer emphasizes the protective aspects of packaging because of the fragile, expensive nature of computer systems.

Another illustration would be a company that recently completed construction of a fully automated warehouse. Such a facility would be very concerned with handling ability, cube utilization, and the ability to convey information in such a way so that it could be read by the equipment.

In contrast, a company doing business in the European Union (EU) generally, or Germany specifically, would be very concerned with reusability and recyclability aspects of packaging due to the very strict environmental laws there. The packaging decision requires using a systems approach in order to understand the true total cost picture.

There are many factors that influence the product package, such as the channel of distribution and/or institutional requirements. This is often true in retail channels. For

---

Box 11–2

Designing the Optimal Package

The ultimate goal is to develop a package that optimizes service, cost, and convenience factors for all elements of the marketing and logistics systems. In the broadest sense, good packaging begins with the design of the product, and it ends with the re-use or disposal of the package.

More narrowly, it concentrates on the shipping container, which might be a corrugated box, cargo cage, van container, truck, covered hopper, or tank car. It also covers any inner containers or protectors, as well as the individual consumer package.

Design of the package involves proper product identification with the size, type, and location of the item code or Universal Product Code, and with other package information to assure correct selection, sorting, and shipping. It relates to transportation through package density and efficient cube use. It satisfies warehousing requirements through dimension and stackability for good pallet patterns and efficient storage. It also affects materials handling in terms of load stability and compatibility with the different forms of mechanization and automation. Finally, it has impact on the customer's distribution system in terms of their ability to receive and integrate merchandise into their warehouse operating system, particularly with less-than-full-case order picking.

The interactions of distribution packaging become complex with product protection, which applies not only in the manufacturer warehouse but also in rail or truck or other forms of transport, in the customer warehouse with many different forms of mechanized or automated materials handling, and in the consumer outlet or other end-use environment.

Packaging must also consider total logistics costs, including freight rates, handling, and storage efficiency, and end-use costs of opening and disposal of the package and assembly or other preparation of the product.

The intangibles of the package are important in terms of customer convenience—those hard-to-measure end-use benefits that allow smooth interface with merchandising, production, or other aspects of the customer's distribution system.

The cost of materials and producing a package, of course, is also a prime factor in any packaging system, but the optimum system is one that considers all the requirements we have outlined at the lowest total cost. Obviously, this involves a good deal more than simple design.

It means that you have to mediate conflicts, evaluate trade-offs, and reach a fair balance. It means that you have to question basic manufacturing, marketing, and logistics assumptions so that invalid claims can be eliminated in favor of meaningful requirements.

It means that you have to measure warehousing and transportation and handling costs against packaging costs and all of them against product protection. And it means that you have to weigh manufacturing efficiencies and marketing decisions against distributor and retailer needs. It means that you have to be willing to pay a premium in one area in order to introduce badly needed benefits in another area—and thereby gain a very real marketing edge.

Source: Adapted from John F. Spencer, "A Picture of Packaging in the Context of Physical Distribution," *Handling & Shipping* 18, no. 10 (October 1977), p. 54. Reprinted with permission from the October 1977 issues of *Handling & Shipping*. Copyright © Penton Publishing.

---

example, when compact discs (CDs) first came out, retailers were concerned that they be able to use the racks they had used for albums. There was also concern related to potential pilferage due to the small size. The large, environmentally unfriendly packages were chosen as a way to address those concerns. In the oil industry, there was initial difficulty in selling the concept of oil packaged in plastic bottles. Retailers did not want to stock the product, as they felt that the old cardboard cans made better use of shelf space. In these examples, least-cost packaging was traded off for other considerations.[45]

Procter & Gamble (P&G) is one firm that has examined the full implications of the packaging decision. The company developed a program called Direct Product

---

[45]Examples provided by Dr. William A. Cunningham, Air Force Institute of Technology, Wright-Patterson Air Force Base, Ohio.

Profitability[46] which examined packaging costs through the entire channel of distribution. Some of the results achieved by P&G included the following:

Packaging Changes Implemented at Procter & Gamble

- An Ivory shampoo bottle was redesigned in a squarer configuration that took up less space and saved distributors 29 cents per case.
- Tide powder detergent was reformulated so that P&G was able to shrink the size of the box without reducing the number of washings per box. P&G was able to pack 14 boxes in a case instead of 12, thus reducing handling and storage.[47] During 1990, the firm introduced an even smaller package, while keeping a comparable number of wash loads yet reducing the case size.

Packaging, warehouse handling systems, and all warehousing operations are interrelated within the firm's logistics system, and all must be managed effectively (see Box 11–3 for some examples). The effectiveness of these systems can be enhanced with excellent information systems.

Packaging should be designed to provide the organization with optimal levels of logistics efficiency and effectiveness. Logistics suffers when management does not pay sufficient attention to packaging issues. In the same fashion, the use of computer technology, information, and warehouse management techniques can have very positive effects on logistics operations.

Box 11–3

Carriers Get into the Packaging Act

It may surprise some shippers, but carriers can be excellent sources of information on packaging improvements. Some large trucking companies and small-package carriers offer package testing, analysis, and consulting either as a free service to customers or on a fee-for-service basis.

For example, United Parcel Service, CF MotorFreight, and Federal Express all have package-testing laboratories. Their packaging engineers employ standard testing methods to determine whether shippers' packaging will withstand the rigors of transportation. Federal Express, for example, employs about 50 packaging engineers in the United States. United Parcel Service operates four packaging labs in the United States and Canada. CF MotorFreight has a lab at company headquarters.

It makes sense for carriers to get involved with packaging. By assisting shippers with their packaging concerns, carriers can reduce loss and damage rates and claims payments. They also benefit when changes in package sizing allow for better pallet and trailer utilization.

Carrier-operated laboratories are independent in the sense that they have no ties to the packaging manufacturers. In fact, there are dozens of such independent package-testing labs that have been certified as conforming to specified testing standards by government agencies such as the U.S. Department of Transportation, and industry groups like the International Safe Transit Association (ISTA) and the National Motor Freight Traffic Association (NMFTA). These groups can provide shippers with a list of certified testing facilities.

Source: Toby B. Gooley, "Is There Hidden Treasure in Your Packaging?" *Logistics Management* 35, no. 12 (December 1996), p. 20.

---

[46]See Martin Christopher, "Integrating Logistics Strategy in the Corporate Financial Plan," in *The Logistics Handbook*, ed. James F. Robeson and William C. Copacino (New York: Free Press, 1994), especially pp. 255–57.

[47]"Packaging/Handling Interaction Gets a Boost," *Material Handling Engineering* 40, no. 3 (March 1985), p. 48.

Computer Technology, Information, and Warehouse Management

Computers and Warehouse Management

We saw in Chapter 10 that the basic functions of warehousing were movement, storage, and information transfer. In each of those areas the use of computer technology and information systems has become widespread. Significant gains in production planning and control, inventory management, labor productivity, and customer service have resulted from various kinds of technological innovation and implementation.

The role of information and computer technology in warehousing and throughout logistics is significant, and growing every day. The pace of technological change is quickening and logistics executives often find themselves saying something like the following:

> You've undoubtedly been through it before—you purchase a new piece of technology or software, master it, then six months down the road find that it has become virtually obsolete. After the investment in time, money and energy, it's time to start over again with the latest and greatest to keep your warehouse moving forward.[48]

Of course, staying on top of the latest technology isn't easy, but it has become a necessity for successful warehouse management. Warehousing will move toward more and more computerization, using systems that manage information. Figure 11–15 illustrates the important position of warehousing in a typical supply chain. Relevant flows typically involve purchase order information and order (or complaint) information.

In the modern warehouse of today, the following technologies are often evident:

Warehouse Technology

- Warehouse management systems (WMSs).[49]
- Radio frequency communication and inventory update.
- Bar-code reading and label generation equipment.
- Electronic data interchange (EDI) and the Internet.
- Transportation management systems (TMSs).
- Interface to enterprise requirements planning (ERP) systems.
- Productivity tracking software.
- Activity-based costing software.[50]

Warehouse Management System (WMS)

The warehouse management system (WMS) is a key element in computerizing warehouse operations. In some instances, implementation of a WMS can result in a 50 percent reduction in operational expense. According to one writer: "The best approach to a WMS is to start with a detailed examination of the operation with an eye toward true business requirements. This . . . is not unlike documenting a design for a new software system. The objective . . . is to document what results are needed."[51]

---

[48]"Mastering Technology," *WERCSheet* 22, no. 1 (January 1999), p. 14.

[49]For a general overview of WMSs, see Mohamed Y. Amer, Chris Brumett, and Ronald D. Chase, "Zen and the Art of WMS Package Selection," *Proceedings of the Annual Conference of the Council of Logistics Management* (Oak Brook, IL: Council of Logistics Management, 1998), pp. 631–41. For a specific example of how a WMS was installed at Kraft Foods, see "A Network Redesign Spells Good Things for Kraft Foods," *WERCSheet* 22, no. 1 (January 1999), pp. 11, 16.

[50]Arnold Maltz, *The Changing Role of Warehousing* (Oak Brook, IL: Warehousing Education and Research Council, 1998), p. 18.

[51]Robert L. Olsen, "WMS—To Buy or Build," article published by Tompkins Associates (1999), unnumbered.

FIGURE 11–15

Information flows in the supply chain

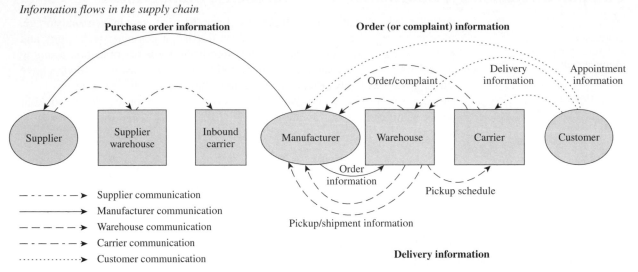

Source: Arnold Maltz, *The Changing Role of Warehousing* (Oak Brook, IL: Warehousing Education and Research Council, 1998), p. 27.

Examples of WMS Applications

Table 11–4 identifies many of the elements or components that would be included in a WMS.

There are many examples of the use of WMS and other technology in warehousing, such as those systems installed at Hewlett-Packard, Malaysia Airlines, Texas Instruments, and Unilever Italia.

Hewlett-Packard (HP) manufactures ink-jet printers at its Camas, Washington, production facility. Parts are stored at an on-site warehouse and an off-site facility 12 miles away. In order to manage the inflow of parts to the manufacturing plant, HP used a warehouse management system (WMS). The WMS tracks the movement of inbound materials through the warehouse and into production. Besides tracking inbound items, the WMS determines which specific parts will be pulled in response to factory orders.

HP runs two separate WMSs that talk to one another. One system runs the on-site warehouse and the other oversees the off-site facility. The systems provide accurate, up-to-date inventory levels and storage locations of all parts. As a result, more than 90 percent of orders now get to the production line 10 minutes after they are requested.[52]

Malaysia Airlines, Southeast Asia's largest airline company, was the first Asia-Pacific air carrier to implement advanced bar-code and client/server technology in cargo tracking and warehouse operations.[53] Other companies in a diverse variety of industries—including toy retailing, blood testing laboratories, and textbook manufacturing—are also using similar technology to improve materials handling efficiency and effectiveness.[54]

---

[52]James Aaron Cooke, "Parts to Go!" *Logistics Management* 35, no. 4 (April 1996), p. 87-S.

[53]Airline Adopts Barcoding," *Logistics and Materials Handling* 4, no. 2 (April 21, 1995), p. 39.

[54]See "Accurate Data Cuts Warehouse Costs by $1 Million Annually," *Modern Materials Handling* 50, no. 6 (May 1995), p. S-17; "Barcodes to Track Blood," *Logistics and Materials Handling* 4, no. 2 (April 21, 1995), p. 41; and "Tracking What's Hot in Toys," *Logistics and Materials Handling* 4, no. 2 (April 21, 1995), p. 40.

TABLE 11–4   Model Warehouse Management System Components

1.0 General requirements
1.1 Support multiple geographic locations, warehouses, and sections within each warehouse
1.2 Support item definitions as well as single-item and mixed-item quantity location
1.3 Support definitions of equipment, storage, and human resources
1.4 Support work measurement criteria and track performance against those criteria
1.5 Support random location of inventory, FIFO processing, and multiple items per location
1.6 Provide management reporting capability
1.7 Provide ability to track orders by status
1.8 Provide inquiry capability
1.9 Handle exceptions and unusual situations
1.10 Support interfaces to materials handling equipment and radio-frequency devices
1.11 Support use of bar-code labels

2.0 Inventory location and management requirements
2.1 Item identification and tracking
2.2 Physical inventories
2.3 Support cycle counting
2.4 Inventory accuracy
2.5 Item history
2.6 Product profile analysis (ABC analysis)
2.7 Allocated and available inventory
2.8 Quarantine or "on-hold" inventory
2.9 Storage locations
2.10 Storage location definitions
2.11 Storage location control
2.12 Storage fill rate
2.13 FIFO control
2.14 Support container sizes and equipment
2.15 Reporting capability

3.0 Inventory location/management requirements assumptions

4.0 Receiving requirements
4.1 Advance notice of delivery
4.2 Various types of receipts
4.3 Availability of items
4.4 Exception status, handling, and reporting
4.5 Bar-code labels
4.6 Multiple receipts
4.7 Purchase order reconciliation
4.8 Receipt inspections

5.0 Put-away requirements
5.1 Directed put-away
5.2 Exception handling
5.3 Inventory updating
5.4 Confirmation of put-away
5.5 Cross-docking
5.6 Combined processing

6.0 Order management requirements
6.1 Order groupings
6.2 Order statistics
6.3 Reporting
6.4 Tracking

7.0 Replenishment requirements
7.1 Replenishment on FIFO basis
7.2 Replenishment based on current demand
7.3 Replenishment confirmation

8.0 Picking requirements
8.1 Sequential picking
8.2 Other than wave picking
8.3 Segregation of picks
8.4 Confirmation of picking
8.5 Use of radio-frequency equipment
8.6 Plan warehouseman work
8.7 Order integrity
8.8 Exceptions
8.9 Efficient picking

9.0 Labor management requirements
9.1 Identify source requirements
9.2 Work flow monitoring
9.3 Operating levels
9.4 Management reports

10.0 Shipping requirements
10.1 Fluid loading
10.2 Order staging
10.3 Confirm complete orders and trailers
10.4 Identify exceptions and shortages
10.5 Print manifests and other required documents for a trailer load
10.6 Interface with inventory and invoice systems
10.7 EDI to intended destinations
10.8 Transfer of loads
10.9 De-assign products or orders
10.10 Picking status
10.11 Verification of orders and items

11.0 Work flow management
11.1 Daily and shift workload
11.2 Exceptions
11.3 Work in progress
11.4 Future workload

Source: Ken Ackerman, *Warehousing Profitably: A Manager's Guide [An Update]* (Columbus, OH: Ackerman Publications, 2000), pp. 310–11.

Texas Instruments has linked electronic data interchange (EDI) and bar-coding in the order placement and management of office supplies, with positive results. The company reduced the amount of cash tied up in inventory by $2 million, freed up 40,000 square feet of warehouse space, reassigned 11 office supply control employees, and reduced cycle time by more than one-third.

By bar-coding inbound shipments, the purchasing department and the entire materials function can get more accurate accounts of actual receipts. The bar-code error rate is between 1 in 10,000 and 1 in 1 million, versus 1 in 25 or 30 for manually keyed data. These data can automatically be used by the accounts payable department to automatically generate checks and reconcile invoices with purchase orders and receiving. Thus, bar-coding represents a logical extension of the organization's information systems, and a link with EDI.[55]

Unilever Italia, a consumer products manufacturer, has benefited from the implementation of radio frequency (RF) identification technology. According to one observer: "Just one warehouse worker is now able to process 350 pallets or more a day at the company's Elida-Gibbs plant near Milan. Previously, it would have taken three men a whole day to do just 200 pallets."[56]

The Unilever system utilizes the RF technology to locate specific pallets of products in the warehouse. Data are transmitted by RF to the firm's computer system,

---

Technology

A Complete Overhaul at McKesson

McKesson Corporation, a San Francisco–based pharmaceutical distributor, had 36 warehouses located throughout the United States, containing a total of $2.2 billion of inventory. The firm was using a manual inventory control system and went through a reengineering exercise that changed its warehousing system from a paper-based environment to an automated one.

The firm acquired a Warehouse Management System (WMS), bar-code technology, and radio frequency (RF) equipment. Because of the company's desire to have its employees work in a "hands-free" environment, arm-mounted units (scanner, antenna, and display) were used. The equipment and computer systems allow McKesson to know "who is moving what product where at all times."

Results of the reengineering have been:

- An 8 percent improvement in productivity, translating into an $8 million savings.

- A 70 percent improvement in inventory shortages, or $1.5 million saved.
- A 42 percent improvement in picking mistakes.
- A 26 percent improvement in inventory item matching.
- A 74 percent improvement in plus adjustments (carrying more inventory than realized).
- A 34 percent improvement in minus adjustments (carrying less inventory than realized).
- A $1 million saving in supplies and maintenance.
- A $17 million saving in inventory costs.

Source: "A Complete Overhaul," *WERCSheet* 21, no. 10 (November 1998), pp. 1–2, 5.

---

[55]Ed Hatchett, "Combining EDI with Bar Coding to Automate Procurement," *1992 NAPM* (Tempe, AZ: National Association of Purchasing Management, 1992), pp. 45–50.

[56]Alain Berthon, "Smart Move," *Logistics Europe* 4, no. 4 (September 1996), p. 69.

which stores information from the bar-code label as well as a description of the pallet, how many boxes it holds, where the order is to go, what products are being shipped, and where the pallet is located within the warehouse. When the product is shipped, RF technology alerts personnel as to the truck trailer where the pallet has been loaded. Because data are transmitted electronically, the system "eliminates manual entry and paperwork. A loading list is automatically printed for each trailer shipment."[57]

In the past two decades, the most significant advances in technology have occurred in the information transfer area. The movement and storage functions require computerization at the mechanical level, where machines and equipment are used. There is also an electronic level, which requires computer-to-computer interface and involves data transmission.[58]

E-Commerce, Internet, and Warehousing

Important questions facing warehousing managers specifically, and logistics executives generally, are when and if newer technology will replace old. This is particularly true in the electronic commerce arena, where electronic data interchange (EDI) is being evaluated relative to use of the Internet. Likely, organizations will continue to use both technologies, much as some firms use public versus private warehousing, or contract versus common carriers. Both technologies move data between individuals, departments, organizations, and other members of the supply chain. A recent article makes the following points:

> The goal of the e-commerce initiative is to improve the ability to exchange data between business entities. Methodologies include batch exchange and direct entry of data. Thus, the EDI standards we have known and used for years retain a unique and appropriate position in the initiative. The Internet expands the enabling of EDI by providing faster and less expensive means of communication, reducing a transmission to an attachment to e-mail . . . Further, the Internet introduces popularity and accessibility to e-commerce that is driving a significant retail market and enabling new capabilities to specific industries that rely on immediate access to data. [Thus] to our question we can answer that the two do not vie for the same market, but work as a team to enhance our expanding world commerce.[59]

In warehouse management, information is important. Accurate and timely information allows a firm to minimize inventories, to improve routing and scheduling of transportation vehicles, and to generally improve customer service levels. A typical warehouse management system achieves these improvements in three ways: (1) by reducing direct labor, (2) by increasing materials handling equipment efficiency, and (3) by increasing warehouse space utilization.

This has brought about the rapid development of industrial networks—a hardware and software solution that interconnects computers, peripherals, programmable controllers, and other intelligent devices. In effect, the handling and storage equipment they control are linked together.

Local Area Networks (LANs)

Networks are communications systems that allow transmission of data between a variety of devices such as terminals, word processors, bar-code readers, robots, conveyors, automatic guided vehicles, and AS/RSs. *Local area networks (LANs),* in which devices are located close to one another, are often used in warehousing. Figure 11–16 shows an example of a local area network.

Whichever approach a firm uses, the objectives are the same: to provide better control over information flows and to allow the warehouse facility to maximize effectiveness and efficiency.

---

[57]Ibid., p. 70.

[58]See Amy Zuckerman, "Warehousing at 65 MPH," *Supply Chain Technology News* 2, no. 7 (July 2000), pp. 36–38.

[59]Robert L. Olsen, "EDI versus the Internet, Do We Understand the Question?" article published by Tompkins Associates (1999), unnumbered.

FIGURE 11–16

Example of a local area network (LAN)

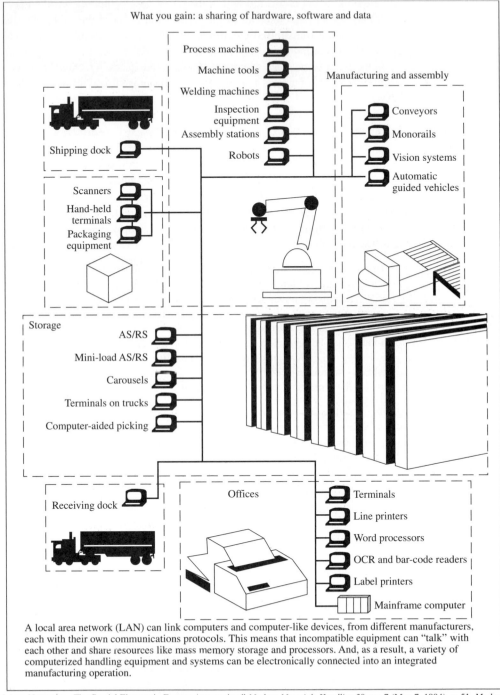

What you gain: a sharing of hardware, software and data

Process machines
Machine tools
Welding machines
Inspection equipment
Assembly stations
Robots

Manufacturing and assembly

Conveyors
Monorails
Vision systems
Automatic guided vehicles

Shipping dock

Scanners
Hand-held terminals
Packaging equipment

Storage

AS/RS
Mini-load AS/RS
Carousels
Terminals on trucks
Computer-aided picking

Receiving dock

Offices

Terminals
Line printers
Word processors
OCR and bar-code readers
Label printers
Mainframe computer

A local area network (LAN) can link computers and computer-like devices, from different manufacturers, each with their own communications protocols. This means that incompatible equipment can "talk" with each other and share resources like mass memory storage and processors. And, as a result, a variety of computerized handling equipment and systems can be electronically connected into an integrated manufacturing operation.

Source: "Local Area Networks—The Crucial Element in Factory Automation," *Modern Materials Handling* 39, no. 7 (May 7, 1984), p. 51, *Modern Materials Handling,* copyright 1984 by Cahners Publishing Company, Division of Reed Holdings, Inc.

Creative Solutions

Design for Payback

Your mission is to improve your distribution operation. Your CEO sets goals for increasing productivity by 20 percent, inventory and order accuracy to 99.9 percent, capacity and throughput to meet the 15 percent annual growth rate, and you must reduce order cycle time for your customers. There is no money for additional space, but you're told to look at automation as a solution.

How do you select the right technology to achieve your goals? How can you improve your project's chances of receiving the necessary capital when it competes with other internal investment proposals?

Design for Payback (DFP) . . . is the concept of requiring payback analysis on every element of an improvement plan, not just measuring the return on investment on the project as a whole . . . DFP is based on putting your investment into those parts of your operation which have the greatest potential for savings due to increases in productivity, accuracy, and throughput.

A large apparel company was considering automating full case picking with "pick-to-belt" technology, picking cases from staged pallets to an adjacent conveyor belt. Using Pareto's Law, they planned to provide pick slots for 900 SKU's (20 percent) with 2–4 pallets per SKU in a three level, pick-to-belt module. The cost was budgeted at $2.9 million, and it required over 35,000 square feet. With the SKU level velocity analysis inherent in DFP, they found that only the first 200 SKU's had the case volume to justify the pick-to-belt technology. On a per SKU basis, the cost of the 200th slot was justified with a two-year payback due to productivity improvements. The entire module for the 200 SKU's cost about $450,000 and experienced a 1.4 year payback. It also occupied less than one-fourth of the space.

Source: Fred Kimball, "Design for Payback: A Model for Selecting Warehouse Automation Technology Based on Return on Investment," *Proceedings of the Annual Conference of the Council of Logistics Management* (Oak Brook, II: Council of Logistics Management, 1998), pp. 643–49.

Summary

In this chapter we discussed materials handling systems and equipment. Both nonautomated and automated equipment issues were examined, and examples were provided of some of the major types of equipment commonly used in warehousing. Nonautomated materials handling equipment can be classified according to the function performed: storage and order picking, transportation and sorting, or shipping. Automated equipment includes items such as AS/RSs, carousels, conveyors, robots, and scanning systems.

In a JIT environment, warehousing and materials handling are important logistics activities. JIT stresses reduced inventory levels and more responsive logistics systems. Thus, greater demands are placed on warehousing to maximize both efficiency and effectiveness.

Packaging decisions often have warehousing and materials handling implications. A number of cost and service aspects of packaging were examined. Environmental concerns are also an issue to logistics executives, specifically the reuse and recycling of packaging materials.

In Chapter 12, we will examine the role of procurement in the logistics process. Because materials that are obtained in the procurement process are often stored in warehouses, our knowledge of warehousing will allow us to more fully understand procurement within the logistics system.

Suggested Readings

Ackerman, Kenneth B. "The Changing Role of Warehousing." *Warehousing Forum* 8, no. 12 (November 1993), pp. 1–4.

————. "Receiving and Shipping Systems." In *The Distribution Management Handbook,* ed. James A. Tompkins and Dale Harmelink. New York: McGraw-Hill, 1994, pp. 17.1–17.33.

"All Wrapped Up." *WERCSheet* 22, no. 2 (January 1999), pp. 1–3.

"Analyze This." *WERCSheet* 22, no. 5 (May 1999), pp. 1–2, 5.

Andel, Tom. "The Environment's Right for a Packaging Plan." *Transportation & Distribution* 34, no. 11 (November 1993), pp. 66–74.

Andersen Consulting. *Warehouse Systems and the Supply Chain: A Survey of Success Factors.* Oak Brook, IL: Warehousing Education and Research Council, 1998.

"An Inside View of the Scanning Market." *WERCSheet* 23, no. 7 (July/August 2000), pp 1–3, 7.

Bhardwaj, S. M. *The Pallet Storage System Selection Process.* Oak Brook, IL: Warehousing Education and Research Council, 1990.

Cooke, James Aaron. "How to Choose the Lift Truck That's Right for You." *American Public Warehouse Register,* 14th ed. (1995), pp. 34–35.

Cooper, Catherine L. "The Human Side of WMS Implementations." *Warehousing Forum* 15, no. 3 (February 2000), pp. 1–3.

Forger, Gary. "We Turned an AS/RS into a Materials Control Center." *Modern Materials Handling* 50, no. 7 (June 1995), pp. 54–55.

Frazelle, Edward H., and James M. Apple, Jr. "Materials Handling Technologies." In *The Logistics Handbook,* ed. James F. Robeson and William C. Copacino. New York: Free Press, 1994, pp. 547–603.

Hall, Craig T. "The Impact of Electronic Commerce on Warehousing." *Warehousing Forum* 13, no. 10 (September 1998), pp. 1–3.

Harmon, Roy L. *Reinventing the Warehouse: World Class Distribution Logistics.* New York: Free Press, 1993.

Harps, Leslie Hansen. "Working Webbed-up Warehouses: WMS Lessons Learned." *Inbound Logistics* 20, no. 5 (May 2000), pp. 48–60.

Moore, Alicia Hills, and Karen Nickel Anhalt. "Manufacturing for Reuse." *Fortune* (February 6, 1995), pp. 102–12.

Napolitano, Maida. *Using Modeling to Solve Warehousing Problems.* Oak Brook, IL: Warehousing Education and Research Council, 1998.

Nofsinger, John B. "Storage Equipment," In *The Distribution Management Handbook,* ed. James A. Tompkins and Dale Harmelink. New York: McGraw-Hill, 1994, pp. 18.1–18.29.

Olson, David R. "Material Handling Equipment." In *The Distribution Management Handbook,* ed. James A. Tompkins and Dale Harmelink. New York: McGraw-Hill, 1994, pp. 19.1–19.29.

"On the Cutting Edge of Fashion. . . and Logistics—boo.com" *Channels* 5, no. 1 (2000), pp. 8–9.

Owens, Greg, and Robert Mann. "Materials Handling System Design." In *The Logistics Handbook,* ed. James F. Robeson and William C. Copacino. New York: Free Press, 1994, pp. 519–45.

Speh, Thomas W.; Jane C. Haley; Kelly A. Logan; and Mindy S. West. *A Guide for Evaluating and Implementing a Warehouse Bar Code System.* Oak Brook, IL: Warehousing Education and Research Council, February 1992.

Stilwell, E. Joseph; R. Claire Canty; Peter W. Kopf; and Anthony M. Montrone. *Packaging for the Environment: A Partnership for Progress.* New York: AMACOM, 1991.

Stock, James R. *Development and Implementation of Reverse Logistics Programs.* Oak Brook, IL: Council of Logistics Management, 1998.

Tompkins, James A. "Measuring Warehousing Performance: How Are You Doing?" *Proceedings of the Annual Conference of the Council of Logistics Management.* Oak Brook, IL: Council of Logistics Management, 1994, pp. 437–49.

"Try to Plan in Orderpicking Productivity." *Modern Materials Handling* 50, no. 5 (April 1995), pp. 19–22.

Twede, Diana, ed. *Logistical Packaging Innovation Symposium Proceedings.* Oak Brook, IL: Council of Logistics Management, 1991.

"What Matters Most." <http://www.manufacturing.net/magazine/mmh/archives/2000> *Modern Materials Handling* (January 1, 2000).

Questions and Problems

1. Identify the major advantages of automated versus nonautomated materials handling systems.

2. What are the major obstacles or problems associated with automated materials handling systems? How do these obstacles impact the use of automated materials handling equipment?

3. In what ways are JIT, warehousing, and materials handling related? In other words, how has JIT affected warehousing and materials handling?

4. Packaging serves two basic functions: marketing and logistics. Identify the role of packaging in each of these functional areas.

5. Discuss some of the general and specific computer and information technologies and trends that have affected warehousing and materials handling.

CHAPTER 12 Procurement

Chapter Outline

Chapter Objectives

- To show how better management of purchasing activities can lead to increased profitability.
- To introduce the activities that must be performed by the purchasing function.
- To describe the impact of just-in-time production on purchasing.
- To show how purchasing costs can be managed.
- To show how to measure and evaluate purchasing performance.
- To introduce the concept of strategic sourcing.
- To describe how e-procurement aids sourcing.
- To describe a model that can be used for developing and implementing partnerships with suppliers.

Introduction

In the United States, purchasing agents for manufacturing firms buy more than $1.6 trillion worth of goods each year.[1] In addition, state and federal purchases are more than $1.2 trillion.[2] How well this money is spent is a question that is of considerable concern to both purchasing agents and top management. The fact that purchases consistently represent the largest single expense of doing business shows that there is a pressing need for reliable measures of purchasing efficiency. Table 12–1 presents purchasing data for the entire U.S. manufacturing sector; purchased materials account for 53 percent of the sales dollar on average and range from 27 to 83 percent. When expenditures for capital equipment are included, the average percentage increases to 56. As firms respond to the mandate to become more efficient if they are to compete with foreign manufacturers, it is likely that additional labor costs will be designed out of the processes used. Also, many companies (examples include Lucent Technologies and Sara Lee Corporation) are outsourcing portions or all of their manufacturing operations. Thus, the material/sales ratio will increase. Any function for which costs amount to over half of a firm's sales is going to attract a great deal of managerial attention. In this chapter we will examine the challenges of purchasing and see how firms are dealing with this important concern.

Purchasing Activities

The terms *purchasing* and *procurement* are often used interchangeably, although they do differ in scope. Purchasing generally refers to the actual buying of materials and those activities associated with the buying process. As we move into the future, purchasing will evolve into the procurement process of supply chain management described in Chapter 2. In procurement the activities are recognized as process-oriented and strategic. Structurally, commodity teams, product supply groups, and cross-functional teams are more prevalent than in the past. The process itself is less transaction-oriented, depends on the implementation of good information systems, and focuses on closer

AlliedSignal's Materials Management Program

supplier relations with fewer suppliers, while considering sources from around the world.[3]

In his address to AlliedSignal shareholders at the 1995 annual meeting, Larry Bossidy provided an example of these changes:

> The second thrust of our productivity program this year is the Materials Management program, which has yielded outstanding results since it was initiated in 1992. Twenty-two multifunctional commodity teams have been charged with overseeing relationships with materials suppliers across our many product lines.
>
> We have culled 3,000 preferred suppliers from a list of 9,500 three years ago, giving them more business in return for better quality, lower prices, greater responsiveness and increased productivity.[4]

---

[1]U.S. Bureau of the Census, *1993 Annual Survey of Manufacturers* (Washington, DC: U.S. Government Printing Office, Statistics for Industry Groups and Industries, M93(AS)-I, 1993), pp. 1–5, 1–8, and Appendix; as reported in Michiel R. Leenders and Harold E. Fearon, *Purchasing and Supply Management,* 11th ed. (Burr Ridge IL: Irwin/McGraw-Hill, 1997), pp. 10–11.

[2]Leenders and Fearon, *Purchasing and Supply Management,* p. 513.

[3]Ibid.

[4]"Chairman's Remarks," in *1995 Annual Meeting/First Quarter Report,* AlliedSignal, Morristown, New Jersey, p. 6, as quoted in Leenders and Fearon, p. 4.

TABLE 12–1   Cost of Materials–Value of Industry Shipments Ratios for Manufacturing Firms, 1993

Standard Industrial Code	Industry	Cost of Materials ($ millions)*	Capital Expenditures, New ($ millions)†	Total Material and Capital Expenditures ($ millions)	Value of Industry Shipments ($ millions)‡	Material/ Sales Ratio	Total Purchase Sales Ratio
20	Food and kindred products	$ 257,293	$ 9,389	$266,682	$423,257	61	63
21	Tobacco products	7,581	388	7,969	28,384	27	28
22	Textile mill products	43,411	2,450	45,861	73,951	59	62
23	Apparel and other textile products	37,169	961	38,130	73,997	50	52
24	Lumber and wood products	57,430	1,951	59,381	94,547	61	63
25	Furniture and fixtures	23,435	973	24,408	47,349	49	52
26	Paper and allied products	74,136	7,364	81,500	133,486	56	61
27	Printing and publishing	55,785	4,874	60,659	172,737	32	35
28	Chemicals, allied products	144,094	15,679	159,773	314,744	46	51
29	Petroleum and coal products	119,863	6,304	126,167	144,715	83	87
30	Rubber, miscellaneous plastics products	59,636	4,995	64,631	122,776	49	53
31	Leather, leather products	5,491	131	5,622	9,991	55	56
32	Stone, clay, glass products	29,509	2,417	31,926	65,574	45	49
33	Primary metal	86,939	4,726	91,665	142,384	61	64
34	Fabricated metal	86,829	4,913	91,742	175,137	50	52
35	Machinery, except electric	138,398	7,931	146,329	277,957	50	53
36	Electric, electronic equipment	105,331	9,985	115,316	233,343	45	49
37	Transportation equipment	250,829	11,408	262,237	414,614	60	63
38	Instruments and related products	44,477	4,431	48,908	136,916	32	36
39	Miscellaneous manufacturing	19,213	933	20,146	42,426	45	47
All Operating Manufacturing Establishments							
1981		$1,193,969	$ 78,632	$1,272,601	$2,017,542	59	63
1983		1,170,238	61,931	1,232,169	2,054,853	57	60
1985		1,276,013	83,237	1,359,250	2,279,132	56	60
1987		1,319,803	78,648	1,398,451	2,475,901	53	57
1989		1,503,558	97,187	1,600,745	2,793,015	54	57
1990		1,554,284	101,953	1,656,237	2,873,502	54	58
1991		1,503,925	98,916	1,602,841	2,826,207	53	57
1992		1,572,520	103,211	1,675,731	3,004,861	52	56
1993		1,646,850	102,201	1,749,051	3,128,284	53	56

*Refers to direct charges actually paid or payable for items consumed or put into production during the year, including freight charges and other direct charges incurred by the establishment in acquiring these materials. Manufacturers included the cost of materials or fuel consumed regardless of whether these items were purchased by the individual establishment from other companies, transferred to it from other establishments of the same company, or withdrawn from inventory. It excludes the cost of services used (such as advertising, insurance, and telephone) and research, developmental, and consulting services of other establishments. It also excludes materials, machinery, and equipment used in plant expansion or capitalized repairs that are chargeable to fixed assets accounts.

†Includes funds spent for permanent additions and major alterations to manufacturing establishments, and new machinery and equipment used for replacement purposes and additions to plant capacity if they are chargeable to a fixed asset account.

‡The received or receivable net selling values, FOB plant, after discounts and allowances, and excluding freight charges and excise taxes. However, where the products of an industry are customarily delivered by the manufacturing establishment, e.g., bakery products, the value of shipments is based on the delivered price of the goods.

Source: U.S. Bureau of the Census, *1993 Annual Survey of Manufacturers* (Washington, DC: U.S. Government Printing Office, Statistics for Industry Groups and Industries, M93(A5)-I, 1993), pp. 1–5, 1–8, and Appendix; as reported in Michiel R. Leenders and Harold E. Fearon, *Purchasing and Supply Management,* 11th ed. (Homewood, IL: Richard D. Irwin, 1997), pp. 10–11.

The Goals of Purchasing

The goals of purchasing are to:

1. Provide an uninterrupted flow of materials, supplies, and services required to operate the organization.
2. Keep inventory investment and loss at a minimum.
3. Maintain and improve quality.
4. Find or develop competent suppliers.
5. Standardize, where possible, the items bought.
6. Purchase required items and services at the lowest total cost.
7. Improve the organization's competitive position.
8. Achieve harmonious, productive working relationships with other functional areas within the organization.
9. Accomplish the purchasing objectives at the lowest possible level of administrative costs.[5]

Among the primary purchasing activities that influence the ability of the firm to achieve its objectives are supplier selection and evaluation (sourcing), quality control, and forward buying.

The Strategic Role of Purchasing

The strategic role of purchasing is to perform sourcing-related activities in a way that supports the overall objectives of the organization. Purchasing can make many contributions to the strategic success of the organization through its key role as one of the organization's boundary-spanning functions.

Access to External Markets.   Through external contacts with the supply market, purchasing can gain important information about new technologies, potential new materials or services, new sources of supply, and changes in market conditions. By communicating this competitive intelligence, purchasing can help reshape the organization's strategy to take advantage of market opportunities.

Supplier Development and Relationship Management.   Purchasing can help support the organization's strategic success by identifying and developing new and existing suppliers. Getting suppliers involved early in the development of new products and services or modifications to existing offerings can reduce development times. The idea of time compression—getting to market quickly with new ideas—can be very important to the success of those ideas and perhaps to the organization's position as a market leader or innovator.

Among the primary purchasing activities that influence the ability of the firm to achieve its objectives are supplier selection, evaluation, and ongoing management (sourcing); total quality management; and purchasing planning and research.

The Role of Purchasing Is Operational and Strategic

Relationship to Other Functions.   Purchasing's role ranges from a support role to a strategic function. To the extent that purchasing provides value to other functional areas, it will be included in important decisions and become involved early in decisions that affect purchasing. Being well informed allows the purchasing function to better

---

[5]Ibid., pp. 35–37.

anticipate and support the needs of other functional areas. This support in turn leads to greater recognition and participation.

Purchasing and logistics need to work closely in coordinating inbound logistics and associated material flows. The following sections apply to purchases of goods and services; thcy apply equally to purchasing of logistics services and managing relationships with logistics service providers.

Supplier Selection and Evaluation

In the acquisition process, perhaps the most important activity is selecting the best supplier from among a number of potential vendors. The buying process is complex because of the variety of actors that must be considered when making such a decision. The process includes both decision makers and decision influencers, which combine to form the decision-making unit (DMU). The process has a number of stages and includes the following 12 steps: identify needs, establish specifications, search for alternatives, establish contact, set purchase and usage criteria, evaluate alternative buying actions, determine budget availability, evaluate specific alternatives, negotiate with suppliers, buy, use, and conduct postpurchase evaluation.[6] It may not be necessary to go through all 12 steps of the buying process unless the decision is a totally new one. If the decision has been made before (routine buying), then many of the steps can be bypassed.

12 Steps in the Buying Process

Purchasing managers may consider some or all of the following attributes when making the purchasing decision:

Variables Used When Making the Purchasing Decision

- Lead time.
- Lead-time variability.
- Percentage of on-time deliveries.
- Percentage in-stock availability.
- Convenience in ordering/communication.
- Ability to expedite.
- Downtime caused by vendor errors, partial shipments, and/or late deliveries.
- Product reliability.
- Ease of maintenance or operation.
- Product failures caused by faulty parts or materials.
- Quality rejects.
- Technical specifications.
- Technical/training services offered.
- Competitiveness of price.
- Confidence in the sales representative.
- Past experience with vendor.
- Overall reputation of the vendor.
- Financing terms.
- Postpurchase sales service.
- Vendor's flexibility in adjusting to the buying company's needs.
- Engineering/design capabilities.

---

[6]Yoram Wind, "The Boundaries of Buying Decision Centers," *Journal of Purchasing and Materials Management* 14, no. 2 (Summer 1978), p. 24.

In a study of purchasing managers, White identified six major product categories that were purchased by most companies: (1) component parts, (2) raw materials, (3) operating supplies, (4) support equipment, (5) process equipment, and (6) services. Each product category could be purchased in any of four buying situations:

Four Buying Situations

1. *Routine order situations*—includes situations where the product has been purchased many times previously and where order routines or procedures are generally established.
2. *Procedural problem situations*—includes purchases that are not routine and that may require that employees learn how to use the product.
3. *Performance problem situations*—includes nonroutine purchases of products that are designed to be substitutes for current products but that must be tested for performance.
4. *Political problem situations*—includes nonroutine purchases of products whose use would affect many departments of the company; thus, a number of individuals throughout the firm will be involved in the decision process.[7]

In the 1980s and 1990s, the increased concern for productivity improvements caused management attention to focus on the purchasing function and on the development of closer ties with a reduced number of suppliers.[8] In order to determine the impact of supplier performance on productivity, performance must be measured and evaluated. Next, the data can be used to identify those suppliers with whom the firm wishes to develop long-term relationships, to identify problems so that corrective action can be taken, and to realize productivity improvements.[9]

The Performance of Individual Suppliers Should Be Evaluated

A variety of evaluation procedures are possible; there is no best method or approach. The important thing is to make certain that some evaluation procedure is used. Table 12–2 presents an example of an evaluation procedure. The manager must identify all potential suppliers for the items being purchased. The next step is to develop a list of attributes by which to evaluate each supplier. Once the attributes have been determined, the performance of individual suppliers should be evaluated on each attribute (e.g., product reliability, price, ordering convenience). A five-point scale (1 = worst rating; 5 = highest rating) is used in the illustration, but other scales may be used.

After evaluating suppliers on each attribute, management must determine the importance of each of the attributes to the firm. If, for example, product reliability was of paramount importance to the firm, that attribute would be given the highest importance rating. If price was not as important as product reliability, management would assign price a lower importance rating. Any attribute that was not important to the firm would be assigned a zero.[10]

The next step is to develop a weighted composite measure for each attribute. This is done by multiplying the supplier's rating for an attribute by the attribute's importance.

[7]Reprinted by permission of the publisher from "Decision Making in the Purchasing Process: A Report," *AMA Management Briefing,* by Phillip D. White, pp. 15–17, © 1978 by AMACOM, a division of American Management Association, New York. All rights reserved.

[8]Robert E. Spekman, "Strategic Supplier Selection: Understanding Long-Term Buyer Relationships," *Business Horizons* (July–August 1988), pp. 75–81; and William F. Given, "Improving Your Supplier Relationships," *NAPDM Insights* (September 1994), pp. 8–9.

[9]Thomas C. Harrington, Douglas M. Lambert, and Martin Christopher, "A Methodology for Measuring Vendor Performance," *Journal of Business Logistics* 12, no. 1 (1991), p. 83.

[10]Some attributes may be of no importance to the firm in one type of buying situation but of moderate or high importance at other times. Therefore, it is necessary that all potential attributes be included in the rating form in order to eliminate the need for a different form for each buying situation.

TABLE 12–2   Evaluating Suppliers in a Typical Manufacturing Firm

Factor	Rating of Supplier (1 = Worst Rating; 5 = Highest Rating) 1 2 3 4 5	(×)	Importance of Attribute to Your Firm (1 = Worst Rating; 5 = Highest Rating) 1 2 3 4 5	(=)	Weighted Composite Rating (0 = Minimum; 25 = Maximum)
Supplier A					
Product reliability					
Price					
Ordering convenience					
.					
.					
.					
After-sale service					
Total for supplier A					_____
Supplier B					
Product reliability					
Price					
Ordering convenience					
.					
.					
.					
After-sale service					
Total for supplier B					_____
Supplier C					
Product reliability					
Price					
Ordering convenience					
.					
.					
.					
After-sale service					
Total for supplier C					_____

Decision Rule: Select the supplier with highest composite rating.

The addition of the composite scores for each supplier provides an overall rating that can be compared to other suppliers. The higher the composite score, the more closely the supplier meets the needs and specifications of the procuring company. One of the major benefits of this approach is that it forces management to formalize the important elements of the purchasing decision and to question existing methods, assumptions, and procedures.

Implementation of a vendor performance evaluation method in a company that assembled kits for the health care industry resulted in a reduction in the number of suppliers, closer relationships with remaining suppliers, and a 34 percent reduction in component inventories within the first few months.[11] After two full years of using the quarterly performance reports, buyers had reduced component inventories by more than 60 percent.

International Sourcing
The process of supplier selection is more difficult when materials are being purchased in international markets. However, more firms are buying raw materials, components, and subassemblies from foreign sources, primarily because of cost and availability. When a company uses foreign suppliers, it should have an understanding of some of the problems associated with international sourcing.

---

[11]Harrington, Lambert, and Christopher, "A Methodology for Measuring Vendor Performance," pp. 97–98.

Global

Implementing a Global Buying Strategy

Based on success of implementing a global sourcing agreement for office supplies, buyers at Elsag Bailey Process Automation N.V. now are purchasing PCs, electronic components, and transportation services from global suppliers for sites located throughout North America and Europe. These global buying agreements have helped to reduce purchasing costs at the automation systems and products manufacturer by $15 million annually. Much of these savings are due to consolidating the buys across a number of Elsag Bailey locations worldwide, says Rich Heider, regional procurement director for the Americas. Future cost savings, he says, will come from increased efforts at standardizing these buys and specification changes. Heider works out of Elsag Bailey's Wickliffe, Ohio, facility.

Based in Amsterdam, The Netherlands, Elsag Bailey manufactures automation systems and services for the process industries—electric power, chemicals, metals & minerals, oil & gas, pulp & paper, food & beverage, and environmental services. In addition to the Wickliffe office, other regional offices are located in Frankfurt, Germany; Genoa, Italy; and Singapore. About 40 operating companies located in 20 countries make up Elsag Bailey Process Automation. In the U.S., these include Fischer & Porter, Warminster, Pa., and Applied Automation, Bartlesville, Okla. Revenues for 1997 were $1.5 billion (U.S. dollars). In the past four years, Elsag Bailey has tripled in size. Like many global companies, Elsag Bailey's recent growth is due mainly to its having acquired a number of smaller businesses. Most recently the company itself was acquired—by the ABB Group, Zurich, Switzerland.

. . . To leverage its growing purchasing power, Elsag Bailey had the foresight to put in place in 1997 a strategy that promises to help reduce buying costs and improve relationships with suppliers. This effort includes formation of a global buying team of which Heider is a member. He and other representatives of Elsag Bailey's U.S. purchasing operation as well as buyers of the company's European operation also worked on the team with two of the company's senior group vice presidents.

One of the benefits that Elsag Bailey hopes to realize through global sourcing is for "geography to become transparent." This, Heider explains, means that the company intends to engineer its products to the exacting requirements of its customers using products procured throughout the world without any disruption in quality or delivery levels.

Not jeopardizing the company's capability to deliver to its customers is of utmost importance to Heider and the other members of the global buying team. Initially, the team evaluated some $120 million in annual purchases of office supplies, personal computers, electronic components, transportation services, and corporate travel. (All told, Elsag Bailey's buying tab amounts to some $500 million annually.) One of the buying team's first initiatives: office supplies.

For its $3.7 million office supplies buy, Elsag Bailey's purchasing strategy is to reduce the supplier base and standardize on the products that requisitioners order every day. At the same time, buyers work to continually improve customer satisfaction and efficiency of internal purchasing processes. "Even with office supplies, there were challenges involved in consolidating the purchase on a global level," says Bob McAvoy, purchasing manager, Fisher & Porter, and leader of the global team for office supplies. These included gathering data on company purchasing activity and meeting customer needs of different organizations. Also on the team representing the U.S. buying operation: Bill Manning of Applied Automation.

"In Germany, we had been purchasing office supplies for seven locations from 27 different suppliers," says Ullrich Neumann, purchasing manager, Hartmann & Braun GmbH & Co. KG, Eschborn, Germany. On the global purchasing team, Neumann represents Elsag Bailey's European purchasing operation.

Another challenge is developing specifications. "It wasn't much of a problem in the U.S.," says Heider, "but we had to take into account the fact that Canada uses the metric system, which complicates price comparisons. And, in Germany, France, and Italy, specs are different for such supplies as binders, paper, and pens and pencils." Then, Elsag Bailey buying operations outside of the U.S. are loyal to local suppliers, recalls Heider. For instance, since the supplier team ultimately selected did not have operations in Canada, it wanted to service the sites from an office in Detroit. "At the country level, including Canada, buyers are nationalistic," says Heider.

Supplier selection criteria varies [sic] by commodity being evaluated by the global buying team. Members determine the criteria. In the team's search for its office-supplies provider, selection criteria included competitive pricing,

---

Implementing a Global Buying Strategy *concluded*

quality, and capability to deliver office supplies to all of the company's U.S. operations as well as those located in Canada and Germany. "With office supplies, it's also important to optimize customer satisfaction," says Neumann.

Ultimately, the team selected BT Office Products International (BT OPI), entering into an agreement with the supplier in January, 1998. Negotiations by the team are conducted in English and U.S. currency is used. Eventually, the team plans to use the euro to do business with suppliers in Europe. The agreement with BT OPI is implemented locally. For instance, locations in Germany purchase office supplies through BT OPI's affiliate in Europe, Hartman & Cie. "As part of our organizational change, we decided to give users responsibility to order directly from the supplier," says Neumann. "This way, purchasing can focus its efforts on more important, strategic issues."

In the U.S. at Elsag Bailey's location in Philadelphia, for instance, requisitioners use an online buying process provided by BT OPI to order office supplies. They make their selection from a standardized list of 400 different items. Requisitioners at other offices phone in or fax their orders using the same standardized list.

"Internally, we learned a lot from consolidating the office supplies purchase, which can be carried over to some of our other buys," says Heider. "We got to know ourselves better. Now, we have an understanding of our annual spends, as well as our supplier base. We have improved communication, gaining a better understanding of specifications. And, in looking at our supplier base, we are taking a closer look at what suppliers can do to help us reduce our costs, aside from offering us rebates on our purchasing volume."

For computer equipment—another of the team's early initiatives—Elsag Bailey's strategy is to improve internal

processes through increased use of the Web to buy PCs that go into the manufacturing of its automation products. Again, capability to deliver quality products at a competitive cost to locations worldwide made up the global buying team's selection criteria for PC suppliers. This time, the team selected Compaq/DEC and Dell. Standardization efforts for PCs include use of products supplied by these providers in its automation systems. "Which is what we are doing unless our customer insists on our using another OEM," says Heider. "We, in turn, will pass our cost savings from consolidating our volume on to our customers."

Setting standards for electronic components and computer equipment "forces us to look at specifications," says Heider. "To do that, we develop a closer relationship with engineering, who then becomes part of the supply management team. With engineering's assistance, we can select alternative products that will help us further reduce our costs." Elsag Bailey also has in place two global agreements for electronic components, as well as three agreements for connectors. The former were negotiated in Germany.

In addition, the team looked at purchasing transportation services globally. "We do a tremendous amount of exporting," says Heider. "We reduced transportation suppliers from 66 freight forwarders down to three. We've had very good success with transportation."

To measure supplier performance, one metric Elsag Bailey uses is capability to meet service requirements. For electronic components, for instance, the company has in place a dock-to-stock quality program with three key suppliers. Orders are shipped to one location, and performance is reviewed formally each month.

Source: Susan Avery, "Office Supplies: First Step in a Global Buying Strategy," *Purchasing* 126, no.4 (1999), pp. 81–84.

When purchasing offshore, it is easy to ignore some of the hidden costs. The buyer must compare total landed cost of the domestic and international supplier. The following checklist is recommended:[12]

Checklist of Cost Factors

- Price in U.S. dollars (if quoted in another currency).
- Commissions to customs brokers.
- Terms of payment costs and finance charges: letter of credit fee, translation costs, exchange rate differentials.

---

[12]Victor H. Pooler, *Global Purchasing: Reaching for the World* (New York: Van Nostrand Reinhold, 1992), p. 41.

- Foreign taxes imposed.
- Extra inventory and the associated inventory carrying costs.
- Extra labor, documentation.
- Obsolescence, deterioration, spoilage, taxes, losses to damage or theft, longer delivery time frames, administrative costs, business travel.
- Packing, marking, and container costs.
- Fees for consultants or inspectors.
- Marine insurance premium.
- Customs documentation charges.
- Import tariffs.
- Transportation costs, including: from manufacturer to port, ocean freight, from port to company plant, freight forwarder's charges, port handling charges, warehouse costs.

The rewards associated with the proper selection and evaluation of suppliers can be significant. As we saw in Chapter 1, logistics cost savings can be leveraged into substantial profit improvements. Similarly, purchasing activities can have positive effects on the firm's profits. Not only will a reduction in the cost of materials increase the profit margin on every unit that is manufactured and sold, but the lower cost associated with the materials purchased will also reduce the investment in inventories. Better logistics service by suppliers will also result in lower inventory in units required and thus dollars invested. In addition, customer service improvements are possible because the manufacturing process can operate smoothly, without slowdowns or shutdowns. The service improvements can result in higher unit sales and in some cases higher prices. And since effective purchasing management results in the acquisition of high-quality materials, there is also less likelihood of customer return of finished goods due to product failure.

Total Quality Management

The Purchase Price of an Item Is Only One Element of the Total Cost

Although cost is an important consideration in materials acquisition, so is quality management. The initial purchase price of an item is only one element of the total cost. For example, some items are easier to work with than others and thus can save production costs. Materials of higher quality may require fewer fabrication processes or have a longer life span, resulting in lower overall product costs or higher prices for finished products. Companies must achieve some balance between the components of the acquisition process—namely, price, cost, and value received.[13]

After the required quality level has been determined and specifications developed, usually by manufacturing, it becomes purchasing's responsibility to secure the proper materials. The correct quality specification must be given to suppliers. The supplier that offers the best cost–quality combination that meets the specifications should be selected.

The firm should never pay higher prices to obtain materials with quality levels greater than those specified by manufacturing unless justifiable marketing or logistics

---

[13]For a comprehensive discussion of total cost issues in purchasing, see Lisa M. Ellram, *Total Cost Modeling in Purchasing* (Tempe, AZ: Center for Advanced Publishing Studies, 1994).

reasons exist for doing so. Purchasing materials that needlessly exceed quality specifications adds unnecessary costs to products.[14]

Supplier Certification Is Better than Inspection Programs

One way that firms might ensure quality is through inspection of incoming materials parts. But this is costly and time-consuming. Inspection requires human resources, space, and perhaps test equipment. In addition, incoming inventory is tied up or delayed awaiting inspection. For these reasons, purchasing managers have turned to supplier certification. In the certification process, the supplier's quality levels and processes are closely evaluated by members of the buying firm. If they "pass," the buying organization no longer inspects that supplier's incoming material.

Quality is even more critical for firms pursuing a just-in-time philosophy, where little or no inventory is held. Improper quality in a JIT environment can shut down processes immediately, creating excessive costs and delays.

Forward Buying

All purchasing activities, except emergency purchases, represent forward buying if materials, component parts, and subassemblies are available in advance of the time they are needed. More accurately, *forward buying* refers to the purchase of materials in quantities exceeding current requirements, well in advance of their need or use.

Reasons for Forward Buying

Essentially, there are two major reasons why a firm would engage in forward buying. First, forward buying minimizes the effects of rising material costs. At least for a time, until the materials are depleted from inventory, the firm is protected from price increases in the marketplace. Second, forward buying provides protection against future availability problems. Forward buying becomes more popular among firms as availability uncertainties become more commonplace. It is particularly prevalent in retailing, where manufacturers offer special prices at the end of the quarter in order to make sales objectives.

Disadvantages of Forward Buying

While there are benefits associated with forward buying, there are also disadvantages. Many companies make forward purchases in anticipation of price increases. There are times, however, when materials prices actually go down because of technological developments, competitive pressures, or other factors. There is a risk that the firm may purchase materials at prices higher than necessary. Another often-overlooked disadvantage of forward buying is the increased inventory carrying cost incurred with holding excess inventory. The savings realized from forward buying must exceed the additional inventory carrying costs.

Table 12–3 presents an example of the role of inventory carrying costs in the forward buying decision. In this example, the firm purchases $2,000 worth of an item once a month. The $2,000 purchase represents the firm's monthly usage of this item. The vendor's salesperson explains that the price will increase by 10 percent next month and encourages the purchasing manager to consider forward buying. If the firm buys for a period of one month, the average level of inventory would be $1,000 for the first month. But there would be no savings in the purchase price. The inventory carrying costs incurred would equal $25 for one month (30 percent of the average level of inventory, which is $1,000 divided by 12), and $302.50 for the next 11 months (30 percent × $1,100 × 11/12). Since the firm would experience a total inventory carrying cost of $327.50 with no forward buying, the net savings from

---

[14]Donald W. Dobler and David N. Burt, *Purchasing and Supply Management,* 6th ed. (New York: McGraw-Hill, 1996), pp. 160–76.

TABLE 12–3   Using Inventory Carrying Costs to Evaluate Forward Buying

| | | | | | | Increase in Inventory Carrying Cost | | |
| | | | | | | --- | --- | --- |
Number of Months Supply Purchased	*Value*	*Average Inventory (1/2 × Order Quantity)*	*Savings in Order Processing Cost from Fewer Orders Being Placed*	*Saving in Purchase Price*	*Inventory Carrying Costs for Buy-Ahead Period 30% × Avg. Inv. × (No. of Months/12)*	*Inventory Carrying Costs for Remaining Months Assuming Purchases of $2,2000/Mo.*	*Less Inventory Carrying Costs if No Forward Buying Takes Place*	*Net Saving from Forward Buying*
1	$ 2,000	$ 1,000	$ —	$ —	$ 25*	$302.50†	$327.50	$ —
2	4,000	2,000	20	200	100	275.00	327.50	172.50
3	6,000	3,000	40	400	225	247.50	327.50	295.00
4	8,000	4,000	60	600	400	220.00	327.50	367.50
5	10,000	5,000	80	800	625	192.50	327.50	390.00
6	12,000	6,000	100	1,000	900	165.00	327.50	362.50
7	14,000	7,000	120	1,200	1,225	137.50	327.50	285.00
8	16,000	8,000	140	1,400	1,600	110.00	327.50	157.50
9	18,000	9,000	160	1,600	2,025	82.50	327.50	–20.00
10	20,000	10,000	180	1,800	2,500	55.00	327.50	–247.50
11	22,000	11,000	200	2,000	3,025	27.50	327.50	–525.00
12	24,000	12,000	220	2,200	3,600‡	—	327.50	–852.50

Assumptions:

1. Monthly usage = 2,000.

2. Expected price increase = 10 percent.

3. Inventory carrying cost = 30 percent.

4. Order cost = $20.00.

5. Vendor pays the freight.

*$1,000 × 30% × 1/12 = $25

†$2,200/2 × 30% × 11/12 = $302.50

‡$1,000 × 30% × 12/12 = $3,600

continuing with the current practice is zero. However, if the purchasing manager obtains a two-month supply, the forward buy of one month's worth of product will result in a $20 savings in ordering costs and a $200 savings in purchase price, for a total savings of $220. The increase in inventory carrying cost would be $47.50 ($375.00 – $327.50), resulting in a net savings of $172.50 ($220.00 – $47.50). If the purchasing manager buys an amount equal to nine months of usage, however, the savings in purchase price and ordering costs is offset entirely by the additional inventory carrying costs.

As shown in Table 12–3, the optimal forward buy would be a five-month supply, which would result in a net savings of $390. However, if the purchasing manager is judged solely on the per-unit purchase price, he or she would purchase a 12-month supply, at a cost to the firm of $852.50. That is, purchasing a 12-month supply would result in a decrease in pretax profits of $852.50. This example illustrates that inventory carrying costs must be included in the forward buying decision. Since the funds expended for inventories are not available for other uses, the firm should anticipate future working capital needs before engaging in forward buying.

Cost trade-offs are a key to successfully managing the purchasing function. By thinking in terms of the cost trade-offs shown in Figure 12–1, management should minimize the total of these costs rather than attempt to minimize the cost of either component. This is critical, as attempts to reduce individual costs may in fact actually increase total costs.

FIGURE 12–1

Cost trade-offs to be considered by the purchasing executive

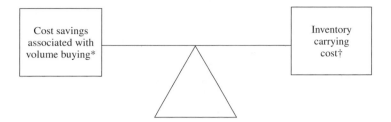

*The savings associated with volume buying include:
    Lower per-unit purchasing prices
    Lower transportation costs
    Lower warehouse handling costs
    Lower order-processing costs
    Lower production lot quantity costs
    Lower stockout costs
†The costs of carrying inventory include:
    Capital costs associated with the inventory investment
    Inventory service costs (insurance and taxes)
    Storage space costs
    Inventory risk costs

Source: Douglas M. Lambert and Jay U. Sterling, "Measuring Purchasing Performance," *Production and Inventory Management Review* 4, no. 6 (June 1984), p. 52. Reprinted with permission form *P&IM Review*, June 1984. Copyright 1984 by T.D.A. Publications, Inc., Hollywood, FL.

Just-in-Time Purchasing

Just-in-time (JIT) manufacturing is more a philosophy of doing business than a specific technique. The JIT philosophy focuses on the identification and elimination of waste wherever it is found in the manufacturing system. The concept of continuous improvement becomes the central managerial focus.

Results of JIT Implementation

Typically, JIT implementation involves the initiation of a "pull" system of manufacturing (matching production to known demand) and the benefits include significant reductions of raw material, work-in-process, and finished goods inventories; significant reductions in throughput time; and large decreases in the amount of space required for the manufacturing process.

A company implementing JIT can usually make the greatest improvement in the area of quality. The JIT focus on the elimination of waste includes the supplier, with the aim of reducing waste and cost throughout the entire supply chain. If a manufacturer decides it will no longer carry a raw materials inventory and that its suppliers must carry this inventory, the cost for the total supply chain is reduced because inventory with lower value-added is being held. Also, when a supplier holds the inventory, the cash value is equal to the supplier's out-of-pocket cost of purchased materials plus manufacturing. The customer's cash value of inventory is equal to the supplier's selling price.

Compaq Uses JIT

One example of this is Compaq, which requires its suppliers to hold a certain amount of inventory at a warehouse near Compaq's production facilities, so suppliers can respond quickly in case of problems. It is preferable that this inventory be eliminated altogether because while those additional inventory carrying costs may be covered in the short term by the seller, eventually they may be passed on to the buyer in the form of higher prices. The supplier needs to reduce its own manufacturing and supplier lead times.

FIGURE 12–2

*Reducing ordering costs
results in a smaller
economic order
quantity (EOQ)*

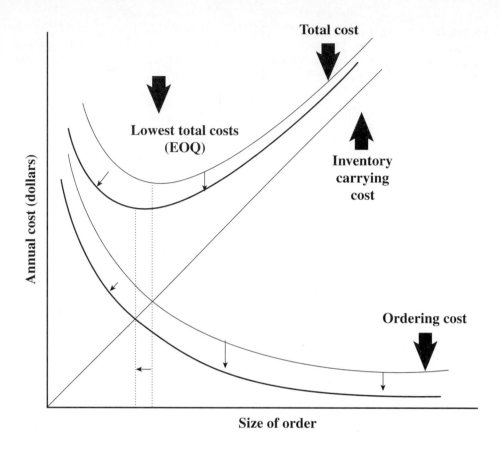

In the JIT system, the ordering costs are reduced so that the savings in inventory carrying cost gained from cutting lot sizes are not offset by increased purchase order cost. Figure 12–2 illustrates how a reduction in ordering costs shifts the total cost curve downward to the left and results in a smaller economic order quantity. In addition, with JIT every effort is made to improve vendor quality levels.

Just-in-time purchasing requires frequent releases of orders and frequent deliveries of products. For this to work, purchasers and suppliers must develop long-term relationships rather than use the multiple sourcing practices popular in the United States.

**Characteristics
of JIT Purchasing**

The JIT characteristics are interrelated and categorized in four groups: suppliers (number, location, longevity, and assistance/advice offered); quantities (product outputs, parts inputs, contracts administered, and purchasing paperwork); quality (specifications coordination, and control); and shipping (inbound freight and freight/storage modes).[15]

Difficulties in Implementing JIT

**Difficulties
in Implementing JIT**

One of the most frequently cited reasons for difficulty in the implementation of JIT is a lack of cooperation from suppliers, due to the changes required in the supplier's system. In addition to changing from traditional quality control inspection practices to the implementation of statistical process control, the supplier is asked to manufacture in

---

[15]Adapted from Richard J. Schonberger and James P. Gilbert, "Just-in-Time Purchasing: A Challenge for U.S. Industry," *California Management Review* 26, no. 1 (Fall 1983), pp. 58–63.

quantities that may differ from the usual lot sizes and to make frequent deliveries of small lots with precise timing. The supplier and buyer are normally required to provide each other with access to their master production planning system, shop floor schedule, and material requirements planning system.

Importance of Buyer–Supplier Communication

Communication Is the Key to Successful JIT

Under JIT, close and frequent buyer–supplier communication is essential. Suppliers are given a long-range view of the buyer's production schedule. Often this view spans months, but the schedule for the nearest several weeks is frozen. The supplier is thus able to acquire raw materials in a stockless production mode and supply the buyer without inventory buildups. Suppliers provide daily updates of progress, production schedules, and problems. Purchasers and suppliers must cooperate and have a trusting relationship in order to convert to JIT operations.

Supplier selection, single sourcing, supply management, and supplier communication become critical issues for purchasing and materials managers in implementing JIT. Issues relating to supplier selection include quality-control methods, supplier proximity, manufacturing flexibility, and lead-time reliability.

JIT manufacturers and their suppliers generally develop close collaborative relationships supported by long-term, single-source contracts. The term *partnership* is often applied to the JIT buyer–supplier relationships. Partnerships will be described in detail later in this chapter.

Once suppliers have been selected, ongoing performance measurement may result in supplier certification, a designation reserved for those suppliers whose quality, on-time delivery, and reliability have proved acceptable over long periods of time.

Under JIT, the focus of the purchasing department is not merely on processing orders but rather on supplier selection and long-term contract negotiation. Many times these close communications are supported by electronic data interchange (EDI) to facilitate the timely and accurate transmittal of information. The following sections apply to purchasing in general and are critical to the success of JIT purchasing.

Supplier Selection

Supplier–Buyer Plant Proximity

Management can facilitate JIT purchasing by developing long-term relationships with a small number of nearby suppliers. The objective is to achieve strong, stable purchase agreements with an uninterrupted supply of materials. The closer the JIT purchasing comes to piece-by-piece delivery, the greater the contribution to productivity and avoidance of defective lots. But piece-by-piece delivery leads to higher transportation costs unless the supplier and seller are close to each other. For example, if a manufacturer builds an assembly plant near suppliers' plants, it can supply its assembly lines with multiple deliveries per day in small vehicles, rather than infrequent deliveries in 40-foot truckloads. Thus, one way to reduce the transportation cost associated with small lots is to reduce the distance between supplier and buyer plants.

The potential advantages of supplier–buyer proximity apply in the United States as well as in Japan. Yet most U.S. industries have considered vertical integration to be a desirable path to corporate growth and success. Nevertheless, a strong case can be made for developing special manufacturing competency in more narrowly focused areas.

Focused Factories

Focused factories offer significant cost savings in areas such as construction and operating costs. This approach downgrades integration in favor of a narrow base of highly competent suppliers. Japanese manufacturers tend to avoid vertical integration. Instead, they develop final assembly competency and contract out as much fabrication as possible to experts. This helps cement stable purchase agreements with reliable suppliers.

Purchase Agreements

JIT Purchase Agreements

JIT purchasing is facilitated by an even, repetitive master production schedule. Repetitive manufacture of products evens out the demand for individual parts. This steady demand for parts has an impact on shipping quantities, containers, and purchasing paperwork. In Japan, JIT purchase agreements usually involve little paperwork. The purchase order, like a blanket order, may specify an overall quantity, but the supplier will deliver in accordance with a schedule or with daily production needs, which are telephoned from the buying plant. The JIT purchase agreement does not permit variability. In most cases, the buyer expects and receives the exact quantity. Having a purchase agreement in place saves much time in negotiating and pricing each order.

Value Analysis

Value Analysis Described

In the United States, *value analysis* is a respected purchasing practice that may receive more attention as a result of the interest in JIT purchasing. When negotiating a purchase agreement, the supplier receives the buyer's specifications and provides a bid price. If the price is too high, the buyer may visit the supplier's plant to review its processes. The objective is to identify areas where the supplier's costs exceed the value added and, if possible, to modify the minimal specifications in order to reduce the supplier's cost and the bid price.

"Loose" Engineering Specifications/Early Supplier Involvement

Traditionally, U.S. engineers would specify tolerances for almost every design feature for which parts were purchased. However, many firms are implementing practices more like the Japanese, who place more importance on how the item actually performs than on conformance to tight design specifications. The supplier is permitted to innovate on the premise that the supplier is the expert.

Early Supplier Involvement Programs

The concept of getting the supplier involved in the design process is often called *early supplier involvement (ESI)*. This concept has been applied successfully by companies like Bose, Chrysler (in the introduction of the Neon), and Harley Davidson. Concurrent engineering is a type of early supplier involvement where the engineers in the buying and selling firms work together on product development or product improvement.

The benefits of closer coordination on engineering and quality matters are significant. Engineers and quality control people may pay frequent visits to a supplier's plant to answer engineering questions and identify potential quality problems before they surface. Xerox Corporation uses these practices with its key suppliers, resulting in better supplier quality, responsiveness, and competitiveness.

Control of Inbound Transportation

Inbound freight decisions such as delivery and routing are frequently left to the supplier's traffic department. This is often the case when materials are purchased "FOB shipping point" and the buyer owns the goods and absorbs the inventory carrying costs from the date of shipment.[16]

---

[16]FOB terms were presented in Chapter 7.

JIT Purchasing Requires Steady, Reliable Incoming Deliveries

JIT purchasing requires steady, reliable incoming deliveries. The objective is to avoid excessive inventory carrying costs for materials that arrive early and to avoid disruptions in manufacturing operations when goods arrive late. Therefore, the buying firms must become involved in selecting both the transportation mode and the specific carrier. For example, CTI and Ryder Integrated Logistics (1) review manufacturers' production schedules, (2) notify the supplier of requirements, (3) schedule pickup of the materials, (4) pick up and time-sequence the materials, and (5) deliver them directly to the JIT production line.[17]

Supplier Development

Supplier development has been defined as

Supplier Development Defined

> a systematic organizational effort to create and maintain a network of competent suppliers and to improve various supplier capabilities that are necessary for the buying organization to meet its increasing competitive challenges.[18]

Sometimes organizations find that their current suppliers are unable to support stringent JIT quality and delivery requirements. Such organizations may search for other suppliers or work with suppliers to develop the skills needed to support JIT. Supplier development efforts are increasing as organizations form longer-term relationships with suppliers. Chrysler is an example of a company that was performing poorly until it adopted innovative purchasing, logistics, and practices such as JIT, supplier development, and early supplier involvement.

Benefits of JIT Purchasing

Benefits to the Buyer

The most important benefit of JIT purchasing to the buyer is the reduction in inventories that it makes possible. There are also scrap/quality and productivity benefits. In addition, purchasing-related paperwork is reduced. Conventional lot size economics suggests that smaller lots mean more orders to process and therefore increased order-processing costs. But the environment in which JIT buying best functions is one in which:

- The buyer's production schedules are relatively level, so that demand for materials is steady and predictable;
- Larger, steadier orders are given to a smaller number of suppliers, thus encouraging excellence and loyalty;
- Purchase agreements are long-term, with minimal paperwork. They provide for frequent small-lot deliveries, thus revealing quality problems sooner; and
- Suppliers are responsive to the need for improved containers and labeling.[19]

Thus, smooth demand, few suppliers, long-term agreements, and fewer quality problems often result in lower order-processing costs.

Benefits to the Supplier

The supplier also benefits from JIT purchasing. The supplier receives a contract that is exclusive (or nearly so), long-term, and invariable, which affords the supplier the opportunity to cut peak capacity, retain a trained labor force, reduce its inventories, and implement purchasing with its suppliers.

---

[17]Information obtained from CTI and Ryder Integrated Logistics.
[18]*NAPM Dictionary* (Tempe, AZ: National Association of Purchasing Management, 1993), p. 22.
[19]Ibid., p. 65.

JIT II

JIT II at Bose Corporation

JIT II is an innovative type of purchasing relationship that aims JIT principles at the purchasing function. Like JIT, JIT II attempts to eliminate waste, redundancy, and excess paperwork, and to improve quality, responsiveness, and innovation in the purchasing arena. It represents a type of alliance relationship between a buying and selling organization. The term *JIT II* was coined by Bose Corporation to describe this type of relationship.[20] The steps in developing JIT II are shown in Table 12–4.

In JIT II, the supplier places one of its employees, called an in-plant representative or in-plant, in the buying company's office, replacing a purchaser, planner, and salesperson. In addition to colocation, the concurrent engineering and continuous improvement aspects of JIT II distinguish it from other supplier relationships. One of the companies with which Bose has established this in-plant relationship is G&F Industries, an injection molder. The in-plant representative places orders, practices concurrent engineering, and has full access to all of Bose's facilities, information, and employees. The supplier benefits include greater integration with the customer, improved communications, more efficient administrative processes, and savings on "sales effort."[21]

TABLE 12–4   Steps in JIT II Information Flow

Steps 1, 2:	Supplier reassigns its sales representative to new duties, and customer reassigns its purchaser.
Step 3:	In full JIT II implementation, the customer reassigns its material planner to new duties.
Step 4:	Supplier replaces purchaser, planner, and salesperson with a full time professional at the customer's location. At Bose Corporation, supplier professionals are called in-plant representatives or in-plants. Although the supplier replaces the purchaser with an in-plant representative, this step actually assists existing purchasing personnel as more people address the overall department workload.
Step 5:	The in-plant representative works 40 hours a week at the customer's location, usually in its purchasing department.
Step 6:	Customer empowers the in-plant within its planning and purchasing systems. The in-plant works directly from the customer's MRP (or similar) system, and uses the customer's purchase order to place material orders on his or her own company. Note: the customer typically prohibits the in-plant from placing purchasing orders with other companies.
Step 7:	Customer provides the in-plant with an employee badge (or equivalent), providing free access to customer engineering and manufacturing personnel. When not planning and ordering material, the in-plant practices concurrent engineering by working with customer's design engineering staff.
Step 8:	Customer and supplier understand that many more steps lie ahead. JIT II will cause change in both organizations.

Source: *Purchasing,* May 6, 1993, p. 17.

---

[20]Lance Dixon and Anne Porter Millen, *JIT II: Revolution in Buying and Selling* (Newton, MA: Cahners, 1994), pp. 9–15.

[21]Ibid., pp. 143–50 and 159–60.

Purchasing Research and Planning

**Important
Environmental
Considerations**

In the business environment, uncertainty makes the purchasing decisions for key items more complex and the effects of these decisions more long lasting.[22] Important environmental considerations include uncertainty of supply and dependence on foreign sources for key commodities, price increases on key commodities, extended and variable lead times, energy shortages or price increases, and increasing worldwide competition.

The changing environment makes it necessary for purchasing management to do a more effective job of researching the supply market and planning. Purchasing needs to provide information about supply conditions, such as availability, lead times, and technology, to different groups within the firm, including top management, engineering and design, and manufacturing. This information is important when formulating long-term strategy and making short-term decisions. Key materials for which availability, pricing, and quality problems may occur should be identified so that management can develop an action plan before problems become critical and costly.

**Strategic Planning
for Purchasing**

Strategic planning for purchasing involves materials screening, risk assessment, strategy development, and implementation. It is important to determine whether (1) materials bottlenecks will jeopardize current or future production, (2) new products should be introduced, (3) materials quality may be expected to change, (4) prices are likely to increase or decrease, and (5) forward buying is appropriate. Management should develop specific plans to ensure that the material supply chain will operate uninterrupted.

Typical criteria to use in identifying critical purchases are percentage of product cost, percentage of total purchase expenditure, and use on high-margin end items. Criteria used for determining the risk in the supply market include number of suppliers, availability of raw materials to suppliers, supplier cost and profitability needs, supply capacity, and technological trends. The more critical the purchase and the riskier the supply market, the greater attention the purchase requires.

Risk Assessment

Risk assessment requires that the purchaser determine the probability of best or worst conditions occurring. Supply strategies should be developed for the predicted events. Asking these questions for any given strategy or situation can help purchasing managers ensure that they have considered the important issues.[23] Implementation of a particular strategy requires the involvement of top management and integration with the firm's overall business plan.

Purchasing Cost Management

Purchasing departments, like other functional areas, must manage and reduce costs. Purchasing can use a number of methods to reduce administrative costs, purchase prices, and inventory carrying costs, but the most prevalent are purchase cost reduction programs, price change management programs, volume (time and/or quantity) contracts, and systems contracts and stockless purchasing.[24]

---

[22]This material is adapted from Robert M. Monczka, "Managing the Purchasing Function," in *The Distribution Handbook,* ed. James F. Robeson and Robert G. House (New York: Free Press, 1985), pp. 478–80. Copyright © 1985 by The Free Press, a Division of MacMillan, Inc. Used by permission of the publisher.

[23] For further discussion of purchasing research and planning, see A. J. van Weele, *Purchasing Management: Analysis, Planning and Practice* (New York: Chapman and Ho, 1994), pp. 97–176; and Leenders and Fearon, *Purchasing and Supply Management,* pp. 463–78.

[24]Monczka, "Managing the Purchasing Function," pp. 480–83.

Cost Reduction Programs

An effective purchasing cost reduction program requires top management support, definition of cost reduction or avoidance, effective goal setting, review and approval of cost reductions or avoidance, measurement of reduction to a specific goal, reporting, and making achievement in individual cost reduction or avoidance part of the performance appraisal process.[25]

For a successful cost reduction program, top management must communicate the need for cost saving accomplishments in both good and bad economic times. It must also adequately define cost reduction objectives so that accomplishments can be measured and performances evaluated. For example, in many firms *cost reduction* is defined as a decrease in prior purchase price, and *cost avoidance* is defined as the amount that would have been paid minus the amount actually paid. Management also has to establish programs with buyers based on opportunities for cost reduction.

Cost reduction and cost avoidance programs may include any of the following:

- Supplier development.
- Development of competition.
- Requirement of supplier cost reduction.
- Early supplier involvement in new-product design and design changes.
- Substitution of materials.
- Standardization.
- Make-or-buy analysis.
- Value analysis, including supplier involvement.
- The reduction of scrap.
- A change in tolerances.
- Improvement of payment terms and conditions.
- Volume buying.
- Process changes.

The appropriateness of each technique will vary with the purchase situation and type of supplier relationship.

Price Change Management

Purchasing managers must challenge vendor price increases and not treat them as pass-through costs. It is important to work with suppliers to restrict price increases to a reasonable and equitable level. Furthermore, purchasing should establish a systematic method of handling all price increase requests from suppliers. At a minimum, the system should require the purchasing department to:

- Determine the reason for the price change request.
- Specify the total dollar-value impact on the firm.
- Ask suppliers to justify the price change.
- Have management review the price change.
- Set strategies to deal with price increases.

[25]Ibid.

In order to restrict price increases, management should require price protection clauses and advance notification of price increases of 30, 60, or 90 days. As part of a program of price change management, purchasing should determine the impact of engineering changes on product costs in order to determine whether engineering changes should be made.

Creative Solutions

How Companies Can Cut Costs by Joining Buying Pools

Kevin Vargas buys $1 million worth of circuit breakers and wiring each year for Comdisco Inc.'s computer refurbishing plant in Schaumburg, Illinois. As a top purchasing manager for the $3.2 billion computer-leasing company, he has the clout to drive a hard bargain with suppliers. But Vargas thinks he has found a way to "supersize" his clout. He's testing online buying groups that purchase equipment in huge volumes for equally big discounts. The potential savings: $200,000 a year.

A mile down the road in another Chicago suburb, Boise Cascade Office Products Corporation is just as excited about online purchasing groups. But the $3 billion supplier of stationery goods isn't simply expecting to save big bucks—it's hoping to make them. With purchasing agents banding together at websites run by Wells Fargo & Company and Chase Manhattan Corporation, Boise suddenly has more people to sell its wares to, and they're all jammed into a few Web locales. Boise estimated it would more than double its $250 million in Net sales in 2000.

Comdisco and Boise Cascade may never do business together. But they are both part of a movement sprouting up all over the Web. Huge buying groups and consortiums are pooling their corporate purchases to get better deals or special treatment. There's a payoff for vendors, too. They lower their costs by gaining quick access to large, well-defined pools of buyers.

Better Prices

The only ones who benefit more are those who pull together the groups of buyers and sellers. Think of them as market makers. They cover the gamut of industries from banking giant Chase Manhattan to telecommunications behemoth Nippon Telegraph & Telephone Corporation to transportation king SAIRGroup. And on October 18, 1999, tiny Internet startup PurchasingCenter.com got into the act, gathering buyers and sellers of industrial goods such as drill bits and motors. Each hopes to take a slice of the action by charging a fee for transactions. But they also get better prices for the goods they need for their own operations. Companies "can not only make money but save money," says Tim Minahan, an e-commerce analyst with Aberdeen Group Inc.

Before the Net, such buying groups simply didn't exist. With the Web, far-flung organizations, sharing nothing more than a need to stock their cafeterias with plastic utensils, can hook up to demand huge discounts. That may sound mundane, but everyday operational goods, including things from janitorial supplies to computer keyboards, typically account for 35 percent of a company's cost of doing business, according to Benchmarking Partners Inc., a research and consulting firm in Cambridge, Massachusetts. By pooling their purchases with other companies that need the same supplies, market makers say they can cut overall procurement costs by as much as 10 percent.

Working on the E-Road

Some companies see cost savings beyond better prices. Jim Limperis, strategic sourcing manager for Motorola Inc.'s Internet and Networking Group in Mansfield, Massachusetts, isn't sure he'll save any up-front costs using PurchasingCenter.com. But Limperis says he's still interested, because it could give him the ability to partly automate his $270 million annual purchases and liberate his workers for other tasks. "If you can help me free up a $50,000-a-year buyer, as opposed to just saving $50,000, I'd put him outside of the department and get him involved with design and development. In the long run, it would produce better cost savings," says Limperis.

Source: Adapted from Kevin Ferguson, "Purchasing in Packs," *Business Week,* November 1, 1999, pp. EB 33, 34, and 38.

Volume Contracts

Volume contracts are a way to leverage purchase requirements over time, between various business units or locations in the company, or on different line-item requirements. As a result of combining purchases, the buyer's leverage with suppliers can lead to reductions in purchase prices and administrative costs. Cumulative volume discounts allow a buyer to combine purchase volume over time, getting lower prices with successive buys as it places additional orders throughout the year. More companies are using this approach to support smaller, more frequent buys in JIT purchasing.

Cumulative Discounts

In noncumulative discounts, the price is based on the amount of each order. A review of purchase prices for a particular item often identifies the opportunity for suppliers to provide quotes on a semiannual or contract basis. An increase in the purchase quantity can enable suppliers to reduce their costs and prices as a result of production or purchasing economies. In addition, the supplier may be willing to accept lower per-unit margins on a higher volume of business.

Past purchase patterns should be available from computer-generated requirement plans and from suppliers. Management needs to review the firm's purchase history systematically and regularly for new opportunities for volume contracting.

Systems Contracts and Stockless Purchasing

Systems contracts, or *blanket orders,* as they are sometimes called, are a means of reducing materials-related costs such as unit purchase price, transportation, inventory, and administration. Systems contracts are arranged for a given volume of purchases over a specified time period. The vendor supplies products to individual plant locations as ordered, and payment is arranged through purchasing. According to one observer, "While this agreed-to quantity is not legally binding, it is generally sufficient assurance for the vendor to seek volume purchase from its sources. These volume purchases help reduce the final cost to the buyer. A key advantage is that a stipulated price is fixed over the period of the contract."[26]

Systems contracts are often referred to as *stockless purchasing,* which implies that the firm does not carry inventory of purchased materials. While a systems contract may or may not result in "zero" inventory, the underlying principles of systems contracting are necessary for stockless purchasing. The objectives of systems contracts and stockless purchasing are to:

Objectives of Systems Contracts and Stockless Purchasing

- Lower inventory levels.
- Reduce the number of suppliers.
- Reduce administrative cost and paperwork.
- Reduce the number of purchases of small dollar value and requisitions that purchasers have to handle (and thereby increase the amount of time available for other key activities).
- Provide the opportunity for larger dollar volumes of business to suppliers.
- Provide for timely delivery of material directly to the user.
- Standardize purchase items where possible.[27]

---

[26]Joseph L. Cavinato, *Purchasing and Materials Management* (St. Paul, MN: West Publishing, 1984), pp. 29–30.

[27]Monczka, "Managing the Purchasing Function," pp. 482–83.

Systems contracts and stockless purchasing systems are best suited to frequently purchased items of low dollar value with administrative processing costs that are relatively large compared to unit prices. In many cases, the combined administrative, processing, and inventory carrying costs may exceed the item's cost. Systems contracting may lead to larger supplier discounts, reduced processing costs, and increased product availability. Both systems require the following: identification of appropriate suppliers; supplier selection; use of a standard-item catalog for availability and ordering; establishment of order communication methods; identification of acceptable receipt areas (docks, warehouses, etc.); monitoring of supplier delivery performance within established delivery parameters (e.g., 4, 8, 24, or 48 hours); and established payment methods to accumulate receipts and pay for all items received over a given time period (e.g., 30 days).[28]

Usually, the length of the contract varies from one to three years and includes price protection clauses. The purchaser should have the right to test-market the items to ensure that suppliers' unit prices are reasonable.

Measurement and Evaluation of Purchasing Performance

Management must identify the information that is required to perform purchasing activities and to measure and evaluate purchasing performance.[29] The following data should be included in the management information system in order to measure and evaluate purchasing performance:

Data for Measuring and Evaluating Purchasing Performance

- Purchase item number and description.
- Quantity required.
- Date on which item is required.
- Date on which purchase requisition is received or authorized.
- Purchase requisition or authorization number.
- Supplier(s) quoted.
- Date on which supplier(s) is quoted.
- Date on which quotes are required from supplier(s).
- Supplier quote(s).
- Supplier price discount schedule.
- Purchase order number.
- Date on which purchase order is placed.
- Purchase price per unit.
- Quantity or percentage of annual requirements purchased.
- Planned purchase price per unit.
- Supplier name.
- Supplier address.
- Supplier's promised ship date.
- Supplier lead time (days or weeks for purchase item).
- Date on which purchase item is received.

---

[28]Ibid., p. 483.

[29]The material in this section is adapted from ibid., pp. 486–92.

- Quantity received.
- Purchase item accepted or rejected (unit/lot).
- Storage location.
- Buyer.
- Work unit.
- Requested price change.
- Effective date of requested price change.
- Date on which price change is approved.
- Ship-to location.[30]

Information Needs Differ by Level of Management

Generally, the primary users of purchasing measurement and evaluation reports include top-level managers, corporate functional managers, operating unit functional managers, and middle managers at plant and operating unit sites.

The information needs of each of these groups are quite different. Top management, for example, may want to know how the firm's purchasing department compares with that of other firms, and how effective it is. Corporate functional managers, such as corporate vice presidents of purchasing, may want complete functional reviews; policy and procedure audits; and a review of key quantitative indicators, such as inventory, minority purchases, and administrative budget measures. The purchasing department manager of the operating unit may want to have a series of regularly reported indicators in order to monitor performance and take corrective action when necessary.

Performance Measures

Key Performance Measures

Monczka, Carter, and Hoagland found that purchasing organizations use a number of key performance measures for purchasing control, including price effectiveness; cost savings; workload; administration and control; efficiency; vendor quality and delivery; material flow control; regulatory, societal, and environmental measures; procurement planning and research; competition; inventory; and transportation.[31]

Price Effectiveness.   Price effectiveness measures are used to determine (1) actual price performance against plan, (2) actual price performance against market, and (3) actual price performance among buying groups and locations. Purchase price variances from plan can be calculated for individual line items and for the total purchasing budget. Typical indicators are price variances measured in terms of (1) actual unit cost minus planned cost, (2) a price variance percentage (actual unit cost over planned cost), or (3) an extended price variance (actual unit cost minus planned cost, multiplied by an estimated annual quantity).

Cost Reduction versus Cost Avoidance

Cost Savings.   Measures of cost savings include both cost reduction and cost avoidance. *Cost reduction* occurs when the new unit cost is lower than the old unit cost on a stock-keeping unit basis. *Cost avoidance* occurs when the new unit price is lower than the average quoted price, even when the new unit price represents an increase over the old price.

---

[30]Ibid., pp. 486–87. From *The Distribution Handbook,* ed. James F. Robeson and Robert G. House. Copyright © 1985 by The Free Press, a Division of Macmillan, Inc. Used by permission of the publisher.

[31]R. M. Monczka, P. L. Carter, and J. H. Hoagland, *Purchasing Performance: Measurement and Control* (East Lansing: Michigan State University, Graduate School of Business Administration, Division of Research, 1979).

Workload.   Workload can be broken down into three categories: (1) *workload in,* which is a measure of the new work coming into the purchasing department; (2) *workload current,* which is a measure of the backlog of work; and (3) *workload completed,* which is a measure of the work accomplished.[32] Measures of workload in include counts of work received, such as purchase requisitions, purchase information requests received, and the number of pricing requests received. Workload current is usually measured in terms of counts of the backlog of work, such as purchase requisitions on hand and items on hand. Measures of workload completed include purchase orders placed, line items ordered, dollars ordered, contracts written, and price proposals written.

Administration and Control.   Administration and control is usually accomplished using an annual administrative budget for the purchasing function. The most common method is to start with the current budget and adjust it up or down, depending on the business forecast, the projected workload, and economic conditions.

Efficiency.   Efficiency measures relate purchasing outputs to purchasing inputs. They range from two-factor measures that have one input and one output, to multifactor measures that relate several outputs to several inputs. Common two-factor measures include purchase orders per buyer, line items per buyer, dollars committed per buyer, change notices per buyer, contracts written per buyer, average open order commitment, worker hours per line item, worker hours per purchase order, worker hours per contract, administrative dollars per purchase order, administrative dollars per contract, and administrative dollars per purchase dollar.[33]

Vendor Quality and Delivery.   Vendor quality measures include the percentage of items (pieces, orders, shipments, or dollar value) that are accepted or rejected; the total cost of purchasing one unit of product from a vendor; and the frequency and severity of defects. Vendor delivery is generally measured in terms of on-time, early, or late deliveries (pieces, orders, shipments, or dollar value).

Material Flow Control.   Reports that measure the flow of material from vendors to the buying organizations can be classified into four groups: (1) open purchase orders and their due dates, (2) past-due open orders, (3) orders that are needed immediately, and (4) ability of buyers and vendors to meet due dates.

Regulatory, Societal, and Environmental Measures.   A number of measures can be used to show how a purchasing department is performing relative to regulatory, societal, and environmental goals. Examples include (1) purchases with small and minority-owned businesses, (2) purchases placed in labor surplus areas, and (3) number and percentage of minority employees.

Procurement Planning and Research.   Generally, procurement planning and research can be evaluated on the basis of the number of procurement plans established per year (including availability and price forecasting); price forecasting accuracy (actual to forecast); lead-time forecasting accuracy (actual to forecast); and the number of make-or-buy studies completed.

---

[32]Ibid., p. 490.
[33]Ibid.

Competition.   Competition measures the extent to which the buying organization has developed alternatives in the supply marketplace and improved purchase prices and terms. Competition measures may include annual purchase dollars, the percentage of purchases on annual contracts, and the volume of purchases placed with single source suppliers (thereby limiting competition).

Inventory.   Inventory measures include inventory turnover, consignments, and inventory levels.

Transportation.   Transportation measures are used to determine the expense incurred for premium transportation. Premium transportation costs are incurred when other-than-normal transportation is used.

Impact of Procurement on Return on Net Worth

Figure 12–3 illustrates the many ways in which procurement contributes to return on net worth. First, better management of procurement can result in higher sales as a result of higher prices, higher volume, or more rapid time-to-market for new-

FIGURE 12–3

How procurement contributes to return on net worth

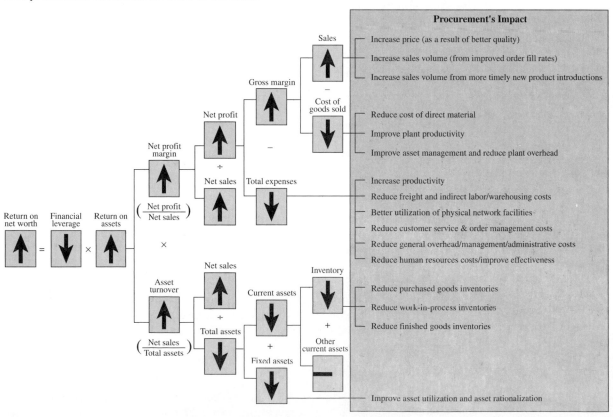

product introductions. Cost of goods sold can be reduced as well as other expenses. These actions will result in much higher profitability. In terms of the balance sheet, excellence in procurement can result in reduction in both current and fixed assets, which leads to increased asset turnover. The higher profitability and higher asset turnover provide two upward pressures on return on assets. This, combined with a reduction in financial leverage as a result of debt repayment, leads to higher return on net worth.

Strategic Sourcing

Executives in many industries are recognizing the value-added role that procurement can bring to their business design.[34] Corporate spending on outside purchases and the changing nature of those purchases are emerging as critical elements for successfully enabling profitable growth. The key to exploiting procurement in the quest for profitable growth is to understand the level of procurement development a company has reached in its sourcing activities and how those capabilities stack up against the requirements of the corporate buy. To gain the full value-added potential of procurement, leading companies are redefining procurement as a key process within the scope of the strategic sourcing. A key underpinning of strategic sourcing is the total cost of ownership concept.

As companies change what they buy, they also must change how they buy in order to unlock savings and growth opportunities. Traditionally, companies have focused on purchase price alone instead of taking a total cost view. Managers who overemphasize purchase price fail to consider several factors that can be the source of innovative, sustainable cost reduction opportunities for suppliers and buyers alike. These factors include:

- Supplier economics and other supply chain costs, such as transportation.
- Buyer's cost of acquiring and managing products and services.
- Quality, inventory, reliability, and other factors of a product or service over its life cycle.
- The value of a product or service to internal and external customers.

Total Cost of Ownership Is a Critical Measure

A critical concept within the total cost perspective is the notion of *total cost of ownership.* Total cost of ownership considers both supplier and buyer activities, and costs over a product or service's complete life cycle in the context of the competitive forces at work in the relevant purchase category. This perspective means understanding a wide range of cost and value relationships associated with individual purchases. For instance, from a competitive economics perspective, it may be more effective for a buyer to rationalize its supply base to enable higher supplier capacity utilization and, in turn, lower acquisition prices while preserving acceptable margins for the surviving suppliers. From a life-cycle ownership standpoint, buying a higher-quality item with a steeper price tag could be justified because the initial purchase cost would ultimately be offset by fewer manufacturing defects, lower inventory requirements, and lower administrative costs.

---

[34]This section is taken from Matthew G. Anderson and Paul B. Katz, "Strategic Sourcing," *The International Journal of Logistics Management* 9, no. 1 (1998), pp. 1–13.

Procurement Pathways

Four Strategic Pathways

Significant savings in total ownership costs can be achieved through a set of four specific strategic pathways. Three of the four pathways—buy for less, buy better, and consume better—represent simple but powerful ways to achieve incremental and overall cost savings by improving procurement. In each case, the magnitude of achievable savings is a function of the company's position along the pathway, the complexity of its purchases, and its commitment to obtaining savings.

The fourth pathway to growth—sell better—embodies an emerging approach in which procurement plays an important role in forging supplier relationships that ultimately enhance corporate revenue streams. As companies reach higher levels of procurement development, the opportunities for cost savings and revenue enhancement along the procurement pathways improve significantly.

Segmenting the Buy

Each company has a unique *buy,* or portfolio of purchased goods and services. There are actually three bases for segmenting the purchase portfolio. The first two deal with the complexity of procurement of the relevant category and nature of the impact on corporate performance. Procurement complexity considers such factors as technical complexity, scope of supply chain integration issues, and the extent to which life-cycle management and costs are relevant. The revenue impact/business risk dimension addresses the degree to which a purchase category can influence customers' perception of value. A third dimension has to do with competitive economic potential, that is, to what extent improvement opportunities are available to the buyer given the cost drivers and competitive dynamics in the industry relevant to the purchase.

**Segmenting
the Purchase Portfolio**

Leaders in procurement have strengthened their focus on value growth by stressing the *segments* of their buy that have the most impact on potential revenue generation or present the greatest risk to corporate performance. For example, the procurement of advertising services could have tremendous risk implications relative to customer perceptions of value, while the purchase of office supplies remains largely a cost issue. Or, in the high-tech arena, the procurement of a new generation of semiconductor technology may essentially be a bet on the company's future. Such segmentation and prioritization of the buy have become increasingly important as corporate purchases have evolved toward greater technical and commercial complexity and come to rely more on the upstream supply chain.

Sourcing Process Excellence

**Practices of the Leaders
in Procurement**

The sourcing value chain is the set of processes through which strategic sourcing decisions are made and value is created for the organization (Figure 12–4). The processes apply to all purchases, although the specific approaches, strategies, and best practices vary and reflect the priorities and opportunities revealed in the segmentation matrix. Leaders in procurement create an annual plan, develop requirements, develop a sourcing strategy, evaluate and select suppliers, procure materials and services, and manage supplier relationships.

FIGURE 12–4

Sourcing value chain

Create annual plan	Develop requirements	Develop sourcing strategy	Evaluate and select suppliers	Procure materials	Manage supplier relationships
• Goals and points of focus during the next year by category and in total	• Item requirements by category across the user base	• Strategy to leverage buying power and minimize total costs by category	• Targeted suppliers and negotiation and contracting	• Systems, procedures, and skills to support strategy and execute efficiently	• Performance metrics, benchmarks, and controls to ensure improvement

Source: Matthew G. Anderson and Paul B. Katz, "Strategic Sourcing," *The International Journal of Logistics Management* 9, no. 12 (1998), p 7.

E-Procurement

The Internet has created numerous opportunities for improving performance in the supply chain, particularly in the area of procurement. Software companies such as Ariba and Commerce One are helping to integrate and streamline the procurement process. The Creative Solutions and Technology boxes in this chapter give examples of how companies in industries from computer products to office products to automobiles are using the Internet to integrate and streamline their purchases. Companies are not just purchasing goods and services using the Internet but also direct materials, which represent the most significant supply chain relationships.

On June 14, 2000, it was announced that 49 leading consumer products companies were uniting to launch Transora.com, a global business-to-business e-marketplace.[35] The companies involved in this effort include: The Cola-Cola Company; Colgate-Palmolive Company; ConAgra, Inc.; Diageo PLC; General Mills, Inc.; Heineken International; Kellogg Company; Kraft Foods, Inc.; M&M/Mars Incorporated; McCain Foods Limited; Nabisco Holdings, Inc.; Pepsi Co, Inc.; The Procter & Gamble Company; Ralston Purina Company; Sara Lee Corporation; Unilever NV; and Wm. Wrigley Jr. Company. In terms of the number of firms involved, many of whom are fierce competitors, it is the largest such effort to date.

Transora will enable consumer products companies to use the Internet to streamline business transactions with their suppliers, buyers, and distributors on a worldwide basis. Transora will be an independent company owned and funded by firms from within the industry. By June 2000, 49 consumer products companies had committed nearly $250 million to fund the venture. A maximum stake for any company is 5 percent. The money will be used to build the infrastructure and fund start-up operations for the new company.

---

[35]<http://www.transora.com>. For up-to-date information on developments related to this major industry initiative, simply visit the Transora website.

E-Procurement

Lou Gerstner, the boss of IBM, dismissively described the thousands of new "dot.com" companies springing up as "fireflies before the storm." The storm would arrive, he said, when the really big firms—the Global 1,000—seized the power of the Internet and used it to transform themselves. This week saw almost simultaneous announcements (funny, that) from the world's two biggest car makers, to say that they are moving their entire supply chains onto the Internet. Mr. Gerstner's storm has arrived with hurricane force.

On November 2, 1999 Ford and then General Motors declared that their huge purchasing operations would swiftly transfer to the Web, connecting suppliers, business partners and customers from all over the world by means of giant online markets. Sadly for Mr. Gerstner, neither company has picked IBM as its technology partner. Instead, Ford will form a joint venture with Oracle, the leader in the database market, to establish AutoXchange. GM has chosen Commerce One, a fast-growing supplier of Web-based procurement software, to build its own MarketSite.

Both sites are expected to be up and running during the first quarter of next year. Oracle will build AutoXchange using its own software and then run it for Ford. (Oracle will be the minority partner, but AutoXchange's management will be drawn from both it and the car maker.) Commerce One will construct GM's site and link it to something it calls "The Global Trading Web," a worldwide network of business-to-business e-commerce portals that use its software.

The sheer scale of both operations marks this as the moment when e-business comes of age. AutoXchange will be the preferred vehicle for all of Ford's $80 billion annual purchases of components and materials, which are ordered from more than 30,000 suppliers. And such business may be only the beginning for the joint venture. Ford's extended supply chain has sales of about $300 billion a year, and the companies that are part of it will be encouraged (not bullied, Ford insists) to do business with each other through AutoXchange. Apart from creating straightforward savings on procurement and inventory—of up to 20 percent, it is claimed—AutoXchange should also encourage shorter product cycles. As well as this, it will help parts of the supply chain to work together, especially when developing new products. Both Oracle and Ford say that rival car makers will be welcome to use the AutoXchange market. Ray Lane, the chief operating officer of Oracle, estimates that within a few years the exchange may be handling transactions worth something like $200 billion.

AutoXchange will make most of its money by taking a small cut on each of potentially billions of transactions. It will earn commissions from companies that use the exchange to hold reverse auctions to liquidate surplus supplies. And it will earn fees for managing the supply chains of firms that use it. As the site expands, it should also be able to attract a lot of advertising.

Mr. Lane predicts that, by its second year, AutoXchange will achieve annual sales of $1 billion; within four years its sales could reach $5 billion. Unsurprisingly, the prospect of taking the business public in fairly short order has quickened pulses at both Ford and Oracle. Even current (relatively) depressed Internet valuations mean that Priceline.com, a name-your-price airline-ticket auctioneer, is worth more than Delta Airlines. It may not be crazy to imagine AutoXchange being worth as much as the traditional businesses of its parents.

GM's MarketSite, which will operate alongside GM SupplyPower, the new portal for the firm's suppliers, is expected to attract broadly the same volume of sales as AutoXchange. GM claims that it will be the world's largest "virtual marketplace" for a wide array of parts, products, raw materials and services. As an incentive, it will also aggregate with its own orders those of smaller firms that do business on the site, to lend them some of its purchasing power.

Jac of E-Trades

Unlike AutoXchange, MarketSite is a GM-only show that is not intended to attract other car makers. GM is saying that it intends to keep control of the portal rather than spin it off in a public offering. But that could change. GM was almost certainly bounced into revealing its plans for MarketSite by the Ford/Oracle announcement. GM is fed up with the campaign of Ford's boss, Jac Nasser, to portray his company as being in the vanguard of the car industry's attempts to embrace the Internet. It was determined to steal a share of the limelight for itself.

Both firms are showing how big companies in a range of industries are likely to use the Internet to put themselves at the centre of new e-business ecosystems that will transform their entire way of doing business. Although big car makers have long used electronic data interchange (EDI) to link with big suppliers, EDI is inherently rigid—it provides basic information about transactions, but it cannot adapt to rapidly changing markets. It is also too expensive for smaller firms.

Source: "Riding the Storm," *The Economist,* November 6, 1999, pp. 63–64.

The investor companies spend approximately $350 billion of the $900 billion in industry purchases of goods and services annually. Purchasing practices are fragmented, with manufacturers making purchases from more than 200,000 suppliers. The industry experiences inflated procurement costs as a result of inconsistent and incomplete information. Inefficient processes, such as lack of integration and paper-laden systems, are challenges facing the industry.

Transora will streamline transactions throughout the supply chain and connect thousands of trading partners. Suppliers will gain access to a much larger customer base at reduced customer acquisition costs. Manufacturers will benefit from improved customer service with retailers and wholesalers. Retailers and wholesalers will be able to simplify their ordering processes and improve order accuracy. Participants throughout the supply chain will benefit from increased connectivity, enhanced automation and improved inventory management.

"With the Internet's borderless connectivity, Transora transcends global boundaries," said Paul Walsh, Group Chief Operating Officer, Diageo PLC. "Economies of the world continue to draw closer together, and our companies increasingly rely on businesses and markets that lie across international boundaries. Transora provides the common marketplace in which our companies can transact and manage business, seamlessly and efficiently."[36]

Consumer packaged goods companies have common customers, suppliers, and processes. Transora will allow universal collaboration across companies, provide singular connectivity to an array of services and exchanges on the Internet, increase efficiencies, and improve interaction with customers and consumers. The e-marketplace promises to lead the transformation of the consumer products industry by delivering breakthrough benefits across the entire supply chain, and ultimately to consumers. The "killer applications" identified for the marketplace include: consumer promotions; collaborative planning forecasting and replenishment/vendor-managed inventory/scanner-based transactions; industry capacity management; and end-to-end logistics.

Forrester Research expects business-to-business transactions over the Internet to reach $1.3 trillion by 2003.[37] Ariba is a leading provider of software; the following quote, from Ariba's website, provides some background information on the company's software solutions:

> Ariba business-to-business eCommerce solutions lower costs and streamline the supply chain, delivering benefits to all trading partners. Buying organizations use Ariba solutions to reduce costs by channeling spend to preferred suppliers and to participate in new revenue opportunities by hosting electronic marketplaces, which provide procurement services to others. Suppliers participate in Ariba eCommerce solutions to increase the revenue potential by more efficiently doing business with existing clients and extending their reach to new prospective clients. Net market makers use Ariba's comprehensive electronic marketplace deployment solution to establish high-performance, fully featured, scalable Net markets. The Ariba solution leverages the Ariba Network platform to deliver reduced costs, increased revenue opportunities, and competitive advantage to buyers, suppliers, value-added service providers, and Net market makers.[38]

---

[36]Ibid.

[37]Dow N. Bauknight, "The Supply Chain's Future in the E-Economy," *Supply Chain Management Review* 4, no. 1 (2000), p. 34.

[38]Ariba, Inc. <http://www.ariba.com>.

The following quote is from Commerce One:

Commerce One offers enterprise customers the most comprehensive and completely interactive e-Procurement solution available today. Through the Commerce One solution, comprised of Commerce One BuySite e-procurement application, and access to a Commerce
One MarketSite global trading portal, the entire procurement cycle from requisition to payment is completely automated. Information moves instantly from the user's desktop directly
to the supplier's back office, with industry-leading XML (extensible markup language)
technology.[39]

Managing Supplier Relationships

Supplier partnerships have become one of the hottest topics in interfirm relationships.
Business pressures such as shortened product life cycles and global competition are
making business too complex and expensive for one firm to go it alone. Despite all the
interest in partnerships, a great deal of confusion still exists about what constitutes a
partnership and when it makes the most sense to have one. This section will present a
model that can be used to identify whether a partnership is appropriate and, if so, the
type of partnership that should be implemented.

While there are countless definitions of *partnership* in use today, we prefer the
following:

Partnership Defined   A partnership is a tailored business relationship based on mutual trust, openness, shared risk
and shared rewards that results in business performance greater than would be achieved by
two firms working together in the absence of partnership.[40]

Types of Partnerships[41]

Relationships between organizations can range from arm's-length relationships (consisting of either one-time exchanges or multiple transactions) to vertical integration of
the two organizations, as shown in Figure 12–5. Most relationships between organizations have been those at arm's length, where the two organizations conduct business
with each other, often over a long period of time and involving multiple exchanges, but
without a sense of joint commitment or joint operations. In arm's-length relationships,
a seller typically offers standard products or services to a wide range of customers, who
receive standard terms and conditions. When the exchanges end, the relationship ends.
While arm's-length relationships are appropriate in many situations, there are times
when a closer, more integrated relationship, called a partnership, would provide significant benefits to both firms.

A partnership is not the same as a joint venture, which involves shared ownership
between the two parties. Nor is it the same as vertical integration. Yet a well-managed
partnership can provide benefits similar to those found in joint ventures or vertical integration. For instance, Pepsi chose to acquire restaurants such as Taco Bell, Pizza Hut,

---

[39]Commerce One, Inc. <http://www.commerceone.com>.

[40]The Global Supply Chain Forum, Fisher College of Business, The Ohio State University, 2000. All
rights reserved.

[41]This section and the following section are taken from Douglas M. Lambert, Margaret A. Emmelhainz,
and John T. Gardner, "Developing and Implementing Supply Chain Partnerships," *The International
Journal of Logistics Management* 7, no. 2 (1996), pp. 1–17.

FIGURE 12–5

Types of relationships

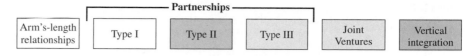

Source: Douglas M. Lambert, Margaret A. Emmelhainz, and John T. Gardner, "Developing and Implementing Supply Chain Partnerships," *The International Journal of Logistics Management* 7, no. 2 (1996), p. 2.

and Kentucky Fried Chicken and by doing so ensured distribution of its products in these outlets. Coca-Cola has achieved a similar result without the cost of vertical integration through its partnership with McDonald's.

While most partnerships share some common elements and characteristics, there is no one ideal or benchmark relationship that is appropriate in all situations. Because each relationship has its own set of motivating factors as well as its own unique operating environment, the duration, breadth, strength, and closeness of the partnership will vary from case to case and over time. Research has indicated that three types of partnerships exist:

> *Type 1.* The organizations involved recognize each other as partners and, on a limited basis, coordinate activities and planning. The partnership usually has a short-term focus and involves only one division or functional area within each organization.
>
> *Type II.* The organizations involved progress beyond coordination of activities to integration of activities. Although not expected to last forever, the partnership has a long-term horizon. Multiple divisions and functions within the firm are involved in the partnership.
>
> *Type III.* The organizations share a significant level of integration. Each party views the other as an extension of its own firm. Typically, no end date for the partnership exists.

Three Types of Partnerships Exist

The Majority of Relationships Will Be Arm's-Length

Normally, a firm will have a wide range of relationships spanning the entire spectrum, the majority of which will not be partnerships but arm's-length associations. Of the relationships that are partnerships, the largest percentage will be Type I, and only a limited number will be Type III partnerships. Type III partnerships should be reserved for those suppliers or customers who are critical to an organization's long-term success. The previously described relationship between Coke and McDonald's has been evaluated as a Type III partnership.

The Partnership Model

Drivers Provide the Motivation to Partner

The partnership model shown in Figure 12–6 has three major elements that lead to outcomes: drivers, facilitators, and components. *Drivers* are compelling reasons to partner. *Facilitators* are supportive corporate environmental factors that enhance partnership growth and development. *Components* are joint activities and processes used to build and sustain the partnership. *Outcomes* reflect the performance of the partnership.

Four Categories of Drivers

Drivers.   Both parties must believe that they will receive significant benefits in one or more areas and that these benefits would not be possible without a partnership. The primary potential benefits that drive the desire to partner include (1) asset/cost efficiencies, (2) customer service improvements, (3) marketing advantage, and (4) profit

FIGURE 12–6

The partnering process

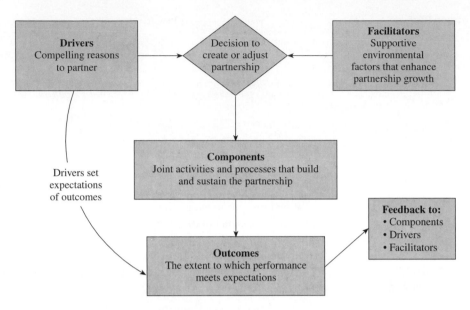

Source: Douglas M. Lambert, Magaret A. Emmelhainz, and John T. Gardner, "Developing and Implementing Supply Chain Partnerships," *The International Journal of Logistics Management* 7, no. 2 (1996), p. 4.

stability/growth. (See Table 12–5 for examples.) While the presence of strong drivers is necessary for successful partnerships, the drivers by themselves do not ensure success. The benefits derived from the drivers must be sustainable over the long term. If, for instance, the marketing advantage or cost efficiencies resulting from the relationship can be easily matched by a competitor, the probability of long-term partnership success is reduced.

In evaluating a relationship, how does a manager know if there are enough drivers to pursue a partnership? First, drivers must exist for each party. It is unlikely that the drivers will be the same for both parties, but they need to be strong for both. Second, the drivers must be strong enough to provide each party with a realistic expectation of significant benefits through a strengthening of the relationship. Each party should independently assess the strength of its specific drivers.

Facilitators Measure Supportiveness of the Environment

Facilitators.   Drivers provide the motivation to partner. But even with a strong desire for building a partnership, the probability of success is reduced if the corporate environments are not supportive of a close relationship. Just as the relationship of a young couple with a strong desire to marry can be derailed by unsupportive in-laws, different communication styles, and dissimilar values, so can a corporate relationship be side-tracked by a hostile environment. In contrast, a supportive environment that enhances integration of the two parties will improve the success of the partnership.

Four Categories of Facilitators

Facilitators are elements of a corporate environment that allow a partnership to grow and strengthen. They serve as a foundation for a good relationship. In the short run, facilitators cannot be developed; they either exist or they do not. And the degree to which they exist often determines whether a partnership succeeds or fails. Facilitators include (1) corporate compatibility, (2) similar managerial philosophy and techniques, (3) mutuality, and (4) symmetry. (See Table 12–5 for details.)

TABLE 12–5   Partnership Drivers, Facilitators, and Components

Partnership Drivers
- *Asset/cost efficiency:* What is the probability that this relationship will substantially reduce channel costs or improve asset utilization, for example, product costs, distribution costs savings, handling costs savings, packing costs savings, information handling costs savings, managerial efficiencies, and assets devoted to the relationship?
- *Customer service:* What is the probability that this relationship will substantially improve the customer service level as measured by the customer, for example, improved on-time delivery, better taking of movement, paperless order processing, accurate order deliveries, improved cycle times, improved fill rates, customer survey results, and process improvements?
- *Marketing advantage:* What is the probability that this relationship will lead to substantial marketing advantages, for example, new market entry; promotion (joint advertising, sales promotion); price (reduced price advantage); product (jointly developed product innovation, branding opportunities); place (expanded geographic coverage, market saturation); access to technology; and innovation potential?
- *Profit stability/growth:* What is the probability that this relationship will result in profit growth or reduced variability in profit, for example, growth, cyclical leveling, seasonal leveling, market share stability, sales volume, and assurance of supply?

Partnership Facilitators
- *Corporate compatibility:* What is the probability that the two organizations will mesh smoothly in terms of (1) culture, for example, both firms place a value on keeping commitments, constancy of purpose, employees viewed as long-term assets, and external stakeholders considered important; and (2) business, for example, strategic plans and objectives consistent, commitment to partnership ideas, and willingness to change?
- *Management philosophy and techniques:* What is the probability that the management philosophy and techniques of the two companies will match smoothly, for example, organizational structure, use of TQM, degree of top management support, types of motivation used, importance of teamwork, attitudes toward "personnel churning," and degree of employee empowerment?
- *Mutuality:* What is the probability both parties have the skills and predisposition needed for mutual relationship building? Is management skilled at two-sided thinking and action, taking the perspective of the other company, expressing goals and sharing expectations, and taking a longer term view, for example, or is management willing to share financial information and integrate systems?
- *Symmetry:* What is the probability that the parties are similar on the following important factors that will affect the success of the relationship: relative size in terms of sales, relative market share in their respective industries, financial strength, productivity, brand image/reputation, and technological sophistication?

Partnership Components
- Planning (style, level, and content).
- Joint operating controls (measurement and ability to make changes).
- Communications (nonroutine and day-to-day: organization, balanced flow, and electronic).
- Risk/reward sharing (loss tolerance, gain commitment, and commitment to fairness).
- Trust and commitment to each other's success.
- Contract style (time frame and coverage).
- Scope (share of partner's business, value added, and critical activities).
- Investment (financial, technology, and people).

Partnership Outcomes
- Global performance outcomes (enhancement of profits, leveling of profits over time).
- Process outcomes (improved service, reduced costs).
- Competitive advantage (market positioning, market share, access to knowledge).

Source: Adapted from Douglas M. Lambert, Margaret A. Emmelhainz, and John T. Gardner, "Developing and Implementing Supply Chain Partnerships," *The International Journal of Logistics Management* 7, no. 2 (1996), pp. 5–13.

Facilitators apply to the combined environment of the two potential partners. Therefore, unlike drivers, which are assessed by managers in each firm independently, facilitators should be assessed jointly. The discussion of corporate values, philosophies, and objectives often leads to an improved relationship even if no further steps toward building a partnership are taken. The more positive the facilitators, the better the chance of partnership success.

Drivers and Facilitators Determine Partnership Type

If both parties realistically expect benefits from a partnership and if the corporate environments appear supportive, then a partnership is warranted. The appropriateness of any one type of partnership is a function of the combined strength of the drivers and facilitators. A combination of strong drivers and strong facilitators would suggest a Type III partnership, while low drivers and low facilitators suggest an arm's-length relationship. While it might seem, from all of the press on the importance of integrated relationships and alliances, that managers should attempt to turn all of their corporate relationships into Type III partnerships, this is not the case. In partnering, more is not always better. The objective in establishing a partnership should not be to have a Type III partnership; rather it should be to have the most appropriate type of partnership given the specific drivers and facilitators. In fact, in situations with low drivers and/or facilitators, trying to achieve a Type III partnership is likely to be counterproductive. The necessary foundation is just not there. Having determined that a partnership of a specific type is warranted and should be pursued, the next step is to actually put the partnership into place. This is done through the components.

An assessment of drivers and facilitators is used to determine the potential for a partnership, but the components describe the type of relationship that has actually been implemented.

Management Controls the Components

Components.   Components are the activities and processes that management establishes and controls throughout the life of the partnership. Components make the relationship operational and help managers create the benefits of partnering. Every partnership has the same basic components, but the way in which the components are implemented and managed varies. Components include planning, joint operating controls, communications, risk/reward sharing, trust and commitment, contract style, scope, and financial investment. (See Table 12–5 for details.)

Outcomes and Feedback.   Whatever type of supplier partnership is implemented, the effectiveness of the relationship must be evaluated and possibly adjusted. The key to effective measurement and feedback is how well the drivers of partnership were developed at the outset. At this beginning point, the measurement and metrics of relating to each driver should have been made explicit. These explicit measures then become the standard in evaluation of the partnership outcomes. Feedback can refer to any step in the model and can take the form of periodic updating of the status of the drivers, facilitators, and components.[42]

Outcomes Measure the Results

---

[42]For more information on how to develop and implement successful partnerships, see John T. Gardner, Douglas M. Lambert, and Margaret A. Emmelhainz, *Partnership Facilitator's Guide: Developing and Implementing Successful Partnerships in the Supply Chain,* The Ohio State University/University of North Florida, 1999 <http://www.logisticssupplychain.org>.

Summary

In this chapter we saw how better management of procurement process can lead to increased profitability. We described the activities that must be performed by the purchasing function and explored the implications of just-in-time purchasing. Because the costs of purchased materials represent a significant cost of doing business, we devoted a considerable amount of attention to the management of purchasing costs and the measurement and evaluation of purchasing performance. Finally, we presented a model that can be used to determine when a partnership is appropriate and, if so, how that relationship should be structured to maximize the benefits for the two organizations.

In Chapter 13 we will see how the concepts that you have learned apply to the global marketplace.

Suggested Readings

Anderson, Matthew G., and Paul B. Katz. "Strategic Sourcing." *The International Journal of Logistics Management* 9, no. 1 (1998), pp. 1–13.

Chandrashekar, Ashok, and Thomas C. Dougless. "Commodity Indexed Surplus Asset Disposal in the Reverse Logistics Process." *The International Journal of Logistics Management* 7, no. 2 (1996), pp. 59–68.

Corini, John. "Integrating e-Procurement and Strategic Sourcing." *Supply Chain Management Review* 4, no. 1 (2000), pp. 70–75.

Dixon, Lance, and Anne Millen Porter. *JIT II: Revolution in Buying and Selling.* Newton, MA: Cahners, 1994.

Dobler, Donald W., and David N. Burt. *Purchasing and Supply Management,* 6th ed. New York: McGraw-Hill, 1996.

Ellinger, Alexander E.; John C. Taylor; and Patricia J. Daugherty. "Automotive Replenishment Programs and Level of Involvement: Performance Implications." *The International Journal of Logistics Management* 10, no. 1 (1999), pp. 25–36.

Festervand, Troy A., and David B. Meinert. "Purchasing Intelligence Systems in Small Manufacturing Firms: Present Status and Future and Future Direction." *The International Journal of Logistics Management* 3, no. 1 (1992), pp. 37–45.

Fontanella, John. "The Web-Based Supply Chain." *Supply Chain Management Review* 3, no. 4 (2000), pp. 17–20.

Harrington, Thomas C.; Douglas M. Lambert; and Martin Christopher. "A Methodology for Measuring Vendor Performance." *Journal of Business Logistics* 12, no. 1 (1991), pp. 83–104.

Hines, Peter. "Network Sourcing in Japan." *The International Journal of Logistics Management* 7, no. 1 (1996), pp. 67–72.

———. "Internationalization and Localization of the Kyoryoku Kai: The Spread of Best Practice Supplier Development." *The International Journal of Logistics Management* 5, no. 1 (1994), pp. 67–72.

Kaplan, Steven, and Mohanbir Sawhney. "E-Hubs: The New B2B Marketplaces." *Harvard Business Review* 78, no. 3 (May–June 2000), pp. 97–103.

Leenders, Michiel R., and Harold E. Fearon. *Purchasing and Materials Management.* 11th ed. Burr Ridge, IL: Irwin/McGraw-Hill, 1997.

Leenders, Michiel R., and Anna E. Flynn. *Value Driven Purchasing.* Burr Ridge, IL: Irwin, 1995.

Newbourne, Paul T. "The Role of Partnerships in Strategic Account Management." *The International Journal of Logistics Management* 8, no. 1 (1997), pp. 67–74.

Raedels, Alan R. *Value Focused Supply Management.* Burr Ridge, IL: Irwin, 1995.

Tersine, Richard J., and Albert B. Schwarzkopf. "Optimal Transition Ordering Strategies with Announced Price Increases." *The International Journal of Logistics Management* 2, no. 1 (1991), pp. 26–34.

Thompson, Kenneth N. "Vendor Profile Analysis." *Journal of Purchasing and Materials Management* 26, no. 1 (Winter 1990), pp. 11–18.

Turban, Efraim; Jae Lee; David King; and H. Michael Chung. *Electronic Commerce: A Managerial Perspective.* Upper Saddle River, NJ: Prentice Hall, 2000.

Questions and Problems

1. Explain why procurement is an area of major importance in most companies.

2. Explain why supplier selection and evaluation is frequently considered to be the most important activity in the procurement function.

3. International sourcing of materials is a much more difficult process than domestic sourcing. What are some of the more significant problems in international sourcing that affect the logistics manager?

4. Explain the concept of forward buying and its relationship to total cost trade-off analysis.

5. Using a format similar to that shown in Table 12–3, determine the optimal forward buy (in months) given the following information:
   - Monthly usage is $4,000.
   - Expected price increase is 10 percent.
   - Inventory carrying cost is 40 percent.
   - The ordering cost is $25 per order.
   - The vendor pays the freight.

6. What are the major advantages of just-in-time purchasing? What difficulties are possible in implementing a JIT system?

7. Why is cost measurement an important purchasing management activity?

8. Which of the 12 purchasing performance measures do you believe would be of the greatest use to management? Why?

9. Explain how e-commerce is likely to revolutionize the way purchasing is conducted in most major corporations.

10. Why is it necessary for two firms to each have strong drivers if they are considering forming a partnership?

11. The chapter stated that the majority of a firm's relationships would be arm's-length. Why do you think this would be the case?

13 Global Logistics

Chapter Objectives

- To describe the major international supply chain channel strategies—exporting, licensing, joint ventures, direct ownership, importing, and countertrade.
- To identify some of the uncontrollable factors that affect global logistics.
- To identify the components and major organizations involved in exporting.
- To define and discuss some of the basic terms associated with global logistics activities.

Introduction

Many organizations have a significant and growing presence in resource and/or demand markets outside their country of origin. Current business conditions blur the distinctions between domestic and international logistics. Successful enterprises have realized that to survive and prosper they must go beyond the strategies, policies, and programs of the past and adopt a global view of business, customers, and competition.

For an ever-growing number of organizations, logistics managers are defining the marketplace globally. Tables 13–1 and 13–2 identify the world's largest manufacturing and service organizations, respectively. The companies may be headquartered in Europe, Asia, or North America, but their markets are international. For example, in 1999 approximately one-half of Procter & Gamble's $38 billion annual revenues were generated from international operations. Approximately 300 P&G brands are sold in more than 140 countries. Similarly, Hewlett-Packard derived about 55 percent of its $43 billion in 1999 revenues from more than 120 countries outside North America.[1]

New markets are opening up and existing markets are expanding worldwide. The economies of industrialized nations have matured; that is, their economic growth rates have slowed. As a result, those countries have sought additional market opportunities in other countries and regions of the world. The development of a global financial network has facilitated this multinational expansion.[2] In addition, manufacturers have increased new material and component acquisitions from other countries (i.e., global sourcing).

Significant changes are under way in the international logistics operations of many organizations. Further deregulation of U.S. ocean liner companies in 1999 created new opportunities for international shippers to redesign their existing supply chains. The results have been some reductions in order cycle time and shipment costs. Furthermore, as the United States continues to shift toward a technology- and service-based economy (i.e., one in which fewer goods will be produced domestically and more will be purchased from abroad), it is clear that for many organizations, global logistics will become more important.

Global Markets May Grow Faster than Domestic Markets

In some instances, global markets may produce more sales than domestic markets. In supporting nondomestic markets, an organization must have a supply chain network and logistics system that satisfies the particular requirements of each market. For example, supply chains in the developing countries of Africa, South America, or Asia are often characterized as having large numbers of intermediaries (middlemen) supplying an even larger number of small retailers. These economies typically have inadequate transportation and storage facilities, a large market comprised mainly of unskilled workers, and an absence of logistics support systems.

In more highly developed countries, such as Japan, Canada, the United States, and most countries in Western Europe, the supply chains and logistics systems are highly sophisticated. A firm entering those countries will find economies with good transportation systems, high-technology warehousing, skilled workers, and a variety of logistics support systems.

---

[1]See Procter & Gamble's 1999 annual report <http://www.pg.com/investor> and Hewlett-Packard's 1999 annual report <http://www.hp.com/abouthp/company_facts/index.html>.

[2]David C. Shanks, "Strategic Planning for Global Competition," *The Journal of Business Strategy* 5, no. 3 (Winter 1985), pp. 80–89.

TABLE 13–1   The World's Largest Corporations—Manufacturing Industries (1998)

Group Rank	Overall Rank	Company	Headquarters	Industry	Sales ($ millions)
1	1	General Motors	United States	Motor vehicles and parts	178,174
2	2	Ford Motor Company	United States	Motor vehicles and parts	153,625
3	5	Royal Dutch/Shell Group	Netherlands/Britain	Petroleum refining	128,922
4	7	Exxon	United States	Petroleum refining	122,379
5	11	Toyota Motor Corporation	Japan	Motor vehicles and parts	95,137
6	12	General Electric Company	United States	Electronics	90,840
7	14	IBM	United States	Computer, office equipment	78,508
8	17	Daimler-Benz	Germany	Motor vehicles and parts	71,561
9	18	Daewoo Group	South Korea	Motor vehicles and parts	71,525
10	20	British Petroleum	Britain	Petroleum refining	71,193
11	21	Hitachi	Japan	Electronics	68,567
12	22	Volkswagen	Germany	Motor vehicles and parts	65,328
13	23	Matsushita Electric Industrial Company	Japan	Electronics	64,281
14	24	Siemens	Germany	Electronics	63,755
15	25	Chrysler Corporation	United States	Motor vehicles and parts	61,147
16	26	Mobil Corporation	United States	Petroleum refining	59,978
17	29	Phillip Morris Companies	United States	Tobacco	56,114
18	30	Sony Corporation	Japan	Electronics	55,033
19	31	Nissan Motor Company	Japan	Motor vehicles and parts	53,261
20	33	Fiat Spa	Italy	Motor vehicles and parts	52,569
21	34	Honda Motor Company	Japan	Motor vehicles and parts	48,876
22	35	Unilever	England	Food	48,761
23	36	Nestlé SA	Switzerland	Food	48,254
24	39	The Boeing Company	United States	Aerospace	45,800
25	40	Texaco Inc.	United States	Petroleum refining	45,185
26	41	Toshiba Corporation	Japan	Electronics	44,467
27	44	Elf Aquitaine	France	Petroleum refining	43,572
28	46	Tokyo Electric Power Company	Japan	Utilities, gas & supply	42,997
29	47	Hewlett-Packard	United States	Computer, office equipment	42,895
30	49	E.I. du Pont de Nemours	United States	Chemicals	41,304
31	52	Fujitsu Limited	Japan	Computer, office equipment	40,613
32	53	RWE Group	Germany	Utilities, gas & supply	40,233
33	54	NEC Corporation	Japan	Electronics	39,927
34	55	Royal Philips Electronics	Netherlands/Britain	Electronics	39,188
35	61	ENI Spa	Italy	Petroleum refining	36,962
36	62	Electricité de France	France	Utilities, gas & supply	36,673
37	63	Chevron Corporation	United States	Petroleum refining	36,376
38	64	Procter & Gamble	United States	Consumer products	35,764
39	65	Renault	France	Motor vehicles and parts	35,624
40	66	Petroleos de Venezuela	Venezuela	Petroleum refining	34,801
41	69	Bayerische Motoren Werke (BMW)	Germany	Motor vehicles and parts	34,692
42	71	SK	South Korea	Petroleum refining	33,816
43	72	Amoco	United States	Petroleum refining	32,836
44	74	TOTAL SA	France	Petroleum refining	32,741
45	75	Suez Lyonnaise des Eaux	France	Energy	32,627
46	77	BASF AG	Germany	Chemicals	32,178
47	78	Peugeot SA	France	Motor vehicles and parts	32,004
48	80	Bayer AG	Germany	Chemicals	31,731
49	83	Asea Brown Boveri	Switzerland	Industrial & farm equipment	31,265
50	85	Mitsubishi Electric Corporation	Japan	Electronics	30,967

Source: Company annual reports and Internet sources, including <http://www.pathfinder.com/fortune>.

TABLE 13–2   The World's Largest Corporations—Service Industries (1998)

Group Rank	Overall Rank	Company	Headquarters	Industry	Sales ($ millions)
1	3	Mitsui & Company	Japan	Trading	142,688
2	4	Mitsubishi Corporation	Japan	Trading	128,922
3	6	Itochu Corporation	Japan	Trading	126,632
4	8	Wal-Mart Stores, Inc.	United States	General merchandisers	119,299
5	9	Marubeni Corporation	Japan	Trading	111,121
6	10	Sumitomo Corporation	Japan	Trading	102,395
7	13	Nissho Iwai Corporation	Japan	Trading	81,894
8	15	Nippon Telegraph & Telephone	Japan	Telecommunications	76,984
9	16	AXA	France	Life and health insurance	76,874
10	19	Nippon Life Insurance	Japan	Life and health insurance	71,388
11	27	U.S. Postal Service	United States	Postal services/delivery	58,216
12	28	Allianz AG	Germany	Insurance	56,785
13	32	AT&T	United States	Telecommunications	53,261
14	37	Crédit Suisse Group	Switzerland	Banking	48,242
15	38	Dai-ichi Mutual Life Insurance	Japan	Life and health insurance	47,442
16	42	State Farm Insurance	United States	Property insurance	43,957
17	43	Veba AG	Germany	Trading	43,881
18	45	Tomen Corporation	Japan	Trading	43,400
19	48	Sumitomo Life Insurance Company	Japan	Life and health insurance	42,279
20	50	Sears, Roebuck and Company	United States	General merchandisers	41,296
21	51	Deutsche Bank	Germany	Banking	40,792
22	56	Deutsche Telekom AG	Germany	Telecommunications	38,969
23	57	ING Group Inc.	Netherlands	Life and health insurance	38,674
24	58	Travelers Group Inc	United States	Diversified financials	37,609
25	59	HSBC Holdings	England	Banking	37,474
26	60	Prudential Insurance Company	United States	Life and health insurance	37,073
27	67	Bank of Tokyo–Mitsubishi Ltd.	Japan	Banking	34,750
28	68	Citicorp	United States	Banking	34,697
29	70	Crédit Agricole Group	France	Banking	34,015
30	73	Metro AG	Germany	Groceries and drugstores	32,790
31	76	Kmart Corporation	United States	General merchandisers	32,183
32	79	Alcatel Alsthom Group	France	Telecommunications	31,847
33	81	Merrill Lynch & Company	United States	Securities	31,731
34	82	Nichimen Corporation	Japan	Trading	31,362
35	84	Meiji Life Insurance Company	Japan	Life and health insurance	31,047
36	86	Assicurazioni Generali Spa	Italy	Property insurance	30,816
37	87	J.C. Penney Company, Inc.	United States	General merchandisers	30,546
38	88	Amedcal International Group	United States	Property insurance	30,520
39	90	Chase Manhattan Corporation	United States	Banking	30,381
40	91	Bell Atlantic Corporation	United States	Telecommunications	30,194
41	94	Teachers Insurance and Annuity Association (TIAA)	United States	Life and health insurance	29,348
42	96	Carrefour	France	Groceries and drugstores	29,003
43	97	ABN-AMRO Holding NV	Netherlands	Banking	28,946
44	98	Gan	France	Banking	28,937
45	99	Société Generale	France	Banking	28,725
46	101	VIAG Aktiengesellschaft	Germany	Trading	28,581
47	104	Prudential Corporation	England	Life and health insurance	27,906
48	105	Hyundai Corporation	South Korea	Trading	27,838
49	106	Federal National Mortgage Association (FNMA or Fannie Mae)	United States	Diversified financials	27,777
50	107	Dayton Hudson Corporation	United States	General merchandisers	27,757

Source: Company annual reports and Internet sources, including <http://www.pathfinder.com/fortune>.

TABLE 13–3   Comparison of Domestic and International Logistics

	Domestic	*International*
Cost	About 10% of U.S. GNP today	Estimated at 16% of world GNP today
Transport mode	Mainly truck and rail	Mainly ocean and air, with significant intermodal activity
Inventories	Lower levels, reflecting short-order, lead-time requirements and improved transport capabilities	Higher levels, reflecting longer lead times and greater demand and transit uncertainty
Agents	Modest usage, mostly in rail	Heavy reliance on forwarders, consolidators, and customs brokers
Financial risk	Minimal	High, owing to differences in currencies, inflation levels, and little recourse for default
Cargo risk	Minimal	High, owing to longer and more difficult transit, frequent cargo handling, and varying levels of infrastructure development
Government agencies	Primarily for hazardous materials, weight, safety laws, and some tariff requirements	Many agencies involved (e.g., customs, commerce, agriculture, transportation)
Administration	Minimal documentation involved (e.g., purchase order, bill of lading, invoice)	Significant paperwork; the U.S. Department of Commerce estimates that paperwork cost for an average shipment is $250
Communication	Voice, paper-based systems adequate, with growing usage of electronic data interchange	Voice and paper costly and often ineffective; movement toward electronic interchange but variations in standards hinder widespread usage
Cultural differences	Relative homogeneity requires little product modification	Cultural differences require significant market and product adaptation

Source: Adapted from William W. Goldsborough and David L. Anderson, "The International Logistics Environment," in *The Logistics Handbook,* ed. James F. Robeson and William C. Copacino (New York: Free Press, 1994), p. 677.

In this chapter we will discuss some of the similarities and differences between domestic and international logistics (see Table 13–3). We will see how to assess the global logistics environment. This knowledge will form the basis for managing global logistics operations, which will be the focus of Chapter 14.

International Supply Chain Strategies

Many factors can influence a company's decision to enter international markets, including:

Factors Influencing Companies to Enter Global Markets

- Market potential.
- Geographic diversification.
- Excess production capacity and the advantage of a low-cost position due to experience-curve economies and economies of scale.
- Products near the end of their life cycle in the domestic market that could generate growth in the international market.
- Source of new products and ideas.
- Foreign competition in the domestic market.[3]

[3]See Vern Terpstra and Ravi Sarathy, *International Marketing,* 7th ed. (Fort Worth, TX: Dryden Press, 1997), p. 24.

An additional reason for a firm to enter international markets is sourcing of raw materials, component parts, or assemblies. For example, some raw materials, such as petroleum, bauxite, uranium, and certain foodstuffs, have limited geographical availability. Organizations may locate facilities overseas or perhaps import items for domestic use, thereby engaging in international operations.

Organizations that become involved in the international marketplace have many strategic options available to them:

**International Market
Entry Strategies**

- Exporting
- Licensing
- Joint ventures
- Ownership
- Importing
- Countertrade and duty drawbacks

Selection of one or more of these market entry strategies involves consideration of several factors, including the organization's commitment to international involvement, the types and levels of risk, the degree of control desired over international operations, and profit potential.[4]

**Major Participants
in International
Logistics Transactions**

There are also several options available within each strategy. Figure 13–1 identifies some of the major participants in an international logistics transaction, including product and information flows. Some of the participants will be discussed in this chapter, others in Chapter 14. Some entities are specifically related to logistics (e.g., inland transportation carrier, international carrier), while others affect some element of the logistics process (e.g., foreign banks, foreign government agencies).

Successful completion of the various logistics activities in the international supply chain can contribute to the development of global markets in many ways. For example, door-to-door freight services that offer speed and reliability of delivery can allow order lead times to be quoted accurately. Logistics also allows companies to reduce delivery costs through consolidation, expand into new world markets that were previously out of reach, and offer a reasonable after-sales service or replacement policy to international markets. Once captured, an overseas market may be held and expanded, despite intense competition, because of high levels of customer service offered through logistics services.

Exporting

The most common form of international involvement is exporting. Exporting requires the least amount of knowledge and commitment, with the lowest risk, because the domestic firm allows an international freight forwarder, distributor, trading company, or some other organization to carry out the logistics and marketing functions.

**Advantages
of Exporting**

There are many advantages associated with exporting, such as greater flexibility and less risk than other international strategies. For example, no additional production facilities or logistics asset investment is needed in the foreign market because the firm

[4]For a discussion of market entry strategies and related topics, see Raphael L. Brown, *A Study of the Relationship Between a Firm's Market Entry Strategy and Environmental Analysis in Foreign-Based Multinational Firms Operating in the United States,* unpublished D.B.A. dissertation, Nova Southeastern University, Ft. Lauderdale, FL (1998).

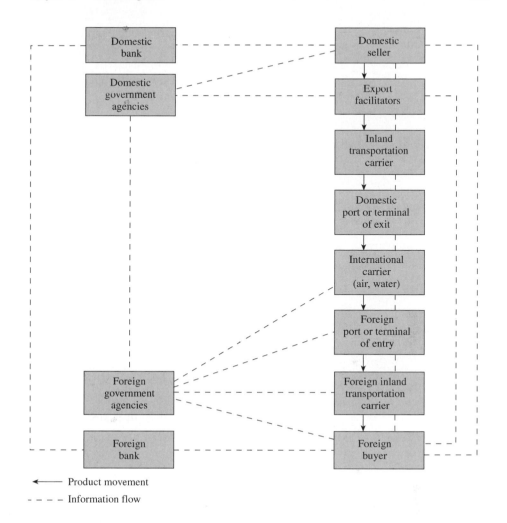

produces the product domestically and allows the exporting intermediary to handle distribution of the product abroad.

Without the presence of direct foreign investment, political uncertainties are a lesser concern; the firm need not worry about the host country nationalizing its operations. Also, it is relatively easy to withdraw if the foreign market does not meet the firm's profit and/or sales expectations. Exporting is also an excellent way for a firm to gain experience and test a market before expanding its own production and marketing operations.

**Disadvantages
of Exporting**

Exporting is not without disadvantages. It is sometimes difficult to compete with other firms located in the foreign market. For example, tariffs (taxes assessed on goods entering a market), import quotas (limitations on the amount of goods that can enter a market), or unfavorable currency exchange rates may adversely affect the export process. In addition, the domestic firm has very little control over the pricing, promotion, or distribution of its product when it exports. Success in international markets depends to a large degree on the capability of export intermediaries.

Management must recognize that the export process is not as simple as it first appears: with or without the help of intermediaries, the firm is responsible for planning, package design, sales negotiation, financial monitoring, banking, insurance, and a variety of documentation. Logistics needs to be involved in the process continually from the planning stage onward. A firm involved in exporting often has to deal with a number of intermediaries that provide a variety of export services.

Licensing

Licensing Defined

Licensing involves agreements that allow a firm in one country (the licensee) "to use the manufacturing, processing, trademark, know-how, technical assistance, merchandising knowledge, or some other skill provided by the licenser located in another country."[5] Licensing allows the domestic firm more control over how the product is distributed, because distribution strategy is usually part of any preliminary discussions with the foreign partner. The specific logistics functions are carried out by the licensee using the established distribution systems of the foreign market.

Advantages of Licensing

Disadvantages of Licensing

Licensing is similar to exporting in that it does not require large capital outlays, thereby reducing risk and increasing flexibility. Licensing is a strategy frequently used by small and medium-sized businesses, and can be an excellent approach if the foreign market has high tariff barriers or strict import quotas. The licensee usually pays the licenser a royalty or a percentage of sales.

Although licensing provides the domestic firm with flexibility, this does not mean that licensing agreements can be terminated quickly. While the agreement with the licensee may include termination or cancellation provisions, there is usually a time lag between the decision to terminate and the actual date of termination, typically much longer than in an exporting situation.

One potentially serious drawback to licensing is that the licensee may become a competitor. As licensees develop their own know-how and expertise, they may end the licensing agreement and begin to compete with the licenser.

Joint Ventures

If an organization wishes to exercise greater control over its international operations than is possible in a licensing agreement, and does not want to establish a freestanding manufacturing plant or other facility in a foreign market, it can enter into a joint venture.

Risks are higher and flexibility lower with this option than with exporting or licensing because an equity position is established in the foreign partner.[6] However, the domestic firm can provide significant management input into the supply chain and logistics strategies of the foreign enterprise because of its financial partnership. This increased management voice does place additional burdens on the domestic firm—namely, it requires a greater knowledge of the international markets the firm is trying to serve. This option also results in greater risks to the domestic firm but, at the same time, can result in higher rewards (i.e., profits).

The joint venture may be the only possible method of market entry if management wishes to exercise a lot of control over the distribution of its products in the foreign

---

[5]David L. Anderson and Dennis Colard, "The International Logistics Environment," in *The Logistics Handbook,* ed. James F. Robeson and William C. Copacino (New York: Free Press, 1994), pp. 658–59.

[6]For a discussion of some of the risks associated with joint ventures, see Eric Farnsworth and Larry Sher, "Protecting Your Interests in a Global Environment," *World Trade* 12, no. 11 (November 1999), pp. 86–90.

market. This would be especially true if wholly owned subsidiaries are prohibited by foreign governments. Such restrictions occur more frequently in less-developed countries (LDCs), which often attempt to promote internal industrial or retail development over outside foreign investment.[7]

Ownership

Ownership Offers the Highest Reward but the Most Risk

Ownership of a foreign subsidiary offers domestic firms the highest degree of control over international marketing and logistics strategies. Ownership can come about through acquisition or expansion. Wal-Mart has successfully used both strategies in its global marketing efforts (see the Global box). Acquisition can be advantageous because it minimizes start-up costs in the foreign market (e.g., locating and building facilities, hiring employees, and establishing supply chain relationships). Ownership requires more knowledge of the international market compared to other forms of market entry and has the most risk of any option. The firm is totally responsible for marketing and distributing its product.

Ownership in the foreign market allows organizations to compete more effectively on price because of the elimination of transportation costs incurred in shipments from domestic plants to foreign points of entry. Customs duties and other import taxes are also eliminated.

Disadvantages of Ownership

Drawbacks to ownership include a loss of flexibility because the firm has a long-term commitment to the foreign market. Fixed facilities and equipment cannot be disposed of quickly in the case of sales or profit declines, increased levels of competition, or other adversities.

Another drawback, especially in politically unstable countries, is the possibility of government nationalization of foreign-owned businesses. Also, exchange rate fluctuations change the relative value of foreign investments, since those investments are valued in local currencies rather than the owner's domestic currency.

Organizations Typically Use More than One Market Entry Strategy

Generally, organizations use more than one market entry strategy. Markets, product lines, economic conditions, and political environments change over time, so it stands to reason that the optimal market entry strategy may also change. Furthermore, a market entry strategy that is good in one country may not be as good in another.

For organizations considering exporting, licensing, joint venture, or ownership, a formal procedure should be established for evaluating each alternative. Each market entry strategy can be evaluated on a set of management-determined criteria. All business functional areas (e.g., accounting, manufacturing, marketing, logistics) must be involved in establishing the criteria and evaluating them. Only after a complete analysis of each market entry strategy should an organization select a method of international involvement.

---

[7]For a discussion of joint ventures in developing countries, see Dianne J. Cyr, "Implications for Learning: Human Resources Management in East-West Joint Ventures," *Organization Studies* 17, no. 2 (Spring 1996), pp. 207–26; Roger W. Mills and Gordon Chen, "Evaluating International Joint Ventures Using Strategic Value Analysis," *Long Range Planning* 29, no. 4 (1996), pp. 552–61; Anthony J. F. O'Reilly, "Establishing Successful Joint Ventures in Developing Nations: A CEO's Perspective," *Columbia Journal of World Business* 23, no. 1 (Spring 1988), pp. 65–71; and Gregory E. Osland and S. Tamer Cavusgil, "Performance Issues in U.S.-China Joint Ventures," *California Management Review* 38, no. 2 (Winter 1996), pp. 106–30.

Importing

Importing involves the purchase of goods from foreign sources. Items being imported can be used immediately in the production process, sold directly to customers, transported to other ports of entry, stored in bonded warehouses (where goods are stored until import duties are paid), or placed in a free trade zone (where goods are exempted from customs duties until they are removed for use or sale).

Customshouse Brokers   Many firms use customshouse brokers for importing products into the United States. These brokers facilitate the movement of imported products and ensure the accuracy and completeness of import documentation. Customshouse brokers are licensed by the U.S. Customs Service of the Department of Treasury. As one textbook notes, "Many . . . brokers help clients choose modes of transportation and appropriate carriers . . . They also provide assistance to importers in assigning shipments the best routes. They handle estimates for landed costs, payments of goods through draft, letters of credit insurance, and redelivery of cargo if there is more than one port of destination."[8]

Countertrade and Duty Drawbacks[9]

Countertrade Defined   *Countertrade* is the term that applies to the requirement that a firm import something from a country in which it has sold something else.[10] Countertrade is essentially any transaction in which part of the payment is made in goods instead of money. The need for countertrade is driven by the balance-of-payments problems of a country, and by weak demand for the country's products. A likely candidate for countertrade is a country with a shortage of foreign exchange or a shortage of credit to finance trade flows. Such a country will be trying to expand its exports or develop markets for its new products.

Five Forms of Countertrade   Five basic forms of countertrade exist: barter, buyback, compensation, counterpurchase, and switch.[11] *Barter,* the simplest form of countertrade, occurs when goods of equal value are exchanged and no money is involved. In *buyback* arrangements, the selling firm provides equipment or an entire plant, and agrees to buy back a certain part of the production; many less-developed countries insist on buyback arrangements, because they ensure access to Western technology and stable markets. If barter is specified as a ratio of the value of goods being traded to the value of the product being sold, this is referred to as a *compensation* arrangement.

Counterpurchase involves more cash in the transaction, smaller volumes of goods flowing to the multinational corporation over a shorter period of time, and goods unrelated to the original deal. A *switch* transaction uses at least one party outside the host country to facilitate the trade. The countertraded goods or the multinational company's

---

[8]R. Neil Southern, *Transportation and Logistics Basics* (Memphis, TN: Continental Traffic Service, Inc., 1997), p. 295.

[9]This section is taken from Lisa M. Ellram and Laura Birou, *Purchasing for Bottom Line Impact* (Burr Ridge, IL: Irwin, 1995), p. 61.

[10]See Kwabena Anyane-Ntow and Santhi C. Harvey, "A Countertrade Primer: A Look at a Growing Trend That Demands Management Accountants' Attention," *Management Accounting* 76, no. 10 (April 1995), pp. 47–50; and John N. Pearson and Laura B. Forker, "International Countertrade: Has Purchasing's Role Really Changed?" *International Journal of Purchasing and Materials Management* 31, no. 4 (Fall 1995), pp. 38–44.

[11]Kenton W. Elderkin and Warren E. Norquist, *Creative Countertrade* (Cambridge, MA: Ballinger, 1987), p. 152.

FIGURE 13–2

How duty drawbacks work

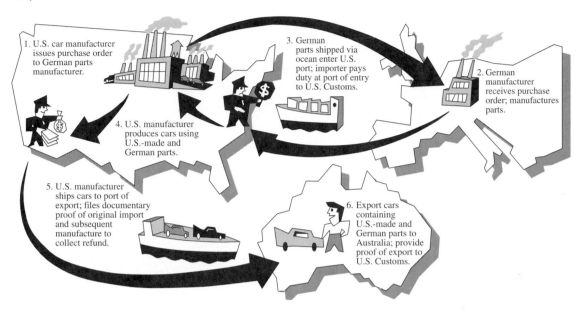

1. U.S. car manufacturer issues purchase order to German parts manufacturer.

2. German manufacturer receives purchase order; manufactures parts.

3. German parts shipped via ocean enter U.S. port; importer pays duty at port of entry to U.S. Customs.

4. U.S. manufacturer produces cars using U.S.-made and German parts.

5. U.S. manufacturer ships cars to port of export; files documentary proof of original import and subsequent manufacture to collect refund.

6. Export cars containing U.S.-made and German parts to Australia; provide proof of export to U.S. Customs.

Source: Lisa H. Harrington, "How to Take Advantage of Duty Drawback," *Traffic Management* 28, no. 6 (June 1989), p. 121A.

goods are sent through a third country, for purchase in hard currency or for distribution. While countertrade agreements may be complex, they do offer an opportunity to develop low-cost sources of supply in the world marketplace. In some cases, they may provide the only means of market entry for the firm.

Duty Drawbacks

Organizations that import goods used in manufacturing or export products that contain imported materials can take advantage of drawbacks. A *drawback,* often referred to as a *duty drawback,* is a refund of customs duties paid on imported items. As illustrated in Figure 13–2, duty drawbacks involve many steps and can be time-consuming. The process typically is automated, though many organizations still handle drawbacks manually. In the United States, more than $3 billion of duty drawback funds are unclaimed every year because the proper paperwork is not filed.[12] However, for organizations that can take advantage of them, duty drawbacks can result in significant cost savings.

The Global Marketplace—Uncontrollable Elements

All forms of international market entry require awareness of the variables that can affect an organization's logistics systems. Some of these factors can be controlled by logistics executives, while others, unhappily, cannot. However, these uncontrollable factors must still be addressed and dealt with in any international marketing undertaking. Figure 13–3 shows the environment in which the logistics executive operates.

---

[12]Martha L. Celestino, "International Trade Logistics Software Solutions," *World Trade* 12, no. 5 (May 1999), p. 62.

FIGURE 13–3

The global logistics environment

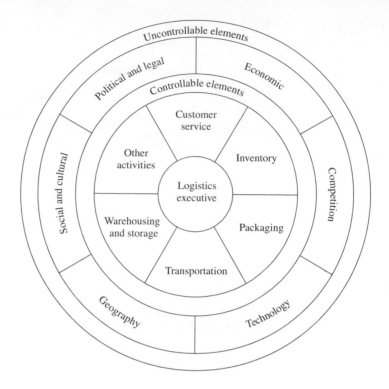

Anything that affects the logistics strategy of the international firm yet is not under the direct control of the logistics executive can be considered an uncontrollable element. The major uncontrollable elements of the environment are political and legal systems of the foreign markets, economic conditions, degree of competition, technology available or accessible, geographic structure of the foreign market, and the social and cultural norms of the various target markets.

Characteristics of the Uncontrollable Environment

The uncontrollable environment is characterized by uncertainty and, many times, volatility.[13] The logistics executive must make decisions within this environment, including making cost–service trade-offs, determining and implementing customer service programs, and measuring cost components of the logistics process.

It is beyond the scope of this chapter to examine in detail each of the various uncontrollable factors of global logistics. Many international marketing and management textbooks address these elements.[14] It is sufficient to say that the uncontrollable elements affect the actions of the logistics executive and must be considered in the planning, implementation, and control of the organization's global supply chain network.

---

[13]A number of books have examined various facets of the uncontrollable environment and have speculated on the impacts they would or have had on organizations. Some of the more interesting and widely read views on this topic include John Naisbitt and Patricia Aburdene, *Megatrends 2000: Ten New Directions for the 1990s* (New York: Avon Books, 1990); and William J. Bennett, *The Index of Leading Cultural Indicators* (New York: William Morrow, 1994).

[14]See Philippe-Pierre Dornier, Ricardo Ernst, Michel Fender, and Panos Kouvelis, *Global Operations and Logistics* (New York: John Wiley & Sons, 1998); Vern Terpstra and Lloyd C. Russow, *International Dimensions of Marketing* (Cincinnati, OH: South-Western, 2000); and Terpstra and Sarathy, *International Marketing,* 7th ed.

The following sections provide a brief look at the multitude of factors that must be considered when making global logistics decisions.

Economic

The economic environment is likely to be the most important of all the external environments. In a global economy, economic activity goes on 24 hours a day, seven days a week. Information is transmitted by satellite and computer technologies without the constraints of national boundaries. Some effects of the economic environment on logistics are the following:

Economic Impacts on Logistics

- Companies may have difficulty in increasing prices and must therefore pay attention to internal efficiency, including the efficiency of logistics expenditures.
- Slow growth rates in some markets make it even more necessary that greater discipline be exercised by logistics executives in planning and ensuring that maximum productivity be achieved for each logistics dollar spent.
- During periods of inflation, high rates of interest on short-term borrowing to meet cash flow requirements often result in greater attention to logistics inefficiencies.
- Poor investment climates in some countries or world regions require strong profit performance, both to provide retained earnings for reinvestment and to attract available investment monies.
- Development of trading blocs can affect all aspects of logistics.[15] (See Table 13–4 for a list of the major trading blocs.)
- Foreign currency exchange rate fluctuations add complexity and uncertainty to decision making.
- Improving economic conditions (i.e., standards of living) in less-developed countries can affect international trade.
- Companies and countries both may change their views on the use of barter and countertrade.
- Long-term pressures exerted on profits by inflation and recession often result in greater corporate emphasis on cost reduction and profits.

Inflation is particularly important to organizations generally and logistics management specifically. The specific impact of inflation on logistics will depend on five factors, discussed below.

Type of Business

Type of Business.   The type of business determines the proportion of assets to revenues employed in cash, receivables, inventories, and fixed assets. For example, some capital-intensive businesses, such as utilities, steel, chemical, and paper companies, require sub-

---

[15]For a discussion how trading blocs can affect global organizations, see Naresh K. Malhotra, James Agarwal, and Imad Baalbaki, "Heterogeneity of Regional Trading Blocs and Global Marketing Strategies: A Multicultural Perspective," *International Marketing Review* 15, no. 6 (1998), pp. 476–506. For a specific discussion of the logistics impacts of Mercosur, see José G. Vantine and Claudirceu Marra, "Logistics Challenges and Opportunities within Mercosur," *The International Journal of Logistics Management* 8, no. 1 (1997), pp. 55–66; and Michael Berzon, "Mercosur Passes Test," *American Shipper* 42, no. 4 (April 2000), pp. 47–58.

TABLE 13–4   Major International Trading Blocs

Trading Bloc	*Member Countries*
Asia-Pacific Economic Cooperation (APEC)	Australia, Brunei, Canada, Chile, China, Indonesia, Japan, South Korea, Malaysia, Mexico, New Zealand, Papua New Guinea, Philippines, Russia, Singapore, Taiwan, Thailand, United States
Association of Southeast Asian Nations (ASEAN)	Brunei, Indonesia, Laos, Malaysia, Myanmar, Philippines, Singapore, Thailand, Vietnam, Burma
European Union (EU)	Austria, Belgium, Denmark, Finland, France, Germany, Greece, Ireland, Italy, Luxembourg, Netherlands, Portugal, Spain, Sweden, United Kingdom
Mercado Comun del Sur (Mercosur)	Argentina, Brazil, Bolivia, Chile, Paraguay, Uruguay
North American Free Trade Agreement (NAFTA)	Canada, Mexico, United States
Southern African Development Community (SADC)	Angola, Botswana, Lesotho, Malawi, Mauritius, Mozambique, Namibia, South Africa, Swaziland, Tanzania, Zambia, Zimbabwe
World Trade Organization (WTO)	134 member countries

Source: Various Internet sources, including <http://www.mercosurinvestment.com/>; <http://europa.eu.int/europedirect>; and <http://www4.nando.net/newsroom/ntn/biz/020997/biz5_10158.html>.

stantial investments in fixed assets in relation to revenues, whereas consumer product manufacturers and financial service companies have more modest fixed-asset requirements.

Inventory Valuation Methods

Inventory Valuation Methods.   The selection of the last-in, first-out (LIFO) or first-in, first-out (FIFO) valuation method can be important in some organizations. In inflationary economies, it is important to use the proper valuation method because of its impact on company profits. The LIFO method would be the most appropriate because the cost of sales is valued closer to the current cost of replacement. On the other hand, the FIFO method gives a larger profit figure than LIFO because old costs are matched with current revenues.

Age of Business and Assets

Age of Business and Assets.   Business age is likely to have an important bearing on the age of the assets employed and the need for the reinvestment of funds. The earnings of new businesses and growth businesses in their early years are often only moderately affected by inflation, because of the relatively recent vintage of much of their plant and equipment.

Inflation can distort the earnings results of older businesses in different ways, depending on whether the fixed assets involved are going to be replaced. Some older businesses (e.g., steel companies and utilities) have major reinvestment requirements. Many of these companies have a large stock of old fixed assets, and the distortions to earnings caused by inflation can be significant. Some enterprises (e.g., coal mines) may go out of business after their resources have been depleted, making price-level-adjusted or current cost depreciation meaningless.

Composition of Expenditures

Composition of Expenditures.   It is axiomatic that inflation does not affect all types of expenditures in the same way. Energy, environmental, and labor costs for some organizations have increased at a rate that far outstrips the growth in the consumer price index. Unit computational costs, however, have decreased, because of technical advances in computer and information systems. Thus, the extent of distortion depends on how much of each type of cost an organization consumes and the inflation rate that applies to that type.

Capital Structure

Capital Structure of the Organization. Capital structure is significant because organizations are hurt by inflation if their monetary assets exceed their liabilities. Enterprises theoretically benefit from inflation if their monetary liabilities exceed their assets.

In general, economic resources act as constraints on enterprises. The availability and cost of economic resources during periods of inflation and recession restrict what the enterprise can and cannot do. For example, increased costs for logistics services can result in a firm's curtailing its customer service activities or reducing expenditures elsewhere if budgets do not grow as quickly as costs. Higher interest rates increase the costs of carrying inventory, thus making it more expensive for an enterprise to provide the same level of customer service in terms of the amount of product in stock and available for sale.

It should also be remembered that the economic environment influences, and is influenced by, other environmental components. Examples of the interrelationships include the following:

Interrelationships between Economics and Other Environmental Factors

- A change in technology (such as the introduction of synthetic fuels) may alter the cost of a major raw material, or perhaps even bring about a change in the type of materials acquired.
- A change in the legal and regulatory environment (such as the election of a new government leader, or a change in monetary policy or tax laws) may alter the rate of inflation or the real cost of money.
- A demographic change (such as an increase in the number of retirement-age individuals) can influence the direction of federal spending.
- A social change (such as changes in attitudes toward the importance of the environment) may alter the manner in which environmental regulations affect product distribution, especially reverse logistics activities.

Competition

Organizations continue to face increasing competitive pressures from many sources. In the United States, manufacturers in certain industries have found themselves at a competitive disadvantage compared to their Asian and European counterparts. For example, the market for microwave ovens, a product invented in the United States in 1945 and introduced commercially to consumers in 1955, has been virtually taken over by Japanese manufacturers. The domestic market share for U.S.-made computers has dropped significantly. Similar trends have been evident in semiconductors, machine tools, apparel, industrial machinery, household appliances, and telephone equipment.

U.S. manufacturers have attempted to respond in several ways in several different areas—manufacturing, research and development, marketing, and logistics. From a logistics perspective, some of the responses have included:

Responding to Competition with Logistics

- Increasing the number of cross-national partnerships, alliances, mergers, and/or acquisitions.
- Expansion of many previously domestic-based organizations into international markets.

Global

Wal-Mart in Europe

With global sales exceeding $165 billion (2000), Wal-Mart is the world's largest retailer. The company is comprised of Wal-Mart stores, Supercenters, and Sam's Club units. In a typical store, 40 percent of sales are hard lines, 20 percent apparel, 25 percent dry groceries, and 15 percent fresh food. Products in a Wal-Mart store include 10,000 SKUs of food and 80,000 SKUs of nonfood products.

In the fiscal year 2000, international sales were $23 billion. By 2005, it is estimated that international sales will be 20 percent of total Wal-Mart revenues. Existing store locations number in the thousands; there are more than 3,000 units domestically and over 1,000 units outside the United States, in countries including Mexico, Canada, Puerto Rico, Argentina, Brazil, United Kingdom, Germany, China, and South Korea. International expansion has occurred through the building of new stores and the acquisition of existing stores of other chains, such as the Wertkauf and Interspar hypermarket chains in Germany, and the Woolco discount department store chain in Canada.

Why has Wal-Mart expanded internationally with such vigor? Financial results appear to indicate that the answer lies in the growth potential of units in foreign markets. Some specific reasons for Wal-Mart's success include:

- Sam Walton's inspirational leadership.
- Associate-focused organizational structure.
- Strong customer service orientation.

- Store-focused and "store-within-a-store" operations adaptable to local markets.
- Low-cost strategy.
- Capacity for innovation and reinvention.
- Continuous merchandising of brands.
- Goal of maximizing inventory turnover.
- Vendor partnering.
- Superefficient logistics system.
- Extensive internal communications.
- Consumer impacts that show Wal-Mart's dominance in location, price, and product assortment.

Although Wal-Mart has been successful on the international front, there are challenges. European competitors such as Carrefour, Metro AG, Ahold, Sainsbury, and Tesco are strong and have significant market shares. Cultural differences between countries may impact Wal-Mart's ability to develop a global brand name to the same level of success as Coca-Cola and McDonald's.

While Wal-Mart faces an increasingly competitive global marketplace, history indicates that it will be up to the challenge.

Sources: Stephen J. Arnold, "Research Note: Wal-Mart in Europe," *International Journal of Retail & Distribution Management* 27, no. 1 (1999), pp. 48–51; and the Internet home page of Wal-Mart <http://www.walmartstores.com>.

- Development of global communications networks operating 24 hours a day.
- Establishment of country and regional warehouses in major world markets.
- Identifying and developing relationships with logistics service providers that offer transportation, storage, materials handling, and other services on a global basis.

Nontraditional Competition

Nontraditional forms of competition are also occurring with greater frequency. For example, in the retail jewelry market, consumers are purchasing more jewelry from outlets such as the Internet, catalog showrooms, discount stores, department stores, and general merchandise stores, and less from traditional outlets such as jewelry stores. Logistics activities must necessarily vary when these nontraditional forms of distribution are used.[16] For example, with Internet sales, service levels become even more

---

[16]For an interesting example of nontraditional logistics management in the grocery sector, see Douglas A. Blackmon, "Launching Barksdale, Version 4.0," *The Wall Street Journal,* September 7, 1999, pp. B1 and B4.

Technology

NAFTA and Technology Combine to Cut Customs Delays

Today, the documentation for more than 1.5 million motor carrier shipments into Canada is processed by customs before the freight even reaches the border, shortening the time spent releasing the freight when it arrives.

Five years ago, going into Mexico meant clearances that could take three or four days. Today, 90 percent of all goods from the United States are cleared by Mexican Customs at the border in 20 seconds or less.

The ultimate goal of [the United States, Canada, and Mexico] is to completely automate the customs clearance process. Canadian Customs is currently implementing Customs 2000 initiatives with the goal of making its customs system paperless. One initiative that has boosted the automation efforts in Canada has been implementation of the Pre-Arrival Review System (PARS) and the Inland Pre-Arrival Review System (INPARS) . . . Through

PARS and INPARS, information on a shipment is sent from the carrier to the broker or designate who prepares the release documentation and forwards it to Canadian Customs for review and processing. These systems allow brokers to prepare release documentation for customs review prior to the freight's arrival . . . This allows paperwork errors to be corrected while the freight is en route instead of delaying the shipment after it arrives at the border.

Automation has helped Mexican Customs . . . Over the last five years, traffic volume through Mexican Customs has increased 300 percent while the agency has been able to reduce its staff by 60 percent through automation.

Source: Robert B. Carr, "Don't Let Borders Be Barriers," *Transportation and Distribution* 36, no. 3 (March 1995), pp. 65–70.

important because customers are not able to physically see and touch merchandise prior to purchase. Rapid delivery systems are often used by organizations engaged in this form of e-commerce.[17]

Technology

In his 1970 book, *Future Shock,* Alvin Toffler explored the changes resulting from advances in technology and foresaw acceleration in the rate of technological advancement. In 1980, in *The Third Wave,* Toffler analyzed the shift from an agricultural economy to an industrial economy and finally to an information economy. Then, in *Powershift,* published in 1990, he examined, among other issues, how technology affected the nature of power and wealth generation in many sectors of the world economy.[18]

John Naisbitt, in *Megatrends,* similarly identified a megashift from an industrial to an information society.[19] Most certainly the advances in technology have been due, in

---

[17]See George Anders, "Virtual Reality: Web Firms Go on Warehouse Building Boom," *The Wall Street Journal,* September 8, 1999, pp. B1 and B8.

[18]Alvin Toffler, *Future Shock* (New York: Random House, 1970); Alvin Toffler, *The Third Wave* (New York: William Morrow & Co., 1980); Alvin Toffler, *Powershift: Knowledge, Wealth, and Violence at the Edge of the 21st Century* (New York: Bantam Books, 1990).

[19]John Naisbitt, *Megatrends: Ten New Directions Transforming Our Lives* (New York: Warner Books, 1982); see also John Naisbitt and Patricia Aburdene, *Megatrends 2000: Ten New Directions for the 1990s* (New York: William Morrow, 1990).

Benefits of Technology

large part, to developments in computers, data communications, and information systems. Significant improvements in computer hardware and software, coupled with a reduction in costs to produce them, have resulted in their widespread adoption and implementation. Technological advancements have had significant impacts on all aspects of commerce, including logistics.

Examples include the use of computer graphics in warehouse layout and design, transportation routing and scheduling, global data transmission through the Internet and electronic data interchange (EDI), computer simulations of logistics systems, data collection and analysis in customer service research, and satellite communications.

Problems Associated with Technology

Advances in technology are not without their problems and concerns, however. New technology speeds up product obsolescence, making logistics system inefficiencies more critical. With products in demand for shorter periods of time, items cannot be held up on transportation equipment or in warehouses, because the loss in sales may be irreplaceable.

As the speed of technology advancement accelerates, it becomes more likely that additional products will undergo technological obsolescence. It is therefore important that an enterprise engage in efforts to monitor the technology components of the environment. This is referred to as "technological forecasting" and should take place as a normal part of the enterprise's environmental scanning activities.

Geography

The varying topography of different geographic areas affects how products can be transported between locations. The distribution of population centers varies significantly from one country to another. As one author has noted, "When intercontinental logistics are considered, the earth's curvature becomes important. Distances are not what they seem on a flat map . . . Locations such as Alaska, that may seem to be at the periphery of the world in a two-dimensional map, may prove to be at the center of things when viewed on a globe."[20]

Air and Water Transport Are Used Extensively

As was discussed in Chapter 8, international transportation occurs primarily by air and ocean shipping, unless the countries are contiguous geographically. In those instances, motor, rail, and inland waterway transport can be used. The distances involved in crossing national borders can range from a few miles to many thousands of miles.

Multiple countries may be traversed in a single product movement. Also, topography can vary significantly within and between countries, such as in Western Europe and Southern Africa. In certain instances, the shortest distance between two points may not be a straight line, especially when a possible transport route must go through mountainous terrain.

Finally, because markets are geographically dispersed in some countries and highly concentrated in others, logistics networks are often different. Mode/carrier selection, warehouse location, and inventory volumes will necessarily be affected by the geographical dispersion of an organization's target markets.

Social and Cultural

The social and cultural environment in which an organization operates is extremely important because it affects how and why individuals, groups, and societies live and

---

[20]Paul S. Bender, "International Logistics," in *The Distribution Management Handbook,* ed. James A. Tompkins and Dale Harmelink (New York: McGraw-Hill, 1994), p. 8.5.

behave as they do. This environment includes how people express themselves, how they think, how they move, how problems are addressed and solved, how employees relate to organizations for which they work, how transportation systems are organized, and how economic and government systems are put together and function.

The task of understanding and scanning the social-cultural environment is becoming increasingly difficult for the logistics executive because of many factors, although the most important are the globalization of markets and the diversity of cultures in those markets.

Components of the Social-Cultural Environment

The social-cultural environment of the global enterprise is comprised of several components: language, education, religion, values, technology, social organization, politics, infrastructure development, and regulatory systems. Each component alone or in combination with the others can affect logistics management in a variety of ways.

For example, variations in language can cause difficulties in developing training manuals, written policies and procedures, and logistics strategies for moving products between and within different countries or regions. Accepted practices vary by region of the world with respect to how products are sold at retail (e.g., large mass merchandisers versus very small family-owned shops). People's perceptions of the family, religion, ethics, values, and education can impact how they as consumers view specific goods and services that are marketed, whether certain types of retail institutions are accepted, and what business practices are considered acceptable.[21]

Different social-cultural environments may require different strategies. Of particular interest to logistics executives are the social and cultural trends that will affect strategies and decisions made on a daily basis. Some of these trends include the following:

Social and Cultural Trends

1. The most valuable commodity to customers will be time rather than money. It will be easier to make money than it will be to "make time" for all of the activities in which people and companies want to engage.

2. A continuing shift from industrial to service economies will alter people's views of the world. The majority of persons in many countries, such as France, Germany, Sweden, the United Kingdom, and the United States, are now employed in the service and/or information sectors. This reflects a continuing trend toward higher levels of consumption of services and information.

3. The ability to obtain information almost instantaneously has already affected such diverse areas of activity as the structure of national and international commodities markets, outsourcing of labor, materials and components used in manufacturing, and individual views of world markets, governments, and products.

Changes in the social-cultural environment must be constantly monitored by an enterprise. Also, in addition to identifying trends that are occurring, it is important to understand their impacts on such corporate issues as profitability, supply chain management strategies, product development strategies, distribution outlets employed, market segmentation policies, and promotion efforts.

---

[21]To illustrate, U.S. executives are prohibited by the Foreign Corrupt Practices Act of 1977 from paying bribes, but foreign competitors have no such limitations. In some parts of the world, bribes and "favors" are standard business practices.

Political and Legal

When a company's operations are limited to a single country, logistics executives need only concern themselves with one set of laws and regulations, although they may be complex. Global companies must operate under many different legal systems with varying laws and regulations. Sometimes there is an overlap between the political and competitive environments when foreign governments own or subsidize local competitors.

In the short run, enterprises are affected by such factors as laws and regulations, the political climate in foreign markets, levels of consumerism activity, judicial interpretation of antitrust laws, trade barriers, and transportation regulations. In the long run, organizations must be aware of trends and changes taking place in the environment. For example, in the United States, transportation carriers, especially motor, air, and rail carriers, had to be aware of what was happening in terms of deregulation during the late 1970s and early 1980s. Economic deregulation of transportation may or may not have taken place in many countries.

Special-interest groups, industry associations, individual firms, governments and government agencies, and the judiciary can influence the political-legal environment. These entities can have indirect influence (such as interest groups lobbying for passage of a particular piece of legislation), or direct influence (such as the English Parliament or U.S. Congress introducing and passing specific logistics-related legislation). Nowhere has this been more evident than in Europe, where environmental legislation has significantly affected all facets of business, including logistics.[22]

Of importance to logistics management is the impact on corporate strategy and operations of the political-legal environment. Typically, three questions must be addressed by logistics executives:

Three Important Questions

1. What specific supply chain, corporate, and/or logistics strategies are affected by the political-legal environment?
2. What are the financial impacts (i.e., costs) of trends and changes occurring or anticipated in the political-legal environment?
3. What opportunities exist for the organization as a result of trends and changes in the political-legal environment?

Political-Legal Impacts on Logistics

The facets of an enterprise's activities affected by the political-legal environment include the marketing mix, international operations, merger and acquisition strategies, competitive responses, and personnel administration decisions. The specific impacts can be one or more of the following: (1) certain marketing and logistics actions may be prohibited, (2) some actions may be mandatory or required, or (3) some actions may be limited in some way.

For example, the majority of business-related legislation in the United States attempts to maintain competition, protect the rights of consumers, and preserve the environment. Various business activities may be mandated, such as listing of product ingredients on the package; maintaining documented evidence to support product and service claims; utilizing government modes of transport within foreign markets for the distribution of products; and complying with host country regulations on exporting, joint ventures, and owned operations. Additionally, communications and joint decision making between supply chain partners may be affected by antitrust regulations.

---

[22]See Judith E. M. Klostermann and Arnold Tukker, eds., *Product Innovation and Eco-Efficiency* (Dordrecht, The Netherlands: Kluwer Academic Publishers, 1998); and James R. Stock, *Development and Implementation of Reverse Logistics Programs* (Oak Brook, IL: Council of Logistics Management, 1998).

The political-legal environment can also affect the enterprise financially. Political risk comes from the many ways in which political forces in a country can negatively affect expected cash flows of an investment and undermine the assumptions on which the investment was made. For example, a new political party in power or the new head of an old governing coalition can decide to change the fundamentals for operating and investing by altering the regulation of licensing, for example, or by changing foreign equity restrictions, local participation requirements, or the basis of corporate taxation.

Political-legal trends and events do not necessarily mean problems and increased costs to an enterprise. Opportunities may exist if management can recognize and respond to them. Because of increasing regulation of the environment, many companies such as Genco Distribution System, Universal Solutions, USF Logistics, and Burnham Corporation have emerged as major providers of reverse logistics services. Historically, international freight forwarders and others involved in global commerce have benefited from the complexity of international documentation, tariff and other trade restrictions, and customs requirements.

Exporting Basics

There are many facilitators or organizations that are involved in the exporting activity. The types of organizations used most extensively are:

Examples of Exporting Companies

- Export distributor.
- Customshouse broker.
- International freight forwarder.
- Trading company.
- Non-vessel-operating common carrier (NVOCC).

Other facilitators are also used to a lesser degree, including export brokers, export merchants, and foreign purchasing agents.[23]

Export Distributor

An organization involved in global marketing often uses the services of an export distributor, sometimes referred to as an export management company. An export distributor (1) is located in the foreign market, (2) buys on his or her own account, (3) is responsible for the sale of the product; and (4) has a continuing contractual relationship with the domestic firm. The distributor frequently is granted exclusive rights to a specific territory and usually refrains from handling the products of competing companies.

The export distributor performs one or more of the following functions:

Functions Performed by Export Distributors

- Obtaining and maintaining agreed-on levels of channel and sales effort.
- Obtaining import business and handling the arrangements for customs clearance.
- Obtaining the necessary foreign exchange for payment to the supplier.
- Maintaining necessary government relations.
- Maintaining inventories.
- Providing warehouse facilities.

---

[23]For a discussion of the decision-making process in selecting export facilitators, see Toby B. Gooley, "Do You Need an Export Intermediary?" *Traffic Management* 34, no. 9 (September 1995), pp. 67A–69A.

- Performing, or overseeing, the inland freight and delivery functions.
- Performing breakbulk operations.
- Managing credit policies.
- Gathering market information.
- Providing after-sale services of various kinds.

Customshouse Broker

Functions Performed

As we briefly discussed earlier in relation to importing, the customshouse broker performs two critical functions: (1) facilitating product movement through customs, and (2) handling the necessary documentation that must accompany international shipments.

For many organizations, the task of handling the many documents and forms that accompany an international shipment can be overwhelming. Coupled with the variety of customs procedures, restrictions, and requirements that differ in each country, the job of facilitating export shipments across international borders requires a specialist—the customshouse broker. In general, if a company is exporting to a number of countries with different import requirements, or if the company has a large number of items in its product line (e.g., automotive parts, electronic components, food products), a customshouse broker should be a part of the organization's international supply chain network.

**Selecting
a Customshouse Broker**

When selecting a customshouse broker, companies should consider a number of factors. Typical of the most important questions or issues that should be addressed are the following:

- Does the broker specialize in certain commodities and/or shipping methods?
- How long has the broker been in business?
- What resources does the broker have to ensure speedy clearance and delivery of the product?
- How does the broker alert his or her clients to delays in handling or clearance?
- What assistance does the broker offer in terms of records maintenance?
- Does the broker have computerized or electronic data interchange (EDI) systems that can expedite document preparation and transmittal and/or expedite customs clearance? What information can it provide?[24]

International Freight Forwarder

Functions Performed

International freight forwarders serve an important role in the export strategies of many firms.[25] They can handle the movement of goods from the site of production to the customer's location. They have an intimate knowledge of the transportation alternatives and can handle documentation responsibilities.[26]

International freight forwarders speed the movement of goods from the site of production to the customer's location by using drop shipments, which eliminates double handling. They may also receive advanced shipping notices that speed clearance of customs and preparation of required documentation.[27] International forwarders also

---

[24]*Freight Facts* (New York: Port Authority of New York and New Jersey, 1989), pp. 28–29.

[25]Freight forwarders can also service significant roles within countries. For an example within Europe, see Robert J. Bowman, "Frans Maas Keeps Parts Flowing to AutoEuropa," *Global Logistics and Supply Chain Strategies* 2, no. 9 (November 1998), pp. 58–64.

[26]*Freight Facts,* p. 9.

[27]William W. Goldsborough and David L. Anderson, "Import/Export Management," in *The Logistics Handbook,* ed. James F. Robeson and William C. Copacino (New York: Free Press, 1994), p. 683.

arrange transportation and carrier routings, coordinate product storage, organize pick-and-pack operations, and provide full-service logistics to their clients. The following describes the services of one such forwarder:

Fritz Companies Provide Forwarder Services to Sears

> The Fritz Companies, a US-based customs broker and freight forwarder, provides a broad base of services for Sears, Roebuck & Company. In addition to performing standard customs brokerage for all Sears products imported from the Far East, Fritz negotiates and manages contracts with eastbound carriers out of Hong Kong and Singapore, books cargo, consolidates merchandise into container loads, manages cargo to Sears distribution facilities in the United States, and provides information regarding cargo disposition as cargo moves through the pipeline.[28]

Firms use freight forwarders for the following reasons: to reduce transportation and distribution costs, to free up or reduce staff, to handle logistics so they can focus on core business, to acquire outside expertise, to improve customer service and satisfaction, to avoid capital expenditures, and to provide logistics information systems.[29]

Nearly every global organization uses the services of an international freight forwarder, even if it has its own export group or department. In such instances, the forwarder helps coordinate shipments at the port or at the final destination.

Trading Company

Functions Performed

Most trading companies are primarily involved in exporting, though some are in the import business as well. Trading companies not only match sellers with buyers of goods or services but also manage export arrangements, paperwork, transportation, and foreign government requirements.

Export Trading Company Act

In the United States, export trading companies became more important as a result of legislation enacted in 1982. The Export Trading Company Act allowed financial institutions (e.g., banks and bank holding companies) to own or participate in export trading companies.[30] That affiliation helped to minimize cash flow, terms of payment, credit, and other financial problems related to exporting. In addition, the act allowed trading companies to export a wide range of services to support global trade, as well as goods.

Trading companies, although not used extensively by U.S. firms, will continue to be an option as a result of the Export Trading Company Act.

Non-Vessel-Operating Common Carrier

NVOCC Functions

The non-vessel-operating common carrier (NVOCC), sometimes referred to as a NVO, "consolidates small shipments from different shippers into full container loads . . . and accepts responsibility for all details of the international shipment from the exporter's dock, including paperwork and transportation" (see Figure 13–4).[31]

NVOCCs differ from freight forwarders in several respects. An ocean freight forwarder usually acts as an agent of the shipper and not as a carrier. Some of its principal activities include preparing and filing export and bank documentation and negotiating freight rates on the shipper's behalf. NVOCCs, on the other hand, act as a common carrier, and freight forwarders are often their biggest customers.

---

[28]Ibid., p. 694.

[29]Gregory E. Burns, "Freight Forwarding/Logistics: Toward a New Era in Transportation," White Paper published by Gerard Klauer Mattison & Co. (1997), Exhibit 24, unnumbered.

[30]See the Export Trading Company Act of 1982, P.L. No. 97-290.

[31]Southern, *Transportation and Logistics Basics,* p. 297.

FIGURE 13–4

How NVOCCs work

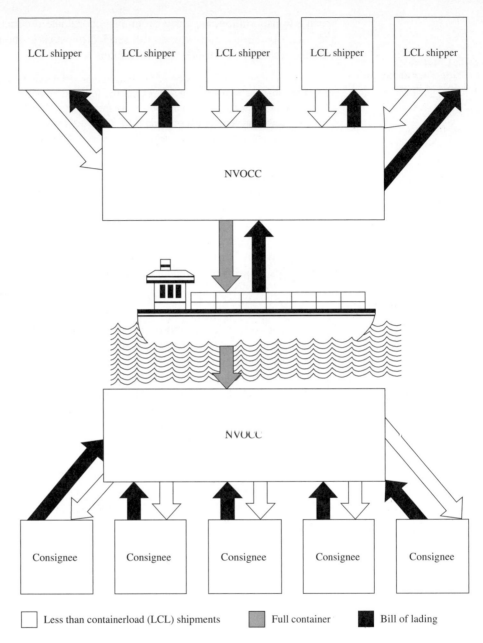

Source: Toby B. Estis, "NVOCC's: A Low-Cost Alternative for LCL Shippers," *Traffic Management* 27, no. 6 (June 1988), p. 87.

Documentation

One of the most important facets of international logistics is the paperwork that must be completed before, during, and after the shipment of a product to a foreign market. While documentation is not a glamorous part of global logistics, it is a necessary part. International documentation is much more complex than domestic documentation because each country or world region has its own specifications and requirements.

Absolute accuracy is required; errors may result in delayed shipments or monetary penalties. It is beyond the scope of this textbook to examine in detail the multitude of export documents that exist. However, some of the more widely used documents are as follows:

Widely Used Export Documents

- *Air waybill.* Issued by: Airline, consolidator. Purpose: Each airline has its own air waybill form, but the format and numbering systems have been standardized by the airline industry to allow computerization. Like the ocean bill of lading, it serves as contract of carriage between shipper and carrier.

- *Certificate of origin.* Issued by: Exporter or freight forwarder on exporter's behalf. Purpose: Required by some countries to certify origin of product components. Used for statistical research or for assessing duties, particularly under trade agreements.

- *Commercial invoice.* Issued by: Seller of goods. Purpose: Invoice against which payment is made. Required for clearing goods through customs at destination.

- *Dock receipt (D/R).* Issued by: Exporter or freight forwarder on exporter's behalf. Purpose: No standard form, but must include shipment description, physical details, and shipping information. Used by both shipper and carrier to verify shipment particulars, condition, and delivery to carrier.

- *Ocean bill of lading (B/L).* Issued by: Steamship line. Purpose: Each carrier has its own bill of lading form. Serves as contract of carriage between carrier and shipper, spelling out legal responsibilities and liability limits for all parties to the shipment. The B/L can be used to transfer title to the goods to a party named in the document. Specifies shipment details, such as number of pieces, weight, and destination.

- *Packing list.* Issued by: Exporter. Purpose: Provides detailed information of contents of each individual package in shipment. Customs authorities at destination use information during clearance and inspection procedures. Invaluable when filing claims for damage or shortage.

- *Shipper's export declaration (SED).* Issued by: Exporter or freight forwarder on exporter's behalf. Purpose: Required by law for any commodity with value over $2,500 or any shipment requiring validated export license.

- *Sight, time drafts.* Issued by: Exporter or freight forwarder on exporter's behalf. Purpose: Request for payment from foreign buyer. Instructs buyer's bank to collect payment; when collected, it (the bank) releases shipping documents to buyer. Buyer's bank then remits to seller's bank. Sight drafts are payable on receipt at buyer's bank. Time drafts extend credit; foreign bank releases documents immediately, but collects payment later.

- *Validated export license.* Issued by: U.S. Department of Commerce. Purpose: Required for commodities deemed important to national security, foreign-policy objectives, or protecting domestic supplies of strategic materials. The validated export license constitutes permission to export a specific product to a specific party.[32]

---

[32]"Ten Key Trade Documents," *Traffic Management* 29, no. 9 (September 1990), pp. 53 and 55.

Terms of Trade

The terms of trade, or terms of shipment, are important inclusions on the actual export documents. The terms of shipment are much more important in international shipping than in domestic shipping because of the uncertainties and control problems that accompany foreign traffic movements. These terms of sale determine who is responsible for the various stages of delivery, who bears what risks, and who pays for the various elements of transportation.

INCOTERMS

A summary of the most commonly used terms of shipment in exporting from the United States is shown below and in Table 13–5. Internationally, INCOTERMS are the equivalent to FOB origin or destination terms and were developed and defined by the International Chamber of Commerce.[33] An overview of INCOTERMS is presented in the appendix to this chapter.

Most Commonly Used Terms of Shipment

- *Ex Origin:* Origin should be identified as factory, plant, etc. Seller bears costs and risks until buyer is obligated to take delivery. Buyer pays for documents, must take delivery when specified, and must pay for any export taxes.
- *FOB (Free on Board) Inland Carrier:* Seller arranges for loading on railcars, trucks, etc. Seller provides a clean bill of lading and is responsible for loss or damage until goods have been placed on inland vehicle.
- *FOB Vessel U.S. Port:* The price quoted covers all expenses involved in delivery of goods upon the vessel designated at the port named. Buyer must give seller adequate notice of sailing date, name of ship, berth, etc. Buyer bears additional costs resulting from late or absent vessels.

TABLE 13–5   **Who's Responsible for Costs under Various Terms of Trade?**

Cost Items/Terms	FOB (Free on Board) Inland Carrier at Factory	FOB (Free on Board) Inland Carrier at Point of Shipment	FAS (Free Alongside) Vessel or Plane at Port of Shipment	CIF (Cost, Insurance, Freight) at Port of Destination
Export packing*	Buyer	Seller	Seller	Seller
Inland freight	Buyer	Buyer	Seller	Seller
Port charges	Buyer	Buyer	Seller	Seller
Forwarders' fee	Buyer	Buyer	Buyer	Seller
Consular fee	Buyer	Buyer	Buyer	Seller
Loading on vessel or plane	Buyer	Buyer	Buyer	Buyer[†]
Ocean freight	Buyer	Buyer	Buyer	Seller
Cargo insurance	Buyer	Buyer	Buyer	Seller
Customs duties	Buyer	Buyer	Buyer	Seller
Ownership of goods passes	When goods are on board an inland carrier (truck, rail, etc.) or in hands of inland carrier	When goods are alongside carrier or in hands of air or ocean carrier	When goods are on board air or ocean carrier at port of shipment	When goods are on board air or ocean carrier at port of shipment

*Who absorbs export packing? This charge should be clearly agreed upon. Charges are sometimes controversial.

†The seller has responsibility to arrange for consular invoices (and other documents requested by buyer's government). According to official definition, buyer pays fees, but sometimes as a matter of practice, seller includes in quotations.

Source: Philip R. Cateora, *International Marketing*, 9th ed. (Burr Ridge, IL: Richard D. Irwin, 1996), p. 367.

---

[33]For a discussion of the basics of international trade law and terms, see James Giermanski, "Can You Talk International Trade?" *Transportation and Distribution* 35, no. 7 (July 1994), pp. 34–36.

- *FAS (Free Alongside) Vessel U.S. Port:* Similar to FOB vessel, but certain additional port charges for the seller, such as heavy lift, may apply. The buyer is responsible for loss or damage while goods are on a lighter (small barge) or within reach of the loading device. Loading costs are also the responsibility of the buyer.

- *FOB Vessel Foreign Port:* The price quoted includes all transportation costs to the point where goods are off-loaded in the destination country. Seller is responsible for insurance to this point. The buyer assumes risk as soon as the vessel is at the foreign port.

- *FOB Inland Destination:* The price quoted includes all costs involved in getting the goods to the named inland point in the country of importation.

- *C&F (Cost and Freight):* The price quoted includes all transportation to the point of destination. Seller also pays export taxes and similar fees. The buyer pays the cost of certificates of origin, consular invoices, or other documents required for importation to the buyer's country. The seller must provide these, but at the buyer's expense. The buyer is responsible for all insurance from the point of vessel loading.

- *CIF (Cost, Insurance, and Freight):* The price quoted under these terms includes the cost of goods, transportation, and marine insurance. The seller pays all taxes or fees, as well as marine and war risk insurance. Buyer pays for any certificates or consular documents required for importation. Although seller pays for insurance, buyer assumes all risk after seller has delivered the goods to the carrier.[34]

Free Trade Zones

Free trade zones (FTZs), sometimes referred to as foreign trade zones, are areas where companies may ship products to postpone or reduce customs duties or taxes. There are more than 225 FTZs in the United States, serving over 3,500 firms and involving more than $160 billion of products.[35] Products remaining in the FTZ are not subject to duties or taxes until they are shipped out of the zone into the country of destination. Within the FTZ, organizations often process, assemble, sort, and repackage products before reshipment.

When products are imported into the United States to be combined with American-made goods and subsequently re-exported, the importer or exporter can avoid payment of U.S. import duties on the foreign portion and eliminate the need for a duty drawback, which, as we explained earlier in the chapter, is a request for a refund from the government of the duties paid on imports that are later re-exported.

Most FTZs Are Underutilized

While there are potentially many benefits in using a FTZ, most FTZs are underutilized, with space going to waste. The facilities, the services offered, and the quality of FTZ management vary significantly. Managers wishing to use an FTZ will have to explore each zone individually in order to determine its potential usefulness.[36]

---

[34]Thomas A. Foster, "Anatomy of an Export," *Distribution* 79, no. 10 (October 1980), pp. 76–77. For a definition of these and other import/export terms, see "Export/Import Terms You Need to Know," *Traffic Management* 19, no. 9 (September 1990), pp. 37–41.

[35]"Is an FTZ Right for You?" *WERCSheet* 22, no. 5 (May 1999), p. 5.

[36]For an examination of the role of FTZs in global marketing strategies, see Tom Andel, "Site Here and Zone Out," *Transportation and Distribution* 37, no. 8 (August 1996), pp. 52–54; and William Armbruster, "The Competitive Edge," *Journal of Commerce and Commercial* 409, no. 28806 (September 11, 1996), pp. 1C–2C. For other information about FTZs, see the website of the National Association of Foreign Trade Zones <http://www.imex.com/naftz/html>.

Creative Solutions

Polaroid's Approach to Global Logistics

Polaroid is a global company with annual sales of $2 billion (2000), of which one-half is from non-U.S. markets. The company is a world leader in instant and digital imaging products, including cameras, film, and digital peripherals.

The company implemented a three-year program beginning in 1997 to improve customer service, inventory turns, and operating efficiencies relative to more than 20 countries located around the world. The specific objectives were as follows:

- Achieve a 95 percent delivered fill rate for customers.
- Achieve a 50 percent reduction in items on back order for more than 10 days.
- Increase inventory turns from 2× to 4× by 1999.
- Improve operating efficiencies to 10 percent in 1997, 8 percent in 1998, and 6 percent in 1999.

The first step taken by Polaroid was to focus more specifically on coordinating and integrating the global operations of the company in transportation, production planning, inventory management, and so on. Second, the company developed logistics programs tailored to its specific product and customer groups. Third, the warehouse and distribution networks were evaluated to ensure that processes would be optimally managed. Fourth, processes were reengineered to be more demand-driven, faster, and more flexible.

Results of Polaroid's efforts have been improvements in order fill rates from 89 percent to 91 percent. Line fill rates have improved by 9 percent, to 94 percent. Additionally, $13 million has been saved in freight and warehousing costs.

Source: "Polaroid's Three-Step Approach to Successful Global Logistics," IOMA's Report on Managing Logistics, Issue 99-09 (September 1999), pp. 4–5; and the Polaroid website <http://www.polaroid.com/index.html>.

Summary

More and more companies are expanding their operations into global markets. As organizations serve customers in various countries, they must establish logistics systems to provide the products and services those customers demand. While the components of a global supply chain system may be the same as in a domestic system, the management and administration of the international network can be vastly different.

To be global, a company must be able to coordinate a complex set of activities—marketing, production, financing, procurement—so that least total cost logistics is realized. This will allow the organization to achieve maximum market impact and competitive advantage in its international target markets.

In this chapter we examined some of the reasons organizations expand into global markets. Companies can enter foreign markets through exporting, licensing, joint ventures, direct ownership, importing, or countertrade and duty drawbacks. As part of the exporting process, we discussed the specific roles of the export distributor, customshouse broker, international freight forwarder, trading company, and NVOCC. In addition, we looked at the importance of documentation and the use of free trade zones.

The international logistics manager must administer the various logistics components in a marketplace characterized by a number of uncontrollable elements—political and legal, economic, competitive, technological, geographical, and social and cultural. Each of these uncontrollable environments was briefly discussed.

With this chapter as background, we are now ready to examine how to manage logistics activities in the global marketplace.

Suggested Readings

Babbar, Sunil, and Sameer Prasad. "International Purchasing, Inventory Management and Logistics Research: An Assessment and Agenda." *International Journal of Physical Distribution and Logistics Management* 28, no. 6 (1998), pp. 403–33.

Bowman, Robert J. "Calling All Partners." *Global Logistics & Supply Chain Strategies* 4, no. 6 (July 2000), pp. 10–20.

Fawcett, Stanley F., and Laura M. Birou. "Exploring the Logistics Interface Between Global and JIT Sourcing." *International Journal of Physical Distribution and Logistics Management* 22, no. 1 (1992), pp. 3–14.

Gillis, Chris. "NVOs Take on Automation." *American Shipper* 42, no. 8 (August 2000), pp. 15–20.

Gilmore, James H. "Designing a Distribution Strategy for Canada." CCA White Paper published by Cleveland Consulting Associates, undated, 12 pages.

Luk, Sherriff T. K. "Structural Changes in China's Distribution System." *International Journal of Physical Distribution and Logistics Management* 28, no. 1 (1998), pp. 44–67.

MacDonald, Mitchell E. "Who Does What in International Shipping." *Traffic Management* 30, no. 9 (September 1991), pp. 38–40.

Murphy, Paul R., and James M. Daley. "EDI Benefits and Barriers: Comparing International Freight Forwarders and Their Customers." *International Journal of Physical Distribution and Logistics Management* 29, no. 3 (1999), pp. 207–16.

Pearson, John N., and Jake Semeijn. "Service Priorities in Small and Large Firms Engaged in International Logistics." *International Journal of Physical Distribution and Logistics Management* 29, no. 3 (1999), pp. 181–91.

Razzaque, Mohammed Abdur. "Challenges to Logistics Development: The Case of a Third World Country—Bangladesh." *International Journal of Physical Distribution and Logistics Management* 27, no. 1 (1997), pp. 18–38.

Sawyer, Richard. "Lost at Sea?" *Operations & Fulfillment* 8, no. 4 (July/August 2000), pp. 12–22.

Stapleton, Drew M., and Virginie Saulnier. "Defining Dyadic Cost and Risk in International Trade: A Review of INCOTERMS 2000 with Strategic Implications." *Journal of Transportation Management* 11, no. 2 (Fall 1999), pp. 25–43.

Ülengin, Füsun, and Nimet Uray. "Current Perspectives in Logistics: Turkey as a Case Study." *International Journal of Physical Distribution and Logistics Management* 29, no. 1 (1999), pp. 22–49.

U.S. Department of Commerce. *A Basic Guide to Exporting.* Washington, D.C.: U.S. Government Printing Office, September 1986.

Zahn, Sherrie E. "Choosing a Market Entry Strategy." *World Trade* 12, no. 5 (May 1999), pp. 40–46.

———. "Top Markets for Trade & Expansion." *World Trade* 12, no. 6 (June 1999), pp. 38–48.

———. "The World Trade Top 100." *World Trade* 12, no. 11 (November 1999), pp. 46–60.

Zinn, Walter, and Robert E. Groose. "Barriers to Globalization: Is Global Distribution Possible?" *The International Journal of Logistics Management* 1, no. 1 (1990), pp. 13–18.

Questions and Problems

1. An increasing number of organizations are becoming involved in international marketing and logistics. Discuss the factors that would influence them to enter international markets.

2. Organizations that choose to enter into the global marketplace have several strategies available to them: (*a*) exporting, (*b*) licensing, (*c*) joint ventures, (*d*) direct ownership, (*e*) importing, and (*f*) countertrade. Briefly discuss each strategy, including advantages and disadvantages of each option.

3. Explain the role each of the following exporting organizations has in global logistics: (*a*) export distributor, (*b*) customshouse broker; (*c*) international freight forwarder, (*d*) trading company, and (*e*) NVOCC.

4. Considering the various uncontrollable environments that affect organizations, identify how each of the following might generally affect international logistics activities: (*a*) economic, (*b*) competition, (*c*) technology, (*d*) geography, (*e*) social and cultural, and (*f*) political and legal.

5. Identify and describe some of the more common terms of shipment or terms of trade used in international logistics.

6. Discuss how organizations can use free trade zones as part of a global logistics network.

7. Briefly define and describe the logistics aspects of countertrade and duty drawbacks.

APPENDIX

THE BASICS: WHAT YOU NEED TO KNOW ABOUT INCOTERMS

Definition

INCOTERMS (for *In*ternational *Co*mmercial *Terms*) are internationally standardized "trade terms" that describe the dyadic obligations of both buyers and sellers in international sales transactions. Moreover, INCOTERMS is a set of 13 terms that clearly allocate the costs, risks, customs and insurance responsibilities of internationally transporting goods between the buyer and the seller. Consequently, it is important to stress that INCOTERMS deal only with the relation between sellers and buyers under a contract of sale; they do not relate directly to the contract of carriage.

Origin

INCOTERMS were first developed in 1936 by the Paris-based International Chamber of Commerce (ICC) as a set of international rules for the interpretation of trade terms. These rules, known as "INCOTERMS 1936," have been subsequently revised. Amendments and additions were later made in 1953, 1967, 1976, 1980, 1990, and presently in 2000 in order to bring the rules in line with current international trade practices.

Use of INCOTERMS

It should be stressed that, when the parties intend to incorporate INCOTERMS into their contract of sale, they should always make an expressed reference to the current version of INCOTERMS. Buyers and sellers willing to use INCOTERMS 2000 should therefore clearly specify that their contract is governed by "INCOTERMS 2000." Further, the correct use of INCOTERMS implies that a named port of destination or named place of destination has to be stipulated to be valid, followed by the INCOTERMS' version governing their use (e.g., EXW La Crosse, WI— INCOTERMS 2000; FAS Norfolk, VA—INCOTERMS 2000).

Four Groups

The terms have been put together in four different groups: E, F, C, and D.

Group E.   Group E stands for "Ex" (from), starts with the minimum responsibility for the seller, and maximum responsibility for the buyer. In this group, the seller is only responsible for making the goods available to the buyer at the agreed place, usually at the seller's premises.

Group F.   Group F continues with "free" of responsibility during the main carriage from the seller's point of view. Thus, the seller is called upon to deliver the goods to a carrier appointed by the buyer. In others words, he is not responsible for the main carriage, but only some pre-shipment charges.

Group C.   Group C stands for "cost" or "carriage" and means that the seller is responsible for contracting and paying for the main carriage, but without assuming the risk of loss, or of damage to the goods, or additional costs due to events occurring after shipment and dispatch.

Group D.   Finally, group D means "delivery" and rallies five "arrival" INCOTERMS where the seller is responsible for the payment and delivery of the goods to the country of destination. The seller has to bear all the costs and risks needed to bring the goods to the country of destination.

Two Categories

Further, INCOTERMS can be classified into two categories from a delivery perspective:

"Departure contracts" are where the seller is responsible for delivering at a named place in the country of export, or departure country. Thus the seller assumes all costs and risks before crossing a border. Departure contracts involve groups E, F, and C. Note that the C terms are frequently misinterpreted as "arrival contracts"; however it must be stressed that under C terms, as under the F terms, the seller fulfils the contract in the country of shipment. Thus, the contracts of sale under the terms C falls within the category of "departure contracts."

"Arrival contracts" under which the seller bears all costs and risks involved in bringing the goods to an overseas point of delivery. In other words, the seller is responsible for the arrival of the goods at the agreed place or point of destination at the border (DAF) or within the country of destination. Hence, the seller assumes most, if not all, of the transportation responsibilities. Arrival contracts only concern D terms.

Furthermore, carriers and freight forwarders may interpret INCOTERMS according to the following alternative:

"Freight Prepaid" is where the seller pays the main carriage charges before the departure. Therefore, the seller is responsible for the costs of the main carriage. It rallies groups C and D.

"Freight Collect" is where the main carriage charges are collected, or payable, at destination; thus the buyer is paying for them. Groups E and F are involved.

INCOTERMS 2000

In response to developing technology and increasing worldwide use of terms, INCOTERMS have been revised for the 21st century. The revisions were made by the Working Party on Trade Terms (WPTT), a group of 40 trade experts from around the world. The WPTT is a subgroup of the Committee on International Practice, which is part of the Paris-based International Chamber of Commerce.

After two years of revision of its sales terms for the new millennium, the ICC is now publishing its new edition: INCOTERMS 2000, since September 1999. INCOTERMS 2000 are in effect with contracts beginning on January 1, and should only be quoted on contracts effective from January 2000.

Standard Obligations of Each Party. As outlined in their definition, INCOTERMS rely on a contract of sale, and do not relate directly to a contract of carriage; therefore, the primary obligations of any party to a contract of international sales should be stressed.

Seller's Standard Obligations.
1. *Packaging & marking.* The seller is obliged to pack the goods in such a manner as is required for the transport, but only to the extent that the circumstances relating to the transport are made known to the seller at the time the contract of sale is concluded. In addition, marking is to be made appropriately (especially when dealing with dangerous goods).
2. *Checking.* The seller supports the costs of any required checking operations, such as checking quality, measuring, weighing, and counting, which are necessary for the purpose of placing the goods at the buyer's disposal.

3. *Goods in conformity with the contract.* The goods provided by the seller must be in conformity with the contract of sale. Moreover, the seller has to enclose the commercial invoice and any other evidence of conformity as required by the contract.

4. *Notice to the buyer.* The seller must inform the buyer when and where the goods will be placed at his disposal.

Buyer's Standard Obligations.

1. *Payment of the price.* The payer must pay the price as provided in the contract of sale.

2. *Take delivery.* The buyer has to take delivery of the goods when they have been placed at his disposal in accordance with the INCOTERM.

Source: Drew Stapleton and Virginia Saulnier. Third Annual International Business and Economics Conference Proceedings, De Pere, WI, USA (2000).

Global Logistics Strategies

Chapter Outline

Chapter Objectives

- To identify some of the controllable factors that affect global logistics activities.
- To identify the organizational, financial, and managerial issues that relate to global logistics.
- To examine logistics aspects within major global markets such as North America, the Pacific Rim, Western Europe, and Eastern Europe.
- To discuss and provide examples of maquiladora operations.

Introduction

One of the most important phenomena of the 20th century was the expansion of business organizations into every region of the world. For example:

- Nearly 37 percent of all ocean cargo entering Europe passes through the port of Rotterdam. This represents 5 million containers and a total cargo volume of 310 million tons.[1]
- U.S. exports to Africa are now 45 percent greater than U.S. exports to all countries of the former Soviet Union combined.[2]
- As a result of the North American Free Trade Agreement (NAFTA), U.S. and Canadian carriers are permitted to provide cross-border truck services to and from Mexico, while Mexican carriers can obtain authority to provide the same services to and from the United States or Canada.[3]

Today, many companies have a significant and growing presence in markets located outside their country of origin. For example, 35 of the largest U.S. retailers are entering a new market every year and, on average, are growing 40 percent faster than single-country retailers.[4] Other examples of global expansion include the following:

Examples of Global Expansion

- Weber-Stephens, a leading manufacturer of quality barbecue grills and accessories, exports more than 15,000 grills to Australia and New Zealand from its distribution center in the United States.[5]
- Circle International, a third-party logistics service provider, opened a 200,000-square-foot distribution center at its Asian headquarters in Singapore. In 2001, DHL Worldwide Express and UPS Worldwide Logistics will also open new distribution facilities of 100,000 and 285,000 square feet, respectively.[6]
- Adobe Systems, Inc., a worldwide provider of publishing and imaging software technologies, has created a partnership with Sykes, a major fulfillment service provider, to manage its 3,000 SKUs in Europe.[7]
- Donaldson Company, a manufacturer of air and liquid filters for vehicle exhaust and emission control, in-plant air-cleaning systems, and specialized filters for computer disk drives, aircraft cabins, and semiconductor processing, sells 40 percent of its products outside the United States, with a large amount of sales in Canada.[8]

---

[1]Thomas A. Foster, "Into the Heart of Europe," *Logistics Management and Distribution Report* 38, no. 7 (July 1999), p. E-7.

[2]Lara Sowinski, "Shipping to Africa Is About More Than Transport," *World Trade* 12, no. 8 (August 1999), p. 56.

[3]David G. Waller, Robert L. D'Avanzo, and Douglas M. Lambert, *Supply Chain Directions for a New North America* (Oak Brook, IL: Council of Logistics Management, 1995), p. 3.

[4]"Bridging Technology & Logistics," *Special Grocery Manufacturers of America Report,* Information Systems and Logistics Distribution Conference (1998), p. 4.

[5]"Weber-Stephens, the World Famous Barbecue Manufacturer, Partners with ANZDL to Ensure Its Third Largest Market Sizzles," *Global Logistics & Supply Chain Strategies* 3, no. 6 (July 1999), p. 63.

[6]Patrick Burnson, "Asia's Economic Rebound Signals Change in Logistics Strategies," *Logistics Management and Distribution Report* 38, no. 9 (September 1999), p. 98.

[7]Hans Kühn, "Making Supply-Chain Planning Work in an Outsourced Environment," *PRTM's Insight* 11, no. 2 (Summer 1999), p. 48.

[8]Toby B. Gooley, "Logistics Boosts Donaldson's Northern Exposure," *Logistics Management and Distribution Report* 37, no. 5 (May 1998), pp. 56–60.

- Jabil Circuit, Inc., designer and manufacturer of electronic circuit boards and systems for original equipment manufacturers (OEMs), has annual revenues of $2 billion. With manufacturing plants in the United States, Scotland, Brazil, China, Hungary, Malaysia, Mexico, and Italy, the company generates approximately 30 percent of its revenues outside North America.[9]

In this chapter we will discuss some of the similarities and differences in the management of logistics in domestic and international environments. We will see how to address and develop meaningful logistics strategies and programs in the global marketplace.

Global Logistics Issues

Key Issues in Global Logistics

Management of a global supply chain is much more complex than that of a purely domestic network. Managers must properly analyze the international environment, plan the foreign logistics system, and develop the correct control procedures to monitor its success or failure. Figure 14–1 identifies some of the questions the international logistics manager must ask—and answer—about the organization's global logistics activities. The questions can be classified into five categories: (1) environmental analysis, (2) planning, (3) structure, (4) plan implementation, and (5) controlling the logistics program.[10]

Global Logistics Management Process

The overall objective of the process diagrammed in Figure 14–1 is to develop the optimal logistics system for each international target market. It involves examining the various characteristics of each market and developing a set of alternatives or strategies that will fulfill the organization's objectives. Given a set of objectives or strategies, management defines the proper organizational and supply chain structures. Once these are established, management implements an optimal logistics network or system. The final step is to measure and evaluate the performance of the system, and provide feedback to the strategic planning process for purposes of adjustment or modification of the system.

As is true in domestic logistics management, an integral part of the global logistics management process is cost/service trade-off analysis. Being able to properly identify, evaluate, and implement the optimal cost/service mix is always important to the organization and its customers, whether operations are domestic or international. The only major difference between the two is in the emphasis placed on each cost and service element.

Some particularly important cost and service considerations relate to response times, order completeness, shipping accuracy, and shipment condition.[11] Compared to domestic markets, sales and costs are less sensitive to the longer *response times* internationally because customers expect longer and less reliable order cycle times. However, this is changing as new technologies enable organizations and third parties to develop and expand their global logistics capabilities.

---

[9]<http://www.jabil.com>.

[10]Warren S. Keegan, *Global Marketing Management,* 5th ed. (Englewood Cliffs, NJ: Prentice Hall, 1995), p. 37.

[11]Paul S. Bender, "International Logistics," in *The Distribution Management Handbook,* ed. James A. Tompkins and Dale Harmelink, (New York: McGraw-Hill, 1994), p. 8.7. Also see Lara Sowinski, "Letters of Credit: Technology Puts a New Spin on an Old Document," *World Trade* 12, no. 11 (November 1999), pp. 80–84.

FIGURE 14–1

The global logistics management process

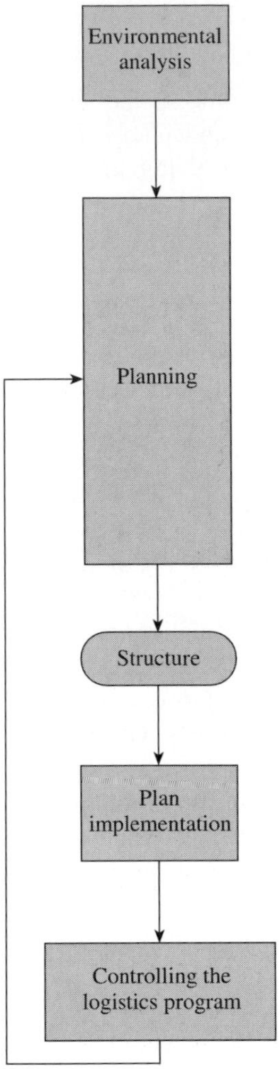

Key Questions for Analysis, Planning, and Control

Environmental analysis

1. What are the unique characteristics of each national market? What characteristics does each market have in common with other national markets?

2. Should the firm cluster national markets for logistics operating and/or planning purposes?

Planning

3. Who should make logistics decisions?

4. What are our major assumptions about target markets? Are they valid?

5. What are the customer service needs of the target markets?

6. What are the characteristics of the logistics systems available to our firm in each target market?

7. What are our firm's major strengths and weaknesses relative to existing and potential competition in each target market?

8. What are our objectives, given the logistics alternatives open to us and our assessment of opportunity, risk, and company capability?

9. What is the balance of payments and currency situation in target markets? What will be their impact(s) on our firm's physical distribution system?

Structure

10. How do we structure our logistics organization to optimally achieve our objectives, given our skills and resources? What is the responsibility of each organizational level?

Plan implementation

11. Given our objectives, structure, and our assessment of the market environment, how do we develop effective operational logistics plans? Specifically, what transportation, inventory, packaging, warehousing, and customer service strategies do we have for each target market?

Controlling the logistics program

12. How do we measure and monitor plan performance? What steps should be taken to bring actual and desired results together?

Source: Adapted from Warren J. Keegan, *Global Marketing Management,* 5th ed., p. 37. Copyright 1996. Reprinted by permission of Prentice Hall, Inc., Upper Saddle River, NJ.

Response Times

There are a number of reasons for longer and less consistent response times in global logistics:

- The distances involved are much longer.
- A substantial fraction of international freight moves by ocean, at a slower speed and with less consistency than land (or air) transportation.
- Additional documentation and arrangements that are usually required, such as letters of credit and consular invoices, may take considerable time to complete.[12]

---

[12]Paul S. Bender, "The International Dimension of Physical Distribution Management," in *The Distribution Handbook,* ed. James F. Robeson and Robert G. House (New York: Free Press, 1985), p. 784.

Order Completeness

Order completeness is much more important in global logistics than in domestic logistics, in part due to the substantially higher costs of back orders and expedited shipments. Processing and shipping costs must be weighed against the cost of improving order completeness. It is more expensive to ship complete orders all the time, but this higher service level may be justified in view of the costs associated with shipping

Shipping Accuracy

incomplete or partial orders. A similar logic can be used in the case of *shipping accuracy*. Because of the higher costs associated with shipping errors in international distribution, it is important to maximize the accuracy of both shipment routing and the

Shipment Condition

items that make up a shipment. Once the shipment is made, *shipment condition* is an important issue. Packages must be protected well in order to reduce the possibility of damage in transit and handling. The time and cost needed to replace damaged items can be significant.

Guidelines in Developing a Global Logistics Strategy

In developing a global logistics strategy, some general management and logistics-specific guidelines apply. With respect to overall management strategies, the following guidelines are relevant:

1. Recognize problems. Logistics problems can relate to maintaining control of global supply chains, obtaining and processing information from suppliers, and responding to various governmental regulatory bodies.

2. Analyze options arising from new situations or opportunities. Logistics-related examples of options include expiration-dated inventory, changes in transportation modes or carriers, consignment, and redirection and reconsolidation of product shipments.

3. Prepare for rapid execution of plans, programs, and strategies, such as those relating to new cross-border constraints or opportunities; electronic information flows; and language, regulatory, and currency variations between markets.[13]

The following list of logistics-specific guidelines is useful to organizations involved in global logistics:

Guidelines for Developing a Global Logistics Strategy

1. *Logistics planning should be integrated into the company's strategic planning process.* For example, DuPont, the $40 billion chemical giant, has recently implemented "total supply chain management" programs throughout its 30 major businesses operating in about 100 countries. The programs' purpose is to focus more on markets and customers, including just-in-time delivery of chemicals and inputs to their product processes. To achieve these objectives, logistics personnel have been added to each business unit to assist in planning activities ranging from site location to customer delivery.

2. *Logistics departments need to be guided by a clear vision and must measure output regularly.* Baxter Healthcare Corporation, an $8 billion global company, accomplished this through its unique arrangement with Trammel Crow, a real estate management firm. In the late 1980s, Baxter set out to rationalize its logistics operations. Its goal was to increase the total space

---

[13]Perry Ziff, "Global Commerce Management: Executing a World of Opportunity," *Global Logistics and Supply Chain Strategies* 3, no. 4 (May 1999), p. 72.

available to handle materials and products from 6.5 million square feet to 9 million square feet. Moreover, Baxter wanted to decrease the number of cities in which it had a facility from 50 to 40, and reduce the total number of facilities from 91 to 49. Baxter entered into a seven-year contract aimed at producing $15 million in savings. All relevant logistics cost and service parameters were measured. The system tracks labor-hour savings, land-cost savings, rental savings, revenue, and tax incentives. A formal steering committee comprised of members from both organizations meets quarterly to monitor performance and suggest improvements.

3. *Import/export management should try to ensure integrated management of all elements of the logistics supply chain, from origin to destination.* This is especially important given that major structural and regulatory changes are under way across the globe. Deregulation in transport, both in the United States and increasingly in Europe, Mexico, Japan, and other areas, permits negotiation of creative "door-to-door" service and price packages with carriers. This allows shippers to design and manage their supply channels so that delivery can be tailored to customer specifications at a reasonable cost.

4. *Opportunities to integrate domestic and international operations should be pursued to leverage total company volumes with globally oriented carriers.* This usually requires change in organizational thinking, but major opportunities exist for companies that can move in this direction. A good starting point is to make a list comparing domestic and international logistics activities.[14]

Managers who approach the global logistics process using the above guidelines, along with good judgment and a determination to succeed, are much more likely to do well than those who don't. While the global marketplace may be undergoing rapid change, it is certainly manageable and offers exciting opportunities and challenges to organizations seeking global markets.

Organizing for Global Logistics

Proper organization and administration of the logistics function is just as important internationally as it is domestically. When a logistics organization operates globally, the best type of organization is usually one in which the planning and control functions are centralized and the operations functions are decentralized. In terms of structure, there is typically a middle- or senior-management executive in charge of global logistics. The key ingredient to success is whether all important international logistics elements are grouped together under a single executive.

As companies enter the international marketplace, initially through exporting or licensing, it is likely that domestic operations will hold the balance of power in the organization. Obviously, that is proper only in the early stages of development. As international operations grow in sales and profits, and thus in importance, the global component of the organization must be given more input into corporate decision making.

Should You Centralize or Decentralize Logistics Globally?

Many companies operating in the global marketplace centralize a large number of logistics activities, while decentralizing others. For example, control and management

---

[14]William W. Goldsborough and David L. Anderson, "Import/Export Management," in *The Logistics Handbook,* ed. James F. Robeson and William C. Copacino (New York: Free Press, 1994), pp. 675–76.

Global

"Localized" Global Distribution

Hoffman–La Roche, the Swiss multinational, has steered a middle course between centralized and decentralized control of logistics for its vitamins and fine-chemicals unit.

The company has given responsibility for distribution and inventories of finished products to the area managers who are responsible for marketing. At the same time, the company has kept carrier selection, rate negotiation, raw-materials supply and intracompany shipments at the Basel headquarters.

Hoffman–La Roche says the "localized" global distribution system is a way to stay close to the customer without surrendering the economies of central control.

Hoffman–La Roche transferred distribution and inventory control to area managers during the second half of 1996.

The company has separate business units (or product divisions) and operates globally, with production facilities in both Europe and in the United States.

The vitamins and fine-chemicals business unit has three regional areas—Europe (which at Hoffman–La Roche also includes Africa and the Near East); the Americas; and the Far East (which includes Australasia).

Before the recent change, managers of these areas already were responsible for marketing.

The head office controlled worldwide logistics and transportation of finished goods from production sites to a "global distribution center" at Venlo, Netherlands; from the global center to "area distribution centers" within each of the three world areas; and from each area center to the area's customers.

In Europe, distribution from the area distribution center to customers is usually by truck and takes only one day at the vitamins and fine-chemicals division. But in Asia, where ocean transportation is used, area distribution can take up to two weeks.

Source: Philip Damas, " 'Localized' Global Distribution," *American Shipper* 39, no. 2 (February 1997), pp. 36 and 38. Reprinted by permission of *American Shipper*.

of customer service tend to work best when it is localized in the foreign market. On the other hand, material flows into the organization are often centralized, primarily because technology is able to overcome distances. Additionally, most information systems tend to be centralized, which allows for integrated logistics decision making across international boundaries.[15]

There are a number of factors that are affecting global logistics strategies and organizational structures:

Factors Affecting Global Logistics Strategies

- Rapid product introduction—bringing new products to market in record time across numerous regions.

- Focused market needs—customized design, packaging, and service offerings to meet varying consumer requirements.

- Quick-response delivery—distributing sufficient product quantities to meet consumer demand as it occurs.

- Expanded services—linking innovative, value-added services (like product kitting or 24–hour customer hot lines) to product offerings.

---

[15]Alan Braithwaite, "Integrating the Global Pipeline: Logistics Systems Architectures," unpublished paper, undated, 19 pages; also see Jonathan Reynolds, "Retailing in Computer-Mediated Environments: Electronic Commerce Across Europe," *International Journal of Retail and Distribution Management* 25, no. 1 (1997), pp. 29–37.

- Innovative channels—using minimal-echelon, direct delivery systems to reach customers rapidly at lower cost.[16]

When these strategies are viewed together, it is both obvious and imperative that logistics organizations be flexible and responsive in order to meet these changing conditions.

Financial Aspects of Global Logistics

An organization involved in global logistics faces a financial environment quite different from that of a strictly domestic one. Whether the organization is involved in importing, exporting, licensing, joint ventures, or direct ownership, there are concerns over currency exchange rates, costs of capital, effects of inflation on logistics decisions and operations, tax structures, and other financial aspects of performing logistics activities in international markets.[17]

Working Capital Considerations

Global logistics activities require financing for working capital, inventory, credit, investment in buildings and equipment, and accommodation of merchandise adjustments that may be necessary. *Working capital* considerations are very important to the international firm owing to time lags caused by distance, border crossing delays, and government regulations that can restrict the smooth movement of goods between and within countries. In general, international operations require larger amounts of working capital than domestic operations.

Inventories

Inventories are an important aspect of global logistics. Higher levels of inventory are often required to service international markets due to greater variability in transit times, port delays, customs delays, and other factors.[18]

Additionally, inventories can have a substantial impact on the global organization due to the rapid inflation that exists in some countries. In inflationary economies, it is very important to use the proper inventory accounting procedure because of its impact on profits. The last-in, first-out (LIFO) method is probably the most appropriate strategy because the cost of sales is valued closer to the current cost of replacements. Conversely, the first-in, first-out (FIFO) method gives a larger profit figure than LIFO because old costs are matched with current revenues.

Managers of an international firm must weigh the cost trade-offs involved in the buildup of inventories, in anticipation of higher costs due to inflation or other factors. The trade-off is between the accumulation of excess inventory and its associated inventory carrying costs, and the reduction of carrying costs by holding less inventory, which would require paying higher acquisition costs at a later date.

Investment in Facilities and Logistics Networks

When management considers direct *investment in facilities and logistics networks,* the capital budgeting aspects of international financial planning become important. One aspect of the capital budgeting process that deserves particular mention is the effect of currency exchange fluctuations on logistics operations.

As is also the case in domestic operations, customers in the international sector do not pay for products until after they are delivered. Many factors can cause the international shipment to take longer to be delivered than a comparable domestic shipment. Exporters must be concerned with exchange rate fluctuations that may occur between

---

[16]David L. Anderson and Dennis Colard, "The International Logistics Environment," in *The Logistics Handbook,* ed. James F. Robeson and William C. Copacino (New York: Free Press, 1994), p. 647.

[17]See Sherrie E. Zahn, "Tips from International Bankers," *World Trade* 12, no. 10 (October 1999), pp. 72–74.

[18]Goldsborough and Anderson, "Import/Export Management," p. 677.

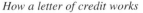

FIGURE 14–2

How a letter of credit works

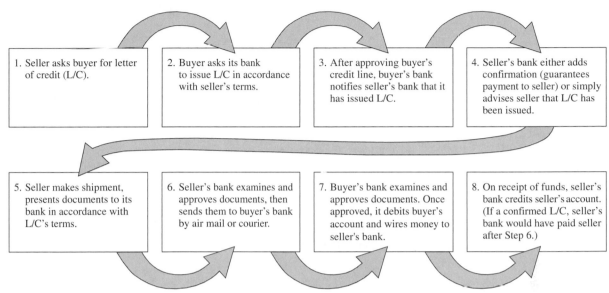

Source: Adapted from James Aaron Cooke, "What You Should Know about Letters of Credit," *Traffic Management* 29, no. 9 (September 1990), pp. 44–45.

the time when the product is shipped, delivered to the consignee, and finally paid for by the customer. Unless steps are taken to protect expected profits, a decline in exchange rate may reduce them or, even worse, result in financial losses.[19]

Letters of Credit

To ensure that international customers pay for products shipped to them, *letters of credit* are often issued. A letter of credit is a document issued by a bank on behalf of a buyer that authorizes payment for merchandise received. Payments are made to the seller by the bank rather than by the buyer. Figure 14–2 shows how a letter of credit works. One writer has cautioned: "Although it might appear to be more the concern of the corporate financial department, it is crucial that logistics managers involved in international trade understand how letters of credit work. If they misinterpret information or fail to diligently follow the shipping instructions contained in the document, it could jeopardize the company's chances of receiving payment for the goods shipped."[20]

Insured Transactions

In recent times, some sellers have used *insured transactions* to make certain that payments are received. This form of payment guarantee is increasing in popularity and has the advantage of lower overhead costs than a comparable letter of credit.

---

[19]See Patrick F. Rossi, "When the Money Comes, What Will It Be Worth?" *World Trade* 12, no. 5 (May 1999), pp. 82–87.

[20]James Aaron Cooke, "What You Should Know about Letters of Credit," *Traffic Management* 29, no. 9 (September 1990), pp. 44–45. Also see Chris Gillis, "Automated Letters of Credit," *American Shipper* 38, no. 2 (February 1996), p. 52; Gordon Platt, "Benchmark Study Finds Letters of Credit Amassed More Than $1 Billion Last Year," *Journal of Commerce and Commercial* 410, no. 28840 (October 30, 1996), p. 9C; and Ira Weissman, "Letters of Credit—Doing Business in a Global Market," *The CPA Journal* 66, no. 1 (January 1996), pp. 46–49.

The Global Marketplace—Controllable Elements

When an organization becomes involved in global operations, the scope of the logistics executive's responsibilities often expands to include international distribution activities. Almost 80 percent of all logistics executives have direct responsibility for their organization's global distribution operations.[21]

Global Logistics Costs Are Often Higher

Management of an organization involved in global marketing must try to administer the logistics components to minimize cost and provide an acceptable level of service to its customers. However, an organization's cost/service mix will vary in international markets. For example, logistics costs as a percentage of sales are higher in Japan and the United States than in Europe, Australia, or the United Kingdom.[22] Managers involved in international logistics—especially in those firms that own foreign subsidiaries—should be aware of the variety of differences between the administration of domestic and foreign logistics activities.

When all factors are considered, global logistics is generally more expensive than domestic distribution. Increased shipping distances, documentation costs, larger inventory levels, longer order cycle times, and other factors combine to increase the expenses associated with international logistics.

Customer Service

Customer Service Consistency Is Harder to Achieve Globally

In most instances, organizations cannot provide the same consistency of service internationally that they are able to provide domestically. For example, because international transportation movements tend to be longer and usually cross multiple international boundaries, require several different transportation carriers, and involve multiple transfers and product handling, time-in-transit often varies significantly from one shipment to the next. As a result, organizations require larger amounts of inventory to meet safety and cycle stock requirements.

In some instances, customer service levels must be higher in global markets, as in the case of Japan, where the order cycle time is shorter on average than in the United States. Due to geographical differences between the two countries, the physical facilities of many wholesalers and retailers, and financial considerations, the majority of all consumer goods orders in Japan can be delivered in 24 hours or less. For that reason, many international organizations have direct investment in owned facilities in foreign markets so that they can compete effectively on the basis of customer service.

Customer Service Costs Vary Widely

Costs of customer service often vary between countries. An organization must examine customer service requirements in each foreign market and develop a logistics program that best serves each area. Sometimes, due to competition, specific customer needs, government regulations and tariff barriers, organizations may have to incur higher logistics costs. This results in lower levels of profitability for those international target markets being served.

Hewlett-Packard Gains Competitive Advantage Internationally

Hewlett-Packard (HP) is an example of a company that was able to gain competitive advantage internationally by improving its level of customer service. HP implemented programs to tightly link R&D and manufacturing and has been successful in

---

[21]Bernard J. La Londe and Terrance L. Pohlen, "The Ohio State University 1999 Survey of Career Patterns in Logistics," *Annual Conference Proceedings of the Council of Logistics Management* (Oak Brook, IL: Council of Logistics Management, 1999), p. 367.

[22]Bender, "International Logistics," pp. 8.15–8.19.

reducing the "concept-to-delivery" time. Its logistics organization has had a key role in this successful program.[23] Improving the order fulfillment process continues to be a key strategic initiative for the company. Objectives have been set that are directed at substantially reducing the cost of taking and processing customer orders, as well as transporting those orders to customers.

Subaru of America (SOA) is another example of a company that was able to gain competitive advantage internationally by improving its customer service levels. SOA improved its customer service by restructuring the logistics network. The company saved thousands of dollars in freight costs and was able to improve warehouse productivity by 50 percent.[24] Subaru was able to maintain its position within the industry through a topflight parts and vehicle support effort.

Inventory

Inventory control in global logistics requires an awareness that international and domestic inventory management systems differ in several respects:

Global Inventories

> International systems usually have more inventory points at more levels between suppliers and customers; thus multilevel inventory systems are more complex and more common than in domestic systems.
>
> In-transit inventories can be substantially higher than for a domestic operation with similar sales volume. This results from the larger number of locations and levels involved, and longer transportation times.[25]

Depending on the distance the shipment must be transported and given the normal type of delays that can occur in international product movements, organizations may have to maintain higher-than-normal levels of inventory in their global markets. Typically, domestic firms have 10 to 20 percent of their assets in inventory. Organizations engaged in international marketing can have inventory levels that comprise up to 50 percent or more of their assets. In the case of high-value products, the inventory carrying costs, as well as the amount of accounts receivable outstanding, can be very high.

In markets where products are sold at retail, the shopping patterns of the population can be very important in determining inventory strategies of global organizations. Companies in the United States can exercise greater control over their inventories because they can influence the amount of product ordered by customers using discounts. This may not be viable in some global markets.

Since conditions may vary in foreign markets, it is important for the firm to develop inventory policies and control procedures that are appropriate for each market area.

Transportation

The selection and management of transportation are much more complex in an international setting than they are domestically. The primary modes of transport between countries or regions are air and water. Within a specific foreign market, the modes and intermodal combinations are basically the same but may possess different characteristics.

Global Differences in Transportation

---

[23]Anderson and Colard, "The International Logistics Environment," pp. 669–70.
[24]Lisa Harrington, "Customer Service Puts Subaru on Fast Track," *Traffic Management* 24, no. 10 (October 1985), pp. 76 and 85.
[25]Bender, "The International Dimension of Physical Distribution Management," pp. 785–86.

Thus, the mode and carrier selection process, and transportation management, must be administered on a country- or region-specific basis.

There can be significant differences between the transportation infrastructure found in nations throughout the world. For example, in the European Union, fewer companies maintain in-house traffic departments. More outsourcing of transportation occurs in Europe.[26] Also, in many countries outside North America, transportation modes are owned and/or operated by the government. At times, domestic shippers are given preferential treatment in terms of lower rates, equipment availability, and other benefits.

Rail service in Europe is usually much better than in the United States because equipment, tracks, and facilities are in better condition due to government ownership and/or subsidies of the rail system. Japan and European countries use water carriage to a much larger degree than the United States or Canada. Due to the length and favorable characteristics of coastlines and inland waterways, water transport is a viable alternative for many shippers. Many organizations shipping between or within the borders of foreign countries need to thoroughly evaluate transport options, costs, and services.

Selecting Global Transport Modes and Carriers

As discussed in Chapter 13, many organizations will use the services of an international freight forwarder. The majority of factors considered to be important in selecting domestic transportation modes and carriers will also be important in global transportation. For example, when organizations select international freight forwarders, expertise, reliability of service, ability to provide relevant information, company reputation, personal attention, reasonable prices, and the forwarder's financial position are the most important factors.[27] The primary differences will be in the abilities and capabilities of the various international transportation options.

In making transportation decisions, logistics decision makers need to consider the many differences between domestic and international transportation. Mode availability, carrier rates, regulatory restrictions, service levels required by customers, service capabilities of carriers, and other aspects of the transportation mix will likely vary from one market to another.

Warehousing

While the basic activities of warehousing are similar throughout the world, many differences exist. Some of the major distinctions between domestic versus international warehousing include size of market area served, types of products stored, and the use of manual versus automated systems.

The following are some basic questions that need to be asked regarding the use of warehouse facilities in global marketing:

Warehousing Questions

- Does the market for the organization's product justify a local warehouse?
- Is good warehouse labor available?
- How quickly do customers need products delivered?
- Are third parties an option?

[26]For a discussion of outsourcing in the UK, see John Fernie, "Outsourcing Distribution in UK Retailing," *Journal of Business Logistics* 20, no. 2 (1999), pp. 83–95.

[27]Paul R. Murphy and James M. Daley, "Investigating Selection Criteria for International Freight Forwarders," *Transportation Journal* 37, no. 1 (Fall 1997), p. 32.

- What are the relevant costs associated with public versus private warehousing?[28]

Market Areas Served by Warehouses

Regarding the size of market areas served by logistics networks, European and Asian markets tend to be smaller and closer together, primarily due to population densities being higher in these regions.[29] In Africa, South America, and Australia, markets served tend to be larger geographically due to population centers being located further apart.

The number and variety of products stored in warehouses and distribution centers tend to vary geographically. In Europe, there are more product-specific storage facilities than in North America, where facilities usually house a larger number and variety of products. For example, convenience product distributors in France have specialty warehouses for fresh foods, beverages, and seafood.[30]

Use of Automation

Automation in warehouse facilities tends to be greater in industrialized countries and regions, and where labor costs are high relative to other costs of production.[31] In countries such as China and India, and in many parts of Africa and Asia, automation is not widespread, owing largely to the cheaper cost of labor. Also influencing the use of automation are differences in the costs of such systems worldwide and the availability of supporting computer and information systems.

Other Activities

Global Shipments Require Greater Protection

Packaging.   Global shipments require greater protection of the product than domestic shipments. The greater distances and number of times products are handled increase the possibility of damage, delays, and pilferage.[32] In general, the amount of loss and/or damage of international shipments is higher than that of domestic shipments. Therefore, global shippers must be much more concerned with the protective aspects of packaging.

Influences on Global Packaging

Among the major factors influencing the design of packaging to be used in international movements are transportation mode/carrier and handling characteristics, climate, possibilities of pilferage, freight rates, customs duties, and, most important, the customer's requirements.

The bottom line of all international packaging decisions is that the item should arrive at its destination undamaged. Logistics executives can help to ensure that goods arrive safely at their international destinations by following some basic guidelines:

International Shipping Guidelines

- Know the merchandise.
- Analyze the transportation environment and pack for the toughest leg of the journey.

---

[28]For a discussion of several of these issues, see Tom Andel, "Making the World Your Warehouse," *Transportation and Distribution* 38, no. 8 (August 1997), pp. 88–92.

[29]See Fernie, "Outsourcing Distribution in UK Retailing," pp. 83–95; and Robert Schipper, "Centralized vs. Distributed Warehousing in Europe: From Make-Hold-Sell to Sell-Source-Deliver," *World Trade* 13, no. 1 (January 2000), pp. 64 and 66.

[30]Philippe-Pierre Dornier, Ricardo Ernst, Michel Fender, and Panos Kouvelis, *Global Operations and Logistics* (New York: John Wiley & Sons, 1998), p. 181.

[31]For an example of warehouse automation in Germany, see Klaus Blumenschein, "Seeds for Germany," *Logistics Europe* 5, no. 4 (September 1997), pp. 56–58.

[32]See Diana Twede, "Packaging," in *The Logistics Handbook,* ed. James F. Robeson and William C. Copacino (New York: Free Press, 1994), pp. 457–58.

- Know the supplier.
- Determine packaging regulations applicable in the country of origin, on each of the carriers, and at the port of entry.
- Arrange for prompt pickup at point of entry.[33]

Containers Are Widely Used Internationally

In order to facilitate product handling and protect the product during movement and storage, many firms have turned to the use of containers. Containers are widely used in global logistics systems, especially when water movements are part of the transport network.[34] Many companies have adopted standard container sizes (8′ × 8′ × 10′, 20′, 30′, or 40′) that allow for intermodal movements of their shipments.[35]

The use of standardized materials handling equipment has also become commonplace. The advantages of containers are numerous:

Advantages of Containers

- Costs due to loss or damage are reduced because of the protective nature of the container.
- Labor costs in freight handling are reduced due to the increased use of automated materials handling equipment.
- Containers are more easily stored and transported than other types of shipments, which results in lower warehousing and transportation costs.
- Containers are available in a variety of sizes, many of which are standardized for intermodal use.
- Containers are able to serve as temporary storage facilities at ports and terminals where warehousing space may be limited.

Disadvantages of Containers

Containerization is not without disadvantages. The major problem with the use of containers is that container ports or terminals may not be available in certain parts of the world. Even when such facilities exist, they may be overburdened with inbound and outbound cargo; long delays are common. Additionally, large capital expenditures are required to initiate a container-based transportation network. Significant capital outlays for port and terminal facilities, materials handling equipment, specialized transport equipment, and the containers themselves are necessary before an organization can use containerization.[36]

Labeling

Related to packaging is labeling. From a cost standpoint, labeling is a relatively minor aspect of global logistics. However, accurate labeling is essential to the timely and efficient movement of products across international borders. Important issues relating to labeling include content, language, color, and location on the package.

Procurement. Firms have historically obtained raw materials, parts, supplies, and components from domestic sources of supply. However, there has been an accelerating

---

[33]Betsy Haggerty, "How to Package Goods for International Transportation," *Inbound Logistics* 5, no. 4 (October 1985), p. 25; also see David A. Clancy, "Develop a Global Package," *Transportation and Distribution* 31, no. 10 (October 1990), pp. 34–36.

[34]For a discussion of how water ports handle ocean containers, see Toby B. Gooley, "Follow That Container!" *Traffic Management* 34, no. 9 (September 1995), pp. 29–35.

[35]For an overview of various types of containers, their usage, and the future of global transportation, see several articles in the section "Container Industry," *World Cargo News* 6, no. 12 (December 1999), pp. 35–43.

[36]See John L. Kent and R. Stephen Parker, "International Containership Carrier Selection Criteria: Shippers/Carriers Differences," *International Journal of Physical Distribution and Logistics Management* 29, no. 6 (1999), pp. 398–408.

trend toward the international sourcing of raw materials. For example, Trek Bicycles in the United States imports 20 containers of finished bicycles and parts each week from suppliers in Taiwan, Singapore, Japan, China, and the Philippines.[37] Canon uses some local sources of supply for products built outside of Japan. In its California facility, the firm uses 30 percent local sources, in Virginia less than 20 percent, and in Germany 40 percent.[38]

The concepts of *integrated logistics management* and *cost trade-off analysis* are still very important in international logistics. However, the relative importance of each logistics component may vary from market to market, as may the costs incurred in carrying out each activity. This results in different cost/service equations for each international market.

Information Systems.   The best advice for the logistics executive whose company is becoming involved in global logistics for the first time is to obtain as much information as possible about business conditions and operating procedures in each market, from as many data sources as possible. The Internet is an especially useful resource for obtaining information about almost any aspect of global commerce and logistics. Web traffic is growing rapidly. In fact, Internet traffic doubles every 100 days, and e-commerce is a multibillion-dollar global industry.[39]

In much the same way that automated information clearinghouses are used by the world banking system to transfer funds and checks among participating banks, the logistics information clearinghouses can provide shipment information to a shipper at any global location, 24 hours a day.[40]

Satellite communication systems are being used more frequently by organizations for such purposes as order processing, transmitting real-time logistics information, private network telephone service, Internet access, and video teleconferencing. Wal-Mart was one of the pioneers in the use of satellite communications, which has helped the company achieve global dominance.[41]

International trade logistics (ITL) software is also being used by organizations involved in international manufacturing and commerce. ITL software is "designed to automate, track, and report on a huge number of activities. These activities are often, but not always, tied into supply chain management, warehouse management, inventory control and transportation management systems."[42] As an example, U.S.-based Xylan Corporation, a global manufacturer of network switching equipment with 60 percent of its revenues from nondomestic sources, uses ITL software to view all of its inventory locations via its own website. The company can also confirm shipping of products, prepare customer profiles, and expedite shipments through customs.[43]

Internet Information Sources *(margin note)*

ITL Software *(margin note)*

---

[37]Toby B. Gooley, "Keeping an Eye on Asia," *Logistics Management and Distribution Report* 37, no. 5 (May 1998), p. 84.

[38]Anderson and Colard, "The International Logistics Environment," p. 666.

[39]Ron Edwards, "Information Technology: The Key to Global Growth," *World Trade* 12, no 7 (July 1999), p. 68. For a discussion of how the Internet is being used in global logistics, see Gerry Dempsey, "A Hands-On Guide for Multilingual Websites," *World Trade* 12, no. 9 (September 1999), pp. 68–70.

[40]For an example of how Unisys Corporation and Mercedes Benz Latina use automated information systems and the Internet to link their worldwide operations, see Lisa H. Harrington, "Traveling the Global Data Highway," *Traffic Management* 29, no. 4 (April 1990), pp. 38–42; and Kurt C. Hoffman, "Mercedes Pares Parts Inventory of Its Latin American Operations," *Global Logistics & Supply Chain Strategies* 4, no. 5 (June 2000), pp. 76–80.

[41]Bruce Elbert, "Satellite Communications," *World Trade* 12, no. 5 (May 1999), p. 35.

[42]Martha L. Celestino, "International Trade Logistics Software Solutions," *World Trade* 12, no. 5 (May 1999), p. 60.

[43]Ibid.

Global Market Opportunities

Three major geographic regions account for the bulk of world economic activity and international trade: North America, Pacific Rim/China (including Japan), and Western Europe. These three areas produce 80 percent of the world's economic output and account for 75 percent of world exports. For this reason, it is necessary to understand the foundations of business and logistics systems in those regions, plus in other developing areas such as Eastern Europe, the former Soviet Union, and South America.

North America

NAFTA Integrates the Markets of Canada, Mexico, and the United States

The North American Free Trade Agreement (NAFTA) created the North American "common market" of Canada, the United States, and Mexico.[44] The annual flow of trade between the United States and Mexico is more than $150 billion, of which about $75 billion is from Mexico to the United States. Between Canada and the United States, the total annual flow of trade is more than $320 billion, with approximately $170 billion flowing south from Canada to the United States.[45] NAFTA's effect on U.S. exports to Canada and Mexico for the period 1993–1998 is shown in Figure 14–3. As an interesting note, in 1999 Mexico surpassed Japan as California's top export market, exceeding $14 billion.[46]

This area has a larger population and domestic economic product than the European Union (EU) and the European Free Trade Association (EFTA) combined. The provisions of NAFTA are significant in that they directly affect not only a variety of

FIGURE 14–3

NAFTA's effect on U.S. exports to Canada and Mexico, 1993–1998*

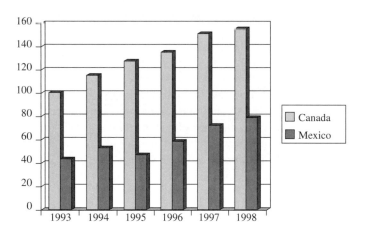

*Figures in $U.S. billions.

Source: U.S. Department of Commerce (1999).

---

[44]The full text of the North American Free Trade Agreement can be found on the Internet at <http://www.sice.oas.org>.

[45]John Sweeney, *NAFTA's Three-Year Report Card: An "A" for North America's Economy* (Washington, DC: Heritage Foundation, May 1997); "Americas Watch: News from the Americas," *Inbound Logistics* 19, no. 9 (September 1999), p. 24; and "Canada: Between Good Neighbors, Fences Are Coming Down," *Global Logistics & Supply Chain Strategies* 4, no. 6 (July 2000), pp. 70–75.

[46]"Americas Watch: California Exports Sunny," *Inbound Logistics* 20, no. 3 (March 2000), p. 14.

logistics activities but also how supply chains are structured when Canadian, U.S., and Mexican companies are involved. Specifically, NAFTA:

Changes Resulting from NAFTA

- Eliminates many tariff and nontariff barriers. (By 2004, most all tariffs will be eliminated.)
- Enhances carriers' ability to operate across borders (especially between the United States and Mexico, where cross-border movements occur much more easily).
- Liberalizes foreign investment. (It allows U.S. and Canadian companies the right to establish firms in Mexico or to acquire existing Mexican companies.)
- Standardizes customs initiatives, local content rules, and packaging and labeling requirements.[47]

Canada and the United States have the most advanced logistics infrastructures and systems in the world. North America offers a wide choice of transportation providers and very good, competitively priced warehousing facilities and ancillary services throughout the continent. It is possible to find common, contract, and private carriers offering transportation services by air, highway, railroad, pipeline, and water. Since practically all modes of transportation in the United States and Canada are non–government owned, in the vast number of instances rates are negotiable, depending on freight type (e.g., hazardous materials, refrigerated goods) and product characteristics (e.g., annual volumes, seasonality, shipment size, type of product).[48]

Canadian Pacific and Union Pacific Partnership

As one example of a result arising from the passage of NAFTA, the Canadian Pacific Railway has partnered with the Union Pacific (U.S.) and the Mexican national rail carrier, TFM, to offer TOFC service between Canada and 16 points in Mexico. Customs clearances for these intermodal shipments will take place primarily at shipping destinations rather than at border crossings.[49]

Unitization (in the form of pallets and slip sheets) and freight containerization have been commonplace for decades. Pallets have been standardized mostly along industry lines (e.g., grocery manufacturers). Containers, mostly 40 or more feet long, with some 20-foot containers, have served as the basis for the International Organization for Standardization's standards.

The use of electronic data interchange (EDI), the Internet, and other information system technologies to support logistics operations was pioneered in North America several decades ago, and the continent is the largest user of such technology in the world today.

Canadian Customs Documents Processed Electronically

According to one source, "the documentation for more than 1.5 million motor carrier shipments into Canada is processed by customs before the freight even reaches the border, shortening the time spent releasing the freight when it arrives. [Additionally] more than 90 percent of all goods from the US are cleared by Mexican Customs at the border in 20 seconds or less."[50] A specific example is the Roadway Express website (www.roadway.com), which allows customers to access the firm's "E-Z Export" system to complete customs documentation online. Over 96 percent of the hundreds of

---

[47]Waller, D'Avanzo, and Lambert, *Supply Chain Directions for a New North America,* pp. 2–3.

[48]For a discussion of how NAFTA has affected the transportation sector, see Michael D. White, "NAFTA Shipping Still Negotiating the Curves," *World Trade* 12, no. 9 (September 1999), pp. 54–56.

[49]Michael D. White, "Wherever You Go, the Tune's the Same," *World Trade* 12, no. 5 (May 1999), p. 72.

[50]Robert B. Carr, "Don't Let Borders Be Barriers," *Transportation and Distribution* 36, no. 3 (March 1995), pp. 65–70.

Technology

Internet Software Cuts Costs

The use of logistics software has been increasing rapidly because of technology development and its subsequent adoption and implementation within organizations and across supply chains. With the Internet adding to the electronic capabilities of companies, many organizations have expanded their use of Web-enabled applications to manage global logistics networks and operations.

One company that has taken advantage of this growth in Internet usage is RockPort Trade Systems. The firm developed a sophisticated client-server system, called RockWeb, that was designed to manage integrated supply chain needs such as global sourcing, purchasing, financials and logistics.

According to an article in *Global Logistics and Supply Chain Strategies:* "In far-flung and undeveloped nations—or in a company that wants to minimize its outlay on information technology—the benefits of the Internet are many. Vendors can be informed of purchase orders, production dates can be changed, notices of letters of credit can be sent, receipt of raw materials can be acknowledged, and forms and invoices can be printed—all without spending a bundle on technology."

Source: Russell W. Goodman, "Internet Cuts Costs, Spreads Availability of Export, Import Software," *Global Logistics and Supply Chain Strategies* 3, no. 1 (January–February 1999), pp. 62–70.

thousands of shipments per year between the United States and Canada are cleared through customs before the freight reaches the border.[51]

Many North American manufacturers, retailers, and logistics service providers are taking advantage of NAFTA opportunities. Those leading-edge, or "best-practice," companies have adopted one or more of the following strategies:

Strategies of Leading-Edge Companies as a Result of NAFTA

- *Customer service.* Best-practice companies manage key accounts in a consistent, coordinated manner in all three countries. They're also working to create more uniform service levels across an integrated North American marketplace.
- *Manufacturing.* Best-practice companies modify their product-development and manufacturing approaches to take advantage of market and tariff advantages inherent in NAFTA.
- *Channel design.* Best-practice companies establish market research groups in each North American country to facilitate distribution channel designs.
- *Sourcing.* Best-practice companies regularly revisit and revise their sourcing strategies. Increasingly, this means moving away from offshore vendors to suppliers in North America.
- *Distribution.* Best-practice companies establish core carrier programs with their major North American carriers. They also develop cross-border shipping programs that include innovative freight consolidation and stacktrain

---

[51]Anne Fitzgibbon, "Two-Way Transportation: US & Canada," *World Trade* 13, no. 2 (February 2000), p. 50.

approaches. Finally, they establish a strong border presence to expedite cross-border product flow.

- *Sales and marketing.* Best-practice companies develop sales and marketing strategies targeted to specific markets and customers within North America.
- *Organization.* Best-practice companies create internal NAFTA units dedicated to managing business in the NAFTA trading area. They also train their own people and their vendors on NAFTA rules and regulations.[52]

Companies that have taken advantage of the opportunities NAFTA has provided include Alamo Iron Works (distributor), Darco Southern (industrial products manufacturer), Loctite Corporation (industrial products manufacturer), NSK-RHP Canada (ball bearing manufacturer), Rich Products (food products), and Yellow Freight (trucking).[53]

Pacific Rim

Firms involved in importing, exporting, outsourcing materials, and entering markets in the Pacific Rim recognize that differences in economics, politics, and culture greatly influence business activities in Asian countries. Ranging from the affluence of Japan to the poverty of Indonesia and China, the region offers a myriad of immense problems and significant opportunities for companies.[54]

Supply Chains in Asia Are Complex

Supply chains in Asia are complex, although manageable. It has been estimated that for every $1 billion of imports from China, at least $150 million could be saved through efficient supply chain management.[55] There are many issues to be addressed in performing logistics activities in Asia, such as vendor selection, mode/carrier choice, consolidation and breakbulk opportunities, use of brokers, identification of ports of entry, number and location of warehouses, and warehousing versus cross-docking.

There are three major logistics hubs in Asia: Singapore, Hong Kong, and Tokyo: "Singapore serves Southeast Asia and the India/Pakistan region, Hong Kong is a sourcing point for North Asia, and Tokyo is the key hub for Japan."[56] Firms marketing products to many parts of Asia will find logistics environments that are similar to those in North America and the European Union. While cultures and politics are different, transportation infrastructures are developed, a variety of warehousing options exist, the use of automated systems is widespread, and customer service concepts are understood and accepted by logistics service providers.

Such cannot be said for underdeveloped countries of the Pacific Rim and Asia, such as China. In China, most logistics activities are administered and/or controlled by the government. Despite some economic and distribution reforms by the government,

[52]Waller, D'Avanzo, and Lambert, *Supply Chain Directions for a New North America,* p. 8.

[53]For a discussion of these and other companies that have benefited from NAFTA, see James H. Gilmore, "Designing a Distribution Strategy for Canada," CCA White Paper (Cleveland, OH: Cleveland Consulting Associates, undated); Toby B. Gooley, "How Rich Products Gets the Best of Both Worlds," *Traffic Management* 35, no. 2 (February 1996), pp. 47–49; "NAFTA's Momentum," *Industrial Distribution* supplement (May 1995), pp. S3–S12; and David Valdez, "Switch to Free Trade," *Transportation and Distribution* 36, no. 1 (January 1995), pp. 53–58.

[54]See Lara Sowinski, "China, India, and Australia: Huge Populations and a US-Friendly Market Urge Trade and Investment," *World Trade* 12, no. 10 (October 1999), pp. 28–32.

[55]John Kao, *Managing the China Supply Chain: A Monograph on Emerging Trends* (Chicago: A. T. Kearney, 1998), p. 2.

[56]Burnson, "Asia's Economic Rebound," p. 98.

FIGURE 14–4

Distribution channels in China for consumer products

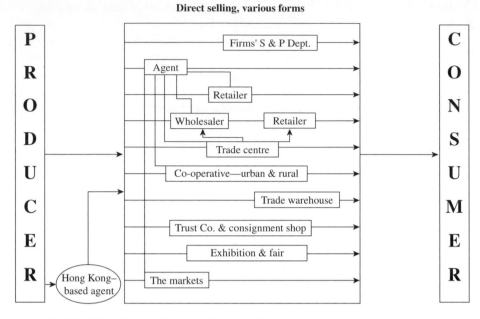

Source: Sherriff T. K. Luk, "Structural Changes in China's Distribution System," *International Journal of Physical Distribution and Logistics Management* 28, no. 1 (1998), p. 59.

the economy is still characterized by materials shortages, planned distribution, and a dual pricing system (planned prices and market prices).[57]

Logistics Options in China

There are more logistics options available to organizations entering China. Figures 14–4 and 14–5 show the distribution channels for consumer products and industrial goods, respectively. Either of two major channel strategies can be used: direct or indirect. As one writer has explained: "Provided that a foreign [organization] decides to deliver its products to target customers through a short, direct channel, [it] can either sell directly to target customers through . . . sales departments, or via retailers, consignment shops, and exhibitions. Alternatively, the [organization] may opt for an indirect channel strategy and sell the products to either sales agents or wholesalers first and let these types of distributors dispatch the products through their own channels to potential customers."[58]

Logistics Challenges in China

Organizations trying to penetrate the Chinese market will find great difficulties logistically. Conditions are changing for the better, albeit slowly, much as in Eastern Europe and the former Soviet Union. However, changes in distribution channels and infrastructures will continue to be very slow, requiring great patience both managerially and financially. Involvement in countries like China will not show significant payback for many years, and firms will not be able to use the same financial criteria in evaluating Chinese logistics efficiencies as in markets located in other parts of the world.

---

[57]For an overview the China's logistics environment, see Sherriff T. K. Luk, "Structural Changes in China's Distribution System," *International Journal of Physical Distribution and Logistics Management* 28, no. 1 (1998), pp. 44–67. Also, for an example in the ocean shipping industry, see "China Opens Shipping Door," *NITL Notice* 64 (March 3, 2000), p. 3.

[58]Luk, "Structural Changes in China's Distribution System," p. 59.

FIGURE 14–5

Distribution channels in China for industrial products and raw materials

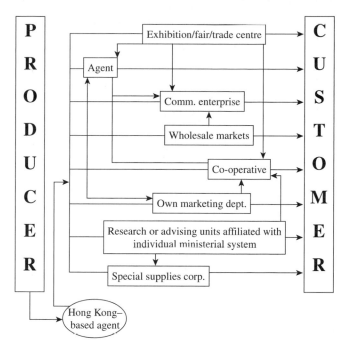

Source: Sherriff T. K. Luk, "Structural Changes in China's Distribution System," *International Journal of Physical Distribution and Logistics Management* 28, no. 1 (1998), p. 60.

Other areas of the Pacific Rim provide logistics challenges to the global organization. The chaotic financial conditions that troubled the Pacific region during the 1990s have abated, resulting in renewed growth and development in the region. Organizations are more cautious regarding the future market potential of Asian countries, but most companies are expanding production, marketing, and logistics operations in the region.[59]

Japanese Distribution Systems

Markets in Japan, South Korea, Australia, and other Asian locations are sophisticated and provide a variety of logistics services common to industrialized nations in North America and Western Europe. For example, Japan has long had efficient transportation and warehousing infrastructures, coupled with good information systems. However, long distribution channels have been the norm for decades, making penetration of the Japanese market difficult for new entrants. This began to change in the 1990s, when there was a movement toward shorter and more direct channels. This greatly improved logistics efficiencies. Direct sales and mail order, for example, have been growing faster than retail sales.[60]

Although Japan is an archipelago comprising more than 5,000 islands, the bulk of its population lives on the four major islands of Hokkaido, Honshu, Kyushu, and Shikoku. Of these, the island of Honshu contains all the major cities and therefore most of the population of Japan.

---

[59]See John Davies, "Trade in the Pacific May Be Poised to Make a Comeback," *Global Logistics and Supply Chain Strategies* 3, no. 4 (May 1999), pp. 62–68; and "Asia: For Asian Supply Chains, Good News and Bad," *Global Logistics & Supply Chain Strategies* 4, no. 6 (July 2000), pp. 58–69.

[60]See John Fahy and Fuyuki Taguchi, "Reassessing the Japanese Distribution System," *Sloan Management Review* (Winter 1995), pp. 49–61; and Lisa M. Ellram and Martha C. Cooper, "The Relationship between Supply Chain Management and Keiretsu," *The International Journal of Logistics Management* 4, no. 1 (1993), pp. 1–12.

Some of the major characteristics of Japanese logistics are the following:

**Characteristics
of Japanese Logistics**

1. *Transportation modes.* Ninety percent of domestically transported tonnage goes by truck, and this is likely to continue. Truck transportation requires licensing from the Ministry of Transport. Licenses distinguish among:

   - Long-distance trucks, which carry loads between major regions (e.g., from plants to distribution centers).
   - Short-distance trucks, which carry loads within a region (e.g., between a wholesaler and a retailer).
   - District trucks, which can carry loads anywhere but whose routes must originate and terminate within a designated district and can carry goods only for a single shipper.
   - Route trucks, which can carry loads along their licensed route for multiple shippers.

2. *Logistics heartland.* The main area for production in Japan is the triangle Tokyo-Nagoya-Osaka, on the island of Honshu; the distance from Tokyo to Osaka is about 500 kilometers. The triangle includes the metropolitan area around Tokyo known as Kanto (including Yokohama and Kawasaki), and that around Osaka, known as Kansai (including Kobe and Kyoto).

3. *Traffic congestion.* Traffic congestion on roads and highways is a critical problem in the triangle, especially in and around the major cities, where traffic speeds average less than 15 kilometers per hour. For this reason, just-in-time systems require many small facilities, and/or substantial fleets of small vehicles, to meet customer requirements quickly, reliably, and economically.

4. *Distribution systems.* Distribution systems for different products are usually very different because of traditional differences in trade practices and channels of distribution.

5. *Distribution channels.* Nontraditional distribution channels, especially nonstore channels, are booming, and often represent the best way to introduce new products into the Japanese market. These channels include mail order, catalog sales, door-to-door sales, teleshopping, and vending machines.

6. *Shared distribution.* Shared distribution is common, with competitors delivering to the same stores sharing delivery facilities and trucks.

7. *Palletization.* Large companies tend to use ISO standard pallet sizes; however, these are not mandatory, and a proliferation of different pallet sizes significantly complicates logistics operations.

8. *Warehousing.* Business warehouses are supervised by the Ministry of Transport and regional transport bureaus. These distinguish among private, agricultural, cooperative, and public warehouses. Public warehouses are further classified into general-purpose, cold storage, open-air, storage tank, floating storage (e.g., for logs), and dangerous goods warehouses. These are each treated differently by the Ministry of Transport, which issues them permits.

**Malaysian Logistics
Activities**

In other regions of the Pacific Rim, markets are also undergoing change, and these changes have significance for logistics. Malaysia has developed a high-growth region called Cyber Jaya that is a part of the $38.5 billion Multimedia Super Corridor (MSC) project. The region is a high-technology center that provides the latest in computer and information systems, coupled with a pro-business economic climate.[61] The establishment of this region allows all facets (e.g., logistics, manufacturing, marketing) of the global organization to benefit from the use of high-technology equipment, software, and systems. While the development of such areas is slow and somewhat limited, it does indicate that the Pacific region will potentially offer a number of opportunities for global organizations. As such development occurs, logistics systems will necessarily develop in sophistication as well.

Western Europe

Geographically, Europe is much smaller than North America; the majority of the European population lives within a 500-mile radius. Therefore, the patterns of transport and distribution are different in Europe and the United States.

Europe 1992

Significant developments are occurring in Western Europe with the creation of a single European market and the adoption of the euro currency throughout the European Union (EU). Referred to as "Europe 1992," the creation of a unified market comprised of over 300 million people has had dramatic impact on business and commerce, not only in Europe but also throughout the world. "Geographically, the European landscape today looks much the same as it did 10 years ago. But from a logistics standpoint, everything has changed."[62]

Changes Occurring in EU Logistics

Changes in the EU have had significant impacts on logistics operations. Since the unification of Europe is ongoing, such changes will likely continue. Some of the major changes have taken place in the following areas: centralization of distribution centers; increasing number of partnerships and strategic alliances;[63] use of outsourcing and third parties; development of pan-European transportation networks; and restructuring of logistics management.

One of the most significant changes has been the use of fewer distribution points servicing larger market areas.[64] For example, Kodak established a logistics network to serve the Scandinavian and Baltic regions. Other companies have followed a similar strategy as border crossings and customs requirements have been streamlined in the EU.[65] In fact, Becton Dickinson, a medical technology company, closed all of its European facilities and centralized its operations into a single location.[66]

Pan-European Logistics Strategies

Organizations in a variety of industries have been able to realize cost and service-level improvements as a result of establishing pan-European logistics strategies. One U.S.-based medical equipment manufacturer consolidated all logistics operations into a single facility in Belgium, resulting in a 50 percent reduction in inventory levels, a 75 percent reduction in stockouts, and a 20 percent cost reduction in total logistics

---

[61]Julian Weiss, "The View from Malaysia . . . The Quest for High, High Tech," *World Trade* 12, no. 8 (August 1999), pp. 43–44.

[62]"Logistics in Europe: Tear Up the Old Maps," *Global Logistics & Supply Chain Strategies* 3, no. 6 (July 1999), p. 38; Lara L. Sowinski, "What's Europe Up To?" *World Trade* 13, no. 1 (January 2000), pp. 34–44; and "Europe: The Single Market Is Coming Together . . . Slowly," *Global Logistics & Supply Chain Strategies* 4, no. 6 (July 2000), pp. 42–57.

[63]See Prabir K. Bagchi and Helge Virum, "Logistical Alliances: Trends and Prospects in Integrated Europe," *Journal of Business Logistics* 19, no. 1 (1998), pp. 191–213.

[64]See Toby B. Gooley, "Pan-European Logistics: Fact or Fiction?" *Logistics Management and Distribution Report* 38, no. 3 (March 1999), pp. 85–91.

[65]"Logistics in Europe," p. 38.

[66]Derek Bell, "Integrated Diagnosis," *Logistics Europe* 5, no. 1 (March 1997), pp. 18–21.

costs.[67] An interesting statistic is that, of the approximately 950 European distribution centers, approximately one-half are located in the Netherlands.[68]

Additionally, the number of cross-national alliances has increased since the unification of Europe. For example, in the Netherlands, KLM Cargo (a Dutch air freight operation), Jan de Rijk (a Dutch transport and logistics firm), and Trailstar (a trans-European intermodal company) have combined services and created scheduled air-rail service between Amsterdam and Milan, Italy.[69]

The use of outsourcing and third parties has always been strong in Europe, but the practice is gaining additional popularity.[70] According to one observer: "Third-party logistics companies, both European and U.S.-based, are making progress toward building Pan-European service networks. The cooperative relationship between Schenker International and its parent company, Stinnes AG, and Sweden's BTL AB, for example, has created a European logistics giant employing more than 20,000 people in 30 European countries with annual revenues of more than $3.5 billion."[71]

Pan-European transportation networks have increased because of transportation deregulation, more optimal routing and scheduling opportunities, and the development of pan-European services. Additionally, the channel tunnel, called the "Chunnel," has linked the United Kingdom with the rest of Europe and facilitated freight movement between England and France.

As a result of the unification of Europe and the addition of some Eastern European countries into the EU, the existing balance of local, regional, and long-distance transport movements has begun to change. Present transport patterns of 50 to 70 percent local (75-km radius), 20 to 30 percent regional (175-km radius), and long-distance traffic (300-km radius) are anticipated to dramatically shift—to 15 to 30 percent local, 20 to 35 percent regional, and 35 to 65 percent long-distance.[72]

Restructuring of Logistics Management

The restructuring of logistics management has occurred in a number of management areas such as the administration of logistics activities. The removal of customs procedures has resulted in greater efficiencies in transportation, packaging, and labeling. Technology improvements have been implemented throughout Europe instead of just within individual countries. More centralization of order processing, inventory control, warehousing, and computer technology has occurred with a unified Europe.

Organizational changes to more centralized control of logistics have affected organization charts and job scopes. Structures put into place since Europe 1992 have tended to be more broad-based, less cognizant of national boundaries, and located at some central point on the continent.

In sum, the competitive situation in Europe has intensified. Penalties for poor performance are greater for manufacturers, retailers, and logistics service providers.

---

[67]Gooley, "Pan-European Logistics," p. 86.

[68]Francesca Cunningham, "Market Analysis: Benelux, Powerhouse of Europe," *Logistics Europe* 5, no. 5 (October 1997), p. 26.

[69]"Air-Rail Shipments Becoming a Reality in Europe," *Logistics Management and Distribution Report* 37, no. 3 (March 1998), p. 83. Also see Michael Babb, "TFGI/NDX Merger to Change European Intermodal Scene," *Logistics Management and Distribution Report* 37, no. 10 (October 1998), pp. 97–98.

[70]Alan Waller, "Forging New Links," *Logistics Europe* 5, no. 1 (March 1997), pp. 12–16.

[71]Gooley, "Pan-European Logistics," p. 89.

[72]Hanspeter Stabenau, "Germany," *New Trends in Logistics in Europe* (Paris: European Conference of Ministers of Transport, 1997), p. 22.

However, the rewards are great for organizations that can effectively implement optimal manufacturing, marketing, and logistics strategies in a unified European economy.

Eastern Europe

At the end of the 20th century, significant changes took place in the former Soviet Union and Eastern Europe, including the fall of the Berlin Wall; the reshaping of political and commercial boundaries in Eastern Europe and Asia; the merging of East and West Germany; and independence movements in many of the republics in the former Soviet Union (e.g., the Baltic states, Georgia).

Commonwealth of Independent States

The Commonwealth of Independent States (CIS), created in 1991, included five basic regions: Baltic States (Estonia, Latvia, Lithuania); Western Frontier (Belarus, Moldova, Ukraine); Transcaucasia (Armenia, Azerbaijan, Georgia); Central Asia (Kazakhstan, Kyrgyzstan, Tajikistan, Turkmenistan, Uzbekistan); and Russia. Many of these countries have moved slowly in the direction of free-market economies.

Investment in Eastern Europe and the CIS has increased, although not as rapidly as envisioned at the time of the breakup of the former Soviet Union. Solvay, Belgium's leading producer of chemicals and pharmaceuticals, has invested 160 million euro dollars (EUR) in Bulgaria. Saint-Globain invested more than 90 million EUR on a new flat-glass plant in Poland. Automaker Renault has had a presence in Slovenia since the 1950s and has invested 230 million EUR in the country since 1992.[73] Annually, the amount of foreign direct investment (FDI) by European Union member countries has amounted to more than 9 billion EUR. Since 1989, the total FDI has exceeded 50 billion EUR. European Union exports to the region have reached 80 billion EUR each year.[74]

Logistics Challenges in Central and Eastern Europe

A study of Central and Eastern Europe by DHL Worldwide Express found that customs clearance procedures are extremely difficult for a majority of countries in the region. Some companies have referred to the customs situation as the "red tape curtain." Fully 90 percent of the companies surveyed indicated that they had experienced customs-clearance problems, including "documents rejected because rubber stamps were in the wrong place or weren't pressed down hard enough [and] documents refused because they were signed in black rather than blue ink."[75]

Coupled with difficult customs-clearance procedures are poor transportation infrastructures resulting from decades of Communist rule and general neglect. The lack of quality transportation carriers; inadequate roads, rail, and port facilities; and uncertain prospects for their improvement all make it hard to transport products throughout Central and Eastern Europe. The concepts of customer satisfaction and customer service are unknown or misunderstood except in a very few instances. Using sophisticated logistics techniques and computerized order processing and information systems is nearly impossible in most areas.

Important Issues Facing Logistics Executives

There are many issues facing organizations marketing and distributing their goods and services in this region. Perhaps the most significant factor is the political instability

---

[73]*The East-West Win-Win Business Experience: Report from the European Round Table of Industrialists* (Brussels, Belgium: ERT, March 1999), pp. 50, 52, and 58.

[74]Ibid., p. 9.

[75]"Survey Finds 'Red Tape Curtain' Slows Trade in Eastern Europe," *Logistics Management and Distribution Report* 37, no. 3 (March 1998), p. 84.

of various countries in Eastern Europe. As evidenced by the military actions that resulted from political turmoil in Bosnia and the Czech Republic during the 1990s, organizations must be aware of the social, economic, and political climates of countries in the region.

Additionally, the attractiveness of individual markets will also depend on other factors, such as:

Factors that Determine the Attractiveness of Individual Markets in Eastern Europe

- Degree of country indebtedness.
- Development of the banking system.
- Level of productivity of industries and individual companies.
- Quality of the workforce.
- Condition of the infrastructure (e.g., transportation, information).
- State of technology.
- Depth of managerial skills.
- Supply of production materials.
- Profit repatriation regulations.[76]

Because of the immense opportunities, many organizations will decide that the benefits of penetrating Eastern Europe and the CIS will outweigh the risks and costs. However, it will be a slow process. Some countries will provide greater opportunities than others. Poland, Hungary, and the Czech Republic have less restrictive customs procedures and more developed logistics systems. Companies such as Hewlett-Packard, McDonald's, Office Depot, Pizza Hut, and Sun Microsystems have penetrated these markets and developed efficient distribution systems and networks.[77] Conditions will change over time, so it will be imperative that organizations examine each market individually and periodically.

Maquiladora Operations

Many firms throughout the world have become involved in global manufacturing; that is, they have manufacturing facilities located in various parts of the world. When firms have multiple plant locations, they face different logistics constraints and opportunities.

The major advantage of producing products throughout the world is that an organization has greater opportunities to reduce the costs of production, especially the labor component. One industry estimate is that the cost of doing business in Mexico, where many manufacturing operations have been established, is one-third as much as in the United States.[78]

Production Sharing Opportunities

Many opportunities for production sharing exist. U.S. manufacturers have traditionally focused on the Pacific Basin countries when establishing production sharing facilities; however, they also set up production sharing facilities in the Caribbean Basin,

---

[76]*The Iron Curtain Rises: Investment Opportunities in East Central Europe,* management report prepared by A. T. Kearney, Inc. (January 1991), p. 6.

[77]Andrea Knox, "Eastern Europe: The Center Holds," *World Trade* 12, no. 7 (July 1999), pp. 24–28.

[78]Martha L. Celestino, "Manufacturing in Mexico," *World Trade* 12, no. 7 (July 1999), p. 36.

Mexico, South America, and some European countries. Japanese firms have established a presence in Mexico. Similarly, some European organizations have set up many production facilities in Mexico and have begun taking advantage of production opportunities available in Eastern Europe.[79]

An example of production sharing is the *maquiladora,* or twin plant, operation. Companies from throughout the world "set up assembly and manufacturing facilities along the Mexican side of the U.S.-Mexican border. The production sharing aspects . . . are encouraged by special tariff provisions that reduce the duties that would normally be assessed on materials that flow across the border."[80]

Three Types of Maquiladoras

There are three types of maquiladoras: manufacturer-owned and operated, shelter operations, and contract manufacturing and assembly. They have been described as follows:

> In *manufacturer-owned operations* the investing company will own the maquiladora subsidiary and assume all of the legal and financial exposure risk. *Shelter organizations* provide a maquila, the building and the labor, do the border transfers, assume the overhead, and take care of insurance and incidentals—all for a flat fee. The manufacturer supplies the materials and components from which the finished goods will be produced, plant equipment, and the technical know-how. Under a shelter, the manufacturer retains a good deal of control of the production aspects, but assumes limited financial risk or legal responsibility. *Contract manufacturing and assembly* maquiladoras are already existing companies in Mexico that produce finished products for a foreign company on either a turn-key basis or with the foreign investor providing materials. The contract maquiladora does the work on a purchase order and the foreign company has no legal or financial exposure risk.[81]

Cost Issues in Maquiladoras

From a logistics perspective, maquiladora operations affect the costs of performing various logistics activities. Generally, costs for documentation, inventory, sourcing, and transportation are higher in maquiladoras than in domestic-only operations. Order processing, packaging, and warehousing costs tend to be the same or slightly lower in maquiladoras.[82] Therefore, the logistics executive will often see logistics costs increase when the firm is involved in maquiladora operations. In total, however, because of the significantly lower labor costs in manufacturing, the total cost to the firm will be lower.

The logistics, as well as manufacturing, implications of maquiladoras need to be considered by any firm planning the establishment of twin plant operations. There are more than 3,100 maquiladora operations in Mexico, and that number is increasing each year. As international sourcing and manufacturing options are evaluated by firms in their search to gain competitive advantage, the maquiladora operation will continue to be a viable option for many companies.[83]

---

[79]Stanley E. Fawcett, "Logistics and Manufacturing Issues in Maquiladora Operations," *International Journal of Physical Distribution and Logistics Management* 20, no. 4 (1990), p. 13.

[80]Ibid.

[81]Celestino, "Manufacturing in Mexico," p. 38.

[82]Theodore P. Stank and Charles W. Lackey, Jr., "Enhancing Performance Through Logistical Capabilities in Mexican Maquiladora Firms," *Journal of Business Logistics* 18, no. 1 (1997), pp. 91–123; also see "Americas Watch: Spotlight on Mexico," *Inbound Logistics* 19, no. 1 (January 1999), p. 40.

[83]For information about maquiladora operations in Mexico, see the following website: <http://www.maqguide.com>.

Creative Solutions

Wanted: Creative Do-It-Yourself Shippers

With so many roadblocks—both figurative and literal—constantly being thrown in a shipper's way, it sometimes takes creative thinking and a can-do attitude to deliver a shipment in the former Soviet Union.

The experience of Houston-based IMC Maritime Group, a ship operator and project-cargo-management company, illustrates the do-it-yourself nature of shipping to the region. IMC had a contract to deliver more than 100,000 tons of oil-field equipment to the new Ardalin oil field in northwestern Siberia. But there were no roads to the remote site. How to get it there?

Because the tundra is waterlogged and mushy in the summer, the brutal Siberian winter was the only time when such heavy shipments could travel overland. IMC first chartered specially built icebreaker vessels to take the oversized shipments to icebound Arkhangel'sk. IMC then used trucks to transfer the cargo to a staging area just north of the Arctic Circle. The final leg of the journey required the company to build its own roads to the site. Rather than dig up the fragile terrain, workers sprayed water over the tundra, forming enough layers of ice to support the heaviest pieces of equipment. The roads are temporary; they melt in summer and leave no permanent damage.

Koch Supplies Inc. of Kansas City, MO, has shown equal creativity in meeting the tough conditions in the former Soviet Union. Koch manufactures and distributes food-handling and -processing equipment. The company has designed a mobile meat-processing plant for sale in the CIS. All the necessary cutting, processing, and packaging equipment is fitted inside a 40-foot ocean container on a chassis with heavy-duty tires. "All the buyer needs to do when it gets there is hook it up to gas or a generator and to a water supply," explains Project Planner Jim Masterson.

Getting there is half the problem, of course, and Koch has found that intermodalism is the answer. Self-contained units move via piggyback from Kansas City to the East or West Coasts, depending on the final destination. From there, the container rolls onto a ship for delivery to the appropriate port, explains Benjamin Khayet, a Russian native who is Koch's export manager and translator for CIS projects. Once overseas, the trailer can continue either by rail or road as dictated by local conditions. "We even shipped a unit to Frankfurt, and then drove it to Kazakhstan," he recalls. The flexibility afforded by the intermodal container and chassis makes modern, sanitary food processing available in even the remotest locations, Khayer says. "It's especially popular for processing reindeer meat in Siberia!" he says with a smile.

Source: Toby B. Gooley, "Shipping to the Wild, Wild East," *Traffic Management* 35, no. 1 (January 1996), p. 70A.

Summary

Successful global marketing and logistics efforts are possible, but not guaranteed. International expansion offers significant potential benefits as well as risks. However, organizations can improve the likelihood of success by following several straightforward steps. Good planning, implementation, and control are important in domestic logistics operations but even more vital in the global arena.

Generally, organizations that accomplish the following activities are more likely to succeed internationally:

- Perform a self-assessment of potential risks and benefits of global expansion.
- Examine the various international target markets in terms of political risk,[84] currency risk, culture, competition, and other factors unique to those markets.

---

[84]For an overview of how organizations can respond to various types of political risk, see Mel Mandell, "Avoiding Overseas Crises: Nothing Beats Being Prepared," *World Trade* 12, no. 10 (October 1999), pp. 44–46.

- Determine the specific market entry strategies to pursue.
- Exercise due diligence regarding the selection of foreign partners.
- Investigate and arrange for all aspects of foreign financing of logistics operations.
- Understand the logistics options available in each target market, including third-party service providers, in-house logistics capabilities, and transportation and warehousing options.
- Ensure that mechanisms exist for timely receipt of payments from foreign customers (e.g., letters of credit).[85]

In summarizing the status of logistics in global commerce, five general trends can be identified:

1. The total supply chain is becoming a greater competitive factor around the world.
2. Shippers are becoming more global in their purchasing, manufacturing, distribution, and after-sales service.
3. Changes are driven by the customer, who is demanding better service, faster deliveries, less inventory, and lower prices.
4. Companies use outsourcing as a primary way to meet these new customer demands.
5. State-of-the-art information technology is critical.[86]

Since logistics management is concerned with the costs associated with supplying a given level of service to foreign customers, it is important to recognize the factors that influence the costs of carrying out the process. Thus, the financial aspects of marketing and logistics are important.

Some global market opportunities for companies in various regions of the world—North America, the Pacific Rim, Western Europe, Eastern Europe, and the CIS—were identified and discussed in this chapter. In addition to identifying some of the opportunities within each of those world regions, we presented the many challenges or disadvantages facing organizations attempting to penetrate those markets.

Finally, maquiladora, or twin plant, operations were examined, with emphasis given to the logistics implications of U.S. firms locating assembly and manufacturing facilities in Mexico.

Suggested Readings

Anderson, David L., and Dennis Colard. "The International Logistics Environment." In *The Logistics Handbook,* ed. James F. Robeson and William C. Copacino. New York: Free Press, 1994, pp. 647–73.

Augustin, Siegfried; Peter G. Klaus; Ernst W. Krog; and Ulrich Mueller-Steinfahrt. "The Evolution of Logistics in Large Industrial Organizations in Europe." *Proceedings of the Annual Conference of the Council of Logistics Management* (Oak Brook, IL: Council of Logistics Management, 1996), pp. 535–53.

---

[85]Adapted from Sherrie E. Zahn, "Building on Your Success: Using Your Strategic Plan for Implementation," *World Trade* 12, no. 10 (October 1999), pp. 50–52.

[86]Robert J. Bowman, "Pulling Together," *Global Logistics & Supply Chain Strategies* 3, no. 6 (July 1999), p. 11.

Aurik, Jonan C., and Jan Van De Dord. "New Priorities in Logistics Services in Europe." *Transportation and Distribution* 35, no. 2 (February 1995), pp. 43–48.

Bagchi, Prabir K., and Helge Virum. "Logistical Alliances: Trends and Prospects in Integrated Europe." *Journal of Business Logistics* 19, no. 1 (1999), pp. 191–213.

Bender, Paul S. "International Logistics." In *The Distribution Management Handbook,* ed. James A. Tompkins and Dale Harmelink. New York: McGraw-Hill, 1994, pp. 8.1–8.21.

Carter, Joseph R.; John N. Pearson; and Li Peng. "Logistics Barriers to International Operations: The Case of the People's Republic of China." *Journal of Business Logistics* 18, no. 2 (1997), pp. 129–44.

Das, Ajay, and Robert B. Handfield. "Just-in-Time and Logistics in Global Sourcing: An Empirical Study." *International Journal of Physical Distribution and Logistics Management* 27, no. 3/4 (1997), pp. 244–59.

Dittmann, Paul. "Planning for Logistics in a Global Corporation." *Proceedings of the Annual Conference of the Council of Logistics Management* (Oak Brook, IL: Council of Logistics Management, 1996), pp. 589–95.

European Round Table of Industrialists. *Improved Investment Conditions: Third Survey on Improvements in Conditions for Investment in the Developing World.* Brussels, Belgium: ERT, 2000.

Fawcett, Stanley; Roger J. Calantone; and Anthony Roath. "Meeting Quality and Cost Imperatives in a Global Market." *International Journal of Physical Distribution and Logistics Management* 30, no. 6 (2000), pp. 472–99.

Fawcett, Stanley E.; Linda L. Stanley; and Sheldon R. Smith. "Developing a Logistics Capability to Improve the Performance of International Operations." *Journal of Business Logistics* 18, no. 2 (1997), pp. 101–27.

Fernie, John. "Quick Response: An International Perspective." *International Journal of Physical Distribution and Logistics Management* 24, no. 6 (1994), pp. 38–46.

Gilmore, James H. "Designing a Distribution Strategy for Canada." CCA White Paper published by Cleveland Consulting Associates, undated, 12 pages.

Goldsborough, William W., and David L. Anderson. "Import/Export Management." In *The Logistics Handbook,* ed. James F. Robeson and William C. Copacino. New York: Free Press, 1994, pp. 675–76.

Harrington, Lisa H. "Point-and-Click to Anyplace on Earth." *Supply Chain Technology News* 2, no. 7 (July 2000), pp. 40–44.

Hoffman, Kurt C. "Building a Global Logistics Network: The Virtual Model." *Global Logistics & Supply Chain Strategies* 4, no. 4 (May 2000), pp. 50–58.

Joung, J. K.; Patrick Lohier; Kevin McGahan; and Samuel Wilkin. "Whither Asia?" *World Trade* 12, no. 8 (August 1999), pp. 36–46.

"Latin America: A Fertile Ground for Efficient Supply Chains." *Global Logistics & Supply Chain Strategies* 4, no. 6 (July 2000), pp. 76–86.

MacDonald, Mitchell E. "Who Does What in International Shipping." *Traffic Management* 30, no. 9 (September 1991), pp. 38–40.

Min, Hokey, and Sean B. Eom. "An Integrated Decision Support System for Global Logistics." *International Journal of Physical Distribution and Logistics Management* 24, no. 1 (1994), pp. 29–39.

Mottley, Robert. "Troika of Third Parties." *American Shipper* 38, no. 11 (November 1996), pp. 47–52.

Mulligan, Robert M. "EDI in Foreign Trade: Case Studies in Utilization." *International Journal of Physical Distribution and Logistics Management* 28, no. 9/10 (1998), pp. 794–804.

Nooyi, Raj, and Rajive Dhar. "Managing Consumer Returns Globally." *PRTM's Insight* 11, no. 2 (Summer 1999), pp. 16–20.

Pellew, Martyn, ed. *Pan-European Logistics.* London: Financial Times' Retail and Commerce Division, 1998.

Rinehart, Lloyd M. "Global Logistics Partnership Negotiation." *International Journal of Physical Distribution and Logistics Management* 22, no. 1 (1992), pp. 27–34.

Rodnikov, Andrei N. "Logistics in Command and Mixed Economies: The Russian Experience." *International Journal of Physical Distribution and Logistics Management* 24, no. 2 (1994), pp. 4–14.

Samiee, Saeed, and Kendall Roth. "The Influence of Global Marketing Standardization on Performance." *Journal of Marketing* 56, no. 2 (April 1992), pp. 1–17.

Schwartz, Beth M. "Asia's Bumpy Road to Recovery." *Transportation & Distribution* 40, no. 10 (October 1999), pp. 43–49.

Skjoett-Larsen, Tage. "European Logistics Beyond 2000." *International Journal of Physical Distribution and Logistics Management* 30, no. 5 (2000), pp. 377–87.

Sohal, Amrik S.; Robert Millen; Michael Maggard; and Simon Moss. "Quality in Logistics: A Comparison of Practices between Australian and North American/European Firms." *International Journal of Physical Distribution and Logistics Management* 29, no. 4 (1999), pp. 267–80.

Terpstra, Vern, and Lloyd C. Russow. *International Dimensions of Marketing.* Cincinnati, OH: South-Western College Publishing, 2000.

Van der Ven, A. D. M., and A. M. A. Ribbers, "International Logistics: A Diagnostic Method for the Allocation of Production and Distribution Facilities." *The International Journal of Logistics Management* 4, no. 1 (1993), pp. 67–83.

Vantine, José G. and Marra, Claudirceu. "Logistics Challenges and Opportunities within MERCOSUR." *International Journal of Logistics Management* 8, no. 1 (1997), pp. 55–66.

Vos, Bart. "Redesigning International Manufacturing and Logistics Structures." *International Journal of Physical Distribution and Logistics Management* 27, no. 7 (1997), pp. 377–94.

Waller, David G.; Robert L. D'Avanzo; and Douglas M. Lambert. *Supply Chain Directions for a New North America.* Oak Brook, IL: Council of Logistics Management, 1995.

Whitehurst, Jr., Clinton H. "Western Australia's Place in a Global Economy: A Logistics Point of View." The Strom Thurmond Institute working paper, Series #022195, February 1995.

Questions and Problems

1. Explain why it is usually more difficult for a firm to provide the same level of customer service in its international markets that it provides in its domestic markets. Under what circumstances may an organization actually be able to provide better customer service to international markets than to domestic markets?

2. Identify the factors that make the packaging component of the logistics process so much more important in international systems than in domestic logistics systems.

3. Discuss the relative importance of inventories in domestic and global logistics. In your response, consider the financial impact of inventory decisions on the strategic position of the firm.

4. Discuss how "letters of credit" are used in international business transactions and identify why they are important.

5. Briefly identify the opportunities and challenges facing firms seeking to perform logistics activities in the following regions:
   • Western Europe
   • Japan
   • Commonwealth of Independent States (CIS) and Eastern Europe
   • China

CHAPTER 15 Organizing for Effective Logistics

Chapter Outline

Chapter Objectives

- To identify how an effective logistics organization can affect a firm.
- To describe various types of logistics organizational structures.
- To explore the factors that can influence the effectiveness of a logistics organization.
- To examine an approach to developing an optimal logistics organization.
- To identify attributes that can be used to measure organizational effectiveness.
- To overview training issues related to the growth and development of logistics personnel.

Introduction

Quality, value, and customer service have become the foci of top management. Embracing these concepts is only the first step, however, in customer satisfaction and long-term corporate profitability. An organization must also be able to implement the strategies, plans, and programs that will deliver acceptable levels of quality, value, and service to customers. Logistics and the people who "do logistics" play vital roles in that process.

In this new millennium, adaptation, continuous improvement, employee autonomy, and unity of purpose have superseded optimum design, consistency of operation, command and control, and economies of scale. Self-organizing teams are taking the place of corporate hierarchies, and creativity is replacing capital as the most important resource of an organization.[1]

Barriers to Implementing Quality Programs

In a study of over 200 European and U.S. organizations, several barriers to instituting a high-quality program were identified; the top six were related to employees and/or organizational issues. In order of importance, these were (1) changing the corporate culture, (2) establishing a common vision throughout the organization, (3) establishing employee ownership of the quality process, (4) gaining senior executive (top-down) commitment; (5) changing management processes, and (6) training and educating employees.[2] This suggests that the roles of individuals and logistics departments are especially important in strategic logistics management, and these roles will be explored in this chapter.

Logistics executives have seen their discipline undergo significant development over the past 40 years. Logistics activities were once dispersed throughout the organization but logistics now is a highly structured, computerized, large-budget functional area. The role of the logistics executive is far different today from what it was, and most probably different from what it will be in the future.

Logistics Executives Face Many Issues

Logistics executives have always had to face a multitude of issues, including economic uncertainty, inflation, product and energy shortages, environmentalism, regulatory constraints, global competition, and rising customer demands and expectations. Logistics as a function is becoming increasingly more complex and hence more difficult to manage successfully, especially within a supply chain management environment.

In this chapter, we will examine the issues of how to organize logistics within a business and how to measure its effectiveness. We will see the importance of an effective logistics organization and the types of organizational structures that exist. Although no single "ideal" structure is appropriate for all companies, we will see how to evaluate various organizational structures and describe the approaches that can be used to develop an efficient and effective logistics organization.

Importance of an Effective Logistics Organization

Effective and efficient logistics organizations are vital elements of supply chain management. The problems and challenges that companies face do not lie primarily in the area of strategic decision making but in systems, structure, mission, people, corporate

---

[1]Thomas Petzinger Jr., "A New Model for the Nature of Business: It's Alive!" *The Wall Street Journal* (February 26, 1999), pp. B1 and B4.

[2]William R. Read and Mark S. Miller, *The State of Quality in Logistics* (Cleveland, OH: Cleveland Consulting Associates, 1991), pp. 12–13.

Global

Organizing for the 21st Century

The Karolinska Hospital in Stockholm, Sweden, underwent a significant reorganization in which it redesigned its traditional structure around patient flow. In other words, the patient stay in the hospital was viewed as a process, with individual steps or components of the process being admitting, surgery, and so on.

The hospital had 47 separate departments and was highly decentralized. Customer service levels for patient care were unacceptable. As an example, some patients spent 255 days between their first contact with the hospital and the time when treatment occurred. Treatment represented only 2 percent of the entire process.

The hospital reduced the number of departments and redesigned those that remained. Eleven departments were formed, and two new positions were created: nurse coor-

dinator and medical chief. Nurse coordinators are responsible for ensuring that all operations within and between departments occur smoothly. Medical chiefs are responsible for maintaining high levels of medical expertise within each department. One of the unique results of the organizational restructuring is that doctors report to nurses on administrative matters.

The results have been significant: "Waiting times for surgery have been cut from six or eight months to three weeks. Three of 15 operating theaters have been closed, yet 3,000 more operations are performed annually, a 25 percent increase."

Source: Adapted from Rahul Jacob, "The Struggle to Create an Organization for the 21st Century," *Fortune* 131, no. 6 (April 3, 1995), pp. 90–99. © 1995 Time, Inc. Reprinted by permission.

culture, and reward structure.[3] In essence, each is an important strategic resource and a corporate asset. The ways they fit together and interact to create a synergistic system are critical. Thus, many organizations have been reengineering, essentially "recreating" their organizations and systems rather than making minor changes.[4]

The challenge of developing the "right" organization can be likened to the challenge facing the military leader who has prepared a superb campaign strategy and must now design the army that will execute that strategy. Without the correct assembly of different battle units and their support services, the campaign cannot proceed, let alone achieve victory. By design we mean not only the selection of the organization structure but also the design of the support, planning, and control systems that deliver the strategy via the organizational structure and its people.

Many Firms Have Reengineered Their Logistics Processes

Atlas Supply has successfully reengineered its processes. Atlas Supply, a distributor of automotive parts, was formed in 1992 to integrate the distribution and logistics of two merged companies. It developed a shared system that allowed the companies to reduce the number of distribution centers by over 50 percent. Transportation costs decreased by more than 20 percent, which included savings of more than $300,000 because of a reduction of empty backhauls. The savings resulted from placing many logistics-related activities under a single organizational unit, and outsourcing some activities to third parties.[5]

---

[3]Tom Peters, *Tom Peters Live* (Boulder, CO: Career Track Publications, 1991).

[4]See Michael Hammer and James Champy, *Reengineering the Corporation: A Manifesto for Business Revolution* (New York: Harper Business, 1993); and James Champy, *Reengineering Management: The Mandate for New Leadership* (New York: Harper Business, 1995).

[5]Helen Richardson and Tom Andel, "Celebrate Best Practices," *Transportation and Distribution* 35, no. 10 (October 1994), p. 28.

FIGURE 15–1

*Traditional approach
to logistics management*

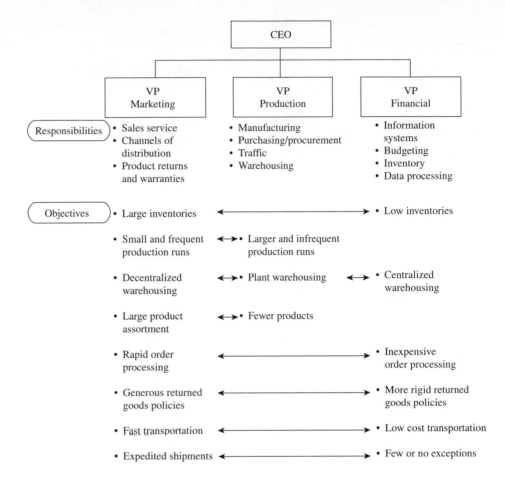

Companies as diverse as Abbott Laboratories, Eastman Kodak, IBM, Karolinska Hospital (Sweden), Maremount Corporation, Mead Johnson, Rohm and Haas, and Uniroyal have undergone similar changes and achieved much the same results as Atlas Supply.

Historically, organizations scattered logistics functions throughout the company, often with no single executive, department, or division responsible for managing the entire logistics process. Such a traditional organizational structure would resemble the one shown in Figure 15–1. Since the 1960s, however, the trend has been to integrate logistics functions under one top-ranking corporate executive and implement the integrated logistics management concept (previously discussed in Chapter 1).

**Trend toward
Integrating Logistics
Functions**

Table 15–1 lists the range of activities over which the logistics executive has had authority. In general, there has been an increase in the logistics executive's span of control to include transportation, warehousing, inventories, order processing, packaging, material handling, forecasting and planning, and purchasing and procurement.[6]

Whether logistics executives are located in North America or elsewhere in the world, the scope of their responsibilities is broadening. Within their organizations,

---

[6]Because the respondent population differs across the surveys, direct comparisons of the results are not possible. However, general trends or tendencies can be determined from the data.

TABLE 15–1   **Control Exercised by Logistics Executives over Selected Logistics Functions**

Activities	Percent of Reporting Companies				
	1966[a]	1976[b]	1985[c]	1990[d]	1999[e]
Transportation	89%	94%	97%	98%	90%
Warehousing	70	93	95	97	88
Inventory control	55	83	81	79	74
Order processing	43	76	67	61	55
Packaging	8	70	37	48	39
Purchasing and procurement	15	58	44	51	41

Sources:

[a]John F. Spencer, "Physical Distribution Management Finds Its Level," *Handling and Shipping* 7, no. 11 (November 1966), pp. 67–69.

[b]Bernard J. La Londe and James F. Robeson, "Profile of the Physical Distribution Executive," in *Proceedings of the Fourteenth Annual Conference of the National Council of Physical Distribution Management* (Chicago, IL: NCPDM, 1976), pp. 1–23.

[c]Data reported are for directors of logistics. From Bernard J. La Londe and Larry W. Emmelhainz, "Where Do You Fit In?" *Distribution* 8, no. 11 (November 1985), p. 34.

[d]James M. Masters and Bernard J. La Londe, "The 1990 Ohio State University Survey of Career Patterns in Logistics," *Proceedings of the Annual Conference of the Council of Logistics Management,* vol. 1 (Oak Brook, IL: Council of Logistics Management, 1990), pp. 33–52.

[e]Bernard J. La Londe and Terrance L. Pohlen, "The 1999 Ohio State University Survey of Career Patterns in Logistics," *Proceedings of the Annual Conference of the Council of Logistics Management* (Oak Brook, IL: Council of Logistics Management, 1999), pp. 359–77.

European logistics executives have primary responsibility for warehousing, transportation, inventory, order processing, and packaging. Additionally, they often manage production planning, purchasing, procurement, information systems, customer service, and production control.[7]

The importance of integrating logistics functions was brought into focus when companies such as Whirlpool, Johnson & Johnson, Hooker Chemicals, and Nabisco established senior logistics executives in their companies with responsibility for managing the major logistics functions. Significant cost savings resulted.[8] Such savings did not go unnoticed by other companies, which quickly saw the opportunities associated with logistics integration and responded by establishing their own senior logistics executives with broad responsibilities.

In the next section, we will examine several of the major types of logistics organizations that have developed in various kinds of companies.

---

[7]Manfred Hessenberger, Nicholas Seiersen, and Frank Straube, "European Logistics Trends and Strategies," *Annual Conference Proceedings of the Council of Logistics Management* (Chicago, IL: Oak Brook, IL: Council of Logistics Management, 1997), p. 125.

[8]Many of these early examples of logistics integration have been reported in various professional journals, conference presentations, and conference proceedings. Specifically, see "Assessing the Organizational Trade-Offs in the Distribution Strategic Planning Process," by Peter H. Soderberg, director of physical distribution and planning, Johnson & Johnson, at the annual meeting of the National Council of Physical Distribution Management, Houston, Texas, in October 1979; Tomas J. Murray, "A Powerful New Voice in Management," *Dun's Review* 107, no. 4 (April 1976), p. 70; and Nicholas J. La Howchic, "Merging the Distribution Operations of Nabisco and Standard Brands, and Customer Service," *Proceedings of the Twenty-Second Annual Conference of the National Council of Physical Distribution Management* (Oak Brook, IL: NCPDM, 1984), pp. 179–96.

Logistics Organizational Structures

To understand how various departments and groups within an organization interact with one another, it is helpful to understand how business organizations have developed. Briefly overviewing this historical development will help you understand the current and future logistics management environments.[9]

Development of Business Structures

Around the time of the founding of the United States, companies tended to be one-person operations. The companies were generally small and specialized, serving a localized region. One or few people controlled the entire operation.

In the mid-19th century, as the industrial revolution was taking place in the United States and many companies began to rapidly grow and develop, it became increasingly difficult for one or a few people to successfully manage all of an organization's operations. Companies began hiring people who specialized in managing specific functions, such as manufacturing, sales, distribution, and accounting. It was believed that this created greater levels of efficiency and effectiveness.

Functional Specialization

By the beginning of 1900, functional specialization was no longer sufficient for effective management, due primarily to increased corporate growth and product/service diversification. Large organizations created divisions or business units, organized vertically around similar product/service offerings. Employees became specialized both in terms of function and product. Government organizations, including the military infrastructure, also expanded tremendously during this period.

In some organizations, functions that did not directly affect the organization's product or service offering and that cut across divisional boundaries were left at a "corporate" level, supporting various divisions of the company. This was common for functions such as human resources, accounts payable, purchasing, and financial reporting. There was no reporting relationship between "line" (or divisional) employees and "staff" (or corporate) employees.

By the 1950s, some large organizations such as Pillsbury Company realized that the division structure was not optimal. It did not provide links among line people in various division and corporate positions, so the synergies of being part of a large organization were being lost. To combat this problem, many organizations began to implement other organizational forms.

The "Hollow Corporation"

As the new millennium begins, there continues to be discussions about optimal organizational forms.[10] With the increasing use of outsourcing as an accepted method for conducting various logistics activities, some experts have speculated that a "hollow corporation" will develop.[11] The hollow corporation will exist as a small organization of

[9]See Lisa M. Ellram and Laura M. Birou, *Purchasing for Bottom Line Impact* (Burr Ridge, IL: Irwin, 1995), pp. 84–87.

[10]See Ian I. Mitroff, Richard O. Mason, and Christine M. Pearson, "Radical Surgery: What Will Tomorrow's Organizations Look Like?" *Academy of Management Executive* 8, no. 2 (1994), pp. 11–21; Thomas A. Stewart, "The Search for the Organization of Tomorrow," *Fortune* 125, no. 10 (May 18, 1992), pp. 92–98; Donald Bowersox et al., *World Class Logistics: The Challenge of Managing Continuous Change* (Oak Brook, IL: Council of Logistics Management, 1995); and Carla Reed, "Becoming a Future Capable Company," *Competitive Edge* (Summer 1999), pp. 5–6.

[11]See Ellram and Birou, *Purchasing for Bottom Line Impact,* pp. 84–87.

managers and "idea people" who hire external companies to perform various types of activities, including manufacturing, logistics, distribution, billing, sales, and marketing.

The "Virtual Corporation"

The rationale for this type of organization is that organizations should specialize and focus efforts on what they do best (i.e., their core competencies), and hire specialists to perform other activities. A variation on this concept is the "virtual corporation," in which a number of companies come together to develop, produce, sell, and distribute a product or a service of limited scope. These organizations establish a very close working relationship, which exists only for as long as the product or service is viable.

An organization may be simultaneously engaged in a number of such relationships across a variety of products and services. These organizations focus on the product or service to be delivered to the customer, relying heavily on interorganizational and interfunctional teams. This type of organization is apparent in alliances, such as the relationship between Apple Computer, IBM, and Motorola to develop a comprehensive microprocessor and operating system for future generations of computers.[12]

Organizations in the E-Commerce Era

In the era of e-commerce, the hollow and virtual corporations are possible scenarios for companies. Of course, customers do not care how companies are organized or integrated; they are concerned with the outputs they see, such as product quality and customer service levels. In an electronic environment, where communications within and between firms are facilitated by e-mail and the Internet, many activities traditionally performed in-house can be outsourced easily. The outsourcing of logistics and other functions affects both organizational structure and the coordination of such activities.[13]

Most executives agree that coordination of logistics activities is essential in any organization, irrespective of size, structure, type of business, or location. Manufacturers, wholesalers, and retailers all perform logistics activities but are often organized differently. Manufacturers may use one of three organizational strategies: process-based, market-based, or channel-based. These strategies have been described as follows:

Process-Based Strategy

Process-based [strategy] is concerned with managing a broad group of logistics activities as a value-added chain. The emphasis of a process strategy is to achieve efficiency from managing purchasing, manufacturing scheduling, and physical distribution as an integrated system.

Market-Based Strategy

Market-based [strategy] is concerned with managing a limited group of logistics activities across a multi-division business or across multiple business units. The logistics organization when following a market-based strategy seeks to: (1) make joint product shipments to customers on behalf of different business units or product groups; and (2) facilitate sales and logistical coordination by a single order-invoice. Often the senior sales and logistics executives report to the same senior manager.

Channel-Based Strategy

Channel-based [strategy] focuses on managing logistics activities performed jointly in combination with dealers and distributors. The channel orientation places a great deal of attention on external control. Firms that concentrate on a channel-based strategy typically have significant amounts of finished inventories forward, or downstream, in the distribution channel.[14]

Wholesalers are structured differently from manufacturers because of their position in the supply chain and the nature of the activities that they perform. In addition to

---

[12]William H. Davidow and Michael S. Malone, *The Virtual Corporation* (New York: Harper Collins Publishers, 1992).

[13]Ann Grackin, "Opportunities Flourish in the E-World," *Competitive Edge* (Winter 1999), pp. 9–11; see also Leslie Hansen Harps, "Outstanding Outsourcing," *Inbound Logistics* 20, no. 7 (July 2000), pp. 78–84, 91–100.

[14]Donald J. Bowersox et al., *Leading Edge Logistics: Competitive Positioning for the 1990s* (Oak Brook, IL: Council of Logistics Management, 1989), pp. 34–35.

the traditional wholesaling functions (e.g., transport, storage), a number of value-added services are being done by wholesalers, including light manufacturing and assembly, pricing, order processing, inventory management, logistics system design, and development of promotional materials.[15]

Retail Logistics

Because of their direct contact with final customers and the high level of competition they face, retailers often place more emphasis on inventory, warehousing, and customer service activities than do manufacturers. They tend to be more centralized than manufacturers and wholesalers. Retail logistics has been described as follows:

> The logistical operations of retailers are geographically focused and highly detailed. Retail distribution warehouses are generally located within one or two days' travel distance from a cluster of store locations. The delivery destinations of retailers' distribution systems are well known, making transportation planning relatively straightforward. Retailers generally ship large numbers of stockkeeping units from their distribution warehouses, creating the need for intricate control systems. The notion of an *inventory pipeline* is critical in retailing due to the high cost of retail space. Proper timing of store deliveries is essential to the maintenance and velocity of store inventory.[16]

Additionally, many retailers are becoming more involved in direct-to-store deliveries from manufacturers and are purchasing many logistics services from third parties rather than performing those activities themselves.

Coordination of the various logistics activities can be achieved in several ways. The basic systems generally take into account the following:

- Strategic versus operational coordination.
- Centralized versus decentralized coordination.
- Line versus staff coordination.

Strategic versus Operational Coordination

Strategic versus operational refers to the level at which logistics activities are positioned within the firm. Strategically, it is important to determine logistics' position in the corporate hierarchy relative to other activities, such as marketing, manufacturing, and finance/accounting. Equally important, however, is the operational structure of the various logistics activities—warehousing, inventory control, order processing, transportation, and others—under the senior logistics executive.

Centralized versus Decentralized Coordination

Centralized distribution reflects a system in which logistics activities are administered at a central location, typically a corporate headquarters, or a system in which operating authority is controlled under a single department or individual. Centrally programming activities such as order processing, traffic, or inventory control can result in significant cost savings due to economies of scale. *Decentralization* of logistics activities can be effective for firms with diverse products or markets. With technological advancements in computer and information systems, high levels of customer service can be delivered with either a centralized or a decentralized logistics network.

Line versus Staff Coordination

Within the three basic types of organizational structures, logistics activities can be *line, staff,* or a *combination of line and staff.* Logistics as a line activity is comparable to sales or production, in that employees are "doing things," that is, performing various tasks. In the staff organization, the line activities, such as order processing, traffic, and warehousing, may be housed under a logistics vice president or under production, marketing, or finance/accounting. The various staff activities assist and coordinate the line

---

[15]Ibid., p. 37.
[16]Ibid., p. 39.

FIGURE 15–2

Organization design for logistics as a function

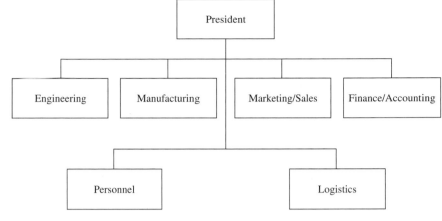

FIGURE 15–3

Organization design for logistics as a program

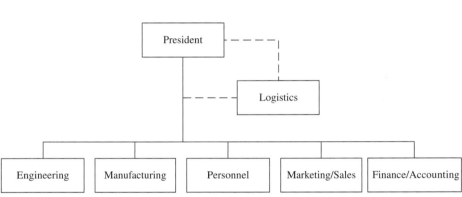

functions. The combination of line and staff activities joins these two organizational types and thus eliminates the shortcomings inherent in systems where line and staff activities are not coordinated.

Other organizational approaches are possible.[17] Examples include logistics as a function, logistics as a program, and the matrix organization approach. Figure 15–2 shows the organizational design for logistics as a *function.* An example of a company that uses a functional approach is the Bechtel Group, a provider of technical, management, and related services, primarily within the transportation, aerospace, power generation, and construction industries.[18]

Logistics as a Function

Some argue that if a firm treats logistics as a functional area, without regard to other activities, the results will be less than optimal. Logistics is cross-functional and therefore requires a different organizational structure, not the "functional silo" approach.

Logistics as a Program

When logistics is organized as a *program* (see Figure 15–3), the distribution activity assumes the role of a program in which the total company participates. Individual functional areas are subordinate to the program.

Logistics in a Matrix Organization

It can be argued that the optimal logistics organization lies between the two extremes represented by the functional and program approaches. One approach has

---

[17]For an examination of a variety of organizational forms, see Robert J. Kramer, *Organizing for Global Competitiveness: The Business Unit Design,* Report No. 1110-95-RR (New York: The Conference Board, 1995).

[18]Ibid., pp. 15–17.

FIGURE 15–4

*Logistics in a matrix
organization*

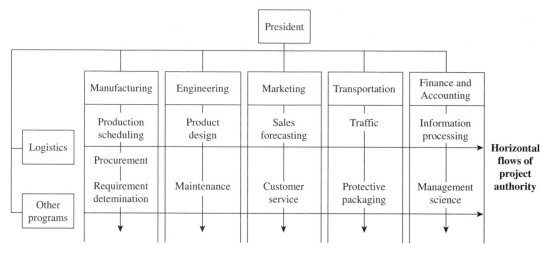

Vertical flows of functional authority

Source: Adapted from Daniel W. DeHayes, Jr., and Robert L. Taylor, "Making 'Logistics' Work in a Firm," *Business Horizons* 15, no. 3 (June 1972), p. 44.
Reprinted by permission from *Business Horizons.* Copyright 1972 by the Board of Trustees at Indiana University, Kelley School of Business.

been termed the *matrix organization* (see Figure 15–4). Firms that use a matrix management approach include Asea Brown Boveri Ltd. (a European company specializing in electrical engineering and equipment), Caterpillar (earthmoving equipment), Dow Chemical (chemicals), and Royal Dutch/Shell Group (petroleum, gas, and chemicals).[19]

The matrix management approach requires the coordination of activities across unit lines in the organization. Therefore, it is essential that top-level management wholeheartedly support the logistics executive. Even with high-level support, however, the complexities of coordination are difficult to master.

For example, when there are multiple reporting responsibilities, as is common in matrix organizations, problems may arise due to conflicts that result from reporting to multiple managers, who may have different goals. As a result of this, many organizations have adopted a team structure.

Rather than replacing the divisional structure, matrix structure overlays the divisional structure. In addition to divisional reporting relationships, managers in matrix organizations report to another person in their function outside the division, often at a corporate level. This structure may also be used to create reporting relationships for special projects that straddle two or more divisions.[20]

Whatever structure is used, however, logistics should be viewed as a process. When managed as a process within a supply chain management context, the specific organizational structure can usually take many forms.

Team Organizations

For some industries, *team organizations* can be very effective. High-technology firms are especially suited to organizing in a team structure because of the high incidence

[19]Robert J. Kramer, *Organizing for Global Competitiveness: The Matrix Design,* Report No. 1088-94-RR (New York: The Conference Board, 1994).
    [20]Ibid.

of task- or project-oriented activities that overlap several functional areas. A team structure also supports the "flattening" of organizational layers many firms are experiencing today.[21]

A team structure involves a small group of people with complementary skills, common goals, mutual accountability, and the resources and empowerment to achieve their goals. This differs from a work group (which is more like the traditional matrix organization) in that people on the team hold themselves mutually accountable, rather than just individually accountable, for results.[22] Because of the number of people involved, it is often difficult to make decisions in matrix organizations. Thus, team structures are becoming increasingly popular.

Teams

The word *team* has been defined as "a small number of people with complementary skills who are committed to a common purpose, set of performance goals and approach for which they hold themselves mutually accountable."[23] Two general types of teams exist: task teams and work teams. Task teams exist for a specific, identifiable purpose with a clear end, whereas work teams are ongoing, much like a divisional structure, with specific, continuing goals.

Task Teams

Task Teams.   While both task teams and ad hoc committees focus on a discrete task, they function differently. The key distinction between a task team and an ad hoc committee is that the members of the latter still function primarily as individuals rather than as a team. Ad hoc committees may meet to decide what has to be done, but then each person individually completes a piece of the whole and is individually accountable for the results. In a task team, there is mutual accountability, and much of the work may even be performed with other team members.

Another important distinction is that the task team "owns" the project it is working on. For example, a task team to implement carrier certification would be fully empowered to design and implement the program without further approvals. However, an ad hoc committee would require approval from parties outside the group, generally top management, before proceeding with each step. Thus, a task team has a much higher level of task and group responsibility than an ad hoc committee.

In the creation of a task team, several issues (applicable to all types of teams) should be addressed:

- *Opportunity:* What is (are) the reason(s) for the team's existence?
- *Process:* What are the steps to be followed, and what are the questions to be answered?
- *Evidence of success:* What results are expected, and how long should it take for the team to achieve success?
- *Resources:* What are the personnel, time, monetary, and other resources required by the team?

---

[21]Donald J. Bowersox, Patricia J. Daugherty, Cornelia Dröge, Richard N. Germain, and Dale S. Rogers, *Logistical Excellence: It's Not Business as Usual* (Burlington, MA: Digital Equipment Corp., 1992).

[22]Jon R. Katzenback and David K. Smith, "The Discipline of Teams," *Harvard Business Review* 71, no. 2 (March/April 1993), pp. 111–23.

[23]Ibid., p. 111.

- *Constraints:* What are the team's time frame, scope of responsibility, scope of authority, and budget?
- *Expectations:* What are the required outputs from the team, and when should those results be produced?[24]

Work Teams

Work Teams.   Returning to the definition of teams above, work teams, also known as self-directed teams, are distinguished from other types of organizations by their commitment to a common purpose and goals, but more importantly by their ongoing mutual accountability to achieve those goals. These cross-functional groups (which may be described as empowered people on empowered teams) are often organized around a product or a service offering, and may be responsible for all aspects of that product/ service, from design and development to customer support.

The work team framework is also unique in that it is not a temporary structure that overlays another organizational form. Work teams are relatively rare in practice, and when they do exist they represent a major change for most organizations. A key question to ask is whether joint performance and extensive cross-functional interaction and participation will likely yield significantly better results than a more traditional approach. Only if the answer is yes should an organization implement work teams. Otherwise, committees may suffice.

One firm that has implemented a work team approach is Chrysler. Each of the automaker's model platform teams is responsible for the design, development, logistics, engineering, and purchasing aspects of a new model, such as the Neon.[25]

Using Teams

Organizations can use more than one type of team at a time. The organizational structure used should fit both the activity to be performed and the culture of the organization. Organizations often use committees first and then task teams before evolving to work teams. Conversely, an organization may decide that work teams would not be a great benefit to its performance.

Problems Associated with Team Structures

Because most people are employed in organizations that consider individual results and accountabilities to be paramount, use of teams can be threatening and even dysfunctional. To combat potential problems, most organizations train employees to function as a contributing group or team member. Training may include such topics as appreciating diversity and individual differences,[26] team interaction, and team accountability, and may even involve team building exercises or activities outside of the workplace. Other issues that must be addressed in developing teams and committees are the degree of accountability, the degree of responsibility and decision-making authority, and the impact of team performance on individual performance appraisals.[27]

---

[24]Jim Tompkins, *Goose Chase* (Raleigh, NC: Tompkins Press, 1997), pp. 79–81.

[25]Thomas T. Stallkamp, "Beyond Reengineering: Developing the Extended Enterprise," *NAPM Insights* (February 1995), p. 76.

[26]See Lisa Harrington, "Why Managing Diversity Is So Important," *Distribution* 92, no. 11 (November 1993), pp. 88–92; and Stephen A. LeMay and John C. Carr, *The Growth and Development of Logistics Personnel* (Oak Brook, IL: Council of Logistics Management, 1999).

[27]See Susan Caminiti, "What Team Leaders Need to Know," *Fortune* 131, no. 3 (February 20, 1995), pp. 93–100; and Dawn R. Deeter-Schmelz, "Applying Teams to Logistics Processes: Information Acquisition and the Impact of Team Role Clarity and Norms," *Journal of Business Logistics* 18, no. 1 (1997), pp. 159–78.

Interfunctional Coordination Is a Key to Success

Regardless of the formal structures chosen, interfunctional relationships remain a key component of the logistics job. Good working relationships with other functions are critical to logistics managers' effectiveness. However, companies that revamp their logistics systems often find that decentralizing authority flies in the face of popular management trends, such as self-directed teams. The reason is that "in an age of delegation and empowerment, logistics demands centralized control."[28] Thus, logistics is often a matrixed team member, retaining both dual reporting to the team and a centralized logistics function, where efficient and effective strategies can be leveraged on a companywide scale.

Is There an Optimal Organizational Structure?

A review of the multitude of organizational types found in companies reveals a variety of structural forms. Firms can be very successful using one or more organizational structures. Which form is optimal for any given company? That is an immensely difficult question to answer. Rather than examining organizational structures of several companies and speculating about "ideal" or "optimal" systems, we need to employ some empirical measures to correlate organizational structure and efficiency/ productivity. Obviously, the best system for a company is one that maximizes its efficiency and effectiveness. The logistics executive must best determine the firm's organizational structure and evaluate the outputs of that structure.

Decision-Making Strategies in Organizing for Logistics

As logistics executives face new challenges in the decades ahead, it will become even more important that logistics systems operate more efficiently and effectively. In the face of higher costs of operation and increasing pressures from customers for better service, logistics organizations must change to meet the challenge. An understanding of the factors that make organizations effective, and knowledge of how these factors interrelate, are the first steps toward developing an organization that will serve the firm's customers.

The Logistics Mission Statement[29]

In general, mission statements provide the foundation or basis from which a company develops strategies, plans, and tactics. The mission statement defines the basic purpose of an organization and identifies the parameters under which it will operate.

As corporate mission statements serve to provide the starting point for developing corporate goals and objectives, so too will logistics mission statements provide direction for developing business strategies. When combined with a specific set of performance goals and measurement systems, the logistics mission statement can help eliminate organizational conflicts and provide direction to logistics personnel.

Components of a Logistics Mission Statement

The components of a corporate mission statement or a logistics mission statement will be similar. They will vary in their specific content because the logistics mission statement is only one element of a firm's total corporate mission, but they will both

---

[28]Ronald Henkoff, "Delivering the Goods," *Fortune* 130, no. 11 (November 28, 1994), p. 70.

[29]This material is based on James R. Stock and Cornelia Dröge, "Logistics Mission Statements: An Appraisal," in *Proceedings of the Nineteenth Annual Transportation and Logistics Educators Conference,* ed. James M. Masters and Cynthia L. Coykendale (Columbus, OH: The Ohio State University, 1990), pp. 79–91.

TABLE 15–2   Components of a Corporate and/or Logistics Mission Statement

- The specification of target customers and markets.
- The identification of principal products and/or services.
- The specification of geographic domain.
- The identification of core technologies.
- The expression of commitment to survival, growth, and profitability.
- The specification of key elements in the company philosophy.
- The identification of the company self-concept.
- The identification of the firm's desired public image.

Source: Adapted from John A. Pearce II and Fred David, "Corporate Mission Statements: The Bottom Line," *Academy of Management Executive* 1, no. 2 (1987), p. 109.

contain similar components. Typically, mission statements will contain eight key components (see Table 15–2).

The similarities between corporate and logistics mission statements based on the eight components identified in Table 15–2 are as follows:[30]

• *Targeted customers and markets.* The selection of target markets and the development of marketing strategies to reach those segments are vital components of a firm's activities. Within corporate mission statements, mention is often made of customers and markets. An examination of logistics mission statements revealed that about one-half of all firms with formal statements included mention of targeted customers and markets. Illustrative of mission statements including such material were the following:

To deliver quality products to our customers and manufacturing groups in the fastest and most cost-effective mode possible. (hospital supply company)

[To] provide integrated logistical support services and facilities to the product groups and field operations units of the division. (communication systems manufacturer)

• *Principal products/services.* Much like corporate mission statements, more than two-thirds of logistics mission statements include discussion of their products and services. In fact, significantly more manufacturers included mention of their principal products and/or services than any other component. Examples of statements that included mention of products/services were the following:

[To] provide timely and effective services for the storage and commercial movement of all company finished products and of materials and supplies necessary for company operations. (tobacco company)

To deliver our furniture to our customers within six weeks of order, in the most efficient manner possible. (furniture company)

• *Geographic domain.* Typically, firms did not specify locations of their target markets within their logistics mission statements.

[To] provide service parts, tools, and test equipment necessary to maintain the company's worldwide installed computer base. (computer manufacturer)

To sell, produce, and deliver the products of the foods business units in the United States. (conglomerate)

---

[30]Ibid., pp. 82–84.

• *Core technologies.* Few firms include mention of core technologies in their logistics mission statements, which perhaps can be attributed to the fact that manufacturing technologies are distinct from logistics technologies. Even when firms include core technologies relevant to their manufacturing operations in the overall corporate mission statement (which occurs infrequently), they may not include such mention in the logistics mission statement. When they do, however, they word the statements similarly to the following:

> Integrated distribution network . . . is managed through a single transportation network structure, common information network, effective facilities network, and performance measurement and control. (computer manufacturer)

> To manage . . . a corporate-wide quality transportation network and supporting multidivisional computer systems that will assure the safe delivery of products. (automobile manufacturer)

• *Survival, growth, and profitability.* Corporate mission statements almost universally include mention of the issues of survival, growth, and profitability. Because some firms may not see any or very little direct correlation between logistics activities and company profits, sales volumes, growth rates, and the like, it is not surprising that only about one-half of all firms include mention of such elements. If logistics is viewed primarily as a way to reduce costs, rather than as a means to improve competitive advantage, corporate management will see only a very indirect link. At best, management will view logistics from the perspective that lower costs can increase bottom-line profitability but cannot increase sales and, ultimately, profits. Examples of logistics mission statements that included mention of a concern for survival, growth, and profitability are the following:

> [To] provide timely, cost-effective shipment and delivery; to enhance our position . . . and to provide career growth for our employees. (metal products manufacturer)

> To provide a cost-effective distribution system to enhance our competitive position and improve our profits. (food company)

• *Company philosophy.* One of the noteworthy findings of the analysis of logistics mission statements was the paucity of statements that included any mention of overall company and/or logistics philosophy. Less than 10 percent of firms include any such statements. When logistics mission statements did mention philosophy, they seemed to include the notion that logistics could create competitive advantage for the firm:

> Logistics will be active in the integration and differentiation strategies that produce competitive advantage. (lighting manufacturer)

> Our mission is to have the right product at the right place at the right time at the right cost. (building products manufacturer)

• *Company self-concept.* Did the logistics mission statement include any statements of how the firm viewed itself? Approximately one-third incorporate mention of self-concept:

> [To] provide our customers the quality product they need when they desire it so that our service is better than our competitors'. (optical manufacturer)

> To be the logistics and distribution vendor of choice by exceeding competitive levels of service at lower cost and increased inventory turns. (office systems manufacturer)

• *Firm's desired public image.* Forty percent of the logistics mission statements identified the firm's desired public image. When firms included mention of public image in their mission statements, only general mention was included. No mention was made of the specific public image the firm was to achieve. Examples included the following statements:

> The goal is to strengthen the company's image, market share, and growth through the excellence of its service and the professionalism of its personnel. (sporting goods manufacturer)

> To promote the firm's image, physical distribution is committed to excellence. (pharmaceutical firm)

Organizations need a clear statement of purpose in order to develop some optimal combination of logistical activities that must be performed in the day-to-day operations of the enterprise. In sum, the logistics mission statement is an important document to guide the planning, implementation, and control of an organization's logistics activities.

Components of an Optimal Logistics Organization

Many factors can influence the effectiveness of a logistics organization. In general, the factors contributing to organizational effectiveness can be summarized as (1) organiza-

---

Technology

New Technologies Are Changing the Way We Work

To more effectively compete in today's global and fast-paced environment, intra- and inter-departmental and organizational communication and coordination are keys to survival. Technology is rapidly impacting how organizations are structured, and how they can most effectively and efficiently communicate and coordinate.

One aspect of technology that will have significant impact on how individuals and firms interrelate will be "Groupware." Groupware is a software technology that has been defined as: "computer-mediated collaboration that increases the productivity or functionality of person-to-person processes." Several categories of groupware exist, including:

1. Electronic mail.
2. Calendaring/scheduling.
3. Group document handling.
4. Workgroup utilities and development tools.
5. Group decisions and meeting support.
6. Information sharing/conferencing.

7. Workflow management and business process design.

Spaulding Sports Worldwide implemented some groupware solutions that resulted in a reduction of their product design/implementation process from one year to six months. Spaulding implemented a document and image management system . . . to streamline the design/implementation process. "Our initial software investment of $100,000 paid for itself overnight," says H. Oldham Brooks in operations research. "We were spending $85,000 a year in copying, mailing, and distributing product specifications."

The use of groupware technology is not an answer to all the problems facing an organization, but it can help a company "find a way to improve collaboration, communication, and coordination within [an] enterprise, department, or workgroup."

Source: David Coleman and Ronni T. Marshak, "Changing Your Organization with Groupware," *Fortune* 130, no. 6 (September 1994), unnumbered advertising supplement.

tional characteristics, (2) environmental characteristics, (3) employee characteristics, and (4) managerial policies and practices.[31]

Structure and Technology Are Most Important

Organizational Characteristics.   Structure and technology are the major components of a firm's organizational characteristics. *Structure* refers to the relationships that exist between various functional areas—interfunctional (marketing, finance, operations, manufacturing, logistics) or intrafunctional (warehousing, traffic, purchasing, customer service). The relationships are most often represented by a company's organization chart. Examples of structural variables are decentralization, specialization, formalization, span of control, organization size, and work-unit size.

Technology has been defined as "the mechanisms used by an organization to transform raw inputs into finished outputs. Technology can take several forms, including variations in the materials used, and variations in the technical knowledge brought to bear on goal-directed activities."[32]

Organizational Climate and Corporate Culture

Environmental Characteristics.   The effectiveness of the organization is influenced by factors internal and external to the firm. Internal factors, which are basically controllable by the logistics executive, are known as *organizational climate.*[33] Sometimes this is referred to as *corporate culture.*

Organizational climate is related to organizational effectiveness. This is particularly evident when effectiveness is measured on an individual level (e.g., job attitudes, performance, satisfaction, involvement).

External factors, sometimes referred to as uncontrollable elements, include the political and legal, economic, cultural and social, and competitive environments.

Employee Characteristics.   The keys to effective organizations are the employees who "fill the boxes" on the organization chart. The ability of individuals to carry out their respective job responsibilities ultimately determines the overall effectiveness of any organization.

Organizational Attachment and Job Performance

All employees have varying outlooks, goals, needs, and abilities. These differences can cause people to behave differently, even when they are in the same work environment. These differences can have a direct bearing on two important organizational processes that affect organizational effectiveness: *organizational attachment,* or the extent to which employees identify with their employer, and *job performance.* Without attachment and performance, effectiveness becomes all but impossible to achieve.[34]

---

[31]See Kim S. Cameron and David A. Whetten, eds., *Organizational Effectiveness: A Comparison of Multiple Models* (New York: Academic Press, 1983); and Richard M. Steers, *Organizational Effectiveness: A Behavioral View* (Santa Monica, CA: Goodyear Publishing, 1977).

[32]Steers, *Organizational Effectiveness,* pp. 7–8.

[33]F. T. Sepic, "Culture, Climate, and Total Quality Management: Measuring Readiness for Change," *Public Productivity & Management Review* 18, no. 4 (Summer 1995), pp. 369–80; B. Schneider, "Creating the Climate and Culture of Success," *Organizational Dynamics* 23, no. 1 (Summer 1994), pp. 17–24; and A. H. Church, "Managerial Behaviors and Work Group Climate as Predictors of Employee Outcomes," *Human Resource Development Quarterly* 6, no. 2 (Summer 1995), pp. 173–82.

[34]See Garry D. Brewer, "Assessing Outcomes and Effects," in *Organizational Effectiveness: A Comparison of Multiple Models,* ed. Kim S. Cameron and David A. Whetten (New York: Academic Press, 1983), pp. 207–14; and Steers, *Organizational Effectiveness,* p. 9.

Managerial Policies and Practices.   Policies at the macro level (i.e., those that apply to the entire company) determine the overall goal structure of the organization. Policies at the micro (departmental) level influence the individual goals of the various corporate functions, such as warehousing, traffic, order processing, and customer service. Macro and micro policies, in turn, affect the procedures and practices of the organization. The planning, coordinating, and facilitating of goal-directed activities—which determine organizational effectiveness—depend on the policies and practices adopted by the firm at the macro and micro levels.

A number of factors can aid the logistics executive in improving the effectiveness of the organization. The following are six of the most important:

Ways of Improving Logistics Organizational Effectiveness

1. Strategic goal setting.
2. Resource acquisition and utilization.
3. Performance environment.
4. Communication process.
5. Leadership and decision-making expertise.
6. Organizational adaptation and innovation.[35]

Strategic Goal Setting

Strategic goal setting involves the establishment of two clearly defined sets of goals: the overall organization goals and individual employee goals. Both sets must be compatible and aimed at maximizing company/employee effectiveness. For example, the company may have an overall goal to reduce order cycle time by 10 percent, but it is the actions of each employee attempting to improve his or her component of the order cycle that brings about achievement of the goal.

Resource Acquisition and Utilization

Resource acquisition and utilization includes the utilization of human and financial resources, as well as technology, to maximize the achievement of corporate goals and objectives. This involves such things as having properly trained and experienced persons operating the firm's private truck fleet, using the proper storage and retrieval systems for the company's warehouses, and having the capital necessary to take advantage of forward buying opportunities, massing of inventories, and other capital projects.

Performance Environment

The *performance environment* is concerned with having the proper organizational climate that motivates employees to maximize their effectiveness and, subsequently, the effectiveness of the overall logistics function. Strategies that can be used to develop a goal-directed performance environment include (1) proper employee selection and placement, (2) training and development programs, (3) task design, and (4) performance evaluation, combined with a reward structure that promotes goal-oriented behavior.[36]

Communication Process

One of the most important factors influencing logistics effectiveness in any organization is the *communication process.* Without good communication, logistics policies and procedures cannot be effectively transmitted throughout the organization, and the feedback of information concerning the success or failure of those policies and procedures cannot take place. Communication flows within the logistics area can be downward (boss-employee), upward (employee-boss), or horizontal (boss-boss or employee-employee).

In a worldwide survey of business executives, it was found that 80 percent of the information needed for making decisions was already available within the organization. However, 38 percent of executives indicated that they wasted substantial amounts of

---

[35]Steers, *Organizational Effectiveness,* p. 136.
[36]Ibid., p. 142.

TABLE 15–3   Comparison of Three Leadership Approaches

Approach to:	Supervisory Leadership	Group Leadership	Team Leadership
Change	React to change	Encourage change	Work with team to create change
People	Direct people	Involve people	Help people grow and obtain synergy
Diversity	Minimize diversity	Allow diversity	Build upon diversity as team asset
Decisions	Explain decisions	Get input for decisions	Facilitate and support team decisions
Development	Train people	Develop people	Develop people and team
Coordination	Manage one-on-one	Coordinate group effort	Build trust and team identity
Conflict	Minimize conflict	Ignore conflict	Use conflict as opportunity to learn

Source: Jim Tompkins, *Revolution: Take Charge Strategies for Business Success* (Raleigh, NC: Tompkins Press, 1998), p. 136.

time trying to locate it, and 68 percent believed the cost of collecting the information outweighed its value to the organization.[37]

Comparable to the importance of effective communication in an organization is the quality of *leadership and decision-making expertise* exercised by the senior logistics executive (see Table 15–3). In many companies the logistics department or division is a mirror image of the top logistics executive. If the top executive is a highly capable and respected individual, and one who makes thoughtful, logical, and consistent decisions, then the logistics organization that reports to him or her will most likely be highly effective. Conversely, a logistics organization led by an executive who lacks the necessary leadership and decision-making skills usually will not be as efficient.

Finally, *organizational adaptation and innovation* is an important attribute of effective organizations. The environment that surrounds the logistics activity requires constant monitoring. As conditions change, logistics must adapt and innovate to continue to provide an optimal cost–service mix to the firm and its markets. Examples of fluctuating environmental conditions include changes in transportation regulations, service requirements of customers, or degree of competition in the firm's target markets, economic and/or financial shifts in the marketplace, and technological advances. It is important, however, that adaptation and innovation not be haphazard and unplanned.

An effective organization must also exhibit stability and continuity. It must not only find a unique offering that the firm can deliver to the market but also stick with it to provide customer value.[38]

Leadership and Decision-Making Expertise

Organizational Adaptation and Innovation

---

[37]Lisa Harrington, "Suddenly Everyone Wants a Portal," *Supply Chain Technology News* 2, no. 1 (January 2000), p. 24.

[38]Michael Treacy and Fred Wiersema, "How Market Leaders Keep Their Edge," *Fortune* 131, no. 1 (February 6, 1995), pp. 88–98.

An Approach to Developing an Optimal Logistics Organization

Organizations change over time. A company may have to modify its design or structure to reflect environmental or corporate changes. As logistics executives attempt to structure a new organizational unit, or perhaps restructure an existing one, they usually proceed through a logical sequence of steps or stages:

1. Research corporate strategy and objectives.
2. Organize functions in a manner compatible with the corporate structure.
3. Define the functions for which they are accountable.
4. Know their management style.
5. Organize for flexibility.
6. Know the available support systems.
7. Understand and plan for human resource allocation so that it complements both the individual and organization objectives.[39]

Corporate Objectives

Corporate Objectives.   Overall corporate strategy and objectives give logistics long-term direction and focus. They provide the underlying foundation and guiding light for each functional component of the firm—finance, marketing, production, and logistics. The logistics structure must support the overall corporate strategy and objectives. Therefore, it is vital that logistics executives completely understand the role their activity will play in carrying out corporate strategy. Furthermore, the logistics organizational structure must be compatible with the primary objectives of the firm.

Corporate Structure

Corporate Structure.   While the specific organizational structure of logistics is affected by overall corporate structure, logistics is increasingly being centralized.[40] In the area of reporting relationships, logistics will typically report to the marketing group if the firm is a consumer goods company, and to manufacturing, operations, or administration if the firm is primarily an industrial goods producer. In many firms with a combination of consumer and industrial goods customers, logistics is often a separate organizational activity reporting directly to the CEO. This practice is growing as the strategic importance of logistics is more widely recognized.[41]

The more successful logistics organization structures have a number of characteristics in common, although they may look quite dissimilar in terms of their organizational chart. In general, they will possess the following characteristics:

Characteristics of Successful Logistics Organizations

- Formal logistics or logistics channel management organization.
- Centralized approach to policy formulation and direction setting.
- Inclusion of activities and processes that are beyond those typically considered to be logistics activities.
- Organization structure to follow logistics strategy.
- Seamless, integrated logistics process.

---

[39]James P. Falk, "Organizing for Effective Distribution," *Proceedings of the Eighteenth Annual Conference of the National Council of Physical Distribution Management* (Chicago, IL: NCPDM, 1980), p. 195.

[40]Henkoff, "Delivering the Goods," p. 70.

[41]See Helen L. Richardson, "Get the CEO on Your Side," *Transportation and Distribution* 36, no. 9 (September 1995), pp. 36–38.

- Elimination of functional silos both within the logistics process and between logistics and other companywide functions/processes.
- Ability to accommodate and facilitate change that is necessary to the continuous improvement of the logistics process.[42]

**Functional
Responsibilities**

Functional Responsibilities.   One writer has argued: "The question causing more conflicts and problems than any other is a clear definition of the *function* of the [logistics] organization, especially if it is being restructured from other substructures having a traditional responsibility."[43] It is important to have all or most logistics subfunctions housed under a single division or department. Such an organizational structure with full functional responsibility allows the firm to implement the concepts of integrated logistics management and cost trade-off analysis. Illustrative of many of the functional responsibilities of the logistics organization are those that were shown in Table 15–1.

An examination of over 100 U.S. companies found that logistics typically had responsibility for outbound transportation, intracompany transportation, warehousing, inbound transportation, materials handling, and inventory management. Because these are basic logistics functions, it is vital that the senior logistics executive administers these areas. Other functions, important but not essential to carrying out the logistics mission of the firm, for which logistics often does not have responsibility, include sales forecasting, raw materials inventory, and international logistics activities.[44]

Management Style

Management Style.   Almost as important as the formal structure of the organization is the management style of the senior logistics executive. Many firms have undergone significant changes in such areas as personnel, employee morale, and productivity as a result of a change in top management. Organizational restructuring does not necessarily have to occur. The management style and personality of the senior logistics executive, and to a lesser degree his or her lower-level managers, have an influence on the attitudes, motivation, work ethic, and productivity of employees at all levels of the organization.

The element of management style is one of those intangibles that can make two companies with identical organizational structures perform at significantly different levels of efficiency, productivity, and profitability. Management style is a vital ingredient to the success of a firm's logistics mission and is one of the primary reasons that many different organizational structures can be equally effective.

Flexibility

Flexibility.   Any logistics organization must be able to adapt to changes, which inevitably occur. Unresponsive and unadaptable organizations typically lose their effectiveness after a period of time. While it may be difficult to anticipate future changes in the marketplace or the firm, the logistics organization must be receptive to those changes and must respond to them in appropriate ways.

Support Systems

Support Systems.   Due to the nature of the logistics activity, support systems are essential. The logistics organization cannot exist on its own. There must be a variety of support services as well as support specialists available to aid the logistics department

---

[42]Robert A. Novack, C. John Langley, Jr., and Lloyd M. Rinehart, *Creating Logistics Value: Themes for the Future* (Oak Brook, IL: Council of Logistics Management, 1995), p. 88.

[43]Falk, "Organizing for Effective Distribution," p. 188.

[44]Bowersox et al., *Leading Edge Logistics,* pp. 74–77.

or division. A good management information system (MIS) is an important facet of an effective logistics network. Other support services or systems that can be used include legal services, computer systems, administrative services, and financial/ accounting services.

Human Resource Considerations

Human Resource Considerations.   Perhaps the most important component of an effective logistics organization is people. It is the people who will ultimately determine how well the company operates. Therefore, it is vital that employees' skills and abilities, pay scales, training programs, selection and retention procedures, and other employee-related issues be considered in the structuring or restructuring of a logistics organization.

Logistics managers are particularly essential to a successful organization. Productive and efficient employees must be effectively led and managers must possess the following qualities or characteristics:

Qualities or Characteristics of Successful Logistics Managers

- Personal integrity and awareness of business ethics.
- Ability to motivate.
- Ability to plan.
- Ability to organize.
- Self-motivation.
- Managerial control.
- Effective oral communication.
- Ability to supervise.
- Problem-solving ability.
- Self-confidence.[45]

Many of the key competencies of successful logistics executives are shown in Table 15–4. Successful organizations are those that successfully blend organizational structure, planning process, people, and style.

Organizational Structures of Successful Companies

Examining Organizational Structures of Successful Companies

While there is no single best organizational form for a firm's logistics activity, there are benefits to be obtained from examining the organizational structures of successful companies.[46] First, as a purely graphical representation, an organization chart allows a person to view how the many functional areas of the firm relate and how the logistics sub-functions are coordinated. Second, viewing several organization charts of companies in a variety of industries illustrates that there is no single ideal structure. Third, because of the commonality of the logistics activities across industry types, there will be marked similarities in the various organization charts. Managers have found through experience that logistics functions should be structured or organized in certain ways.

---

[45]Paul R. Murphy and Richard F. Poist, "Skill Requirements of Senior-Level Logistics Executives: An Empirical Assessment," *Journal of Business Logistics* 12, no. 2 (1991), pp. 83–87; also see Jonathan L. S. Byrnes and William C. Copacino, "Develop a Powerful Learning Organization," *Transportation and Distribution Presidential Issue* 31, no. 11 (October 1990), pp. 22–25.

[46]For a discussion of the importance of organizational structure, see Peter Drucker, *Management Challenges for the 21st Century* (New York: HarperBusiness, 1999).

TABLE 15–4   Required Competencies of Logistics Executives

- Use supervisory, development, recruiting, and selection skills to build and maintain a logistics organization.
- Use training skills and training resources to develop managers and supervisors to operate and manage a variety of logistics offices, facilities, and networks.
- Use decision-making skills to manage a complex, rapidly changing operation.
- Apply basic mathematics, statistics, accounting, budgeting, and human resources to establish goals and measure progress toward goals.
- Use skills in managing and directing meetings to gather information for decision making.
- Use writing and oral communication skills to report on logistics activities to corporate offices, customers, and others.
- Apply knowledge of warehousing, inventory control, transportation, manufacturing, purchasing, and other areas specific to the firm or the industry to operations decision making.
- Apply knowledge of warehousing, inventory control, transportation, manufacturing, and purchasing to developing strategic plans.

Source: Stephen A. LeMay and Jon C. Carr, *The Growth and Development of Logistics Personnel* (Oak Brook, IL: Council of Logistics Management, 1999), p. 56.

Representative organizational charts from three industry groups—chemical manufacturing, consumer and industrial products manufacturing, and mass merchandising—are shown in Figures 15–5 through 15–7. The companies represented are considered to have good logistics organizations by peers within their respective industries.

Logistics Structure at the Rohm and Haas Company

The Rohm and Haas Company is a $6.7 billion manufacturer of specialty chemicals, with operations in 25 countries worldwide.[47] Approximately 40 percent of total sales are from outside North America. In 1999, the company acquired LeaRonal (electronic chemicals) and Morton International (specialty chemicals). Figure 15–5 shows the logistics activity, which was reorganized in 1996 to incorporate all distribution functions under a director of supply chain and logistics. The company has 16 producing locations, 30 warehouses, and 400 employees in the logistics area. With a 1997 logistics budget of $120 million, Rohm and Haas uses all transport modes to ship its chemical products to locations throughout the world.

Logistics Structure at the 3M Company

As a $16 billion manufacturer of innovative high-technology products that are produced in more than 60 countries and sold worldwide,[48] the 3M Company uses the organization structure shown in Figure 15–6. With numerous divisions and products, 3M employs approximately 6,000 logistics personnel throughout the world to serve its customers in nearly 200 countries. The company operates eight warehouses or distribution centers in the United States and has 15 sales or order-entry locations.

As the 3M organization chart shows, some of the functions reporting to logistics include customer service, transportation, supply chain management, and international logistics. Each warehouse makes inventory control decisions. Overall inventory management decisions (i.e., how much product to stock where and when) are a product division responsibility. With such a structure, 3M is well suited for competing in a global marketplace.

Logistics Structure at Target Stores

Target Corporation is comprised of several divisions, including Target Stores, Dayton's, Marshall Field's, Hudson's, Mervyn's California, and target.direct. The

[47]Specific company information available on the Internet at <http//:www.rohmhaas.com>.
[48]Specific company information available on the Internet at <http//:www.mmm.com>.

FIGURE 15–5

Rohm and Haas Company

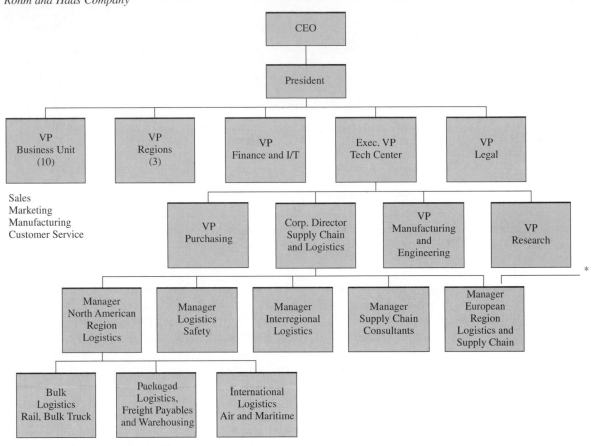

*Also reports to European Region Operations Director

Source: Rohm and Haas Company. Used with permission.

company is primarily an upscale discount retail store in the United States, with more than 1,200 stores located in 44 states. The company is the largest and most successful upscale discounter in the country, with 1999 sales of $33.2 billion.[49] Target employs 8,000 logistics personnel and operates 10 regional distribution centers, which encompass over 10.9 million square feet of space.

As Figure 15–7 shows, the organization chart for Target is significantly different from those in manufacturing companies such as Rohm and Haas and 3M. Retailers and manufacturers often have different organization structures, reflecting their different markets and customers. However, all of the firms illustrated here are extremely efficient in carrying out their logistics activities, and in each case the senior logistics executive is positioned at a high level in the organization.

---

[49]Specific company information available on the Internet at <http//:www.targetcorp.com>.

FIGURE 15–6

3M Company

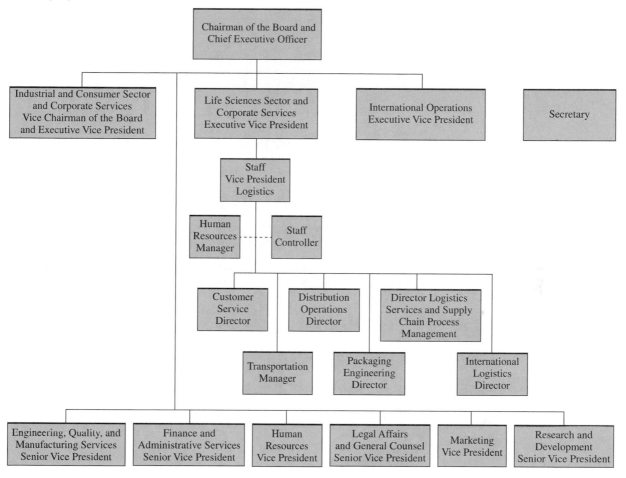

Source: 3M Company. Used with permission.

Effectiveness of the Logistics Organization

Organizational performance can be measured against many criteria. Examples of the multitude of performance dimensions that are presently being measured by organizations include the following:

Examples of Performance Measures

- Outbound freight cost.
- Inventory count accuracy.
- Order fill.
- Finished goods inventory turns.
- On-time delivery.
- Customer complaints.
- Over/short/damaged.
- Out-of-stocks (finished goods).

FIGURE 15–7

Target Stores distribution

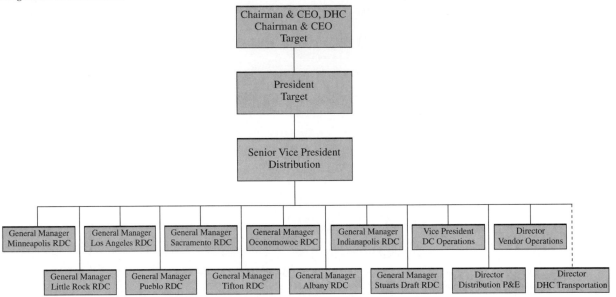

DHC = Dayton Hudson Corp.
DC = Distribution Center
RDC = Regional distribution center
P&E = Planning and Engineering

Source: Target Stores, Inc. Used with permission.

- Returns and allowances.
- Line item fill.
- Inbound freight cost.
- Back orders.
- Inventory obsolescence.
- Order cycle time.
- Incoming material quality.
- Overall customer satisfaction.
- Inventory carrying costs.
- Logistics cost per unit versus budget.
- Invoice accuracy.[50]

Of course, it is not enough to merely identify dimensions or elements of organizational effectiveness, although this is a necessary first step. The next step is to prioritize these elements and develop specific measuring devices to evaluate their respective levels of effectiveness. It is vital that management identify the measures of organizational effectiveness it wishes to use, and prioritize them. It is impractical in most instances to

---

[50]CSC/University of Tennessee Logistics Survey (1998) published in James S. Keebler, Karl B. Manrodt, David Durtsche, and D. Michael Ledyard, *Keeping Score: Measuring the Business Value of Logistics in the Supply Chain* (Oak Brook, IL: Council of Logistics Management, 1999), p. 59.

TABLE 15–5   Logistics Management Evaluation Measures
---

1. Logistics cost as a percent of sales
   a. Compared internally (e.g., among divisions)
   b. Compared externally (between similar companies)
2. Cost of specific logistics functions as a percent of sales or of logistics cost
   a. Compared internally (e.g., among divisions)
   b. Compared externally (between similar companies)
3. Performance
   a. Budget versus actual, expressed in terms of dollars, labor-hours, headcount, or other appropriate measures
   b. Productivity, output compared to input in appropriate terms
      (1) Service provided
      (2) Time (order cycle, invoice cycle)
      (3) On-time dependability
      (4) Customer complaint level
      (5) Errors (invoice, shipping)
   c. Project management within
      (1) Time constraints
      (2) Dollar limitations
      (3) Benefits projected (dollar savings, productivity improvements, etc.)

Source: A. T. Kearney, Inc., *Measuring and Improving Productivity in Physical Distribution* (Oak Brook, IL: National Council of Physical Distribution Management, 1984), pp. 307–8.

employ every effectiveness measure in the evaluation process. Time and monetary constraints impede the collection and monitoring of all the data needed for such evaluation.

In addition, it is usually sufficient to examine only a portion of the available measures, because patterns or trends are often exhibited very early in the evaluation process. The selection of particular logistics organizational effectiveness measures must depend on a firm's particular characteristics and needs. Perhaps the most difficult process is developing the techniques or procedures needed to measure the effectiveness criteria. In this regard, there are a number of alternatives.

Cost-to-Sales Ratios

Cost-to-sales ratios are used extensively by businesses to evaluate organizational effectiveness. As with any measure used by a company, there are issues that must be addressed, especially with regard to which costs to include under each logistics activity. For example: "Were net or gross sales used? What logistics functions were included in the cost total? Were management salaries included? Was inventory carrying cost included? Has there been a change in order mix or service levels?"[51] There are no simple answers to these questions, except to say that all costs that are rightfully logistics costs should be included when computing cost effectiveness measures. If management has adopted and implemented the integrated logistics management concept, there is greater likelihood that all relevant costs will be included.

Logistics Performance Measures Must be Evaluated Against a Standard

Every measure identified in Table 15–5 must be evaluated against some *predetermined standard*. The standard may be generated internally; that is, it may be developed within the organization so as to be compatible with corporate hurdle rates, return on investment percentages, and other financial performance measures. In some instances, logistics performance standards may be externally generated.

---

[51]A. T. Kearney, Inc., *Measuring and Improving Productivity in Physical Distribution* (Oak Brook, IL: National Council of Physical Distribution Management, 1984), pp. 307–8; and Novack et al., *Creating Logistics Value,* pp. 116–75.

Many logistics executives believe that their firm's standards should be based on those of other firms within the same industry, or the leaders in other industries with similar characteristics. There are many arguments in favor of this approach, but the major one states that an organization should be most concerned with its position in relation to its competition, and therefore the competition should influence the way management evaluates the firm's effectiveness. After all, in the marketplace customers are indirectly evaluating a firm's level of performance effectiveness through their day-to-day buying decisions. (For an expanded discussion of logistics performance measurement, see Chapter 16.)

A limitation of this approach is that each competitor has a different marketing mix and perhaps slightly different target markets. One firm may spend substantially more on logistics than another firm, yet realize higher profits and sales. Therefore, direct comparisons between competitors must be approached cautiously.[52]

How Logistics Executives Are Evaluated

Performance measurement is critical for *logistics executives.* Typically, managers are evaluated on three attributes:

1. *Line management ability.* This criterion considers the executive's ability to manage the department's day-to-day operations and meet goals that have been established for productivity, utilization, and all aspects of performance, including budget.

2. *Problem solving ability.* This deals with the ability to diagnose problems within the operation, and identify opportunities for savings, service improvement, or increased return on investment.

3. *Project management ability.* This refers to the ability to structure and manage projects designed to correct problems, improve productivity, and achieve improvement benefits.[53]

360-Degree Evaluation

Many organizations have used an approach known as a *360-degree evaluation* to assess their logistics executives. Decision making usually involves anonymous inputs from the boss, workers/peers, and subordinates. While the results generated are more qualitative than quantitative, the approach generates a clear picture of how the employee is perceived at all levels and identifies areas of ambiguity and conflict between participants. Once those problems are overcome, the manager becomes much more efficient and effective. Done effectively, the end result is better managers.[54]

If management is to measure organizational effectiveness, it must employ a variety of factors. In addition, the factors must be measurable, and standards of performance need to be established. Finally, management should compare the organization with others in its industry. It is likely that there is no single ideal organizational structure that every company should adopt. The most logical approach to organizing logistics activities to maximize their effectiveness is to understand the factors that contribute to organizational performance and include them in the planning, implementation, and control of the organization.

---

[52]An interesting approach to measurement with implications for measuring organizational effectiveness within a supply chain can be found in Alan Braithwaite and Edouard Samakh, *The Cost-to-Serve Method* (Berkhamsted, UK: Logistics Consulting Partners Ltd., 1997).

[53]A. T. Kearney, *Measuring and Improving Productivity,* p. 305.

[54]Stratford Sherman, "Leaders Learn to Heed the Voice Within," *Fortune* 130, no. 4 (August 22, 1994), pp. 92–100.

Logistics Training

Logistics training of employees is a key ingredient of successful organizations. Employee training has been shown to improve individual performance, morale, company loyalty, efficiency and effectiveness. Organizations with comprehensive training programs tend to provide higher customer service levels, retain employees for longer periods, and achieve greater overall profitability than those without such programs. The following statistics provide evidence of the importance of training, especially as it relates to the costs associated with hiring and retaining employees:[55]

Importance of Training

- The U.S. Department of Labor estimates that it costs a company one-third of a new hire's annual salary to replace an employee.
- In the trucking industry, managers estimate the per-driver replacement expense at $3,000 to $5,000. Some large trucking firms use $6,000 per driver as a planning estimate, and all of these numbers may be too low.
- A major insurance company estimated that its average cost per hire was $35,000.

Many environmental factors have highlighted the need to locate, hire, and retain the best employees. Outsourcing, downsizing, employee turnover, legal issues, and many other factors have made it vital that organizations have people who can be as effective and efficient as possible. While this has always been important, it becomes even more so in today's highly competitive and technologically advanced global society.

Logistics Training Themes

Several themes have been identified relative to logistics training. The following themes have significant implications for employee hiring, retention, efficiency, and effectiveness:

- The structure of logistics organizations today is not the structure of the past— or the structure of tomorrow. Logistics managers must create organizations that adapt quickly to rapid change and quickly add to the organizational knowledge base.
- Firms can no longer guarantee long-term employment, and most employees expect to change jobs and firms several times before they retire.
- Operating- and executive-level jobs in logistics are expanding and taking on new tasks, even as technology and competitive pressure reduce the middle level of logistics organizations.
- Inventory control and customer service are diminishing as distinct functions because they are becoming part of the larger supply chain organization.[56]

The following quote summarizes these themes:

> Logistics organizations cannot take the growth and development of logistics personnel lightly. Training should be more formal and systematic to bring employees to competence quickly in a field where tasks are changing, jobs are changing, and the available workforce is changing. Adaptation is the watchword when the only certainty is uncertainty. Logistics

---

[55]See Joan Brannick, *Decreasing the Staggering Costs of Turnover in Your Organization.* See the website <http://www.florida-speakers.com/turnover-costs.htm>.

[56]LeMay and Carr, *The Growth and Development of Logistics Personnel,* pp. 2–3.

Creative Solutions

Logistics Training at MegaProducts

The rules for access to training programs at MegaProducts are simple—anyone who wants to attend a training program offered at MegaProducts can go. Work time may be released for job-related training and many programs are offered at times convenient to the majority of employees.

The director of logistics offered a training program on basic logistics management. The program lasted several weeks, covering the subject matter of an introductory college logistics course—with a twist—these employees could look at hands-on, directly applicable examples. Attendees included a manager newly transferred to logistics from marketing, a longtime operating employee from the warehouse, and a middle manager just promoted from one functional area and now responsible for several. The text for the training was customized from a major textbook publisher. The company covered the cost for all participants.

Training was even taken beyond the walls of the organization—to suppliers and customers. Some middle managers were certified as trainers in root cause failure analysis (RCFA). They offered the course to their own employees and to customers, but they required their transportation suppliers to take the course. MegaProducts covers the expenses, but trains all its carriers worldwide in RCFA.

There were other required training courses—especially for those taking over a new job. Supervisors went through several training courses prior to promotion and consistently took new programs to maintain their skills. Some years, managers at MegaProducts spend one working day in ten in training programs.

Personal development programs were encouraged—stress management, time management, and communications skills for example. The director of logistics favors training that develops people and that affects their behavior at home and at work.

The MegaProducts approach may sound costly—but it is even more valuable. Consider these numbers. On-time delivery is over 98% worldwide for all non-rail transportation. Voluntary turnover at the operating, supervisory, and managerial levels is non-existent. Can it be claimed that these results come solely from training? Probably not, at least not in a scientific or academic sense. However, the training adds value to already valuable employees. The top managers in this organization consider the training worth the investment—in the warehouse, throughout the organization, and beyond.

Source: Stephen A. LeMay and Jon C. Carr, *The Growth and Development of Logistics Personnel* (Oak Brook, IL: Council of Logistics Management, 1999), pp. 8–9.

---

managers must assume responsibility for developing training relationships and working with human resource professionals to build the human side of logistics systems.[57]

Forms of Training

Many organizations have recognized the need for employee training. They have used various forms of logistics training listed in Table 15–6: videos, specialized training firms, universities and community colleges, the Internet, and other sources. All of the sources shown in the table can be used effectively. The training results of each source must be measured in order to determine its usefulness and effectiveness. However, about two-thirds of all organizations perform training needs assessments and only one-quarter of all firms develop employee competency models.[58]

Web-Based Training

Web-based training, while the least used presently, is likely to increase significantly as individuals and organizations incorporate this medium into their affairs.

---

[57]Ibid., p. 15.
[58]Ibid., p. 35.

TABLE 15–6   **Training Sources Used by Logistics Organizations**

Training Source	Percent Using
Training videos	61%
Training firms	55
Universities	42
Consulting firms	37
Community colleges	36
Other sources (e.g., internal)	22
Web-based training	12

Source: Adapted from Stephen A. LeMay and Jon C. Carr, *The Growth and Development of Logistics Personnel* (Oak Brook, IL: Council of Logistics Management, 1999), p. 34.

Incorporating the Internet into education and training will involve both stand-alone logistics-related coursework and the integration of the technology into other, more traditional, media.[59]

Logistics employees at all levels benefit from training programs that provide information, skills, and competencies that affect their jobs and general well-being. The consensus among logistics executives in most organizations is that training enhances an employee's ability to carry out his or her logistics functions in a more efficient and effective manner.

Summary

A biblical verse reads, "Where there is no vision, the people will perish."[60] Logistics organizations with clear statements of purpose, specific and measurable objectives, strategies and plans for achieving those objectives, and a committed workforce undoubtedly achieve higher levels of efficiency than those organizations without them.

Logistics organizations must, of necessity, become more cost- and service-efficient. An understanding of the factors that affect a firm's organizational effectiveness, along with strategies to improve the factors that reveal weakness or deficiencies, can help create more efficient logistics systems. Organizational changes form the basis for procedural modifications that can reduce costs or improve service.

This chapter discussed the importance to a firm of an effective logistics organization. Many firms have shown significant improvements in their logistics cost/service mix as a result of organizational improvements. The most important ingredient in successful management is integration of all of the logistics activities under a single individual, department, or division.

Logistics organizations can be structured in several ways, including strategic versus operational, centralized versus decentralized, line versus staff, and various combinations of these. There is probably no single ideal organizational structure. However, there are important elements that comprise an effective organization. In general, the

---

[59]Laurie Joan Aron, "Online Learning Anytime, Anywhere," *Inbound Logistics* (February 1999), pp. 19–24.

[60]Proverbs 29:18.

factors contributing to organizational effectiveness include the following: organizational, environmental, and employee characteristics and managerial policies and practices.

A number of approaches can be used to measure the effectiveness of logistics organizations. Each approach requires management to identify the elements that impact effectiveness, and then to evaluate their relative importance. Next, the elements must be measured and performance evaluated. Evaluation requires that standards of performance be established. Related to effectiveness is logistics training. Employee training is especially valuable in the creation and maintaining of an efficient and effective workforce.

With this and the preceding chapters as background, the concepts and principles already learned can be applied to measuring the performance of logistics activities. This is the subject of Chapter 16.

Suggested Readings

Bartlett, Christopher A., and Sumantra Ghoshal. "Changing the Role of Top Management: Beyond Strategy to Purpose." *Harvard Business Review* 72, no. 6 (November–December 1994), pp. 79–88.

Bowersox, Donald J.; David J. Closs, and Theodore P. Stank. *21st Century Logistics: Making Supply Chain Integration a Reality.* Oak Brook, IL: Council of Logistics Management, 1999.

Bowersox, Donald J.; Patricia J. Daugherty; Cornelia L. Dröge; Richard N. Germain; and Dale S. Rogers. *Logistical Excellence: It's Not Business as Usual.* Burlington, MA: Digital Equipment Corp., 1992.

Cooke, James Aaron. "CEO's Seize Logistics Opportunities." *Traffic Management* 34, no. 3 (March 1995), pp. 29–35.

Covey, Stephen R. *The Seven Habits of Highly Effective People.* New York: Simon and Schuster, 1989.

———. *Principle-Centered Leadership.* New York: Simon and Schuster, 1991.

Doctoroff, Susan. "Reengineering Negotiations." *Sloan Management Review* 39, no. 3 (Spring 1998), pp. 63–71.

Ellinger, Alexander E.; Patricia J. Daugherty; and Scott B. Keller. "The Relationship between Marketing/Logistics Interdepartmental Integration and Performance in U.S. Manufacturing Firms: An Empirical Study." *Journal of Business Logistics* 21, no. 1 (2000), pp. 1–22.

Ellram, Lisa M., and Laura M. Birou. *Purchasing for Bottom Line Impact.* Burr Ridge, IL: Irwin, 1995, pp. 80–92.

Fishman, Shirley R., and Allon Bross. "Developing a Global Workforce." *Canadian Business Review* 23, no. 1 (Spring 1996), pp. 18–21.

Gooley, Toby B. "Logistics in the Boardroom." *Logistics Management* 35, no. 5 (May 1996), pp. 51–52.

Gunn, Thomas G. *In the Age of the Real-Time Enterprise.* Essex Junction, VT: Oliver Wight Publications, 1994.

Henkoff, Ronald. "Delivering the Goods." *Fortune* 130, no. 11 (November 28, 1994), pp. 64–78.

Hoffman, Lowell M., and John Thompson. "Building Bridges between the Supply Chain by Creating a Flexible Organization Supported by Portable Executives." *Proceedings of the Annual Conference of the Council of Logistics Management.* Oak Brook, IL: Council of Logistics Management, 1997, pp. 361–67.

Jackson, Thomas L., and Constance E. Dyer. *Corporate Diagnosis: Setting the Global Standard for Excellence.* Portland, OR: Productivity Press, 1996.

Kanter, Rosabeth M.; Barry A. Stein; and Todd D. Jick. *The Challenge of Organizational Change—How Companies Experience It and Leaders Guide It.* New York: Free Press, 1992.

Kohn, Jonathan W., and Michael A. McGinnis. "Advanced Logistics Organization Structures: Revisited." *Journal of Business Logistics* 18, no. 2 (1997), pp. 147–62.

"Learning and Leadership." *Warehousing Forum* 14, no. 8 (July 1999), pp. 1–2.

Lynch, Clifford F. *Logistics Outsourcing—A Management Guide.* Oak Brook, IL: Council of Logistics Management, 2000.

Mitroff, Ian I.; Richard O. Mason; and Christine M. Pearson. "Radical Surgery: What Will Tomorrow's Organizations Look Like?" *Academy of Management Executive* 8, no. 2 (1994), pp. 11–21.

Ornatowski, Gregory K. "The End of Japanese-Style Human Resource Management?" *Sloan Management Review* 39, no. 3 (Spring 1998), pp. 73–84.

Pagonis, William G. *Moving Mountains: Lessons in Leadership and Logistics from the Gulf War.* Boston, MA: Harvard Business School Press, 1992.

Petzinger, Thomas, Jr. *The New Pioneers: The Men and Women Who Are Transforming the Workplace and Marketplace.* New York: Simon & Schuster, 1999.

Pfohl, Hans-Christian, and Hans Peter Buse. "Inter-organizational Logistics Systems in Flexible Production Networks: An Organizational Capabilities Perspective." *International Journal of Physical Distribution and Logistics Management* 30, no. 5 (2000), pp. 388–408.

Riggs, John. "Building a Core Strategic Vision." *PRTM's Insight* 11, no. 1 (Spring 1999), pp. 30–32.

Senge, Peter M. *The Fifth Discipline: The Art and Practice of the Learning Organization.* New York: Doubleday, 1990.

Stewart, Thomas A. "The Search for the Organization of Tomorrow." *Fortune* 125, no. 10 (May 18, 1992), pp. 92–98.

———. "Welcome to the Revolution." *Fortune* 128, no. 15 (December 13, 1993), pp. 66–78.

Williams, Lisa R.; Avril Nibbs; Dimples Irby; and Terence Finely. "Logistics Integration: The Effect of Information Technology, Team Composition, and Corporate Competitive Positioning." *Journal of Business Logistics* 18, no. 2 (1997), pp. 31–41.

Questions and Problems

1. Discuss the relationship between a firm's organizational structure and the integrated logistics management concept.

2. Coordination of the various logistics activities can be achieved in a variety of ways. Within the context of logistics organizational structure, explain each of the following

   a. Process-based versus market-based versus channel-based strategies.

   b. Strategic versus operational coordination.

   c. Centralized versus decentralized coordination.

   d. Line versus staff coordination.

3. It has been frequently stated that there is no single ideal or optimal logistics organizational structure. Do you think that statement is accurate? Briefly present the arguments for and against it.

4. How do personnel affect the degree of organizational effectiveness and/or productivity of a firm's logistics function?

5. What is the major value of a logistics mission statement? A corporate mission statement?

6. Identify how a firm's logistics management can be evaluated on each of the following factors:

   a. Total logistics cost.

   b. Cost-specific logistics functions.

   c. Performance.

7. Identify the role that employee training has in influencing logistics efficiency and effectiveness.

Chapter Objectives

- To show how logistics costs affect customer and product profitability.
- To show the limitations of current profitability reports in most companies.
- To show the importance of accurate cost data.
- To show how to use logistics costs for decision making.
- To show how to measure and control performance of the logistics function.

Introduction

In Chapter 1 we saw that logistics costs can exceed 25 percent of the cost of doing business at the manufacturing level. For this reason, better management of the logistics function offers the potential for large savings, which can contribute to improved corporate profitability. In mature markets—in which large sales increases are difficult to achieve and corporate profitability is continuously being eroded by increasing costs and competition—it is necessary to look for ways to improve productivity.

In the final analysis a business is about selling products and services to customers. Without accurate measures of the profitability of the company's products/services and its customers, management is running the business blind. However, evidence suggests that in many companies the required cost data are not available.[1] Depending on the industry, logistics costs may be a key determinant of customer and product profitability.[2] Also, the accurate measurement and the control of logistics costs offer significant potential for improving cash flow and return on assets. In this chapter we will concentrate on the financial impact of logistics performance.

The Impact of Logistics on Customer and Product Profitability

Management Must Measure the Profitability of Customers and Products

Knowledge of the profitability of customers and products is a requirement for informed management of a business. Table 16–1 illustrates the recommended framework for judging segment profitability using revenues and avoidable costs. From revenues it is necessary to deduct only the variable manufacturing costs to determine the manufacturing contribution. Next, variable marketing and logistics costs, such as sales commissions, transportation, warehousing, and order processing, along with a charge for investment in accounts receivable must be deducted. Management should apply the corporate cost of money to accounts receivable. Then it must attach to each segment assignable nonvariable costs incurred for the segment, including expenses like bad debts, sales promotion, salaries, and inventory carrying costs. Finally, management should use the corporate opportunity cost of money as a charge for all other assets required by the segment being evaluated. The size of the net segment margin will determine the relative contribution of each product (product group) or customer (customer group) from the standpoint of financial performance. This information, combined with estimates of future growth for each segment, enables management to develop strategies that will maximize profitability. The cost/revenue analysis shown in Table 16–1 also can be used to measure the performance of lines of trade.

Traditional Accounting Gives Few Clues Regarding Poor Performance

The following example illustrates the recommended approach. Traditional accounting data showed a net profit of $2.5 million before taxes on sales of $42.5 million. While management believed that this profit was not adequate, traditional accounting gave few clues with regard to the specific problem. In the absence of fact,

[1]Douglas M. Lambert and Jay U. Sterling, "What Types of Profitability Reports Do Marketing Managers Receive?" *Industrial Marketing Management* 16, no. 4 (1987), pp. 295–303; Stephen Barr, "The Big Picture," *CFO* 12, no.7 (1996), pp. 37–42; and Dick A. van Damme and Frank L. A. van der Zon, "Activity Based Costing and Decision Support," *The International Journal of Logistics Management* 10, no. 1 (1999), pp. 71–82.

[2]William C. Copacino, "A Cost-to-Serve Analysis Can Be an Eye-Opener," *Logistics Management and Distribution Report* 38, no.4 (1999), p. 4.

TABLE 16–1   Contribution Approach with a Charge for Assets Employed

	Total Company	*Segment A*	*Segment B*	*Segment C*
Net sales				
Cost of goods sold (variable manufacturing cost)	———	———	———	———
Manufacturing contribution	———	———	———	———
Variable marketing and logistics costs				
Sales commissions				
Transportation				
Warehousing (handling in and out)				
Order processing				
Charge for investment in accounts receivable	———	———	———	———
Segment contribution margin	———	———	———	———
Assignable nonvariable costs				
Salaries				
Segment-related advertising				
Bad debts				
Inventory carrying costs	———	———	———	———
Segment controllable margin	———	———	———	———
Charge for assets used by segment	———	———	———	———
Net segment margin	———	———	———	———

Assumption: Public warehouses are used for field inventories.

the managers representing the various business functions would have conflicting ideas about how profitability could be improved. A marketing manager would like to increase the advertising budget to increase sales. The vice president of finance might argue that the company is spending twice as much as it should on advertising. The sales representatives would like more products but the manufacturing manager argues there are too many SKUs now and that it is impossible to achieve the necessary efficiencies in production. Salespeople want lower prices but the finance vice president argues that prices are too low and a 5 percent increase would solve the profitability problems of the division. Everyone has a suggestion for improving profitability that is based on his or her experience and area of expertise. Without good information it is difficult if not impossible to determine the course of action that will have the desired impact on the bottom line. However, a contribution approach to profitability analysis by type of account can be used to diagnose areas where performance is inadequate (see Table 16–2).

In this example, drugstores were the largest of the manufacturer's four customer types, but the segment controllable margin-to-sales ratio was the lowest; it was less than one-half that of the second most profitable segment, and only 37 percent of the most profitable segment. Nevertheless, at $3.1 million the segment controllable margin is substantial, and it is doubtful that elimination of drugstores would be a wise decision. A product-channel matrix analysis showed that product mix was not the source of the problem. However, all drugstores were not the same. The company sold to national drug chains, regional drug chains, and independent pharmacies. Further segmentation of the drugstore channel revealed that national drugstore chains had a segment controllable margin-to-sales ratio almost as large as that of the grocery chains and somewhat better than discount stores, that regional drugstore chains were almost

TABLE 16–2   Profitability by Type of Account: A Contribution Approach ($ 000)

	Type of Account				
	Total Company	Department Stores	Grocery Chains	Drugstores	Discount Stores
Sales	$42,500	$6,250	$10,500	$19,750	$6,000
Less discounts, returns, and allowances	2,500	250	500	1,750	—
Net sales	40,000	6,000	10,000	18,000	6,000
Cost of goods sold (variable manufacturing costs)	20,000	2,500	4,800	9,200	3,500
Manufacturing contribution	20,000	3,500	5,200	8,800	2,500
Variable selling and distribution costs:					
Sales commissions	800	120	200	360	120
Transportation costs	2,500	310	225	1,795	170
Warehouse handling	600	150	—	450	—
Order-processing costs	400	60	35	280	25
Charge for investment in accounts receivable	700	20	50	615	15
Contribution margin	15,000	2,840	4,690	5,300	2,170
Assignable nonvariable costs (costs incurred specifically for the segment during the period):					
Sales promotion and slotting allowances	1,250	60	620	400	170
Advertising	500	—	—	500	—
Bad debts	300	—	—	300	—
Display racks	200	—	—	200	—
Inventory carrying costs	1,250	150	200	800	100
Segment controllable margin	$11,500	$2,630	$ 3,870	$ 3,100	$1,900
Segment controllable margin-to-sales ratio	27.1%	42.1%	36.9%	15.7%	31.7%

Note: This approach could be modified to include a charge for the assets employed by each of the segments, as well as a deduction for the change in market value of these assets. The result would be referred to as the net segment margin (residual income).

Source: Douglas M. Lambert and Jay U. Sterling, "Educators Are Contributing to Major Deficiencies in Marketing Profitability Reports," *Journal of Marketing Education* 12, no. 3 (Fall 1990), pp. 43–44.

as profitable as discount stores, and that small independent pharmacies were losing money (see Table 16–3).

The primary reason that the independent pharmacies were losing $85,000 per year was the result of logistics costs associated with overnight package service, third-party warehousing, inventory carrying costs, and small orders. Also, these customers were slow paying their bills and some never paid, which resulted in the high bad debts. With this information, management could determine the impact on corporate profitability if the independent pharmacies were served by drug wholesalers or by field warehouses supported by inside sales and scheduled deliveries. The alternative that would lead to the greatest improvement in long-term profitability should be selected.

Rather than contribution reports, most firms use a full-cost accounting system, which assigns fixed costs to individual segments.[3] However, a full-cost system provides incorrect information because costs "common" to multiple segments are allocated to

[3]Lambert and Sterling, "What Types of Profitability Reports Do Marketing Managers Receive?" pp. 295–303.

TABLE 16–3   Profitability by Type of Account: A Contribution Approach ($ 000)

	Type of Account			
	Drugstore Channel	National Drug Chains	Regional Drug Chains	Independent Pharmacies
Sales	$19,750	$4,250	$5,500	$10,000
Less discounts, returns, and allowances	1,750	250	500	1,000
Net sales	18,000	4,000	5,000	9,000
Cost of goods sold (variable manufacturing costs)	9,200	2,100	2,600	4,500
Manufacturing contribution	8,800	1,900	2,400	4,500
Variable selling and distribution costs:				
Sales commissions	360	80	100	180
Transportation costs	1,795	120	200	1,475
Warehouse handling	450	—	100	350
Order-processing costs	280	25	55	200
Charge for investment in accounts receivable	615	20	35	560
Contribution margin	5,300	1,655	1,910	1,735
Assignable nonvariable costs				
(costs incurred specifically for the segment during the period:)				
Sales promotion and slotting allowances	400	90	110	200
Advertising	500	—	—	500
Bad debts	300	—	—	300
Display racks	200	—	—	200
Inventory carrying costs	800	80	100	620
Segment controllable margin	$ 3,100	$1,485	$1,700	($85)
Segment controllable margin-to-sales ratio	15.7%	34.9%	30.9%	—

Note: This approach could be modified to include a charge for the assets employed by each of the segments, as well as a deduction for the change in market value of these assets. The result would be referred to as the net segment margin (residual income).

Source: Douglas M. Lambert and Jay U. Sterling, "Educators Are Contributing to Major Deficiencies in Marketing Profitability Reports," *Journal of Marketing Education* 12, no. 3 (Fall 1990), pp. 44–45.

segments according to some arbitrary measure of activity. Vital information about the controllability and behavior of segment costs is lost. For example, if a segment is found to be unprofitable under a full-cost approach and as a result is discontinued, the fixed costs will simply be reallocated to the remaining segments.

Research has identified the following shortcomings of the profitability reports used by executives in major corporations:

Shortcomings of Corporate Profitability Reports

1. Full manufactured costs (which sometimes included a profit for the plant) were used in calculating costs of goods sold.

2. Operating costs such as development, selling, and administration were fully allocated to products often on a percentage-of-sales basis.

3. Costs such as transportation, warehousing, sales commissions, and sales promotions were not reported as separate line items.

4. When marketing and logistics costs were identified explicitly as expenses, they usually were allocated to products on a percentage-of-sales basis.

TABLE 16–4   Profitability by Type of Account: A Full-Cost Approach ($000)

			Type of Account		
	Total Company	Department Stores	Grocery Chains	Drugstores	Discount Stores
Net sales	$40,000	$6,000	$10,000	$18,000	$6,000
Cost of goods sold (full manufacturing costs)	25,000	3,750	6,250	11,250	3,750
Manufacturing margin	15,000	2,250	3,750	6,750	2,250
Less expenses:					
Sales commissions	800	120	200	360	120
Transportation costs ($/case)	2,500	375	625	1,125	375
Warehouse handling ($/cu.ft)	600	90	150	270	90
Order-processing costs ($/order)	400	30	50	300	20
Sales promotion (% of sales)	1,250	187	312	563	188
Advertising (% of sales)	500	75	125	225	75
Bad debts (% of sales)	300	45	75	135	45
General overhead and administrative expense (% of sales)	6,150	922	1,538	2,768	922
Net profit (before taxes)	$ 2,500	$ 406	$ 675	$ 1,004	$ 415
Profit-to-sales ratio	6.3%	6.8%	6.8%	5.6%	6.9%

Source: Douglas M. Lambert and Jay U. Sterling, "Educators Are Contributing to Major Deficiencies in Marketing Profitability Reports," *Journal of Marketing Education* 12, no. 3 (Fall 1990), p. 49.

5. Inconsistencies in terminology were common. When executives referred to contribution margins, often the numbers used were actually manufacturing contribution.

6. Opportunity costs such as inventory carrying costs, a charge for accounts receivable, and a charge for other assets employed did not appear on profitability reports.

7. Reports that covered more than one year were not adjusted for inflation.

8. Reports were not adjusted to reflect replacement costs.[4]

Cost Allocations Distort Profitability

In summary, cost allocations can seriously distort a segment's profitability. "Seriously distorted product costs can lead managers to choose a losing competitive strategy by de-emphasizing and overpricing products that are highly profitable and by expanding commitments to complex, unprofitable lines. The company persists in the losing strategy because executives have no alternative sources of information to signal when product costs are distorted."[5]

Table 16–4 illustrates how the customer profitability analysis contained in Table 16–2 would change if it were calculated using average costs. Drugstores would show by far the largest dollar profit. The profit-to-sales ratio for drugstores would compare favorably with that of the other customer groups (82 percent of the profit-to-sales ratio for grocery chains), whereas the controllable margin-to-sales ratio of the drugstores was less than half

[4]Ibid.
[5]Robert S. Kaplan, "One Cost System Isn't Enough," *Harvard Business Review* 66 (January–February 1988), pp. 61–66.

(43 percent) of that earned by the grocery stores. The differences in the results obtained using the two methods of accounting could be much greater in a product profitability analysis because manufacturing, marketing, and logistics costs can vary more across products. If the costs in Table 16–4 had been allocated on a percentage-of-sales basis, as is the practice in many firms, the profit-to-sales ratios for the four groups of customers would have been equal.

Limitations of Current Profitability Reports

Research has shown that gross inadequacies exist in the segment profitability reports used by managers in the majority of U.S. corporations.[6] Most segment profitability reports are based on average cost allocations rather than on the direct assignment of costs at the time a transaction occurs. Period costs (e.g., fixed plant overhead and general/administrative costs) are arbitrarily allocated to customers and products using bases such as direct labor hours, sales revenue, or cost of sales. Opportunity costs to cover investments in inventories and accounts receivable are not included. Finally, key marketing and distribution cost components are frequently ignored. In fact, only 16 percent of the Fortune 1,000 firms surveyed reported having relatively comprehensive and accurate profitability reports, as determined by the cost categories included in these reports and the methods used to assign costs to segments. It is interesting that these firms also reported an average return on assets that was 50 percent higher than that reported by the other 84 percent of the respondents.

One Culprit Is "Full Costing"

Many of the problems encountered by manufacturers result from the use of a "full costing" approach where all indirect costs (such as overhead and general administrative expenses) are allocated to each product or customer group on some arbitrary basis. As a result, many companies use management controls that focus on the wrong targets: direct manufacturing labor or sales volume. Reward systems based on such controls drive behavior toward either simplistic goals that represent only a small fraction of total cost (labor) or single-minded sales efforts (volume). They ignore more effective ways to compete, such as emphasizing product quality, on-time delivery, short lead times, rapid product innovations, flexible manufacturing and distribution, and efficient deployment of scarce capital.

Why Accounting Systems Are Inadequate

Unfortunately, most managers do not know the true cost of their company's products or services, how to most effectively reduce expenses, or how to allocate resources to the most profitable business segments because of the following factors:[7]

- Accounting systems are designed to report the aggregate effects of a firm's operations to its stockholders, its creditors, and government agencies.

- Accounting costs are computed to provide a historical record of the company's operations. Because the costs are not captured by segment, all of the firm's costs are allocated to the various business segments. Since costs common to multiple segments are allocated, the process is necessarily subjective and arbitrary.

---

[6]Lambert and Sterling, "What Types of Profitability Reports Do Marketing Managers Receive?" pp. 295–303.

[7]Ibid., pp. 96–103; Thomas S. Dudick, "Why SG&A Doesn't Always Work," *Harvard Business Review* 65, no. 1 (January–February 1987), pp. 30–35; Robert S. Kaplan, "How Cost Accounting Distorts Product Costs," *Management Account,* April 1988, pp. 20–27; John J. Wheatley, "The Allocation Controversy in Marketing Cost Analysis," *University of Washington Business Review* 30, no. 4, (Summer 1971), pp. 61–70; Ford S. Worthy, "Accounting Bores You? Wake Up," *Fortune,* October 12, 1987, pp. 43–50; and Lambert and Sterling, "What Types of Profitability Reports Do Marketing Managers Receive?" pp. 295–303.

- Accounting systems typically record marketing and logistics costs in aggregated natural accounts. Seldom is an attempt made to attach the costs to functional responsibilities and to individual products or customers. Accounting systems are not capable of identifying these costs at the time transactions are recorded or incurred. When the detail is captured, it is frequently lost because only aggregated data are carried forward to subsequent accounting periods. Once data are aggregated, the only way to disaggregate them is by allocation methods that distort the profitability.
- Profitability reports do not show a segment's contribution to profitability but, rather, include fixed costs, joint product/service costs, and corporate overhead costs. Often top management encourages this approach because of the fear that knowledge of variable costs will lead to unrealistically low prices. However, in most cases prices are set by the marketplace and not on the basis of costs.
- In most standard cost systems, fixed costs are often treated as variable costs, which masks the true behavior of the fixed costs.

The Importance of Accurate Cost Data

Accurate Cost Data Are Required for Integrated Logistics

Computers, operations research techniques, and the systems approach brought high-speed processing and the logic of mathematics to the field of logistics and led not only to changes in transportation strategy, inventory control techniques, warehousing location policy, order processing systems, and logistics communication, but also to the desire to manage the costs associated with these functions in an integrated format. However, the lack of adequate cost data has prevented logistics management from reaching its full potential. In general, accountants have not kept pace with developments in logistics. Consequently, much of the necessary cost analysis has not been carried out.

Accurate cost data are required for development of product and customer profitability reports and for successful implementation of the integrated logistics management concept using total cost analysis. They are also required for the management and control of logistics operations.

Total Cost Analysis

Total Cost Analysis Is the Key to Managing Logistics

The key to managing the logistics function is *total cost analysis*.[8] That is, at a given level of customer service, management should minimize total logistics costs rather than attempt to minimize the cost of individual activities. The major shortcoming of a non-integrative approach to logistics cost analysis is that attempts to reduce specific costs within the logistics function may be less than optimal for the system as a whole, leading to greater total costs.

Total logistics costs do not respond to cost-cutting techniques individually geared to warehouse, transportation, or inventory costs. Reductions in one cost invariably result in increases in one or more of the others. For example, aggregating all finished goods inventory into fewer distribution centers may minimize warehousing costs and increase inventory turnover, but it will lead to increased transportation expense. Similarly, savings resulting from favorable purchase prices on large orders may be entirely

---

[8]This section is adapted from Douglas M. Lambert and Howard M. Armitage, "Distribution Costs: The Challenge," *Management Accounting* 60, no.11 (May 1979), pp. 33–34; and Lambert and Sterling, "What Types of Profitability Reports Do Marketing Managers Receive?" pp. 295–303.

offset by greater inventory carrying costs. Thus, to minimize total cost, management must understand the effect of trade-offs within the distribution function.

Cost Trade-Offs Are Essential

Cost trade-offs between and among the various components of the logistics system are essential. Profit can be enhanced, for example, if the reduction in inventory carrying cost is more than the increase in the other functional costs (Figure 16–1), or if improved customer service yields greater overall revenue. If knowledgeable trade-offs are to be made, however, management must be able to account for the costs associated with each component, and to explain how changes in each cost contribute to total costs.

Many Management Decisions Require Good Cost Data

The quality of the accounting data influences management's ability to exploit new markets, take advantage of innovative transportation systems, choose between common carriers and private trucking, increase deliveries or increase inventories, make changes

FIGURE 16–1

Cost trade-offs required in marketing and logistics

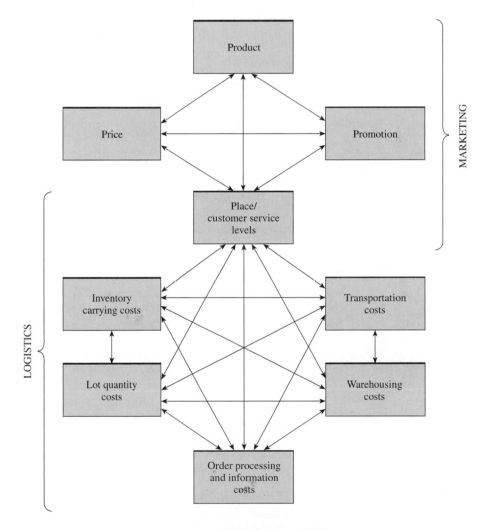

Marketing objective: Allocate resources to the marketing mix in such a manner as to maximize the long-term profitability of the firm.

Logistics objective: Minimize total costs given the customer service objective where Total costs = Transportation costs + Warehousing costs + Order processing and information costs + Lot quantity costs + Inventory carrying costs.

Source: Adapted from Douglas M. Lambert, *The Development of an Inventory Costing Methodology: A Study of the Cost Associated with Holding Inventory* (Chicago: National Council of Physical Distribution Management, 1976), p. 7.

in distribution center configuration, restructure the echelon of inventories, make changes in packaging, and determine to what extent the order processing system should be automated. The accounting system must be capable of providing information to answer questions such as the following:

- How do logistics costs affect contribution by product, by territory, by customer, and by salesperson?
- What are the costs associated with providing additional levels of customer service? What trade-offs are necessary, and what are the incremental benefits or losses?
- What is the optimal amount of inventory? How sensitive is the inventory level to changes in warehousing patterns or to changes in customer service levels? How much does it cost to hold inventory?
- What mix of transport modes/carriers should be used?
- How many field warehouses should be used and where should they be located?
- How many production setups are required? Which plants will be used to produce each product? What are the optimum manufacturing plant capacities based on alternative product mixes and volumes?
- What product packaging alternatives should be used?
- To what extent should the order processing system be automated?
- What distribution channels should be used?

Only Consider Relevant Costs

To answer these and other questions, management must know what costs and revenues will change if the logistics system changes. That is, the determination of a product's contribution should be based on how corporate revenues, expenses, and hence profitability would change if the product were dropped. Any costs or revenues that are unaffected by this decision are irrelevant to the problem. For example, a relevant cost is the public warehouse handling charges associated with a product's sales. An irrelevant cost is the overhead associated with the firm's private trucking fleet.

Implementation of this approach to decision making is severely hampered by the unavailability of accounting data, or the inability to use the right data when they are available. The best and most sophisticated models are only as good as the accounting input. A number of studies attest to the inadequacies of logistics cost data.[9]

Controlling Logistics Activities

Cost Data Are Essential for Control

One of the major reasons for improving the availability of logistics cost data is to control and monitor logistics performance. Without accurate cost data, performance analysis is next to impossible. How can a firm expect to control the cost of shipping a product to a customer if it does not know what the cost should be? How can management determine if distribution center costs are high or low in the absence of performance measurements? What is "good" performance for the order processing function? Are inventory levels sat-

---

[9]See, for example, David Ray, "Distribution Costing and the Current State of the Art," *International Journal of Physical Distribution* 6, no. 2 (1975), pp. 75–107; Michael Schiff, *Accounting and Control in Physical Distribution Management* (Chicago: National Council of Physical Distribution Management, 1971), p. 4-21; Douglas M. Lambert, *The Distribution Channels Decision* (New York: The National Association of Accountants, and Hamilton, Ontario: The Society of Management Accountants of Canada, 1978), pp. 88–91, 102–11; and Douglas M. Lambert, *The Product Abandonment Decision* (New York: The National Association of Accountants, and Hamilton, Ontario: The Society of Management Accountants of Canada,1985), pp. 98, 127–32.

Global

One Common System

When Eastman Kodak decided to play hardball in the global competition arena, the film and imaging company focused on an integrated logistics approach. The initiative launched across the global Kodak enterprise was founded on one common system that would handle 90 percent of the world audience's demand for Kodak products and services. To facilitate the initiative, Kodak converted its largest warehouses around the world from multiple mainframes to a single client/server-based warehouse management system, which it viewed as more cost effective.

The driving factors for the Kodak Worldwide Warehouse Information Center (KWWIC) program were the development of both consistent business processes to ensure that all warehouses operated in the same manner and a matrix for monitoring internal and external performance. KWWIC aimed for higher levels of accuracy and productivity, real-time data interfaces, data for ABC costing, improved metrics, reduced systems, and the ability to run 24 hours a day, seven days a week, to meet customer requirements. The program also dictated a change in software and, in turn, expanded radio frequency data collection (RF/DC).

"Around the world in Kodak logistics, each country was pursuing its own systems initiative to automate local warehouses," explains Gus Holderer, manager, international product handling development. "We were seeing multi-initiatives throughout our plants, resulting in duplications of

effort and significant expenditures by geography, all of which needed to be addressed. At the same time, we were very interested in changing our computer architecture and required an RF partner that could make the change with us."

To facilitate the initiative, Kodak converted the computer systems in its largest warehouses around the world from multiple mainframes to a single client/server-based warehouse management system (WMS), which it viewed as more cost-effective. This was to support the new global supply chain tactic and capitalize on advances in warehouse automation technology. Client/server applications can speed up the distribution process and streamline labor-intensive warehousing tasks.

"Our goal was to configure each warehouse to take on additional value-added responsibilities such as flexible labeling, kitting/assembly, lot tracing, dating, crossdocking, and variable picking strategies," says Holderer. "We also wanted to utilize an array of logistics technologies including RF terminals, AGVs (automated guided vehicles), bar coding, high-speed conveyors, and electronic commerce."

Source: Adapted from "Focusing on a Successful System," *Automatic I.D. News* 14, no. 11 (October 1998), pp. 40–43. Reproduced by permission from *Auto ID News.* Copyright 1998 by Advanstar Communications, Inc. Advanstar Communications, Inc. retains all rights to this article.

isfactory, too high, or too low? These questions are not the only ones we can ask, but they serve to illustrate the need for accurate cost data.

The following quotes describe the importance of a good measurement program for the management and control of logistics:

> If no measurement program exists, the "natural" forces shaping the behavior of busy managers tend to place the emphasis on the negative.
>
> Issues only attract management attention when something is "wrong." In this type of situation, there is often little reinforcement of positive results. A formal measurement program helps focus attention on the positive and helps improve employee moral . . . Once a plan has been established, actual results can be measured and compared with the plan to identify variances requiring management attention.[10]

---

[10]A. T. Kearney, *Measuring Productivity in Physical Distribution* (Chicago: National Council of Physical Distribution Management, 1978), pp. 18–19.

Case Studies

As the cost of logistics continues to rise, the need for management to be able to account for the costs associated with each component becomes increasingly critical.[11] It is also necessary to know how changes in the costs of each component affect total costs and profits. Estimates of logistics costs ranging from 15 to 50 percent of total sales are not uncommon, depending on the nature of the company. However, these are at best only educated guesses since logistics costs are usually incorrectly computed by management. From a corporate standpoint, the inability to measure and manage logistics costs leads to missed opportunities and expensive mistakes. The following four actual examples will serve to highlight the problems associated with most logistics accounting systems.

Average Freight Costs Distort Segment Profitability

Case 1: The Effect of Average Freight Costs on Customer/Product Profitability. Freight costs are a major expense in most companies, yet few accounting systems track actual freight costs by customer or by product. When management does try to determine these costs, it usually relies on national averages. These averages, however, do not indicate the actual costs of moving each product to its destination; hence, profitability calculations based on them are erroneous.

For example, management of Company A used a national average freight rate when calculating customer and product profitability. It determined the rate by taking the total corporate transportation bill as a percentage of total sales revenue. It applied the same cost—4 percent of sales—to products moving by common carrier from Chicago to New York and from Chicago to Los Angeles, as well as to deliveries in the Chicago area, where the company used its own vehicles. It used the 4 percent figure for transportation cost regardless of the product being shipped, the size of the shipment, or the distance involved.

The fallacy of this approach is threefold. First, management was unable to determine the profitability of individual products or customers. The averaging process hid the fact that delivery of small quantities and deliveries to distant customers may be highly unprofitable, thereby reducing the overall corporate rate of return. Second, using the same percentage rate for all products ignores the impact of product characteristics such as weight, cube, and distance on freight rates and consequently on product and customer profitability. Finally, management did not know actual delivery costs for customers, which made it more difficult to perform a trade-off analysis between the cost of the current system and the cost of an alternative system, where carload shipments would go first to a regional warehouse on the West Coast, and then on to the customers in that market by motor carrier. In this company, the allocation of freight costs on a percentage-of-sales basis led to erroneous profitability figures for customers and products, and lower overall performance.

Separating Fixed and Variable Costs Can Be a Problem

Case 2: Inability to Distinguish between Fixed and Variable Costs. Management of Company B used a product reporting statement that deducted manufacturing, logistics, and marketing costs from sales to arrive at a net income for each product. It used the profit statement for making decisions about the acceptability of product performance, the assignment of marketing support, and the deletion of products. The allocation of logistics costs to each product was carried out using ABC analysis, in which A

[11]This material is adapted from Douglas M. Lambert and Howard M. Armitage, "Managing Distribution Costs for Better Profit Performance," *Business* 30, no. 5 (September–October 1980), pp. 46–52. Reprinted by permission from *Business* magazine.

products were allocated a certain amount of logistics costs, B products twice as much as A, and C products three times as much as A. These allocations contained costs that varied with activity, such as warehouse labor, supplies, and freight expenses. They also included costs that remained fixed regardless of activity levels (e.g., corporate allocations, depreciation, and administration costs of the corporate fleet). Several of the company's products, including one that was among the company's top 10 in terms of sales performance, were showing negative profits and were therefore candidates for being discontinued. However, analysis revealed that a large proportion of the total distribution cost, along with approximately 30 percent of the manufacturing cost, was fixed and would not be saved if the products were eliminated. In fact, by discontinuing these products, total corporate profitability would decline, since all of the revenues related to these products would disappear, but all of the costs would not. Although the variable costs and the specifically identifiable fixed costs would be saved, the company would continue to incur the majority of fixed costs—which in this case were substantial— regardless of the product deletion being considered. If the firm discontinued the products, the existing fixed costs would be redistributed to the remaining products, leading to the very real possibility that even more products would appear to be unprofitable.

Most Logistics Costing Systems Rely on Allocations

Case 3: The Pitfalls of Allocation.   Most logistics costing systems are in their infancy and rely heavily on allocations to determine the performance of segments such as product, customers, territories, divisions, or functions. In Company C such allocations led to erroneous decision making and loss of corporate profits. The firm was a multidivision corporation that manufactured and sold high-margin pharmaceutical products, as well as a number of lower-margin packaged goods. The company maintained a number of field warehouse locations managed by corporate staff. These climate-controlled facilities were designed for the pharmaceutical business and required security and housekeeping practices far exceeding those necessary for packaged goods. In order to fully utilize the facilities, however, the corporation encouraged nonpharmaceutical divisions to store their products in these distribution centers. The costs of operating the warehouses were primarily fixed, although overtime and/or additional warehouse employees were necessary if the throughput increased. The corporate policy was to allocate costs to user divisions on the basis of the square footage occupied. Due to the pharmaceutical warehousing requirements, this charge was relatively high. Furthermore, the corporate divisions were managed on a decentralized profit center basis.

The vice president of logistics in a division that marketed relatively bulky and low-value consumer products realized that similar services could be obtained at a lower cost to his division by using a public warehouse. For this reason, he withdrew the division's products from the corporate facilities and began to use public warehouses in these locations. Although the volume of product handled and stored in the corporate distribution centers decreased significantly, the cost savings were minimal in terms of the total costs incurred by these facilities due to the high proportion of fixed costs. Consequently, approximately the same cost was allocated to fewer users, making it even more attractive for the other divisions to change to public warehouses in order to obtain lower rates.

The result was higher, not lower, total company warehousing costs. The corporate warehousing costs were primarily fixed. Whether or not the space was fully occupied would not significantly alter these costs. When the nonpharmaceutical divisions moved to public warehouses, the company continued to incur approximately the same total expense for the corporate-owned and operated warehouses, as well as the additional public warehousing charges. In effect, the logistics costing system motivated the divisional logistics managers to act in a manner that was not in the company's best interests, and total costs escalated.

Case 4: Control Deficiencies.   Control of costs and motivation of key personnel are both critical in every business activity. Logistics is no exception. However, the control concepts successfully used by other functional areas have not been widely adopted for logistics activities. Some have argued that logistics is different from other disciplines and cannot be evaluated with the same tools. In most cases, however, the application has never been attempted. A particular case in point is the application of the flexible budgeting concept.

The Application of Control Techniques Is Lacking in Logistics

Company D maintained an annual budget for its branch warehousing costs. These costs consisted of variable and fixed expenses. Each month, the budget was divided by 12 and compared to the actual costs of that month. Differences from the budget were recorded as variances, and management took action on these. However, Company D's sales were seasonal, and some months were far more active than others. During peak periods, the variances were virtually always unfavorable, while during slow months the variances were favorable. Productivity ratios, in contrast, gave different results. Productivity ratios were high during peak periods and dropped during slower periods.

In such a situation, neither cost control nor employee motivation is being adequately addressed. Dividing the annual budget by 12 and comparing it to actual monthly costs means that management is trying to compare costs at two different activity levels. However, the costs should be the same only if actual monthly activity is equal to $\frac{1}{12}$ of the planned annual activity. A far more acceptable approach is to recognize that some of the costs are variable and will rise or fall with the level of output. Flexing the budget to reflect what the costs should have been at the operating activity level experienced permits a true measure of efficiency and productivity, and provides more meaningful evaluations of performance.

Solving the Problem of Insufficient Cost Data

Logistics Costs Are Often Grouped into Natural Accounts

One of the difficulties in obtaining logistics costs is that they may be grouped under a series of natural accounts rather than by functions. *Natural accounts* are used to group costs for financial reporting on the firm's income statement and balance sheet. For example, all payments for salaries might be grouped into a salaries account. Whether they apply to production, marketing, logistics, or finance, they usually are lumped together and the total shown on the financial statements at the end of the reporting period.[12] Other examples of natural accounts include rent, depreciation, selling expenses, general and administrative expenses, and interest expense. It is entirely possible that in a firm with a strong financial accounting orientation, logistics costs such as warehousing and transportation may not be given separate headings in the natural accounts. Instead they may be lumped into such diverse catchalls as overhead, selling, or general expense. Furthermore, there has been a tendency, particularly in the case of freight, to abandon the accrual-accounting concept so that costs of one period are matched with revenues of another period. This occurs, for instance, when freight bills are charged directly to an expense account as they are paid—regardless of when the orders are recognized as revenue. These conditions make it difficult to determine logistics expenditures, control costs, or perform trade-off analyses.

---

[12]Wilbur S. Wayman, "Harnessing the Corporate Accounting System for Physical Distribution Cost Information," *Distribution System Costing: Concepts and Procedures,* Proceedings of the Fourth Annual James R. Riley Symposium on Business Logistics (Columbus, OH: Transportation and Logistics Research Foundation, 1972), p. 35.

FIGURE 16–2

Controlling logistics activities

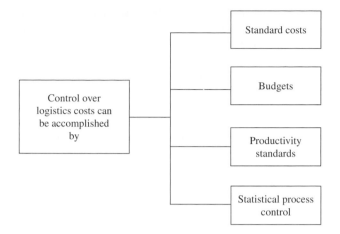

Accounting Data Must Be Tailored to Meet Needs of Logistics

    The challenge is not so much to create new data, since much of the information needed already exists in one form or another, but to tailor the existing data in the accounting system to meet the needs of the logistics function.[13] By improving the *availability* of logistics cost data, management is in a better position to make both operational and strategic decisions. Abnormal levels of costs can be detected and controlled only if management knows what they ought to be for various levels of activity. As Figure 16–2 shows, logistics performance can be monitored by using standard costs, budgets, productivity standards, and/or statistical process control.[14] Other methods of addressing the problem of insufficient cost data include a computerized management information system, activity-based costing, and an automated order processing system.

Standard Costs and Flexible Budgets

Standard Costs and Flexible Budgets Improve Control

Control of costs through predetermined standards and flexible budgets is the most comprehensive type of control system available. *Standard* can be defined as a benchmark or "norm" for measuring performance; standard costs are what the costs should be if the firm is operating efficiently. Using management by exception, managers direct their attention to variances from the standard. A flexible budget is geared to a range of activity. Given the level of activity that occurs, managers can determine what the costs should have been. The use of standard costs represents a direct, effective approach to the logistics costing problem because it attempts to determine what the costs should be, rather than basing future cost predictions on past cost behavior.

    A decision to use standard costs requires a systematic review of logistics operations to determine the most effective means of achieving the desired output. Accounting, logistics, and engineering personnel must work together, using regression analysis, time and motion studies, and efficiency studies, so that a series of flexible budgets can be drawn up for various operating levels in different logistics cost centers. Standards

---

[13]We will describe a system for recording accounting data in the necessary format on pp. 640–43.

[14]The following sections on standard costs, budgets, and productivity standards are adapted from Lambert and Armitage, "Managing Distribution Costs for Better Profit Performance," pp. 50–51. Reprinted by permission from *Business* magazine.

can and have been set for such warehouse operations as stock picking, loading, receiving, replenishing, storing, and packing merchandise. In addition, standards have been used successfully in order processing, transportation, and even clerical functions. However, the use of standards has not been widespread, due in part to the belief that logistics costs are quite different from those in other areas of the business. While there may be some merit to this argument, logistics activities are, by nature, repetitive operations, and such operations lend themselves to control by standards. A more compelling reason why standard costs have not achieved widespread acceptance is that it is only recently that the importance of logistics cost control has been recognized. However, management accountants and industrial engineers say most firms have a wealth of experience in installing standard costs in the production area, which, with some effort, could be expanded into logistics.

Standard costs for logistics may be more complex to develop because the output measures can be considerably more diverse than in the case of production. For example, in developing a standard for the picking function, it is possible that the eventual control measure could be stated as a standard cost per order, a standard cost per order line, a standard cost per unit shipped, or a standard cost per shipment. Despite the added complexities, work measurement does appear to be increasing in logistics activities.[15]

A Computerized System of Freight Standards

In one example of a successful applications, a firm used a computerized system with standard charges and routes for 25,000 routes and eight different methods of transportation. Up to 300,000 combinations were possible, and the system was updated regularly. Clerks at any location could obtain from the computer the optimum method of shipment. A monthly computer printout listed the following information by customer:

- Destination.
- Standard freight cost to customer.
- Actual freight charges paid for shipments to customer.
- Standard freight to warehouse cost.
- Total freight cost.
- Origin of shipment.
- Sales district office.
- Method of shipment.
- Container used.
- Weight of shipment.
- Variance in excess of a given amount per hundredweight.

Another monthly report listed the deviation from standard freight cost for each customer and the amount of the variance. This system obviously provided the firm with a measure of freight performance. Equally important, the standards provided the means for determining individual customer profitability and identifying opportunities for logistics cost trade-offs. Because this firm used standards as an integral part of its management information system, it could fairly easily determine the impact of a system change—such as an improved, automated order processing system—on transportation costs.[16]

---

[15]See, for example, Ernst and Whinney, *Transportation Accounting and Control: Guidelines for Distribution and Financial Management* (Chicago: National Council of Physical Distribution Management, and New York: National Association of Accountants, 1983); Ernst and Whinney, *Warehousing Accounting and Control: Guidelines for Distribution and Financial Managers* (Chicago: National Council of Physical Distribution Management, and New York: National Association of Accountants, 1985).

[16]Schiff, *Accounting and Control in Physical Distribution Management,* pp. 4-63–4-70.

The use of standards as a management control system is depicted in Figure 16–3. As the figure indicates, standards may result from either formal investigation, philosophy/intuition, or both. Once standards have been set, the firm must compare actual performance with the particular standard to see if it is acceptable. If performance is acceptable, the system is deemed to be under control, and that is the end of the control process. Inherent in this notion is that management operates under the principle of exception—exerting no changes in the system so long as it operates satisfactorily (and the measure of "satisfactory" is found in the standard).

Variances Must Be Analyzed to Identify the Causes

It is highly unlikely that performance will exactly equal standard. Where there is a departure, the procedure is to break the variance down into its component parts to try to ascertain its sources. For example, the standard may be a budgeted amount

FIGURE 16–3

The use of standards as a management control system

The control system

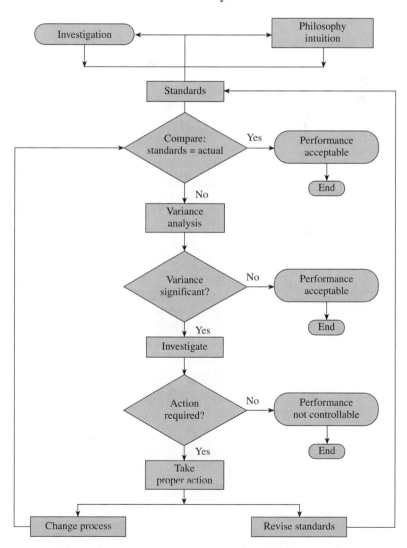

Source: Richard J. Lewis and Leo G. Erickson, "Distribution System Costing: An Overview," in *Distribution System Costing: Concepts and Procedures,* ed. John R. Grabner and William S. Sargent (Columbus, OH: Transportation and Logistics Research Foundation, 1972), p. 17A.

TABLE 16–5   **Summary of Warehouse Picking Operation Week of** _____

Item picked during week	14,500
Hours accumulated on picking activities	330
Standard hours allowed for picks performed	
based on 50 items per hour	290
Variation in hours	40
Standard cost per labor hour	$8
Variation in cost due to inefficiency	$320*

*The cost was $320 over budget because of 40 picking hours in excess of the standard number of hours allowed for efficient operation.

for transportation in a territory. If the actual exceeds the budget, management would like to see the variance analyzed into separate measures of volume and efficiency. It is impossible to know how to proceed unless the variance is analyzed into meaningful sources.

The next question is whether the observed variance is great at enough to be deemed significant. It is possible to handle such a question in strictly statistical terms, setting quality control limits about the standard. This may be done in terms of standard deviations; an acceptable limit may be established on the downside only, or the limit may be on either side of the standard. In the latter case, if performance exceeds standard, management may decide to raise the standard or reward the performer accordingly. Probably of greater concern are those departures in which performance is below standard.

Much of logistics lends itself to measures of statistical significance in departures from standard. However, as with demand-obtaining activities, it is probably more meaningful to judge departures from standard in terms of their practical significance. A form of sensitivity analysis goes on here, in which managers must ask, How critical is the departure in its effects on bottom-line performance or net profit? Regardless of how the assessment is made, the variance will be termed either significant or not significant. If it is not significant, performance is judged acceptable and the control process is ended. If it is significant, the next question is whether action is required.

The variance may be significant but, in analyzing it and explaining it, managers may judge it as not controllable. If so, no action may be indicated and the control process may be terminated. If action is indicated, it will be one of two broad kinds: Either the standard is held to be wrong and must be changed, or the process itself is not producing the results it should and thus must be changed. The feedback goes up to the appropriate levels. If the process is changed and the standard is held, comparisons are again made. If the standard is changed and the process remains unchanged, the feedback is to the standard. It is possible that both would be changed. Thus, both sets of feedback may result from the action phase, and the system cycles through again.[17]

Advantages of Standard Costs

A standard tells management the expected cost of performing selected activities and allows comparisons to be made to determine whether there have been operating inefficiencies. For example, Table 16–5 shows a sample of a report that is useful at the operating level. It shows why the warehouse labor for the picking activity was $320 over budget. The costs of logistics activities can be reported by department, division, function, product group, or total; compared to the standard costs; and included as part of regular

[17]Richard J. Lewis and Leo G. Erickson, "Distribution System Costing: An Overview," in *Distribution System Costing: Concepts and Procedures,* ed. John R. Grabner and William S. Sargent (Columbus, OH: Transportation and Logistics Research Foundation, 1972), pp. 18–20.

TABLE 16–6   Segmental Analysis Using a Contribution Approach ($000)

	Budget	Variance Due to Ineffectiveness	Standard Allowed for Output Level Achieved	Variance Due to Inefficiency	Actual Results
			Explanation of Variation from Budget		
Net sales	$90,000	$10,000	$80,000	—	$80,000
Cost of goods sold (variable manufacturing cost)	40,500	4,500	36,000	—	36,000
Manufacturing contribution	49,500	$ 5,500	$44,000	—	$44,000
Variable marketing and logistics costs (out-of-pocket costs that vary directly with sales to the segment)*	22,500	2,500	20,000	$1,400	21,400
Segment contribution margin	$27,000	$ 3,000	$24,000	$1,400	$22,600
Assignable nonvariable costs (costs incurred specifically for the segment during the period)†	6,000	—	6,000	—	6,000
Segment controllable margin	$21,000	$ 3,000	$18,000	$1,400	$16,600

Notes: This analysis can be performed for segments such as products, customers, geographic areas, or divisions.

Assumption: Actual sales revenue decreased, a result of lower volume. The average price paid per unit sold remained the same. (If the average price per unit changes then an additional variance—the marketing variance—can be computed.)

Difference in income of $4,4000 ($21,000 – 16,600) between budgeted and actual results can be explained by the following variances:

*a.*Ineffectiveness—inability to reach target sales objective	$3,000
*b.*Inefficiency at operating level achieved of $80,000	1,400
	$4,400

*These costs might include sales commissions, transportation costs, warehouse handling costs, order processing costs, and a charge for accounts receivable.

†These costs might include salaries, segment-related advertising, bad debts, and inventory carrying costs. The fixed costs associated with corporate-owned and -operated facilities would be included if, and only if, the warehouse was solely for this segment of the business.

weekly or monthly performance reports. Table 16–6 shows a level of aggregation that would be of interest to the firm's president. This report allows the president to see at a glance why targeted net income has not been reached. On the one hand, there is a $3 million difference due to ineffectiveness, which indicates the net income the company has forgone because of its inability to meet its budgeted level of sales. On the other hand, there is also an inefficiency factor of $1.4 million. The difference between $18 million and the actual outcome of $16.6 million is a $1.4 million variation due to inefficiency within the marketing and logistics functions.

The appendix to this chapter provides an example of how to develop standard costs and flexible budgets for warehousing.

Budgetary Practices

Control Can Be Achieved Using Budgets

Conceptually, standard costs are generally superior for control purposes. However, sometimes the use of standards is inappropriate. This is particularly true in situations that involve essentially nonrepetitive tasks and for which work-unit measurements are difficult to establish. In these situations, control can still be achieved through budgetary practices. The extent to which the budget is successful depends on whether individual cost behavior patterns can be predicted and whether the budget can be flexed to reflect changes in operation conditions.

Most logistics budgets are static. That is, they are a plan developed for a budgeted level of output. If actual activity happens to be the same as budgeted activity, management can make a realistic comparison of costs and establish effective control. However, this is seldom the case. Seasonal or internal factors invariably lead to different levels of activity, the efficiency of which can be determined only if the reporting system can compare the actual costs with what they should have been at the operating level achieved.

For instance, a firm's warehousing unit may have an estimated or budgeted level of activity of 10,000 line items per week, but the actual level of activity may be only 7,500. Comparing the budgeted costs at 10,000 line items against the actual costs at 7,500 leads to the erroneous conclusion that the operation has been efficient, since items such as overtime, temporary help, packing, postage, and order processing are less than budget. A flexible budget, in contrast, indicates that the costs should have been at the 7,500 line items level of activity, and a true dollar measure of efficiency results.

The key to successful implementation of a flexible budget lies in the analysis of cost behavior patterns. In most firms little of this analysis has been carried out in the logistics function. The expertise of the management accountant and industrial engineer can be invaluable in applying tools such as scatter diagrams and regression analysis to determine the fixed and variable components of costs. These techniques use previous cost data to determine a variable rate per unit of activity and a total fixed cost component. Once this is accomplished, the flexible budget for control becomes a reality. Unlike engineered standards, however, the techniques are based on past cost behavior patterns, which undoubtedly contain inefficiencies. The predicted measure of cost, therefore, may not be a measure of what the activity should cost but an estimate of what it will cost, based on the results of previous periods.

Productivity Standards

Productivity Ratios

Logistics costs also can be controlled by the use of productivity ratios. These ratios take the following form:

$$\text{Productivity} = \frac{\text{Measure of output}}{\text{Measure of input}}$$

For example, a warehouse operation might make use of such productivity ratios as the following:

$$\frac{\text{Number of orders shipped this period}}{\text{Number of orders received this period}}$$

$$\frac{\text{Number of orders shipped this period}}{\text{Average number of orders shipped this period}}$$

$$\frac{\text{Number of orders shipped this period}}{\text{Number of direct labor hours worked this period}}$$

Productivity ratios for transportation might include:[18]

$$\frac{\text{Ton-miles transported}}{\text{Total actual transportion costs}}$$

$$\frac{\text{Stops served}}{\text{Total actual transportation costs}}$$

$$\frac{\text{Shipments transported to destination}}{\text{Total actual transportation costs}}$$

---

[18]A. T. Kearney, Inc., *Measuring and Improving Productivity in Physical Distribution* (Oak Brook, IL: National Council of Physical Distribution Management, 1984), p. 170.

TABLE 16–7   **Transportation Activity/Input Matrix**

Activities	Labor	Facilities	Equipment	Energy	Overall (cost)
Transportation strategy development	—	—	—	—	X
Private fleet over-the-road trucking					
Loading	X	—	—	—	X
Line-haul	X	—	—	X	X
Unloading	X	—	—	—	X
Overall	X	—	X	X	X
Private fleet pickup/delivery trucking					
Pre-trip	X	—	—	—	X
Stem driving	X	—	—	X	X
On-route driving	X	—	—	X	X
At-stop	X	—	—	—	X
End-of-trip	X	—	—	—	X
Overall	X	—	X	X	X
Purchased transportation operations					
Loading	—	—	—	—	X
Line-haul	—	—	—	—	X
Unloading	—	—	—	—	X
Rail/barge fleet management	—	—	—	—	X
Transportation/traffic management	—	—	—	—	X

Source: A. T. Kearney, Inc., *Measuring and Improving Productivity in Physical Distribution* (Oak Brook, IL: National Council of Physical Distribution Management, 1984), p. 144.

The transportation resource inputs for which productivity ratios can be generated include labor, equipment, energy, and cost. Table 16–7 illustrates the specific relationships between these inputs and transportation activities. An *X* in a cell of the matrix denotes an activity/input combination that can be measured. Table 16–8 illustrates an activity/input matrix for warehousing.

Productivity measures of this type can and have been developed for most logistics activities. In the absence of a standard costing system, they are particularly useful with budgetary practices and flexible budgeting, since they do provide some guidelines on operating efficiencies. Furthermore, such measures are easily understood by management and employees.[19] However, productivity measures are not without their shortcomings:

Three Shortcomings of Productivity Measures

1. Productivity measures are expressed in terms of physical units and actual dollar losses due to inefficiencies, and predictions of future logistics costs cannot be made. This makes it difficult to cost-justify any system changes that will result in improved productivity.

2. The actual productivity measure calculated is seldom compared to a productivity standard. For example, a productivity measure may compare the number of orders shipped this period to the number of direct labor-hours worked this period, but it does not indicate what the relationship ought to be.

---

[19]For more information on the development of productivity ratios refer to A. T. Kearney, Inc., *Measuring and Improving Productivity in Physical Distribution;* and Howard M. Armitage, "The Use of Management Accounting Techniques to Improve Productivity Analysis in Distribution Operations," *International Journal of Physical Distribution and Materials Management* 14, no.1 (1984), pp. 41–51.

TABLE 16–8   Warehouse Activity/Input Matrix

Activities	Labor	Facilities	Equipment	Energy	Financial	Overall (cost)
Company-operated warehousing						
Receiving	X	X	X	—	—	X
Put-away	X	—	X	—	—	X
Storage	—	X	—	X	—	X
Replenishment	X	—	X	—	—	X
Order selection	X	—	X	—	—	X
Checking		—	X	—	—	X
Packing and marking	X	X	X	—	—	X
Staging and order consolidation	X	X	X	—	—	X
Shipping	X	X	X	—	—	X
Clerical and administration	X	—	X	—	—	X
Overall	X	X	X	X	X	X
Public warehousing						
Storage	—	—	—	—	—	X
Handling	—	—	—	—	—	X
Consolidation	—	—	—	—	—	X
Administration	—	—	—	—	—	X
Overall	—	—	—	—	—	X

Source: A. T. Kearney, Inc., *Measuring and Improving Productivity in Physical Distribution* (Oak Brook, IL: National Council of Physical Distribution Management, 1984), p. 195.

Without work measurement or some form of cost estimation, it is impossible to know what the productivity standard should be at efficient operations.

3. Finally, changes in output levels may in some cases distort measures of productivity. This distortion occurs because the fixed and variable elements are seldom delineated. Consequently, the productivity measure computes utilization, not efficiency. For example, if 100 orders shipped represents full labor utilization and 100 orders were received this period, then productivity as measured by the following ratio:

$$\frac{\text{Number of orders shipped this period}}{\text{Number of orders received this period}}$$

In this case, productivity is 100 percent. However, if 150 orders had been received and 100 orders shipped, productivity would have been 66.67 percent, even though there was no real drop in either efficiency or productivity.

Statistical Process Control

Statistical Process Control Is Gaining in Popularity

In Japan, there is a high level of sophistication in the use of statistical methods to enhance the quality of products and services.[20] The use of such approaches is increasing in North America with the automobile industry, with high-tech firms, and with

---

[20]This material is adapted from C. John Langley, Jr., "Information-Based Decision Making in Logistics Management," *International Journal of Physical Distribution and Materials Management* 15, no. 7 (1985), pp. 48–52.

many consumer products manufacturers. The output of successful logistics is the level of customer service provided. Although many firms measure the proportion of shipments that arrive on time or the average length of the order cycle from a particular vendor, further insight into these areas is seldom obtained through the use of statistical process control techniques.

The use of statistical methods offers an alternative to conventional management control processes. Statistical process control (SPC) requires an understanding of the variability of the process itself prior to making management decisions. For example, to analyze delivery times from several vendors, it is necessary to know the mean, or average, time, elapsed from the issuance of a purchase order to the receipt of a shipment and the likely variation in delivery times.

Figure 16–4 illustrates the steps of SPC. As with classical approaches to control, the first three steps are:

FIGURE 16–4

Statistical process control (SPC)

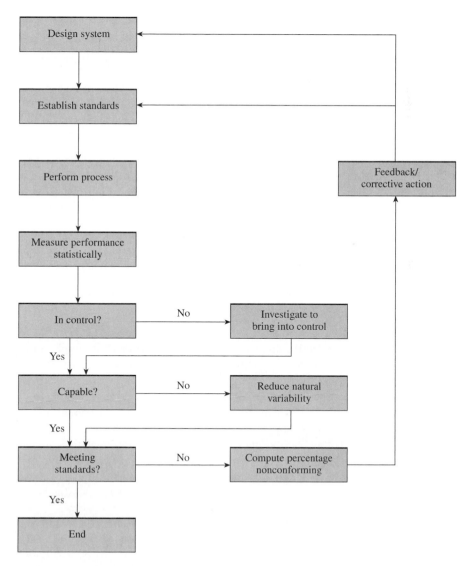

Source: C. John Langley, Jr., "Information-Based Decision Making in Logistics Management," *International Journal of Physical Distribution and Materials Management* 15, no. 7 (1985), p. 50. Copyright MCB University Press Limited.

1. Design system.
2. Establish standards.
3. Perform process.

Once the first three steps are accomplished, SPC requires that the following questions be raised: First, are the measurements "in control"? That is, do they all fall within reasonable proximity of the mean? Second, is the process capable; that is, is the observed variability less in magnitude than a prespecified range? Third, do the measurements meet standards? Only if the answers to these three questions are yes is the process itself said to be in control.

The Control Chart Is Used to Identify Significant Variances

The *control chart* is perhaps the most widely used statistical approach to gain insight into these questions. The control chart permits an examination of process behavior measurements in relation to both upper and lower *control limits*. These limits are statistically derived and are used to identify instances where the observed behavior differs significantly from what was expected, and where a problem is likely to exist. The search for explanations can then proceed in an organized, efficient manner.

[Figure 16–5] shows two control chart applications, which were developed using actual logistics-related data. Part A resulted from an examination of transit time data (in minutes) of shipments traveling between two cities which were 260 miles apart. Once the three out-of-control points (i.e., those located outside the control limits) were identified and isolated, an inquiry was undertaken to determine their causes and assure removal of those causes.

Part B of Figure 16–5 shows the percentages of carrier freight bills, which were found by a particular shipper to contain errors. In this particular example the only error percentages which would be of concern are those which are excessively high, and an inspection of Part B shows that only one such point was sufficiently high as to be labeled out-of-control in a statistical sense. In this instance, subsequent investigation resulted in the identification and removal of the cause of the problem at hand.

Although these two examples are relatively simple, any one of a number of activities in logistics management could have been selected for purposes of illustration. Areas having significant applications potential include not only transportation, but warehousing, materials handling, packaging, inventory control, order processing, and customer service. There is strong evidence to suggest that large cost savings can be captured in areas such as these through the appropriate use of statistical method.[21]

Prerequisites to Success

There are a number of prerequisites to success with SPC. First, it is important to recognize that the use of statistical methods is simply a tool that can assist in improving quality. SPC provides valuable insight into the behavior of the various processes under scrutiny. Second, top management support is necessary for success. The effective use of SPC approaches may involve a cultural change.

Statistical Methods Must Be Part of an Overall Quality

Successful firms have involvement and commitment from top management and require that all of those involved have a high level of familiarity with and knowledge of the various approaches. Finally, the use of statistical methods should be viewed as a key component of an overall quality management program. Other elements of the quality program may include the establishment of quality policies, the setting of goals and objectives, supervisory training, quality awareness and error cause removal programs, and performance management.

The issue of quality in logistics is frequently addressed in conjunction with the topic of productivity. However, attention has been focused on the identification of spe-

---

[21]Langley, "Information-Based Decision Making," pp. 49–52.

FIGURE 16–5

Control chart example

A. Transit time performance

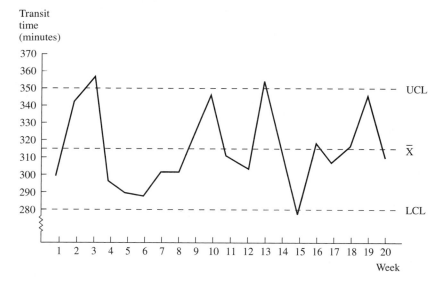

B. Freight bill accuracy

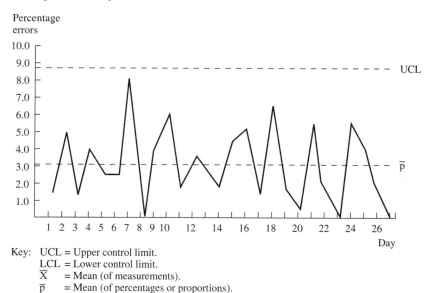

Key: UCL = Upper control limit.
LCL = Lower control limit.
$\overline{X}$ = Mean (of measurements).
$\overline{p}$ = Mean (of percentages or proportions).

Source: C. John Langley, Jr., "Information-Based Decision Making in Logistics Management," *International Journal of Physical Distribution and Materials Management* 15, no. 7 (1985), p. 51. Copyright MCB University Press Limited.

cific data and information needs rather than on what to do with the information once it has been acquired. Until more progress is made in this direction, the benefits of improved productivity will continue to represent a largely untapped resource.

Successful implementations of SPC approaches are dependent on the timely availability of appropriate information. For this reason, SPC provides an opportunity for the logistics and information systems areas to work together to enhance productivity and improve quality.

Technology

Enabling Managers to Develop Performance Metrics

Whether it's creating performance metrics or tracking material flows, no one disputes that it will be technology that gets the job done . . . It looks as if technology and logistics are finally on the same path and it couldn't come at a better time. "Companies are looking beyond their own organizations so there's a lot of interest in collaboration. There are a lot of frontiers beyond enterprise resource planning," said Yossi Sheffi, director of the Center for Transportation Studies at Massachusetts Institute of Technology. "They want to integrate their systems back to their suppliers."

Ann Tomlanovich, manager of corporate material control for the MOPAR Parts Division of Chrysler Corp., agrees that technology has taken substantial leaps in the last five years. MOPAR always has made extensive use of performance metrics and is stepping up its activity in this area even more. It has just established a Material and Order Flow team whose number one objective is to get metrics. "Technology is really enabling us to do this," Tomlanovich said. "Five years ago it would have been possible to get some of this information but it would have

been more cumbersome and we wouldn't have been able to get some metrics, like event tracking."

In the past, MOPAR's metrics were more like historical snapshots of the company. That wasn't good enough. "We knew our metrics weren't telling the story anymore," Tomlanovich said. "The supply chain takes on a variety of flavors and relying on static metrics doesn't tell us where we should be heading." Today the company is moving the static historical snapshots and those that show performance over time. "We're now saying that it doesn't matter where inventory comes from but what's important is when it arrives. So warehousing becomes secondary in terms of where inventory is stored if it can be moved quickly," she said.

According to Tomlanovich: "Everybody's been reengineering their information systems. Now we want to start using them and optimizing what we do. That will be the tell-tale sign of how well companies did their reengineering in the 1990s."

Source: Adapted from Ann Saccomano, "Technology Meets Logistics," *Traffic World* 256, no. 2 (1998), pp. 30–32.

Logistics Costs and the Corporate Management Information System

Accurate Costs Are Required for Informed Decision Making

While substantial savings can be generated when management is able to compare its actual costs to a set of predetermined standards or budgets, there are even greater opportunities for profit improvement in the area of decision making. If management is to make informed decisions, it must be able to choose between such alternatives as hiring additional common carrier transportation or enlarging the company's private fleet, increasing deliveries or increasing inventories, expanding or consolidating field warehouses, and automating the order processing and information system. The addition or deletion of territories, salespeople, products, or customers requires a knowledge of how well existing segments are currently performing, and how revenues and costs will change with the alternatives under consideration. For this purpose, management needs a database capable of aggregating data so that it can obtain routine information on individual segments such as customers, salespeople, products, territories, or channels of distribution. The system must also be able to store data by fixed and variable components so that the incremental revenues and costs associated with alternative strategies can be developed.

Source Documents

Several types of transactions occur in every business, and each transaction results in the creation of source documents (such as customer orders, shipment bill of lading, sales invoices to customers, and invoices from suppliers/vendors). In addition, compa-

FIGURE 16–6

A modular database system for reporting cost and revenue flows

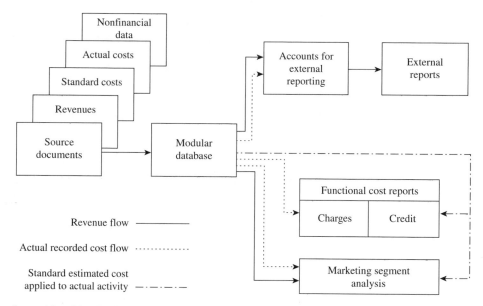

Source: Adapted from Frank H. Mossman, Paul M. Fischer, and W. J. E. Crissy, " New Approaches to Analyzing Marketing Profitability," *Journal of Marketing* 38, no. 2 (April 1974), p. 45.

nies perform a variety of internal transactions and activities that are documented (e.g., "trip reports" for private fleet activities, salespeople's "call reports," and warehouse labor time cards). Other costs may be recognized by means of standard cost systems, engineering time studies, or statistical estimating (e.g., multiple regression techniques). The key to success is computerization of source documents.

The Modular Database System

One of the most promising database systems for generating logistics cost information and profit contribution reports is the modular database (Figure 16–6).[22] It is a central storage system in which source documents are fed into the database in coded form. Inputs can be coded according to function, subfunction, customer, territory, product, revenue or expense, channel of distribution, transportation mode, carrier, revenue, or expense, or a host of other possibilities. For example, the information that may be recorded by customer order as shown in Table 16–9. The system is capable of storing large amounts of data and allows rapid aggregation and retrieval of various modules of information for decision making or external reporting. The modular database, combined with standard costs, is capable of generating both function cost reports and segment contribution reports. The system works by charging functions, such as warehousing and transportation, with actual costs; the costs are then compared to predetermined standards. Individual segments such as customers or products are credited with segment revenues and charged the standard cost, plus controllable variances.

The modular database is capable of collecting all of the revenues and costs for every transaction and aggregating them by functional activity (e.g., selling, advertising/promotion, transportation, warehousing, and order processing). This technique is

---

[22]See Frank H. Mossman, Paul M. Fischer, and W. J. E. Crissy, "New Approaches to Analyzing Marketing Profitability," *Journal of Marketing* 38, no. 2 (April 1974), pp. 43–48.

TABLE 16–9   **Information That May Be Recorded in the Modular Database by Customer Order**

Customer number	Salesperson number
Customer name	Territory
Order number	Region
Previous order number	Partial ship back order number
Customer order number	Credit limit
Customer billing address	Credit outstanding
Customer shipping address	Prepaid/collect freight
Customer order date	Terms
Requested shipping date	Instructions regarding shipping and product
Date product reserved	substitutions
Date released to distribution center	Quantity, product number, price
Date picked/packed	Packing and shipping instructions
Ship date	Transportation commodity classification
Date, time, and operator	Carrier
Priority code	Bill of lading number

commonly referred to as *responsibility accounting* and is used primarily to develop annual budgets and monthly variance reports by major categories and subcategories of corporate activities, such as manufacturing, research development, marketing/sales, and logistics. In addition to being able to evaluate the profitability of individual customers, product line, territories, and/or channels of distribution, the database permits the user to simulate trade-off decisions and determine the effect of proposed system changes on total costs. Figure 16–7 summarizes the report-generating capabilities of the modular database. In order to implement the modular database approach, it is necessary to collect the raw cost data and break them down into fixed-variable and direct-indirect components. In other words, the data must be sufficiently refined to permit the formulation of meaningful modules. Full implementation of the integrated logistics management concept and knowledgeable decision making in the areas of strategic and operational planning require a sophisticated management information system.

Even though the modular database concept has been described in the literature for more than 25 years, surveys of corporate practices and a review of marketing management texts indicate that there are relatively few integrated operating systems that report segment profits on a timely and accurate basis.[23] Why does this condition exist? Many managers mistakenly feel that the same accounting practices (i.e., the allocation of all costs) used to value inventories and report results to the Internal Revenue Service or Securities and Exchange Commission are required to generate reports for managing the business. Managers may also feel that using only variable and direct fixed costs might encourage suboptimal pricing by salespeople. A separate management accounting system is frequently opposed by accountants. Top management and accountants may feel more comfortable if they can tie the cumulative results of the various segments to total company profit-and-loss data. Managers often fail to recognize the behavioral differences of fixed and variable costs, as well as the distinction between direct and indirect expenses. As a result, they fail to understand the usefulness and purpose of contribution

---

[23]Douglas M. Lambert and Jay U. Sterling, "Educators Are Contributing to Major Deficiencies in Marketing Profitability Reports," *Journal of Marketing Education* 12, no. 3 (Fall 1990), pp. 42–52.

FIGURE 16–7

*Report generating
capabilities of the
modular database*

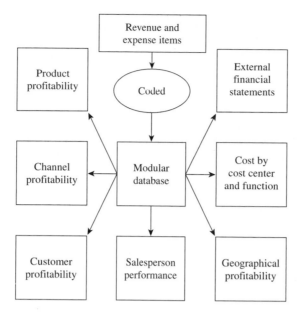

reports. Finally, data processing personnel often discourage the development of such reports by citing the difficulties in creating the databases and operating systems required to assign direct costs to specific product and market segments. In today's information technology environment, these reasons are no longer valid.

With the information from the modular database, management is in a position to evaluate the profitability of various segments. In addition, the database permits the user to simulate trade-off situations and determine the effect of proposed strategic and system changes on total cost.

**The Key to Measuring
Logistics Performance**

The key to measuring logistics performance is an integrated, broad-based computer data file. In order to track an order and its associated costs—for example, from origin to receipt by customer—it is necessary to access a number of files in the logistics information system:

- Open orders (for back orders).
- Deleted orders (order history file).
- Shipped manifest (bills of lading).
- Transportation freight bills paid.

With today's data processing capabilities, it is possible to automatically access desired information from these and other necessary files (such as inventory, customer retail feedback data, damage reports/claims, and billing/invoicing files). From these files, a condensed "logistics performance" database file can be constructed. This will provide all of the information required to measure overall as well as individual activities on a regular basis. What used to take several man-years of concerted programming effort and large sums of resources can be developed in a matter of weeks or months using personal computers and standard statistical packages. A major consumer products company uses this approach to construct a series of more than 50 reports using a common "logistics performance file." More than just logistics costs are reported. However, the same data files are used to report financial, customer service, or productivity-related reports.

Activity-Based Costing

Activity-Based Costing Requires Identification of Cost Drivers

One method of solving the problem of insufficient cost data that has been receiving increased attention is activity-based costing.[24] Traditional accounting systems in manufacturing firms allocate factory/corporate overhead to products based on direct labor. In the past, this method of allocation may have resulted in minor distortions. However, product lines and channels have proliferated and overhead costs have increased dramatically, making traditional allocation methods dangerous. Cooper and Kaplan recommend identification of an activity-based system to examine the demands that are made by particular products (or customers) on indirect resources.[25] They recommend the following three rules when examining the demands made by individual products on indirect resources:

- Focus on expensive resources.
- Emphasize resources whose consumption varies significantly by product and product type.
- Focus on resources whose demands are uncorrelated with traditional allocation methods such as direct labor or materials cost.[26]

They believe that the process of tracing costs, first from resources to activities and then from activities to specific products (or customers), cannot be done with surgical precision. But they also believe it is better to be basically correct with activity-based costing, say within 5 percent or 10 percent of the actual demands a product (or customer) makes on organizational resources than to be precisely wrong (perhaps by as much as 200 percent) using outdated allocation techniques or including indirect, common costs.

One of the biggest challenges to activity-based costing/management (ABC/M) adoption has been the increase in enterprise resource planning (ERP) implementations. Installation of this software, which runs all the operations of a company, has diverted attention and resources away from "change enablers" like ABC/M and toward infrastructure applications such as financials, human resources, and manufacturing/logistics. Afraid of clashing with powerful ERP implementations, many of those in charge of ABC/M implementations have delayed or abandoned their projects. However, once the ERP systems have been implemented, the emphasis will shift to using the data being collected. ERP vendor SAP AG has made a substantial equity investment in ABC Technologies, developer and producer of Windows-based ABC/M applications. The combination of ABC Technologies' Oros application and SAP's R/3 CO-ABC demonstrates how an enterprisewide ABC/M environment can be constructed.[27]

Activity-Based Costing Is Another Method of Allocation

The major shortcoming of activity-based costing is that it is simply another method of allocation, and by definition any method of allocation is arbitrary. The potential problems associated with using activity-based costing for logistics was made

[24]Terrance L. Pohlen and Bernard J. La Londe, "Implementing Activity-Based Costing (ABC) in Logistics," *Journal of Business Logistics* 15, no. 2 (1994), pp. 1–23; and van Damme and van der Zon, "Activity Based Costing and Decision Support," pp. 71–82.

[25]Cooper and Kaplan, "Measure Costs Right: Make the Right Decisions," pp. 96–103.

[26]Ibid., p. 98.

[27]Russell Shaw, "ABC and ERP: Partners at Last?" *Management Accounting* 80, no. 5 (1998), pp. 56–58.

Creative Solutions

Activity-Based Costing at Pitney Bowes Inc.

An eight-member team at Pitney Bowes Inc. set out to determine how much money the Stamford, Connecticut–based mailing-systems company was spending on logistics from order management and the sourcing of raw materials through installation of finished products at customer sites.

"We were forced to look inside the organization at what it is that we really do here, and come up with a cost where people close to the process might not see a cost," says Bill O'Loughlin, executive director for supply chain integration at the $3.5 billion company. O'Loughlin supervised the work of the cross-functional team, which included members from finance, manufacturing, sales, and other functional areas.

Many of Pitney Bowes's transportation costs were in fact easy to find—they were in the general ledger. So were the costs associated with warehousing and distribution. The real challenge was uncovering the rework costs related to the company's rather dismal first-time yield of 30 percent. How do you assign a cost to unplanned scheduling changes and frequent assembly-line reconfigurations? What about the costs associated with holding raw materials and finished goods in inventory? And what about the additional customer installation costs when orders were wrong or missing critical parts?

The solution, for Pitney Bowes, was activity-based costing. ABC is "the most correct way to cost the process," says O'Loughlin. With the help of ABC, it took O'Loughlin's team little more than a month to come up with a preliminary number, the "total installed cost." Then, it spent several more months rechecking and massaging it until, finally, Pitney Bowes had what it was after: a benchmark against which improvement initiatives can be measured, and a message about the importance of looking at the supply chain in an integrated fashion.

"We wanted one common number, and we want to improve that number over time," says O'Loughlin. "Our objective is to make logistics decisions in concert with fixing our supply chain processes, rather than in a vacuum where in the short-term we save a few dollars here or there but ignore the impact on other parts of the process."

Source: Adapted from Stephen Barr, "The Big Picture," *CFO* 12, no. 7 (July 1996), pp. 37–42.

---

very clear in a 1991 article in *Management Accounting.*[28] The article described the use of activity-based costing for marketing and made the claim that physical distribution is the most effective area for application. However, the examples used were simply average costs where selling costs were reported as 5 percent of sales, advertising costs were 40 cents per unit sold, warehousing costs were 10 cents per pound shipped, packing and shipping costs were 20 cents per unit sold, and general office expenses were allocated at $20 per order.[29] Clearly, activity-based costing implemented in this manner represents an average cost system that contains the problems described earlier in this chapter. For example, transportation costs need to be identified by origin and destination zip codes and by shipment size categories before they can be assigned to customers and/or products.

Only Revenues and Costs That Will Change with a Decision Are Relevant

The overriding rule is to *include, in segment reports, only those costs that would disappear if the revenues of the segment were lost.* With this philosophy in mind, we recommend a hybrid system that combines the detailed manufacturing cost structure provided by an activity-based system with the marketing and distribution cost components recognized in the contribution approach to measure segment profits.

---

[28]Ronald J. Lewis, "Activity-Based Costing for Marketing," *Management Accounting* 73, no. 5 (November 1991), pp. 33–38.

[29]Ibid., p. 35.

Segment Profitability Reports

Managers responsible for product and customer business segments need to understand the financial implications of their decisions. Executives must be able to talk the language of accountants, understand the benefits of contribution analysis, recognize the difference between good and bad accounting data, and have the capability of accessing relevant data files on an ongoing basis. The support and active participation by top management, including the chief executive, is necessary since resistance to change is one of the major barriers facing U.S. manufacturers in their quest to become world-class operations.

Segment Contribution Reports Are Required to Manage the Business

Once segment contribution reports are implemented, managers can begin to accurately assess strategic options such as which product lines to drop or whether prices can be raised on inelastic products or reduced on high-volume products. Added emphasis can be placed on those segments that are most profitable. Product lines can be accurately assessed using 80–20 analyses in order to eliminate unprofitable items. The firms that have developed and implemented segment profitability reports have been able to identify products and customers that were either unprofitable or did not meet corporate financial objectives. Ironically many of these products/customers were previously thought to be profitable, due either to their sales volumes or to manufacturing margins. It is difficult for U.S. firms to compete with foreign competitors even when the U.S. firms have good financial information. It is almost impossible to compete effectively with bad information.

One company that has developed customized profitability analysis is 3M. Managers are now able to see how manufacturing, distribution, and marketing costs affect segment profitability by product and customer. According to Karen Madsen, manager of logistics planning and analysis for 3M, the key enablers are data availability, data accuracy, and state-of-the-art system capabilities. An extensive data warehouse combined with activity-based costing allows 3M to track the costs associated with serving customers and selling individual products.[30]

The Role of the Order Processing System

The Order Processing System Can Affect Logistics in Two Major Ways

The order processing system can affect the performance of the logistics function in two major ways. First, the system can improve the quality of the management information system by providing such data as customer names, location of customers, items demanded by customer, sales by customer, sales patterns (when items are ordered), order size, sales by salesperson, and sales data for the company's sales forecasting package.

Second, the customer order is the message that sets the logistics function in motion. The speed and quality of the information provided by the order processing system have a direct impact on the cost and efficiency of the entire logistics process. Slow and erratic communication can lead to lost customers or excessive transportation, inventory, and warehousing costs. It can also bring about possible production inefficiencies because of frequent line changes. Implementation of the latest technology in order processing and communications systems can lead to significant improvements in logistics performance.

---

[30]Karen K. Madsen, "Integrated Supply Chain Metrics: An Industry Perspective," Measuring Logistics Performance Seminar, The Ohio State University/University of North Florida, May 17–19, 2000.

Summary

Logistics costs can have a significant impact on the profitability of a firm's customers and products. Yet many firms do not have accurate data for judging customer and product profitability. Accurate cost data also are required to achieve least-cost logistics. Successful implementation of integrated logistics management depends on a full knowledge of the costs involved. And cost data are required to manage logistics operations.

In this chapter, we saw how logistics costs can make a business segment unprofitable and how contribution reports can point the direction for improvement. We also saw how to use logistics costs for decision making and how erroneous decisions result when inaccurate costs are used. We examined the measurement and control of logistics performance using standard costs and flexible budgets, budgetary practices, productivity standards, and statistical process control. Finally, we described how the modular database system and activity-based costing can be used to generate segment profitability reports.

In Chapter 17 we will see how management can measure and sell the value provided by logistics.

Suggested Readings

Armitage, Howard M. "The Use of Management Accounting Techniques to Improve Productivity Analysis in Distribution Operations." *International Journal of Physical Distribution and Materials Management* 14, no. 1 (1984), pp. 41–51.

Braithwaite, Alan, and Edouard Samakh. "The Cost-to-Serve Method." *The International Journal of Logistics Management* 9, no.1 (1998), pp. 69–84.

Cooper, Robin. "You Need a New Cost System When . . ." *Harvard Business Review* 67, no. 1 (January–February 1989), pp. 77–82.

Cooper, Robin, and Robert S. Kaplan. "Measure Costs Right: Make the Right Decisions." *Harvard Business Review* 66, no. 5 (September–October 1988), pp. 96–103.

Davies, Gary, and Eliane Brito. "The Relative Cost Structures of Competing Grocery Supply Chains." *The International Journal of Logistics Management* 7, no. 1 (1996), pp. 49–60.

Ellram, Lisa M. "Framework for Total Cost of Ownership." *The International Journal of Logistics Management* 4, no. 2 (1993), pp. 49–60.

Ellram, Lisa M., and Arnold B. Maltz. "The Use of Total Cost of Ownership Concepts to Model the Outsourcing Decision." *The International Journal of Logistics Management* 6, no. 2 (1995), pp. 55–66.

Ernst and Whinney. *Transportation Accounting and Control: Guidelines for Distribution and Financial Management.* Oak Book, IL: National Council of Physical Distribution Management, and New York: National Association of Accountants, 1983.

————. *Warehouse Accounting and Control: Guidelines for Distribution and Financial Managers.* Chicago: National Council of Physical Distribution Management, and New York: National Association of Accountants, 1985.

Kaplan, Robert S. "One Cost System Isn't Enough." *Harvard Business Review* 66, no. 1 (January–February 1988), pp. 61–66.

————. "How Cost Accounting Distorts Product Costs." *Management Accounting* 70 (April 1988), pp. 20–27.

Keebler, James S.; Karl B. Manrodt; David A. Durtsche; and D. Michael Ledyard. *Keeping Score: Measuring the Business Value of Logistics in the Supply Chain.* Oak Brook, IL: Council of Logistics Management, 1999.

La Londe, Bernard J., and Terrance L. Pohlen. "Issues in Supply Chain Costing." *The International Journal of Logistics Management* 7, no. 1 (1996), pp. 1–12.

Lambert, Douglas M., and Jay U. Sterling. "What Types of Profitability Reports Do Marketing Managers Receive?" *Industrial Marketing Management* 16, no. 4 (1987), pp. 295–303.

McIntyre, Kristie; Hugh A. Smith; Alex Henham; and John Pretlove. "Logistics Performance and Greening Supply Chains: Diverging Mindsets." *The International Journal of Logistics Management* 9, no. 1 (1998), pp. 57–68.

Mentzer, John T., and Brenda Ponsford Konrad. "An Efficiency/Effectiveness Approach to Logistics Performance Analysis." *Journal of Business Logistics* 12, no. 1 (1991), pp. 33–62.

Mossman, Frank H.; W. J. E. Crissy; and Paul M. Fischer. *Financial Dimensions of Marketing Management.* New York: John Wiley and Sons, 1978.

Novack, Robert A. "Quality and Control in Logistics: A Process Model." *International Journal of Physical Distribution and Materials Management* 19, no. 11 (1989), pp. 1–44.

Roth, Harold P., and A. Faye Borthick. "Are You Distorting Costs by Violating ABC Assumptions?" *Management Accounting* 71 (November 1991), pp. 39–42.

Tyndall, Gene R., and John R. Busher. "Improving the Management of Distribution with Cost and Financial Information." *Journal of Business Logistics* 6, no. 2 (1985), pp. 1–18.

Webber, Mary Margaret. "Calculating the Cost of Variances in the Supply Chain." *Industrial Marketing Management* 29, no. 1 (2000), pp. 57–64.

Worthy, Ford S. "Accounting Bores You? Wake Up." *Fortune,* October 12, 1987, pp. 43–44, 48–50.

Questions and Problems

1. Explain why it is important to include logistics costs in profitability reports for customers and products.
2. What are the problems associated with the segment profitability reports of most companies?
3. Why is it so important to have accurate cost data for management of the logistics function?
4. What problems are associated with the use of average cost data for decision making?
5. How does the inability to distinguish between fixed and variable costs hamper good management practice?
6. What are the problems associated with the arbitrary allocation of logistics costs?
7. How does having accurate cost data contribute to the motivation of personnel?
8. Why is it difficult to obtain logistics cost data in many firms?
9. Explain the four methods that can be used for controlling logistics activities. What are the advantages and disadvantages of each?
10. What is activity-based costing? What are the advantages of activity-based costing? What are the potential limitations associated with activity-based costing?
11. How can the order processing system improve the quality of the logistics information system?
12. The shipping department of Company A has recently converted to a standard cost system for cost control and performance measurement. For every 1,000

containers packed and shipped, the department expects the following variable cost pattern:

Materials: 1,000 containers at $5	$ 5,000
20,000 cartons at 20 cents	
(each container holds 20 cartons)	4,000
Labor: 200 hours at $5	1,000
Variable overhead (varies with	
direct labor-hours)	200
Total	$10,200

The budgeted level of activity for the previous reporting period was 1,000 containers packed and shipped. The actual results for the period are as follows:

Actual shipments: 1,100 containers	
Materials purchased and used:	
Containers: 1,100 at $5.10	$ 5,610
Cartons: 22,300 at 22 cents	4,906
Labor: 210 hours at $5.00	1,050
Variable overhead	230
Total	$11,796

Show the variances due to ineffectiveness and inefficiency for containers, cartons, labor, variable overhead, and the total variable cost of the shipping department. Explain how your answer provides management with more useful information than would be obtained by simply comparing budgeted figures with actual results.

13. Find the impact on return on net worth of a new order processing system, given the following information about the Southland Manufacturing Company:

    a. Sales are $200 million.

    b. Net profit is $8 million after taxes.

    c. Asset turnover rate is 2.5.

    d. Financial leverage is 2.

    e. Taxes are 50 percent of net income.

    f. The new system will provide management with four additional days for planning logistics operations.

    g. Inventories will be reduced by $3 million, valued at variable costs delivered to the storage location.

    h. The company's inventory carrying cost is 45 percent, which is comprised of a pretax cost of money of 40 percent, and non-cost-of-money components of 5 percent of the inventory value.

    i. Transportation consolidations made possible by the additional planning time will reduce transportation costs by $850,000 per year.

   j. Warehousing costs of $200,000 will be eliminated.

   k. The new order processing system will cost $300,000 per year more than the existing system.

   l. Software costs associated with the new system will increase the first-year costs by $100,000.

14. What percentage increase in sales would be necessary in order to realize the same increase in return on net worth (from your answer to Question 13) that is possible by implementing the new order processing system for Southland Manufacturing Company?

DEVELOPING STANDARD COSTS AND FLEXIBLE BUDGETS FOR WAREHOUSING[31]

The first step is to define operating characteristics. Possible units of measure of activities in warehousing might be order, case, shipment, SKU, line item, arrival, or overpacked carton. The basic elements of this warehouse operation consist of receiving (unloading and clerical), shipping (clerical and order consolidation), stock put-away, stock replenishment, order picking, and overpacking. A description of the process is shown in Figure 16A–1.

All of the basic functions of warehousing are present. A 45-day sample was obtained and data were accumulated for the various important functions of the operation. The results of the sample are shown in Table 16A–1. Also included is the average number of occurrences observed per day

FIGURE 16A–1

Operating characteristics

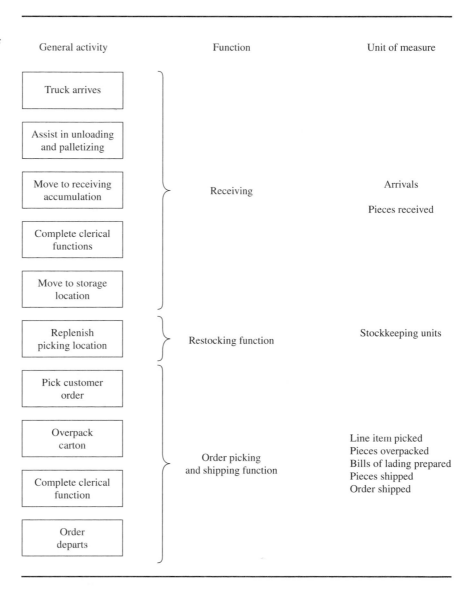

[31]This material is adapted from Howard M. Armitage and James F. Dickow, "Controlling Distribution with Standard Costs and Flexible Budgets," in *Proceedings of the Seventeenth Annual Conference of the National Council of Physical Distribution Management* (Chicago: NCPDM, 1979), pp. 116–20.

TABLE 16A–1   **Activity Levels (45-Day Sample)**

Function	Unit of Measure	Average (units of measure per day)	Standard Deviation (units of measure per day)
Receiving functions:			
Arrivals	Arrivals	18	14
Unloadead	Pieces	735	731
Stock put away	Pieces	735	731
Replenishment functions:			
Volume	SKU	200	0
Shipping functions:			
Order picking	Line items	279	72
Overpacking	Pieces	85	37
Orders	Orders	113	31
Freight shipments	Bill of lading	61	14
Small shipments	Pieces	83	24
Load	Pieces	863	198

TABLE 16A–2   **Activity Standards—Empirical**

Operating Function	Unit of Measure (per labor-hour)	Time Standard (units of measure per labor-hour)
Warehouse:		
Receiving		
Unload truck	Pieces	250
Check receipts	Pieces	167
Clerical function	Pieces	500
Put-away stock	Pieces	150
Shipping		
Order picking	Line item	30
Order packing	Pieces	22.7
UPS/small shipment	Pieces	100
Freight shipping	Bills of lading	15
Stockkeeping		
Bulk items	Skill	70
QA and shelf items	Skill	50

and the standard deviation, which is a measure of central tendency or variation around the average. The larger the standard deviation, the more variation there is in day-to-day activity. For instance, the receiving function has higher standard deviations than the order-picking function. This is logical, since receiving activities tend to fluctuate. Shipping, on the other hand, is more consistent, and the standard deviation of the number of lines picked per day is small.

Now that the process has been described—its operating characteristics and activity levels known—the next step is to develop activity standards. These were developed using empirical standards. These standards could have been developed based on industry standards, engineering studies, or historical data, but the empirical method of observing the operation and using judgment to develop estimates was thought to be the most appropriate in this case (see Table 16A–2).

Now that the daily activities, the approximate levels of activity, and knowledge of the process have been determined, this information is used to develop standard costs (see Table 16A–3).

The information in Table 16A–3, which includes the standard times and hourly wage rates, allows an incremental cost per unit of measure to be calculated. The unit of measure for each one

TABLE 16A–3   Standard Cost

Function	Unit of Measure	Daily Activity (units of measure)	Standard Time (units of measure per L-H)	Hourly Rate ($ per L-H)	Standard Cost ($ per unit of measure)
Receiving:					
Unload truck	Pieces	735	250	7.50	3.0¢/Piece
Check receipts	Pieces	735	167	7.50	4.5¢/Piece
Clerical function	Pieces	735	500	7.50	1.5¢/Piece
Put-away stock	Pieces	735	150	7.50	5.0¢/Piece
					14.0¢/Piece
Replenishment:					
Replenish	SKU	200	50	7.50	15.0¢/SKU
Shipping:					
Order picking	Line item	279	30	8.00	26.7¢/Line
Order packing	Pieces	85	23	7.50	32.6¢/Piece
Small shipping	Pieces	83	100	8.00	8.0¢/Piece
Freight shipping	Shipments	61	15	8.25	55.0¢/Shipment

L-H = Labor hour.

TABLE 16A–4   Application to a Flexible Budget

Function	Unit of Measure (U/M)	Standard Cost ($/U/M)	Weekly Summary			
			Activity (U/M)	Std. Cost ($)	Actual Cost ($)	Variance ($)
Receiving	Piece	0.14	4,200	588	800	212 U
Replenishment	SKU	0.15	1,000	150	100	50 F
Shipping:						
Order picking	Line item	0.27	1,430	386	450	64 U
Order packing	Piece	0.33	350	116	100	16 F
Small shipping	Piece	0.08	500	40	25	15 F
Freight shipping	Shipment	0.55	400	220	150	70 F
				1,500	1,625	125 U

of the activities might be different, and in this case they are different—that is, piece, SKU, line item, and freight shipment. In some cases it is possible to lump activities together as they are in the receiving function, but this is not possible in every situation. The standard cost per unit of measure is obtained by dividing the labor costs per labor-hour by the estimated standard time.

If this warehousing operation were using flexible budgeting, the standard costs would be used to develop the flexible budget. An example is contained in Table 16A–4.

In this week, 4,200 cases were received, 1,000 stockkeeping units were replenished, and so on. These activity levels, when multiplied by the standard cost per unit, give the total standard cost for each activity. The actual costs incurred during the week also are shown, and variances favorable or unfavorable—are calculated. For the activity levels achieved during the week, a net unfavorable variance of $125 was calculated. Since this activity level was significantly higher than the average level of activity, the unfavorable variance would have been larger if a fixed budget approach had been used. Developing standard costs and using them to develop a flexible budget gives management a tool to measure the performance of individuals. The minimization of unfavorable variances is a goal that, when achieved, will yield increased profits.

Measuring and Selling the Value of Logistics

Chapter Outline

Chapter Objectives

- To show the various methods of measuring the value of logistics.
- To identify the advantages and disadvantages of each of these measures.
- To show how logistics affects shareholder value.
- To demonstrate how failure to measure and sell the value of logistics leads to suboptimal performance.
- To show that value creation is a moving target.

Introduction[1]

What is similar about the following scenarios?

1. A major manufacturer of consumer durable goods implemented a rapid delivery system for its independent dealers whereby these customers could receive deliveries in 48–72 hours anywhere in the United States. Third-party logistics providers operated the company's regional distribution centers and delivery vehicles. After implementing economic value-added (EVA) measures in an effort to improve financial performance, the company reduced the service to 24–48 hours and switched to a single third-party provider who was not one of the original three.

2. A major chemical company eliminated its corporate logistics function after being advised by a logistics consulting firm that it was not necessary to have a corporate logistics group when each of the company's divisions had a logistics function. As a result, the 55-year-old vice president of corporate logistics, formerly the president of one of the company's divisions, and a number of his staff were looking for work.

In both cases, the value that was being provided by logistics was not being measured and sold. In the first case the company's sales force was not trained to sell the economic benefits to the customer—that is, the potential for much higher inventory turns and therefore lower inventory carrying costs per unit on every unit sold. In fact, the marketing organization still provided these customers with incentives to purchase in large volumes. Also, logistics neglected to estimate how much of the increase in sales was the result of the rapid delivery system. Consequently, marketing took all of the credit for the sales increases achieved. In this situation the value of logistics was not sold externally to the customer or internally to top management.

In the second case, it was a failure to sell the value internally. The corporate logistics organization was not doing an adequate job of showing how it contributed to the financial performance of the company, and therefore it was expendable.

Logistic Value Must Be Measured and Sold Internally and Externally

It cannot be taken for granted that customers (in this chapter we are referring to business customers, not consumers) will understand the value being provided and be willing to compensate the supplier for it. Customers must be shown on a regular basis the value that is being created by logistics, and so must top management within the organization. It is easy for management within the firm to ignore logistics and to underestimate its importance when things are going well. For this reason logistics management must measure and sell the value created by logistics internally as well as externally throughout the supply chain. In this chapter we will review the various methods of measuring value; describe the advantages and disadvantages of each method; and provide suggestions on how the value, once recognized, can be sold.

Key Value Metrics

As customers place demands on suppliers for more value-added services, it is becoming increasingly important to be able to measure the value of these services in terms that are meaningful to the customer. Failure to do so will result in erosion of profitability

---

[1]This chapter is based on Douglas M. Lambert and Renan Burduroglu, "Measuring and Selling the Value of Logistics," *The International Journal of Logistics Management* 11, no. 1 (2000), pp. 1–17.

since it will cost to provide the services to customers, but the firm may not receive adequate compensation for these services. In most cases, it will be necessary to spend more money in order to achieve higher levels of customer satisfaction. However, if customers do not purchase more or are not prepared to pay more, providing more for the customers will leave the company's shareholders with less. Failure to justify a premium price as a result of offering value-added services will lead to profit erosion. It is not good enough to simply enumerate the superior levels of customer service that are being provided to the customer and assume that the customer will understand the financial benefits of this service. For example, the buyer might acknowledge the shorter lead times, better fill rates, and higher levels of on-time performance that the firm is providing over its competitors but still say that the prices of the company's products are too high. In order to justify charging a premium price, it is necessary to convert the higher levels of customer service into a financial benefit such as an inventory turn improvement and use the associated reduction in inventory carrying costs per unit to offset the premium price. Alternatively, it may be possible to show how the higher levels of customer service are contributing to increased sales for customers through better service to their customers or consumers. The most common options for measuring value are:

Options for Measuring Value

1. Customer satisfaction.
2. Customer value-added (CVA).
3. Total cost analysis.
4. Profitability analysis (includes revenue considerations).
5. Strategic profit model.
6. Shareholder value.

Each of these methods will be described in detail in the following sections. Note first, however, that customer satisfaction measures are the least quantitative in financial terms, and shareholder value is the most comprehensive financial measure. In corporations such as Coca-Cola and General Electric, top management has bought into the idea that shareholder value is the best measure of how a corporation is performing. Shareholder value is a better measure than profitability because profitability can be manipulated in the short term and earnings per share do not consider the investment in assets required to achieve those earnings. Shareholder value considers all cash flows related to the profit and loss statement as well as the balance sheet, now and in the future. Future cash flows are discounted to a net present value on a risk-adjusted basis. So shareholder value considers not just earnings but also the investment required to generate those earnings both now and in the future. This long-term orientation means that management is less likely to make myopic decisions.

Customer Satisfaction

Customer satisfaction occurs when businesses successfully fulfill their obligations on all components of the marketing mix: product, price, promotion, and place. As described in Chapter 1, the place component represents the manufacturer's expenditure for customer service, which can be thought of as the output of the logistics system.

Four Reasons to Focus on Customer Satisfaction

There are at least four reasons why companies should focus on customer service. First, satisfied customers are typically loyal and make repeat purchases. Second, it can be up to five times as costly to attract a new customer as it is to keep an old one. Third, customers who decide to defect are very likely to share their dissatisfaction with others.

Fourth, it is more profitable to sell more to existing customers than it is to find new customers for this same level of sales increase.[2] Therefore, in many businesses research is periodically conducted in order to determine customers' needs and set customer service levels so that managers can recognize trade-off efficiencies in revenues and total logistics costs.

Management can use customer service audits, which were described in Chapter 3, to identify the elements of service that are important in customers' purchasing decisions, and to evaluate the level of services being provided by each of the major suppliers in the market. These data can be used to identify ways of improving customers' perceptions of the firm's service. Customer satisfaction is a critical measurement, because it allows management to align the company's service package with customers' needs. Higher levels of customer satisfaction can have a direct impact on customers' financial performance through higher revenues as well as lower costs as a result of the better service. However, providing higher levels of customer service will often increase costs for the supplier. Furthermore, businesses can improve their market share significantly and cost-effectively by investing in logistics to achieve higher levels of customer service than their competitors. The advantages of customer satisfaction measures are that (1) they are not complicated to implement and (2) they enable management to align the company's service package with customers' needs.

Measure the Company's Performance Relative to Competitors

While there are a number of approaches to the measurement and management of customer satisfaction, it is generally considered best to measure the firm's performance relative to specific competitors and identify gaps that represent opportunities for differentiating the company. Usually, customer satisfaction measures are collected using surveys. Table 17–1 illustrates the type of information that can be provided. This survey evaluated both customer service and other marketing mix attributes and is similar to those described in Chapter 3. The two columns on the left side of the table show that the ranking of the attributes was not influenced by the order in which the questions appeared on the questionnaire.

In this example, 12 of the 18 attributes with the highest mean customer importance scores were customer service (logistics-related) attributes. This result highlights the importance of customer service within the firm's marketing mix. A small standard deviation in customer importance ratings means that there was little variation in the respondents' individual evaluations of an attribute's importance. For attributes with a large standard deviation, it is important to use the demographic information to determine which customers want which services.

Higher Customer Service May Not Be Adequately Rewarded

Customers may recognize a firm's superior service performance but still may not be willing to pay a premium price or reward the firm with a larger percentage of their purchases. They may say, for example, "Yes, you are providing better service than your competitors and that's great, but your prices are too high." If the service improvement is not translated into a financial benefit for the customer, the increase in sales or the price premium will not be as large as possible and the improvement may even go unrewarded. High fill rates, on-time deliveries, and short lead times have financial consequences for the customer in terms of costs and revenues that must be estimated. If management does not measure and sell these financial benefits to the customer, it is relying on the customer alone to recognize them.

---

[2]James L. Heskett; W. Earl Sasser, Jr.; and Leonard A. Schlesinger, *The Service Profit Chain* (New York: The Free Press, 1997), pp. 57–79.

TABLE 17–1   Importance Compared to Performance of Suppliers of a Retail Consumer Product

| | | | | | Performance | | | | | | | | | | |
| | | | Importance | | Supplier 1 | | Supplier 2 | | Supplier 3 | | Supplier 4 | | Supplier 5 | |
Rank	Item	Description	Mean	Std. Dev.	Mean	Std. Dev.	Mean	Std. Dev.	Mean	Std. Dev.	Mean	Std. Dev.	Mean	Std. Dev.
1	30d	Quality of sales force: honesty	6.6	1.0	5.8	1.3	6.1	1.4	5.9	1.5	5.4	1.8	5.6	1.7
2	19	Competitiveness of price	6.5	0.8	5.3	1.6	5.9	1.2	5.9	1.2	5.1	1.8	5.3	1.7
3	40	Accuracy in filling orders	6.5	0.8	6.0	1.3	6.1	1.0	5.8	1.3	5.7	1.2	6.0	1.1
4	10	Responsiveness of vendor to competitor's price reductions	6.4	1.0	5.1	1.6	5.0	1.8	5.2	1.8	4.6	1.8	4.8	1.9
5	33	Supplier's freight terms: prepaid	6.3	1.3	6.4	0.9	6.5	0.8	6.8	0.4	6.5	1.0	6.2	1.3
6	6c	Length of promised lead times on ASAP or emergency orders	6.3	1.9	5.6	1.4	5.8	1.4	5.7	1.2	5.6	1.3	5.6	1.5
7	4	Supplier absorbs cost of freight and handling on returns due to shipping damages or product shipped in error	6.3	1.4	5.9	1.6	6.1	1.8	5.9	1.7	5.6	1.8	5.8	1.7
8	15	Adequate advance notice of price changes	6.3	1.0	5.2	1.5	5.1	1.5	5.0	1.5	4.8	1.7	5.2	1.6
9	43c	High fill rate on emergency/ ASAP orders	6.2	1.2	5.8	1.3	6.0	0.9	5.6	1.3	5.6	1.3	5.9	1.1
10	25b	Ability of supplier to handle defective product returns	6.2	1.2	5.5	1.7	5.8	1.8	5.4	1.5	5.4	1.8	5.5	1.5
11	3	Ability to expedite emergency orders	6.2	1.0	5.4	1.6	5.0	2.0	5.6	1.1	5.1	1.8	5.5	1.6
12	43b	High fill rate on ad promotional orders	6.2	1.4	5.5	1.5	5.8	1.0	5.6	1.2	5.3	1.4	5.8	1.1
13	43a	High fill rate on normal reorders	6.2	1.3	5.6	1.4	5.7	1.0	5.7	1.2	5.5	1.1	5.8	1.1
14	6a	Length of promised lead times on normal reorders	6.1	1.1	5.4	1.5	5.7	1.6	5.8	1.0	5.3	1.2	5.5	1.4
15	2	Quality/durability of packaging	6.1	1.2	5.7	1.4	5.7	1.3	6.0	0.8	5.9	1.1	5.8	1.2
16	47	Supplier's adherence to your specific shipping instructions	6.1	1.2	5.4	1.5	5.5	1.6	5.3	1.5	5.3	1.5	5.5	1.5
17	6b	Length of promised lead times on ad/promotional orders	6.1	1.5	5.4	1.5	5.5	1.5	5.5	1.2	5.5	1.2	5.6	1.4
18	34	Timely responses to requests for assistance from supplier's sales rep	6.1	1.2	5.5	1.0	5.9	1.3	5.8	1.1	5.4	1.6	5.6	1.5

Source: Douglas M. Lambert and Renan Burduroglu, "Measuring and Selling the Value of Logistics," *The International Journal of Logistics Management* 11, no. 1 (2000), p. 4.

Our research in a number of industries has shown that some customers who give high satisfaction ratings to a supplier will purchase a greater percentage of their requirements for the product category from that supplier and/or are more likely to pay a price premium. However, this typically occurs in only a small number of firms, which indicates that generally suppliers are not adequately compensated for incrementally better performance. As good as customer satisfaction measures are, they do not show the financial benefit of what the firm is providing for the customer and therefore may not enable management to redirect the firm's efforts in the most profitable manner.

Customer satisfaction measures by themselves are not adequate to sell the value of logistics internally. It is important to relate levels of customer service performance and the associated costs with revenue streams as well as costs. Failure to do so will result in top management's recognizing the costs of logistics but not the revenue-generating capabilities associated with outstanding customer service.

Customer Value-Added

Another popular value metric, customer value-added (CVA), also focuses on the customer satisfaction concept. CVA measures were developed in the marketing literature as measures of value for end consumers but are now being used by consultants such as Gale with clients in business-to-business settings.[3] Customer satisfaction, as captured by CVA, is accomplished by providing value to the customer beyond price. In fact, as Naumann showed in his book *Creating Customer Value: The Path to Competitive Advantage,* price is only one component of value.[4] Customers are interested in obtaining quality at a good price. They use product and service attributes to evaluate the benefits that will be received. The perceived benefits are divided by the perceived sacrifice (i.e., associated costs and risks) to calculate expected customer value (see Figure 17–1).

Management can increase value for the customer by increasing the quality associated with product attributes or service attributes or by reducing transaction costs, life cycle costs, or risk. Product quality and service quality provide the foundation that supports price. If a company either produces poor-quality products or provides bad service, the value-based price will fall. By the same token, if management sets prices too high

FIGURE 17–1

Components of customer value

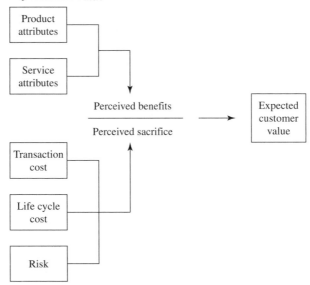

Source: Earl Naumann, *Creating Customer Value: The Path to Sustainable Competitive Advantage* (Cincinnati, OH: Thomson Executive Press, 1995), p. 103.

---

[3]Bradley T. Gale, *Managing Customer Value* (New York: The Free Press, 1994).

[4]Earl Naumann, *Creating Customer Value: The Path to Competitive Advantage* (Cincinnati, OH: Thompson Executive Press, 1995).

for a given level of product and service quality, value is decreased and sales will suffer. Hence, from the company's perspective, "the focus is on finding ways of adding value to a product where the price premium generated by the additional value is greater than the incremental cost to produce the value added."[5]

Value Equals Quality Relative to Price

Gale also linked market-perceived quality (both product and customer service quality) to exceptional customer value where value is defined as the market-perceived quality adjusted for the relative price of the company's products (see Figure 17–2).[6] According to Gale, the customer buys based on value. Value equals quality relative to price. Quality includes all nonprice attributes of both the product and customer service. Quality, price, and value are relative; that is, a customer's evaluation of the quality, price, and value of a product offering depends on a firm's performance relative to its competitors.

Figure 17–3 shows Gale's perspective on how firms create value for the customer as well as how doing so leads to business results such as profitability, growth, and shareholder value. The first step is to understand customer needs in a well-defined market. That is, management should identify segments of customers and determine how the customers in each segment make the decision to buy. With that information, and effective design and quality control, the company can provide superior quality in areas that matter to the customer. Next, management will use advertising and other communications to inform customers that it has listened to them and met their needs, which will result in market-perceived quality. Together, effective design and quality control result in low "cost of quality" and cost leadership, which leads to exceptional customer value and, in turn, to higher profitability, growth, and shareholder value.

Many Major Corporations Use CVA Measures

Companies whose products and services represent a better value than those customers could purchase from competitive companies will have higher sales figures, higher profit margins, higher market shares, and higher shareholder value than competitors. Customer value-added is the perceived value of the company's offer divided by the perceived value of the best competitive offers. Companies such as Lucent Technologies, Texas Instruments, and Fletcher Challenge (New Zealand) use this metric to

FIGURE 17–2

How customers select among competitive suppliers

- Customer buys on value
- Value equals quality relative to price
- Quality includes all nonprice attributes
  — Product   — Customer service
- Quality, price, and value are relative

Source: Bradley T. Gale, *Managing Customer Value* (New York: The Free Press, 1994), p. 29.

---

[5]Ibid., p. 101.
[6]Gale, *Managing Customer Value.*

FIGURE 17–3

Creating value that customers can see

Source: Bradley T. Gale, *Managing Customer Value* (New York: The Free Press, 1994), p. 19.

provide products and services to customers that are perceived as better value than those they can purchase from competitive companies in similar markets (see Figure 17–4).

To measure CVA, managers collect data on specific attributes at a level of detail that allows them to make the necessary changes. In the example shown in Table 17–2, management wanted to identify the firm's comparative performance on "delivering material when you wanted it." On this attribute the company scored 3.35 on average, and the best other vendor scored 3.32. When the company's score was divided by the best competitor's score, the result was above 1.0 (1.01). The company's score on "having the necessary information on all shipping documentation" was 3.67, but management was not able to obtain a best-competitor score and so could not compute a ratio. The company received a score of 4.00 for "having the correct materials delivered relative to what you ordered," and the best other vendor scored a 3.76, for a ratio of 1.05. With this approach, the company's performance is compared to the best vendor for each attribute. However, the "best other vendor" is not the same vendor each time. In fact, since various competitors will most probably have different areas of strength, the best other vendor is unlikely to be the same firm each time, but rather the sum of the best traits of a number of suppliers. The firm must keep in mind that the overall "best other vendor" score is a composite and does not represent a single entity. Overall, on "delivery of materials," the company highlighted in Table 17–2 received a score of 3.89 and competitors received a score of 3.74, resulting in a ratio of 1.04.

FIGURE 17–4

Calculating CVA

THE VALUE QUESTION

Considering the products and services that you purchased, how would you rate them as being worth what you paid for them?

$$CVA = \frac{\text{Perceived value of company's offer}}{\text{Perceived value of competitive offers}}$$

Source: Douglas M. Lambert and Renan Burduroglu, "Measuring and Selling the Value of Logistics," *The International Journal of Logistics Management* 11, no. 1 (2000), p. 5.

TABLE 17–2   Order Fulfillment Customer Satisfaction Survey Results: Delivering Material

	Performance (1 poor . . . 5 excellent)		
Questions/Attributes	*Company*	*Best Other Vendor*	*Company/Best Other Vendor*
Delivering material when you wanted it	3.35	3.32	1.01
Having the necessary information on all shipping documentation	3.67	NA	—
Having the correct materials delivered relative to what you ordered	4.00	3.76	1.05
Overall quality of delivery of materials	3.89	3.74	1.04

Source: Douglas M. Lambert and Renan Burduroglu, "Measuring and Selling the Value of Logistics," *The International Journal of Logistics Management* 11, no. 1 (2000), p. 6.

The next step in calculating CVA is to multiply the ratio scores by 100 and compare them to the results from the Profit Impact of Marketing Strategies (PIMS) database. Since 1975, the Strategic Planning Institute (SPI) has developed and maintained the PIMS database for use in strategy analysis and research. SPI member companies contribute detailed profiles of thousands of businesses in many industries in regional, national, and international markets. These profiles include financial data as well as information on competitive environments, customers, markets, and operations. The PIMS unit of analysis is the strategic business unit (SBU). Each business is a division, product line, or other profit center within its parent company. Businesses in the database can be separated into groups such as producers of: (1) consumer durables, (2) consumer nondurables, (3) capital goods, (4) raw and semifinished materials, (5) components, (6) supplies or consumables, (7) services, and (8) wholesale and retail distribution. Sample results are shown in Table 17–3.[7] If a firm's score is greater than 10 percent better than that of the best of its competitors, the firm is

---

[7]For an explanation of the PIMS database, see Robert D. Buzzell, Bradley T. Gale, and Ralph G. M. Sultan, "Market Share—a Key to Profitability," *Harvard Business Review* 55, no. 1 (January–February 1975), p. 105. A more recent update on PIMS can be found at <www.thespinet.org/db.html>.

TABLE 17–3   Distribution of CVA Levels

Calibration Category	CVA Levels	% of Businesses by Category
World class	>110	15%
Above parity	103–110	25
Parity	98–102	20
Below parity	<98	40

Source: PIMS database.

considered to be "world class"; 15 percent of the businesses in the PIMS database are in this category. A firm with a score of 3 to 10 percent better is considered to be "above parity"; 25 percent of businesses in the database are in this category. "Parity" and "below parity" firms make up 20 percent and 40 percent, respectively, of the businesses in the database.

CVA Scores Do Not Easily Convert to a Financial Benefit for the Customer

The problem is that, though it will cost money to become "world class," these CVA scores do not convert easily into customer benefits that justify a premium price or lead to increased purchase volumes. For example, how much above 1.0 does a firm need to score in order to justify a 1 percent increase in price? And what will it cost to achieve this level of performance?

Total Cost Analysis

In terms of selling value to the customer, the weakness in the first two measures is that they leave it up to the customer to determine the economic benefit of customer service or the CVA. Many customers will not do this. As we noted earlier, some will admit that the service the firm provides is superior but will argue that the firm's prices are too high. If management expects the customer to pay more for better service, then it is management's responsibility to express to the customer the benefits of the higher levels of customer service in financial terms.

Customers Must Evaluate All Costs Associated with Suppliers

As we have defined it in this book, *total cost analysis* involves figuring out how to minimize the total costs of logistics—including transportation, warehousing, inventory, order processing and information systems, and purchasing and production-related lot quantity costs—while achieving a given customer service level. The basic principle of total cost analysis is that managers should consider the *total* cost of all logistics activities instead of trying to reduce the cost of one or more individual logistics activities. Cost reductions in one logistics activity can lead to cost increases in others, and this may result in increased total costs. From a customer value standpoint, the purchase price alone is not good enough; customers must evaluate all of the costs associated with purchasing a product and make their selection among suppliers on the basis of purchase price plus the logistics costs associated with delivering that product. Total cost analysis can be expanded to include all of the costs of ownership, not just those related to logistics. This is referred to as the "total cost of ownership."[8]

[8]Lisa M. Ellram, "Framework for Total Cost of Ownership," *The International Journal of Logistics Management* 4, no. 2 (1993), pp. 49–60; and Lisa M. Ellram and Arnold B. Maltz, "The Use of Total Cost of Ownership Concepts to Model the Outsourcing Decision," *The International Journal of Logistics Management* 6, no. 2 (1995), pp. 55–66.

Technology

Allegiance Healthcare Corporation

Based in McGraw Park, Illinois, Allegiance Healthcare Corporation manufactures and distributes both its own surgical products and those of more than a thousand manufacturers worldwide. A spinoff of Baxter Healthcare Corporation, Allegiance first implemented its stockless inventory program known as "ValueLink" in 1988. Currently in service at over 150 acute-care hospitals in the United States, this program supplies hospital personnel with the products they need when they need them and where they are needed. Twenty customers in the rapidly expanding health care provider market outside of the hospital are already signed up as well (subacute surgery centers and other diagnostic and therapeutic care delivery sites).

Allegiance ships products to each facility in units of measurement that are ready for use in the customer's departments. In each of approximately a dozen hospitals, some 30 Allegiance employees are actually on the customer's premises full-time, 365 days a year, to hand-deliver products to emergency rooms, laboratories, and other areas.

Using the most sophisticated technology available, the ValueLink program achieves a fill rate in excess of 98 percent on the first shipment. Pricing accuracy is in the 99 percent range, much higher than a customer would likely expect when using several different suppliers. Allegiance attributes this accuracy to its cooperative customers and integrated EDI network, a flexible system for handling all orders and invoices electronically. According to Tony Kesman, corporate vice president of distribution at Allegiance, "About 96 percent of the order lines we receive from our customers now come through the EDI network. An equal amount of orders that we make to our suppliers are also handled electronically."

The key to Allegiance's success in processing orders is the integrated system that meets the needs of customers who are dealing with life-and-death situations every minute. In the traditional distribution system, an 18-wheeler simply dropped off a week's or even a month's worth of supplies at the back door of the hospital for central storage. As important items were used, there were various mechanisms for keeping track of the inventory. "We found out," says Kesman, "that the items in most demand often were the ones that the hospital was out of, whereas there were large quantities on hand of certain supplies they seldom needed. The caregiver, however, always had one thing on his or her mind relative to supplies: They wanted it on the shelf when they reached for it."

To design a new system, one that would provide the syringe when and where it was needed, a company undertakes a feasibility study that includes on-site interviews, data collection, needs assessment, and projections of trends. Once a customer decides to adopt the ValueLink program, an implementation team drives the process. A steering committee comprising both hospital employees and Allegiance personnel oversees the installation and assesses how effectively it is processing orders.

Allegiance estimates that the ValueLink system saves its customers an average of $500,000 or more each year. These savings come from improved replenishment processes, the consolidation of multiple vendors, and the reuse of space that is no longer needed to warehouse inventory for other hospital needs.

In providing a sophisticated inventory technology and working in close contact with each customer, Allegiance Healthcare has mastered the techniques of processing orders. The logical extension of this subprocess, as Allegiance so clearly recognizes, is product standardization. The company hires clinical project managers, often nurses or clinicians with business expertise, to observe the flow and consumption of materials. If a hospital is using three different types of catheters, for example, Allegiance suggests a single type that would work in any medical situation. As Kesman points out, "Our ability to standardize these items further creates value for our customers and simultaneously improves our productivity and returns. It's business-to-business marketing."

Source: Robert Hiebeler, Thomas B. Kelly, and Charles Ketteman, *Best Practices: Building Your Business with Customer-Focused Solutions* (New York: Simon & Schuster, 1998), pp. 125–27.

Table 17–4 shows the costs that might be included in total cost analysis. With total cost analysis, the goal is to show the customer the financial benefits associated with the firm's higher service performance. For example, it is necessary to convert fill rates, lead times, and on-time performance that are better than those of competitors to an inventory turn advantage and thereby lower carrying costs per unit. In addition to purchase price, we would want to consider differences in customer-paid freight between the firm and its competitors. Rather than telling customers that the firm provides better on-time delivery performance than competitors, that its fill rates are better and its lead time is shorter, management needs to show the customer how this performance affects its inventory investment. For example, if an item costs the customer $100 and the customer's inventory carrying cost is 36 percent, the cost associated with one inventory turn is $36. Dividing this number by inventory turns actually achieved allows us to calculate the cost on a per unit basis. If the firm's better service results in 12 inventory turns for the customer compared to 6 turns for a competitor's product, the inventory carrying cost per unit would be $3 ($36 ÷ 12) versus $6 ($36 ÷ 6) for the competitor. The $3 per unit savings can be used to justify a price premium over that competitor.

Total cost analysis can be used as a measure of logistics performance internally as well as externally. Logistics costs are a major cost of doing business, and logistics assets represent a significant portion of a firm's total assets. Thus, reducing the total costs associated with logistics represents value creation for the company.

However, the ultimate goal should not be to reduce one entity's costs simply by shifting them to another form. The goal should be to reduce total costs for the supply chain. A shortcoming of total cost analysis as a measure of value creation either externally (from a customer's perspective) or internally (from top management's perspective) is that revenue implications are ignored. Also, the more logistics professionals concentrate on cost savings to justify their existence, the more top management will view logistics as simply a cost reduction opportunity. If logistics professionals want to receive full recognition for their accomplishments, total cost analysis falls short.

Profitability Analysis

From the customer's standpoint, total cost analysis assumes that the suppliers under consideration are revenue-neutral, that is, that the choice of supplier will not affect the level of sales achieved. If this is not the case, then total cost analysis does not go far

TABLE 17–4   Total Cost Analysis

Purchase Price, Plus:
Transportation costs
Inventory carrying costs
Costs associated with alternative terms of sale
Ordering costs
Receiving costs
Quality costs (returns, etc.)
Returned goods costs
Other costs (will depend on situation)

Source: Douglas M. Lambert and Renan Burduroglu, "Measuring and Selling the Value of Logistics," *The International Journal of Logistics Management* 11, no. 1 (2000), p. 7.

enough. For example, if Toshiba sells more laptop computers because the computer has an "Intel Inside" label on it, then Intel would not want the customer to compare the total cost of an Intel microprocessor to the total cost of an Advanced Micro Devices microprocessor.

Segment Profitability Analysis Considers Revenue Implications

Segment profitability analysis using a contribution approach is a much better value metric when there are revenue implications to supplier selection. With this approach only the variable out-of-pocket costs and the avoidable fixed costs are deducted from revenue. In order for a cost to appear in the report, it must disappear if the revenue is lost. Segment profitability analysis, which was described in Chapter 16, helps managers accurately evaluate strategic options such as which product lines to add or drop as well as whether prices can be raised on products with inelastic demand or reduced on high-volume products. Segment profitability analysis considers the impact not just on cost but on revenue as well since the customer service levels can influence the customer's sales volume. Consequently, the firm can allocate scarce resources to those segments that are most profitable while either eliminating unprofitable segments or revitalizing them (see Table 17–5). The segments might be Supplier A, Supplier B, and Supplier C. The questions are: What revenue does the customer generate from the products of each of these suppliers? And what are the out-of-pocket costs associated with each supplier?

TABLE 17–5   Segment Profitability Analysis: A Contribution Approach with Charge for Assets Employed

	Supplier A	Supplier B	Supplier C	Supplier D
Sales				
Cost of goods sold	_____	_____	_____	_____
Gross margin	_____	_____	_____	_____
Plus				
Discounts and allowances				
Market development funds				
Slotting allowances				
Co-op advertising	_____	_____	_____	_____
Net margin	_____	_____	_____	_____
Variable marketing and logistics costs:				
Transportation				
Receiving				
Order processing				
Other costs				
(will depend on situation)	_____	_____	_____	_____
Contribution margin	_____	_____	_____	_____
Assignable nonvariable costs:				
Salaries				
Advertising				
Inventory carrying costs less:				
Charge for accounts payable				
Other costs				
(will depend on situation)	_____	_____	_____	_____
Controllable margin	_____	_____	_____	_____

Source: Douglas M. Lambert and Renan Burduroglu, "Measuring and Selling the Value of Logistics," *The International Journal of Logistics Management* 11, no. 1 (2000), p. 8.

Segment profitability reports can be used to capture both the revenue and cost implications of the firm's value proposition for the customer. The same approach can be used internally to measure the impact of logistics on the profitability of business segments such as customers, class of trade, geographic area, sales territory, and product.

The Strategic Profit Model

The Strategic Profit Model Considers Asset Utilization

A potential limitation of total cost analysis and segment profitability analysis is that they do not measure the cost of assets other than inventory and accounts receivable that might be involved in the business. The strategic profit model demonstrates how asset management and margin management will influence both return on assets and return on net worth, which is the return on shareholders' investment plus retained earnings (see Figure 17–5). The most common practices of asset and cash flow management are to reduce accounts receivable and to reduce the investment in inventory. However, it is important to note that both of these practices, when used without any changes in logistics systems' efficiency or effectiveness, can lead to disastrous results on corporate profit performance. Indeed, large reductions in inventory levels, without considering the impact on other logistics costs, may increase the total cost of logistics significantly. Likewise, reducing accounts receivable without any change in the logistics system can affect the customers negatively, resulting in lower sales revenue. The strategic profit model helps managers determine the overall impact of decisions with regard to cash flows and asset use.

Figure 17–5 illustrates the many ways in which logistics contributes to return on net worth. First, better management of logistics (as measured by length of lead time, in-stock availability, and fill rates, for example) can result in higher sales as a result of higher prices, higher volume, or more rapid time-to-market for new-product introductions. Cost of goods sold can be reduced as a result of taking cash from an inventory reduction and/or accounts receivable and investing it in new manufacturing equipment that will enable quick production changeover and be more efficient (lower labor costs, less material waste, and less energy use). Cost of goods sold also can be **Logistics Can Reduce Both Current and Fixed Assets** reduced through purchasing cost reductions as a result of logistics. Total expenses can be reduced by improved logistics in a number of expense categories. These actions will result in much higher profitability. In terms of the balance sheet, excellence in logistics can result in a reduction in both current and fixed assets, which leads to increased asset turnover. The higher profitability and higher asset turnover provide two upward pressures on return on assets. This, combined with a reduction in financial leverage as a result of debt repayment, leads to higher return on net worth though the increase is not as high as that from reinvesting the cash in the business would be. Generally, companies that are flush with cash are not those with high price earnings ratios.

Reinvestment of the cash in the business is the option used most frequently by companies. The cash from asset reductions related to logistics is invested more productively in plant modernization, new products, or other investments that meet the firm's minimum acceptable rate of return on new investments. In this case all of the impact on return on net worth would be due to changes on the profit and loss statement. Asset turnover would remain the same since the cash made available from reductions in inventories and accounts receivable is reinvested in other, more productive assets. Consequently, financial leverage remains the same. However, the impact on sales and the size of the cost reductions would be much greater with this option, and the increase

FIGURE 17–5

Impact of logistics on return on net worth

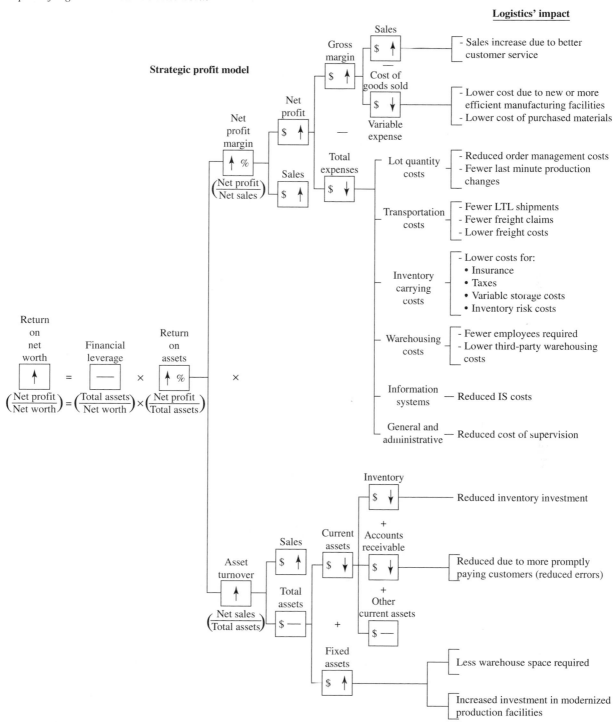

in return on net worth would be larger than in the previous example (debt repayment). It should be noted that if fixed costs increase, then operating leverage increases, which may result in higher risk and a lower valuation.

The strategic profit model can be used to measure and sell the value of logistics to customers. It is equally useful in showing top management the role that logistics is playing in corporate success. However, it is not without problems. First, it is necessary to estimate the impact of logistics in generating revenue. Customer satisfaction surveys can be very useful in this regard. Cost measurement systems of the type described in Chapter 16 can provide the cost data. Information on inventory levels and other assets can come from the logistics information system.

Although the strategic profit model has many strengths over the methods of measuring value described thus far, recent literature on corporate finance has shown a strong consensus among researchers that shareholder value is a better performance metric of the financial consequences of strategies than traditional accounting measurements.

Shareholder Value

Shareholder value has become popular as a reliable and consistent way to look at the value of many businesses and to measure how alternative strategies and investments will affect the company's total value.[9] According to shareholder value theory, a business creates value when it meets or exceeds a cost of capital that correctly reflects its investment risk.[10] It is built on the key assumption that a business is worth the net present value of its future cash flows, discounted at the appropriate cost of capital. By focusing on cash flow, shareholder value overcomes the inadequacies of the traditional financial measurements. Also, by using a present value approach, the model recognizes the time preference for money and the risk of an investment. It links management decisions to value in a clear objective framework, which analyzes management decisions in value terms through the planning horizon and several key value drivers.

A Business Is Worth the Net Present Value of Its Future Cash Flows

For many years the traditional focus of attention in accounting has been criticized because of its inappropriateness for the purposes of assisting in decision making. Traditional measures are backward-looking and short-sighted, whereas decision making is forward-looking and concerned with the long-term outcomes.

Copeland, Koller, and Murrin gave the following explanation for why shareholder value should be the measure of choice:

Why Value Value?

> Empirical evidence indicates that increasing shareholder value does not conflict with the long-run interest of other stakeholders. Winning companies seem to create relatively greater value for all stakeholders: customers, labor, the government (via taxes paid), and suppliers of capital. Yet, there are additional reasons—more conceptual in nature, but equally compelling—to adopt a system that emphasizes shareholder value. First, value is the best metric for performance that we know. Second, shareholders are the only stakeholders of a corporation who simultaneously maximize everyone's claim in seeking to maximize their own. And finally, companies that do not perform will find that capital flows toward their competitors.[11]

---

[9]Martin Christopher and Lynette Ryals, "Supply Chain Strategy: Its Impact on Shareholder Value," *The International Journal of Logistics Management* 1, no. 1 (1999), pp. 1–10.

[10]Francis V. McCrory and Peter G. Gerstberger, "The New Math of Performance Measurement," *The Journal of Business Strategy* 13, no. 2 (March–April 1992), pp. 33–38.

[11]Tom Copeland, Tim Koller, and Jack Murrin, *Valuation: Measuring and Managing the Value of Companies* (New York: John Wiley and Sons, 1994), p. 22.

They provide the additional argument for why value is the best metric:

Value Is the Best Metric

Value (discounted cash flows) is best because it is the only measure that requires complete information. To understand value creation one must use a long-term point of view, manage all cash flows on both the income statement and the balance sheet, and understand how to compare cash flows from different time periods on a risk-adjusted basis. It is nearly impossible to make good decisions without complete information, and no other metric uses complete information.[12]

Every decision that managers make is reflected in the valuation of the company. No other single metric is this comprehensive. According to Copeland, Koller, and Murrin, value cannot be short-term if properly implemented, but the other measures can be short-term:

Value Compared to Other Financial Measures

Earnings per share or return on equity are usually used in a myopic way—requiring information about only the next few years at best. Furthermore, earnings tends to focus mainly on managing the income statement and places low weight on the actual amount and timing of cash flows. Even the spread between the return on invested capital (ROIC) and the cost of capital can be a bad metric if used only for the short term and because it encourages underinvestment (harvesting the business to increase ROIC). If the value manager does the job well, the results are reflected in MVA (market value added). Other performance measures, such as the growth in earnings, return on equity, and the spread between the return on capital and the cost of capital are less comprehensive than value creation and less well correlated with the actual market value of companies.[13]

In addition to measuring value to the firm, it is also possible to measure value to the customer:

Value to Customers

The value to customers is the present value of the difference between what they would be willing to pay for the company's goods and services minus what the company receives as revenues. Economists call this consumer's surplus. If the company increases its prices, and nothing else changes, the value of consumer's surplus decreases, and the value of equity increases. Of course, price increases often result in lower sales volume, so that the value impact on customers and equity holders depends heavily on the price-quantity relationship embedded in the demand curve for the product.[14]

Table 17–6 contains pro forma income statements and balance sheets showing forecasts into the distant future. These are the building blocks of information that are necessary to value the claims that various stakeholders have on the company.

The ability to create wealth for shareholders is crucial to the survival of companies in today's turbulent environment. The increasing number and sophistication of financing approaches now available to companies make it imperative for executives to link their financing and operating strategies. Alfred Rappaport of Northwestern University and Joel Stern of Stern & Stewart brought the theoretical concept of valuation to business applications and made the practical knowledge available to many companies. Indeed, a thorough scanning of the literature supports the fact that two of the most accepted schools of thought on how management should link corporate performance to the creation of shareholder value are shareholder value analysis (SVA), established by

[12]Ibid., p. 23.
[13]Ibid.
[14]Ibid., p. 24.

TABLE 17–6   Pro Forma Financials ($ Millions)

	Today	Distant future	Present value of
Value to customers	1,100	4,400	
Income statement			Consumer's surplus
Sales revenue	1,000	4,000	
– Labor costs	(400)	(1,600)	Labor's claim
– Cost of goods and services	(300)	(1,200)	Supplier's claim
– Depreciation	(100)	(400)	
Operating income	200	800	
– Interest expense	(50)	(200)	Debt claim
Taxable income	150	600	
–Taxes	(75)	(300)	Government claim
Net income			
– Retained earnings	(40)	(160)	
Dividends	35	140	Equity claim
Balance sheet			
Assets			
Cash	50	200	
Accounts receivable	200	800	Uses of working capital
Inventories	250	1,000	
Net property, plant, equipment	1,000	4,000	Uses of physical capital
Total assets	1,500	6,000	
Liabilities			
Accounts payable	100	400	Sources of working
Accruals	150	600	capital
Debt	500	2,000	Sources of debt
Retained earnings	500	2,000	Sources of equity
Common equity	250	1,000	
Total liabilities	1,500	6,000	

Source: Tom Copeland, Tim Koller, and Jack Murrin, *Valuation: Measuring and Managing the Value of Companies* (New York: John Wiley and Sons, 1994), p. 24.

Rappaport,[15] and economic value-added (EVA), established by Stern.[16] Showing customers how the company's logistics operations affect the shareholder value of their firms would be the ultimate measure of the financial impact of logistics.

Shareholder Value Method

Seven Key Generic Value Drivers

In expressing the fundamental assumption of SVA, Rappaport notes that "a business is worth the net present value of its cash flows discounted at the appropriate cost of capital" and identifies seven key generic value drivers that are expected to drive the value of any business: sales growth rate, operating profit margin, cash tax rate, fixed capital needs, working capital needs, cost of capital, and planning period.[17] The aim is to think

---

[15]Alfred Rappaport, *Creating Shareholder Value: The New Standard for Business Performance* (New York: The Free Press, 1986).

[16]Joel M. Stern, "One Way to Build Value in Your Firm, à la Executive Compensation," *Financial Executive* (November–December 1990), pp. 51–54.

[17]Rappaport, *Creating Shareholder Value.*

the strategic alternatives through in value terms so that value can be maximized. The approach recognizes the importance of better reporting of historic cash flows and asserts that a better relationship exists between shareholder returns and cash flow measurements than traditional accounting measurements. SVA derives the total shareholder value by discounting free cash flows at the cost of capital, for the period over which a particular strategy is expected to be in use. Furthermore, in order to calculate the cash flows beyond the planning period, a perpetuity model is used in which the last year's forecasted operating profit is divided by the company's weighted cost of capital. The calculation considers the opportunity cost of capital and value is only increased if returns exceed that cost of capital. While the approach possesses the advantage of recognizing the value beyond the present planning period of a strategy and leads to a better judgment among alternative investments from the company's perspective, it may fail to show the real value beyond the planning period since the returns are assumed to be equal to the company's cost of capital, ignoring the fact that additional sales beyond the planning period may generate value returns higher than the cost of capital.

EVA Theory Is That Shareholders Measure Value Creation

EVA is an alternative approach to SVA. EVA derives the total shareholder value by determining a performance spread—that is, the excess of the return on invested capital above the cost of capital—which when multiplied by the invested capital produces the EVA for each period in the forecast. These individual EVA figures are then discounted and summed to produce a premium. This premium plus the invested capital determines the common equity value. The detailed steps in EVA calculation are very well documented by Stewart,[18] Mills and Print,[19] and Ehrbar.[20] The EVA approach theorizes that shareholders measure value creation, not value preservation. It deducts out all capital expenditures designed to maintain plant and equipment, as well as dividends, since the shareholder has invested the funds for superior investment returns.[21]

Several other studies also attempted to shed some light on the shareholder valuation concept. Copeland, Koller, and Murrin, after working on a special research project in their corporate finance practice at McKinsey & Company Inc., developed several approaches to valuation.[22] In fact, they presented two frameworks based on discounted cash flow (DCF) for valuing a business, including the entity DCF model and the economic profit model. The entity DCF model values the equity of a company as the discounted value of a company's operations (which equals the discounted value of expected future cash flow) less the discounted value of debt and other investor claims that are superior to common equity. In the economic profit model, in contrast, the value of a company is the amount of capital invested plus a premium or discount equal to the present value of the cash flows created each year going forward. In other words, economic profit is equal to the spread between the return on invested capital and the cost of capital, times the amount of invested capital. The economic profit model is especially useful for understanding a company's performance in a single year, while the entity model is not.

The Economic Profit Model

---

[18]G. Bennett Stewart III, *The Quest for Value: A Guide for Senior Managers,* 2nd ed. (New York: HarperCollins, 1999).

[19]Roger Mills and C. Print, "Strategic Value Analysis," *Management Accounting* 73, no. 2 (February 1995), pp. 35–36.

[20]Al Ehrbar, *EVA: The Real Key to Creating Wealth* (New York: John Wiley and Sons, 1998).

[21]Jeffrey M. Kanter and Matthew P. Ward, "Long-Term Incentives for Management, Part 4: Performance Plans," *Compensation and Benefits Review* 22, no. 1 (January–February 1990), pp. 36–49.

[22]Tom Copeland, Tim Koller, and Jack Murrin, *Valuation: Measuring and Managing the Value of Companies,* 2nd ed. (New York: John Wiley & Sons, Inc., 1995).

Creative Solutions

Calculating EVA

Economic value-added (EVA) forces managers to pay attention to their capital cost by explicitly accounting for it as a dollar charge, thus establishing a clear mandate for a company's leaders to earn more than their cost of capital.

How is this done? Three means of value creation exist, although they go by a variety of titles: stopping activities that consume rather than generate value, improving processes that already are value-creating, and investing in assets or operations that return more than their cost of capital.

The basic EVA calculation starts with a firm's net operating profits after taxes and adjusts that to eliminate any accounting distortions. For example, accounting rules stipulate that R&D costs be expensed; Stern Stewart & Co., which created EVA, advocates amortizing them over several years, given their longer-term impact.

The optimal number and type of adjustments vary with the company and its industry. Al Ehrbar, senior vice president with Stern Stewart, offers three criteria for deciding whether to make an adjustment: Will operating managers understand the change? Will it influence their decisions? Finally, can the necessary data be obtained? If the answer to any of these questions is no, the company may be better off leaving the numbers alone.

Next is a calculation of the amount of capital invested in the business. This number includes both fixed assets (such as machinery and equipment) and working capital assets (such as cash, inventory, and receivables).

Now determine the capital charge, which is the weighted average cost of the firm's debt and equity. The debt portion is simply the interest charged on a firm's loans. The cost of equity is more difficult to pin down, as it varies with a firm's performance and the riskiness of the markets and industries in which it operates. Normally, the accountants and analysts take the lead on this task.

The final step: Multiply total capital invested in the business by the capital charge. Subtract this number from adjusted net operating profits. A positive result means the firm is creating value for its shareholders. A negative number means that there is work to be done.

Source: Karen M. Kroll, "EVA and Creating Value," *Industry Week*, April 7, 1997, p. 102. Reprinted from various editions of *Transportation & Distribution* and *Industry Week*. Copyright 1995 permission granted by Penton, Cleveland, Ohio.

How Logistics Drives Value

Although expressed in somewhat different forms and known by different names, these models are almost identical to SVA and EVA, respectively. Copeland, Koller, and Murrin stress the importance of value-based management and identify three levels of value drivers within this concept: generic, business-unit-specific, and operating. While the generic ones are consistent with the key value drivers that are mentioned in Rappaport's work, these authors go one step further in specifying the other levels of drivers and linking all of them to operational-level strategies and decisions. If logistics is viewed as a business-unit-specific measure, for example, then generic value drivers may consist of sales growth rate, cash tax rate, operating profit margin, fixed and working capital needs, cost of capital, and planning horizon. Business-unit-specific value drivers for logistics may contain logistics service quality, total cost of logistics, and order-to-delivery cycle time. Operating value drivers may include items like ability to mix products in a truckload, order-fill rate, order cycle consistency, inventory carrying costs, transportation costs, and warehousing costs.

---

[23]Enrique R. Arzac, "Do Your Business Units Create Shareholder Value?" *Harvard Business Review* 64, no. 1 (January–February 1986), pp. 121–26.

Arzac developed a formula to evaluate the potential for value creation or destruction at the level of business units rather than the whole corporation.[23] The value creation is expressed in terms of the expected return on equity (ROE), the cost of equity capital, the expected growth of the company, and the period during which the company is expected to maintain a positive spread between its ROE and its cost of equity. However, in order to translate this method to the business-unit level, the spread between ROE and a unit's weighted-average cost of equity and debt capital (WACC) is calculated. Furthermore, to estimate the unit's contribution to the value of shareholder equity, return on investment is added to the spread between ROI and the after-tax cost of debt, multiplied by the debt–equity ratio.

Valuation Requires Three Stages of Cash Flows

Wiggins, Kare, and Madura developed a valuation model based on four tenets: investors will pay only for future expected returns from an investment, the return that investors are seeking is cash, money has time value, and investors are risk averse.[24] The valuation of business is done by adding three stages of cash flows: cash flows that would occur at or soon after the purchase of the business being appraised, cash flows that would occur in each year of the short-run period, and cash flows that would occur in the first year after the short-run period. The model has several advantages over other valuation techniques. It is very flexible and easily adjustable to many different conditions, such as risk, through varying the required rate of return. It can handle almost any growth pattern of sales, costs, or cash flows. Relationships between factors, such as decreasing cost of goods sold as a percentage of sales over time, can be specifically adjusted over different time periods. The business valuation model developed by Wiggins, Kare, and Madura is presented in Figure 17–6.

FIGURE 17–6

Valuation model

Business value = Present value of the short run + Present value of the long run

$$= CF_0 + \left[\sum_{t=1}^{n} \frac{CF_t}{(1+k_e)^t} + \left(\frac{CF_{n+1}}{k_e - g_l} \times \frac{1}{(1+k_e)^n} \right) \right] \times IPAF$$

where:

CF_0 = Initial cash inflows or outflows to equity holders from the asset or business.

CF_t = Independently forecast cash flow to equity holders in each year t of the short-run period n.

n = Number of years in the short run where cash flow patterns are expected to be different from the long run.

k_e = Return required by investors on equity investment given the risk level of the business.

CF_{n+1} = Cash flow available to equity holders in the first year of the long run.

g_l = Long-run growth rate in cash flow.

IPAF = Intrayear cash flow pattern adjustment factor.

Source: C. Donald Wiggins, Dilip D. Kare, and Jeff Madura, "A Universal Valuation Model for Closely Held Businesses," *Valuation* 40, no. 1 (1996), p. 42. Reprinted by permission of the American Society of Appraisers.

Advantages of Shareholder Valuation over Traditional Accounting Measures

Some very impressive results have been reported for firms where management embraced the shareholder valuation technique. For example, Bank America Corporation made a dramatic turnaround from losing money, having to suspend payment of dividends on its common stock, and facing a hostile takeover attempt by First Interstate Bank Corporation.[25] On the road to recovery, in addition to paying attention to

---

[24]C. Donald Wiggins, Dilip D. Kare, and Jeff Madura, "A Universal Valuation Model for Closely Held Businesses," *Valuation* 40, no. 1 (1996), pp. 38–57, at p. 39.

[25]A. W. Clausen, "Strategic Issues in Managing Change: The Turnaround at Bank America Corporation," *California Management Review* 32, no. 2 (Winter 1990), pp. 98–105.

fundamental concepts, the bank focused on how to generate maximum value for its shareholders. It immediately improved its capital ratios by selling assets and issuing capital securities. In three years, Bank America's primary capital ratio increased from 6.29 percent to 9.60 percent and its common stock rose from a price of $6.88 per share to $30 per share.

Wilde, Tunstall, and Smist studied the financial standing of Regional Bell Operating Companies (RBOCs) after their divestiture from AT&T.[26] They found that although the RBOCs' earnings in constant dollars remained essentially flat during the first six years after the breakup, their stock prices increased on average more than 125 percent. The authors explored the issue of linking stock performance to operating performance and found that focusing on the creation of shareholder value through factors at the strategic, operational, and industry levels rather than focusing on the accrual-based accounting measures contributed to the RBOCs' success.

Using EVA in Resource Allocation Decisions

George Lorsch, the chairman and CEO of Armstrong World Industries Inc., explained how using EVA in resource allocations and investment decisions helped his company.[27] In its simplest form, EVA is a measurement that holds a management accountable for the cost of capital it uses to expand and operate the business, and shows whether management is creating value for the company's shareholders. It forces management to focus on important matters such as growth, operating margins, taxes, and cost of capital. Lorsch favored EVA because it contains a lot of common elements that are used in return on assets (ROA) calculation, making it easier for managers to implement it.

Stern stated that the best way to maximize shareholder returns was to provide management with EVA bonuses to make decisions that increase long-term value.[28] He gave the example of a company named Applied Power, a $420 million manufacturer of hydraulic equipment based in Wisconsin, which after using EVA as the foundation of its planning and incentive compensation received a 56.9 percent compound average annual return for investors between 1987 and 1989 versus only 6.6 percent for the S&P 500.

Disadvantages of Shareholder Valuation

Three Concerns about Shareholder Valuation

Although many researchers favor the shareholder valuation technique over traditional financial measurements, there are some disadvantages. The three most mentioned concerns about the technique are all related to its application and include the areas of discount rates, planning periods, and projected cash flows.

Michel criticized a number of popular business theories, including the SVA method developed by Alfred Rappaport.[29] He suggested that the shareholder-value-based quantitative system encourages CEOs to judge businesses on how well they can enhance value for shareholders, sometimes reaching success at the expense of the best

---

[26]Dean L. Wilde II, Brooke W. Tunstall, and James P. Smist, "Investing for the Future: Assessing Shareholder Value of the Regional Bell Operating Companies," *Interfaces* 22, no. 4 (July–August 1992), pp. 60–69.

[27]"George Lorsch Explains Economic Value Added," *Management Review* 84, no. 9 (September 1995), pp. 50–52.

[28]Stern, "One Way to Build Value in Your Firm."

[29]Robert Michel, "Times Change, but Do Strategists?" *Journal of Business Strategy* 14, no. 2 (March–April 1993), pp. 12–15.

interests of the business. It is suggested that the best way to satisfy both the shareholders and the business itself is to focus on the best interests of the customers.

Likewise, Devlin[30] and Day and Fahey[31] stressed the importance of selecting discount rates, planning periods, and projected cash flows properly. They emphasized the critical role of the planning period, since some of the value measured through SVA lies in the residual value at the end of the planning period. They attempted to solve these problem areas by linking shareholder value to the company's strategic objectives. Although these two concepts use different notions of value (that is, SVA tries to maximize returns to shareholders and strategic analysis attempts to establish superior value in the eyes of the customer), they are bound to merge in the long run. In fact, the authors claimed that a successful business strategy is able to lead the company to both a stronger competitive advantage and a higher shareholder value.

How Logistics Affects EVA

Logistics can affect EVA in four areas: revenue growth, operating cost reduction, working capital efficiency, and fixed asset efficiency (see Figure 17–7).[32]

Revenue Growth

The customer service provided by logistics can have a major impact on sales volume and customer retention. While it is not generally possible to calculate the exact correlation between service and sales, there have been many studies that have indicated a positive relationship.[33] Certainly the effect of an out-of-stock situation can be dramatic. Compaq, for example, reported that in 1994 the company lost between half a billion and a billion dollars in sales because one of its top-selling products was not available when customers wanted it.[34]

Superior Customer Service Strengthens Customer Loyalty

Superior customer service (in terms of reliability and responsiveness) can strengthen the likelihood that customers will remain loyal to a supplier. Evidence suggests that higher levels of customer retention lead to greater sales. Typically this occurs because the customer is more likely to place a greater proportion of its purchases with that supplier.

Operating Cost Reductions

A Large Portion of Costs Is Driven by Logistics

The potential for operating cost reductions through logistics is considerable. A large proportion of costs in a typical business is driven by logistics practices. Transportation cost, warehousing costs, lot quantity costs, information systems costs, and the non-cost-of-money components of inventory carrying costs must be considered. Often the

---

[30]Godfrey Devlin, "A Strategy for Shareholder Value," *Accountancy* 103, no. 1146 (February 1989), pp. 89–90.

[31]George S. Day and Liam Fahey, "Putting Strategy into Shareholder Value Analysis," *Harvard Business Review* 68, no. 2 (March–April 1990), pp. 156–62.

[32]This material is adapted from Christopher and Ryals, "Supply Chain Strategy: Its Impact on Shareholder Value," pp. 3–5.

[33]Eugene W. Anderson, Claes Fornell, and Donald R. Lehmann, "Customer Satisfaction, Market Share and Profitability: Findings from Sweden," *Journal of Marketing* 58 (July 1994), pp. 53–64; and Coca-Cola Retailing Research Council and Andersen Consulting, *The Retail Problem of Out-of-Stock Merchandise,* 1996.

[34]*Fortune,* November 28, 1994.

Figure 17–7

How logistics affects EVA

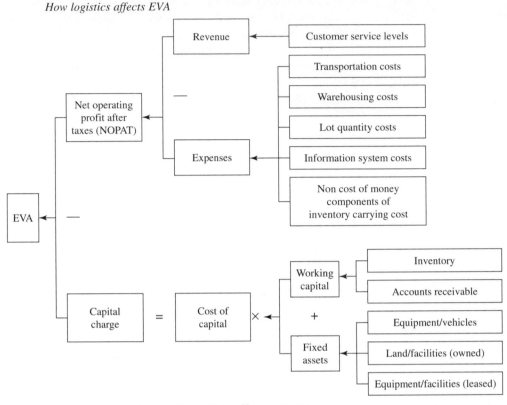

Source: Douglas M. Lambert and Renan Burduroglu, "Measuring and Selling the Value of Logistics," *The International Journal of Logistics Management* 11, no. 1 (2000), p. 13.

upstream logistics costs can represent a significant proportion of total supply chain costs embedded in the final product.

There is also a recognition that time compression in the supply chain not only enhances customer service but also can reduce costs through the reduction of non-value-adding activities.[35]

Working Capital Efficiency

Long Pipelines Generate More Inventory

Logistics management is fundamentally linked to the working capital requirement within the business. Long supply chains, by definition, generate more inventory. Order-fill rates and invoice accuracy directly affect accounts receivable, and procurement

---

[35]Thomas H. Davenport, *Process Innovation* (Cambridge, MA: Harvard Business School Press, 1993).

policies affect cash flow. Working capital requirements can be reduced through time compression in the supply chain and subsequently reducing cash-to-cash cycle times.

Surprisingly few companies know the cash-to-cash cycle time for their products (i.e., the elapsed time from the payment for materials or components through to sale of the finished product and collection of cash). The cash-to-cash cycle time can be six months or longer in many manufacturing industries. By focusing on eliminating time in the supply chain that does not add value, reductions in working capital can be achieved.

Fixed Capital Efficiency

Logistics Is Fixed-Asset Intensive

Logistics by its very nature tends to be "fixed-asset intensive." Trucks, distribution centers, and automated handling systems involve considerable investment and consequently will often depress return on investment. In conventional multiechelon logistics systems, it is not unusual to find factory warehouses, regional distribution centers, and local warehouses—all of which represent significant fixed investment.

One of the main drivers behind the growth of the third-party logistics service sector has been the desire to reduce fixed-asset investment. Decisions to rationalize distribution networks and production facilities are increasingly being driven by the realization that the true cost of financing that capital investment is sometimes greater than the return that it generates.

Selling the Value Advantage

It is critical to measure value from the customer's perspective. Once value has been measured, it must be sold to the customer. It is important at this stage to identify who in the customer organization should receive this information; the sales force must seek out executives at the appropriate level.

For planning purposes it is important to remember that value is a moving target. Customers can be expected to pay a premium only for service that is incrementally better than that of competitors. As competitors improve, so must the company. What represents value-added this year will not represent it next year if competitors can match the level of service provided.

The Role of the Sales Force Is Changing

In addition, the role of the sales force is changing. Increasingly, salespeople must be consultants for the customer. In terms of the products and services that they are selling, they must know the customer's business better than the customer. And they must be constantly searching for new ways to add value for the customer. For these reasons, knowledge of how to measure and sell the value of logistics should be a necessary part of the training of the sales force.

It is also critical to sell the value provided by logistics inside the firm. Customer satisfaction surveys should be used to estimate the impact of logistics on revenue. Logistics performance metrics should be designed to capture the impact that logistics is making on operating expenses, working capital, and fixed assets. Failure to do so will put the logistics organization and its programs at risk. Everyone on the top management team should know how logistics is contributing to the performance of the company's share price.

Summary

Value Must Be Measured in Financial Terms

The advantages and disadvantages of the various methods of measuring value are summarized in Table 17–7. The most common measures of value used in corporations are customer satisfaction measures.[36] However, these are the least financially oriented metrics and only in rare cases will they result in customers paying premium prices or rewarding the supplier with sufficiently large increases in volume. In some cases total cost analysis is used, but if customers are expected to pay for value-added services, then total cost analysis is not an acceptable measure of the value of a supplier's performance. Total cost analysis when used within the organization to show the value of logistics reinforces the view that logistics is simply a cost center.

In cases where there are revenue implications associated with logistics performance, total cost analysis falls short. For example, if the firm is selling a consumer product through retailers, the measure of value should be profit contribution. Increasingly, anything that a supplier can do to help its customers better serve their customers or consumers adds value. But every attempt should be made to show the financial impact of these value-creation efforts. If the buyer is being judged only on margin and inventory turns, then it will be necessary to sell at a higher level in the organization. There will be an education process that must take place. Buyers are going to buy the way they are rewarded for buying. If they are judged on gross margin, and not on profitability, that is how they will buy. However, increasingly firms will have the capability to generate contribution reports by stockkeeping unit and measure the costs and revenues associated with different suppliers. Once that happens, buyers are going to be more willing to consider all the cost and revenue implications of supplier alternatives. They are going to look at transportation costs, warehousing costs, and the other costs that show up in their reports as well as attempt to estimate the impact that suppliers have on revenue.

We believe that shareholder value is the most comprehensive measure. Research is necessary to determine what it will take to measure the impact of logistics on shareholder value and what the cost of doing so would be. What are the time and cost implications of attempting to specify the impact of logistics operations on the value of the customer's firm as well as on the value of the supplier's firm? Is it possible to segment the market based on value? Another important point is that value is a moving target and customers can be expected to pay only for the incremented value received. What represents incremental value this year may not represent it next year if competitors improve. It is constantly necessary for firms to innovate and look for new ways to add value for their customers. Once this has been accomplished, customers must be shown in financial terms the benefits that they are receiving. Finally, executives from other functional areas within the company must be shown how this value being provided for customers creates value for the company's own shareholders. Only then will situations like the ones described at the beginning of this chapter be avoided.

---

[36]James S. Keebler, Karl B. Manrodt, David A. Durtsche, and D. Michael Ledyard, *Keeping Score: Measuring the Business Value of Logistics in the Supply Chain* (Oak Brook, IL: Council of Logistics Management, 1999), p. 61.

TABLE 17–7   Comparative Advantages and Disadvantages of Various Value Metrics

Value Metric	Advantages	Disadvantages
Customer satisfaction	• Direct impact on the bottom line through revenues and total logistics costs • Improves market share • Enables alignment of services with customer needs • Relatively easy to obtain these measures • Customer does the work by filling out the survey	• Relies on the customer to determine if the level of satisfaction justifies paying a premium price or purchasing more from the supplier • Relies on management outside of logistics to identify the impact on revenues, which typically does not happen
Customer value-added	• Based on the notion that value beyond price leads to higher sales figures, higher profit margins, and higher shareholder value • Relatively easy to obtain these measures • Customer does the work by filling out the survey	• Relies on the customer to determine if the level of customer value-added justifies paying a premium price or purchasing more from the supplier • Fails to measure the financial impact of providing higher levels of customer value-added
Total cost analysis	• Price and related costs are considered • Managers can improve profits by reducing total cost of logistics	• Does not consider revenue implications of logistics-related service • More time-consuming since it has to be done on an individual customer basis • Requires access to cost information • Perpetuates the myth that logistics is simply a cost that must be reduced
Segment profit-ability analysis	• Revenue and out-of-pocket costs are considered	• Does not measure the cost of assets employed with the exception of inventory and accounts receivable • Need revenue and cost data by supplier; customer may not have these data or be willing to share supplier data • Requires sophisticated accounting system
Strategic profit model	• Measures net profit, ROA, return on net worth • Assists managers in the evaluation of cash flows and asset utilization decisions	• Fails to consider the timing of cash flows • Subject to manipulation in the short run • In addition to revenues and costs, assets dedicated to the relationship must be known
Shareholder value	• Recognizes the time value of money and the risk of an investment • Focus on cash flow overcomes the inadequacies of traditional financial measures	• Implementation-related concerns in the areas of discount rates, planning period, and projected cash flows (missing linkage between the business strategy and shareholder value) • Most data-intensive method • Time and cost required

Source: Douglas M. Lambert and Renan Burduroglu, "Measuring and Selling the Value of Logistics," *The International Journal of Logistics Management* 11, no. 1 (2000), p. 15.

Suggested Readings

Bovet, David, and Joseph Martha. *Value Nets.* New York: John Wiley & Sons, 2000.

Christopher, Martin, and Lynette Ryals. "Supply Chain Strategy: Its Impact on Shareholder Value." *The International Journal of Logistics Management* 10, no. 1 (1999), pp. 1–10.

Copeland, Tom; Tim Koller; and Jack Murrin. *Valuation: Measuring and Managing the Value of Companies,* 2nd ed. New York: John Wiley & Sons, 1995.

Day, George S. *The Market Driven Organization: Understanding, Attracting and Keeping Valuable Customers.* New York: The Free Press, 1999.

Heskett, James L.; W. Earl Sasser Jr.; and Leonard A. Schlesinger. *The Service Profit Chain.* New York: The Free Press, 1997.

Hiebeler, Robert; Thomas B. Kelly; and Charles Ketternor. *Best Practices: Building Your Business with Customer-Focused Solutions.* New York: Simon & Schuster, 1998.

Kaplin, Robert S., and David P. Norton. *The Balanced Scorecard.* Boston, MA: Harvard Business School Press, 1996.

Keebler, James S.; David A. Durtsche; Karl B. Manrodt; and D. Michael Ledyard. *Keeping Score: Measuring the Business Value of Logistics in the Supply Chain.* Oak Brook, IL: Council of Logistics Management, 1999.

Simchi-Levi, David; Philip Kaminsky; and Edith Simchi-Levi. *Designing and Managing the Supply Chain.* Burr Ridge, IL: Irwin/McGraw-Hill, 2000.

Slywotzky, Adrian J., and David J. Morrison. *The Profit Zone.* New York: Times Books, 1997.

Steward, G. Bennett III. *The Quest for Value.* New York: HarperCollins, 1999.

Wiggins, C. Donald; Dilip D. Kare; and Jeff Madura. "A Universal Valuation Model for Closely Held Businesses." *Valuation* 40, no. 1 (1996), pp. 38–57.

Questions and Problems

1. Why is it necessary to measure the value that logistics is providing for the customer?

2. Why are customer service and customer satisfaction measures the most widely used measures of the value that is being provided to customers?

3. For each of the methods of measuring value described in this chapter, give an example of a situation in which the method would be an acceptable measure.

4. Which components of logistics are likely to have the greater impact on value as measured by return on net worth? Why?

5. Which financial measure of value (total cost analysis, segment profitability analysis, strategic profit model, shareholder value) do you believe is the best? Why?

6. What problems would you expect to encounter in implementing financially oriented measures of value? Please consider both internal and external perspectives.

7. It was mentioned in the chapter that value is a moving target. What exactly does this mean? Give an example of how value might be a moving target.

Chapter Outline

Chapter Objectives

- To show how to develop a strategic logistics plan.
- To show how the logistics audit can be used to formulate logistics objectives and strategy.
- To identify challenges that the logistics professional will face in the future.

Introduction

A number of factors promise to make the next decade a period of challenge and opportunity for the logistics executive. The fact that most firms are competing in mature markets, the desire to create customer loyalty, and knowledge of the impact of logistics costs and assets on corporate profitability have resulted in increased top management awareness of the importance of logistics in achieving shareholder value. In addition, the globalization of supply sources, production, demand, and competition has led to increased interest in logistics on the part of top management. The challenges and opportunities for the logistics professional have never been greater. In order to successfully meet these challenges and capitalize on the opportunities, logistics executives must become involved in the strategic planning process. In this chapter we will look at the importance of the logistics audit and trace the development of a strategic logistics plan. In addition, we will identify and explore the key challenges that the logistics executive will face in the future.

What Is Strategic Planning?

Cooper, Innis, and Dickson define strategic planning as follows:

> The process of identifying the long-term goals of the entity (where we want to be) and the broad steps necessary to achieve these goals over a long-term horizon (how to get there), incorporating the concerns and future expectations of the major stakeholders.[1]

The mission statement and strategic plan provide direction and control for tactical plans and daily operations. The company's management may decide that the long-term goal is to achieve a sustainable competitive advantage by focusing on customer requirements and capitalizing on opportunities in the marketplace. "The strategic plan should anticipate the service expectations of both current and future customers."[2] The strategic planning process should also include the financial implications of major shifts in strategy and the resources required.

Logistics strategic planning has been defined as follows:

Logistics Strategic Planning Defined

> A unified, comprehensive, and integrated planning process to achieve competitive advantage through increased value and customer service, which results in superior customer satisfaction (where we want to be), by anticipating future demand for logistics services and managing the resources of the entire supply chain (how to get there). This planning is done within the context of the overall corporate goals and plan.[3]

This definition comprises three major elements: "(1) the long-term goals (customer satisfaction, competitive advantage, supply chain management); (2) the means to achieving these goals (value, customer service); and (3) the process for achieving these goals (anticipate, manage, relate to company's goals)."[4] The strategic plan covers a period of five or more years.

---

[1]Martha C. Cooper, Daniel E. Innis, and Peter Dickson, *Strategic Planning for Logistics* (Oak Brook, IL: Council of Logistics Management, 1992), p. 3.

[2]Ibid.

[3]Ibid., pp. 4–5.

[4]Ibid., p. 5.

The Importance of Planning

Strategic Planning Minimizes Risks in a Changing Environment

The development of a strategic plan, along with its continued evaluation and modification, is essential to long-run profitable business development.[5] The rate of change in the business environment increases the risk of business failure or loss of market position for firms whose management has neglected to consider alternative future scenarios. In the absence of planning, managers must spend a disproportionate amount of their time as "firefighters"—reacting to crises rather than anticipating change and developing strategies to deal with it.

The Operating Plan and the Strategic Plan

There are basically two types of plans: the operating plan, which covers a period of one or two years, and the strategic plan, which covers a period of five or more years. The strategic plan "can be thought of as a set of guideposts which keep the operating plan on the path to meeting objectives. It is the operating plan which must be programmed in fine detail to demonstrate how the objectives will be reached and to justify the expenditures of the . . . budget."[6]

Planning requires that managers evaluate the probability of various scenarios and anticipate possible problems and opportunities. In the process, management's outlook shifts from crisis management, or reacting to changes in the environment, to planning for change. By planning for change, management can anticipate capital requirements and, when necessary, arrange financing. Consider the case of a manufacturer that has built its entire freight consolidation program around shipments to the more than 2,000 individual stores of a major retail chain. How should marketing react if, in next year's negotiation, the chain wants deliveries made to its distribution centers in return for a price reduction? A number of questions need to be answered. How important is the chain's business to the firm's overall market penetration objectives? Is the business profitable? Will it be profitable if the new conditions are accepted? What will happen to the cost or frequency of deliveries to the firm's other customers if the chain's conditions are accepted? What will happen to the profitability of non-chain accounts? How important are these accounts to the firm's long-run profitability? What is the chain likely to demand in the future? To respond to the retailer's request in a knowledgeable way, management must answer these questions in advance and include logistics in the planning process. The traditional emphasis on sales might cause many managers, when faced with a similar situation, to protect sales volume and accept the chain's conditions without considering the impact on overall corporate profitability.

A major advantage of planning is that when managers establish benchmarks, they can measure their firm's progress and take corrective action as needed. Thus, as Stern has stated, "The plan provides a management philosophy, a day-to-day operating guide, and a basis for measuring both individual and total company performance."[7]

The Corporate Planning Process

Marketing, Manufacturing, and Logistics Must Be Closely Coordinated in the Planning Process

The logistics plan is an important component of the overall corporate plan. As we saw in Chapters 1 and 2, marketing and logistics must be closely coordinated in the planning process as must production. The logistics plan is deeply rooted in the marketing plan, which must be based on corporate objectives and strategy. Figure 18–1 provides a useful framework for visualizing logistics planning within the context of the overall

---

[5]Portions of this section are adapted from Douglas M. Lambert and James R. Stock, "Strategic Planning for Physical Distribution," *Journal of Business Logistics* 3, no. 2 (1982), pp. 26–46.
[6]Mark E. Stern, *Marketing Planning: A Systems Approach* (New York: McGraw-Hill, 1966), p. 4.
[7]Ibid.

FIGURE 18–1

A model for design, evaluation, and modification of a supply chain

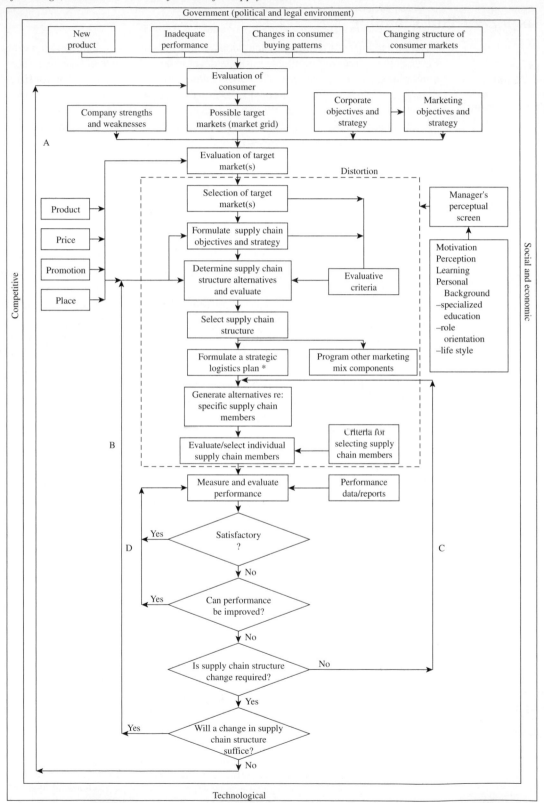

*Also, formulate strategic plans for manufacturing and procurement.
Source: Adapted from Douglas M. Lambert, *The Distribution Channels Decision* (New York: National Association of Accountants, and Hamilton, Ontario: The Society of Management Accountants of Canada, 1978), pp. 44–45, 112–13.

corporate planning process, the supply chain, and the firm's environment. It illustrates that all planning must take place within the following constraints:

- The political and legal environment.
- The social and economic environment.
- The technological environment.
- The competitive environment.

The following steps must be performed in the corporate planning process before the strategic logistics plan can be formulated:

Steps in the Corporate Planning Process

- Evaluate consumer and/or industrial customer needs.
- Identify possible target markets.
- Evaluate target markets.
- Select target markets.
- Formulate supply chain objectives and strategy.
- Identify and evaluate supply chain structure alternatives.
- Select the supply chain structure.

While the example used to illustrate the planning process is a consumer good viewed from the manufacturer's perspective, the model applies equally to other members of the supply chain such as retailers and wholesalers as well as to industrial products and services.

Evaluation of the Consumer and Identification of Potential Target Markets

Evaluation of the consumer can be triggered by one or more of the following: a new-product introduction; inadequate performance in terms of market share, sales volume, profitability, and return on investment; changing consumer buying patterns; or the changing structure of consumer markets. To begin the evaluation, management must determine if it will be possible to satisfy the needs of a large enough segment of customers (the target market) to generate the desired rate of return. Meaningful customer groups or segments have to be defined so that the following questions can be answered:

- Who buys or will buy?
- Why do they buy?
- When do they buy?
- Where do they buy?
- What services do they require?
- How do they buy?
- What is the competitive environment in each of these segments?

A competitive analysis by market segment is more meaningful than an overall competitive analysis, since a competitor's strengths and weaknesses usually vary depending on the market segment in question.

Evaluation and Selection of Target Markets

Once identified, potential target markets must be evaluated and actual target markets selected giving full consideration to company strengths and weaknesses, such as production capabilities, marketing strengths, and financial resources; corporate objectives and strategy; marketing objectives and strategy; environmental considerations; and the

Selection of Target Markets Requires a Preliminary Profitability Analysis

marketing mix required for successful market development. Selection of target markets requires a preliminary profitability analysis of the type introduced in Chapter 16 and shown in Table 16–1 (see page 617). The analysis is based on the cost trade-off framework that we have used throughout this text; it is illustrated once again in Figure 18–2. The total dollars committed to the marketing mix—that is, for product development, promotion, price, and place—influence the ultimate market share, sales volume, and profitability of the firm. The total amount spent on logistics (customer service) is equal to the place expenditure. Management should allocate dollars to the marketing mix and the individual logistics activities in a way that will improve marketing effectiveness and

FIGURE 18–2

Cost trade-offs required in logistics

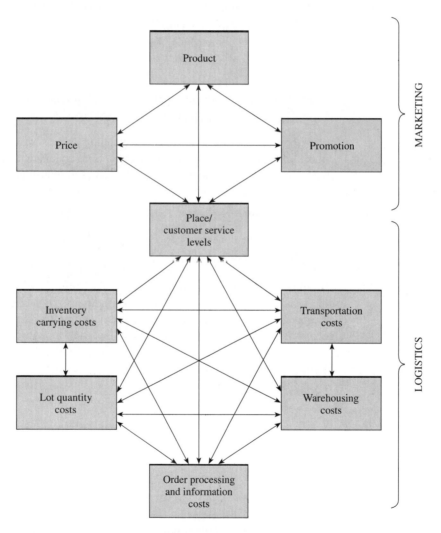

Marketing objective: Allocate resources to the marketing mix in such a manner as to maximize the long-term profitability of the firm.

Logistics objective: Minimize total costs given the customer service objective where
Total costs = Transportation costs + Warehousing costs + Order processing and information costs + Lot quantity costs + Inventory carrying costs

Source: Adapted from Douglas M. Lambert, *The Development of an Inventory Costing Methodology: A Study of the Cost Associated with Holding Inventory* (Chicago: National Council of Physical Distribution Management, 1976), p. 7.

efficiency and result in greater profitability. For example, the decision to use wholesalers to reach retail accounts may lower advertising, selling, and logistics expenditures, but the manufacturer will receive a lower price per unit for its products. The channel of distribution selected by the firm will have a significant impact on its profitability.

The goal is to select target markets that promise to generate the highest net segment margin. Only those costs that would change by adding or dropping a segment should be included in the profitability analysis.

Global

If Procter & Gamble Isn't Global, Who Is?

Is there such a beast as a truly global company? Ask a brand-name, multinational company and the likely answer will be no.

Take Procter & Gamble Co., maker of such beloved consumer products as Tide detergent, Pringles potato chips, and just about any product to be found under a kitchen sink. With operations in 160 countries and $38 billion in annual revenue, P&G sure looks like a global company. It acts like one, too. Its annual transportation budget alone is $2 billion. Each day P&G ships 29 million cases of product using 350 ocean containers, 9,000 rail cars, and 97,000 trucks. That translates to 130,000 ocean containers shipped worldwide each year, and 800,000 cross-border shipments.

Even with all that, P&G balks at describing itself as global. "We're working on becoming a global company," said Michael Barr, international services manager for Procter & Gamble. "There are some things we do globally. We negotiate ocean freight globally but we still don't have a system that would allow me to determine whether a plant manager in Japan, for example, is using the right carrier." That will change as P&G doggedly pursues an all-encompassing corporate strategy known as Organization 2005. P&G is counting on the initiative to spur long-term annual sales growth of 6 to 8 percent. The company intends to boost earnings per share growth (excluding costs associated with the initiative) to 13 to 15 percent annually through fiscal 2004.

As part of the initiative, P&G will transform its global structure from one based on four geographic regions into one based on product lines. The new structure will create seven global business units responsible for building markets at the local level and raising brand awareness among consumers. On the production end, P&G said it will standardize production lines worldwide to better align them with overall manufacturing capacity.

The company is even changing how it pays for advertising. Beginning next July P&G will pay its advertising

agencies a percentage of its global brand sales instead of the commissions based on media spending, as it does now. P&G said the switch is in keeping with the Organization 2005 restructuring and is intended to spur sales of its top product lines through greater brand awareness worldwide. Organization 2005 represents a substantial investment for P&G. The total cost of the initiative after tax will be $1.9 billion. It will affect 15,000 jobs worldwide.

Organization 2005 also represents a significant challenge to P&G's corporate culture, Barr said. "It's about stretch, innovation, and speed. Part of that has to do with the creation of the global business units. By [managing] brands globally it makes it easier for us to deal with transportation," he said.

The global business units will get administrative support from shared service centers. These centers will act as the logistics and administrative arms of the business units. The creation of the service centers means that P&G's in-house staff "must justify what we do," Barr said. "We must make them happy or they can go to someone else."

Although P&G's business units now have the choice of outsourcing their logistics, Barr said he doesn't see a truly global contender among third-party logistics providers. "If they have any credibility at all, they will readily admit that they are not as strong in some areas as other companies," he said.

That's a fair assessment, agrees a third-party logistics executive. "There's a lot of talk in this business about globalization but few companies are truly global. They may have global brands but in reality they operate on a regional basis. Even Exel isn't global, though we operate in 30 countries," said Chris Munro, senior vice president of Exel Logistics.

Source: Ann Saccomano, *Traffic World* 260, no. 2 (October 11, 1999), pp. 22–24.

Formulation of Supply Chain Objectives and Strategy

With target markets selected, the next step is to formulate the objectives and strategy for the supply chain. As part of this process it is necessary to identify the channel of distribution that will be used and the supplier network. A channel of distribution can be defined as the collection of organizational units, internal and external to the firm, that performs the functions involved in product marketing. These functions are pervasive; they include buying, selling, transportation, sorting, grading, financing, bearing market risk, and providing marketing information.[8] These functions are also performed to varying degrees by the supplier network. A firm that performs one or more of the marketing functions becomes a member of the supplier chain.

Supply chain objectives flow from the firm's marketing objectives. Specific marketing objectives include market coverage and customer service levels at the retail level that give full consideration to product characteristics that may limit supply chain alternatives. Supply chain strategy is the specific plan that management will use to achieve its objectives. For example, consumer advertising can be used to "pull" the product through the supply chain, or discounts can be offered in order to encourage wholesalers and retailers to "push" the product to consumers. In addition, management may wish to perform certain functions internally and "spin off" other functions to external members of the supply chain. There are a number of potential strategies available. It is important that logistics executives be involved in the formulation of supply chain objectives and strategy, since logistics costs affect the efficiency of the supply chain and logistics considerations affect supply chain effectiveness.

Identification and Evaluation of Supply Chain Structure Alternatives

Marketing Functions May Be Performed Internally or Externally

The nature of the supply chain structure affects the speed and consistency of delivery and communications, the control of the functions' performance, and the cost of operations. In selecting supply chain structure, management may choose to perform all of the marketing functions internally, or it may choose to have one or more of the functions performed by external members of the supply chain. A number of alternatives are presumed to be available to the supply chain designer. However, in most cases not all alternatives are known or available when the decisions must be made. Consequently, the decisions may be less than optimal. Even if management makes the optimal supply chain decision at a particular time, unforeseen environmental changes may lead to a reevaluation of the decision.

Selection of the Supply Chain Structure

Potential Profitability Is Important When Selecting Channel Structure

Various supply chain structures should be evaluated in detail, using segment profitability reports in the format introduced in Table 16–1 (page 617). Management should select the alternatives that best satisfy corporate and marketing objectives. Multiple supply chains may be used to satisfy an objective of national coverage. For example, in some geographic areas the volume of business may permit direct sales to retailers,

---

[8]Fred E. Clark, *Principles of Marketing* (New York: Macmillan, 1923), p. 11; and Robert Bartels, *Marketing Theory and Metatheory* (Homewood, IL: Richard D. Irwin, 1970), pp. 166–75.

while in other areas corporate return on investment objectives can be met only when wholesalers or distributors are used. Also, as in the case of companies such as Cisco Systems and Nortel Networks, suppliers might ship directly to customers. Logistics considerations affect both the efficiency and effectiveness of individual supply chain structures, and must be included in the selection process.

Finally, management must program the various components of the marketing mix. It is at this point that the strategic logistics plan is formulated.

Formulation of the Strategic Logistics Plan

The development of an effective logistics plan depends on several key inputs from marketing, manufacturing, finance/accounting, and logistics.

Marketing Input

Marketing must provide the proposed product, pricing, and promotional strategies for each supply chain used. This will include full knowledge of the product line, complete with planned product introductions and product deletions; pricing programs, including volume discounts and terms of sale; planned promotions and sales incentive programs; forecasts of monthly sales volumes by geographic area, by type of account, and by customer, if available; and customer service policies by type of account and geographic area. The planned customer service policies are especially significant to the logistics strategist, who should be involved in establishing them. Customer service policies should include the following elements on a customer-class or geographic basis: the method of order transmittal, order entry, and order processing; the desired order cycle time; the acceptable level of variability in order cycle time; the level of in-stock availability; policies on expediting and transshipment; and product substitution policies.

Manufacturing Input

Manufacturing should provide a list of production facilities, including manufacturing capabilities and the planned production for each product. When products can be manufactured at more than one plant, logistics and manufacturing must determine where products can be produced most economically, giving full consideration to the sales forecast and the necessary cost trade-offs.

Purchasing Input

Purchasing should perform sourcing-related activities in a way that supports the overall objectives of the organization. Purchasing can provide information about new technologies, potential new materials or services, and new sources of supply that will enable the firm to take advantage of market opportunities. Purchasing must identify the supplier network and select individual suppliers after receiving input from logistics and the other functional areas.

Finance/Accounting Input

Finance/accounting is the source of the cost data required to perform segmental analysis and cost trade-off analysis. In addition, finance/accounting must provide information on corporate hurdle rates and the availability of capital to finance logistics assets such as inventory, facilities, and equipment.

Logistics Input

Logistics must provide information that describes the existing logistics network in terms of product storage locations at plants and in the field; transportation links between suppliers and plants, plants and distribution centers, and distribution centers and customers; and the operating characteristics of the distribution centers in terms of size, volume, and product mix. In addition, logistics must identify the costs associated with materials flow and storage.

Typically, the costs required from logistics include fixed and variable costs for storage and handling by location; transportation costs by link in the supply chain; order processing costs; inventory carrying costs; and purchasing/acquisition costs.

The strategic logistics plan should consist of the following:[9]

**Components of the
Strategic Logistics Plan**

1. A *management overview,* describing the logistics strategy in general terms and its relationship to the other major business functions.

2. A *statement of the logistics objectives* related to cost and service for both products and customers.

3. A *description of the individual customer service, inventory, warehousing, order processing, and transportation strategies* necessary to support the overall plan.

4. An *outline of the major logistics program or operational plans* described in sufficient detail to document plans, related costs, timing, and their business impact.

5. A *forecast* of the necessary workforce and capital requirements.

6. A *logistics financial statement* detailing operating costs, capital requirements, and cash flow.

7. A *description of the business impact of the logistics strategy,* in terms of corporate profits, customer service performance, and the impact on other business functions.

Evaluation and Selection of Individual Logistics Members of the Supply Chain

Once it establishes the strategic logistics plan, management must develop operational procedures or methods for carrying it out. It is at this stage that management must develop alternatives with respect to individual supply chain members such as carriers and warehousers. Managers must evaluate supply chain members and select those that satisfy the evaluative criteria. Criteria for selection and evaluation were discussed in previous chapters of this text, beginning with Chapter 2.

Performance Evaluation and Supply Chain Modification

Logistics Input

Successful implementation of the strategic logistics plan requires that performance be measured on a timely basis and changes made when performance is not satisfactory. Total supply chain performance should be measured by customer segments using the profitability analysis framework shown in Table 16–1 (page 617).

When performance is not satisfactory, management must determine whether performance can be improved with existing supply chain members. If performance can be improved, management must make the required changes and continue to monitor performance (see Loop D in Figure 18–1). If performance cannot be improved with the existing participants and a structural change is not required, management should consider alternative supply chain members and select a replacement (see Loop C in Figure 18–1). If a replacement is not available or a change in the supply chain structure is required, supply chain objectives and strategy must be reviewed, and the planning process repeated at that point (see Loop B in Figure 18–1). However, if a change in the supply chain structure does not yield the necessary level of performance, management must repeat the entire planning process (see Loop A in Figure 18–1). In any case, the strategic logistics plan should be reevaluated each year to accommodate changes in consumer needs, marketing

[9]Adapted from Robert E. Murray, "Strategic Distribution Planning: Structuring the Plan," *Proceedings of the Eighteenth Annual Conference of the National Council of Physical Distribution Management,* 1980, pp. 220–21.

Technology

What's in a Name?

2000 Logistics, a third-party logistics start-up, says it can handle just about any task an e-tailer throws its way.

"We handle everything, from the time the consumer checks out his shopping cart to when the goods are delivered. And we also handle reverse logistics," said Douglas Kowalchuk, senior vice president of logistics, for the White Plains, N.Y.–based company.

2000 Logistics began as the in-house logistics operation of Internet retailer WorldSpy.com, which was created [in 1999] as an online mall to help traditional manufacturers compete with e-tailers by selling products directly to consumers. 2000 Logistics has honed its services for the past 18 months managing WorldSpy's logistics operations.

"WorldSpy is probably the worst-case customer that 2000 Logistics will ever have," Kowalchuk said. "WorldSpy has goods they want to purchase and put in a warehouse; goods they want the manufacturer to continue to own in the warehouse, while WorldSpy acts as a third-party warehousing agent on the manufacturer's behalf; goods that are going to ship directly from the manufacturer's warehouse; and goods where the manufacturer said, 'Just go through a regular distributor and we will support you on the back end.' "

2000 Logistics says it can provide credit card processing; fraud check; authorization; pick, pack, and ship; customer service; call center; reverse logistics; and packaging services.

The company has developed proprietary information technology to settle online payments, which is essential to the e-tailer because of the speed of sales, Kowalchuk said. "The benefit for the merchant . . . is that they get paid in real time. As soon as the goods are shipped, the funds are in their merchant account within 6 hours, and, on the very outside, 48 hours. So, there are no receivables."

Traditional manufacturers face a number of disadvantages when it comes to competing against online rivals. Channel conflict—a benign name for the thorny problems that arise when manufacturers skip their distributors, wholesalers, and retail stores—and customer service are two serious issues, Kowalchuk said.

Those problems will eventually fall away as the retailing world adjusts to a new style of business. But there remains one problem that isn't going to go away without a fight.

"Major manufacturers can't get one piece to your house today," Kowalchuk said. "Electronics companies, for example—it is near impossible for them to ship one Walkman to your home today. The cost is almost as much as it is to fulfill a full truckload."

WorldSpy spun 2000 Logistics off into a stand-alone subsidiary in October. Kowalchuk said venture capitalists are beginning to show interest, and that the company has a list of more than 1,000 prospective clients.

Source: Gordon Forsyth, *American Shipper* 42, no. 1 (January 2000), p. 15. Reprinted by permission of *American Shipper*.

Outsourcing Fulfillment Services

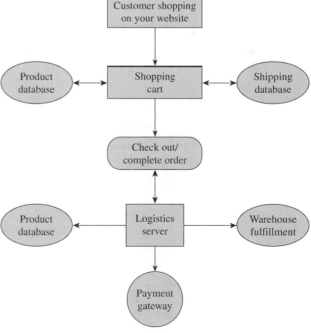

Source: 2000 Logistics.

strategy, the economic environment, the competitive environment, government regulation, and available corporate resources.

The logistics planning process is a natural extension of the corporate planning process. The remainder of this chapter is devoted to a detailed discussion of how to develop a strategic logistics plan.

Developing a Strategic Logistics Plan

The development of a strategic logistics plan requires the following:[10]

Requirements of a Strategic Logistics Plan

- A thorough understanding and appreciation of corporate strategies and marketing plans, in order to provide sound strategic planning recommendations and move toward a logistics system that balances cost and service effectiveness.

- A customer service study to determine what elements of service are key, how service is measured, what levels of performance are expected, and how the firm's performance compares to that of specific competitors.

- Identification of the total costs associated with alternative logistics systems to select the lowest-cost network that meets corporate, marketing, and customer requirements.

When overall corporate strategies and marketing plans have been determined, the logistics planner must evaluate basic alternatives and recommend the system configuration that satisfies customer requirements at the lowest total cost. Consequently, the process must begin with identifying and documenting customer service goals and strategies. Management can use a customer service survey to determine the specific needs and requirements of the firm's customers—as well as the firm's performance compared to that of competitors. The survey can be supplemented with face-to-face interviews. The plan must consider the specific requirements of customers, competitive service levels, changing environmental conditions, and the amount of service that the company is willing to offer.

In many companies, collecting such information may be a difficult process. It is here that the logistics audit, first described in Chapter 3, can be of significant benefit.

The Logistics Audit[11]

An audit program should be conducted on a routine basis, although the length of time between audits may vary among firms. One reason for the logistics audit is to develop a database that can be used to evaluate the various components of the logistics operating system in order to identify productivity improvements. Consequently, it is necessary to identify, collect, and analyze the data that will best describe current costs and customer service levels. When conducting a logistics audit in a manufacturing environment, management should take the following steps:

The Steps That Should Be Taken When Conducting a Logistics Audit

1. A task force should be established to assist in the review process.
2. Current corporate strategies and objectives that could affect, or be affected by, logistics must be determined.

---

[10]Murray, "Strategic Distribution Planning," p. 216.

[11]This section is adapted from Jay U. Sterling and Douglas M. Lambert, "A Methodology for Assessing Logistics Operating Systems," in *International Journal of Physical Distribution and Materials Management* 15, no. 6 (1985), pp. 1–44.

3. Key questions should be constructed by the task force to serve as a basis for both internal and external audit interviews, for identifying weaknesses in the current system, and for recommending improvements.

4. Critical variables and measurements that are accurate, reliable, and efficient must be identified and conceptualized by major customer segments.

5. An external audit of customer perspectives and requirements should be undertaken to determine the firm's performance, competitive practices and performance, and the specific levels of service required.

6. An internal audit of current logistics performance should be conducted. This audit involves two distinct processes:
   a. Personal interviews with representatives from various functions throughout the firm.
   b. Sampling of firm records and transaction data so that the existing operating system can be statistically analyzed and performance accurately described.

7. Cost and service trade-off alternatives must be identified and analyzed.

8. The questions identified in step 3 must be addressed, and improvements and changes to the current system identified and recommended to management.

9. The system that will exist after the recommended changes should be described, and expected performance predicted.

Figure 18–3 summarizes these steps. The process is described in the following sections.

The Logistics Task Force.   Firms should use a task force approach because members of the task force are directly involved in the decision-making process and recognize that they are responsible for implementing the recommendations. The task force approach leads to a level of commitment that is not possible when recommended strategies and system changes are proposed by an outside agency, or by an individual within the firm who is not involved in the actual day-to-day operations of the function.

The Task Force Should Include Representatives from Logistics and Other Corporate Functions

Two types of individuals need to be included in the task force: those involved in managing logistics activities such as traffic, warehousing, private fleet operations, customer service, and inventory management; and those representing other corporate functions that regularly interact with logistics. Consequently, representatives from the controller's office, marketing/sales, manufacturing, and purchasing should be asked to participate. Also, representation from the management information systems area is important. The participation of these functions offers several advantages: corporatewide data and information will be more accessible; cooperation across organizational areas will be facilitated; broader perspectives will evolve; and final recommendations will be more practical and more easily implemented.

Review of Company Strategies.   Too frequently, one function of a company may develop objectives, strategies, and operating systems without considering their impact on the company's overall mission and stated goals. For example, a firm may desire to grow 15 percent a year, achieve a 10 percent profit before taxes, target new investment returns at 25 percent after taxes, and introduce a minimum of five new products each year. These objectives will have an impact on every activity and output controlled by the logistics function. It is useless to propose an expanded warehouse network if the projected return on investment (ROI) would be only 10 percent or the additional inventories would decrease profits below the targeted level.

Therefore, the corporate mission, the firm's goals and objectives, and the firm's manufacturing, marketing, and purchasing strategies must be analyzed during the

FIGURE 18–3

The logistics audit: a conceptual model

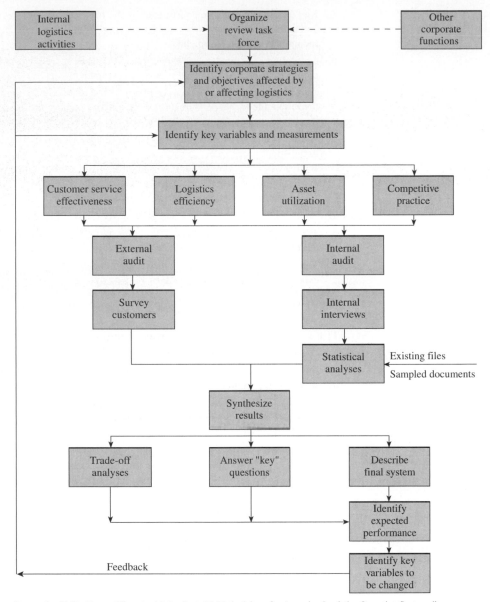

Source: Jay U. Sterling and Douglas M. Lambert, "A Methodology for Assessing Logistics Operating Systems," *International Journal of Physical Distribution and Materials Management* 15, no. 6 (1985), p. 13.

Three Good Reasons for Reviewing Company Strategies

preliminary phases of a logistics audit. This procedure helps to identify: (1) critical questions that need to be addressed during subsequent interview phases of the audit; (2) key measurements that will be used to compare current logistics performance with customer requirements; and (3) potential alternative strategies.

Construction of Key Questions.   Before attempting to interview customers and internal operating personnel, and before measuring current logistics performance, the task force should prepare a list of questions that, if properly resolved, will enable the company to achieve a distinct competitive advantage in the markets it serves. These questions should be broad in scope, so that they do not restrict the task force's charter. They must consider the corporate mission and goals, and address the individual concerns of top management. The following questions can serve as examples:

- What changes are likely to occur in the structure of each market segment, and how will these changes affect the relative importance of each segment?
- What supply chains are competitors currently using, and where might the firm gain a differential advantage?
- Will achievement of the company's current order cycle time and fill rate standards make it a leader in its industry?
- What overall customer service strategies should be developed, and how will these differ by customer (market) segment?
- How should the firm respond in a proactive way to the desire of customers to reduce inventories or other costs?
- What order processing system requirements must the company meet in order to lead the industry in responding to customer needs?
- Should the company utilize a centralized or decentralized/regional warehousing network?
- How can the company improve productivity in its warehouses, and what measurements are required?
- How can transportation costs be reduced without adversely influencing customer service levels?
- Are small orders a problem? How is this likely to change in the future, and what strategies should management employ to minimize the associated costs?
- Should the company expand, contract, or retain its current investment in private carriage?
- What are the best cost-reduction opportunities for the firm's logistics operation?
- How can the company's logistics organization best interface with manufacturing, marketing, purchasing, and finance/accounting organizations?
- Are there opportunities for consolidating logistics operations of the firm's subsidiaries/independent operating divisions?

Four Categories of Variables Must Be Identified

Identification of Critical Variables.   Once the key questions have been identified, the task force can identify specific variables and measurements that, if available, will enable it to successfully answer the questions and begin to restructure the firm's logistics strategies. These variables involve both quantitative and qualitative data, and can be grouped into four broad categories:

1. *Customer service effectiveness,* such as:
   - Order cycle time, in total and for each component of the order cycle.
   - Fill rate (percent ordered versus delivered).
   - Order cycle consistency (variance in delivery time).
   - Response capabilities to customer inquiries.
   - Ability to adjust order quantities.
   - Ability to change requested delivery dates.
   - Ability to interact with production schedules.
   - Ability to substitute or back-order line items.

2. *Logistics efficiency,* or costs associated with each of the following functional activities:
   - Transportation.
   - Warehousing.
   - Inventory management.
   - Production planning and scheduling.
   - Purchasing.
   - Order entry and order processing.
3. *Utilization of assets,* such as:
   - Inventories.
   - Warehousing facilities.
   - Private carriage operations.
4. *Competitive practices* and performance with respect to customer service attributes and asset utilization.

External Audit.   The external audit may be comprised of a comprehensive mail survey, as described in Chapter 3, or selected in-depth interviews with customers who represent the different market segments served, such as original equipment manufacturers, private-label retailers, wholesalers, or large mass-merchant retailers; differences in annual dollar volumes purchased; and geographic location. A primary purpose is to replicate the firm's overall business/product mix. This is accomplished by collecting specific information regarding the interaction between vendor and customer logistics systems, as well as determining the logistics/customer service effectiveness of major competitors. Inquiries should be made concerning both the current and future competitive environment and customer service requirements. The logistics audit will include a number of basic questions as well as unique industry/situation-specific questions. Table 18–1 provides a sample of the basic inquiries that need to be included in a competitive analysis.

Many of the questions in Table 18–1 can be further segregated by customer segment, make-to-order versus make-to-stock products, channel segments, or product line/product group. Ideally, the identity of the firm should not be disclosed during the interview process, so that objective industrywide data can be collected. For this reason, the assistance of university researchers or consultants is frequently preferable when conducting a logistics audit. The in-depth interviews may provide enough data to proceed with the development of a logistics strategy, or management may use them as the basis of a comprehensive mail survey.

Internal Audit: Personal Interviews.   In addition to using the external audit, those analyzing logistics performance should collect information from in-depth interviews with the firm's management. Specifically, formal interview guides need to be prepared for each of the following management functions:

Formal Interview Guides Need to Be Prepared for Each of These Functions

   - Customer service/order administration.
   - Transportation (inbound and outbound).
   - Warehousing operations.
   - Inventory management and forecasting.
   - Production planning and scheduling.
   - Purchasing/procurement.
   - Marketing/sales.
   - Financial control/accounting.
   - Data processing.

TABLE 18–1   Sample Questions in a Competitive Analysis

1. How often do you order products from your major suppliers?
2. What are the typical sizes of these orders?
3. What are the typical lead times encountered when replenishing inventories from your major suppliers?
4. What percentage of the product ordered is normally delivered by your requested delivery date?
5. What lead time would you prefer?
6. What percentage of your orders is eventually delivered, and how long does it typically take to receive all of your order?
7. What is the current performance by each of your major suppliers with respect to order cycle (lead) time and fill rate?
8. If a supplier is unable to commit to an order by your requested "date wanted," what percentage of the time do you:
   a. Cancel your order?
   b. Back-order with supplier?
   c. Request substitution?
   d. Back-order and also submit to a second source?
9. What percentage of the time do you use the following techniques to transmit orders to your major suppliers:
   a. Online terminal?
   b. Internet
   c. Inward WATS telephone service (800-number service)?
   d. Telephone paid by you?
   e. Mail?
   f. Fax?
   g. Hand-deliver to salesperson?
10. Do any of your suppliers use a "scheduled delivery" program? Which one(s)?
11. What percentage of your orders would you classify as emergency (ship as soon as possible)?
12. Do any of your major suppliers furnish you with any of the following written information/reports on a regular basis:
    a. Confirmation notices on orders submitted?
    b. Open order status reports?
    c. Product availability/inventory status data?
    d. Advance notice of shipping information?
13. Do any of your major suppliers offer incentives, such as prepaid freight, quantity discounts, claims handling for damage, or extended payment terms, for ordering in larger quantities?
14. What type of terms do your major suppliers offer? What terms do you prefer?
15. How many supplier sources do you normally use when purchasing your major components/products?
16. What criteria do you use to select suppliers?
17. How has the number of suppliers with whom you regularly do business changed in the past three years?
18. How do you anticipate this will change in the future?
19. What are the distinguishing features or services of those suppliers who consistently provide you with desired/satisfactory customer service as compared to those who do not?
20. How have your major suppliers improved their customer service, deliveries, and information with respect to your orders in the past 12 to 18 months?
21. What services would you like suppliers to provide with respect to logistics/customer service that are not presently available to you?
22. What are the normal/published lead times that you provide to your customers?
23. What method do your customers use to submit their orders to you?
24. Have you experienced, or are you experiencing, any changes in the ordering characteristics of your customers?
25. Do you have a computerized inventory record-keeping/customer order status system that identifies balance on hand, on order, and on back order by individual items?
26. What are your annual inventory turnovers by SKU, product, and product line?
27. Do you use, or are you contemplating using, a "just-in-time/zero inventory" concept in managing your inventories, or when ordering from your major vendors?
28. Do you perform trade-off analysis to weigh the economics of quantity discounts or forward buys against the added inventory carrying costs?
29. Do you attempt to carry different levels of safety stock for fast movers as compared to low-volume items?
30. What has been your average annual growth rate during the past five years? What do you anticipate this percentage will be in the next five years?
31. Have you made any significant changes in the way you order materials from your major suppliers during the past 12 to 18 months?

Sample interview guides are included in Appendixes A through I at the end of this chapter. They include the most important questions that need to be answered during the internal audit interviews.

Internal Audit: Sampling of Firm's Records.   Various types of source documents can serve as a basis for the quantitative phase of a logistics audit. They can be obtained by extracting data from existing files, or they can be compiled by using sampling techniques. The following represent possible data sources:

**Internal Audit:
Possible Data Sources**

1. Existing files.
   a. Order history and/or open order files.
   b. Bills of lading and/or shipment manifest data files.
   c. Paid transportation freight bills for both inbound and outbound shipments.
   d. Private fleet trip reports.
   e. Warehouse labor time cards or payroll records.

2. Original documents.
   a. Trailer contents of all incoming and outgoing shipments for a selected time span, by origin and destination zip codes, contents, weight, trailer cube percentages, and damage condition upon arrival.
   b. Warehouse labor-hours for receiving, put-away, picking, packing, shipping, housecleaning, and stocking rearrangement.
   c. Private fleet data, including routes, miles driven, empty miles, trailer cube percentages, shipment weight, and fixed and variable costs incurred.
   d. Freight charges (pro-bills) paid to common, contract, and rail carriers, compiled by commodity codes, actual weight, deficit weight, mode, carrier name, and origin/destination zip codes.
   e. Order cycle and fill rate information extracted from individual orders and/or line items shipped and compiled by customer segment, product group, quantities shipped and ordered, date ordered by customer, date received, date inventory committed/reserved, date released to distribution center, date picked, and date shipped.

The source documents outlined above, and a computer-based statistical package, will make it possible to efficiently perform a wide range of analyses. The output reports from this phase of the methodology can be grouped into the following broad categories:

**Categories of Reports
That Can Be Developed**

- The weight, cube, and commodities/product categories of trailers, boxcars, or vans received at, or shipped from, each of the firm's facilities.
- Supply chain flow and configuration volumes into and out of each company facility.
- Warehouse labor hours and dollar accounts by company facility and internal activities.
- Geographic dispersions of receipts (origins) and shipments (destinations).
- Where applicable, routes, miles driven, cost/revenue, and composition of trailers transported by private fleet or contract carriage.
- Inbound and outbound freight volumes shipped by, and paid to common and contract carriers, grouped by mode, individual carrier, geographic area, and weight break categories.
- Order-history data regarding cycle time and service measurements, such as fill rates and on-time delivery.

An Example
of a Coding Structure

To facilitate the various analyses, common coding structures should be developed for all source documents. Common codes provide the ability to identify product flows as well as applicable logistics costs and key customer service measurements, for segments such as geographic area, company location, product group, customer, customer segment, and in total. Any problems in data collection should be fully documented. The following represents a sample of common coding structures:

1. All transactions should include the first three digits of the postal zip code(s) involved.

2. A single-digit table of transportation modes involved in all shipments can be compiled, such as:
   a. Private fleet.
   b. Contract carrier.
   c. Common carrier.
   d. Local cartage.
   e. Rail.
   f. TOFC.
   g. Air freight.
   h. Air express parcel service.
   i. Broker.
   j. Freight forwarder.

3. Each of the company's shipping and receiving locations should be identified by a unique code.

4. The name of the carrier involved with the shipment should be identified. This can be accomplished by constructing a three- or four-digit cross-reference coding system.

5. Customers should be reviewed so that a logic can be developed to regroup customers into meaningful market segments.

6. Inbound receipts should be classified into a representative range of commodities, such as steel, copper, plastics, motors, packaging, and returns. A single-digit alpha code has proven to be most useful in this respect.

7. Stock-keeping units (SKUs) should be categorized by:
   a. Fast versus slow movers.
   b. Brand.
   c. Customer group.
   d. Product class/group.

   SKU categorization can often be accomplished by selecting certain fields in the model or stock number, in conjunction with customer number classifications.

Synthesis Process. Once the internal and external audit phases have been completed, it is necessary to identify cost and service trade-off opportunities; address the questions originally constructed in the key-question phase of the methodology; and describe the recommended strategy, including required changes to the existing measurements in order to accurately report the effectiveness of the logistics system.

If the sampling process is sufficiently comprehensive, it should be possible to perform statistical analyses that will accurately predict the impact of alternative strategies and trade-offs. For example, regression analysis can be used to predict the expected order cycle time, given a range of fill rates. Or fill rates can be accurately predicted based on the actual level of safety stock. Similarly, shipment costs and transit times can

FIGURE 18–4

Making logistics decisions

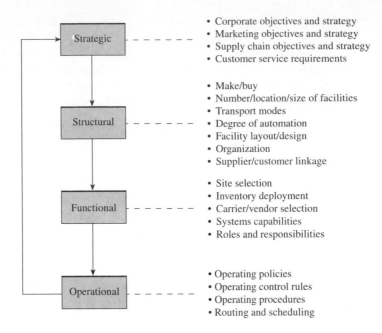

| Strategic | - - - - - | • Corporate objectives and strategy
• Marketing objectives and strategy
• Supply chain objectives and strategy
• Customer service requirements |

| Structural | - - - - - | • Make/buy
• Number/location/size of facilities
• Transport modes
• Degree of automation
• Facility layout/design
• Organization
• Supplier/customer linkage |

| Functional | - - - - - | • Site selection
• Inventory deployment
• Carrier/vendor selection
• Systems capabilities
• Roles and responsibilities |

| Operational | - - - - - | • Operating policies
• Operating control rules
• Operating procedures
• Routing and scheduling |

Logistics decisions are generally made hierarchically, but in an iterative manner.

be predicted for shipments of various size or weight. This analysis is useful in determining how long to hold less-than-truckload (LTL) orders at the firm's distribution center for consolidation into truckload (TL) shipments. Likewise, management can use analysis of variance (ANOVA) statistics to identify if various customer, product, or other segments require or use significantly different order cycle times, fill rates, order sizes, product mixes, expedited/emergency orders, transport modes, make-to-order versus in-stock product, and damage prevention techniques.

All of these data are necessary for the development of an efficient and effective logistics strategy. The previously described analyses make it possible to recommend a strategy that will identify specific changes that need to be made to the current logistics operating system, describe which key variables require adjustment, and provide the firm with a competitive/differential advantage in the marketplace.

The external audit allows management to benchmark the firm's performance relative to that of major competitors on those attributes rated to be most important by customers. Combined with the internal audit, the external audit enables management to identify the key gaps in performance. Then, every effort should be made to identify world-class practices and processes, regardless of the industry in which they have been successfully implemented, in order to close the gaps and build a competitive advantage over industry rivals.

The Logistics Plan

Logistics decisions are generally made hierarchically, but in an iterative manner from strategic (business objectives, marketing strategy, service requirements) to structural (make/buy, number/location/size of facilities, transportation modes, etc.) to functional (site selection, inventory deployment, carrier/vendor selection, etc.) to operational (operating policies, operating control rules, operating procedures, and routing and scheduling). This process is shown in Figure 18–4. Developing a logistics strategy involves

FIGURE 18–5

*Logistics strategy
integrates eight key areas*

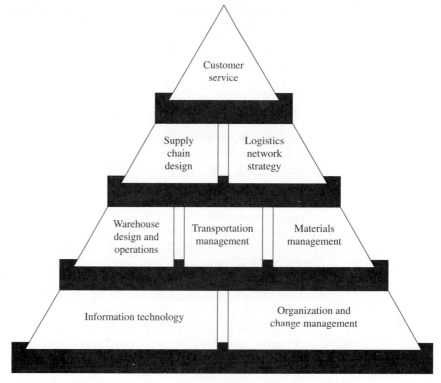

Source: William C. Copacino, Andersen Consulting, 2000. All rights reserved by the author.

**The Logistics Plan
Starts with Customer
Service Goals
and Strategies**

the integration of eight key areas: (1) customer service, (2) supply chain design, (3) network strategy, (4) warehouse design and operations, (5) transportation management, (6) materials management, (7) information technology, and (8) organization and change management (see Figure 18–5).

The corresponding questions representing each of the eight key areas addressed by the logistics strategy include the following:[12]

**Eight Corresponding
Questions**

1. What are the service requirements for each customer segment?
2. How can operational integration be achieved among the various supply chain members?
3. What is the supply chain structure that best minimizes costs and provides competitive levels of service?
4. What materials handling/storage technologies will facilitate attaining the service objectives with optimum levels of investment in facilities and equipment?
5. Are there opportunities to reduce transportation costs in both the short run and the long run?
6. Can current inventory management procedures support more stringent service demands?
7. What information technology is required to gain maximum efficiency in logistics operations?

---

[12]William C. Copacino, Andersen Consulting, 2000.

8. How should resources be organized to best achieve service and operating objectives?

The answers to these questions in the order illustrated in Figure 18–4 provide the basis for the logistics plan.

An Industry Example

A strategic logistics plan was developed for a $500 million division of a billion-dollar firm that manufactured and distributed industrial products used in the manufacture of home appliances.[13] A major objective was to identify the firm's current customer service performance. The company operated manufacturing and warehousing facilities in the Midwest, Southwest, and West Coast. It sold its products to original equipment manufacturers (OEM) and to wholesalers and retailers.

The company was under growing pressure for local warehousing from OEM customers who were attempting to implement just-in-time inventory management concepts in their own firms. Large OEM accounts wanted the firm to place warehouses near their plants in order to reduce lead times. Management was concerned about the effect this decision would have on the firm's inventory levels and logistics operations. In fact, the increased inventory necessary to provide local warehousing for two large OEM customers would be approximately $2 million.

Initially, management believed that the best way to determine if a regional network of distribution centers was feasible would be to purchase the services of a consulting firm that had a simulation model. However, the cost and time required by this approach proved to be unacceptable.

After initial discussion with the firm's management, the project was refocused into a study of the company's current customer service capabilities, as well as the recommended logistics strategies it should pursue in the future. To facilitate this task, management identified the following key questions:

Key Questions That Must Be Answered

- What changes will likely occur in the structure of trade (consumer) and OEM (industrial) markets?
- How will these changes affect the relative importance of trade and OEM segments of the business?
- What logistics systems are currently used by competitors? Are they likely to change?
- How can a differential advantage be achieved in the marketplace?
- How does the current order processing and information system compare to state-of-the-art information processing technology?
- What customer service system capabilities are required to lead the industry?
- What customer service strategies should be implemented? How will these strategies differ by customer segment, product class, and order size?
- Will an order cycle standard of three weeks lead the industry?
- What is the extent of the small-order problem? How is it likely to change in the future? What strategies are required to deal with this problem?
- What changes are required to proactively respond to just-in-time inventory programs or requirements?

---

[13]This example is adapted from Douglas M. Lambert and Jay U. Sterling, "Developing a Logistics Strategy: A Case Study," unpublished manuscript.

Creative Solutions

Collaboration Is the Way to Go

"Collaboration is the new competitive imperative," declares Michael Dell, founder and CEO of Dell Computer and *Industry Week*'s CEO of the Year for 1998. In fact, Dell is using an entirely new collaborative supply chain model for durable-goods production to dominate the PC industry.

Collaboration has become the watchword for many supply chain initiatives. But talking about collaborative behavior is easy; achieving it (as Dell has done) is hard.

The move toward collaboration began with a forecasting technique called Collaborative Forecasting and Replenishment (CFAR). CFAR, in turn, led to Collaborative Planning, Forecasting, and Replenishment (CPFR). This latter approach recognized that forecasting alone was an insufficient basis for improved supply chain management. After all, forecasts are predictions about the future, and no one can know what the future holds. The most we can do is analyze what happened in the past, and consider how circumstances differ today. From that point, we can collaborate to form an opinion about how the future will differ from the past.

Information sharing is essential to collaboration. Unless there is liberal information sharing across all of the "boundaries"—both intercompany and intracompany—supply chain collaboration is hindered or stopped. In his column in the fall 1998 issue of *Supply Chain Management Review,* Bernard La Londe noted that sharing of information was one of the five building blocks that characterized solid supply chain relationships. Without collaborative information sharing, La Londe wrote, the collective wisdom of the businesses and functions was not applied to solve the problems. The people must be willing to work together and improve the operation of each part of the supply chain they influence.

The Internet can have a profound effect on the ability to share information, yet many people still don't trust the Web enough to use it for mission-critical applications. One who does is Michael Dell, who says: "The real potential lies in its [the Internet's] ability to transform relationships within the traditional supplier-vendor-customer chain and to create value that can be shared across organizational boundaries. The companies that position themselves to build 'information partnerships' with suppliers and customers and make the Internet an integral part of their strategy—not just an add-on—have the potential to fundamentally change the face of global competition" (*Industry Week,* November 16, 1998).

But collaboration above all is about people working together in an environment of trust to collectively leverage their knowledge. Collaboration requires extensive sharing. Early leaders in a concept called JIT-II, pioneered at the Bose Corporation, approached this requirement by placing employees of the supplier in the offices of the customer. This kind of close contact is advantageous on two fronts. It builds trust because the day-to-day personal contact helps take the secrecy and hidden agendas out of the relationship. It also enables the supplier and customer to respond more quickly to problems and opportunities. Leading companies like IBM, Honeywell, and Allied Signal have embraced JIT-II in their efforts to foster higher levels of trust.

When companies are able to combine collaboration and trust with technology, their supply chain performance will take a giant step forward.

Source: John L. Mariotti, *Supply Chain Management Review* 3, no. 1 (Spring 1999), p. 75.

- Should the firm implement centralized warehousing or a decentralized/regional warehousing strategy?
- How can distribution center productivity be improved? What performance measurements are required?
- How can the logistics organization best interface with manufacturing and marketing?

In order to answer these questions, an internal audit and an external audit were conducted. The objectives of the internal audit were to quantify the firm's actual performance in key customer service areas such as the order cycle and levels of in-stock availability; and to identify current and potential problems/conflicts between the various logistics operating departments as well as between logistics and other corporate functions such as manufacturing, marketing/sales, and finance/accounting. The goals of the external audit were to identify the elements of customer service that customers used in their evaluation of vendors, and to determine the relative performance of the firm and its competitors.

The Internal Audit

The internal audit was completed in two phases. In the first phase, 7 in-depth interviews were conducted within the customer service, transportation, and warehousing functions, and 11 interviews were conducted with finance/accounting, forecasting, manufacturing, production planning, inventory management, purchasing, and marketing. Comprehensive interview guides were constructed and used in the interviews;[14] all interviews were tape-recorded. After the interviews were completed, the information was synthesized and key comments and issues were summarized.

The second phase of the internal audit was comprised of a two-month sample of customer order shipments. This was necessary because the company did not possess an order-history file that contained all of the data required to identify order cycle times, order cycle variability, and fill rates. Orders were tracked through the system from shipment back to receipt of the order. The sample was comprised of all shipments made during the two-month period. For each of the shipments, the firm's records were reviewed to determine the following times:

- Order received until accumulated in customer service.
- Order accumulated until released to distribution center.
- Order released to distribution center until picked at the distribution center.
- Order picked until packed at the distribution center.
- Order packed until shipped

This information was collected by stock class, type of customer, zip code, date wanted, date promised, date shipped, weight, shipment location, and mode. The sample may not have been totally representative of annual business, but if a bias existed, management believed it was conservative because more stockouts and longer lead times were likely to occur at other times of the year during peak periods.

The External Audit

The external audit was comprised of in-depth interviews with selected OEM and trade customers. The customers were selected so that they would be representative of the firm's business. The individuals interviewed were told that the interviewers were conducting research on just-in-time inventory management systems. Information was collected concerning the methods vendors were using to reduce customer inventories. The interviews were designed to collect specific information with respect to the interaction between vendor and customer logistics systems, as well as the effectiveness of major vendors. Interviewers also asked questions about the current and future competitive environment and customer service requirements.

---

[14]See Appendixes A through G at the end of this chapter.

By matching the output from the internal and external audits, management was able to identify the firm's current performance, customer expectations, and areas that required improvement for the following customer service categories:

- Order cycle time by internal function, as well as for order transmission and outbound transit times.
- Range in order cycle times.
- On-time delivery performance.
- Percentage of product shipped versus ordered.
- Split order quantities and frequencies.
- Shipment quantities by size categories (weight).

Based on the audit results and the division's stated mission to "maintain both a leading position in key markets and required profit margins in an environment characterized by increasing competition, rapid technological changes, and increasing emphasis on product quality and service," the following logistics strategy was recommended:

Recommended Logistics Strategy

Support the division's strategic emphasis by providing dependable lead times for customer orders, high levels of in-stock availability for "A" items, consistency of service on all orders, and responsiveness and flexibility to customers' inquiries and emergency needs in a cost-effective manner. Customer service improvements will be achieved by improving logistics productivity using appropriate state-of-the-art technologies.

It was recommended that the strategy be implemented for "A" items by establishing a two-week order cycle, measured from the time the customer initiated the order to customer receipt of the ordered products. The two-week order cycle was to be accompanied by an in-stock availability standard of 98 percent. That is, customers would receive their orders 98 percent complete within two weeks of order placement and with a high level of on-time performance. The corresponding standard for "B" items was six weeks with 99 percent order completeness.

In order to implement this strategy the following changes were recommended:

Recommended Changes

- Implement an automated order processing system.
- Implement an inside sales/telemarketing program.
- Modify current terms of sale for wholesale/retail customers.
- Implement formal production and inventory strategies and establishment of procedures and responsibilities between customer service and production planning.
- Revise the system used to transmit orders to distribution centers.
- Implement a scheduled delivery program.
- Implement inbound transportation programs.
- Upgrade the warehouse management system.
- Design and implement integrated performance measurements for logistics.

Estimated Savings

Successful implementation of the recommended changes would make the firm the industry leader in customer service. In addition, the firm would achieve annual cost savings conservatively estimated to be in the range of $2 to $4 million as a result of cost reductions in order entry and order processing; reductions in production downtime; consolidation of outbound freight shipments; consolidation and routing of inbound transportation; productivity improvements in warehouse handling activities and techniques; reductions in raw materials, work-in-process, and finished product inventories; and reductions in overtime at month's end due to changes in payment terms. More optimistic estimates placed the annual savings at $10 million.

Additional Benefits   In addition to quantifiable benefits, the study identified a number of opportunities that were not quantified in financial terms but would enable the firm to achieve further improvements in its ability to serve both trade and OEM customers more effectively. These included:

- Reducing the effort required to schedule production.
- Reducing raw material and work-in-process inventories.
- Reducing administrative costs that resulted from excessive expediting of parts orders.
- Eliminating duplicative efforts with respect to routing and planning warehouse shipments.
- Eliminating customer safety stocks due to shorter and more consistent order cycle times.
- Increasing order quantities due to online substitution and more accurate availability information.
- Implementing scheduled deliveries and revised terms of sale, in order to smooth shipment activity.
- Providing more reliable and consistent service to customers.
- Reducing both inbound and outbound damage.
- Reducing transit times for inbound and outbound shipments.
- Improving control over vendor transportation policies.
- Reducing vendor packaging, routing, and timing errors.

Costs to the Firm   The one-time costs associated with implementing the changes were estimated at $1.3 to $1.5 million. These costs primarily reflected new online interactive order processing and warehouse management information systems. The firm's out-of-pocket cost for the study was about $30,000.

Future Challenges

A number of topics that represent future challenges for logistics professionals received considerable attention in the previous chapters of this book. However, there are two emerging issues that represent particularly significant challenges and at the same time opportunities for those in logistics: supply chain management and e-commerce.

Supply Chain Management[15]

While many management teams have been successful at implementing the integrated logistics management concept within the boundaries of their corporations, there are relatively few examples of successful implementation throughout the supply chain. However, executives are becoming aware of the emerging paradigm of internetwork compe-

---

[15]Adapted from Douglas M. Lambert and Martha C. Cooper, "Issues in Supply Chain Management," *Industrial Marketing Management* 29, no. 1 (2000), pp. 81–82.

tition, and know that the successful integration and management of key business processes across members of the supply chain will determine the ultimate success of the single enterprise. Managing the supply chain cannot be left to chance. For this reason, executives are striving to interpret and determine how to manage the company's supply chain network, and achieve the potential of supply chain management. Logistics executives must play a key role in the cross-functional teams that are necessary to implement the process approach to supply chain management that was described in Chapter 2.

As was described, supply chain management involves three closely interrelated elements: (1) the supply chain network structure; (2) the supply chain business processes; and (3) the management components. The structure of activities/processes within and between companies is vital for creating superior competitiveness and profitability. Successful supply chain management requires integrating business processes with key members of the supply chain. Much friction, and thus waste of valuable resources, results when supply chains are not integrated, appropriately streamlined, and managed. A prerequisite for successful supply chain management is to coordinate activities within the firm. One way to do this is to identify the key business processes and manage them using cross-functional teams as described in Chapter 2.

Marketing researchers were in the forefront of studying critical aspects of what we now call supply chain management, particularly with respect to identifying the members of a channel of distribution. However, they focused on the manufacturer to the customer and neglected the supplier network. Our approach to supply chain management ensures inclusion of suppliers and customers. While marketing strategy formulation has always considered internal and external constraints, supply chain management makes the explicit evaluation of these factors even more critical. Additionally, traditional roles of marketing and sales employees are changing. Team efforts are becoming more common for developing and marketing new products, as well as managing current ones. The role of the firm's sales force is changing to one of measuring and selling the value proposition for the customer (see Chapter 17). Increasingly, the salesperson must act as a consultant understanding what brings value to the customer, working with those within his or her company to provide value to the customer and then sell that value to the customer.

The implementation of supply chain management involves identifying the supply chain members, with whom it is critical to link, what processes need to be linked with each of these key members, and what type/level of integration applies to each process link. The objective is to create the most value not simply for the company but the whole supply chain network, including the end customer. Consequently, supply chain process integration and reengineering initiatives should be aimed at boosting total process efficiency and effectiveness across members of the supply chain.

A top priority should be the development of a normative model that can guide managers in the effort to identify and manage their supply chains. It is much easier to write a definition of supply chain management than it is to implement the definition. Many challenges face managers wanting to implement supply chain management. The following represent key questions that must be answered by those wanting to implement supply chain management and therefore research opportunities for educators:[16]

1. What are the relationships among the key business processes introduced in Chapter 2? How do you obtain buy in from the functional silo owners in

---

[16]Ibid.

order to implement a process approach within the firm? How can the various participants in a company be encouraged to work toward a common goal? Marketing and manufacturing reward structures often tend to be counter to one another, yet the firm has overall profitability goals. Does the answer lie in similar reward structures, or rewards tied to overall performance, or will process teams provide the mechanism for integration? Beyond internal integration, how should interorganizational change management be implemented?

2. How should the existing supply chain be mapped? Should the map include all connected firms or only the primary firms? Are there other means of determining who should and should not be part of the supply chain map? What are the implications for good supply chain management practice based on the shape of the supply chain—that is, horizontal structure, vertical structure, and focal company position in the supply chain? (See Chapter 2.)

3. What is the value proposition at the consumer level or end point of the supply chain? What supply chain configuration is best for achieving the value proposition? How should the various firms in the supply chain share the costs and the benefits?

4. What metrics should be used to evaluate the performance of the entire supply chain, individual members, or subsets of members? What are the potential barriers to implementation, and how should they be overcome?

5. What is the process to take the map of the existing supply chain and modify it to obtain the best supply chain given the desired outputs?

6. How should the role of the sales force change to contribute where stronger buyer–seller relationships exist and when the purchase function is mechanized?

7. What determines the processes to link with these key members? How should the firm decide which internal process to link with which suppliers and customers? What decision criteria determine whose internal business processes prevail across all or part of the supply chain?

8. What determines the type/level of integration that should be applied to each process link? It is important to provide firms with some guidelines regarding what level of management components to apply to achieve the desired relationship and management of a link.

In order to achieve the most efficient and effective product flows within the supply chain, it is necessary to integrate the key business processes across firms in the supply chain network. Failure to do so will result in a fragmented and destructive approach to the marketplace. For example, there may be marketing programs such as end-of-quarter loading of customers that undermine quick response logistics programs designed to reduce customer inventories, improve service to consumers, and increase profitability for customers and the supplier. Implementation of supply chain management is key to achieving integrated logistics management, that is, integrated materials and information flows from point-of-origin to point-of-consumption. Information is a key enabler for both supply chain management and logistics, which brings us to the second future challenge, e-commerce.

E-Commerce[17]

The Internet makes it possible to access a broad range of trading partners and exchange detailed information quickly and inexpensively. Information and communication technologies are forcing managers to redefine their business strategies, rethink their use of technology, and examine their relationships with suppliers and customers. The Internet is allowing many firms that were not able to participate in information exchange using EDI to electronically share data.

E-businesses are providing value through the power of information networks linking suppliers and customers while redefining and/or eliminating activities in the physical network. Supply-and-demand auctions, collaborative product design, cross-enterprise workflow processes, and demand management collaboration are examples of how information is reshaping the supply chain. However, stockouts during the 1999 Christmas season made it clear to electronic retailers (e-tailers) and others that fulfillment processes are critical for success.

Companies such as Dell, Cisco, and IBM have discovered that low inventories, lean production, demand collaboration, and make-to-order operations result in lower costs and greater responsiveness to changing customer needs. For example, IBM has realized significant benefits from supply chain integration and e-commerce. Since 1994, IBM has reduced inventory write-offs by $800 million, increased ontime delivery from 90 to 98 percent, and reduced order commit time from two weeks to real time. In addition, IBM has reduced the cost of purchased goods and services by $4.2 billion. In 1999, IBM bought approximately $12 billion worth of goods over the Internet and expects that its electronic purchases will approximate $29 billion in 2000.[18]

The Boston Consulting Group predicts that Internet-based e-commerce between businesses will grow from $92 billion in 1999 to $2.0 trillion in 2003. During that same period, EDI transactions over private networks are estimated to grow from $579 billion to $780 billion. By 2003 approximately one-third of all U.S. business-to-business transactions will be done online.[19]

Figure 18–6 provides an example from the apparel industry in the United States that illustrates how four levels of the supply chain (fiber suppliers, fabric manufacturers, apparel manufacturers, and retailers) can use point-of-sales data to synchronize manufacturing and logistics operations to provide higher levels of service to consumers as well as reduce costs. Internet-enabled tools will facilitate other supply chain activities such as design, postponement, sourcing, and collaborative planning forecasting and replenishment.

The Internet's broad bandwidth and availability allow migration from a supply chain with a single, threaded, serial flow of information to trading networks where information is potentially available in a usable form to all members of the supply chain. For example, trading partners will be able to link their planning and execution systems across networks.

The following are three initiatives by industry associations and consortiums to shape the use of the Internet for their industries:

---

[17]Adapted from Gary J. Cross, "How E-Business Is Transforming Supply Chain Management," *The Journal of Business Strategy* 21, no. 2 (March–April 2000), pp. 36–39.

[18]Ibid., p. 37.

[19]Ibid.

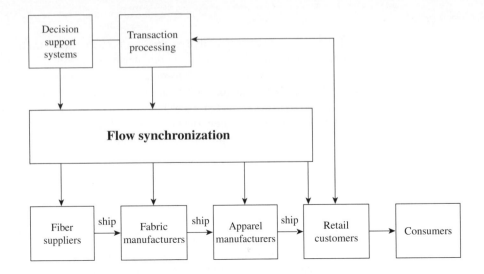

FIGURE 18–6

Using information to enable supply chain integration

- The Automotive Network Exchange (ANX), the initiative from an association of automobile manufacturers and their suppliers, plans to develop a secure, high-performance, and highly reliable extranet that members can use to exchange the large volumes of design data their computer-assisted design and manufacturing systems generate. Executives in the auto industry believe that collaborative design of automobiles and their components will take time and cost out of the automotive supply chains.

- Rosettanet, the initiative of the high-technology and electronics industry, is focused on building the standards and tools for business process integration through standard interface processes that allow more complex exchanges of knowledge between members of the supply chain. An example is the automated update of manufacturers' product information on distributors' online catalogs. Automating the process benefits the whole industry by increasing speed and accuracy.

- Transora,[20] the initiative of the customer packaged goods industry, is a global business-to-business e-marketplace that will enable manufacturers to use the Internet to streamline business transactions with their suppliers, buyers, and distributors on a worldwide basis. Transora will be an independent company owned and funded by firms from within the industry. By June 2000, 49 consumer products companies had committed nearly $250 million to fund the venture. These companies have common customers, suppliers, and processes. Transora will allow universal collaboration across companies, provide singular connectivity to an array of services and exchanges on the Internet, increase efficiencies, and improve interaction with customers and consumers. The e-marketplace promises to lead the transformation of the consumer products industry by delivering breakthrough benefits across the entire supply chain, and ultimately to consumers in areas such as: consumer promotions; collaborative planning forecasting and replenishment/vendor-managed inventory/scanner-based transactions; industry capacity management; and end-to-end logistics.

---

[20]www.transora.com. For up-to-date information on developments related to this major industry initiative, visit the Transora website.

In the future, supply chains will use networked technologies and business processes to respond to dynamic consumer and customer demands, optimizing their structure and performance at higher levels of efficiency and responsiveness. Future supply chains will display three characteristics:[21]

- They will have access to substantial amounts of information on capabilities, capacities, inventories, and plans that can be exchanged between tools, servers, and optimizing agents that will augment the capabilities of management.
- They will be designed to meet customer needs and provide product exactly when the customer wants it.
- They will serve customer needs with a minimum of wasted effort or assets through collaboration and sharing of knowledge.

New approaches are being developed between members of the supply chain, across supplier networks, and across whole industry segments. Corporate success will require a vision of the organization's future e-business role, a capability to execute that vision, and the ability to make adjustments over time. Logistics needs to be involved in this entire process if its full potential is to be realized.

Those firms in which management responds proactively to these challenges will realize marketing advantages in terms of market share improvements and/or premium prices. In addition, the potential negative effects on profitability will be minimized since high-cost, short-term responses will be avoided.

Summary

Four decades have elapsed since the integrated logistics management concept (originally called integrated physical distribution management) was recognized and the first courses were offered in the area. The emphasis in the years ahead will be on the profitable development of business segments, and the lack of growth in many markets combined with globalization will make the logistics function a focal point within the majority of firms. The challenges and opportunities for the logistics professional have never been greater. The rewards for accepting these challenges and finding creative solutions will be significant. It is our hope that we have presented the material in this text in a manner that will encourage bright young men and women to seek careers within the profession and will provide practitioners with a reference source that will help them in their day-to-day management activities.

Suggested Readings

Anderson, David L., and Hau L. Lee. "The Internet-Enabled Supply Chain: From the 'First Click' to the 'Last Mile.'" In *Achieving Supply Chain Excellence Through Technology*, vol. 2. San Francisco: Montgomery Research, Inc., 2000, pp. 15–20.

Bovet, David, and Joseph Martha. *Value Nets*. New York: John Wiley & Sons, Inc., 2000.

Bowersox, Donald J.; David J. Closs; and Theodore P. Stank. *21st Century Logistics: Making Supply Chain Integration a Reality*. Oak Brook, IL: Council of Logistics Management, 1999.

---

[21]Ibid., p. 39.

Chandrashekar, Ashok, and Philip B. Schary. "Toward the Virtual Supply Chain: The Convergence of IT and Organization." *The International Journal of Logistics Management* 10, no. 2 (1999), pp. 27–40.

Christopher, Martin, and Lynette Ryals. "Supply Chain Strategy: Its Impact on Shareholder Value." *The International Journal of Logistics Management* 10, no. 1 (1999), pp. 1–10.

Cooper, Martha C.; Daniel E. Innis; and Peter Dickson. *Strategic Planning for Logistics.* Oak Brook, IL: Council of Logistics Management, 1992.

Davis, Stan, and Christopher Meyer. *BLUR: The Speed of Change in the Connected Economy.* Reading, MA: Addison-Wesley, 1998.

Davis, Stanley M. *Future Perfect.* Reading, MA: Addison-Wesley, 1987.

Day, George S. *The Market Driven Organization: Understanding, Attracting, and Keeping Valuable Customers.* New York: The Free Press, 1999.

Gudmundsson, Sveinn Vidar, and Rita Walczuck. "The Development of Electronic Markets in Logistics." *The International Journal of Logistics Management* 10, no. 2 (1999), pp. 99–114.

Hamel, Gary. *Leading the Revolution.* Cambridge, MA: Harvard University Press, 2000.

Hanman, Stephen. "Benchmarking Your Firm's Performance with Best Practice." *The International Journal of Logistics Management* 8, no. 2 (1997), pp. 1–18.

Holmström, Jan; William E. Hoover, Jr.; Eero Eloranta; and Antti Vasara. "Using Value Reengineering to Implement Breakthrough Solutions for Customers." *The International Journal of Logistics Management* 10, no. 2 (1999), pp. 1–12.

Porter, Michael E. *Competitive Advantage: Creating and Sustaining Superior Performance.* New York: The Free Press, 1998.

———. *Competitive Strategy: Techniques for Analyzing Industries and Competitors.* New York: The Free Press, 1998.

Quick Response in the Apparel Industry. Boston, MA: Harvard Business School, 1990, pp. 1–18.

Stank, Theodore P.; Patricia J. Daugherty; and Alexander E. Ellinger. "Marketing/Logistics Integration and Firm Performance." *The International Journal of Logistics Management* 10, no. 1 (1999), pp. 11–24.

Sterling, Jay U., and Douglas M. Lambert. "A Methodology for Assessing Logistics Operating Systems." *International Journal of Physical Distribution and Logistics Management* 15, no. 6 (1985), pp. 3–44.

Taylor, David H. "Measurement and Analysis of Demand Amplification Across the Supply Chain." *The International Journal of Logistics Management* 10, no. 2 (1999), pp. 55–70.

Towill, Denis R., and Peter McCullen. "The Impact of Agile Manufacturing on Supply Chain Dynamics." *The International Journal of Logistics Management* 10, no. 1 (1999), pp. 83–96.

Questions and Problems

1. Why is planning an important activity for logistics managers?

2. What is the role of the marketing plan in the development of a strategic logistics plan?

3. What do you believe to be the most important elements of the strategic planning process for logistics? Why?

4. What audits need to be performed to formulate a logistics strategy?

5. Explain the importance of measuring and evaluating the performance of individual channel members.

6. What do you believe to be the most significant challenge facing logistics managers in the coming years? Why?

7. What are the benefits of synchronizing manufacturing and logistics operations throughout the supply chain?

APPENDIX A

CUSTOMER SERVICE/ORDER ADMINISTRATION AUDIT

1. Do you have a written customer service policy?
2. Do customers receive a copy of this policy?
3. Can you provide us with a definition of customer service as viewed by your company?
4. Do you provide different levels of customer service by product or customer? Explain.
5. Do your customer service standards change? How frequently?
6. If your company designates a particular area as customer service (or customer relations, distribution services, etc.):
   a. How many people are assigned to the area?
   b. Describe the major responsibilities of these individuals.
   c. To what department does this area report?
   d. If possible, please provide us with all job descriptions that include customer service/customer relations in the title.
7. How frequently do you measure your company's order cycle time?
8. Indicate (by circling the appropriate letters from the choices below) which of the following dates are part of your measurement:
   a. Order prepared by customer.
   b. Order received by you.
   c. Order processed and released by customer service.
   d. Order received at the distribution center.
   e. Order picked and/or packed.
   f. Order shipped by the distribution center.
   g. Order received by customer.
9. Is order processing centralized in one location or decentralized?
10. On average, how many orders do you process each day, week, month?
11. What is the dollar value of a typical order? Number of line items?
12. What percentage of customer orders are placed by company field salespeople?
13. What percentage of total customer orders are placed by inside salespeople/order clerks who call the customer to get the order?
14. What percentage of total customer orders are placed by customers online unaided by either company field or inside salespeople?
15. In terms of methods of order entry: How does each customer segment enter orders? If they use multiple methods, please indicate the percentage of their total entered via each method.
16. How many order entry locations exist in the company?
17. Once received by the firm, does the order taker:
    _____ Fill out a preprinted order form? If yes, ask for a copy.
    _____ Enter the order into the computer via a data terminal offline?
    _____ Enter the order into the computer via a data terminal online?

Source: Appendixes A–G are adapted from Jay U. Sterling and Douglas M. Lambert, "A Methodology for Assessing Logistics Operating Systems," *International Journal of Physical Distribution and Materials Management* 15, no. 6 (1985), pp. 29–44, adapted and expanded by the authors from Douglas M. Lambert and M. Christine Lewis, "Meaning, Measurement and Implementation of Customer Service," *Proceedings of the Nineteenth Annual Conference of the National Council of Physical Distribution Management,* 1981 (Chicago: National Council of Physical Distribution Management, 1981), pp. 569–95.

Order Entry Methods	Field Salespeople		Customers		Inside Sales Order Clerks	
	Total Company	*This Location*	*Total Company*	*This Location*	*Total Company*	*This Location*
Mail	_____%	_____%	_____%	_____%	_____%	_____%
Telephone (paid by customer)	_____	_____	_____	_____	_____	_____
Free telephone (800 number)	_____	_____	_____	_____	_____	_____
Online using the Internet	_____	_____	_____	_____	_____	_____
EDI	_____	_____	_____	_____	_____	_____
Fax	_____	_____	_____	_____	_____	_____
Hand-delivered to field sales rep/office	_____	_____	_____	_____	_____	_____
Other (specify)	_____	_____	_____	_____	_____	_____
Total	100%	100%	100%	100%	100%	100%

18. Does the ordering system automatically:
    _____ Verify credit?
    _____ Verify inventory availability?
    _____ Assign inventory to the order?
    _____ Make product substitutions?
    _____ Price the order?
    _____ Confirm delivery date?
    _____ Attempt to increase order size to achieve an efficient quantity?

19. Are the following reference files manual or computerized? (Check one.)

	Manual	*Computerized*
File	_____	_____
Customer	_____	_____
Product model dictionary	_____	_____
Prices (standard data)	_____	_____
Prices (special quotes/projects data)	_____	_____
Promotions	_____	_____
Inventory balances	_____	_____
Ship schedules	_____	_____
Order history	_____	_____
Bills of lading	_____	_____
Freight payment data	_____	_____
Production schedules	_____	_____
Credit	_____	_____
Other (please specify)	_____	_____

20. How are orders processed?
    _____ Batch processed
    _____ Individually processed (online, real-time environment)

21. How does the order processing system provide order information to:
    a. Transportation, for determining route loading sequence, and ship date?
    b. Warehouse, for picking and packing?

22. Do salespeople or customers receive an order acknowledgment? (Check and write in responses.)

    Sales _____   When? _____   How transmitted?_____
    Customers _____   When? _____   How transmitted? _____
    Both _____   When? _____   How transmitted? _____
    Neither _____

23. Do you have a single point of contact for customers, or do certain departments handle different types of inquiries/complaints?

24. Do you provide customers with a website? If so, how do you make them aware of it?

25. Do your competitors have an established method of communication for their customers who want to contact them about some aspect of their order after the order has been entered?

26. Do you have a precalculated cost for processing a customer order?

27. Do you compute a standard cost for a stockout (cost of lost sales)?

28. Do you use a standard cost for a back order?

29. Describe the exact procedures used in assigning transportation routes.

30. How do you determine that you will comply with a customer's request to change to a nonstandard carrier on prepaid shipments?

31. Who determines if an expedite charge will be assessed?

32. What percentage of orders require expedited service?

33. What criteria are used to process the following types of orders/order adjustments?
    a. Requests for premium and/or special, nonstandard transport mode.
    b. Revisions/adjustments to production schedules.
    c. Split shipments.

34. Do you attempt to differentiate service to different customers (prioritize)?

35. Has marketing told customer service the service standards it expects for various customers—specific and/or distinct groups of customers?

36. What distinguishes "cooperative" from "noncooperative" customer accounts?

37. How do you view your interface with production planning and scheduling?

38. What data do you provide to production planning?

39. What effort is made to encourage a scheduled delivery program with customers—particularly for those with LTL shipments?

40. How are orders physically transmitted to the distribution center(s)?

41. Please describe the exact procedures followed in sorting/preparing (picking lists) for submission to the distribution center(s).

APPENDIX B

TRANSPORTATION (INBOUND AND OUTBOUND) AUDIT

1. What is the total amount spent annually for transportation?
   a. Inbound shipments from suppliers $_____
   b. Outbound shipments to customers $_____

2. What percentage of your total inbound freight liability is accounted for by the following terms:
   a. Collect (paid by you)?
   b. Prepaid by supplier and included in piece price?
   c. Prepaid by supplier and added to invoice and/or rebilled to you separately?

3. Are outbound transportation costs for finished product assigned to individual customers and product lines?

4. What is the basis used to assign outbound transportation costs to products/customers or other meaningful segments (directly from freight bills, or allocated based on sales volume, unit sales volume, or some other basis)?

5. Are the costs applicable to various modes (common carrier and private fleet) accounted for differently?

6. Who selects the modes, routes, and carriers for outbound shipments to customers?

7. Who communicates carrier instructions to warehouses?

8. How frequently are routes and carriers reviewed and selected: at time of order shipment or periodically?

9. Is carrier selection for each order based on the size of the shipment?

10. What is the basis used for determining a "preferred carrier"?

11. How do order changes and expedited or "rush" orders affect the mode/route/carrier selection process? Frequency of occurrence?

12. Are inbound orders for raw material and parts reviewed by corporate traffic personnel prior to receipt, in order to:
    a. Determine and communicate least-cost mode and carrier to supplier?
    b. Determine opportunities for consolidation of LTL quantities in high-volume metropolitan areas for shipment into factories in truckload increments?
    c. Plan warehouse labor and materials handling equipment needs?
    d. Identify "priority" material that will require expedited service to meet scheduled production runs?
    e. Identify candidates for "cover-off" return loads (backhauls) via private fleet or contract carrier?

13. Are outbound LTL customer shipments consolidated to most market areas, and/or is a "scheduled delivery" program used to ensure timely, consistent outbound transit times?

14. To what extent, if any, are rates negotiated with common carriers, for inbound, outbound, and/or intercompany transfers?

15. How are these rates negotiated?

16. What is the number of carriers with whom you currently do business?
    a. Common _____
    b. Contract _____
    c. Rail _____

17. In your opinion, could this current pool of common/contract carriers be reduced to a workable handful and still realize acceptable service to all geographical areas?

18. If contract carriage is not currently used, could a viable contract service be structured to supplement the firm's current transport network in order to further reduce current common carrier costs and improve transit times?

19. Are bills of lading prepared by some type of computerized program?

20. Does a computerized "bill of lading" file exist? If so, what information could be readily accessed to provide planning and performance measurement tools regarding:
    a. Transportation routes, modes, and costs?
    b. Warehouse processing and transit cycle times?
    c. Channel product flow?
    d. Inbound and outbound consolidation?

21. What percentages of total outbound shipments are sent by:
    a. Rail?
    b. Truck?
    c. Will call?
    d. Other (please specify)?

22. As a percentage of total product shipped this year, how much product was transshipped?

23. How often do diversions in route occur? Causes? Decision process?

24. What is your procedure for delays in route? Decision process? Communications process? Order tracing capability?

25. Do you backhaul goods? Please explain nature of the backhaul, the scheduling process, economic justification.

26. Are freight charges built into the product's price, or does the customer pay freight separately?

27. Does the customer choose the transport mode? Carrier?

28. How much did you pay in demurrage this year? Causes of demurrage?

29. How much did you pay in detention this year? Causes of detention?

30. What are your terms of sale for outbound shipments to customers?

31. What percentage of the freight bill is attributed to company-operated transportation (private fleet)?

32. What cost categories are included in transportation costs associated with company-operated vehicles?

33. What do you use company-operated vehicles for? Intracompany hauling? Company to customers? Please explain.

34. Regarding management and administration of the private fleet operation:
    a. What are the annual miles driven?
    b. What are the empty miles driven (miles and percentage of total)?
    c. What percentage of inbound and outbound product is shipped via private fleet?
    d. What is the ratio of trailers to tractors? If greater than 3:1, what are trailers used for?
    e. How are routes configured?

35. Are private fleet trailer movements, usage, and nonusage identified in order to reduce nonproductive uses to a minimum? (Examples: trailers used as storage and duplicative, intercompany transfers.)

36. Are optimum routes and loading techniques developed to maximize utilization of private fleet trailer capacities, minimize empty miles, increase warehouse labor efficiency, and maximize savings versus common carrier modes?

37. Are inbound LTL raw material and parts orders consolidated either in major metropolitan areas, or locally, for delivery in volume to plant sites?

APPENDIX C

WAREHOUSE OPERATIONS AUDIT

1. How many warehouses do you use?
   a. Number _____
   b. Location _____
   c. Total square feet _____
   d. Ceiling height (ft.) _____

2. Do manufacturing and/or traffic personnel contact key vendors for the purpose of scheduling and routing receipts into the appropriate facility?

3. What percentage of raw materials/in-process and finished product inventories move more than once before final disposition?

4. Are there specific firm facilities, product categories, and/or geographical origins/destinations that account for a majority of these movements?

5. What criteria are used for selecting existing warehouse facilities and sites?

6. What is the company's policy regarding consolidation or relocation of existing facilities?

7. Are warehouse administrative policies, procedures, and financial record keeping uniform throughout the firm? Are they adequate to serve both present and future needs?

8. What costs are included in warehousing expense?
   a. Direct labor.
   b. Materials handling equipment.
   c. Utilities.
   d. Administrative salaries:
      (1) Clerical.
      (2) Management.
   e. Fixed depreciation/lease payments for:
      (1) Building/facility.
      (2) Automated conveyors, etc.
   f. Miscellaneous office supplies and expense.
   g. Maintenance:
      (1) Building.
      (2) Equipment.
   h. Data processing:
      (1) Terminals.
      (2) Corporate computer charges.
      (3) Telephone lines.
      (4) Corporate overhead charges.

9. Are the following costs used to measure warehouse performance?
   a. Cost per square foot.
   b. Cost per unit.
   c. Cost of direct labor per unit.
   d. Overtime as a percentage of direct labor.
   e. Fixed costs versus variable costs.
   f. Other: _____.

10. Are systems and/or controls used to manage warehouse activities (in total) and schedule/plan manpower and materials handling equipment requirements? (Circle where used.)
   a. Unloading receipts.
   b. Unpacking.
   c. Packing.
   d. Loading trucks.
   e. Processing returns from customers.
   f. Processing returns to vendors.
   g. Put-away into storage.
   h. Pull orders from storage.
   i. Writing bill of lading.
   j. Stock relocation/rearrangement/verification.
   k. Housekeeping.
   l. Utility (materials handlers).
   m. Maintenance.

11. What are your total annual warehousing costs?

12. What percentage of total warehousing costs can be attributed to:
   a. In-plant warehouses? _____%
   b. Field (private)? _____%
   c. Field (public)? _____%

13. Are standard costs utilized to expense warehousing costs, such as the following?
   a. Total cost.
   b. Direct labor.
   c. Materials handling equipment.
   d. Public warehousing.

14. What type of payment arrangement do you have with public warehouse(s) for handling charges? For storage charges?

15. What are the per-unit handling charges at public warehouse(s)? Per-unit storage costs?

16. What techniques and/or systems, if any, are used to measure performance of departments within each distribution center, as well as individual employees performing direct labor activities?

17. What percentage of trailers received and shipped at each location are less than truckload (LTL), and what are current procedures and tools for consolidation into truckload increments?

18. Is damage a problem? If so, what types of prevention or minimization techniques are used?

19. Are shortages and damage recognized, recorded, and accounted for regarding:
    a. Inbound receipts?
    b. Internal distribution center activities?
    c. Outbound transit?
    d. Customer receipts?

20. For purchases of raw materials, parts, and/or finished product, are vendors' errors documented and are vendors charged for variances in quantity received versus purchase order, failure to comply with packing and routing instructions, and quality problems? (Circle if yes and explain.)
    a. Raw materials.
    b. Work in process.
    c. Service parts.
    d. Finished product.

21. What logic and procedures and/or operating systems are employed to assign receipts to storage locations and extract orders from storage?

22. Is some logic (such as ABC analysis) used to lay out storage locations and assign products to storage (e.g., fast movers are placed in storage locations closest to shipping docks)?

23. How are inventories controlled by SKU regarding:
    a. Storage location assignment?
    b. Storage location balance on hand?
    c. Preparation of picking lists?
    d. Preparation of bill of lading?
    e. Preparation of packing list?
    f. Preparation of serial number listings?
    g. Identification of slow movers?
        (1) By location.
        (2) By SKU.

24. How frequently are warehouse inventories physically counted (including periodic test counts)?

25. Are warehouse locations periodically checked for inventory verification?

26. How frequently are warehouse inventories relocated or consolidated?

27. Are orders batch-picked? If so, how are picking lists developed, and by whom are they developed?

28. After picking, is a copy of the packing list transmitted to:
    a. Invoicing?
    b. Transportation?
    c. Sales?
    d. Customer service?

APPENDIX D

INVENTORY MANAGEMENT AND FORECASTING AUDIT

1. What is your average annual raw material inventory?
    a. Units _____
    b. Delivered cost per unit _____
    c. Annual turns _____

2. What is your average annual finished goods inventory?
   a. Units _____
   b. Variable delivered cost per unit _____
   c. Annual turns _____

3. From how many vendors does your firm purchase raw materials and parts? Where are they located?

4. How frequently do you typically order material (by major commodity category and geographical territory)?

5. Are minimum or fixed quantities used in determining order release quantities on purchase orders (for each major product class)? How are these quantities computed (by computer or manually)?

6. What are average lead times, by product class, for major vendors (from date purchase order is released to vendor until receipt at factories)?

7. Is time-phased, on-order information available on a regular basis? If so, how frequently are these reports published?

8. Are these on-order reports automatically generated from a data processing system? Is the information provided to distribution center personnel?

9. What are purchase order policies with regard to blanket purchase orders with periodic releases; specification of carrier; charge backs (packing/quantity errors, damages/rejects, misrouting, and late deliveries)?
   a. Blanket purchase orders.
   b. Carrier specs.
   c. Charge backs.
   d. Packing/quantity.
   e. Damages/rejects.
   f. Misroutings.
   g. Late deliveries.

10. Describe the exact responsibilities of each of the following corporate functions in the forecasting/production planning/production scheduling/finished goods inventory control process:
    a. Purchasing.
    b. Master scheduling.
    c. Production (title).
    d. Sales.
    e. Marketing.
    f. Logistics.
    g. Other (describe).

11. Are finished goods inventory level targets established on a regular basis? By whom? And at what level (SKU, product, product line)?

12. What are your standard product availability/service levels, by major product category?

Category	*Percent Available from Existing Inventory*	**Percent Available from Current/Future Production**	
		Percent	*Number of Weeks*

13. Who is responsible for establishing product level forecasts? What time frame do these forecasts cover? And how frequently are they compiled?

14. How are inventory levels at the distribution centers (DCs) set? Weeks of supply? Average inventory in units? Variable delivered cost of one unit of product?

15. How is the inventory file updated to reflect product received and product shipped?

16. With reference to the replenishment of inventory at distribution centers, how do you know when it is time to order product? How do you know how much to order? How do you communicate your replenishment need to the plant? Explain.

17. What formal reports are generated regarding inventory?

18. What cost categories do you include in inventory carrying costs?

Cost Category	Check if Included in Carrying Costs	Cost as Percentage of Inventory at Cost
Cost of money	_____	_____ %
Taxes	_____	_____ %
Insurance	_____	_____ %
Variable storage	_____	_____ %
Obsolescence	_____	_____ %
Shrinkage	_____	_____ %
Damage	_____	_____ %
Relocation costs	_____	_____ %
Total carrying costs	_____	_____ %

Average monthly inventory valued at variable costs delivered to the distribution center _____

19. Do financial departments analyze industries to which the firm's products are sold?

20. Describe the statistical forecasting system and its component parts.

21. How frequently are short-range forecasts, by SKU, released to production?

22. Are incoming orders monitored daily from reports generated by the order processing system?

23. Which department determines or sets inventory levels? Are inventory levels based on coverage/fill rate objectives?

24. How are fill rates measured by SKU and category?

25. Are there problems encountered in reviewing daily/weekly order receipt reports from customer service?

26. What types of problems are encountered when forecasting sales to large customers?

27. Are short-range forecasts derived from customer orders? If so, explain the process.

28. What are the major reasons why customers change order quantities and forecasts or request expedited service?

29. Who determines ABC product categories?

30. How many adjustments to your forecast do you average per week?

31. How could forecast accuracy be improved?

Appendix E

Production Planning/Scheduling Audit

1. Describe the production scheduling process in detail: steps in the process, inputs (type and source), outputs, all interfaces—where information comes from and goes to, decision points.

2. Describe the exact responsibilities of each of the following corporate functions in the forecasting/production planning/production scheduling/finished goods inventory control process:
   a. Purchasing.
   b. Production (title).
   c. Remote master scheduling.
   d. Sales.

     e. Marketing.

     f. Logistics.

     g. Finance and administration.

3. Are there any bottlenecks or other problems in exchanging information relevant to production scheduling?

4. How much downtime did you incur this year as a percentage of available production time? Causes? Cost?

5. How long does an average production run take? What is the yield?

6. Does this vary significantly between products and/or customers?

7. Are there any bottlenecks or other problems in exchanging information relevant to materials scheduling?

8. How are A, B, and C product categories determined? What criteria are used? Who determines A, B, and C categories?

9. Are finished goods inventory level targets established on a regular basis? By whom? And at what level (SKU, product, product line)?

10. What are normal manufacturing lead times, by major product category? How frequently are schedule requirements established?

11. For what period of time, from initial release (establishment of production requirements) for a specific period to actual production, are adjustments permitted (re: additions, deletions, quantity changes, push/pull adjustments)?

12. How frequently and to what extent are changes currently made to production schedules? Who is involved in this decision?

13. What are your standard product availability/service levels, by major product category?

14. Which functions are best qualified to make the necessary decisions/trade-offs regarding requests for changes in the production schedule?

15. What percentage of the time are schedules changed during first, second, third week before actual production?

16. What cost savings could be realized if changes were not made in week 1, 2, or 3?

17. What is the typical percentage that line rate is adjusted?

18. What are major causes of changes in production quantities?
    a. Inventory shortages (record-keeping errors and/or late-arriving parts).
    b. Line rate changes (added parts do not arrive in time).
    c. Production changes inside firm periods.

19. What percentage of your production scheduling problems are related to:
    a. A items?
    b. B items?
    c. C items?

20. How frequently are A items typically produced?

21. What customer groups give you the most problems with regard to production changes?

22. What type of reports not presently available would be most beneficial to you?

23. What problems are caused by production changes inside the firm period?

24. What percentage of purchase requisitions (number) are expedited (i.e., requested inside the vendor's stated lead time)?

25. What are the different categories of expedited orders from vendors?

26. What percentage of your requisitions are delivered on time (either standard lead time or negotiated lead time for expedited orders)?

27. How can the percentage of expedited orders be reduced?

28. How do you determine routing instructions and freight terms on requisitions?

Appendix **F**

Marketing/Sales Audit

1. Please describe the marketing/sales organization.
2. Does your division have a formal, written long-range strategic plan?
   - *a.* If yes, please describe this strategy/plan.
   - *b.* How often is it updated?
   - *c.* Is input provided by organizations outside the marketing division, and does marketing provide input to other divisional plans?
   - *d.* May we have a copy of this plan to review?
3. From a marketer's perspective, what do you believe are your firm's major strengths and weaknesses in each of your major market segments?
4. What percentage of your business is derived from each of the following major market segments?
   - *a.* OEM _____%
   - *b.* Trade/wholesale _____%
   - *c.* Commercial _____%
   - *d.* International _____%
   - *e.* Retail _____%
5. Please describe your role, responsibilities, and function in the forecasting/production planning/scheduling process.
   - *a.* What do you particularly like about the current process?
   - *b.* What do you believe are the weaknesses/shortcomings that you would like corrected? How would you implement these corrections?
   - *c.* How successfully do you believe the current process performs and how could it be improved with regard to:
     - (1) Forecast accuracy? (Please state the actual percent achieved versus your preferred standard.)
     - (2) Timing (planned versus actual performance)?
     - (3) Lead times/firm periods for major production categories?
     - (4) Machine downtime? (Is this a problem?)
     - (5) Parts shortages? (Is this a problem?)
     - (6) Production changes inside the firm X-week period?
     - (7) Late deliveries of vendor parts?
     - (8) Shifting demand/order patterns?
     - (9) Customer service—willingness to meet specific customer needs?
     - (10) Information system database?
     - (11) Use of customer sales to forecast (versus factory shipments to customers)?
     - (12) Other? (Describe.)
6. How frequently does your organization intercede on behalf of a customer with customer service regarding:
   - *a.* Adjusting orders?
   - *b.* Reallocating available inventory between competing customers?
   - *c.* Production schedule changes to handle emergency/key orders?
   - *d.* Waivers of freight terms and/or premium freight charges (for expedited shipments)?
   - *e.* Returned goods requests/problems?
   - *f.* Products/orders shipped in error?
   - *g.* Orders damaged in transit to customers (including both visible and concealed damage)?
7. With respect to customer service, what does each of your major customer market segments require in terms of:
   - *a.* Order cycle times (from the time a customer releases an order to receipt of the product)?
   - *b.* Order fill rate (the initial percentage of the order received by the customer's requested delivery date)?

   c. Order completeness percentage (the percentage of the order that the customer eventually receives)?

   d. Order cycle consistency (the variability in the lead time experienced across time as compared to the requested delivery date)?

8. How do you believe the firm is currently performing with respect to each of these measurements, and how could performance be improved?

9. Who establishes the ABC classifications for the products comprising the various product groups/families?

   a. What are the criteria and analytical tools used to determine the ABC classifications?

   b. How do you interface with the other departments in this process?

10. Who is responsible for establishing "terms and conditions of sale" for each of your major market segments, regarding:

   a. Payment period/discounts?

   b. Truckload/quantity discounts?

   c. Freight terms?

   d. Returned goods policies?

   e. Damage and freight terms policies?

11. How effective are your terms in general, and how could each of the above components be improved? In your opinion, is the large volume of business shipped by distribution centers at month's end a problem? If so, how could it be leveled?

12. What do you perceive to be the major problems of your organization with respect to the activities performed by or in conjunction with logistics? What would you like to see changed with respect to the issues stated above?

13. From a marketer's perspective, what changes do you see occurring in your industry over the next 5 to 10 years with regard to:

   a. Market/market segment growth?

   b. Shifts in demographic and/or geographic characteristics?

   c. Shifts, growth, declines in product groups?

   d. New products/product deletions?

   e. Customer service requirements?

   f. Competitive environment?

   g. Emphasis placed on the individual components of the marketing mix?

14. How do you believe customer service should be organized to better serve customers?

15. Do you provide input to other functions with reference to their long-range plans?

16. Do you receive input from any other area in developing your long-range plans?

17. What are the reasons for any production problems you may encounter?

18. Describe the current and projected five-year marketing environment for each market segment with regard to:

   a. Trade/channel structure.

   b. Competitive environment.

   c. Product line/mix.

   d. Pricing strategies.

   e. Promotional programs.

   f. Sales/support organization.

19. With respect to promotional programs, please describe how you communicate/interface with logistics/customer service regarding:

   a. Timing (including phase in/phase out).

   b. Coordination of programs between different product managers/customer segment managers.

   c. Pricing allowances administration.

   d. Inventory requirements to support increased volumes from a promotion program.

e. Special shipment/freight terms.

f. Special payment, dating terms.

g. SKUs to be covered.

APPENDIX G

FINANCIAL CONTROL/ACCOUNTING AUDIT

1. Are standards established for each function, so that overall performance of the logistics system is measured and compared to these standards?
   a. Customer service.
   b. Inventory management.
   c. Transportation.
   d. Warehousing.
   e. Order processing.
   f. Other (describe).

2. What are the components of logistics costs that are recognized by your firm, and how are they currently captured or otherwise computed?

3. What was your firm's approximate gross sales volume last year?

4. What was the average annual percentage increase in gross sales that your firm experienced over the past five years?

5. What was the after-tax net profit as a percentage of sales for your firm last year?

6. What was the average annual after-tax profit as a percentage of sales that your firm experienced over the past five years?

7. What was the return on net worth for your firm last year?

8. What was the average annual return on net worth that your firm experienced over the past five years?

9. What percentage of your firm's total assets is represented by cash?

10. What percentage of your firm's total assets is represented by inventory (raw, in-process, and finished goods)?

11. What is your average annual inventory turnover rate on finished goods inventories? How did you calculate it?

12. What percentage of total assets is represented by accounts receivable?

13. What is the firm's minimum acceptable rate of return on new investments (after taxes)?

14. What is your firm's approximate overall market share? (Please include your major business activities.)

15. Do you use standard costs in controlling logistics expense?

16. If there is a variance, what corrective actions are initiated, and how frequently?

17. In your opinion, what are specific reports that your firm should compile, on an ongoing basis, to effectively measure the performance of its overall logistics organization, as well as key individual functions?

18. Please describe what, if any, steps, procedures, systems, and so on are currently being employed to:
    a. Set up department standards regarding head count, budgets, and performance measurements.
    b. Secure viable, least-cost contract/common carrier services.
    c. Provide management reports/controls.
    d. Minimize use of expensive, duplicative product movements.
    e. Use automated freight bill audit and/or payment techniques.

APPENDIX H

PURCHASING AUDIT

1. What is your average investment in raw materials and in-process inventories and average inventory turns for each major commodity category?

2. From how many vendors does your firm purchase raw materials and parts?
   a. How many vendors account for 80 percent of your purchases?
   b. How has the number of vendors and the amount of business done with your top-volume vendors changed during the past two years?

3. How many vendors do you use for each major category/commodity, and where are they located?

Commodity Category	Number Used	Location

4. How frequently do you typically order material (by major commodity category)?

Commodity Category	Frequency	Order Quantity/Weight

5. Are minimum or fixed quantities used in determining order release quantities on purchase orders (for each major product class)? How are these quantities computed (by computer or manually)?

Commodity Category	Basis	How Computed

6. What are average lead times, by product class, for major vendors (from date purchase order is released to vendor until receipt at factories)?

Commodity Category	Average Lead Time

7. Is time-phased order information for raw materials and parts available on a regular basis? If so, how frequently are these reports published? Describe.

8. Are these recommended order reports automatically generated from a data processing system?

9. What are purchase order policies with regard to the following: blanket orders with periodic releases; specification of order; and charge back to vendors (packing/quantity errors, damages/rejects, misroutings, and late deliveries)?

10. What is the typical lead time encountered in replenishing your inventories (days/weeks from time order is placed to times product is received)? Please list by major vendor or product category.

11. What amount of lead time do you require/desire (from order submission to receipt of order)?
    a. Major suppliers _____
    b. Other suppliers _____

Source: Professor Jay U. Sterling, University of Alabama.

12. What percentage of line items you order are normally delivered by the date requested by you? Please list by major vendor or product category.

13. What percentage of your orders would you classify as emergency/ship ASAP orders? Does this vary significantly by vendor and/or product category? (Explain.)

14. If a supplier is unable to commit to an order by the desired date, what percentage of the time do you:
    a. Cancel the order and seek an alternate supplier? _____%
    b. Back-order with the supplier? _____%
    c. Request substitutions? _____%
    d. Other? (Please specify.) _____%

15. Does this vary by vendor source? (Explain.)

16. What percentage of your purchase requisitions are expedited (i.e., requested inside the vendor's stated lead time)? _____%
    a. Please describe the different categories of expedited orders from vendors (e.g., orders processed around normal system by phone, request delivery ASAP, small emergency quantities order, etc.).
    b. Is the percentage of expedited orders too high?

17. Do you receive periodic reports from your major vendor sources that give you the:
    a. Status of orders?   Yes _____   No _____
    b. Availability of individual items?   Yes _____   No _____
    c. Recommended stocking balances, by model (based on your inventory levels)?
       Yes _____   No _____

18. If any answer to question 17 is yes, how do you obtain this information? How frequently do you receive these data?

19. How have your suppliers improved their deliveries and information (orders, etc.) processing systems in the last 12 months?

20. Are you able to determine the availability of product that you would like to order from your major manufacturing source?   Yes _____   No _____ If yes, how?

21. If parts/materials are not available, are you able to determine what and when your major manufacturing source will produce the desired products?   Yes _____   No _____

22. How are you able to communicate with your major manufacturing sources to obtain the above information?

23. What percentage of your parts/materials is received by each of the following modes of transportation?
    a. Private carriage _____%
    b. Common/contract carrier _____%
    c. UPS _____%
    d. Rail _____%
    e. TOFC (piggyback) _____%
    f. Air express _____%

24. Do you use a scheduled delivery program with any of your suppliers (i.e., order the bulk of your requirements on a regularly scheduled day each week)? If so, with whom? How does the program work? How effective is it in helping you to manage your inventories?

25. Do any of your suppliers offer incentives (e.g., prepaid freight, quantity discounts, claims handling for damage) for ordering in larger quantities? (If so, explain, by supplier.)

26. Do you attempt to carry different levels of safety stock inventories (e.g., fast movers versus low-volume product)? If yes, what type of logic do you use in establishing which product will be maintained in inventory versus ordered only as needed?

27. What are the average days/weeks/months of supply that you typically maintain in your on-hand inventory?
    a. Is this: Too high? _____   Too low? _____
    b. Does this percentage vary by major commodity and/or vendor? (Explain.)

28. Do you perform any type of trade-off analysis to weigh the economies of quantity discounts/forward buys versus the added carrying costs to be incurred?

29. What type of terms do your major suppliers offer?

Vendor	Commodity	Terms

30. What payment terms would you prefer from your major vendors?

31. Do you regularly measure the performance of your major vendors? (Explain.)

32. How is the performance of the purchasing function measured by your management?

33. What are the major criteria that you use when:
    a. Selecting vendors?
    b. Evaluating performance of vendors?

34. What are the distinguishing features of those vendors/suppliers who consistently provide you with desired/satisfactory customer service versus those who do not?

35. How have your major vendors/suppliers improved their customer service, deliveries, and information with respect to orders over the past 12 to 18 months?

36. What services would you like vendors/suppliers to provide that presently are not available to you (with respect to logistics/customer service)?

37. Have you made, or are you contemplating making, any changes in the way you order product from your vendors (e.g., stock orders versus make-to-order product, reductions in lead time, higher expected fill rates)?

38. What percentage of the time do you use the following techniques to transmit orders to your major suppliers?

	Supplier			
Order Transmittal Techniques	*A*	*B*	*C*	*D*
On-line communication terminal				
Fax				
800 number				
Telephone paid by you				
Mail				
Hand-delivered to sales representative				
EDI				
Internet				
Other (specify)				
Total	100%	100%	100%	100%

APPENDIX I

GENERAL/SENIOR MANAGEMENT AUDIT

1. How many product lines do you sell?

   _____ *Product Line* _____ *Annual Sales* _____ *Percentage of Your Business*

2. Describe the overall competitive environment in the major industries you serve.

3. What is your overall marketing strategy?

4. Who are your major competitors? What products do they sell? To whom?

Source: Professor Jay U. Sterling, University of Alabama.

5. How do your major competitors distribute their products?

6. Do any of your major competitors offer any unique marketing/distribution services? Explain.

7. Why would your customers purchase products from your competitors rather than from you?

8. What are the estimated market shares in your major markets?

9. Describe the marketing channels (intermediaries and/or retailers) used in the major industries you service.

10. Are your firm's logistics-related strategies identified and/or specified in writing?
    Yes _____ No _____ If yes, please summarize them.

11. How is the physical distribution/logistics function organized?

12. Activities typically associated with distribution/logistics are listed in the table below. For each activity, please indicate with a (√) whether your firm:
    a. Includes these activities/functions in an overall, firmwide, and/or centralized distribution/logistics organization (e.g., corporate).
    b. Includes these activities/functions in a decentralized distribution/logistics organization (e.g., divisional or business unit operating group).
    It is permissible to check both columns.

Activity	*Included in Decentralized Organization*	*Included in Centralized Organization*	*If Neither, to Whom Do These Activities Report?*
Development of logistics strategies			
Logistics audit			
System modeling and/or simulation			
Logistics performance measurement reports			
Accounting/financial reporting systems unique to the logistics organization			
Development of customer service strategies			
Customer service audit			
Development of transportation strategies			
Traffic system/network analysis			
Private fleet management			
Common and/or contract carrier management			
Transportation cost accounting system			
Rating/rate books/rate maintenance			
Rate negotiation			
Vehicle routing and scheduling			
Freight payment/audit system			
Transportation claims management			
Vehicle dispatching			
Vehicle training			
Vehicle financing (e.g., lease versus buy)			
Development of warehousing strategies			
Warehouse site location			
Warehouse layout and design			
Warehouse space forecast studies			
Automated storage and retrieval (AS/AR) systems			
Warehouse conveyor systems			
Warehouse handling systems design and specification			
Warehousing labor management			
Warehouse space management			
Warehouse slot location record keeping			
Warehouse storage and handling rate calculations/negotiations			

Activity	Included in Decentralized Organization	Included in Centralized Organization	If Neither, to Whom Do These Activities Report?
Public vs. private (company-owned) warehousing analyses	_____	_____	_____
Automated order entry/processing	_____	_____	_____
Online communication network/systems	_____	_____	_____
Demand forecasting	_____	_____	_____
Official product level forecasting	_____	_____	_____
Inventory deployment to distribution centers and/or customers	_____	_____	_____
Inventory tracking/record keeping	_____	_____	_____
Distribution requirements planning (DRP) systems	_____	_____	_____
Energy management	_____	_____	_____
Hazardous materials	_____	_____	_____
Labor management			
Recruitment/placement	_____	_____	_____
Training	_____	_____	_____
Supervision	_____	_____	_____
Incentives	_____	_____	_____
Work measurement/productivity	_____	_____	_____
Safety compliance	_____	_____	_____
Law and industrial relations	_____	_____	_____
International logistics			
U.S. to P.O.E.	_____	_____	_____
Overseas distribution	_____	_____	_____
Data processing (MIS) dedicated and/or assigned to logistics	_____	_____	_____
Packaging design	_____	_____	_____
Computer-aided design and manufacturing (CAD/CAM) systems	_____	_____	_____
Purchasing systems	_____	_____	_____

13. Diagram your company's organizational chart (or provide a photocopy). Show the functions of logistics, marketing, production, purchasing, and top management, or their equivalents. Include any function your company presently defines as customer service (or customer relations, distribution services, etc.). If your company subdivides the logistics activities, show where they report. Show staff responsibility with a dashed line, and line responsibility with a solid line. If appropriate, you may describe only a division or subsidiary of your company if most of the corporate functional areas described above are included within it.

14. Are standards established for each logistics function so that overall performance of the logistics system is measured and compared to these standards?

15. Do you have automated files that record distribution-related transactions?
    a. Orders.
       Yes _____ No _____ Comments: _____
    b. Bills of lading.
       Yes _____ No _____ Comments: _____
    c. Freight bills.
       Yes _____ No _____ Comments: _____
    d. Inventory by SKU.
       Yes _____ No _____ Comments: _____
    e. Warehouse activity.
       Yes _____ No _____ Comments: _____

16. In your opinion, what are specific reports that your firm should compile, on an ongoing basis, to effectively measure the performance of its overall logistics organization, as well as key individual functions?

Report	*Key Measurements Included*
_____	_____
_____	_____
_____	_____

17. What kinds of performance data that are not currently available would you like to receive?

18. What problems do you perceive with respect to marketing/production/logistics?

19. Please describe what, if any, steps, procedures, systems, and so on are currently being employed to:

    a. Develop department organizational standards.
    b. Secure viable, least cost contract/common carrier services.
    c. Establish efficient warehouse handling and loading procedures.
    d. Provide management reports/controls.
    e. Use state-of-the-art logistics concepts and services.
    f. Be responsive to regulatory requirements and changes.
    g. Minimize use of expensive, complex multiple distribution channels.
    h. Establish customer service standards.
    i. Install warehouse manpower planning procedures.
    j. Use managed/scheduled shipping programs
    k. Use automated freight bill audit and/or payment techniques.
    l. Negotiate/implement beneficial freight terms on inbound purchase orders (re: materials and parts).
    m. Design and implement online order entry systems.
    n. Install telephone communications with regard to order entry.
    o. Design automated time-phased production and inventory planning programs by SKU and model.

HORIZON FOODS CORPORATION

"So, why are we calling this meeting?" Roger Bennett asked. "Are we finally beginning to recognize that we have a distribution problem?" As a newly appointed brand manager, Roger had just been promoted from the sales force and was interested in clearing up some of the problems that had appeared during his customer contacts. "How can we continue to sell our products when we can't tell our customers when our products will be delivered?"

"I think you have guessed the problem," replied Sally Ryan, the production scheduling manager. "We have so many requests for special production runs to supply inventory that we can't seem to plan a decent normal schedule." It seemed that the production scheduling desk had become a crisis center, and there was a continuing series of requests from sales.

Mel Young, the financial director, looked up as they entered the conference room. "Maybe one of you can tell me what's happening out there. I pay some pretty large bills to those public warehouses to store our products. I have had to increase our working capital in order to have enough inventory on hand. Yet we never seem to have enough. Can't we get some kind of control out there?"

Roger spoke first. "Mel, you know how we are organized. We let Production take care of supplying the market, and let Marketing take care of dealing with the customer. My apologies to Sally, but when I was in the field, I was never sure if Production would be able to back me up."

Sally began to burn a little at that last comment. "Roger, I can't blame you, because you haven't been in the corporate office very long, but it always seemed to me that Marketing was always a little out of control. You guys wanted everything—the full product line and lots of inventory—but you really couldn't tell me what the customers wanted to buy and when they planned to take it."

Background

Horizon Foods is a relatively small specialty foods processor serving a national market with a broad product line and sales of $300 million per year. It markets its products through a network of food brokers who represent the company to retail food chains. Horizon's product lines have focused on ethnic food specialties including salad dressings, sauces for Italian pasta, and condiments such as specialty pickles. The Company advertises at a low level—about 2 percent of sales, placing most of its promotional efforts on supporting the brokers with point-of-sale displays and cooperative advertising with local retailers, and couponing for special promotions. Retailers have generally liked Horizon's products because of their high quality. However, Horizon is not alone in this market; there is intense competition for retail shelf space. Competition has become more intense in recent years as other companies are beginning to offer complete product lines that compete directly with Horizon's. The brokers report that there is strong pressure to increase service to retail chain stores. They report that the retail buyers are raising questions about the number of stockouts that they have been recently experiencing. These buyers have occasionally even suggested that they might switch to other brands if service is not improved.

This case was written by Professor Philip Schary, College of Business, Oregon State University.

Products are produced in two plants: one in the Central Valley of California at Fresno and the other in Illinois about 60 miles south of Chicago. They buy ingredients from other food suppliers, avoiding the peak seasonal characteristics encountered by food packers. Production takes place in large batch quantities in order to maintain low production costs and assure consistent product quality. As items are packed, they are generally transported to the market in mixed truckload volumes using contract carriers. Product inventories are normally spotted around the country in about 20 public warehouses. The food brokers call on customers and generate orders, which are telexed to these warehouses. These public warehouses then arrange transportation. Horizon's products are packaged and are not considered perishable items. Orders are generally small, amounting to five to six cases per order, or about 150 to 200 pounds at a time. These are then delivered using carriers selected individually by each public warehouse. The costs of delivery are billed to Horizon. Transportation costs are high, because of these small shipments. Delivery schedules vary by carrier; some provide fast, reliable service, while others have been erratic to the point that customers have commented on poor delivery service. Even though Horizon's two plants are located in agricultural areas, many of the ingredients are shipped over long distances, depending on the season.

Horizon's management is divided into two major departments. One is Marketing and Sales; the other is Production. There are also several smaller staff units for personnel, purchasing, and finance. Production is the oldest of the two. Marketing came in almost as an afterthought and had a difficult time establishing credibility within the company. Production is responsible for scheduling production runs, as well as arranging transportation to and maintaining inventory in the plant warehouses.

Within Marketing and Sales, two brand managers are responsible for marketing the product line. They are responsible for promotion, product inventory at the public warehouses, providing sales support, and merchandising. There is also a national sales manager who has responsibility for maintaining contact with food brokers, coordinating public warehouses, and arranging for delivery. This split between delivery from production and service from the warehouse has often led to problems in holding enough inventory on many items to meet customer demand.

The Challenge

At that minute the president, Harold Sessions, came in. "I'm glad to see that we are finally getting this problem out in the open. Maybe we can do something about it at last. We need some better control over this product movement process. I chose you people because you seem to have a real interest in doing something about it. Now, how do you suggest that we eliminate this problem?"

Questions

1. What are the characteristics of the market served by the Horizon Foods Corporation?
2. What problems exist at the Horizon Foods Corporation?
3. Why do you think the problems exist?
4. What would you suggest the task force recommend in order to gain "control over this product movement process"?

CASE 2

UNICHEMA

On May 15, 1992, Mr. Jan Löwik, general manager of Unichema BV, Gouda, the Netherlands, was discussing operational strategy with his senior management staff. The group was reviewing the importance of meeting customer needs, the role of inventory control in meeting these demands, the problem of changeover times, and the constraints of the firm's asset base.

The following are excerpts from their conversation:

H. H. Ott, Commercial/Finance Manager:

My most recent analysis of the company's performance indicates some progress in cost reduction. However, we are still not managing our assets as effectively as we need to, and I cannot stress hard enough the pressures put on us in this respect.

H. G. ten Barge, Manager of Logistics:

The new logistics system we have put in place is helping us in this respect. It also enables us to talk directly with customers. This has helped us in producing what customers need, but with some problems still remaining. Just last week we had a situation which shouldn't have occurred.

We were running product number 1761 (a special product sold to a small number of customers) and asked the salespeople to determine how much of this product customers needed over the next few months. The response from sales was that 10 tons were needed, so we made 10 tons and then cleaned the equipment and prepared a batch run for another product. A few days later, a valued customer called to order 40 tons of 1761 ASAP. In order to meet his needs, we lost two days of production due to changeovers with obvious cost consequences. We must find ways to avoid these kinds of unpleasant surprises!

Mr. Griem, Sales Manager:

I agree that we have to respond to our customers and anticipate their needs, but we will always face unpleasant surprises. We just need to be able to respond to these situations either by carrying more inventory or by being more flexible in manufacturing. Moreover, I am concerned that the direct contact which Logistics is developing with customers takes the sales department out of the loop. I believe that sales should be the primary customer contact in the company to ensure the ongoing relationship.

Jan Löwik studied each of his managers as he thought about the changing nature of the business. Responding to customer needs had to remain a top priority, as did asset utilization, but balancing these issues with achievement of volume and good margins would clearly affect the way in which the entire organization functioned. Leaning back in his chair, he said:

Gentlemen, these are all valid concerns. But, to complicate matters, some of our larger customers have an expressed interest in initiating aspects of just-in-time (JIT) in their businesses. They too recognize the need for a higher return on assets employed and see inventory reduction as a key means to this end. Our job is determining how best to meet this requirement . . . while, at the same time, achieving a higher return on *our* assets employed.

EXHIBIT 1

Unilever Turnover and Operating Profit by Operation

Turnover by operations 1990
($ million)

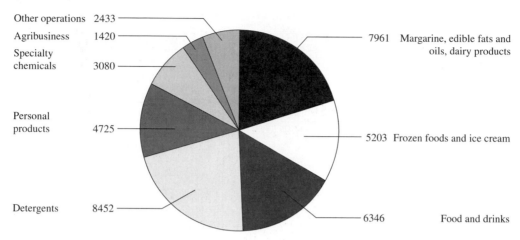

Other operations	2433
Agribusiness	1420
Specialty chemicals	3080
Personal products	4725
Detergents	8452

7961 Margarine, edible fats and oils, dairy products

5203 Frozen foods and ice cream

6346 Food and drinks

Operating profit by operations 1990
($ million)

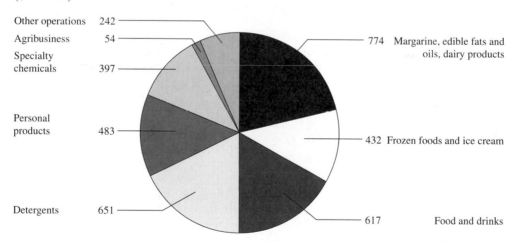

Other operations	242
Agribusiness	54
Specialty chemicals	397
Personal products	483
Detergents	651

774 Margarine, edible fats and oils, dairy products

432 Frozen foods and ice cream

617 Food and drinks

Unilever

In 1992, Unichema was a subsidiary of Unilever, one of the world's largest food and personal care companies. Total Unilever turnover (sales) in 1990 was $39.6 billion: 21 percent from detergents; 20 percent from margarines, dairy products, and edible oils; 16 percent from food and drinks; 13 percent from frozen foods and ice cream; 12 percent from personal products; 8 percent from specialty chemicals; and 10 percent from agribusiness and other operations. (Refer to Exhibit 1 for a breakdown of turnover by operations and operating profits.) Within specialty chemicals, the companies were National Starch, Quest International, Crosfield Chemical, and Unichema International (see Exhibit 2). The greater part of Unilever's business was in branded consumer goods primarily in the areas of foods, drinks, detergents, and personal products.

EXHIBIT 2

Unilever, Specialty Chemicals

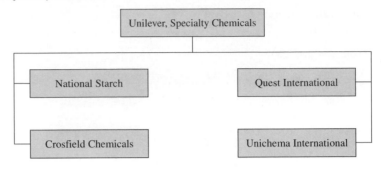

EXHIBIT 3

Unichema Production and Sales

Volume '000 tons

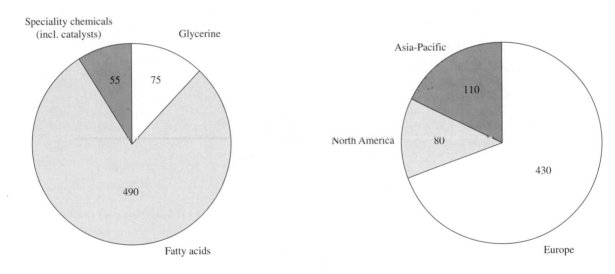

Unichema International

Unichema International, with headquarters in Gouda, the Netherlands, produced over half a million tons of oleochemicals yearly for customers worldwide (see Exhibit 3). Oleochemicals were derived from natural biodegradable oils and fats from vegetable or animal sources. They were environmentally friendly and very versatile products that could be used in a number of diverse applications. Oleochemicals were the starting point for the production of distilled and fractioned fatty acids, stearine, oleine, glycerine, and performance products like esters, amides, dimeric fatty acids, and soap noodles. Esters, among many other applications, were the basic raw materials for biodegradable synthetic lubricants. The oleochemical products produced by Unichema had a large application area—in polymers, cosmetics, rubber, textiles, leather, paper and lubricants. (Refer to Exhibit 4 for a list of products.) Unichema International produced these products in nine sites located on four continents. Unichema Chemie BV in Gouda was the largest of the production sites, employing approximately 430 people and host-

EXHIBIT 4

Unichema Products

Unilever, Specialty Chemicals	Performance Products
Glycerine	Polymer chemicals
Catalysts	Lubricants
Fatty acids	Personal care ingredients
Soap noodles	

ing an additional 120 employees who reported to the corporate center, also located on the site (development, marketing, etc.).

Unichema Chemie BV

The candle factory Gouda, established in 1858, used animal tallow for its stearines. This was the beginning of the activities on the site. After a merger with another candle factory in 1929, production of candles continued under the name of Gouda Apollo. Gradually, from this base in tallow processing for the manufacture of candle wax and wool smoothing oil, a modern oleochemical process industry developed. In 1960, Unilever and the American company Emery Industries founded Unilever-Emery, with Gouda Apollo becoming the center of the joint venture. This venture subsequently developed several unique processes and products. In 1980, Unilever took over Emery's share and adopted its present name, Unichema Chemie BV, 100 percent owned by Unilever. Production of candles ceased in 1983; in 1992 the company produced over 200 industrial oleochemical products, which were sold throughout the world.

The Oleochemical Industry

The oleochemical industry was being affected by globalization and a concentration within the industry itself. Tightening legislation with regard to product liability, environmental issues, and high operating fixed-cost levels resulted in declining overall industry profitability. Pressure was also being exercised by overcapacity and imports of low-priced materials from Southeast Asian producers. Refer to Exhibit 5 for a five-year view of European prices.

The European oleochemical industry produced more than one-third of all global oleochemical products in 1991. Large multinational groups were the leading producers in the industry, although there were still some small and highly specialized producers with a strong market niche. From a strategic point of view, the European industry was concentrating on a two-pronged approach. The first was to develop alliances with companies in Asia that had access to low-cost supplies of oleochemical raw materials. The second was to accelerate the degree of sophistication in developing new product derivatives and process technology, delivering total quality and service, and exploiting market desires for natural and biodegradable products. Future success was believed to depend on company flexibility and a strong technological base to optimize opportunities.

The Need for Efficiencies

Customer demands and market pressures were forcing the oleochemical industry participants to become more competitive and more responsive to customer requirements.

EXHIBIT 5

Fatty Acid and Glycerine Prices, Europe (1985 = 100)

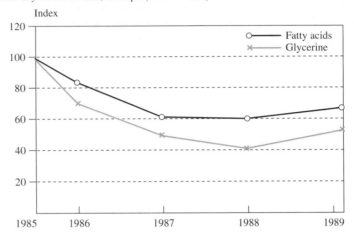

Customers were demanding lower prices, shorter lead times on deliveries, precise timings for deliveries, better quality, and increased reliability over time. Oleochemical manufacturers increasingly found themselves in a position where they had to provide better response to customers, with lower prices, while maintaining and improving their own businesses.

Just-in-Time

The concept of just-in-time (JIT) was being adopted by more and more manufacturers to enhance efficiencies in their manufacturing environments. The ultimate objectives of JIT were zero inventory, zero lead time, zero failures, enhanced flow processes, flexible manufacturing, and elimination of waste. Cost savings were achieved through reduction in the manufacturing cycle time, reduction in inventories, reduction in labor costs, reduction in space requirements, reduction in quality costs, reduction in transaction costs, and reduction in material costs. JIT implementation affected all areas of manufacturing planning and control systems, as well as redefining manufacturing processes and how performance was evaluated.

Pressures on Unichema

All of these forces led Unichema managers to a fundamental evaluation of how they were conducting their business. From a financial point of view, there was increasing pressure to maximize return on assets. The push to maximize profits, the narrowing of profit margins, increasing competition in the marketplace, and relatively flat sales necessitated that Unichema become more efficient. Analysis by the logistics and financial departments targeted material costs and investments in inventories as areas where *real* savings could be achieved. This targeting soon focused on areas in logistics planning and inventory control, where greater efficiencies could lead to cost savings. However, more than cost savings were required to achieve the desired financial return. After considerable analysis, Mr. Löwik and his management team became convinced that cost cutting could raise the return on assets by about 6 to 7 percent, but the goal was a 15 percent increase. This would only be possible with an improvement in market conditions. In other words, to reach the ultimate goal, cost cutting would not be sufficient. It was necessary to become more customer driven—to increase volume and/or provide new products and services to the customers. In determining how best to meet these new demands, Unichema realized that it was necessary to have a greater understanding of the customers' business needs, their product needs, and their information needs.

Capacity Utilization

Unichema had invested significantly in new equipment over the last five years. The primary reason for the investments was to provide higher quality, more specialized products (with higher margins). Capital investments in the chemical industry typically were for large chunks of capacity, considerably in excess of present market requirements. The expectation was that new business would be attracted before long, thus utilizing the capacity at higher levels.

This was clearly the situation at Unichema. Indeed, there was considerable pressure to, in fact, find the business to utilize the equipment and increase the return on the assets invested. Similarly, Unichema wanted to utilize its equipment as efficiently as possible in order to not only ensure but maximize the return on assets. Exhibit 6 shows the operating results for four ester production units in 1991. As can be seen, the maximum operating time for each of the four plants is 8,736 hours. From this amount, public holidays (and startup hours after holidays) need to be deducted, as well as hours for which there are no customer orders (ester units 1 and 4). The net result is then further reduced by various causes for lost capacity, both planned (standard) and actual. Logistical losses are the result of one piece of equipment in the ester production unit being idle while waiting for a batch of production to be completed in a previous or subsequent piece of equipment. The last row shows the overall variances (in hours) for each of the four ester units.

EXHIBIT 6

1991 Ester Unit Production

	Ester Unit # 1		Ester Unit # 2		Ester Unit # 3		Ester Unit # 4	
	Standard	*Actual*	*Standard*	*Actual*	*Standard*	*Actual*	*Standard*	*Actual*
Maximum operating time	8,736	8,736	8,736	8,736	8,736	8,736	8,736	8,736
Public holidays	192	225	192	255	192	232	192	241
Number of orders		1,178		0		0		1,413
Available capacity	8,544	7,333	8,544	8,481	8,544	8,504	8,544	7,082
Factory holidays	0	0	0	0	0	0	0	0
Planned overhaul	0	24	336	868	336	729	281	310
Variety changes	468	685	133	523	133	335	218	577
Breakdowns	126	1049	124	288	124	261	125	433
Logistical losses	678	1,163	682	684	682	907	678	641
Achieved capacity	7,272	4,412	7,269	6,118	7,269	6,272	7,242	5,121
Variance (Standard − Actual)	−2,860		−1,151		−997		−2,121	

Unichema's Response

Having determined that achieving efficiencies depended on the plant becoming more customer driven and less production driven, Unichema set out to identify areas where changes could be effected. In doing so, upper management consciously tried to support changes that drove a customer orientation within the company. The biggest change affected the areas of production, logistics, sales, and customer service. Production—which had traditionally driven the company—became a secondary process, while logistics assumed a primary function. In real terms, this meant that the logistics department dealt directly with the customers and established a process whereby customer needs determined production runs. The process created a major shift in company priorities as well as in the functions of various departments.

Logistics, Production, and Sales

In the new system, the logistics department assumed a coordinating role between the customer and production. Logistics served sales and production served logistics, which enabled customer needs to drive the manufacturing process. However, this change in orientation also forced a change in the traditional role of the sales force. Sales had historically provided the major, and sometimes the only, contact between the customer and the company. Under the new system, logistics assumed the role of providing customer service on a day-to-day basis, interacting directly with customers to determine their specific needs and the exact timing of these needs. This information was essential if economies were to be obtained in the production cycle with minimal inventory levels. Knowing what products customers needed and the times at which they needed these products enabled production to schedule the most efficient production runs. This approach, in effect, created the heart of the new program.

Close order coupling of customer needs and production schedules were one cornerstone of Unichema's response. But it was not the only one. Many just-in-time fundamentals were also implemented. Attempts to reduce changeover times were another part of these efforts. In ester production, for example, there were four ester units, which were somewhat interchangeable. But ester 1, which had been recently built, had twice the capacity of each of the ester units 2, 3, and 4. One of the remaining units was dedicated to additives for edible products, and one other unit was being focused toward smaller lots and faster changeovers. It was believed that achieving high flexibility in this unit would allow the others to be run at maximum effectiveness.

Other aspects of a JIT philosophy were also being pursued. Total quality management was being adopted with a goal of zero mistakes, minimum variability, and no surprises. Formulations were being made more exact so that processing times could be better predicted. Workers were being cross-trained to be able to take on more job activities, particularly in a grouping (or cell) of equipment that produced a "family" of products. Other changes in work practices combined activities formerly done by staff personnel—such as maintenance and quality inspection—with "direct labor" activities.

After the new logistics process changed the role of the sales team—removing them from day-to-day customer service—it gave them an opportunity to concentrate on fostering partnerships and helping customers identify new product areas where Unichema could provide research and development as well as other kinds of support. One example of this kind of arrangement occurred with a customer that specialized in environmentally friendly personal care products. Unichema and the customer developed a relationship where it was Unichema—with its extensive knowledge of oleochemicals—instead of the customer that provided the basic research and development. The customer's role was to determine what properties would be desirable in the products rather than how to best achieve those properties. However, resistance to the partnership concept with logistics managing day-to-day interactions was strong in some parts of the sales department. One of the salespeople stated:

> Although I realize that customers want shorter and shorter delivery times, I believe that the sales team should manage day-to-day contact and maintain order responsibility with the customers. I do not like logistics assuming the lead role in this area. If I am going to establish a partnership with my customers, I cannot let someone else come between me and my customer.

Data Processing

Through JIT and logistics, changes at Unichema also depended on a more fully automated plant, enhanced technical processes, foolproof operations, and an upgraded computer control system. This was seen as an ongoing effort. Many of the computer programs had to be changed and adapted to reflect those changes. The software was crucial for running production units efficiently—in order to more closely couple plant scheduling with actual customer needs—and for providing the data necessary to analyze and self-correct problems occurring on the production floor. Moreover, data were generated that tied into finance and pinpointed specific areas where cost savings might be achieved.

Personnel

Implementing Unichema's response created changes in the way people did their jobs as well as changes in the personnel department in terms of performance measures and job descriptions. Performance measures, which had traditionally been based on costs associated with producing the product, now had to place a value on better responsiveness to customer needs. Moreover, the old distinction between direct and indirect labor costs became less important in the new environment. At the same time, customer satisfaction measures came to be increasingly important in evaluating how successfully individuals and the company were performing. Personnel evaluation and career development needed to reflect these new directions, and performance measures had to be changed to correspond to the new priorities.

Job functions and roles also changed under the JIT system. Functions became more flexible. Enhancement of the computer system reduced dependence on the human element. The personnel manager stated:

> We need to focus more on quality and product predictability, which will change the way we define specific jobs.

Partnerships

The initiation of better responses to customer requirements enabled the company to identify other areas where changes had to occur. In order to become more customer driven, Unichema had to consider all areas that made an impact on its ability to deliver the correct products to its customers in a timely fashion. As an example, one area where Unichema had to excel was in shipping the products exactly as the customer wished. The products had to arrive on time, in good condition, and the drivers had to be able to take the products through customs in a number of different countries. Since Unichema contracted with haulers, one way to ensure that the best tariffs were obtained and the best service delivered was to form partnerships with a select number of haulers. This enabled Unichema to establish a mutual relationship where both partners focused on the customer. Unichema began to evaluate trucker complaints on a yearly basis, and to monitor and set standards of cleanliness in the trucks being used. Based on these measures, Unichema was able to improve shipping performance to customers.

Unichema was even more interested in forming partnerships with certain customers. By knowing precisely how each customer was using its products, Unichema could tailor the products (solutions) to individual customer problems more effectively. Moreover, these partnerships allowed Unichema to understand which product features/parameters were most critical to particular customers.

Unichema also worked to establish partnerships with suppliers so that joint problem solving could be achieved. These partnerships included sharing information on production schedules, anticipated needs, critical parameters, and problems at Unichema that might be jointly addressed.

The partnership program allowed Unichema to serve customer needs better as well as establish efficiencies in costs and in the production cycle. Working with a limited number of customers, suppliers, vendors, and haulers enabled Unichema to develop better production schedules, integrate with actual customer needs, and coordinate logistics. Dealing directly with customers so as to fully understand their needs and problems in product, packaging, delivery, and service areas allowed Unichema to produce more products to order instead of stocking them in anticipation of order, thus saving time and inventory holding costs and enhancing the production cycle.

The importance of fully understanding customer needs involved truly knowing how the customer used the product. Mr Löwik gave an example:

> A long-standing customer had been receiving regular shipments of a product in a color that required special and costly production runs. One day a production run resulted in the product being produced in an off-spec color. Due to time constraints and customer time demands, the product was sent to the customer. However, I became concerned and decided to visit the customer to apologize for the off-spec product color. I discovered that the customer used this particular product in a waste water treatment plant and was totally unconcerned about its color. Had the customer's business been better understood in the first place, the product could have been made in a regular production run, saying changeover time and money.

In an effort to further strengthen its relationship with customers, Unichema developed a Partnership Evaluation Program. This program involved development of a booklet for each customer in which specific needs and requirements were defined. The sales team then used the booklet with customers to further develop joint problem solving. The booklet was part of the companywide quality drive directed toward providing improved service and products for customers.

ABC Analysis

Unichema recently developed an ABC analysis of its customers and products. ABC, or Pareto, analysis was based on the idea that a minority of the customers typically comprised a majority of the sales.[1]

The ABC analysis for Unichema *customers* found that, in 1992, the firm had approximately 250 customers. Of these, the top 50 (20 percent) accounted for more than 80 percent of sales. Purchases of the next 50 customers amounted to an additional 15 percent,

---

[1]The concept was widely applied:
- In quality management, a few defects account for the majority of the scrap.
- A minute percentage of a university's alumni donate the vast proportion of alumni gifts.
- 20 percent of the beer drinkers consume more than 80 percent of the beer in many countries.

Exhibit 7

Sample ABC Analysis of Customers (10 Percent Sample)

Customer Number	1992 Total Purchases (Guilders)
Customer Class A	
1	3,548
2	1,072
3	513
4	320
5	216
Customer Class B	
6	115
7	91
8	75
9	55
10	42
Customer Class C	
11	31
12	26
13	20
14	14
15	9
16	6
17	5
18	3
19	2
20	1
21	1
22	1
23	0
24	0
25	0

while the remaining 150 customers accounted for only 5 percent of the annual sales. Unichema was attempting to form partnerships with the first 50 ("A") customers, providing special services and actively trying to promote joint problem solving. Exhibit 7 shows a 10 percent sample of the 250 Unichema customers.

The ABC analysis for *products* found that Unichema produced 61 major products: 16 of these accounted for 80 percent of the total sales in 1991. Another 11 accounted for the next 15 percent, while the remaining 34 products comprised the last 5 percent of sales. Exhibit 8 provides an abbreviated version of Unichema's product ABC analysis. As shown, the 1992 sales (in tons) are not completely consistent with the earlier ABC classification (e.g., product 6, an A product, was not purchased in 1992).

Three Challenges

Unichema, like many companies throughout the world, was faced with increasing competition, shrinking markets, global customers, and changing technology. These forces pushed the management to reevaluate the way in which the company was being run both internally and externally. Although strides had been made in understanding the

Exhibit 8

ABC Analysis of Products

	Customer Class Buying	1992 Tons
A Products		
1	A, B	2,890
2	A, C	867
3	A, B, C	1,686
4	A	1,572
5	A, C	406
6	A, B	0
7	A	1,256
8	A	1,080
9	A, B, C	821
10	A	1,161
11	A	789
12	A, B	629
13	A	287
14	A, C	357
15	A, B, C	408
16	A	272
B Products		
17	A, C	394
18	A, C	238
19	A	297
20	A	255
21	A	204
22	A	340
23	A, C	17
24	A	129
25	A, B	294
26	A	17
27	A, C	141
C Products		
28	C	212
29	A, B	102
30	A, C	68
31	A, C	54
32	A, B	43
33	A	0
34	A, C	177
35	A	54
36	C	1,836
37	C	26
38	C	680
39	B	9
40	B, C	17
41	A	9
42	A, C	0
43	A	340
44	A, C	0
45	C	0
46	C	0
47	A, C	17
48	A, B	0
49	A, B	2

Exhibit 8 *(continued)*

	Customer Class Buying	1992 Tons
50	B	0
51	C	0
52	C	0
53	C	0
54	C	0
55	B, C	0
56	C	0
57	C	0
58	C	0
59	C	0
60	C	0
61	C	0

customer, it was evident that further understanding of customers' businesses was necessary. This would necessitate greater involvement of the technical staff with customers, further complicating the roles of the sales team and the technical personnel. With changes occurring in customer businesses as well, Unichema also had to be responsive to changing product needs and prepared to provide increasing research and development support for customers. Cost pressures and stagnant markets put pressure on Unichema's customers that, in turn, affected Unichema.

As customers demanded totally reliable products delivered on time, Unichema was faced with continuous improvement of technology, better evaluation of the fit between products and markets, elimination of all mistakes, and a quicker response based on techniques such as reduced changeover times. At the same time, logistics (and production scheduling) managers were faced with the challenge of utilizing equipment as effectively as possible in order to maximize the return on assets. All of these issues required new solutions. However, better software programs were leading to better problem definitions and the development of improved solutions. Automated data collation in the factory was being tied to financial numbers that could pinpoint problem areas to be targeted for cost savings. In addition, logistics was now the lead contact with customers, undertaking sales activities that encompassed more than just typical order taking. The underlying objective was to become very knowledgeable in helping customers define *their* needs and how Unichema could meet them more effectively.

As noted earlier, partnerships were increasingly important in providing a network for meeting customer requirements. Establishing exclusive relationships with customers, suppliers, vendors, and so on, led to a further redefinition of personnel functions within the company. But these relationships were expensive in terms of employee time and effort. Specific people needed to be deployed to specific customer partnerships. Unichema wanted to achieve a good return from these partnership efforts. With exclusive relationships, the role of the sales team in particular underwent a transformation. The traditional role of order taking and problem identification became institutionalized within other divisions, such as logistics. Unichema wanted to target its sales efforts for maximum effectiveness. Attracting new customers became increasingly difficult in an environment where many of the large competitors had already established partnership relationships. Unichema needed to find ways to overcome these hurdles— while, at the same time, making them even greater for their competitors.

Unichema sought to establish its own partnerships in a timely fashion, to develop unique partnership features that customers would find attractive, and to make those partnerships ever more impervious to competitive actions.

The Assignment

Jan Löwik was pleased with the progress made to date and wanted to build on this base of accomplishments. His first thoughts for the group were:

> I think we have been doing a great job and we should all be proud of our accomplishments. But now is not the time to sit back and relax. We need to redouble our efforts and link the various individual efforts in ways that will achieve even greater synergies. Let me hear your views on how to accomplish this goal.

CASE 3

L. L. BEAN, INC.

L. L. Bean, Inc., a specialty-merchandise direct marketer based in Freeport, Maine, was founded in 1912 by Leon L. Bean. An avid outdoorsman, Bean started the company bearing his name when he acquired a mailing list of Maine hunting-license holders and began advertising a superior, lightweight dry boot, the "Maine hunting shoe." In the initial three-page brochure promoting the boot, Bean guaranteed "perfect satisfaction in every way." The beginnings of a company founded on product quality and superior service were established.

In the following years, L. L. Bean has grown into a company that mails over 150 million catalogs yearly (including 50 different catalogs), and whose annual sales in 1998 were over $1.03 billion. Catalogs are seasonal and range from full catalogs presenting the entire product line to specialty catalogs, including hunting, fly fishing, sporting goods, and home furnishings. Over the last 20 years or so, L. L. Bean's sales have grown at rates that have far exceeded average growth rates in the mail order business generally. Between 1965 and 1979, the company grew at an average annual rate of 30 to 35 percent. The late 1980s saw growth rates in the range of 20 to 25 percent, and the figures for the early 1990s were in the range of 17 to 18 percent. Overall sales increased from a total of $850 million in 1993 to the figure quoted above for year 1998.

In order to meet customer demand, L. L. Bean stocks more than 16,000 different items for sales through the catalogs, retail and factory stores, and its website. To support this variety of different items, L. L. Bean manages a total of approximately 100,000 stock-keeping units (SKUs). More than 11 million packages were shipped to

---

Note: The background material on L. L. Bean, Inc., is based on, but has been revised significantly from, the content of a case study that appeared in Bernard J. La Londe, Martha C. Cooper, and Thomas G. Noordewier, *Customer Service: A Management Perspective* (Oak Brook, IL: Council of Logistics Management, 1988), pp. 117–20. The content of this document has been updated from information in publicly available materials from L. L. Bean, Inc., and from the company's website at <www.llbean.com>.

customers during 1998, with 199,196 shipped on the busiest day, December 11. All incoming and outgoing packages are processed through the Order Fulfillment Center, in Freeport, Maine, which at peak season employs 2,800 people.

Product/Service Philosophy

L. L. Bean competes with companies ranging from general merchandise direct marking giants (such as Nordstrom, J. C. Penney, and Sears) to a host of specialty direct marketers (such as Lands' End, Eddie Bauer, Orvis, Lillian Vernon, and The Gap). In 1995, L. L. Bean launched its own website, www.llbean.com, and in 1996, offered online commerce. The company experiences competition from a growing number of e-commerce retailers carrying similar product lines, some of which are new ventures of traditional retail firms. L. L. Bean's main retail store is in Freeport, Maine, while factory stores are located in Maine, New Hampshire, Delaware, and Oregon. In 1992, L. L. Bean opened a retail store in Tokyo, Japan, through a partnership with the Seiyu, Ltd., and Matsushita Electric Industrial Company. The company now has over 20 retail stores in Japan. L. L. Bean's catalog and store operations are supported by its distribution facilities located either in or close to Freeport, including Portland, Brunswick, Lewiston, and Waterville, Maine. The company's main retail store, in Freeport, Maine, has nearly 109,000 square feet of selling space and attracts 3.5 million visitors a year. The new L. L. Kids Store, adjacent to the flagship retail store, attracted more than 680,000 visitors in 1998.

The heart of L. L. Bean's success has been the company's dual philosophy of premium quality in both product and service. Informally, this philosophy is embodied by what is referred to as "L. L. Bean's Golden Rule":

> Sell good merchandise at a reasonable profit, treat your customers like human beings, and they'll always come back for more.

Formally, the quality product/service philosophy finds expression in L. L. Bean's statement of corporate purpose:

> To market high-quality recreational products of the best functional value directly to outdoor-oriented consumers with the kind of superior personal service we would like to receive. We will fulfill this mission in a productive and efficient manner, consistent with our total quality management principles.

Customer Service

Although product quality is a key to the success of L. L. Bean, the company's ability to attract and retain customers is a direct result of Bean's emphasis on customer service (e.g., "treat your customers like human beings," "provide superior personal service"). At the the heart of Bean's service is its "100 percent guarantee." All products sold by the company come with an unconditional guarantee of satisfaction. If for any reason a customer is dissatisfied with a product, L. L. Bean pledges to replace it or refund the purhcase price. In fact the L. L. Bean guarantee is as follows:

> Our products are guaranteed to give 100 percent satisfaction in every way. Return anything purchased from us at any time if it proves otherwise. We will replace it, refund your purchase price, or credit your credit card, as you wish. We do not want you to have anything from L. L. Bean that is not completely satisfactory.

At the company's Maine-based Customer Satisfaction Department, multilingual representatives are available 24 hours a day, 365 days a year. In addition to assisting customers with questions regarding order status, returns, and special requests, customer satisfaction representatives provide checklists of outdoor gear and apparel for specific needs. In 1998, the company received more than 15 million toll-free catalog and customer service calls. During its busiest week in 1998, the order department at L. L. Bean received more than 800,000 calls, with 148,506 calls coming on the single busiest day, December 7. In 1998, L. L. Bean added customer services to its website, including monogramming, engraving, pant alterations, gift boxes and cards, and multiple forms of payment.

L. L. Bean handles product returns from its customers at its special product returns facility in Freeport, Maine. Most returns are because the products received are the wrong size. A large portion of the company's shipping is via Federal Express, to ensure the fastest delivery. L. L. Bean ships to all foreign countries except Cuba and North Korea.

Questions

1. Based on the information contained in the preceding paragraphs, and on your own observations, what do you feel are the most essential "customer requirements" that must be met by L. L. Bean?
2. For each of the requirements identified above pertaining to customer service, please suggest an appropriate "example measurement" that could be used to determine whether the requirement is/is not being met. Be sure to carefully define your measurement needs, and to consider a strategy for acquiring the needed measurement information. What do you feel might be a reasonable "target value" for each of the measurements you select?

L. L. Bean, Inc.
Customer Service: Key Measurements

Customer Requirements	Example Measurements	Target Values

3. What further information do you feel that executives at L. L. Bean would want to have before making the final determination of high-priority customer needs, and the specific measurement strategies associated with each?

CASE 4

METALCO: THE SAP PROPOSAL

On March 23, 1996, the senior executives (known as the G14 group) of Metalco Inc. gathered in Perth, Western Australia, for their regular quarterly meeting. A number of items were on the agenda for the meeting, but one in particular had garnered most of the attention on this day. The specific item was a $23.5 million proposal for a new, companywide integrated management information system (the IMI project) supplied by SAP AG. The project was being championed by Andrew Murray, the general manager of Western Australian Operations (see Exhibit 1).

Metalco was established in Australia in 1933. It is controlled and owned predominantly by Australians, and is one of Australia's largest enterprises. Metalco produces a traditional range of mineral products with relatively low-value-added content. Its main business is the discovery, development, production, and processing of minerals and petroleum, with particular emphasis on nickel and gold. The 1995 sales revenue was just over $2.2 billion Australian dollars (AUS) with assets of AUS $6.0 billion (Exhibit 2). The company has approximately 6,300 employees, including contractors. Operations are primarily in Australia with some interests overseas.

Under four executive directors, the corporation is organized as three relatively autonomous business units, with a small corporate office. Lloyd Jones is the managing director. The operations personnel reported to Keith Smythe, the executive director of operations. The primary operating units are Western Australian Operations (WA Ops), Metalco Americas, and Eastern Australian Operations (EA Ops), each of which is run by a general manager. WA Ops and Metalco Americas each contains many individual operations—mines, smelters, and refineries—with WA Ops having by far the most. The corporate staff groups are responsible to Don Matheson, the executive director of finance. Exploration personnel report to Roy Woodside, the executive director of exploration. The executive team (the G14) consists of the managing director, the executive directors, and the general managers.

Metalco grew significantly during the 1980s, a consequence of its exploration successes in the 1960s and 1970s, and had been very profitable for several years. There was a high corporate value placed on exploration excellence. In contrast to this commitment to exploration, technical and operational innovation had not been as highly valued. The company was very conservative with respect to technical choices for new plant and equipment. Metalco's mineral processing and process control technologies lagged the state of the art by a number of years in most operations. While some mines were highly

Elspeth Murray prepared this case under the supervision of Professor Sid Huff solely to provide material for class discussion. The authors do not intend to illustrate either effective or ineffective handling of a managerial situation. The authors may have disguised certain names and other identifying information to protect confidentiality.

mechanized and efficient, others were not. Research and development spending was a small proportion of revenues as was that for information systems. In fact, Metalco's information systems were generally acknowledged to be seriously lagging those of industry leaders.

In an attempt to remedy the information systems issue, Metalco had initiated a number of information systems projects in the early 1990s. These projects included:

- Better Use of Existing Systems Project—a project designed to get better use of the existing information systems (initiated by Finance).
- Removal of Bottlenecks Project—a project aimed at improving the turnaround time for management reporting (initiated by Finance).
- Workforce Management System—a completely new payroll and personnel system (initiated by Human Resources).
- Maintenance Management System Rewrite—a joint venture with another large Australia-based metals company to completely rewrite this core system to make it more user-friendly (initiated by joint venture partner).
- Communication Network Upgrade—a project to enable a client–server environment (initiated by Management Information Systems [MIS]).

But by far the largest and most ambitious of the projects initiated by Metalco to date was the Total Operations System (TOS) project, started up in 1992. The project was set up with the following objectives:

- To provide a set of standard definitions and procedures for relevant aspects of the business—to ensure that the information was recorded, analyzed, and reported consistently, and that effort was expended in the most economical way.
- To implement the system and procedures in a timely and efficient manner—this would take into account the physical implementation, end-user training, implementation support, and standard information.
- To assist in improving the timeliness of corporate reporting.
- To promote Metalco policies with respect to management information and reporting.

The original budget and time frame for companywide implementation of TOS were $5 million and two years, respectively. As of July 1, 1996, the system was fully operational at only one-third of the sites and had already cost Metalco $12 million. At those sites where the system was operational, there was widespread dissatisfaction with its performance. In fact Metalco's operations managers, who had never had much respect for Metalco's information systems (IS) group and its products, were openly comparing notes about which outside consulting firms they had engaged to fix up the TOS system in their own operations.

Metalco had recently reorganized the MIS group. Up until 1994, the MIS group had been a central corporate group responsible for setting the information technology (IT) strategy for Metalco as well as for building information systems within Metalco. The group had had a rocky history within Metalco and had never been able to recover fully from the reputation it earned in the early days of computing in the company, as being unable to deliver information systems on time or on budget. In January 1995, the head of the group, Des Hanson, resigned over a dispute with senior management over the future direction of information systems within Metalco. Hanson had generally advocated a strong, centralized IS group, while Jones maintained that such an organization had not been effective in the past.

Jones saw Hanson's resignation as an opportunity to radically change the MIS organization within Metalco. Responsibility for information systems was completely devolved into the operating groups, and the organization itself was decentralized, with former IS group employees becoming members of the various operations. A small corporate group was, however, retained to coordinate IS activities among the various operations and to set companywide standards. In addition to these structural changes, a new policy was put in place to ensure that Metalco would no longer build systems in-house. Packaged software solutions were the first choice, and if any custom software development was required, it would be done by a third party.

Despite the problems experienced with the TOS project, and indeed information systems in general within Metalco, Andrew Murray, the general manager of Western Australian Operations, felt confident that the project he was proposing—coined the Integrated Management Information (IMI) project—would not experience the same challenges. Murray acknowledged that the IMI project would introduce not only new ways of doing business but also new computer hardware and software to support these new ways. He felt, however, that the choice of SAP AG, globally the leading supplier of enterprisewide integrated information systems, as the software supplier would mitigate some of the risks associated with trying to introduce all of these things simultaneously. In any case, Murray felt that the benefits far outweighed the risks.

Not all the senior managers shared Murray's enthusiasm for the project, and the executive team had heard rumors of significant disagreement among the senior ranks. While no one disputed the importance of containing costs, several felt that the benefits of the proposed system in no way justified the $23.5 million price tag. Several plant executives believed that their existing information systems were already better than anything the IMI project could provide. Other managers expressed concern about Metalco's ability to successfully implement such a large system, and also about the ability of Metalco employees to actually use the system to its full potential if and when it actually became fully operational. In essence, they felt that $23.5 million would be better spent elsewhere. One senior manager was quite open in stating that he was going to have a very difficult time explaining to his operations managers that there was going to be significantly less money available for what he perceived to be important upgrades to existing production assets.

Despite these rumblings within the management group, Murray felt the up-front assessment for the project clearly identified the payoff for Metalco and the risks inherent in the project. Although the project team was still working on the details of the project plan, Murray had no doubts about the team's ability to deliver the new information systems on time and on budget. And just as important, Murray believed very strongly that the project was critical for taking Metalco into the 21st century and that proceeding with it was the right thing to do.

Exhibit 1

Memorandum to G14 Members

To:	All G14 Members
Date:	March 23, 1996
From:	A. D. Murray
Subject:	Proposal for Integrated Management Information (IMI) Project

The attached document outlines a proposal for a new enterprisewide information system for Metalco. In conjunction with an organizationwide review of our business processes, this new information system will enable Metalco to enter the next century as a low-cost producer.

We have conducted a thorough cost–benefit analysis as well as an assessment of the risks associated with this investment, and I am pleased to wholeheartedly endorse this proposal. A summary of our analyses is included in this document.

At a total cost of $23.5 million, this project represents a significant expenditure for Metalco. We believe, however, that it is critical to make this investment in our future now. Without it, we will have difficulty delivering on our primary strategic objective of becoming a lowest quartile cost producer by the year 2000.

As most of you are aware, the state of our information technology lags that of industry leaders such as BHP. Their low-cost position is instrumental in insulating their share price against the dip in metal prices we are currently experiencing. We believe their information systems are key to their continuing position as one of the lowest-cost producers.

I ask that you approve this proposal, to ensure that Metalco continues its strong financial performance.

Sincerely,

Andrew Murray
General Manager, WA Ops

Executive Project Summary
Integrated Management Information Project

Description

The IMI project represents a significant investment of information systems development resources for Metalco. In the past, Metalco has not invested heavily in information systems, and the IMI project represents a significant departure from past practices. In the past, Metalco has developed information systems on an operation-by-operation basis, with little attention paid to the sharing of information among the various operations. As a result, Metalco has 32 separate information systems within its operations, none of which can share information. There are no standard definitions across operations, and there is considerable duplication of effort in managing the data. In addition, the information systems are used primarily for reporting purposes and not for managing operations on a day-to-day basis. The IMI project has been initiated to rectify this situation. The specific objectives are:

Exhibit 1 *(continued)*

Executive Project Summary
Integrated Management Information Project *(continued)*

Objectives

- On-line, real-time, access to production data
- On-line, real-time, management reporting capability
- Standard definitions across operations

Preliminary Benefits

Tangible:
- $10M in labor savings over a 5-year period
- $50M in improved margins over a 5-year period

Intangible:
- Spearhead effort to become more business-like

Preliminary Cost Estimates

$23.5M—development

Project Scoring Synopsis

Category	Weight	×	Score	=	Weighted Score
Economic Impact	10		5.0		50
Strategic Match	2		4.0		8
Competitive Advantage	2		5.0		10
Management Information	2		5.0		10
Competitive Response	2		5.0		10
Organizational Risk	−1		1.0		−1
Strategic IS Architecture	3		5.0		15
Definitional Uncertainty	−2		2.0		−4
Technical Uncertainty	−2		4.0		−8
IS Infrastructure Risk	−2		5.0		−10
Final project score					80*

*See attached forms for details of project scoring.

G14 Action Requested

This synopsis represents an accurate estimate of the costs and benefits of implementing the proposed project, based on the preliminary requirements. Consideration by the G14 is requested.

_____
Mr. Jones
Managing Director

_____
Mr. Smythe
Executive—Operations

_____
Mr. Smythe
Executive Director—Operations

_____
Mr. Woodside
Executive Director—Exploration

Exhibit 1 *(continued)*

IMI Project Scoring Procedure

Economic Impact

	Development	Year 1	Year 2	Year 3	Year 4	Year 5
Cost	$23,500.00					
Benefit		$24,100.00	$11,695.00	$11,695.00	$11,695.00	$11,695.00
Total benefit	$70,880.00					
NPV @ 10%	$55,610.52					
Simple ROI	60.32%					

Economic Impact Score: 5

Note: The IMI project, when compared with other information systems investments, scored significantly higher than any others with respect to its financial benefits; therefore, the project received the top score of five points for economic impact.

Strategic Match

The strategic match score depends on the degree to which the proposed project corresponds to established strategic goals. Projects that are integral and a critical part of the organization's strategy will be assigned a higher strategic match score. Strategic Planning will list the strategic goals contained in the current plan for use by those scoring this category. The scoring is as follows:

Score	Description
0	The project has no direct or indirect relationship to the achievement of any stated organizational or departmental strategic goal.
1	The project has no direct or indirect relationship to the achievement of any stated organizational or departmental strategic goals, but will achieve greater operational efficiencies.
2	The project has no direct or indirect relationship to the achievement of any stated organizational or departmental strategic goals, but the project is a prerequisite system (a necessary precursor) to another system (or systems) that achieves a portion of a strategic goal.
3	The project has no direct or indirect relationship to the achievement of any stated organizational or departmental strategic goals, but the project is a prerequisite system (a necessary precursor) to another system (or systems) that does achieve a strategic goal.
4	The project directly achieves a portion of stated strategic goal.
5	The project directly achieves a stated strategic goal.

Strategic Match Score: 4

E<small>XHIBIT</small> **1** *(continued)*

Competitive Advantage

Competitive advantage scoring depends on the degree to which the proposed project directly, or indirectly, provides the organization with an increased ability to compete. For example, projects that provide information that increases the operations' ability to measurably decrease operating costs would be assigned a higher competitive advantage score.

Score	*Description*
0	The project does not support increased competitiveness of the organization. It has little or no impact on operating costs.
1	The project indirectly improves the competitive positions of the operating units by improving operating efficiencies. It has no impact on the effectiveness of the organization.
2	The project directly improves the competitive position of the organization by improving operating efficiencies in a key strategic area.
3	The project materially reduces operating costs so that the organization is marginally more competitive.
4	The project materially reduces operating costs so that the organization is moderately more competitive.
5	The project materially reduces operating costs so that the organization is substantially more competitive.

Competitive Advantage Score: 5

Management Information

The scoring in this category depends on the degree to which the project provides management information to managers and vice presidents that will allow them to assess their operations and make their function more effective in such a way that it materially benefits the organization. The score also depends on the extent to which this management information supports the organization's key activities.

Score	*Description*
0	The project is unrelated to management information support of core activities (MISCA).
1	The project is unrelated to MISCA, but does provide some data on functions that bear on core activities in the enterprise.
2	The project is unrelated to MISCA, but does provide information on functions that directly support core activities.
3	The project is unrelated to MISCA, but provides essential information identified as core activities. Such information is operational in character.
4	The project is essential to providing MISCA in the future.
5	The project is essential to providing MISCA in a current period.

Management Information Score: 5

Exhibit 1 *(continued)*

Competitive Response

The scoring in this category reflects the organizational risk of *not* undertaking this project.

Score	Description
0	The project can be postponed for at least 12 months without affecting competitive position; or existing systems and procedures can produce substantially the same result and will not affect competitive position.
1	The postponement of the project does not affect competitive position, and minimal labor costs are expected to be incurred to produce substantially the same result.
2	The postponement of the project does not affect competitive position; however, labor costs may escalate to produce substantially the same result.
3	If the project is postponed, the organization remains capable of responding to the needed change without affecting its competitive position; lacking the new system, the organization is not substantially hindered in its ability to respond rapidly and effectively to change in the competitive environment.
4	The postponement of the project may result in further competitive disadvantage to the enterprise; or in a loss of competitive opportunity; or existing successful activities in the enterprise may be curtailed because of the lack of the proposed system.
5	The postponement of the project will result in further competitive disadvantage to the enterprise; or in a loss of competitive opportunity; or existing successful activities in the enterprise must be curtailed because of the lack of the proposed system.

Competitive Response Score: 5

Organizational Risk

This category is rated on the degree to which the system is dependent on new or untested skills, management capabilities, and experience.

Score	Description
0	The business domain organization has a well-formulated plan for implementing the proposed system. Management is in place, and processes and procedures are documented. Contingency plans exist for the project, there is a project champion, and the product or competitive value added is well defined for a well-understood market.
1 through 4	Values for 1–4 may be adopted for situations that blend elements of preparedness with elements of risk. The following checklist can be used for this purpose.

	Yes	No	Not known
Well-formulated business domain plan	X		
Business domain management in place	X		
Contingency plans in place	X		
Processes and procedures in place		X	
Training for users planned	X		
Management champion exists	X		
Product is well defined		X	
Well-understood market need	X		

For each "no" or "not known," .5 point may be added.

Eʜɪʙɪᴛ 1 *(continued)*

Organizational Risk *(continued)*

5   The business domain organization has no plan for implementing the proposed system. Management is uncertain about responsibility. Processes and procedures have not been documented. No contingency plan is in place. There is no defined champion for the initiative. The product or competitive value added is not well defined. There is no well-understood market.

Organizational Risk Score: 1

Strategic IS Architecture

The scoring in this category reflects the degree to which the system is aligned with the IS and IT strategy, as reflected by the IS and IT blueprints.

Score	Description
0	The proposed project is unrelated to the blueprint.
1	The proposed project is a part of the blueprint, but its priorities are not defined.
2	The proposed project is a part of the blueprint, and has a low dollar payout; it is not a prerequisite to other blueprint projects, nor is it closely linked to other prerequisite projects.
3	The proposed project is an integral part of the blueprint and has medium dollar payoff; it is not a prerequisite to other blueprint projects, but is loosely linked to other prerequisite projects.
4	The proposed project is an integral part of the blueprint and has a high dollar payoff; it is not a prerequisite to other blueprint projects, but is closely linked to other prerequisite projects.
5	The proposed project is an integral part of the blueprint and is one that is to be implemented first; it is a prerequisite project to other blueprint projects.

Strategic IS Architecture Score: 5

Definitional Uncertainty

This category measures the degree to which the specifications for the project are ill-defined and/or unapproved.

Score	Description
0	Requirements are firm and approved. Specifications are firm and approved. Investigated area is straightforward. High probability of no changes.
1	Requirements are moderately firm. Specifications are moderately firm. No formal approvals. Investigated area is straightforward. Low probability of nonroutine changes.
2	Requirements are moderately firm. Specifications are moderately firm. Investigated area is straightforward. Reasonable probability of nonroutine changes.
3	Requirements are moderately firm. Specifications are moderately firm. Investigated area is straightforward. Changes are almost certain and close to immediately.
4	Requirements are not firm. Specifications are not firm. Area is quite complex. Changes are almost certain, even during the project period.
5	Requirements are unknown. Specifications are unknown. Area may be quite complex. Changes may be ongoing, but the key here is unknown requirements.

Definitional Uncertainty Score: 2

Technical Uncertainty

This category measures the degree to which the system is dependent on new or untested skills, hardware, software and systems.

Skills Required
1. No new skills for staff, management. Both have experience.
2. Some new skills for staff, none for management.
3. Some new skills required for staff and management.
4. Some new skills required for staff, extensive for management.
5. Extensive new skills required for staff, some for management.
6. Extensive new skills required for staff and management.

Hardware Dependencies
1. Hardware is in use in a similar application.
2. Hardware is in use, but this is a different application.
3. Hardware exists and has been tested, but not operationally.
4. Hardware exists, but not utilized yet within organization.
5. Some key features are not tested or implemented.
6. Key requirements are not now available in MIS configuration.

Software Dependencies (other than application software)
1. Standard software, or straightforward or no programming required.
2. Standard software is used, but complex programming is required.
3. Some new interfaces between software are required, and complex programming may be required.
4. Some new features are required in operating software; some complex interfaces between software may be required.
5. Features not now supported are needed, and moderate advances in local state of the art are required.
6. Significant advances in the state of the art are required.

Application Software
1. Programs exist with minimal modifications required.
2. Programs are available commercially with minimal modifications, or programs available in-house with moderate modifications, or software will be developed in-house with minimal complexity.
3. Programs are available commercially with moderate modifications, or in-house programs are available but modifications are extensive, or software will be developed in-house with minimal design complexity but with moderate programming complexity.
4. Software is available commercially but the complexity is high, or software will be developed in-house and the difficulty is moderate.
5. No package or current in-house software exists. Complex design and programming are required, with moderate difficulty.
6. No package or current in-house software exists. Complex design and programming is required, even if contracted outside.

Skills required	5
Hardware dependencies	5
Software dependencies	3
Application software	3
Total	16

Technical Uncertainty Score: 16/4 = 4

EXHIBIT 1 *(continued)*

IS Infrastructure Risk

The score in this category depends on the degree to which technology domain investment in other prerequisite service or environmental facilities is required.

Score	Description
0	The system uses existing services and facilities. No investment in IS prerequisite facilities (e.g., database management) is required; no up-front costs not directly a part of the project itself are anticipated.
1	Change in one element of the computer service delivery system is required for this project. The associated up-front investment other than direct project costs is relatively small.
2	Small changes in several elements of the computer service delivery system are required. Some up-front investment is necessary to accommodate this project. Some later investment for subsequent integration of this project into the mainstream of the IS environment may be necessary.
3	Moderate changes in several elements of the computer service delivery system are required. Some up-front investment is necessary to accommodate this project; some later investment for subsequent integration of this project into the mainstream of the IS environment will be necessary.
4	Moderate changes in elements of computer service delivery are required, in multiple areas. Moderate to high up-front investment in staff, software, hardware, and management is necessary to accommodate the project. This investment is not included in the direct project cost, but represents IS facilities investment to create the needed environment for the project.
5	Substantial change in elements of computer service delivery is required, in multiple areas. Considerable up-front investment in staff, software, hardware, and management is necessary to accommodate the project. This investment is not included in the direct project cost, but represents IS facilities investment to create the needed environment for the project.

IS Infrastructure Score: 5

Exhibit 2

Consolidated P&L accounts ($ Millions)

	1995	1994
Operating revenue	2242.5	1697.2
Operating profit (loss) before abnormal items:		
Group	433.9	127.8
Associated bodies corporate	0	0
	433.9	127.8
Abnormal items	0	(0.7)
Operating profit (loss) before income tax:		
Group	433.9	127.1
Associated bodies corporate	0	0
	433.9	127.1
Income tax (charge) credit attributable to operating profit including abnormal items:		
Group	(109.8)	(3.5)
Associated bodies corporate	0	0
Abnormal income tax (charge)/credit		
Group	(18.6)	5.8
Associated bodies corporate	0	0
	(128.4)	9.3
Operating profit after income tax	305.5	136.4
Outside equity interests in operating (profits) losses and extraordinary items after income tax	(7.5)	(4.4)
Operating profit and extraordinary items after income tax attributable to members of Metalco Inc.	298	132
Retained profits at the beginning of the financial year		
Group	186	132.4
Associated bodies corporate	0	0
	186	132.4
Total available for appropriation	484	264.4
Dividends provided for or paid	(221.9)	(78.4)
Retained profits at the end of the financial year		
Group	262.1	186
Associated bodies corporate	0	0
	262.1	186
Basic earnings per share	26.9 cents	13.2 cents
Basic earnings per share before abnormal	28.6 cents	12.6 cents
Capital expenditures	613	769

GILES LABORATORIES

Paul McNaughton, director of distribution services for Giles Laboratories, a wholly owned subsidiary of the worldwide Thurber Pharmaceutical group of companies, was under strong pressure from top management to reduce the number of field warehouses that the company maintained throughout the United States. Top management believed that the company could manage on fewer distribution facilities without hurting sales operations. They were concerned about Giles having more warehouses than the parent company even though the parent carried more products at a higher unit-sales volume. They were also disturbed by the fact that Giles' main competitor had fewer warehouses giving the same national market coverage.

At the beginning of 1996, Giles Laboratories had 37 field warehouses, of which 33 were public. Four warehouses were owned by the parent company, but contractual arrangements with them paralleled those with public warehouses. In addition to the 37 field warehouses, Giles owned four plant warehouses that served the field warehouses and customers located in areas where these plant warehouses were situated.

By March 1996, McNaughton was faced with the decision to phase out the public warehouse at Columbus, Ohio, and serve the customers in the area directly from the main plant warehouse at Indianapolis, Indiana. This meant extending the service area of the Indianapolis facility beyond Dayton, Ohio. The contract with the Columbus warehouse was up for renewal in mid-April.

Thurber Pharmaceuticals

Giles was part of a group of companies that was controlled by Thurber Pharmaceuticals. Although the parent corporation specialized in a variety of prescription drugs, the products of the subsidiary companies ranged from food items to consumer sundries.

Each subsidiary operated as an autonomous corporate entity with its own set of executive officers and was relatively free to set its own policies in marketing, research, and manufacturing activities. Control by Thurber took the form of broad intercorporate policies and close monitoring of significant investment decisions. With the exception of the products of one or the subsidiary companies, an international division supervised the manufacture and marketing of all products in foreign countries.

Background on Giles Laboratories

Giles and its major competitor enjoyed about 75 percent of the nutrient and dietary-food market, with Giles' share of the total market approximately 40 percent.

Product Lines

The company manufactured 35 variations of one basic mixture of raw materials, and product differences were determined primarily by additives and calorie content. Finished products came in both a liquid concentrate and a powder packed in cans of

---

This case was made possible by the cooperation of a business firm that remains anonymous. It was written by Albert M. Ladores under the direction of Bernard J. La Londe of the faculty of Marketing and Logistics, The Ohio State University. Revised by Douglas M. Lambert.

various sizes. The Indianapolis plant, which was the largest and oldest of the company's four plants, produced 25 items of the product line. Each of the other plants manufactured as many of 12 of the products.

Sales Operations

Approximately 90 percent of the company's sales were derived from consumer outlets, the most significant of which were department stores, wholesale drug houses, drug chains, and supermarket chains. The balance was sold directly to hospitals for patient use while recovering from illness. Demand for the company's products was not subject to seasonal variations.

Salespeople concentrated their selling efforts on medical practitioners, hospitals, and the major retail outlets. Their function was to promote product awareness by improving the sales distribution of the product lines and to assist retailers in merchandising. With minor exceptions, they did not act as order takers.

Distribution Organization

Mr. McNaughton, as the company's director of distribution services, reported to the vice president of operations and shared the same rank and status as the comptroller and the director of manufacturing. He had responsibility for four major areas: distribution, operations planning, purchasing, and production planning, each headed by a manager reporting directly to him. The director had control over most of the logistics functions with the exceptions of plant shipping and receiving, which were the responsibility of each plant manager, who reported to the director of manufacturing.

All of the distribution personnel were located at the company's central headquarters in Indianapolis. The coordination of receiving and shipping activities at the plants was accomplished by the plant manager.

Distribution Policies and Practices

Giles Laboratories followed their traditional practice of distributing all products through public warehouses, which was in direct contrast to the parent company's system of ownership and control of warehouses. However, efforts had been initiated by Giles to determine the utility of continuing with its system of dealing exclusively with public warehouses.

Giles currently owned four plant warehouses, dealt with four warehouses owned by the parent company, and, as mentioned, maintained 33 public warehouses specializing in grocery products and servicing other companies in the grocery trade. In no instance did Giles totally occupy the leased space of a specific field warehouse, and individual field warehouse allocation ranged from 3,000 to 100,000 hundredweight. Giles did not share a public warehouse with any of its sister companies.

Most public warehouse rates were negotiated at least every 12 months, and rarely did a contract extend beyond two years. In all cases, a one-shot billing system applied whereby a composite rate for storage and handling was set for every 100 pounds delivered to a warehouse. Accessorial charges for such things as damaged products and telephone expenses were billed separately. The public warehouses would assess a small penalty charge for every hundredweight in excess of the stipulated storage level per month. In plant warehouses, the rule of thumb was to assess storage and handling costs at 1.5 percent per month of the manufactured cost of average monthly inventory that was valued at the full cost of production. Full cost included allocations of overhead and other fixed charges in addition to the direct variable cost of manufacturing, which at Giles represented 80 percent of the full cost.

Top management felt that it was necessary to maintain a 100 percent service level with respect to hospitals. This was a reflection of their belief that hospitals in general had poor inventory management. In actual experience, the achieved customer service level was about 98 percent. Consumer products enjoyed a 96 percent service level, which compared favorably to the target of 98 percent. The distribution manager said that studies were being conducted to determine the optimum service levels considering distribution costs (including the inventory holding costs) and actual service requirements. He explained that prior to 1996, the company did not have a documented inventory carrying cost figure and although a number had been used in plant expansion proposals he was not sure how it had been arrived at. ("Perhaps it was the cost of money at that time applied to the full manufactured cost of the inventory.") However, a study has just been completed by a distribution analyst who recently completed his MBA degree in the evenings while working at Giles. A memo outlining the results of this study is given as Exhibit 1.

Shipments from field warehouses to customers were carried by motor carriers at prevailing cartage rates or negotiated contract carrier rates with the exception of a few of the field warehouses that operated their own truck fleets. These customer deliveries were FOB destination. No orders below 15 cases were accepted, and truckload orders (40,000 pounds) were referred to the head office by field warehouse personnel for possible direct service from the nearest plant warehouse. Unit-sales prices for the company's products were quoted at two price break ranges: at 15 to 49 cases, and at 50 cases and over.

Shipping schedules from plant warehouses to field warehouses were initiated from central headquarters. Supervisors who reported to the distribution manager analyzed warehouse delivery receipts, in-transit stock levels, and bill-of-lading figures that indicated deliveries to customers, in order to initiate corrective action if required. Stocking requirements were determined according to normal usage levels (versus inventory levels) for each field warehouse and were reviewed periodically and changed if required.

Although most communication with public warehouses was by telephone or fax, the company had begun to install direct data-transmission connections with warehouses located in major market areas. The lead time for processing and consolidating orders was targeted at three days for consumer outlets, but an actual average of five days was experienced. For hospital deliveries, the usual experience was two days compared to a target of one day.

Columbus Warehouse Facts and Data

The Columbus field warehouse was serving the metropolitan area and neighboring municipalities within a 40-mile radius. The outlying areas were being serviced by wholesalers that drew stock from Columbus. The distribution manager estimated that shipments to Columbus would average in excess of 15,000 cases per month for the next year. One-third of the present shipments came from the Michigan plant and were consolidated at 40,000 pounds for shipment at a freight rate of 70 cents per hundredweight. The rest of the shipments were sent out of the Indianapolis plant warehouse in truckload quantities (40,000 pounds) by public motor carrier at a rate of 60 cents per hundredweight. The 60 cents per hundredweight was based on a contract mileage rate of $1.40 per mile for truckload shipments from Indianapolis to Columbus. In this case, motor carrier rates

Exhibit 1

Giles Laboratories Interoffice Memo

GILES LABORATORIES
INTEROFFICE MEMO

Date: January 30, 1996
To: Mr. Paul McNaughton, Director of Distribution Services
From: Wesley Scott, Distribution Analyst
Subject: A Documented Inventory Carrying Cost

The following four basic cost categories must be considered when calculating inventory carrying costs: (1) capital costs, (2) inventory service costs, (3) storage space costs, and (4) inventory risk costs.

The money invested in inventory has a very real cost attached to it. Holding inventory ties up money that could be used for other types of investments. This reasoning holds for internally generated funds as well as those obtained from outside sources. Consequently, the company's opportunity cost of capital should be used in order to accurately reflect the true cost involved.

In order to establish the opportunity cost of capital for Giles Laboratories, the comptroller, Mr. John Munroe, was interviewed. Giles' cost of capital was the charge paid to the parent company, Thurber Pharmaceuticals. Currently, this rate is 10 percent before taxes for working capital. However, due to capital rationing, the current hurdle rate on new investments is 30 percent before taxes (15 percent after taxes). The company conducts a postaudit of most projects in order to substantiate the rate of return. This is required by corporate policy, and in the majority of cases the desired return is achieved. Occasionally a 40 percent hurdle rate is employed by Giles' management to ensure that the required corporate rate of 30 percent is realized.

Although it would seem that the 30 percent hurdle rate also should be applied to inventory since Thurber Pharmaceuticals is not cash rich and in times of capital rationing an investment in inventory precludes other investments at the 30 percent rate. Thurber Pharmaceuticals only requires a 10 percent return on inventory investments. Consequently, 10 percent before taxes is used as the cost of money in this study. However, this is an issue that must be resolved at the top management level.

The opportunity cost of capital should be applied to only the out-of-pocket investment in inventory. This is the direct variable expense incurred up to the point at which the inventory is stored. In other words, it was necessary to obtain the average variable cost of products, FOB the distribution center. The individual cost component and the final carrying cost percentages are shown below.

Inventory Carrying Costs

Cost Component	Percentage of Inventory Value
Capital costs	10.00
Inventory services costs	
Taxes	1.80
Insurance	0.26
Warehousing costs	
Public warehouses (recurring storage only)	2.94
Plant warehouses	nil
Inventory risk costs	
Obsolescence	0.80
Shrinkage	0.58
Damage	0.63
Relocation (transshipment) costs	N.A.
Total	17.01†

*Not available
†Inventory is valued at variable cost FOB the distribution center

---

were more favorable than railroad rates. Shipments from Michigan represented products that were not manufactured in Indianapolis.

Mr. McNaughton was reviewing a plan that would phase out the Columbus public warehouse. Michigan shipments would be diverted to Indianapolis and could be expected to be transported at the same freight rate. Indianapolis would then serve

Columbus customers by motor carrier under new rates. The new rates and mix of shipment sizes are set forth in the following schedule:

Percent of Total Weight Shipped	Cost per Hundredweight
40% @	$0.60 (TL)
35	1.50 (LTL)
25	2.40 (LTL)

Under the new plan another trucking firm would be contracted to provide local delivery to Columbus customers. This company was willing to offer better rates for LTL shipments and cartage (intracity) rates. Moreover, it had suggested allocating 100 square feet of space at its Columbus terminal for transit storage at no additional expense to Giles Laboratories. The lower cartage rates would result in a small saving to the company. If the contract with the Columbus warehouse was renegotiated, it was estimated that the throughput rate could be fixed at 25 cents per case plus a storage penalty when inventory turns fell below 12 times per annum.

A case of Giles products averaged 25 pounds and had a full manufactured cost of about $18. The selling price to wholesalers and chain retail accounts averaged $24.90 per case. The variable cost of marketing, such as sales commissions, promotional allowances, and local delivery costs, averaged $1.66 per case.

While reviewing the proposal, Mr. McNaughton became aware that there would be a one-time reduction in total system inventory of $135,000 valued at full manufactured cost as a result of elimination of the Columbus facility. Although this figure represented an estimate, he felt somewhat encouraged by the fact that it was the consensus among members of his department. The reduction would be comprised primarily of Indianapolis-produced products.

The phase-out possibility was not without its uncertainties. It was not clear whether additional personnel would be needed to process the orders emanating from the Columbus area. It appeared that the existing system was operating at capacity. There was also the matter of convincing the sales department to lengthen the service time from one day to two or three days. The main competitor was serving Columbus out of Pittsburgh, which is 190 miles northeast of Columbus, while the distance from Indianapolis is 171 miles. Mr. McNaughton has been advised by the president to attempt to phase out at least five field facilities within the year, and the Columbus warehouse was the first to come up for lease renewal.

Questions

1. What are the financial implications associated with closing the Columbus warehouse?
2. How would your analysis differ if:
   - freight rates changed?
   - warehousing rates changed?
   - additional personnel were required at Indianapolis?
3. Which option would you prefer if you were responsible for transportation? For inventory?
4. How would you incorporate customer service considerations into your analysis? How much would sales volume have to change in order to change your answer to question 1?
5. Is there a better way to service the Columbus customers?
6. Should the carrier plan at Giles be changed? If so, what recommendations would you suggest?
7. What other issues need to be addressed?

HEWLETT-PACKARD SPOKANE DIVISION

Chrissy Ransom collapsed into her chair and stared at the piles of documents littering her desk. It was only 4:00 P.M., but the cubes on the second floor were nearly empty. July in Spokane meant a time to quickly grab the best part of summer before the weather changed. Especially on Fridays, the office would be crowded by 7:00 A.M. with employees coming early so they could leave by 3:00 P.M. Ransom had planned to get out early herself to spend the weekend with her new husband at their nearby lakeside cottage. Somehow the events of the day had not cooperated, and with pressing deadlines approaching, she aborted her plans for a relaxing weekend.

The past six months had been as crazy as Ransom could ever remember. It seemed unbelievable that only two months ago she was rushing to prepare for her wedding. Meanwhile at work, new projects mounted on her desk. Hewlett-Packard's Spokane Division had survived many tough times in the past, but now business was looking up. Orders were strong during the first half of 1994, and the improving business outlook had energized the division. But with the improving business came increased inventory and stubbornly poor order fulfillment. Order fulfillment had always been an issue for the division that produced instruments in a primarily make-to-order environment. Despite multiple initiatives over the past 10 years, Spokane had been unable to improve on-time delivery performance beyond 70 percent (shipment from factory to customer acknowledgment date). Now, to make matters worse, HP as a company was pushing hard to reduce inventories. A cash scare earlier that year forced traditionally cash-rich HP to float short-term loans in order to make payroll. The cash crisis had become a rallying cry for CEO Lew Platt in his fight to reduce inventories.

Hewlett-Packard Company

Hewlett-Packard Company was founded in 1939 by William Hewlett and David Packard, with headquarters in Palo Alto, California. It grew steadily over the next 50 years, diversifying from its base in electronic test and measurement equipment into computer and peripheral products, which had become a dominant portion of the company's sales. In 1994 HP had over 50 operations worldwide with projected revenues of $25 billion.

HP was organized partially by product group and partially by function. The Test and Measurement Organization (TMO) was the second largest of the five groups, with orders estimated at $2.8 billion for 1994. While the early 1990s witnessed a continuing decline in the worldwide aerospace/defense market, TMO showed strong growth in the first half of 1994, and there was much optimism for a strong year. Moreover, through-

---

This case was written by M. Eric Johnson, who is a member of the faculty at the Tuck School of Business, Dartmouth College. It was written for class discussion and not to illustrate either effective or ineffective management practices. Some names and facts have been changed.

© M. Eric Johnson. Revised 2/28/00.

out the company there was steady progress in improving asset structures—as a percentage of revenue, accounts receivable, property, plant and equipment, and inventories all showed declines over the same period in 1993. "We're starting to see some payoff from our focus on inventories," said Platt. "But we still have a lot of work to do in this area."

Spokane Division

The Spokane Division produced a variety of radio-frequency (RF) test instruments including signal generators, communication test sets, modulation analyzers, measuring receivers, audio analyzers, and transceiver systems. These products were used to test and calibrate RF communications equipment such as two-way radios (e.g., CB, police, marine), cellular phones, and pagers. Spokane's customers were generally large international vendors of wireless communication equipment such as AT&T, Motorola, Ericsson, Nokia Mobira, and Pacific Telesis. Other large customers included the U.S. military, General Electric, Sony, Panasonic, and Hitachi.

Spokane Division was part of the Test and Measurement Group of HP, led by Dick Anderson. The changing business climate had left the group struggling to maintain profitability over the past five years. Spokane closed the 1993 fiscal year in October with raw material inventories in excess of $22 million on sales of $142 million. Finished goods inventories were nonexistent in their make-to-order business, where customers could specify thousands of different option configurations on any of their 10 major product lines. Alarmingly, inventories were growing as sales grew and were near $24 million by March 1994.

Doug Scribner, the group manufacturing manager, was working hard within the group to reduce manufacturing costs, which in many cases meant reducing inventories. Earlier that year, Spokane's manufacturing manager, Dan Nelson, had begun initiatives to both reduce inventory and improve order fulfillment. Chrissy Ransom, who was the procurement and planning manager reporting to Nelson, had been charged with leading a team to attack the inventory problem. Procurement was responsible for maintaining inventories of more than 18,000 components through a network of over 700 suppliers. The problem-solving team, called RID for Reduce Inventory Debt, comprised members from manufacturing, planning, finance, marketing, and procurement.

Dan Nelson, who had served as the manufacturing manager for over 10 years, had initiated many changes and improvements to the manufacturing process. Most recently, Spokane had begun using teams of workers to produce whole families of instruments rather than using dedicated lines. This had required extensive effort in manufacturing to make production more flexible and to eliminate setup requirements between different instruments. While Spokane had struggled with inventory issues in the past, progress on reducing inventory had been scant. Nelson believed that opportunities to reduce inventory existed but had eluded him. He had recently heard presentations by other divisions who had reduced inventories by analyzing their entire manufacturing process from product design and supplier relationships through distribution—referred to as supply chain analysis. Nelson believed such an approach held promise for Spokane, and that spring he had sponsored a supply chain seminar conducted by a corporate group called Strategic Planning and Modeling (SPaM).

Supply Chain Analysis and SPaM

SPaM had become known throughout the company for conducting and facilitating successful supply chain initiatives, with particularly notable successes in divisions responsible for computer peripherals such as laser and inkjet printers. The two-day seminar had been developed by SPaM to help divisions initiate supply chain projects. An instrumental part of the seminar was the concluding half day, where participants formed groups to attack a business problem using ideas they had seen in the seminar. Chrissy Ransom planned to use that time to focus the RID team and to refine their mission.

The seminar was held in May and resulted in an initiative to begin examining the supply chain for one particular product—the 10031. That particular product was Spokane's largest and most important. The supply chain of the 10031 was relatively straightforward (see Exhibit 1). Printed circuit boards containing HP proprietary technology were produced by HP's Surface Mount Technology Center (SMTC) located next door to the Spokane division. SMTC had at one time been part of the Spokane division, but had recently become an independent operation, assembling boards for other divisions along with those produced for Spokane. Many other components for the 10031 were purchased from various vendors, with Spokane assembling the final instruments and shipping them directly to end customers.

The core members of the supply chain steering committee were Dan Nelson, Jack Condor (physical distribution and order fulfillment manager), Rick Duran (procurement manager), and Blake Green (SMTC materials manager). Chrissy Ransom acted as the project leader and coordinated information between the new supply chain project and the other existing teams. The plan was to use a short study of the 10031 as a pilot for a full-scale supply chain study to be conducted during 1995. SPaM agreed to support Ransom's team through the summer, visiting every other week for working meetings. Members of Ransom's RID team were assigned the task of gathering much of the necessary data for the short project.

Throughout June and into July the team worked to gather data on the planning and manufacturing process for the 10031. It became apparent, only a few weeks into the process, that SMTC was too distracted to fully participate. SMTC was in the midst of moving its operation to a new building on the Spokane site, and felt it could not make any strong staff commitments to the project. Consequently, the focus of the project centered on Spokane's own processes.

Exhibit 1

Supply chain for the 10031

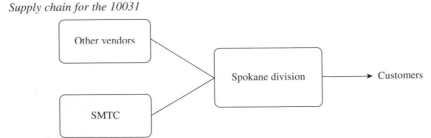

Inventory Control at Spokane

While it was widely believed by the group that Spokane held too much inventory, there was little hard evidence that it could reduce inventories without eroding order fulfillment. In fact, there were those who felt the focus on order fulfillment required Spokane to hold even more inventory. Many of the components used in the instruments had exceedingly long lead times of 16 to 20 weeks and the high option mix required Spokane to hold many components for different configurations. Others argued that certain unreliable vendors caused most of the order fulfillment problems. They believed that inventory on many components supplied by reliable vendors could be reduced while those from unreliable vendors should be increased. Still others felt that production capacity issues along with scheduling problems resulted in many of the order fulfillment problems. Finally, it was also suggested that many times production was held up simply because component inventory could not be found (even though the system indicated that the inventory was available).

After the first meeting, it became clear that many of the important processes in the supply chain were not well understood. Local experts within the division understood their own process, but no one understood how the different processes interacted, nor did anyone have a full view of the whole system. Thus the group established their first goal of understanding the whole process and the relationship between inventory and order fulfillment. In particular they felt that it was important to understand:

1. The order forecasting process.
2. The order processing process.
3. The manufacturing planning process.
4. The procurement process.

They also wanted to investigate the inventory levels on particular components for the 10031 as reported by the information systems and through cycle counts. Finally, they planned to investigate the manufacturing process itself, hoping to identify the root causes for order fulfillment problems and determine if inventory was a key driver.

The group met regularly through June and July, collecting and discussing information about the supply chain. While the Spokane team gathered data and developed flowcharts of each process, the SPaM project group, led by Marguerita Sasser, developed an aggregate inventory model of the division to estimate Spokane's inventory needs, given their order fulfillment goals (see Exhibit 2).

Pulling the Information Together

With late afternoon quietness, Chrissy Ransom settled back into her chair and began poring over the reports. With only one week left before the group's July 30 deadline for a preliminary report, she struggled to pull all the information together. Earlier that morning, Sasser had called Ransom to discuss the initial results of SPaM's inventory model. Sasser mentioned that they still had much sensitivity analysis to perform, but that the model had indicated that Spokane should be able to cut its inventory in half while improving order fulfillment. At first these results seemed shocking, but Ransom wasn't surprised. She had long suspected that Spokane had far more inventory than necessary. In fact, the group had determined early in the project that many of the order fulfillment problems were not related to inventories (see Exhibit 3). One operator on the shop floor said she couldn't remember the last time the line stopped because they had really run out of a component. More likely they simply couldn't find the component quickly.

EXHIBIT 2

Spokane Product Demand and Cost Data

review (mn)		1						
fill rate		0.9						

Product	Target item fill rate	Avg monthly demand	Leadtime (weeks)	Review period (months)	Forecast Std Dev (monthly)	Mat'l cost ($/unit)	ICOEM cost ($/unit)	Total cost ($/unit)
10001	90%	2	12	1	1.23	$5,343	$3,182	$8,525
10002	90%	0	4	1	0.24	$897	$9,782	$10,679
10003	90%	0	4	1	0.24	$349	$11,375	$11,724
10004	90%	0	4	1	0.37	$897	$12,837	$13,734
10005	90%	5	14	1	2.65	$2,759	$0	$2,759
10006	90%	4	7	1	2.47	$152	$12,153	$12,305
10007	90%	1	15	1	0.41	$11,273	$1,119	$12,392
10008	90%	1	14	1	0.77	$13,229	$352	$13,581
10009	90%	1	12	1	0.15	$35	$7,351	$7,386
10010	90%	1	12	1	0.33	$5,337	$7,927	$13,264
10011	90%	8	13	1	1.94	$683	$0	$683
10012	90%	22	10	1	5.66	$429	$744	$1,173
10013	90%	3	11	1	4.10	$633	$1,052	$1,685
10014	90%	3	14	1	3.36	$1,642	$565	$2,207
10015	90%	2	6	1	1.03	$82	$799	$881
10016	90%	14	11	1	8.47	$3,588	$0	$3,588
10017	90%	29	11	1	11.57	$4,431	$206	$4,637
10018	90%	9	18	1	5.13	$5,401	$1,340	$6,741
10019	90%	1	9	1	3.42	$1,111	$598	$1,709
10020	90%	0	12	1	0.78	$5,379	$0	$5,379
10021	90%	2	12	1	2.08	$3,470	$151	$3,621
10022	90%	80	10	1	24.32	$1,983	$0	$1,983
10023	90%	10	10	1	3.05	$1,535	$0	$1,535
10024	90%	41	16	1	12.24	$1,340	$0	$1,340
10025	90%	157	15	1	22.20	$94	$0	$94
10026	90%	48	15	1	9.84	$119	$0	$119
10027	90%	31	19	1	13.13	$2,341	$0	$2,341
10028	90%	9	19	1	3.50	$2,449	$0	$2,449
10029	90%	26	12	1	5.00	$49	$0	$49
10030	90%	6	19	1	1.25	$2,244	$0	$2,244
10031	90%	169	15	1	11.75	$3,621	$0	$3,621
10032	90%	1	15	1	0.50	$2,961	$0	$2,961
10033	90%	1	15	1	0.50	$10,800	$0	$10,800
10034	90%	12	19	1	5.09	$6,197	$0	$6,197
10035	90%	30	17	1	23.15	$3,862	$0	$3,862
10036	90%	1	17	1	0.50	$6,400	$0	$6,160
10037	90%	11	16	1	7.67	$6,227	$0	$6,227
10038	90%	0	15	1	0.86	$5,465	$340	$5,805
10039	90%	1	14	1	1.01	$6,043	$555	$6,598
10040	90%	1	14	1	1.77	$6,115	$359	$6,474
10041	90%	2	16	1	8.12	$6,123	$158	$6,281
10042	90%	8	13	1	5.84	$5,689	$702	$6,391
10043	90%	3	13	1	1.39	$6,081	$702	$6,783
10044	90%	3	8	1	3.36	$699	$0	$699
10045	90%	0	12	1	0.39	$12	$0	$12
10046	90%	0	12	1	1.09	$514	$0	$514
10047	90%	1	14	1	0.82	$121	$0	$121
10048	90%	1	12	1	0.84	$124	$0	$124
10049	90%	1	12	1	0.63	$124	$0	$124
10050	90%	1	9	1	0.72	$579	$133	$712
10051	90%	2	12	1	2.46	$96	$624	$720
10052	90%	0	14	1	1.64	$6,035	$6,535	$12,570
10053	90%	0	6	1	0.27	$8,447	$13,895	$22,342
10054	90%	0	8	1	0.20	$12,361	$35,210	$47,571
10055	90%	0	6	1	0.41	$13,657	$15,860	$29,517
10056	90%	70	13	1	20.67	$925	$0	$925
10057	90%	0	16	1	2.37	$4,588	$702	$5,290
10058	90%	0	14	1	4.88	$8,762	$864	$9,626
10059	90%	0	13	1	0.19	$6,087	$702	$6,789
10060	90%	12	12	1	1.62	$4,888	$527	$5,415
10061	90%	11	16	1	2.20	$5,946	$951	$6,897
10062	90%	2	13	1	1.32	$6,428	$1,132	$7,560
10063	90%	10	18	1	3.30	$8,670	$1,117	$9,787
10064	90%	3	18	1	1.68	$9,278	$1,140	$10,418
10065	90%	7	14	1	1.81	$9,141	$1,309	$10,450
10066	90%	1	12	1	0.38	$667	$0	$667
10067	90%	3	18	1	3.83	$136	$0	$136
10068	90%	1	12	1	0.45	$1,064	$0	$1,064
10069	90%	5	11	1	4.56	$12,734	$1,381	$14,115
10070	90%	5	12	1	2.13	$16,487	$1,609	$18,096
10071	90%	2	12	1	1.59	$9,344	$702	$10,046
10072	90%	5	12	1	1.95	$11,711	$702	$12,413
10073	90%	62	15	1	20.59	$2,834	$0	$2,834

EXHIBIT 3

Delays Causing Order Reacknowledgments

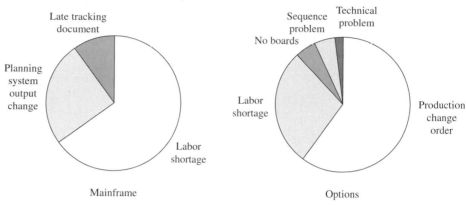

The cycle count information revealed what many had suspected. Physical inventories often significantly deviated from system inventories (see Exhibit 4 for an example). Sometimes this occurred because components could not be found, but other times the database was simply wrong.

However, Ransom believed that the most fascinating findings had come from the group's efforts to document the processes. Magi Queen, a financial analyst who was part of the RID team, had stopped by earlier with new drafts of flowcharts that she and Cindy Black had been working on. Black was an MBA summer intern who spent most of her summer digging through and charting the processes (shown in Exhibits 5 to 8 with an overview in Exhibit 9 and a glossary in Exhibit 10). Throughout the planning processes there appeared to be processes that redundantly added safety stock. Beginning with forecasts that were padded for potential "big deals" straight through to component buyers who placed component orders earlier than necessary, the total safety stock snowballed. While some of the processes were transparent and easy to understand, others had subtle impacts on safety stock.

For example, during the master scheduling process, planners purposely created capacity and component inventory for additional products beyond the forecast. A model (called the FLEX model), based on statistical variations in demand, added requirements to the master schedule, allowing for flexibility in production capability each month. When these added products were added to the forecast, they drove increased component demand through the MRP explosion. The output of the MRP system drove the procurement system (POPLAN), which also added safety stock at the component level. The buyers used the recommendations from POPLAN to alert them of component needs, but also used their own judgment as to exact quantity and timing of orders. Finally, there were questions concerning the integrity of parameters used in the MRP system that may have been causing overexplosion of some components.

More puzzling was a process that projected different option requirements, referred to as MIN/MAX. Since forecasts were made on a generic instrument level, forecasting the option mix was an important step in maintaining appropriate component inventories. For each option, the MAX parameter represented the (forecast) proportion of the products that would require the option—driving optional component demand. When an optional component was included in a product, it would often displace a standard one. The MIN parameter was used to specify the number of standard components not needed, reducing standard component demand. Since the MAX parameter was almost always

EXHIBIT 4
Cycle Count Example for a Typical Component of the 10031

Cycle Count Comparison for Six Components of the 10031

Date	A System Onhand	A Actual Onhand	B System Onhand	B Actual Onhand	C System Onhand	C Actual Onhand	D System Onhand	D Actual Onhand	F System Onhand	F Actual Onhand	G System Onhand	G Actual Onhand
6/20 8:00 AM	473		48		389		203		369		3130	
6/20 12:00 PM	473		48		389		203		363		3121	
6/20 4:00 PM	473		48		389		203		363		3121	
6/21 8:00 AM	473	476	48	49	389	322	203	250	361	377	3121	2925
6/21 12:00 PM	472		48		371		196		351		3029	
6/21 4:00 PM	472		48		371		196		351		3029	
6/22 8:00 AM	471		41		371		196		359		2995	
6/22 12:00 PM	471		41		371		196		359		2995	
6/22 4:00 PM	471		41		371		191		357		2920	
6/23 8:00 AM	470	569	35	36	362	361	178	248	347	297	2835	2776
6/23 12:00 PM	470		35		392		178		347		2825	
6/23 4:00 PM	470		35		393		178		347		2825	
6/24 8:00 AM	467		35		386		169		332		2764	
6/24 12:00 PM	467		35		392		169		332		2764	
6/24 4:00 PM	467		35		392		169		332		2764	
6/27 8:00 AM	458		35		394		449		317		2683	
6/27 12:00 PM	458		35		378		445		317		2618	
6/27 4:00 PM	458		35		378		445		317		2618	
6/28 8:00 AM	458	562	35	28	378	126	445	665	311	386	2603	2496
6/28 12:00 PM	458		35		372		437		307		2553	
6/28 4:00 PM	454		29		372		435		298		2531	
6/29 8:00 AM	454		29		372		435		297		2533	
6/29 12:00 PM	454		29		372		435		297		2531	
6/29 4:00 PM												

EXHIBIT 5

Flowchart of Order Processing

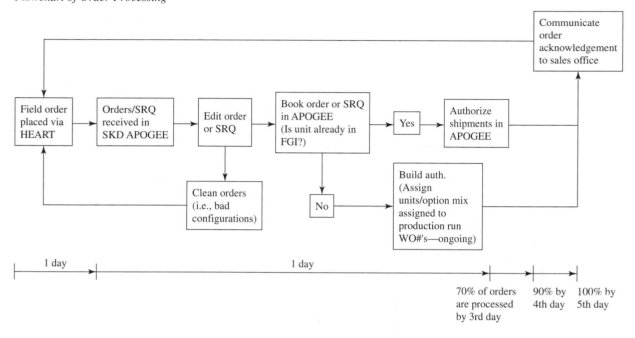

EXHIBIT 6

Flowchart of the Order Forecasting Process

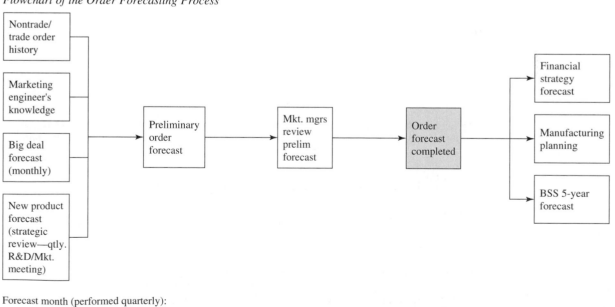

Exhibit 7

Flowchart of Manufacturing Planning Process

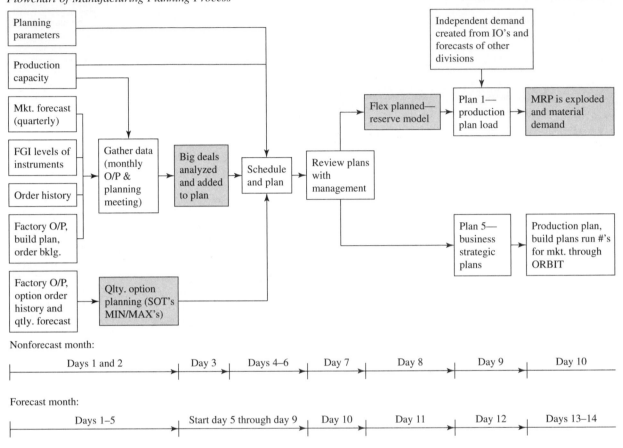

☐ Denotes areas where buffer inventory is added.

specified to be larger than the MIN, component requirements would always be exaggerated. Moreover, fractional component requirements were always rounded up, thus further exaggerating requirements. This rounding was often significant since demand for some options was relatively small. Exhibit 11 shows an example of a MIN/MAX calculation.

During the last project meeting, the group began discussing which of the processes caused the most problems and how to go about eliminating the redundancies. Unfortunately, throughout the Spokane organization, different groups controlled each process and each group had an interest in not running short. For years component buyers had learned that while having too much inventory may cause occasional grumbling, running out of a component created a major incident. As one buyer put it, "If I have too much inventory, my boss may casually mention it, but if I run out I get my arms broken!" The master schedulers felt much the same. They believed that their FLEX model enabled them to protect against changes in demand and allowed them to respond to urgent requests from marketing.

To make matters worse, a few weeks ago Dan Nelson had surprised the division with his resignation. A search was underway for a new Manufacturing Manager. Without a strong project sponsor, significant changes would be particularly challenging. Chrissy Ransom knew the redundancies had to be eliminated and replaced with a single safety-stock strategy; but agreeing on that strategy and gaining support and a sponsor would not be easy.

EXHIBIT 8

Flowchart of the Procurement Process

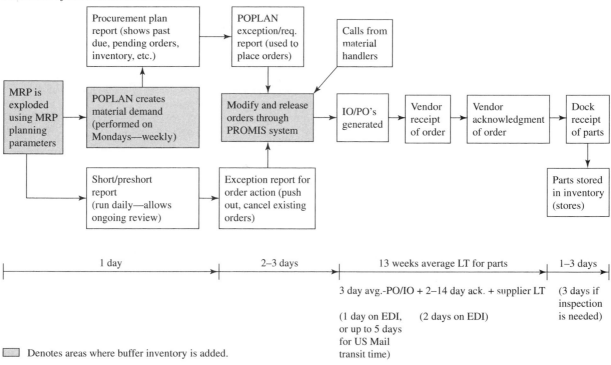

1 day | 2–3 days | 13 weeks average LT for parts | 1–3 days

3 day avg.-PO/IO + 2–14 day ack. + supplier LT | (3 days if inspection is needed)

(1 day on EDI, or up to 5 days for US Mail transit time) | (2 days on EDI)

Denotes areas where buffer inventory is added.

EXHIBIT 9

Overview of Entire Process

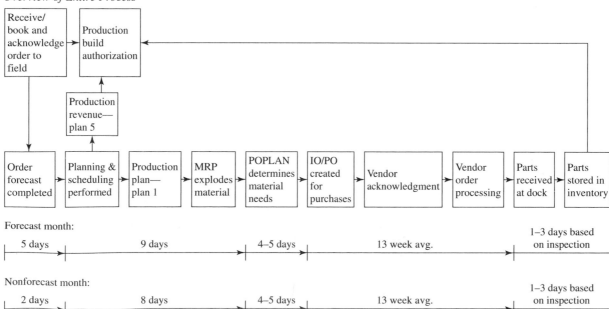

Forecast month:

5 days | 9 days | 4–5 days | 13 week avg. | 1–3 days based on inspection

Nonforecast month:

2 days | 8 days | 4–5 days | 13 week avg. | 1–3 days based on inspection

Exhibit 10

Glossary of Terms Used in Flowcharts

Order Entry

HEART is HP's order-entry system. Salespeople throughout the world enter customer orders into HEART for all of HP's products. The system processes the orders and notifies the appropriate HP division. Later the division acknowledges the customer order and notifies the salesmen concerning delivery dates.

SRQ stands for Scheduled Request. This is an order reservation placed by a sales office pending a firm order. Such requests are made to ensure timely customer delivery.

(SKD) APOGEE is HP's order booking system. It is a phased replacement for the ORBIT booking system.

WO#s—Work order number.

Forecasting

Big Deals are large sales to a single customer.

BSS—Business Strategy Summary (HP's term for a business plan).

Manufacturing Planning Process

Planning parameters include current levels of finished goods inventory, backorders, forecast order quantities, production capacity, material leadtimes, and planning objectives.

FGI—finished goods inventory.

O/P—order processing.

MIN/MAX is the option planning process (see Exhibit 11).

FLEX model (or reserve model) is performed by master schedulers (see text).

ICOEM are customizing parts that HP buys and inventories. These components are sold with certain instruments as shown in Exhibit 2.

Plan 1—Material plan in the master schedule (Build plan plus units added by FLEX).

Plan 5—Build plan in the master schedule.

MRP—Material requirements planning.

IOs—Internal orders.

ORBIT is an HP order booking system. The acronym stands for Order Requirements, Backlog, and Inventory Tracking.

Procurement Process

POPLAN is a system that processes component demand from MRP along with inventory information and recommends component purchase schedules to buyers.

Short/Preshort report—Daily expedite report for buyers.

PROMIS is a system designed to help HP monitor and manage its procurement activities both divisionally and on a companywide basis.

EDI—electronic data interchange (used to transfer orders and forecast electronically).

Exhibit 11

Example of a MIN/MAX Calculation

Functionality of MIN/MAX% in creating material demand for options.

Example:

In this example both part A and part B are used in the standard instrument. However, in Option #001, part A is not used and is replaced by part D. The MAX% is used to create the material demand for the positive part(s) of an option by taking its percent times the size of each run. It states that "MAX" percent of every run of an option X will be built. The MIN% is used to remove and return to stock the part(s) from the standard instrument not used in option X. It states that a minimum "MIN" percent of the time an option X will be built, and it is calculated by subtracting its percent times the size of each run from the total run size.

Assumptions: Quantity per for each part is one.

Run Size = 10

Option #001:   MAX% = 70%

MIN% = 35%

EXHIBIT 11 *(continued)*

Instrument Structure:

8920A Standard   Option #001

$$+A \qquad +D$$
$$+B \qquad -A$$

Option #001 explodes and shows buyers a demand for:

$+D$ = 7 part Ds (MAX% at 70% of 10)

$-A$ = 6 part Ds (MIN% at 35% of 10 is 3.5 units. This then rounds to 4 and is subtracted from the run size of 10. The net shows buyers a demand for 6 part As.)

Therefore, this allows flexibility for option mix so that it is possible to build 6 whole option #001s and a possible 7th option #001 because that 7th part D has been purchased and is unique to that option. From a material perspective, the unique part of an option is what would constrain its production.

CASE 7

LADNER BUILDING PRODUCTS

Gordon Stephens, logistics analyst for Ladner Building Products (Ladner), a building materials distributor located in Montreal, Quebec, had been asked by Doug Turner, vice president, logistics and materials management, to prepare a report analyzing the company's logistics practices. Doug was especially interested in where changes could be made to reduce costs, improve company performance, or accomplish both simultaneously:

> We spend a lot of money on logistics at Ladner—especially in the distribution end of our business. Right now I am not at all satisfied that our area is performing as well as it could. Our delivery performance is getting better, but we still have a ways to go. What troubles me most, however, is that our costs are too high. I'm not sure if we should simply charge more for customer deliveries or take another approach.

It was Monday, August 24, 1998, and Gordon knew Doug did not want a report that simply summarized Ladner's logistics costs—he was expecting Gordon to offer specific recommendations on how to address the problems uncovered. Although Doug wasn't expecting the report for another two weeks, Gordon felt that he would easily need all of that time to analyze the information that he had collected over the past few days and to gather any additional data he might need.

The Building Materials Industry

The Canadian building materials industry comprised three main product segments: commodities, industrial, and allied products. The domestic forest products industry

---

P. Fraser Johnson prepared this case solely to provide material for class discussion. The author does not intend to illustrate either effective or ineffective handling of a managerial situation. The author may have disguised certain names and other identifying information to protect confidentiality.

provided a competitive supply base for commodity products, including lumber and plywood. Prices for these products were based on commodity exchanges, such as the Chicago Board of Trade and the Winnipeg Commodity Exchange.

Some industrial products, such as hardwood plywoods and particleboard, were essentially commodities. However, others, such as formica countertops, were manufactured goods with well-established pricing structures. Canadian building materials distributors typically used domestic suppliers as their main source of supply for industrial products.

Allied products included hardware, fasteners, and exterior and interior home repair and maintenance items. Typically, only about half of the allied products sold by Canadian building materials distributors were sourced domestically. U.S. companies supplied products for approximately 40 percent of this market segment, while the remaining 10 percent were purchased from offshore suppliers. Building materials distributors were usually able to negotiate pricing arrangements with allied products suppliers that fixed prices for a one-year period.

Building materials distribution companies in Canada served two main customer groups: dealers and industrial. Dealers included large buying groups and retail chains. The buying group segment, such as Home Hardware, represented independent retailers that combined purchases in an effort to lower acquisition costs and gain access to a wider range of products. Large retail chains included companies such as The Home Depot and Wal-Mart.

There were a wide variety of firms in the industrial segment, including prefab home construction companies, boat and recreational vehicle manufacturers, and cabinet and furniture manufacturers. Most companies in this segment had one manufacturing location.

Dealers and industrial customers typically made purchases from each of the three main product segments. Demand was mostly seasonal, with approximately two-thirds of sales occurring between May and November.

Competition within the building products distribution industry was fierce, and margins were low. Operating margins, representing the difference product acquisition costs and customer purchase prices, averaged 10.5 percent. Most firms competed on a regional basis, with some specializing in a narrow product segment, thereby creating a market that was fragmented both geographically and by product lines. No single firm had a dominant position in the marketplace, and Ladner was one of the few national firms in the Canadian building material industry. Its market share was estimated at 4 to 5 percent.

Ladner Building Products

Ladner began operations in 1986 for the purposes of selling and distributing products for a large forest product company. Initially, Ladner's product line was limited to the products manufactured by its parent company, such as plywood sheets and wood panels. In 1989, new management was hired as part of an effort to improve Ladner's financial performance and expand its market presence. As a result, Ladner's product base grew dramatically to include a broader range of building product materials, particularly in the allied and industrial product segments.

In August 1998, Ladner had 15 distribution centers, located across Canada. The company's distribution network was divided into five regions: British Columbia, Prairies, Ontario, Quebec, and Atlantic. Each region was headed by a general manager, who had profit and loss accountability for the region. Ladner had a total of 385 employees in its distribution centers and 35 staff in the Montreal, Quebec, head office. Exhibit 1 provides a corporate organization chart.

Ladner had sales of $495 million in 1997, with an operating loss of $1.9 million. Although the general economic climate had been strong in Canada, the company had generated losses in each of its last four years.

Ladner offered over 15,000 brand-name and private-label products. Although Ladner's shareholder was still its largest supplier, the company had a supplier base of approximately 500 organizations. Company products were grouped into seven categories: commodity, industrial, exterior, interior decor, fasteners, storage and shelving, and security products. Exhibit 2 provides examples of each product group.

Each region carried approximately 3,000 stock-keeping units (SKUs). However, because of differences among the regions, only 3 percent of the company's SKUs were common across all five regions.

Exhibit 1

Organization Structure

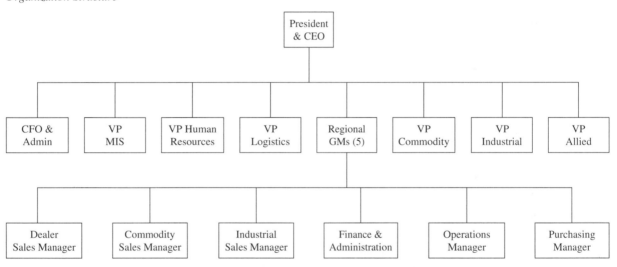

Exhibit 2

Product Categories

Product Category	Examples
Commodity products	Plywood, oriented strandboard, lumber
Industrial products	Formica, particleboard, hardwood plywood
Allied products	
Exterior	Vinyl siding, vinyl fencing, asphalt shingles
Interior decor	Moldings, spindles, columns, wall paneling
Fasteners	Nails, screws
Storage and shelving	Wood shelving, wire shelving, closet organizers
Security	Door locks, dead bolts, door knobs

The company had three product vice presidents: commodity, industrial, and allied. The product vice presidents were responsible for sourcing, promotions, and negotiating supplier contracts. The regions placed orders and scheduled deliveries on the basis of these contracts.

The sales mix among product groups varied substantially. For example, commodity products represented 40 percent of annual dollar volume and 10 percent of Ladner's SKUs, while industrial products accounted for 20 percent of the annual dollar volume and 30 percent of the SKUs.

Customer Base

Ladner served 5,120 customers and 8,525 customer shipping locations. A single customer could have several shipping locations, each with different requirements in terms of products, delivery, and volume. These differences made it difficult to establish minimum order sizes, even for large, national retail chains. Both customer orders and deliveries were made on the basis of the individual shipping locations, with very few customers requiring deliveries to central distribution centers.

The company dealt with approximately 20 buying groups and 1,000 large retailers, which accounted for $365 million in sales and 4,360 shipping locations. Customers in the dealer segment used their purchasing power to negotiate volume discounts that averaged 1 percent.

Sales to the 4,100 firms in the industrial segment varied substantially—some were among Ladner's largest customers, while others were quite small. Most customers in this segment had only one shipping location per customer.

Ladner's regional industrial and dealer sales groups handled requirements for their respective customer segments, with the exception of commodity products. Regional sales groups had both inside and outside sales representatives. The inside sales staff processed customer orders placed over the telephone or by fax, while the outside sales representatives met with customers to solicit new orders, address customer complaints, and collect information on market activities.

Prices for commodity products were based on published prices in international commodity exchanges and were therefore managed differently from other sales activities. It was not unusual for a Ladner commodity trader to be on the phone with both the supplier and customer negotiating the purchase and selling prices simultaneously. Margins for commodity products ranged from 7 to 9 percent.

Industrial and allied products had higher margins than commodities. Margins for industrial products ranged from 12 to 15 percent, while allied products were 12 to 28 percent. Generally, products with higher volumes had lower margins.

Large orders for commodity, industrial, and allied products could be shipped directly from Ladner's suppliers, bypassing its distribution centers. These "direct mill" shipments were full truckload (FTL), and freight was paid by the customer.

In 1997, total sales from direct mill shipments amounted to $130 million. Margins on these shipments were usually 4 percent lower than those shipped from a distribution center.

Doug Turner wondered if the company could do a better job managing the diversity of Ladner's customers and products:

> Should we set some parameters regarding our customer base? Maybe we should not accept certain small orders, and send some customers to The Home Depot, which is better at handling small orders. Right now we give too much flexibility to our salespeople, who like to

get on the phone and play "dial-a-deal." The difficulty is that the sales staff gets evaluated on the basis of product gross margins, which ignores the costs of handling, storage, and transportation.

Regional Operations

Ladner's decentralized organization structure provided a great deal of authority to the five regional general managers and their staff (see again Exhibit 1). Regional management was given flexibility when negotiating arrangements with customers and establishing distribution policies based on the competitive climate within each region.

Each region had an operations manager, a small purchasing staff, product sales managers, and a financial manager, all of whom reported to the regional general manager. The sales staff negotiated the terms of customer orders, including pricing and delivery. The regional operations manager had responsibility for inventory control, warehouse operations, and outbound transportation. As part of Ladner's financial planning process, operations managers negotiated annual operating budgets in these three areas and were held accountable for their performance. Budgets were typically based on historical performance and adjusted based on expected changes to regional sales.

The regional purchasing manager was responsible for arranging supplier deliveries, including inbound transportation. The purchasing managers worked off the national contracts negotiated at the head office, with the exception of certain unique, small-volume requirements for their region.

The regional sales department established delivery charges when negotiating customer orders. Sales representatives could rebate all or part of the delivery charge to customers, depending on circumstances. Rebates could be made for any number of reasons, including high volume orders, promotions, or simply price pressures.

Logistics and Materials Management

Doug Turner headed Ladner's logistics and materials department. He joined Ladner in 1990 in a newly created position in charge of companywide logistics activities. Doug had extensive experience in transportation and logistics before joining Ladner.

Doug reported to the president and CEO, Ken Jacobs. Ken had joined Ladner in January 1997 from a large industrial manufacturer, located in Ontario, and had extensive experience in product marketing. Ken was hired with a mandate to turn around Ladner's poor financial performance.

Responsibility for logistics activities at Ladner was shared among several members of the organization. The corporate logistics staff consisted of Doug Turner, Gordon Stephens, and Bill Jenkins, the transportation manager. Gordon had been with the company for about a year. He had experience with a major consulting firm before returning to school to complete his MBA, and he joined Ladner immediately after graduation.

Doug's head office group was responsible for establishing logistics-related performance objectives, guidelines, and policies for the regions, and assisting with their implementation. For example, Doug worked with Ken Jacobs to develop target customer service levels of 95 percent for the company, as measured by line fill rates (LFR).[1] It was up to Doug to work with the regional general managers and their staff to achieve this objective.

---

[1]$LFR = \dfrac{\text{Number of lines filled}}{\text{Number of lines ordered}}$

The Distribution System

Freight charges tended to reflect the industry pricing practices within each region. Consequently, differences existed between regions regarding customer freight policies. Doug had asked Gordon to focus on the Ontario Region when preparing his report. He was particularly interested in this region since it represented 40 percent of total company freight costs.

The Ontario Region had sales of $117 million in 1997, including $28 million in direct mill orders. The balance of the region's sales was handled through one of its four distribution centers. In Ontario, Ladner delivered 91.5 percent of its sales from its distribution centers, charging customers a flat rate of 1.5 percent of sales for delivery fee. According to the region's financial report, Gordon determined that the Ontario Region delivered 81,346 orders from its distribution centers in 1997, and rebated $418,000 in customer delivery charges that year.

Ladner did not have its own truck fleet, but contracted with three regional carriers to handle deliveries for different geographic regions of the province. The Ontario Region classified its deliveries into two groups: local and rural. Both local and rural shipments were handled by highway transport tractor-trailer units with a capacity of 72,000 pounds. Because some of Ladner's products were heavy, trucks that were properly loaded would typically reach the maximum weight before running out of available space.

Gordon knew that in Ontario, carriers were paid $34 per hour and $0.37 per kilometer for local runs, while costs for rural runs were $17 per drop and $0.87 per kilometer. Gordon had collected one fairly typical example of a local run (see Exhibit 3) and another typical example of a rural run (see Exhibit 4). In 1997, the Ontario Region paid $2.827 million to its carriers for customer deliveries.

Some of Ladner's customers preferred to pick up their orders rather than use the company's delivery system. During 1997, 8.5 percent of distribution center sales in the Ontario region were pickup orders, representing a total of 11,224 orders during that year.

Ladner did not have many policies regarding pickup orders, other than payment conditions. Established customers were able to negotiate appropriate credit limits and charge their orders. Other customers were expected to pay at the distribution center with cash or a check.

Additional Considerations

Gordon felt that Ladner's transportation volume allowed it to negotiate competitive freight rates. Since logistics, including transportation, were a significant expense to Ladner, Gordon understood why Ken Jacobs had identified logistics and materials management as a critical area in his efforts to improve the company's financial performance.

Gordon knew that a couple of years earlier Ladner moved its freight cost charged to customers from one to 1.5 percent of sales. There had been strong market resistance, particularly from the dealers in Ontario. Some of them even went as far as to boycott Ladner. However, eventually most of Ladner's competitors followed.

As Gordon sat down to review the information, he recognized that it was important to consider how his recommendations might affect other activities in the company such as marketing and sales, regional operations, and purchasing. Since Ken Jacobs was a

EXHIBIT 3

Example of One Local Run for One Ontario Regional Distribution Center

Activity	Invoice Number	Weight[1]	Km	Time[2]	Sales	Customer Charge	Total Cost
Load			0	2.0	$ 0	$ 0	$ 68.00
Drop 1	35061	14,399	8	2.25	1,120.46	0	79.46
	35069				457.64	0	
Drop 2	34243	795	40	1.25	287.20	4.31	57.30
Drop 3	33673	467	25	1.0	286.08	4.29	43.25
Drop 4	34920	132	15	0.75	525.60	7.88	31.05
Drop 5	34977	215	4	0.75	64.50	0.97	26.98
Drop 6	33617	4,425	4	0.75	960.00	14.40	26.98
	35104				806.40	12.10	
Drop 7	35085	15,322	10	0.75	4,778.28	71.67	29.20
Return			51	1.5		0	69.87
Total		35,755	157	11.0	$9,286.16	$115.62	$432.09

[1]lbs.

[2]hours

EXHIBIT 4

Example of One Rural Run for One Ontario Regional Distribution Center

Activity	Invoice Number	Weight[1]	Km	Time[2]	Sales	Customer Charge	Total Cost
Load			0	1.25	$ 0	$ 0	$ 0
Drop 1	35974	5,040	31	1.5	1,680.00	25.20	43.97
Drop 2	36069	744	67	1.75	616.80	9.25	75.29
	34834				218.42	3.28	
	36202				92.55	1.39	
Drop 3	36354	216	27	1.0	153.00	2.29	40.49
Drop 4	35497	8,884	37	1.25	1,519.00	0	49.19
	35738				34.10	0.51	
Drop 5	35876	368	17	0.5	153.09	2.30	31.79
	35766				112.80	1.69	
Drop 6	36383	1,366	8	0.75	509.74	7.65	23.96
Drop 7	31266	5	13	0.5	143.27	2.15	28.31
Drop 8	34941	3,888	4	0.5	658.80	9.88	20.48
Drop 9	31202	1,385	23	0.75	2,595.84	38.94	37.01
	35376				364.32	5.47	
Drop 10	36007	10	42	1.0	80.80	1.21	53.54
Return			160	2.75			139.20
Total		21,906	429	13.5	$8,933.03	$111.21	$543.23

[1]lbs.

[2]hours

strong proponent of the decentralized structure of the company, Gordon knew that he should be prepared to address the concerns raised by other members of the organization when recommending changes to Ladner's logistics practices. He wondered if he should collect additional information and of what kind to bolster potential changes that he might recommend.

CASE 8

KKC COMPUTER CONSOLIDATION

The firm is a major electronics manufacturer that produces two categories of high value, high technology computers (A and B) and distributes these products from two production facilities (Los Angeles and San Francisco) respectively to seven U.S. markets: Atlanta (ATL); Denver (DEN); Detroit (DTW); Houston (HOU); Terre Haute (HUF); Little Rock (LIT); and Minneapolis (MSP) (see Exhibit 1). Since the computers are manufactured far from markets, a major firm objective is to deliver the products on-time while minimizing the transportation expense. Historically, the firm has utilized daily direct air shipments from each production facility to all major U.S. markets. Table 1 shows the daily demand for each product for major markets.

The customer is billed immediately upon receipt of the individual computer shipment. Since a majority of sales are on the basis of delivered cost, the firm assumes the risk of transportation damage and theft and the cost of financing in-transit inventory. Thus, in addition to minimizing transportation expense, the terms of sale and high product values dictate that the firm have transportation objectives of (1) maximizing accounts receivable turnover, (2) minimizing damage and theft related to extended transit time and multiple handlings, and (3) minimizing in-transit inventory investment. The firm's desire for a distribution system characterized by high speed transportation and low in-transit inventory levels has resulted in the following distribution policies or actions:

1. All time lags have been removed from the controllable portion(s) of the order cycle including order processing.
2. No warehouse facilities are used since they would increase inventories and the potential for damage.
3. Freight consolidation at production facilities for greater than one day is undesirable because plant storage capacity is limited; delays in billing would decrease accounts receivable turnover, and longer order cycle times would result in unacceptable customer service levels.

Given these assumptions, transportation costs make up a major percentage of the distribution system cost and become the major objective criteria for evaluating alternative distribution system strategies.

Analysis Methodology

The analysis objective is to evaluate and identify the consolidation strategy alternative between plants and markets that results in the lowest total *daily* (consolidation cost + air transport cost + truck transport cost + cost of lost sales).

A. Capacity

Flights from each location and number of trucks at each location are *not* limited. Air and truck capacity is also *not* limited.

This case was written by Professor Robert L. Cook, Central Michigan University.

EXHIBIT 1

Major western markets

TABLE 1   *Average daily demand by product/market in units**

	Market							
Product	*DTW†*	*HOU*	*LIT*	*DEN*	*MSP*	*ATL*	*HUF*	*Total*
A(LAX)	31	20	11	22	11	23	10	128
B(SFO)	24	13	9	18	9	22	5	100
Market Total	55	33	20	40	20	45	15	228

*Each unit weighs 100 pounds.

†Key to cities: DTW, Detroit; HOU, Houston; LIT, Little Rock; DEN, Denver; MSP, Minneapolis; ATL, Atlanta; HUF, Terre Haute.

B. Transit Times
   1. Air transit times are: one day between all locations (products may not be flown between markets).
   2. Consolidation transit times: one day if any consolidations occur.
   3. Truck transit times (see Table 2):
      Transit times are calculated from city to city; same-day delivery can be made in cities where shipments land; therefore, local delivery is zero days transit time.

      Transit example: All products are flown to San Francisco (SFO), sorted, and then flown San Francisco (SFO) to Minneapolis (MSP), where a truckload

TABLE 2   *Truck transit time (in days)*

From \ To	LAX*	SFO	DTW	HOU	LIT	DEN	MSP	ATL	HUF
LAX	0	1	7	7	6	4	6	7	6
SFO	1	0	7	7	6	4	6	7	6
DTW			0	3	2	3	2	2	1
HOU			3	0	1	3	4	2	2
LIT			2	1	0	2	3	1	1
DEN			3	3	2	0	2	3	2
MSP			2	4	2	2	0	3	2
ATL			2	2	1	3	3	0	1
HUF			1	2	1	2	2	1	0

* See Table 1 for identification of cities.

[Minneapolis (MSP), Terre Haute (HUF), Atlanta (ATL) freight] is routed Minneapolis (MSP), Terre Haute (HUF), Atlanta (ATL). A second truck is sent to Denver (DEN), Houston (HOU). The transit times would be as follows:

	Air (LAX to SFO)	Consolidation	Air (SFO to MSP)	Truck (MSP to HUF)	Truck (HUF to ATL)	Total Time
To MSP	1	1	1	—	—	3 DAYS
To HUF	1	1	1	2	—	5 DAYS
To ATL	1	1	1	2	1	6 DAYS

The transit times for the second truck would be:

	Air (LAX to SFO)	Consolidation	Air (SFO to MSP)	Truck (MSP to DEN)	Truck (DEN to HOU)	Total Time
To DEN	1	1	1	2	—	5 DAYS
To HOU	1	1	1	2	3	8 DAYS

C. Current Customer Service

One-day service for 100 percent of units is the current service level (one day air transport of 14 shipments directly from plant to market and local LTL delivery).

D. Costs

1. *Air Freight Costs.* Table 3 summarizes the air rates from Los Angeles (LAX) and San Francisco (SFO) to each city for four weight groups.

2. *Truck Freight Costs.* Table 4 depicts the LTL truck rates/100 lbs between city pairs. Truckload rates are calculated by taking 50 percent of the rates shown in Table 4.

TABLE 3 *Air rates per 100 lbs**

100–1,200 lbs*

From \ To	LAX†	SFO	DTW	HOU	LIT	DEN	MSP	ATL	HUF
LAX	—	8	40	43	46	44	48	45	50
SFO	7	—	42	45	46	45	50	44	53

1,201–2,399 lbs

From \ To	LAX	SFO	DTW	HOU	LIT	DEN	MSP	ATL	HUF
LAX	—	7	35	38	43	39	46	40	49
SFO	6	—	37	40	44	41	47	41	52

2,400–13,499 lbs

From \ To	LAX	SFO	DTW	HOU	LIT	DEN	MSP	ATL	HUF
LAX	—	7	28	30	34	29	37	29	40
SFO	5	—	30	32	36	31	38	33	44

13,500–25,000 lbs

From \ To	LAX	SFO	DTW	HOU	LIT	DEN	MSP	ATL	HUF
LAX	—	6	21	23	28	22	30	24	34
SFO	4	—	25	27	30	26	30	26	36

* Each product weighs 100 lbs.
† See Table 1 for identification of cities.

TABLE 4 *LTL truck rates between cities (rates per 100 lbs)**

From \ To	LAX†	SFO	DTW	HOU	LIT	DEN	MSP	ATL	HUF
LAX	6	7	39	36	40	34	38	41	39
SFO	7	6	40	38	41	36	39	45	42
DTW			6	15	13	14	11	10	8
HOU			15	6	10	14	16	11	13
LIT			13	10	6	12	13	9	9
DEN			14	14	12	6	11	15	12
MSP			11	16	13	11	6	15	13
ATL			10	11	9	15	15	6	9
HUF			8	13	9	12	13	9	6

* Rates are dollars per 100 pounds.
† See Table 1 for identification of cities.

Truckload rates may be applied to all shipments in a truck that begins at its origin point with 60 or more computers. For example, if the market demand for Minneapolis (MSP), Terre Haute (HUF), and Atlanta (ATL) were flown to Minneapolis (MSP) and loaded into a truck for delivery, it would be a truckload (80 units) and the truckload rate would apply to all three shipments.

In addition, the freight rate used for each shipment is always based on the origin point [i.e., for the truckload in the previous paragraph, the three rates to use would be: Minneapolis (MSP) to Minneapolis (MSP), Minneapolis (MSP) to Terre Haute (HUF), and Minneapolis (MSP) to Atlanta (ATL)]. Note that unlike transit times, the freight rates are not cumulative from city to city [i.e., Minneapolis (MSP) to Atlanta (ATL) is $15 not $22].

The correct truck freight calculation for the truckload in this example would be:

(TL)	*(MSP to MSP)*	*(MSP to HUF)*	*(MSP to ATL)*
.5	[(20 units × $6 per day) +	(15 × $13) +	(45 × $15)] = $495.00

3. *Consolidation Costs.* Each time units are brought together (different products or units headed for different markets), those units involved incur a $1.00/unit charge. For example, if all Products A and B were flown consolidated to Minneapolis (MSP) and then sorted by city for delivery by truck, the consolidation costs would be 228 units × $1/day = $228. This is the maximum consolidation cost for any scenario.

4. *Lost Sales.* This cost is based on the percentage of customer sales lost due to slow delivery. The price of each product is $100 per unit.

- Seven day service is unacceptable to 100 percent of customers.
- Six-day service is unacceptable to 20 percent of customers.
- Five-day service is unacceptable to 5 percent of customers.
- Four-day service is unacceptable to 1 percent of customers.
- Three-day service is unacceptable to .5 percent of customers.

Calculation example: Delivery of 45 units to Atlanta (ATL) on day 6:

$$(45 \times \$100/unit)\ .20 = \$900 \text{ lost sales}$$

CASE 9

FAVORED BLEND COFFEE COMPANY

The Favored Blend Coffee Company is a prominent manufacturer of coffee sold on a nationwide basis to the consumer and institutional markets. Sales to the consumer market are achieved through wholesalers, chain stores, and other grocery product retailers under the brand name *Favored Blend*. Sales to the institutional market are achieved by

This case was provided by Donald J. Bowersox of the Graduate School of Business Administration, Michigan State University. All rights reserved to the contributor. The case was updated in 1993.

direct account coverage and by the efforts of brokers under the brand name *Best Blend.* With the exception of packaging size and style, the two product lines are identical. Both Favored Blend and Best Blend offer ground and instant coffee in a variety of packages. Both blends are manufactured and distributed in the same production plants and logistics systems.

Until 1990, the Favored Blend Coffee Company prospered and expanded. Sales growth averaged 5 percent annually. Profits, while not increasing in the same proportion as sales, reflected a favorable growth. At the year-end management meeting in 1990, the management group was optimistic about continued growth in both sales and profits. By mid-1992 this optimism had given way to a serious situation. While the sales of Favored Blend's two product lines continued to grow, profits dropped sharply in 1991, and for the first quarter of 1992 a loss was experienced for the first time since 1929. Analysis of the operating figures clearly indicated that increased costs in logistics constituted the major reason for the profit decline. Transportation costs had increased by 4 percent in 1991, as compared to 1990, and warehousing costs were up by 3 percent. Despite a rigorous cost-control program instituted in the last half of 1991, the cost trend had not been reversed during the first quarter of 1992. Year-end finished goods inventory in 1991 was 8 percent higher than in 1990. By the end of the first quarter of 1992, inventory had been forced in line as a result of a reduced production schedule.

In April 1992, Mr. Smith, president and chief executive officer of Favored Blend, called a general management meeting. While the entire group was aware of the fact that a logistics problem existed, the problem reached a new climax when Big Food Chain dropped Favored Blend Coffee from its product line. Mr. Smith had been informed by Big Food Chain's chief executive officer that Big was forced into the decision by alleged poor inventory availability and erratic delivery of orders placed with Favored Blend Coffee. Based upon the apparent inability of Favored Blend's management group to correct the adverse situation, Smith had decided, with the advice of his board of directors, to call in an independent consultant to study and analyze the company and its distribution structure.

At the April meeting Smith presented his decision to retain the services of Able Management Consultants—a firm of logistics specialists. The marketing vice president was in full agreement with the decision. The director of distribution services and the financial vice president were opposed. In their opinion, the problem could be corrected if proper marketing and customer service polices were implemented on a corporatewide basis. They questioned if a so-called high-powered specialist would in fact have sufficient knowledge of food product distribution to conduct a meaningful investigation. At one point in a heated discussion the vice president of manufacturing added to the general argument with the comment, "The last thing we need is some more theory; the last group of so-called experts spent three weeks here and then told us things we already knew and had told them. We need action, not research." After about two hours of discussion, Smith concluded the meeting with the following comment:

> Some of you may be right about consultants, but frankly I feel you're defensive, and the figures just don't support standing by while the situation further deteriorates. I am going to call the head of Able, give him the facts as I know them, and see what he would do if we give him the job.

Case Situation

You are the head of Able Management Consultants. Mr. Smith has reviewed the background of Favored Blend's problem and provided you with the briefing below. Your immediate assignment is to answer questions as instructed at the end of this case.

Smith's Briefing to the Head of Able Management Consultants

In serving its nationwide market, Favored Blend Company operates processing facilities in Philadelphia, New Orleans, and Los Angeles. Each plant supplies a relatively fixed geographical portion of the United States. Operations at each of these fully integrated plants consist of receiving shipments of green coffee from overseas and then blending, roasting, grinding, processing, and packaging the product for customer shipment. As the packaging process is completed, the coffee moves into a shipment either directly to customers or to warehouses throughout the territory of distribution. The production process consists of running a single-size package until estimated weekly requirements are satisfied and then processing other packs in scheduled sequence.

The space devoted to storage and shipping at each plant is small, having been whittled down in recent years by the expansion of space devoted to production facilities for instant coffee. A continuing search for additional space in the plants, on plant property, or on property contiguous to the plants has proven fruitless. As an expedient for making space, the Distribution Services Department has come to favor rail shipments, principally because they find empty boxcars can be used as auxiliary storehouses while being loaded. This added storage space is provided at moderate cost by reason of 48-hour free-time provisions in the demurrage tariff, coupled with the fact that switching is performed at 8:00 A.M. at all plants. As a result, almost three days' loading time is provided on free time before demurrage accrues. Mr. H. J. Speedy, director of distribution services of Favored Blend Coffee Company, is very proud of his accomplishments in this area and has presented the concept several times at industry meetings.

Although coffee consumption in general is fairly predictable, orders from customers tend to be sporadic, so that shipments both direct from the plant and from the warehouses are rather irregular. Attempts have been made at predicting orders; however, the results have not been particularly accurate. The Distribution Services Department has tended to utilize warehouses as outlet valves when the storage problem became burdensome at the plant. In total, 30 public warehouses are utilized by the firm for distribution.

Consequently, though there is a planned supply program, some warehouses have tended to become greatly overstocked, others considerably understocked. The mixture of Favored Blend and Best Blend products at any single time at any single warehouse often lacks the proper combination of package sizes and grinds. Frequently, cross-hauling between warehouses and emergency shipments from plants has been necessary in order to fill customer orders.

The physical pattern of distribution has been a source of friction between the Marketing and Distribution Services departments for a number of years. In general, it consists of two principal methods:

1. Direct shipments from the plants to the customer in truckload or carload quantities, with less-frequent shipments in LTL quantities.
2. Shipments in carload and truckload quantities to public warehouses located in the market area, with LTL shipments from the warehouse to the customer.

Quantity shipments direct from the plant to customers were at one time of considerable significance and are, in general, lowest cost and most desirable from the Distribution Services Department's standpoint. However, in line with a general trend in business philosophy in recent years toward lower inventory levels, customers have been hesitant to purchase in large enough quantities to warrant delivery in carload and truckload lots. The Distribution

Services Department has confronted an increasing demand on the part of customers to order in small lots on an immediate delivery basis, with requested truck delivery. The degree to which this trend has progressed is illustrated by tonnage reports for 1991 in comparison to 1981. In 1981, 80 percent of all coffee, from all locations combined, was shipped to customers by rail, and 20 percent was shipped by truck. By 1991, these figures had reversed.

Mr. Smith has spent considerable time with the Distribution Services and Marketing departments in the attempt to solve the problem of increasing costs. In general, the Distribution Services Department feels that marketing has not instituted realistic price incentives to encourage quantity purchasing and that salespersons allowed customers to unduly dictate terms and routing of shipments. The Marketing Department, in contrast, points to increased competition from private as well as other national branded coffee as the source of the problem. "Competitors provide the service desired by customers, and we have little choice but to try to meet this service if we want the business."

Questions

1. What principles of logistics system design will be helpful to guide Able in approaching a revamping of Favored Blend's operation if they get the assignment? Be specific.

2. Is there sufficient similarity among logistics systems in general to support Mr. Smith's feeling that Able Management Consultants should be capable of handling a food industry assignment? What factors, principles, or general reasons would you as the president of Able present to the management group of Favored Blend to help get the assignment?

3. With 30 warehouses across the nation, why do you feel Favored Blend is constantly faced with the need to cross-haul between warehouses and make emergency shipments to customers from plants? Be as specific as possible regarding current practices that result in poor inventory assortments in individual warehouses.

4. What in your opinion is the total system impact of the Distribution Services Department's policy of using boxcars as warehouses? Keep in mind that both transportation and warehouse costs have recently increased.

CASE 10

COASTAL LOGISTICS INC.: ESTABLISHING THIRD-PARTY LOGISTICS SERVICES

The management of Coastal Logistics Inc. (CLI), a start-up company with plans to provide logistics services to offshore petroleum platform operators in the Gulf of Mexico, must decide the company's next steps. Traditionally each petroleum company provides

Developed for Council of Logistics Management by Associate Professor E. Powell Robinson Jr. and Assistant Professor Anthony D. Ross of Texas A&M University.

logistics services in-house. CLI claims that by consolidating logistics operations for multiple petroleum firms, it can lower logistics costs through "resource sharing." The case challenge is to evaluate the economic feasibility of the resource-sharing concept, to determine whether CLI should proceed with plans to establish itself as a major logistics service provider in the Gulf of Mexico, and to establish an implementation plan, should CLI decide to pursue this new venture.

Problem Definition

Joe Ross, director of business development for Coastal Logistics Inc. (CLI), looked up from the cargo manifest when he heard the *Miss Ellie* sound off, announcing her departure for the Eugene Island Area of the Gulf of Mexico. Several members of Affiliated Oil Company's (AOC) logistics staff had just left Joe's temporary office at the Morgan City shore base. For most of the afternoon, and well into the night, they had explored a proposal that would, with AOC's help, establish CLI as a third-party provider of marine logistics services in the gulf. The proposal represented a radical departure from AOC's current logistics strategy of servicing its own platforms. Not only did the proposal call for the transfer of AOC's logistics assets to CLI, but it would create a new philosophy for logistics operations. Joe knew that by the time *Miss Ellie* returned from her three-day delivery route, he would have either clinched the deal, and be celebrating with a large bowl of gumbo at the Crawfish Cavern, or be on his way back to corporate offices in Cleveland.

Joe returned his attention to *Miss Ellie's* cargo manifest. On this route, she used 55 percent of her outbound deck space and 30 percent of her bulk cargo capacity. These load factors were typical of supply boats operating in the Gulf of Mexico, and played a key role in CLI's proposal to establish itself as a third-party supplier of logistics services in the region. Joe poured himself another cup of coffee and settled in among the stacks of manifests, maps, boat routes, and other operational data. It was going to be a long night, but by tomorrow afternoon's meeting he had to clearly demonstrate the economic benefits of asset sharing and come up with an implementation plan for establishing CLI as a logistics service provider. Joe knew that, although they all agreed in principle, this would be his best chance to convince AOC's logistics team that the numbers were right and that it could be pulled off. He couldn't afford to blow it.

Company Overview

The offshore oil industry is composed of several major oil companies, such as AOC, and a multitude of smaller, independent operators. Once an oil field is targeted for development, the oil company identifies exploration drilling sites, often 20 to 100 nautical miles from shore, and constructs drilling platforms. If exploration activities are successful, the platform is converted into a production platform to extract crude oil and natural gas. Otherwise, the platform is moved to another site to continue exploration.

Like its competitors, AOC traditionally focused on exploration and production activities, paying little attention to operating costs. However, flat oil prices since the 1986 crash and rapid cost increases since 1990 pushed the need to control operating costs to the forefront. Logistics costs account for approximately 16 percent of total operating costs, making this a significant area for generating cost savings. In 1996 AOC spent $1.0 million for shore base operations and $12 million for boat operations at its Morgan City shore base alone. In addition, a slight upward fluctuation in oil prices had sparked exploration and production activity, increasing demand for the already scarce marine logistics assets. Boat lease costs had risen 200 to 300 percent from 1993 to 1996.

In the early 1990s, Aberdeen Service Co. Ltd. established third-party contract logistics services (CLS) for petroleum platform operators in the North Sea and demonstrated its potential economic benefit to the industry. CLS transfers responsibility for the provision of logistics support from the oil company to a logistics specialist. This permits the oil company to focus management energy and capital investment on core exploration and production business activities. The contractor manages the logistics resources, which are shared across its customer base, with a focus on reducing the total logistics costs of each participating oil company. CLS applications by Aberdeen Service Co. Ltd. yielded logistics cost reductions of approximately 30 percent, equating to a 12 percent increase in profit margins for the participating oil firms. These benefits were derived from the release of working capital, economies of scale, better resource utilization, and improved management position. While some of these benefits could be derived individually by any oil company, the balance of savings could not have been achieved without the drive to attain synergy and economies of scale with other oil companies. Given the constraints on competition and antitrust law, which hampers resource sharing agreements among major oil companies, relying on a third party to provide logistics services is one way to unlock these potential benefits.

In early 1996, Coastal Logistics Inc. was formed as a joint venture to explore opportunities for establishing logistics services to support offshore petroleum exploration and production operations in the Gulf of Mexico. Both of CLI's parents had established records in the offshore petroleum industry, and viewed the Gulf of Mexico as a fertile area for applying the resource-sharing concept that was successfully implemented in the North Sea. CLI's long-term vision was to become the "UPS of the Gulf." In order to attain this objective, CLI would attempt to establish shore base operations in all of the major ports in the Gulf of Mexico.

CLI started operations with a bare-bones management staff consisting of a president, logistics and information systems director, systems analyst, and marketing director. Other personnel would be added as needed. The firm would draw on its parents for software development and technical support during its start-up years. The parent companies established a board of directors consisting of representatives of each parent firm to monitor CLI's progress. The board expected CLI to show a profit within three years. CLI immediately began promoting the shared-resources concept at industry trade shows and contacted platform operators. At the same time, it began the development of a geographic information system (GIS) software program titled Integrated Logistics Management System (ILMS) for managing shore bases and marine vessels. ILMS would be a critical component for integrating both the information and physical flows associated with establishing coordinated logistics services.

AOC expressed early interest in the shared-resource concept and met with CLI's management several times to explore its potential benefits and how it might be implemented. Where traditionally each oil company provided its own logistics services at low capacity utilization, CLI proposed that AOC turn over its shore bases and marine assets to CLI. In turn, CLI would use these assets to provide logistics services for AOC and other platform operators in the region. This would expand the customer base using the assets and lower the logistics costs. CLI and the platform operators would share the logistics savings associated with the increased efficiencies. In addition, the oil companies would be relieved from managing their own logistics activities, permitting them to focus on their core competencies in exploration and production. The proposal followed the general concepts implemented by Aberdeen Service Company Ltd. in the North Sea.

By mid-1996, AOC and CLI had formed a research team to validate the economic feasibility of the resource-sharing concepts. At their first meeting, the team decided to study the shore base operations in Morgan City, Louisiana, as a test case. In addition to AOC, several other major and independent platform operators maintained shore bases there and had expressed an interest in the project. In particular, two independent operators, Petroleum Resources (PR) and Gulf Energy Inc. (GEI), had previously contacted CLI about the need to lower their logistics costs and encouraged CLI to establish third-party operations in their production areas. Both firms pledged to participate in the task force's feasibility study.

Business Situation: Logistics Activities in Morgan City

Production platforms are either manned or unmanned. Manned platforms are staffed by a crew size ranging from 2 to 10 workers. The platform crew provides all the activities necessary to extract oil and gas from the ground and route it to onshore facilities for processing. These activities include controlling the production processes and maintaining capital-intensive production equipment. Unmanned platforms are serviced from the nearest manned platform. Platform crews work a variety of shift schedules. A typical work shift is seven days on and seven days off, working 12 hours per day. Crew changes are performed by helicopter or boat shuttle to and from the shore base.

Production platforms generate demand for a variety of products. These include potable water, fuel, lubricants, equipment, spare parts, and groceries, among others. Due to the limited storage space on the platform, weekly replenishments of many items are necessary. In addition, emergency shipments of spare parts are sometimes required. All production by-products (e.g., used parts, trash, and broken tools) are transported back to the shore base for disposal. Exhibit 1–6 provides the boat cargo capacities needed to support the average weekly requirements of AOC's, PR's, and GEI's production platforms. The data indicate the square feet of outbound boat deck space required for platform delivery, inbound deck space required for returning by-products to the shore base, and the outbound bulk capacities required for the delivery of potable water and diesel fuel to the platforms. In the table, *outbound* refers to shipments originating at the shore base, and *inbound* refers to shipments originating at the platforms. Delivery requirements vary among platforms depending on the number of unmanned platforms supported, the crew size, equipment age, whether or not the platform is equipped with a water maker, and whether the platform is fueled by natural gas extracted during production or diesel fuel that must be delivered from shore.

The manned platform supervisor schedules and coordinates all production and maintenance activities for his platform group. He identifies demand requirements, places replenishment orders with onshore vendors, and schedules product deliveries with the onshore boat dispatcher.

Onshore facilities consist of boat docks, warehouses, boat loading and unloading equipment, and administrative offices. Shore base staff includes a supervisor, logistics coordinator, two or three dispatchers, several yard workers, and secretarial staff. The shore base dispatcher is the primary interface with the platforms. He receives land-based shipments destined for the platforms, stages them by destination platform in the shore base warehouse, and coordinates their shipment to the platform. AOC provides complete onshore logistics activities for their platforms. However, intermediate-sized firms typically just maintain a shore base office and lease dock space, warehousing, and loading/unloading services from larger operators. The smaller operators often buy dock services as needed.

EXHIBIT 1

Typical Weekly Demand by Platform

Platform ID#	Outbound Deck Space	Inbound Deck Space	Potable Water	Diesel Fuel
EI105	328	244	820	0
EI126	163	50	0	0
EI128	616	450	974	0
EI240	236	190	1,820	0
GC18	400	281	2,600	0
GI20	153	114	0	0
GI76	59	37	1,281	0
GI94	328	244	820	0
SM10	335	284	0	810
SM132	426	293	2,200	284
SM205	163	150	2,716	0
SM243	177	200	1,845	0
SP10	426	293	2,614	284
SS182	177	166	1,845	960
SS219	16	0	974	0
SP72	335	260	1,281	810
VR215	300	244	1,200	750
VR271	410	250	900	920
WD34	29	24	256	0

Two main categories of boats—crew boats and supply boats—provide logistics services to the platforms. Both boat types are equipped to handle a variety of cargo characteristics. Boats contain bulk storage tanks for hauling potable water, fuel, and drilling mud; open deck space for transporting drilling pipe, large equipment, and tools; and enclosed cargo bins for shipping groceries, small parts, and tools. Crew boats are smaller than supply boats, with an average deck space of 1,450 square feet of cargo space. However, they are faster and burn less fuel per unit distance traveled. Crew boats are primarily used to support production platforms and run regularly scheduled routes. Each route typically serves from one to six platforms depending on the volume demanded by each platform, their distance from the shore base, and the capacity of the delivery vessel. Emergency deliveries to platforms occur as needed. Supply boats average 3,300 square feet of cargo deck space. Due to their large capacity and relatively slow speed, they are primarily used to support drilling platforms. It takes approximately two dedicated supply boats and 1.25 crew boats to support a drilling platform.

Each platform is equipped with cranes for loading/unloading cargo. The boats have pumps for unloading liquid bulk products. Boats are capable of loading and unloading cargo 24 hours a day depending on the crew's familiarity with the platform, weather conditions, and platform docking facilities. When possible, deliveries are scheduled to occur during daylight hours. Boat crews consist of a captain, first mate, and deck hands. Typical crew size is four to six workers. Boat crews operate a variety of work shifts with routes lasting up to two weeks in duration. Typical routes last one to three days. Most oil companies acquire boats through long-term leases, which include boat maintenance and crew costs. However, for emergencies and one-time needs, boats can be leased by the day at the "spot" rate. The spot rate is a function of boat availability and demand. The spot rate is typically twice the long-term lease daily rate. Due to a decline in ship building activity in the late 1980s and early 1990s, boat supply in the late 1990s is tight.

Current lead times to obtain a long-term boat lease average 24 months. Exhibit 2 provides typical operating characteristics and lease rates for the 135-foot crew boats and 180-foot supply boats operating out of Morgan City shore bases.

A delivery route begins at the shore base when the boat is loaded. Bulk cargo such as potable water, fuel, and drilling mud are pumped into the boat's storage tanks at dedicated loading facilities. These bulk liquid items are stored in large compartmentalized tanks in the vessel's hull. Other materials such as pipe, drilling bits, and production equipment are loaded onto the boat's deck at the shore base with cranes. Upon release by the dispatcher, the boat travels down the river to the intercoastal sea buoy, where it begins its delivery route. The sea buoy is approximately 42 miles and 2.5 hours transit time from the Morgan City Pass shore base. The delivery route follows a specified sequence of platform deliveries. After making its last delivery, the boat returns to the sea buoy and then goes back up river to the shore base, where it unloads the material returned from the platforms.

Analysis: The Benchmark Study

The first task of the research team was to document the current logistics procedures and costs of AOC, PR, and GEI to provide a benchmark for comparison. The research team directed its efforts on the delivery system for the production platforms. The team identified two major cost categories: delivery route costs and shore base operating costs. It then devised a strategy to collect the relevant data from the firms. In order to gather boat costs and operating data, each boat captain filled in a daily Boat Log that documented the boat's activities over a 24-hour period. The boat logs were kept over a two-month period. The boat logs captured data on boat loading and unloading times, running time, standby time at platforms and shore bases, down time for repairs, and inclement weather standby times. Additionally, the logs tracked all diesel fuel and lubricant usage. This enabled fuel consumption while running and consumption while on standby to be calculated. Using the boat logs, average utilization rates for the delivery boats were computed. The summarized data are presented in Exhibit 3.

During August 1996, AOC, PR, and GEI ran the regularly scheduled delivery routes identified in Exhibit 4. Each route began and terminated at a Morgan City shore base. In assigning platforms to routes, the objective is to minimize the cost of the deliv-

EXHIBIT 2

Operating Characteristics of Typical Crew and Supply Boats

Characteristics	Crew Boat	Supply Boat
Length	135 feet	180 feet
Open deck space	1,450 square feet	3,300 square feet
Diesel fuel capacity	10,800 gallons	43,700 gallons
Potable water	15,000 gallons	15,000 gallons
Running fuel consumption	100 gallons per hour	160 gallons per hour
Standby fuel consumption	50 gallons per hour	50 gallons per hour
Average running speed	18 miles per hour	10 miles per hour
Fuel cost	$.75 per gallon	$.75 per gallon
Long-term boat lease	$2,100 per day	$7,250 per day
Spot rate boat lease	$4,200 per day	$14,500 per day

ery routes, including boat lease costs and operating costs. To ensure adequate deck space is available to pick up by-products from the platforms, the outbound cargo is limited to 85 percent of the boat's deck space. In addition, the three firms attempt to assign their boats to 24-hour-duration daily delivery routes with at least three hours per route scheduled for loading, unloading, and standby at the shore base. Exhibit 4 provides the sequence of platforms served and the capacity utilization of the boats.

AOC held the long-term lease on *Miss Ellie,* a 135-foot crew boat, but subleased her to another platform operator three days per week. AOC ran three scheduled routes: AOC-1 on Wednesday, AOC-2 on Thursday, and AOC-3 on Saturday. In addition, about once a month *Miss Ellie* made a delivery to a jack-up barge in one of the oil fields. A jack-up barge is a shallow water structure that can be moved from platform to platform to temporarily expand the storage or work space at a permanent platform site. Delivery requirements for the jack-up barge averaged 200 square feet of deck space. The location of the jack-up barge varied over time. Its delivery was worked into a regularly scheduled delivery route.

PR and GEI shared *Miss Janice,* a 135-foot crew boat. PR controlled the long-term lease. Each firm used the boat two days per week to service their production platforms. In addition, PR used the boat to serve one of its drilling platforms two days per week. Each firm had an option to use the boat on Sundays when the need arose. The firm using the boat on Sunday paid that day's lease rate, otherwise the lease for Sunday was split with PR paying 70 percent of the lease cost and GEI paying 30 percent. On average each firm used the boat one Sunday per month.

Exhibit 5 presents an analysis of the seven delivery routes listed in Exhibit 4. The exhibit indicates the boat used on each route, the number of platform deliveries, the total route distance, the boat running (in-transit) times, and times at the platforms and

EXHIBIT 3

Average Utilization of Boat

Activity	Production Routes	Drilling Routes
Standby at shore base	40%	18%
Loading/unloading at shore base	2	14
Running time	37	23
Loading/unloading at platform	13	17
Standby at platform	8	28
Standby for maintenance/weather	0	0

EXHIBIT 4

Boat Utilization on Current Delivery Routes

Route Name	Delivery Route	Outbound Deck Space	Inbound Deck Space	Water	Fuel
AOC-1	SB-EI240-SM205-GC18-SB	55%	43%	61%	0%
AOC-2	SB-SP10-SP72-SB	59	40	49	3
AOC-3	SB-SS182-GI94-GI20-SB	45	36	25	6
PR-1	SB-SM10-SM132-SB	53	40	20	6
PR-2	SB-SS219-GI76-SB	6	3	21	0
GEI-1	SB-EI105-EI128-WD34-SB	75	55	19	0
GEI-2	SB-SM243-VR215-VR271-EI126-SB	81	57	37	11

Exhibit 5

Analysis of Current Delivery Routes

Route Name	Boat Name	Number of Platforms	Route Miles	Route Duration (hours)	Platform Standby (hours)	Shorebase Standby (hours)	Boat Lease	Intransit Fuel Cost	Platform Standby Fuel Cost	Shorebase Standby Fuel Cost	Total Route Cost
AOC-1	ELLIE	3	319	14.5	4.5	5.0	$2,100	$1,088	$169	$188	$3,544
AOC-2	ELLIE	2	213	9.7	3.0	11.3	2,100	726	113	424	3,363
AOC-3	ELLIE	3	345	15.7	4.5	3.8	2,100	1,176	169	143	3,588
PR-1	JANICE	2	226	12.6	3.0	8.4	2,100	1,036	113	317	3,565
PR-2	JANICE	2	306	17.0	3.0	4.0	2,100	1,403	113	150	3,765
GEI-1	JANICE	3	333	18.5	4.5	3.0	2,275	1,526	169	113	4,083
GEI-2	JANICE	4	284	15.8	6.0	3.0	2,168	1,302	225	113	3,807

Exhibit 6

Shore Base and Interplatform Distances

From/To	EI105	EI126	EI128	EI240	GC18	GI20	GI76	GI94	SM10	SM132	SM205	SM243	SP10	SP72	SS182	SS219	VR215	VR271	WD34
EI105	0																		
EI126	6	0																	
EI128	6	3	0																
EI240	39	42	45	0															
GC18	84	87	90	60	0														
GI20	102	108	111	119	116	0													
GI76	95	107	110	105	88	28	0												
GI94	91	92	95	98	74	46	20	0											
SM10	35	38	35	35	95	133	123	123	0										
SM132	70	74	77	35	74	154	133	126	53	0									
SM205	79	76	79	47	56	146	128	119	72	25	0								
SM243	42	38	41	56	116	137	133	133	25	70	94	0							
SP10	49	54	54	67	77	56	46	49	81	98	109	91	0						
SP72	36	42	49	67	81	53	45	53	81	102	105	88	14	0					
SS182	39	42	42	39	49	81	63	60	67	70	74	77	35	38	0				
SS219	46	49	49	35	39	91	70	63	67	67	91	81	42	45	11	0			
VR215	60	63	66	46	98	158	147	140	28	32	60	46	105	108	84	81	0		
VR271	81	84	87	56	98	175	158	151	52	25	49	70	119	122	95	88	25	0	
WD34	109	112	115	130	123	11	35	52	144	165	165	144	63	66	91	98	168	186	0
Shorebase	56	59	62	84	132	147	140	149	69	104	132	70	95	104	92	96	102	91	156

shore base. Boat lease and fuel costs associated with the routes are also provided. Assumptions for the calculations are: 1.5 hours for unloading, loading, and standby at each platform served; a minimum of 3 hours for unloading, loading, and standby at the platform for each delivery route; $.75 per gallon fuel cost; and $2,100 per day boat lease cost. Note that in Exhibit 5 boat lease costs are assigned according to the actual number of hours used on the route with a minimum charge of 24 hours. *Miss Ellie's* average running speed is 22 miles per hour with a fuel consumption rate of 100 gallons per hour while running and 50 gallons per hour while idling at a platform or at the shore base. *Miss Janice's* average running speed is 18 miles per hour with a fuel consumption rate of 110 gallons per hour while running and 50 gallons per hour while idling at a platform or at the shore base.

While the benchmark study did not consider emergency supply runs for the delivery of spare parts, or delivery requirements to support drilling platforms, the research team felt that any savings obtained from improving production platform supply would be matched from improved efficiencies in supporting the drilling operations.

A second area for potential cost savings was in shore base consolidation. Annual operating costs for AOC's shore base including wages, insurance, taxes, amortized facility and equipment costs, and so on, were approximately $1 million per year. This included support for both production and drilling operations. The research team determined that 40 percent of the shore base overhead costs should be allocated to support logistics operations associated with production platforms. PR leased dock space and loading/unloading services from AOC for $6,000 per month, but maintained its own shore base office for an annual cost of $140,000. GEI's annual shore base operating costs for production platforms totaled $180,000. The annual cost of providing shore base services from a single consolidated operation was projected to be $620,000. The savings were attributed to the elimination of duplicated staff, facilities, and equipment.

Consolidation of the Current System and Implementation

Joe reviewed the route information in Exhibit 4 and Exhibit 5 once again. He knew there had to be a better way. He immediately set about redesigning the seven routes assuming that CLI was the sole service provider for the three firms. Once this was accomplished, he would analyze their performance and compare them to the current routes. To aid him in his efforts he constructed a table showing the distances between the shore base and all platforms, and all inter-platform distances. These are given in Exhibit 6. After he finished this part of the analysis, he would direct his attention toward developing an implementation plan. An important component of this plan would be the pricing strategy for each platform served. Funda Sila, logistics coordinator of PR, had already suggested that platform WD34 might be served more efficiently by adding it to route AOC-3, and she wanted to know what the delivery price would be assuming it was appended to route AOC-3. It was going to be a long night, but Joe was looking forward to that large bowl of gumbo at the Crawfish Cavern.

SUPPLIER MANAGEMENT AT SUN MICROSYSTEMS (A)

Dick Allen looked through the most recent quarterly results: Sun Microsystems had continued to grow rapidly to record levels of revenue and profit. As Global Commodity Manager for Memory, he and his team now managed over a billion dollars of purchases

---

This case was prepared by David Farlow (MBA '95), Glen Schmidt (Ph.D. candidate), and Andy Tsay (Ph.D. '95) under the supervision of Charles A. Holloway, Kleiner, Perkins, Caufield, and Byers Professor of Management, Stanford University Graduate School of Business, as the basis for class discussion rather than to illustrate either effective or ineffective handling of an administrative situation.

each year. He reflected on Sun's very close relationship with its suppliers: Sun needed the suppliers' products in order to remain on the leading edge, and the suppliers needed Sun to bring their new technologies to market.

He put the quarterly results to one side and moved on to his next task, which was to calculate the aggregate global performance scores for his suppliers. This was part of the Scorecard process that Sun used to help manage its relationship with its suppliers. The program had been a great success: Some of Sun's suppliers had even started to use it with their own suppliers, while others went so far as to base 50 percent of their senior executives' bonuses on their company's Scorecard performance. However, Dick pondered whether the Scorecard process really was the best way that he could work with his suppliers.

Company Background

Sun Microsystems is a leading supplier of enterprise computing products that feature networked workstations and servers that store, process, and distribute information. Sun's computer systems are used for many demanding commercial and technical applications. The company's objective is to be a leading provider of open technologies for general purpose computing. Competitors and market shares are given in Exhibit 1, and Sun's financial performance is shown in Appendix 1.

There is a very strong cost focus at Sun. Although the company continues to grow rapidly, its stock trades at a price/earnings ratio that is more typical of a mature company. Sun believes it should trade at a much higher multiple due to its future growth prospects, while Wall Street analysts believe that workstation growth will be threatened by the technological advance of personal computers.[1] Therefore, there is significant pressure for Sun to maintain earnings growth, through both increasing revenue and lowering costs. In order to maximize operational efficiency, Worldwide Operations (WWOPS) management commits to achieving cost and headcount reductions annually. Performance versus these targets is reviewed quarterly, and monthly updates are sent to ensure management is on track.

EXHIBIT 1

Workstation Market Share, Worldwide (second quarter 1995; total shipments = 220,000)

Vendor	Market Share
Sun	34%
HP	20
IBM	14
DEC	11
Silicon Graphics	7
Other	14

Source: Dataquest.

---

[1]Sun's main competitors (Hewlett-Packard, IBM, and DEC) have a portfolio of products and therefore are less exposed to this market risk.

Business Model

Sun strives for its products to have two to three key differentiators, on which they are leading edge. On everything else, Sun wants to be competitive vis-à-vis cost and quality, as it is unable to afford the resources to differentiate every aspect of its products. This drives it to use industry standards, as well as standard components and standardized suppliers. Standardization leads to lower costs due to economies of scale that are achieved by having many products share the same components. If Sun invests in the right set of leading edge differentiators, and matches competition on the other criteria, then Sun feels it will be successful. Its key product differentiators are:

- *Scalability.* From laptops up to large systems (commonality in product features up and down Sun's product line)
- *Open system.* Commonality with industry standards.
- *Proprietary Sun technologies.* SPARC microprocessor architecture and Solaris operating software.

At the heart of Sun's strategy is the decision to use the "leverage model" for manufacturing. While achieving $4.7 billion in sales in 1994 with 13,000 employees worldwide, internal manufacturing involved fewer than 1,000 line employees. Parallel with Sun's decision to outsource the bulk of its manufacturing is its view that this strategy is an investment in its suppliers, thus increasing the manufacturing and technological capabilities of its supply base. Most decisions on scope are not driven by cost analyses; they are made for strategic reasons. Additionally, it is crucial that Sun and its suppliers have a solid relationship with aligned strategies.

Within the leveraged manufacturing model, there are three alternative levels of "make versus buy" to be considered:

1. *Buy components/systems; assemble in-house.* This leveraged strategy, in which Sun manufactures relatively little (mainly "clicking" the final product together), was adopted early in Sun's life. Unlike DEC, for instance, Sun does not have Integrated Circuit "foundries." Instead, Sun partners with suppliers who have been willing to make integrated circuits, networks, or other components necessary to keep Sun's products leading edge. Sun believes that not having to bear the investment cost of supporting capital infrastructure makes Sun faster on its feet. In return Sun will help its partners, by sharing information about Sun's intended technical direction, and by being the largest purchaser of new technology.

2. *Make and buy components/systems; assemble in-house.* Despite Sun's commitment to outsourcing, it has adopted a "make-*and*-buy" approach for some components, such as CPU boards. Sun's purpose in using this dual model is not just to provide extra capacity but to ensure it understands the technology, and can effectively perform design for manufacturability (DFM) and testability (DFT). (If the product is not designed appropriately for the manufacturing and test processes, the yields will be poor.) This strategy reduces the risk that as more components and activities are outsourced, Sun's capability to support the product internally is diminished. Also there is an occasional need to develop a new product in total secrecy, which is easier to accomplish with internal manufacturing. Furthermore, this approach may also allow Sun to maintain higher utilization of its manufacturing capacity (outsourcing only that portion of demand that exceeds internal capacity).

3. *Buy fully finished systems.* This approach has generally been avoided, except for mature products, for several reasons. First, by maintaining final assembly in-house, Sun maintains ultimate control over the customer satisfaction level, as it is able to conduct the final quality check before shipment. Since assembly is not particularly capital intensive, this can be achieved with a relatively low expenditure. Second, Sun maintains skills related to systems integration, and is reluctant to rely on suppliers for this expertise. And third, Sun is closer to demand information, and can thereby provide faster response. While suppliers' lead times are typically 14 to 16 weeks for parts, Sun's goal is to ship finished product within five days of customer order. By assembling internally (and configuring systems to allow flexibility in the product mix), Sun believes it can achieve faster response with lower inventory levels, as compared to positioning final assembly at multiple suppliers.

It should be noted that the above leveraged strategy refers to the manufacturing process, as distinguished from the design and development process. Sun maintains design and development responsibility for those components/systems where it is important to be first to market, in order to maintain technical leadership, as well as for systems integration.

Supplier Management Organization

Sun Microsystems is organized as a loosely coupled, highly aligned set of companies building off their core technologies: the SPARC microprocessor and the Solaris operating system. The hardware is focused in Sun Microsystems Computer Corporation (SMCC), which is organized in a matrix structure with product and functional axes. Sun's manufacturing organization was recently consolidated from a model emphasizing geographic independence into a centralized group called Worldwide Operations. By moving to a global operations unit Sun hoped to improve coordination both internally and throughout the supply chain. The reorganization resulted in approximately 20 percent fewer employees due to removal of duplication from operations. The importance of headcount goes beyond cost, as sales per employee is viewed as an important measure of efficiency by Wall Street analysts.

The vice president of supplier management lies three levels below Scott McNealy (chairman, president, and CEO), and reports to McNealy through the vice president of worldwide operations and the president of SMCC. There are six global commodity managers (GCMs) reporting to the vice president of supplier management, each with multimillion-dollar purchasing responsibility, to cover the following commodity areas: Memory; Mass Storage; Displays; ASICs; I/O & Power Conversion; External Manufacturing; and Noncore.[2]

Just three of these commodity groups are truly commodities (Memory, Mass Storage, and Displays), as the other groups' products are customized for use in Sun products. For these various "commodities," there is a significant difference in the number of devices per product or per board. For example, there may be only one to five ASICs per motherboard but as many as 300 memory devices.

---

[2]Noncore covers all other commodities that do not have a GCM. It includes PCBs, back plates, board level components (e.g., logic crystals, complex silicon), interconnect products (cables), and software duplication.

The GCMs, who each has between 10 and 30 years' industry experience, have no direct reports, but each acts as team leader for his or her respective Commodity Team. The Commodity Team has responsibility for its commodity components all the way through the process from "procure-to-pay," including the following:

- Acting as point of contact between Sun and its suppliers.
- Building relationships with suppliers.
- Understanding technological and manufacturing capability of the supply base.
- Understanding future technological developments in its commodity area.

Exhibit 2 shows the company's matrix structure, with line responsibility divided into four product groups: (1) Desktop Products; (2) Deskside Products & Servers; (3) Graphics; and (4) Peripherals.

Most people at Sun have two bosses. As Dick said: "This [matrix structure] can be somewhat troublesome due to conflicting demands of the bosses . . . however when I stand back and look at it the system works as well as one could expect and these difficulties really are minor."

Each GCM has multiple Commodity Managers (as well as other team members) on the Commodity Team. The direct line supervisor for a commodity manager (CM) is the corresponding product group manager. While the product group managers have design responsibility, the GCMs control the design guidelines that Sun uses with its

EXHIBIT 2

SMCC's Matrix Organization

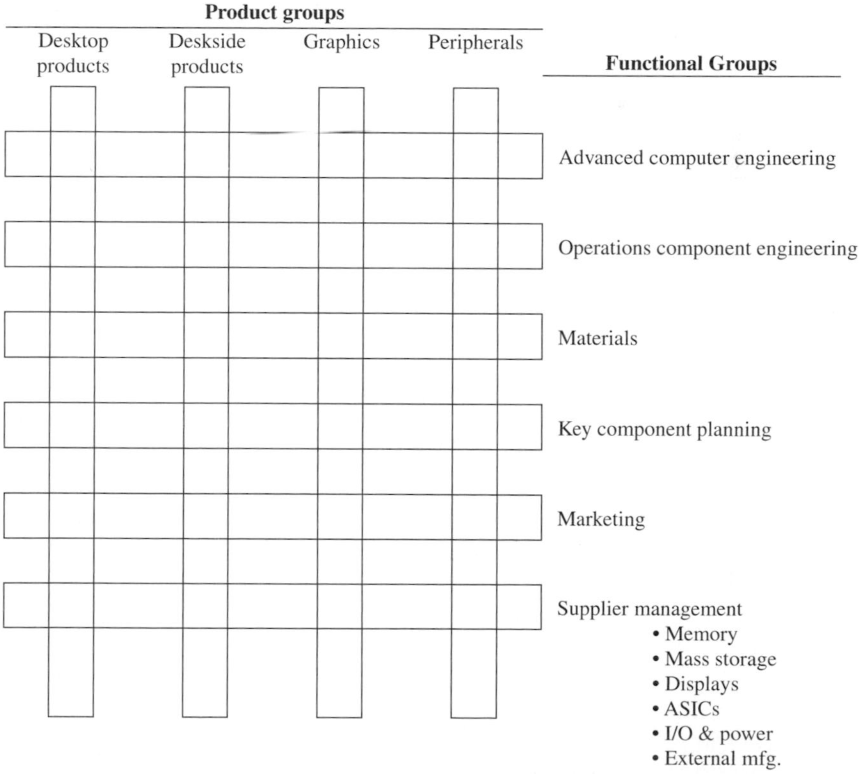

suppliers. The organization of Dick's Memory Commodity Team (detailed in Exhibit 3) consists of parallel Strategy, Project, and Site Teams (individual teams in the United States and Scotland).

Commodity Manager (CM) Responsibilities

The CM has responsibility for a given set of components (and thereby a set of suppliers) at the assembly site at which he or she is located (Milpitas, California, or Linlithgow, Scotland). Additionally, each CM has global responsibility for several of these suppliers. If a global supplier has a delivery problem that affects only one site, the local CM would handle the problem, but if the issue affected both sites the CM with global responsibility would deal with the problem.

CMs not only are responsible for managing the relationship with suppliers but are expected to fully understand the suppliers' technological and manufacturing capabilities. They also have responsibility for monitoring the capabilities of a set of future potential suppliers. Dick viewed their responsibilities as follows:

- Gather information on future technology trends and future supplier capabilities.
- Build relationships with suppliers.
- Monitor suppliers through Scorecards and detailed "action item" lists.
- Act as a point of contact/liaison between Sun and supplier.
- Act as an internal advocate for the supplier.

CMs endeavor to spend most of their time working directly with Sun's suppliers. One CM stated: "I probably spend about 60 percent of my time focusing on supplier issues . . . Another 30 percent of my time is spent on internal meetings. I have many standing meetings: Supply Planning, U.S. Operations, Qualifications. The final 10 percent is spent performing documentation."

CMs at Sun are viewed as nontraditional, as they typically come from nonprocurement backgrounds and often have general business or technical backgrounds. They act as gate keepers between the design team and suppliers, by arranging meetings between the two parties when requested. "I don't want the engineers being distracted by suppli-

Exhibit 3

Organization of Memory Commodity Team

Team	Team members
Strategy team (Meets 2 hours/week on average)	• Advanced component engineering • Operations component engineering • Materials • Key component planning • Marketing • Supplier management
Site team (Meets 1 hours/week on average)	• Operations component planning • Materials • Supplier management
	Milpitas, CA ◄—— Intersite teleconference ——► Linlithgow, Scotland
Project teams (Multiple teams as needed to address tactical issues)	• Key component planning • Materials • Supplier management • Other (as needed)

ers all the time. I prefer to keep control of the process by ensuring that the commodity managers set up any meetings between suppliers and Sun engineers," Dick Allen said.

Supplier Management Process

Exhibit 4 outlines the activities typically undertaken in supplier management, and lists some of the tasks that Sun performs in each area. Each of these activities is also discussed in more detail below.

Identification of Needs

Each commodity area typically has a core group of "tier 1" suppliers (each providing at least 15 percent of a commodity area's dollar volume) with whom it works closely, in what Sun views as a symbiotic relationship. Sun shares its development information, and suppliers are involved at the earliest stages of identifying Sun's technology needs. Sun is an early adopter of new technology and often is the major buyer of new component technology. Hence, Sun benefits from maintaining its position on the cutting edge, and suppliers benefit from access to the market at an early stage.

The early development phases where Sun and a supplier work on product development are generally not covered by any contract, and do not involve any exchange of money, but are based on the good intentions of both sides. In some cases where the supplier expends significant resources on a component that Sun eventually does not use, Sun has paid compensation.

Despite the pressure for Sun to continually improve quarterly results, the supplier management organization also needs to focus on the longer term (five-year) strategy to

EXHIBIT 4

Supply Base Management Model

Building long-term relationships		• Sharing information and strategy • Developing technical capabilities • Listening to voice-of-the-supplier			
Identification of needs	**Supplier identification**	**Supplier communication**	**Negotiation of terms**	**Supplier liaison**	**Logistics management**
"What we need"	*"Who can provide it"*	*"Here's what we want"*	*"How much, when, at what price . . ."*	*"Here's how it's going"*	*"Control the flow"*
• Establish product requirements	• Determine make-vs.-buy	• Document product requirements	• Develop contract agreements	• Manage the scorecard	• Convey forecasts
• Understand technical direction	• Pick sole-vs.-multiple suppliers	• Formulate an RFQ		• Communicate with suppliers	• Control inventory costs
• Formulate 3–5 yr. strategy	• Understand supplier capabilities; technical & mfg				• Manage end-of-life cycle

ensure that it identifies future technologies. In helping develop this strategy, Dick visited all his major suppliers around the world, to increase Sun's understanding of future technology trends and permit Sun to communicate and influence the direction in which it would like to see technology develop.

Sun takes open architecture to an extreme when it "gives away" new technologies, in the belief that the more general the use of the technology, the lower the cost to Sun. Sun perceives that it will maintain a competitive advantage because it has more experience in utilizing the technology and therefore will be able to stay ahead of the competition. For example the Memory group recently introduced a new technology called 3D-RAM. The 3D-RAM architecture was designed by Sun, but the design at the silicon level and the production are done by Mitsubishi. Sun is encouraging Mitsubishi to commercialize 3D-RAM and make it available to the open market, including Sun's competitors.

"Good ideas will get out anyway, and all that Sun really needs is a head start," Dick Allen said.

Supplier Identification

Dick Allen sees himself as part of the "old school" of supplier management, where "competition keeps people honest . . . Suppliers become sloppy when they consider *when* they will win a contract rather than *if*." He stated it was possible to have a strategic relationship where information was shared, and still encourage competition. He has three tier 1 suppliers in the Memory commodity area whom he will involve in most of his major outsourcing. He then gives each tier 1 supplier a "slice of the pie" (10 to 40 percent of the program) based on its competitiveness on price, capacity, technology, and previous performance as measured by the Scorecard process. At times, however (for example, when 16 MB DRAM replaced 4 MB DRAM), the combined capacity of the suppliers was insufficient to meet Sun's volume needs.

It takes from six months to a year to bring on a new supplier, as the qualification process involves significant management time and site visits to the supplier's manufacturing and engineering sites. The estimated direct cost of this process is approximately $500,000 of management time and travel.

In Mass Storage, where there are three main suppliers, the relationship is described as being a traditional one where each supplier is played off against the others.

In Displays and ASICs, sole suppliers are the norm. Displays uses only one company for the vast majority of its monitors, which are a Sun-specified (customized) version of a standard model. For ASICs, any one of a number of suppliers can supply the entire volume, such as Mitsubishi, LSI, or AT&T. Because of the "application-specific" nature of this product, a single supplier is chosen to minimize development costs for a given project. However, across projects there are multiple suppliers.

As the ASICs Commodity Team tenders for sole suppliers for each ASIC at the start of the design process, there is increased exposure to supplier failure. However, Sun tries to minimize this risk by assessing the supplier's manufacturing capacity and engineering capability as part of the decision process. Once the contract is awarded Sun will provide the supplier with 12-month rolling forecasts, thus enabling the supplier to begin producing wafer starts before the initial orders are made. (It takes 12 weeks to produce an ASIC from the initial wafer.)

When a GCM and his or her Commodity Team select a new supplier, Sun forms a Project Team to work with engineering and the supplier on design verification, process verification, and ramp-up of production, in order to deliver the component to Sun at the stated quality, delivery, performance, and price targets.

Supplier Communication

Sun details its component specifications, which are produced by the Engineering Department, in a Request for Quotation (RFQ) document. In the Memory Commodity area the RFQ is typically 15 to 20 pages long consisting of electrical, mechanical, and environmental specifications. The Commodity Team decides which suppliers receive the RFQ, based on perceptions of their capabilities. Since Sun works closely with its suppliers, this should not be the first time the suppliers have seen the specification.

When the supplier quotations are received, the Commodity Team "racks and stacks" them. The quotations are screened for compliance with the RFQ. Caveats to the specification are compiled and supplier bids are assessed on cost and availability.

Negotiation of Terms

Dick views his suppliers as equal partners; they are in business to make each other competitive: "Both Sun and our suppliers sign a letter of agreement and put it in a drawer." He likes to keep his agreements down to 3 to 4 pages, as opposed to the 30- or 40-page documents the legal staff would prefer in order to cover all contingencies. The Commodity Team feels the key to a successful ongoing relationship is based on trust that has been built up over many years rather than in the words of a legal contract.

Once the Commodity Team has gathered all the suppliers' bids, areas of negotiation are pursued and suppliers are asked for their "best and final" offer. Some Commodity Teams multiply the bid price by the Total Cost of Ownership as shown in the supplier's Scorecard (further described in the following section) to calculate an "effective price." Although the Commodity Team is unlikely to decide a bid based on just this adjusted price, it acts as an important signal to the suppliers that they should act to improve their performance as measured by the Scorecard.

Sun and the supplier agree on delivery and performance targets, including rolling four-quarter price targets set by Sun that typically stipulate a 3 to 6 percent reduction per quarter.

Supplier Liaison (The Scorecard)

According to Dick, "Instead of using contracts and litigation, Sun prefers to use Scorecards to influence supplier behavior."

The Scorecard is the highest-profile tool used in managing the supplier relationship. The process is clearly defined, with each supplier being rated on several criteria. Each criterion carries a separate weighting, and scores are determined by a clear series of guidelines, which may differ by commodity group. The supplier is rated against performance targets that are established and documented by the Commodity Team, and discussed with the supplier. Targets are to be achievable, challenging, and slanted toward achieving goals of greater significance.

A Scorecard synopsis is given in Appendix II, based on Sun's *WWOPS: Scorecard Calculation for Electronic Components* (a 60-page document). There are four main criteria that contribute a maximum of 100 points to this Performance Matrix Total: Quality (30 points), Leadtime/Delivery/Flexibility (30), Technology (25), and Support (15).

Since a given supplier may ship multiple part numbers to a given site, and in addition may ship to multiple sites, a "roll-up" procedure is used to calculate a global score for that supplier. To do this for, say, the Quality criterion, each part number is first given a Quality score using the established guidelines. The Quality score for that part number is then weighted by its number of units purchased (relative to total unit purchases of the commodity from that supplier), yielding a Quality roll-up score for each part number. (In some cases, this weighting may be done by dollar volume.) The individual roll-up scores are summed to obtain the site commodity score for the supplier. Next, a global roll-up procedure, again using a unit (or dollar) volume weighting, is applied to obtain the global Quality score for the commodity for the supplier.

The global scores are obtained for each of the four major criteria, and then are added to obtain the Performance Matrix Total, which in turn is multiplied by a Price Index (which introduces price as the fifth major criterion) to determine the overall score. Finally, the Total Cost of Ownership (TCOO) is calculated: TCOO = $[(100 - \text{Score})/100] + 1$.

TCOO is interpreted quite literally. If a supplier had a score of, say, 86, corresponding to a TCOO of 1.14, the commodity manager might inform the supplier that every dollar Sun spends with the supplier actually costs Sun $1.14. It is "better to buy from people with a score closer to 1," according to Dick Allen.

Sun reviews the Scorecard with each of its suppliers every quarter, and each meeting results in an action plan. The Scorecard is also reviewed with the supplier at a vice-president level every six months. This conversation handles higher level issues, such as the overall state of the relationship. Some companies even prepare their own Scorecard on their performance and compare this to Sun's scores.

Each supplier is given its Scorecard results graphically displayed against the highest scores of the other suppliers in that commodity area, thus highlighting relative performance: "The Scorecards are very high profile within supplier organizations. There is often a large fear factor with managers in local supplier organizations, as they are concerned about the reaction of their bosses to a poor score."

The Scorecard rating does not always affect the level of business. Factors such as technology or capacity that another supplier may be unable to match can lead to a contract being awarded to a supplier whose performance on the Scorecard is relatively weak: "In one area the supplier with the lowest score (and therefore the highest Cost of Ownership) has the largest dollar volume. The process in this case does not work due to differing technological capabilities of our suppliers," according to one commodity manager.

The process used to be highly secretive, but Sun recently made the process public, as suppliers were keen to use the Scorecard with their own suppliers. Sun updates the Scorecard criteria and weightings every year, and this year, suppliers also provided feedback to Sun.

Supplier liaison work also involves the New Product Introduction (NPI) process, which is under the control of a dedicated NPI program manager. "NPI is a very difficult process to manage. Often the design team members are keen to move on to the next hot product; therefore the NPI manager loses some of the engineering expertise from her team," Dick Allen said.

Working with suppliers on NPI creates its own set of challenges: "For us to qualify a particular memory chip we have to run 100 chips down the line. At a price of $5,000 each, simple math tells you that this is quite a lot of money. We don't put a burden onto the supplier to give us parts for qualification, like some other companies do; we issue a purchase order that is contingent on them passing qualification. If they don't pass then they have to credit us . . . Earlier this year I canceled a multi-tens-of-million-dollar contract as they didn't meet spec . . . It's not as if we didn't give them enough chances: we let them try three times; they just couldn't do it."

Logistics Management

Forecasts for high-volume products are developed by the Key Component Planning group (the 80–20 rule applies; 80 percent of Sun's dollar purchases come from 20 percent of the components). These forecasts (typically on a 12- or 18-month rolling basis) are used by the Materials Organization, which is responsible for managing the day-to-day inventory flow through Sun's MRP system, and are relayed to suppliers by the CMs. While forecasts are continually shifting, CMs usually wait until changes are significant before communicating them to suppliers.

The commodity teams still have to deal with managing the end of the product life cycle: "Sun is its own worst enemy—we are very bad at managing end-of-life. We often announce products too soon, thus creating demand for products that are not yet ready, and demand for our existing products falls close to zero."

While the Materials Group manages day-to-day aspects of inventory, it is the responsibility of the GCMs to establish inventory strategy, and their performance is measured in part by inventory costs. One of the most difficult times to manage inventory is at end-of-life, due to the difficulty in predicting how quickly product volumes will decline. As volume does not always decline slowly but instead may collapse to zero, WWOPS can often be left with orders for components that it no longer needs (due to the long lead times involved). Sun works with its suppliers to overcome these problems when they arise. Sun may be able to cancel some part of these orders, and identify new channels for Sun's unwanted supplies.

Building Long-Term Relationships

Sun's suppliers are critical in helping the company remain on the cusp of the technology curve. The relationship is based heavily on trust, and Sun shares a lot of technological and strategic information with its suppliers. This relationship is not based on contracts or monetary exchange during the development phase, but on the common goal of profitably bringing new technology to market.

Supplier Management recently started a "Voice of the Supplier" initiative, where it gathers its suppliers together and asks them to identify and rank major issues surrounding their relationship with Sun. The suppliers appreciated this opportunity to provide feedback, and now the Commodity Teams are individually addressing the issues raised. The number one issue is dissatisfaction with Sun's component forecasts.

Issues Surrounding the Scorecard

Dick realized he was dealing with a complex process in a complex organization and he wondered whether the Scorecard motivated suppliers to focus on the mechanics (to "achieve the numbers") rather than focus on the substance. For example, one concern was: "Suppliers get good scores if they quote long lead times . . . others who help Sun out by taking on upside demand and miss their target get hurt."

Another issue facing Dick was the management of core commodity suppliers that delivered a large volume of product not directly to Sun, but rather to Sun's suppliers. How can Sun ensure these suppliers are properly motivated and recognized relative to their contribution to Sun's product and bottom line?

Dick noted that his management attendance was higher at Scorecard reviews when the supplier was experiencing problems, and suppliers were being ignored when their Scorecard performance was high. He wondered how suppliers were perceiving this behavior.

Finally, the Scorecard process seemed to require an inordinate amount of time for development and implementation. Establishing consistent criteria, collecting the data, reporting results to management, and giving feedback to suppliers were never-ending tasks. Dick did not have concrete numbers to determine what the payback was from the Scorecard process, and wondered how it could be improved.

Appendix 1: Financial Information for Sun Microsystems ($ in millions, except per share amounts. For year ended June 30.)

	1990	1991	1992	1993	1994	1995	Growth
Revenue	$2,646	$3,221	$3,589	$4,309	$4,690	$5,902	15%/yr.
United States	51%	49%	50%	52%	49%	49%	
Europe	27%	30%	28%	27%	26%	26%	
Rest of world	22%	21%	22%	22%	25%	25%	
Cost of sales	1,399	1,758	1,963	2,518	2,753	3,399	18%/yr.
Research and development	302	356	382	445	455	520	11%/yr.
Selling, general, and administration	588	812	983	1,105	1,205	1,483	20%/yr.
Operating income	177	295	261	241	277	500	12%/yr.
Interest expense	23	11	6	2	(6)	(23)	
Taxes	43	94	82	67	88	167	
Net income	$111	$190	$173	$157	$196	$356	15%/yr.
Earnings per share	$1.21	$1.85	$1.71	$1.49	$2.02	$3.61	14%/yr.
Share price (high)	$34.38	$38.63	$35.88	$41.00	$31.38	$51.38	
Share price (low)	$13.00	$15.00	$20.75	$25.00	$18.25	$19.25	

Consolidated Balance Sheet (June 30)

	1993	1994	1995
Assets			
Current assets			
Cash, cash equivalents, & short-term investments	$1,139	$ 883	$1,228
Accounts receivable, net	627	853	1,042
Inventories	256	295	320
Other	250	274	345
Total current assets	$2,272	$2,305	$2,934
Plant, property, and equipment, net	348	360	429
Other assets, net	147	233	181
Total assets	$2,768	$2,898	$3,545
Liabilities and Stockholders' Equity			
Current liabilities			
Short-term borrowings	$ 91	$ 79	$ 51
Accounts payable	270	364	304
Accrued liabilities	393	501	688
Income taxes payable	93	94	143
Other current liabilities	100	110	145
Total current liabilities	$ 947	$1,148	$1,331
Long-term debt and other obligations	178	122	91
Stockholders' equity	1,643	1,628	2,123
Total liabilities and stockholders' equity	$2,768	$2,898	$3,545

Appendix 2: Scorecard Synopsis (Based on Sun's *WWOPS: Scorecard Calculation for Electronic Components*)

The SMCC Scorecard Summary for Electronic Components is at the end of this appendix. As shown, four criteria contribute a maximum of 100 points to the supplier's Performance Matrix Total:

- **Quality** contributes up to 30 points, as the sum of Receiving Inspection (0 to minus 8 points), Total Failure Rate (0 to 20 points), Failure Verification/Retest (0 to 2 points), FA/Corrective Action (0 to 8 points), Purge or Stop Ship (0 to minus 10 points), and PPA, DOA, or Field Problems (0 to minus 10 points).
- **Leadtime/Delivery/Flexibility** are worth up to 10, 15, and 5 points, respectively.
- **Technology** is comprised of Product Technology (0 to 9 points) and Manufacturing Technology (0 to 16 points).
- **Support** is broken down into Materials/Purchasing (0 to 10 points) and Sustaining Technical Support (0 to 5 points).

As an example of the rating scheme and roll-up procedure, below find an abbreviated description of the Lead Time category.

The delivery lead time rating scheme compares the supplier's demonstrated lead time to the committed lead time. *Committed lead time* is the delivery time agreed to by the supplier, *demonstrated lead time* is the actual delivery time, and *targeted lead time* is the goal set by the Commodity Team. Lead-time rating points are calculated as follows:

Lead-Time Rating Scheme

Demonstrated Lead Time	Award Points for Lead Time (max. = 10)
At or below committed lead time	10.0
Less than 5% above committed lead time	6.6
5 to 9.9% above committed lead time	5.0
10 to 14.9% above committed lead time	3.3
15 to 24.9% above committed lead time	2.0
25% or more above committed lead time	0.0

The Commodity Teams set lead-time goals, based on competitive lead-time benchmarks, value chain analysis, and SMCC factory and customer lead-time requirements. There is one target for all suppliers of a part, reflecting the technology that offers the shortest lead time.

When the demonstrated delivery lead time is regularly better than the committed delivery lead time, SMCC still scores the supplier based on the committed delivery lead times. Additionally, the responsible GCM, CM, or buyer/planner should negotiate with the supplier to improve the supplier's committed delivery lead times to reflect the demonstrated lead times.

Based on the above rating scheme, below find a sample calculation of lead time points for parts in a single commodity. For this example, the lead-time goal is 30 days.

Calculation of Lead Time Award Points and Site Roll-up Score

Sun Part No.	No. of Line Items	Average Demonstrated in Days	Difference Compared to Commitment of 30 Days	% Above Target of 30 Days	Award Points for Lead Time (max = 10)	Site Roll-up Score for Lead Time
17560	20	30	0	0%	10	(20/210)10 = 0.95
17575	70	30	0	0%	10	(70/210)10 = 3.33
17585	10	45	15	50%	0	(10/210)0 = 0.00
17590	30	37	7	20%	2	(30/210)2 = 0.29
17595	80	30	0	0%	10	(80/210)10 = 3.81
Total	210					8.4

The GCM performs the global roll-up procedure for lead time by weighting the individual site roll-up scores. Global roll-up scores are obtained similarly for all four major criteria, and added to obtain the performance matrix total.

The price index is determined for each part number for each supplier as follows, with site roll-ups and global roll-ups calculated from relative dollar volume:

Price Index, as Determined by Ratio of Target Price to Actual Price

(Target Price)/(Actual Price) Is Greater Than or Equal To	*(Target Price)/(Actual Price) Is Less Than*	*Price Index*
1.00	n/a	1.00
0.99	1.00	0.99
0.98	0.99	0.97
0.97	0.98	0.94
0.96	0.97	0.91
0.95	0.96	0.88
0.94	0.95	0.85
0.93	0.94	0.83
0.92	0.93	0.81
0.91	0.92	0.80
0.90	0.91	0.79
0.89	0.90	0.79
0.88	0.89	0.78
0.87	0.88	0.77
0.86	0.87	0.76
0.85	0.86	0.75
0.84	0.85	0.74
0.83	0.84	0.73
0.82	0.83	0.72
0.81	0.82	0.71
0.80	0.81	0.70
0.00	0.80*	Target/Actual − 0.12

*Minimum price index is 0.50.

The scorecard-score is calculated by multiplying the price index by the sum of the four global roll-up scores for Quality, Lead Time/Delivery/Flexibility, Technology, and Support.

Sample Calculation of the Scorecard Score

Category	*Global Scores*
Quality	27 points
Lead time/delivery/flexibility	26 points
Technology	20 points
Support	15 points
Total for performance matrix	**88 points**
Price index	0.98
Scorecard score	88(0.98) = **86.24**

Finally, total cost of ownership (TCOO) is calculated:

$$TCOO = [(100 - Score)/100] + 1$$

The calculation for TCOO in the above example is as follows:

$$TCOO = [(100 - 86.24)/100] + 1 = \textbf{1.14.}$$

SMCC Scorecard Summary for Electrical Components

SMCC Scorecard Electrical Components			Quarter:		
Summary Supply unit or Global Results			FY:		
Scorecard for:	Commodity rated:		Done on:		
Category	**Subcategory**	**Data or comments**	**Max points**	**Actual points**	**Score**
Quality	Receiving inspection		(8.0)		
	Total failure rate (RPM/DPM)		20.0		
	Failure verification/ retest		2.0		
	FA/corrective action		8.0		
	Purge or stop ship		(10.0)		
	PPA, DOA, or field problems		(10.0)		
	Quality subtotal:		**30.0**		pts
Lead Time/ Delivery/ Flexibility	Lead time		10.0		
	On-time delivery		15.0		
	Flexibility		5.0		
	L/D/F subtotal:		**30.0**		pts
Technology	Product		9.0		
	Manufacturing		16.0		
	Technology subtotal:		**25.0**		pts
Support	Materials/ Purchasing		10.0		
	Sustaining technical		5.0		
	Support subtotal:		**15.0**		100 pts
Performance matrix total			**100.0**		
Price index			**1.0**		
Score = performance matrix × price index			100.0		
Total cost of ownership = [(100 — Score)/100] + 1			Goal: 1.0		
Prior performance matrix score:					
Prior price performance:					
Prior total cost of ownership:					

CASE 12

THE LAURA ASHLEY AND FEDERAL EXPRESS STRATEGIC ALLIANCE

On March 20, 1992, Laura Ashley (LA), a global clothing and furnishings retailer based in the United Kingdom, and logistics leader Federal Express's Business Logistics Service

Research Associate Robert Anthony prepared this case under the supervision of Professor Gary Loveman as the basis for class discussion rather than to illustrate either effective or ineffective handling of an administrative situation. It was adapted from "Laura Ashley: The Strategic Alliance with Federal Express," HBS No. 493-018, originally written by Dr. Gloria Schuck, with Professor Shoshana Zuboff.

(BLS) announced a strategic alliance that would result in BLS taking over LA's worldwide distribution. The arrangement was preceded by a letter to the LA board of directors by newly arrived chief executive officer Jim Maxmin in December of 1991 that described "the gross inadequacies of our current distribution and warehousing operations . . . (including inadequate) systems to control our stockouts, stock levels, margins, stock replenishment requirements, etc." The objective of the alliance was to transform LA customer service levels by offering improved reliability, speed, and frequency of deliveries. An aggressive implementation schedule would result in the integration of warehouse systems by September 1992, integration of shop systems by February 1993, and an expanded mail order business offering delivery within 48 hours to any destination by September 1993.

The prospective alliance held exciting potential, as well as risks, for both parties. For LA the alliance promised more effective, lower-cost distribution, which would enhance its competitiveness in the market as well as facilitate a transformation of the way in which it did business at the retail level. For BLS the alliance represented an opportunity to effectively utilize all of its capabilities on a global basis, thereby refining its skills and opening up large new potential markets for the future. On the other hand, a failure of the alliance could mean continuing distribution ineffectiveness for LA, and, for BLS, a tremendous setback for the idea of partnership, which possibly could be a large part of the future of BLS. The alliance would be visible, and any difficulties would be highly embarrassing for both companies.

Even as the alliance was announced, managers participating in its development on both sides wondered what its eventual impact on LA and BLS would be, and, if it succeeded, in what creative directions it might evolve.

Laura Ashley

Laura Ashley, founded in 1953 by Bernard and Laura Ashley when they began printing textiles on the kitchen table of their London attic flat, was a specialty retailer, primarily of upscale women's fashions, fabrics, and home furnishing products. The company was known for products that typified the tradition of English rural life. As Jim Maxmin observed:

> Few great brands have been created in the last 50 years and fewer still have achieved global renown. Laura Ashley is quintessentially English, and therein lies its timeless appeal. It is synonymous with English Romanticism.

LA segmented its market in terms of customer lifestyles. As opposed to many of its competitors who targeted specific demographic or age groups, LA offered styles that would be appropriate for a customer from an early age to an older age. This customer tended to be an upscale consumer who was "fashion conscious but not fashion forward." Market research concluded in 1991 revealed similarities in the company's customer base, as described in the fiscal year 1992 annual report:

> The typical Laura Ashley customer is a well-educated, relatively affluent woman. She is confident, concerned, and interested in ideas, travel, and natural beauty, as well as fashion. She cares about family, health, home, the countryside, relationships, and responsibilities. Generous but not extravagant, the Laura Ashley customer believes in quality, service, value, and things that last. Her loyalty to Laura Ashley is based on her perception that we share those values.

A high level of in-store personal service was important to Laura Ashley's customer base and integral to maintaining the image of the brand. The company encouraged interpersonal interplay between customers and its store employees, although it avoided "hard-sell" approaches. In general, shops were staffed with women who shared the tastes and interests of the LA customer base and had the ability to develop a personal rapport with customers.

The Late 1980s and the Arrival of Jim Maxmin

In 1990 LA operated 481 retail stores throughout the world, up from 231 in 1986 (Exhibits 1 and 2). However, despite the continuing success of LA branded products in the market, financial performance during the late 1980s was disastrous (Exhibit 3).

EXHIBIT 1

1990 LA Shop Statistics (retail space in thousands of square feet)

	1986	1987	1988	1989	1990
Number of shops	231	292	365	439	481
Net retail space	357	492	630	738	816

Source: 1990 annual report.

EXHIBIT 2

1989/1990 Geographical Analysis (retail space in square feet)

	Number of Shops	Retail Space
United Kingdom	184	393,700
North America	185	255,600
Europe	65	99,000
Australia	23	34,800
Japan	24	33,300

Source: 1990 annual report.

EXHIBIT 3

Laura Ashley Financial Overview (in millions of English pounds)

	For the 52 Weeks Ended January 25				
	1992	1991	1990	1989	1988
Sales	260.7	327.5	296.6	252.4	201.5
Operating profit	1.1	5.3	6.1	23.6	23.8
Profit (loss) from associates	3.6	0.1	(0.2)	—	—
Royalty income	0.3	0.3	1.1	1.6	1.7
Net interest payable	(2.3)	(12.4)	(8.6)	(4.9)	(2.4)
Profit (loss) before exceptional items	2.7	(6.7)	(1.6)	20.3	23.1
Exceptional items*	(11.8)	(4.8)	(6.7)	—	—
Profit (loss) before taxation	(9.1)	(11.5)	(8.3)	—	—

*Includes charges for restructuring costs, systems costs, inventory writedowns, and other one-time events.
Source: 1992 annual report.

Andrew Higginson, financial director appointed in 1990, summarized: "Sales went up, profits were flat, and capital employed rose out of control. All of our problems were internal."

As early as 1986, "at the height of the stores' euphoria," an LA report identified fundamental weaknesses in the company. These included an overdependence on in-house manufacturing, significant currency exposure, working capital intensity, excessive short-term debt, and rapid cash outflow. Still, growth continued to strain the management of the business, and by the end of the 1980s, LA had developed an expensive hierarchy with an inappropriate structure. Information technology investments lagged growth and, where systems did exist, they were totally inadequate.

Also, by 1990 specific changes in the LA supply chain had added to the complexity of the company. In an effort to reduce dependency on in-house manufacturing, an extensive, worldwide network of third-party product sources was developed, limiting company-owned factories to 42 percent of sales by 1990, down from 100 percent in 1986. However, systems and management practices were not aligned to optimize the transition. The result was a hodgepodge of logistics relationships and arrangements that were difficult to manage and were often ineffective.

Explained Maxmin:

> The organization was overcomplicated. Each operating region (Continental Europe, the United Kingdom, and the United States) had its vertical hierarchy, so functions and systems were triplicated and communications were erratic. Overhead levels were not supported by gross margins or sales. Despite the brand's global appeal, less than 5 percent of our range was common to all stores and operations worldwide. In all this we had lost sight of our customers' real wishes and lifestyle, as well as our heritage.

In September 1991 Bernard Ashley handed chief executive responsibilities to Maxmin, who was former chief executive of Thorn EMI Home Electronic International. Maxmin immediately introduced strategic and organizational initiatives aimed at building the LA brand and restoring the company to profitability. They included an aggressive campaign to streamline the business and decentralize decision making, which was called *S*implify, *F*ocus, and *A*ct (SFA), and a three-pronged strategic focus on branding, distribution, and systems development. Maxmin's goal for LA was to become "strategically led, competitively focused, market oriented, employee driven, and operationally excellent."

A first step in the revitalization process was a restructuring of the company to emphasize its global coordination. A Global Operations Executive (GOE) team consisting of managers from across the business was formed to oversee global interrelationships, and two layers of field management in the United Kingdom and one layer in the United States were removed. In total, 100 senior- and support-level managers departed. In addition, bonuses were linked to global performance, common merchandising was developed, and uniform financial systems were implemented. The pyramidal reporting structure in the stores was flattened to two levels in the United Kingdom and one in the United States.

The SFA initiative involved empowerment of frontline service providers, enhanced training at all levels, and the integration of information technology to simplify and improve service. A Profit Improvement Program (PIP) scheme was implemented in 10 trial stores, wherein store employees came up with a number of new ideas to increase sales, from special events such as fashion shows and decorating demonstrations to special window displays that reflected the local customer mix. The PIP shops were 62 to 70 percent over sales forecast for the trial period. Training involved in-store training for frontline personnel, as well as time spent in the store for others throughout the organization. Technology would be focused on providing stores with the capabilities to make decisions with timely, accurate information. Maxmin noted:

> I've told everybody that you must challenge complexity . . . We need to simplify our approach to business and all our operations . . . [With the PIP] we let the staff have more say about how they do things by letting them come up with ideas to attract customers into the store. I only asked four things of them: (1) Love the customer absolutely and keep seeing the problems through the eyes of the customer. If something we do doesn't contribute to our service, we have to get rid of it. (2) Use your common sense. If you get instructions that are dumb, then you should point it out to the people concerned and suggest a better way of doing it. (3) Bring forward your ideas. (4) Each of us must create an open, honest, and trusting structure. In that way we can reduce costs.

The strategic focus on brand management was designed to rectify weaknesses in the brand that had developed, as well as expand its prominence globally. While LA appealed to a 6 to 7 percent share of local markets, it was felt that the brand had not grown with its traditional customer base. There was too much repetition in the product line (e.g., floral dresses), which also lacked sufficient breadth to reflect customers' career and leisure-based lifestyles. As a result, Maxmin decided to extend coverage of the LA brand in existing clothing and furnishing categories, as well as to identify licensing opportunities in such areas as tableware, bridal wear, and china, which would be sold outside of LA's own retail distribution structure.

The strategic focus on systems development was designed to provide retail shops with information flows and to make the business more "transparent." It was felt that transparency, when coupled with empowerment, would be the key to superior customer service.

Historically, LA systems had been designed to provide information to independent business units. Duplicate systems designed to serve independent business units caused LA to spend twice the industry average on systems in 1990. Over the next two years significant efforts would be undertaken to implement common systems across the business. Major software systems to be introduced in 1992–93 included a merchandise planning system, a group finance/executive information system, an electronic point-of-sale (EPOS) system, a global purchase ordering system, and a manufacturing and UK distribution system. PC-based POS registers would be installed in every shop, which would make the data in the company accessible by everyone. LA expected to make a large investment to convert to common systems, but it expected annual systems costs to reduce greatly thereafter.

The strategic focus on distribution aimed at overhauling warehousing, replenishment, and delivery operations, which were, in the words of Maxmin, "a disaster, out of control." A global team headed by Phil Baker, Special Projects Director in Global Finance, was formed to evaluate options for fixing the problems. The objectives of the team were to develop a system capable of providing 99 percent availability, 24- to 48-hour delivery, and a 50 percent reduction of working capital. Currently, availability was roughly 80 percent, and the company maintained an extended, working capital-intensive supply chain, which housed an average of 18 months' worth of inventory from product design through store sale. The strategic alliance with BLS resulted from LA's distribution initiative.

Federal Express and Business Logistics Services

Federal Express (FedEx) was incorporated in 1971 by Frederick W. Smith Jr. He designed a nationwide air service network to resemble the spokes of a wheel, with Memphis, Tennessee, as hub. Utilizing the hub as a central processing center for all packages, FedEx pioneered next-day delivery, and by 1991 the company had become the premier carrier in the overnight delivery business.

FedEx was renowned for its logistics expertise and tracking systems. It employed 90,000 people worldwide, operated 444 aircraft and 30,000 collection and delivery vehicles, with more than 1,300 facilities serving 176 countries. FedEx created the American overnight delivery market and was expanding overseas, mostly in the Far East, with a smaller portion of its business in Europe, where its operations were unprofitable in 1991. FedEx posted operating income in 1991 of $280 million on sales of $7.7 billion, with operating margins down significantly from the prior year. While FedEx had been hurt by recessionary business conditions, it was also dissatisfied with the underlying performance of its business, and, in fiscal year 1992, it undertook several initiatives to reduce overhead and control expenses.

FedEx created the Business Logistics Services Division in December 1987 to provide specialized logistics services to businesses throughout the world. It had operations in the United States, Europe, and the Far East. BLS had earned a reputation for providing quality services, and its long-term strategy was "one of synergy with FedEx's other mainstream operations: to develop pan-European business logistics services that enhance the total range of FedEx services available, and enhance those business logistics services by making maximum use of FedEX global networks." As one BLS manager explained, "BLS is the boutique, the custom shop. We're the people who do it your way in the big contractual context as opposed to doing it in the totally standard way, one package at a time." BLS employed 4,000 people worldwide (940 in the United Kingdom), and its European operations included 1,100 road vehicles and 1,750,000 square feet of warehouse space, made up of 75 contract locations and distribution centers. BLS worldwide revenues were approximately 6 to 7 percent of Federal Express revenues.

BLS UK had three major operations. Through its "Systemline" service, BLS planned, implemented, and operated sophisticated information technology-based inventory management systems under contract. Systemline services tailored to the needs of individual clients included warehouse location and specification, inventory systems, vehicles, routing, and scheduling, as well as provision of a highly trained workforce. Markets for the service included automotive, consumer electronics, computers, and toys, with clients including industry leaders in each category.

The "Partsbank" service provided global, low-risk, and rapid start-up distribution for high-value products by operating pay-as-you-go distribution centers shared by approximately 200 users. Clients, including leading international high-tech manufacturers, purchased services from a menu that included collection, storage, inventory control, customs/administration, customer service support, international forwarding and air freight, and delivery. BLS's Systemcare service provided home delivery of large, bulky, and heavy items such as furniture and household appliances. Systemcare offered both dedicated delivery operations and shared facility operations for smaller clients.

BLS provided three elements where logistics expertise offered a competitive advantage: transportation, primarily through the FedEx network; warehousing; and information systems. BLS's international business development director, Bill Parsons, identified warehousing and information systems as the "real value-added":

> Quite often warehousing is at the back end of the client organization. Since it's at the front end of what we do, we developed systems and productivity that the client can't match. But where we really score, what puts us ahead of the competition is systems. There's no ques-

tion that information is vitally important, as important as product flows. Information flows should go before product flows, then you can get your physical operation as sophisticated as possible and optimize it.

BLS's vice president for Europe, Charles Kirks, explained that BLS offered clients umbrella information systems that would "take care of the inventory system end-to-end":

> We have systems for managing inventories. We have systems for running warehouses that are like shop floor control. Mainly, and most importantly, we have this ubiquitous network that lets you know where parcels are as they flow through the system, . . . [can] tell you where every single item is every day . . . We have it all.
>
> Sometimes a customer comes and says he's already narrowly predetermined what he wants from BLS. He says he wants "transportation." There are plenty of good transportation providers out there, and given how soft the market is right now there are some extremely low prices. If he just wants computer systems, there are other people who might be able to do that, too. If he just wants warehousing services, there are other people. But if he wants somebody to put all three of those things together and to hook them to an international transportation network that FedEx represents, there's nobody out there to do that except BLS! If he wants all three services and he wants us to manage it for him, too—that's the very best scenario. We end up acting like a general contractor, drawing first upon the resources of BLS worldwide and next upon the resources that FedEx has all over the world.

The Laura Ashley Opportunity

As 1991 came to a close, it was apparent to all in Laura Ashley that its distribution performance was abysmal. Its distribution structure and systems were excessively complicated, and its operations and logistics track record was horrible. Problems LA had with its distribution system included inefficient goods flows, outdated inventory ordering practices, long lead times, and broken promises to customers. Anecdotes of distribution nightmares abounded. As distribution team coordinator Phil Baker stated at the outset of the project, "Right now, we're the opposite of service maximization and cost minimization."

LA maintained eight warehouses. The largest was in Newtown (the United Kingdom), and others were in Milton Keynes (the United Kingdom), Veldhoven (Holland), Mahwah (New Jersey), California, Canada, Paris, and Australia. The company had been geographically organized, and regional Strategic Business Units (SBUs) in the United States, United Kingdom, and continental Europe operated as stand-alone businesses, with independent inventory, systems, and merchandising. This resulted in a number of problems in the distribution system. First, the SBUs' parochial perspectives led to inventory turns of less than two and an out-of-control working capital situation. SBUs maintained, as an objective, filling up their allocations of the warehouses with inventory.

Second, because SBUs independently managed logistics, the transportation system was suboptimal. Maxmin characterized as "dumb" distribution product flows that, for instance, would involve "manufacturing a T-shirt in Hong Kong, moving it to Newtown, and sending it back to Japan to be sold!" Notwithstanding the fact that LA had inventory throughout the supply chain, its out-of-stock position neared 20 percent on average. Commented Baker:

> All the routes have different transporters. We have numerous distribution contractors and different suppliers. Trying to control this is a nightmare. We're continually renegotiating so that we get the best price. Individual markets don't understand global supply and demand.

We have locations all over the world, and we have numerous echelons of stock for different markets. The supply chain has stock, the market has stock, and the factory has stock.

Maxmin offered an anecdote related to this kind of distribution ineffectiveness, which he had heard from a shop employee in California:

A customer waited a year for a fabric pattern called "cornflower," and she still thought that we were the greatest people in the world for getting it for her! That shop had been out of stock and had faxed the home office 17 times and never got a reply. The shop rang around and finally located the fabric in San Diego. When I returned to the United Kingdom, the factory manager told me that he had 27,000 meters of the fabric, and he'd had it for a year.

Baker discovered that the replenishment system was based on ineffective historic practices and outdated priorities:

The replenishment system was based on what happened when the company was a lot smaller. It was based on custom and practice and the belief that you could only know the demand and merchandise of a shop by looking individually at that shop from headquarters and telling them the products that they needed. If a shop was given 10 of an item last year, when one sold it would automatically be replaced. It could have taken a whole year to sell only one, but it would be replenished! They ignored the rate of sale in their algorithm.

At the Oxford Circus shop they're selling 25 items a week and they've got 100 in stock; they'll place an order for 25 more each week. At the Cardiff shop they may have five in stock and sell them all, and place an order for five more. The warehouse has only 20 items, and the current priority says ship it to Oxford Circus because that's the fastest-selling shop.

Delivery problems also multiplied. Delivery pallets often looked like "leaning towers of Pisa," garments could be wrinkled and soiled, and shops would receive deliveries at times when they were not staffed to handle them, or when there was not room for them in storerooms. The result would be shops that were a mess. Perhaps the most disturbing aspect for LA of distribution ineffectiveness was the fact that it often resulted in broken promises to customers. Baker observed that "people thought that 80 percent on time was good; they never challenged it, standards were nonexistent. The customer was an inconvenience, their needs and concerns were a source of irritation." An operations update for the week ending October 11, 1991, summed up this mentality for LA at the time:

Can *all* managers please ensure that when furniture orders are taken, customers are told that the delivery date given is only *approximate* and not the guaranteed delivery date? The customer should be told that the delivery arrangements will be confirmed nearer the time. This is very important as many customers think that the date given is the date on which the furniture will arrive, thus causing a considerable amount of bad feeling when a different date is given.

SFA, new structures that provided an enhanced focus on global coordination, and the strategic distribution initiative all were LA responses to its costly and ineffective distribution system.

The Strategic Alliance

Between October 1991 and March 1992, when implementation would commence, LA and BLS reached a comprehensive agreement that would result in BLS taking over LA's Newtown, Wales, warehouse, and all of LA's distribution activities. The process was initiated by Jim Maxmin, who quickly turned the project over to the Global Operations Executive team to implement. The GOE team worked with a BLS team led by the business development director, Bill Parsons, to produce initial solutions, and in December 1991 a joint operating and systems team was formed to detail the solutions and prepare them for planned March 1992 implementation.

Solutions would include the formation of a new company that would be owned and managed by BLS, the creation of new management systems and the integration of existing systems, and ongoing evaluation of the arrangement. The alliance was purposefully created with a loose structure that would allow it to evolve in appropriate directions as a baseline of experience was garnered, and that was intended to keep both companies focused on the strategic nature of their partnership. The anticipated timetable of the integration activities was:

- September 1992: Completion of global reorganization of warehousing.
- February 1993: Integration of BLS/LA information technology systems.
- September 1993: 24- or 48-hour delivery of LA products throughout the world.
- September 1993: Development of global mail order capability.

LA expected that the alliance would result in significant working capital savings, lower cost distribution, and improved customer service levels. BLS anticipated that the alliance would help define its business in an area with tremendous future growth potential.

Initiation of the Alliance

Upon his arrival at LA, Jim Maxmin sorted out his options for fixing the distribution mess at the company. They boiled down to reorganizing existing operations and writing new integrated distribution systems or withdrawing from warehousing and distribution altogether and handing them to a third-party expert. Feeling that "it would take 100 years" to write the necessary systems from scratch and recognizing that distribution was not a "core competence" of the company, Maxmin decided to go outside of LA for help. In October 1991 he approached FedEx to explore pooling the two companies' resources:

> I got the idea of a "strategic alliance" between LA and FedEx. I had met [FedEx Senior Vice President] Tom Oliver and was hugely impressed by him. As you go through your business life you meet certain people, and you just register that these people are extraordinary. I picked up the phone and told him my idea. He was interested and said we should form the alliance. That was the essence of our conversation; the rest of it has been left to our organizations.

Maxmin then met with the GOE team and explained his concept of the strategic alliance. LA would not solicit competitive bids for distribution but, instead, it would form a "win–win business partnership" with BLS. The partnership would have no defined end point, lasting a minimum of 10 years. Maxmin described the reaction of the GOE team to his idea:

> There was huge skepticism to start with . . . Their expectation was that within a few weeks they needed to get a contract with FedEx and have every *i* dotted and *t* crossed. I told them that I wanted to do it differently and that I didn't want to be bothered with lawyers, contracts, and all kinds of complications. The partnership was to be an open book—no secrets, no surprises. I kept saying that you have got to have faith and embrace a new way of doing business . . . a different way to compete . . . Look out to the 21st century, not back to the 19th.

In November 1991, Charles Kirk, BLS's vice president for Europe, had a meeting at LA to pursue a deal. Kirk was pleasantly surprised by the attitudes he found at LA:

> We try very hard to have strategic alliances, but typically you go to a company and it turns into "traffic manager court." The traffic manager says he wants the cheapest price per kilogram to ship, and then you don't have a deal. Traffic managers don't buy value added. But in LA I never met a traffic manager . . . They had already decided that they were going to make drastic changes in their distribution and the way they served the customer before we ever met them . . . They just wanted us to get on with it. This was a real marriage made in heaven. These guys really want us to do what we're good at doing.

By November 29, LA's Baker and BLS's Parsons produced a presentation of "first-look" solutions for the GOE team and a gross schedule of activities, responsibilities, and deadlines. The companies would work toward signing a "global contract" by March 1992, at which time implementation would commence. Prior to the presentation, LA and BLS participants agreed to a policy for sharing information in the development of the final deal. The intent was to build trust and to keep the parties focused on areas of mutual interest. Then, on December 3, 1991, LA sent a letter acknowledging its intent to develop with BLS a "worldwide logistics partnership," subject to board approval and completion of a definitive agreement.

Solutions

Forming the alliance involved stipulating the means by which the LA distribution system would be organized, planning implementation of the transition to BLS, and creating the integrated systems that would be the core of the new distribution enterprise. This would be the work of a joint, cross-functional project team, comprised of key managers from both companies. The team organized into subcommittees, under the auspices of a steering committee, with Baker and Parsons leading the work of developing the final arrangement.

In order to achieve the goals, a new company, LA Distribution Ltd., would be formed and "sold" to BLS, which would then manage all aspects of LA distribution. LA would then close the Mahwah and Veldhoven warehouses. The Newtown facility was designated central "processing center" for all product flows, with a satellite processing center for the U.S. market being established in Memphis. Shipments to shops could be through the warehouse system or, if it made sense, directly from manufacturers to shops. As Parsons explained, "You can have a single warehouse worldwide if you've got the links. FedEx has the links, the airplanes. We've also got the logistics and inventory accounting systems to back it up."

LA distribution employees would be transferred to the new company. Both BLS and LA resolved to make the transition as painless as possible for them. Jim Maxmin personally got involved in assuring employees that they would be taken care of, and BLS made its complete program of induction and training available to them. While there was some skepticism and disappointment among former LA employees, many also recognized that they would be joining an excellent company that had managing distribution as its core business.

Two BLS systems would be central to the operation of the new company. BLAST prepared invoices and tracked cartons for dispatch, and Federal Express's COSMOS tracking system provided information on package location through a bar coding system. These would be linked with LA's Shop Stock and Warehouse Inventory System, to provide for complete information on inventory from order through delivery. The integration was slated to occur by the end of 1992. At the same time, BLS was developing a Warehouse Management System (WMS), which would "dynamically" manage labor scheduling and control, storage management, quality of performance, and product protection. By February of 1993, the WMS would be integrated with LA Merchandise Planning System, Purchase Order Management System, and core retail system (used for shop inventory, replenishment, and shop financial management) to provide for decision making related to inventory and inventory management. Baker explained:

> The shops and warehouses will be linked by BLAST and COSMOS. The movements between those will be goods in transit movements, and we'll have the ability to actually track where something is at any point in time. I call it GIT, Goods in Transit Control. What we've actually got is a closed loop. These movements then update the shop stock. Then by looking at linking in the warehouse inventory, the shop inventory, and the GIT inventory, what you've actually got is "global inventory."

Once the system was complete (completion was planned for 1993), LA would be able to resupply its shops throughout the world within 24 to 48 hours. Each shop would be online to the global inventory control system, by which it would have total visibility of goods in the supply chain. It was anticipated that simplification of the supply chain would lead to a reduction of 10 to 12 percent in distribution costs. Baker explained the significance:

> With the BLS and Federal Express systems we'll have transparency. At the moment we are looking at our business through a fog. The fog is our own internal organization. We're using the FedEx systems as one of the mechanisms to make the fog clear. We have a multitude of suppliers and distribution contracts all over the world . . . We are willing to pay a premium to get the clarity and the simplicity that the technology will give us.

Coming to Terms

While BLS and LA reached a rough agreement on the mechanics of the alliance, the process of forming the partnership was challenging for both. Specific challenges included structuring the incentives of the deal and decisions regarding how tightly to define the arrangement. Kirk elaborated:

> There's hardly a price in the whole agreement. It's all relative. Everything is a function of something else and, therefore, over time that base factor changes. It's only possible that we got it done this quickly for an agreement of this size because we have dealt with things as generalities. Things that are values in other contracts are variables in this contract. There are no numbers in there; everything is a function of everything else. It doesn't give the answer. It gives the formula because over time the specifics change.

The project team toyed with the idea of defining Service Quality Indicators and attaching penalties in the agreement, but in the end it decided only to use the indicators, which would be mutually determined, to measure progress. Baker explained why penalties were rejected:

> It does us no good at all to get penalties built in because what they've done is missed the service. No penalty can satisfy a customer that we've lost. At the end of the day, if we have a penalty structure it is meaningless because we still lost the customer.

Developing the final contract was a challenge due to a lack of consensus among counsel advising both parties on how tightly the arrangement should be defined. Throughout the process lawyers on both sides grappled with how to define issues without obscuring the mutual interests on which the success of the alliance would depend. Said one attorney:

> At the start we had two different approaches, ours and theirs. I believe that they thought it would be much more straightforward and simple, perhaps because of talk of cooperation and working together. However, I've been present at the start of many marriages and also at the end! A partnership is a marriage. No matter how positive, cooperative, and helpful the partners are at the start, it is essential that they see their relationship in the cold light of the practicalities. They have to look at it as if it doesn't work and walk through the consequences.

BLS and LA agreed on a "transparent, cooperative venture" to last a minimum of 10 years. Each had a right to inspect the other party's business, and there were mechanisms built in to deal with matters that could not be agreed upon. In essence, the companies had "agreed to agree" on issues that would arise in the course of doing business. Higginson, LA's financial director, stated:

> We hope that the contract is just a fallback position. The intention is to put the contract in the drawer and never get it out again, because the day you get it out again you have to admit that there is a problem with the relationship.

Said Maxmin:

> Problems will come up, and people will say, "I told you so." I'll be totally sympathetic to the problems and do everything I can, but I'll just turn my mind off of the negativism, because I know this alliance is going to work.
>
> We lifted this above just distribution and logistics and formed a strategic alliance. It's a systems partnership. It's a business partnership. We're affecting in an integral way the processes of LA, and, therefore, it doesn't have a time scale to it. It doesn't have a time span to it, and nobody is worried. You set standards of operations that have to be achieved, but it's not about having a contract and going back and saying that you violated line 82. It's not the spirit in which it was conceived.

Given the loose nature of the alliance, development of a high level of trust among the parties involved was the critical ingredient. "We have all gone through the trust hoop," said one LA manager, "but at the end of the day you have to believe that you're all working for the same end objective." Said another, "You need to trust, not in a naive sort of way, but in an open-minded sort of way—you trust, but skeptically. You know what could go wrong and you work all the more to make sure that trust is maintained." This was not always easy.

At times, project team progress became bogged down in disagreement over the details of the arrangement. At such times leaders from both companies stepped in to refocus the project on the win–win aspects of the partnership. Maxmin recalled one day in January 1992 when he met with the team to keep them focused on the strategic aspects of the alliance:

> I stayed away other than to attend one meeting. Basically, I've watched it evolve with the vacillations and vicissitudes of management inside the business. Everyone is coming up with all of their reservations. In January they started worrying about the size of boxes for delivery and got bogged down. I had to sit down with the team and get them to focus on the real issues. I asked them if there were any systems, political, business process, or commercial issues that say we shouldn't proceed with the alliance. Do you see anything that would actually inhibit our operation? And I asked them to be sure that we can get the rundown on incremental costs. Those were the only things I was interested in.

Other reasons for skepticism existed. Managers from both companies at times wondered if they were being taken advantage of in the negotiation process, and, if they were, when and how they would know it. Jim Maxmin began to receive what he called "defense documents" from some LA managers who were keen to point out all of the risks in the deal. One LA team member described the reaction to the defense documents:

> Jim has refused to listen to any other argument. We all got bogged down in the trucks and sheds issues, but Jim ignored all of it and said that the alliance was going to happen. He's driven it through. Jim takes risk and he takes our blinders off so we can see new possibilities.

On the basis of this support, project team members would return to acknowledging the possibilities for both parties that might accrue from joint efforts, ignoring many of the detailed allocations of risks and rewards. Nonetheless, some project team members had lingering doubts down to the signing of the agreement. "Is this too good to be true?" they thought.

Still, at the end of the process, managers on both sides lauded the concept of strategic alliance as a means of gaining a competitive advantage in the market and felt confident that their alliance would succeed. Said one LA team member:

> The concept of a strategic alliance is that we both work together to get a competitive edge. But the outcomes aren't really defined, because to define them suggests an endpoint . . . Jim's view is that we don't know how good we can be and we don't know where that's actually going to take us. Where we're going specifically isn't as important as figuring out how we'll work together to get a competitive advantage.

BLS's president, Robert May, who was responsible for BLS worldwide operations, summarized:

> [This] was just the sort of program that BLS had been striving for—an alliance where both parties worked together to develop each other's business. It represented a step forward for both companies, each recognizing the other's skills and harnessing them to move forward on a truly global level. BLS has always been highly successful in its individual economic markets around the world. With LA we had the opportunity to demonstrate to the global community that FedEx/BLS was the only company worldwide that was capable of providing a tailored global solution. LA had the vision to see that capability and want to use it to their competitive advantage.

LA and FedEx considered the specifics of its deal to be confidential. They viewed the alliance as a unique opportunity for both parties, and, accordingly, the structure of the highly complicated arrangement was unique in their experience. Basically, LA would pay the direct costs that BLS incurred in managing LA's global logistics requirements and a management fee to BLS as a percentage of cost. LA would pay BLS for freight, with some discount to the market price offered in consideration of LA's large volume. Formulas were then determined to provide incentives for BLS to improve operations. After two years during which BLS would stabilize the logistics operation, if LA agreed to pick up the capital costs of an improvement project, the benefits, for the most part, would be split by the two parties. Longer term, a larger proportion of the benefits, growing to 100 percent, would begin to accrue to LA in consideration of its funding. In addition, the deal specified certain safety nets for LA in case the alliance failed, which would ease its transition to another option.

Conclusion

Both LA and BLS expected to realize "substantial and real" benefits from the alliance. For LA these included access to new systems in a compressed time frame, new ways of doing business, improved performance, and ability to focus resources on activities where it could add the most value. Also, LA had come to be seen as somewhat of a turn-around story in England, and the positive momentum gained from the alliance could help it consolidate investor confidence. For BLS the alliance would be trend setting, provide entry into the clothing business, provide entry into Europe, utilize existing international loading capacity, establish the global nature of its business, and align it with a well-respected consumer franchise.

On the other hand, the failure of either business, together or separately, would result in dramatically poor consequences for both. At risk for FedEx was the value of its reputation for reliability, which supported an $8 billion business. LA risked its entire operations infrastructure.

In addition to the opportunities and risks, there was the potential for the alliance to evolve in creative directions. For instance, LA had planned to utilize its new distribution capabilities by greatly expanding its mail order business in 1993. Also, the new capabilities would support the empowerment of frontline service providers and lead to improved levels of customer service, as well as make it possible to simultaneously reduce inventories and expand the LA product lines. Clearly, the idea of global partnership could be leveraged by BLS with other customers in other industries. As the potential of the deal was assessed, it was left open by both parties that there were other unique forms of competitive advantage that could be gained by LA and that could be sold in the future by BLS to other customers.

CASE 13

SKF

Svenska Kullagerfabriken (SKF), one of the world's biggest manufacturers of bearings, was established in Sweden in 1907. By 1910, sales offices had been set up in France and Germany and agents had been appointed as far apart as Helsinki and Melbourne. Subsidiary companies had also been set up in the United Kingdom and the United States.

The first UK factory opened in 1911, while 1913 saw the opening of the first manufacturing unit in Germany. SKF bought its own steelworks in 1916. The rapid development of the U.S. motor industry led to the setting up of SKF's first manufacturing company in the United States at Hartford, Connecticut, in 1916. Between the two wars there was further expansion of the business, including the purchase of another competi-

---

This case was written by Professor Martin Christopher, Cranfield School of Management, Cranfield, England.

tor in the United States and the opening of a second factory in France. World War II brought a halt to the booming expansion, and like other international engineering groups, SKF was placed on a war footing. The task of getting back to normal after five years of war was formidable, although SKF's position was probably no worse than that of other international groups at the same time. The German factories, over which SKF had exercised little control since the 1930s, were largely in ruins. SKF's French installations had also been badly bombed.

Increasing Competition

Competition in the early 1960s was becoming even fiercer. SKF decided to strengthen its Common Market operations. This was partially achieved by the takeover, in 1965 in Italy, of RIV, a bearing manufacturer with 10 local plants and one each in Spain and Argentina. After a decade, 67 percent of the Italian bearing market was supplied by RIV-SKF. At the same time, the French SKF company started expanding, partly to meet the needs of its own increasing exports. Two new subsidiaries, Les Applications du Roulement (ADR) and RKS developed satisfactorily, before major interests were taken in La Technique Integrale and Compagnie Generale du Roulement (CGR).

Throughout the 1960s and 1970s, SKF bought up many companies, both inside and outside the bearing business. Despite the diversification of interest, roller bearings still accounted for 70 percent of SKF's business.

In 1973, a corporate audit of SKF's position in the European bearings industry showed them to be a fragmented organization, comprising five largely uncoordinated manufacturing and marketing operations in Sweden, West Germany, the United Kingdom, France, and Italy. SKF had a strong position in the market, in part because they had developed a very large product range (50,000 variants) to cater for every need of their customers. Many of these were low-volume products, tailored for the specific requirements of individual customers. Also, the majority of the range was manufactured at all or several of the European locations. This marketing policy necessitated the use of low-volume batch production.

In the early 1970s, SKF came under competitive pressure from a hitherto unknown area, that of Japan. Two of Japan's largest general machinery manufacturers, Fuyo and Sumitomo, poured vast amounts of resources into bearing companies such as Koyo Seiko, Tsubakimoto Precision Products, and many others. This meant that the Japanese manufacturers could pursue an aggressive pricing strategy to penetrate the European market. Using line production, that is, high volumes of each variant, the production costs were much lower than those of SKF. Although the Japanese produced fewer variants—only 10,000 compared to 50,000 of SKF—they were able to sell products of equivalent quality at prices equal to SKF's manufacturing costs.

Question

Discuss the courses of action open to SKF to counter the Japanese competitive threat in Europe.

PROCTER & GAMBLE: IMPROVING CONSUMER VALUE THROUGH PROCESS REDESIGN

Procter & Gamble Worldwide (P&G) is one of the largest manufacturers supplying grocery retailers and wholesalers and a leader in designing how branded consumer-goods manufacturers go to market. P&G's process innovations are driven by its focus on improving consumer value by eliminating non-value-added processes in the channel. Changes at P&G in organization, systems, procedures, and policies affected both the company and the entire channel. These changes were governed by the recognition that manufacturers, distributors, and retailers have to cooperate in creating industrywide approaches to drive inefficiency out of the grocery distribution system.

Many changes leading to organizational and channel transformation were initially viewed as information systems innovations (e.g., developing systems to automate existing practices). Breakthrough change came with the realization that the success of P&G brands depended on eliminating all processes that didn't deliver value to brand-loyal consumers. The promotional frenzy of the late 1970s and 1980s that characterized the retail industry had produced a backlash among brand-loyal consumers, who felt they weren't getting fair value day in, day out. P&G studies showed that less than half of the company's promotional dollars were passing through to the consumer and that swings in price were creating variability and massive inefficiency, not only in P&G's manufacturing and distribution systems but throughout the entire grocery supply chain.

As a result, P&G redesigned how it went to market as a branded consumer-goods maker. Its actions fell into two broad categories—participation in industrywide efficiency improvements and pricing policy changes—both necessary to improve the value of its brands. As its new pricing strategy was implemented, P&G also took a leadership role in working with the grocery industry—including other manufacturers—to significantly accelerate the adoption of more efficient systems, policies, and practices in the grocery channel (Exhibit 1). These industrywide changes resulted in dramatic improvements in P&G's and retailers' effectiveness in delivering value to the consumer.

Company and Industry Background

P&G's sales of $30 billion in 1993 were evenly divided between the United States and the rest of the world. P&G had developed a reputation for aggressive and successful "world-class" development and marketing of high-quality consumer goods over more than 150 years of operations. Throughout its history, the company focused on providing superior-performing brands that gave consumers good value.

EXHIBIT 1

The ECR Vision—A Continuous Channel Process

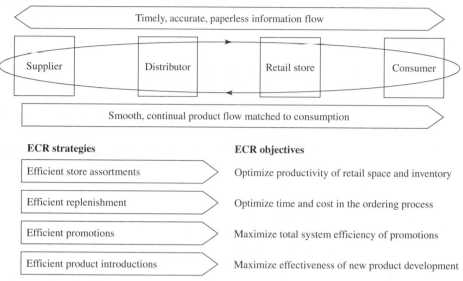

Source: Procter & Gamble.

P&G's post–World War II growth came from three sources: acquisitions, development and marketing of new brands, and international expansion. Its acquisitions included Duncan Hines and Hines-Park Foods (food products), W. T. Young Foods (peanut butter and nuts), J. A. Folger (coffee), and Clorox Chemical Co. (bleach). In 1957, the U.S. Federal Trade Commission (FTC) sued P&G to force the divestiture of its Clorox subsidiary. This effectively terminated the growth by acquisition strategy for two decades, forcing P&G management to grow through new-product development and international expansion.

P&G's international strategy was to take core U.S. businesses—soap, toothpaste, diapers, and shampoo—and replicate them to the rest of the world. International sales increased from virtually zero in 1953 to $4 billion in 1985. During this expansion period, new geography was conquered for existing brands, and P&G rotated managers to different locations between the United States, Europe, and Asia. During the 1980s, P&G International shifted to developing and marketing products tailored to the needs of each market. This increased focus on understanding and meeting consumer needs worldwide enabled P&G to expand international sales from about $4 billion (31 percent of sales) in 1985 to $15 billion (50 percent of sales) in 1993. Ed Artzt, president of P&G International from 1983 to 1990, was appointed CEO of the company in 1990.

By 1993, P&G's product lines included a wide assortment of products, with the company organized into five product sectors: Health/Beauty; Food/Beverage; Paper; Soap; and Special Products (e.g., chemicals). Each sector was organized into product categories, and each category was responsible for a group of brands. Most new-brand introductions were based on improvements or extensions of existing products. Several new products, such as Pampers disposable diapers and Pringles potato chips, were developed to meet basic consumer needs not yet served by existing products. Extensive market research, low-cost and effective advertising, and aggressive R&D investments enabled P&G to increase sales in the U.S. market from $1 billion in 1955 to almost $9 billion by 1985.

Competition for most of P&G product categories was concentrated, with two or three branded product producers controlling more than 50 percent of total branded product sales in each category. This concentration for the top three brands in any product category was typical for other manufacturers as well, although increasing sales of private-label products were eroding market share for the major brands in some categories. For some products, such as soaps or diapers, P&G and one competitor controlled more than 70 percent of the market. The strong consumer pull for P&G products provided the company with an advantage in dealing with retailers and wholesalers.

P&G products were sold through multiple channels, with grocery retailers, wholesalers, mass merchandisers, and club stores the most important in product sales volume. While relationships with retailers and wholesalers had not always been harmonious, P&G management recognized the need to serve the needs of both the consumer and the channel in order to be successful in the market. Demand for P&G products was primarily driven by pull through the channel by end consumers, rather than by trade push, with the trade frequently carrying P&G products because of consumer demand and competitive necessity rather than due to the trade's strong loyalty to P&G as a channel partner. Relationships between P&G and the trade through 1980 had primarily been based on negotiations over short-term initiatives and promotions. Increased use of promotions was part of the trend during this period, with P&G competing with other manufacturers for retail shelf space and promotional displays through various types of periodic promotions. Forward buying of promoted merchandise by 1985 had become the norm of the industry, with many brands stocked with over three months' supply.

Pricing and Promotions

Product promotions had existed to a limited extent for decades but expanded dramatically during the 1970s, partly due to President Nixon's imposition of price controls in 1971 as part of an attempt to reduce inflation. The combination of high inflation, relatively low interest costs, and large promotional discounts made the economics of forward buying very attractive for chains. Product procurement cost depended upon so many different allowances and other incentives provided by manufacturers that the actual cost of a single product at any one time on the shelf was impossible to determine. Inability to understand costs and the discounts and allowances available from aggressive purchasing resulted in a focus in the channel on "buying for profit" rather than "selling for profit."

This reliance on a multitude of promotional programs coupled with forward buying increased retailer inventories and required manufacturers to also maintain large inventories in order to be able to meet the high demand artificially created by forward buying during these promotional periods. Variation in consumer demand was increased by store promotions, and variation in manufacturer demand was further increased by retailer forward buying activities, making changes in demand difficult to forecast accurately for manufacturers. This uncertainty about total demand and large fluctuations in periodic demand not only increased manufacturer inventory requirements but also resulted in higher manufacturing costs than would have been possible in a direct pull through demand environment.

One of the objectives of channel-transforming innovations in the 1990s was to develop more collaborative and mutually productive relationships with channel partners, replacing negotiations with cooperative efforts to better serve consumer needs efficiently. By combining consumer loyalty with improved channel efficiency and relationships, P&G believed that market share for P&G products would increase and the cost to serve the channel and the end consumer would decline, enabling all members of the channel to benefit.

Retail Distribution Channels

Retail grocery was the most important channel for the sale of P&G products and consisted of manufacturers, distributors, and retail stores (Exhibit 2). Approximately half of all retail grocery sales volume went through chains of stores that provided their own distribution and warehousing of products, and half through wholesalers who primarily served small chains and independent retail stores.

Profit margins for grocery retailers were low, typically 1 to 3 percent of gross sales before tax. With low unit prices and high volumes, store operating profits were highly dependent on providing efficient operations. Total sales volume per store and per square foot of retail space were critical factors influencing retailer profitability. Since advertising was a significant cost for most retailers, regional market share was a critical factor influencing retailer profitability by leveraging the fixed costs of regional (e.g., newspaper) advertising.

Mass-merchandise (e.g., Wal-Mart) and club-store (e.g., Sam's Club) retailers supplied a limited assortment of P&G and other grocery-channel products at low margins, enabling them to offer attractive prices to consumers. These formats grew rapidly during the 1980s. Even though club stores offered a limited product selection and provided less service than traditional grocery retailers, a significant segment of consumers was willing to replace grocery-store shopping with club-store purchases, with the attraction of lower prices at the club stores more than offsetting the inconveniences involved. A McKinsey study of alternative distribution channels for grocery products, published by the Food Marketing Institute in 1992, demonstrated that the more efficient distribution and merchandising of these alternative formats enabled them to offer lower

Exhibit 2

Simplified Grocery Industry Functional Value Chain

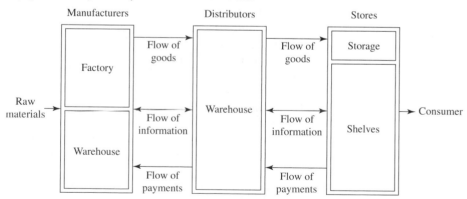

Flow of goods is frequent and high-volume and may be provided by trucks owned by one of the channel members or by a third party.

Flow of information was minimal for most channel members in the early 1990s, mostly conducted via voice telephone, paper mail, and face-to-face communications.

Source: Procter & Gamble.

prices to consumers than traditional grocery retailers. This study served as a wakeup call to the grocery industry, suggesting that existing processes needed to be improved to enable it to meet the challenge of these rapidly growing alternative formats.

Improving Channel Efficiency and Service

In the mid-1980s, P&G management launched several projects to improve service and reduce costs across the channel. The first effort focused on improving supply logistics and reducing channel inventory via a continuous replenishment program (CRP). The second was a project to revise the ordering and billing system to improve total ordering and service quality for channel customers.

The Early Logistics Improvement Trials

In 1985, P&G tested a new approach to channel logistics for replenishment ordering with a moderate-sized grocery chain. This test involved using electronic data interchange (EDI) to transmit data daily from the retailer to P&G on warehouse product shipments to each store. P&G then determined the quantity of products to be shipped to the retailer's warehouse by using shipment information rather than shipping based on retailer-generated orders. Product order quantities were computed by P&G with the objectives of providing sufficient safety stock, minimizing total logistics costs, and eliminating excess inventory in the retailer's warehouse.

The results of this initial trial were impressive in inventory reductions, service level improvements (e.g., fewer stockouts), and labor savings for the retailer. Besides other savings, the retailer was able to eliminate several buyer positions through this process restructuring. However, the benefits for P&G were unclear, and the new ordering process was more costly for P&G than the old one where the retailer determined order quantities.

The second test of the new ordering process was with a large mass merchandiser. In 1986, P&G approached this retailer's management with a proposal to dramatically change the way diapers were ordered and distributed in an effort to reduce retail store stockouts, lower product acquisition costs, and minimize total inventories. Limited warehouse capacity forced the retailer to purchase P&G diaper products in small quantities to be delivered directly to each retail store. Retail stores had frequent stockout problems, and the cost of these small orders delivered directly to the store was high for both P&G and the retail chain. Diapers were an important product category for this retailer, and it wanted to price diapers lower than other retailers in their markets. Unfortunately, the distribution system used for procurement resulted in higher acquisition cost for diaper products than many of its competitors (e.g., supermarkets), who were able to order in truckload quantities.

P&G proposed that the retailer inventory diaper products in the chain's distribution warehouse, provide P&G with daily data on warehouse orders received from the stores, and allow P&G to use the daily warehouse shipment data to determine warehouse replenishment volumes needed. This new replenishment process would limit the retailer's warehouse inventory to acceptable levels, eliminate costly less-than-truckload (LTL) shipments, and reduce stockouts for retail stores. Both P&G and the retailer would benefit by reducing costs and increasing sales. Sales increases would result from lower retail prices enabled by lower costs and from providing better service to consumers through greater product availability.

The new replenishment process resulted in substantially lower product acquisition costs through truckload volume purchases, enabling lower retail pricing. Without increasing inventory levels or stockouts, the retail chain was able to expand P&G's diaper SKUs in the stores. The combination of lower prices, reduced stockouts, and expanded SKUs in the stores dramatically increased P&G's diaper sales through this retailer's stores. This new process represented a major change in channel ordering and logistics and established the basic principles of what eventually became known as the continuous replenishment program (CRP). This second trial demonstrated the potential for logistics innovations to offer mutual benefits to retailers and manufacturers by reducing channel costs and increasing consumer sales.

In early 1988, top executives from P&G and another mass-merchandise chain met to discuss ways to improve logistics in the channel. The retailer was warehouse constrained due to rapid growth and was relying heavily on costly LTL shipments to meet demand. LTL shipments were expensive for both partners, and made it difficult for the retailer to increase diaper sales. During the meeting, the CEO of the mass-merchandise chain suggested that P&G simply ship products on a just-in-time basis when needed using the retailer's actual sales data. Deals and promotions would be replaced by a constant allowance that resulted in an equivalent net price for the retailer to remove forward-buy incentives.

A multifunctional team worked together to work out many of the details of implementing the new process. With top executives from both companies committed to rapid adoption, and building on P&G's experience with two other retailers, implementation of CRP took less than two months in total. In April 1988, P&G began shipping products based on retail demand data, placing orders automatically for the retailer. Information on demand was transmitted via fax and phone until EDI links were established.

Expanding the CRP Innovation

The success of CRP with leading mass merchandisers generated interest from other retailers in the new process. By 1990, most large mass merchandisers had fully implemented CRP. In 1990 and 1991, three grocery chains adopted CRP with P&G, and the innovation proved highly successful in reducing inventory and stockout levels for these early grocery pioneers. CRP adoption started with diapers and then expanded rapidly to other products as the potential for mutual cost reduction was demonstrated across the channel. CRP's success with early partners led the head of the diaper product group to commit $1.5 million in development funding during 1991 to expand the initial CRP system into a more robust production system that could be expanded to as many customers as needed. The increased sales and profits from the initial adopters of CRP were enough to justify the entire development cost being funded by this single product category!

The diaper product group then used CRP as a tool in selling an expanded diaper product line (boy and girl diapers) to retail chains. The new product line doubled the total number of SKUs in an already crowded product category but was needed to better respond to customer needs and meet competitive pressures. CRP enabled the diaper product sales force to offer customers a solution that managed the increased number of SKUs while reducing both inventory levels and stockouts for the retailer. Since a barrier to expanding product SKUs was the resulting increase in inventory required, CRP proved helpful in marketing the new diaper product line.

During 1992, 14 additional grocery chains implemented CRP with P&G, and existing CRP customers continued to expand CRP usage to new product lines. During 1993, an additional 15 new grocery chains or divisions of grocery chains adopted CRP. By July of 1994, a total of 47 channel customers had adopted CRP with P&G, and more than 26 percent of P&G sales volume was ordered via CRP. As these customers expanded use of CRP to new product lines and across multiple distribution centers, total CRP demand from these customers alone was expected to increase to 35 percent of P&G sales by the end of 1994. Ralph Drayer, vice president of customer services, expected use of CRP to reach 50 percent or more of total U.S. product shipment volume by the end of 1995.

Increased retail sales were an important benefit of the CRP program for P&G and its distributors. Sales of P&G products through CRP retailers increased 4 percent more on average during 1993 than sales through non-CRP retailers. Although some of this difference could be attributed to faster-growing retailers adopting CRP, Drayer believed that some of the gain was due to sales gained from competing products due to reduced stockouts, lower retail pricing, and expanded product selection in the store. However, even if only 1 percent of the 4 percent sales increase was due to competitive share gains, this represented a huge competitive and economic gain for P&G. One food division manager said he would "gain more market share by expanding CRP than through [product] line extensions."

The Role of EDI

When P&G began expanding the use of EDI with retailers to improve ordering efficiency, problems with order quality increased significantly. The sales representative or customer service representative in the manual process was often able to catch some of the problems and manually adjust retailers' orders to work in the P&G systems. Some of these adjustments later resulted in errors in the collections phase, but at least the order was entered and shipped. Removal of this human buffer created problems, for most EDI orders could not be processed without manual intervention. These early EDI trials with customers increased costs for P&G instead of providing savings since most orders had to be manually reworked and rekeyed into the ordering, shipping, and billing (OSB) system. Without process redesign, using EDI for ordering offered little benefit for P&G or customers, although it did highlight problems and misunderstandings.

EDI represented an important part of P&G's strategy to improve the efficiency of the ordering process and was essential for CRP implementation, but EDI alone was not viewed as particularly important in the effort to improve efficiency and order quality. One P&G manager described EDI as "an enabling technology" that, if implemented without changes in interorganizational processes and policies, represented little more than "a fancy electronic fax." Another manager explained: "EDI is simply an electronic envelope, not a system. It does not fix anything and, by itself, is not a solution. However, when implemented in parallel with process and systems reengineering, it can become a powerful tool."

An important role for EDI at P&G was to provide an essential platform for CRP operations. One manager described CRP as "two-way EDI with tight links into the systems of both companies." Of course, CRP required more than system changes, but the degree of interconnection with the systems of each organization was much tighter with CRP than was required for EDI with non-CRP customers. This linkage between systems across the two companies, enabled by the EDI link, resulted in error-free interchange of large amounts of data automatically between the companies. CRP dramatically increased the amount of data shared by companies in the channel, which made EDI essential for effective operations. Although early CRP trials had used fax and phone for data transmission, several P&G managers expressed the view that CRP without EDI was not viable:

> The problem [with manual entry of data] is that any error would probably result in an out-of-stock condition. The risk of [data entry] keying errors in a non-EDI environment is just too great. You also have a lot of data that need to be entered, which would require extensive manual support. CRP without EDI is just not viable.

EDI offered companies economic benefits by reducing transaction costs, which encouraged EDI adoption, even without making the commitment to CRP. Although the potential benefits from CRP were much larger than the benefits from EDI ordering alone, the challenges in shifting to CRP were greater than many retailers were willing to face. EDI provided an easy first step for companies that wanted to be technologically prepared for the new era without committing to the management and policy changes required to implement CRP.

Drayer observed that successful implementation of CRP required both senior management commitment to the innovation and a relationship of trust between management at the two organizations linking their systems:

> Companies that have made the choice to be interdependent will move to CRP. You can't remain independent with CRP . . . This is not something you can just connect between customers and suppliers. You need to understand the management changes required.

The Ordering, Shipping, and Billing Systems

In 1987, P&G management approved a major rewrite of the entire ordering, shipping, and billing (OSB) system, which took several years and cost tens of millions of dollars to complete. The systems in use at the time had been developed during the 1960s and had been upgraded many times. The batch processing system was both inefficient and ineffective; upgrading it was considered a competitive requirement for P&G to be able to provide the level of service required by customers. The OSB system supported all P&G activities in serving channel customers, including pricing, ordering, shipping, invoicing, and separate credit systems. The OSB project integrated many separate systems that did not work well together across functions and product sectors, enabling P&G to improve consistency and overall service levels.

The charter of the OSB development team was to understand how the business worked and then to automate the existing processes with sufficient flexibility to meet the various needs of the different sectors and functions. In some cases, standardization was allowed to simplify design and improve practices to a common level across the organization. The system absorbed a lot of the complexity of the existing processes that contributed to the cost of development, and was designed to eliminate manual processing steps but not to redesign the existing processes.

The rewrite of the system and the simultaneous upgrade of the hardware infrastructure were necessary, but significant additional performance improvement opportunities remained because of complex pricing and promotion practices. The process and performance levels in 1988 (prior to OSB rewrite) are shown in Exhibit 3, with comparable data for 1992 (after OSB rewrite) shown in Exhibit 4. Invoice deductions by customers were still quite large in 1992, although the new system had helped some in this area. Although the new system did improve order shipment quality, problems with the existing pricing and promotion policies and processes still created deductions. It was clear that the front end of the OSB system, which involved pricing and promotions policies, needed to be revised.

EXHIBIT 3

Total Order Management Process before New OSB (1988)

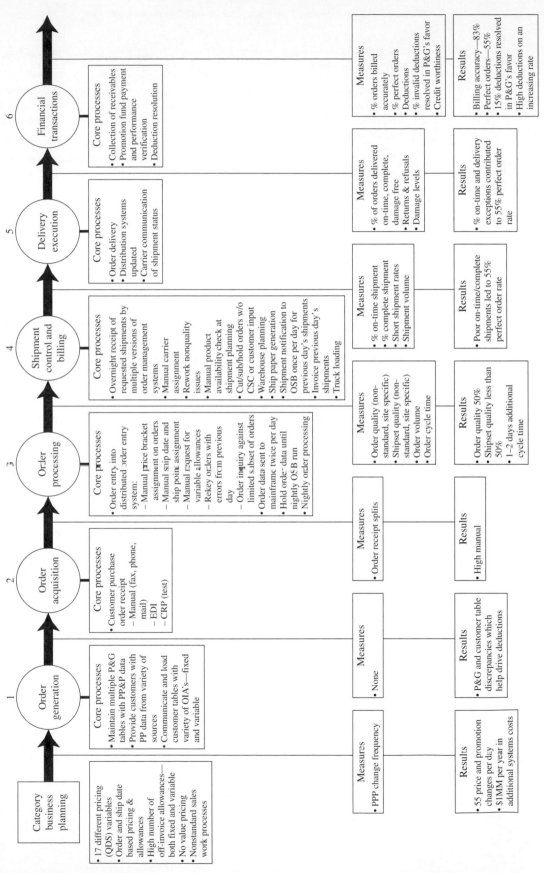

Source: Procter & Gamble.

EXHIBIT 4

Total Order Management Process after New OSB (1992)

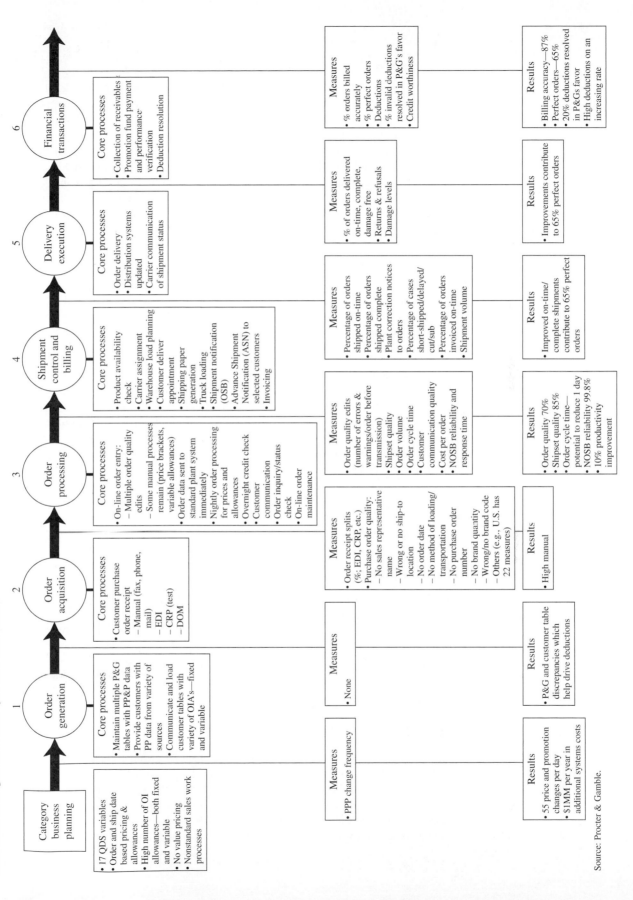

	Category business planning	1 Order generation	2 Order acquisition	3 Order processing	4 Shipment control and billing	5 Delivery execution	6 Financial transactions
Core processes	• 17 QDS variables • Order and ship date based pricing & allowances • High number of OI allowances—both fixed and variable • No value pricing • Nonstandard sales work processes	• Maintain multiple P&G tables with PP&P data • Provide customers with PP data from variety of sources • Communicate and load customer tables with variety of OIA's—fixed and variable	• Customer purchase order receipt – Manual (fax, phone, mail) – EDI – CRP (test) – DOM	• On-line order entry: – Multiple order quality edits – Some manual processes remain (price brackets, variable allowances) • Order data sent to standard plant system immediately • Nightly order processing for prices and allowances • Overnight credit check • Customer communication • Order inquiry/status check • On-line order maintenance	• Product availability check • Carrier assignment • Warehouse load planning • Customer deliver appointment • Shipping paper generation • Truck loading • Shipment notification (OSB) • Advance Shipment Notification (ASN) to selected customers • Invoicing	• Order delivery • Distribution systems updated • Carrier communication of shipment status	• Collection of receivables • Promotion fund payment and performance verification • Deduction resolution
Measures	• PPP change frequency	• None	• Order receipt splits (%; EDI, CRP, etc.) • Purchase order quality: – No sales representative name – Wrong or no ship-to location – No order date – No method of loading/ transportation – No purchase order number – No brand quantity – Wrong/no brand code – Others (e.g., U.S. has 22 measures)	• Order quality edits (number of errors & warnings/order before transmission) • Shipset quality • Order volume • Order cycle time • Customer communication quality • Cost per order • NOSB reliability and response time	• Percentage of orders shipped on-time • Percentage of orders shipped complete • Plant correction notices to orders • Percentage of cases short-shipped/delayed/ cut/sub • Percentage of orders invoiced on-time • Shipment volume	• % of orders delivered on-time, complete, damage free • Returns & refusals • Damage levels	• % orders billed accurately • % perfect orders • Deductions • % invalid deductions resolved in P&G's favor • Credit worthiness
Results	• 55 price and promotion changes per day • $1MM per year in additional systems costs	• P&G and customer table discrepancies which help drive deductions	• High manual	• Order quality 70% • Shipset quality 85% • Order cycle time— potential to reduce 1 day • NOSB reliability 99.8% • 10% productivity improvement	• Improved on-time/ complete shipments contribute to 65% perfect orders	• Improvements contribute to 65% perfect orders	• Billing accuracy—87% • Perfect orders—65% • 20% deductions resolved in P&G's favor • High deductions on an increasing rate

Source: Procter & Gamble.

Redesigning the Complete Ordering Process

P&G managers realized they needed to improve the total ordering process, starting with pricing policies and practices. Improving ordering quality required a simpler pricing structure that customers could both understand and track in their systems. A new pricing structure, introduced by Durk Jager, executive vice president responsible for all U.S. operations, dramatically simplified expansion of the new OSB system capabilities and represented a significant change in corporate strategy and policies. Pricing policy changes were critical for improving consumer value and building brand loyalty and facilitated expansion of the OSB systems to allow improvements in billing accuracy and reductions in invoice deductions. The combination of pricing policy changes and systems improvements benefited both P&G and channel customers.

The standardization and simplification of processes and policies across the organization accelerated under the leadership of Artzt and Jager. Challenging traditional practices and policies became acceptable and welcome, as long as suggested changes could be shown to improve consumer value by eliminating processes or costs that did not add value to the channel or products. One manager observed:

> Jager made it okay to make change happen faster. The ideas were bubbling in the organization and the pace of change accelerated dramatically.

Redesigning the ordering process involved a combination of systems and business process changes that had to be carefully integrated. A key element of the new ordering process was the development of common databases for product pricing and product specifications. This shared vision of business simplification and a common database was solidly grounded in the philosophy of "simplify, standardize, then mechanize." The common databases developed to support simplified pricing were designed to provide data directly to the customer's own system electronically. This resulted in dramatic reductions in invoice deductions for retailers using the new pricing database to verify or confirm purchase order information.

The combined changes in systems, strategy, organization, and policies resulted in a dramatic improvement in total order quality at P&G (Exhibit 5). Billing errors decreased by more than 50 percent from 1992 to 1994, and the percentage of billing disputes resolved in P&G's favor increased by more than 300 percent during the same period. The first-year savings from increased collections on invoices alone were enough to pay for the entire cost of development of the new pricing systems. P&G's customer teams were also able to concentrate on providing better service and marketing new products instead of spending time resolving billing problems. P&G's redesign of the total ordering process required fundamental changes in its structure, policies, and systems but yielded dramatic benefits in cost reduction and quality improvement. In addition to reducing invoice deductions, the redesigned business process allowed P&G to reduce costs throughout the entire ordering process.

Radical Restructuring of Pricing

The long-term strategic goal of increasing consumer value and brand loyalty, CRP's need for simple and stable pricing, and the need to reduce pricing complexity to improve quality in the ordering process all supported the decision to replace existing pricing structures with a simplified "value-pricing" program. This new pricing program was introduced initially for dishwashing liquids, where this new pricing approach was accepted, generally without much resistance. As the pricing change became accepted

EXHIBIT 5

Total Order Management Process after Redesign (1994)

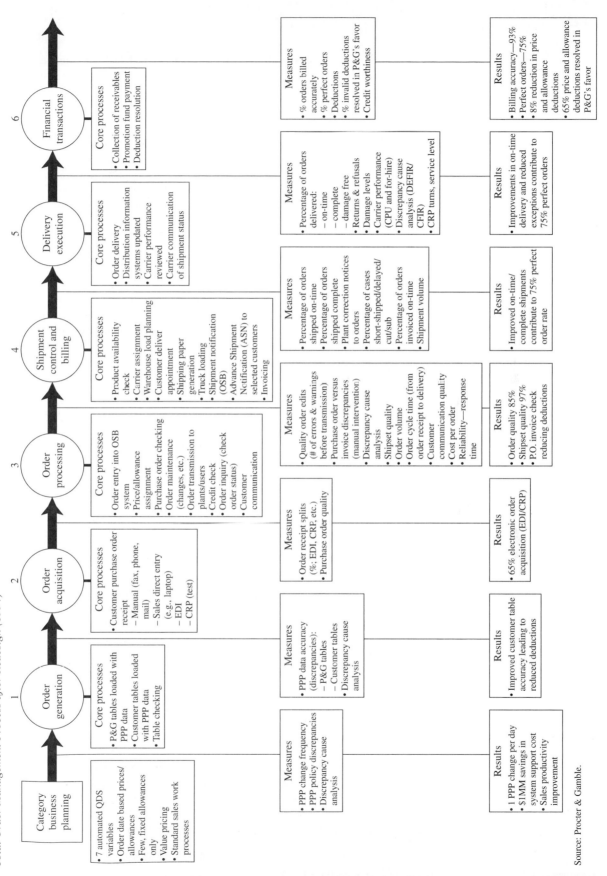

Source: Procter & Gamble.

generally, although not universally, value pricing was gradually implemented for more products (Exhibit 6). By late 1993, almost all P&G products were on some form of value-pricing plan.

The shift to value pricing represented a radical change in policies and was driven mostly by concern that frequent and complex promotions were eroding the value of P&G's brands. Brand loyalty declined in the United States during the 1970s and 1980s, due to the wild price swings that came with constant promotional activity. Frequent promotions rewarded only those consumers most sensitive to price and acted as a disincentive to brand-loyal consumers. Value pricing eliminated incentives for retailer forward buying and essentially offered constant procurement costs combined with some flexible allowances or funds provided for retail store promotions.

Value pricing offered important benefits for CRP customers, encouraging increased CRP adoption. Implementation of CRP with the first few customers required prototyping new net-pricing terms that eliminated variable discounts and promotions in order to remove incentives for forward buying. There was little benefit in trying to improve channel logistics efficiency while using a pricing structure that encouraged inefficient purchasing practices (e.g., forward buying). Until P&G restructured pricing, efforts to extend CRP were constrained because it lacked a standardized pricing structure that would eliminate forward-buying incentives.

Implementation of value pricing reduced the number of pricing changes at P&G from 55 per day in 1992 to less than 1 per day in early 1994. In July 1994, all remaining variable promotional allowances were eliminated for the last few product categories using these incentives, and geographic pricing differences were eliminated as well. Temporary price reductions or special promotions were allowed only to meet significant competitive threats to P&G brands, and they had to be approved by Jager.

Exhibit 6

Value Pricing Timing and Product Volume

Value Pricing Initial Date	Product Brands or Categories	% of Total P&G Shipment Volume
July 1991	All liquid dishwashing products, some bar soap products, some Duncan Hines products	8.2%
August 1991	Metamucil	0.6
November 1991	Bold, Liquid Bold, Solo, Cascade, Liquid Cascade, all Bounce products, Downy Sheets, all Comet products, Mr. Clean, all Spic and Span products, Top Job, Lestoil, Gain, Ivory Snow, Dash, Dreft, Oxydol	11.3
February 1992	Pantene, Liquid Safeguard	1.0
April 1992	Luvs, Pampers	7.0
July 1992	Old Spice Deodorant, Downy Ultra and Regular, Secret, Sure, Bounty	12.8
October 1992	Always, Attends (retail)	2.0
November 1992	Liquid Cheer, Liquid Tide	4.3
January 1993	Prell, Cinch	0.5
March 1993	Tide Powder, Cheer Powder, Era	10.2
May 1993	Puffs	1.0
July 1993	Head & Shoulders, Charmin/White Cloud, Scope	8.9
August 1993	Hawaiian Punch	1.3
Total product volume with no off-invoice allowances in August 1993		69.1

Source: Procter & Gamble.

There was considerable resistance to the change in pricing philosophy from some P&G senior managers, in spite of the obvious advantages, since this was completely the opposite of the high-low pricing strategies many executives had used to create new brands and strengthen P&G product market throughout their careers. Jager noted that the new pricing did cost P&G sales over the period, but that this incremental revenue actually cost P&G more to generate than the income created by the promotions. Thus, while sales were lower than would have been possible using promotional pricing, profits were stronger, and the company was better positioned to build a future based on value-priced products for brand-loyal consumers.

Leading the Grocery Channel Transformation

Working with retailers, wholesalers, other manufacturers, industry trade associations, and consulting firms, P&G participated in the development of the efficient consumer response (ECR) vision of channel innovations that would enable grocery chains to compete effectively with low-cost alternative retail formats. ECR became a banner for a wide variety of innovations in the grocery channel that would improve efficiency (see again Exhibit 1). Various joint industry ECR committees were established in a coordinated effort to explore opportunities for channel process improvement.

CRP was an important element of the ECR vision. The ECR report by Kurt Salmon Associates, published in January 1993, suggested that 38 percent of the $30 billion in savings projected from implementing ECR in the grocery industry could be realized through more efficient replenishment ordering. Many grocery channel members were able to realize significant savings immediately by adopting CRP without waiting for the remainder of the ECR proposals to be fully developed. P&G was a clear leader in the implementation of CRP and other ECR programs and wanted to increase the pace of ECR and CRP adoption in the industry overall.

The Change from Brand to Category Management

In the late 1980s, P&G management made a significant change in its brand management structure to improve coordination and efficiency. Multiple brands were combined into product categories, under the responsibility of a category manager, who managed individual brands as part of the overall category portfolio. For more than 50 years, the brand management approach had served P&G well, and the company had been recognized as the benchmark for excellence in brand management. The introduction of category management was a dramatic shift for a company that had pioneered brand management in the 1930s.

The category management approach provided more flexibility in restructuring the P&G product line. Brand restructuring or consolidation would have been more difficult to achieve under the prior structure. Brand managers maintained responsibility for advertising and limited promotional programs, but category managers established overall pricing and product policies, which enabled P&G to eliminate weaker brands. For example, the elimination of the White Cloud brand by merging the product into the Charmin line would have been resisted by a White Cloud brand manager but was strongly supported by the toilet-tissue category manager, who reported to the paper products sector manager. Category management also avoided conflicts between similar branded products in the same channel for advertising and distribution resources.

The shift to category management was consistent with the company's efforts to simplify and standardize operations and product lines. Many unnecessary SKUs were eliminated when SKU differences did not provide significant incremental value to the consumer. At the same time, new SKUs were added as new products and innovative extensions of existing product lines were developed. In total, the number of SKUs P&G offered remained about the same during the early 1990s, but the restructuring of SKUs provided consumers with greater choice of products that were specifically tailored to their needs, and eliminated a proliferation of product variety that was based simply on labeling or packaging differences.

Manufacturing and Planning Improvements

Although the initial benefits of CRP were reductions in inventory, stockouts, and handling and transportation costs, increased adoption of CRP by P&G customers offered dramatic cost saving opportunities for production and raw-material purchasing. P&G managers estimated that at least 10 percent of the cost of production for paper products was the cost of excess capacity required to handle product demand variations. Value pricing reduced demand uncertainty by eliminating forward-buy distortions, and CRP further reduced demand uncertainty and allowed almost instant feedback on demand resulting from product innovations or pricing changes.

The potential benefits of CRP for production cost and inventory savings were quite large. Savings in inventory or production were not automatic, but the shift to a more stable environment enabled P&G to negotiate more attractive pricing with suppliers and to use internal production capacity more efficiently. In some cases, the efficiency gains from value pricing, rationalized product lines, CRP ordering, and dramatic improvements in process reliability resulted in sufficient excess production capacity to eliminate entire production plants. During the 1990s, many P&G plants were expected to close as a result of improved operations due to the new policies and processes. In 1993, P&G took an extraordinary charge of almost an entire year's profits to reflect the actual and expected costs of closing unneeded plants and reducing total employment levels for the company (Exhibit 7).

The CRP savings for diaper production were estimated based on experiences of multiple plants with different levels of CRP ordering by customers. The results of this analysis are shown in Exhibit 8 and represent the early results of CRP adoption on the production process. Paper product managers believed that further cost savings could be realized as P&G teamed to better use the improved information about demand that was available through CRP ordering data. Through more effective negotiating with vendors and better use of actual demand data for planning and scheduling, additional savings could be realized in production.

Customers and Category Management

The second most important aspect of the joint industry ECR vision was the retailers' shift from buyers to category managers that was taking place among leaders in the industry during the early 1990s. Although the cost savings from this shift were not as dramatic or easily quantified as the savings from CRP adoption, the potential profit improvement of the shift to category management could easily exceed the cost savings from CRP. Category managers in retail chains were ideally responsible for the entire profit of a product category across all stores. Replacing buyers, who were primarily focused on cost or promotional deals, with category managers responsible for both profits and meeting consumer needs required new skills and capabilities. The shift from buyer to category manager represented a new mind-set, for both the individuals in the

Exhibit 7

Selected P&G Financial Statistics

	1987	1988	1989	1990	1991	1992	1993
Net sales	$17,000	$19,336	$21,398	$24,081	$27,026	$29,362	$30,433
Net earnings	$786	$1,020	$1,206	$1,602	$1,773	$1,872	$2,015
Net earnings per share	$1.13	$1.49	$1.78	$2.25	$2.46	$2.62	$1.87
Net earnings as % of sales	4.6%	5.3%	5.6%	6.7%	6.6%	6.4%	6.6%
Dividends per common stock	$0.68	$0.69	$0.75	$0.88	$0.98	$1.03	$1.10

Note: These numbers exclude extraordinary charges of $459 in 1987 and $1746 in 1993 for costs of restructuring (plant closings and staff reductions), and a charge of $925 to reflect accounting changes in 1993.

Source: Procter & Gamble.

Exhibit 8

Projected Manufacturing Cost Savings Using CRP Ordering

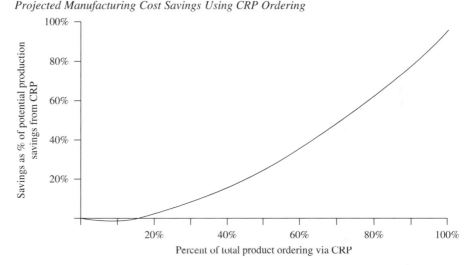

Source: Estimates based on interviews with P&G manufacturing and product category executives.

role and the overall organization. Few buyers were able to make the transition to the new role, and few organizations could make the shift in procurement and merchandising strategy without a strong CEO vision and mandate for change.

The shift to category management benefited both retailers and P&G Category managers were better positioned to understand the true costs and profits generated from each product in their category. P&G customer teams were able to use solid economic analysis with category managers to demonstrate that their brands should be given additional shelf space or variety because the retail profit per unit of shelf space for P&G brands was higher than most other products in the category. In addition, category managers were able to appreciate the storage and handling savings provided by P&G's simplified pricing policies and logistics programs.

Sale of CRP to IBM

In late 1993, P&G announced the sale of its CRP to IBM's Integrated Systems Solutions Corporation (ISSC) subsidiary. The P&G program was to be offered by IBM to all manufacturers as a service provided by IBM, with P&G outsourcing support and operations of its CRP systems to ISSC. Within two weeks, Ralston Purina signed up as IBM's first customer, and five other manufacturers had become IBM CRP clients by mid-1994. Many other large manufacturers had expressed interest in the IBM service offering, which offered manufacturers CRP capabilities quickly, at low cost, and with experienced operating personnel. This IBM CRP service offering allowed retailers to interact with multiple vendors in a common format, creating a powerful force in the industry for standardization. The availability of the IBM CRP also increased the attractiveness of CRP for manufacturers and retailers by reducing barriers to CRP adoption.

The decision to sell CRP to IBM was primarily based on strategic, not economic, justification. The net benefits to P&G and its customers of implementing CRP increased as the total number of customers and other manufacturers using CRP increased. Therefore, it was more important for P&G to be sure this innovation was rapidly adopted by the industry overall than to try to gain advantage from being the technological leader of the innovation. The sale to IBM increased the probability of other manufacturers adopting CRP by providing them access to a complete CRP service offering with quick start-up capability.

In addition, the agreement with IBM reduced P&G's cost of operating CRP, since the IBM service contract cost was less than the cost of operating the system using P&G's internal staff and systems. IBM planned to run the applications using excess capacity at the Kodak operations center that IBM was managing under an IT service contract. Thus, IBM was able to operate the outsourced CRP operations on capacity that would otherwise be underutilized from another outsourced MIS operations client. The outsourcing of CRP services to large manufacturers also gave IBM an opportunity to demonstrate the potential benefits of MIS services outsourcing to multiple potential clients, who might be interested in further outsourcing services that could be linked with the CRP applications over time. In summary, P&G's sale of CRP to IBM offered important strategic and operational benefits for both companies and provided the credibility of a third-party platform offering to increase the attractiveness of CRP for the industry.

Jager believed that any technological advantage P&G lost by selling the proprietary CRP to IBM would be more than offset by the benefits for consumers and for the company of having the grocery industry fully embrace CRP. Increased adoption of CRP by P&G's customers would allow the company and its customers to improve internal processes and reduce costs. Jager explained:

> By eliminating non-value-added processes, we will ultimately win in the market by providing the best product to the consumer at the lowest cost through the channel.

Questions

1. What were the key decisions taken by Procter & Gamble in relation to the distribution channel? Could a mid-sized manufacturer have used this approach? Describe implementation problems facing retailers.
2. How important are the new information technologies in Procter & Gamble's efforts?
3. To what extent has Procter & Gamble changed its strategy to take advantage of ECR?
4. What are the next steps for Procter & Gamble?

CASE 15

FORD MOTOR COMPANY: SUPPLY CHAIN STRATEGY

Teri Takai, Director of Supply Chain Systems, had set aside this time on her calendar to contemplate recommendations to senior executives. The question they'd asked was widely agreed to be extremely important to Ford's future: How should the company use emerging information technologies (e.g., Internet technologies) and ideas from new high-tech industries to change the way it interacted with suppliers? Members of her team had different views on the subject.

Some argued that the new technology made it inevitable that entirely new business models would prevail, and that Ford needed to radically redesign its supply chain and other activities or risk being left behind. This group favored "virtual integration," modeling the Ford supply chain on that of companies like Dell, which had aggressively used technology to reduce working capital and exposure to inventory obsolescence.[1] Proponents of this approach argued that although the auto business was very complex, both for historical reasons and because of the inherent complexity of the automotive product, there was no reason such business models could not provide a conceptual blueprint for what Ford should attempt.

Another group was more cautious. This group believed that the differences between the auto business and relatively newer businesses like computer manufacturing were important and substantive. Some noted, for example, that relative to Dell the Ford supplier network had many more layers and many more companies, and that Ford's purchasing organization had historically played a more prominent and independent role than Dell's. These differences and others posed complications when examined closely, and it was difficult to determine the appropriate and feasible scope for redesign of the process.

As she read through the documents provided by her team, she thought about CEO Jac Nasser's recent companywide emphasis on shareholder value and customer responsiveness. It was widely acknowledged that Dell had delivered on those dimensions, but would the same methods deliver results for Ford?

Company and Industry Background

Based in Dearborn, Michigan, the Ford Motor Company was the second largest industrial corporation in the world, with revenues of more than $144 billion and about 370,000 employees. Operations spanned 200 countries. Although Ford obtained significant revenues and profits from its financial services subsidiaries, the company's core business had remained the design and manufacture of automobiles for sale on the consumer market.

Professor Robert D. Austin prepared this case as the basis for class discussion rather than to illustrate either effective or ineffective handling of an administrative situation.

[1]Information on Dell included in this case was obtained by Ford from public sources, including the 1997 Dell Annual Report, the Dell website (www.dell.com), and from "The Power of Virtual Integration: An Interview with Dell Computer's Michael Dell" by Joan Magretta, *Harvard Business Review,* March–April 1998 (reprint 98208).

Since Henry Ford had incorporated in 1903, the company had produced in excess of 260 million vehicles.

The auto industry had grown much more competitive over the last two decades. Since the 1970s, the Big Three U.S. automakers—General Motors (GM), Ford, and Chrysler—had seen their home markets encroached upon by the expansion of foreign-based auto manufacturers, such as Toyota and Honda. The industry was also facing increasing overcapacity (estimated at 20 million vehicles) as developing and industrialized nations, recognizing the wealth and job-producing effects of automobile manufacturing, encouraged development and expansion of their own export-oriented auto industries.

Although manufacturers varied in their degree of market presence in different geographical regions, the battle for advantage in the industry was fast becoming global. Faced with the need to continue to improve quality and reduce cycle times while dramatically lowering the costs of developing and building cars, Ford and the other large automakers were looking for ways to take advantage of their size and global presence. One element of the effort to achieve advantage in size and scale was a movement toward industry consolidation. In the summer of 1998, Chrysler merged with Daimler-Benz to form a more global automaker. In early 1999, Ford announced that it would acquire Sweden's Volvo, and there were rumors of other deals in the works.

Previously, in 1995, Ford had embarked on an ambitious restructuring plan called Ford 2000, which included merging its North American, European, and International automotive operations into a single global organization. Ford 2000 called for dramatic cost reductions to be obtained by reengineering and globalizing corporate organizations and processes. Product development activities were consolidated into five Vehicle Centers (VCs), each responsible for development of vehicles in a particular consumer market segment (one VC was in Europe). By making processes and products globally common, Ford intended to eliminate organizational and process redundancies and realize huge economies of scale in manufacturing and purchasing. Major reengineering projects were initiated around major company processes, such as Order-to-Delivery (OTD) and Ford Production System (FPS), with goals such as reducing OTD time from more than 60 days to less than 15.

Ford's new global approach required that technology be employed to overcome the constraints usually imposed by geography on information flow. Teams on different continents needed to be able to work together as if they were in the same building. Furthermore, in virtually every reengineering project, information technology (IT) had emerged as a critical enabler. The link between reengineering success and the company's IT groups was made explicit in the Ford 2000 restructuring—IT was placed within the process reengineering organization. In the supply chain area, there was general agreement that IT could also be deployed to dramatically enhance material flows and reduce inventories—substituting information for inventory, as the expression went.

As Ford 2000 unfolded, the Internet revolution unfolded in parallel, creating new possibilities for reengineering processes within and between enterprises. Ford launched a public Internet site in mid-1995; by mid-1997 the number of visits to the site had reached more than 1 million per day. A companywide *intra*net was launched in mid-1996, and by January of 1997 Ford had in place a Business-to-Business (B2B) capability through which the intranet could be extended in a secure manner beyond company boundaries into an *extra*net, potentially connecting Ford with its suppliers. Ford teamed with Chrysler and General Motors to work on the Automotive Network Exchange (ANX), which aimed to create consistency in technology standards and processes in the supplier network, so that suppliers, already pressed to lower costs, would not have to manage different means of interaction with each automaker.

On January 1, 1999, Jac Nasser took over the CEO job from Alex Trotman. Nasser had been Trotman's second-in-command throughout the Ford 2000 rollout, and had a long-standing reputation as a tough-minded cost-cutter and a capable leader. Even before taking the helm, he had begun to focus Ford senior management on shareholder value. In the period between 1995 and 1999, Ford had seen companies with fewer physical assets and much lower revenues and profits achieve market capitalization well in excess of Ford's. Corporate staff members began to study models such as Cisco and Dell to try to understand whether Ford could produce shareholder value in the ways that these newer companies had.

As the end of 1998 approached, Ford had amassed profits of $6.9 billion, employees enjoyed record profit sharing, and return on sales (3.9 percent in 1997) was trending solidly upward. The company was the world leader in trucks. It had taken over the U.S. industry lead in profit per vehicle ($1,770) from Chrysler, and it was the most improved automaker on the 1997 J. D. Power Initial Quality Study (in fourth place overall, behind Honda, Toyota, and Nissan).

Ford's Existing Supply Chain and Customer Responsiveness Initiatives

Ford had a number of initiatives underway that were aimed at positioning the company favorably for success in integrating with the extended enterprise that also included suppliers and customers. In addition, there were historical factors that would need to be taken into account in any virtual integration strategy.

Ford's Existing Supply Base

The existing supply base was, in many respects, a product of history. As the company had grown over the years so had the supply base, to the point where in the late 1980s there were several thousand suppliers of production material in a complex network of business relationships. Suppliers were picked primarily based on cost, and little regard was given to overall supply chain costs, including the complexity of dealing with such a large network of suppliers.

Beginning in the early 1990s, Ford had begun to actively try to decrease the number of suppliers the company dealt with directly. Rather than fostering strong price competition among suppliers for individual components, there was a shift toward longer-term relationships with a subset of very capable suppliers who would provide entire vehicle subsystems. These "tier one" suppliers would manage relationships with a larger base of suppliers of components of subsystems—tier two and below suppliers. Ford made its expertise available to assist suppliers in improving their operations via a range of techniques, including just-in-time (JIT) inventory, total quality management (TQM), and statistical process control (SPC). In exchange for the closer relationships and long-term commitments, Ford expected yearly price reductions from suppliers. While tier one suppliers had fairly well-developed IT capabilities (many interacted with Ford via electronic data interchange links), they were not able to invest in new technologies at the rate Ford itself could. Also, the IT maturity (understanding and modernity of technology) decreased rapidly in lower tiers of the supply chain. As more cautious members of Takai's staff had often observed, this supply base was different in its nature and complexity from Dell's supply base.

Another major difference between Dell and Ford was organizational. At Dell, purchasing activities reported into the product development organization. At Ford, purchasing was organizationally independent of product development and had been—historically and up to the present—a powerful force within Ford. Because of the sheer volume of materials and services that Ford purchased, a very slim reduction in purchasing cost could result in very significant savings. Consequently, purchasing was involved closely in nearly every product decision. Engineers were counseled to avoid discussing prices in interactions with suppliers, as price negotiation was the sole province of purchasing agents. How this might work in a more virtually integrated system was unclear.

Ford Production System

The Ford 2000 initiative produced five major, corporationwide reengineering projects. One of these was Ford Production System (FPS). Modeled roughly on the Toyota Production System, FPS involved a multiyear project that drew on internal and external expertise worldwide. FPS was an integrated system aimed at making Ford manufacturing operations leaner, more responsive, and more efficient. It focused on key attributes of the production process, aspiring to level production and move to a more pull-based system, with synchronized production, continuous flow, and stability throughout the process. One important part of FPS was Synchronous Material Flow (SMF), which Ford defined as "a process or system that produces a continuous flow of material and products driven by a fixed, sequenced, and leveled vehicle schedule, utilizing flexibility and lean manufacturing concepts." One key to SMF was In-Line Vehicle Sequencing (ILVS), a system that used vehicle in-process storage devices (such as banks and ASRSs)[2] and computer software to assure that vehicles were assembled in order sequence. By assuring assembly in order sequence, Ford could tell suppliers exactly when and where certain components would be needed days in advance, and buffer stocks could be dramatically reduced. If such sequenced assembly could be kept level and if it was well-forecasted, the benefits would be felt throughout the supply chain. The vision was of trucks constantly in motion throughout their lives, in continuous circuits between suppliers and Ford, stopping only to refuel or change drivers, feeding a process that worked like a finely tuned and smoothly running precision instrument.

Order to Delivery

Another key process Ford reengineering initiative was Order to Delivery (OTD). The purpose of the OTD project was to reduce to 15 days the time from a customer's order to delivery of the finished product—a significant reduction versus the present performance of 45–65 days. Ford took a holistic approach to the reengineering. Pilot studies in 1997 and 1998 identified bottlenecks throughout Ford's supply chain, including its marketing, material planning, vehicle production, and transportation processes. Ford's approach to implementing improved OTD processes relied on several elements: (1) ongoing forecasting of customer demand from dealers—before OTD Ford had never officially involved dealers in forecasting demand; (2) a minimum of 15 days of vehicles in each assembly plant's order bank to increase manufacturing stability—gaps

---

[2]A "bank" is a storage area into which partially assembled vehicles can be directed, for the purpose of removing them in a different order than the order in which they entered (i.e., resequencing). An Automated Storage and Retrieval System (ASRS) is essentially a multilevel bank (vehicles are literally stored on top of each other); whereas an ordinary bank provides some resequencing flexibility, an ASRS provides the ability to access any vehicle in the bank at any time. As might be imagined, to hold a large number of vehicles and allow them to be accessed randomly, an ASRS must be very large (roughly the size of a several-story building).

in the order bank are filled with "suggested" dealer orders based on historical buying patterns; (3) regional "mixing centers" that optimize schedules and deliveries of finished vehicles via rail transportation; and (4) a robust order amendment process to allow vehicles to be amended for minor color and trim variations without having to submit new orders. The OTD vision was to create a lean, flexible, and predictable process that harmonized the efforts of all of Ford's components to enable it to provide consumers with the right products in the right place at the right time. Ford believed that success in achieving this vision would provide better quality, higher customer satisfaction, improved customer selection, better plant productivity, stability for its supply base, and lower dealer and company costs.

Ford Retail Network

On July 1, 1998, Ford launched the first of its Ford Retail Network (FRN) ventures in Tulsa, Oklahoma, under the newly formed Ford Investment Enterprises Company (FIECo). Ford Investment Enterprises was formed to take advantage of the changing face of retail vehicle distribution systems in North America. FIECo had two primary goals: (1) to be a test bed for best practices in retail distribution and drive those practices throughout the dealer network, and (2) to create an alternate distribution channel to compete with new, publicly owned retail chains such as AutoNation. Ownership in the FRN varied from market to market; in some Ford would be the majority owner and in others Ford would be the minority owner. In Rochester, New York, Ford was partnering with Republic—another large, publicly owned corporation. One of the principles of the FRN was to buy all the Ford dealers in a local market so that the dealers were in competition against the "real" competition (i.e., GM, Toyota, Honda), rather than with each other. The overriding goal was for the consumer to receive the highest level of treatment and to create an experience they would want to come back to again and again. Showrooms would have a consistent look on the outside, with customized interiors for the different Ford brands—Ford, Mercury, Lincoln, and Jaguar. The number of showrooms would be consolidated to focus resources on creating a superior selling experience, while the number of service outlets would increase to be closer to customer population centers. Ford expected personnel and advertising cost savings, as well as inventory efficiencies due to economies of scale and greater use of the Internet. Ford also believed that the FRN would provide an opportunity to increase business not just in new and used vehicles but also in parts and service, body shop operations, and Ford Credit.

Dell's Integrated Supply Chain

See "The Power of Virtual Integration: An Interview with Dell Computer's Michael Dell," *Harvard Business Review,* March–April 1998, pages 72–84.

The Decision

Takai perused the neatly prepared documents that had been provided by her staff. There was a broad-based comparison between Dell and Ford on many important dimensions (Exhibit 1). Virtual integration would require changes in fundamental operations; some of the changes, framed as a shift from "push" to "pull" processes, were identified in another document (Exhibit 2). Whatever she decided, she would have to do it soon. Meetings were already scheduled with the vice president of Quality and Process Leadership, and from there the recommendations would move upward, eventually to Nasser.

Case 15

Exhibit 1

Dell and Ford Compared

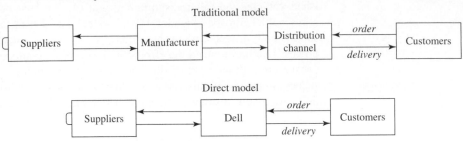

Traditional model

Direct model

Comparative metrics (latest fiscal year)

	Dell	Ford Automotive	Fin. Services
Employees	16,100	363,892	
Assets ($mils)	4,300	85,100	194,000
Revenue ($mils)	12,300	122,900	30,700
Net income ($mils)	944	4,700	2,200
Return on sales	7.7%	3.8%	7.2%
Cash ($mils)	320	14,500	2,200
Manufacturing facilities	3 (Texas, Ireland Malaysia)	180 (in North and South America, Europe, Asia, Australia)	
Market capitalization ($mil)	58,469	66,886	
P/E	60	10*	
Five year average revenue growth	55% per year	6% per year	
Five year average stock price growth	133% per year	33.4% per year	

* Excludes earnings from Associates spin-off.

Sources: Dell 1998 financial report, Ford 1997 annual report, *Wall Street Journal Interactive.*

EXHIBIT 1 *(continued)*

Enterprise Model Comparison
A high-level comparison of the Dell and Ford Motor enterprise models is shown below. Besides the lack of a dealer distribution channel, other key differences are Dell's ownership of assembly plants only—all component/subassembly manufacturing is done by its supply base—and the more integrated nature of Dell's Sales, R&D, and Manufacturing Operations. All of the operating principles that underlie Dell's success have counterparts in Ford's breakthrough objectives and key business plan initiatives.

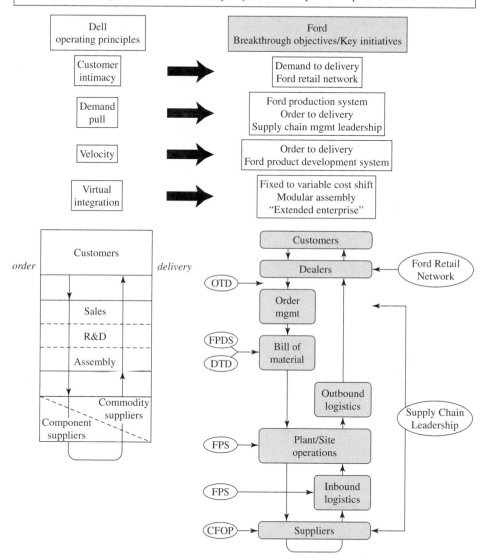

Exhibit 1 *(continued)*

Dell processes	Ford
Suppliers own inventory until it is used in production	
Suppliers maintain nearby ship points, delivery time 15 minutes to 1 hour	✓
External logistics supplier used to manage inbound supply chain	✓
Customers frequently steered to PCs with high availability to balance supply and demand	✓
Demand forecasting is critical—changes are shared immediately within Dell and with supply base	
Demand pull throughout value chain—"information for inventory" substitution	
Focused on strategic partnerships: suppliers down from 200 to 47	✓
Complexity is low: 50 components, 8–10 keys, 100 permutations	

Exhibit 2

Moving from Push to Pull

	Process	Push	Pull
Design	Design strategy	Please everyone	Mainstream customer wants
	Vehicle combinations	More is better	Minimal
Marketing	Pricing strategy	Budget-driven	Market-driven
	Vehicle purchase incentives	Higher	Lower
Manufacturing and Supply	Capacity planning	Multiple material/capacity constraints, driven by program budget	Market-driven (no constraints, FPV/CPV + 10% for vehicle, +15% for components)
	Schedule and build stability	Maximize production—make whatever you can build	Schedule from customer-driven order bank, build to schedule
Dealer Network	Dealer ordering	Orders based on allocations and capacity constraints	Orders based on customer demand
	Order to delivery times	Longer (60+ days)	Shorter (15 days or less)
	Inventory	High with low turnover	Low with rapid turnover
	Dealership model	Independent dealerships, negotiations with company	Company controlled dealerships (Ford Retail Network)

Name Index

Abdullah, Adini, 309
Abrahamsson, Mats, 92
Aburdene, Patricia, 526n, 531n
Ackerman, Kenneth B., 394n, 396n, 398n,
    423n–424n, 429, 469n, 474
Ackoff, R. L., 4n
Agarwal, James, 527n
Alderson, Wroe, 58n
Aljian, George W., 194n
Allen, Mary Kay, 174n–175n
Allenby, Greg M., 309
Allessie, Martijn, 380
Allison, Donald J., 152n, 155n
Amer, Mohamed Y., 467n
Andel, Tom, 40n, 399n, 421n, 458n, 462n,
    474, 541n, 561n, 583n
Anders, George, 403n, 531n
Andersen, Matthew G., 503n
Anderson, David L., 343n, 519n, 522n,
    537n, 554n, 556n, 559n, 563n,
    577–578, 713
Anderson, Eugene W., 677n
Anderson, Matthew G., 505n, 513
Andersson, Jesper, 50
Andraski, Joseph C., 50, 92
Andrews, Dorine C., 77n
Anhalt, Karen Nickel, 474
Anthony, Robert, 815n
Anyane-Ntow, Kwabena, 524n
Apple, James M., Jr., 417n, 442n, 452n,
    454n, 474
Aquilano, Nicholas J., 177n–178n, 241n,
    256n, 260n, 267, 309
Armbruster, William, 541n
Armitage, Howard M., 129n, 622n, 626n,
    629n, 635n, 647, 651n
Armstrong, Gary, 6n
Arnold, Stephen J., 530n

Arntzen, Bruce C., 56n, 79n
Aron, Laurie Joan, 611n
Arzac, Enrique R., 674n
Aspinwall, Leo, 59n
Augello, William J., 339n
Augustin, Siegfried, 577
Auguston, Karen A., 459n–461n
Aurik, Jonan C., 578
Austin, Robert D., 846n
Avery, Susan, 485
Ayers, Allan F., 173n, 282n

Baalbaki, Imad, 527n
Babbar, Sunil, 543
Bagchi, Prabir K., 365n–366n, 571n, 578
Baker, C.M., 430, 449n
Bakker, Ben A., 578
Ballou, Ronald H., 92, 430
Bancroft, Nancy H., 177n
Bardi, Edward J., 346, 413n
Barks, Joseph V., 319n, 367n
Barr, Michael, 689
Barr, Stephen, 616n, 645n
Barry, Jack, 3n, 51, 319n
Bartels, Robert, 690n
Bartlett, Christopher A., 612
Bauknight, Dow N., 507n
Bechtel, Christian, 56n, 92
Becker, S.W., 283n
Bell, Derek, 571n
Bender, Paul S., 174n, 342n–343n, 376n,
    532n, 551n–552n, 558n–559n, 578
Bennett, William J., 526n
Bennion, Mark L., 107n–108n, 217n
Berg, Michael J., 463n
Bergin, Sarah A., 308
Berry, Danny, 92

Berthon, Alain, 470n
Bertrand, H.E., 287n
Berzon, Michael, 527n
Beskow, Martin J., 361n
Bhardwaj, S.M., 474
Bhattacharya, Arindam K., 88n, 92
Bicheno, John, 93
Bier, Frederick J., 267
Bigness, Jon, 346
Billington, Corey, 56n, 79n
Birou, Laura M., 159n, 176n, 524n, 543,
    586n, 612
Blackmon, Douglas A., 530n
Blain, Jonathan, 177n
Blanchard, Benjamin S., 287n
Blanchard, Dave, 50
Blomquist, James A., 432n, 436n
Bloomberg, David J., 380
Blore, F. Robert, 281n
Blumenschein, Klaus, 561n
Boey, Peter, 430
Bohman, Ray, 339n
Bookbinder, James H., 182
Borsodi, Ralph, 11n
Borthick, A. Faye, 648
Bossidy, Larry, 478
Bovet, David, 682, 713
Bowers, Jim, 367n
Bowersox, Donald J., 12n, 38n, 50,
    56n–57n, 73n, 81n, 92, 586n–587n,
    591n, 601n, 612, 713, 790n
Bowman, Robert J., 319n, 367n, 536n, 577n
Boyson, Sandor, 359n, 380
Bozer, Yavuz A., 397n
Brace, Gordon, 88n, 92
Bradley, Peter, 47n, 330n, 339n–340n, 373n
Braithwaite, Alan, 93, 555n, 608n, 647
Bramble, Gary M., 175n

Subject Index